CPA

Comprehensive Exam Review

Financial Accounting & Reporting

Nathan M. Bisk, JD, CPA

ACKNOWLEDGEMENTS

CONTRIBUTING EDITORS

J. Ralph Byington
PhD, CPA
University of South Carolina, Aiken

Ivan Fox
JD, LLM
Pace University

Anne Keaty
JD
University of Louisiana at Lafayette

Robert L. Monette
JD, CPA
Philadelphia CPA Review

Paul Munter
PhD, CPA
KPMG

Thomas A. Ratcliffe
PhD, CPA
Troy University

C. William Thomas
MBA, PhD, CPA
Baylor University

Mark A. Turner
DBA, CPA, CMA
Texas State University

We wish to thank the **American Institute of Certified Public Accountants** and other organizations for permission to reprint or adapt the following copyrighted © materials:

1. Uniform CPA Examination Questions and Unofficial Answers, Copyright © American Institute of Certified Public Accountants, Inc., Harborside Financial Center, 201 Plaza Three, Jersey City, NJ 07311-3881.
2. Accounting Research Bulletins, APB Opinions, Audit and Accounting Guides, Auditing Procedure Studies, Risk Alerts, Statements of Position, and Code of Professional Conduct, Copyright © American Institute of Certified Public Accountants, Inc., Harborside Financial Center, 201 Plaza Three, Jersey City, NJ 07311-3881.
3. FASB Statements, Interpretations, Technical Bulletins, and Statements of Financial Accounting Concepts, Copyright © Financial Accounting Standards Board, 401 Merrit 7, P.O. Box 5116, Norwalk, CT 06856.
4. GASB Statements, Interpretations, and Technical Bulletins, Copyright © Governmental Accounting Standards Board, 401 Merritt 7, P.O. Box 5116, Norwalk CT 06856-5116.
5. Statements on Auditing Standards, Statements on Standards for Consulting Services, Statements on Responsibilities in Personal Financial Planning Practice, Statements on Standards for Accounting and Review Services, Statements on Quality Control Standards, Statements on Standards for Attestation Engagements, and Statements on Responsibilities in Tax Practice, Copyright © American Institute of Certified Public Accountants, Inc., Harborside Financial Center, 201 Plaza Three, Jersey City, NJ 07311-3881.
6. ISB Standards, Copyright © Independence Standards Board, 6th Floor, 1211 Avenue of the Americas, New York, NY 10036-8775

THIRTY-SIXTH EDITION

PREFACE

Our texts provide comprehensive, complete coverage of <u>all</u> the topics tested on all <u>four</u> sections of the CPA Examination, including **Financial Accounting & Reporting, Auditing & Attestation, Regulation,** and **Business Environment & Concepts.** Used effectively, our materials will enable you to achieve maximum preparedness for the Uniform CPA Examination. Here is a brief summary of the **features** and **benefits** that our texts will provide for you:

1. **Information on the Computer-Based Exam**...The Uniform CPA Examination is administered at secure testing centers on computers. See Appendix B for a full discussion of this issue. This edition contains up-to-date coverage, including complete coverage of all exam changes. This edition also includes all the latest pronouncements of the AICPA and FASB, the current tax rates, governmental and nonprofit accounting, and other topics that are tested on the CPA exam. Our coverage is based on the most recent **AICPA Content Specification Outlines for the Uniform CPA Exam.**

2. **Separate and Complete Volumes**...Each volume includes text, case based simulations, and multiple choice questions with solutions. There is no need to refer to any other volume.

3. **More than 3,500 Pages of Text**...Including a selection of more than 4,000 recent CPA Examination and exclusive Bisk Education multiple choice questions, and simulations with Unofficial Answers from past CPA Examinations. Solving these questions under test conditions with immediate verification of results instills confidence and reinforces our **SOLUTIONS APPROACH™** to solving exam questions.

4. **Complete Coverage**...No extra materials are required to be purchased. We discuss and explain all important AICPA, FASB, GASB, and ISB pronouncements, including all significant ARBs, APBs, SASs, SSARs, SFACs, and FASB materials. We also cite and identify all authoritative sources including the dates of all AICPA Questions and Unofficial Answers covered in our materials.

5. **Detailed Summaries**...We set forth the significant testable concepts in each CPA exam topic. These highly readable summaries are written in complete sentences using an outline format to facilitate rapid and complete comprehension. The summaries isolate and emphasize topics historically tested by the CPA examiners.

6. **Emphasis on "How to Answer Questions" and "How to Take the Exam"**...We teach you to solve free response and simulations using our unique and famous **SOLUTIONS APPROACH™.**

7. **Discussion and Development of**...AICPA grading procedures, grader orientation strategies, examination confidence, and examination success.

8. **Unique Objective Question Coverage and Unofficial Answers Updated**...We explain ***why*** the multiple choice alternatives are either right or wrong. Plus, we clearly indicate the changes that need to be made in the Unofficial Answers to correctly reflect current business and tax laws and AICPA, FASB, GASB, and other authoritative pronouncements.

9. **Writing Skills**...Each volume contains a section to help you brush up on your writing skills for the CPA exam.

10. **Indexes**...We have included a comprehensively compiled index for easy topic reference in all four sections.

11. **Cross References**...If you do decide to use our other materials, the software uses the same chapter numbering system as the book to allow for easy synchronization between the two formats. Our video and audio programs also are referenced to those same chapters.

12. **Diagnostic Exam to Test Your Present Level of Knowledge**...And we include a **Practice Exam** to test your exam preparedness under actual exam conditions. These testing materials are designed to help you single out for concentrated study the exam topic areas in which you are dangerously deficient.

Our materials are designed for the candidate who previously has studied accounting. Therefore, the rate at which a candidate studies and learns (not merely reads) our material will depend on a candidate's background and aptitude. Candidates who have been out of school for a period of years might need more time to study than recent graduates. The point to remember is that <u>all</u> the material you will need to know to pass the exam is here, except for the professional databases available for free from www.cpa-exam.org to candidates with a notice to schedule. All you need to do is apply yourself and learn this material at a rate that is appropriate to your situation. **As a final thought,** keep in mind that test confidence gained through disciplined preparation equals success.

OUR EDITORIAL BOARD INCLUDES THE NATION'S LEADING CPAs, ATTORNEYS AND EDUCATORS!

The Only CPA Review Texts Developed By Full-Time Experts.

YOU WILL LEARN FROM OUR OUTSTANDING EXPERTS… WITHOUT LEAVING YOUR HOME OR OFFICE.

Consulting Editor
RICHARD M. FELDHEIM, MBA, JD, LLM, CPA (NY), is a New York CPA as well as an attorney in New York and Arizona. He holds a Master's in Tax Law from New York University Law School. Mr. Feldheim is a member of the AICPA, New York State Society of CPAs, American Bar Association, New York State Bar Association, and Association of the Bar of the City of New York. His background includes practice as both a CPA with Price Waterhouse & Co. and as a Senior Partner with the Arizona law firm of Wentworth & Lundin. He has lectured for the AICPA, the Practising Law Institute, Seton Hall University, and the University of Arizona.

Consulting Editor
WILLIAM J. MEURER, CPA (FL), is former Managing Partner for both the overall operations in Central Florida and the Florida Audit and Business Advisory Services sector of Arthur Andersen LLP. During his 35-year career with the firm, Mr. Meurer developed expertise in several industries, including high technology, financial services, real estate, retailing/distribution, manufacturing, hospitality, professional services, and cable television. A graduate of Regis University, Mr. Meurer is a member of both the American Institute of CPAs and the Florida Society of CPAs.

Consulting Editor
THOMAS A. RATCLIFFE, PhD, CPA (TX), is the Director of Accounting and Auditing at Wilson, Price, Barranco, Blankenship & Billingsley, P.C. [Montgomery, AL]. In that role, Dr. Ratcliffe is responsible for quality control within the firm. Dr. Ratcliffe is Director Emeritus of the School of Accountancy at Troy University and also serves as accounting/auditing technical advisor to three different associations of CPA firms (CPA America, Leading Edge, and PKF North American Network). Continuing his involvement in service roles within the accounting profession, Dr. Ratcliffe serves on the AICPA Council and is the current chair of the AICPA Accounting and Review Services Committee. He also is a member of the AICPA Private Company Financial Reporting Task Force.

Consulting Editor
C. WILLIAM THOMAS, MBA, PhD, CPA (TX), is J.E. Bush Professor and former chairman of the Department of Accounting and Business Law at Baylor University. He is a member of the AICPA, the Texas Society of CPAs, the Central Texas Chapter of CPAs, and the American Accounting Association, where he is past Chairperson for the Southwestern Regional Audit Section. In addition, he has received recognition for special Audit Education and Curriculum projects he developed for Coopers & Lybrand. His background includes public accounting experience with KPMG Peat Marwick.

CHANGE ALERTS

SFAS 155, Accounting for Certain Hybrid Financial Instruments—an amendment of FASB Statements No. 133 and 140 (Issued 2/06)

The objective of this Statement is to improve the financial reporting of certain hybrid financial instruments by requiring more consistent accounting that eliminates exemptions and provides a means to simplify the accounting for these instruments. Specifically, it allows financial instruments that have embedded derivatives to be accounted for as a whole if the holder elects to account for the whole instrument on a fair value basis.

This Statement is effective for all financial instruments acquired or issued after the beginning of an entity's first fiscal year that begins after September 15, 2006. (Chapter 2)

Editor's Note: The editors do not expect this Statement to be tested heavily on the exam, if it is tested at all.

SFAS 156, Accounting for Servicing of Financial Assets—an amendment of FASB Statement No. 140 (Issued 3/06)

The objective of this Statement is to simplify the accounting for servicing assets and liabilities, such as those common with mortgage securitization activities. Specifically, it addresses the recognition and measurement of separately recognized servicing assets and liabilities and provides an approach to simplify efforts to obtain hedge-like (offset) accounting.

This Statement is effective for all separately recognized servicing assets and liabilities acquired or issued after the beginning of an entity's fiscal year that begins after September 15, 2006. (Chapter 2)

Editor's Note: The editors do not expect this Statement to be tested heavily on the exam, if it is tested at all.

SFAS 157, Fair Value Measurements (Issued 9/06)

The objective of this Statement is to increase consistency and comparability in fair value measurements and to expand disclosures about fair value measurements. Specifically, it defines fair value, establishes a framework for measuring fair value in generally accepted accounting principles (GAAP), and expands disclosures about fair value measurements.

This Statement is effective for financial statements issued for fiscal years beginning after November 15, 2007, and interim periods within those fiscal years. Early application is encouraged. (Chapter 1)

SFAS 158, Employers' Accounting for Defined Benefit Pension and Other Postretirement Plans—an amendment of FASB Statements No. 87, 88, 106, and 132(R) (Issued 9/06)

The objective of this Statement is to improve the reporting of employers' obligations for pensions and other postretirement benefits by recognizing the overfunded or underfunded status of defined benefit postretirement plans as an asset or a liability in the statement of financial position. Specifically, this means that a sponsoring entity would recognize all previously unrecognized items even when the plan is fully funded.

This Statement is effective for a public entity with its fiscal year ending after December 15, 2006. (Chapter 9)

Editor's Note: The editors expect these changes to be tested beginning in the July/August 2007 test cycle.

FINANCIAL ACCOUNTING & REPORTING

VOLUME I of IV

TABLE OF CONTENTS

PAGE

Foreword: Getting Started F-1

Chapter 1: Overview 1-1
Chapter 2: Cash, Marketable Securities & Receivables 2-1
Chapter 3: Inventory 3-1
Chapter 4: Property, Plant & Equipment 4-1
Chapter 5: Intangible Assets, R&D Costs & Other Assets 5-1
Chapter 6: Bonds 6-1
Chapter 7: Liabilities 7-1
Chapter 8: Leases 8-1
Chapter 9: Postemployment Benefits 9-1
Chapter 10: Owners' Equity 10-1
Chapter 11: Reporting the Results of Operations 11-1
Chapter 12: Reporting: Special Areas 12-1
Chapter 13: Accounting for Income Taxes 13-1
Chapter 14: Statement of Cash Flows 14-1
Chapter 15: Financial Statement Analysis 15-1
Chapter 16: Foreign Operations 16-1
Chapter 17: Consolidated Financial Statements 17-1
Chapter 18: Governmental Overview 18-1
Chapter 19: Governmental Funds & Transactions 19-1
Chapter 20: Nonprofit Accounting 20-1

Appendix A: Practice Examination A-1
Appendix B: Practical Advice B-1
Appendix C: Writing Skills C-1
Appendix D: Compound Interest Tables D-1
Appendix E: Recently Released AICPA Questions E-1
Index I-1

The editors recommend that candidates remain cognizant of the depth of coverage of a topic and their proficiency with it when studying for the exam. Ensure you review the AICPA Content Specification Outline and make informed decisions about your study plan by reading the information in the **Getting Started** and **Practical Advice** sections of this volume.

QUICK TEXT REFERENCE

AICPA Content Specification Outline B-29

Audio Tutor 12-18

Authoritative Pronouncements Cross-References B-31

Boards of Accountancy B-4

Checklist 20-50, B-15

Computerized CPA Exam F-31, B-5, B-9

Diagnostic Examination F-20, C-8

Examination Schedule B-3

Examination Strategies B-12

Granting of Credit B-5

Out of State Candidates B-4

Post-Exam Diagnostics 16-24, B-9

Question Reference Numbers B-36

Registration Process B-5

Research 18-40, B-8, B-20

Simulations 6-36, B-7

Study Tips F-1, F-11, 10-30, 15-16, B-1, B-10

Testable Topics 8-37, B-29, B-35

Time Management 3-14, F-3, B-9, E-22

Updating Supplements I-10

Video Cross Reference F-13

Video Descriptions 4-38, 7-18, 10-66, 17-50, 20-26, A-32

Written Communications 18-58, B-3, B-17, B-24, C-1

The editors strongly recommend that candidates read the entire **Getting Started**, **Practical Advice**, and **Writing Skills** sections of this volume. The references on this page are intended only for conveniently relocating selected parts of the volume. Add items to this list that you find yourself revisiting frequently.

FOREWORD: GETTING STARTED

Step One: Read Section One of the Practical Advice Section

Section One of the **Practical Advice** section (Appendix B) is designed to familiarize you with the CPA examination. Included in **Practical Advice** are general comments about the exam, a schedule of exam dates, addresses and numbers of state boards of accountancy, and attributes required for exam success.

Step Two: Take the Diagnostic Exam

The diagnostic exam in this foreword is designed to help you determine your strong and weak areas. This in turn will help you design your personalized training plan so that you spend more time in your weak areas and do not waste precious study time in areas where you are already strong. You can take the exams using either the books or CPA Review Software for Windows™. Don't mark answers in the book; then you can use the diagnostic as a second practice exam, if you want. The books provide you with a worksheet that makes self-diagnosis fast and easy. CPA Review Software for Windows™ automatically scores your exams for you and gives you a personalized analysis of your strong and weak areas.

NOTE: If you took a previous CPA exam and passed some, but not all the sections, also analyze these exam sections to help you determine where you need to concentrate your efforts this time.

NOTE: If you purchase a package that includes software, you will also want to go through all of the software tutorials prior to beginning intensive study. They are each only a few minutes long, but they are loaded with valuable information. There is simply no better way to prepare yourself to study. The software programmers assumed candidates would take the diagnostic exam before beginning studying; take the diagnostic exam to get full benefit from the software.

Step Three: Develop a Personalized Training Plan

Based on the results from your diagnostic exams, develop your personalized training plan. If you are taking all four exam sections, are sitting for the exam for the first time, and are an "average" CPA candidate, we recommend that you train for 20 weeks at a minimum of 20 hours per week. This level of intensity should increase during the final four weeks of your training and peak at 40 hours the final week before the exam. Designed to complete your study program, our Intensive Video Series is a concentrated and effective "cram course" that targets the information you must know to pass. The videos will refresh your memory on subjects you covered weeks earlier and clarify topics you haven't yet fully grasped.

If you took the exam previously and did not condition (you will take all four sections), and you are the "average" CPA candidate, we recommend that you train for 12 weeks at a minimum of 20 hours per week. Again, this level of intensity should increase during the final four weeks of your training and peak during the final week before the exam.

The Bisk Education editors expect that most candidates will write less than four sections at once. If you are writing less than four sections, you should adjust these guidelines accordingly.

You may wonder what we mean by an "average" candidate. We are referring to a candidate who is just finishing or has just finished her/his academic training, attended a school that has a solid accounting curriculum, and received above average grades in accounting and business law courses. (An "average" candidate's native language is English.) Remember, "average" is a benchmark. Many candidates are not "average," so adjust your training plan accordingly.

Time Availability

	MON	TUES	WED	THURS	FRI	SAT	SUN
1:00 AM							
2:00 AM							
3:00 AM							
4:00 AM							
5:00 AM							
6:00 AM							
7:00 AM							
8:00 AM							
9:00 AM							
10:00 AM							
11:00 AM							
12:00 PM							
1:00 PM							
2:00 PM							
3:00 PM							
4:00 PM							
5:00 PM							
6:00 PM							
7:00 PM							
8:00 PM							
9:00 PM							
10:00 PM							
11:00 PM							
12:00 AM							

How to Find 20 Hours a Week to Study

The typical CPA candidate is a very busy individual. He or she goes to school and/or works full or part time. Some candidates have additional responsibilities such as a spouse, children, a house to take care of—the list can go on and on. Consequently, your first reaction may be, "I don't have 20 hours a week to devote to training for the CPA exam." Using the chart on the previous page, we will show you how to "find" the time that you need to develop your training schedule.

1. Keeping in mind what you would consider to be a typical week, first mark out in black the time that you know you won't be able to study. For example, mark an "X" in each block which represents time that you normally sleep, have a class, work, or have some other type of commitment. Be realistic.

2. Next, in a different color, put a "C" in each block that represents commute time, an "M" in each block that represents when you normally eat, and an "E" in each block that represents when you exercise.

3. Now pick one hour each day to relax and give your mind a break. Write "BREAK" in one block for each day. Do not skip this step. By taking a break, you will study more efficiently and effectively.

4. In a third color, write "STUDY" in the remaining blocks. Count the "STUDY" blocks. Are there 20? If not, count your "C", "M", and "E" blocks; if needed, these blocks of time can be used to gain additional study time by using Bisk Education CPA Review audio lectures and video programs. For example, our audio tutor is ideal for candidates on the go, you can listen to lectures whenever you're in the car or exercising and gain valuable study time each week.

5. If you still do not have 20 "STUDY" blocks, and you scored 70% or more on your diagnostic exams, you may still be able to pass the exam even with your limited study time. If, however, you scored less than 70% on your diagnostic exams, you have several options: (1) re-prioritize and make a block that has an "X" in it available study time; (2) concentrate on fewer exam sections; or (3) study more weeks but fewer hours per week.

How to Allocate Your 20 Weeks

Develop your overall training plan. We outline a sample training plan based on 20 hours per week and 20 weeks of study for all four sections. The time allocated to each topic was based on the length of the chapter, the difficulty of the material, and how heavily the topic is tested on the exam (refer to the exam specifications and our frequency analysis found in the **Practical Advice** section of your book). Keep in mind that this plan is for the "average" CPA candidate. You should **customize one of these plans** based on the results of your diagnostic exams and level of knowledge in each area tested. Given the AICPA examiner's stated intent to make the BEC exam section integrative, the editors recommend that candidates review for the BEC section after, or concurrently with, other exam sections. **Warning:** When studying, be careful not to fall into the trap of spending too much time on an area that rarely is tested. Note: There are Hot•Spot™ videos and audio lectures corresponding to each chapter for more in-depth study. Call 1-888-CPA-BISK.

Sample Training Plan (all 4 sections)*

		Hours
Week 1:	Read **Getting Started** and **Practical Advice** sections	1
	Take Diagnostic Exams under exam conditions (see page F-19)	10
	Read **Writing Skills** section and get organized	1
	Chapter 1—Overview	2
	Chapter 2—Cash, Marketable Securities & Receivables	6

* Candidates should make modifications to this plan to suit their individual circumstances. For instance, this plan repeats Chapter 18. Candidates may not need to return to Chapter 18, particularly those who took a governmental accounting course. Training plans for candidates sitting for one or two sections start on page F-13. The online classes incorporate different training plans within the weekly assignments posted on the online class web site. These different plans take advantage of the additional material provided online.

		Hours
Week 2:	Chapter 2—Cash, Marketable Securities & Receivables	4
	Chapter 3—Inventory	5
	Chapter 4—Property, Plant & Equipment	6
	Chapter 5—Intangible Assets, R&D Costs & Other Assets	4
	Chapter 6—Bonds	1
Week 3:	Weekly review of weeks 1 - 2	1
	Chapter 6—Bonds	5
	Chapter 7—Liabilities	6
	Chapter 8—Leases	5
	Chapter 9—Postemployment Benefits	3
Week 4:	Weekly review of weeks 1 - 3	1
	Chapter 9—Postemployment Benefits	2
	Chapter 10—Owners' Equity	8
	Chapter 21—Standards & Related Topics	4
	Chapter 22—Planning	5
Week 5:	Weekly review of weeks 1 - 4	1
	Chapter 22—Planning	2
	Chapter 23—Internal Control: General	7
	Chapter 24—Internal Control: Transaction Cycles	8
	Chapter 25—Evidence & Procedures	2
Week 6:	Weekly review of weeks 1 - 5	1
	Chapter 11—Reporting the Results of Operations	4
	Chapter 25—Evidence & Procedures	8
	Chapter 26—Audit Programs	7
Week 7:	Weekly review of weeks 1 - 6	1
	Chapter 11—Reporting the Results of Operations	8
	Chapter 27—Audit Sampling	7
	Chapter 28—Auditing IT Systems	4
Week 8:	Weekly review of weeks 1 - 7	1
	Chapter 12—Reporting: Special Areas	6
	Chapter 13—Accounting for Income Taxes	6
	Chapter 14—Statement of Cash Flows	5
	Chapter 28—Auditing IT Systems	2
Week 9:	Weekly review of weeks 1 - 8	1
	Chapter 14—Statement of Cash Flows	1
	Chapter 15—Financial Statement Analysis	4
	Chapter 16—Foreign Operations	2
	Chapter 29—Reports on Audited Financial Statements	12
Week 10:	Weekly review of weeks 1 - 9	1
	Chapter 16—Foreign Operations	1
	Chapter 17—Consolidated Financial Statements	8
	Chapter 30—Other Types of Reports	3
	Chapter 31—Other Professional Services	7

		Hours
Week 11:	Weekly review of weeks 1 - 10	1
	Chapter 18—Governmental Overview	3
	Chapter 19—Governmental Funds & Transactions	9
	Chapter 32—Accountant's Professional Responsibilities	3
	Chapter 33—Accountant's Legal Responsibilities	4
Week 12:	Weekly review of weeks 1 - 11	1
	Chapter 18—Governmental Overview (after Chapter 19)	3
	Chapter 20—Nonprofit Accounting	6
	Chapter 34—Contracts	8
	Chapter 35—Sales	2
Week 13:	Weekly review of weeks 1 - 12	1
	Chapter 35—Sales	4
	Chapter 36—Negotiable Instruments & Documents of Title	5
	Chapter 37—Secured Transactions	2
	Chapter 50—Economic Theory	8
Week 14:	Weekly review of weeks 1 - 13	1
	Chapter 38—Debtor & Creditor Relationships	7
	Chapter 42—Property	1
	Chapter 51—Financial Management	11
Week 15:	Weekly review of weeks 1 - 14	1
	Chapter 41—Other Regulations	2
	Chapter 42—Property	4
	Chapter 51—Financial Management	2
	Chapter 52—Decision Making	4
	Chapter 53—Cost Accounting	7
Week 16:	Weekly review of weeks 1 - 15	1+
	Chapter 39—Agency	2
	Chapter 43—Federal Taxation: Property & Other Topics	5
	Chapter 44—Federal Taxation: Individuals	4
	Chapter 52—Decision Making	2
	Chapter 54—Planning & Control	6
Week 17:	Weekly review of weeks 1 - 16	1+
	Chapter 44—Federal Taxation: Individuals	6
	Chapter 46—Federal Taxation: Corporations	7
	Chapter 49—Corporations	6
Week 18:	Weekly review of weeks 1 - 17	1
	Chapter 45—Federal Taxation: Estates & Trusts	6
	Chapter 46—Federal Taxation: Corporations	3
	Chapter 47—Federal Taxation: Partnerships	5
	Chapter 48—Partnerships	5
Week 19:	Review areas in which you still feel weak	10+
	Chapter 40—Federal Securities Regulation	3
	Chapter 55—Information Technology	7
Week 20:	Take Practice Exams under exam conditions (see page A-1)	10
	Do final reviews	10+

Your Personalized Training Plan:

WEEK	TASK	DIAGNOSTIC SCORE	EST. HOURS	DATE COMPLETE	Chapter SCORE	FINAL SCORE
1						
2						
3						
4						
5						
6						
7						
8						
9						

WEEK	TASK	DIAGNOSTIC SCORE	EST. HOURS	DATE COMPLETE	Chapter SCORE	FINAL SCORE
10						
11						
12						
13						
14						
15						
16						
17						

WEEK	TASK	DIAGNOSTIC SCORE	EST. HOURS	DATE COMPLETE	Chapter SCORE	FINAL SCORE
18						
19						
20						

Step Four: Read the Rest of the Practical Advice Section

In Section Two of the **Practical Advice** section of the book, we discuss examination strategies. Section Three will familiarize you with how the CPA examination is graded and tell you how you can earn extra points on the exam simply by knowing what the grader is going to seek. In addition, in Section Four we explain our Solutions Approach™, an approach that will help you maximize your grade. In Section Five, we provide information on the AICPA exam content specifications and point distribution.

Step Five: Integrate Your Review Materials

In this step, we demonstrate how to integrate the Bisk Education CPA Review products to optimize the effectiveness of your training plan. Find and read the section that corresponds to the package that you purchased. (To facilitate easy reference to your package guidance, you may want to strike through the sections corresponding to other packages.)

Videos

The video programs are designed to supplement all of the study packages. Note how we recommend using the audio lectures in the following review plans. These recommendations also apply to the Hot•Spot™ video lectures. FYI: The videos have similar content as the online video lectures, but they are not exactly the same. Each of the Hot•Spot™ video programs concentrates on a few topics. Use them to help you study the areas that are most troubling for you. Each of the Intensive video programs is designed for a final, intensive review, after a candidate already has done considerable work. If time permits, use the Intensive programs at both the very beginning (for an overview) and set them aside until the final review one or two weeks before your exam. They contain concise, informative lectures, as well as CPA exam tips, tricks, and techniques that will help you to learn the material needed to pass the exam.

Online Package: Books, Video Lectures & CPA Review Software for Windows™

This is our most comprehensive review package. This combination provides the personal advice, discipline, and camaraderie of a classroom setting with the convenience of self-study. It is intended for those candidates who want to make sure that they pass the exam the **first** time. By using this package, you are eligible to qualify for Bisk Education's money-back guarantee. Contact a customer representative for details on the components of this package. Contact your online faculty advisor if you have questions about integrating your materials after viewing the web site guidance. (The editors strongly recommend that candidates working full-time take a maximum of 2 sections concurrently.)

Books, Audio Tutor & CPA Review Software for Windows™

This is our most comprehensive self-study review package. This combination is designed expressly for the serious CPA candidate. It is intended for those candidates who want to make sure that they pass the exam the **first** time (or *this* time, if you have already taken the exam). In addition, by using this package, you are eligible to qualify for Bisk Education's money-back guarantee.

How to Use This Package:

1. First take the diagnostic exams using CPA Review Software for Windows™. CPA Review Software for Windows™ automatically scores your exams and tells you what your strong and weak areas are. Then view the short tutorial to learn how to use the software features to their fullest.

In chapters where you are strong (i.e., you scored 65% or better on the diagnostic exam):

2. Answer the multiple choice questions using CPA Review Software for Windows™.
3. Read the subsections of the chapter that correspond to your weak areas.
4. Listen to the audio tutor for topics covered in this chapter to reinforce your weak areas and review your strong areas.
5. Now, using CPA Review Software for Windows™, answer the multiple choice questions that you previously answered incorrectly. If you answer 70% or more of the questions correctly, you are ready to move to the next chapter. If you answer less than 70% of the questions correctly, handle this chapter as if you scored less than 65% on the diagnostic exam.
6. Answer at least one simulation (if there are any) and review essay questions and solutions in any other simulations.

In chapters where you are weak (i.e., you scored less than 65% on the diagnostic exam):

2. Read the chapter in the book.
3. Listen to the audio lectures on topics covered in the chapter.
4. Re-read the subsections of the chapter that correspond to your weak subtopics.
5. Using CPA Review Software for Windows™, answer the multiple choice questions for this chapter. If you answer 70% or more of the questions correctly, you are ready to move on to the next chapter. If you get less than 70% of the questions correct, review the subtopics where you are weak. Then answer the questions that you previously answered incorrectly. If you still do not get at least 70% correct, check the exam specifications in the Practical Advice section to find out how heavily the area is tested. If this is an area that is heavily tested, continue reviewing the material and answering multiple choice questions until you can answer at least 70% correctly. Allocate more time than you originally budgeted, if necessary. If this is not a heavily tested area, move on, but make a note to come back to this area later as time allows.
6. Answer at least one simulation (if there are any) and review essay questions and solutions in any other simulations.

Books & CPA Review Software for Windows™

This combination allows you to use the books to review the material and CPA Review Software for Windows™ to practice exam questions. You can also use the books to practice exam questions when you do not have access to a computer. In addition, by using this package, you are eligible to qualify for Bisk Education's money-back guarantee.

How to Use This Package:

1. Take the diagnostic exams using CPA Review Software for Windows™. CPA Review Software for Windows automatically scores your exams and tells you what your strong and weak areas are. Then view the short tutorial to learn how to use the software features to their fullest.

In chapters where you are strong (i.e., you scored 65% or better on the diagnostic exam):

2. Answer the multiple choice questions using CPA Review Software for Windows™.

3. Read the subsections of the chapter that correspond to your weak areas.

4. Now using CPA Review Software for Windows™, answer the multiple choice questions that you previously answered incorrectly. If you answer 70% or more of the questions correctly, you are ready to move on to the next chapter. If you answer less than 70% of the questions correctly, handle this chapter as if you scored less than 65% on the diagnostic exam.

5. Answer at least one simulation (if there are any) and review essay questions and solutions in any other simulations.

In chapters where you are weak (i.e., you scored less than 65% on the diagnostic exam):

2. Read the chapter in the book.

3. Using CPA Review Software for Windows™, answer the multiple choice questions for this chapter. If you answer 70% or more of the questions correctly, you are ready to move on to the next chapter. If you get less than 70% of the questions correct, review the subtopics where you are weak. Then answer the questions that you previously answered incorrectly. If you still do not get at least 70% correct, check the exam specifications in the Practical Advice section to find out how heavily the area is tested. If this is an area that is heavily tested, continue reviewing the material and answering multiple choice questions until you can answer at least 70% correctly. Allocate more time than you originally budgeted, if necessary. If this is not a heavily tested area, move on, but make a note to come back to this area later as time allows.

4. Answer at least one simulation (if there are any) and review essay questions and solutions in any other simulations.

Books & Audio Tutor

This combination is designed for the candidate who has a strong preference for hard copy, who spends time commuting or doing other activities that could take valuable time away from studying, and for those who like to reinforce what they read by listening to a lecture.

How to Use This Package:

1. Take the diagnostic exams found in your book. Using the worksheets provided, score your exams to determine your strong and weak areas.

In chapters where you are strong (i.e., you scored 65% or better on the diagnostic exam):

2. Do the multiple choice questions for that chapter. Using the worksheet provided, analyze your strong and weak areas.

3. Read the subsections of the chapter that correspond to your weak subtopics.

4. At this point, listen to the audio tutor on topics covered in this chapter to reinforce weak areas and review strong areas.

5. Answer the multiple choice questions that you previously answered incorrectly. If you answer 70% or more of the questions correctly, you are ready to move on to the next chapter. If you answer less than 70% of the questions correctly, handle this chapter as if you scored 65% or less on the diagnostic exam.

6. Answer at least one simulation (if there are any) and review essay questions and solutions in any other simulations.

In chapters where you are weak (i.e., you scored less than 65% on the diagnostic exam):

2. First read the chapter in the book.

3. Now listen to the audio lectures covering topics in this chapter.

4. Re-read the subsections of the chapter that correspond to your weak subtopics.

5. Do the multiple choice questions and score yourself using the worksheet provided. If you answer 70% or more of the questions correctly, you are ready to move on to the next chapter. If you answer less than 70% of the questions correctly, review the subtopics that are still giving you trouble. Then answer the questions that you previously answered incorrectly. If you still do not get at least 70% of the questions correct, check the exam specifications in the Practical Advice section to find out how heavily this area is tested. If this is an area that is heavily tested, continue reviewing the material and answering questions until you can answer at least 70% of them correctly. Allocate more time than you originally budgeted, if necessary. If this area is not heavily tested, move on, but make a note to come back to this topic later as time allows.

6. Answer at least one simulation (if there are any) and review essay questions and solutions in any other simulations.

Step Six: Use These Helpful Hints as You Study

- MAKE FLASHCARDS OR TAKE NOTES AS YOU STUDY

  Make flashcards for topics that are heavily tested on the exam or that are giving you trouble. By making your own flashcards, you learn during their creation and you can tailor them to your individual learning style and problem areas. You will find these very useful for weekly reviews and your final review. Replace flashcards of information you know with new material as you progress through your study plan. Keep them handy and review them when you are waiting in line or on hold. This will turn nonproductive time into valuable study time. Review your complete set during the last two weeks before the exam.

  Make notes and/or highlight when you read the chapters in the book. When possible, make notes when you listen to the lectures. You will find these very useful for weekly reviews and your final review.

- DO NOT MARK THE OBJECTIVE QUESTION ANSWERS IN THE BOOK.

  Do not circle the answer to objective questions in the book. You should work every multiple-choice question at least twice and you do not want to influence later answers by knowing how you previously answered.

  Date your answer sheets to facilitate tracking your progress.

- SPEND YOUR WEEKLY REVIEW TIME EFFECTIVELY. DURING EACH WEEKLY REVIEW:

  Answer the objective questions that you previously answered incorrectly or merely guessed correctly.

  Go through your flashcards or notes.

  Pick at least one simulation to work. Even if you are studying BEC and are sure that simulations will not appear on your exam, the practice that you gain will be useful. (Do not wait until the end of your review to attempt a simulation with an essay question.) Read the essay questions and solutions for this week's topics that you do not answer this week.

- MARK THE OBJECTIVE QUESTIONS THAT YOU ANSWER INCORRECTLY OR MERELY GUESS CORRECTLY.

  This way you know to answer this question again at a later time.

- EFFECTIVELY USE THE VIDEO PROGRAMS

  Watch the video lectures in an environment without distractions. Be prepared to take notes and answer questions just as if you were attending a live class. Frequently, the instructors will have you stop the program to work a question on your own. This means a 2-hour program may take 2½ hours or more to view.

- EFFECTIVELY USE THE AUDIO TUTOR

  Use Audio Tutor to turn nonproductive time into valuable study time. For example, play the lectures when you are commuting, exercising, getting ready for school or work, doing laundry, etc. Audio Tutor will help you to memorize and retain key concepts. It also will reinforce what you have read in the books. Get in the habit of listening to the lectures whenever you have a chance. The more times that you listen to each lecture, the more familiar you will become with the material and the easier it will be for you to recall it during the exam.

Step Seven: Implement Your Training Plan

This is it! You are primed and ready. You have decided which training tools will work best for you and you know how to use them. As you implement your personalized training plan, keep yourself focused. Your goal is to obtain a grade of 75 or better on each section and, thus, pass the CPA exam. Therefore, you should concentrate on learning new material and reviewing old material only to the extent that it helps you reach this goal. Also, keep in mind that now is not the time to hone your procrastination skills. Utilize the personalized training plan that you developed in step three so that you do not fall behind schedule. Adjust it when necessary if you need more time in one chapter or less time in another. Refer to the AICPA content specifications to make sure that the adjustment is warranted. Above all else, remember that passing the exam is an **attainable** goal. Good luck!

Video Cross Reference

The video programs are designed to supplement all of our study packages. They contain concise, informative lectures, as well as CPA exam tips, tricks, and techniques to help you learn the material needed to pass the exam. The **HotSpots**™ videos concentrate on particular topics. Use them to study the areas that are most troubling for you. Each of the **Intensive** video programs covers one of the four exam sections. The Intensive videos are designed for a final review, after you already have done considerable work. Alternatively, the Intensive videos may be used as both a preview and a final review. Please see page F-8 of this volume and page iii of any HotSpots™ or Intensive viewer guide for a discussion on integrating videos into your study plan. This information, with approximate times, is accurate as we go to press, but it is subject to change without notice.

Video Title	Text Chapter	Time
Hot•Spots™ Cash, Receivables & Marketable Securities	2	2:30
Hot•Spots™ Inventory, Fixed Assets & Intangible Assets	3, 4, 5	2:25
Hot•Spots™ Bonds & Other Liabilities	6, 7	3:00
Hot•Spots™ Leases & Pensions	8, 9	2:45
Hot•Spots™ Owners' Equity & Miscellaneous Topics	10, 15, 16	2:10
Hot•Spots™ Revenue Recognition & Income Statement Presentation	1, 11, 12	3:55
Hot•Spots™ FASB 109: Accounting for Income Taxes	13	2:10
Hot•Spots™ FASB 95: Statement of Cash Flows	14	1:55
Hot•Spots™ Consolidations	2, 17	4:40
Hot•Spots™ Governmental & Nonprofit Accounting	18 - 20	5:15
Hot•Spots™ Audit Planning & Standards	21, 22, 29	2:40
Hot•Spots™ Internal Control	23, 27	1:55
Hot•Spots™ Audit Evidence	24, 25	2:45
Hot•Spots™ Statistical Sampling	26	1:30
Hot•Spots™ Standard Audit Reports	28	2:50
Hot•Spots™ Other Reports, Reviews & Compilations	30, 31	1:50
Hot•Spots™ Professional & Legal Responsibilities	32, 33	1:45
Hot•Spots™ Contracts	34	2:25
Hot•Spots™ Sales	35	1:50
Hot•Spots™ Commercial Paper & Documents of Title	36	2:00
Hot•Spots™ Secured Transactions	37	0:55
Hot•Spots™ Bankruptcy & Suretyship	38	2:10
Hot•Spots™ Fiduciary Relationships	39, 45	0:55
Hot•Spots™ Government Regulation of Business	40, 41	2:00
Hot•Spots™ Property & Insurance	42	1:20
Hot•Spots™ Property Taxation	43	1:25
Hot•Spots™ Individual Taxation	44	3:10
Hot•Spots™ Gross Income, Tax Liabilities & Credits	44, 46	2:55
Hot•Spots™ Corporate Taxation	46	3:00
Hot•Spots™ Partnerships & Other Tax Topics	45, 47	2:15
Hot•Spots™ Business Entities	48, 49	2:25
Hot•Spots™ Economics	50	3:25
Hot•Spots™ Financial Management	51	3:00
Hot•Spots™ Cost & Managerial Accounting	52 - 54	3:30
Hot•Spots™ Information Technology	55	3:00

Intensive Video Review	FAR	AUD	REG	BEC	Total
Text Chapters	1 - 20	21 - 31	32 - 47	48 - 55	
Approximate Time	9:15	4:15	6:45	4:45	25:00

Supplement to Step Three: Alternative Sample Training Plans

The editors strongly recommend that candidates develop personalized training plans. Several training plans are outlined for candidates to modify. The time allocated to each topic was based on the length of the chapter, the difficulty of the material, and how heavily the topic is tested on the exam (refer to the exam specifications found in the **Practical Advice** section). You should **customize one of these plans** based on the results of your diagnostic exams and level of knowledge in each area tested.

FAR Sample Training Plan (1 exam section)

		Hours
Week 1:	Read **Getting Started** and **Practical Advice** sections (if not yet done)	1
	Take Diagnostic Exam under exam conditions (see page F-20)	3
	Read **Writing Skills** section and get organized (if not yet done)	1
	Chapter 1—Overview	2
	Chapter 2—Cash, Marketable Securities & Receivables	10
	Chapter 3—Inventory	3
Week 2:	Chapter 3—Inventory	5
	Chapter 4—Property, Plant & Equipment	6
	Chapter 5—Intangible Assets, R&D Costs & Other Assets	4
	Chapter 6—Bonds	5
Week 3:	Weekly review of weeks 1 - 2	1
	Chapter 6—Bonds	1
	Chapter 7—Liabilities	6
	Chapter 8—Leases	5
	Chapter 9—Postemployment Benefits	5
	Chapter 10—Owners' Equity	2
Week 4:	Weekly review of weeks 1 - 3	1
	Chapter 10—Owners' Equity	6
	Chapter 11—Reporting the Results of Operations	12
	Chapter 12—Reporting: Special Areas	1
Week 5:	Weekly review of weeks 1 - 4	1+
	Chapter 12—Reporting: Special Areas	5
	Chapter 13—Accounting for Income Taxes	6
	Chapter 14—Statement of Cash Flows	6
	Chapter 15—Financial Statement Analysis	2
Week 6:	Weekly review of weeks 1 - 5	1+
	Chapter 15—Financial Statement Analysis	2
	Chapter 16—Foreign Operations	3
	Chapter 17—Consolidated Financial Statements	8
	Chapter 18—Governmental Overview	2
	Chapter 19—Governmental Funds & Transactions	4
Week 7:	Review areas in which you still feel weak	5+
	Chapter 19—Governmental Funds & Transactions	5
	Chapter 18—Governmental Overview (after Chapter 19)	4
	Chapter 20—Nonprofit Accounting	6
Week 8:	Take Practice Exams under exam conditions (see page A-1)	3
	Do final reviews and check for Updating Supplement	17+

Bisk Education's updating supplements are small publications available from either customer representatives or our CPA Review website (http://www.cpaexam.com/content/support.asp). The editors recommend checking the website for new supplements once a month and again a week before your exam. Version 36 updating supplements are appropriate for candidates with the 36th edition. Information from earlier supplements (for instance, Version 35.2) is already incorporated into this edition of the book. Supplements are issued no more frequently than every three months. Supplements are not necessarily issued every three months; supplements are issued only as information appropriate for supplements becomes available.

FAR & AUD Sample Training Plan (2 exam sections)

		Hours
Week 1:	Read **Getting Started** and **Practical Advice** sections (if not yet done)	1
	Take Diagnostic Exams under exam conditions (see page F-20)	5
	Read **Writing Skills** section and get organized (if not yet done)	1
	Chapter 1—Overview	2
	Chapter 2—Cash, Marketable Securities & Receivables	10
	Chapter 3—Inventory	1
Week 2:	Chapter 3—Inventory	4
	Chapter 4—Property, Plant & Equipment	6
	Chapter 5—Intangible Assets, R&D Costs & Other Assets	4
	Chapter 6—Bonds	6
Week 3:	Weekly review of weeks 1 - 2	1
	Chapter 7—Liabilities	6
	Chapter 8—Leases	5
	Chapter 9—Postemployment Benefits	5
	Chapter 10—Owners' Equity	3
Week 4:	Weekly review of weeks 1 - 3	1
	Chapter 10—Owners' Equity	5
	Chapter 21—Standards & Related Topics	4
	Chapter 22—Planning	7
	Chapter 23—Internal Control: General	3
Week 5:	Weekly review of weeks 1 - 4	1
	Chapter 23—Internal Control: General	4
	Chapter 24—Internal Control: Transaction Cycles	8
	Chapter 25—Evidence & Procedures	7
Week 6:	Weekly review of weeks 1 - 5	1
	Chapter 11—Reporting the Results of Operations	9
	Chapter 25—Evidence & Procedures	3
	Chapter 26—Audit Programs	7
Week 7:	Weekly review of weeks 1 - 6	1
	Chapter 11—Reporting the Results of Operations	3
	Chapter 12—Reporting: Special Areas	3
	Chapter 27—Audit Sampling	7
	Chapter 28—Auditing IT Systems	6
Week 8:	Weekly review of weeks 1 - 7	1
	Chapter 12—Reporting: Special Areas	3
	Chapter 13—Accounting for Income Taxes	6
	Chapter 14—Statement of Cash Flows	6
	Chapter 15—Financial Statement Analysis	4

		Hours
Week 9:	Weekly review of weeks 1 - 8	1+
	Chapter 16—Foreign Operations	3
	Chapter 17—Consolidated Financial Statements	4
	Chapter 29—Reports on Audited Financial Statements	12
Week 10:	Weekly review of weeks 1 - 9	1+
	Chapter 17—Consolidated Financial Statements	4
	Chapter 18—Governmental Overview	4
	Chapter 19—Governmental Funds & Transactions	1
	Chapter 30—Other Types of Reports	3
	Chapter 31—Other Professional Services	7
Week 11:	Weekly review of weeks 1 - 10	4+
	Chapter 19—Governmental Funds & Transactions	8
	Chapter 18—Governmental Overview (after Chapter 19)	2
	Chapter 20—Nonprofit Accounting	6
Week 12:	Review areas in which you still feel weak	10+
	Take Practice Exams under exam conditions (see page A-1)	5
	Do final reviews and check for Updating Supplement	5+

FAR & REG Sample Training Plan (2 exam sections)

		Hours
Week 1:	Read **Getting Started** and **Practical Advice** sections (if not yet done)	1
	Take Diagnostic Exams under exam conditions (see page F-20)	5
	Read **Writing Skills** section and get organized (if not yet done)	1
	Chapter 1—Overview	2
	Chapter 2—Cash, Marketable Securities & Receivables	10
	Chapter 3—Inventory	1
Week 2:	Chapter 3—Inventory	4
	Chapter 4—Property, Plant & Equipment	6
	Chapter 5—Intangible Assets, R&D Costs & Other Assets	4
	Chapter 6—Bonds	6
Week 3:	Weekly review of weeks 1 - 2	1
	Chapter 7—Liabilities	6
	Chapter 8—Leases	5
	Chapter 9—Postemployment Benefits	5
	Chapter 10—Owners' Equity	3
Week 4:	Weekly review of weeks 1 - 3	1
	Chapter 10—Owners' Equity	5
	Chapter 11—Reporting the Results of Operations	12
	Chapter 12—Reporting: Special Areas	2
Week 5:	Weekly review of weeks 1 - 4	1
	Chapter 12—Reporting: Special Areas	4
	Chapter 13—Accounting for Income Taxes	2
	Chapter 42—Property	5
	Chapter 43—Federal Taxation: Property & Other Topics	5
	Chapter 44—Federal Taxation: Individuals	3

		Hours
Week 6:	Weekly review of weeks 1 - 5	1
	Chapter 13—Accounting for Income Taxes	4
	Chapter 14—Statement of Cash Flows	6
	Chapter 15—Financial Statement Analysis	2
	Chapter 44—Federal Taxation: Individuals	7
Week 7:	Weekly review of weeks 1 - 6	1
	Chapter 15—Financial Statement Analysis	2
	Chapter 16—Foreign Operations	3
	Chapter 17—Consolidated Financial Statements	8
	Chapter 46—Federal Taxation: Corporations	6
Week 8:	Weekly review of weeks 1 - 7	1
	Chapter 18—Governmental Overview	3
	Chapter 19—Governmental Funds & Transactions	9
	Chapter 32—Accountant's Professional Responsibilities	3
	Chapter 33—Accountant's Legal Responsibilities	4
Week 9:	Weekly review of weeks 1 - 8	1+
	Chapter 18—Governmental Overview (after Chapter 19)	3
	Chapter 20—Nonprofit Accounting	6
	Chapter 34—Contracts	8
	Chapter 35—Sales	2
Week 10:	Weekly review of weeks 1 - 9	1+
	Chapter 35—Sales	4
	Chapter 36—Negotiable Instruments & Documents of Title	5
	Chapter 37—Secured Transactions	2
	Chapter 38—Debtor & Creditor Relationships	7
	Chapter 39—Agency	1
Week 11:	Weekly review of weeks 1 - 10	1+
	Chapter 39—Agency	1
	Chapter 40—Federal Securities Regulation	3
	Chapter 41—Other Regulations	2
	Chapter 45—Federal Taxation: Estates & Trusts	6
	Chapter 46—Federal Taxation: Corporations	4
	Chapter 47—Federal Taxation: Partnerships	3
Week 12:	Review areas in which you still feel weak	8+
	Chapter 47—Federal Taxation: Partnerships	2
	Take Practice Exams under exam conditions (see page A-1)	5
	Do final reviews and check for Updating Supplement	5+

FAR & BEC Sample Training Plan (2 exam sections)

		Hours
Week 1:	Read **Getting Started** and **Practical Advice** sections (if not yet done)	1
	Take Diagnostic Exams under exam conditions (see page F-20)	5
	Read **Writing Skills** section and get organized (if not yet done)	1
	Chapter 1—Overview	2
	Chapter 2—Cash, Marketable Securities & Receivables	10
	Chapter 3—Inventory	1

		Hours
Week 2:	Chapter 3—Inventory	4
	Chapter 4—Property, Plant & Equipment	6
	Chapter 5—Intangible Assets, R&D Costs & Other Assets	4
	Chapter 6—Bonds	6
Week 3:	Weekly review of weeks 1 - 2	1
	Chapter 7—Liabilities	6
	Chapter 8—Leases	5
	Chapter 50—Economic Theory	8
Week 4:	Weekly review of weeks 1 - 3	1
	Chapter 9—Postemployment Benefits	5
	Chapter 10—Owners' Equity	3
	Chapter 48—Partnerships	5
	Chapter 49—Corporations	6
Week 5:	Weekly review of weeks 1 - 4	1
	Chapter 10—Owners' Equity	5
	Chapter 11—Reporting the Results of Operations	1
	Chapter 51—Financial Management	13
Week 6:	Weekly review of weeks 1 - 5	1
	Chapter 11—Reporting the Results of Operations	11
	Chapter 12—Reporting: Special Areas	6
	Chapter 13—Accounting for Income Taxes	2
Week 7:	Weekly review of weeks 1 - 6	1
	Chapter 13—Accounting for Income Taxes	4
	Chapter 14—Statement of Cash Flows	6
	Chapter 15—Financial Statement Analysis	4
	Chapter 52—Decision Making	5
Week 8:	Weekly review of weeks 1 - 7	1+
	Chapter 16—Foreign Operations	3
	Chapter 17—Consolidated Financial Statements	8
	Chapter 52—Decision Making	1
	Chapter 53—Cost Accounting	1
	Chapter 54—Planning & Control	6
Week 9:	Weekly review of weeks 1 - 8	1+
	Chapter 18—Governmental Overview	3
	Chapter 19—Governmental Funds & Transactions	9
	Chapter 20—Nonprofit Accounting	1
	Chapter 53—Cost Accounting	6
Week 10:	Weekly review of weeks 1 - 9	5+
	Chapter 18—Governmental Overview (after Chapter 19)	3
	Chapter 20—Nonprofit Accounting	5
	Chapter 55—Information Technology	7
Week 11:	Review areas in which you still feel weak	10+
	Take Practice Exams under exam conditions (see page A-1)	5
	Do final reviews and check for Updating Supplement	5+

DIAGNOSTIC EXAMINATION

Editor's Note: There is only one practice (or final) examination. Mark your answers for the diagnostic examination on a separate sheet of paper and then these questions can be used again as a second "final" exam at the end of your review.

Problem 1 MULTIPLE CHOICE QUESTIONS (120 to 150 minutes)

1. According to the FASB conceptual framework, an entity's revenue may result from
a. A decrease in an asset from primary operations
b. An increase in an asset from incidental transactions
c. An increase in a liability from incidental transactions
d. A decrease in a liability from primary operations
(3436)

2. According to the FASB conceptual framework, the usefulness of providing information in financial statements is subject to the constraint of
a. Consistency
b. Cost-benefit
c. Reliability
d. Representational faithfulness (6084)

3. The following information pertains to Grey Co. at December 31 of the previous year:

Checkbook balance	$12,000
Bank statement balance	16,000
Check drawn on Grey's account, payable to a vendor, dated and recorded last 12/31 but not mailed until 1/10 of the current year	1,800

On Grey's December 31, previous year balance sheet, what amount should be reported as cash?
a. $12,000
b. $13,800
c. $14,200
d. $16,000 (4827)

4. Park Co. uses the equity method to account for its January 1 current year purchase of Tun, Inc.'s common stock. On this date, the fair values of Tun's FIFO inventory and land exceeded their carrying amounts. How do these excesses of fair values over carrying amounts affect Park's reported equity in Tun's current year earnings?

	Inventory excess	*Land excess*
a.	Decrease	Decrease
b.	Decrease	No effect
c.	Increase	Increase
d.	Increase	No effect

(2015)

5. When the equity method is used to account for investments in common stock, which of the following affect(s) the investor's reported investment income?

	A change in market value of investee's common stock	*Cash dividends from investee*
a.	Yes	Yes
b.	Yes	No
c.	No	Yes
d.	No	No

(6275)

6. Walt Co. adopted the dollar-value LIFO inventory method as of January 1 of the current year, when its inventory was valued at $500,000. Walt's entire inventory constitutes a single pool. Using a relevant price index of 1.10, Walt determined that its December 31 inventory was $577,500 at current year cost, and $525,000 at base year cost. What was Walt's dollar-value LIFO inventory at December 31 of the current year?
a. $525,000
b. $527,500
c. $552,500
d. $577,500 (5547)

7. Herc Co.'s inventory at December 31 of the previous year was $1,500,000, based on a physical count priced at cost, and before any necessary adjustment for the following:

- Merchandise costing $90,000, shipped F.O.B. shipping point from a vendor on December 30 of the previous year, was received and recorded on January 5 of the current year.
- Goods in the shipping area were excluded from inventory although shipment was not made until January 4. The goods, billed to the customer F.O.B. shipping point on December 30 had a cost of $120,000.

What amount should Herc report as inventory in its December 31, previous year balance sheet?
a. $1,500,000
b. $1,590,000
c. $1,620,000
d. $1,710,000 (5278)

8. During periods of inflation, a perpetual inventory system would result in the same dollar amount of ending inventory as a periodic inventory system under which of the following inventory valuation methods?

	FIFO	LIFO
a.	Yes	No
b.	Yes	Yes
c.	No	Yes
d.	No	No

(7062)

9. Samm Corp. purchased a plot of land for $100,000. The cost to raze a building on the property amounted to $50,000 and Samm received $10,000 from the sale of scrap materials. Samm built a new plant on the site at a total cost of $800,000 including excavation costs of $30,000. What amount should Samm capitalize in its land account?
a. $150,000
b. $140,000
c. $130,000
d. $100,000 (6898)

10. On January 1, year 1, Crater Inc. purchased equipment having an estimated salvage value equal to 20% of its original cost at the end of a 10-year life. The equipment was sold December 31, year 5, for 50% of its original cost. If the equipment's disposition resulted in a reported loss, which of the following depreciation methods did Crater use?
a. Double-declining-balance
b. Sum-of-the-years'-digits
c. Straight-line
d. Composite (4215)

11. In an exchange with commercial substance, Slate Co. and Talse Co. exchanged similar plots of land with fair values in excess of carrying amounts. In addition, Slate received cash from Talse to compensate for the difference in land values. As a result of the exchange, Slate should recognize
a. A gain equal to the difference between the fair value and the carrying amount of the land given up
b. A gain in an amount determined by the ratio of cash received to total consideration
c. A loss in an amount determined by the ratio of cash received to total consideration
d. **Neither** a gain **nor** a loss (5566)

12. Roro Inc. paid $7,200 to renew its only insurance policy for three years on March 1, the effective date of the policy. At March 31, Roro's unadjusted trial balance showed a balance of $300 for prepaid insurance and $7,200 for insurance expense. What amounts should be reported for prepaid insurance and insurance expense in Roro's financial statements for the three months ended March 31?

	Prepaid insurance	Insurance expense
a.	$7,000	$300
b.	$7,000	$500
c.	$7,200	$300
d.	$7,300	$200

(5550)

13. Which of the following is an example of activities that would typically be excluded in research and development costs?
a. Design, construction, and testing of preproduction prototypes and modes
b. Laboratory research aimed at discovery of new knowledge
c. Quality control during commercial production, including routine testing of products
d. Testing in search for, or evaluation of, product or process alternatives (7789)

14. On July 31 of the current year, Dome Co. issued $1,000,000 of 10%, 15-year bonds at par and used a portion of the proceeds to call its 600 outstanding 11%, $1,000 face value bonds, due in ten years on July 31, at 102. On that date, unamortized bond premium relating to the 11% bonds was $65,000. In its year-end income statement, what amount should Dome report as gain or loss, before income taxes, from retirement of bonds?
a. $ 53,000 gain
b. $0
c. $ (65,000) loss
d. $ (77,000) loss (5304)

15. Jent Corp. purchased bonds at a discount of $10,000. Subsequently, Jent sold these bonds at a premium of $14,000. During the period that Jent held this investment, amortization of the discount amounted to $2,000. What amount should Jent report as gain on the sale of bonds?
a. $12,000
b. $22,000
c. $24,000
d. $26,000 (4858)

16. On July 1 of the current year, Eagle Corp. issued 600 of its 10%, $1,000 bonds at 99 plus accrued interest. The bonds are dated April 1 of the current year, and mature in 10 years. Interest is payable semiannually on April 1 and October 1. What amount did Eagle receive from the bond issuance?
a. $579,000
b. $594,000
c. $600,000
d. $609,000 (5555)

17. Ace Co. settled litigation on February 1 of the current year for an event that occurred during the prior year. An estimated liability was determined as of December 31 of the prior year. This estimate was significantly less than the final settlement. The transaction is considered to be material. The financial statements for prior year-end have not been issued. How should the settlement be reported in Ace's prior year-end financial statements?
a. Disclosure only of the settlement
b. Only an accrual of the settlement
c. Neither a disclosure nor an accrual
d. Both a disclosure and an accrual (7065)

18. Cali Inc. had a $4,000,000 note payable due on March 15 of the current year. On January 28 of the current year, before the issuance of its prior year financial statements, Cali issued long-term bonds in the amount of $4,500,000. Proceeds from the bonds were used to repay the note when it came due. How should Cali classify the note in its prior year December 31 financial statements?
a. As a current liability, with separate disclosure of the note refinancing
b. As a current liability, with no separate disclosure required
c. As a noncurrent liability, with separate disclosure of the note refinancing
d. As a noncurrent liability, with no separate disclosure required (5541)

19. In its current year financial statements, Cris Co. reported interest expense of $85,000 in its income statement and cash paid for interest of $68,000 in its cash flow statement. There was no prepaid interest or interest capitalization either at the beginning or end of the current year. Accrued interest at December 31 of the prior year was $15,000. What amount should Cris report as accrued interest payable in its current year December 31 balance sheet?
a. $ 2,000
b. $15,000
c. $17,000
d. $32,000 (5282)

20. Ace Corp. entered into a troubled debt restructuring agreement with National Bank. National agreed to accept land with a carrying amount of $75,000 and a fair value of $100,000 in exchange for a note with a carrying amount of $150,000. Disregarding income taxes, what amount should Ace report as extraordinary gain in its income statement?
a. $0
b. $25,000
c. $50,000
d. $75,000 (6905)

21. In a sale-leaseback transaction, a gain resulting from the sale should be deferred at the time of the sale-leaseback and subsequently amortized when

I. The seller-lessee has transferred substantially all the risks of ownership.
II. The seller-lessee retains the right to substantially all of the remaining use of the property.

a. I only
b. II only
c. Both I and II
d. Neither I nor II (6093)

22. On January 1 of the current year, Marx Co. as lessee signed a 5-year noncancelable equipment lease with annual payments of $200,000 beginning December 31. Marx treated this transaction as a capital lease. The five lease payments have a present value of $758,000 at January 1, based on interest of 10%. What amount should Marx report as interest expense for the year on December 31?
a. $0
b. $48,400
c. $55,800
d. $75,800 (6277)

23. Winn Co. manufactures equipment that is sold or leased. On December 31 of the current year, Winn leased equipment to Bart for a 5-year period ending December 31, in five years, at which date ownership of the leased asset will be transferred to Bart. Equal payments under the lease are $22,000 (including $2,000 executory costs) and are due on December 31 of each year. The first payment was made on December 31 of the current year. Collectibility of the remaining lease payments is reasonably assured, and Winn has no material cost uncertainties. The normal sales price of the equipment is $77,000, and cost is $60,000. For the current year ended December 31, what amount of income should Winn realize from the lease transaction?
a. $17,000
b. $22,000
c. $23,000
d. $33,000 (1193)

24. The following information pertains to the current year activity of Ral Corp.'s defined benefit pension plan:

Service cost	$300,000
Return on plan assets	80,000
Interest cost on pension benefit obligation	164,000
Amortization of actuarial loss	30,000
Amortization of remaining net obligation	70,000

Ral's current year pension cost was
a. $316,000
b. $484,000
c. $574,000
d. $644,000 (1221)

Items 25 and 26 are based on the following:

The following information pertains to Hall Co.'s defined benefit pension plan at December 31, year 4:

Unfunded accumulated benefit obligation	$25,000
Unrecognized prior service cost	12,000
Net periodic pension cost	8,000

Hall made no contributions to the pension plan during the year.

25. At December 31, year 4, what amount should Hall record as additional pension liability?
a. $ 5,000
b. $13,000
c. $17,000
d. $25,000 (6096)

26. In its December 31, year 4, other comprehensive income, what amount should Hall report as excess of additional pension liability over unrecognized prior service cost?
a. $ 5,000
b. $13,000
c. $17,000
d. $25,000 (6097)

27. Plack Co. purchased 10,000 shares (2% ownership) of Ty Corp. on February 14 of the current year. Plack received a stock dividend of 2,000 shares on April 30 when the market value per share was $35. Ty paid a cash dividend of $2 per share on December 15. In its current year income statement, what amount should Plack report as dividend income?
a. $20,000
b. $24,000
c. $90,000
d. $94,000 (6980)

28. Selected information from the accounts of Row Co. at December 31 follows:

Total income since incorporation	$420,000
Total cash dividends paid	130,000
Total value of property dividends distributed	30,000
Excess of proceeds over cost of treasury stock sold, accounted for using the cost method	110,000

In its December 31 financial statements, what amount should Row report as retained earnings?
a. $260,000
b. $290,000
c. $370,000
d. $400,000 (6274)

29. During the current year, Young and Zinc maintained average capital balances in their partnership of $160,000 and $100,000, respectively. The partners receive 10% interest on average capital balances, and residual profit or loss is divided equally. Partnership profit before interest was $4,000. By what amount should Zinc's capital account change for the year?
a. $ 1,000 decrease
b. $ 2,000 increase
c. $11,000 decrease
d. $12,000 increase (6105)

30. For interim financial reporting, a company's income tax provision for the second quarter should be determined using the
a. Effective tax rate expected to be applicable for the full year as estimated at the end of the first quarter
b. Effective tax rate expected to be applicable for the full year as estimated at the end of the second quarter
c. Effective tax rate expected to be applicable for the second quarter of the year
d. Statutory tax rate for the year (4536)

31. In which of the following situations should a company report a prior-period adjustment?
a. A change in the estimated useful lives of fixed assets purchased in prior years
b. The correction of a mathematical error in the calculation of prior years' depreciation
c. A switch from the straight-line to double-declining balance method of depreciation
d. The scrapping of an asset prior to the end of its expected useful life

(7787)

32. On October 1, year 3, Wand Inc. committed itself to a formal plan to sell its Kam division's assets. Wand estimated that the loss from the disposal of assets in February of year 4 would be $25,000. Wand also estimated that Kam would incur operating losses of $100,000 for the period of October 1 through December 31, year 3, and $50,000 for the period January 1 through February 28, year 4. These estimates were materially correct. Disregarding income taxes, what should Wand report as loss from discontinued operations in its comparative year 3 and year 4 income statements?

	Year 3	*Year 4*
a.	$175,000	$0
b	$125,000	$ 50,000
c.	$100,000	$ 75,000
d.	$0	$175,000

(5313)

33. At December 31 of the current year, Off-Line Co. changed its method of accounting for demo costs from writing off the costs over two years to expensing the costs immediately. Off-Line made the change in recognition of an increasing number of demos placed with customers that did not result in sales. Off-Line had deferred demo costs of $500,000 at December 31 of the previous year, $300,000 of which were to be written off in the current year and the remainder in the following year. Off-Line's income tax rate is 30%. In its current year income statement, what amount should Off-Line report as cumulative effect of change in accounting principle?

a. $140,000
b. $200,000
c. $350,000
d. $500,000

(6781)

34. The following data pertaining to Pell Co.'s construction jobs, which commenced during the current year:

	Project 1	Project 2
Contract price	$420,000	$300,000
Costs incurred during the year	240,000	280,000
Estimated costs to complete	120,000	40,000
Billed to customers during the year	150,000	270,000
Received from customers during the year	90,000	250,000

If Pell used the completed contract method, what amount of gross profit (loss) would Pell report in its current year income statement?

a. $ (20,000)
b. $0
c. $340,000
d. $420,000

(4079)

35. Rill Co. owns a 20% royalty interest in an oil well. Rill receives royalty payments on January 31 for the oil sold between the previous June 1 and November 30, and on July 31 for oil sold between the previous December 1 and May 31. Production reports show the following oil sales:

June 1, year 1—November 30, year 1	$300,000
December 1, year 1—December 31, year 1	50,000
December 1, year 1—May 31, year 2	400,000
June 1, year 2—November 30, year 2	325,000
December 1, year 2—December 31, year 2	70,000

What amount should Rill report as royalty revenue for year 2?

a. $140,000
b. $144,000
c. $149,000
d. $159,000

(6112)

36. Financial statements prepared under which of the following methods include adjustments for both specific price changes and general price-level changes?

a. Historical cost/nominal dollar
b. Current cost/nominal dollar
c. Current cost/constant dollar
d. Historical cost/constant dollar

(6139)

37. Quinn Co. reported a net deferred tax asset of $9,000 in its December 31, year 1 balance sheet. For year 2, Quinn reported pretax financial statement income of $300,000. Temporary differences of $100,000 resulted in taxable income of $200,000 for year 2. At December 31, year 2, Quinn had cumulative taxable differences of $70,000. Quinn's effective income tax rate is 30%. In its December 31, year 2 income statement, what should Quinn report as deferred income tax expense?

a. $12,000
b. $21,000
c. $30,000
d. $60,000

(5578)

38. For the current year ended December 31, Tyre Co. reported pretax financial statement income of $750,000. Its taxable income was $650,000. The difference is due to accelerated depreciation for income tax purposes. Tyre's effective income tax rate is 30%, and Tyre made estimated tax payments during the year of $90,000. What amount should Tyre report as income tax expense for the year?

a. $105,000
b. $135,000
c. $195,000
d. $225,000

(5577)

39. On its current year December 31 balance sheet, Shin Co. had income taxes payable of $13,000 and a current deferred tax asset of $20,000 before determining the need for a valuation account. Shin had reported a current deferred tax asset of $15,000 at December 31 of the previous year. No estimated tax payments were made during the current year. At December 31, current year, Shin determined that it was more likely than not that 10% of the deferred tax asset would not be realized. In its current year income statement, what amount should Shin report as total income tax expense?
a. $ 8,000
b. $ 8,500
c. $10,000
d. $13,000 (6118)

40. In its cash flow statement for the current year, Ness Co. reported cash paid for interest of $70,000. Ness did not capitalize any interest during the current year. Changes occurred in several balance sheet accounts as follows:

Accrued interest payable	$17,000 decrease
Prepaid interest	23,000 decrease

In its income statement for the current year, what amount should Ness report as interest expense?
a. $ 30,000
b. $ 64,000
c. $ 76,000
d. $110,000 (7749)

41. During the current year, Xan Inc. had the following activities related to its financial operations:

Payment for the early retirement of long-term bonds payable (carrying amount $370,000)	$375,000
Distribution of cash dividend declared in previous year to preferred shareholders	31,000
Carrying amount of convertible preferred stock in Xan, converted into common shares	60,000
Proceeds from sale of treasury stock (carrying amount at cost, $43,000)	50,000

In Xan's current year statement of cash flows, net cash used in financing operations should be
a. $265,000
b. $296,000
c. $356,000
d. $358,000 (4377)

42. Alp Inc. had the following activities during the year:

- Acquired 2,000 shares of stock in Maybel Inc. for $26,000
- Sold an investment in Rate Motors for $35,000 when the carrying amount was $33,000
- Acquired a $50,000, 4-year certificate of deposit from a bank (During the year, interest of $3,750 was paid to Alp.)
- Collected dividends of $1,200 on stock investments

In Alp's statement of cash flows, net cash used in investing activities should be
a. $37,250
b. $38,050
c. $39,800
d. $41,000 (1237)

43. The following data pertain to Thorne Corp. for the current calendar year:

Net income	$240,000
Dividends paid on common stock	120,000
Common stock outstanding (unchanged during year)	300,000 shares

The market price per share of Thorne's common stock at December 31 was $12. The price-earnings ratio at December 31 was
a. 9.6 to 1
b. 10.0 to 1
c. 15.0 to 1
d. 30.0 to 1 (1255)

44. The following information pertains to Jet Corp.'s outstanding stock for the current year:

<u>Common stock, $5 par value</u>	
Shares outstanding 1/1	20,000
2-for-1 stock split 4/1	20,000
Shares issued 7/1	10,000
<u>Preferred stock, $10 par value, 5% cumulative</u>	
Shares outstanding 1/1	4,000

What are the number of shares Jet should use to calculate earnings per share?
a. 40,000
b. 45,000
c. 50,000
d. 54,000 (4099)

45. Kline Co. had the following sales and accounts receivable balances at the end of the current year:

Cash sales	$1,000,000
Net credit sales	3,000,000
Net accounts receivable, 1/1	100,000
Net accounts receivable, 12/31	400,000

What is Kline's average collection period for its accounts receivable?
a. 48.0 days
b. 30.0 days
c. 22.5 days
d. 12.0 days (7058)

46. On October 1, Velec Co., a U.S. company, contracted to purchase foreign goods requiring payment in euros one month after their receipt at Velec's factory. Title to the goods passed on December 15. The goods were still in transit on December 31. Exchange rates were one dollar to 2.2 euros, 2.0 euros, and 2.1 euros on October 1, December 15, and December 31 respectively. Velec should account for the exchange rate fluctuation in the year as
a. A loss included in net income before extraordinary items
b. A gain included in net income before extraordinary items
c. An extraordinary gain
d. An extraordinary loss (4222)

Items 47 and 48 are based on the following:

On January 2, Year 3, Pare Co. purchased 75% of Kidd Co.'s outstanding common stock. Selected balance sheet data at December 31, Year 3, is as follows:

	Pare	Kidd
Total assets	$420,000	$180,000
Liabilities	$120,000	$ 60,000
Common stock	100,000	50,000
Retained earnings	200,000	70,000
	$420,000	$180,000

During year 3, Pare and Kidd paid cash dividends of $25,000 and $5,000, respectively, to their shareholders. There were no other intercompany transactions.

47. In its December 31, Year 3, consolidated statement of retained earnings, what amount should Pare report as dividends paid?
a. $ 5,000
b. $25,000
c. $26,250
d. $30,000 (6131)

48. In Pare's December 31, Year 3, consolidated balance sheet, what amount should be reported as minority interest in net assets?
a. $0
b. $ 30,000
c. $ 45,000
d. $105,000 (6132)

49. Perez, Inc. owns 80% of Senior, Inc. During the current year, Perez sold goods with a 40% gross profit to Senior. Senior sold all of these goods in this year. For year-end consolidated financial statements, how should the summation of Perez and Senior income statement items be adjusted?
a. Sales and cost of goods sold should be reduced by the intercompany sales.
b. Sales and cost of goods sold should be reduced by 80% of the intercompany sales.
c. Net income should be reduced by 80% of the gross profit on intercompany sales.
d. No adjustment is necessary. (4516)

50. According to GASB 34, *Basic Financial Statements and Management's Discussion and Analysis for State and Local Governments*, certain budgetary schedules are required supplementary information. What is the minimum budgetary information required to be reported in those schedules?
a. A schedule of unfavorable variances at the functional level
b. A schedule showing the final appropriations budget and actual expenditures on a budgetary basis
c. A schedule showing the original budget, the final appropriations budget, and actual inflows, outflows, and balances on a budgetary basis
d. A schedule showing the proposed budget, the approved budget, the final amended budget, actual inflows and outflows on a budgetary basis, and variances between budget and actual (7075)

51. Hill City's water utility fund held the following investments in U.S. Treasury securities at June 30, year 5:

Investment	Date purchased	Maturity date	Carrying amount
3-month T-bill	5/31, Yr 5	7/31, Yr 5	$ 30,000
3-year T-note	6/15, Yr 5	8/31, Yr 5	50,000
5-year T-note	10/1, Yr 1	9/30, Yr 6	100,000

In the fund's balance sheet, what amount of these investments should be reported as cash and cash equivalents at June 30, year 5?
a. $0
b. $ 30,000
c. $ 80,000
d. $180,000 (4448)

52. GASB Statement No. 34, *Basic Financial Statements—and Management's Discussion and Analysis—for State and Local Governments,* requires governments to include which of the following in management's discussion and analysis (MD&A)?
a. Analysis of significant budget variances
b. Comparisons of current year to prior year, based on government-wide information
c. Currently known facts, decisions, or conditions that are expected to have a significant effect on financial position or results of operations
d. All of the above (6894)

53. The following information pertains to Spruce City's current year liability for claims and judgments:

Current liability at January 1	$100,000
Claims paid during the year	800,000
Current liability at December 31	140,000
Noncurrent liability at December 31	200,000

What amount should Spruce report for current year claims and judgments expenditures?
a. $1,040,000
b. $ 940,000
c. $ 840,000
d. $ 800,000 (4436)

54. Lake County received the following proceeds that are legally restricted to expenditure for specified purposes:

Levies on affected property owners to install sidewalks	$500,000
Gasoline taxes to finance road repairs	900,000

What amount should be accounted for in Lake's special revenue funds?
a. $1,400,000
b. $ 900,000
c. $ 500,000
d. $0 (2659)

55. Japes City issued $1,000,000 general obligation bonds at 101 to build a new city hall. As part of the bond issue, the city also paid a $500 underwriter fee and $2,000 in debt issue costs. What amount should Japes City report as other financing sources?
a. $1,010,000
b. $1,008,000
c. $1,007,500
d. $1,000,000 (6994)

56. A not-for-profit hospital issued long-term tax exempt bonds for the hospital's benefit. The hospital is responsible for the liability. Which fund may the hospital use to account for this liability?
a. Enterprise
b. Specific purpose
c. General
d. General long-term debt account group (4663)

57. Valley's community hospital normally includes proceeds from sale of cafeteria meals in
a. Deductions from dietary service expenses
b. Ancillary service revenues
c. Patient service revenues
d. Other revenues (4665)

58. In hospital accounting, restricted funds are
a. **Not** available unless the board of directors removes the restrictions
b. Restricted as to use only for board-designated purposes
c. **Not** available for current operating use; however, the income generated by the funds is available for current operating use
d. Restricted as to use by the donor, grantor, or other source of the resources (4136)

59. Oz, a nongovernmental not-for-profit organization, received $50,000 from Ame Company to sponsor a play given by Oz at the local theater. Oz gave Ame 25 tickets, which generally cost $100 each. Ame received no other benefits. What amount of ticket sales revenue should Oz record?
a. $0
b. $ 2,500
c. $47,500
d. $50,000 (7066)

60. Which of the following classifications is required for reporting of expenses by all not-for-profit organizations?
a. Natural classification in the statement of activities or notes to the financial statements
b. Functional classification in the statement of activities or notes to the financial statements
c. Functional classification in the statement of activities and natural classification in a matrix format in a separate statement
d. Functional classification in the statement of activities and natural classification in the notes to the financial statements (6545)

SIMULATIONS

Problem 2 (7 to 13 minutes)

Scenario & Responses | Research Task

Items 1 through 6 represent various commitments and contingencies of Town, Inc. at December 31, Year 4, and events subsequent to December 31, Year 4, but prior to the issuance of the Year 4 financial statements. Town, Inc. is preparing its financial statements for the year ended December 31, Year 4. For each item, select the reporting requirement from the choices below. Place the letter in the space provided.

Reporting Requirement Choices	
A. Accrual only	D. Disclosure only
B. Both accrual and disclosure	N. Neither accrual nor disclosure

A choice may be selected once, more than once, or not at all.

1. ______ On December 1, Year 4, Town was awarded damages of $75,000 in a patent infringement suit it brought against a competitor. The defendant did not appeal the verdict, and payment was received in January Year 5.

2. ______ A former employee of Town has brought a wrongful-dismissal suit against Town. Town's lawyers believe the suit to be without merit.

3. ______ At December 31, Year 4, Town had outstanding purchase orders in the ordinary course of business for purchase of a raw material to be used in its manufacturing process. The market price is currently higher than the purchase price and is not anticipated to change within the next year.

4. ______ A government contract completed during Year 4 is subject to renegotiation. Although Town estimates that it is reasonably possible that a refund of approximately $200,000-$300,000 may be required by the government, it does not wish to publicize this possibility.

5. ______ Town has been notified by a governmental agency that it will be held responsible for the cleanup of toxic materials at a site where Town formerly conducted operations. Town estimates that it is probable that its share of remedial action will be approximately $500,000.

6. ______ On January 5, Year 5, Town redeemed its outstanding bonds and issued new bonds with a lower rate of interest. The reacquisition price was in excess of the carrying amount of the bonds. (6152)

Scenario & Responses | Research Task

Research Question: An estimated loss from a loss contingency shall be accrued by a charge to income if both of what conditions are met?

Paragraph Reference Answer: ______________

Problem 3 (30 to 40 minutes)

Scenario	Schedule of Interest Expense	Essay	Research Task

Chris Green, CPA, is auditing Rayne Co.'s year 2 financial statements. The controller, Dunn, has provided Green with the following information:

- At December 31, year 1, Rayne had a note payable to Federal Bank with a balance of $90,000. The annual principal payment of $10,000, plus 8% interest on the unpaid balance, was paid when due on March 31, year 2.
- On January 2, year 2, Rayne leased two automobiles for executive use under a capital lease. Five annual lease payments of $15,000 are due beginning January 3, year 2. Rayne's incremental borrowing rate on the date of the lease was 11% and the lessor's implicit rate, which was known by Rayne, was 10%. The lease was properly recorded at $62,500, before the first payment was made.
- On July 1, year 2, Rayne received proceeds of $538,000 from a $500,000 bond issuance. The bonds mature in 15 years and interest of 11% is payable semiannually on June 30 and December 31. The bonds were issued at a price to yield investors 10%. Rayne uses the effective interest method to amortize bond premium.
- Dunn has prepared a schedule of all differences between financial statement and income tax return income. Dunn believes that as a result of pending legislation, the enacted tax rate at December 31, year 2, will be increased for year 3. Dunn is uncertain which differences to include and which rates to apply in computing deferred taxes under FASB 109, *Accounting for Income Taxes.* Dunn has requested an overview of FASB 109 from Green. (4975)

Scenario	Schedule of Interest Expense	Essay	Research Task

Prepare a schedule of interest expense for the year ended December 31, year 2.

Rayne Co.
Schedule of Interest Expense
For the Year Ended December 31, Year 2

Note payable	
Capital lease obligation	
Bonds payable	
Total interest expense	

Scenario	Schedule of Interest Expense	Essay	Research Task

Prepare a brief memo to Dunn from Green:

- Identifying the objectives of accounting for income taxes,
- Defining temporary differences,
- Explaining how to measure deferred tax assets and liabilities, and
- Explaining how to measure deferred income tax expense or benefit.

Scenario | Schedule of Interest Expense | Essay | Research Task

Research Question: In which part of the income statement should deferred tax liabilities and assets be reported?

Paragraph Reference Answer: ____________

ANSWERS TO MULTIPLE CHOICE QUESTIONS

Solution 1:

1.	d	11.	a	21.	b	31.	b	41.	c	51.	c
2.	b	12.	b	22.	d	32.	b	42.	d	52.	d
3.	b	13.	c	23.	a	33.	d	43.	c	53.	c
4.	b	14.	a	24.	b	34.	a	44.	b	54.	b
5.	d	15.	b	25.	c	35.	c	45.	b	55.	a
6.	b	16.	d	26.	a	36.	c	46.	b	56.	c
7.	d	17.	d	27.	b	37.	c	47.	b	57.	d
8.	a	18.	c	28.	a	38.	c	48.	b	58.	d
9.	b	19.	d	29.	a	39.	c	49.	a	59.	b
10.	c	20.	a	30.	b	40.	c	50.	c	60.	b

SIMULATION SOLUTIONS

Solution 2:

Research: FAS 5, Par. 8

1. B
2. N
3. N
4. D
5. B
6. D

(Ch 7, Problem 4)

Solution 3:

Research: FAS 109, Par. 27

1. $6,600
2. $4,750
3. $26,900
4. $38,250

Memo: See page 13-54 for Essay Solution
(Ch 13, Problem 4)

EXPLANATIONS OF ANSWERS

The editors strongly recommend that candidates **not** spend much time on the answers to specific questions that they answered incorrectly on the diagnostic exam, particularly at the beginning of their review. Instead, study the related chapter.

PERFORMANCE BY TOPICS

Diagnostic exam question numbers corresponding to each chapter of the Financial Accounting & Reporting text are listed below. To assess your preparedness for the CPA exam, record the number and percentage of questions you correctly answered in each topic area. Multiple choice questions are worth one point. The multiple choice question point distribution (not counting the simulations) approximates that of the exam.

The numbers in parenthesis refer to similar question numbers and corresponding explanations in the related chapters. We strongly recommend that candidates not spend much time on the answers to specific questions that they answered incorrectly on the diagnostic exam, particularly at the beginning of their review. Instead, study all of the related chapter.

Chapter 1: Overview

Question #	Correct √
1 (6)	
2 (11)	
# Points	2
# Correct	________
% Correct	________

Chapter 2: Cash, Marketable Securities & Receivables

Question #	Correct √
3 (67)	
4 (72)	
5 (22)	
# Points	3
# Correct	________
% Correct	________

Chapter 3: Inventory

Question #	Correct √
6 (38)	
7 (2)	
8 (37)	
# Points	3
# Correct	________
% Correct	________

Chapter 4: Property, Plant & Equipment

Question #	Correct √
9 (1)	
10 (21)	
11 (10)	
# Points	3
# Correct	________
% Correct	________

Chapter 5: Intangible Assets, R&D Costs & Other Assets

Question #	Correct √
12 (23)	
13 (12)	
# Points	2
# Correct	________
% Correct	________

Chapter 6: Bonds

Question #	Correct √
14 (19)	
15 (10)	
16 (28)	
# Points	3
# Correct	________
% Correct	________

Chapter 7: Liabilities

Question #	Correct √
17 (33)	
18 (40)	
19 (58)	
20 (46)	
# Points	4
# Correct	________
% Correct	________

Chapter 8: Leases

Question #	Correct √
21 (30)	
22 (20)	
23 (25)	
# Points	3
# Correct	________
% Correct	________

Chapter 9: Postemployment Benefits

Question #	Correct √
24 (7)	
25 (31)	
26 (32)	
# Points	3
# Correct	________
% Correct	________

Chapter 10: Owners' Equity

Question #	Correct √
27 (26)	
28 (33)	
29 (92)	
# Points	3
# Correct	________
% Correct	________

Chapter 11: Reporting the Results of Operations

Question #	Correct √
30 (75)	
31 (40)	
32 (9)	
33 (28)	
# Points	4
# Correct	________
% Correct	________

Chapter 12: Reporting: Special Areas

Question #	Correct √
34 (23)	
35 (44)	
36 (46)	
# Points	3
# Correct	________
% Correct	________

Chapter 13: Accounting for Income Taxes

Question #	Correct √
37 (50)	
38 (1)	
39 (27)	
# Points	3
# Correct	________
% Correct	________

Chapter 14: Statement of Cash Flows

Question #	Correct √
40 (21)	
41 (42)	
42 (37)	
# Points	3
# Correct	________
% Correct	________

Chapter 15: Financial Statement Analysis

Question #	Correct √
43 (21)	
44 (25)	
45 (16)	
# Points	3
# Correct	________
% Correct	________

Chapter 16: Foreign Operations

Question #	Correct √
46 (14)	
# Points	1
# Correct	________
% Correct	________

Chapter 17: Consolidated Financial Statements

Question #	Correct √
47 (19)	
48 (20)	
49 (30)	
# Points	3
# Correct	________
% Correct	________

Chapter 18: Governmental Overview

Question #	Correct √
50 (38)	
51 (35)	
52 (23)	
# Points	3
# Correct	________
% Correct	________

Chapter 19: Governmental Funds & Transactions

Question #	Correct √
53 (10)	
54 (21)	
55 (24)	
# Points	3
# Correct	________
% Correct	________

Chapter 20: Nonprofit Accounting

Question #	Correct √
56 (37)	
57 (34)	
58 (50)	
59 (63)	
60 (7)	
# Points	5
# Correct	________
% Correct	________

PERFORMANCE BY AICPA CONTENT SPECIFICATIONS OUTLINE

Diagnostic exam question numbers corresponding to each section of the AICPA Financial Accounting and Reporting Content Specifications Outline are listed below. To assess your preparedness for the CPA exam, record the number and percentage of questions you correctly answered in each topic area. To simplify the self-evaluation, the simulations are excluded from the Performance By AICPA Content Specifications Outline. Multiple choice questions are worth one point. The multiple choice question point distribution (not counting the simulations) approximates that of the exam.

CSO I: Concepts and Standards for Financial Statements (17% - 23%)

Question #	Correct √
1	
2	
16	
36	
40	
41	
43	
44	
47	
48	
49	
# Points	11
# Correct	______
% Correct	______

CSO II: Typical Items: Recognition, Measurement, Valuation, and Presentation in Financial Statements in Conformity With GAAP (27% - 33%)

Question #	Correct √
3	
4	
5	
6	
7	
8	
9	
10	
11	
12	
14	
15	
18	
19	
27	
28	
29	
34	
35	
# Points	19
# Correct	______
% Correct	______

CSO III: Specific Types of Transactions and Events: Recognition, Measurement, Valuation, and Presentation in Financial Statements in Conformity With GAAP (27% - 33%)

Question #	Correct √
13	
17	
20	
21	
22	
23	
24	
25	
26	
30	
31	
32	
33	
37	
38	
39	
42	
45	
46	
# Points	19
# Correct	______
% Correct	______

CSO IV: Accounting and Reporting for Governmental Entities (8% - 12%)

Question #	Correct √
50	
51	
52	
53	
54	
55	
# Points	6
# Correct	______
% Correct	______

CSO V: Accounting and Reporting for Nongovernmental Not-for-Profit Organizations (8% - 12%)

Question #	Correct √
56	
57	
58	
59	
60	
# Points	5
# Correct	______
% Correct	______

THE NATURE OF THE COMPUTER-BASED CPA EXAM

See the **Practical Advice** section of this volume for detailed information about the types of questions and point value of various topics.

The editors strongly encourage candidates to visit the AICPA's website (www.cpa-exam.org) and practice the free tutorial and sample exam there. The multiple choice questions in this book include letters (a, b, c, d, etc.) next to the response options. On the actual exam, these will be radio buttons, rather than letters. Candidates will click on the radio button corresponding to their answer to indicate their selection.

What will the actual exam be like? The questions throughout this book are either former exam questions or based on former exam questions. General predictions of future exams can be made based on previously disclosed exams. Specific predictions about which topics will be stressed on a particular candidate's exam are mere speculation and rather useless. (The examiners try not to make the exam predictable.) Don't waste time with mere speculation; instead, study and be prepared!

CHANGE ALERTS

SFAS 157, Fair Value Measurements (Issued 9/06)

In September 2006, the FASB issued Statement of Financial Accounting Standard No. 157, *Fair Value Measurements*.

The objective of this Statement is to increase consistency and comparability in fair value measurements and to expand disclosures about fair value measurements. Specifically, it defines fair value, establishes a framework for measuring fair value in generally accepted accounting principles (GAAP), and expands disclosures about fair value measurements.

This Statement is effective for financial statements issued for fiscal years beginning after November 15, 2007, and interim periods within those fiscal years. Early application is encouraged, provided that the reporting entity has not yet issued financial statements for that fiscal year, including any financial statements for an interim period within that fiscal year.

Editor's Note: Accounting and auditing pronouncements are eligible to be tested on the Uniform CPA Examination in the testing window beginning six months after an announcement's effective date, unless early application is permitted. When early application is permitted, the new pronouncement is eligible to be tested in the window beginning six months after the issuance date. The material in this Statement would be eligible for testing in the April/May 2007 test cycle.

CHAPTER 1

OVERVIEW

I. **Accounting Environment** ... 1-2
- A. Financial Accounting ... 1-2
- B. Underlying Environmental Assumptions ... 1-2
- C. Basic Accounting Principles ... 1-2
- D. Accounting Model ... 1-3

II. **Financial Position—Balance Sheet** ... 1-4
- A. Description ... 1-4
- B. Format ... 1-4
- C. Valuation ... 1-5
- D. Fair Value Measurements (SFAS 157) ... 1-6
- E. Off-Balance-Sheet Risk ... 1-8

III. **Reporting of Operations—Income Statement** ... 1-9
- A. Description ... 1-9
- B. Format ... 1-9
- C. Elements ... 1-9
- D. Statement of Retained Earnings ... 1-10

IV. **Statement of Comprehensive Income** ... 1-10
- A. Description ... 1-10
- B. Format ... 1-11

V. **Statement of Cash Flows** ... 1-11
- A. Description ... 1-11
- B. Format ... 1-11

VI. **Statements of Financial Accounting Concepts** ... 1-12
- A. Objectives ... 1-12
- B. *Objectives of Financial Reporting by Business Enterprises* (SFAC 1) ... 1-12
- C. *Qualitative Characteristics of Accounting Information* (SFAC 2) ... 1-12
- D. *Recognition & Measurement in Financial Statements of Business Enterprises* (SFAC 5) ... 1-15
- E. *Elements of Financial Statements* (SFAC 6) ... 1-16
- F. *Using Cash Flow Information & Present Value in Accounting Measurements* (SFAC 7) ... 1-17

VII. **Authority of Pronouncements** ... 1-17
- A. Accounting Standard-Setting Bodies & Their Pronouncements ... 1-17
- B. GAAP Hierarchy ... 1-18

EXAM COVERAGE: Historically, exam coverage of the topics in Chapter 1 has been 1 to 3 percent of the FAR section. More information regarding exam coverage is included in Appendix B, *Practical Advice*.

CHAPTER 1

OVERVIEW

I. Accounting Environment

A. Financial Accounting

Accounting is a service activity. Its function is to provide quantitative information, primarily financial in nature, about economic entities that is intended to be useful in making economic decisions—in making reasoned choices among alternative courses of action. These objectives are met primarily by the presentation of financial statements. Financial statements purport to present in a condensed form the economic events affecting an entity during a specific period of time and the cumulative effect of such events. The most important criterion to meet in a financial statement presentation is that the information provided be useful for decision making. Examples of useful information include information that helps a user of the financial statements predict cash flows and earning power, as well as information that increases management's ability to use resources efficiently and to understand contingencies that may have an effect on future operations.

B. Underlying Environmental Assumptions

Accounting operates in an environment almost as varied as the many types of entities which accounting serves. To provide a basis for comparison, it has been necessary to formulate certain underlying environmental assumptions on which financial accounting theory is based. The most important of these assumptions are as follows:

1. **Economic Entity** In order to properly report those economic events affecting an entity, the specific economic entity must be defined and separated from other entities. A distinction is also made between a business concern and its owners.

2. **Going Concern** The business is not expected to liquidate in the near future. Where there is a reasonable expectation of an upcoming liquidation, the going concern assumption is abandoned. Liquidation accounting, characterized by the use of net realizable values rather than historical costs, is then employed.

3. **Unit-of-Measure** Monetary units are used for the measurement and reporting of economic activity. Costs incurred at different points in time are intermingled in the accounts and, thus, it must be assumed that the purchasing power of the dollar remains constant over time. Inflation makes this assumption questionable. SFAS 89, *Financial Reporting and Changing Prices,* encourages enterprises to issue voluntary supplementary reports based on current costs and dollars of constant purchasing power. This information is furnished in addition to the usual historical cost financial statements.

4. **Periodicity** This assumption recognizes the necessity of providing financial accounting information on a periodic, timely basis, so that it is useful in decision making.

C. Basic Accounting Principles

Based upon these underlying environmental assumptions, a set of basic accounting principles has evolved. These assumptions and principles are implemented through the use of the basic accounting model, upon which the accounting for most profit-oriented entities is based. This model is composed of three main sub-models, each focusing on a different aspect of the economic activities of an enterprise.

1. **Historical Cost** Assets acquired, as well as liabilities incurred by an enterprise, are recorded at cost. Cost is generally defined as the cash equivalent amount that would be paid in an

arm's-length transaction. When costs benefit more than one period, they are apportioned among the periods benefited through depreciation or amortization.

2. **Revenue Recognition** Revenue generally is recognized when both of the following conditions are met:

   a. The earnings process is complete or virtually complete.

   b. An exchange has taken place. This implies that revenues are usually recognized at the point of sale. Under certain conditions, however, revenue recognition takes place on a different basis, such as a percentage of completion, production, installment, or cost recovery basis.

3. **Matching** For income to be stated fairly, all expenses incurred in generating the revenues for a period must be recognized in that same period.

4. **Objectivity** Accounting data should be both (a) objectively determined and (b) verifiable. While this does not preclude the use of estimates, they must be verifiable in the sense that an independent, knowledgeable person would find such estimates reasonable.

5. **Materiality** The relative importance of data, the cost-benefit relationship of additional accuracy, and the possible confusion resulting from the use of too much detail are considerations that must be weighed in determining the materiality of accounting information. When an item is immaterial, good accounting theory can be abandoned.

6. **Consistency** The usefulness of accounting information is enhanced when the information is presented in a manner consistent with that used in prior periods. This provides for interperiod comparability and the identification of trends. Consistency in the application of accounting principles also prevents income manipulation by management.

7. **Full Disclosure** Financial statements should be presented in a manner that will reasonably assure complete and understandable communication of all relevant accounting information useful for decision making. When the nature of relevant information is such that it cannot appear in the accounts, this principle dictates that such relevant information be included in the accompanying notes to the financial statements.

8. **Conservatism** Where use of the most appropriate accounting treatment is uncertain, when making estimates, or when data conflicts, the favored accounting treatment should be that which understates rather than overstates income or net assets. Conservatism, however, should not be used in place of a more conceptually sound approach when the difference in results is of a material nature.

D. Accounting Model

1. **Financial Position** Assets = Liabilities + Owners' equity. The financial position sub-model purports to present the economic resources, the economic obligations, and the resulting residual interest in the assets of the entity to its owners. This information is reported by means of a balance sheet.

2. **Results of Operations** Revenues – Expenses = Net income. The purpose of the results of operations sub-model is to report on the relative success of the profit-directed activities of an entity. The revenues obtained through the sale of goods and services are compared to the expenses incurred in providing those goods and services. The resulting difference is the operating income or loss for the period. To arrive at net income, gains, losses, and the effect of accounting changes must be incorporated into the sub-model. The results of operations sub-model is formally represented by the income statement and the statement of changes in comprehensive income.

3. **Statement of Cash Flows** Cash flows from operating activities +(–) Cash flows from investing activities +(–) Cash flows from financing activities = Change in cash. The objective of this sub-model is to provide information about the cash receipts and cash payments of an entity during the period. The statement of cash flows reports the net cash provided or used by operating, investing, and financing activities, and the aggregate effect of those flows on cash during the period.

II. Financial Position—Balance Sheet

A. Description

The balance sheet presents the assets, liabilities, and owners' equity of an entity at a specific point in time, measured in conformity with generally accepted accounting principles (GAAP).

B. Format

The formats most commonly used are the account format and the report format.

Exhibit 1 ▸ Balance Sheet Formats (assumed amounts)

Account Format		Report Format	
Assets $50,000	Liabilities $35,000	Assets	$50,000
		Liabilities	$35,000
	Owners' equity $15,000	Owners' equity	$15,000

1. **Assets** SFAC 6 defines assets as probable future economic benefits obtained or controlled by a particular entity as a result of past transactions or events. Assets are classified in their order of liquidity and intended use.

   a. **Current Assets** Current assets are assets that are reasonably expected to be converted into cash or used during the normal operating cycle of the business or one year, whichever is longer.

   b. **Investments** Investments are assets that are held for control, appreciation, regular income, or a combination of the above. Examples include stocks, bonds, subsidiaries, land held as a future plant site, and the cash surrender value of life insurance. Also in this category are special purpose funds such as bond sinking funds and plant expansion funds.

   c. **Operational Assets** Operational assets are assets that are directly used by the enterprise in generating revenues.

   d. **Valuation Accounts** Valuation accounts are reductions or increases in an asset account to reflect adjustments beyond the historical cost or carrying amount of the asset. Valuation accounts are part of the related asset; they are neither assets nor liabilities in their own right.

2. **Liabilities** SFAC 6 defines liabilities as probable future sacrifices of economic benefits arising from present obligations of a particular entity to transfer assets or provide services to other entities in the future as a result of past transactions or events. Liabilities are classified according to their due date as either current or long-term.

   a. **Current Liabilities** Current liabilities are obligations whose liquidation is expected to require the use of existing current assets or the creation of other current liabilities.

   b. **Long-Term Liabilities** Long-term liabilities are obligations not requiring the use of existing current assets or the creation of current liabilities for their extinguishment.

c. **Valuation Accounts** Valuation accounts may increase or decrease the carrying amount of a liability. Examples include the premium or discount on outstanding bonds payable. Valuation accounts are part of the related liability; they are neither assets nor liabilities in their own right.

3. **Owners' Equity** SFAC 6 defines owners' equity as the residual interest in the assets of an entity that remains after deducting its liabilities.

a. **Equity of Business Enterprises** An equity interest derives its value from being a potential source of distribution of cash or other assets to its owner. In case of liquidation, all liabilities must be satisfied first.

(1) Equity is originally created by the initial investment of the enterprise owners. Subsequent investments by the owners, or the admission of new owners, increase equity, while distributions to owners decrease it.

(2) Equity is also changed as a result of the operating activities of the enterprise and other events and circumstances affecting it. This combined effect constitutes comprehensive income.

Financial position
Results of operations
Stat of cash flows.

b. **Proprietorship** Proprietorship's equity consists of a single proprietor's equity account.

c. **Partnership** Partnership's equity consists of one capital account for each partner. Each individual partner's capital account records her/his investment and subsequent allocations of income and withdrawals.

d. **Corporation** Corporation's equity consists of several accounts that are segregated according to source.

(1) **Contributed Capital** Par or stated value represents minimum legal required capital as determined by articles of incorporation and state law. Additional paid-in capital reflects the amount received in excess of the par or stated value of the stock at the time of issuance.

(2) **Retained Earnings** Retained earnings are accumulated earnings less losses and dividends. They represent resources retained by the entity for use in expansion and growth.

(3) **Accumulated Other Comprehensive Income** SFAS 115, *Accounting for Certain Investments in Debt and Equity Securities,* requires adjustments to accumulated other comprehensive income (OCI) for unrealized gains and losses on available-for-sale securities. SFAS 52, *Foreign Currency Translation,* also requires that certain translation adjustments be reported in OCI. In addition, SFAS 87, *Employers' Accounting for Pensions,* also requires that adjustments from recognizing certain additional pension liabilities be reported in OCI.

e. **Net Assets** The net assets of a nonprofit organization represent a residual, but are not an ownership interest.

C. Valuation

1. Assets

a. **Historical Cost** The acquisition cost less depreciation or amortization to date. While this method of valuation is both verifiable and systematic, it often fails to reflect either the current value of the asset or changes due to the purchasing power of the dollar.

b. **Market Value** The hypothetical selling price that could be obtained in an arm's-length transaction.

c. **Replacement Cost** Attempts to value assets on the basis of their current replacement cost. Current replacement cost is defined as the price of a new, similar item after allowance for use and depreciation. This method is used in the primary financial statements only in certain cases where the utility of inventory items has diminished.

d. **Price-Level Adjusted** Historical cost adjusted to reflect changes in the general purchasing power of the dollar.

e. **Discounted Cash Flows** Valuation of assets in terms of the present value of the future benefits associated with the ownership of the asset. Notes receivable and bond investments are valued at present value upon acquisition.

2. **Liabilities** Liabilities are valued at their current debt equivalent. For long-term liabilities this implies discounting to their present value the future sums required to satisfy the liability. Due to materiality considerations, short-term liabilities are usually presented at their face amount.

3. **Owners' Equity** The valuation of owners' equity depends on the amounts presented for assets and liabilities.

D. **Fair Value Measurements (SFAS 157)**
SFAS 157 defines fair value, establishes a framework for measuring fair value, and expands disclosures about fair value measurements

1. **Definition** Fair value is the price that would be received to sell an asset or paid to transfer a liability in an orderly transaction between market participants at the measurement date.

2. **Assumptions**

a. **Basic** The measurement should consider attributes particular to the asset or liability.

b. **Orderly Transaction** The exchange is a transaction that assumes exposure to the market for a period prior to the measurement date to allow for marketing activities that are usual and customary for transactions involving such assets or liabilities; it is not a forced transaction (for example, a forced liquidation or distress sale).

c. **Market** The transaction occurs in the principle market for the asset or liability, or in the absence of such, the most advantageous market for the asset or liability The principle market is the market with the greatest volume and level of activity for the asset or liability. The most advantageous market is the market with the price that maximizes the amount that would be received for the asset or minimizes the amount that would be paid to transfer the liability.

d. **Price** The price in the market used to measure the fair value of the asset or liability shall not be adjusted for transaction costs. Transaction costs represent the incremental direct costs to sell the asset or transfer the liability and should be accounted for in accordance with the provisions of other accounting pronouncements.

e. **Market Participants** Buyers and sellers in the market for the asset or liability that are independent of the reporting entity, knowledgeable, able to transact for the asset or liability, and willing to transact for the asset or liability (not forced to do so).

f. **Application to Assets** The highest and best use of the asset by market participants, considering the use of the asset that is physically possible, legally permissible, and financially feasible at the measurement date. The highest and best use of the asset establishes the valuation premise used to measure the fair value of the asset.

(1) **In-use** The highest and best use of the asset is in-use if the asset would provide maximum value to market participants principally through its use in combination with other assets as a group.

(2) **In-exchange** The highest and best use of the asset is in-exchange if the asset would provide maximum value to market participants principally on a stand-alone basis.

g. **Application to Liabilities** The liability is transferred to a market participant at the measurement date and the nonperformance risk relating to that liability is the same before and after its transfer. Nonperformance risk refers to the risk that the obligation will not be fulfilled and affects the value at which the liability is transferred.

3. **Initial Recognition** The transaction price represents the price paid to acquire an asset or received to assume a liability, an entry price. In contrast, the fair value of the asset or liability represents the price that would be received to sell the asset or paid to transfer the liability, an exit price. Conceptually entry and exit prices are different, but in many cases the transaction price will equal the exit price and, therefore, represent the value of the asset or liability at initial recognition.

4. **Valuation Techniques** Valuation techniques consistent with the market approach, income approach, and/or cost approach shall be used to measure fair value. The technique(s) used shall be the best appropriate in the circumstance and for which sufficient data are available. The valuation techniques used to measure fair value shall be consistently applied.

a. **Market Approach** The market approach uses prices and other relevant information generated by market transactions involving identical or comparable assets or liabilities.

b. **Income Approach** The income approach uses valuation techniques to convert future amounts to a single present amount. The measurement is based on the value indicated by current market expectations about those future amounts.

c. **Cost Approach** The cost approach is based on the amount that currently would be required to replace the service capacity of an asset, often referred to as the current replacement cost.

5. **Inputs to Valuation Techniques** There are two types of inputs to valuation techniques, observable and unobservable. Observable inputs are those that reflect the assumptions market participants would use in pricing the asset or liability based on market data obtained from sources independent of the reporting entity. Unobservable inputs are those that reflect the entity's own assumptions about the assumptions the market participants would use in pricing the asset or liability based on the best information available in the circumstances.

6. **Fair Value Hierarchy** To increase consistency and comparability in fair value measurements and related disclosures, the fair value hierarchy prioritizes the inputs to valuation techniques used to measure fair value into three broad categories. The highest priority, Level 1, is given to quoted prices in active markets for identical assets or liabilities. The lowest priority, Level 3, is given to unobservable inputs. Level 2 inputs are other than quoted prices included within Level 1 that are observable for the asset or liability, either directly or indirectly.

7. **Bid and Ask Prices** If an input used to measure fair value is based on bid and ask prices, the price within the bid-ask spread that is most representative of fair value in the circumstances shall be used to measure fair value, regardless of which level in the fair value hierarchy the input falls. This does not preclude the use of mid-market pricing or other pricing conventions as a practical expedient for fair value measurement in a bid-ask spread.

8. **Disclosures** The reporting entity shall disclose information that enables users of its financial statements to assess the inputs used to develop fair value. To meet that objective, the reporting entity shall disclose information for each interim and annual period separately for each category of assets and liabilities. The reporting entity is encouraged, but not required, to combine the fair value information disclosed under SFAS 157 with the fair value information disclosed under other accounting pronouncements.

a. **Recurring Basis** For assets and liabilities that are measured at fair value on a recurring basis in periods subsequent to initial recognition and for recurring fair value measurements using significant unobservable inputs, the reporting entity shall disclose information that enables users of its financial statements to assess the effect of the measurements on earnings for the period. Disclosures specific to assets and liabilities measured on a recurring basis include:

(1) The fair value measurements at the reporting date

(2) The level within the fair value hierarchy in which the fair value measurements in their entirety fall, segregating fair value measurements using quoted prices in active markets for identical assets or liabilities (Level 1), significant other observable inputs (Level 2), and significant unobservable inputs (Level 3)

(3) For fair value measurements using significant unobservable inputs (Level 3), a reconciliation of the beginning and ending balances, separately presenting changes during the period attributable to the following:

(a) Total realized and unrealized gains or losses for the period

(b) Purchases, sales, issuances, and settlements (net)

(c) Transfers in and/or out of Level 3

(4) The amount of total gains or losses for the period included in earnings (or changes in net assets) that are attributable to the change in unrealized gains or losses relating to those assets and liabilities still held at the reporting date and a description of where those unrealized gains or losses are reported in the statement of income (or activities).

(5) In annual periods only, the valuation techniques(s) used to measure fair value and a discussion of any changes in valuation techniques during the period.

b. **Nonrecurring Basis** For assets and liabilities that are measured at fair value on a nonrecurring basis in periods subsequent to initial recognition, the reporting entity shall disclose the following information:

(1) The fair value measurements recorded during the period and the reasons for the measurements

(2) The level within the fair value hierarchy in which the fair value measurements in their entirety fall, segregating fair value measurements using quoted prices in active markets for identical assets or liabilities (Level 1), significant other observable inputs (Level 2), and significant unobservable inputs (Level 3)

(3) For fair value measurements using significant unobservable inputs (Level 3), a description of the inputs and the information used to develop inputs

(4) In annual periods only, the valuation techniques(s) used to measure fair value and a discussion of any changes in valuation techniques used to measure similar assets and/or liabilities in prior periods.

E. Off-Balance-Sheet Risk

Off-balance-sheet risk is the risk of accounting loss from a financial instrument that exceeds the amount recognized for the instrument in the balance sheet. Examples include standby loan commitments written, options, letters of credit, and noncancelable operating leases with future minimum lease commitments. Recent pronouncements attempt to eliminate off-balance-sheet risk by requiring that more risks are reflected within the balance sheet.

III. Reporting of Operations—Income Statement

A. Description

The income statement for a period presents the revenues, expenses, gains, losses, and net income (net loss) recognized during the period and thereby presents an indication, in conformity with GAAP, of the results of the enterprise's profit-directed activities during the period.

B. Format

Two basic formats are used to present the income statement.

1. **Single-Step Format** Focuses on two classifications of items: revenues and expenses. All revenues are added together to arrive at a total revenue figure. The sum of all expenses is subtracted from this figure. The resultant amount is "Income Before Extraordinary Items."

2. **Multiple-Step Format** Focuses on multiple classifications of revenue and expense items. This format is characterized by several intermediate subtotals, such as gross margin and operating income, which together produce "Income Before Extraordinary Items."

Exhibit 2 ▸ Income Statement Formats (assumed amounts)

Single-Step Format

Revenues:		
Sales revenue	$500,000	
Other revenues, gains	20,000	
Total revenues		$520,000
Expenses:		
CGS	350,000	
Selling	80,000	
Administrative	30,000	
Other expenses, losses	10,000	
Income taxes	5,000	
Total expenses		475,000
Income from continuing operations		45,000
Extraordinary gain, net of $1,200 applicable taxes		7,000
Net income		$ 52,000

Multiple-Step Format

Net sales	$500,000	
Less CGS	350,000	
Gross margin		$150,000
Less operating exp.		
Selling	80,000	
Administrative	30,000	
Total operating exp.		110,000
Operating income		40,000
Other revenues, gain	20,000	
Other exp., losses	10,000	10,000
Income from continuing operations before taxes		50,000
Income taxes		5,000
Income from continuing operations		45,000
Extraordinary gain, net of $1,200 applicable taxes		7,000
Net income		$ 52,000

C. Elements

1. **Revenues** Revenues are inflows or other enhancements of assets of an entity or settlements of its liabilities (or a combination of both) during a period from delivering or producing goods, rendering services, or other activities that constitute the entity's ongoing major or central operations.

   a. **Inflows** Revenues represent actual or expected cash inflows (or equivalents) resulting from the entity's major or central operations.

   b. **Recognition** Revenues usually are recognized at the point of sale, in conformity with the basic accounting principle of revenue realization. Several exceptions to this principle are permitted under very specific circumstances.

2. **Expenses** Expenses are outflows or other use of assets or incurrence of liabilities (or a combination of both) from delivering or producing goods, rendering services, or carrying out other activities that constitute the entity's ongoing major or central operations during a period. Expenses represent actual or expected cash outflows (or equivalents) resulting from the

entity's major or central operations. Expenses generally are recognized in accordance with one of three principles.

a. **Associating Cause and Effect** Some costs are presumed to be directly related to specific revenues. Examples are cost of goods sold and sales commissions.

b. **Systematic and Rational Allocation** If a direct association between costs and revenues is not apparent, costs must be allocated on a systematic and rational basis among the periods benefited. Depreciation of fixed assets, amortization of intangible assets, and allocation of prepaid rent and insurance are applications of this principle.

c. **Immediate Recognition** Costs that are deemed to provide no discernible future benefits are expensed in the current period. Likewise, costs recorded as assets in prior periods that no longer have discernible benefits are expensed in the current period.

3. **Gains and Losses** Gains and losses are defined by SFAC 6 as increases (or decreases) in equity—i.e., net assets—from peripheral or incidental transactions of an entity and from all other transactions and other events and circumstances affecting the entity during a period, except those that result from revenues (expenses) or investments (withdrawals) by owners.

a. **Operating** Gains and losses related to the business enterprise's central operations (e.g., write-down of inventory to lower of cost or market) are classified as operating.

b. **Nonoperating** Gains and loses not attributable to operations are classified as nonoperating.

D. Statement of Retained Earnings

This statement is presented as a supplement to the income statement and serves as a link between beginning and ending retained earnings.

Exhibit 3 ▸ Statement of Retained Earnings

Beginning balance, as reported	$ XXX
+/– Prior period adjustments, net of $______ tax	XXX
Beginning balance, as adjusted	XXX
+ Net income (– Net loss)	XXX
– Dividends	(XXX)
Ending balance	$ XXX

IV. Statement of Comprehensive Income

A. Description

SFAC 6 defines comprehensive income as "the change in equity of a business enterprise during a period from transactions and other events and circumstances from nonowner sources." SFAS 130, *Reporting Comprehensive Income,* requires that comprehensive income be displayed prominently within a financial statement in a full set of general-purpose financial statements. Comprehensive income must be shown on the face of a statement, not just in the notes to the statements.

1. Comprehensive income includes all changes in equity during a period except those resulting from investments by owners and distributions to owners.

2. Over the life of the business, comprehensive income equals the net difference between cash receipts and outlays, excluding cash investments by owners and cash distributions to owners, regardless of whether cash or accrual accounting is used.

3. SFAS 130 divides comprehensive income into the components of net income and other comprehensive income.

4. Other comprehensive income (OCI) refers to revenues, expenses, gains, and losses that are included in comprehensive income, but excluded from net income.

B. Format

There are three acceptable means of reporting comprehensive income: a statement of income and comprehensive income, a statement of income and a separate statement of comprehensive income, and a statement of changes in equity.

1. **Classification** Comprehensive income is comprised of two components, net income and other comprehensive income. An entity must classify items of other comprehensive income by their nature: foreign currency items, minimum pension liability adjustments, unrealized gains and losses on certain investments in debt and equity securities, and certain gains and losses on hedging activities.

2. **Accumulated Balance of OCI** An entity must also display the accumulated balance of other comprehensive income separately from retained earnings and additional paid-in capital in the equity section of a statement of financial position. An entity must disclose accumulated balances for each classification in that separate component of equity on the face of the statement of financial position, in the statement of changes in equity, or in the notes to the financial statements.

Exhibit 4 ▸ Comprehensive Income Reporting (Separate Statement)

Net Income			$XXX
Foreign currency adjustments, net of tax of $XXX		$XXX	
Unrealized holding gain/loss arising during period, net of tax of $XX	$XXX		
Reclassification adjustment, net of tax of $XX, for gain/loss included in net income	XXX		
Unrealized Gain/Loss on Marketable Securities		XXX	
Minimum pension liability adjustment, net of tax of $XX		XXX	
Other Comprehensive Income			XXX
Comprehensive Income			$XXX

V. Statement of Cash Flows

A. Description

SFAS 95, *Statement of Cash Flows,* requires that a statement of cash flows be issued whenever a balance sheet and an income statement are issued. This financial statement provides relevant information about the cash receipts and cash payments of an enterprise during a period.

1. **Classification** The statement of cash flows classifies cash receipts and cash payments resulting from operating, investing, and financing activities.

2. **Noncash Investing and Financing Transactions** Noncash investing and financing transactions are not reported in the statement of cash flows because the statement reports only the effects of operating, investing, and financing activities that directly affect cash flows. If significant, noncash investing and financing transactions are reported in related disclosures.

B. Format

Net cash from operating activities can be determined under either the direct or indirect method. Under the direct approach, operating cash payments are deducted from operating cash receipts, effectively resulting in a cash basis income statement. The indirect approach converts net income to net cash flow from operating activities by adding back noncash charges in the income statement to net income and subtracting noncash credits from net income.

VI. Statements of Financial Accounting Concepts

A. Objectives

Statements of Financial Accounting Concepts (SFACs) are intended by the FASB to set forth objectives and fundamentals that will be the basis for future development of financial accounting and reporting standards. The idea is to create a conceptual framework consisting of coherent interrelated objectives and principles that will lead to consistent standards of accounting and reporting. SFACs, however, do **not** establish standards prescribing accounting procedures or disclosures, nor supersede, amend, or otherwise modify present GAAP. Therefore, SFACs are **not** considered authoritative pronouncements in the context of Rule 203 of the AICPA Code of Professional Conduct. Since their promulgation, SFACs have been a constant, although limited, source of CPA exam questions.

B. *Objectives of Financial Reporting by Business Enterprises* (SFAC 1)

Financial statements are most significant in the scheme of financial reporting. Although financial reporting may consist entirely of financial statements, a financial report may or may not include financial statements.

1. **Limitations** Financial reports are based on information that is expressed in units of money and often are based on approximations or estimations. These expressions document transactions that have already occurred. Given these limitations, financial reporting is simply one element to be considered in a total understanding of a business enterprise.

2. **Benefits vs. Costs** The benefits accruing to the users of financial reports must outweigh the production costs of the reports.

3. **Needs of Users** The objectives of SFAC 1 stem primarily from the needs of external users (e.g., investors and creditors) who lack the authority to prescribe the information they desire. The kind and quality of information needed by investors and creditors is indicative of the kind and quality of information that should generally be helpful to the broad economic community.

4. **Decision Making** The objectives focus on establishing goals for financial reporting that will enable financial reports to aid investors, creditors, and others in making sound economic decisions. The objectives are not meant to determine directly the resolution of those decisions. Users must be willing to expend a reasonable amount of time in order to understand the information and use it properly.

5. **Scope of Information** Financial reports should provide information about an enterprise's economic resources, obligations, and owners' equity. They should provide information concerning financial performance and earnings. Financial reports should indicate how an enterprise obtains and spends cash, how it borrows, and how it distributes dividends. The majority of the wide variety of users of financial information are interested in the capacity of an enterprise to generate favorable cash flow.

6. **Management Performance** Information concerning the performance of management in guiding the enterprise should also be included in financial reporting. Management is responsible for the earnings of an enterprise. Consequently, management's performance can be closely correlated to increases or decreases in earnings. Financial reports, in and of themselves, are limited in their capacity to precisely measure the effect of management policy on the enterprise. Therefore, management is in a unique position to fairly explain and interpret financial reports.

C. *Qualitative Characteristics of Accounting Information* (SFAC 2)

The purpose of SFAC 2 is to examine the characteristics that make accounting information useful for decision making. Once these desired characteristics have been isolated, accountants can choose among alternate accounting methods the one that maximizes these qualitative criteria, subject to cost-benefit and materiality constraints.

1. **Usefulness** Information useful for decision making should be both relevant and reliable.

   a. **Relevance** Information is relevant if it is capable of making a difference in a decision by helping users to form predictions about the outcomes of past, present, and future events or to confirm or correct prior expectations. In other words, relevant information must be timely and must have either predictive or feedback value.

      (1) **Timeliness** Information is timely if it is available to a decision maker before it loses its capacity to influence decisions.

      (2) **Predictive Value** Information has predictive value if it helps users increase the likelihood of correctly forecasting the outcome of past or present events.

      (3) **Feedback Value** Information has feedback value if it enables users to confirm or correct prior expectations.

   b. **Reliability** Information is reliable when it represents what it purports to represent, coupled with an assurance for the user that it has that representational quality. Reliability must often be measured by degrees; information is rarely either absolutely reliable or unreliable. Reliability is increased when—in addition to being representationally faithful—the information is both verifiable and neutral.

      (1) **Representational Faithfulness** Correspondence or agreement between a measure or description and the phenomenon that it purports to represent.

      (2) **Verifiability** Information can be said to be verifiable when a large number of independent observers derive similar results using the same measurement methods.

      (3) **Neutrality** Neutrality means that the information is free from bias towards a predetermined result.

2. **User-Specific Factors** The degree of usefulness of information to individual users—particularly the relevancy of information—may vary according to the specific needs of the user. It is virtually impossible to provide information that will completely satisfy the needs of all users; thus, the information provided usually represents a compromise among the perceived needs of the various users (i.e., general purpose financial statements).

3. **Constraints**

   a. **Cost** In determining the kind and amount of information to be provided, the cost of obtaining the information must be considered. Information is valuable only to the extent that the cost of procuring and analyzing it is less than the benefits derived from its use.

   b. **Materiality** The kind and amount of information to be provided is also restricted by materiality considerations. Information is immaterial if the amounts involved are too small to make a difference in the decision. The concept of materiality applies to both relevance and reliability.

Exhibit 5 ▸ Hierarchy of Accounting Qualities (SFAC 2)

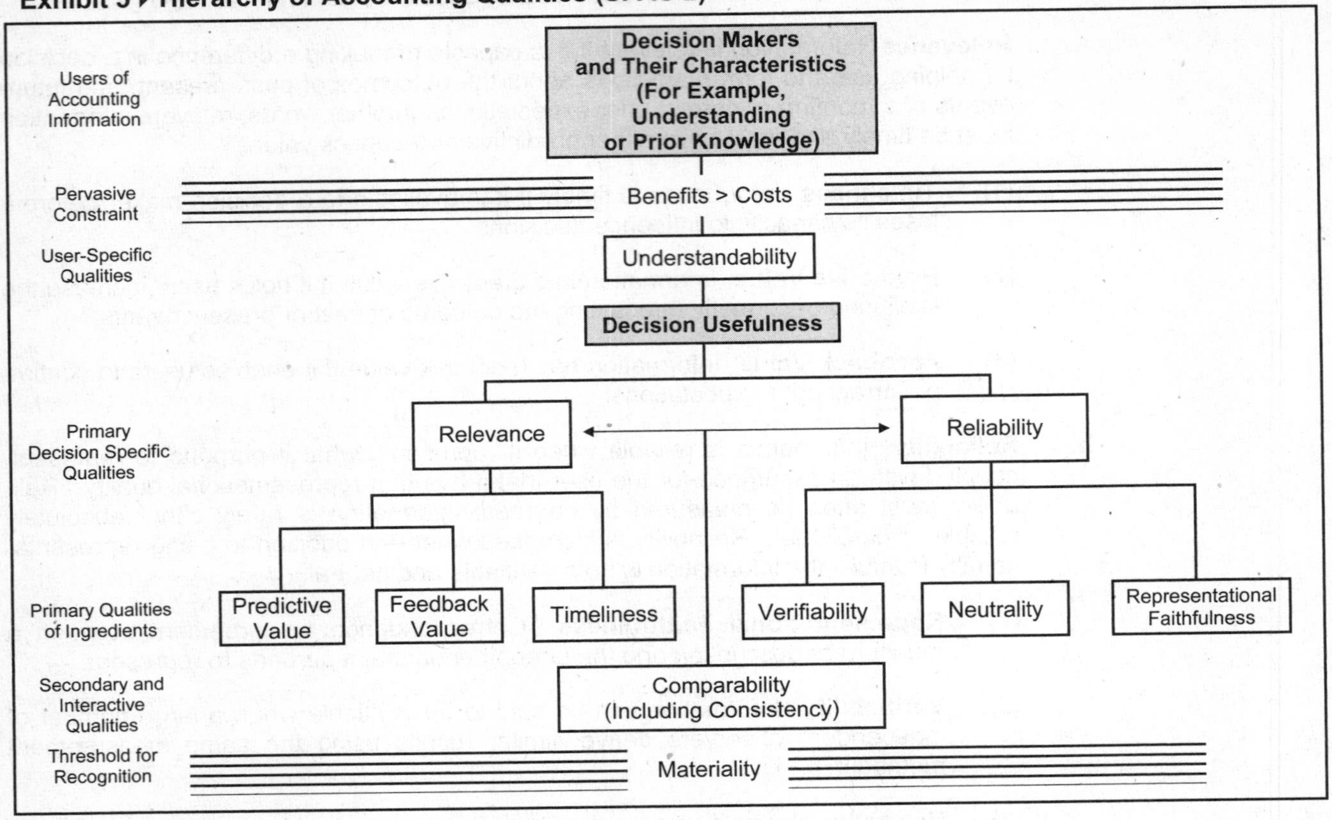

Exhibit 6 ▸ Types of Information Used in Investment, Credit, and Similar Decisions

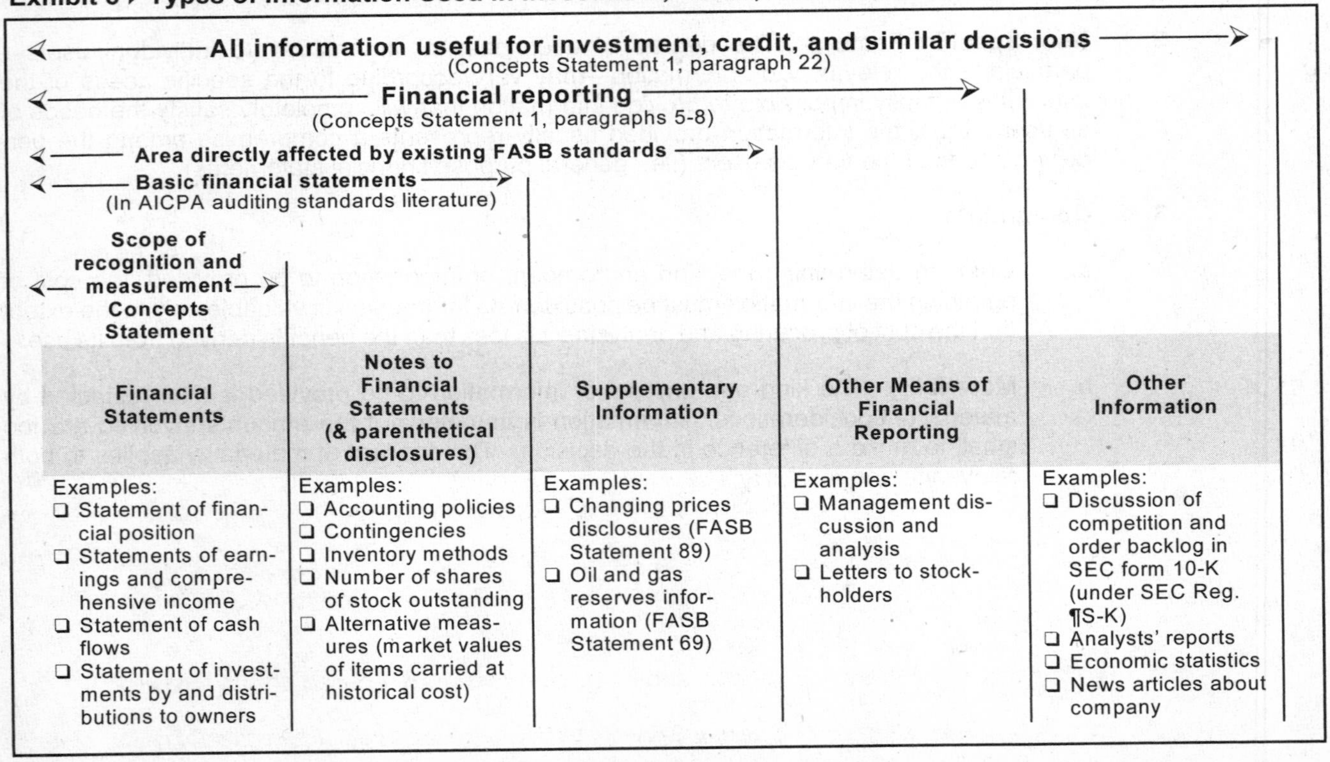

D. ***Recognition & Measurement in Financial Statements of Business Enterprises* (SFAC 5)**
Some information is provided better by financial statements, and some is provided better or can only be disclosed in notes to financial statements, parenthetically, or by supplementary information or other means of financial reporting. The scope of SFAC 5 is limited to recognition and measurement in financial statements.

1. **Completeness** A full set of financial statements provides information that is necessary to satisfy the broad purposes of financial reporting, as described in SFAC 1. A full set of financial statements includes information (some of which may be combined in a single statement) showing the financial position at the end of the period, earnings (net income) for the period, comprehensive income (total nonowner changes in equity) for the period, cash flows during the period, and investments by and distributions to owners during the period.

2. **Maintenance Concepts** The full set of articulated financial statements discussed in SFAC 5 is based on the concept of financial capital maintenance. The main difference between the two concepts involves the effect of price changes during the period. Under the financial capital concept, if the effects of price changes are recognized, they are reported as holding gains or losses, (i.e., included in income). Under the physical capital concept, such changes are considered adjustments to equity.

   a. **Financial Capital** Under this concept, a return on financial capital results only if the financial (money) amount of an enterprise's net assets at the end of a period exceeds the corresponding amount at the beginning of the period, after excluding the effects of transactions with owners. The financial capital concept is the traditional view and is the capital maintenance concept in present financial statements and comprehensive income.

   b. **Physical Capital** Under this concept, a return on physical capital results only if the physical productive capacity of the enterprise at the end of the period exceeds its capacity at the beginning. Thus, the physical capital concept can be implemented only if the enterprise's productive assets, inventory, etc., are measured by their current cost.

3. **Recognition** The process of formally recording or incorporating an item into the financial statements of an entity as an asset, liability, revenue, expense, or the like. An item and information about it must meet four fundamental recognition criteria to be recognized, subject to cost-benefit and materiality considerations.

   a. **Definition** The item meets the definition of an element of financial statements.

   b. **Measurability** The item has a relevant attribute measurable with sufficient reliability.

   c. **Relevance** The information may make a difference in user decisions.

   d. **Reliability** The information is representationally faithful, verifiable, and neutral.

4. **Revenues and Gains** Revenues and gains are recognized when they are both realized and earned.

   a. **Realized** Revenues and gains generally are not recognized until realized or realizable.

   b. **Earned** Revenues are not recognized until earned. For gains, being earned is generally less significant than being realized or realizable, since gains commonly involve no "earning process."

5. **Expenses and Losses** Expenses and losses are recognized based on the following:

   a. **Consumption of Economic Benefits** May be recognized either directly or by relating them to revenues recognized during the period.

b. **Loss or Lack of Benefit** Expenses or losses are recognized if it becomes evident that previously recognized future economic benefits of assets have been reduced or eliminated, or that liabilities have been incurred or increased, without associated economic benefits.

E. ***Elements of Financial Statements* (SFAC 6)**

1. **Elements** SFAC 6 identifies ten elements of financial statements. Seven elements of financial statements of both business enterprises and not-for-profit organizations—assets, liabilities, equity (business enterprises) or net assets (not-for-profit organizations), revenues, expenses, gains, and losses. Three elements of business enterprises only—investment by owners, distributions to owners, and comprehensive income.

2. **Accrual Accounting** Accrual accounting attempts to record the financial effects on an entity of transactions and other events and circumstances that have cash consequences for the entity in the periods in which those transactions, events, and circumstances occur, rather than only in the periods in which cash is received or paid by the entity. Accrual accounting is characterized by the use of accruals, deferrals, allocations, and amortizations.

   a. **Accrual** Accrual is the accounting process of recognizing assets or liabilities and the related liabilities, assets, revenues, expenses, gains, or losses for amounts expected to be received or paid, usually in cash, in the future.

   b. **Deferral** Deferral is the accounting process of recognizing a liability resulting from a current cash receipt or an asset resulting from a current cash payment with deferred recognition of revenues, expenses, gains, or losses.

   c. **Allocation** Allocation is the accounting process of assigning or distributing an amount according to a plan or a formula.

   d. **Amortization** Amortization is the accounting process of reducing an amount by periodic payments or write-downs. It is an allocation process for accounting for prepayments and deferrals by reducing a liability or an asset and recognizing a revenue or an expense.

3. **Realization and Recognition**

   a. **Realization** Realization is the process of converting noncash resources and rights into money. This term is most precisely used in accounting and financial reporting to refer to sales of assets for cash or claims to cash. The related terms realized and unrealized, therefore, identify revenues or gains or losses on assets sold and unsold, respectively.

   b. **Recognition** Recognition is the process of formally recording or incorporating an item in the financial statements of an entity. Thus, an asset, liability, revenue, expense, gain, or loss may be recognized (recorded) or unrecognized (unrecorded).

4. **Matching** Combined or simultaneous recognition of the revenues and expenses that result directly and jointly from the same transactions and other events.

   a. **Period Costs** Some costs cannot be directly related to particular revenues, yet result in benefits that are exhausted in the same period in which the cost was incurred. These costs are usually recognized as expenses in the period in which incurred. Examples: administrative salaries, store utilities, etc.

   b. **Cost Allocation** Other costs yield their benefits over two or more periods of time. These costs are usually allocated to the periods benefited through a systematic and rational cost allocation method (e.g., depreciation and amortization).

F. ***Using Cash Flow Information & Present Value in Accounting Measurements* (SFAC 7)**
SFAC 7 presents the FASB's conclusions about the use and approach to making interest computations in financial reporting. It is limited to measurement issues and does not address recognition.

1. **Present Value Measurement of Assets and Liabilities** Most accounting measurements use an observable marketplace-determined amount, such as cash exchanged, current cost, or current market value. However, in other instances, estimates of future cash flows must be used as the basis for measuring an asset or a liability. SFAC 7 provides a framework for using future cash flows as the basis for accounting measurements at initial recognition or fresh-start measurements as well as for the interest method of amortization. Additionally, it provides general principles that govern the use of present value computations, particularly when the amount and/or timing of future cash flows are uncertain.

2. **Present Value as Surrogate for Market Value** In order to provide more relevant information (a primary qualitative characteristic of financial reporting), present value must represent some observable measurement attribute of assets or liabilities. In the absence of observed transaction prices, accounting measurements at initial recognition and fresh-start measurements should attempt to capture the elements that taken together would comprise a market price if one existed (fair value). While the expectations of management are often useful and informative, ultimately, it is the market that dictates market price when exchanges occur. However, for certain assets or liabilities, management's estimates may be the only information available on which to value the asset or liability. In that case, the use of present value can be seen as a surrogate for market value.

3. **Uncertainties** An accounting measurement that uses present value should reflect the uncertainties inherent in the estimated cash flows. This means that risk should be specifically incorporated into the computation. SFAC 7 provides guidance on how to incorporate risk into the analysis, including its effect on both the timing and amount of future cash flows.

4. **Projection of Future Cash Flows** In the past, present value computations have relied on a single estimate of cash flows and a single interest rate. SFAC 7 calls for the use of expected cash flows, which incorporates uncertainty, use of ranges, and probabilistic computations in the projection of future cash flows.

5. **Measuring Liabilities** In measuring liabilities, the SFAC 7 indicates that there are different issues at hand. Nonetheless, the ultimate objective remains the same—to reflect fair value. SFAC 7 provides additional guidance for measuring liabilities.

6. **Credit Risk** Credit risk can affect a variety of components in the present value computation and should be incorporated in the present value computation. Additionally, in measuring liabilities, the entity's credit standing should always be incorporated into that measurement.

VII. Authority of Pronouncements

A. Accounting Standard-Setting Bodies & Their Pronouncements

1. **Committee on Cooperation With Stock Exchanges (1932-1934)** The American Institute of Accountants (known today as the American Institute of Certified Public Accountants, or AICPA) created in 1932 a Committee on Cooperation With Stock Exchanges. The Committee made a series of recommendations, which later were adopted by the AICPA.

2. **Committee on Accounting Procedure and Accounting Research Bulletins (1939-19**
In 1939, the Institute formed a second committee, the Committee on Accounting Procedu (CAP), with the objective of narrowing the areas of differences and inconsistencies ir practice of accounting. During its existence, CAP issued 51 pronouncements, know Accounting Research Bulletins (ARBs). ARB No. 43 consisted of a rewrite of the 42 pronouncements.

3. **Accounting Principles Board and Opinions and Statements (1959-1973)** CAP was replaced in 1959 by the Accounting Principles Board (APB). From 1959 through 1973, the APB promulgated 31 pronouncements known as Opinions. In addition, the Board issued four Statements. Unlike Opinions, APB Statements were simply recommendations, not requirements.

4. **Financial Accounting Standards Board and Statements, Interpretations, Concepts, Technical Bulletins, and Emerging Issues Task Force Statements (1973-Present)** The APB was substituted in 1973 by the Financial Accounting Standards Board (FASB), an independent private-sector body composed of seven full-time members and a 35 member Advisory Council. The promulgations issued by the FASB have the same authority as the prior APB Opinions, but are known as Statements of Financial Accounting Standards. A new statement is issued only after a majority vote by the members of the FASB. In addition, the FASB also issues Interpretations of prior pronouncements. FASB Interpretations have as much force as ARBs, Opinions, and FASB Statements. Beginning in 1978, the FASB started a new series, Statements of Financial Accounting Concepts, with the purpose of setting forth fundamental concepts upon which financial accounting and reporting standards would be based. Unlike a Statement of Financial Accounting Standards or Interpretation, a Statement of Financial Accounting Concepts does not establish generally accepted accounting principles. In addition, the FASB issues Emerging Issues Task Force Consensus and FASB Technical Bulletins that are less authoritative than FASB Statements of Financial Accounting Standards and Interpretations.

B. GAAP Hierarchy

SAS 69 establishes a hierarchy for applying accounting principles to financial statements in conformity with GAAP. The hierarchy is presented in Exhibit 7.

Exhibit 7 ▸ GAAP Hierarchy

1. FASB Statements and Interpretations, APB Opinions, and AICPA Accounting Research Bulletins
2. FASB Technical Bulletins, AICPA Industry Audit and Accounting Guides, and AICPA Statements of Position cleared by the FASB
3. Consensus positions of the FASB's EITF, and AcSEC Practice Bulletins cleared by the FASB
4. AICPA accounting interpretations, "Qs&As" published by the FASB staff, as well as industry practices widely recognized and prevalent
5. Other accounting literature, including FASB Concepts Statements; APB Statements; AICPA Issues Papers; AcSEC Practice Bulletins; minutes of FASB EITF; International Accounting Standards Committee statements; pronouncements of other professional associations or regulatory agencies; and accounting articles and textbooks

---

ASB ancial Accounting Standards Board

CHAPTER 1—OVERVIEW

Problem 1-1 MULTIPLE CHOICE QUESTIONS (44 to 55 minutes)

1. Reporting inventory at the lower of cost or market is a departure from the accounting principle of
a. Historical cost
b. Consistency
c. Conservatism
d. Full disclosure (5/94, FAR, #3, 4818)

2. What is the underlying concept that supports the immediate recognition of a contingent loss?
a. Substance over form
b. Consistency
c. Matching
d. Conservatism (11/94, FAR, #3, 5268)

3. What is the purpose of information presented in notes to the financial statements?
a. To provide disclosures required by generally accepted accounting principles
b. To correct improper presentation in the financial statements
c. To provide recognition of amounts **not** included in the totals of the financial statements
d. To present management's responses to auditor comments (5/94, FAR, #6, 4821)

4. According to the FASB conceptual framework, which of the following is an essential characteristic of an asset?
a. The claims to an asset's benefit are legally enforceable.
b. An asset is tangible.
c. An asset is obtained at a cost.
d. An asset provides future benefits. (5/92, Theory, #2, 2694)

5. According to the FASB's conceptual framework, asset valuation accounts are
a. Assets
b. Neither assets **nor** liabilities
c. Part of stockholders' equity
d. Liabilities (11/88, Theory, #1, 9001)

6. According to the FASB conceptual framework, an entity's revenue may result from
a. A decrease in an asset from primary operations
b. An increase in an asset from incidental transactions
c. An increase in a liability from incidental transactions
d. A decrease in a liability from primary operations (11/92, Theory, #3, 3436)

7. According to the FASB conceptual framework, comprehensive income includes which of the following?

	Loss on discontinued operations	*Investments by owners*
a.	Yes	Yes
b.	Yes	No
c.	No	Yes
d.	No	No

(5/98, FAR, #1, 6604)

8. What are the Statements of Financial Accounting Concepts intended to establish?
a. Generally accepted accounting principles in financial reporting by business enterprises
b. The meaning of "Present fairly in accordance with generally accepted accounting principles"
c. The objectives and concepts for use in developing standards of financial accounting and reporting
d. The hierarchy of sources of generally accepted accounting principles (5/94, FAR, #2, 4817)

9. During a period when an enterprise is under the direction of a particular management, its financial statements will directly provide information about
a. Both enterprise performance and management performance
b. Management performance but **not** directly provide information about enterprise performance
c. Enterprise performance but **not** directly provide information about management performance
d. Neither enterprise performance nor management performance (5/94, FAR, #4, 4819)

10. According to the FASB conceptual framework, the objectives of financial reporting for business enterprises are based on
a. Generally accepted accounting principles
b. Reporting on management's stewardship
c. The need for conservatism
d. The needs of the users of the information (11/95, FAR, #1, 6083)

11. According to the FASB conceptual framework, the usefulness of providing information in financial statements is subject to the constraint of
a. Consistency
b. Cost-benefit
c. Reliability
d. Representational faithfulness (11/95, FAR, #2, 6084)

12. According to the FASB conceptual framework, predictive value is an ingredient of

	Reliability	*Relevance*
a.	Yes	Yes
b.	No	Yes
c.	No	No
d.	Yes	No

(5/92, Theory, #3, 2695)

13. According to the FASB conceptual framework, which of the following situations violates the concept of reliability?
a. Data on segments having the same expected risks and growth rates are reported to analysts estimating future profits.
b. Financial statements are issued nine months late.
c. Management reports to stockholders regularly refer to new projects undertaken, but the financial statements never report project results.
d. Financial statements include property with a carrying amount increased to management's estimate of market value. (5/95, FAR, #1, 5537)

14. According to the FASB conceptual framework, what does the concept of reliability in financial reporting include?
a. Effectiveness
b. Certainty
c. Precision
d. Neutrality (R/05, FAR, 1001F, #17, 7761)

15. According to the FASB conceptual framework, which of the following relates to both relevance and reliability?
a. Comparability
b. Feedback value
c. Verifiability
d. Timeliness (11/92, Theory, #2, 3435)

16. FASB's conceptual framework explains both financial and physical capital maintenance concepts. Which capital maintenance concept is applied to currently reported net income, and which is applied to comprehensive income?

	Currently reported net income	*Comprehensive income*
a.	Financial capital	Physical capital
b.	Physical capital	Physical capital
c.	Financial capital	Financial capital
d.	Physical capital	Financial capital

(11/91, Theory, #1, 2509)

17. Which of the following disclosures should prospective financial statements include?

	Summary of significant accounting policies	*Summary of significant assumptions*
a.	Yes	Yes
b.	Yes	No
c.	No	Yes
d.	No	No

(R/99, FAR, #3, 6772)

18. According to the FASB conceptual framework, which of the following statements conforms to the realization concept?
a. Equipment depreciation was assigned to a production department and then to product unit costs.
b. Depreciated equipment was sold in exchange for a note receivable.
c. Cash was collected on accounts receivable.
d. Product unit costs were assigned to cost of goods sold when the units were sold. (11/93, Theory, #6, 4511)

19. Some costs cannot be directly related to particular revenues but are incurred to obtain benefits that are exhausted in the period in which the costs are incurred. An example of such a cost is
a. Salespersons' monthly salaries
b. Salespersons' commissions
c. Transportation to customers
d. Prepaid insurance (5/85, Theory, #2, 1775)

20. According to the FASB conceptual framework, the process of reporting an item in the financial statements of an entity is
a. Allocation
b. Matching
c. Realization
d. Recognition (5/94, FAR, #1, 4816)

21. In the hierarchy of generally accepted accounting principles, APB Opinions have the same authority as AICPA
a. Statements of Position
b. Industry Audit and Accounting Guides
c. Issues Papers
d. Accounting Research Bulletins (11/94, FAR, #2, 5267)

22. Which of the following accounting pronouncements is the most authoritative?
a. FASB Statement of Financial Accounting Concepts
b. FASB Technical Bulletin
c. AICPA Accounting Principles Board Opinion
d. AICPA Statement of Position (11/92, Theory, #1, 3434)

SIMULATION

Note: The editors recommend that candidates who are unfamiliar with researching the AICPA's database of professional literature review the sample research question in the Practical Advice appendix before answering their first research question. Candidates typically should start developing their research skills at least a month before their exams. While essay responses must be on the specified topic and should not conflict with guidance, essays on the computer-based exam are scored mainly for writing skills, rather than content. The large (and high point value) essays presented in these simulations are atypical of those you probably will see on the exam; however, essay questions that you see on the exam probably will be similar to these except any one essay question will address fewer issues and earn fewer points than these do. Further, the content presented in these large and atypical essays is important to learn, as it may be asked in any question format, either in multiple choice questions or within simulations.

Problem 1-2 (15 to 25 minutes)

Essay | Research Task

Mono Tech Co. began operations in year 1 and confined its activities to one project. It purchased equipment to be used exclusively for research and development on the project, and other equipment that is to be used initially for research and development and subsequently for production. In year 2, Mono constructed and paid for a pilot plant that was used until December of year 3 to determine the best manufacturing process for the project's product. In December of year 3, Mono obtained a patent and received cash from the sale of the pilot plant. In year 4, a factory was constructed and commercial manufacture of the product began.

a. 1. According to the FASB conceptual framework, what are the three essential characteristics of an asset?

2. How do Mono's project expenditures through year 3 meet the FASB conceptual framework's three essential characteristics of an asset? Do **not** discuss why the expenditures may **not** meet the characteristics of an asset.

3. Why is it difficult to justify the classification of research and development expenditures as assets?

b. How should Mono report:

1. The effects of equipment expenditures in its income statements and balance sheets from year 1 through year 4?

2. Pilot plant construction costs and sale proceeds in its year 2 and year 3 statements of cash flows using the direct method? (11/93, Theory, #5, amended, 6186)

Essay | Research Task

Research Question: A business enterprise that prepares its financial statements in U.S. dollars and in accordance with U.S. generally accepted accounting principles is encouraged, but not required, to disclose supplementary information on the effects of what?

Paragraph Reference Answer: ________________

Solution 1-1 MULTIPLE CHOICE ANSWERS

Accounting Environment

1. (a) The accounting principle of historical cost requires assets as well as liabilities to be recorded and carried on the books at cost. Therefore, reporting inventory at the lower of cost or market is a departure from this principle.

2. (d) While a contingent loss may be recognized *before* it is realized, a contingent gain cannot be recognized *until* it is realized. Therefore, the underlying concept that supports the immediate recognition of a contingent loss is conservatism. The convention of conservatism urges the accountant to refrain from overstatement of net income or net assets.

3. (a) The notes to the financial statements provide disclosures required by generally accepted accounting principles. The notes may be used to amplify or explain items presented in the main body of the financial statements but not to correct errors or omissions in the statements. Management's responses to auditor comments would normally be reported in a separate letter to the auditors and not as part of the financial statements.

Financial Statements

4. (d) SFAC 6, par. 26, states, "An asset has three essential characteristics: (1) it embodies a probable future benefit that involves a capacity, singly or in combination with other assets, to contribute directly or indirectly to future net cash inflows, (2) a particular entity can obtain the benefit and control others' access to it, and (3) the transaction or other event giving rise to the entity's right to or control of the benefit has already occurred." The legal enforceability of a claim to a benefit is not a prerequisite for a benefit to qualify as an asset if the entity has the ability to obtain and control the benefit in other ways (par. 26). Assets may be intangible and they may be acquired without cost (par. 26).

5. (b) Per SFAC 6, par. 34, "A separate item that reduces or increases the carrying amount of an asset is sometimes found in financial statements. For example, an estimate of uncollectible amounts reduces receivables to the amount expected to be collected, or a premium on a bond receivable increases the receivable to its cost or present value. Those 'valuation accounts' are part of the related assets and are neither assets in their own right nor liabilities."

6. (d) Revenues are inflows or other enhancements of assets or settlements of liabilities from activities that constitute the entity's major or central operations (SFAC 6, par. 78). An expense would result from an outflow or other using up of assets from activities that constitute the entity's major or central operations (par. 78). Gains and losses result from changes in net assets from an entity's peripheral or incidental transactions (par. 84).

7. (b) Comprehensive income includes all changes in equity during a period except those resulting from investments by owners and distributions to owners. Loss on discontinued operations is part of comprehensive income.

SFAC

8. (c) The Statements of Financial Accounting Concepts are intended by the FASB to set forth objectives and fundamentals that will be the basis for future development of financial accounting and reporting standards. SFACs do not establish standards prescribing accounting procedures or disclosures, nor supersede, amend, or otherwise modify present GAAP.

9. (c) Financial statements provide information about an enterprise's economic resources, obligations, and owner's equity. In addition, they should provide information concerning financial performance, earnings, how the entity spends and receives cash, and how it distributes dividends. The objective of financial reporting is to aid investors, creditors, and others in making sound economic decisions. Information regarding management performance is also part of financial reporting. Since management is responsible for the earnings of an enterprise, management performance can be closely correlated to increases or decreases in earnings. However, this information is not *directly* provided for, but rather inferred from the financial data contained in the financial statements.

10. (d) According to SFAC 1, "Objectives of Financial Reporting by Business Enterprises," the need for information on which to base investment, credit, and similar decisions underlies the objectives of financial reporting. The objectives of financial reporting are not based upon the need for conservatism, reporting on management's stewardship, or GAAP.

Ceramic Tools

Qualitative Characteristics

11. (b) A specific constraint in terms of the usefulness of information in financial statements pertains to the cost-benefit relationship. In determining the kind and amount of information to be provided, the cost of obtaining the information must be considered. Information is valuable only to the extent that the cost of procuring and analyzing it is less than the benefits derived from its use. While consistency, reliability, and representational faithfulness are important aspects of financial information, they are not associated with constraints.

12. (b) Per SFAC 2, relevance and reliability are the two primary qualities of information. The "ingredients" of relevance are predictive value, feedback value, and timeliness. The "ingredients" of reliability are verifiability, neutrality, and representational faithfulness.

13. (d) Reliability is increased when, in addition to being representationally faithful, the information is both verifiable and neutral. Increasing the carrying amount of property to management's estimate of market value is not verifiable or neutral. Answer (a) relates to comparability; answers (b) and (c) relate to relevance.

14. (d) Neutrality, verifiability and representational faithfulness are concepts of reliability. Effectiveness, certainty and precision are not concepts of reliability.

15. (a) Comparability is a secondary quality of information that interacts with both relevance and reliability to contribute to the usefulness of the information (SFAC 2, par. 33). Feedback value and timeliness are ingredients of relevance and not of reliability. To be relevant, information must be timely and it must have predictive value, feedback value, or both. Verifiability is an ingredient of reliability and not of relevance. To be reliable, information must have representational faithfulness and it must be verifiable and neutral.

Recognition & Measurement

16. (c) The financial capital maintenance concept defines income as the change in net resources other than from owner transactions. The financial capital maintenance concept is the capital maintenance concept used in present financial statements and comprehensive income. In contrast, under the physical capital maintenance concept, a return on physical capital results only if the physical productive capacity of the enterprise at the end of the period exceeds its capacity at the beginning of the period, also after excluding the effects of transactions with owners. The physical capital maintenance concept can be implemented only if inventories and property, plant, and equipment are measured by their current costs.

17. (a) To assist in understanding prospective financial statements, summaries of both significant accounting policies and significant assumptions should be included in the disclosures.

Elements of Financial Statements

18. (b) Per SFAC 6, par. 143, "Realization in the most precise sense means the process of converting noncash resources and rights into money and is most precisely used in accounting and financial reporting to refer to sales of assets for cash or *claims to cash.*" Thus, the sale of the depreciated equipment for a note (i.e., a claim to cash) conforms to the realization concept. None of the transactions in the other choices involve the conversion of a noncash resource or right into cash or claims to cash.

19. (a) SFAC 6, par. 148, specifically mentions *salesmen's monthly salaries* as an example that fits the description of a cost that cannot be directly related to particular revenues, but rather it is incurred in order to obtain benefits that are exhausted during the period. Salespersons' commissions and transportation to customers are mentioned as examples of items that are *directly* related to sales revenues. Prepaid insurance is mentioned as an asset yielding benefits over several periods.

20. (d) Recognition is the process of formally recording or incorporating an item in the financial statements of an entity.

Authority of Pronouncements

21. (d) The AICPA Code of Professional Conduct requires that members prepare financial statements in accordance with generally accepted accounting principles (Rule 203). Pronouncements of an authoritative body designated by the AICPA Council to establish accounting principles have greater authority than pronouncements of bodies composed of expert accountants that follow a due process procedure for the intended purpose of establishing accounting principles or describing existing practices that are generally accepted (SAS 69). Therefore, FASB Statements on Financial Accounting Standards and Interpretations, APB Opinions and Interpretations, and CAP (Committee on Accounting Procedure) Accounting Research Bulletins have greater authority than AICPA Statements of Position, AICPA Industry Audit and Accounting Guides, and AICPA Issue Papers.

22. (c) Rule 203 of the AICPA Code of Professional Conduct requires that members prepare financial statements in accordance with generally accepted accounting principles. Generally accepted accounting principles are construed to be FASB Statements of Financial Accounting Standards and FASB Interpretations, AICPA Accounting Principles Board (APB) Opinions and Interpretations, and CAP (Committee on Accounting Procedure) Accounting Research Bulletins. FASB Statements of Financial Accounting Concepts, FASB Technical Bulletins, and AICPA Statements of Position are less authoritative than APB Opinions because they do not establish GAAP.

PERFORMANCE BY SUBTOPICS

Each category below parallels a subtopic covered in Chapter 1. Record the number and percentage of questions you correctly answered in each subtopic area.

Accounting Environment

Question #	Correct √
1	
2	
3	
# Questions	3
# Correct	
% Correct	

SFAC

Question #	Correct √
8	
9	
10	
# Questions	3
# Correct	
% Correct	

Recognition & Measurement

Question #	Correct √
16	
17	
# Questions	2
# Correct	
% Correct	

Authority of Pronouncements

Question #	Correct √
21	
22	
# Questions	2
# Correct	
% Correct	

Financial Statements

Question #	Correct √
4	
5	
6	
7	
# Questions	4
# Correct	
% Correct	

Qualitative Characteristics

Question #	Correct √
11	
12	
13	
14	
15	
# Questions	5
# Correct	
% Correct	

Elements of Financial Statements

Question #	Correct √
18	
19	
20	
# Questions	3
# Correct	
% Correct	

SIMULATION SOLUTION

Solution 1-2

Essay—Asset Characteristics

a. 1. According to the FASB conceptual framework, the three essential characteristics of an asset are:

- It embodies a **probable future benefit** that involves a capacity to contribute to future net cash inflows.
- A particular entity can obtain the benefit and control others' access to it.
- The **transaction or other event** giving rise to the entity's right to or control of the benefit has **already occurred.**

2. Mono's project expenditures through Year 3 meet the FASB conceptual framework's three essential characteristics of an asset as follows:

- Since Mono intends to produce the product, it presumably **anticipates future net cash inflows.**
- Mono has obtained a patent that will enable it to **control the benefits** arising from the product.
- The control is a consequence of past events.

3. It is difficult to justify the classification of research and development expenditures as assets because at the time expenditures are made the **future benefits are uncertain,** and **difficult to measure.**

b. 1. Expenditures for equipment to be used exclusively for research and development should be reported as research and development **expense in the period incurred.** Expenditures for equipment to be used both for research and development and for production should be **capitalized and reported as fixed assets,** less accumulated depreciation, on Mono's balance sheets from Year 1 through Year 4. An appropriate depreciation method should be used, with depreciation from Year 1 through Year 3 reported as research and development expense. Depreciation for Year 4 should be **added to cost of inventory,** via factory overhead, and expensed as cost of goods sold.

2. **Cash payments** for the pilot plant construction should be reported as **cash outflows from operating activities** on Mono's Year 2 statement of cash flows. **Cash received from the sale** of the pilot plant should be reported as a **cash inflow from operating activities** on Mono's Year 3 statement of cash flows.

Research

FAS 89, Par. 3

3. A business enterprise that prepares its financial statements in U.S. dollars and in accordance with U.S. generally accepted accounting principles is encouraged, but not required, to disclose supplementary information on the effects of changing prices. Appendix A provides measurement and presentation guidelines for disclosure. Entities are not discouraged from experimenting with other forms of disclosure.

CHANGE ALERTS

SFAS 155, Accounting for Certain Hybrid Financial Instruments—an amendment of FASB Statements No. 133 and 140 (Issued 2/06)

In February 2006, the FASB issued Statement of Financial Accounting Standard No. 155, *Accounting for Certain Hybrid Financial Instruments.* This statement is an amendment of FASB Statements No. 133 and 140.

The objective of this statement is to improve the financial reporting of certain hybrid financial instruments by requiring more consistent accounting that eliminates exemptions and provides a means to simplify the accounting for these instruments. Specifically, it allows financial instruments that have embedded derivatives to be accounted for as a whole if the holder elects to account for the whole instrument on a fair value basis.

This Statement is effective for all financial instruments acquired or issued after the beginning of an entity's first fiscal year that begins after September 15, 2006. Earlier adoption is permitted as of the beginning of an entity's fiscal year, provided the entity has not yet issued financial statements, including financial statements, for any interim period for that fiscal year.

Editor's Note: The editors do not expect this statement to be tested heavily on the exam, if it is tested at all.

SFAS 156, Accounting for Servicing of Financial Assets—an amendment of FASB Statement No. 140 (Issued 3/06)

In March 2006, the FASB issued Statement of Financial Accounting Standards No. 156, *Accounting for Servicing of Financial Statements Costs.* This statement is an amendment of FASB Statement No. 140.

The objective of this statement is to simplify the accounting for servicing assets and liabilities, such as those common with mortgage securitization activities. Specifically, it addresses the recognition and measurement of separately recognized servicing assets and liabilities and provides an approach to simplify efforts to obtain hedge-like (offset) accounting.

This Statement is effective for all separately recognized servicing assets and liabilities acquired or issued after the beginning of an entity's fiscal year that begins after September 15, 2006. Earlier adoption is permitted as of the beginning of an entity's fiscal year, provided the entity has not yet issued financial statements, including financial statements, for any interim period for that fiscal year.

Editor's Note: The editors do not expect this statement to be tested heavily on the exam, if it is tested at all.

CHAPTER 2

CASH, MARKETABLE SECURITIES & RECEIVABLES

I. **Current Assets** 2-2
- A. Definition 2-2
- B. Examples 2-2

II. **Cash & Cash Equivalents** 2-2
- A. Presentation 2-2
- B. Exclusions 2-2
- C. Bank Reconciliation 2-3

III. **Investments in Securities** 2-4
- A. Uses 2-4
- B. Acquisition Cost 2-5
- C. Accounting Methods for Equity Securities 2-5
- D. Cost Method 2-5
- E. Equity Method 2-6

IV. **Investments in Marketable Securities (SFAS 115)** 2-11
- A. Applicability 2-11
- B. Classification 2-11
- C. Acquisition Cost 2-11
- D. Year-End Valuation 2-12
- E. Other Than Temporary Decline in Fair Value 2-13
- F. Transfers Between Categories 2-13
- G. Sale 2-14

V. **Financial Instruments & Derivatives** 2-14
- A. Definitions 2-14
- B. Derivative Instruments & Hedging Activities (SFAS 133, 138, 149 & 155) 2-16
- C. Disclosures (SFAS 107) 2-23
- D. Transfers & Servicing of Financial Assets & Extinguishments of Liabilities (SFAS 140 & 156) ... 2-24

VI. **Accounts Receivable** 2-27
- A. Definition 2-27
- B. Valuation 2-27

VII. **Notes Receivable** 2-30
- A. Definition 2-30
- B. Types 2-30
- C. Valuation 2-30
- D. Impairment (SFAS 114) 2-31

VIII. **Receivables as Immediate Sources of Cash** 2-34
- A. Overview 2-34
- B. Discounting 2-34
- C. Assignment 2-35
- D. Factoring 2-35
- E. Pledging 2-36

EXAM COVERAGE: Historically, exam coverage of the topics in Chapter 2 has been 10 to 15 percent of the FAR section. More information regarding exam coverage is included in Appendix B, *Practical Advice.*

CHAPTER 2

CASH, MARKETABLE SECURITIES & RECEIVABLES

I. Current Assets

A. Definition

Current assets are economic benefits owned by a firm that are reasonably expected to be converted into cash or consumed during the entity's operating cycle or one year, whichever is longer.

B. Examples

Include cash, temporary investments in marketable securities, accounts and notes receivable, inventories, and most prepaid expenses (ARB 43).

II. Cash & Cash Equivalents

A. Presentation

Cash is by definition the most liquid asset of an enterprise; thus, it is usually the first item presented in the current assets section of the balance sheet. The following are components of cash.

1. Coin and currency on hand, including petty cash funds

2. Negotiable paper (i.e., transferable by endorsement). Examples include claims to cash such as bank checks, money orders, traveler's checks, bank drafts, and cashier's checks

3. Money market funds

4. Passbook savings accounts (although banks have the legal right to demand notice before withdrawal, they seldom exercise this right)

5. Deposits held as compensating balances against borrowing arrangements with a lending institution that are **not** legally restricted

6. Checks written by the enterprise, but not mailed until **after** the financial statement date, should be *added back* to the cash balance

7. Time certificates of deposit with **original** maturities of three months or less

B. Exclusions

1. **Certain Time Certificates of Deposit** Time certificates of deposit with original maturities of longer than three months are classified as either temporary or long-term investments depending upon maturity dates and managerial intent.

2. **Compensating Balances** Legally restricted deposits held as compensating balances against borrowing arrangements with a lending institution are classified as follows:

   a. If held as a compensating balance against a short-term borrowing arrangement, the restricted deposit is classified as a current asset but segregated from unrestricted cash.

   b. If held as a compensating balance against a long-term borrowing arrangement, the restricted deposit is classified as a noncurrent asset in either the investments or other assets section and should be disclosed in the financial statements.

3. **Restricted Cash** Restricted cash is classified based upon the date of availability or disbursement.

a. **Current** If restricted for a current asset or current liability, the restricted cash is classified as a current asset, but segregated from unrestricted cash.

b. **Noncurrent** If restricted for a noncurrent asset or noncurrent liability (e.g., cash to be used for plant expansion or the retirement of long-term debt), the restricted cash is classified as a noncurrent asset in either the investments or other assets section regardless of whether the cash is expected to be disbursed within one year of the financial statement date. This accounting policy should be disclosed in the financial statements.

4. **Overdrafts** Overdrafts in accounts with no available cash in another account at the same bank to offset are classified as current liabilities.

5. **Certain Deposits** Deposits in banks under receivership or in foreign banks that are restricted as to conversion into dollars and/or transfer are segregated from unrestricted cash and are classified as current or noncurrent assets depending upon expected dates of availability.

6. **Postdated Checks** Postdated checks received from customers are classified as receivables.

7. **IOUs** IOUs from officers or employees are classified as receivables.

8. **Postage** Postage stamps are classified as supplies or prepaid expenses.

C. **Bank Reconciliation**

1. **Periodic Reconciliation**

a. **Control** Errors can be uncovered and corrected on a timely basis.

b. **Information** Appropriate amounts are provided for entries in books.

2. **Reasons for Differences**

a. **Items in Books and Not in Bank Statement** Deposits in transit and cash on hand should be added to the bank balance. Outstanding checks should be subtracted from the bank balance.

b. **Items in Bank Statement and Not in Books** Interest earned and collections by the bank should be added to the book balance. Bank service charges, returned checks (i.e., NSF checks), and payments by the bank should be subtracted from the book balance.

c. **Errors** Differences may also result from errors in books or bank statement.

d. **Certified and Cashier's Checks** As both the bank and the enterprise have deducted the amounts of these checks from the enterprise's account, they do not represent reconciling items.

3. **Format** A common format of the bank reconciliation statement is to reconcile both book and bank balances to a common amount known as the "true balance." This approach has the advantage of providing the cash figure to be reported in the balance sheet. Furthermore, journal entries necessary to adjust the books can be taken directly from the "book balance" section of the reconciliation.

Example 1 ▸ Bank Reconciliation

On July 31 of the current year, The Company's bank statement showed a balance of $4,056, whereas the book balance was $4,706. Deposits in transit and cash on hand amounted to $588 and $456, respectively. During July, the bank collected a $215 note for The Company and charged the account $15 for service fees; neither of these transactions had been recorded by The Company. In addition, a check for $110 received from a customer and deposited by The Company was returned on July 31 for lack of funds. The following checks were outstanding at the end of July:

#320	$ 24.00
#321	$235.00
#325	$ 45.00

Required: Reconcile both balances to the true cash amount at July 31.

Solution:

BANK			BOOKS		
7/31 balance per bank		$4,056	7/31 balance per books		$ 4,706
Deposit in transit	$588		Note collected by bank	$215	
Cash on hand	456		Add		215
Add		1,044	Subtotal		4,921
Subtotal		5,100			
Outstanding checks:			Bank service charge	15	
#320	24		Returned NSF check	110	
#321	235		Less		(125)
#325	45				
Less		(304)	True cash		$ 4,796
True cash		$4,796			

Entries to adjust the books are taken directly from the reconciliation:

Cash	215	
Notes Receivable		215
Bank Service Charge Expense	15	
Cash		15
Special Receivable—NSF Check	110	
Cash		110

III. Investments in Securities

A. Uses

Funds not needed for the daily operations of the business are usually invested in short-term marketable securities to generate additional income. Some funds may be committed for longer periods by investing in securities to be held long term. Equity investments are assets that may be acquired for future income potential, appreciation, or control over the investee. As such, they generally occupy an auxiliary position in relation to a firm's primary activities. Investments may be classified as either temporary or long-term. SFAS 115, *Accounting for Certain Investments in Debt and Equity Securities,* does **not** apply to investments accounted for by the equity method nor to investments in consolidated subsidiaries.

1. **Temporary** Temporary investments are those that meet two tests: (a) marketability, and (b) intention by management to dispose of the investment for cash or other current assets if the need arises.

2. **Long-Term** Long-term investments are all other investments not meeting these two criteria. Investments in the form of common or preferred stock represent an equity interest in the investee, and are discussed in this chapter.

B. Acquisition Cost

All securities initially are recorded at cost, which includes broker's fees, taxes, and any other direct costs of acquisition.

C. Accounting Methods for Equity Securities

An investment in the equity securities of a corporation confers upon the investor the right to share in the earnings of the investee. If the investment is in the voting common stock of the investee, the investor is also entitled to participate, at least indirectly, in the investee's management. The degree of influence that the investor is deemed to have over the investee by virtue of the investment determines the method of accounting for that investment. Under the cost method, the investor recognizes dividends as income when received. Under the equity method, an investor recognizes as income its share of an investee's earnings or losses in the periods in which they are reported by the investee. The equity method is more consistent with accrual accounting than the cost method, because the equity method recognizes income when earned rather than when dividends are received. When a company owns stock in another corporation, its investment should be accounted for under one of three methods.

1. **Cost Method** The cost method is appropriate where the investor is **not** deemed to have a significant level of influence over the investee by virtue of the investment (generally, less than 20% ownership of the outstanding common stock). In this case, income will be recognized as cash dividends are received and the investment is accounted for in accordance with SFAS 115.

2. **Equity Method** The equity method is required where the investor is deemed to have significant influence over the investee by virtue of the investment, but consolidated financial statements are not appropriate (generally 20%-50% ownership of the outstanding common stock). Under the equity method, the investor recognizes as income its pro rata share of the investee's earnings, while cash dividends received reduce the carrying amount of the investment. APB 18, *The Equity Method of Accounting for Investments in Common Stocks,* provides accounting and reporting standards.

3. **Consolidated Financial Statements** Consolidated financial statements are required by ARB 51, *Consolidated Financial Statements,* when a company owns more than 50% of the voting stock of another firm, with few exceptions. SFAS 141, *Business Combinations,* provides accounting and reporting standards.

Exhibit 1 ▸ Accounting for Investments

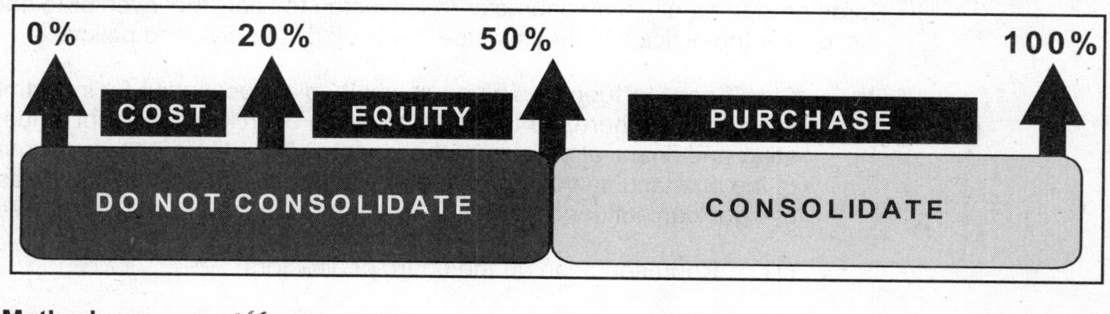

D. Cost Method

1. **Cost Method Criteria** The cost method is appropriate when the investor is **not** deemed to be able to exercise significant influence over the investee by virtue of the investment. Factors such as participation in policy-making or directorship indicate significant influence. In the absence of other evidence, ownership of 20% or more of the voting stock of an investee indicates significant influence. The cost method typically is used in the following situations.

a. **Nonvoting Stock** The investment is in nonvoting stock, such as preferred stock.

b. **Less Than 20% Ownership** The number of shares of voting common stock owned represent less than 20% of the common stock outstanding.

c. **Temporary** The investment is of a temporary nature due to circumstances outside the investor's control.

2. **Upon Acquisition** Upon acquisition, the investment is recorded at cost. "Cost" also includes broker's fees and other direct costs of acquisition. In a lump-sum purchase, the purchase price is allocated to the various types of securities on the basis of their relative fair values.

3. **Trading and Available-for-Sale Securities** In accordance with SFAS 115, investments in equity securities are classified as either (1) trading securities or (2) available-for-sale (AFS) securities. Dividends received are accounted for in current income. Changes in fair value (at year-end) of trading or AFS securities' portfolios are recorded through a valuation allowance account's addition or subtraction for both unrealized holding gains and losses. For trading securities, these changes are reported in current income. For AFS securities, these changes are reported in other comprehensive income.

4. **Investment Account** The investment account is not adjusted to reflect the investor's share of the investee's earnings or dividend distributions of earnings subsequent to acquisition. An adjustment must be made, however, for liquidating dividends (i.e., dividend distributions in excess of earnings subsequent to acquisition). Stock dividends and splits are recorded only by a memo entry, the carrying amount of the investment being allocated to the total number of shares owned.

5. **Stock Rights** If stock rights are received (rights to buy additional shares usually received to satisfy the investor's preemptive right to maintain its existing level of ownership in the investee), the carrying amount of the investment should be allocated between the investment and the rights. The allocation should be based on the ratio of the market value of the stock to the market value of the rights. This procedure is also used for the receipt of stock warrants. A stock warrant is physical evidence of stock rights.

6. **Upon Disposal** Upon disposal, a realized gain or loss should be recognized to the extent that the proceeds received differ from the carrying amount of the investment. The carrying amount of the shares sold may be determined by specific identification, FIFO, or the average method.

E. **Equity Method**

1. **Criteria** The equity method is based upon the premise that the investor owns a sufficiently large proportion of voting shares of the investee to allow the investor to exert significant influence over the policies of the investee, particularly the dividend policy.

a. **Significant Influence** The equity method of accounting for investments is required for investments where the investor is able to exercise significant influence over the operating and financial policies of the investee by virtue of the investment. If 20% or more of the outstanding voting stock of the investee is owned by the investor, a presumption of significant influence exists. Significant influence may be indicated by the following.

(1) Representation on the board of directors

(2) Participation in policy-making decisions

(3) Level of intercompany transactions or dependency

(4) Concentration of ownership in the hands of a small group of stockholders

b. **Consolidation** ARB 51, Consolidated Financial Statements (as amended by SFAS 94, *Consolidation of All Majority-Owned Subsidiaries*), requires consolidation of all majority-owned subsidiaries. The equity method is not a valid substitute for consolidation.

2. **Exceptions** The exception to APB 18's presumption that an investor owning 20% or more of the voting stock of an investee has significant influence over the investee is if the investment is operating in a foreign country where severe operating restrictions exist. Additionally, FASB Interp. 35, *Criteria for Applying the Equity Method of Accounting for Investments in Common Stock,* indicates sample situations where the 20% ownership presumption may be overcome.

   a. **No Significant Influence** Opposition by the investee, such as litigation or complaints to governmental regulatory authorities, challenges the investor's ability to exercise significant influence.

   b. **By Agreement** The investor and investee sign an agreement under which the investor surrenders significant rights as a shareholder.

   c. **Other Owners** Majority ownership of the investee is concentrated among a small group of shareholders who operate the investee without regard to the views of the investor.

   d. **Lack of Information** The investor needs or wants more financial information to apply the equity method than is available to the investee's other shareholders (for example, the investor wants quarterly financial information from an investee that publicly reports only annually), tries to obtain that information, and fails.

   e. **No Representation** The investor tries and fails to obtain representation on the investee's board of directors.

3. **Upon Acquisition** Upon acquisition, the investment should be recorded at cost. If the investor owned less than 20% of the voting stock of the investee and subsequently increased the ownership percentage to 20% or more, the equity method should be retroactively applied in a manner consistent with the accounting for a step-by-step acquisition of a subsidiary. APB 18 requires a retroactive adjustment to the investor's *Investment* and *Retained Earnings* accounts.

4. **Subsequent to Acquisition** Subsequent to acquisition, the *Investment* and the *Investment Income* accounts periodically must be adjusted in a manner analogous to a consolidated investment. (The equity method is sometimes referred to as a "one line consolidation.") Steps an investor would follow in applying the equity method include:

   a. **Investee's Earnings** Periodically, the investor recognizes its share of the investee's earnings. This is done by debiting the *Investment* account and crediting *Investment Income* for an amount proportionate to the ownership interest. The investor's share of investee earnings or losses is computed after deducting any cumulative preferred dividends of the investee. If the investor also owns shares of preferred stock, the investor should account for them under the cost method because they are nonvoting securities. Income on preferred stock would be recorded simply as dividend income as the preferred dividends are declared. Finally, when the investor's and the investee's fiscal years do not coincide, the investor may report its share of investee income from the most recent financial statements of the investee, so long as the time lag is consistent from period to period.

   b. **Dividends** Dividends declared by the investee represent a distribution of earnings previously recognized. The investor records the declaration of dividends by debiting a receivable and crediting the *Investment* account, since the distribution reduces the owners' equity of the investee. Dividends declared by the investee do not affect the *Investment Income* account.

c. **Goodwill** The price paid for the common stock of the investee will seldom, if ever, equal the book value of the shares acquired. Any excess purchase price over the underlying equity is usually regarded as purchased goodwill.

d. **Excess Purchase Price** Specific investee assets may have fair values that differ from their book values. Any excess purchase price identified directly with individual assets (e.g., inventory, buildings, equipment, patents) having a limited useful life is amortized over the appropriate time period. The proper entry is to debit *Investment Income* and credit the *Investment* account for the amortization amount. The opposite entry is made if the fair value of the asset is less than its book value.

e. **Intercompany Profits & Losses** Intercompany profits and losses are eliminated until realized.

Example 2 ▸ Intercompany Profits & Losses

Investee Co. sells inventory to Investor, Inc., and recognizes a profit on the sale. At year-end Investor has not resold 25% of this inventory. Investor, Inc., must then reduce both its *Investment Income* and *Investment* accounts by an amount equal to 25% of the intercompany profits contained in the ending inventory.

f. **Intercompany Receivables and Payables** Intercompany receivables and payables between affiliates should not be eliminated unless the requirements for consolidation are met (i.e., > 50% ownership).

g. **Capital Transactions** Investee's capital transactions are accounted for as if the investee were a consolidated subsidiary. For instance, a sale by the investee of its common stock to third parties, at a price greater than book value, results in an increase in the carrying amount of the investment and a corresponding increase in the investor's additional paid-in capital. No income is recorded if the investee declares stock dividends or splits since the investor continues to own the same portion of the investee as before the stock split or dividend. The investor needs only to make a memo entry.

h. **Deferred Income Taxes** Deferred income taxes should be recognized for the temporary difference caused by the difference between the income recognized using the equity method and the dividends received from the investee. Corporate shareholders that own 20% or more (but less than 80%) of the stock of the distributing corporation are allowed an 80% dividend deduction. This portion of the dividends received is an event recognized in the financial statements that does not have a tax consequence because it is exempt from taxation. Events that do not have tax consequences do not give rise to temporary differences and are often referred to as "permanent differences."

i. **Changes in Common Stock Market Value** Changes in the market value of the investee's common stock do **not** affect the *Investment* account or the *Investment Income* account.

Example 3 ▸ Equity Method Application

On January 2 Company R purchased 20% of the outstanding common stock of Company E for $25,000. Any excess of the purchase price over the book value of the securities acquired is attributable to goodwill. Company E's net income for the year was $10,000. Cash dividends amounting to $4,000 were declared and paid. During the year, Company E sold inventory to R for $8,000, recording a $2,000 profit on the sale; 50% of this inventory ($4,000) had not been resold by Company R at year-end. The owners' equity section of Company E at the time of acquisition is summarized below.

Common stock ($1 par)	$ 10,000
Additional paid-in capital	40,000
Retained earnings	50,000
Book value of Company E's net assets, Jan. 2	$100,000

Required: Provide the journal entries to record the acquisition and subsequent accounting for Company R's investment in Company E.

Solution: Entry to record acquisition of the 20% interest in E's common stock outstanding.

Investment in E	25,000	
Cash		25,000

Entry to record R's share of E's net income for the year.

Investment in E (20% × $10,000)	2,000	
Investment Income		2,000

Entry to reduce the investment in E for the amount of the dividend distribution received.

Cash ($4,000 × 20%)	800	
Investment in E		800

E's profit on sale of inventory to R	$2,000
Sale price of inventory	/ 8,000
E's gross margin ratio	25%
E's inventory still in R's ending inventory (in dollars)	× 4,000
E's recorded profit on R's ending inventory	$1,000

Entry to adjust for Co. R's share of intercompany unrealized profits.

Investment Income ($1,000 × 20%)	200	
Investment in E		200

Note: The $5,000 of goodwill attributable to the investment in E is not recorded separately. It is recognized as a portion of the investment price that should be tested periodically for impairment.

5. **Changes From Equity Method** Upon disposal of an equity method investment, the investor should recognize a gain or loss equal to the difference between the carrying amount of the investment and its sale price. Note that the carrying amount of the investment must be adjusted to the date of disposal. If, as a result of a partial disposal, the ownership percentage becomes less than 20%, the investor should stop accruing its share of investee income. A change in the method of accounting must be made to the cost method. The cost basis for accounting purposes is the carrying amount of the investment at the date of the change. Any dividends in future years that exceed the investor's share of the investee's income for such future years (i.e., liquidating dividends) should be applied to reduce the *Investment* account.

6. **Changes to Equity Method** Where the investor's level of ownership increases, so that use of the equity method is required, the investment account, results of operations, and retained earnings of the investor must be retroactively adjusted. This adjustment must be consistent with the accounting for a step-by-step subsidiary acquisition. The amount of the adjustment to prior periods is for the difference between the amounts that were recognized in prior periods under the cost method and the amounts that would have been recognized if the equity method had been used. The adjustments are made based on the ownership interest that existed at the time the income was earned.

Example 4 ▸ Changes to Equity Method

On January 2, year 1, Amsted Corporation purchased 10% of the outstanding shares of Cable Company common stock for $250,000 and recorded the investment using the cost method. On January 2, year 3, Amsted purchased an additional 20% of Cable's stock for $600,000. Now having a 30% interest and significant influence, Amsted uses the equity method. Cable Co.'s net income and dividends paid are as follows.

Year	Cable Co. net income	Cable Co. dividends paid to Amsted
1	$250,000	$10,000
2	500,000	15,000
3	600,000	60,000

Required: Provide the journal entry for the January 2, year 3, transaction retroactively reflecting the change from the cost to equity method.

Solution:

	Dr.	Cr.
Investment in Cable Co. Stock	650,000	
Cash		600,000
Retained earnings		50,000*

***Computations:**	Year 1	Year 2	Total
Amsted Corp. equity in earnings of Cable Co., 10%	$ 25,000	$ 50,000	$ 75,000
Dividends received	(10,000)	(15,000)	(25,000)
Prior period adjustment	$ 15,000	$ 35,000	$ 50,000

7. **Losses** A loss in the value of an equity method investment should be recognized if such loss is other than temporary. A loss in value may be evidenced by a poor earnings record, inability to recover the carrying amount of the investment, or similar causes. An investor should reduce its investment for its pro rata share of investee losses. However, if the investee continuously reports net losses, the investor should discontinue applying the equity method after the investment has been written down to zero. The investor should then record her/his share of further investee losses by memo entry only. If the investee becomes profitable in the future, the investor should resume applying the equity method only after its share of net income equals its share of net losses not previously recognized.

8. **Financial Statement Presentation** The investor's investment in common stock should be disclosed as a single line item on the balance sheet. The investor's share of investee's earnings is disclosed as a single line item on the income statement. An **exception** arises for investee's extraordinary items and prior period adjustments. If material, these items should be separately reported in the investor's financial statements.

Exhibit 2 ▸ T-Account Summary of the Equity Method

Equity Investment in X Co. (balance sheet)	
Original cost of investment	
Pro rata share of investee's income since acquisition	Pro rata share of investee's losses since acquisition
Retroactive adjustment due to change from cost to equity method (dr. or cr.)	Pro rata share of investee's dividends declared
	Disposal of investee stock

Investment Income, X Co. (income statement)	
Pro rata share of investee's losses since acquisition	Pro rata share of investee's income since acquisition

NOTE: The investment income account is **not** affected by dividends declared by the investee.

IV. Investments in Marketable Securities (SFAS 115)

A. Applicability

SFAS 115 applies to investments in equity securities that have a readily determinable fair value and to all investments in debt securities. SFAS 115 does **not** apply to investments accounted for under the equity method nor to investments in consolidated subsidiaries. The focus of guidance in SFAS 115 is on portfolios (groups of stocks) rather than individual stocks.

B. Classification

SFAS 115, *Accounting for Certain Investments in Debt and Equity Securities,* classifies securities in one of three categories: trading securities, available-for-sale (AFS) securities, or held-to-maturity (HTM) securities.

1. **Trading Securities** Debt and equity securities that are bought and held principally for the purpose of selling them in the near term. Generally used with the objective of generating profits on short-term differences in price.

   a. They are reported at fair value (market value).

   b. Unrealized holding gains and losses are included in current earnings.

2. **Available-for-Sale (AFS) Securities** Debt and equity securities not classified as either held-to-maturity or trading securities.

   a. They are reported at fair value (market value).

   b. Unrealized holding gains and losses are excluded from current earnings and are instead reported in other comprehensive income (OCI).

3. **Held-to-Maturity (HTM) Securities** Debt securities that the enterprise has the positive intent and the ability to hold to maturity.

   a. They are reported at amortized cost.

   b. They are not adjusted for unrealized holding gains and losses, although fair value must be disclosed.

C. Acquisition Cost

Marketable debt and equity securities are recorded at cost, which includes the purchase price and other direct costs of acquisition, such as broker's fees and taxes. For debt securities purchased between interest dates, accrued interest is **not** part of the cost of the securities. Generally, the discount or premium on temporary investments in debt securities is not recorded separately in the accounts and not amortized because the investment is ordinarily held for only a short time and hence any amortized amount would be immaterial.

Example 5 ▸ Marketable Securities

On November 1, securities are purchased for $500. At year end, the fair value is $400. The entries are as follows:

	Trading Securities			Available-for-Sale Securities (AFS)		
11/1	Investment in Securities	500		Investment in Securities	500	
	Cash		500	Cash		500
12/31	Unrealized Holding Gain or Loss on Securities (Income)	100		Unrealized Holding Gain or Loss on Securities (OCI)	100	
	Market Adjustment—Trading		100	Market Adjustment—AFS		100

D. Year-End Valuation

HTM securities are reported at amortized cost. Trading securities and AFS securities are accounted for at fair value, determined at the balance sheet date. The excess of cost over fair value or fair value over cost is recorded as a credit or debit in a *Market Adjustment* account. The offsetting entry goes to an income statement account for trading securities, and to an *Other Comprehensive Income* (OCI) account for AFS securities.

Example 6 ▶ Available-for-Sale Portfolio, Unrealized Gain

The aggregate cost and fair value (FV) of Zeta Corp.'s investments (all classified as available-for-sale) in marketable securities at 12/31 for years 1 and 2 are given below.

	December 31, Year 1		December 31, Year 2	
	Cost	FV	Cost	FV
Security W	$ 800	$1,300	$ 800	$1,100
Security X	800	1,000	800	700
Security Y	900	600	1,000*	900
Security Z	900	600	1,000*	1,400
	$3,400	$3,500	$3,600	$4,100

* Increases reflect net acquisitions during the period.

Required: Determine the following:

a. Amount to report for these investments on the 12/31, year 1 balance sheet.

b. Amount of unrealized gain or loss to be recognized in year 2.

c. Amount to report for these investments on the 12/31, year 2 balance sheet.

Solution:

a. The fair value of the securities at 12/31, year 1 ($3,500) is greater than its aggregate cost ($3,400). Therefore, the *Market Adjustment—AFS* account would have a $100 debit balance at 12/31, year 1 and the *Unrealized Holding Gain or Loss* (OCI) account would have a $100 credit balance at 12/31, year 1. The securities portfolio is presented in the asset section of the 12/31, year 1 balance sheet.

Investment in securities at fair value	$3,500

b. At the end of year 2, the fair value of the portfolio ($4,100) is $500 greater than its aggregate cost ($3,600). An additional $400 debit is required to bring the year-end balance in the valuation account to $500, resulting in the following journal entry:

Market Adjustment—AFS	400	
Unrealized Holding Gain or Loss (OCI)		400

This brings the *Market Adjustment—AFS* account balance up to the $500 ($4,100 – $3,600) difference between cost and fair value at year end. Since it pertains to the AFS portfolio, the net unrealized holding gain of $500 is reported in *Accumulated Other Comprehensive Income.*

c. The securities portfolio is presented in the asset section of the 12/31, year 2 balance sheet.

Investment in securities at fair value	$4,100

NOTE: If the securities are classified as current, they would appear in the current asset section of the balance sheet. If they are classified as noncurrent, they would appear in the long-term investment section.

Example 7 ▸ Available-for-Sale Portfolio, Unrealized Loss

Assume the fair value of the portfolio at 12/31, year 1 in Example 6 was $3,100 rather than $3,500 ($300 less than its aggregate cost). Therefore, the *Market Adjustment—AFS* account would have a $300 credit balance at 12/31, year 1 and the *Unrealized Holding Gain or Loss* (OCI) account would have a $300 debit balance at 12/31, year 1.

At 12/31, year 2, assume the fair value of the portfolio was $3,500 (only $100 *less* than its $3,600 aggregate cost). Therefore, the *Market Adjustment—AFS* account must be reduced by $200 with a corresponding reduction of the balance in the *Unrealized Holding Gain or Loss* (OCI) account. The journal entry is as follows:

Market Adjustment—AFS	200	
Unrealized Holding Gain or Loss (OCI)		200

This brings the *Market Adjustment—AFS* account balance down to the $100 ($3,600 – $3,500) difference between cost and fair value at year end. Because it applies to the AFS category, the net unrealized loss of $100 is reported in OCI. The security portfolio is presented in the asset section of the 12/31, year 2 balance sheet.

Investment in securities at fair value	$3,500

Example 8 ▸ Trading Securities Portfolio

With the same facts as Examples 6 and 7, the solutions for the trading securities category are the same, except that the changes in the *Market Adjustment—Trading* account flow through the current income statement, rather than through other comprehensive income.

In Example 6, the unrealized holding gain of $400 would appear in the year 2 income statement.

Market Adjustment—Trading	400	
Unrealized Holding Gain or Loss (Income)		400

E. Other Than Temporary Decline in Fair Value

If the decline in fair value for AFS or HTM securities is determined to be other than temporary, the cost basis of the individual security is written down to fair value that becomes the new cost basis and a realized loss is recognized in current earnings.

1. **Subsequent Increases** The new cost basis is not changed for subsequent recoveries in fair value. Subsequent increases in fair value of AFS securities are accounted for as unrealized gains by debiting the *Market Adjustment* account and crediting the *Unrealized Holding Gain or Loss* (OCI) account.

2. **Subsequent Decreases** Subsequent decreases in fair value of AFS securities, if not other-than-temporary, are accounted for as unrealized losses by debiting the *Unrealized Holding Gain or Loss* (OCI) account and crediting the *Market Adjustment* account.

F. Transfers Between Categories

Securities may be transferred among the three classifications: trading, AFS, and HTM. Reclassification should be rare under the guidelines of SFAS 115.

1. **Transfers From Trading** If a security is transferred from the trading category, any previously recognized unrealized holding gain or loss should not be reversed. Additionally, the security should be transferred at fair value with a gain or loss recognized upon transfer.

2. **Transfers to Trading** If a security is transferred into the trading category, any unrealized holding gain or loss related to this security should be recognized in earnings immediately.

3. **Transfers From HTM to AFS** If a debt security is transferred from HTM to AFS category, any unrealized holding gain or loss related to this security should be recognized in an *Other Comprehensive Income* account consistent with the treatment for AFS securities.

4. **Transfers From AFS to HTM** If a debt security is transferred from AFS to HTM category, any unrealized holding gain or loss related to this security should still be reported in an *Other Comprehensive Income* account and amortized over the security's remaining life.

G. **Sale**

The realized gain or loss from the sale of a debt or equity security is the difference between the net proceeds received from the sale (i.e., the gross selling price of the security less brokerage commissions and taxes) and the cost or unamortized cost of the security (not its fair value at the most recent balance sheet date).

1. **Previously Recognized Losses or Recoveries** In determining the realized gain or loss on the sale, no regard is given to previously recognized unrealized losses or recoveries or to the amount accumulated in the *Market Adjustment* account.

2. **Reclassification Adjustments** Reclassification adjustments, required by SFAS 130, are made to avoid double counting in comprehensive income gains or losses realized and included in net income of the current period that were previously included in other comprehensive income as unrealized gains or losses. Reclassification adjustments for unrealized gains and losses on certain investments in debt and equity securities may be summarized on the face of the financial statement in which comprehensive income is reported or disclosed in the notes to the financial statements.

Exhibit 3 ▸ SFAS 115 Summary

	Trading	Available-for-Sale	Held-to-Maturity
Type of security	Debt or Equity	Debt or Equity	Debt
Accounting at acquisition	Cost (purchase price plus other direct costs of acquisition)	Cost (purchase price plus other direct costs of acquisition)	Cost (purchase price plus other direct costs of acquisition)
End-of-year valuation	Fair value	Fair value	Amortized cost
Valuation adjustments	Market adjustment account	Market adjustment account	Not adjusted for fair value
Change in fair value	Reported in income	Reported in OCI	Not applicable
Other than temporary declines in fair value below cost	Reported in income	Reported in income	Reported in income
Balance sheet classification	Current asset	Either current or noncurrent asset	Noncurrent asset (Unless maturing within one year)
Dividends and interest earned	Reported in income using interest method to amortize associated premium or discount*	Reported in income using interest method to amortize associated premium or discount	Reported in income using interest method to amortize associated premium or discount

* Generally, the amount of amortization for short-term investments is immaterial and therefore not recorded.

V. Financial Instruments & Derivatives

A. Definitions

1. **Financial Instrument** A financial instrument is cash, evidence of an ownership interest in an entity, or a contract that does both of the following:

a. **Contractual Obligation** Imposes on one entity a contractual obligation (1) to deliver cash or another financial instrument to a second entity or (2) to exchange other financial instruments on potentially unfavorable terms with the second entity.

b. **Contractual Right** Conveys to that second entity a contractual right (1) to receive cash or another financial instrument from the first entity or (2) to exchange other financial instruments on potentially favorable terms with the first entity.

2. **Derivative Instrument** A derivative instrument is an instrument or other contract that has the following three characteristics:

   a. **Underlying and Notional Amount or Payment Provision** A derivative instrument has at least one underlying and at least one notional amount or payment provision or both.

   b. **Zero or Small Investment** A derivative instrument either requires no initial net investment, or one that is smaller than would be required for other types of contracts expected to have a similar response to market factor changes.

   c. **Net Settlement** A derivative instrument requires or permits net settlement, can be readily settled net by a means outside the contract, or provides for delivery of an asset that puts the recipient in a position not substantially different from net settlement.

3. **Underlying** An underlying is a specified interest rate, security price, commodity price, foreign exchange rate, index of prices or rates, or other variable (including the occurrence or nonoccurrence of a specified event such as a scheduled payment under a contract). An underlying may be a price or rate of an asset or liability, but it is not the asset or the liability.

4. **Notional Amount** A notional amount is a number of currency units, shares, bushels, pounds, or other units specified in a derivative instrument. The notional amount is called a face amount in some contracts.

5. **Fair Value** Fair value is the amount at which an asset (liability) could be bought (incurred) or sold (settled) in a current transaction between willing parties other than in a forced or liquidation sale. Generally, quoted market prices, if available, are the best evidence of fair value. If quoted market prices are unavailable, the estimate of fair value should be based on the best information available in the circumstances.

6. **Hedging** Hedging is a risk management strategy to protect against the possibility of loss, such as from price fluctuations. Generally, the strategy involves counterbalancing transactions in which a loss on one financial instrument or cash flow stream would be offset by a gain on the related derivative.

7. **Firm Commitment** A firm commitment is an agreement with an unrelated party, binding on both parties and usually legally enforceable, with the following characteristics:

   a. **Significant Terms** The agreement specifies all significant terms, including the quantity to be exchanged, the fixed price, and the timing of the transaction. The fixed price may be expressed as a specified amount of an entity's functional currency or of a foreign currency, or as a specified interest rate or specified effective yield.

   b. **Nonperformance** The agreement includes a disincentive for nonperformance that is sufficient to make performance probable.

8. **Forecasted Transaction** A forecasted transaction is a transaction that is expected to occur for which there is no firm commitment, and does not give an entity any present rights to future benefits or a present obligation for future sacrifices.

B. Derivative Instruments & Hedging Activities (SFAS 133, 138, 149 & 155)

1. **Standards** SFAS 133, *Accounting for Derivative Instruments and Hedging Activities,* and SFAS 138 establish standards for derivative instruments and for hedging activities. SFAS 133 and 138 require that companies include derivatives in financial statements. SFAS 149 amends SFAS 133 by requiring contracts with comparable characteristics to be accounted for similarly. SFAS 155 amends SFAS 133 to simplify accounting for certain hybrid financial instruments by permitting fair value remeasurement for any hybrid financial instrument that contains an embedded derivative that would otherwise require bifurcation.

Exhibit 4 ▸ Highlights of Accounting for Derivative Instruments & Hedging Activities

- Derivatives are recognized as assets or liabilities on the financial statements.
- **Fair value** is used to measure derivatives.
- Changes in fair value of **non-hedge derivatives** are reported as **gains or losses in earnings.**
- Accounting for the unrealized gains or losses from the changes in fair value of **hedge derivatives** depends on the intended use of the derivative.
  1. **Fair Value Hedge**—Reported in **earnings.**
  2. **Cash Flow Hedge**—Effective portion reported in **other comprehensive income;** ineffective portions reported in earnings.
  3. **Hedge of a Net Investment in a Foreign Operation**—Effective portion reported in **other comprehensive income;** ineffective portion reported in earnings.

2. **Recognition at Fair Value** An entity must recognize in the statement of financial position all derivatives as either assets or liabilities and measure them at fair value. Recognizing derivative assets and liabilities makes financial statements more complete and informative.

   a. **Rights and Obligations** Derivatives are assets and liabilities because they are rights and obligations. The ability to settle a derivative in a gain position by receiving cash is evidence of the right to a future economic benefit and indicates the instrument is an asset. Similarly, the fact that a cash payment is required to settle a derivative in a loss position is evidence of the duty to sacrifice assets in the future and indicates the instrument is a liability.

   b. **Embedded Derivatives** Some contracts may not meet the definition of a derivative instrument in their entirety, but may contain "embedded" derivative instruments. Embedded derivatives could be separately valued if their economic characteristics and risks are not clearly and closely related to the economic characteristics and risks of the host contract. SFAS 155 allows an entity to value the host, and embedded derivative, in its entirety at fair value (initially or when subject to remeasurement).

3. **Hedging Derivatives**

   a. **Types** If certain conditions are met, the derivative may be designated as one of three categories of hedges, depending on its intended use: fair value hedge, cash flow hedge, or foreign currency hedge.

      (1) **Fair Value Hedge** A hedge of the exposure to changes in the fair value of an asset or liability, or an unrecognized firm commitment.

      (2) **Cash Flow Hedge** A hedge of the exposure to variable cash flows on an existing, recognized asset or liability (such as all or certain future interest payments on variable-rate debt) or a forecasted transaction (such as a forecasted purchase or sale).

(3) **Foreign Currency Hedge** A hedge of the foreign currency exposure of a net investment in a foreign operation, an unrecognized firm commitment, an AFS security, or a foreign-currency-denominated forecasted transaction.

b. **Criteria** Derivatives that are intended to be fair value or cash flow hedges and are effective as fair value or cash flow hedges must meet all of the following criteria.

(1) **Formal Documentation** At the inception of the hedge, there must be formal documentation of the hedging relationship and the entity's risk management objective and strategy for undertaking the hedge, including identification of the hedging instrument, the related hedged item, the nature of the risk being hedged, and how the hedging instrument's effectiveness in offsetting the hedged item's exposure attributable to the hedged risk will be assessed. There must be a reasonable basis for how the entity plans to assess the hedging instrument's effectiveness.

(2) **Effectiveness Expectation** Both at the inception of the hedge and on an ongoing basis, the hedging relationship must be expected to be highly effective in achieving offsetting changes in fair value or cash flows attributable to the hedged risk, consistent with the originally documented risk management strategy for that particular hedging relationship, during the period that the hedge is designated. An assessment of effectiveness is required whenever financial statements or earnings are reported, and at least every three months.

(3) **Gain Potential** If a net written option is designated as hedging a recognized asset or liability, the combination of the hedged item and the written option must provide at least as much potential, for a fair value hedge, for gains as a result of a favorable change in the fair value of the combined instruments as exposure to losses from an unfavorable change in their combined fair value; or for a cash flow hedge, favorable cash flows as exposure to unfavorable cash flows.

c. **Fair Value Hedge Criteria** The following are the primary criteria; there are other specific exclusions provided for in SFAS 133.

(1) The hedged item is specifically identified as either all or a specific portion of a recognized asset or liability or of a firm commitment.

(2) The hedged item is a single asset or liability, or is a portfolio of similar assets or a portfolio of similar liabilities. If similar assets or similar liabilities are aggregated and hedged as a portfolio, the individual assets or individual liabilities must share the risk exposure for which they are designated as being hedged.

(3) The hedged item presents an exposure to changes in fair value for the hedged risk that could affect reported earnings.

d. **Cash Flow Hedge Criteria** A forecasted transaction is eligible for designation as a hedged transaction in a cash flow hedge if all of the following primary criteria are met:

(1) The forecasted transaction is a single transaction or a series of individual transactions. If individual forecasted transactions are aggregated and hedged as a group, either (a) the individual transactions must be projected to occur within a short period of time from a single identified date for the group or (b) the date at which the variability of the cash flows of each of the individual transactions is projected to cease must be within a short period of time from a single identified date for the group. Additionally, the individual transactions must share the same risk exposure for which they are designated as being hedged.

(2) The forecasted transaction is probable and there is a positive expectation that the forecasted transaction, or group of similar forecasted transactions, will occur

within an insignificant variance from the initially projected date of the forecasted transaction relative to the original length of time from the inception of the hedge to that projected date.

(3) The forecasted transaction is a transaction with a third party external to the reporting entity and presents an exposure to variations in cash flows for the hedged risk that could affect reported earnings.

Example 9 ▸ Hedge of Commodity Price Risk on Purchase of Inventories

Cereal Co. manufactures breakfast cereals and is concerned about the volatility of grain prices, since such volatility will significantly impact its profit margins on sales of cereal products. Cereal Co. anticipates acquiring 10 million bushels of grain in six months at the then current spot rate. To protect against future price changes in the commodity on May 1, Cereal Co. acquires grain futures for 10 million bushels at the current spot rate for delivery in six months. The current price is $0.40 per bushel. Cereal Co. acquires the 10 million bushels of grain on October 1 at $0.45 per bushel. It then sells the finished products over the following three months. All of the hedging criteria are met.

Required: Provide the journal entries to record the commodity futures on the current date, prior to the settlement of the contract and a summary entry for the realization of the gain over the following three months as the inventory is sold. The entries to record the actual settlement of the contract and acquisition of inventory are not required.

Solution:

5/1	Investment in Grain Futures	4,000,000	
	Due to Broker		4,000,000
10/1	Investment in Grain Futures	500,000	
	Unrealized Gain on Derivative—OCI		500,000

Settlement of contract and acquisition of inventory: Cereal Co. would settle the contract and purchase inventory at the current market price. This results in inventory of $4,500,000.

3 months following, in proportion to sales of inventory:		
Unrealized Gain on Derivative—Accumulated OCI	500,000	
Gain on Derivatives		500,000

4. **Unrealized Gains and Losses** Unrealized gains and losses resulting from changes in the fair value of a derivative will be accounted for in either current earnings or in other comprehensive income, depending on the intended use of the derivative.

a. **Non-Hedging Derivative** The gain or loss is recognized in earnings in the period of change for derivatives not held for hedging purposes.

b. **Fair Value Hedge** The gain or loss is recognized in earnings in the period of change, together with the offsetting loss or gain in the hedged item. Net losses or gains in the hedging activity indicates the effectiveness of the hedge; i.e., if the net loss or gain is zero, then the hedge was highly effective. The effect of that accounting is to reflect in earnings the extent to which the hedge is not effective in achieving offsetting changes in fair value. Thus both overhedged and underhedged positions will be included in income.

c. **Cash Flow Hedge** The effective portion of the gain or loss is initially reported as a component of other comprehensive income (OCI) and subsequently reclassified into earnings when the forecasted transaction affects earnings. The overhedged ineffective portion of the gain or loss is reported in earnings immediately. For example, if the derivative is a hedge of anticipated cash flows associated with the acquisition of inventory, the gain or loss on the derivative would be included in income when the cost of sales is recognized. If, however, the forecasted cash flow were the acquisition of property and equipment, the gain or loss on the derivative would be recognized based on the depreciation of the property and equipment.

d. **Foreign Currency Hedges**

(1) **Foreign Currency Fair Value Hedge** The gain or loss on an unrecognized firm commitment or an available-for-sale security designated as a fair value foreign currency hedge is recognized currently in *earnings.* The gain or loss on the hedged item adjusts the carrying amount of the hedged item and is also recognized currently in earnings. (Note that this is the same treatment as for a fair value hedge.) If the hedged item is an available-for-sale security, the recognition of gain or loss in earnings rather than in other comprehensive income is an exception to the normal accounting treatment of gains and losses on available-for-sale securities, in order to offset the gain or loss on the hedging instrument that is reported in current earnings.

(2) **Foreign Currency Cash Flow Hedge** The *effective portion* of the gain or loss on a forecasted foreign-currency-denominated transaction or a forecasted inter-company foreign-currency-denominated transaction designated as a cash flow hedge is reported in other comprehensive income, and the ineffective portion is reported in earnings. Effectiveness is defined as the degree that the gain (loss) for the hedging instrument offsets the loss (gain) on the hedged item.

(3) **Hedge of Net Investment in Foreign Operation** The gain or loss on a hedging derivative instrument, or the foreign currency transaction gain or loss on a non-derivative hedging instrument, that is designated as an economic hedge, and is effective as an economic hedge, of the net investment in a foreign operation is reported in other comprehensive income, as part of the cumulative translation adjustment, to the extent it is effective as a hedge.

Example 10 ▸ Hedge of Foreign Currency Exchange Rate Risk on Equipment Acquisition

On March 1, an entity anticipates acquiring equipment from a foreign manufacturer. The equipment is expected to be delivered in three months and will cost 1,200,000 FCU (Foreign Currency Units). The equipment will have a 5-year useful life and straight-line depreciation will be used. To hedge the foreign currency exchange rate exposure, the entity acquires forward contracts on the currency for delivery in three months. The current forward rate is $1 = 0.5 FCU. The spot (forward) rate for June 1 (at settlement) is $1 = 0.3 FCU. All of the hedging criteria are met. The entity takes a full year's depreciation in the year of requisition.

Required: Provide the journal entries to record the acquisition of the foreign currency derivative, unrealized gain, realization of gain, and depreciation expense.

Solution:

3/1	Due from Broker (1,200,000/0.5)	2,400,000	
	Foreign Currency Derivative		2,400,000

Prior to settlement of contract:

6/1	Due from Broker		
	[(1,200,000 FCU × $1/0.3 FCU) – $2,400,000]	1,600,000	
	Unrealized Gain on Derivative—OCI		1,600,000

Settlement of contract and acquisition of equipment: The entity would settle the contract and purchase the equipment, resulting in equipment recorded at $4,000,000.

Recorded each year for five years:

Unrealized Gain on Derivative—OCI ($1,600,000/5)	320,000	
Gain on Derivatives		320,000
Depreciation Expense ($4,000,000/5)	800,000	
Accumulated Depreciation		800,000

5. **Disclosures**

a. **Objectives** An entity that holds or issues hedging instruments must disclose its objectives for holding or issuing those instruments, the context needed to understand those objectives, and its strategies for achieving those objectives.

b. **Type** The description must distinguish between instruments designated for fair value hedges, cash flow hedges, foreign currency hedges, and all other derivatives.

c. **Risk Policy** The description must indicate the entity's risk management policy for each type of hedge, including a description of the items or transactions for which risks are hedged.

d. **Purpose** For non-hedge derivatives, the description must indicate the purpose of the derivative activity.

e. **Additional Disclosures Encouraged** The entity is encouraged, but not required, to provide additional qualitative disclosures, including the entity's objectives and strategies within the context of an entity's overall risk management profile.

f. **Fair Value Hedges** For fair value hedges, the net gain or loss recognized in earnings during the reporting period representing the amount of the hedges' ineffectiveness and the component of the derivative instruments' gain or loss, if any, excluded from the assessment of hedge effectiveness and a description of where the net gain or loss is reported in the financial statements must be disclosed. When a hedged firm commitment no longer qualifies as a fair value hedge, the amount of net gain or loss recognized in earnings must be disclosed.

g. **Cash Flow Hedges** For cash flow hedges, disclosure must include:

(1) The net gain or loss recognized in earnings during the reporting period representing the amount of the hedges' ineffectiveness and the component of the derivative instruments' gain or loss, if any, excluded from the assessment of hedge effectiveness and a description of where the net gain or loss is reported in the financial statements.

(2) A description of the transactions or other events that will result in the reclassification into earnings of gains and losses reported in accumulated other comprehensive income, and the estimated net amount of the existing gains or losses at the reporting date expected to be reclassified into earnings within the next 12 months.

(3) The maximum length of time over which the entity is hedging its exposure to the variability in future cash flows for forecasted transactions excluding those forecasted transactions related to the payment of variable interest on existing financial instruments.

(4) The amount of gains and losses reclassified into earnings as a result of the discontinuance of cash flow hedges because it is probable that the original forecasted transactions will not occur.

h. **Foreign Currency Hedges** For foreign currency hedge instruments, the net amount of gains or losses included in the cumulative translation adjustment during the reporting period must be disclosed.

i. **Other Comprehensive Income (OCI)** An entity must display as a separate classification within other comprehensive income the net gain or loss on derivative instruments designated and qualifying as cash flow hedging instruments that are reported in comprehensive income.

j. **Accumulated OCI** An entity must separately disclose, as part of the accumulated OCI disclosures, the beginning and ending accumulated derivative gain or loss, the related net change associated with current period hedging transactions, and the net amount of any reclassification into earnings.

6. **Terminology** This list is not intended to be all inclusive. It includes a sample of derivatives and instruments that contain embedded derivatives. **NOTE:** CPA candidates do not need to memorize the following list. It is included so that candidates may become familiar with terminology that could be used in questions regarding derivative instruments.

   a. **Benchmark Interest Rate** The benchmark interest rate is a widely recognized and quoted rate in an active financial market as a rate associated with no risk of default. It is widely used as an underlying basis for determining the interest rates of individual financial instruments and commonly referenced in interest-rate-related transactions. In some markets, government borrowing rates may be used. In other markets, an interbank offered rate may be used. Currently in the US, only the interest rates on direct Treasury obligations of the US government and, for practical reasons, the LIBOR swap rate are considered to be benchmark interest rates.

   b. **LIBOR Swap Rate** LIBOR (London Interbank Offered Rate) swap rate is the fixed rate on a single-currency, constant-notional interest rate swap that has its floating-rate leg referenced to the LIBOR. The fixed rate is derived as the rate that would result in the swap having a zero fair value at inception; the rate at which the present value of the fixed cash flows are equal to the present value of the floating cash flows.

   c. **Interest Rate Swap Agreement** An interest rate swap agreement is an arrangement used to limit interest rate risk. Two companies swap interest payments, but not the principal, in an interest rate swap agreement. A company with a substantial amount of variable rate debt may wish to swap into fixed-rate debt to limit its exposure to rising interest rates. A company with a high fixed rate may wish to swap to a floating rate in anticipation of falling interest rates. Companies with lower credit ratings often cannot borrow in the fixed-rate market but can swap into it. Such transactions were previously considered off-balance sheet financing because only the original borrowings were reported on the balance sheet and the rights and obligations related to the interest payments per the swap agreement were not reported on the balance sheet, but only in the disclosures. Under SFAS 133, this is an example of a derivative required to be reported on the balance sheet.

   d. **Swaption** A swaption is an option to require delivery of a swap contract, which is a derivative.

   e. **Embedded Derivative** A derivative embedded in a host contract in a hybrid instrument.

   f. **Host Contract** A hybrid contract that contains an embedded derivative.

   g. **Inverse Floater** A bond with a coupon rate of interest that varies inversely with changes in specified general interest rate levels or indexes (such as LIBOR).

   h. **Levered Inverse Floater** A bond with a coupon that varies indirectly with changes in general interest rate levels and applies a multiplier (greater than 1.00) to the specified index in its calculation of interest.

   i. **Delevered Floater** A bond with a coupon rate of interest that lags overall movements in specified general interest rate levels or indices.

   j. **Range Floater** A bond with a coupon that depends on the number of days that a reference rate stays within a preestablished collar; otherwise, the bond pays either zero percent interest or a below-market rate.

k. **Ratchet Floater** A bond that pays a floating rate of interest and has an adjustable cap, adjustable floor, or both that move in sync with each new reset rate.

l. **Fixed-to-Floating Note** A bond that pays a varying coupon (first-year coupon is fixed; second- and third-year coupons are based on LIBOR, Treasury bills, or prime rate).

m. **Indexed Amortizing Note** A bond that repays principal based on a predetermined amortization schedule or target value. The amortization is linked to changes in a specific mortgage-backed security index or interest rate index. The maturity of the bond changes as the related index changes. This instrument includes a varying maturity.

n. **Equity-Indexed Note** A bond for which the return of interest, principal, or both is tied to a specified equity security or index (such as the Standard and Poor's 500 index).

o. **Variable Principal Redemption Bond** A bond whose principal redemption value at maturity depends on the change in an underlying index over a predetermined observation period. A typical example would be a bond that guarantees a minimum par redemption value of 100% and provides the potential for a supplemental principal payment at maturity as compensation for the below market rate of interest offered with the instrument.

p. **Crude Oil Knock-in Note** A bond that has a 1% coupon and guarantees repayment of principal with upside potential based on the strength of the oil market.

q. **Gold-Linked Bull Note** A bond that has a fixed 3% coupon and guarantees repayment of principal with upside potential if the price of gold increases.

r. **Step-up Bond** A bond that provides an introductory above-market yield and steps up to a new coupon, which will be below then-current market rates or alternatively, the bond may be called in lieu of the step-up in the coupon rate.

s. **Credit-Sensitive Bond** A bond that has a coupon rate of interest that resets based on changes in the issuer's credit rating.

t. **Inflation Bond** A bond with a contractual principal amount that is indexed to the inflation rate but cannot decrease below par; the coupon rate is typically below that of traditional bonds of similar maturity.

u. **Disaster Bond** A bond that pays a coupon above that of an otherwise comparable traditional bond; however, all or a substantial portion of the principal amount is subject to loss if a specified disaster experience occurs.

v. **Certain Purchases in a Foreign Currency** A U.S. company enters into a contract to purchase corn from a local American supplier in six months for yen; the yen is the functional currency of neither party to the transaction. The corn is expected to be delivered and used over a reasonable period in the normal course of business.

w. **Participating Mortgage** A mortgage in which the investor receives a below-market interest rate and is entitled to participate in the appreciation in the market value of the project that is financed by the mortgage upon sale of the project.

x. **Convertible Debt** An investor receives a below-market interest rate and receives the option to convert its debt instrument into the equity of the issuer at an established conversion rate. The terms of the conversion require that the issuer deliver shares of stock to the investor. Generally, the written option is not considered to be a derivative instrument for the issuer. However, the investor generally should separate the embedded option contract from the host contract and account for the embedded option contract as a derivative instrument, unless the stock is privately held and not readily convertible to cash.

7. **Exceptions** The following contracts are not subject to the requirements of SFAS 133:

   a. **Regular-Way Security Trades** Regular-way security trades are contracts with no net settlement provision and no market mechanism to facilitate net settlement. They provide for delivery of a security within the time generally established by regulations or conventions in the marketplace or exchange in which the transaction is being executed.

   b. **Normal Purchases and Sales** Normal purchases and normal sales are contracts with no net settlement provision and no market mechanism to facilitate net settlement. They provide for the purchase or sale of something other than a financial instrument or derivative instrument that will be delivered in quantities expected to be used or sold by the reporting entity over a reasonable period in the normal course of business.

   c. **Certain Insurance Contracts** An insurance contract that entitles the holder to be compensated only if, as a result of an identifiable insurable event (other than a change in price), the holder incurs a liability or there is an adverse change in the value of a specific asset or liability for which the holder is at risk. Examples include traditional life insurance contracts, traditional property and casualty contracts.

C. Disclosures (SFAS 107)

1. **Fair Value** An entity must disclose, either in the body of the financial statements or in the accompanying notes, the fair value of financial instruments for which it is practicable to estimate that value and the method(s) and significant assumptions used to estimate the fair value of financial instruments.

2. **Evidence of Fair Value** Quoted market prices, if available, are the best evidence of the fair value of financial instruments. If quoted market prices are not available, management's best estimate of fair value may be based on the quoted market price of a financial instrument with similar characteristics or on valuation techniques.

3. **Trade Receivables and Payables** For trade receivables and payables, no disclosure is required under SFAS 107 when the carrying amount approximates fair value.

4. **Practicability** In the context of SFAS 107, practicable means that an estimate of fair value can be made without incurring excessive costs. If it is not practicable to estimate the fair value of a financial instrument or a class of financial instruments, the following should be disclosed.

   a. **Pertinent Information** Information pertinent to estimating the fair value of that financial instrument or class of financial instruments, such as the carrying amount, effective interest rate, and maturity

   b. **Reasons** The reasons why it is not practicable to estimate fair value

5. **Concentration of Credit Risk** An entity must disclose all significant concentrations of *credit risk* arising from **all** financial instruments, whether from an individual counterparty or groups of counterparties. Credit risk is the possibility that a loss may occur from the failure of another party to perform according to the terms of a contract.

   a. **Group Concentrations** Group concentrations of credit risk exist if a number of counterparties are engaged in similar activities and have similar economic characteristics that would cause their ability to meet contractual obligations to be similarly affected by changes in economic or other conditions.

   b. **Significant Concentrations** For each significant concentration, disclosure must be made as follows:

      (1) Information about the (shared) activity, region, or economic characteristic that identifies the concentration.

(2) The maximum amount of loss exposure due to credit risk if all parties to the financial instruments failed completely to perform and the amounts due proved to be of no value to the entity.

(3) The entity's policy of requiring collateral or other security to support financial instruments subject to credit risk, information about the entity's access to that collateral or security, and the nature and a brief description of the collateral or other security.

(4) The entity's policy of entering into master netting arrangements to mitigate the credit risk and information about such arrangements and the extent the arrangements reduce the credit risk.

6. **Market Risk** An entity is encouraged, but not required to disclose quantitative information about the market risks of financial instruments that is consistent with the way it manages or adjusts those risks. *Market* risk is the possibility that future changes in market prices may make a financial instrument less valuable or more onerous.

7. **Exclusions** The disclosures prescribed by SFAS 107 are not required for employers' and plans' obligations for pension benefits, other postretirement benefits, and employee stock option and stock purchase plans, substantially extinguished debt subject to the disclosure requirements of SFAS 140, lease contracts, warranty obligations and rights, unconditional purchase obligations, investments accounted for under the equity method, minority interests in consolidated subsidiaries, equity investments in consolidated subsidiaries, and equity instruments issued by the entity and classified in stockholders' equity in the statement of financial position.

D. **Transfers & Servicing of Financial Assets & Extinguishments of Liabilities (SFAS 140 & 156)** SFAS 140 establishes standards for transfers and servicing of financial assets and extinguishments of liabilities. The standards focus on control; an entity must recognize the financial and servicing assets it controls and the liabilities it has incurred, derecognize financial assets when control has been surrendered, and derecognize liabilities when extinguished. SFAS 140 establishes guidelines to determine transfers of financial assets that are sales and transfers that are secured borrowing. SFAS 140 is based on a financial-components approach, which is the recognition that financial assets and liabilities can be divided into a variety of components. A transaction may be treated partially as a sale and partially as collateralized borrowing.

1. **Accounting for Transfers and Servicing of Financial Assets** A transfer in which control is surrendered by the transferor shall be accounted for as a sale to the extent that consideration other than beneficial interests in the transferred assets is received in exchange. For control to be surrendered, *all of the following conditions* must be met.

   a. The transferred assets must be isolated from the transferor and must be beyond the reach of the transferor and its creditors, even in bankruptcy.

   b. Either the transferee obtains the rights to pledge or exchange the transferred assets, or the transferee is a qualified special purpose entity and the holders of the beneficial interest of that special purpose entity can pledge or exchange the interest. The transferor cannot place restrictions or conditions on what the transferee does with the transferred assets.

   c. The transferor does not maintain effective control over the transferred assets through repurchase or redemption agreements.

2. **Sale vs. Collateralized Borrowing** If the above conditions are met, the transfer is accounted for as a sale and the assets received and liabilities incurred in the exchange are measured at fair value. If not all of the above conditions are met, the exchange would be accounted for as collateralized borrowing.

3. **Recognition** An entity shall recognize and initially measure a servicing asset or servicing liability at fair value when entering a service contract in any of the following situations.

   a. A transfer of the financial assets that meets the requirements for sale accounting.

   b. A transfer of financial assets to a qualifying SPE in a guaranteed mortgage securitization in which the transferor retains all of the resulting securities and classifies them as either available-for-sale or trading securities.

   c. An acquisition or assumption of a servicing obligation that does not relate to financial assets of the servicer or its consolidated affiliates.

4. **Measurement** An entity shall subsequently measure each class of servicing assets and servicing liabilities using one of the following methods.

   a. *Amortization method:* Amortize in proportion to and over the period of estimated net servicing income or loss and assess for impairment or increased obligation based on fair value at each reporting date

   b. *Fair value measurement method:* Measure at fair value each reporting date and report changes in fair value in earnings in the period in which the change occurs.

5. **Reporting** An entity shall report recognized servicing assets and servicing liabilities measured using the fair value measurement method in a manner that separates their carrying amounts from the carrying amounts of those measured using the amortization method.

Example 11 ▸ Transfer & Servicing of Financial Assets

Assume that ABC Company originates $50,000 of loans that can be prepaid. These loans yield 10% interest income over their expected lives. ABC transfers 80% of the principal plus interest of 8.5% to another entity. ABC will continue to service the loans and will receive the interest income not sold. Additionally, ABC has an option to purchase the loans, and there is a recourse obligation requiring ABC to repurchase delinquent loans.

ABC receives the following in the transfer (each amount represents fair value):

Cash	$40,000
Call option (to repurchase loans)	3,500
Recourse obligation	2,500
Servicing asset	3,000
20% interest retained	10,000

The fair value of the net proceeds received in the transfer is:

Cash	$40,000
Call option	3,500
Recourse obligation	(2,500)
Net proceeds	$41,000

Required:

a. Allocate the carrying amount of the loan ($50,000) between the portion sold and the portion retained based upon the relative fair values.

b. Calculate the gain or loss on the sale.

c. Show the journal entries required for ABC to record the transfer and to recognize the servicing asset.

d. Show how the amounts would appear on ABC's balance sheet after the transfer.

Solution:

a. Allocation of the carrying amount of the loan, based upon relative fair values, is calculated as follows:

Interest	Fair Value	% Allocation of Total Fair Value	Carrying Amount
Interest sold	$41,000	75.9%	$37,950
Servicing asset	3,000	5.6%	2,800
20% interest retained	10,000	18.5%	9,250
Total	$54,000	100.0%	$50,000

b. The gain/loss on the sale is calculated as follows:

Net proceeds	$41,000
Carrying amount of loans sold	37,950
Gain on sale	$ 3,050

c. ABC would record the transfer and the servicing asset as follows:

	Debit	Credit
Cash	40,000	
Call option	3,500	
Loans		37,950
Recourse obligation		2,500
Gain on sale		3,050
Servicing asset	2,800	
Loans		2,800

d. Since the loans retained have an assigned carrying amount of $9,250, the following amounts appear on ABC's balance sheet after the transfer:

Assets:		Liabilities:	
Cash	$40,000	Recourse obligation	$2,500
Loans	9,250		
Call option	3,500		
Servicing asset (fair value)	2,800		

6. **Terminology**

a. **Interest-Only Strip** A contractual right to receive some or all of the interest due on a bond, mortgage loan, collateralized mortgage obligation, or other interest-bearing financial asset.

b. **Cleanup Call** An option held by the servicer, which may be the transferor, to purchase transferred financial assets when the amount of outstanding assets falls to a level at which the cost of servicing those assets becomes burdensome.

c. **Securitization** The process by which financial assets are transformed into securities.

d. **Wash Sales** A situation where the same financial asset is purchased soon before or after the sale of the asset. Wash sales are accounted for as sales, unless there is a concurrent contract to repurchase in which the entity retains control of the asset.

e. **Factoring** Arrangements to discount accounts receivable on a nonrecourse, notification basis. If the arrangements meet the criteria for surrendering control (SFAS 140), the transactions are accounted for as sales.

VI. Accounts Receivable

A. Definition

Accounts receivable is used for claims arising from the sale of goods or the performance of services. Receivables not arising from normal operations, such as amounts due from stockholders, officers, or employees, should be reported separately from trade accounts receivable.

B. Valuation

Accounts receivable should be reported at their **net realizable value**—the net amount expected to be received in cash. This raises two major problems: (1) determining the amount due, and (2) estimating the extent to which receivables will not be collected.

1. **Determining the Amount Due**

   a. **Discounts for Prompt Payment** Conceptually, sales and receivables should be recorded net of any discounts for prompt payment. Failure by the purchaser to take advantage of the discount offered should not be regarded as additional consideration received for the goods or services provided. These additional amounts should be considered as interest revenue. If receivables are recorded at gross, such discounts should be anticipated at year-end and deducted from the accounts receivable.

   b. **Trade and Quantity Discounts** Sales and accounts receivable should be recorded net of any trade or quantity discounts. The actual consideration agreed upon should be the amount recorded for the transaction. Sometimes the list price of a product is subject to several trade discounts. When more than one discount is given, each discount is applied to the declining balance successively. If a product has a list price of $100 and is subject to trade discounts of 20% and 10%, the actual amount recorded for the sale would be: $100 – 20%($100) = $80; $80 – 10%($80) = $72.

   c. **Sales Returns and Allowances** Future returns and allowances associated with accounts receivable outstanding at the balance sheet date should be anticipated. An allowance account should be credited for the estimated amount. The offsetting debit is to a special inventory account to reflect the expected net realizable value of returned items and the balance is charged to the sales return expense account (a "plug" amount).

   d. **Freight Charges** The treatment of freight charges depends on the terms of the sale. If they are to be borne by the seller, an expense account is charged; however, if the seller pays the freight but the amount is ultimately charged to the customer, the freight charges are included in the receivable.

      (1) **FOB Shipping Point** When goods are shipped FOB shipping point, the buyer is responsible for paying the freight charges.

      (2) **FOB Destination** When goods are shipped FOB destination, the seller is responsible for paying the freight charges.

2. **Estimating Uncollectible Receivables** There are basically two generally accepted allowance methods of recognizing the amount of uncollectible receivables and the related bad debt expense.

   a. **Percentage-of-Sales Method** Under this approach, bad debt expense is calculated as a percentage of credit sales for a period. This percentage is determined on the basis of the company's overall experience with credit sales over a period of time and is then adjusted for any relevant conditions. The amount thus estimated is charged to *Bad Debt Expense* and credited to the *Allowance for Uncollectible Accounts,* a contra-account to *Accounts Receivable.* Any previous balance in the allowance account is **not** considered in determining the amount of bad debt expense recognized for the period. The percentage-of-sales method is income statement oriented because it attempts to match bad debt expense with the revenues generated by the credit sales in the same period.

b. **Percentage-of-Outstanding-Receivables Method** This approach is based on the balance in the trade receivables accounts and attempts to value the accounts receivable at their future collectible amounts. A percentage of uncollectible accounts in the gross accounts receivable is determined based on the company's overall experience with uncollectible accounts over a period of time, and is then adjusted for any relevant conditions. This percentage is applied to the ending balance of the gross accounts receivable to obtain the desired ending balance of the allowance for uncollectible accounts. The amount of bad debt expense recognized is the difference between the *existing* balance in the allowance account and the *desired* ending balance. A more refined version of this method entails the *aging* of the gross accounts receivable. Under this approach, gross accounts receivable are classified by age intervals and a different percentage is applied to each age group. After the desired ending balance of the allowance group is determined, the amount of bad debt expense recognized is determined in exactly the same manner as when only one percentage is used—the amount of bad debt expense recognized is the difference between the *existing* balance in the allowance account and the *desired* ending balance. The percentage-of-outstanding-receivables method is balance sheet oriented because it attempts to achieve a proper carrying amount for the accounts receivable at the end of a period because they are reported at their net realizable value.

c. **Interim** Some companies estimate bad debt expense during the year using the percentage-of-sales method and then age their accounts receivable at the end of the year to determine the desired ending balance of the allowance for uncollectible accounts. In this situation, the total amount of bad debt expense recognized for the year is the amount of bad debt expense recognized during the year **plus** the amount recognized at the end of the year to adjust the existing balance in the allowance account to its desired ending balance.

Example 12 ▸ Estimating Uncollectible Receivables

Beginning balances:

Accounts receivable	$10,000
Allowance for uncollectible accounts	(750)
Accounts receivable, net	$ 9,250

During the period, there were credit sales of $60,000 and collections on credit sales of $55,000. Also, accounts receivable amounting to $1,000 were written off as uncollectible, bringing the allowance for uncollectible accounts to a $250 debit balance.

Aging of Accounts Receivable, Year-End:

		Days Outstanding			
	Total	0-30	31-60	61-90	Over 90
Accounts receivable*	$14,000	$9,000	$3,000	$1,000	$1,000
Est. % uncollectible		× 2%	× 6%	× 20%	× 50%
Est. amount uncollectible	$ 1,060	$ 180	$ 180	$ 200	$ 500

* [$10,000 + ($60,000 – $55,000 – $1,000) = $14,000]

Required: Estimate uncollectible receivables using the following methods.

a. Percentage-of-Sales: 3% of credit sales is the estimated bad debt expense.

b. Simple Percentage-of-Outstanding-Receivables: 6% of outstanding accounts receivable is estimated to be uncollectible.

c. Aged Percentage-of-Outstanding-Receivables

Solution:

a. Percentage-of-Sales Method: The balance of the allowance for uncollectible accounts would be $1,550 ($1,800 – $250) at the end of the period.

Bad Debt Expense (3% × $60,000)	1,800	
Allowance for Uncollectible Accounts		1,800

b. Percentage-of-Outstanding-Receivables Method—Simple Percentage

Desired balance in allowance, credit (6% × $14,000)	$ 840
Present balance, debit	250
Bad debt expense to be recognized	$1,090

Bad Debt Expense	1,090	
Allowance for Uncollectible Accounts		1,090

c. Percentage-of-Outstanding-Receivables Method—Aged Accounts Receivable

Desired balance, credit [total column of aging]	$1,060
Present balance, debit	250
Bad debt expense to be recognized	$1,310

Bad Debt Expense	1,310	
Allowance for Uncollectible Accounts		1,310

3. **Recording Valuation Adjustments**

a. **Recording Bad Debt Expense** Regardless of the allowance method used, the same entry is used to record bad debt expense (see Example 12). **NOTE:** This entry decreases net income, net accounts receivable, current assets, and working capital.

b. **Recording Accounts Written Off** Regardless of the allowance method used to estimate uncollectible receivables, the following journal entry should be made to record accounts written off during the period. **NOTE:** This entry has no effect on net income, net accounts receivable, current assets, or working capital.

Allowance for Uncollectible Accounts	XX	
Accounts Receivable—Joe Doe		XX

c. **Recording Subsequent Collections** Journal entries to record the collection of an account previously written off as uncollectible are as follows. These entries have no net effect on net income, current assets, or working capital.

Accounts Receivable—Joe Doe	XX	
Allowance for Uncollectible Accounts		XX
To reopen the individual account to the balance it had when written off.		

Cash	XX	
Accounts Receivable—Joe Doe		XX
To record the receipt of cash in partial payment of the receivable.		

d. **Direct Write-Off Method** The direct write-off method of recognizing bad debt expense requires the identification of specific balances that are deemed to be uncollectible before any bad debt expense is recognized. At the time that a specific account is deemed uncollectible, the account is removed from accounts receivable and a corresponding amount of bad debt expense is recognized. Since the direct write-off method does not recognize bad debt expense until a specific amount is deemed uncollectible, it does not match the cost of making a credit sale with the revenues generated by the sale, and it does not achieve a proper carrying amount for the accounts receivable at the end of a period because they are reported at more than their net realizable value.

VII. Notes Receivable

A. Definition

Notes receivable are claims usually **not** arising from sales in the ordinary course of business. Legally, the claim is evidenced by a note representing an unconditional promise to pay. Typically, notes receivable result from the following transactions.

1. Sale of property other than in the ordinary course of business—for instance, disposition of operating assets
2. Special arrangements concerning overdue accounts receivable
3. Loans to stockholders, employees, and affiliates

B. Types

Notes can be classified as either *interest-bearing,* in which case the maker of the note pays an interest amount in addition to the face amount of the note, or *noninterest-bearing,* in which case the interest is included in the face amount.

C. Valuation

APB 21 generally requires the recording of notes receivable at their present value.

1. **Interest-Bearing Notes** For interest-bearing notes calling for the prevailing rate of interest at the time of issuance, the present value of the note is the same as the face amount of the note.
2. **Exchanged for Cash** Where a note is exchanged *solely* for cash and no other rights or privileges are exchanged, it is presumed to have a present value at issuance equal to the cash proceeds exchanged. When a note is exchanged for cash and a promise to provide merchandise at a discount from market price, the issuer records the note at present value. The difference between fair value and cash payments is recognized as interest revenue over the contract life and is recorded as part of the cost of the related merchandise.
3. **Noninterest-Bearing or Other Notes** For noninterest-bearing notes and those with an unrealistic stated rate of interest, the receivable must be reported at its present value or the fair value of the property, good, or service exchanged, whichever is more clearly determinable. If material, the resultant discount or premium should be amortized over the life of the note by use of the *interest method.* Under this method, interest is calculated by applying the prevailing rate at the time of issuance to the carrying amount of the note at the beginning of the period. The prevailing rate of interest is usually defined as the cost of borrowing for a specific debtor.
4. **Loan Origination Fees** Loan origination fees are deferred and amortized over the life of the loan as an adjustment to interest income. Such amounts, if material, are amortized using the interest method.

Example 13 ▶ Recording Notes Receivable, Interest Method

On January 1, year 1, Company X received a $10,000 note in exchange for equipment sold. The stated rate of interest was 5%, payable yearly on December 31. The prevailing interest rate at the time of the exchange was determined to be 8%. The note matures on December 31, year 5.

Required: Compute the discount and interest income. Prepare the journal entries required to record the sale, the discount amortization, and the collection of the note, assuming no gain or loss on the sale of equipment.

Solution:

Determine the present value (PV) of the note at the time of acquisition.

Obtaining the interest factors from the tables in Appendix D, the calculation is:

PV = \$10,000 (0.681)* + \$500 (3.993)** = \$8,807

* The present value of \$1 for 5 periods at 8%.
** The present value of an annuity of \$1 in arrears for 5 periods at 8%.

NOTE: Interest factors are provided in the CPA examination. Memorizing the present value interest factor and annuity interest factor formulas is not necessary. The ability to select the correct interest factor is necessary.

Construct a discount amortization table. (\$8 difference due to rounding.)

1 Date	2 Interest Income (8% × Col. 5)	3 Interest Payment (5% × \$10,000)	4 Discount Amortiz. (2 – 3)	5 Present Value (PV + 4)
1/1, year 1	--	--	--	\$ 8,807
12/31, year 1	\$705	\$500	\$205	9,012
12/31, year 2	721	500	221	9,233
12/31, year 3	739	500	239	9,472
12/31, year 4	758	500	258	9,730
12/31, year 5	770	500	270	\$10,000

Provide the entries required to record the sale of the equipment, the discount amortization, and the collection of the note.

Date	Account	Debit	Credit
1/1, year 1	Notes Receivable	10,000	
	Discount on Note Receivable		1,193
	Equipment		8,807
	To record the exchange of the equipment for the note receivable.		
12/31, year 1	Cash	500	
	Discount on Note Receivable	205	
	Interest Income		705
	To record the receipt of a \$500 nominal interest payment and amortize the discount on the note. (This entry would be repeated at the end of each year until maturity, using the amounts from the amortization table.)		
12/31, year 5	Cash	500	
	Discount on Note Receivable	270	
	Interest Income		770
	To record receipt of interest and amortization (as before).		
12/31, year 5	Cash	10,000	
	Notes Receivable		10,000
	To record the receipt of the \$10,000 principal.		

D. Impairment (SFAS 114)

A creditor considers a loan to be impaired when, "based on current information and events, it is probable that the creditor will be unable to collect all amounts due according to the contractual terms of the loan agreement."

1. Initial Recognition

a. **Measurement** The creditor measures the impaired loan using one of three methods.

(1) **Present Value Method** The present value of future principal and interest cash inflows, net of discounted disposal costs, all discounted at the loan's effective interest rate

(2) **Market Price Method** The loan's observable market price

(3) **Fair Value of Collateral Method** The fair value of collateral pledged, if the loan is collateral-dependent; if foreclosure is probable, this method is to be used.

b. **Valuation Allowance Account** If the measure of the impaired loan is **less** than the recorded investment in the loan (excluding any existing valuation allowance, but including accrued interest and net deferred loan fees/costs and unamortized premium or discount), the creditor creates or adjusts an existing valuation allowance account (Allowance for Impaired Loan) with a corresponding charge or debit to the bad debt expense account.

c. **Net Carrying Amount** The loan's net carrying amount shall not exceed the loan's recorded investment at any time.

Example 14 ▸ Initial Recognition of Impairment

On January 1, year 1, Risky Developers Inc. borrowed $100,000 from Easymoney Corp. The promissory note called for 10% interest, payable annually on Dec. 31, with a maturity date of December 31, year 3. Risky made the first interest payment on time but, due to financial difficulties, defaulted on the payment due Dec. 31, year 2. On July 1, year 3, Risky and Easymoney reached an agreement to reduce the principal amount to $60,000, and the interest rate to 6%, with the payment of principal and interest due December 31, year 5. The discounted present value of the principal and interest is $54,000, net of discounted related costs, and discounted at the loan's effective interest rate.

Required: Provide the journal entry to record the initial recognition of impairment on the creditor's (Easymoney's) books.

Solution:

7/1, year 3	Bad Debt Expense	61,500	
	Allowance for Impaired Loan		61,500

Principal		$100,000
12/31, year 2 ($100,000 × 10%)	$10,000	
6/30, year 3 ($100,000 + $10,000)(10%)(1/2)	5,500	
Accrued interest		15,500
Investment in loan		115,500
PV of principal and interest		(54,000)
Allowance for impaired loan		$ 61,500

2. **Subsequent Recognition of Income or Expense**

a. **Present Value Method** If the initial impairment was measured by the discounted future cash flows method, use any of the following three methods:

(1) An *increase* in present value attributable to *time passage* is reported as interest income accrued on the net carrying amount of the loan, using the same effective interest rate used in discounting the future cash flows.

(2) The entire change in the present value in amounts or timing of future cash flows is reported as an increase or reduction in bad debt expense.

(3) A cost recovery basis of accounting may be used for income recognition purposes. Thus, an impaired loan on which no amounts of cash are collected would result in no income recognition. Use of the cost recovery method does not, of course, alter the total income recognized on the loan; it merely delays the timing of the income recognition.

b. **Other Methods** If the initial impairment was measured by the observable market price of the impaired loan, or by the fair value of the collateral:

(1) A decrease in the measure of the impaired loan is an addition to the bad debt expense.

(2) An increase in the measure of the impaired loan is a reduction of the bad debt expense.

Example 15 ▸ Subsequent Recognition of Income or Expense

Refer to Example 14, and add the following information: At December 31, year 3, based upon the effective rate of interest, income to be recognized on creditor's books is $2,700.

Required: Provide the journal entry to record the recognition of income at December 31, year 3.

Solution:

Allowance for Impaired Loan	2,700	
Interest Income (or Bad Debt Expense)		2,700

3. **Subsequent Change** If there is a subsequent material change in the future cash flows' amounts or timing, or in the loan's market price or the collateral's fair value, the creditor should remeasure the impairment amount, and adjust accordingly the valuation allowance and the bad debt expense accounts.

Example 16 ▸ Subsequent Material Change in Cash Flows

Refer to Examples 14 and 15, and add the following information: At July 1, year 4, there is a further change to extend the term to June 30, year 6. The new discounted future cash flows is $53,000.

Required: Provide the journal entry to record the revised recognition of impairment on creditor's books.

Solution: ($115,500 – $61,500 + $2,700) – $53,000 = $3,750

Bad Debt Expense	3,750	
Allowance for Impaired Loan		3,750

4. **Disclosures**

a. **Receivables** The total receivable, differentiating between the receivables with related allowances and receivables without allowances, must be disclosed. The amounts of the related allowances must also be disclosed. The reconciliation of the allowance account must be disclosed, because of the possibility of additional changes from cash flows charged against the allowance or direct write-offs.

b. **Interest Income** How the interest income was recognized must be disclosed; whether all in bad debt or broken into an interest income component and a bad debt component. The company's policy for recognizing income on impaired loans must also be disclosed.

c. **Cash Received** The amount of cash received for the period and how the cash was recognized must be disclosed.

VIII. Receivables as Immediate Sources of Cash

A. Overview

It may become desirable for the holder of receivables to immediately convert them into cash. This can be accomplished by any of four methods discussed below: discounting, assignment, factoring, and pledging. If the conversion into cash meets SFAS 140 criteria, the transaction is accounted for as a sale. If the criteria are not met, the transfer is accounted for as a secured borrowing.

B. Discounting

Discounting refers to the sale of a note to a third party, usually a bank or other financial institution. These sales are usually on a "with recourse" basis, which means that upon default of the debtor, the seller of the note becomes liable for its maturity value. The contingent liability assumed by the seller of a note "with recourse" must be disclosed. Either a footnote disclosure or a "contra asset" to notes receivable is used. Two calculations are necessary prior to discounting.

1. **Interest** Interest accrued prior to discounting must be determined

2. **Proceeds** The proceeds to be received from discounting must be calculated

Example 17 ▸ Discounting

Y Company has a $4,000, 90-day, 8% interest-bearing note; 30 days after acquiring the note, Y Company decides to discount it at a bank that charges a 10% discount rate.

Required: Determine the accrued interest income for the 30 days that Y Company held the note. Determine the proceeds Y Company received from the bank.

Solutions:

Accrued interest income: $4,000 × 8% × 1/12 = $26.67

Face amount	$4,000
Interest ($4,000 × 8% × 3/12)	80
Maturity value	4,080
Discount charged by bank ($4,080 × 10% × 2/12)	(68)
Proceeds from discounting the note receivable	$4,012

Example 18 ▸ Contingent Liability

The note in Example 17 was discounted with recourse. Provide the entries to record the discounting, and the repayment or default, for each of the two approaches.

	Footnote disclosure		Contra asset	
	Dr.	Cr.	Dr.	Cr.
a. *Discounting of N/R*				
Cash	4,012.00		4,012.00	
Interest Expense*	14.67		14.67	
Interest Income*		26.67		26.67
N/R		4,000.00		--
N/R Discounted		--		4,000.00
b. *Repayment of note by maker*				
N/R Discounted	(no entry)		4,000.00	
N/R				4,000.00

c. *Default by maker on note discounted "with recourse"*

N/R Overdue	4,080.00		4,080.00	
Cash		4,080.00		4,080.00
N/R Discounted	(no entry)		4,000.00	
N/R				4,000.00

* For greater disclosure, interest income and expense are recorded separately, rather than as a net amount.

C. Assignment

The assignment of accounts receivable represents a formal arrangement whereby the rights to accounts receivable are assigned to a financial institution in exchange for cash. Recording the transaction involves the transfer of the receivables to a special account, *Accounts Receivable Assigned.* At the same time, a liability is entered for the amount of cash received from the financial institution. Assignment usually includes "with recourse" and "non-notification" clauses. "With recourse" means that the assignor remains liable for the collection of the receivables. "Non-notification" means that the debtors are not notified of the assignment, and therefore continue making their payments to the seller. These payments are forwarded by the seller to the financial institution, thus reducing the original liability. At any point, the seller's equity in the receivables is represented as the difference between the accounts assigned and the related liability.

Example 19 ▸ Assignment of Accounts Receivable

Retro Co. assigns accounts receivable having a net carrying amount of $10,000 to Finn Inc. in exchange for $7,000 cash. Interest of 1% per month is charged on the outstanding balance of the obligation. Collections on accounts receivable are to be remitted to Finn Inc. on a monthly basis; $2,000 is collected during the first month.

Required: Record these transactions in Retro Co.'s books.

Solution:

Accounts Receivable Assigned	10,000	
Accounts Receivable		10,000
Cash	7,000	
Note Payable—Finn Inc.		7,000
Cash	2,000	
Accounts Receivable Assigned		2,000
Note Payable—Finn Inc.	1,930	
Interest Expense	70	
Cash		2,000

Following these transactions, Retro Company would present accounts receivable in its balance sheet as follows:

A/R assigned (net) ($10,000 – $2,000)	$ 8,000
Less: N/P on A/R assigned ($7,000 – $1,930)	(5,070)
Equity in A/R assigned	$ 2,930

D. Factoring

Factoring is similar to a sale of receivables because it is generally without recourse (i.e., the financing institution or "factor" assumes the risk of collectivity) and the factor generally handles the billing and collection function. A transfer of receivables to a factor without recourse is accounted for as any other sale of an asset: debit cash, credit the receivables, and record a gain or loss for the difference. If the factoring is *with recourse,* it may be accounted for as a sale of the receivables or as secured borrowing, depending on whether certain criteria are met.

E. **Pledging**

Receivables may be pledged as security for loans. Collections on the receivables are usually required to be applied to a reduction of the loan. Where receivables are pledged, adequate disclosure must be made in the financial statements.

Exhibit 5 ▸ Sale of Receivables

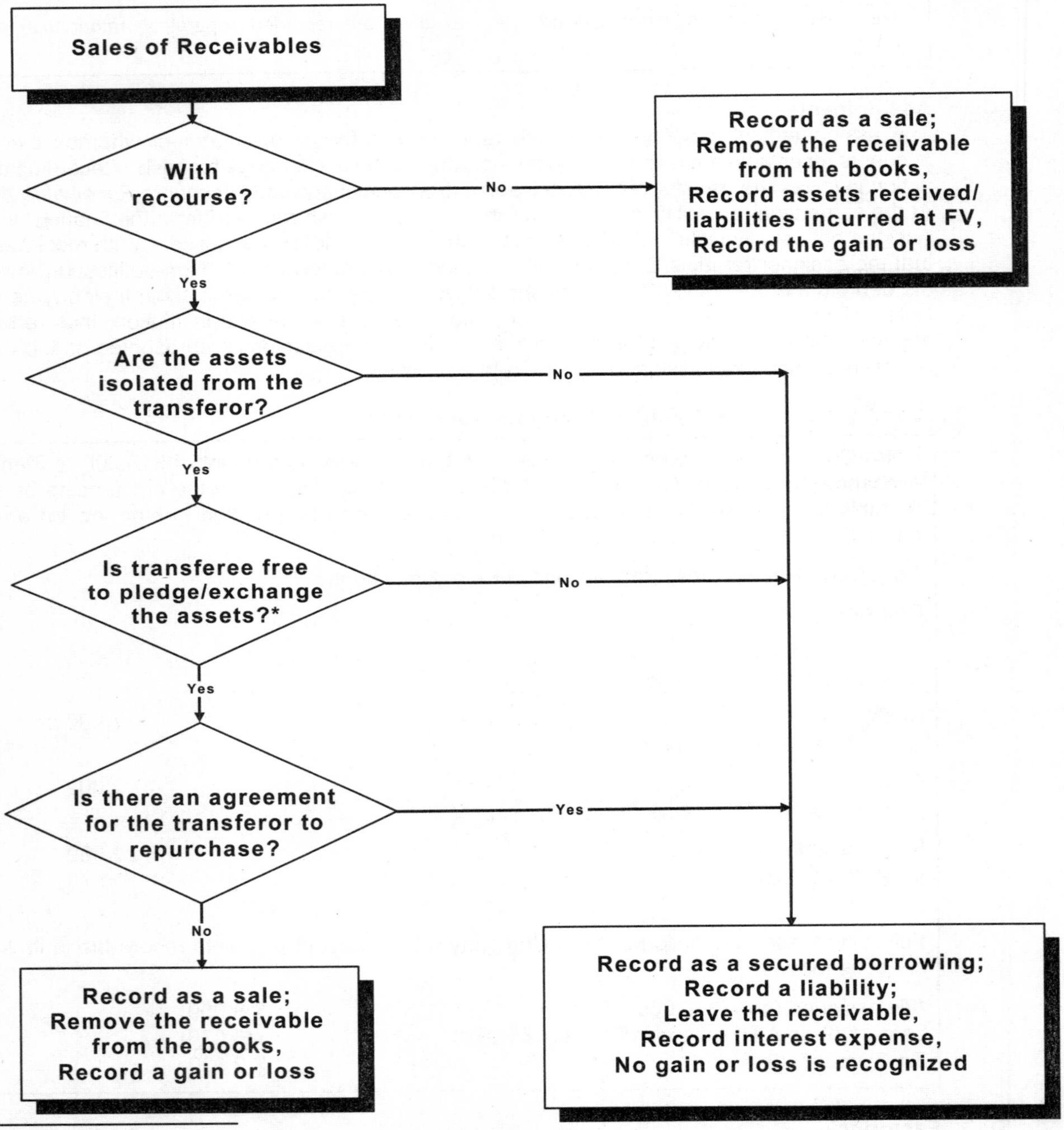

* or if transferee is a special purpose entity, does it have standing at law?

CHAPTER 2—CASH, MARKETABLE SECURITIES & RECEIVABLES

Problem 2-1 MULTIPLE CHOICE QUESTIONS (128 to 160 minutes)

1. The following trial balance of Trey Co. at December 31 of the current year has been adjusted except for income tax expense.

	Dr.	Cr.
Cash	$ 550,000	
Accounts receivable, net	1,650,000	
Prepaid taxes	300,000	
Accounts payable		$ 120,000
Common stock		500,000
Additional paid-in capital		680,000
Retained earnings		630,000
Foreign currency translation adjustment	430,000	
Revenues		3,600,000
Expenses	2,600,000	
	$5,530,000	$5,530,000

- During the year, estimated tax payments of $300,000 were charged to prepaid taxes. Trey has not yet recorded income tax expense. There were no differences between financial statement and income tax income, and Trey's tax rate is 30%.
- Included in accounts receivable is $500,000 due from a customer. Special terms granted to this customer require payment in equal semi-annual installments of $125,000 every April 1 and October 1.

In Trey's December 31 year-end balance sheet, what amount should be reported as total current assets?

a. $1,950,000
b. $2,200,000
c. $2,250,000
d. $2,500,000 (11/94, FAR, #8, amended, 5273)

2. The following are held by Smite Co.:

Cash in checking account	$20,000
Cash in bond sinking fund account	30,000
Post-dated check from customer dated one month from balance sheet date	250
Petty cash	200
Commercial paper (matures in two months)	7,000
Certificate of deposit (matures in six months)	5,000

What amount should be reported as cash and cash equivalents on Smite's balance sheet?

a. $57,200
b. $32,200
c. $27,450
d. $27,200 (R/05, FAR, A0303F, #42, 7786)

3. Burr Company had the following account balances at December 31 of the current year:

Cash in banks	$2,250,000
Cash on hand	125,000
Cash legally restricted for additions to plant (expected to be disbursed in the following year)	1,600,000

Cash in banks includes $600,000 of compensating balances against short-term borrowing arrangements. The compensating balances are not legally restricted as to withdrawal by Burr. In the current assets section of Burr's December 31 year-end balance sheet, total cash should be reported at

a. $1,775,000
b. $2,250,000
c. $2,375,000
d. $3,975,000 (11/88, PI, #1, amended, 9002)

Items 4 and 5 are based on the following data:

Poe Inc. had the following bank reconciliation at March 31 of the current year:

Balance per bank statement, 3/31	$ 46,500
Add: Deposit in transit	10,300
	56,800
Less: Outstanding checks	(12,600)
Balance per books, 3/31	$ 44,200

Data per bank for the month of April:	
Deposits	$ 58,400
Disbursements	49,700

All reconciling items at March 31 cleared the bank in April. Outstanding checks at April 30 totaled $7,000. There were no deposits in transit at April 30.

4. What is the cash balance per books at April 30?

a. $48,200
b. $52,900
c. $55,200
d. $58,500 (5/90, PI, #1, amended, 0875)

5. What is the amount of cash disbursements per books in April?

a. $44,100
b. $49,200
c. $54,300
d. $56,700 (Editors, 9003)

6. Mint Co.'s cash balance in its balance sheet is $1,300,000, of which $300,000 is identified as a compensating balance. In addition, Mint has classified cash of $250,000 that has been restricted for future expansion plans as "other assets." Which of the following should Mint disclose in notes to its financial statements?

	Compensating balance	Restricted cash
a.	Yes	Yes
b.	Yes	No
c.	No	Yes
d.	No	No

(R/03, FAR, #17, 7619)

7. Peel Co. received a cash dividend from a common stock investment. Should Peel report an increase in the investment account if it uses the cost method or the equity method of accounting?

	Cost	Equity
a.	No	No
b.	Yes	Yes
c.	Yes	No
d.	No	Yes

(11/93, Theory, #9, 4514)

8. Green Corp. owns 30% of the outstanding common stock and 100% of the outstanding noncumulative nonvoting preferred stock of Axel Corp. In the current year, Axel declared dividends of $100,000 on its common stock and $60,000 on its preferred stock. Green exercises significant influence over Axel's operations. What amount of dividend revenue should Green report in its income statement for the current year ended December 31?

a. $0
b. $30,000
c. $60,000
d. $90,000 (5/92, PI, #42, amended, 2613)

9. Pal Corp.'s current year dividend income included only part of the dividend received from its Ima Corp. investment.. The balance of the dividend reduced Pal's carrying amount for its Ima investment. This reflects that Pal accounts for its Ima investment by the

a. Cost method, and only a portion of Ima's current year dividends represent earnings after Pal's acquisition
b. Cost method, and its carrying amount exceeded the proportionate share of Ima's market value
c. Equity method, and Ima incurred a loss in the current year
d. Equity method, and its carrying amount exceeded the proportionate share of Ima's market value

(11/92, Theory, #30, amended, 3463)

10. Wood Co. owns 2,000 shares of Arlo, Inc.'s 20,000 shares of $100 par, 6% cumulative, nonparticipating preferred stock, and 1,000 shares (2%) of Arlo's common stock. During the current year, Arlo declared and paid dividends of $240,000 on preferred stock. No dividends had been declared or paid the previous year. Also, Wood received a 5% common stock dividend from Arlo when the quoted market price of Arlo's common stock was $10 per share. What amount should Wood report as dividend income in its year-end income statement?

a. $12,000
b. $12,500
c. $24,000
d. $24,500 (5/95, FAR, #29, amended, 5565)

11. An investor uses the cost method to account for an investment in common stock classified as an available-for-sale security. Dividends received this year exceeded the investor's share of investee's undistributed earnings since the date of investment. The amount of dividend revenue that should be reported in the investor's income statement for this year would be

a. The portion of the dividends received this year that were in excess of the investor's share of investee's undistributed earnings since the date of investment
b. The portion of the dividends received this year that were **not** in excess of the investor's share of investee's undistributed earnings since the date of investment
c. The total amount of dividends received this year
d. Zero (11/91, Theory, #10, amended, 2518)

12. Information pertaining to dividends from Wray Corp.'s common stock investments for the current year ended December 31 follows:

- On September 8, Wray received a $50,000 cash dividend from Seco, Inc., in which Wray owns a 30% interest. A majority of Wray's directors are also directors of Seco.
- On October 15, Wray received a $6,000 liquidating dividend from King Co. Wray owns a 5% interest in King Co.
- Wray owns a 2% interest in Bow Corp., which declared a $200,000 cash dividend on November 27, to stockholders of record on December 15, payable on January 5 of next year.

What amount should Wray report as dividend income in its income statement for the current year ended December 31?

a. $60,000
b. $56,000
c. $10,000
d. $ 4,000 (11/92, PI, #44, amended, 3277)

13. On January 2 of the current year, Well Co. purchased 10% of Rea, Inc.'s outstanding common shares for $400,000. Well is the largest single shareholder in Rea, and Well's officers are a majority on Rea's board of directors. Rea reported net income of $500,000 for the year and paid dividends of $150,000. In its December 31 balance sheet, what amount should Well report as investment in Rea?
a. $450,000
b. $435,000
c. $400,000
d $385,000 (11/94, FAR, #16, amended, 5281)

14. Pare, Inc. purchased 10% of Tot Co.'s 100,000 outstanding shares of common stock on January 2 of the current year for $50,000. On December 31, Pare purchased an additional 20,000 shares of Tot for $150,000. There was no goodwill as a result of either acquisition, and Tot had not issued any additional stock during the year. Tot reported earnings of $300,000 for the year. What amount should Pare report in its December 31 balance sheet as investment in Tot?
a. $170,000
b. $200,000
c. $230,000
d. $290,000 (11/93, PI, #14, amended, 4383)

15. Band Co. uses the equity method to account for its investment in Guard, Inc. common stock. How should Band record a 2% stock dividend received from Guard?
a. As dividend revenue at Guard's carrying value of the stock
b. As dividend revenue at the market value of the stock
c. As a reduction in the total cost of Guard stock owned
d. As a memorandum entry reducing the unit cost of all Guard stock owned (R/99, FAR, #8, 6777)

16 Puff Co. acquired 40% of Straw, Inc.'s voting common stock on January 2 of the current year for $400,000. The carrying amount of Straw's net assets at the purchase date totaled $900,000. Fair values equaled carrying amounts for all items except equipment, for which fair values exceeded carrying amounts by $100,000. The equipment has a five-year life. During the year, Straw reported net income of $150,000. What amount of income from this investment should Puff report in its year-end income statement?
a. $40,000
b. $52,000
c. $56,000
d. $60,000 (R/01, FAR, #6, 6981)

Items 17 through 19 are based on the following:

Grant, Inc. acquired 30% of South Co.'s voting stock for $200,000 on January 2, year 3. Grant's 30% interest in South gave Grant the ability to exercise significant influence over South's operating and financial policies. During year 3, South earned $80,000 and paid dividends of $50,000. South reported earnings of $100,000 for the six months ended June 30, year 4, and $200,000 for the year ended December 31, year 4. On July 1, year 4, Grant sold half of its stock in South for $150,000 cash. South paid dividends of $60,000 on October 1, year 4.

17. Before income taxes, what amount should Grant include in its year 3 income statement as a result of the investment?
a. $15,000
b. $24,000
c. $50,000
d. $80,000 (11/95, FAR, #26, amended, 6108)

18. In Grant's December 31, year 3, balance sheet, what should be the carrying amount of this investment?
a. $200,000
b. $209,000
c. $224,000
d. $230,000 (11/95, FAR, #27, amended, 6109)

19. In its year 4 income statement, what amount should Grant report as gain from the sale of half of its investment?
a. $24,500
b. $30,500
c. $35,000
d. $45,500 (11/95, FAR, #28, amended, 6110)

20. On January 1 of the current year, Point, Inc. purchased 10% of Iona Co.'s common stock. Point purchased additional shares bringing its ownership up to 40% of Iona's common stock outstanding on August 1. During October, Iona declared and paid a cash dividend on all of its outstanding common stock. How much income from the Iona investment should Point's year-end income statement report?
a. 10% of Iona's income for January 1 to July 31, plus 40% of Iona's income for August 1 to December 31
b. 40% of Iona's income for August 1 to December 31 only
c. 40% of Iona's total year income
d. Amount equal to dividends received from Iona (11/93, Theory, #8, amended, 4513)

21. Birk Co. purchased 30% of Sled Co.'s outstanding common stock on December 31 of the current year for $200,000. On that date, Sled's stockholders' equity was $500,000, and the fair value of its identifiable net assets was $600,000. On December 31, what amount of goodwill should Birk attribute to this acquisition?
a. $0
b. $20,000
c. $30,000
d. $50,000 (R/00, FAR, #4, 6899)

22. When the equity method is used to account for investments in common stock, which of the following affect(s) the investor's reported investment income?

	A change in market value of investee's common stock	*Cash dividends from investee*
a.	Yes	Yes
b.	Yes	No
c.	No	Yes
d.	No	No

(5/96, FAR, #2, 6275)

23. At year end, Rim Co. held several investments with the intent of selling them in the near term. The investments consisted of $100,000, 8%, five-year bonds, purchased for $92,000, and equity securities purchased for $35,000. At year end, the bonds were selling on the open market for $105,000 and the equity securities had a market value of $50,000. What amount should Rim report as trading securities in its year-end balance sheet?
a. $ 50,000
b. $127,000
c. $142,000
d. $155,000 (R/05, FAR, 0394F, #7, 7751)

24. Nola has a portfolio of marketable equity securities which it does not intend to sell in the near term. How should Nola classify these securities, and how should it report unrealized gains and losses from these securities?

	Classify as	*Report as a*
a.	Trading securities	Component of income from continuing operations
b.	Available-for-sale securities	Component of other comprehensive income
c.	Trading securities	Component of other comprehensive income
d.	Available-for-sale securities	Component of income from continuing operations

(5/94, FAR, #14, amended, 4829)

25. For a marketable trading securities portfolio, which of the following amounts should be included in the period's net income?

I. Unrealized losses during the period
II. Realized gains during the period
III. Changes in the Market Adjustment account during the period

a. III only
b. II only
c. I and II
d. I, II, and III (5/91, Theory, #22, amended, 4573)

26. The following information was extracted from Gil Co.'s December 31, year-end balance sheet:

Noncurrent assets:	
Investments in available-for-sale marketable equity securities (carried at market)	$ 96,450
Accumulated other comprehensive income:	
Net unrealized loss on investments in marketable equity securities	(19,800)

Historical cost of the long-term investments in marketable equity securities was
a. $ 63,595
b. $ 76,650
c. $ 96,450
d. $116,250 (5/91, PII, #18, amended, 4566)

Items 27 and 28 are based on the following:

Sun Corp. had investments in equity securities classified as trading costing $650,000. On June 30 of the current year, Sun decided to hold the investments indefinitely and accordingly reclassified them from trading to available-for-sale on that date. The investment's fair value was $575,000 at December 31 of the previous year; $530,000 at this June 30; and $490,000 at December 31 of the current year.

27. What amount of loss from investments should Sun report in its current year income statement?
a. $ 45,000
b. $ 85,000
c. $120,000
d. $160,000 (5/93, PI, #3, amended, 4045)

28. What amount should Sun report as net unrealized loss on investments in equity securities in other comprehensive income at the end of the current year?
a. $ 40,000
b. $ 45,000
c. $ 85,000
d. $160,000 (5/93, PI, #4, amended, 4046)

29. When the fair value of an investment in debt securities exceeds its amortized cost, how should each of the following debt securities be reported at the end of the year?

	Debt securities classified as	
	Held-to-maturity	*Available-for-sale*
a.	Amortized cost	Amortized cost
b.	Amortized cost	Fair value
c.	Fair value	Fair value
d.	Fair value	Amortized cost

(11/96, FAR, #6, 6452)

30. During the current year, Scott Corp. purchased marketable equity securities and classified them as available-for-sale. Pertinent data follow:

Security	Cost	Fair value 12/31
D	$ 36,000	$ 40,000
E	80,000	60,000
F	180,000	186,000
	$296,000	$286,000

Scott appropriately carries these securities at fair value. The amount of unrealized loss on these securities in Scott's current year income statement should be

a. $20,000
b. $14,000
c. $10,000
d. $0 (5/90, PI, #2, amended, 4568)

31. During the previous year, Wall Co. purchased 2,000 shares of Hemp Corp. common stock for $31,500 as an available-for-sale investment. The market value of this investment was $29,500 at December 31 of the previous year. Wall sold all of the Hemp common stock for $14 per share on December 15 of the current year, incurring $1,400 in brokerage commissions and taxes. On the sale, Wall should report a realized loss of

a. $4,900
b. $3,500
c. $2,900
d. $1,500 (5/90, PI, #57, amended, 0978)

32. Which of the following risks are inherent in an interest rate swap agreement?

I. The risk of exchanging a lower interest rate for a higher interest rate
II. The risk of nonperformance by the counterparty to the agreement

a. I only
b. II only
c. Both I and II
d. Neither I nor II (11/96, FAR, #8, 6454)

33. Whether recognized or unrecognized in an entity's financial statements, disclosure of the fair values of the entity's financial instruments is required when

a. It is practicable to estimate those values.
b. The entity maintains accurate cost records.
c. Aggregated fair values are material to the entity.
d. Individual fair values are material to the entity.

(R/99, FAR, #15, 6784)

34. If it is not practicable for an entity to estimate the fair value of a financial instrument, which of the following should be disclosed?

I. Information pertinent to estimating the fair value of the financial instrument
II. The reasons it is not practicable to estimate fair value

a. I only
b. II only
c. Both I and II
d. Neither I nor II (11/96, FAR, #9, 6455)

35. Disclosure of information about significant concentrations of credit risk is required for

a. All financial instruments
b. Financial instruments with credit risk only
c. Financial instruments with market risk only
d. Financial instruments with risk of accounting loss only (5/95, FAR, #4, amended, 5540)

36. Where in its financial statements should a company disclose information about its concentration of credit risks?

a. No disclosure is required.
b. The notes to the financial statements
c. Supplementary information to the financial statements
d. Management's report to shareholders

(R/05, FAR, 0376F, #6, 7750)

37. In its previous year-end balance sheet, Fleet Co. reported accounts receivable of $100,000 before allowance for uncollectible accounts of $10,000. Credit sales during the year were $611,000, and collections from customers, excluding recoveries, totaled $591,000. In the year, accounts receivable of $45,000 were written off and $17,000 were recovered. Fleet estimated that $15,000 of the accounts receivable at December 31 were uncollectible. In its December 31 current year balance sheet, what amount should Fleet report as accounts receivable before allowance for uncollectible accounts?

a. $58,000
b. $67,000
c. $75,000
d. $82,000 (R/00, FAR, #2, amended, 6897)

38. Delta Inc. sells to wholesalers on terms of 2/15, net 30. Delta has no cash sales but 50% of Delta's customers take advantage of the discount. Delta uses the gross method of recording sales and trade receivables. Delta's trade receivables balances at December 31 revealed the following:

Age	Amount	Collectible
0-15 days	$100,000	100%
16-30 days	60,000	95%
31-60 days	5,000	90%
Over 60 days	2,500	$500
	$167,500	

In its December 31 balance sheet, what amount should Delta report for allowance for discounts?
a. $1,000
b. $1,620
c. $1,675
d. $2,000 (5/94, FAR, #15, amended, 4830)

39. On the December 31 balance sheet of Mann Co., current receivables consisted of the following:

Trade accounts receivable	$ 93,000
Allowance for uncollectible accounts	(2,000)
Claim against shipper for goods lost in transit (November)	3,000
Selling price of unsold goods sent by Mann on consignment at 130% of cost (**not** included in Mann's ending inventory)	26,000
Security deposit on lease of warehouse used for storing some inventories	30,000
Total	$150,000

At December 31, the correct total of Mann's current net receivables was
a. $ 94,000
b. $120,000
c. $124,000
d. $150,000 (11/90, PI, #5, amended, 0887)

40. In its December 31 balance sheet, Butler Co. reported trade accounts receivable of $250,000 and related allowance for uncollectible accounts of $20,000. What is the total amount of risk of accounting loss related to Butler's trade accounts receivable, and what amount of that risk is off-balance sheet risk?

	Risk of accounting loss	*Off-balance sheet risk*
a.	$0	$0
b.	$230,000	$0
c.	$230,000	$20,000
d.	$250,000	$20,000

(R/99, FAR, #6, 6775)

41. The following accounts were abstracted from Roxy Co.'s unadjusted trial balance at December 31:

	Debit	Credit
Accounts receivable	$1,000,000	
Allowance for uncollectible accounts	8,000	
Net credit sales		$3,000,000

Roxy estimates that 3% of the gross accounts receivable will become uncollectible. After adjustment at December 31, the allowance for uncollectible accounts should have a credit balance of
a. $90,000
b. $82,000
c. $38,000
d. $30,000 (5/90, PI, #9, amended, 0894)

42. Foster Co. adjusted its allowance for uncollectible accounts at year end. The general ledger balances for the accounts receivable and the related allowance account were $1,000,000 and $40,000, respectively. Foster uses the percentage-of-receivables method to estimate its allowance for uncollectible accounts. Accounts receivable were estimated to be 5% uncollectible. What amount should Foster record as an adjustment to its allowance for uncollectible accounts at year end?
a. $10,000 decrease
b. $10,000 increase
c. $50,000 decrease
d. $50,000 increase
(R/05, FAR, 1183F, #25, 7769)

43. Hall Co.'s allowance for uncollectible accounts had a credit balance of $24,000 at December 31 of the previous year. During the current year Hall wrote off uncollectible accounts of $96,000. The aging of accounts receivable indicated that a $100,000 allowance for doubtful accounts was required at December 31 of the current year. What amount of uncollectible accounts expense should Hall report for the current year?
a. $172,000
b. $120,000
c. $100,000
d. $ 96,000 (5/93, PI, #47, amended, 4088)

44. A method of estimating uncollectible accounts that emphasizes asset valuation rather than income measurement is the allowance method based on
a. Aging the receivables
b. Direct write-off
c. Gross sales
d. Credit sales less returns and allowances
(11/89, Theory, #7, 1816)

45. Marr Co. had the following sales and accounts receivable balances, prior to any adjustments at year end:

Credit sales	$10,000,000
Accounts receivable	3,000,000
Allowance for uncollectible accounts	50,000

Marr uses 3% of accounts receivable to determine its allowance for uncollectible accounts at year end. By what amount should Marr adjust its allowance for uncollectible accounts at year end?
a. $0
b. $ 40,000
c. $ 90,000
d. $140,000 (R/05, FAR, 1254F, #28, 7772)

46. On March 31, Vale Co. had an unadjusted credit balance of $1,000 in its allowance for uncollectible accounts. An analysis of Vale's trade accounts receivable at that date revealed the following:

Age	Amount	Estimated uncollectible
0-30 days	$60,000	5%
31-60 days	4,000	10%
Over 60 days	2,000	$1,400

What amount should Vale report as allowance for uncollectible accounts in its March 31 balance sheet?
a. $4,800
b. $4,000
c. $3,800
d. $3,000 (11/93, PI, #18, amended, 4387)

47. Inge Co. determined that the net value of its accounts receivable at December 31 of the current year, based on an aging of the receivables, was $325,000. Additional information is as follows:

Allowance for uncollectible accounts—1/1	$ 30,000
Uncollectible accounts written-off during the year	18,000
Uncollectible accounts recovered during the year	2,000
Accounts receivable at 12/31	350,000

For the current year ending December 31, what would be Inge's uncollectible accounts expense?
a. $ 5,000
b. $11,000
c. $15,000
d. $21,000 (11/94, FAR, #45, 9005)

48. When the allowance method of recognizing uncollectible accounts is used, the entry to record the write-off of a specific account
a. Decreases both accounts receivable and the allowance for uncollectible accounts
b. Decreases accounts receivable and increases the allowance for uncollectible accounts
c. Increases the allowance for uncollectible accounts and decreases net income
d. Decreases both accounts receivable and net income (11/94, FAR, #12, 5277)

49. Bee Co. uses the direct write-off method to account for uncollectible accounts receivable. During an accounting period, Bee's cash collections from customers equal sales adjusted for the addition or deduction of the following amounts:

	Accounts written-off	*Increase in accounts receivable balance*
a.	Deduction	Deduction
b.	Addition	Deduction
c.	Deduction	Addition
d.	Addition	Addition

(5/91, Theory, #9, 1784)

50. Leaf Co. purchased from Oak Co. a $20,000, 8%, 5-year note that required five equal annual year-end payments of $5,009. The note was discounted to yield a 9% rate to Leaf. At the date of purchase, Leaf recorded the note at its present value of $19,485. What should be the total interest revenue earned by Leaf over the life of this note?
a. $5,045
b. $5,560
c. $8,000
d. $9,000 (11/94, FAR, #38, 5300)

51. On December 30 of the current year, Chang Co. sold a machine to Door Co. in exchange for a noninterest-bearing note requiring ten annual payments of $10,000. Door made the first payment on that same date. The market interest rate for similar notes at date of issuance was 8%. Information on present value factors is as follows:

Period	Present value of $1 at 8%	Present value of ordinary annuity of $1 at 8%
9	0.50	6.25
10	0.46	6.71

In its December 31 year-end balance sheet, what amount should Chang report as note receivable?
a. $45,000
b. $46,000
c. $62,500
d. $67,100 (5/95, FAR, #8, amended, 5544)

52. Jole Co. lent $10,000 to a major supplier in exchange for a noninterest-bearing note due in three years and a contract to purchase a fixed amount of merchandise from the supplier at a 10% discount from prevailing market prices over the next three years. The market rate for a note of this type is 10%. On issuing the note, Jole should record

	Discount on note receivable	Deferred charge
a.	Yes	Yes
b.	Yes	No
c.	No	Yes
d.	No	No

(R/01, FAR, #4, 6979)

53. On August 15 of the current year, Benet Co. sold goods for which it received a note bearing the market rate of interest on that date. The four-month note was dated this July 15. Note principal, together with all interest, is due November 15. When the note was recorded on August 15, which of the following accounts increased?
a. Unearned discount
b. Interest receivable
c. Prepaid interest
d. Interest revenue
(5/92, Theory, #21, amended, 2714)

54. Frame Co. has an 8% note receivable dated June 30, year 1, in the original amount of $150,000. Payments of $50,000 in principal plus accrued interest are due annually on July 1, year 2, year 3, and year 4. In its June 30, year 3, balance sheet, what amount should Frame report as a current asset for interest on the note receivable?
a. $0
b. $ 4,000
c. $ 8,000
d. $12,000 (11/93, PI, #17, amended, 4386)

Items 55 and 56 are based on the following:

On January 2 of the current year, Emme Co. sold equipment with a carrying amount of $480,000 in exchange for a $600,000 noninterest-bearing note due on January 2 in three years. There was no established exchange price for the equipment. The prevailing rate of interest for a note of this type at January 2 of the current year, was 10%. The present value of 1 at 10% for three periods is 0.75.

55. In Emme's current year income statement, what amount should be reported as interest income?
a. $ 9,000
b. $45,000
c. $50,000
d. $60,000 (11/93, PI, #46, amended, 4415)

56. In Emme's current year income statement, what amount should be reported as gain (loss) on sale of machinery?
a. ($ 30,000) loss
b. $ 30,000 gain
c. $120,000 gain
d. $270,000 gain (11/93, PI, #47, amended, 4416)

57. When a loan receivable is impaired but foreclosure is **not** probable, which of the following may the creditor use to measure the impairment?

I. The loan's observable market price
II. The fair value of the collateral if the loan is collateral dependent

a. I only
b. II only
c. Either I or II
d. Neither I nor II (11/96, FAR, #7, 6453)

58. Ace Co. sold to King Co. a $20,000, 8%, 5-year note that required five equal annual year-end payments. This note was discounted to yield a 9% rate to King. The present value factors of an ordinary annuity of $1 for five periods are as follows:

8%	3.992
9%	3.890

What should be the total interest revenue earned by King on this note?
a. $9,000
b. $8,000
c. $5,560
d. $5,050 (5/92, PI, #41, 2612)

59. After being held for 40 days, a 120-day, 12% interest-bearing note receivable was discounted at a bank at 15%. The proceeds received from the bank equal
a. Maturity value less the discount at 12%
b. Maturity value less the discount at 15%
c. Face value less the discount at 12%
d. Face value less the discount at 15%
(11/92, Theory, #4, 3437)

60. Roth Inc. received from a customer a one-year, $500,000 note bearing annual interest of 8%. After holding the note for six months, Roth discounted the note at Regional Bank at an effective interest rate of 10%. What amount of cash did Roth receive from the bank?
a. $540,000
b. $523,810
c. $513,000
d. $495,238 (11/93, PI, #15, 4384)

61. Rand Inc. accepted from a customer a $40,000, 90-day, 12% interest-bearing note dated August 31 of the current year. On September 30, Rand discounted the note at the Apex State Bank at 15%, however, the proceeds were not received until October 1. In Rand's September 30 balance sheet, the amount receivable from the bank, based on a 360-day year, includes accrued interest revenue of

a. $170
b. $200
c. $300
d. $400 (5/90, PI, #12, amended, 0896)

62. A note receivable bearing a reasonable interest rate is sold to a bank with recourse. At the date of the discounting transaction, the notes receivable discounted account should be

a. Decreased by the proceeds from the discounting transaction
b. Increased by the proceeds from the discounting transaction
c. Increased by the face amount of the note
d. Decreased by the face amount of the note

(5/89, Theory, #3, 1823)

63. On November 1 of the current year, Davis Co. discounted with recourse at 10% a one-year, non-interest-bearing, $20,500 note receivable maturing on January 31 of next year. What amount of contingent liability for this note must Davis disclose in its financial statements for the current year ended December 31?

a. $0
b. $20,000
c. $20,333
d. $20,500 (11/93, PI, #41, amended, 4410)

64. Gar Co. factored its receivables without recourse with Ross Bank. Gar received cash as a result of this transaction, which is best described as a

a. Loan from Ross collateralized by Gar's accounts receivable.
b. Loan from Ross to be repaid by the proceeds from Gar's accounts receivable.
c. Sale of Gar's accounts receivable to Ross, with the risk of uncollectible accounts retained by Gar.
d. Sale of Gar's accounts receivable to Ross, with the risk of uncollectible accounts transferred to Ross. (5/95, FAR, #7, 5543)

Problem 2-2 ADDITIONAL MULTIPLE CHOICE QUESTIONS (50 to 63 minutes)

65. Mare Co.'s December 31 year-end balance sheet reported the following current assets:

Cash	$ 70,000
Accounts receivable	120,000
Inventories	60,000
Total	$250,000

An analysis of the accounts disclosed that accounts receivable consisted of the following:

Trade accounts	$ 96,000
Allowance for uncollectible accounts	(2,000)
Selling price of Mare's unsold goods out on consignment, at 130% of cost, **not** included in Mare's ending inventory	26,000
Total	$120,000

At December 31, the total of Mare's current assets is

a. $224,000
b. $230,000
c. $244,000
d. $270,000 (11/94, FAR, #11, amended, 5276)

66. At October 31 of the current year, Dingo Inc. had cash accounts at three different banks. One account balance is segregated solely for a November 15 payment into a bond sinking fund. A second account, used for branch operations, is overdrawn. The third account, used for regular corporate operations, has a positive balance. How should these accounts be reported in Dingo's October 31 classified balance sheet?

a. The segregated account should be reported as a noncurrent asset, the regular account should be reported as a current asset and the overdraft should be reported as a current liability.
b. The segregated and regular accounts should be reported as current assets, and the overdraft should be reported as a current liability.
c. The segregated account should be reported as a noncurrent asset, and the regular account should be reported as a current asset net of the overdraft.
d. The segregated and regular accounts should be reported as current assets net of the overdraft.

(11/92, Theory, #13, amended 3446)

67. The following information pertains to Grey Co. at December 31 of the previous year:

Checkbook balance	$12,000
Bank statement balance	16,000
Check drawn on Grey's account, payable to a vendor, dated and recorded last 12/31 but not mailed until 1/10 of the current year	1,800

On Grey's December 31, previous year balance sheet, what amount should be reported as cash?

a. $12,000
b. $13,800
c. $14,200
d. $16,000 (5/94, FAR, #12, amended, 4827)

68. Cobb Co. purchased 10,000 shares (2% ownership) of Roe Co. on February 12 of the current year. Cobb received a stock dividend of 2,000 shares on March 31 when the carrying amount per share on Roe's books was $35 and the market value per share was $40. Roe paid a cash dividend of $1.50 per share on September 15. In Cobb's income statement for the year ended October 31, what amount should Cobb report as dividend income?

a. $98,000
b. $88,000
c. $18,000
d. $15,000 (11/93, PI, #48, amended, 4417)

69. For the last 10 years, Woody Co. has owned cumulative preferred stock issued by Hadley, Inc. During year 12, Hadley declared and paid both the year 12 dividend and the year 11 dividend in arrears. How should Woody report the year 11 dividend in arrears that was received in year 12?

a. As a reduction in cumulative preferred dividends receivable
b. As a retroactive change of the prior period financial statements
c. Include, net of income taxes, after year 12 income from continuing operations
d. Include in year 12 income from continuing operations (5/92, Theory, #43, amended, 2736)

70. On July 1 of the current year, Denver Corp. purchased 3,000 shares of Eagle Co.'s 10,000 outstanding shares of common stock for $20 per share. On December 15, Eagle paid $40,000 in dividends to its common stockholders. Eagle's net income for the current year ended December 31 was $120,000, earned evenly throughout the year. In its year-end income statement, what amount of income from this investment should Denver report?

a. $36,000
b. $18,000
c. $12,000
d. $ 6,000 (5/93, PI, #43, amended, 4084)

71. Sage, Inc. bought 40% of Adams Corp.'s outstanding common stock on January 2 of the current year for $400,000. The carrying amount of Adams' net assets at the purchase date totaled $900,000. Fair values and carrying amounts were the same for all items except for plant and inventory, for which fair values exceeded their carrying amounts by $90,000 and $10,000, respectively. The plant has an 18-year life. All inventory was sold during the year. Goodwill, if any, will be tested for impairment each year. During the year, Adams reported net income of $120,000 and paid a $20,000 cash dividend. What amount should Sage report in its income statement from its investment in Adams for the current year ended December 31?

a. $48,000
b. $42,000
c. $36,000
d. $32,000 (5/92, PI, #40, amended, 2611)

72. Park Co. uses the equity method to account for its January 1 current year purchase of Tun, Inc.'s common stock. On this date, the fair values of Tun's FIFO inventory and land exceeded their carrying amounts. How do these excesses of fair values over carrying amounts affect Park's reported equity in Tun's current year earnings?

	Inventory excess	Land excess
a.	Decrease	Decrease
b.	Decrease	No effect
c.	Increase	Increase
d.	Increase	No effect

(5/91, Theory, #20, amended, 2015)

73. The following information pertains to Smoke Inc.'s investments in marketable equity securities, classified as available-for-sale:

- On December 31 of the current year, Smoke has a security with a $70,000 cost and a $50,000 fair value. (No Market Adjustment account exists.)
- A marketable equity security costing $50,000, has a $60,000 fair value on December 31 of the current year. Smoke believes the recovery from an earlier lower fair value is permanent.

What is the net effect of the above two items on the balances of Smoke's Market Adjustment account for available-for-sale marketable equity securities as of December 31 of the current year?

a. No effect
b. Creates a $10,000 debit balance
c. Creates a $20,000 credit balance
d. Creates a $10,000 credit balance (5/92, PI, #14, amended, 4578)

74. On December 29 of the current year, BJ Co. sold a marketable equity security that had been purchased on January 4 of the previous year. BJ owned no other marketable equity security. An unrealized loss was reported in the previous year income statement. A realized gain was reported in the current year income statement. How was the marketable equity security classified, and did its previous year market price decline exceed its current year market price recovery?

	Classification	Previous year market price decline exceeded current year market price recovery
a.	Trading	Yes
b.	Available-for-sale	No
c.	Held-to-maturity	Yes
d.	Trading	No

(11/90, Theory, #6, amended, 4574)

75. Lee Corp. reported the following marketable equity security on its December 31 previous year balance sheet, classified as an available-for-sale security:

Neu Corp. common stock, at cost	$100,000
Market adjustment to reflect decline in fair value	(20,000)
Balance	$ 80,000

At December 31 of the current year, the fair value of Lee's investment in the Neu Corp. stock was $85,000. As a result of the current year increase in this stock's fair value, Lee's current year income statement should report

a. An unrealized gain of $5,000
b. A realized gain of $5,000
c. An unrealized loss of $15,000
d. No gain or loss (11/89, PII, #3, amended, 9004)

76. A marketable equity security is transferred from the trading category to the available-for-sale category. At the transfer date, the security's cost exceeds its market value. What amount is used at the transfer date to record the security in the available-for-sale category?

a. Market value, regardless of whether the decline in market value below cost is considered permanent or temporary
b. Market value, only if the decline in market value below cost is considered permanent
c. Cost, if the decline in market value below cost is considered temporary
d. Cost, regardless of whether the decline in market value below cost is considered permanent or temporary (5/92, Theory, #42, amended, 4581)

77. A marketable debt security was purchased on September 1 of the current year between interest dates, and classified as an available-for-sale security. The next interest payment date was February 1 of next year. Because of a permanent decline in market value, the cost of the debt security substantially exceeded its market value at December 31. On the balance sheet at December 31 of the current year, the debt security should be carried at

a. Market value plus the accrued interest paid
b. Market value
c. Cost plus the accrued interest paid
d. Cost (11/88, Theory, #3, amended, 4575)

78. A company should report the marketable equity securities that it has classified as trading at

a. Lower of cost or market, with holding gains and losses included in earnings
b. Lower of cost or market, with holding gains included in earnings only to the extent of previously recognized holding losses
c. Fair value, with holding gains included in earnings only to the extent of previously recognized holding losses
d. Fair value, with holding gains and losses included in earnings (5/95, FAR, #6, amended, 5542)

79. On June 1 of the current year, Pitt Corp. sold merchandise with a list price of $5,000 to Burr on account. Pitt allowed trade discounts of 30% and 20%. Credit terms were 2/15, n/40 and the sale was made F.O.B. shipping point. Pitt prepaid $200 of delivery costs for Burr as an accommodation. On June 12, Pitt received from Burr a remittance in full payment amounting to

a. $2,744
b. $2,940
c. $2,944
d. $3,140 (5/90, PI, #10, amended, 0895)

80. Lew Co. sold 200,000 corrugated boxes for $2 each. Lew's cost was $1 per unit. The sales agreement gave the customer the right to return up to 60% of the boxes within the first six months, provided an appropriate reason was given. It was immediately determined, with appropriate reason, that 5% of the boxes would be returned. Lew absorbed an additional $10,000 to process the returns and expects to resell the boxes. What amount should Lew report as operating profit from this transaction?

a. $170,000
b. $179,500
c. $180,000
d. $200,000 (R/02, FAR #8, 7063)

81. The following information relates to Jay Co.'s accounts receivable for the current year:

Accounts receivable, 1/1	$ 650,000
Credit sales for the year	2,700,000
Sales returns for the year	75,000
Accounts written off during year	40,000
Collections from customers during year	2,150,000
Estimated future sales returns at 12/31	50,000
Estimated uncollectible accounts at 12/31	110,000

What amount should Jay report for accounts receivable, before allowances for sales returns and uncollectible accounts, at December 31 of the current year?

a. $1,200,000
b. $1,125,000
c. $1,085,000
d. $ 925,000 (5/93, PI, #12, amended, 4054)

82. For the current year ended December 31, Beal Co. estimated its allowance for uncollectible accounts using the year-end aging of accounts receivable. The following data are available:

Allowance for uncollectible accounts, 1/1	$42,000
Provision for uncollectible accounts (2% on credit sales of $2,000,000)	40,000
Uncollectible accounts written-off, 11/30	46,000
Estimated uncollectible accounts per aging, 12/31	52,000

After year-end adjustment, the uncollectible accounts expense for the current year should be

a. $46,000
b. $48,000
c. $52,000
d. $56,000 (5/90, PI, #54, amended, 0897)

83. At January 1 of the current year, Jamin Co. had a credit balance of $260,000 in its allowance for uncollectible accounts. Based on past experience, 2% of Jamin's credit sales have been uncollectible. During the year, Jamin wrote off $325,000 of uncollectible accounts. Credit sales for the year were $9,000,000. In its December 31 year-end balance sheet, what amount should Jamin report as allowance for uncollectible accounts?

a. $115,000
b. $180,000
c. $245,000
d. $440,000 (5/95, FAR, #9, amended, 5545)

84. Which method of recording uncollectible accounts expense is consistent with accrual accounting?

	Allowance	*Direct write-off*
a.	Yes	Yes
b.	Yes	No
c.	No	Yes
d.	No	No (5/95, FAR, #35, 5571)

Items 85 and 86 are based on the following:

On December 1, year 5, Money Co. gave Home Co. a $200,000, 11% loan. Money paid proceeds of $194,000 after the deduction of a $6,000 nonrefundable loan origination fee. Principal and interest are due in 60 monthly installments of $4,310, beginning January 1, year 6. The repayments yield an effective interest rate of 11% at a present value of $200,000 and 12.4% at a present value of $194,000.

85. What amount of income from this loan should Money report in its year 5 income statement?

a. $0
b. $1,833
c. $2,005
d. $7,833 (5/96, FAR, #5, amended, 6278)

86. What amount of accrued interest receivable should Money report in its year 5 balance sheet?

a. $0
b. $1,833
c. $2,005
d. $7,833 (6278a, Editors)

87. On December 31 of the current year, Jet Co. received two $10,000 notes receivable from customers in exchange for services rendered. On both notes, interest is calculated on the outstanding principal balance at the annual rate of 3% and payable at maturity. The note from Hart Corp., made under customary trade terms, is due in nine months and the note from Maxx Inc. is due in five years. The market interest rate for similar notes on this date was 8%. The compound interest factors to convert future values into present values at 8% follow:

Present value of $1 due in nine months:	.944
Present value of $1 due in five years:	.680

At what amounts should these two notes receivable be reported in Jet's December 31 balance sheet?

	Hart	*Maxx*
a.	$ 9,440	$6,800
b.	$ 9,652	$7,820
c.	$10,000	$6,800
d.	$10,000	$7,820

(5/92, PI, #15, amended, 2582)

88. On May 1 of the current year, Lane Corp. bought a parcel of land for $100,000. Seven months later, Lane sold this land to a triple-A rated company for $150,000, under the following terms: 25% at closing, and a first mortgage note (at the market rate of interest) for the balance. The first payment on the note, plus accrued interest, is due December 1 of next year. Lane reported this sale on the installment basis in its current year tax return. In its current year income statement, how much gain should Lane report from the sale of this land?
a. $0
b. $12,500
c. $37,500
d. $50,000 (5/87, PII, #13, amended, 0902)

89. On July 1 of the previous year, Kay Corp. sold equipment to Mando Co. for $100,000. Kay accepted a 10% note receivable for the entire sales price. This note is payable in two equal installments of $50,000 plus accrued interest on December 31 of the previous and current year. On July 1 of the current year, Kay discounted the note at a bank at an interest rate of 12%. Kay's proceeds from the discounted note were
a. $48,400
b. $49,350
c. $50,350
d. $51,700 (11/90, PII, #1, amended, 0890)

SIMULATIONS

Problem 2-3 (15 to 25 minutes)

Scenario #1 and Response	Scenario #2 and Response	Research Task

Items 1 through 4 are based on the following:

Camp Co. purchased various securities during the current year to be classified as held-to-maturity securities, trading securities, or available-for-sale securities.

These items describe various the securities purchased by Camp. For each item numbered **1 through 4,** select the appropriate category for each security. A category may be used once, more than once, or not at all.

Categories	
H.	Held-to-maturity
T.	Trading
A.	Available-for-sale

1. ____ Debt securities bought and held for the purpose of selling in the near term.

2. ____ U.S. Treasury bonds that Camp has both the positive intent and the ability to hold to maturity.

3. ____ $3 million debt security bought and held for the purpose of selling in three years to finance payment of Camp's $2 million long-term note payable when it matures.

4. ____ Convertible preferred stock that Camp does not intend to sell in the near term.
(11/95, FAR, #61 - 70, amended, 6143)

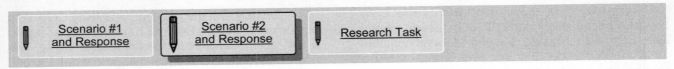

Scenario #1 and Response	Scenario #2 and Response	Research Task

Items 5 through 10 are based on the following chart: The following information pertains to Dayle Inc.'s portfolio of marketable investments for the current year ended December 31. Security ABC was purchased at par. All declines in fair value are considered to be temporary.

	Cost	Fair value, 12/31 previous year	Current year activity		Fair value, 12/31 current year
			Purchases	*Sales*	
Held-to-maturity securities Security ABC			$100,000		$ 95,000
Trading securities Security DEF	$150,000	$160,000			155,000
Available-for-sale securities Security GHI	190,000	165,000		$175,000	
Security JKL	170,000	175,000			160,000

Answer choices for responses					
A.	$0	E.	$ 25,000	I.	$155,000
B.	$ 5,000	F.	$ 95,000	J.	$160,000
C.	$10,000	G.	$100,000	K.	$170,000
D.	$15,000	H.	$150,000		

Items 5 through 10 describe amounts to be reported in Dayle's current year financial statements. For each item, select the correct numerical response. A choice may be selected once, more than once, or not at all. Ignore income tax considerations.

5. ____ Carrying amount of security ABC at 12/31 of the current year.

6. ____ Carrying amount of security DEF at 12/31 of the current year.

7. ____ Carrying amount of security JKL at 12/31 of the current year.

Items 8 through 10 require two responses. For each item, indicate whether a gain (G) or a loss (L) is to be reported and the amount of that gain or loss.

8. ___ ______ Recognized gain or loss on sale of security GHI.

9. ___ ______ Unrealized gain or loss to be reported in current year income statement.

10. ___ ______ Unrealized gain or loss to be reported at December 31 of the current year in accumulated other comprehensive income.

Scenario #1 and Response | Scenario #2 and Response | Research Task

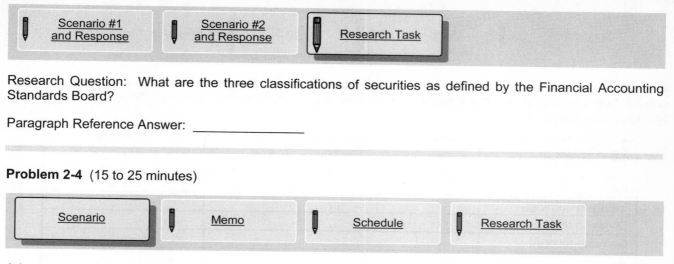

Research Question: What are the three classifications of securities as defined by the Financial Accounting Standards Board?

Paragraph Reference Answer: ______________

Problem 2-4 (15 to 25 minutes)

Scenario | Memo | Schedule | Research Task

Johnson, an investor in Acme Co., asked Smith, CPA, for advice on the propriety of Acme's financial reporting for two of its investments. Smith obtained the following information related to the investments from Acme's December 31, current year financial statements:

- 20% ownership interest in Kern Co., represented by 200,000 shares of outstanding common stock purchased on January 2 of the current year for $600,000.
- 20% ownership interest in Wand Co., represented by 20,000 shares of outstanding common stock purchased on January 2 of the current year for $300,000.
- On January 2, the carrying values of the acquired shares of both investments equaled their purchase price.
- Kern reported earnings of $400,000 for the current year ended December 31, and declared and paid dividends of $100,000 during the year.
- Wand reported earnings of $350,000 for the current year ended December 31, and declared and paid dividends of $60,000 during the year.
- On December 31, Kern's and Wand's common stock were trading over-the-counter at $18 and $20 per share, respectively.
- The investment in Kern is accounted for using the equity method.
- The investment in Wand is accounted for as available-for-sale securities.

Smith recalculated the amounts reported in Acme's December 31, current year financial statements, and determined that they were correct. Stressing that the information available in the financial statements was limited, Smith advised Johnson that, assuming Acme properly applied generally accepted accounting principles, Acme may have appropriately used two different methods to account for its investments in Kern and Wand, even though the investments represent equal ownership interests.

Scenario | Memo | Schedule | Research Task

Prepare a detailed memorandum from Smith to Johnson supporting Smith's conclusion that, under generally accepted accounting principles, correctly applied, Acme may have appropriately used two different methods to account for its investments representing equal ownership interests.

Do not discuss SFAS No. 115, *Accounting for Investments in Certain Debt and Equity Securities.*

Scenario	Memo	**Schedule**	Research Task

Prepare a schedule indicating the amounts Acme should report for the two investments in its December 31, current year balance sheet and statement of income and comprehensive income. Show all calculations. Ignore income taxes.

Calculations		
Kern:		
Equity in earnings		
Dividend rec'd		
Carrying amount		
Wand:		
Investment in Wand		
Divided income		
Unrealized gain		

Kern:

Balance Sheet

Acme reported its investment in Kern at a carrying amount of $____________

Statement of Income and Comprehensive Income

Acme's equity in Kern's earnings $__________

Wand:

Balance Sheet

Acme reported its investment in Wand at a fair value of $____________

Statement of Income and Comprehensive Income

Dividend income $____________

Unrealized gain $____________

(11/98, FAR, #2, amended, 6750)

Scenario	Memo	Schedule	**Research Task**

Research Question: What are the criteria for applying the Equity Method to Investments?

Paragraph Reference Answer: ______________

Problem 2-5 (15 to 25 minutes)

Essay | Research Task

Coyn, CPA, has been approached by Howe, the chief financial officer of Chatham Co. Howe is aware that the Financial Accounting Standards Board is engaged in an ongoing project to improve disclosure of information about financial instruments. Howe has prepared the following footnote for Chatham's financial statements:

Note 12: Financial Instruments

The Company is party to financial instruments with risk of accounting loss in the normal course of business. The Company uses various financial instruments with market risk, including derivative financial instruments, to manage its interest rate and foreign currency exchange rate risks. Other financial instruments that potentially subject the Company to concentrations of credit risk consist principally of trade receivables.

Howe will be meeting with Chatham's board of directors to review the financial statements, and has asked Coyn to prepare a handout for the board explaining the terms used in the footnote.

(5/97, FAR, #1, amended, 6614-6617)

a. What is a financial instrument? Define and give an example of derivative financial instruments.

b. Define *off-balance-sheet risk of accounting loss.*

c. Define both *market risk* and *credit risk.* What is meant by the term *concentration of credit risk?*

d. Define *fair value.* Discuss the methods management might use to estimate the fair values of various financial instruments.

Essay | Research Task

Research Question: Where and when shall accumulated other comprehensive income be displayed in financial statements?

Paragraph Reference Answer: _______________

Problem 2-6 (15 to 25 minutes)

Scenario | Allowance Schedule | Provision Schedule | Research Task

Sigma Co. began operations on January 1 of the previous year. On December 31 of the previous year, Sigma provided for uncollectible accounts based on 1% of annual credit sales. On January 1 of the current year, Sigma changed its method of determining its allowance for uncollectible accounts by applying certain percentages to the accounts receivable aging as follows:

Days past invoice date	Deemed to be uncollectible
0-30	1%
31-90	5%
91-180	20%
Over 180	80%

→

In addition, Sigma wrote off all accounts receivable that were over one year old. The following additional information relates to the previous and current years ended December 31:

	Current year	Previous year
Credit sales	$3,000,000	$2,800,000
Collections	2,915,000	2,400,000
Accounts written-off	27,000	None
Recovery of accounts previously written-off	7,000	None
Days past invoice date		
0-30	300,000	250,000
31-90	80,000	90,000
91-180	60,000	45,000
Over 180	25,000	15,000

Scenario	Allowance Schedule	Provision Schedule	Research Task

a. Prepare a schedule showing the calculation of the allowance for uncollectible accounts at December 31 of the current year.

Sigma Co.
Schedule of Calculation of
Allowance for Uncollectible Accounts
December 31, Current Year

	A/R Amount	Percentage	Allowance
0 to 30 days			
31 to 90 days			
91 to 180 days			
Over 180 days			
Accounts receivable			
Allowance for uncollectible accounts			

Scenario	Allowance Schedule	Provision Schedule	Research Task

b. Prepare a schedule showing the computation of the provision for uncollectible accounts for the year ended December 31 of the current year. (5/92, PI, #4, amended, 9918)

Sigma Co.
Schedule of Calculation of
Provision for Uncollectible Accounts
For Year Ended December 31, Current Year

Balance December 31, previous year	
Write-offs during the current year	
Recoveries during the current year	
Balance before the current year provision	
Required allowance at December 31 of current year	
Current year provision	

Scenario | Allowance Schedule | Provision Schedule | Research Task

Research Question: What was the Board's opinion concerning presentation of allowances?

Paragraph Reference Answer: _______________

Problem 2-7 (45 to 55 minutes)

Scenario | Schedules | Research Task

Kern Inc. had the following long-term receivable account balances at December 31, year 3:

Note receivable from the sale of an idle building	$750,000
Note receivable from an officer	200,000

Transactions during year 4 and other information relating to Kern's long-term receivables follows:

- The $750,000 note receivable is dated May 1, year 3, bears interest at 9%, and represents the balance of the consideration Kern received from the sale of its idle building to Able Co. Principal payments of $250,000 plus interest are due annually beginning May 1, year 4. Able made its first principal and interest payment on May 1, year 4. Collection of the remaining note installments is reasonably assured.

- The $200,000 note receivable is dated December 31, year 1, bears interest at 8%, and is due on December 31, year 6. The note is due from Frank Black, president of Kern Inc., and is collateralized by 5,000 shares of Kern's common stock. Interest is payable annually on December 31, and all interest payments were made through December 31, year 4. The quoted market price of Kern's common stock was $45 per share on December 31, year 4.

- On April 1, year 4, Kern sold a patent to Frey Corp. in exchange for a $100,000 noninterest-bearing note due on April 1, year 6. There was no established exchange price for the patent, and the note had no ready market. The prevailing interest rate for this type of note was 10% at April 1, year 4. The present value of $1 for two periods at 10% is 0.826. The patent had a carrying amount of $40,000 at January 1, year 4, and the amortization for the year ended December 31, year 4 would have been $8,000. Kern is reasonably assured of collecting the note receivable from Frey.

- On July 1, year 4, Kern sold a parcel of land to Barr Co. for $400,000 under an installment sale contract. Barr made a $120,000 cash down payment on July 1, year 4, and signed a four-year 10% note for the $280,000 balance. The equal annual payments of principal and interest on the note will be $88,332, payable on July 1 of each year from year 5 through year 8. The fair value of the land at the date of sale was $400,000. The cost of the land to Kern was $300,000. Collection of the remaining note installments is reasonably assured.

(5/91, PI, #4, amended, 9919)

Scenario | Schedules | Research Task

Prepare a long-term receivables section of Kern's December 31, year 4 balance sheet.

Kern Inc.
Long-Term Receivables Section of Balance Sheet
December 31, Year 4

9% note receivable from sale of idle building, due in annual installments of $250,000 to May 1, year 6, less current installment	________
8% note receivable from officer, due December 31, year 6, collateralized by 5,000 shares of Kern Inc. common stock with a fair value of $225,000	________
Noninterest-bearing note from sale of patent, net of 10% imputed interest, due April 1, year 6	________
Installment contract receivable, due in annual installments of $88,332 to July 1, year 7, less current installment	________
Total long-term receivables	________

Prepare a schedule showing current portion of long-term receivables and accrued interest receivable to be reported in Kern's December 31, year 4 balance sheet.

Kern Inc.
Selected Balance Sheet Accounts
December 31, Year 4

Current portion of long-term receivables:	
Note receivable from sale of idle building	________
Installment contract receivable	________
Total	________
Accrued interest receivable:	
Note receivable from sale of idle building	________
Installment contract receivable	________
Total	________

Prepare a schedule showing interest revenue from long-term receivables and gains recognized on sale of assets to be reported in Kern's year 4 income statement.

Kern Inc.
Interest Revenue From Long-Term Receivables
and Gains Recognized on Sale of Assets
For the year ended December 31, Year 4

Interest revenue:	
Note receivable from sale of idle building	________
Note receivable from sale of patent	________
Note receivable from officer	________
Installment contract receivable from sale of land	________
Total interest revenue	________
Gains recognized on sale of assets:	
Patent	________
Land	________
Total gains recognized	________

Scenario | Schedules | Research Task

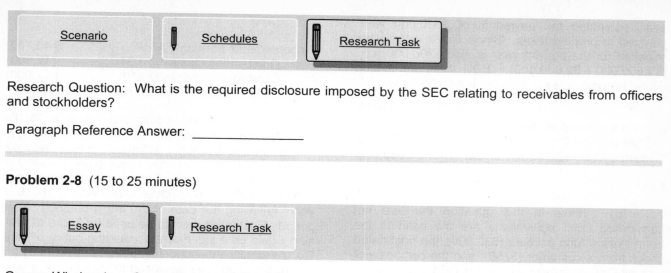

Research Question: What is the required disclosure imposed by the SEC relating to receivables from officers and stockholders?

Paragraph Reference Answer: _______________

Problem 2-8 (15 to 25 minutes)

Essay | Research Task

Gregor Wholesalers Co. sells industrial equipment for a standard three-year note receivable. Revenue is recognized at time of sale. Each note is secured by a lien on the equipment and has a face amount equal to the equipment's list price. Each note's stated interest rate is below the customers' market rate at date of sale. All notes are to be collected in three equal annual installments beginning one year after sale. Some of the notes are subsequently discounted at a bank with recourse, some are subsequently discounted without recourse, and some are retained by Gregor. At year-end, Gregor evaluates all outstanding notes receivable and provides for estimated losses arising from defaults. (11/93, Theory, amended, #3, 6187)

a. What is the appropriate valuation basis for Gregor's notes receivable at the date it sells equipment?

b. How should Gregor account for the discounting, without recourse, of a February 1, year 2 note receivable discounted on May 1, year 2? Why is it appropriate to account for it in this way?

c. At December 31, year 2, how should Gregor measure and account for the impact of estimated losses resulting from notes receivable that it

   1. Retained and did **not** discount?
   2. Discounted at a bank with recourse?

Essay | Research Task

Research Question: Is restoration of a previously recognized impairment loss allowed?

Paragraph Reference Answer: _______________

Solution 2-1 MULTIPLE CHOICE ANSWERS

Current Assets

1. (a) The operating cycle of an enterprise is the *average* period of time between expenditures for goods and services and the date those expenditures are converted into cash. Since there is no indication that Trey's operating cycle is greater than one year, a twelve month time period should be used as the basis for determining the amount to be reported as total current assets. Included in Trey's accounts receivable is $500,000 due from a customer. *Special terms* granted to this customer require payment in equal semiannual installments of $125,000 every April 1 and October 1. Therefore, $250,000 (i.e., $125,000 semiannual payments to be received on 4/1 and 10/1 in two years) of this receivable should be excluded from current assets at 12/31 of the current year because this amount would be received after 12/31 of the following year. During the current

year, estimated tax payments of $300,000 were charged to prepaid taxes. Since Trey's income tax expense for the current year is also $300,000 [i.e., ($3,600,000 – $2,600,000) × 30%], there are, in fact, no net prepaid taxes at 12/31 of the current year.

Cash	$ 550,000
Accounts receivable, net ($1,650,000 – $250,000)	1,400,000
Current assets, 12/31 current year	$1,950,000

Cash

2. (d) Items in this question that are not considered cash equivalents are the cash in the bond sinking fund account ($30,000), the post dated check from a customer ($250), and the certificate of deposit that matures in six months ($5,000).

Cash in checking account	$20,000
Petty cash	200
Commercial paper (matures in two months)	7,000
Total cash and cash equivalents	$27,200

3. (c) The $600,000 of compensating balances against short-term borrowing arrangements is properly includible in unrestricted cash in current assets because the compensating balances are not legally restricted as to withdrawal by Burr. The $1,600,000 of cash legally restricted for additions to plant should *not* be included in cash in current assets because it is not readily available to meet current obligations. Cash that is restricted as to withdrawal or use for other than current operations, designated for expenditure in the acquisition or construction of noncurrent assets, or segregated for the liquidation of long-term debts should be excluded from current assets (ARB 43).

Cash in banks	$2,250,000
Cash on hand	125,000
Cash reported in current assets section	$2,375,000

4. (a) The cash balance per books at April 30, is computed by subtracting the outstanding checks at April 30, from the balance per bank.

Cash balance per bank 3/31	$ 46,500
Add: Deposits per bank, April	58,400
Less: Disbursements per bank, April	(49,700)
Cash balance per bank, 4/30	55,200
Less: Outstanding checks, 4/30	(7,000)
Cash balance per books, 4/30	$ 48,200

5. (a)

Disbursements per bank, April	$ 49,700
Less: Outstanding checks at 3/31	(12,600)
Add: Outstanding checks at 4/30	7,000
Cash disbursement per books, April	$ 44,100

6. (a) A compensating balance is a legally restricted deposit held against borrowing arrangements with a lending institution. SFAS No. 47 requires that the combined aggregate amount of maturities and sinking fund requirements for all long-term borrowings be disclosed for each of the five years following the date of the latest balance sheet period. Restricting cash to be used for future expansion would be a significant accounting policy of Mint Co. All significant accounting policies followed by an enterprise should be disclosed in its financial statements. No specific disclosure format is required. APB 22 prefers a *separate* note, or a summary preceding the notes entitled *Summary of Significant Accounting Policies.* The accounting policy disclosures should identify and describe the principles and methods that materially affect the financial position and operations.

Cost Method

7. (a) The receipt of a cash dividend from a common stock investment should not be reported as an increase in the *Investment* account under either the cost or equity methods. Under the cost method, (1) dividends received up to the investor's share of the investee's earnings subsequent to the date of the investment are recorded as dividend income and (2) dividends received in excess of the investor's share of the investee's earnings since the date of the investment represent a liquidating dividend and are recorded as a decrease to the *Investment* account. Under the equity method, the receipt of a cash dividend from the investee always is recorded as a decrease to the *Investment* account.

8. (c) The investment in the *nonvoting* preferred stock must be accounted under the cost method because Green does not have the ability to significantly influence the financial and operating policies of the investee by virtue of the preferred stock investment. Therefore, the $60,000 dividend declared on the preferred stock is reported as dividend revenue by Green. The 30% investment in the common stock should be accounted for under the equity method because Green has the ability to exercise significant influence over the investee by virtue of the investment. Under the equity method, the investor recognizes as income its share of the investee's earnings in the periods in which they are reported by the investee. These amounts are

20% or more equity mtd.

recognized as equity in the earnings of the investee and not as dividend revenue.

9. (a) Dividend income is not recognized under the equity method of accounting for investments in common stock. Under this method, the investor's share of dividends declared by the investee reduce the carrying amount of the investment. Pal recognized dividend income from the investment in the current year. Hence it must account for the investment by the cost method. Under this method, investment income reported for the year is usually the investor's share of dividends declared by the investee during the year. The exception is where the investor's share of dividends declared by the investee exceeds the investor's share of investee earnings subsequent to the date of the investment. In this case, the excess amount represents a liquidating dividend that is recorded as a reduction of the carrying amount of the investment and not as dividend income. Since only part of the dividends that Pal received in the current year was recorded as dividend income, only a portion of the current year dividends represent earnings subsequent to the date of Pal's investment (i.e., the balance of the current year dividends represent liquidating dividends).

10. (c) Wood owns 10% of Arlo's preferred stock and would have received $24,000 ($240,000 dividends × 10%) in dividends in the current year on this preferred stock. Although this amount represents the dividend preference for the previous year, due to the 6% cumulative feature of the stock, as well as for the current year, the revenue is not recognized until the dividends are actually declared in the current year. Per ARB 43, Ch. 7, stock dividends received are not recognized as income because they are not a distribution, division, or severance of the corporate assets.

11. (b) When the cost method is used to account for investments in common stock, dividends received up to the investor's share of the investee's earnings subsequent to the date of investment are recorded as dividend income. Dividends received in excess of the investor's share of the investee's earnings since the date of investment represent a liquidating dividend and should be recorded as a decrease to the investment account.

12. (d) Of the dividends listed, only the $4,000 (i.e., $200,000 × 2%) cash dividend receivable from Bow should be reported as dividend income. Wray owns only a 2% interest in Bow; thus, Wray does not have the ability to exercise significant influence over Bow by virtue of the investment. Therefore, the investment should be accounted for under the cost method. The cash dividend received from Seco should be recorded as a reduction of the carrying amount of the investment in Seco reported in Wray's balance sheet because the investment should be accounted for under the equity method (i.e., Wray owns a 30% interest in Seco and a majority of Wray's directors are also directors of Seco). The liquidating dividend received from King should be recorded as a reduction of the carrying amount of the investment in King reported in Wray's balance sheet.

Equity Method

13. (b) Although Well does not own 20% or more of Rea's common shares, Well should use the equity method to account for its investment in Rea because it can exercise significant influence over the operating and financial policies of Rea.

Purchase price, 1/2	$400,000
Add: Share of Rea's income ($500,000 × 10%)	50,000
Less: Share of dividends ($150,000 × 10%)	(15,000)
Investment carrying amount, 12/31	$435,000

14. (c) When Pare purchased an additional 20,000 shares of Tot at 12/31, it increased its investment in Tot's common stock from 10% to 30%. Thus, at 12/31, Pare gained the ability to exercise significant influence over the financial and operating policies of Tot and accordingly should report its investment in Tot using the equity method in its 12/31 balance sheet. The change from the cost method of reporting the investment in Tot to the equity method should be made by retroactively restating all prior periods in which the investment was held as if the equity method were used from inception. Thus, Pare should report the investment in Tot in its 12/31 balance sheet at $230,000, the sum of the amounts paid for Tot's shares (i.e., $50,000 and $150,000) and Pare's equity in Tot's reported earnings for the year (i.e., $300,000 × 10%).

15. (d) Stock dividends are recorded as memorandum entries only, reducing the unit cost of the stock owned. No dividend revenue is recorded and the total cost of the stock owned remains the same.

16. (b) If fair value exceeds the net assets' carrying value, the excess is allocated among most undervalued assets. Then consideration is given to the existence of goodwill. As the related undervalued asset is depreciated or sold, the investment account is adjusted. Straw's fair value is $900,000 + $100,000 = $1,000,000. Puff's investment in Straw is 40% × $1,000,000 = $400,000, the same as the purchase price. Puff offsets its share of Straw's income with the depreciation of its share of the difference in the carrying and fair value of equipment. {[$150,000 – ($100,000 / 5 years)] × 40% = $52,000}

17. (b) As Grant has 20% or more ownership in South, the amount of investment income in Grant's income statement is Grant's percentage of ownership times South's earnings. [$80,000 × 30% = $24,000]

18. (b) As Grant has 20% or more ownership in South, the carrying amount of the investment is the original purchase price plus Grant's share in South's earnings ($80,000 × 30% = $24,000), less the dividends paid to Grant ($50,000 × 30% = $15,000). [$200,000 + $24,000 – $15,000 = $209,000]

19. (b) The balance in Grant's Investment in South account at the beginning of year 4 is $209,000. Grant has equity in South's earnings of $30,000 ($100,000 × 30%), which increases the investment account. South did not pay any dividends during the first six months of year 4, so the balance in Investment in South is $239,000 at the date of sale. Half of the investment was sold, so half of the balance in the account is Grant's carrying value for the stock sold ($239,000 × 50% = $119,500). The gain is the sale price less the carrying value ($150,000 – $119,500 = $30,500).

20. (a) On 8/1, when Point increased its investment in Iona's common stock from 10% to 40%, Point gained the ability to exercise significant influence over the financial and operating policies of Iona and accordingly should report its investment using the equity method. The change from the cost method to the equity method should be made by retroactively restating all prior periods in which the investment was held as if the equity method were used from inception. Therefore, the amount Point should report as income from the Iona investment in its year-end income statement is 10% of Iona's income from 1/1 to 7/31, plus 40% of Iona's income for 8/1 to 12/31.

21. (b) Goodwill is recognized at an amount equal to the excess of the cost of the enterprise acquired over the fair value of the identifiable net assets (INA).

Purchase price of 30% of Sled Co's O/S common stock		$ 200,000
Fair value of Sled's INA	$600,000	
Times: % acquired by Birk	× 30%	
Less: Sled's INA acquired by Birk		(180,000)
Goodwill		$ 20,000

22. (d) Under the equity method of accounting for investments in common stock, the investment is recorded at cost. Changes in the market value of the investee's common stock do not affect the Investment account or the Investment Income account. The investor recognizes as income its share of the investee's earnings or losses in the periods in which they are reported by the investee. Dividends declared by the investee represent a distribution of earnings previously recognized and, thus, do not affect the Investment Income account.

Investments in Marketable Securities

23. (d) Trading securities can be debt and/or equity securities that are bought and held principally for the purpose of selling in the near term. Trading securities are reported at fair value and unrealized holding gains and losses are included in current earnings.

24. (b) Marketable securities which an entity does not intend to sell in the near future are classified as available-for-sale (AFS) securities. Unrealized gains and losses for AFS securities are reported in other comprehensive income. If the entity did intend to sell the securities in the near future, then they would be classified as trading securities and any unrealized gains or losses would be reported as a component of income from continuing operations.

25. (d) Realized gains and losses related to marketable equity securities should always be included in net income. In addition, with trading marketable securities, unrealized losses and other changes in the *Market Adjustment* account flow through the income statement.

26. (d) The carrying amount of an available-for-sale marketable equity securities portfolio should be its market value. The amount by which aggregate cost of the portfolio exceeds market value should be accounted for as a valuation allowance. An amount equal to the valuation allowance is reported in accumulated other comprehensive income within owners' equity. Since the portfolio in question has a valuation allowance, its market value is less than cost. Thus, the historical cost of the portfolio is the sum of the amount of the valuation allowance of the portfolio and the market value of the portfolio. [($19,800 + $96,450 = $116,250)]

27. (a) Per SFAS 115, the transfer of a security from the trading category of investments shall be accounted for at fair value. The unrealized holding loss resulting from the decrease in market value while classified as trading securities shall be included in earnings. As of the date of transfer, June 30 of the current year, the securities had experienced a decline in fair value of $45,000 ($575,000 – $530,000) from the end of the prior year. Upon transfer to a different category of investment, this unrealized loss is required to be included in earnings. (The decline from $650,000 to $575,000 would have been

included as an unrealized loss on the previous year income statement.)

28. (a) Unrealized holding losses for available-for-sale (AFS) securities shall be excluded from earnings and reported in other comprehensive income until realized. The decrease in fair value over the time period in which the securities were classified as trading securities would have been reported in earnings. However, the decrease occurring after the transfer to the AFS category, $40,000 ($530,000 – $490,000), would be reflected in OCI.

29. (b) In accordance with SFAS 115, at year-end, held-to-maturity securities are reported at amortized cost. Trading securities and available-for-sale (AFS) securities are accounted for at fair value. Unrealized holding gains and losses are included in current earnings for trading securities, and in other comprehensive income for AFS securities.

30. (d) Marketable securities classified as available-for-sale (AFS) are to be reported at fair value. The amount by which aggregate cost of an AFS portfolio exceeds its fair value should be accounted for as a credit to the *Market Adjustment—AFS* account. In addition, an amount equal to the balance of the *Market Adjustment—AFS* account should be reported separately within equity in accumulated other comprehensive income. The balance in the *Market Adjustment—AFS* account at year-end is a $10,000 credit ($296,000 – $286,000). An increase in the *Market Adjustment—AFS* account is recognized in other comprehensive income, not in net income; only changes in the *Market Adjustment—Trading* account are recognized in income.

31. (a) The realized loss reported from the sale of the marketable securities is determined as the difference between the proceeds received (i.e., the gross selling price of the shares less any brokerage commissions and taxes incurred in the sale) and the cost of the securities.

Gross selling price of 2,000 share @ $14	$ 28,000
Less: Brokerage commissions and taxes incurred	(1,400)
Proceeds received from sale of securities	26,600
Less: Cost of securities sold	(31,500)
Recognized loss on sale	$ (4,900)

Financial Instrument Disclosure

32. (c) An interest rate swap agreement is an arrangement used to limit interest rate risk. Two companies swap interest payments, but not the principal, in an agreement, such as an exchange of a variable interest rate for a fixed rate. The risk of accounting loss from an interest rate swap includes both (1) the risk of exchanging a lower interest rate for a higher rate and (2) the risk of nonperformance by the other party.

33. (a) SFAS 107 requires an entity to disclose the fair value of financial instruments for which it is practicable to estimate that value. If it would be excessively costly to estimate fair values, an entity is not required to disclose the fair values. If the entity does not disclose fair value, it must disclose information relating to the financial instruments, including the reasons why it is not practicable to estimate fair value.

34. (c) SFAS 107 requires that, if it is not practicable to estimate the fair value of a financial instrument, disclosures include (1) the information pertinent to estimating the fair value of that financial instrument, such as the carrying amount, effective interest rate, and maturity; and (2) the reasons why it is not practicable to estimate fair value.

35. (a) SFAS 107 requires an entity to disclose all significant concentrations of credit risk arising from *all* financial instruments.

36. (b) A disclosure about concentration of credit risks is required in the notes to the financial statements.

Accounts Receivable

37. (c) The A/R balance was increased by credit sales and decreased by collections from customers and by accounts written off. Accounts recovered resulted in an increase and a decrease of equal amount to the A/R balance.

Accounts Receivable			
Balance, 1/1	100,000		
Credit sales	611,000	591,000	Customer collections
Accounts reinstated	17,000	45,000	Accounts written-off
		17,000	Accounts recovered
Balance, 12/31	75,000		

38. (a) Only the receivables which have aged 0-15 days are eligible for the discount. The discount is computed using 50% of the dollar amount eligible, not 50% of the discount. Only 50% of the customers take advantage of the discount.

Amount eligible for discount	$100,000
% of customers that take discount	× 50%
Amount of eligible amount taken	50,000
Discount allowed	× 2%
Allowance for discount	$ 1,000

39. (a) The goods out on consignment have not yet been sold and, thus, must be included in Mann's *inventory* at their *cost* of $20,000 ($26,000 /

130%). The security deposit on lease of the warehouse should be classified as a noncurrent asset.

Trade accounts receivable	$93,000
Less: Allowance for uncollectible accounts	(2,000)
Plus: Claim against shipper for goods lost in transit	3,000
Current net receivables, 12/31	$94,000

40. (b) The total risk of accounting loss is the amount of potential loss the entity would suffer if all parties to the financial instruments failed completely to perform and the amounts due proved to be of no value to the entity. Butler Co. had already recorded an allowance for uncollectible accounts of $20,000 on its trade accounts receivable of $250,000, so the net of $230,000 is the risk of accounting loss. The entire amount is shown on the balance sheet, thus there is no off-balance sheet risk involved.

Uncollectible Accounts

41. (d) Under the percentage-of-receivables method, the allowance for uncollectible accounts is determined at the end of the period by multiplying the ending A/R balance by an estimate of the percentage of gross A/R that will become uncollectible.

Accounts receivable, 12/31	$1,000,000
Estimated percentage of uncollectible accounts	× 3%
Allowance for uncollectible accounts, 12/31	$ 30,000

42. (b) The allowance account balance would increase by the difference between the required amount and the balance at the end of the year.

Accounts receivable balance	$1,000,000
Times: % uncollectible	× 5%
Balance required	50,000
Less: End of year balance in allowance account	(40,000)
Adjustment to increase balance	$ 10,000

43. (a) The *Allowance for Uncollectible Accounts* had a credit balance of $24,000 at 12/31 of the previous year. During the current year, $96,000 of uncollectible accounts were written-off. Therefore, the allowance account had a debit balance of $72,000 (i.e., $96,000 – $24,000) before recognition of uncollectible account expense for the current year. Since the aging of accounts receivable indicated that a credit balance of $100,000 was required at 12/31 of the current year, Hall recognizes uncollectible account expense of $172,000 (i.e., $72,000 + $100,000).

44. (a) The allowance method based on aging the receivables attempts to value the receivables at their future collectible amounts. Thus, it emphasizes asset valuation rather than income measurement. Allowance methods based on sales attempt to match bad debts with the revenues generated by the sales in the same period. Therefore, they emphasize income measurement rather than asset valuation. The direct write-off method is not an allowance method. The direct write-off method does not recognize bad debt expense until a specific amount is deemed uncollectible and, therefore, does not report the receivables at their net realizable value.

45. (b) The balance in the allowance account would change by the difference between the required amount and the balance at the end of the year because the percentage of receivables method is used.

Accounts receivable	$3,000,000
Times: Percentage	× 3%
Required balance	90,000
Less: Balance in allowance account at year end	(50,000)
Adjustment required	$ 40,000

46. (a) While the unadjusted credit balance in the allowance accounts would be used to compute the uncollectible account expense for the period ending 3/31, the amount is not used to compute the balance of the allowance for uncollectible accounts at 3/31.

Age	Accounts receivable	Estimated % uncollectible	Allowance for uncollectible accounts
0-30 days	$60,000	5%	$3,000
31-60 days	4,000	10%	400
Over 60 days	2,000	*	1,400
			$4,800

* The dollar amount is given in the data.

47. (b) After the allowance for uncollectible accounts at 12/31 is determined, uncollectible accounts expense can be analyzed.

Accounts receivable, 12/31	$ 350,000
Net realizable value of the receivables	(325,000)
Allowance for uncollectible accounts, 12/31	$ 25,000

Allowance for Uncollectible Accounts

Debit		Credit
		30,000 Balance, 1/1
Current year write-offs	18,000	2,000 Uncollectible accounts recovered, current year
		14,000 Subtotal
		11,000 Uncollectible accounts expense, current year (forced)
		25,000 Balance, 12/31

Direct Write-Off

48. (a) The entry to record the write-off of a specific account receivable using the allowance method involves a debit to *Allowance for Uncollectible Accounts* and a credit to *Accounts Receivable.* This affects balance sheet accounts, but not net income.

49. (a) An increase in A/R indicates that there was an excess of sales over cash collections. A write-off of receivables will offset the gross increase in A/R without affecting cash. Regardless of the accrual method used to account for uncollectible accounts, the cash collections from customers equal sales adjusted for a deduction for an increase in A/R balance and a deduction for accounts written-off during the period.

Notes Receivable

50. (b) Total interest revenue earned over the life of the note is determined as the excess of the summation of the required annual year-end payments over the present value of the note.

Summation of required annual year-end payments ($5,009 × 5)	$ 25,045
Less: Present value of note	(19,485)
Interest revenue earned over life of note	$ 5,560

51. (c) APB 21 generally requires the recording of notes receivable at their present value. At December 31, Chang is owed 9 more annual payments of $10,000. The appropriate factor to apply is the present value of ordinary annuity of $1 at 8% for 9 periods, which is given as 6.25. $10,000 × 6.25 = $62,500.

52. (a) Notes receivable are reported net of any discount. If a non-interest-bearing (or low) note is exchanged for cash and a promise to provide future goods at lower-than-usual market prices, the issuer values the note at present value. APB 21 (¶7) requires the difference between present value and the cash payments be recognized as a part of the future goods' cost, i.e., a deferred charge.

53. (b) When an interest-bearing instrument is sold between interest payment dates, the seller collects accrued interest from the buyer. The buyer will later collect interest for a full interest period at the next interest payment date. In the case at hand, inventory is being exchanged for the note. Because the market rate of interest is equal to the note's stated rate, the note's present value is equal to the face amount of the note plus the one month's accrued interest. The journal entry to record the exchange involves a debit to *Note Receivable* for its face amount, a debit to *Interest Receivable* for the one month of accrued interest, and a credit to Sales Revenue for the sum of the note's face amount and the one month of accrued interest.

54. (c) The note can be recorded at its face amount of $150,000 because there is no indication that the rate of interest (8%) stipulated by the parties to the transaction does not represent fair and adequate compensation for the use of the funds. Payments of $50,000 in principal plus accrued interest are due annually on July 1, year 2, year 3, and year 4. Frame should report the interest receivable as a current asset in its 6/30, year 3 balance sheet, because the amount is to be received within one year of the balance sheet date (i.e., it is to be received 7/1, year 3).

Carrying amount of note, 6/30, year 1	$150,000
Less: Principal payment, 7/1, year 2	(50,000)
Carrying amount of note, 7/1, year 2	100,000
Times: Stated interest rate	× 8%
Interest receivable, 6/30, year 3	$ 8,000

55. (b) A noninterest-bearing note exchanged for property, goods, or services should not be recorded at its face amount. Since there is not an established exchange price for the equipment and the question does not indicate the fair value of the note, the note should be recorded at its present value, which is computed by discounting all future payments of the note at the prevailing rate of interest for a note of this type.

Face amount of note	$600,000
Less: Imputed interest [$600,000 × (1 – 0.75)]	(150,000)
Carrying amount of note, 1/2	450,000
Times: Effective interest rate	× 10%
Interest income	$ 45,000

56. (a) A noninterest-bearing note exchanged for property, goods, or services should not be recorded at its face amount. Since there is not an established exchange price for the equipment and the question does not indicate the fair value of the note, the note should be recorded at its present value, which is computed by discounting all future payments of the note at the prevailing rate of interest for a note of this type.

Present value of note ($600,000 × 0.75)	$ 450,000
Carrying amount of machinery	(480,000)
Loss on sale of machinery	$ (30,000)

Impairment

57. (c) SFAS 114 states that a creditor should consider a loan to be impaired when, "based on

current information and events, it is probable that the creditor will be unable to collect all amounts due according to the contractual terms of the loan agreement." If foreclosure is not probable, the creditor measures the impaired loan at one of the following: (1) the loan's observable market price, (2) the fair value of collateral pledged, or (3) the present value of future principal and interest cash inflows, net of discounted disposal costs all discounted at the loan's effective interest rate. If foreclosure is probable, the second method is to be used to value a collateral dependent impaired loan.

Discounting

58. (c) The total amount of interest revenue to be earned by King over the life of the note is determined as the excess of the summation of the required annual year-end payments over the present value of the note discounted to yield 9% to King.

Summation of required annual year-end payments [5 × $5,010 (as determined below)]	$25,050	
Face amount of note		$ 20,000
Divide by: PV factor of an ordinary annuity of $1 for 5 periods at 8%	/ 3.992	
Required equal annual year-end payments under note		5,010
Times: PV factor of an ordinary annuity of $1 for 5 periods at the yield rate of 9%	× 3.890	
Less: Present value of note		(19,490)
Interest revenue to be earned over note's life		$ 5,560

59. (b) Determining the proceeds received from discounting a note receivable consists of three steps:

(1) Determine the maturity value of the note. This amount is based on the face amount, the stated rate of interest, and the time of maturity of the note.

(2) Apply the bank's discount rate to the maturity value of the note to obtain the amount of the discount charged by the bank.

(3) Subtract the discount charged by the bank from the maturity value of the note to obtain the proceeds received from the bank.

60. (c)

Face amount of note	$500,000
Add: Interest to maturity ($500,000 × 8%)	40,000
Maturity value of note	540,000
Less: Bank discount ($540,000 × 10% × 6/12)	(27,000)
Proceeds from discounted note	$513,000

61. (a)

Face amount of note	$ 40,000
Add: Interest to maturity ($40,000 × 12% × 90/360)	1,200
Maturity value of note	41,200
Less: Bank discount ($41,200 × 15% × 60/360)	(1,030)
Proceeds from discounted note	40,170
Less: Face amount of note	(40,000)
Accrued interest revenue, 9/30	$ 170

With/Without Recourse

62. (c) A company that discounts a note receivable with recourse is contingently liable to the lender. It must pay the lender the amount due at maturity, if the maker of the note fails to pay the obligation. The contingent liability is usually shown in the accounts by recording the note discounted in a *Notes Receivable Discounted* account at the note's face amount. The *Notes Receivable Discounted* account is reported as a contra asset and deducted from *Notes Receivable* in the balance sheet.

Notes receivable	$ XXX	
Less: Notes receivable discounted	(XXX)	$XXX

63. (d) Davis discounted the note receivable with recourse. If the maker fails to pay at maturity, the note is presented to Davis, who is then liable for $20,500, the amount due at maturity. Davis should disclose this contingent liability in its 12/31 financial statements.

64. (d) Factoring of receivables is in substance a sale of receivables when the transfer is without recourse (i.e., the financing institution or "factor" assumes the risk of collection).

Problem 2-2 ADDITIONAL MULTIPLE CHOICE ANSWERS

Current Assets

65. (c) Since the goods out on consignment have not yet been sold, two adjustments are required. Accounts receivable decreases by the $26,000 selling price of the unsold goods that was included in its balance. Inventories increases by the $20,000 (i.e., $26,000 / 130%) cost of the unsold goods which was not included in its balance.

Cash	$ 70,000
Accounts receivable ($120,000 – $26,000)	94,000
Inventories ($60,000 + $20,000)	80,000
Current assets, 12/31	$244,000

Cash

66. (a) Cash that is segregated for the liquidation of long-term debts should be excluded from current assets (ARB 43, Ch. 43A, par. 6). Hence, the account balance which is segregated solely for payment into the bond sinking fund should be reported as a noncurrent asset. The bank overdraft should be reported as a current liability because there is no available cash in another account at that bank to offset the overdrawn account (i.e., the bank overdraft should not be netted against the account used for regular operations held at the third bank). The cash in the regular account at the third bank is to be used for current operations, hence it should be reported as a current asset.

67. (b) The $1,800 check was not mailed as of 12/31 of the previous year and needs to be added back to the checkbook balance to arrive at the true cash balance as of 12/31 that year. The starting point is the checkbook, not the bank statement, because the bank statement does not include checks in transit.

Cost Method

68. (c) Cobb owns only a 2% interest in Roe. Thus, Cobb does not have the ability to exercise significant influence over Roe by virtue of the investment, and the investment should be accounted for under the cost method. Therefore, Cobb should report the cash dividend received from Roe as dividend income. No income is recognized from the receipt of the stock dividend from Roe, since Cobb's proportionate interest in Roe has not changed and Roe's underlying assets and liabilities have also not changed.

Shares of Roe purchased 2/12	10,000
Add: Shares of Roe from stock dividend, 3/31	2,000
Shares of Roe held, 9/15	12,000
Times: Cash dividend per share	× $1.50
Dividend income, year ended 10/31	$18,000

69. (d) The preferred stock investment should be accounted for under the cost method since it is highly unlikely that the investor has the ability to exercise significant influence over the operating and financial policies of the investee by virtue of the investment. Preferred stock is usually nonvoting. Under the cost method, dividends are normally not recognized as income until they are declared by the investee. By definition, dividends in arrears have not yet been declared. Dividend income is a component of income from continuing operations.

Equity Method

70. (b) This investment should be accounted for under the equity method because Denver's purchase of 30% (i.e., 3,000 / 10,000) of Eagle's common stock gives Denver the ability to exercise significant influence over the operating and financial policies of Eagle by virtue of the size of the investment. Denver should recognize investment income only for its share of Eagle's net income subsequent to the date of the investment. While dividends declared by Eagle reduce the carrying amount of the investment, they do not affect the amount of investment income that Denver recognizes. Therefore, Denver should report income from the equity method investment of $18,000 (i.e., $120,000 × 6/12 × 30%).

71. (b) The common stock investment should be accounted for under the equity method since Sage has the ability to exercise significant influence over the operating and financial policies of Adams by virtue of the investment. To determine Sage's reported amount of equity in income in Adams, the cost of the investment must first be allocated. The amount that Sage should report in its income statement from its investment in Adams can then be determined. The cash dividends paid by Adams to Sage reduce the carrying amount of the investment in Sage's balance sheet. They do not effect Sage's reported amount of equity in income in Adams.

Purchase price	$ 400,000
Percentage of carrying amount acquired ($900,000 × 40%)	(360,000)
Cost in excess of carrying amount of net assets acquired	40,000
Excess payment associated with specific assets:	
Plant assets ($90,000 × 40%)	(36,000)
Inventory ($10,000 × 40%)	(4,000)
Goodwill	$ 0

Interest in Adams net income ($120,000 × 40%)	$ 48,000
Less: Amortization of excess payment associated with plant assets ($36,000 / 18)	(2,000)
Excess payment associated with inventory sold	(4,000)
Equity in income of Adams	$ 42,000

72. (b) When using the equity method, a difference between the cost of the investment and the amount of underlying equity in net assets of an investee should be accounted for as if the investee were a consolidated subsidiary [APB 18]. In a consolidated situation, the excess of the investee's FIFO inventory over its carrying amount would have been charged to cost of goods sold while the excess of the fair value of the land over its carrying amount would not affect consolidated income because land is not depreciated. Thus, the excess of the fair value of Tun's FIFO inventory over its carrying amount would decrease

Park's reported equity in Tun's earnings but the excess of the fair value of Tun's land over its carrying amount would have no effect on Park's reported equity in Tun's earnings.

Investments in Marketable Securities

73. (d) The securities are measured at their fair value, with a *Market Adjustment* account established for the difference from cost. A $20,000 loss difference is offset by a $10,000 gain difference; the net is a $10,000 credit balance needed in the *Market Adjustment* account.

74. (d) An unrealized loss was reported in the previous year income statement for a temporary decline in the market value of an investment in a marketable equity security; hence, the investment must have been classified as a trading security. (An unrealized loss on an investment in marketable securities classified as available-for-sale would be shown in other comprehensive income rather than as an income statement item.) The market price decline in the previous year was *less* than the increase in market price during the current year because there was a realized gain reported on the current year income statement which means that the security was sold for a price exceeding its cost. Thus, in the current year, the market price increased enough to recover the unrealized loss experienced in the previous year and to produce a gain on the sale of the investment.

75. (d) At 12/31 of the previous year, the required balance of the *Market Adjustment—AFS* account was a $20,000 credit ($100,000 – $80,000). At 12/31 of the current year, the required balance of the *Market Adjustment—AFS* account is a $15,000 credit ($100,000 – $85,000). Thus, in the current year, the required balance of the *Market Adjustment—AFS* account decreased by $5,000. Although changes in the *Market Adjustment* account related to a trading category of marketable securities are included in the determination of net income in the period in which they occur, changes in the *Market Adjustment* account related to the available-for-sale category are included in other comprehensive income. Thus, Lee does not recognize any gain or loss from a change in the *Market Adjustment—AFS* account on its income statement.

76. (a) If there is a change in the classification of a marketable equity security between trading and available-for-sale, the security is transferred between the corresponding portfolios at the fair value at the date of transfer. If fair value is less than cost, the fair value becomes the new cost basis, and the difference is accounted for as if it were a realized loss and included in the determination of net income.

77. (b) Subsequent to purchase, debt securities classified as available-for-sale are carried in the investment account at cost, net of premium or discount amortization to date, with a separate valuation account for any difference between unamortized cost and fair value. If there is a decline in market value which is deemed *permanent,* then the security should be written down to *fair value* by a credit to the investment account and a realized loss is recognized. Debt securities purchased between interest dates should be recorded separately from accrued interest.

Investment in Marketable Debt Securities	XX	
Accrued Interest Receivable	XX	
Cash (cost of security plus accrued interest)		XX

78. (d) According to SFAS 115, trading securities are reported at fair value and unrealized holding gains and losses are included in current earnings.

Accounts Receivable

79. (c)

List price of merchandise	$ 5,000
Less: Trade discount—30%	(1,500)
Balance	3,500
Less: Trade discount—20%	(700)
Balance	2,800
Less: 2% cash discount, remittance received within 15 days of sale ($2,800 × 2%)	(56)
Amount received for merchandise	2,744
Add: Reimbursement of prepayment of delivery costs	200
Remittance received from Burr in full payment	$ 2,944

80. (c) SFAS 5, ¶8, provides that an estimated loss from a loss contingency shall be accrued by a charge to income if both of the following conditions are met: (1) it is probable that an asset has been impaired or a liability has been incurred, and (2) the amount of the loss can be reasonably estimated. FIN 14, ¶3 states that when the reasonable estimate of loss is a range and some amount within the range appears at the time to be a better estimate than any other amount within the range, that amount shall be accrued. "When no amount within the range is a better estimate than any other amount, however, the minimum amount in the range shall be accrued."

Future returns and allowances should be anticipated. Accounting treatment depends on the likelihood that future events will confirm the contingent loss **and** whether the amount can be reasonably estimated. Where the likelihood of confirmation of a loss is considered probable and the loss can be reasonably estimated, the estimated loss should be accrued. If, however, only a range of possible loss can be estimated—and no amount in the range is a better estimate than the others—the minimum amount in the range should be accrued.

Estimated returns
($200,000 × 5% = $10,000) × $1 = <u>$10,000</u>

Sales revenue (200,000 × $2)	$ 400,000
Less: Cost (200,000 × $1)	(200,000)
	200,000
Less: Processing costs	(10,000)
	190,000
Less: Estimated returns	(10,000)
Operating profit	$ 180,000

81. (c) Credit sales increase accounts receivable (A/R). Collections from customers, accounts written-off, and sales returns decrease A/R. Since the estimated future sales returns and the estimated uncollectible accounts are recorded in allowance accounts to A/R, they do not directly decrease the balance of the *Accounts Receivable* account.

Accounts Receivable

Balance, 1/1	650,000		
Credit sales	2,700,000	2,150,000	Collections from customers
			Accounts written-off
		40,000	Sales returns
		75,000	
Balance, 12/31	1,085,000		

Uncollectible Accounts

82. (d) The uncollectible accounts expense for the current year is <u>$56,000</u> ($40,000 + $16,000). The uncollectible accounts expense can be determined by an analysis of the allowance for uncollectible accounts.

Allowance for Uncollectible Accounts

		42,000	Balance, 1/1 (given)
Write-offs (given)	46,000	40,000	Uncollectible accounts expense recorded during year ($2,000,000 × 2%)
		36,000	Balance before adjustment
		16,000	Adjustment to increase allowance account to desired ending balance
		52,000	Desired ending balance per aging (given)

83. (a) Based on the information given, Jamin uses the percentage of sales method, under which bad debt expense is calculated as a percentage of credit sales, charged to *Bad Debt Expense,* and credited to the *Allowance for Uncollectible Accounts.* The allowance account balance is not considered in determining the amount of bad debt expense.

Allowance for Uncollectible Accounts

		260,000	Beg. bal. 1/1
Write-offs	325,000		
		180,000	Bad debt expense*
		115,000	12/31 balance

* Credit sales of $9,000,000 × 2% = $180,000

84. (b) The allowance method of recording uncollectible account expense matches uncollectible account expense with the revenues generated by credit sales in the same period. Therefore, the allowance method of recording uncollectible account expense is consistent with accrual accounting. Since the write-off of an account receivable often occurs in a period after the revenues were generated, the direct write-off method of recording uncollectible account expense does not necessarily match uncollectible account expense with the revenues generated by credit sales in the same period. Therefore, the direct write-off method is not consistent with accrual accounting.

Notes Receivable

85. (c) Where a note is exchanged solely for cash and no other rights or privileges are exchanged, it is presumed to have a present value at issuance equal to the cash proceeds exchanged (APB 21). The note receivable is recorded at its present value, which in the case of Money Co. is $194,000. Income on this loan for December year 5 is calculated based on the effective rate of interest on the present value of the loan; $194,000 × 12.4% = $24,056 × 1/12 = <u>$2,005</u>.

86. (b) Accrued interest receivable is calculated by multiplying the face amount of the note by the stated rate for the applicable period of time; $200,000 × 11% × 1/12 = <u>$1,833</u>. A helpful way of clearly seeing the difference between accrued interest receivable (balance sheet account) and interest income (income statement account) is by preparing the journal entries at December 1 and 31.

12/1		
Notes Receivable	200,000	
Loan Origination Fee		6,000
Cash		194,000
12/31		
Accrued Interest Receivable (face value × stated rate × time)	1,833	
Amortization of Loan Origination Fees (plug)	172	
Interest Income (PV × effective rate × time)		2,005

87. (d) Both notes were received on the balance sheet date. Since the note from Hart arose from a transaction with a customer in the normal course of business and is due in customary trade terms not exceeding one year, it can be reported at its face amount of $10,000 despite the fact that the 3% stated interest rate of the note differs from the prevailing market interest rate of 8% for similar notes at the transaction date [APB 21, ¶3(a)]. On the other hand, the note from Maxx is due in more than one year. Therefore, the note from Maxx cannot be reported at its face amount because the 3% stated interest rate of the note differs from the prevailing market interest rate of 8% for similar notes at the transaction date. Because neither the fair value of the services performed by Jet nor the fair value of the note received from Maxx is indicated, the note is reported at its present value, determined by discounting all future cash payments of the note at the prevailing (i.e., market) rate of interest for a note of this type.

Principal amount	$10,000
Interest on outstanding principal balance due on maturity date [($10,000 × 3%) × 5]	1,500
Amount due on maturity date	11,500
Present value factor of $1 at 8% for 5 periods	× 0.680
Present value of note received from Maxx	$ 7,820

88. (d) ARB 43 states that profit is deemed to be realized when a sale in the ordinary course of business is effected, unless the circumstances are such that the collection of the sale price is not reasonably assured. APB 10 states, "in absence of these circumstances, the installment method of recognizing revenue is not acceptable." Because the company purchasing the land has a triple-A credit rating, the gain is recognized fully in the period of sale. Since the mortgage note bears interest at the market rate, it is recorded at its face amount.

Cash ($150,000 × 25%)	$ 37,500
Mortgage note ($150,000 × 75%)	112,500
Fair value of proceeds received	150,000
Carrying amount of land	(100,000)
Gain realized and recognized	$ 50,000

Discounting

89. (d)

Face amount of note, 7/1 of previous year	$100,000
Less: Payment of first installment, 12/31 of previous year	(50,000)
Face amount of note, 12/31 of previous year (due 12/31 of current year)	50,000
Add: Interest to maturity ($50,000 × 10% × 12/12)	5,000
Maturity value of remaining portion of note	55,000
Less: Bank discount ($55,000 × 12% × 6/12)	(3,300)
Proceeds from discounted note	$ 51,700

PERFORMANCE BY SUBTOPICS

Each category below parallels a subtopic covered in Chapter 2. Record the number and percentage of questions you correctly answered in each subtopic area.

Current Assets

Question#	Correct √
1	
# Questions	1
# Correct	______
% Correct	______

Cash

Question #	Correct √
2	
3	
4	
5	
6	
# Questions	5
# Correct	______
% Correct	______

Cost Method

Question #	Correct √
7	
8	
9	
10	
11	
12	
# Questions	6
# Correct	______
% Correct	______

Equity Method

Question #	Correct √
13	
14	
15	
16	
17	
18	
19	
20	
21	
22	
# Questions	10
# Correct	______
% Correct	______

Investments in Marketable Securities

Question #	Correct √
23	
24	
25	
26	
27	
28	
29	
30	
31	
# Questions	9
# Correct	______
% Correct	______

Financial Instrument Disclosure

Question #	Correct √
32	
33	
34	
35	
36	
# Questions	5
# Correct	
% Correct	

Accounts Receivable

Question #	Correct √
37	
38	
39	
40	
# Questions	4
# Correct	
% Correct	

Uncollectible Accounts

Question #	Correct √
41	
42	
43	
44	
45	
46	
47	
# Questions	7
# Correct	
% Correct	

Direct Write-Off

Question #	Correct √
48	
49	
# Questions	2
# Correct	
% Correct	

Notes Receivable

Question #	Correct √
50	
51	
52	
53	
54	
55	
56	
# Questions	7
# Correct	
% Correct	

Impairment

Question #	Correct √
57	
# Questions	1
# Correct	
% Correct	

Discounting

Question #	Correct √
58	
59	
60	
61	
# Questions	4
# Correct	
% Correct	

With/Without Recourse

Question #	Correct √
62	
63	
64	
# Questions	3
# Correct	
% Correct	

SIMULATION SOLUTIONS

Solution 2-3

Responses 1-10—Marketable Securities

1. T Trading securities are debt and equity securities that are bought and held principally for the purpose of selling them in the near term.

2. H Held-to-maturity (HTM) securities are debt securities that the enterprise has the positive intent and the ability to hold to maturity.

3. A Available-for-sale (AFS) securities are debt and equity securities not classified as either HTM or trading securities.

4. A AFS securities are debt and equity securities not classified as either HTM or trading securities.

5. G $100,000. HTM securities are reported at amortized cost and are not adjusted for unrealized holding gains and losses, although fair value must be disclosed.

6. I $155,000. Trading securities are reported at fair market value.

7. J $160,000. AFS securities are reported at fair market value.

8. L,D The recognized gain or loss from the sale of a debt or equity security is the difference between the net proceeds received from the sale and the cost or amortized cost of the security. $175,000 – $190,000 = $15,000 loss.

9. L,B The $5,000 unrealized loss pertains to the trading securities, as these are the only securities for which unrealized holding gains and losses are included in current earnings. $155,000 fair value at 12/31 of the current year – $160,000 fair value at 12/31 of the previous year = $5,000 unrealized loss.

10. L,C The $10,000 loss pertains to security JKL as AFS securities are the only securities for which net unrealized holding gains or losses are reported in accumulated other comprehensive income. $160,000 fair value at 12/31 of the current year – $170,000 cost = $10,000 net unrealized loss.

Research

FAS 115, Par. 6

At acquisition, an enterprise shall classify debt and equity securities into one of three categories: held-to-maturity, available-for-sale, or trading. At each reporting date, the appropriateness of the classification shall be reassessed.

Solution 2-4

Memo—Equity Method

To: Johnson

From: Smith, CPA

Re: Acme Co. Investments in Kern Co. and Wand Co.

The purpose of this memorandum is to explain to you that although Acme's investment in Wand and Kern represent equal ownership interests of 20%, the use of different accounting methods may be appropriate under generally accepted accounting principles.

Under those principles, Acme **must use the equity method** to account for an investment if Acme's ownership interest allows it to **exercise significant influence** over the investee company.

Generally, an investor is presumed to be able to exercise significant influence when it has an ownership interest of 20% or more, and is presumed to be unable to exercise significant influence when it has an ownership interest of less than 20%. However, either **presumption may be overcome by predominant evidence to the contrary**. The determination of whether an investor can exercise significant influence is not always clear and often requires **judgment** in light of such factors as an investor's **representation** on the investee's board of directors, **participation** in policymaking activities, and/or the extent of ownership as **compared to that investee's other shareholders**.

Acme used the **equity method** to account for its investment in Kern which indicates that its **20% ownership interest** allowed it to **exercise significant influence over Kern's** operating and financial policies.

Acme accounted for its investment in Wand as available-for-sale securities. Apparently, despite its 20% ownership interest, there was evidence that Acme could **not exercise significant influence over Wand's** operating and financial policies, hence, Acme did not use the **equity method** to account for its investment in Wand.

Schedule

Prepare a schedule indicating the amounts Acme should report for the two investments in its December 31 current year balance sheet and statement of income and comprehensive income. Show all calculations. Ignore income taxes. Do not discuss SFAS No. 115, *Accounting for Investments in Certain Debt and Equity Securities*.

Calculations:		
Kern:		
Equity in earnings	$40,000 × 20%	$ 80,000
Dividend rec'd	$100,000 × 20%	$ 20,000
Carrying amount	$600,000 + $80,000 – $20,000	$660,000
Wand:		
Investment in Wand	20,000 shares × $20 per share	$400,000
Dividend income	$60,000 × 20%	$ 12,000
Unrealized gain	$400,000 – $300,000	$100,000

Kern

Balance Sheet—Acme reported its investment in Kern at a carrying amount of $660,000

Statement of Income and Comprehensive Income

Acme's equity in Kern's earnings $80,000

Wand

Balance Sheet

Acme reported its investment in Wand at a fair value of $400,000

Statement of Income and Comprehensive Income

Dividend income $12,000

Unrealized gain $100,000

Research

General Standards

I82.104

The equity method of accounting for an investment in common stock also shall be followed by an investor whose investment in voting stock gives it the ability to exercise significant influence over operating and financial policies of an investee even though the investor holds 50 percent or less of the voting stock. Ability to exercise that influence may be indicated in several ways, such as representation on the board of directors, participation in policymaking processes, material intercompany transactions, interchange of managerial personnel, or technological dependency. Another important consideration is the extent of ownership by an investor in relation to the concentration of other shareholdings, but substantial or majority ownership of the voting stock of an investee by another investor does not necessarily preclude the ability to exercise significant influence by the investor. Determining the ability of an investor to exercise such influence is not always clear and applying judgment is necessary to assess the status of each investment. In order to achieve a reasonable degree of uniformity in application, an investment (direct or indirect) of 20 percent or more of the voting stock of an investee shall lead to a presumption that in the absence of evidence to the contrary an investor has the ability to exercise significant influence over an investee. Conversely, an investment of less than 20 percent of the voting stock of an investee shall lead to a presumption that an investor does not have the ability to exercise significant influence unless such ability can be demonstrated. 3 [APB18, ¶17]

Solution 2-5

Essay—Financial Instruments

a. **A financial instrument is cash, evidence of an ownership interest in an entity, or a contractual right to receive or deliver cash or another financial instrument**. A **derivative financial instrument** is a product whose **value is derived, at least in part, from the value and characteristics of one or more underlying assets**. Examples of derivative financial instruments include: futures; forward, swap, or options contracts; interest-rate caps; and fixed-rate loan commitments.

b. **Off-balance-sheet risk** of accounting loss is the **risk of accounting loss from a financial instrument that exceeds the amount recognized for the financial instrument in the balance sheet**.

c. **Market risk** is the **possibility that future changes in market prices may make a financial instrument less valuable or more burdensome. Credit risk is the possibility that a loss may occur from the failure of the other party to perform** according to the terms of a contract. **Concentrations of credit risk** exist when receivables have **common characteristics that may affect their collection**. One common characteristic might be that the receivables are due from companies in the same industry or in the same region of the country.

d. The **fair value** of a financial instrument is the amount at which the instrument could be exchanged in a current transaction between **willing parties, other than in a forced or liquidation sale**. **Quoted market price**, if available, is the best evidence of the fair value of a financial instrument. If quoted prices are not available, the best estimate of fair value might be based on **valuation techniques** or on the quoted market price of a financial instrument with similar characteristics.

Research

FAS 130, Par. 26

26. The total of other comprehensive income for a period shall be transferred to a component of equity that is displayed separately from retained earnings and additional paid-in capital in a statement of financial position at the end of an accounting period. A descriptive title such as accumulated other comprehensive income shall be used for that component of equity. An enterprise shall disclose accumulated balances for each classification in that separate component of equity on the face of a statement of financial position, in a statement of changes in equity, or in notes to the financial statements. The classifications shall correspond to classifications used elsewhere in the same set of financial statements for components of other comprehensive income.

Solution 2-6

Allowance Schedule

Sigma Co.
Schedule of Calculation of Allowance for Uncollectible Accounts
December 31, Current Year

0 to 30 days	$300,000 × 1%		**$ 3,000**	1
31 to 90 days	80,000 × 5%		**4,000**	2
91 to 180 days	60,000 × 20%		**12,000**	3
Over 180 days	25,000 × 80%		**20,000**	4
Accounts receivable	$465,000			5
Allowance for uncollectible accounts			**$39,000**	6

Provision Schedule

Balance December 31, previous year	**$ 28,000**	7
Write-offs during current year	(27,000)	8
Recoveries during current year	7,000	9
Balance before current year provision	**8,000**	10
Required allowance at December 31, current year	39,000	11
Current year provision	**$ 31,000**	12

1. Accounts receivable 0 - 30 days past invoice date × percent deemed to be uncollectible (1%) = Amount to include in allowance for uncollectible accounts.

2. Accounts receivable 31 - 90 days past invoice date × percent deemed to be uncollectible (5%) = Amount to include in allowance for uncollectible accounts.

3. Accounts receivable 91 - 180 days past invoice date × percent deemed to be uncollectible (20%) = Amount to include in allowance for uncollectible accounts.

4. Accounts receivable over 180 days past invoice date × percent deemed to be uncollectible. (80%) = Amount to include in allowance for uncollectible accounts.

5. Total Accounts receivable.

6. Total allowance for uncollectible accounts.

7. Balance of allowance for uncollectible accounts 12/31 of previous year: ($2,800,000 × .01)

8. Accounts written off during the current year given in scenario information.

9. Recoveries during the current year given in scenario information.

10. Balance of allowance for uncollectible accounts before provision.

11. Required allowance at 12/31 of the current year from part A

12. Current year provision: Required provision less balance before provision ($39,000 – $8,000)

Research

APB 12, Par. 3

It is the Board's opinion that such allowances should be deducted from the assets or groups of assets to which the allowances relate, with appropriate disclosure.

Solution 2-7

Schedules

Kern Inc.
Long-Term Receivables Section of Balance Sheet
December 31, Year 4

9% note receivable from sale of idle building, due in annual installments of $250,000 to May 1, year 6, less current installment	$250,000	(1)
8% note receivable from officer, due December 31, year 6, collateralized by 5,000 shares of Kern Inc. common stock with a fair value of $225,000	200,000	(2)
Noninterest-bearing note from sale of patent, net of 10% imputed interest, due April 1, year 6	88,795	(3)
Installment contract receivable, due in annual installments of $88,332 to July 1, year 7, less current installment	219,668	(4)
Total long-term receivables	$758,463	(5)

Kern Inc.
Selected Balance Sheet Accounts
December 31, Year 4

Current portion of long-term receivables:		
Note receivable from sale of idle building	$250,000	(6)
Installment contract receivable	60,332	(7)
Total	$310,332	(8)
Accrued interest receivable:		
Note receivable from sale of idle building	$ 30,000	(9)
Installment contract receivable	14,000	(10)
Total	$ 44,000	(11)

Kern Inc.
Interest Revenue From Long-Term Receivables
and Gains Recognized on Sale of Assets
For the year ended December 31, Year 4

Interest revenue:		
Note receivable from sale of idle building	$ 52,500	(12)
Note receivable from sale of patent	6,195	(13)
Note receivable from officer	16,000	(14)
Installment contract receivable from sale of land	14,000	(15)
Total interest revenue	$ 88,695	(16)
Gains recognized on sale of assets:		
Patent	$ 44,600	(17)
Land	100,000	(18)
Total gains recognized	$144,600	(19)

Explanations

Explanation of Amounts:

[1,6]	Long-term portion of 9% note receivable at 12/31, year 4	
	Face amount, 5/1, year 3	$ 750,000
	Less: Installment received 5/1, year 4	(250,000)
	Balance, 12/31, year 4	500,000
	Less: Installment due 5/1, year 5	(250,000)
	Long-term portion, 12/31, year 4	$ 250,000
[2]	Note receivable is reported at book value	
[3, 13]	Noninterest-bearing note, net of imputed interest at 12/31, year 4	
	Face amount, 4/1, year 4	$ 100,000
	Less: Imputed interest [$100,000 – $82,600 ($100,000 × 0.826)]	(17,400)
	Balance, 4/1, year 4	82,600
	Add: Interest earned to 12/31, year 4 [$82,600 × 10% × 9/12]	6,195
	Balance, 12/31, year 4	$ 88,795
[4, 7]	Long-term portion of installment contract receivable at 12/31, year 4	
	Contract selling price, 7/1, year 4	$ 400,000
	Less: Cash down payment	(120,000)
	Balance, 12/31, year 4	280,000
	Less: Installment due 7/1, year 5 [$88,332 – $28,000 ($280,000 × 10%)]	(60,332)
	Long-term portion, 12/31, year 4	$ 219,668
[5]	Sum of amounts entered in #1 through #5	
[9]	Accrued interest—note receivable, sale of idle building at 12/31, year 4	
	Interest accrued from 5/1 to 12/31, year 4 [$500,000 × 9% × 8/12]	$ 30,000
[10, 15]	Accrued interest—installment contract at 12/31, year 4	
	Interest accrued from 7/1 to 12/31, year 4 [$280,000 × 10% × 1/2]	$ 14,000
[11]	Sum of amounts entered in #6 through #10	
[12]	Interest revenue—note receivable, sale of idle building, for year 4	
	Interest earned from 1/1 to 5/1, year 4 [$750,000 × 9% × 4/12]	$ 22,500
	Interest earned from 5/1 to 12/31, year 4 [$500,000 × 9% × 8/12]	30,000
	Interest revenue	$ 52,500
[14]	Interest revenue—note receivable, officer, for year 4	
	Interest earned 1/1 to 12/31, year 4 [$200,000 × 8%]	$ 16,000

[16]	Sum of amounts entered in #12 through #15		
[17]	Gain recognized on sale of patent		
	Stated selling price		$ 100,000
	Less: Imputed interest		(17,400)
	Actual selling price		82,600
	Less: Cost of patent (net)		
	Carrying amount 1/1, year 4	$40,000	
	Less amortization 1/1 to 4/1, year 4 [$8,000 × 1/4]	(2,000)	(38,000)
	Gain recognized		$ 44,600
[18]	Gain recognized on sale of land		
	Selling price		$ 400,000
	Less: Cost		(300,000)
	Gain recognized		$ 100,000
[19]	Sum of amounts entered in #17 through #18		

Research

Statement of Financial Accounting Concepts

Con 2: Qualitative Characteristics of Accounting Concepts

Par 166:

Receivables from officers and stockholders

SEC Regulation S-X, Rule 5-04

Disclose details of receivables from any officer or principal stockholder if it equals or exceeds $20,000 or 1% of total assets.

Solution 2-8

Essay—Notes Receivable Valuation

a. The appropriate valuation basis of a note receivable at the date of sale is its **discounted present value** of the future amounts receivable for **principal and interest** using the **customers' market rate of interest**, if known or determinable, at the date of the equipment's sale.

b. Gregor should **increase** the **carrying amount** of the note receivable by the **effective interest revenue earned** for the period February 1 to May 1, year 2. Gregor should account for the discounting of the note receivable without recourse by **increasing cash** for the **proceeds received, eliminating the carrying amount of the note receivable**, and **recognizing a loss (gain)** for the resulting difference.

This reporting is appropriate since the note's carrying amount is correctly recorded at the date it was discounted and the discounting of a note receivable without recourse is **equivalent to a sale** of that note. Thus the difference between the cash received and the carrying amount of the note at the date it is discounted is reported as a loss (gain).

c. 1. For notes receivable not discounted, Gregor should **recognize an uncollectible notes expense**. The expense **equals the adjustment** required to bring the balance of the allowance for uncollectible notes receivable **equal to the estimated uncollectible amounts less the fair values of recoverable equipment**.

2. For notes receivable discounted with recourse, Gregor should recognize an uncollectible notes expense. The expense equals the estimated amounts payable for customers' defaults less the fair values of recoverable equipment.

Research

FAS 144, Par. 15

15. If an impairment loss is recognized, the adjusted carrying amount of a long-lived asset shall be its new cost basis. For a depreciable long-lived asset, the new cost basis shall be depreciated (amortized) over the remaining useful life of that asset. Restoration of a previously recognized impairment loss is prohibited.

CHAPTER 3

INVENTORY

I.	**Overview**	3-2
A.	Definition	3-2
B.	Ownership Criteria	3-2
II.	**Measuring Inventories**	3-2
A.	Physical Quantities	3-2
B.	Acquisition & Production Cost	3-3
C.	Cost Flow Assumptions	3-4
D.	Lower-of-Cost-or-Market (LCM)	3-8
III.	**Inventory Estimation Methods**	3-10
A.	Gross Margin Method	3-10
B.	Retail Method	3-11

EXAM COVERAGE: Historically, exam coverage of the topics in Chapter 3 has been 5 to 10 percent of the FAR section. More information regarding exam coverage is included in Appendix B, *Practical Advice.*

CHAPTER 3

INVENTORY

I. Overview

A. Definition

ARB 43, *Inventory Pricing,* defines inventory as items of tangible personal property that are held for sale in the ordinary course of business, in the process of production for such sale, or which are to be currently consumed in the production of goods or services to be available for sale. The measuring of inventories involves two distinct problems: (1) determining **physical quantities** and (2) determining an appropriate **dollar valuation**.

B. Ownership Criteria

Only items that are *owned* by the enterprise should be included in inventory. Ownership is determined by possession of title, rather than mere physical possession of the goods.

1. **Goods in Transit From Vendor** If shipped "F.O.B. destination," the goods are **not** inventoriable until *received.* However, if shipped "F.O.B. shipping point," the goods should be inventoried when *shipped* by the vendor.

2. **Goods in Transit to Customer** The cost of inventory items sold "F.O.B. destination" should remain in inventory until the goods are *received* by the purchaser, while the cost of inventory items sold "F.O.B. shipping point" should be removed from inventory when the goods are *shipped.*

3. **Goods on Consignment** Goods *out* on consignment should be included in inventory at cost because title to the goods has not changed. Conversely, goods *held* on consignment should **not** be included in inventory. Costs incurred by a consignor on a transfer of goods to a consignee (e.g., shipping costs, warehousing costs, and in-transit insurance premiums) should be considered as inventory cost to the consignor.

4. **Transportation Charges** F.O.B. means "free on board" and requires the seller, at her/his expense, to deliver the goods to the destination indicated as F.O.B. Therefore, if goods are shipped F.O.B. *shipping point,* transportation charges are buyer's responsibility; if F.O.B. *destination,* they are seller's responsibility.

II. Measuring Inventories

A. Physical Quantities

Determination of physical inventory quantities is accomplished by the use of one or both of the following systems:

1. **Periodic Inventory System** This system is characterized by no entries being made to the inventory account during the period. Acquisitions of inventory goods are debited to "Purchases" while issuances are not recorded, so that at any point in time the balance in the inventory account reflects the amount at the *beginning* of the period. The inventory on hand is *periodically* determined by physical count. Cost of goods sold (CGS) is a residual amount obtained by subtracting the ending inventory from the sum of beginning inventory and net purchases.

2. **Perpetual Inventory System** A continuous record is maintained of items entering into and issued from inventory. The balance in the inventory account at any time reveals the inventory that should be on hand.

B. Acquisition & Production Cost

1. **Cost Method** The primary basis of accounting for inventories is cost. The cost of an inventory item is the cash price or fair value of other consideration given in exchange for it.

   a. **Merchandise Inventory** With respect to merchandise inventory, this cost figure is net of trade and/or cash discounts, if any, but should include freight-in, taxes, insurance while in transit, warehousing costs, and similar charges paid by the purchaser to bring the article to its existing condition and location.

   b. **Finished Goods Inventory** The finished goods inventory of a manufacturer must include the cost of direct materials, direct labor and *both* variable and fixed manufacturing overhead. Interest cost should **not** be capitalized for inventories that are routinely manufactured or otherwise produced in large quantities on a repetitive basis.

   c. **Freight-Out** Freight-out is a selling expense and, thus, should **not** be included in the cost of inventory.

   d. **Abnormal Costs** Paragraph 5 of ARB 43, Chapter 4, provides guidance on allocating certain costs to inventory. SFAS 151 amended ARB 43, Chapter 4 to clarify that abnormal amounts of idle facility expense, freight, handling costs, and wasted materials (spoilage) should be recognized as current-period charges rather than as a portion of the inventory cost. In addition, SFAS 151 requires that allocation of fixed production overheads to the costs of conversion be based on the normal capacity of production facilities.

   e. **Discounts** A *trade discount* is a deduction from the list or catalog price of merchandise to arrive at the gross selling price. Trade discounts are not recorded in the seller's or purchaser's accounting records. A *chain discount* occurs when a list price is subject to several trade discounts. In this situation, the amount of each trade discount is determined by multiplying (1) the list price of the merchandise **less** the amount of prior trade discounts by (2) the trade discount percentage.

Example 1 ▶ Chain Discount

Cairns Corp. purchased merchandise with a list price of $20,000, subject to trade discounts of 10% and 5%. Cairns should record the cost of this merchandise as $17,100, computed as follows:

List price	$20,000
Less: Trade discount—10%	(2,000)
Balance	18,000
Less: Trade discount—5%	(900)
Cost of the merchandise	$17,100

2. **Relative Sales Value Method** When a group of varying units are purchased at a single lump-sum price (sometimes called a "basket purchase"), the total cost of the units should be allocated to the various units on the basis of their relative sales value.

Example 2 ▶ Relative Sales Value Method

On May 1, Brevard Development Company purchased a tract of land for $600,000. Additional costs of $100,000 were incurred in subdividing the land during May through December. Of the tract acreage, 80% was subdivided into residential lots as shown below and 20% was conveyed to the city for roads and a park.

Lot class	Number of lots	Sales price per lot
A	100	$2,000
B	200	4,000
C	200	5,000

Under the relative sales value method, the cost allocated to each lot is determined as follows:

(A) Lot class	(B) Number of lots	(C) Sales price per lot	(D) (B × C) Total Sales price	(E) Relative sales price	(F) Total cost	(G) (E × F) Cost allocated to lots	(H) (G / B) Cost per lot
A	100	$2,000	$ 200,000	10.0%	$700,000	$ 70,000	$ 700
B	200	4,000	800,000	40.0%	700,000	280,000	1,400
C	200	5,000	1,000,000	50.0%	700,000	350,000	1,750
			$2,000,000			$700,000	

3. **Cost Rule Exceptions**

   a. **Decline in Market Value** When the utility of an inventory item is impaired, the pricing of the item is at cost or market, whichever is lower.

   b. **Replacement Cost** This departure from the cost basis is justified for used, damaged, or repossessed inventory items. The valuation of these goods is based upon the hypothetical replacement cost of similar items in similar conditions of use.

   c. **Valuation at Sale Price** ARB 43 provides specific guidelines for valuation of inventories at sale price. This valuation method is justifiable only by inability to determine appropriate approximate costs, immediate marketability at quoted market price, and the characteristic of units' interchangeability. Examples commonly given include precious metals and agricultural products with assured sales prices. When inventories are stated above cost, this fact is disclosed in the financial statements.

   d. **Losses on Purchase Commitments** When there is a firm commitment to purchase goods in a future period at a set price (i.e., an enforceable contract exists), any loss resulting from a drop in the market value of such goods should be recognized in the current period.

Exhibit 1 ▸ Journal Entries for a Loss on Purchase Commitment

Account	Debit	Credit
Loss on Purchase Commitment	(Contract price – FV)	
Allowance for Loss on PC		(Contract price – FV)
To record estimated loss at the end of the period.		
Inventory (or purchases)	(Current FV)	
Allowance for Loss on PC	(Allowance account balance)	
Cash		(Contract price)
To record purchase in subsequent period. Had there been a further change in FV, it would be recorded by crediting or debiting an unrealized income (or loss) account, as appropriate.		

C. **Cost Flow Assumptions**

The per-unit cost of inventory items purchased at different times will often vary. In order to allocate the total cost of goods available for sale (i.e., beginning inventory plus net purchases) between cost of goods sold and ending inventory, either the cost of specific items must be tracked or a *cost flow* method must be adopted.

1. **Specific Identification** This costing method requires the ability to identify each unit sold or in inventory. The cost of goods sold is the cost of the specific items sold, and the ending inventory is the cost of the specific items still on hand. It is used when inventory goods are few in number, have individually high costs, and can be clearly identified.

2. **First-In, First-Out (FIFO)** This method assumes that the goods first acquired are the first sold. Hence, the earliest costs are charged to CGS and the ending inventories are stated in terms of the most recent costs. Use of FIFO necessitates maintaining records of separate lot prices (layers).

Example 3 ▸ FIFO

During the year, ABC Inc. determined ending inventory and cost of goods sold under the FIFO cost flow assumption as follows:

	Units	Unit cost	Total
Beginning inventory	100	$5	$ 500
Purchase, 1/12	200	6	1,200
Purchase, 8/25	150	7	1,050
Goods available for sale	450		2,750
Ending inventory	200*		1,350**
Cost of goods sold	250		$1,400

* Determined by physical count of inventory
** Determined by applying the most recent prices to the ending inventory quantity, as below:

8/25 layer	150	@ $7	$1,050
1/12 layer	50	@ 6	300
EI,	200		$1,350

a. **Impact** FIFO is balance sheet-oriented, since it tends to report ending inventories at their approximate replacement cost. Income, however, may be misstated because old costs are matched to current revenues.

b. **Calculation** The easiest way to determine the cost of ending inventory under FIFO involves 4 simple steps: (a) determine the number of units in ending inventory; (b) segregate ending inventory into price layers, beginning with the most recent purchase prices; (c) determine the cost of each layer (i.e., unit cost multiplied by number of units); and (d) add up the cost of all the layers.

3. **Last-In, First-Out (LIFO)** This method charges CGS with the latest acquisition costs, while ending inventories are reported at the older costs of the earliest units. The objective of LIFO is to charge against current revenues the cost of the goods acquired to replace those sold, rather than the original cost of the goods actually sold. Therefore, LIFO provides a better measure of earnings, particularly during periods of rising prices. However, balance sheet presentation may suffer because the inventory is presented at the oldest unit costs that may substantially differ from current replacement cost.

a. **Effect of Changing Prices** During periods of rising prices, the LIFO inventory cost-flow method reports a *higher* cost of sales and a lower amount for ending inventory than FIFO. During periods of falling prices, the reverse is true; the LIFO inventory cost flow method would report a lower cost of sales and a higher amount for ending inventory.

b. **Perpetual vs. Periodic** Under the FIFO cost-flow method, a perpetual system would result in the same dollar amount of ending inventory as a periodic inventory system. Under the LIFO cost-flow method, however, a perpetual system would generally **not** result in the same dollar amount of ending inventory as a periodic inventory system.

c. **LIFO Methods** LIFO is generally applied by one of two different methods.

(1) **Quantity LIFO** This classical application of LIFO is generally limited to use in small businesses or where there is a small number of different inventory items. Application of quantity LIFO requires that records of separate lot prices be kept for each inventory item. At the end of the period, inventory items are valued at the oldest costs. Note that the same 4 steps used to value ending inventory under FIFO can be used for LIFO, except that step (b) now involves the **oldest** inventory layers.

Example 4 ▸ Quantity LIFO

Consider this data at the end of year 3:

	Quantity		Amount	
Beginning inventory (@ unit price):				
Year 1, base layer (@ $2.00)	120		$240	
Year 2 layer (@ $2.10)	40	160	84	$ 324
Year 3 Purchases:				
Jan. (@ $2.15)	100		215	
Apr. (@ $2.20)	200		440	
Aug. (@ $2.30)	250		575	
Nov. (@ $2.30)	300	850	690	1,920
Goods available for sale		1,010		2,244
Ending inventory, year 3		(290)		(605)*
Cost of goods sold		720		$1,639

* Computed as follows:

Base layer	120	@	$2.00	=	$240
Year 2 layer	40	@	2.10	=	84
Jan. purchase	100	@	2.15	=	215
Apr. purchase	30	@	2.20	=	66
EI Year 3	290				$605

(2) **Dollar-Value LIFO** Widely used in practice, this procedure is designed to reduce clerical costs usually associated with LIFO and to minimize the probability of liquidating the LIFO inventory layers. The application of dollar-value LIFO is based on the use of the dollar value of inventory pools of similar items, rather than physical units, as a basis for allocating inventory costs. A *base year dollar cost* is determined in the year of adoption by dividing total inventory cost by number of units. The ending inventory in each subsequent period is costed at both the base year dollar amount and current year dollar costs. The ratio obtained by dividing these two amounts (Ending Inventory [EI] valued at *current year costs* over EI at *base year cost),* is the *price index* for the current period. A layer of inventory is added every time the ending inventory stated at base year dollars exceeds the beginning inventory (also stated at base year dollars). This new layer is costed by multiplying it by the specific price index for the current period. If an inventory liquidation has occurred, the reductions are taken from the most recent layers acquired.

Example 5 ▸ Dollar-Value LIFO

On the basis of the quantity and price information in Table 1, columns 1 and 2, a price index is computed (columns 3, 4, and 5). This price index is used to value each inventory layer in Table 2. The price indices in Table 1 are figured by comparing current year prices to the base year prices.

Table 1—Price Indices

Ending Inventory		1	2	3	4	5
Year	Item	Quantity	@*	Base Year Amount (1A × $2.50) (1B × $4.00)	Current Year Amount (1 × 2)	Price Index (4 / 3)
Year 1 (base)	A	10,000	$2.50	$25,000	$25,000	--
	B	6,000	4.00	24,000	24,000	--
Year 1 Total				$49,000	$49,000	1.00
Year 2	A	11,600	2.60	$29,000	$30,160	--
	B	6,100	4.25	24,400	25,925	--
Year 2 Total				$53,400	$56,085	1.05
Year 3	A	12,200	2.95	$30,500	$35,990	--
	B	6,200	4.45	24,800	27,590	--
Year 3 Total				$55,300	$63,580	1.15
Year 4	A	10,600	**	$26,500	**	--
	B	5,800	**	23,200	**	--
Year 4 Total				$49,700		**

* These unit prices may represent the weighted average of all purchase prices paid during the year or the latest price paid.

** No price indices are computed nor new layers added due to inventory liquidation.

Table 2—Valuation of the Ending Inventory, year 2 to year 4:

	12/31/yr 2	Layers	Index	Valuation
Total	$ 53,400			
Year 1 layer	(49,000)	$49,000	1.00	$49,000
Year 2 layer	$ 4,400	4,400	1.05	4,620
Total 12/31 year 2		$53,400		$53,620

	12/31/yr 3	Layers	Index	Valuation
Total	$ 55,300			
Year 1 layer	(49,000)	$49,000	1.00	$49,000
Year 2 layer	(4,400)	4,400	1.05	4,620
Year 3 layer	$ 1,900	1,900	1.15	2,185
Total 12/31 year 3		$55,300		$55,805

	12/31/yr 3	Reduction	12/31/yr 4	Index	Valuation
Year 1 layer	$49,000		$49,000	1.00	$49,000
Year 2 layer	4,400	$ 3,700	700	1.05	735
Year 3 layer	1,900	1,900	0	1.15	0
Total 12/31 year 4	$55,300	$ 5,600	$49,700		$49,735

Chain-link (or link-chain) method The chain-link method may also be used. In the chain-link method, a price change index is figured from year-beginning to year-end each year. To arrive at the price index for a current layer of inventory, the indices for all the intervening years from the current to the base year are multiplied together.

4. **Average Inventory Methods** These assume that cost of goods sold and ending inventory should be based on the average cost of the inventories available for sale during the period. A *weighted average* is generally used with a *periodic* inventory system while a *moving average* requires the use of a *perpetual* system. The weighted-average method costs inventory items on the basis of average prices paid, weighted according to the quantity purchased at each price. The moving average requires computation of a new average after each purchase. Issues are priced at the latest average unit cost.

Example 6 ▸ Average Inventory Methods

During the year, ABC Inc. purchased and sold several lots of inventory item X, as follows:

Purchases:	Units	Unit Cost	Extended Cost
2/15	10,000	$3.00	$30,000
6/1	5,000	3.30	16,500
8/10	6,000	3.38	20,280
Goods available	21,000		$66,780
Sales:			
7/1	7,000		
9/10	9,000		
Goods sold	16,000		
Ending inventory	5,000		

The cost of the ending inventory of item X using the *weighted-average* method is $15,900 determined as follows:

Ending inventory in units	5,000
Weighted average cost per unit ($66,780 / 21000)	× $3.18
Ending inventory	$15,900

The cost of the ending inventory of item X using the *moving-average* method is $16,100, determined as follows:

	1	2	3	4
Date	Units	@	Extended	Moving Avg. (3 / 1)
2/15	10,000	$3.00	$ 30,000	$3.00
6/1	5,000	3.30	16,500	--
	15,000		46,500	3.10
7/1	(7,000)	3.10	(21,700)	--
	8,000		24,800	3.10
8/10	6,000	3.38	20,280	--
	14,000		45,080	3.22
9/10	(9,000)	3.22	(28,980)	--
End inventory	5,000		$ 16,100	3.22

D. **Lower-of-Cost-or-Market (LCM)**

The cost basis (specific identification or cost flow assumption) ordinarily achieves the objective of properly matching inventory costs and revenue. This is only satisfactory, however, as long as the utility of the inventory equals or exceeds its cost. When the utility of inventory is impaired or otherwise reduced by damage, deterioration or any other cause, the decline in value should be charged against revenue in the period in which the decline occurred. The measurement of this decline is accomplished by pricing the inventory at cost or market, whichever is lower (ARB 43).

1. **Market** As used in the phrase lower-of-cost-or-market, market means current replacement cost (by purchase or reproduction) except for the following:

   a. Market should not exceed the net realizable value (estimated selling price in the ordinary course of business less reasonably predictable costs of completion and disposal). This would be the *maximum,* or *ceiling,* amount at which market could be valued.

   b. Market should not be less than the net realizable value minus normal profit. This would be the *minimum,* or *floor,* amount at which market could be valued.

Exhibit 2 ▸ Market Under Lower-of-Cost-or-Market Rule

Rule of thumb:

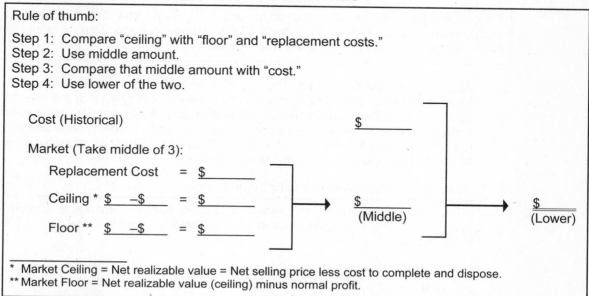

Step 1: Compare "ceiling" with "floor" and "replacement costs."
Step 2: Use middle amount.
Step 3: Compare that middle amount with "cost."
Step 4: Use lower of the two.

Cost (Historical) $______

Market (Take middle of 3):

Replacement Cost = $______

Ceiling * $ –$ = $______ → $______ (Middle) → $______ (Lower)

Floor ** $ –$ = $______

* Market Ceiling = Net realizable value = Net selling price less cost to complete and dispose.
** Market Floor = Net realizable value (ceiling) minus normal profit.

Example 7 ▸ Cost or Market, Whichever Is Lower Computation

Information related to Ellis Company's inventory at December 31 is given in columns 1 through 6. Lower-of-cost-or-market inventory calculations are illustrated in columns 7 through 10. The format shown in Exhibit 2 is also shown for inventory Item 1.

(1) Item	(2) Cost	(3) Replacement Cost (Market)	(4) Selling Price	(5) Cost of Completion	(6) Normal Profit	(7) Ceiling Maximum (4) - (5)	(8) Floor Minimum (7) - (6)	(9) Market: Limited by Floor and Ceiling	(10) Lower-of-Cost-or-Market
1	$20.50	$ 19.00	$ 25.00	$ 1.00	$ 6.00	$ 24.00	$18.00	$ 19.00	$19.00
2	25.00	17.00	30.00	2.00	10.00	28.00	18.00	18.00	18.00
3	10.00	12.00	15.00	1.00	3.00	14.00	11.00	12.00	10.00
4	40.00	55.00	60.00	6.00	4.00	54.00	50.00	54.00	40.00
	$95.50	$103.00	$130.00	$10.00	$23.00	$120.00	$97.00	$103.00	$87.00

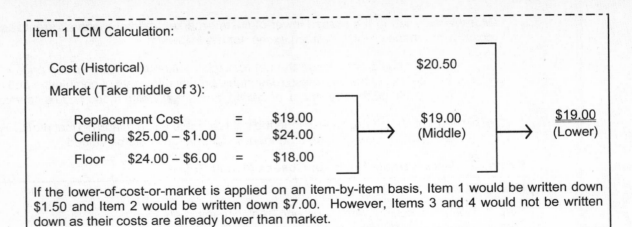

Item 1 LCM Calculation:

Cost (Historical)			$20.50	
Market (Take middle of 3):				
Replacement Cost		= $19.00		
Ceiling	$25.00 – $1.00	= $24.00	$19.00 (Middle)	$19.00 (Lower)
Floor	$24.00 – $6.00	= $18.00		

If the lower-of-cost-or-market is applied on an item-by-item basis, Item 1 would be written down $1.50 and Item 2 would be written down $7.00. However, Items 3 and 4 would not be written down as their costs are already lower than market.

2. **Applied Per Item or Groups** The rule of "cost or market, whichever is lower" may properly be applied either directly to each item or to one or more groups of the inventory. If LCM is applied item by item to each component in inventory, the lowest possible inventory balance is computed. If the inventory items are grouped into one or more groups and the LCM applied to each, decreases below cost of some items can be partially offset by increases above cost of others, resulting in a higher inventory balance.

Example 8 ▸ LCM Applied to Entire Inventory

Based on the information in Example 7, if lower-of-cost-or-market is applied to the entire inventory of Ellis Company, there is no write-down because the total cost of $95.50 is lower than the market of $103.00.

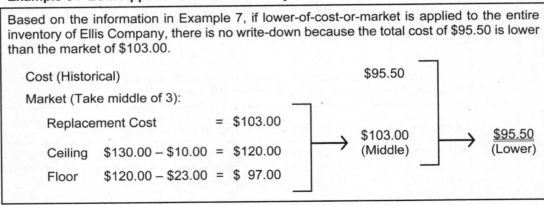

Cost (Historical)			$95.50	
Market (Take middle of 3):				
Replacement Cost		= $103.00		
Ceiling	$130.00 – $10.00	= $120.00	$103.00 (Middle)	$95.50 (Lower)
Floor	$120.00 – $23.00	= $ 97.00		

3. **Conservatism and Matching Concepts** The LCM produces a realistic estimate of future cash flows to be realized from the sale of inventories. This is consistent with the principle of conservatism, and recognizes (matches) the anticipated loss in the income statement in the period in which the price decline occurs.

III. Inventory Estimation Methods

A. Gross Margin Method

This method rests on the assumption that the gross margin (GM) percentage is relatively stable. Cost of goods sold (CGS) is determined by applying the gross margin ratio to sales and subtracting this amount from the sales figure. Ending inventory is computed by subtracting the estimated CGS from the actual goods available for sale (GAFS), obtained from the beginning inventory and purchases accounts.

1. **Not GAAP** The gross margin method is **not** generally accepted for annual financial reporting purposes.

2. **Gross Margin Method Use** This method is used to (a) verify the accuracy of the year-end physical count, (b) estimate ending inventory and cost of goods sold for interim financial reporting, and (c) estimate inventory losses from theft and casualties (fires, floods).

Example 9 ▸ Gross Margin (Profit) Method

Maggie Company has a recent gross profit history of 40% of net sales. The following data are available from Maggie's accounting records for the three months ended March 31:

Inventory at 1/1	$ 650,000
Purchases	3,200,000
Net sales	4,500,000
Purchase returns	25,000

Required: Using the gross profit method, estimate the cost of the inventory at March 31.

Solution:

Beginning inventory		$ 650,000
Purchases		3,200,000
Purchase returns		(25,000)
Goods available for sale		3,825,000
Less: Estimated cost of goods sold:		
Net sales	$ 4,500,000	
Less: Gross margin (40% × $4,500,000)	(1,800,000)	(2,700,000)
Estimated ending inventory		$ 1,125,000

B. **Retail Method**

This method of inventory estimation is often used by department stores and other retailers whose inventory goods are usually labeled upon receipt at their retail sales prices. Application of this method requires that records be kept of beginning inventory and purchases for the period, both at cost and retail, additional markups and markdowns, and sales for the period. The ending inventory at cost is estimated by converting the ending inventory expressed in retail dollars to cost dollars, through the use of a cost/retail ratio. The retail method is generally applied under one of three following methods:

1. **Weighted Average, LCM** The weighted average is accomplished by combining beginning inventory and net purchases to determine a single cost/retail ratio. The LCM effect is achieved by including net markups, but **not** net markdowns, in the denominator of the ratio. This results in a larger denominator for the ratio and, thus, a lower ratio is obtained. Applying this lower ratio to ending inventory at retail, the inventory is reported at an amount below cost. This amount is intended to approximate lower of average cost or market.

2. **LIFO Retail** As a LIFO cost flow is assumed, (a) separate cost/retail ratios must be computed for beginning inventory and net purchases, and (b) LCM need not be used. Therefore, both net markups and net markdowns are included in the denominator of the purchases' cost/retail ratio. This results in a smaller denominator for the ratio and, thus, a higher ratio is obtained.

3. **Dollar-Value LIFO Retail** Combines retail and dollar-value LIFO methods. Under this method

   a. Ending inventory at retail is determined in the same manner as LIFO retail.

   b. Ending inventory at retail is then divided by the current price index to determine ending inventory at retail at base year dollars.

   c. Ending inventory at retail at base year dollars is then compared to beginning inventory at base year dollars. If the ending inventory at retail at base year dollars is larger, a new layer has been added; this layer is converted to current dollars by applying the current price index. If ending inventory at retail at base year dollars is smaller, liquidation takes place by layers, in LIFO order.

d. Any incremental layer for the year, as determined in c. above, is then converted to cost by multiplying it by the cost/retail for purchases for the period. This layer is then added to the previous LIFO ending inventory at cost.

Example 10 ▸ Retail Methods

The LFGW Company commenced operations on January 1. An external price index is used for dollar-value LIFO computations. This index was 125 at January 1, and 150 at December 31. The following data was available from the records of the Company for the year ended December 31:

	Cost	Retail
Merchandise inventory January 1	$120,000	$200,000
Purchases, net	720,000	990,000
Markups, net		10,000
Markdowns, net		40,000
Sales, net		860,000

Required: Using the retail method, estimate merchandise inventory at December 31 under the following methods:

a. Weighted average, LCM
b. LIFO retail
c. Dollar-value LIFO retail

Solution:

a. Weighted Average, LCM:

	Cost		Retail		
Beginning inventory	$120,000		$ 200,000		
Purchases, net	720,000		990,000		
Markups, net	--		10,000		
WA/LCM cost/retail ratio	$840,000	/	$1,200,000	=	70%
Less: Sales, net			(860,000)		
Markdowns, net			(40,000)		
Ending inventory at retail			$ 300,000		
Ending inventory at cost ($300,000 × 70%)	$210,000				

b. LIFO Retail:

	Cost		Retail		
Beginning inventory	$120,000	/	$ 200,000	=	60%
Purchases, net	720,000		990,000		
Markups, net			10,000		
Markdowns, net			(40,000)		
Purchases cost/retail ratio	$720,000	/	$ 960,000	=	75%
Goods available for sale			$1,160,000		
Less: Sales, net			(860,000)		
Ending inventory at retail			$ 300,000		

Inventory layer	EI at retail		Cost/Retail ratio		EI at retail cost
Beginning	$200,000	×	60%	=	$120,000
Purchases	100,000	×	75%	=	75,000
	$300,000				$195,000

NOTE: Under a LIFO cost-flow assumption, the sum of ending inventory in retail dollars is composed of beginning inventory retail dollars (to the extent available) and a layer of purchase retail dollars for any increase in retail dollars for the period. The beginning inventory retail dollars and the purchase layer retail dollars are then converted to cost dollars by their separate cost/retail ratios.

c. Dollar-Value LIFO Retail:

	Cost	Retail
Ending inventory at retail at base year dollars ($300,000 / 1.20*)		$ 250,000
Base layer, January 1 year 1	$120,000	(200,000)
Incremental year 1 layer at base year dollars		$ 50,000
Incremental year 1 layer at current year dollars ($50,000 × 1.20)		$ 60,000
Incremental year 1 layer at cost ($60,000 × 75%)	45,000	
Ending inventory, dollar-value LIFO	$165,000	

*Current year external price index (150 / 125 = 1.20)

Wondering how to allocate your study time?

In your excitement to answer multiple choice questions, don't forget that the examiners ask questions in simulation format as well!

The first pass through a chapter:

1. Strive to answer **all** the multiple choice questions and the objective elements of the simulations, except for research elements.

2. Choose one or more of the simulations to answer completely. Read the questions and responses for the simulation elements that you don't answer.

3. At the very beginning of your review, don't worry about whether you finish questions within the time allocated. As you become more familiar with the content and the way the examiners ask questions, your speed will increase. Start concerning yourself about time when you are on the first pass through your fourth or fifth chapter.

When you review the chapter later:

1. Answer **at least** those objective questions that you did not understand the first time. (If you had a lucky guess, did you really understand?)

2. Select a new simulation to answer completely. Read the questions and responses for the simulation elements that you don't answer.

When you review the chapter for the final time (for some chapters, the second time may **be** the final time):

1. Answer the questions "cold turkey" (without reviewing the text materials just before answering questions). Before answering questions, only review the notes you would review just before the exam. For a whole exam section, this should take less than five minutes.

2. Answer **at least** those objective questions that you did not understand the first time.

3. Select a new simulation, if available, to answer completely. Read the questions and responses for the simulation elements that you don't answer.

Remember, with the techniques and information in your material,

A passing score is well within reach!

CHAPTER 3—INVENTORY

Problem 3-1 MULTIPLE CHOICE QUESTIONS (64 to 80 minutes)

1. On December 30 of the previous year, Astor Corp. sold merchandise for $75,000 to Day Co. The terms of the sale were net 30, F.O.B. shipping point. The merchandise was shipped on December 31 and arrived at Day on January 5 of the current year. Due to a clerical error, the sale was not recorded until January and the merchandise, sold at a 25% markup, was included in Astor's inventory at December 31. As a result, Astor's cost of goods sold for the previous year ended December 31 was
   a. Understated by $75,000
   b. Understated by $60,000
   c. Understated by $15,000
   d. Correctly stated

(11/93, PI, #51, amended, 4420)

2. Herc Co.'s inventory at December 31 of the previous year was $1,500,000, based on a physical count priced at cost, and before any necessary adjustment for the following:

- Merchandise costing $90,000, shipped F.O.B. shipping point from a vendor on December 30 of the previous year, was received and recorded on January 5 of the current year.
- Goods in the shipping area were excluded from inventory although shipment was not made until January 4. The goods, billed to the customer F.O.B. shipping point on December 30 had a cost of $120,000.

What amount should Herc report as inventory in its December 31, previous year balance sheet?
   a. $1,500,000
   b. $1,590,000
   c. $1,620,000
   d. $1,710,000 (11/94, FAR, #13, amended, 5278)

3. The following items were included in Opal Co.'s inventory account at December 31:

Merchandise out on consignment, at sales price, including 40% markup on selling price	$40,000
Goods purchased, in transit, shipped F.O.B. shipping point	36,000
Goods held on consignment by Opal	27,000

By what amount should Opal's inventory account at December 31 be reduced?
   a. $103,000
   b. $ 67,000
   c. $ 51,000
   d. $ 43,000 (5/93, PI, #20, amended, 4062)

4. Southgate Co. paid the in-transit insurance premium for consignment goods shipped to Hendon Co., the consignee. In addition, Southgate advanced part of the commissions that will be due when Hendon sells the goods. Should Southgate include the in-transit insurance premium and the advanced commissions in inventory costs?

	Insurance premium	*Advanced commissions*
a.	Yes	Yes
b.	No	No
c.	Yes	No
d.	No	Yes

(5/92, Theory, #23, 2716)

5. Bren Co.'s beginning inventory at January 1 was understated by $26,000, and its ending inventory was overstated by $52,000. As a result, Bren's cost of goods sold for the year was
   a. Understated by $26,000
   b. Overstated by $26,000
   c. Understated by $78,000
   d. Overstated by $78,000

(11/94, FAR, #43, amended, 5305)

6. Which of the following statements regarding inventory accounting systems is true?
   a. A disadvantage of the perpetual inventory system is that the inventory dollar amounts used for interim reporting purposes are estimated amounts.
   b. A disadvantage of the periodic inventory system is that the cost of good sold amount used for financial reporting purposes includes both the cost of inventory sold and inventory shortages.
   c. An advantage of the perpetual inventory system is that the record keeping required to maintain the system is relatively simple.
   d. An advantage of the periodic inventory system is that it provides a continuous record of the inventory balance. (R/05, FAR, 0827F, #15, 7759)

7. A company records inventory at the gross invoice price. Theoretically, how should the following affect the costs in inventory?

	Warehousing costs	*Cash discounts available*
a.	Increase	Decrease
b.	No effect	Decrease
c.	No effect	No effect
d.	Increase	No effect

(11/87, Theory, #1, 1844)

8. On July 1, Casa Development Co. purchased a tract of land for $1,200,000. Casa incurred additional costs of $300,000 during the remainder of the year in preparing the land for sale. The tract was subdivided into residential lots as follows:

Lot Class	Number of lots	Sales price per lot
A	100	$24,000
B	100	16,000
C	200	10,000

Using the relative sales value method, what amount of costs should be allocated to the Class A lots?
a. $300,000
b. $375,000
c. $600,000
d. $720,000 (5/95, FAR, #10, amended, 5546)

9. According to the FASB conceptual framework, which of the following attributes would **not** be used to measure inventory?
a. Historical cost
b. Replacement cost
c. Net realizable value
d. Present value of future cash flows
(11/95, FAR, #5, 6087)

10. Town Inc. is preparing its financial statements for the current year ended December 31. At December 31, Town had outstanding purchase orders in the ordinary course of business for purchase of a raw material to be used in its manufacturing process. The market price is currently higher than the purchase price and is not anticipated to change within the next year. What is the reporting requirement?
a. Disclosure only
b. Accrual only
c. Both accrual and disclosure
d. Neither accrual nor disclosure
(11/95, FAR, #80, amended, 6154)

11. A company decided to change its inventory valuation method from FIFO to LIFO in a period of rising prices. What was the result of the change on ending inventory and net income in the year of the change?

	Ending inventory	*Net income*
a.	Increase	Increase
b.	Increase	Decrease
c.	Decrease	Decrease
d.	Decrease	Increase

(11/95, FAR, #9, 6091)

12. Generally, which inventory costing method approximates most closely the current cost for each of the following?

	Cost of goods sold	*Ending inventory*
a.	LIFO	FIFO
b.	LIFO	LIFO
c.	FIFO	FIFO
d.	FIFO	LIFO

(11/91, Theory, #7, 2515)

13. The UNO Company was formed on January 2, year 1, to sell a single product. Over a two-year period, UNO's acquisition costs have increased steadily. Physical quantities held in inventory were equal to three months' sales at December 31, year 1, and zero at December 31, year 2. Assuming the periodic inventory system, the inventory cost method which reports the highest amount for each of the following is

	Inventory December 31, Year 1	*Cost of sales Year 2*
a.	LIFO	FIFO
b.	LIFO	LIFO
c.	FIFO	FIFO
d.	FIFO	LIFO

(11/89, Theory, #9, amended, 9006)

14. Drew Co. uses the average cost inventory method for internal reporting purposes and LIFO for financial statement and income tax reporting. At December 31, the inventory was $375,000 using average cost and $320,000 using LIFO. The unadjusted credit balance in the LIFO Reserve account on December 31 was $35,000. What adjusting entry should Drew record to adjust from average cost to LIFO at December 31?

		Debit	*Credit*
a.	Cost of Goods Sold	$55,000	
	Inventory		$55,000
b.	Cost of Goods Sold	$55,000	
	LIFO Reserve		$55,000
c.	Cost of Goods Sold	$20,000	
	Inventory		$20,000
d.	Cost of Goods Sold	$20,000	
	LIFO Reserve		$20,000

(11/93, PI, #19, amended, 4388)

15. Estimates of price-level changes for specific inventories are required for which of the following inventory methods?
a. Conventional retail
b. Dollar-value LIFO
c. Weighted average cost
d. Average cost retail (11/93, Theory, #3, 4508)

16. When the double-extension approach to the dollar-value LIFO inventory method is used, the inventory layer added in the current year is multiplied by an index number. Which of the following correctly states how components are used in the calculation of this index number?

a. In the numerator, the average of the ending inventory at base year cost and at current year cost
b. In the numerator, the ending inventory at current year cost, and, in the denominator, the ending inventory at base year cost
c. In the numerator, the ending inventory at base year cost, and, in the denominator, the ending inventory at current year cost
d. In the denominator, the average of the ending inventory at base year cost and at current year cost (11/91, Theory, #28, 2536)

17. Nest Co. recorded the following inventory information during the month of January:

	Units	Unit cost	Total cost	Units on hand
Balance on 1/1	2,000	$1	$2,000	2,000
Purchased on 1/8	1,200	3	3,600	3,200
Sold on 1/23	1,800			1,400
Purchased on 1/28	800	5	4,000	2,200

Nest uses the LIFO method to cost inventory. What amount should Nest report as inventory on January 31 under each of the following methods of recording inventory?

	Perpetual	*Periodic*
a.	$2,600	$5,400
b.	$5,400	$2,600
c.	$2,600	$2,600
d.	$5,400	$5,400

(R/01, FAR, #2, 6977)

18. Brock Co. adopted the dollar-value LIFO inventory method as of January 1, year 1. A single inventory pool and an internally computed price index are used to compute Brock's LIFO inventory layers. Information about Brock's dollar value inventory follows:

	Inventory		
Date	At base year cost	At current year cost	At dollar-value LIFO
1/1, year 1	$40,000	$40,000	$40,000
Year 1, layer	5,000	14,000	6,000
12/31 year 1	45,000	54,000	46,000
Year 2, layer	15,000	26,000	?
12/31, year 2	$60,000	$80,000	$?

What was Brock's dollar-value LIFO inventory at December 31, year 2?

a. $80,000
b. $74,000
c. $66,000
d. $60,000 (11/93, PI, #20, amended, 4389)

19. Bach Co. adopted the dollar-value LIFO inventory method as of January 1, year 1. A single inventory pool and an internally computed price index are used to compute Bach's LIFO inventory layers. Information about Bach's dollar value inventory follows:

	Inventory	
Date	At base year cost	At current year cost
1/1, year 1	$90,000	$90,000
Year 1 layer	20,000	30,000
Year 2 layer	40,000	80,000

What was the price index used to compute Bach's year 2 dollar value LIFO inventory layer?

a. 1.09
b. 1.25
c. 1.33
d. 2.00 (R/01, FAR, #1, amended, 6976)

Items 20 and 21 are based on the following:

During January, Metro Co., which maintains a perpetual inventory system, recorded the following information pertaining to its inventory:

	Units	Unit cost	Total cost	Units on hand
Balance on 1/1	1,000	$1	$1,000	1,000
Purchased on 1/7	600	3	1,800	1,600
Sold on 1/20	900			700
Purchased on 1/25	400	5	2,000	1,100

20. Under the moving-average method, what amount should Metro report as inventory at January 31?
a. $2,640
b. $3,225
c. $3,300
d. $3,900 (5/93, PI, #18, amended, 4060)

21. Under the LIFO method, what amount should Metro report as inventory at January 31?
a. $1,300
b. $2,700
c. $3,900
d. $4,100 (5/93, PI, #19, amended, 4061)

22. The original cost of an inventory item is below the net realizable value and above the net realizable value less a normal profit margin. The inventory item's replacement cost is below the net realizable value less a normal profit margin. Under the lower of cost-or-market method, the inventory item should be valued at
a. Original cost
b. Replacement cost
c. Net realizable value
d. Net realizable value less normal profit margin (5/97, FAR, #1, 6473)

23. The original cost of an inventory item is below both replacement cost and net realizable value. The net realizable value less normal profit margin is below the original cost. Under the lower-of-cost-or-market method, the inventory item should be valued at
a. Replacement cost
b. Net realizable value
c. Net realizable value less normal profit margin
d. Original cost (11/92, Theory, #14, 3447)

24. Which of the following statements are correct when a company applying the lower-of-cost-or-market method reports its inventory at replacement cost?

I. The original cost is less than replacement cost.
II. The net realizable value is greater than replacement cost.

a. I only
b. II only
c. Both I and II
d. Neither I nor II (11/94, FAR, #14, 5279)

25. Rose Co. sells one product and uses the last-in, first-out method to determine inventory cost. Information for the month of January follows:

	Total Units	*Unit Cost*
Beginning inventory, 1/1	8,000	$8.20
Purchases, 1/5	12,000	7.90
Sales	10,000	

Rose has determined that at January 31 the replacement cost of its inventory was $8 per unit and the net realizable value was $8.80 per unit. Rose's normal profit margin is $1 per unit. Rose applies the lower of cost or market rule to total inventory and records any resulting loss. At January 31 what should be the net carrying amount of Rose's inventory?
a. $79,000
b. $79,800
c. $80,000
d. $81,400 (R/03, FAR, #10, amended, 7612)

26. Based on a physical inventory taken on December 31, Chewy Co. determined its chocolate inventory on a FIFO basis at $26,000 with a replacement cost of $20,000. Chewy estimated that, after further processing costs of $12,000, the chocolate could be sold as finished candy bars for $40,000. Chewy's normal profit margin is 10% of sales. Under the lower-of-cost-or-market rule, what amount should Chewy report as chocolate inventory in its December 31 balance sheet?
a. $28,000
b. $26,000
c. $24,000
d. $20,000 (11/93, PI, #21, amended, 4390)

27. The lower-of-cost-or-market rule for inventories may be applied to total inventory, to groups of similar items, or to each item. Which application generally results in the lowest inventory amount?
a. All applications result in the same amount
b. Total inventory
c. Groups of similar items
d. Separately to each item

(11/93, Theory, #4, 4509)

28. Dart Company's accounting records indicated the following information:

Inventory, 1/1	$ 500,000
Purchases during the year	2,500,000
Sales during the year	3,200,000

A physical inventory taken on December 31 resulted in an ending inventory of $575,000. Dart's gross profit on sales has remained constant at 25% in recent years. Dart suspects some inventory may have been taken by a new employee. At December 31, what is the estimated cost of missing inventory?
a. $ 25,000
b. $100,000
c. $175,000
d. $225,000 (11/87, PI, #9, amended, 9009)

29. The following information was obtained from Smith Co.:

Sales	$275,000
Beginning inventory	30,000
Ending inventory	18,000

Smith's gross margin is 20%. What amount represents Smith purchases?
a. $202,000
b. $208,000
c. $220,000
d. $232,000 (R/05, FAR, A0151F, #41, 7785)

30. The retail inventory method includes which of the following in the calculation of both cost and retail amounts of goods available for sale?
a. Purchase returns
b. Sales returns
c. Net markups
d. Freight in (11/90, Theory, #16, 1796)

31. Hutch Inc. uses the conventional retail inventory method to account for inventory. The following information relates to current year operations:

	Average	
	Cost	Retail
Beginning inventory and purchases	$600,000	$920,000
Net markups		40,000
Net markdowns		60,000
Sales		780,000

What amount should be reported as cost of sales for the current year?
a. $480,000
b. $487,500
c. $520,000
d. $525,000 (5/92, PI, #49, amended, 2620)

32. Union Corp. uses the first-in, first-out retail method of inventory valuation. The following information is available:

	Cost	Retail
Beginning inventory	$12,000	$ 30,000
Purchases	60,000	110,000
Net additional markups		10,000
Net markdowns		20,000
Sales revenue		90,000

If the lower-of-cost-or-market rule is disregarded, what would be the estimated cost of the ending inventory?
a. $24,000
b. $20,800
c. $20,000
d. $19,200 (5/90, PI, #13, 0910)

Problem 3-2 ADDITIONAL MULTIPLE CHOICE QUESTIONS (26 to 33 minutes)

33. On December 1, Alt Department Store received 505 sweaters on consignment from Todd. Todd's cost for the sweaters was $80 each, and they were priced to sell at $100. Alt's commission on consigned goods is 10%. At December 31, 5 sweaters remained. In its December 31 balance sheet, what amount should Alt report as payable for consigned goods?

a. $49,000
b. $45,400
c. $45,000
d. $40,400 (5/93, PI, #29, amended, 4071)

34. During the current year, Kam Co. began offering its goods to selected retailers on a consignment basis. The following information was derived from Kam's current year accounting records:

Beginning inventory	$122,000
Purchases	540,000
Freight in	10,000
Transportation to consignees	5,000
Freight out	35,000
Ending inventory—held by Kam	145,000
—held by consignees	20,000

In its current year income statement, what amount should Kam report as cost of goods sold?

a. $507,000
b. $512,000
c. $527,000
d. $547,000 (5/95, FAR, #33, amended, 5569)

35. On December 28, Kerr Manufacturing Co. purchased goods costing $50,000. The terms were F.O.B. destination. Some of the costs incurred in connection with the sale and delivery of the goods were as follows:

Packaging for shipment	$1,000
Shipping	1,500
Special handling charges	2,000

These goods were received on December 31. In Kerr's December 31 balance sheet, what amount of cost for these goods should be included in inventory?

a. $54,500
b. $53,500
c. $52,000
d. $50,000 (11/91, PI, #12, amended, 2400)

36. Jones Wholesalers stocks a changing variety of products. Which inventory costing method will be most likely to give Jones the lowest ending inventory when its product lines are subject to specific price increases?

a. Specific identification
b. Weighted average
c. Dollar-value LIFO
d. FIFO periodic (11/92, Theory, #15, 3448)

37. During periods of inflation, a perpetual inventory system would result in the same dollar amount of ending inventory as a periodic inventory system under which of the following inventory valuation methods?

	FIFO	*LIFO*
a.	Yes	No
b.	Yes	Yes
c.	No	Yes
d.	No	No

(R/02, FAR #7, 7062)

38. Walt Co. adopted the dollar-value LIFO inventory method as of January 1 of the current year, when its inventory was valued at $500,000. Walt's entire inventory constitutes a single pool. Using a relevant price index of 1.10, Walt determined that its December 31 inventory was $577,500 at current year cost, and $525,000 at base year cost. What was Walt's dollar-value LIFO inventory at December 31 of the current year?

a. $525,000
b. $527,500
c. $552,500
d. $577,500 (5/95, FAR, #11, amended, 5547)

39. The dollar-value LIFO inventory cost flow method involves computations based on

	Inventory pools of similar items	*A specific price index for each year*
a.	No	Yes
b.	No	No
c.	Yes	No
d.	Yes	Yes

(11/86, Theory, #6, 1865)

40. On January 1, year 1, Poe Company adopted the dollar-value LIFO inventory method. Poe's entire inventory constitutes a single pool. Inventory data for year 1 and year 2 are as follows:

Date	Inventory at current year cost	Inventory at base year cost	Relevant price index
01/01, year 1	$150,000	$150,000	1.00
12/31, year 1	220,000	200,000	1.10
12/31, year 2	276,000	230,000	1.20

Poe's LIFO inventory value at December 31, year 2, is
a. $230,000
b. $236,000
c. $241,000
d. $246,000 (5/88, PI, #22, amended, 0916)

41. Ashe Co. recorded the following data pertaining to raw material X during January:

	Units			
Date	Received	Cost	Issued	On Hand
1/01 Inventory		$8.00		3,200
1/11 Issue			1,600	1,600
1/22 Purchase	4,800	9.60		6,400

The moving-average unit cost of X inventory at January 31 is
a. $8.80
b. $8.96
c. $9.20
d. $9.60 (11/90, PI, #8, amended, 9007)

42. Kahn Co., in applying the lower-of-cost-or-market method, reports its inventory at replacement cost. Which of the following statements are correct?

	The original cost is greater than replacement cost	*The net realizable value, less a normal profit margin, is greater than replacement cost*
a.	Yes	Yes
b.	Yes	No
c.	No	Yes
d.	No	No

(5/92, Theory, #25, 2718)

43. The following information pertains to an inventory item:

Cost	$12.00
Estimated selling price	13.60
Estimated disposal cost	.20
Normal gross margin	2.20
Replacement cost	10.90

Under the lower-of-cost-or-market rule, this inventory item should be valued at
a. $10.70
b. $10.90
c. $11.20
d. $12.00 (11/89, PII, #10, 0913)

44. Dean Company uses the retail inventory method to estimate its inventory for interim statement purposes. Data relating to the computation of the inventory at July 31 are as follows:

	Cost	Retail
Inventory, 2/1	$ 180,000	$ 250,000
Purchases	1,020,000	1,575,000
Markups, net		175,000
Sales		1,705,000
Estimated normal shoplifting losses		20,000
Markdowns, net		125,000

Under the approximate lower-of-average-cost-or-market retail method, Dean's estimated inventory at July 31 is
a. $ 90,000
b. $ 96,000
c. $102,000
d. $150,000 (11/87, PI, #53, amended, 0919)

45. On December 31 of the previous year, Jason Company adopted the dollar-value LIFO retail inventory method. Inventory data are as follows:

	LIFO Cost	Retail
Inventory, 12/31 previous year	$360,000	$500,000
Inventory, 12/31 current year	--	660,000
Increase in price level for current year		10%
Cost to retail ratio for current year		70%

Under the LIFO retail method, Jason's inventory at December 31 of the current year should be
a. $437,000
b. $462,000
c. $472,000
d. $483,200 (5/86, PI, #12, amended, 0927)

SIMULATIONS

Problem 3-3 (15 to 25 minutes)

Essay | Research Task

Huddell Company, which is both a wholesaler and retailer, purchases merchandise from various suppliers FOB destination, and incurs substantial warehousing costs. The dollar-value LIFO method is used for the wholesale inventories. Huddell determines the estimated cost of its retail ending inventories using the conventional retail inventory method, which approximates lower of average cost or market.

a. When should the purchases from various shippers generally be included in Huddell's inventory? Why?

b. How should Huddell account for the warehousing costs? Why?

c. 1. What are the advantages of using the dollar-value LIFO method as opposed to the traditional LIFO method?

2. How does the application of the dollar-value LIFO method differ from the application of the traditional LIFO method?

d. 1. In the calculation of the cost to retail percentage used to determine the estimated cost of its ending retail inventories, how should Huddell use

- Net markups?
- Net markdowns?

2. Why does Huddell's retail-inventory method approximate lower of average cost or market?

(5/90, Theory, #4, 9911)

Essay | Research Task

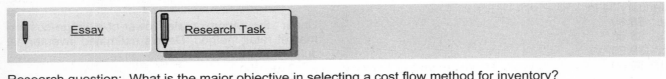

Research question: What is the major objective in selecting a cost flow method for inventory?

Paragraph Reference Answer: _______________

Problem 3-4 (40 to 50 minutes)

Scenario | Schedule | Research Task

On January 1, year 1, Silver Industries Inc. adopted the dollar-value LIFO method of determining inventory costs for financial and income tax reporting. The following information relates to this change:

- Silver has continued to use the FIFO method, which approximates current costs, for internal reporting purposes. Silver's FIFO inventories at December 31, year 1, year 2, and year 3 were $100,000, $137,500, and $195,000, respectively.
- The FIFO inventory amounts are converted to dollar-value LIFO amounts using a single inventory pool and cost indices developed using the link-chain method. Silver estimated that the current year cost change indices, which measure year-to-year cost changes, were 1.25 for year 2 and 1.20 for year 3.

Prepare a schedule showing the computation of Silver's dollar-value LIFO inventory at December 31, year 2 and year 3. Show all calculations. (11/92, PI, #4(b), amended, 6188)

Scenario | Schedule | Research Task

Silver Inc.
Computation of Dollar-Value LIFO Inventory
December 31, Year 2 and Year 3

Year	FIFO inventory	Current year cost change index	Link-chain cost index	Inventory at base year costs
1	$100,000	1.00	1.00	$100,000
2	137,500	1.25	______ (a)	______ (c)
3	195,000	1.20	______ (b)	______ (d)

Year	LIFO inventory layers at base year costs	Link-chain cost index	Year 2 dollar-value LIFO inventory	Year 3 dollar-value LIFO inventory
1	$100,000	1.00	$100,000	$100,000
2	______ (e)	______ (a)	______ (h)	______ (j)
3	______ (f)	______ (b)		______ (k)
	______ (g)		______ (i)	______ (l)

Scenario | Schedule | Research Task

Research question: When does a LIFO inventory temporary difference become taxable or deductible?

Paragraph Reference Answer: ______________

Problem 3-5 (15 to 25 minutes)

Essay | Research Task

Happlia Co. imports expensive household appliances. Each model has many variations and each unit has an identification number. Happlia pays all costs for getting the goods from the port to its central warehouse in Des Moines. After repackaging, the goods are consigned to retailers. A retailer makes a sale, simultaneously buys the appliance from Happlia, and pays the balance due within one week. To alleviate the overstocking of refrigerators at a Minneapolis retailer, some were reshipped to a Kansas City retailer where they were still held in inventory at December 31. Happlia paid the costs of this reshipment. Happlia uses the specific identification inventory costing method.

a. In regard to the specific identification inventory costing method
   1. Describe its key elements.
   2. Discuss why it is appropriate for Happlia to use this method.

b. 1. What general criteria should Happlia use to determine inventory carrying amounts at December 31? Ignore lower-of-cost-or-market considerations.
   2. Give four examples of costs included in these inventory carrying costs.

c. What costs should be reported in Happlia's year-end income statement? Ignore lower-of-cost-or-market considerations.

(5/91, Theory, amended, #3, 9911)

Essay	Research Task

Research question: When shall goodwill of a reporting unit be tested for impairment?

Paragraph Reference Answer: ______________

Problem 3-6 (30 to 40 minutes)

Scenario	Inventory Response	Essay	Research Task

York Co. sells one product, which it purchases from various suppliers. York's trial balance at December 31 included the following accounts:

Sales (33,000 units @ $16)	$528,000
Sales discounts	7,500
Purchases	368,900
Purchase discounts	18,000
Freight-in	5,000
Freight-out	11,000

York Co.'s inventory purchases during the year were as follows:

	Units	Cost per unit	Total cost
Beg. inventory, Jan. 1	8,000	$8.20	$ 65,600
Purchases, quarters ended:			
March 31	12,000	8.25	99,000
June 30	15,000	7.90	118,500
September 30	13,000	7.50	97,500
December 31	7,000	7.70	53,900
	55,000		$434,500

Additional information:

York's accounting policy is to report inventory in its financial statements at the lower of cost or market, applied to total inventory. Cost is determined under the last-in, first-out (LIFO) method.

York has determined that, at December 31, the replacement cost of its inventory was $8 per unit and the net realizable value was $8.80 per unit. York's normal profit margin is $1.05 per unit.

Prepare York's schedule of cost of goods sold, with a supporting schedule of ending inventory. York uses the direct method of reporting losses from market decline of inventory. (5/94, FAR, #4, amended, 4974)

Scenario | Inventory Response | Essay | Research Task

York Co.
Schedule of Cost of Goods Sold
For the Year Ended December 31, YYYY

Beginning inventory	
Add: Purchases	
Less: Purchase discounts	
Add: Freight-in	
Goods available for sale	
Less: Ending inventory	
Cost of Goods Sold	

York Co.
Supporting Schedule of Ending Inventory
December 31, YYYY

Inventory at cost (LIFO):

	Units	Cost per unit	Total cost
Beg. inventory, Jan. 1			
Purchases, quarters ended:			

Scenario | Inventory Response | Essay | Research Task

Explain the rule of lower-of-cost-or-market and its application in this situation.

Scenario | Inventory Response | Essay | Research Task

Research question: What does the term *market* mean as used in the phrase lower of cost or market?

Paragraph Reference Answer: ________________

Solution 3-1 MULTIPLE CHOICE ANSWERS

Ownership Criteria

1. (b) Goods should be removed from the seller's inventory when legal title passes to the purchaser. Therefore, Astor should exclude the cost of the goods shipped F.O.B. shipping from inventory at 12/31 because title of these goods passed to Day when the goods were picked up by the common carrier on 12/31. Since the goods were erroneously in Astor's inventory at 12/31, Astor's previous year ending inventory and cost of goods sold were overstated and understated, respectively, by the $60,000 (i.e., $75,000 / 125% cost of the goods).

2. (d) Goods should be included in the purchaser's inventory when legal title passes to the purchaser. Therefore, Herc should include the $90,000 cost of goods shipped to it F.O.B. shipping point in inventory at 12/31 because title of these goods passed to Herc when the goods were picked up by the common carrier on 12/30. Herc should also include the $120,000 cost of goods in its shipping area in inventory at 12/31. These goods should be included in inventory because shipment of these goods to the customer was not made until the following year.

3. (d) Opal's inventory account should be reduced by <u>$43,000</u> (i.e., $16,000 + $27,000) at 12/31. The merchandise out on consignment should be included in Opal's inventory at cost. Therefore, Opal's inventory must be reduced by the amount of the markup. Note that the question states that the merchandise out on consignment includes 40% *markup on selling price,* not a 40% markup on cost. The markup is easily calculated because the selling price is given. Selling price of $40,000 times 40% equals a markup of $16,000. Since Opal does not have title to the $27,000 of goods held on consignment, the cost of these goods should also be excluded from Opal's inventory. The cost of the $36,000 of goods in transit at 12/31, purchased F.O.B. shipping point, are properly included in Opal's inventory because title of the goods passed to Opal when the goods were shipped.

4. (c) The goods shipped to the consignee remain the property of the consignor. The consignor should include the in-transit insurance premium for the goods out on consignment in inventory costs because it is a cost necessary to get the goods in the place and condition for their intended sale. The consignor should charge the advanced commissions to a prepaid commissions expense account. The commissions should not be included in inventory costs because they were not necessary to get the merchandise ready for sale. When the goods are sold by the consignee, the consignor should report the commissions as a selling expense.

Measuring Inventories

5. (c) An understatement of beginning inventory understates the cost of goods available for sale, thereby understating cost of goods sold. An overstatement of ending inventory also understates cost of goods sold. Therefore, cost of goods sold for the year is understated by the sum of the understatement of beginning inventory and the overstatement of ending inventory.

6. (b) In the periodic system cost of goods sold (CGS) is a residual amount obtained by subtracting the ending inventory from the sum of beginning inventory and net purchases. The periodic system is characterized by no entries being made to the inventory account during the period. This amount would also include shortages as well as items actually sold, thus inaccurately reporting the true cost of goods sold. In a perpetual inventory system, record keeping is not simple; inventory dollar amounts are not estimated. The balance in the inventory account at any time reveals the inventory that should be on hand.

7. (a) Warehousing costs are usually treated as an expense in the period in which they are incurred, although conceptually they comprise part of the total cost of merchandise made ready for sale. Conceptually, the cost of inventory should be reduced for cash discounts available, because the acquisition cost of an asset should not exceed its cash equivalent price.

8. (c) Under the relative sales value method, the total cost of the individual units purchased at a single lump-sum price should be allocated to the various units on the basis of their relative sales value. The total cost includes the purchase price of $1,200,000 plus the additional costs of $300,000 to prepare the land for sale.

Lot Class	Number of lots	Sales price per lot	Total sales for class
A	100	$24,000	$2,400,000
B	100	16,000	1,600,000
C	200	10,000	2,000,000
Total			$6,000,000

Class A lots ($2,400,000) / Total sales value ($6,000,000) = 40%.

Purchase price of entire tract	$1,200,000
Additional costs of preparing land for sale	300,000
Total cost	1,500,000
Class A lots relative value percentage	× 40%
Costs allocated to Class A lots	$ 600,000

9. (d) The primary basis for accounting for inventories is cost. The cost of an inventory item is the cash price or fair value of other consideration given in exchange for it. Historical cost, replacement cost, and net realizable value are all appropriate methods for measuring inventory. The present value of future cash flows (which would include profits not yet earned) pertains to the time value of money and is not appropriate for measuring inventory.

Losses on Purchase Commitments

10. (d) Because the outstanding purchase orders occurred in the ordinary course of business and the raw materials have not yet been received, the purchase is not required to be accrued. Because the price difference is only a market price difference occurring in the ordinary course of business, disclosure it not required.

Cost Flow Assumptions

11. (c) During periods of rising prices, the LIFO inventory cost flow method reports a higher cost of sales and a lower amount for ending inventory than FIFO. Therefore, a change from FIFO to LIFO during this period would result in a decrease in net income and a decrease in ending inventory.

12. (a) In using LIFO, the cost of the last goods in are used in pricing the cost of goods sold. In using FIFO, the cost of the last goods in are used in pricing the ending inventory. Therefore, the LIFO method will result in having cost of goods sold most closely approximate current cost and the FIFO method will result in having ending inventory most closely approximate current cost.

13. (c) Under the last-in, first-out (LIFO) method of inventory valuation, the units remaining in ending inventory are costed at the oldest unit costs available. On the other hand, under the first-in, first-out (FIFO) method of inventory valuation, the units remaining in ending inventory are costed at the most recent unit costs available. Therefore, because inventory acquisition costs increased steadily during year 1, the FIFO method of inventory valuation would report a higher amount for ending inventory than the LIFO method. The question indicates that there were no goods in inventory at 12/31 year 2. Therefore, cost of goods sold for year 2 is comprised of the cost of inventory purchases made in year 2 and the cost of ending inventory at 12/31 year 1. Because the cost of the ending inventory at 12/31 year 1 is higher under FIFO, cost of goods sold for year 2 would also be higher under FIFO.

14. (d) Some companies use LIFO for tax and external reporting purposes, but they maintain a FIFO, average cost, or standard cost system for internal reporting purposes. The difference between the inventory method used for internal reporting purposes and LIFO is often referred to as the LIFO reserve. The LIFO reserve is a contra-inventory account that must be adjusted to its required balance at the financial statement date. At 12/31 Drew's inventory was $375,000 using average cost and $320,000 using LIFO. The required balance in the LIFO reserve at 12/31 is $55,000 (i.e., $375,000 – $320,000). Since the unadjusted LIFO reserve balance was $35,000, the reserve must be increased by $20,000 (i.e., $55,000 – $35,000).

Cost of Goods Sold	20,000	
LIFO Reserve		20,000

15. (b) As a general rule, dollar-value LIFO uses a "double-extension method" to compute: (1) the value of the ending inventory in terms of base year prices, and (2) the value of ending inventory at current prices. The ratio of (2) over (1), above, provides the specific price index for valuing any layers of inventory added in the period. None of the other inventory methods require estimates of price-level changes for specific inventories.

16. (b) The inventory layer added in the current year is computed in terms of base year prices. It then must be converted to current year cost because the layer was added during the current year. Because we are converting *to* current year cost *from* base year cost, the index is computed by dividing the ending inventory at current year cost by the ending inventory at base year cost.

17. (b) Under the perpetual method, only 1,400 beginning inventory units remain, as 600 units were sold on 1/23, along with all units purchased on 1/8: (1,400 × $1) + (800 × $5). Under the periodic method, the beginning inventory and inventory first-in for the period is assumed to remain in inventory: (2,000 × $1) + (200 × $3).

18. (c) The price index is computed by dividing the ending inventory at current year cost by its base year cost.

Date	Layers at base year cost	Price index	Ending inventory at LIFO cost
01/01 Yr 1	$40,000	1.0000 [1]	$ 40,000
12/31 Yr 1	5,000	1.2000 [2]	6,000
12/31 Yr 2	15,000	1.3333 [3]	20,000
	$60,000		$ 66,000

[1] $40,000 / $40,000. [2] $54,000 / $45,000. [3] $80,000 / $60,000.

19. (d) The price index is the year 2 layer current year cost divided by the base year cost, $80,000 / $40,000.

Date	Base year cost	Current year cost
01/01, year 1	$ 90,000	$ 90,000
Year 1 layer	20,000	30,000
Year 2 layer	40,000	80,000

20. (b) Under the moving-average method, a new average unit price is computed every time a purchase is made. The inventory is then priced on the basis of this "moving average."

	Units	Unit cost	Total cost
Balance on 1/1	1,000	$1.00	$1,000
Purchased on 1/7	600	3.00	1,800
Balance after purchase	1,600	1.75*	2,800
Sold on 1/20	(900)	1.75	1,575
Balance after sale	700	1.75	1,225
Purchased on 1/25	400	5.00	2,000
Balance after purchase	1,100		$3,225

*$2,800 / 1,600 units

21. (b) Where the LIFO cost flow method is used in conjunction with a perpetual inventory system, the cost of the last goods purchased are matched against revenue every time a sale is made ($700 + $2,000 = $2,700).

Date	Purchased	Sold	Balance
1/1			(1,000 @ $1) $1,000
1/7	(600 @ $3) $1,800		(1,000 @ 1) 1,000 (600 @ 3) 1,800
1/20		(600 @ $3) $1,800 (300 @ 1) 300	
1/25	(400 @ 5) 2,000		(700 @ 1) 700 (400 @ 5) 2,000

Lower of Cost or Market

22. (d) Under the lower-of-cost-or-market rule, market means current replacement cost with the exception that market value should not exceed the net realizable value (ceiling) and should not be less than the net realizable value minus normal profit (floor). Because in this question replacement cost is below the floor, this would be the minimum amount at which market could be valued. This market value is then compared to the original cost and the lower amount is used for the value of the inventory item. The question states that the original cost is above the net realizable value less a normal profit margin, thus, the market value is the lower amount.

23. (d) According to the lower-of-cost-or-market rule, market is defined as replacement cost. Market cannot exceed net realizable value and cannot be less than net realizable value less normal profit margin. In this instance, original cost is between net realizable value and net realizable value less normal profit margin. Since original cost is within the parameters for replacement cost and is less than replacement cost, the inventory should be reported at original cost.

24. (b) The answer to this question assumes that the original cost, replacement cost, and net realizable value of the inventory differ in amount. Statement II is correct. Under lower-of-cost-or-market (LCM) procedures for inventory valuation, market value cannot exceed a "ceiling" of net realizable value and cannot be below a "floor" of net realizable value reduced by a normal profit margin. Since the inventory is reported at its replacement cost, the net realizable of the inventory exceeds its replacement cost. Statement I is incorrect. Under LCM procedures, inventory is reported at the lower of original cost or market value (which is replacement cost in this case). Since the inventory is reported at replacement cost, the original cost of the inventory is greater than its replacement cost.

25. (c) The market *maximum,* or *ceiling,* should not exceed the net realizable value (NRV), which is the estimated selling price in the ordinary course of business less reasonably predictable costs of completion and disposal. Market minimum, or floor should not be less than the net realizable value minus normal profit.

Market:	
Ceiling (NRV)	$8.80
Replacement cost	8.00
Floor (NRV minus normal profit)	7.80

LIFO charges Cost of Goods Sold with the latest acquisition costs, while ending inventories are reported at the older costs of the earliest units. The 10,000 units sold reduce the 1/5 purchases, leaving 8,000 units from the beginning inventory and 2,000 units purchased on 1/5.

Cost [(8,000 × \$8.20) + (2,000 × \$7.90)]	\$81,400
Market (10,000 × \$8.00)	80,000

\$80,000 is the lowest of cost or market.

26. (c) Under the lower-of-cost-or-market rule, replacement cost cannot exceed a "ceiling" of net realizable value (estimated selling price less estimated cost of completion and disposal) and cannot be below a "floor" of net realizable value reduced by a normal profit margin.

	Replacement Cost Parameters		
Cost	Replacement Cost	Ceiling (NRV)	Floor (NRV - NP)
\$26,000	\$20,000	\$28,000 [1]	\$24,000 [2]

[1] \$40,000 – \$12,000. [2] \$28,000 – (\$40,000 × 10%).

The replacement cost is below the prescribed range [i.e., \$20,000 < (\$24,000 to \$28,000)]. Therefore, the "floor" of \$24,000 is the assigned market value. Because the assigned market value of \$24,000 is below the historical cost of \$26,000, the inventory should be valued at \$24,000.

27. (d) The application of the lower-of-cost-or-market (LCM) rule directly to each inventory item generally results in the lowest inventory amount because unrealized losses on inventory items cannot be offset by unrealized gains on other inventory items. Generally, a different inventory amount would be reported when the LCM rule is applied to (1) total inventory, (2) groups of similar inventory items, or (3) each inventory item. Answers (b) and (c) are incorrect. These methods of applying the LCM rule for inventories would allow unrealized losses on some inventory items to be offset by unrealized gains on others. This would result in a higher inventory amount than if the LCM rule were applied to each inventory item.

Gross Margin Method

28. (a) The missing inventory is estimated by determining the difference between the estimated ending inventory using the gross margin method and the actual physical inventory on hand at year-end.

Beginning inventory		\$ 500,000
Purchases		2,500,000
Goods available for sale		3,000,000
Sales	\$ 3,200,000	
Less gross margin (25% × \$3,200,000)	(800,000)	
Less: Estimated CGS		(2,400,000)
Estimated ending inventory		600,000
Less: Actual physical inventory		(575,000)
Estimated cost of missing inventory		\$ 25,000

29. (b)

Net Sales	\$275,000
Less: Gross margin (20% × 275,000)	(55,000)
Estimated COGS	\$220,000

Solve for Goods Available for Sale: (GAFS – COGS = EI)
GAFS – \$220,000 = \$18,000
GAFS = \$238,000

Solve for Purchases: (BI – Purch = GAFS)
\$30,000 – Purch = \$238,000
Purchases = \$208,000

Retail Method

30. (a) When the retail method is employed, purchase returns is included in the calculation of both cost and retail amounts of goods available for sale (AFS). Sales returns does not appear in the computation of the cost amount of goods AFS. Net markups appears in the retail amount of goods AFS (assuming the retail method is used to approximate a lower-of-average-cost-or-market figure) but not in the cost amount of goods AFS. Freight in appears in the cost amount of goods available for sale but not in the retail amount of goods AFS.

31. (d) Cost of sales is determined by subtracting the estimated ending inventory at cost from the cost of the beginning inventory and purchases (i.e., \$600,000 – \$75,000 = \$525,000).

	Cost	Retail
Beg. inventory and purchases	\$600,000	\$920,000
Net markups		40,000
Close-to-retail amounts	\$600,000	960,000
Less: Sales		(780,000)
Net Markdowns		60,000
Estimated EI at retail		120,000
Cost-to-retail ratio (\$600,000 / \$960,000)		× 62.5%
Estimated ending inventory at cost		\$ 75,000

32. (a) Under the first-in, first-out (FIFO) retail method of inventory valuation, the goods in beginning inventory are charged to cost of goods sold during the period; therefore, the cost/retail ratio is based only on the purchases for the period. If the lower-of-cost-or-market rule is disregarded, both net additional markups and net markdowns are included in the purchases cost-to-retail ratio.

	Cost	Retail
Purchases	\$60,000	\$110,000
Net additional markups	--	10,000
Net markdowns	--	(20,000)
Purchases cost-to-retail ratio amts.	60,000	100,000
Beginning inventory	12,000	30,000
Goods available for sale	\$72,000	130,000
Less: Sales		(90,000)
Estimated ending inventory at retail		40,000
Cost-to-retail ratio (\$60,000 / \$100,000)		× 60%
Estimated ending inventory at cost		\$ 24,000

Solution 3-2 ADDITIONAL MULTIPLE CHOICE ANSWERS

Ownership Criteria

33. (c) Goods held on consignment remain the property of the consignor. The consignee does not incur a liability for consigned goods until the goods are sold to a third party.

Consignment sales (500 × $100)	$50,000
Less: Alt's commission on consignment sales ($50,000 × 10%)	(5,000)
Payable for consigned goods, 12/31	$45,000

34. (b) Goods out on consignment remain the property of the consignor and must be included in the consignor's inventory at purchase price or production cost, including freight and other costs incurred to process the goods up to the time of sale.

Beginning inventory		$ 122,000
Purchases	$540,000	
Freight in	10,000	
Transportation to consignees	5,000	
Add: Inventoriable costs		555,000
Goods available for sale		677,000
Less: EI ($145,000 + $20,000)		(165,000)
Cost of goods sold		$ 512,000

35. (d) The term *F.O.B. destination* means free on board at destination; that is, the goods are shipped to their destination without charge to the buyer. Thus, the costs incurred in connection with the sale and delivery of the goods (i.e., packaging for shipment, shipping, and special handling charges) are borne by the seller. Thus, Kerr's cost of the goods purchased is $50,000.

Cash Flow Assumptions

36. (c) The last-in, first-out (LIFO) methods of inventory valuation assign the oldest costs available to ending inventory. Therefore, when inventory is subject to specific price increases, the dollar-value LIFO method would report the lowest ending inventory of the inventory methods listed.

37. (a) Under the FIFO cost-flow method, a perpetual system would result in the same dollar amount of ending inventory as a periodic inventory system. Under the LIFO cost-flow method, however, a perpetual system would generally **not** result in the same dollar amount of ending inventory as a periodic inventory system.

38. (b) The 20X4 layer is determined by the difference of the ending inventory at base year cost and the beginning inventory (which is the base year in this case) at base year cost and applying the relevant price index to the difference.

Ending inventory at base year cost	$ 525,000
Less: Beginning inventory at base year cost	(500,000)
Current year layer at base year cost	25,000
Times: Relevant price index	× 1.10
Current year layer at current year prices	27,500
Beginning inventory (1/1/X4) at DV LIFO	500,000
Dollar-value LIFO inventory, 12/31	$ 527,500

39. (d) The dollar-value LIFO method, by definition, is based on the aggregation of similar inventory items into pools. Acquisitions and issuances of similar materials are recorded in the same pool, even if the substitute items are not exactly the same as the replaced items. As a general rule, dollar-value LIFO uses a "double-extension method" to determine: (1) the value of the ending inventory in terms of base year prices, and (2) the value of the ending inventory at current prices. The ratio of (2) over (1), above, provides the specific price index for valuing any layers of inventory added in the period.

40. (c)

Date	Layers at base year cost	Price index	Ending inventory at LIFO cost
01/01 Year 1	$150,000	1.00	$150,000
12/31 Year 1	50,000 [1]	1.10	55,000
12/31 Year 2	30,000 [2]	1.20	36,000
	$230,000		$241,000

[1] $200,000 – $150,000. [2] $230,000 – $200,000.

41. (c)

$$\frac{\$12{,}800^{*} + \$46{,}080^{**}}{1{,}600 + 4{,}800} = \$9.20$$

* Cost of 1,600 (3,200 – 1,600) units of 1/1 inventory on hand at date of last purchase (1,600 units × $8.00 = $12,800).
** Cost of latest purchase (4,800 units × $9.60 = $46,080).

Lower of Cost or Market

42. (b) ARB 43, Chapter 4, requires valuation of inventory items at the lower of cost or market. As used in this context, market means current replacement cost. Since the goods in question are reported at replacement cost, original cost is greater than replacement cost. Replacement cost cannot exceed the net realizable value of the goods (ceiling) and cannot be less than the net realizable value reduced by an allowance for a normal profit margin (floor). Therefore, the net realizable value of the goods, less

a normal profit margin, must be less than replacement cost.

43. (c) Under the lower-of-cost-or-market rule, replacement cost cannot exceed a "ceiling" of net realizable value (estimated selling price less estimated cost of disposal) and cannot be below a "floor" of net realizable value reduced by a normal profit margin.

	Replacement Cost Parameters		
Cost	Replacement Cost	Ceiling (NRV)	Floor (NRV - NP)
$12.00	$10.90	$13.40 [1]	$11.20 [2]

[1] $13.60 – $.20. [2] $13.40 – $2.20.

The replacement cost is below the prescribed range; therefore, the "floor" of $11.20 is the assigned market value. Because the assigned market value of $11.20 is below the historical cost of $12.00, the inventory item should be valued at $11.20.

Retail Method

44. (a)

	Cost	Retail
Inventory, 2/1	$ 180,000	$ 250,000
Purchases	1,020,000	1,575,000
Markups, net		175,000
Cost ratio	$1,200,000	2,000,000
Less: Sales		(1,705,000)
Markdowns, net		(125,000)
Est. normal shoplifting losses		(20,000)
Estimated ending inventory at retail		150,000
Cost-to-retail ratio ($1,200,000 / $2,000,000)		× 60%
Estimated ending inventory at cost		$ 90,000

45. (a)

Inventory at retail, 12/31 current year adjusted for price level increase ($660,000 / 1.1)	$600,000
Beginning inventory at retail, base year price	(500,000)
New layer added in current year	100,000
Times: Price level adjustment	× 1.1
Current year layer, at LIFO retail	110,000
Times: Cost to retail ratio	× 0.70
Current year layer, at LIFO cost	77,000
Add: Beg. inventory, at LIFO cost	360,000
Ending inventory, 12/31 current year	$437,000

PERFORMANCE BY SUBTOPICS

Each category below parallels a subtopic covered in Chapter 3. Record the number and percentage of questions you correctly answered in each subtopic area.

Ownership Criteria

Question #	Correct √
1	
2	
3	
4	
# Questions	4
# Correct	______
% Correct	______

Measuring Inventories

Question #	Correct √
5	
6	
7	
8	
9	
# Questions	5
# Correct	______
# Correct	______

Losses on Purchase Commitments

Question #	Correct √
10	
# Questions	1
# Correct	______
% Correct	______

Cost Flow Assumptions

Question #	Correct √
11	
12	
13	
14	
15	
16	
17	
18	
19	
20	
21	
# Questions	11
# Correct	______
% Correct	______

Lower of Cost or Market

Question #	Correct √
22	
23	
24	
25	
26	
27	
# Questions	6
# Correct	______
% Correct	______

Gross Margin Method

Question #	Correct √
28	
29	
# Questions	2
# Correct	______
% Correct	______

Retail Method

Question #	Correct √
30	
31	
32	
# Questions	3
# Correct	______
% Correct	______

SIMULATION SOLUTIONS

Solution 3-3

Essay—Accounting For Inventories

a. Purchases from various suppliers generally should be included in Huddell's inventory when Huddell **receives the goods.** Title to goods purchased F.O.B. destination is assumed to pass when the goods are received.

b. Huddell should account for the warehousing costs as **additional cost of inventory.** All necessary and reasonable costs of readying goods for sale should be included in inventory.

c. 1. The advantages of using the dollar-value LIFO method are to **reduce the cost of accounting** for inventory and to **minimize** the **probability of reporting** the **liquidation** of LIFO inventory layers.

2. The application of dollar-value LIFO is based on **dollars of inventory,** an inventory **cost index for each year,** and **broad inventory pools.** The **inventory layers are identified** with the inventory cost index for the year in which the layer was added. In contrast, traditional LIFO is applied to individual units at their cost.

d. 1. Huddell's net markups should be included only in the retail amounts (denominator) to determine the cost to retail percentage.

Huddell's net markdowns should be **ignored** in the calculation of the cost to retail percentage.

2. By **not deducting net markdowns** from the retail amounts to determine the cost to retail percentage, Huddell produces a **lower cost to retail percentage** than would result if net markdowns were deducted. Applying this lower percentage to ending inventory at retail, the inventory is **reported at an amount below cost.** This amount is intended to approximate lower of average cost or market.

Research

ARB 43, Ch. 4, Statement 4

Cost for inventory purposes may be determined under any one of several assumptions as to the flow of cost factors (such as first-in first-out, average, and last-in first-out); the major objective in selecting a method should be to choose the one which, under the circumstances, most clearly reflects periodic income.

Solution 3-4

Worksheet Solution

Silver Inc.
Computation of Dollar-Value LIFO Inventory
December 31, Year 2 and Year 3

Year	FIFO inventory	Current year cost change index	Link-chain cost index		Inventory at base year costs	
1	$100,000	1.00	1.00		$100,000	
2	137,500	1.25	**1.25**	(a)	**110,000**	(c)
3	195,000	1.20	**1.50**	(b)	**130,000**	(d)

Year	LIFO inventory layers at base year costs		Link-chain cost index		Year 2 dollar-value LIFO inventory		Year 3 dollar-value LIFO inventory	
1	$100,000		1.00		$100,000		$100,000	
2	**10,000**	(e)	**1.25**	(a)	**12,500**	(h)	**12,500**	(j)
3	**20,000**	(f)	**1.50**	(b)			**30,000**	(k)
	$130,000	(g)			**$112,500**	(i)	**$142,500**	(l)

Explanations

a. 1.00 × 1.25 = 1.25

In the link chain method, the current year indices are multiplied to arrive at the link chain indices.

b. 1.25 × 1.20 = 1.50

In the link chain method, the current year indices are multiplied to arrive at the link chain indices.

c. $137,500 / (1.00 × 1.25) = $110,000

FIFO inventory amounts converted to dollar-value LIFO using the year 2 link-chain index applied to year 2 FIFO inventory

d. $195,000 / (1.00 × 1.25 × 1.20) = $130,000

FIFO inventory amounts converted to dollar-value LIFO using the year 3 link-chain index applied to year 3 FIFO inventory

e. $110,000 – $100,000 = $10,000

Year 2 LIFO layer

f. $130,000 – $110,000 = $20,000

Year 3 LIFO layer

g. $100,000 + $10,000 + $20,000 = $130,000

Sum of LIFO layers for year 1, year 2, and year 3

h. $10,000 × 1.25 = $12,500

Year 2 dollar value LIFO layer

i. $100,000 + $12,500 = $112,500

Dollar-value LIFO inventory at December 31, year 2

j. See explanation for h.

k. $20,000 × 1.5 = $30,000

Year 3 dollar value LIFO layer

l. $100,000 + $12,500 + $30,000 = $142,500

Dollar-value LIFO inventory at December 31, year 3

Research

FASB 109, Accounting for Income Taxes

Par. 228, Pattern of Taxable or Deductible Amounts

A LIFO inventory temporary difference becomes taxable or deductible in the future year that inventory is liquidated and not replaced.

Solution 3-5

Essay—Accounting for Inventories

a. 1. The specific identification method requires **each unit to be clearly distinguished** from similar units either by description, identification number, location, or other characteristic. **Costs are accumulated for specific units** and **expensed as the units are sold.** Thus, the specific identification method results in recognized cost flows being identical to actual physical flows. Ideally, **each unit is relatively expensive** and the number of such units **relatively few** so that recording of costs is not burdensome. Under the specific identification method, if similar items have different costs, cost of goods sold is influenced by the specific units sold.

2. It is appropriate for Happlia to use the specific identification method because **each appliance is expensive,** and **easily identified** by number and description. The specific identification method is feasible because Happlia **already maintains records** of its units held by individual retails. Management's ability to manipulate cost of goods sold is minimized because once the inventory is in retailer's hands Happlia's management cannot influence the units selected for sales.

b. 1. Happlia should include in inventory carrying amounts **all necessary and reasonable costs** to get an appliance into a useful condition and place for sale. **Common (or joint) costs** should be **allocated** to individual units. Such costs **exclude** the **excess costs** incurred in transporting refrigerators to Minneapolis and their reshipment to Kansas City. These unit costs should only **include normal freight** costs from Des Moines to Kansas City. In addition, **costs incurred to provide time utility** to the goods, i.e., ensuring that they are available when required, will also be **included in inventory** carrying amounts.

2. Examples of inventoriable costs include the **unit invoice price,** plus an allocated proportion of the **port handling fees, import duties, freight costs** to Des Moines and to retailers, **insurance costs, repackaging,** and **warehousing costs.**

c. The year-end income statement should report in **cost of goods sold all inventory costs** related to units **sold during the year,** regardless of when cash is received from retailers. **Excess freight costs** incurred for shipping the refrigerators from Minneapolis to Kansas City should be included in determining operating income.

Research

FAS 142, Par. 26

26. Goodwill of a reporting unit shall be tested for impairment on an annual basis and between annual tests in certain circumstances (refer to paragraph 28). The annual goodwill impairment test may be performed any time during the fiscal year provided the test is performed at the same time every year. Different reporting units may be tested for impairment at different times.

Solution 3-6

Worksheets with Explanations

York Co.
Schedule of Cost of Goods Sold
For the Year Ended December 31, YYYY

Beginning inventory	$ 65,600	1
Add: Purchases	368,900	2
Less: Purchase discounts	(18,000)	3
Add: Freight-in	5,000	4
Goods available for sale	421,500	5
Less: Ending inventory	(176,000)	6
Cost of Goods Sold	$ 245,500	7

York Co.
Supporting Schedule of Ending Inventory
December 31, YYYY

Inventory at cost (LIFO):

	A Units	B Cost per unit	C Total cost	
Beg. inventory, Jan. 1	8,000	$8.20	$ 65,600	8
Purchases, quarters ended:				9
March 31	12,000	8.25	99,000	10
June 30	2,000	7.90	15,800	11
	22,000		$180,400	

1. Beginning inventory given in scenario.
2. Purchases given in scenario.
3. Purchase discounts given in scenario.
4. Freight in given in scenario.
5. Sum of inventory adjustments.
6. Inventory at market: 22,000 units @ $8 = $176,000
7. Total cost of goods sold.

8 A. Units in beginning inventory given in scenario.

8 B. Cost per unit given in scenario.

8 C. Total cost: Beginning inventory × cost per unit = Total given in scenario.

9 A. Purchases for quarter ended March 31 given in scenario.

9 B. Cost per unit given in scenario.

9 C. Total cost of purchases for quarter ended March 31: Units × cost = Total given in scenario.

10 A.

Total units purchased for year	55,000
Less total units sold	33,000
Total units left in inventory	22,000
Units left in inventory (Beg. + March 31)	(20,000)
Units left in inventory purchased in quarter ended 6/30	2,000

10 B. Cost per unit given in scenario

10 C. Units left in inventory purchased in quarter ended 6/30 × cost per unit (2,000 × $7.90)

11 A. Number of units remaining in LIFO inventory.

11 C. Total cost of units remaining in LIFO inventory.

Research

ARB 43, Ch. 4, Inventory Pricing, Statement 6

As used in the phrase lower of cost or market, the term market means current replacement cost (by purchase or by reproduction, as the case may be) except that:

(1) Market should not exceed the net realizable value (i.e., estimated selling price in the ordinary course of business less reasonably predictable costs of completion and disposal); and

(2) Market should not be less than net realizable value reduced by an allowance for an approximately normal profit margin.

CHAPTER 4

PROPERTY, PLANT & EQUIPMENT

I. **Introduction** 4-2
   A. Expensing vs. Capitalizing 4-2
   B. Classification 4-2

II. **Acquisition** 4-2
   A. Acquisition Cost 4-2
   B. Costs Incurred Subsequent to Acquisition 4-8

III. **Cost Recovery** 4-8
   A. Depreciation 4-8
   B. Depletion 4-11

IV. **Impairment or Disposal of Long-Lived Assets (SFAS 144)** 4-11
   A. Categories 4-11
   B. Classification 4-12

V. **Fixed Asset Disposal** 4-12
   A. Voluntary 4-12
   B. Involuntary 4-12

EXAM COVERAGE: Historically, exam coverage of the topics in Chapter 4 has been 5 to 10 percent of the FAR section. More information regarding exam coverage is included in Appendix B, *Practical Advice*.

CHAPTER 4

PROPERTY, PLANT & EQUIPMENT

I. Introduction

A. Expensing vs. Capitalizing

Property, plant, and equipment (PP&E) are tangible assets acquired for long-term use in the normal operations of a business. If an outlay will provide a service benefit beyond the current period, it is a capital expenditure and is recorded as an asset. Expenditures that benefit only the current period are charged to expense as incurred and are referred to as revenue expenditures. The concept of materiality influences the decision whether to capitalize expenditures. Most companies expense all items costing less than a certain amount, regardless of their estimated useful lives. This is permissible as long as the total effect is immaterial **and** this policy is consistently applied.

B. Classification

Productive assets are classified according to their characteristics, as follows:

1. **Limited Lives** Plant and equipment have limited service lives; thus, their costs must be allocated to the periods benefited by the application of depreciation charges.

2. **Indefinite Life** Land is deemed to have an indefinite life and, therefore, is not depreciated.

3. **Natural Resources** Natural resources are wasting (nonregenerative) assets such as mineral, gas, and oil deposits, and standing timber. Their costs must be allocated to inventory by the application of depletion charges because these resources are subject to exhaustion through extraction.

II. Acquisition

A. Acquisition Cost

Assets are to be recorded at their acquisition cost. Acquisition cost is defined as the cash price, or its equivalent, plus all other costs reasonably necessary to bring it to the location and to make it ready for its intended use. Examples of these additional costs include transportation, insurance while in-transit, special foundations, installation, test runs, and the demolition of an old building, less any scrap proceeds received. Property, plant, and equipment may be acquired in various ways.

1. **Purchase for Cash** Record the asset net of any trade or quantity discounts available.

2. **Purchase on Deferred Payment Plan** The fixed asset should be recorded at its cash equivalent price. If the cash equivalent price is unavailable, an imputed interest rate should be used to record the asset at the present value of the payments to be made.

3. **Purchase by Issuance of Securities** The asset should be recorded at its fair value or the fair value of the securities issued, whichever is more clearly determinable. If there is an active market for the security and the additional securities issued can be reasonably expected to be absorbed without a decline in their value, the fair value of the securities should be used. If the securities exchanged are bonds and no established market exists, the asset should be recorded at the present value of the interest and principal payments to be made, discounted by use of an implicit or "imputed" rate. If equity securities are issued and no fair value is determinable, the appraisal value of the asset acquired should be used for the recording of the transaction.

4. **Self-Construction** The cost of assets constructed for the use of the business should include all directly related costs, such as direct materials, direct labor, and additional overhead incurred.

5. **Interest Costs** SFAS 34, *Capitalization of Interest Cost,* requires capitalization of interest costs incurred during the construction period. The interest cost capitalized is a part of the cost of acquiring the asset and is written off over the estimated useful life of the asset.

   a. Assets qualifying for interest capitalization include assets constructed or produced for self-use on a repetitive basis, assets acquired for self-use through arrangements requiring down payments or progress payments, and assets constructed or produced as discrete projects for sale or lease (e.g., ships or real estate developments). Assets **not** qualifying for interest capitalization include inventories that are routinely manufactured on a repetitive basis, assets in use or ready for use, and assets not in use and not being prepared for use.

   b. The amount of interest cost to be capitalized is the interest cost incurred during the acquisition period that could have been avoided if expenditures for the asset had not been made. If a specific interest rate is associated with the asset, that rate should be used to the extent that the average accumulated expenditures on the asset do not exceed the amount borrowed at the specific rate. If the average accumulated expenditures on an asset exceed the amount of specific new borrowings associated with the asset, the excess should be capitalized at the weighted average of the rates applicable to other borrowings of the enterprise.

   c. The interest rate determined above is applied to the *average* amount of accumulated expenditures for the asset during the period. For example, if construction of a qualifying asset begins in January and the accumulated expenditures at year-end amount to $400,000, the interest rate is applied to the $200,000 average accumulated expenditure [($0 + $400,000) / 2]. (**NOTE:** The preceding assumes that construction expenditures take place *evenly* throughout the period. If expenditures fluctuate widely, the average accumulated expenditure should be computed monthly.)

Example 1 ▸ Capitalizing Interest on Assets Constructed for Self-Use

On January 1 of last year, Expansions Inc. borrowed $1,000,000 to finance the construction of a warehouse for its own use. The loan was to be repaid in 10 equal payments of $199,250, including interest of 15%, beginning on January 1 of this year. No other loans are presently outstanding. The total cost of labor, materials, and overhead assigned to the warehouse was $1,000,000. Construction was completed on December 30 last year. The warehouse is depreciated using the straight-line method over an estimated useful life of 20 years, with no salvage value. The proceeds borrowed were invested in short-term liquid assets until needed to pay construction expenditures, yielding $24,000 interest income.

Required: Determine the capitalized cost of the asset, as of December 30 last year the interest expense for last year (assume no other debt outstanding), and the depreciation expense for this year.

Solution:

Materials, labor, overhead, etc.	$1,000,000
Capitalized interest cost, [($0 + $1,000,000) / 2] × 0.15	75,000
Capitalized cost of asset	$1,075,000
Total interest cost incurred, 20X1 ($1,000,000 × 0.15)	$ 150,000
Less capitalized interest cost	(75,000)
Interest expense last year	$ 75,000
Capitalized cost of asset	$1,075,000
Estimated useful life	/ 20
Depreciation expense this year	$ 53,750

Example 2 ▸ Partial Amount Borrowed

The same as in Example 1, except that Expansions Inc., needed to borrow only $300,000 (at 15%) to finance construction of the $1,000,000 warehouse. The remaining cash was provided from operations and from the sale of miscellaneous investments. During all of last year, Expansions' only other long-term liabilities consisted of $2,000,000, 10%, 20-year bonds (sold at par in 20X0) and a $500,000, 14%, interest-bearing note payable due in three years.

Required: Determine the amount of interest that should be capitalized in 20X1.

Solution: Total interest cost incurred during the year is ($300,000 × 15%) + ($2,000,000 × 10%) + ($500,000 × 14%) = $315,000.

Accumulated average expenditures ($0 + $1,000,000) / 2	$500,000
Interest on new borrowings specifically associated with asset ($300,000 × 0.15)	$ 45,000
Weighted average rate on other borrowings, applied to accumulated average expenditures in excess of $300,000 ($200,000 × 0.108*)	21,600
Total interest cost capitalized during last year	$ 66,600

*Computation of weighted average rate:

$$\frac{\text{Total interest}}{\text{Total principal}} = \frac{(\$2{,}000{,}000 \times 10\%) + (\$500{,}000 \times 14\%)}{\$2{,}000{,}000 + \$500{,}000} = 0.108$$

d. The total interest cost capitalized in a period may **not** exceed the total interest cost incurred during that period.

e. Interest *earned* by the enterprise during the period is **not** offset to interest costs incurred in determining the amount of interest to be capitalized.

6. **Gifts** Donated assets should be recorded at their fair value along with any incidental costs incurred. When the asset is received from a governmental entity, no income is recognized, and the offsetting credit is to an owners' equity account, *Additional Paid-In Capital—Donated Assets.* Assets donated by entities other than governmental units are included in revenue in the period of receipt (SFAS 116).

7. **Group Purchases** If several dissimilar assets are purchased for a lump sum, the total amount paid should be allocated to each individual asset on the basis of its relative fair value.

Exhibit 1 ▸ Allocation Formula

Asset Y = Total cost of assets × FV of Y / Total FV

8. **Acquisition by Exchange** APB 29, *Accounting for Nonmonetary Transactions,* provides the standards for the accounting of nonmonetary transactions and nonreciprocal transfers. SFAS 153 has amended APB 29 and eliminated the guidance that provided an exception for nonmonetary exchanges of similar productive assets. The exception in SFAS 153 applies to exchanges of nonmonetary assets that do not have commercial substance.

   a. **Exchange** An exchange transaction is a reciprocal transfer between one reporting entity and another reporting entity that results in the transferor entity acquiring assets (or services) or satisfying liabilities through the surrender of other assets (or services) or through incurring liabilities. These types of reciprocal transfers of nonmonetary assets are considered to be "exchanges" only if the transferor has no substantial continuing involvement in the transferred assets (i.e., the usual risks and rewards of ownership have been transferred to the transferee).

   b. **Conversion** Nonmonetary assets that are involuntarily converted to monetary assets that are then reinvested in other nonmonetary assets are considered monetary transactions since the recipient is not obligated to reinvest the monetary consideration in other nonmonetary assets.

c. **Nonreciprocal Transfers** A transfer of a nonmonetary asset to a stockholder or to another entity, such as in charitable contributions, in a **nonreciprocal** transfer should be recorded at the fair value of the asset transferred, and a gain or loss should be recognized on the disposition of the asset.

d. **Exceptions** As amended by SFAS No. 153, the accounting guidance in APB Opinion No. 29 does not apply to the following transactions (in the following circumstances):

(1) Business combinations that are accounted for utilizing the provisions of SFAS No. 141, titled *Business Combinations.*

(2) Transfers of nonmonetary assets solely between companies (or persons) under common control. Examples of these types of transactions would be transfers between a parent company and subsidiaries of the parent, or between/among multiple subsidiaries of the same parent, or between a corporate joint venture and its owners.

(3) Acquisitions of nonmonetary assets (or services) that were acquired through issuance of capital stock of the reporting entity.

(4) Stock that was issued/received in stock dividends/stock splits.

(5) Transfers of assets to an entity for an equity (ownership) interest in the other entity.

(6) The pooling of assets in a joint undertaking intended to find, develop, or produce oil or gas from a particular property or group of properties.

(7) Exchange of a part of an oil or gas operating interest owned for a part of an operating interest owned by another party, commonly called a joint venture in the oil and gas industry.

(8) Transfer of a financial asset within the scope of SFAS No. 140, titled *Accounting for Transfers and Servicing of Financial Assets and Extinguishments of Liabilities.*

e. **Gains and Losses** In general, accounting for nonmonetary transactions should be based on the fair values of the assets involved. The acquisition is recorded at the fair value of the asset surrendered or the FV of the asset received, whichever is more clearly determinable, and gains or losses should be recognized. The rationale associated with the immediate gain/loss recognition (recording the transactions at fair value) is that the exchange of assets represents the culmination of the earnings process associated with the assets surrendered.

f. **Based on Recorded Amounts** Nonmonetary exchanges should be based on recorded amounts (rather than fair values) of the exchanged assets if *any* of the following conditions apply:

(1) Neither the fair value of the assets received nor the fair value of the assets surrendered is determinable within reasonable limits. For purposes of applying this literature, fair values should be determined by referring to estimated realizable values in cash transactions of the same (or similar) assets, quoted market prices, independent appraisals, estimated fair values of assets (or services) received in exchange for the transferred assets, and/or any other available evidence. If either party involved in the nonmonetary exchange could have elected to receive cash (rather than the nonmonetary asset) in the transaction, the amount of cash that could have been received may be evidence of the fair value of the nonmonetary assets exchanged.

(2) The transaction is an exchange of a product or property held for sale in the ordinary course of business for a product or property to be sold in the same line of business to facilitate sales to customers (other than the parties to the exchange).

(3) The transaction lacks commercial substance.

g. **Commercial Substance** A nonmonetary exchange has commercial substance if the entity's future cash flows are expected to change significantly as a result of the exchange. The entity's future cash flows are expected to significantly change if either of the following criteria is met:

(1) The configuration (risk, timing, and amount) of the future cash flows of the asset(s) received differs significantly from the configuration of the future cash flows of the asset(s) transferred.

(2) The entity-specific value of the asset(s) received differs from the entity-specific value of the asset(s) transferred, and the difference is significant in relation to the fair values of the assets exchanged. (A conclusive determination related to whether a transaction or exchange involves commercial substance, in some cases, can be based on a qualitative assessment rather than detailed calculations associated with the transaction or exchange.)

h. **No Commercial Substance** In a nonmonetary exchange that has no commercial substance, the assets exchanged are accounted for at book value (after reduction, if appropriate, for an indicated impairment of value) of the nonmonetary asset(s) given up; therefore, no gains or losses are normally recognized on the exchange itself. However, if the asset's carrying amount exceeds its fair value when exchanged, an impairment loss should be recognized. Also, the recipient of any boot would realize some amount of gain.

Example 3 ▸ Nonmonetary Exchange of Assets – No Commercial Substance

Axel Company exchanged an asset with a fair value of $15,000 and a carrying value of $12,000 for an asset from Berry Company with a fair value of $17,000 and a carrying value of $18,000.

Required:

(a) Prepare the journal entry Axel Company would make for the exchange.
(b) Prepare the journal entry Berry Company would make for the exchange.

Solutions:

(a)	Asset received	12,000	
	Asset given up		12,000
	To record the exchange		
(b)	Loss on impairment	1, 000	
	Asset given up		1,000
	To record the reduction for impairment		
	Asset received	17,000	
	Asset given up		17,000
	To record the exchange		

i. **Boot** A small monetary consideration that is sometimes included in exchanges of nonmonetary assets, even though the exchange is essentially nonmonetary. Exchanges of nonmonetary assets that would otherwise be based on recorded amounts may include an amount of boot.

(1) The recipient of the boot realizes a gain on the exchange to the extent the monetary receipt exceeds a proportionate share of the recorded amount of the assert surrendered. The portion of the cost applicable to the realized amount should be based on the ratio of the monetary consideration to the total consideration received or, if more clearly evident, the fair value of the nonmonetary asset transferred.

(2) The entity paying the monetary consideration should not recognize any gain but should record the asset received at the amount of the monetary consideration paid plus the recorded amount of the nonmonetary asset surrendered.

(3) If the terms of the transaction indicate a loss, the entire loss on the exchange should be recognized.

Example 4 ▸ Nonmonetary Exchange With Boot – No Commercial Substance

Beta Company exchanges asset A to Delta Company for asset C. Asset C has a book value of $12,000.

Required: Prepare journal entries to record this exchange under the following different conditions.

(a) Asset A has a book value of $11,000 and $3,000 cash is received.
(b) Asset A has a book value of $16,000 and $3,000 cash is received.

Solutions:

(a) *Beta's journal entry:*

Asset C (see note 2)	8,800	
Cash	3,000	
Asset A		11,000
Gain on Exchange (see note 3)		800

Delta's journal entry:

Asset A	11,000	
Loss on exchange (see note 4)	4,000	
Asset C		12,000
Cash		3,000

Note (1): BV of old asset x [boot / (boot + BV of new asset)] = portion of BV sold; $11,000 x [$3,000 / ($3,000 + $12,000)] = $2,200
Note (2): BV of old asset - portion of BV sold = carrying amount of new asset; $11,000 - $2,200 = $8,800
Note (3): Cash received – portion of BV sold = gain on sale of old asset; $3,000 - $2,200 = $800
Note (4): BV of new asset – [BV of old asset + cash given] = gain (loss) on exchange; $11,000 – [$12,000 + $3,000] = ($4,000)

(b) *Beta's journal entry:*

Asset C (see note 5)	12,000	
Cash	3,000	
Loss on Exchange (see note 6)	1,000	
Asset A		16,000

Delta's journal entry:

Asset A (see note 7)	15,000	
Asset C		12,000
Cash		3,000

Note (5): BV of old asset x [boot / (boot + BV of new asset)] = portion of BV sold; $16,000 x [$3,000 / ($3,000 + $12,000)] = $3,200.
Note (6): The portion of BV sold being greater than cash received indicates a loss. [BV of old asset + cash received] – BV of new asset = gain (loss) on exchange; [$12,000 + $3,000] – $16,000 = $1,000. If a loss is indicated, the entire amount of loss is recognized ($1,000).
Note (7): BV of new asset – [BV of old asset + cash given] = gain (loss) on exchange; $16,000 – [$12,000 + $3,000] = $1,000. The entity paying the boot does not recognize gain, but instead records the asset received at the amount of cash given plus recorded amount of asset given.

B. Costs Incurred Subsequent to Acquisition

The continued use of fixed assets will require further outlays to maintain their given level of services. These costs are in the nature of maintenance and repairs and are expensed as incurred or charged to overhead and hence to production, as appropriate. Some costs, however, extend the service life of the asset, increase its output rate, or lower production costs. These are known as betterments or improvements and are *capitalized* (i.e., added to the assets' book value).

Exhibit 2 ▸ Summary of Costs Subsequent to Acquisition of PP&E

Type of Expenditure	Expense	Capitalize	Comments
Additions		X	
Betterment and replacement (book value known)		X	• Remove cost and accumulated depreciation of old asset • Recognize any gain or loss • Capitalize replacement
Betterment and replacement (book value unknown)		X	• If the useful life is extended, debit accumulated depreciation for the cost of the replacement • If productivity is increased, capitalize the cost of the replacement
Ordinary repairs	X		
Extraordinary repairs		X	

III. Cost Recovery

A. Depreciation

Depreciation is the process of allocating the depreciable cost of fixed assets over their estimated useful lives in a systematic and rational manner. This process matches the depreciable cost of the asset with revenues generated from its use. Depreciable cost is the capitalized cost less its estimated residual (salvage) value. Depreciation accounting recognizes both physical and functional causes of declining service potential. Physical causes include wear and tear, deterioration, and decay. Examples of functional factors are obsolescence and inadequacy. Depreciation is recorded by charging expense (or manufacturing overhead) and crediting accumulated depreciation. Property, plant, and equipment is not written up to reflect appraisal, market, or current values above cost (APB 6, par. 17). Various depreciation methods are used.

1. **Straight-Line Depreciation (SL)** The straight-line depreciation method is a fixed charge method where an equal amount of depreciable cost is allocated to each period. This method should be used when approximately the same amount of an asset's service potential is used up each period. If the reasons for the decline in service potential are unclear, then the selection of the straight-line method could be influenced by the ease of recordkeeping, its use for similar assets, and its use by others in the industry.

Exhibit 3 ▸ SL Depreciation Formula

$$\text{SL depreciation} = \frac{\text{Historical Cost (HC)} - \text{Salvage value (SV)}}{\text{Estimated useful life (EUL)}}$$

2. **Accelerated Depreciation** The rationale for using accelerated depreciation methods is based on two assumptions. First, an asset is more productive in the earlier years of its estimated useful life. Therefore, larger depreciation charges in the earlier years would be matched against the larger revenues generated in the earlier years. Second, an asset may become technologically obsolete prior to the end of its originally estimated useful life. The risk associated with estimated long-term cash flows is greater than the risk associated with near-term cash flows. Accelerated depreciation recognizes this condition.

   a. **Sum-of-the-Years'-Digits (SYD)** A decreasing fraction is applied each year to the depreciable base (i.e., HC – SV). The denominator of the fraction is obtained by adding the number of years of EUL at the *beginning* of the asset's life (n). For instance, the denominator for an asset with n years would be computed as [n + (n – 1) + (n – 2) + ... + 1]. The use of the equation [n(n+1)/2] provides the same result and is more practical when n is a large number. Once determined, the denominator remains unchanged for all future computations. The numerator of the fraction is given by the remaining years of EUL, including the current year, and thus it decreases with time.

Example 5 ▸ Sum-of-the-Years'-Digits Depreciation

Historical Cost (HC)	$1,000
Salvage Value (SV)	$ 100
Estimated Useful Life (EUL)	3 years

Required: Calculate the depreciation using the SYD method.

Solution: Depreciable base (HC – SV): $1,000 – 100 = $900

Fraction denominator (remains unchanged): 3 + 2 + 1 = 6, or 3(3 + 1) / 2 = 6

Fraction numerator: Remaining years of life at the beginning of each period: 3, 2, 1

	Fraction	×	Depreciable base	=	Depreciation charge
Year 1	3/6		$900		$450
Year 2	2/6		900		300
Year 3	1/6		900		150

   b. **Double-Declining-Balance (DDB)** A rate of depreciation twice the SL rate is applied to the *book value* (i.e., declining balance) of the asset to obtain the depreciation expense for the period. (Note that the SV is not used in the calculation of depreciation expense under DDB except as a lower bound for the asset's BV.)

Exhibit 4 ▸ DDB Formula

$$\textit{Depreciation for current period} = \frac{2}{\text{EUL}} \times (\text{HC} - \text{AD})$$

Where: AD = Accumulated depreciation

   c. **Fixed-Percentage-of-Declining-Balance** A fixed percentage (usually 125 percent to 175 percent of the SL rate) is applied to the decreasing book value of the asset. It is similar to the DDB method in b., above, except that instead of double (i.e., 200 percent) the SL rate, a lower percentage is used.

Example 6 ▸ Double-Declining-Balance Depreciation

Historical Cost (HC)	$1,200
Salvage Value (SV)	$ 100
Estimated Useful Life (EUL)	3 years

Required: Calculate the depreciation using the DDB method.

Solution: Original depreciable base = $1,200

	Fraction	×	Depreciable base	=	Depreciation Charge
Year 1	2/3		$1,200		$800
Year 2	2/3		$1,200 – $800 = $400		$267
Year 3	2/3		$1,200 – $1,067 = $133		$ 33*

* May not depreciate below the salvage value ($133 × 2/3 = $89)

3. **Multiple-Asset Depreciation** In order to reduce the number of computations needed, assets are sometimes depreciated in groups, rather than individually. Two types are used.

   a. **Group Depreciation** Homogeneous assets having similar service lives are lumped together and one depreciation rate is applied to the entire group. Retirements are recorded by a credit to the asset for the amount of cost and a debit to accumulated depreciation for the same amount less any proceeds received in disposition. Note that **no** gains or losses are recognized.

   b. **Composite Depreciation** Similar to the group system but applied to groups of assets having a wider range of service lives. The composite rate is determined by calculating the annual depreciation expense for each asset, adding up these amounts, and expressing this as a percentage of the total cost of all the assets.

Example 7 ▸ Composite Depreciation

Asset class	Asset cost	–	Salvage value	=	Depr'n. base	/	EUL (yrs.)	=	SL Depr'n.
A	$120,000		$20,000		$100,000		10		$10,000
B	60,000		10,000		50,000		5		10,000
C	30,000		5,000		25,000		5		5,000
	$210,000		$35,000		$175,000				$25,000

Composite depreciation rate: ($25,000 / $210,000) = 11.905%
Composite life: ($175,000 / $25,000) = 7 years

The annual composite depreciation charge for the group of assets above would be $25,000 ($210,000 × 11.905%) and, assuming no additions or retirements, the group would be depreciated to the salvage value of its assets at the end of their seven-year average life. Additions are debited to the group at cost. Retirements are recorded by a credit to the asset account, a debit to cash or receivable for the consideration received, and the balance is debited to accumulated depreciation. No gains or losses are recognized.

4. **Variable Charge Methods** Depreciation is based upon the actual **usage** of the asset. Both of the two commonly used methods are represented by same formula.

Exhibit 5 ▸ Variable Charge Depreciation Formula

$$\text{Depreciation expense} = \frac{HC - SV}{\text{Total expected output or usage}} \times \text{Current output or use}$$

a. **Service Hours** The expected useful life (EUL) of the asset is determined on the basis of service hours, rather than years. Depreciation expense for the current period is a proportion of current hours of service to EUL (in service hours).

b. **Units-of-Output** The EUL is stated in units of output, rather than years.

5. **Fractional-Year Depreciation** Assets are seldom acquired or disposed of at the exact date of the beginning or the end of the entity's accounting period. Fractional-year depreciation is generally accounted for under one of three different approaches.

a. Depreciation for one entire year in the year of acquisition and none in the year of disposal.

b. Half-year's depreciation in the year of acquisition and the year of disposal.

c. Proportional depreciation based on the number of months the asset was used, both for the year of acquisition and disposal. When assets are acquired or retired during the year, the amount of depreciation for a given period is determined by allocating the annual depreciation based on the number of months (weeks, days) that the asset was held during the period.

B. **Depletion**

Depletion refers to periodic allocation of acquisition costs of natural resources. A per-unit depletion rate is computed by dividing the depletable base of the natural resource (i.e., purchase price, exploring, drilling, and other development costs), less any estimated residual value, by the estimated number of units of the resource available for extraction. This unit rate is applied to the number of units extracted during the period to obtain the total amount of depletion for the period (i.e., inventoried and expensed). The unit rate is applied to the number of units sold during the period to determine the amount of depletion to be recognized as an expense.

IV. Impairment or Disposal of Long-Lived Assets (SFAS 144)

A. **Categories**

SFAS 144, *Accounting for the Impairment or Disposal of Long-Lived Assets,* divides assets into three categories of impaired assets: held for use, held for disposal by sale, and held for disposal other than by sale. An asset group is a group of assets and liabilities that represents the unit of accounting for a long-lived asset to be held for use.

1. **Held for Sale** Criteria to determine when long-lived assets are held for sale, include requirements that (a) the asset is available for prompt sale as is, subject only to customary and usual sales terms for such assets; and (b) the asset sale is probable, and generally, to be completed within 12 months. The same accounting model is used for all long-lived assets to be sold, whether previously held and used or newly acquired. A long-lived asset to be sold is measured at the lower of its book or fair value less cost to sell and its depreciation (or amortization) discontinues. Therefore, discontinued operations are no longer valued at net realizable value (NRV) and future operating losses are no longer recognized before they occur.

2. **Assets Held for Use** SFAS 144 defines impairment as the condition that exists when the carrying amount of a long-lived asset, or asset group, exceeds its fair value. An impairment loss shall be recognized only if the carrying amount of a long-lived asset, or asset group, is not recoverable and exceeds its fair value. The carrying amount (book value) is not recoverable if it exceeds the sum of the undiscounted cash flows expected to result from the use and eventual disposition of the asset. The amount of an impairment loss is the difference between an asset's book and fair value. The new book value is used as a basis for depreciation. Goodwill need not be allocated to long-lived assets to be tested for impairment.

3. **Disposals Other Than by Sale** SFAS 144 provides guidance for long-lived assets that will be abandoned, exchanged for a similar productive asset (exchanged), or distributed to owners in a spin-off (distributed). SFAS 144 requires that these long-lived assets be considered held and used until disposal, plus (a) revision in the depreciable life of a long-lived asset to be

abandoned, or (b) recognition of an impairment loss when a long-lived asset is exchanged or distributed if book value exceeds fair value (amending APB Opinion No. 29, *Accounting for Nonmonetary Transactions*).

Example 8 ♦ Impairment of Long-Lived Asset

In Joan Co.'s review of long-lived assets to be held and used, an asset with a cost of $10,000 and accumulated depreciation of $5,500 was determined to have a fair value of $3,500.

Required: Determine the amount of impairment loss to be recognized if the expected future (undiscounted) cash flows is (a) $5,000, and (b) $3,000.

Solution a: The carrying value of $4,500 is less than the future cash flows of $5,000, so no loss is recognized even though the carrying value is greater than the fair value.

Solution b: The amount of impairment loss to be recognized is determined by calculating the difference between the carrying amount and the fair value. The carrying value of $4,500 is greater than future cash flows of $3,000 so an impairment loss of $1,000 is recognized.

B. Classification

1. **Retroactive Classification** SFAS 144 prohibits retroactive classification of the asset when the criteria for classification as held for sale are met before financial statement issuance, but after the balance sheet date.

2. **Reclassification** If a long-lived asset classified as held for sale is reclassified as held and used, the reclassified asset is valued at the lower of (a) fair value at the date that the asset is reclassified as held and used; or (b) book value before being classified as held for sale, adjusted for any depreciation (or amortization) that would have been recognized had the asset classification continuously been held and used.

V. Fixed Asset Disposal

A. Voluntary

Accounting for the voluntary disposal of an operational asset usually involves crediting the asset account for the cost of the asset, removing the accumulated depreciation by a debit to that account, debiting the appropriate account for any proceeds received, and recognizing a gain or loss on disposal (balancing figure). (Exceptions to this treatment are when multiple-asset depreciation methods are used. If the disposal qualifies as an exchange of nonmonetary assets, accounting should follow the guidelines of an acquisition by exchange.)

B. Involuntary

Property, plant, and equipment may be totally or partially destroyed by storm, fire, flood, or other similar causes. Damaged assets should be written down to their remaining value in use, if any, and a loss recognized in the current period. This loss is reported in accordance with SFAS 144.

1. **Casualty Losses** Property, plant, and equipment are usually insured against casualty losses. A gain or loss should be recognized depending on whether the amount due from the insurer exceeds the carrying amount of the loss.

2. **Recognition of Gain or Loss Regardless of Replacement** Per FASB Interp. 30, *Accounting for Involuntary Conversions of Nonmonetary Assets to Monetary Assets,* an interpretation of APB 29, a gain or loss on the involuntary conversion (e.g., due to casualty, condemnation, theft, etc.) of a nonmonetary asset should be recognized even if the proceeds received as a result of the involuntary conversion (e.g., insurance settlement, condemnation award, etc.) are reinvested in a replacement nonmonetary asset. Removal and clean-up costs are used to determine the gain or loss recognized on the involuntary conversion. Incidental costs incurred in the acquisition of replacement property are capitalized as costs of acquiring the replacement property (i.e., they do not affect the gain or loss recognized on involuntary conversion).

CHAPTER 4—PROPERTY, PLANT & EQUIPMENT

Problem 4-1 MULTIPLE CHOICE QUESTIONS (74 to 93 minutes)

1. Samm Corp. purchased a plot of land for $100,000. The cost to raze a building on the property amounted to $50,000 and Samm received $10,000 from the sale of scrap materials. Samm built a new plant on the site at a total cost of $800,000 including excavation costs of $30,000. What amount should Samm capitalize in its land account?
a. $150,000
b. $140,000
c. $130,000
d. $100,000 (R/00, FAR, #3, 6898)

2. Land was purchased to be used as the site for the construction of a plant. A building on the property was sold and removed by the buyer so that construction on the plant could begin. The proceeds from the sale of the building should be
a. Netted against the costs to clear the land and expensed as incurred
b. Netted against the costs to clear the land and amortized over the life of the plant
c. Deducted from the cost of the land
d. Classified as other income
(5/92, Theory, #12, 2705)

3. Theoretically, which of the following costs incurred in connection with a machine purchased for use in a company's manufacturing operations would be capitalized?

	Insurance on machine while in transit	*Testing and preparation of machine for use*
a.	Yes	Yes
b.	Yes	No
c.	No	Yes
d.	No	No

(5/95, FAR, #12, 5548)

4. Tomson Co. installed new assembly line production equipment at a cost of $175,000. Tomson had to rearrange the assembly line and remove a wall to install the equipment. The rearrangement cost $12,000 and the wall removal cost $3,000. The rearrangement did not increase the life of the assembly line but it did make it more efficient. What amount of these costs should be capitalized by Tomson?
a. $175,000
b. $178,000
c. $187,000
d. $190,000 (R/05, FAR, 1036F, #20, 7764)

5. Herr Inc. has a fiscal year ending April 30. On May 1, of the previous year, Herr borrowed $10,000,000 at 15% to finance construction of its own building. Repayments of the loan are to commence the month following completion of the building. During the current year ended April 30, expenditures for the partially completed structure totaled $6,000,000. These expenditures were incurred evenly throughout the year. Interest earned on the unexpended portion of the loan amounted to $400,000 for the year. How much should be shown as capitalized interest on Herr's financial statements at April 30?
a. $0
b. $ 50,000
c. $ 450,000
d. $1,100,000 (5/83, PII, #14, amended, 0966)

6. During the year, Bay Co. constructed machinery for its own use and for sale to customers. Bank loans financed these assets both during construction and after construction was complete. How much of the interest incurred should be reported as interest expense in the year-end income statement?

	Interest incurred for machinery for own use	*Interest incurred for machinery held for sale*
a.	All interest incurred	All interest incurred
b.	All interest incurred	Interest incurred after completion
c.	Interest incurred after completion	Interest incurred after completion
d.	Interest incurred after completion	All interest incurred

(5/91, Theory, #23, amended, 1788)

7. On January 2 of the current year, Cruises, Inc. borrowed $3 million at a rate of 10% for three years and began construction of a cruise ship. The note states that annual payments of principal and interest in the amount of $1.3 million are due every December 31. Cruises used all proceeds as a down payment for construction of a new cruise ship that is to be delivered two years after start of construction. What should Cruise report as interest expense related to the note in its income statement for the second year?
a. $0
b. $300,000
c. $600,000
d. $900,000 (R/05, FAR, A0636F, #44, 7788)

8. Cole Co. began constructing a building for its own use in January of the current year. During the year, Cole incurred interest of $50,000 on specific construction debt, and $20,000 on other borrowings. Interest computed on the weighted-average amount of accumulated expenditures for the building during the year was $40,000. What amount of interest cost should Cole capitalize?
a. $20,000
b. $40,000
c. $50,000
d. $70,000 (5/94, FAR, #17, amended, 4832)

9. Yola Co. and Zaro Co. are fuel oil distributors. To facilitate the delivery of oil to their customers, Yola and Zaro exchanged ownership of 1,200 barrels of oil without physically moving the oil. Yola paid Zaro $30,000 to compensate for a difference in the grade of oil. On the date of the exchange, cost and market values of the oil were as follows:

	Yola Co.	Zaro Co.
Cost	$100,000	$126,000
Market values	120,000	150,000

In Zaro's income statement, what amount of gain should be reported from the exchange of the oil?
a. $0
b. $ 4,800
c. $24,000
d. $30,000 (5/92, PII, #11, 2643)

10. In an exchange with commercial substance, Slate Co. and Talse Co. exchanged similar plots of land with fair values in excess of carrying amounts. In addition, Slate received cash from Talse to compensate for the difference in land values. As a result of the exchange, Slate should recognize
a. A gain equal to the difference between the fair value of the total consideration received and the carrying amount of the land given up
b. A gain in an amount determined by the ratio of cash received to total consideration
c. A loss in an amount determined by the ratio of cash received to total consideration
d. **Neither** a gain **nor** a loss
(5/95, FAR, #30, amended, 5566)

11. Pine Football Company had a player contract with Duff that is recorded in its books at $500,000 on July 1. Ace Football Company had a player contract with Terry that is recorded in its books at $600,000 on July 1. On this date, Pine traded Duff to Ace for Terry and paid a cash difference of $50,000. The fair value of the Terry contract was $700,000 on the exchange date. After the exchange, the Terry contract should be recorded in Pine's book as
a. $550,000
b. $600,000
c. $650,000
d. $700,000 (5/89, PI, #28, amended, 0945)

12. In an exchange with commercial substance, Vey Co. traded equipment with an original cost of $100,000 and accumulated depreciation of $40,000 for similar productive equipment with a fair value of $120,000. In addition, Vey received $30,000 cash in connection with this exchange. What should be Vey's carrying amount for the equipment received on the day of exchange?
a. $ 90,000
b. $ 60,000
c. $ 48,000
d. $120,000 (5/92, PI, #19, amended, 2586)

13. Dahl Co. traded a delivery van and $5,000 cash for a newer van owned by West Corp. The following information relates to the values of the vans on the exchange date:

	Carrying value	Fair value
Old van	$30,000	$45,000
New van	40,000	50,000

Dahl's income tax rate is 30%. What amounts should Dahl report as gain on exchange of the vans?
a. $15,000
b. $ 1,000
c. $ 700
d. $0 (11/92, PI, #46, 3279)

14. On July 1, in an exchange with commercial substance, Balt Co. exchanged a truck for 25 shares of Ace Corp.'s common stock. On that date, the truck's carrying amount was $2,500, and its fair value was $3,000. Also, the book value of Ace's stock was $60 per share. On December 31, Ace had 250 shares of common stock outstanding and its book value per share was $50. What amount should Balt report in its December 31 balance sheet as investment in Ace?
a. $3,000
b. $2,500
c. $1,500
d. $1,250 (11/92, PI, #20, amended, 3253)

15. Pine City owned a vacant plot of land zoned for industrial use. Pine gave this land to Medi Corp. solely as an incentive for Medi to build a factory on the site. The land had a fair value of $300,000 at the date of the gift. This nonmonetary transaction should be reported by Medi as
a. Extraordinary income
b. Additional paid-in capital
c. A credit to retained earnings
d. A memorandum entry (11/91, PII, #9, 2457)

16. Derby Co. incurred costs to modify its building and to rearrange its production line. As a result, an overall reduction in production costs is expected. However, the modifications did not increase the building's market value, and the rearrangement did not extend the production line's life. Should the building modification costs be capitalized?

	Building modification costs	*Production line rearrangement costs*
a.	Yes	No
b.	Yes	Yes
c.	No	No
d.	No	Yes

(5/92, Theory, #11, 2704)

17. An expenditure to install an improved electrical system is a

	Capital expenditure	*Revenue expenditure*
a.	No	Yes
b.	No	No
c.	Yes	No
d.	Yes	Yes

(5/88, Theory, #8, 1832)

18. A building suffered uninsured water and related damage. The damaged portion of the building was refurbished with upgraded materials. The cost and related accumulated depreciation of the damaged portion are identifiable. To account for these events, the owner should
a. Capitalize the cost of refurbishing and record a loss in the current period equal to the carrying amount of the damaged portion of the building
b. Capitalize the cost of refurbishing by adding the cost to the carrying amount of the building
c. Record a loss in the current period equal to the cost of refurbishing and continue to depreciate the original cost of the building
d. Record a loss in the current period equal to the sum of the cost of refurbishing and the carrying amount of the damaged portion of the building (11/90, Theory, #13, 1794)

19. Dell Printing Co. incurred the following costs for one of its printing presses:

Purchase of collating and stapling attachment	$84,000
Installation of attachment	36,000
Replacement parts for overhaul of press	26,000
Labor and overhead in connection with overhaul	14,000

The overhaul resulted in a significant increase in production. Neither the attachment nor the overhaul increased the estimated useful life of the press. What amount of the above costs should be capitalized?
a. $0
b. $ 84,000
c. $120,000
d. $160,000 (5/90, PI, #16, amended, 0940)

20. On January 2, Lem Corp. bought machinery under a contract that required a down payment of $10,000, plus 24 monthly payments of $5,000 each, for total cash payments of $130,000. The cash equivalent price of the machinery was $110,000. The machinery has an estimated useful life of 10 years and estimated salvage value of $5,000. Lem uses straight-line depreciation. In its year-end income statement, what amount should Lem report as depreciation for this machinery?
a. $10,500
b. $11,000
c. $12,500
d. $13,000 (5/94, FAR, #45, amended, 4860)

21. On January 1, year 1, Crater Inc. purchased equipment having an estimated salvage value equal to 20% of its original cost at the end of a 10-year life. The equipment was sold December 31, year 5, for 50% of its original cost. If the equipment's disposition resulted in a reported loss, which of the following depreciation methods did Crater use?
a. Double-declining-balance
b. Sum-of-the-years'-digits
c. Straight-line
d. Composite (5/93, Theory, #27, amended, 4215)

22. Spiro Corp. uses the sum-of-the-years'-digits method to depreciate equipment purchased in January of the current year for $20,000. The estimated salvage value of the equipment is $2,000 and the estimated useful life is four years. What should Spiro report as the asset's carrying amount as of December 31 in the third year?
a. $1,800
b. $2,000
c. $3,800
d. $4,500 (R/99, FAR, #7, amended, 6776)

23. A machine with a 5-year estimated useful life and an estimated 10% salvage value was acquired on January 1, of the current year. On December 31 of the fourth year, accumulated depreciation using the sum-of-the-years'-digits method would be
a. (Original cost less salvage value) multiplied by 1/15.
b. (Original cost less salvage value) multiplied by 14/15.
c. Original cost multiplied by 14/15.
d. Original cost multiplied by 1/15.
(5/92, Theory, #16, amended, 2709)

24. The graph below depicts three depreciation expense patterns over time.

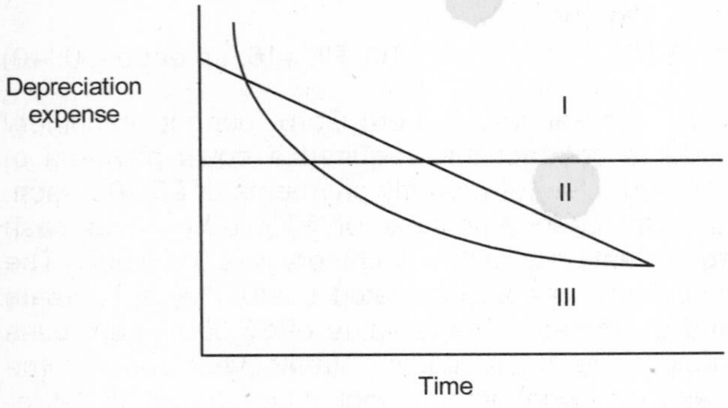

Which depreciation expense pattern corresponds to the sum-of-the-years'-digits method and which corresponds to the double-declining-balance method?

	Sum-of-the-years'-digits	*Double-declining-balance*
a.	III	II
b.	II	I
c.	I	III
d.	II	III

(11/90, Theory, #14, 9013)

25. Turtle Co. purchased equipment on January 2, year 1, for $50,000. The equipment had an estimated five-year service life. Turtle's policy for five-year assets is to use the 200% double-declining depreciation method for the first two years of the asset's life, and then switch to the straight-line depreciation method. In its December 31, year 3 balance sheet, what amount should Turtle report as accumulated depreciation for equipment?
a. $30,000
b. $38,000
c. $39,200
d. $42,000 (5/94, FAR, #18, amended, 4833)

26. Rye Co. purchased a machine with a four-year estimated useful life and an estimated 10% salvage value for $80,000 on January 1 of the current year. In its income statement for the third year, what would Rye report as the depreciation expense using the double-declining-balance method?
a. $ 9,000
b. $10,000
c. $18,000
d. $20,000 (5/95, FAR, #37, amended, 5573)

27. A fixed asset with a five-year estimated useful life and no residual value is sold at the end of the second year of its useful life. How would using the sum-of-the-years'-digits method of depreciation instead of the double-declining-balance method of depreciation affect a gain or loss on the sale of the fixed asset?

	Gain	*Loss*
a.	Decrease	Decrease
b.	Decrease	Increase
c.	Increase	Decrease
d.	Increase	Increase

(5/90, Theory, #20, 1808)

28. Which of the following uses the straight-line depreciation method?

	Group depreciation	Composite depreciation
a.	No	No
b.	Yes	No
c.	Yes	Yes
d.	No	Yes

(5/93, Theory, #28, 4216)

29. When equipment is retired, accumulated depreciation is debited for the original cost less any residual recovery under which of the following depreciation methods?

	Composite depreciation	Group depreciation
a.	No	No
b.	No	Yes
c.	Yes	No
d.	Yes	Yes

(11/84, Theory, #15, 1888)

30. Depreciation is computed on the original cost less estimated salvage value under which of the following depreciation methods?

	Double-declining-balance	Productive output
a.	No	No
b.	No	Yes
c.	Yes	Yes
d.	Yes	No

(5/88, Theory, #25, 1842)

31. On January 3, Quarry Co. purchased a manufacturing machine for $864,000. The machine had an estimated eight-year useful life and a $72,000 estimated salvage value. Quarry expects to manufacture 1,800,000 units over the life of the machine. During the year, Quarry manufactured 300,000 units. Quarry uses the units-of-production depreciation method. In its December 31 balance sheet, what amount of accumulated depreciation should Quarry report for the machine?
a. $ 99,000
b. $108,000
c. $132,000
d. $144,000 (R/03, FAR, #15, amended 7617)

32. What factor must be present to use the units-of-production (activity) method of depreciation?
a. Total units to be produced can be estimated.
b. Production is constant over the life of the asset.
c. Repair costs increase with use.
d. Obsolescence is expected.
(5/92, Theory, #15, 2708)

33. In January, Vorst Co. purchased a mineral mine for $2,640,000 with removable ore estimated at 1,200,000 *tons*. After it has extracted all the ore, Vorst will be required by law to restore the land to its original condition at an estimated cost of $180,000. Vorst believes it will be able to sell the property afterwards for $300,000. During the year, Vorst incurred $360,000 of development costs preparing the mine for production and removed and sold 60,000 tons of ore. In its year-end income statement, what amount should Vorst report as depletion?
a. $135,000
b. $144,000
c. $150,000
d. $159,000 (5/95, FAR, #36, amended, 5572)

34. In January, two years ago, Winn Corp. purchased equipment at a cost of $500,000. The equipment had an estimated salvage value of $100,000, an estimated 8-year useful life, and was eing depreciated by the straight-line method. Two ears later, it became apparent to Winn that this quipment suffered a permanent impairment of alue. In January of the current year, management termined the carrying amount should be only 75,000, with a 2-year remaining useful life, and salvage value should be reduced to $25,000. In nn's current year December 31 balance sheet, the uipment should be reported at a carrying amount of
$350,000
$175,000
$150,000
100,000 (5/91, PI, #26, amended, 0932)

35. On January 2, year 2, Reed Co. purchased a machine for $800,000 and established an annual depreciation charge of $100,000 over an eight-year life. During year 4, after issuing its year 3 financial statements, Reed concluded that: (1) the machine suffered permanent impairment of its operational value, and (2) $200,000 is a reasonable estimate of the amount expected to be recovered through use of the machine for the period January 1, year 4 through December 31, year 8. In Reed's December 31, year 4 balance sheet, the machine should be reported at a carrying amount of
a. $0
b. $100,000
c. $160,000
d. $400,000 (5/93, PI, #24, amended, 4066)

36. On July 1 one of Rudd Co.'s delivery vans was destroyed in an accident. On that date, the van's carrying amount was $2,500. On July 15, Rudd received and recorded a $700 invoice for a new engine installed in the van in May, and another $500 invoice for various repairs. In August, Rudd received $3,500 under its insurance policy on the van, which it plans to use to replace the van. What amount should Rudd report as gain (loss) on disposal of the van in its year-end income statement?
a. $1,000
b. $ 300
c. $0
d. $ (200) (5/92, PI, #45, amended, 2616)

37. On December 31 of the current year a building owned by Carr Inc. was destroyed by fire. Carr paid $12,000 for removal and clean-up costs. The building had a book value of $250,000 and a fair value of $280,000 on December 31. What amount should Carr use to determine the gain or loss on this involuntary conversion?
a. $250,000
b. $262,000
c. $280,000
d. $292,000 (5/91, PI, #27, amended, 0933)

Problem 4-2 ADDITIONAL MULTIPLE CHOICE QUESTIONS (38 to 48 minutes)

38. During the year, Burr Co. had the following transactions pertaining to its new office building:

Purchase price of land	$ 60,000
Legal fees for contracts to purchase land	2,000
Architects' fees	8,000
Demolition of old building on site	5,000
Sale of scrap from old building	3,000
Construction cost of new building (fully completed)	$350,000

In Burr's December 31 balance sheet, what amounts should be reported as the cost of land and cost of building?

	Land	*Building*
a.	$60,000	$360,000
b.	$62,000	$360,000
c.	$64,000	$358,000
d.	$65,000	$362,000

(5/91, PI, #24, amended, 0931)

39. On October 1 of the current year, Shaw Corp. purchased a machine for $126,000 that was placed in service on November 30. Shaw incurred additional costs for this machine as follows:

Shipping	$3,000
Installation	4,000
Testing	5,000

In Shaw's December 31 balance sheet, the machine's cost should be reported as

a. $126,000
b. $129,000
c. $133,000
d. $138,000 (5/91, PI, #23, amended, 0930)

40. Town Company purchased for $540,000 a warehouse building and the land on which it is located. The following data were available concerning the property:

	Current appraised value	Seller's original cost
Land	$200,000	$140,000
Warehouse building	300,000	280,000
	$500,000	$420,000

Town should record the land at

a. $140,000
b. $180,000
c. $200,000
d. $216,000 (11/85, PI, #12, amended, 0959)

41. In an exchange with commercial substance, Amble Inc. exchanged a truck with a carrying amount of $12,000 and a fair value of $20,000 for a truck and $4,000 cash. The fair value of the truck received was $16,000. At what amount should Amble record the truck received in the exchange?

a. $ 8,000
b. $ 9,600
c. $12,000
d. $16,000 (5/93, PII, #10, amended, 4119)

42. An asset is being constructed for an enterprise's own use. The asset has been financed with a specific new borrowing. The interest cost incurred during the construction period as a result of expenditures for the asset is

a. Interest expense in the construction period
b. A prepaid asset to be written off over the estimated useful life of the asset
c. A part of the historical cost of acquiring the asset to be written off over the estimated useful life of the asset
d. A part of the historical cost of acquiring the asset to be written off over the term of the borrowing used to finance the construction of the asset (5/86, Theory, #17, 1878)

43. A company is constructing an asset for its own use. Construction began in the previous year. The asset is being financed entirely with a specific new borrowing. Construction expenditures were made last year and this year at the end of each quarter. The total amount of interest cost capitalized in the current year should be determined by applying the interest rate on the specific new borrowing to the

a. Total accumulated expenditures for the asset in both years
b. Average accumulated expenditures for the asset in both years
c. Average expenditures for the asset in the current year
d. Total expenditures for the asset in the current year (11/87, Theory, #4, amended, 1847)

44. In an exchange with commercial substance, Beam Co. paid $1,000 cash and traded inventory, which had a carrying amount of $20,000 and a fair value of $21,000, for other inventory in the same line of business with a fair value of $22,000. What amount of gain (loss) should Beam record related to the inventory exchange?

a. $ 2,000
b. $ 1,000
c. $0
d. $(1,000) (5/93, PII, #9, amended, 4118)

45. Madden Company owns a tract of land which it purchased four years ago for $100,000. The land is held as a future plant site and has a fair market value of $140,000 on July 1 of the current year. Hall Company also owns a tract of land held as a future plant site. On this date, Madden exchanged its land and paid $50,000 cash for the land owned by Hall. At what amount should Madden record the land acquired in the exchange?

a. $150,000
b. $160,000
c. $190,000
d. $200,000 (11/83, PI, #16, amended, 9010)

46. An entity disposes of a nonmonetary asset in a nonreciprocal transfer. A gain or loss should be recognized on the disposition of the asset when the fair value of the asset transferred is determinable and the nonreciprocal transfer is to

	Another entity	*A stockholder of the entity*
a.	No	Yes
b.	No	No
c.	Yes	No
d.	Yes	Yes

(11/88, Theory, #36, 9011)

47. During the previous year, Yvo Corp. installed a production assembly line to manufacture furniture. In the current year, Yvo purchased a new machine and rearranged the assembly line to install this machine. The rearrangement did not increase the estimated useful life of the assembly line, but it did result in significantly more efficient production. The following expenditures were incurred in connection with this project:

Machine	$75,000
Labor to install machine	14,000
Parts added in rearranging the assembly line to provide future benefits	40,000
Labor and overhead to rearrange the assembly line	18,000

What amount of the above expenditures should be capitalized in the current year?

a. $147,000
b. $107,000
c. $ 89,000
d. $ 75,000 (11/90, PII, #4, amended, 0934)

48. Parke Corp. replaced its boiler with a more efficient one. The following information was available on that date:

Purchase price of new boiler	$60,000
Carrying amount of old boiler	5,000
Fair value of old boiler	2,000
Installation cost of new boiler	8,000

The old boiler was sold for $2,000. What amount should Parke capitalize as the cost of the new boiler?

a. $68,000
b. $66,000
c. $63,000
d. $60,000 (5/89, PI, #25, amended, 0943)

49. A depreciable asset has an estimated 15% salvage value. At the end of its estimated useful life, the accumulated depreciation would equal the original cost of the asset under which of the following depreciation methods?

	Straight-line	*Productive output*
a.	Yes	No
b.	Yes	Yes
c.	No	Yes
d.	No	No

(5/89, Theory, #4, 9012)

50. On April 1, year 1, Kew Co. purchased new machinery for $300,000. The machinery has an estimated useful life of five years, and depreciation is computed by the sum-of-the-years'-digits method. The accumulated depreciation on this machinery at March 31, year 3 should be

a. $192,000
b. $180,000
c. $120,000
d. $100,000 (5/90, PI, #17, amended, 0941)

51. South Co. purchased a machine that was installed and placed in service on January 1 of the current year, at a cost of $240,000. Salvage value was estimated at $40,000. The machine is being depreciated over 10 years by the double-declining-balance method. For the second year ended December 31, what amount should South report as depreciation expense?

a. $48,000
b. $38,400
c. $32,000
d. $21,600 (5/92, PI, #50, amended, 2621)

52. A machine with a four-year estimated useful life and an estimated 15 percent salvage value was acquired on January 1. Would depreciation expense using the sum-of-the-years'-digits method of depreciation be higher or lower than depreciation expense using the double-declining-balance method of depreciation in the first and second years?

	First year	Second year
a.	Higher	Higher
b.	Higher	Lower
c.	Lower	Higher
d.	Lower	Lower

(5/84, Theory, #10, 9014)

53. A company using the composite depreciation method for its fleet of trucks, cars, and campers retired one of its trucks and received cash from a salvage company. The net carrying amount of these composite asset accounts would be decreased by the
a. Cash proceeds received and original cost of the truck
b. Cash proceeds received
c. Original cost of the truck less the cash proceeds
d. Original cost of the truck

(5/88, Theory, #9, 1833)

54. Weir Co. uses straight-line depreciation for its property, plant, and equipment, which, stated at cost, consisted of the following:

	12/31/Yr2	12/31/Yr1
Land	$ 25,000	$ 25,000
Buildings	195,000	195,000
Machinery and equipment	695,000	650,000
	915,000	870,000
Less: Accumulated depreciation	(400,000)	(370,000)
	$ 515,000	$ 500,000

Weir's depreciation expense for year 2 and year 1 was $55,000 and $50,000, respectively. What amount was debited to accumulated depreciation during year 2 because of property, plant, and equipment retirements?
a. $40,000
b. $25,000
c. $20,000
d. $10,000

(11/93, PI, #23, amended, 4392)

55. A state government condemned Cory Co.'s parcel of real estate. Cory will receive $750,000 for this property, which has a carrying amount of $575,000. Cory incurred the following costs as a result of the condemnation:

Appraisal fees to support a $750,000 value	$2,500
Attorney fees for the closing with the state	3,500
Attorney fees to review contract to acquire replacement property	3,000
Title insurance on replacement property	4,000

What amount of cost should Cory use to determine the gain on the condemnation?
a. $581,000
b. $582,000
c. $584,000
d. $588,000

(11/91, PI, #19, 2407)

56. Lano Corp.'s forest land was condemned for use as a national park. Compensation for the condemnation exceeded the forest land's carrying amount. Lano purchased similar, but larger, replacement forest land for an amount greater than the condemnation award. As a result of the condemnation and replacement, what is the net effect on the carrying amount of forest land reported in Lano's balance sheet?
a. The amount is increased by the excess of the replacement forest land's cost over the condemned forest land's carrying amount.
b. The amount is increased by the excess of the replacement forest land's cost over the condemnation award.
c. The amount is increased by the excess of the condemnation award over the condemned forest land's carrying amount.
d. No effect, because the condemned forest land's carrying amount is used as the replacement forest land's carrying amount.

(5/92, Theory, #13, 2706)

SIMULATIONS

Problem 4-3 (15 to 25 minutes)

Research Task | Responses 1-6 | Responses 7-10 | Responses 11-14

Research Question: What requirement must be met for an asset to qualify for capitalization of interest costs?

Paragraph Reference Answer: ____________

Research Task | Responses 1-6 | Responses 7-10 | Responses 11-14

Items 1 through 6 represent expenditures for goods held for resale and equipment. Determine for each item whether the expenditure should be capitalized (C) or expensed as a period cost (E).

1. _____ Freight-in charges paid for goods held for resale.
2. _____ In-transit insurance on goods held for resale purchased F.O.B. shipping point.
3. _____ Interest on note payable for goods held for resale.
4. _____ Installation of equipment.
5. _____ Testing of newly-purchased equipment.
6. _____ Cost of current year service contract on equipment.

Research Task | Responses 1-6 | Responses 7-10 | Responses 11-14

Items 7 through 10 are based on the following transactions:

- Link Co. purchased an office building and the land on which it is located by paying $800,000 cash and assuming an existing mortgage of $200,000. The property is assessed at $960,000 for realty tax purposes, of which 60% is allocated to the building.
- Link leased construction equipment under a 7-year capital lease requiring annual year-end payments of $100,000. Link's incremental borrowing rate is 9%, while the lessor's implicit rate, which is not known to Link, is 8%. Present value factors for an ordinary annuity for seven periods are 5.21 at 8% and 5.03 at 9%. Fair value of the equipment is $515,000.
- Link paid $50,000 and gave a plot of undeveloped land with a carrying amount of $320,000 and a fair value of $450,000 to Club Co. in exchange for a plot of undeveloped land with a fair value of $500,000. The land was carried on Club's books at $350,000.

For items 7 through 10, calculate the amount to be recorded for each item. Enter the amounts as numeric values in the space provided.

7. _____ Building
8. _____ Leased equipment
9. _____ Land received from Club on Link's books
10. _____ Land received from Link on Club's books

Research Task | Responses 1-6 | Responses 7-10 | Responses 11-14

Items 11 through 14 are based on the following information:

On January 2, year 1, Half Inc. purchased a manufacturing machine for $864,000. The machine has an eight year estimated life and a $144,000 estimated salvage value. Half expects to manufacture 1,800,000 units over the life of the machine. During year 2, Half manufactured 300,000 units.

Items 11 through 14 represent various depreciation methods. For each item, calculate depreciation expense for year 2 (the second year of ownership) for the machine described above under the method listed.

11. _____ Straight-line
12. _____ Double-declining-balance
13. _____ Sum-of-the-years'-digits
14. _____ Units of production

(11/94, FAR, #2, amended, 5321)

Problem 4-4 (30 to 40 minutes)

Research Task | Scenario | Responses | Essay

Research Question: When is land not a qualifying asset for capitalization of interest costs?

Paragraph Reference Answer: _______________

Research Task | Scenario | Responses | Essay

During the year, Sloan Inc. began a project to construct new corporate headquarters. Sloan purchased land with an existing building for $750,000. The land was valued at $700,000 and the building at $50,000. Sloan planned to demolish the building and construct a new office building on the site.

Research Task | Scenario | Responses | Essay

1. _____ Purchase of land for $700,000.
2. _____ Interest of $147,000 on construction financing incurred after completion of construction.
3. _____ Interest of $186,000 on construction financing paid during construction.
4. _____ Purchase of building for $50,000.
5. _____ $18,500 payment of delinquent real estate taxes assumed by Sloan on purchase.
6. _____ $12,000 liability insurance premium during the construction period.
7. _____ $65,000 cost of razing existing building.
8. _____ Moving costs of $136,000.

For each expenditure in items **1 through 8,** select from the list below the appropriate accounting treatment.

L. Classify as land and do not depreciate.
B. Classify as building and depreciate.
E. Expense.

(11/92, P1, #4(a), amended, 3292)

Research Task	Scenario	Responses	Essay

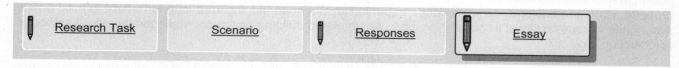

Portland Co. uses the straight-line depreciation method for depreciable assets. All assets are depreciated individually except manufacturing machinery, which is depreciated by the composite method.

During the year, Portland exchanged a delivery truck with Maine Co. for a larger delivery truck. It paid cash equal to 10% of the larger truck's value.

a. What factors should have influenced Portland's selection of the straight-line depreciation method?

b. How should Portland account for and report the truck exchange transaction?

c. 1. What benefits should Portland derive from using the composite method rather than the individual basis for manufacturing machinery?

2. How should Portland have calculated the manufacturing machinery's annual depreciation expense in its first year of operation?

(11/91, Theory, #3, 6189)

Problem 4-5 (40 to 50 minutes)

Directions	Situation	Accounting Treatment	Capitalized Cost

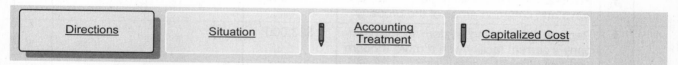

In the following simulation, you will be asked various questions regarding the accounting and reporting for property, plant and equipment. The simulation will provide you with all of the information necessary to answer the questions. For full credit, be sure to answer all questions

Remember

- Information and data necessary to complete the simulation are found by clicking information tabs, i.e., those **without** a pencil icon.
- All tasks that you should complete before leaving the simulation are found on work tabs, i.e., those tabs **with** a pencil icon
- An unshaded pencil icon means that you have **not** yet responded to anything on a particular work tab.
- A shaded pencil icon indicates that you have responded to some or all of the requirements on a work tab; it does **not** necessarily mean that you have completed the requirements on the tab.

To start this simulation, click on the Situation tab.

To respond to the tasks or questions, click on the work tabs.

Directions	Situation	Accounting Treatment	Capitalized Cost

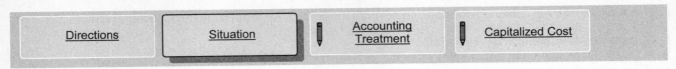

Sherman Inc. uses the calendar year as its reporting period. During year 1, the company completed numerous property, plant and equipment transactions. In particular, Sherman Inc. incurred long-term debt to build a new warehouse storage facility at its current location. An unrelated building contractor managed the new warehouse construction project.

Sherman Inc. has a policy of capitalizing expenditures with a unit cost of at least $1,000 and a useful life greater than one year. The company prorates depreciation expense in the year of acquisition based on the date of purchase.

Directions	Situation	Accounting Treatment	Capitalized Cost

Sherman Inc. had the following property, plant and equipment transactions during the year. For each transaction, double-click on the shaded space and choose the correct accounting treatment from the drop-down list. Each accounting treatment may be used once, more than once, or not at all.

	A	B	C
1	**Asset**	**Cost**	**Accounting treatment**
2	Cost of parking lot for new warehouse	$8,500	
3	Painting all of the ceiling tiles in the hallways and common areas of the property	$8,500	
4	Replace the cooling system in the company's current facility with a more modern and fuel efficient model.	$33,000	
5	15 new desk-top computers for support personnel	$22,500	
6	New process costing software—this software will need to be replaced in 5 years	$12,000	
7	Replacing office windows cracked as a result of an explosion at a neighboring manufacturing plant.	$16,000	

Selection List

A. Capitalize and depreciate

B. Capitalize, but do not depreciate

C. Capitalize and amortize

D. Expense at time incurred

E. Expense monthly

F. Partially capitalize and partially expense

Directions	Situation	Accounting Treatment	Capitalized Cost

Sherman Inc. purchased or constructed the following assets during year 1. Use the spreadsheet below to calculate the amount that the company should capitalize for each of the following property, plant and equipment assets. Enter your answer in the appropriate shaded cell below. Note: To use a formula in the spreadsheet, it must be preceded by an equal sign e.g., =B1+B2. Any negative numbers should be entered with a leading minus (–) sign.

	A	B
1	**Land for the new warehouse**	
2	Purchase price	$325,000
3	Demolition of existing structures on property	120,000
4	Proceeds from the sale of scrap from the old buildings on the site	65,000
5	Costs incurred to grade and pave driveways and parking lots	40,000
6	Lawn and garden sprinkler systems for the property	18,500
7	Legal fees incurred to purchase the property and paid at settlement	24,000
8	**Capitalized cost of the land**	$404,000
9	**Construction of new warehouse**	
10	Construction began March 15 and ended August 31	
11	Borrowings to finance construction	$265,000
12	Interest incurred from 3/15 through 8/31	11,000
13	Interest incurred from 9/1 through 12/31	8,500
14	Total cost of labor, materials, and overhead to construct the warehouse	305,000
15	Costs incurred to grade and pave driveways and parking lots	40,000
16	Costs to repair water line ruptured during excavation	8,000
17	**Capitalized cost of the warehouse**	$316,000
18	**New machine**	
19	Cost of machine	$ 36,000
20	Sales tax paid on machine	2,100
21	Installation costs	3,700
22	Finance charges on purchase loan	2,900
23	**Capitalized cost of the new machine**	$ 41,800

(4/06, FAR, #2, amended, 8118)

Solution 4-1 MULTIPLE CHOICE ANSWERS

Valuation

1\. (b) Land must be recorded at its acquisition cost. Generally, acquisition cost is defined as the cash price, or its equivalent, plus all other costs reasonably necessary to make it ready for its intended use. Such additional costs include demolition of an old building, less any scrap proceeds received.

Purchase price of land	$100,000
Add: Cost to raze old building	50,000
Less: Proceeds from sale of scrap	(10,000)
Capitalized value of land	$140,000

2\. (c) Sometimes a structure is constructed on a newly acquired site with an existing building on it. If the existing building is sold and the buyer assumes the costs for its removal, the entire amount of the proceeds from the sale of the building should be deducted from the cost of the land.

3. (a) The acquisition cost of a machine for use in a company's manufacturing operations includes all costs reasonably necessary to bring the asset to the location where it is to be used and to make it ready for its intended use, including insurance while in-transit and test runs.

4. (d) Assets are to be recorded at their acquisition cost. Acquisition cost is defined as the cash price, or its equivalent, plus all other costs reasonably necessary to bring it to the location and to make it ready for its intended use.

Cost	$175,000
Rearrangement	12,000
Removal of wall	3,000
Total amount to be capitalized	$190,000

Interest

5. (c) The amount of interest to be capitalized in accordance with SFAS 34 is determined by applying an interest rate to the average amount of accumulated expenditures for the asset during the period. The interest rate to be used is the rate on new borrowings which are specifically associated with the acquisition of the new asset, or a weighted average of the interest rates on all debt outstanding during the period (SFAS 34, ¶13). The amount of interest thus determined is *not* reduced or in any way offset by interest income earned during the construction period (FASB Technical Bulletin 81-5).

Average expenditure during year ($6,000,000 / 2)	$3,000,000
Interest (capitalization) rate	× 0.15
Capitalized interest	$ 450,000

6. (d) According to SFAS 34, interest cost during construction is to be capitalized on assets that are constructed for an enterprise's own use or assets intended for sale or lease that are constructed as discrete projects. However, interest cost shall not be capitalized for inventories that are routinely manufactured or otherwise produced in large quantities on a repetitive basis. Once the constructed assets are completed, all interest should be expensed as incurred. In the question at hand, it is not clear, but it is assumed that the machinery constructed for sale is routinely manufactured in large quantities on a repetitive basis. Therefore, the interest during construction should be capitalized only for the equipment constructed for Bay's own use. The interest incurred during construction of the inventory items should be expensed. The interest incurred after completion should be expensed on both groups of equipment.

7. (a) Assets qualifying for interest capitalization include assets constructed or produced for self-use on a repetitive basis, assets acquired for self-use through arrangements requiring down payments or progress payments, and assets constructed or produced as discrete projects for sale or lease (e.g., ships or real estate developments).

8. (b) The amount of interest that may be capitalized is based on the weighted-average amount of accumulated expenditures. The weighted-average amount of accumulated expenditures applies the avoidable interest concept. This concept limits the amount of interest to be capitalized to the lower of the actual interest cost incurred during the period or avoidable interest. Avoidable interest is the amount of interest cost incurred during the period that theoretically could have been avoided if expenditures for the asset had not been made.

Exchange

9. (b) The transaction is an exchange of a product held for sale in the ordinary course of business for a product to be sold in the same line of business to facilitate sales to customers other than parties to the exchange and does not result in the culmination of an earnings process. The nonmonetary exchange shall be measured based on the recorded amount of the nonmonetary assets relinquished. Only to the extent cash (boot) has been received has a portion of the asset exchanged been sold and a gain can be recognized. The fair value of the asset acquired is reduced by the portion of the gain realized which is not recognized. The gain recognized on the exchange is determined by the ratio of the cash to the total consideration received (asset received and cash).

Cash received		$ 30,000
Fair value of inventory received		120,000
Total fair value received		150,000
Carrying amount of inventory exchanged		(126,000)
Gain realized on exchange		$ 24,000
Cash	$ 30,000	
Total fair value received	/ 150,000	
Extent earnings process culminated		× 20%
Gain recognized on exchange		$ 4,800
Fair value of inventory acquired		$ 120,000
Unrecognized gain ($24,000 – $4,800)		(19,200)
Recorded cost of inventory acquired		$ 100,800

10. (a) In general, accounting for nonmonetary transactions should be based on the fair values of the assets involved. The acquisition is recorded at the fair value of the asset surrendered or the FV of the asset received, whichever is more clearly determinable, and gains or losses should be recognized. The amount would be the difference between the fair value received and the carrying value of the consideration given up.

11. (d) In an exchange with commercial substance, the transaction is recorded at the fair value of the asset received or the asset given up, whichever is greater (more clearly evident), and a gain or loss is recognized on the exchange. The Terry contract would be recorded at $700,000 and a gain would be indicated as follows:

Cash paid	$ 50,000
Book value of contract given up	500,000
Total fair value received	550,000
Fair value of contract received	(700,000)
Gain on exchange	$ 150,000

The journal entry to be recorded in Pine's books is:

Terry Contract	700,000	
Duff Contract		500,000
Cash		50,000
Gain		150,000

12. (d) In an exchange with commercial substance, the exchange is recorded at the fair value of the asset received or the asset given up, whichever is greater (more clearly evident), and a gain or loss is recognized on the exchange.

Cash received		$ 30,000
Fair value of equipment received		120,000
Total fair value received		150,000
Cost	$100,000	
Accumulated depreciation	(40,000)	
Carrying amount of equipment exchanged		(60,000)
Gain on exchange		$ 90,000

The journal entry to be recorded in Vey's books is:

Cash	30,000	
New Equipment	120,000	
Accumulated Depreciation	40,000	
Old Equipment		100,000
Gain on Exchange		90,000

13. (a) Dahl is giving boot in an exchange with commercial substance. Dahl has a realized gain on its old van of $15,000:

Cash paid	$ 5,000
Book value of truck given up	30,000
Total consideration given up	35,000
Fair value of truck received	(50,000)
Gain on exchange	$ 15,000

The journal entry to be recorded in Dahl's books is:

Truck received	50,000	
Cash paid		5,000
Truck given up		30,000
Gain		15,000

14. (a) In an exchange with commercial substance, the new asset is recorded at the fair value of the asset received or the fair value of the asset surrendered, whichever is more clearly evident. Balt should record its investment in Ace at the fair value of the truck given because the fair value of the shares acquired is not given.

Carrying amount of truck	$ 2,500
Fair value of truck	(3,000)
Gain on exchange	$ 500

The journal entry to be recorded in Balt's books is:

Investment in Ace	3,000	
Truck given up		2,500
Gain		500

Nonreciprocal Transfer

15. (b) The contribution of land by a governmental unit to an enterprise for industrial use is an example of a nonreciprocal transfer. A nonmonetary asset received in a nonreciprocal transfer should be recorded at the fair value of the asset received. The corresponding credit for a corporation is *Additional Paid-In Capital—Donated Assets.* Donated assets should *not* be recorded as income or gain or added to retained earnings when received from governmental entities. Assets donated by entities other than governmental units should be included in revenue in the period of receipt (SFAS 116).

Post-Acquisition Costs

16. (b) Both the building modification costs and the production line rearrangement costs should be capitalized because they have resulted in an overall reduction of production costs, the benefits of which extend beyond the current period.

17. (c) The expenditure to install an improved electrical system represents a betterment (or improvement); that is, the substitution of a better asset for an existing asset. The expenditure increases the service potential of the electrical system. Because this increased service potential is a benefit that will be enjoyed throughout the life of the electrical system, the expenditure should be capitalized and depreciated over the life of the system. Revenue expenditures, on the other hand, are recurring expenditures that do not add to the service potential of a plant asset; they serve merely to maintain a given level of services. Revenue expenditures should be expensed when incurred.

18. (a) The damaged portion of the building was refurbished with upgraded materials which indicates that a "betterment" is involved. There are future benefits due to the refurbishing expenditures; thus, they should be capitalized. The cost and related accumulated depreciation of the damaged portion of the building are identifiable so they should be removed from the books (with a resulting debit to "loss" for the difference) because this portion of the building has been replaced and upgraded.

19. (d) The collating and stapling attachment is an addition to the printing press and so its cost (including installation cost) should be capitalized. The overhaul resulted in a significant increase in the productivity of the printing press; therefore, its cost (replacement parts, labor and overhead) should also be capitalized. The total cost capitalized is $160,000 (i.e., $84,000 + $36,000 + $26,000 + $14,000).

Straight-Line Depreciation

20. (a) Assets are recorded at their acquisition cost. Acquisition cost is the cash price, or its equivalent. [($110,000 – $5,000) / 10 years = $10,500/year]

21. (c) The carrying amount of the equipment at the date of sale is computed by subtracting the accumulated depreciation on the equipment from the cost of the equipment. Under the straight-line method, the accumulated depreciation on the equipment at the date of sale is equal to 40% of the original cost of the equipment [i.e., (100% – 20%) × 1/10 × 5]. Thus, under the straight-line method, the carrying amount of the equipment at the date of sale is 60% (i.e., 100% – 40%) of the original cost of the equipment. Since the equipment was sold for only 50% of its original cost, use of the straight-line depreciation method would have resulted in a loss being recognized on the sale equal to 10% (i.e., 60% – 50%) of the original cost of the equipment.

SYD Depreciation

22. (c)

Asset cost		$ 20,000
Year 1 [(4/10)($20,000 – 2,000)]	$7,200	
Year 2 [(3/10)($20,000 – 2,000)]	5,400	
Year 3 [(2/10)($20,000 – 2,000)]	3,600	
Depreciation		(16,200)
Carrying amount, 12/31, year 3		$ 3,800

23. (b) On December 31, of the fourth year, four years of depreciation would have been recorded. The accumulated depreciation would be 14/15 (i.e., 5/15 + 4/15 + 3/15 + 2/15) multiplied by the machine's depreciable base (i.e., cost less salvage value).

Year	Depreciation fraction	×	Depreciable base
1	5/15		Cost less salvage value
2	4/15		Cost less salvage value
3	3/15		Cost less salvage value
4	2/15		Cost less salvage value
5	1/15		Cost less salvage value
15			Cost less salvage value

24. (d) The depreciation pattern corresponding to the sum-of-the-years'-digits (SYD) method is the straight sloping line (II) and the pattern corresponding to the double-declining-balance (DDB) method is the curved line (III). The straight line parallel with the horizontal axis describes the pattern of the straight-line (SL) method of depreciation because the SL method results in a constant amount of depreciation each period. The line for the pattern of the SYD method is a straight sloping line because the method results in a decreasing depreciation charge based on a decreasing fraction of depreciable cost where each fraction has the same denominator (sum of the years). The line for the pattern of the DDB method will be a curved sloping line because that type of method employs a constant percentage multiplied by a decreasing balance to obtain a decreasing charge for depreciation.

DDB Depreciation

25. (b) On December 31, year 3, Turtle reports $32,000 + $6,000 = $38,000 as accumulated depreciation. Double-declining-balance is computed using twice the straight-line rate, which in this case is 40% (1/5 = 0.20; 0.20 × 2 = 0.40). In year 3, depreciation is computed by dividing the remaining book value of $18,000 by the remaining life of 3 years = $6,000.

	Book value beginning of year	Rate	Depreciation expense	Accumulated depreciation	Book value end of year
Year 1	$50,000	40%	$20,000	$20,000	$30,000
Year 2	30,000	40%	12,000	32,000	18,000

26. (b) Under the double-declining-balance method of depreciation, the annual depreciation charge is computed by multiplying the carrying amount of the plant asset (i.e., cost minus accumulated depreciation) by a rate equal to 200% of the straight-line rate (e.g., 200% × 25% = 50%). Salvage value is not used in the depreciation formula, but the plant asset cannot be depreciated below its salvage value.

Year 1 expense [50% × ($80,000 – $0)]	$40,000
Year 2 expense [50% × ($80,000 – $40,000)]	$20,000
Year 3 expense [50% × ($80,000 – $60,000)]	$10,000

27. (b) This question requires the determination of how using the sum-of-the-years'-digits (SYD) method of depreciation, instead of the double-declining-balance (DDB) method of depreciation, affects the gain or loss on the sale of a fixed asset with a five-year estimated useful life and no residual value that is sold at the end of the second year of its useful life. A gain or loss on the sale of a fixed asset is computed by comparing the proceeds received from its sale to its carrying amount at the date of sale. To determine the carrying amount of the fixed asset at the sale date, two years of depreciation must be subtracted from its cost. Because the cost of the fixed asset is not given, there are two options: (1) determine depreciation as a percent or fraction of the unknown cost of the fixed asset, "x," or (2) plug in any value for the cost of the machine and simply compute depreciation under both methods based on this amount. We chose the latter approach, assigning to the machine a cost of $300. Now we can compare the carrying amount of the fixed asset at the sale date under both methods. The fixed asset has a greater carrying amount at the date of sale under the SYD method. Therefore, using the SYD method of depreciation, instead of the DDB method of depreciation, decreases any gain and increases any loss recognized on the sale of the fixed asset.

Cost of fixed asset	$ 300
Depreciation to date of sale:	
Yr. 1: 5/15 × ($300 – $0)	(100)
Yr. 2: 4/15 × ($300 – $0)	(80)
Carrying amount, date of sale, SYD	$ 120

Cost of fixed asset	$ 300
Depreciation to date of sale:	
Yr. 1: 2/5 × ($300 – $0)	(120)
Yr. 2: 2/5 × ($300 – $120)	(72)
Carrying amount, date of sale, DDB	$ 108

Multiple Asset Depreciation

28. (c) The composite depreciation method refers to the depreciation of a collection of assets that are dissimilar. The group depreciation method refers to the depreciation of a collection of assets that are similar in nature. From an accounting standpoint, there is no distinction between the two methods. The same procedures are followed for both, and both utilize the straight-line depreciation method.

29. (d) Under both the group depreciation and the composite depreciation methods, assets are depreciated on the basis of their average lives. New assets are recorded at cost, and retirements are accounted for by crediting *Assets* for the original cost of the equipment and debiting *Accumulated Depreciation* for the original cost less proceeds received; thus, no gain or loss is recognized on disposal. The theoretical justification for this is that some assets will be retired early, while some will be used longer than originally estimated. The same approach is used under both group and composite depreciation—the only difference is that "group depreciation" refers to pools of assets that are similar in nature, whereas "composite" refers to essentially dissimilar assets.

Variable Charge Methods

30. (b) It is important to note that although an estimated salvage value is not directly incorporated into the formula for computing annual depreciation expense under the double-declining-balance (DDB) method, total depreciation expense over the life of the plant asset under this method cannot exceed the depreciable base (i.e., Historical cost minus salvage value) of the plant asset. An estimated salvage value is directly incorporated into the formula for computing annual depreciation expense under the productive output method.

$$\text{Depreciation expense} = \frac{\text{Historical cost} - \text{Estimated salvage value}}{\text{Estimated productive output}} \times \text{Productive output current period}$$

An estimated salvage value is not directly incorporated into the formula for computing annual depreciation expense under the DDB method:

$$\text{Depreciation expense} = \frac{2}{\text{Estimated useful life}} \times \left[\text{Historical cost} - \text{Accumulated depreciation}\right]$$

31. (c) Units-of-output depreciation takes into account salvage value and the number of units produced by the asset. Cost – salvage/expected output × current output:

$$\frac{\$864{,}000 - \$72{,}000}{1{,}800{,}000} = \frac{\$792{,}000}{\$1{,}800{,}000} = \$0.44 \times 300{,}000 = \$132{,}000$$

32. (a) The units-of-production depreciation method allocates the cost of plant assets on the basis of units produced (i.e., activity). Depreciation for a period is computed by multiplying the number of units produced during the period by the amount of depreciation per unit. The amount of depreciation per unit is determined by dividing the depreciable base of the plant asset (i.e., cost minus estimated salvage value) by the estimated number of total units to be produced. Thus, an estimate of total units to be produced must be available to use this method. Production does not have to be at a constant level over the life of the asset in order to use this method. Expected repair costs do not affect this method. Obsolescence does not have to be expected to use this method.

Depletion

33. (b)

Purchase price of mine	$2,640,000
Development costs to prepare for production	360,000
Estimated restoration costs	180,000
Estimated residual value	(300,000)
Depletion base of mine	2,880,000
Estimated tons of removable ore	/ 1,200,000
Depletion charge per ton	2.40
Tons sold in the year	× 60,000
Depletion expense for the year	$ 144,000

Impairment

34. (d) In January of the current year, the equipment was written down to a new cost basis of $175,000 due to a permanent impairment of its operational value. Since the estimated salvage value of the equipment on the date of the write-down is $25,000, the $150,000 ($175,000 – $25,000) depreciable base of the equipment should be allocated over the equipment's remaining estimated useful life of 2 years. At 12/31 of the current year, the carrying amount of the equipment is $100,000 [$175,000 – ($150,000 / 2)].

35. (c) During year 4, the machine was written down to $200,000 due to a permanent impairment of its operational value. Thus, $200,000 is the new cost basis of the machine, which is depreciated over the machine's remaining estimated useful life of five years. At 12/31 year 4, the carrying amount of the machine is $160,000, i.e., ($200,000 – $0) × 4/5.

Disposals

36. (b) FASB Interpretation 30 provides that a gain or loss on the involuntary conversion (e.g., casualty, condemnation, theft) of a nonmonetary asset should be recognized in income even if the proceeds received as a result of the involuntary conversion are reinvested in a replacement nonmonetary asset. The normal maintenance performed on the van (i.e., the various repairs) should not be capitalized. Normal maintenance does not enhance the service potential of the van, it serves only to maintain a given level of services from the van. On the other hand, the cost of the new engine should be capitalized because the expenditure for the new engine is nonrecurring in nature, enhances the service potential of the van, and is expected to yield benefits over a number of accounting periods.

Insurance proceeds		$ 3,500
Carrying amount, 7/1	$2,500	
Cost of new engine installed prior to conversion	700	
Carrying amount of van		(3,200)
Gain recognized on involuntary conversion		$300

37. (b)

Building carrying amount, 12/31	$250,000
Removal and clean-up costs	12,000
Amount to determine gain or loss on involuntary conversion	$262,000

Solution 4-2 ADDITIONAL MULTIPLE CHOICE ANSWERS

Valuation

38. (c) The cost of demolishing the old building (net of any scrap proceeds) is a reasonable and necessary cost to get the land ready for its intended use.

Demolition of old building on site	$ 5,000
Purchase price of land	60,000
Legal fees for contracts to purchase land	2,000
Sale of scrap from old building	(3,000)
Cost of land	$ 64,000
Architect's fees	$ 8,000
Construction cost of new building	350,000
Cost of building	$358,000

39. (d) The acquisition cost of the machine includes all of the costs incurred to get it ready for its intended use. Thus, the costs incurred in shipping, installing, and testing the machine are capitalized and added to its purchase price, resulting in an acquisition cost for the machine of $138,000 ($126,000 + $3,000 + $4,000 + $5,000).

40. (d) When several dissimilar assets are purchased for a lump sum, the amount paid should be allocated to each asset on the basis of its relative fair value. Land cost = (Total cost of assets) × (FMV of land) / Total FMV. Land = $540,000 × $200,000 / $500,000 = $216,000.

41. (d) The $16,000 fair value of the truck received is the amount that should be recorded in Amble's books because it is known and equal to or greater than the assets given up. A gain is indicated as follows:

Cash received	$ 4,000
Fair value of truck received	16,000
Total fair value received	20,000
Carrying amount of truck exchanged	(12,000)
Gain on exchange	$ 8,000

The journal entry to be recorded in Amble's books is:

Truck received	16,000	
Cash	4,000	
Truck given up		12,000
Gain		8,000

Interest

42. (c) SFAS 34 requires the capitalization of interest cost incurred during the construction of most assets having an extended construction period. Capitalized interest is included in the cost of the asset in the same manner as any other construction cost; it is then written off over the life of the asset as part of the periodic depreciation charges.

43. (b) The amount of interest cost to be capitalized is that portion of interest cost incurred during the asset's acquisition period that theoretically could have been avoided if expenditures for the asset had not been made. In this question, the amount of interest cost to be capitalized in the current year is determined by applying the interest rate on the specific new borrowing to the average accumulated expenditures for the asset in both years (SFAS 34).

Exchange

44. (b) Beam has a $1,000 gain on the exchange because the inventory it received has a fair value in excess of the consideration given up: (i.e., $20,000 + $1,000).

Book value of inventory given up	$20,000
Plus cash paid	1,000
Total consideration given up	21,000
Fair value of inventory received	22,000
Gain on exchange	$ 1,000

45. (c) In an exchange with commercial substance, the transaction is accounted for at the fair value of the asset received or the asset given up, whichever is more clearly evident, and a gain or loss is recognized on the exchange.

Fair value of land given up	$140,000
Plus cash paid	50,000
Total consideration given up	$190,000

Nonreciprocal Transfer

46. (d) A transfer of a nonmonetary asset to a stockholder or to another entity in a nonreciprocal transfer should be recorded at the fair value of the asset transferred, and a gain or loss should be recognized on the disposition of the asset.

Post-Acquisition Costs

47. (a) All of the expenditures related to the purchase of the new machine ($75,000 + $14,000) and the rearrangement of the assembly line to install this machine ($40,000 + $18,000) should be capitalized. The costs associated with the rearrangement of the assembly line are capitalized because the rearrangement has resulted in significantly more efficient production, the benefits of which extend beyond the current period.

48. (a) The replacement of the boiler with a more efficient boiler is a betterment (or improvement) as it is the substitution of a better asset for an existing

asset. The amounts associated with the old boiler do *not* affect the new boiler acquisition cost.

Purchase price	$60,000
Plus: Installation cost	8,000
Acquisition cost	$68,000

Straight-Line Depreciation

49. (d) At the end of the estimated useful life of a depreciable plant asset, the amount of accumulated depreciation would equal the depreciable base of the plant asset (i.e., its acquisition cost less any estimated salvage value), regardless of the depreciation method used.

SYD Depreciation

50. (b)

Year 1: 4/1, year 1 to 3/31, year 2	
[5/15 × ($300,000 – $0)]	$100,000
Year 2: 4/1, year 2 to 3/31, year 3	
[4/15 × ($300,000 – $0)]	80,000
Accumulated depreciation, 3/31, year 3	$180,000

DDB Depreciation

51. (b) Under the double-declining-balance method of depreciation, a rate equal to twice the straight-line rate (e.g., 2 × 10%) is applied against the remaining carrying amount of the plant asset (i.e., cost – accumulated depreciation). Salvage value is ignored, except that the plant asset cannot be depreciated below this amount.

Current year depreciation expense	
[($240,000 – $0) × 20%]	$48,000
Second year depreciation expense	
[($240,000 – $48,000) × 20%]	38,400

52. (c) Because the purchase price of the machine is not given, there are two options: (1) determine depreciation as a percent or fraction of the unknown cost of the machine "x," or (2) plug in any value for the cost of the machine, and then simply compute depreciation under both methods based on this amount. We chose to assign to the machine a $200 cost and a $30 salvage value (i.e., 15%).

SYD Yr. 1: 4/10 × ($200 – $30) = $ 68
SYD Yr. 2: 3/10 × ($200 – $30) = $ 51

DDB Yr. 1: 2/4 × ($200 – $0) = $100
DDB Yr. 2: 2/4 × ($200 – $100) = $ 50

Multiple Asset Depreciation

53. (b) Under the composite or group method of depreciation, no gain or loss is recognized upon the retirement of a plant asset. This practice is justified because some assets will be retired before the average service life and others after the average service life. Accumulated depreciation is debited for the difference between original cost and the cash received; no gain or loss is recorded on the disposition. The net carrying amount of these composite asset accounts is decreased by the cash proceeds received of $3,000 (cost removed of $18,000 minus accumulated depreciation removed of $15,000).

Cash	3,000	
Accumulated Depreciation	15,000	
Truck		18,000
To record sale of truck.		

Disposals

54. (b) Weir's *Accumulated Depreciation* account increased by $30,000 ($400,000 – $370,000) during year 2, despite the fact that $55,000 of depreciation expense was recorded during year 2. Therefore, the debit to accumulated depreciation during year 2 because of plant and equipment retirements was $25,000 (i.e., 55,000 – $30,000).

55. (a) The amount of cost that should be used to determine the gain on condemnation is $581,000 (i.e., the property's carrying amount of $575,000 plus the $2,500 appraisal fee plus the $3,500 attorney fees for the closing with the state). The attorney fees to review the contract and the title insurance are costs of acquiring the replacement property.

56. (a) The condemnation of the forest land represents an example of an involuntary conversion of a nonmonetary asset to a monetary asset. FASB Interpretation 30 requires that any gain or loss realized on the property converted be recognized in income even though the enterprise reinvests or is obligated to reinvest the monetary assets in replacement nonmonetary assets. Since any gain or loss realized on the property converted is recognized in income, the replacement nonmonetary asset is recorded at cost. Because the cost of the replacement forest land exceeds the condemnation award which exceeds the condemned forest land's carrying amount, the debit to *Forest Land* to record the cost of the replacement property exceeds the credit to *Forest Land* to remove the carrying amount of the condemned property, and, thus, the carrying amount of *Forest Land* in the balance sheet increases by the amount of this excess.

PERFORMANCE BY SUBTOPICS

Each category below parallels a subtopic covered in Chapter 4. Record the number and percentage of questions you correctly answered in each subtopic area.

Valuation

Question #	Correct √
1	
2	
3	
4	
# Questions	4
# Correct	
% Correct	

Interest

Question #	Correct √
5	
6	
7	
8	
# Questions	4
# Correct	
% Correct	

Exchange

Question #	Correct √
9	
10	
11	
12	
13	
14	
# Questions	6
# Correct	
% Correct	

Nonreciprocal Transfer

Question #	Correct √
15	
# Questions	1
# Correct	
% Correct	

Post-Acquisition Costs

Question #	Correct √
16	
17	
18	
19	
# Questions	4
# Correct	
% Correct	

Straight-Line Depreciation

Question #	Correct √
20	
21	
# Questions	2
# Correct	
% Correct	

SYD Depreciation

Question #	Correct √
22	
23	
24	
# Questions	3
# Correct	
% Correct	

DDB Depreciation

Question #	Correct √
25	
26	
27	
# Questions	3
# Correct	
% Correct	

Multiple Asset Depreciation

Question #	Correct √
28	
29	
# Questions	2
# Correct	
% Correct	

Variable Charge Methods

Question #	Correct √
30	
31	
32	
# Questions	3
# Correct	
% Correct	

Depletion

Question #	Correct √
33	
# Questions	1
# Correct	
% Correct	

Impairment

Question #	Correct √
34	
35	
# Questions	2
# Correct	
% Correct	

Disposals

Question #	Correct √
36	
37	
# Questions	2
# Correct	
% Correct	

SIMULATION SOLUTIONS

Solution 4-3

Research

I67 Summary

Interest cost shall be capitalized as part of the historical cost of acquiring certain assets. To qualify for interest capitalization, assets must require a period of time to get them ready for their intended use. Examples are assets that an enterprise constructs for its own use (such as facilities) and assets intended for sale or lease that are constructed as discrete projects (such as ships or real estate projects). Interest capitalization is required for those assets if its effect, compared with the effect of expensing interest, is material. If the net effect is not material, interest capitalization is not required. However, interest cannot be capitalized for inventories that are routinely manufactured or otherwise produced in large quantities on a repetitive basis, or on qualifying assets acquired using gifts or grants that are restricted by the donor or grantor to acquisition of those assets to the extent that funds are available from such gifts or grants.

Responses 1-14—Acquisition Costs/Depreciation Methods

1. C The freight charges should be capitalized as an inventory cost because all reasonable and necessary costs of bringing goods for sale to their existing condition and location should be included in inventory.

2. C Since title to goods purchased F.O.B. shipping point passes when the goods are shipped, the purchaser incurs any in-transit insurance charges on the goods. In-transit insurance charges should be capitalized as an inventory cost because all reasonable and necessary costs of bringing goods for sale to their existing condition and location should be included in inventory.

3. E Interest cost should not be capitalized for inventories routinely manufactured or otherwise produced on a repetitive basis (SFAS 34, ¶10). Therefore, interest cost on the note payable for goods held for resale should be expensed as a period cost.

4. C Expenditures to install equipment should be capitalized because the capitalized cost of equipment includes all reasonable and necessary costs of preparing the equipment for its intended use.

5. C Expenditures to test newly-purchased equipment should be capitalized because the capitalized cost of equipment includes all reasonable and necessary costs of preparing the equipment for its intended use.

6. E The cost of the current year service contract on the equipment should be expensed as a period cost. Expenditures to maintain plant assets in operating condition should be charged to repair and maintenance expense.

7. $600,000

The cost of the office building and land on which it is located is $1,000,000, the sum of the $800,000 cash payment made and the $200,000 existing mortgage assumed by Link. Since 60% of the property tax assessment on the building and land is allocated to the building, it can be inferred that the fair value of the building is 60% of the sum of the fair values of the building and the land. Thus, Link should record the building at $600,000, 60% of the $1,000,000 cost of the building and land.

8. $503,000

At the inception of a capital lease, the lessee records an asset and the corresponding lease liability at the lesser of the present value of the minimum lease payments or the fair value of the leased property. Although the lessor's implicit rate in the lease of 8% is lower than the lessee's incremental borrowing rate of 9%, it is not known to the lessee. Therefore, the present value of the minimum lease payments should be computed using the lessee's incremental borrowing rate of 9%. The leased equipment is recorded at the present value of the minimum lease payments of $503,000 (i.e., $100,000 × 5.03) because this amount is less than the $515,000 fair value of the equipment.

9. $500,000

In an exchange with commercial substance, the transaction is recorded at the fair value of the asset received or the asset given up, whichever is greater (more clearly evident), and a gain or loss is recognized on the exchange.

Book value of land given up	$320,000
Cash paid	50,000
Total consideration given up	370,000
Fair value of land received	500,000
Gain on exchange of land	$130,000

10. $450,000

In an exchange with commercial substance, the transaction is recorded at the fair value of the asset received or the asset given up, whichever is greater (more clearly evident), and a gain or loss is recognized on the exchange.

FV of land received	$450,000
Cash received	50,000
Total consideration received	500,000
Book value of land given up	350,000
Gain on exchange of land	$150,000

11. $90,000

Cost of machine	$864,000
Less: Estimated salvage value	(144,000)
Depreciable base of machine	720,000
Divide by: Estimated useful life in years	/ 8
Annual depreciation charge	$ 90,000

12. $162,000

Under the double-declining-balance method (DDB), the depreciation charge for the first year must be computed before the depreciation charge for the second year can be computed.

Cost of machine, 1/2, year 1	$ 864,000
Less: Accumulated depreciation, 1/2, year 1	(0)
Carrying amount of machine, 1/2, year 1	864,000
Times: Twice the SL rate [(100% / 8) × 2]	× 25%
Depreciation charge for year 1	$ 216,000

Cost of machine, 1/2, year 1	$ 864,000
Less: Accumulated depreciation, 1/1, year 2	(216,000)
Carrying amount of machine, 1/1, year 2	648,000
Times: Twice the SL rate	× 25%
Depreciation charge for year 2	$ 162,000

13. $140,000

Cost of machine, 1/2, year 1	$864,000
Less: Estimated salvage value	(144,000)
Depreciable base of machine	720,000
Times: Fraction for second year of 8 year life*	× 7/36
Depreciation charge for year 2	$140,000

* The numerator of the fraction is the number of years of useful life remaining at 1/1, year 2 (i.e., 8 – 1). The denominator is the sum of the years of the estimated useful life of the machine.

14. $120,000

Cost of machine	$ 864,000
Less: Estimated salvage value	(144,000)
Depreciable base of machine	720,000
Divide by: Estimated useful life in units	/ 1,800,000
Depreciation charge per unit of output	0.40
Times: Units produced in year 2	× 300,000
Depreciation charge recorded for year 2	$ 120,000

Solution 4-4

Research

I67.107

.107 Land that is not undergoing activities necessary to get it ready for its intended use is not a qualifying asset. If activities are undertaken for the purpose of developing land for a particular use, the expenditures to acquire the land qualify for interest capitalization while those activities are in progress. The interest cost capitalized on those expenditures is a cost of acquiring the asset that results from those activities. If the resulting asset is a structure, such as a plant or a shopping center, interest capitalized on the land expenditures is part of the acquisition cost of the structure. If the resulting asset is developed land, such as land that is to be sold as developed lots, interest capitalized on the land expenditures is part of the acquisition cost of the developed land. [FAS34, ¶11]

Responses 1-8—Acquisition Costs

1. L The purchase price of the land should be capitalized in the *Land* account.

2. E The interest cost on the construction financing incurred *after* completion of the construction should be expensed. Interest capitalization ceases when the asset is substantially complete and ready for its intended use (SFAS 34, ¶18).

3. B The new office building requires a period of time to get it ready for its intended use. Therefore, the interest cost on the construction financing incurred during the construction period should be capitalized as part of the historical cost of constructing the building.

4. L Where a building is to be constructed on a newly acquired site with an existing building on it, the amount paid for the existing building should be capitalized in the Land account.

5. L The payment of accrued or delinquent property taxes on the land at the time of purchase should be capitalized in the Land account.

6. B The liability insurance premium incurred during the construction period should be capitalized in the Building account because it was a reasonable and necessary cost of constructing the building.

7. L Since the existing building was torn down to prepare the site for the new building, the cost of demolition of the existing building, less any salvage proceeds, is a cost of getting the land ready for its intended use and should be included in the cost of the land.

8. E The moving costs should be expensed as incurred; they should not be included in the cost of the land or building.

Essay—Depreciation & Nonmonetary Exchanges

a. Portland should have selected the straight-line depreciation method when approximately the **same amount of an asset's service potential is used up each period.** If the reasons for the decline in service potential are unclear, then the selection of the straight-line method could be influenced by the **ease of record keeping,** its use for **similar assets,** and its use by **others in the industry.**

b. Portland should record **depreciation expense to the date** of the exchange. If the **original** truck's **carrying amount is greater than its fair value,** a **loss** results. The truck's **capitalized cost** and **accumulated depreciation** are **eliminated,** and the loss on the trade-in is reported as part of **income from continuing operations.** The newly acquired truck is recorded at fair value. If the original truck's **carrying amount is less than its fair value** at trade-in, then there is an **unrecognized gain.** The newly acquired truck is recorded at **fair value less the unrecognized gain. Cash** is **decreased** by the **amount paid.**

c. 1. By associating depreciation with a group of machines instead of each individual machine, Portland's **bookkeeping** process is greatly **simplified.** Also, since actual **machine lives vary** from the average depreciable life, **unrecognized net losses** on **early dispositions** are expected to be **offset** by **continuing depreciation** on machines **usable beyond** the **average** depreciable life. Periodic income does not fluctuate as a result of recognizing gains and losses on manufacturing machine dispositions.

2. Portland should **divide the depreciable cost** (capitalized cost less residual value) of each machine by its **estimated life** to obtain its annual depreciation. The **sum** of the individual annual depreciation amounts should then be **divided by** the **sum of the individual capitalized costs** to obtain the annual composite depreciation rate.

Solution 4-5

Response 1—Accounting Treatment Tab

	A	B	C
1	**Asset**	**Cost**	**Accounting treatment**
2	Cost of parking lot for new warehouse	$8,500	Capitalize and depreciate
3	Painting all of the ceiling tiles in the hallways and common areas of the property	$8,500	Expense at time incurred
4	Replace the cooling system in the company's current facility with a more modern and fuel efficient model.	$33,000	Capitalize and depreciate
5	15 new desk-top computers for support personnel	$22,500	Capitalize and depreciate
6	New process costing software—this software will need to be replaced in 5 years	$12,000	Capitalize and amortize
7	Replacing office windows cracked as a result of an explosion at a neighboring manufacturing plant.	$16,000	Expense at time incurred

Response 2—Capitalized Cost Tab

		A	B
1	**Land for the new warehouse**		
2	X	Purchase price	$325,000
3	X	Demolition of existing structures on property	120,000
4	X	Proceeds from the sale of scrap from the old buildings on the site	65,000
5		Costs incurred to grade and pave driveways and parking lots	40,000
6		Lawn and garden sprinkler systems for the property	18,500
7	X	Legal fees incurred to purchase the property and paid at settlement	24,000
8		**Capitalized cost of the land**	$404,000
9	**Construction of new warehouse**		
10		Construction began March 15 and ended August 31	
11		Borrowings to finance construction	$265,000
12	X	Interest incurred from 3/15 through 8/31	11,000
13		Interest incurred from 9/1 through 12/31	8,500
14	X	Total cost of labor, materials, and overhead to construct the warehouse	305,000
15		Costs incurred to grade and pave driveways and parking lots	40,000
16		Costs to repair water line ruptured during excavation	8,000
17		**Capitalized cost of the warehouse**	$316,000
18	**New machine**		
19	X	Cost of machine	$ 36,000
20	X	Sales tax paid on machine	2,100
21	X	Installation costs	3,700
22		Finance charges on purchase loan	2,900
23		**Capitalized cost of the new machine**	$ 41,800

Editor's Note: Items marked "X" are included in the related calculations.

Select Hot•Spots™ Video Descriptions

CPA 3255 Cash, Receivables & Marketable Securities
This video program provides comprehensive coverage of cash and cash equivalents, accounts and notes receivable, investments in marketable debt and equity securities, fair value disclosure of financial instruments, derivative financial instruments and hedging activities...and more!

CPA 3248 Inventory, Fixed Assets & Intangible Assets
This program provides extensive coverage of accounting for inventory, including measurement, valuation, cost flow assumptions, lower of cost or market, and estimation methods. Specific identification, moving and weighted averages, FIFO, and LIFO are illustrated under periodic and perpetual methods. Fixed asset capitalization, classification, exchange, cost recovery, and impairment are illustrated with several examples. Intangible assets, research and development, and other related topics are also covered.

Call our customer representatives toll-free at 1 (800) 874-7877 for more details about videos.

Subject to Change Without Notice

CHAPTER 5

INTANGIBLE ASSETS, R&D COSTS & OTHER ASSETS

I. Intangible Assets 5-2

A. Overview 5-2

B. Initial Recognition & Measurement 5-3

C. After Acquisition 5-3

D. Presentation 5-5

II. Research & Development (SFAS 2) 5-5

A. Overview 5-5

B. Accounting 5-6

C. Disclosures 5-7

III. Computer Software 5-7

A. To Be Sold, Leased, or Otherwise Marketed (SFAS 86) 5-7

B. Developed or Obtained for Internal Use (SOP 98-1) 5-8

IV. Other Assets 5-9

A. Prepaid Expenses 5-9

B. Cash Surrender Value of Life Insurance Policies 5-9

C. Special Purpose Funds 5-10

EXAM COVERAGE: Historically, exam coverage of the topics in Chapter 5 has been 2 to 7 percent of the FAR section. More information regarding exam coverage is included in Appendix B, *Practical Advice.*

CHAPTER 5

INTANGIBLE ASSETS, R&D COSTS & OTHER ASSETS

I. Intangible Assets

A. Overview

Intangible assets are assets without physical substance that provide economic benefits through the rights and privileges associated with their possession. While goodwill is an intangible asset, the term intangible asset is used to refer to an intangible asset other that goodwill. Intangibles may be classified as identifiable or unidentifiable and externally acquired or internally developed. Examples of identifiable intangible assets include patents, franchises, licenses, leaseholds, leasehold improvements, copyrights, and trademarks.

1. **Patent** A patent represents a special right to a particular product or process that has value to the holder of the right. Only the external acquisition costs of a patent are capitalized; research and development costs incurred to internally develop a patent are expensed as incurred. In addition, the cost of a competing patent acquired to protect an existing patent and the cost of a successful legal defense of an existing patent also should be capitalized. The cost of an unsuccessful defense, along with any amounts previously capitalized for the patent, is expensed in the period in which an unfavorable court decision is rendered.

2. **Franchise** A franchise represents a special right to operate under the name and guidance of another enterprise over a limited geographic area. A franchise is always externally purchased; it cannot be internally developed. Capitalize all significant costs incurred to acquire the franchise (e.g., purchase price, legal fees, etc.). If the acquisition cost of the franchise requires future cash payments, these payments should be capitalized at their present value using an appropriate interest rate. On the other hand, periodic service fees charged as a percentage of revenues are not capitalized; these costs represent a current operating expense of the franchisee.

3. **License** A license is a permit issued by a governmental agency allowing an entity to conduct business in a certain specified geographical area. Capitalize significant costs incurred to acquire the license and amortize the cost over the lesser of its useful or legal life.

4. **Leasehold** A leasehold is a right to use rented properties, usually for a number of years. In some situations, for example, a ten-year lease may require the immediate cash payment of the annual rent for the first and tenth years. The prepayment of the rent for the tenth year would be recorded as a leasehold and would be classified as an intangible asset until the tenth year, when it would be charged to rent expense.

5. **Leasehold Improvement** A leasehold improvement is an improvement made by the lessee to leased property for which benefits are expected beyond the current accounting period. Leasehold improvements are not separable from the leased property and revert to the lessor at the end of the lease term. The cost of leasehold improvements should be capitalized and amortized over the lesser of their estimated useful life or the remaining term of the lease. If a lease has a renewal option, which the lessee intends to exercise, the leasehold improvement should be amortized over the *lesser* of its estimated useful life or the sum of the remaining term of the lease **and** the period covered by the renewal option.

6. **Copyright** A copyright is an exclusive right granted by the federal government giving the owner protection against the illegal reproduction by others of the owner's written works, designs, and literary productions. Although the copyright period is for the life of the creator plus 70 years, the cost of a copyright should be amortized over its useful life.

7. **Trademark** A trademark is a symbol, design, or logo that is used in conjunction with a particular product, service, or enterprise. Generally, only the external acquisition costs of trademarks are capitalized; internal acquisition costs usually are expensed when incurred. Amortize any capitalized costs over the useful life of the trademark.

B. Initial Recognition & Measurement

1. **Externally Acquired** Acquired intangible assets initially are recognized and measured based on fair value, except those acquired in a business combination. If acquired as a group of assets, the cost is allocated to individual assets based on their relative fair values, without recognizing goodwill. Intangible assets acquired in a business combination are discussed in the chapter on consolidated financial statements.

2. **Internally Developed** The costs of internally developing, maintaining, or restoring intangible assets (including goodwill) that are not specifically identifiable and that have indeterminate lives, are expensed when incurred.

C. After Acquisition

1. **Finite Useful Life** An intangible asset with a finite useful life is amortized. Intangible assets with finite useful lives are amortized over their useful lives, without the constraint of an arbitrary ceiling. The useful life is the period over which the asset is expected to contribute directly or indirectly to future cash flows. The estimate of the useful life should take into consideration all pertinent factors, including the expected use of the asset by the entity; any legal, regulatory, or contractual provisions that may limit the useful life and such provisions that might result in renewal or extension of the useful life without substantial cost; the effects of obsolescence, demand, competition, and other economic factors; and the expected maintenance expenditures required.

   a. **Amortization Period** An intangible asset shall be amortized over the best estimate of its useful life.

   b. **Amortization Method** The method of amortization should reflect the pattern in which the economic benefits are consumed or used up. If that pattern cannot be reliably determined, a straight-line amortization shall be used.

   c. **Residual Value** The amount of an intangible asset to be amortized shall be the amount initially assigned to the asset less any residual value.

   d. **Reevaluation** Each reporting period, the remaining useful life should be evaluated to determine whether events and circumstances warrant a revision to the remaining period of amortization.

      (1) If the remaining useful life changes, the remaining amount of the intangible asset should be amortized prospectively over the revised remaining useful life.

      (2) If the remaining useful life is indefinite, the asset is no longer amortized and is tested for impairment annually.

2. **Indefinite Useful Life** An intangible asset with an indefinite useful life is not amortized. If no legal, regulatory, contractual, competitive, economic, or other factors limit the useful life, it is considered to be indefinite. The term indefinite does not mean infinite. Goodwill and intangible assets with indefinite useful lives are not amortized, but rather are tested at least annually for impairment.

3. **Impairment Loss** SFAS 142, *Goodwill and Other Intangible Assets,* requires an impairment-only approach for accounting for goodwill, rather than an amortization approach. SFAS 142 does not presume that intangible assets are wasting assets.

a. **Annually** At least annually, all intangible assets should be tested for impairment. SFAS 142 provides specific guidance on testing for impairment of intangible assets that are not amortized. The testing is done at least annually by comparing the fair values of those intangible assets with their recorded amounts.

b. **Impairment Recognition** An impairment loss is recognized if the carrying amount of an intangible asset is not recoverable and its carrying amount exceeds its fair value. After an impairment loss is recognized, the adjusted carrying amount of the asset is its new accounting basis. Subsequent reversal of a previously recognized impairment loss is prohibited.

4. **Goodwill Impairment Testing** Goodwill is tested for impairment at least annually, using a two-step process, beginning with an estimation of a reporting unit's fair value. If certain criteria are met, the annual requirement can be satisfied without a remeasurement of the reporting unit's fair value. The goodwill impairment test may be performed any time during the fiscal year, provided the test is performed at the same time every year.

a. **Reporting Unit** Accounting for goodwill is based on reporting units, (the units of the combined entity into which an acquired entity is integrated) as an aggregate view of goodwill. Goodwill is tested for impairment at a reporting unit level. A reporting unit is an operating segment or one level below an operating segment, referred to as a component. A component of an operating segment is a reporting unit if the component constitutes a business for which discrete financial information is available and segment management regularly reviews the operating results of that component.

b. **Two-Step Impairment Test** The first step is a screen for potential impairment, and the second step measures the amount of impairment, if any.

(1) **Step One** The first step used to identify potential impairment compares reporting unit's fair value with its carrying amount, including goodwill. If the fair value exceeds its carrying amount, the reporting unit's goodwill is considered not impaired and the second step is unnecessary. If the carrying amount exceeds its fair value, the second step is performed.

Compare carrying amt with fair value

- **Fair Value Measurements** The fair value is the amount at which the asset could be bought or sold in a current transaction between willing parties. Quoted market prices are the best evidence of fair value and should be used if available. Otherwise, the best information available should be used, including prices for similar assets and results of using other valuation techniques, such as present value. The estimates should be based on reasonable and supportable assumptions and consider all available evidence. If a range is estimated, the likelihood of possible outcomes shall be considered. Other techniques include multiples of earnings or revenue or similar performance measurements.

(2) **Step Two** The second step compares the implied fair value of reporting unit's goodwill with its carrying amount. If the carrying amount exceeds the implied fair value of that goodwill, an impairment loss is recognized in an amount equal to that excess. The loss recognized cannot exceed the goodwill's carrying amount. After an impairment loss is recognized, the adjusted carrying amount of goodwill is its new accounting basis. Subsequent reversal of a previously recognized goodwill impairment loss is prohibited.

compare implied FV with carrying amt

D. Presentation

Goodwill is presented as a separate line item. At a minimum, all other intangible assets are aggregated and presented as a separate line item in the statement of financial position. This does not preclude presentation of more detailed information.

1. **Expense & Losses** The amortization expense and impairment losses for intangible assets are presented in income statement line items within continuing operations. Goodwill impairment losses are presented as a separate line item in the income statement before the subtotal of income from continuing operations unless the impairment is associated with a discontinued operation. An impairment loss resulting from impairment testing is **not** recognized as a change in accounting principle.

2. **Disclosures**

   a. **Acquisition Period**

      (1) **Intangible Assets Subject to Amortization** The total amount assigned and the amount assigned to any major intangible asset class, the amount of any significant residual value and the weighted-average amortization period, in total and by major intangible asset class.

      (2) **Intangible Assets Not Subject to Amortization** The total amount assigned and the amount assigned to any major intangible asset class.

      (3) **Other Information** The amount of research and development assets acquired and written off in the period and the line item in the income statement in which the amounts written off are aggregated.

   b. **Subsequent Periods** Disclosures include the carrying amount of intangible assets by major intangible asset class for those assets subject to amortization and for those not subject to amortization.

      (1) **Intangible Assets Subject to Amortization** The gross carrying amount and accumulated amortization, in total and by major intangible asset class, the aggregate amortization expense for the period, and the estimated aggregate amortization expense for each of the five succeeding fiscal years.

      (2) **Intangible Assets Not Subject to Amortization** The total carrying amount and the carrying amount for each major intangible asset class.

      (3) **Goodwill** Information about the changes in the carrying amount of goodwill from period to period (in the aggregate and by reportable segment), the aggregate amount of impairment losses recognized, and the amount of goodwill included in the gain or loss on disposal of all or a portion of a reporting unit.

   c. **Periods When Impairment Loss is Recognized** The disclosures for periods that impairment loss is recognized include descriptions of the impaired asset, the facts and circumstances leading to the impairment, the amount of the impairment loss and the method for determining fair value, the caption in the income statement that includes the impairment loss, and any other potentially significant information.

II. Research & Development (SFAS 2)

A. Overview

Research activities are those aimed at the discovery of knowledge that will be useful in developing or significantly improving products or processes. *Development* activities are those concerned with translating research findings and other knowledge into plans or designs for new or significantly improved products or processes.

1. **R&D Examples** Examples of activities that are typically included in R&D

   a. Laboratory research aimed at discovery of new knowledge

   b. Searching for applications of new research findings or other knowledge

   c. Conceptual formulation and design of product or process alternatives

   d. Testing in search for or evaluation of product or process alternatives

   e. Modification of the formulation or design of a product or process

   f. Design, construction, and testing of pre-production prototypes and models

   g. Design of tools, jigs, molds, and dies involving new technology

   h. Pilot plant costs if **not** of a scale economically feasible for commercial production

   i. Engineering activities until product meets specific functional and economic requirements and is ready for manufacture

2. **Non-R&D Examples** Examples of activities that are excluded from R&D

   a. Engineering follow-through in early stages of commercial production

   b. Quality control during commercial production including routine testing of products

   c. Troubleshooting in connection with breakdowns during commercial production

   d. Routine, ongoing efforts to improve existing products

   e. Adaptation of existing capability to meet particular requirements or customer's needs as part of continuing commercial activity

   f. Seasonal or other periodic design changes to existing products

   g. Routine design of tools, jigs, molds, and dies

   h. Construction, relocation, rearrangement, or start-up activities (including design and construction engineering) of facilities or equipment other than (1) pilot plants; and (2) facilities or equipment whose only use is for a particular R&D project

   i. Legal work to secure, sell, or license patents

B. Accounting

1. **Expense R&D Costs** Future economic benefits deriving from R&D activities, if any, are uncertain in their amount and timing. Due to these uncertainties, SFAS 2, *Accounting for Research and Development Costs,* requires that most R&D costs be charged to expense the year in which incurred. Capitalization of R&D costs, except as indicated below, is not acceptable.

2. **Alternative Future Uses** Materials, equipment, facilities, or intangibles purchased from others that are acquired for a particular R&D project and have *no alternative use* in other R&D projects or in normal operations should be *expensed* in the period in which acquired. However, these items should be recorded as *assets* if *alternative future uses* are expected, whether in other R&D activities or in normal operations. Assets recorded for R&D costs with alternative future uses should be amortized over their useful lives by periodic charges to R&D expense. If, at any point, these assets are no longer deemed to have alternative future uses, the remaining unamortized cost is charged to R&D expense for the period.

Example 1 ▸ Research & Development

In the current year, Futura Inc. began an extensive research and development program. The following R&D related costs were incurred during the year:

Jan. 2:	Purchase of general purpose lab building (10-year life)	$150,000
Jan. 5:	Purchase of general purpose lab equipment (5-year life)	25,000
Jan. 7:	Purchase of a machine to be used exclusively on Project X (4-year life)	8,000
Jan. 30:	Acquired materials and supplies, as follows:	
	Materials to be used in Project X	10,000
	Miscellaneous lab supplies for several projects	12,000

In addition, $40,000 of direct labor costs was incurred on various R&D projects and $3,000 of overhead costs was appropriately allocated to R&D activities during the year. All but $4,000 of the materials purchased for Project X and $5,000 of the general purpose supplies were consumed during the year.

Required: Determine Futura's R&D expense for the year.

Solution: The cost of equipment and materials to be used on a single R&D project (i.e., having no alternative future uses) should be expensed as R&D when incurred.

Depreciation on lab building ($150,000 / 10)	$15,000
Depreciation on general purpose lab equipment ($25,000 / 5)	5,000
Machine to be used exclusively on Project X	8,000
Materials for Project X	10,000
Miscellaneous lab supplies ($12,000 – $5,000)	7,000
Direct labor	40,000
Appropriately allocated overhead	3,000
Total R&D expense for the year	$88,000

3. **Other Issues** R&D costs conducted for others under contract may be carried as assets. Contractually reimbursable R&D costs are not expensed as R&D (SFAS 2).

C. Disclosures

Total R&D costs expensed in each period for which an income statement is presented must be clearly disclosed.

III. Computer Software

A. To Be Sold, Leased, or Otherwise Marketed (SFAS 86)

1. **R&D Costs** Costs incurred internally in creating a computer software product are charged to expense when incurred as research and development until technological feasibility has been established for the product. Technological feasibility is established only upon completion of a detailed program design or, in its absence, completion of a working model. All costs of planning, designing, coding, and testing activities that are necessary to establish technological feasibility are expensed as research and development when incurred.

2. **Production Costs** The costs of producing product masters incurred subsequent to establishing technological feasibility are capitalized. Capitalized software costs are amortized on a product-by-product basis. These costs include coding and testing performed subsequent to establishing technological feasibility. Capitalization of computer software costs ceases when the product is available for general release to customers. Capitalized software production costs are reported at the lower of unamortized cost or net realizable value.

3. **Inventory Costs** Costs incurred for (1) duplicating the computer software and training materials from product masters and (2) physically packaging the product for distribution are capitalized as inventory. Capitalized inventory costs are expensed when the inventory is sold.

4. **Amount to Amortize** The annual amortization is the **greater** of the amount computed using the percent of revenue or the straight-line approach.

   a. **Percent of Revenue** The ratio that current gross revenues for a software product bear to the total of current and anticipated future gross revenue for that product

   b. **Straight-Line** The straight-line method over the remaining estimated economic life of the product, including the current period

Greater amortisation charge.

Example 2 ▶ Amortization Expense

On December 31 of last year, the Clone Company had $200,000 of capitalized costs for a new computer software product with an economic useful life of five years. Sales for this year were thirty percent of expected total sales of the software.

Required: Determine the amortization expense for this year.

Solution: Under the percent of revenue approach, the amortization expense for this year would be $60,000 ($200,000 × 30%). Under the straight-line approach, the amortization would be $40,000 ($200,000 / 5 years). The amortization for this year is $60,000, determined under the percent of revenue approach, because it results in a greater amortization charge.

5. **When to Begin** Amortization starts when the product is available for release to customers.

B. **Developed or Obtained for Internal Use (SOP 98-1)**

1. **Preliminary Project Stage** Computer software costs that are incurred in the preliminary project stage should be expensed as incurred. Activities in this stage include conceptual formulation and evaluation of alternatives, determination of existence of needed technology, and final selection of alternatives.

2. **Application Development Stage**

   a. **Capitalized Costs** Most costs in this stage are capitalized, including external direct costs, payroll and payroll-related costs for those who are directly involved with the project, and interest costs. Activities in this stage include design of the chosen path, design of the software configuration, coding, installation to hardware, and testing. Capitalization of the costs should cease when the software project is substantially complete and ready for its intended use, which generally is after all substantial testing is completed.

   b. **Expensed Costs** Training costs and data conversion costs are generally expensed.

3. **Post-Implementation/Operation Stage**

   a. **Costs** Internal and external training and maintenance costs should be expensed as incurred. The costs of upgrades are capitalized.

   b. **Amortization** Capitalized costs are amortized over the estimated useful life, and adjusted periodically with changes in the estimates of the useful life or when the value of the asset is impaired.

   c. **Other Considerations** If, after the development of internal-use software is completed, the entity decides to market the software, net proceeds received from the license should be applied against the carrying amount of the software.

IV. Other Assets

A. Prepaid Expenses

Under accrual accounting, revenues and expenses are recognized when earned or incurred, respectively. Thus when a firm pays in advance for a good or service such as insurance, rent, interest, etc., the cost of the item is first recorded as an asset—*Prepaid Expense.*

Example 3 ▸ Prepaid Insurance

On April 1, Denso Co. purchased for $120,000 a 4-year blanket casualty insurance policy covering all its buildings, equipment, and inventory. Denso is a calendar year corporation that issues a classified balance sheet.

Required: Provide the journal entries if Denso Co. initially records this policy as an asset and as an expense. Show the proper balance sheet presentation at December 31.

Solution: Premium, $120,000 / Number of months, 48 = Monthly expense, $2,500

1. Journal entries if initially recorded as an asset

4/1	Prepaid Insurance	120,000	
	Cash		120,000
12/31	Insurance Expense ($2,500/month × 9 months)	22,500	
	Prepaid Insurance		22,500

2. Journal entries if initially recorded as an expense

4/1	Insurance Expense	120,000	
	Cash		120,000
12/31	Prepaid Insurance [$120,000 – ($2,500 × 9)]	97,500	
	Insurance Expense		97,500

3. Balance sheet presentation, December 31

Current Assets	
Prepaid insurance (12 mos. × $2,500)	$30,000
Noncurrent Assets	
Prepaid insurance (27 mos. × $2,500)	$67,500

1. **Current vs. Noncurrent** In a classified balance sheet, a prepaid expense should be separated into a current and a noncurrent portion. In general, the current portion of the prepaid expense is the amount that expires within the next 12 months.

2. **Realized Expense** As the benefits from the prepayment are realized (i.e., the costs expire), the prepaid expenses are reduced and charged to an appropriate expense account, such as insurance expense, rent expense, interest expense, etc.

B. Cash Surrender Value of Life Insurance Policies

Companies frequently insure the lives of key executives. Insurance premiums paid on many such life insurance policies consist of an amount for life insurance and a balance that constitutes a form of savings. The savings portion is manifested in the growing cash surrender value (amount realizable by the owner of the policy should the policy be canceled). Cash surrender value of life insurance policies are usually classified as noncurrent assets, among *Investments and Funds.*

1. **Asset** The savings portion is manifested in the growing *cash surrender value* or amount realizable by the owner of the policy should the policy be canceled. Cash surrender value of life insurance policies are usually classified as noncurrent assets, among Investments and Funds.

2. **Expense** The amount to be reported as life insurance expense for a year is the annual premium paid, less (a) the increase in cash surrender value and (b) any dividends received.

C. **Special Purpose Funds**

These funds result from the setting aside of specific assets, usually under the custody of a trustee for a particular purpose. Some funds may be voluntarily created, such as preferred stock acquisition funds and plant expansion funds. Other funds result from contractual obligations, such as debt retirement funds. The funds may or may not be under the custody of a separate trustee. The accounting depends on the specific nature of the fund, legal requirements, etc.

1. **Asset** The fund initially is established by crediting cash or other assets and debiting the fund account. The fund is affected by (a) additions or withdrawals to the fund, (b) earnings on the fund, (c) gains or losses on the disposal of assets in the fund, and (d) expenses of operating the fund. The exchange of one asset for another within the fund (such as the exchange of cash for an investment) will not have any net effect on the balance of the fund. The fund balance at the end of the period is presented as a net amount, a separate line item, generally under *Investments and Funds.*

2. **Expense** The fund accounts for its own investments and generally records its own revenues and expenses.

CHAPTER 5—INTANGIBLE ASSETS, R&D COSTS & OTHER ASSETS

Problem 5-1 MULTIPLE CHOICE QUESTIONS (64 to 80 minutes)

1. Which of the following statements concerning patents is correct?
   a. Legal costs incurred to successfully defend an internally developed patent should be capitalized and amortized over the patent's remaining economic life.
   b. Legal fees and other direct costs incurred in registering a patent should be capitalized and amortized on a straight-line basis over a five-year period.
   c. Research and development contract services purchased from others and used to develop a patented manufacturing process should be capitalized and amortized over the patent's economic life.
   d. Research and development costs incurred to develop a patented item should be capitalized and amortized on a straight-line basis over 17 years. (5/93, Theory, #25, 4213)

2. On June 30, Union Inc. purchased goodwill of $125,000 when it acquired the net assets of Apex Corp. During the year, Union incurred additional costs of developing goodwill, by training Apex employees ($50,000) and hiring additional Apex employees ($25,000). Union's December 31 balance sheet should report goodwill of
   a. $200,000
   b. $175,000
   c. $150,000
   d. $125,000 (5/91, PI, #28, amended, 0998)

3. On January 2, Year 1, Lava Inc. purchased a patent for a new consumer product for $90,000. At the time of purchase, the patent was valid for 15 years; however, the patent's useful life was estimated to be only 10 years due to the competitive nature of the product. On December 31, Year 4, the product was permanently withdrawn from sale under governmental order because of a potential health hazard in the product. What amount should Lava charge against income during year 4, assuming amortization is recorded at the end of each year?
   a. $ 9,000
   b. $54,000
   c. $63,000
   d. $72,000 (11/93, PI, #54, amended, 4423)

4. Gray Co. was granted a patent on January 2, Year 1, and appropriately capitalized $45,000 of related costs. Gray was amortizing the patent over its estimated useful life of fifteen years. During year 4, Gray paid $15,000 in legal costs in successfully defending an attempted infringement of the patent. After the legal action was completed, Gray sold the patent to the plaintiff for $75,000. Gray's policy is to take no amortization in the year of disposal. In its year 4 income statement, what amount should Gray report as gain from sale of patent?
   a. $15,000
   b. $24,000
   c. $27,000
   d. $39,000 (11/95, FAR, #33, amended, 6115)

5. On January 2, Gant Co. purchased a franchise with a useful life of five years for $60,000 and an annual fee of 1% of franchise revenues. Franchise revenues were $20,000 during the year. Gant projects future revenues of $40,000 next year and $60,000 per year for the following three years. Gant uses the straight-line method of amortization. What amount should Gant report as intangible asset-franchise, net of related amortization in its December 31 balance sheet?
   a. $48,000
   b. $48,160
   c. $49,920
   d. $56,000 (R/03, FAR, #16, amended 7618)

6. On January 1, Year 1, Nobb Corp. signed a 12-year lease for warehouse space. Nobb has an option to renew the lease for an additional 8-year period on or before January 1, Year 5. During January of year 3, Nobb made substantial improvements to the warehouse. The cost of these improvements was $540,000, with an estimated useful life of 15 years. At December 31, Year 3, Nobb intended to exercise the renewal option. Nobb has taken a full year's amortization on this leasehold. In Nobb's December 31, Year 3 balance sheet, the carrying amount of this leasehold improvement should be
   a. $486,000
   b. $504,000
   c. $510,000
   d. $513,000 (5/91, PI, #25, amended, 0997)

7. Star Co. leases a building for its product showroom. The ten-year non-renewable lease will expire on December 31, Year 6. In January of year 1, Star redecorated its showroom and made leasehold improvements of $48,000. The estimated useful life of the improvements is 8 years. Star uses the straight-line method of amortization. What amount of leasehold improvements, net of amortization, should Star report in its June 30, Year 1 balance sheet?

a. $45,600
b. $45,000
c. $44,000
d. $43,200 (5/93, PI, #22, amended, 4064)

8. On January 1, Year 1, Bay Co. acquired a land lease for a 21-year period with no option to renew. The lease required Bay to construct a building in lieu of rent. The building, completed on January 1, Year 2, at a cost of $840,000, will be depreciated using the straight-line method. At the end of the lease, the building's estimated market value will be $420,000. What is the building's carrying amount in Bay's December 31, Year 2 balance sheet?

a. $798,000
b. $800,000
c. $819,000
d. $820,000 (11/91, PI, #16, amended, 2404)

9. On December 1, of the current year, Clark Co. leased office space for five years at a monthly rental of $60,000. On the same date, Clark paid the lessor the following amounts:

First months' rent	$ 60,000
Last months' rent	60,000
Security deposit (refundable at lease expiration)	80,000
Installation of new walls and offices	$360,000

What should be Clark's current year expense relating to utilization of the office space?

a. $ 60,000
b. $ 66,000
c. $120,000
d. $140,000 (11/92, PI, #56, amended, 3288)

10. On January 2, Judd Co. bought a trademark from Krug Co. for $500,000. Judd retained an independent consultant, who estimated the trademark's remaining life to be 50 years. Its unamortized cost on Krug's accounting records was $380,000. In Judd's December 31 balance sheet, what amount should be reported as accumulated amortization?

a. $ 7,600
b. $ 9,500
c. $10,000
d. $12,500 (11/93, PI, #25, amended, 4394)

11. Tech Co. bought a trademark on January 2, two years ago. Tech accounted for the copyright as instructed under the provisions of FASB #142 during the current year. The intangible was being amortized over 40 years. The carrying value at the beginning of the year was $38,000. It was determined that the cash flow will be generated indefinitely at the current level for the trademark. What amount should Tech report as amortization expense for the current year?

a. $0
b. $ 922
c. $ 1,000
d. $38,000 (R/05, FAR, 1814F, #38, 7782)

12. Which of the following is an example of activities that would typically be excluded in research and development costs?

a. Design, construction, and testing of preproduction prototypes and modes
b. Laboratory research aimed at discovery of new knowledge
c. Quality control during commercial production, including routine testing of products
d. Testing in search for, or evaluation of, product or process alternatives

(R/05, FAR, C01282F, #45, 7789)

13. During the year, Jase Co. incurred research and development costs of $136,000 in its laboratories relating to a patent that was granted on July 1. Costs of registering the patent equaled $34,000. The patent's legal life is 20 years, and its estimated economic life is 10 years. In its December 31 balance sheet, what amount should Jase report as patent, net of accumulated amortization?

a. $ 32,300
b. $ 33,000
c. $161,500
d. $165,000 (5/95, FAR, #13, amended, 5549)

14. Wizard Co. purchased two machines for $250,000 each on January 2 of the current year. The machines were put into use immediately. Machine A has a useful life of five years and can only be used in one research project. Machine B will be used for two years on a research and development project and then used by the production division for an additional eight years. Wizard uses the straightline method of depreciation. What amount should Wizard include in research and development expense for the year?

a. $ 75,000
b. $275,000
c. $375,000
d. $500,000 (11/98, FAR, #11, amended, 6738)

15. Cody Corp. incurred the following costs during the year:

Design of tools, jigs, molds, and dies involving new technology	$125,000
Modification of the formulation of a process	160,000
Troubleshooting in connection with breakdowns during commercial production	100,000
Adaptation of an existing capability to a particular customer's need as part of a continuing commercial activity	110,000

In its year-end income statement, Cody should report research and development expense of

a. $125,000
b. $160,000
c. $235,000
d. $285,000 (11/90, PI, #42, amended, 1000)

Items 16 and 17 are based on the following:

During the year, Pitt Corp. incurred costs to develop and produce a routine, low-risk computer software product, as follows:

Completion of detail program design	$13,000
Costs incurred for coding and testing to establish technological feasibility	10,000
Other coding costs after establishment of technological feasibility	24,000
Other testing costs after establishment of technological feasibility	20,000
Costs of producing product masters for training materials	15,000
Duplication of computer software and training materials from product masters (1,000 units)	25,000
Packaging product (500 units)	9,000

16. In Pitt's December 31 balance sheet, what amount should be reported in inventory?

a. $25,000
b. $34,000
c. $40,000
d. $49,000 (5/91, PI, #21, amended, 0995)

17. In Pitt's December 31 balance sheet, what amount should be capitalized as software cost, subject to amortization?

a. $54,000
b. $57,000
c. $59,000
d. $69,000 (5/91, PI, #22, amended 0996)

18. Miller Co. incurred the following computer software costs for the development and sale of software programs during the current year:

Planning costs	$ 50,000
Design of the software	150,000
Substantial testing of the project's initial stages	75,000
Production and packaging costs for the first month's sales	500,000
Costs of producing product masters after technology feasibility was established	200,000

The project was not under any contractual arrangement when these expenditures were incurred. What amount should Miller report as research and development expense for the current year?

a. $200,000
b. $275,000
c. $500,000
d. $975,000 (R/02, FAR #9, 7064)

19. On December 31 of the previous year, Byte Co. had capitalized software costs of $600,000 with an economic life of four years. Sales for the current year were 10% of expected total sales of the software. At December 31 of the current year, the software had a net realizable value of $480,000. In its December 31, current year balance sheet, what amount should Byte report as net capitalized cost of computer software?

a. $432,000
b. $450,000
c. $480,000
d. $540,000 (R/01, FAR, #3, amended, 6978)

20. Brill Co. made the following expenditures during the current year.

Costs to develop computer software for internal use in Brill's general management information system	$100,000
Costs of market research activities	75,000

What amount of these expenditures should Brill report in its current year income statement as research and development expenses?

a. $175,000
b. $100,000
c. $ 75,000
d. $0 (11/93, PI, #56, amended, 4425)

21. An analysis of Thrift Corp.'s unadjusted prepaid expense account at December 31, Year 2, revealed the following:

- An opening balance of $1,500 for Thrift's comprehensive insurance policy. Thrift had paid an annual premium of $3,000 on July 1, Year 1.
- A $3,200 annual insurance premium payment made July 1, Year 2.
- A $2,000 advance rental payment for a warehouse Thrift leased for one year beginning January 1, Year 3.

In its December 31, Year 2 balance sheet, what amount should Thrift report as prepaid expenses?
a. $5,200
b. $3,600
c. $2,000
d. $1,600 (5/93, PI, #27, amended, 4069)

22. On May 1 of the current year, Marno County issued property tax assessments for the fiscal year ending the following June 30. The first of two equal installments was due on November 1 of this year. On September 1, Dyur Co. purchased a 4-year old factory in Marno subject to an allowance for accrued taxes. Dyur did not record the entire year's property tax obligation, but instead records tax expenses at the end of each month by adjusting prepaid property taxes or property taxes payable, as appropriate. The recording of the November 1, payment by Dyur should have been allocated between an increase in prepaid property taxes and a decrease in property taxes payable in which of the following percentages?

	Percentage Allocated to	
	Increase in prepaid property taxes	*Decrease in property taxes payable*
a.	66-2/3%	33-1/3%
b.	0%	100%
c.	50%	50%
d.	33-1/3%	66-2/3%

(5/91, Theory, #13, amended, 2045)

23. Roro Inc. paid $7,200 to renew its only insurance policy for three years on March 1, the effective date of the policy. At March 31, Roro's unadjusted trial balance showed a balance of $300 for prepaid insurance and $7,200 for insurance expense. What amounts should be reported for prepaid insurance and insurance expense in Roro's financial statements for the three months ended March 31?

	Prepaid insurance	*Insurance expense*
a.	$7,000	$300
b.	$7,000	$500
c.	$7,200	$300
d.	$7,300	$200

(5/95, FAR, #14, amended, 5550)

24. On January 1, Year 1, Sip Co. signed a 5-year contract enabling it to use a patented manufacturing process beginning in Year 1. A royalty is payable for each product produced, subject to a minimum annual fee. Any royalties in excess of the minimum will be paid annually. On the contract date, Sip prepaid a sum equal to two years' minimum annual fees. In year 1, only minimum fees were incurred. The royalty prepayment should be reported in Sip's December 31, Year 1 financial statements as
a. An expense only
b. A current asset and an expense
c. A current asset and noncurrent asset
d. A noncurrent asset
(11/92, Theory, #28, amended, 3461)

25. Ott Company acquired rights to a patent from Grey under a licensing agreement that required an advance royalty payment when the agreement was signed. Ott remits royalties earned and due, under the agreement, on October 31 each year. Additionally, on the same date, Ott pays, in advance, estimated royalties for the next year. Ott adjusts prepaid royalties at year-end. Information for the current year ended December 31 is as follows:

Date		Amount
01/01	Prepaid royalties	$ 65,000
10/31	Royalty payment (charged to royalty expense)	110,000
12/31	Year-end credit adjustment to royalty expense	25,000

In its December 31 balance sheet, Ott should report prepaid royalties of
a. $25,000
b. $40,000
c. $85,000
d. $90,000 (11/86, PI, #1, amended, 0986)

26. In year 1, Chain Inc. purchased a $1,000,000 life insurance policy on its president, of which Chain is the beneficiary. Information regarding the policy for the year ended December 31, Year 6, follows:

Cash surrender value, 1/1, year 6	$ 87,000
Cash surrender value, 12/31, year 6	108,000
Annual advance premium paid 1/1, year 6	40,000

During year 6, dividends of $6,000 were applied to increase the cash surrender value of the policy. What amount should Chain report as life insurance expense for year 6?
a. $40,000
b. $25,000
c. $19,000
d. $13,000 (11/92, PI, #51, amended, 3284)

27. On January 2, Year 1, Jann Co. purchased a $150,000 whole-life insurance policy on its president. The annual premium is $4,000. The company is both the owner and the beneficiary. Jann charged officers' life insurance expense as follows:

Year 1	$ 4,000
Year 2	3,600
Year 3	3,000
Year 4	2,200
Total	$12,800

In its December 31, Year 4, balance sheet, what amount should Jann report as investment in cash surrender value of officers' life insurance?

a. $0
b. $ 3,200
c. $12,800
d. $16,000 (5/97, FAR, #2, amended, 6474)

28. Upon the death of an officer, Jung Co. received the proceeds of a life insurance policy held by Jung on the officer. The proceeds were not taxable. The policy's cash surrender value had been recorded on Jung's books at the time of payment. What amount of revenue should Jung report in its statements?

a. Proceeds received
b. Proceeds received less cash surrender value
c. Proceeds received plus cash surrender value
d. None (11/95, FAR, #35, 6117)

29. An increase in the cash surrender value of a life insurance policy owned by a company would be recorded by

a. Decreasing annual insurance expense
b. Increasing investment income
c. Recording a memorandum entry only
d. Decreasing a deferred charge

(11/94, FAR, #46, 5307)

30. An issuer of bonds uses a sinking fund for the retirement of the bonds. Cash was transferred to the sinking fund and subsequently used to purchase investments. The sinking fund

I. Increases by revenue earned on the investments
II. Is **not** affected by revenue earned on the investments
III. Decreases when the investments are purchased

a. I only
b. I and III
c. II and III
d. III only (11/91, Theory, #36, 2544)

31. The following information relates to noncurrent investments that Fall Corp. placed in trust as required by the underwriter of its bonds:

Bond sinking fund balance, 12/31, year 1	$ 450,000
Year 2 additional investment	90,000
Dividends on investments	15,000
Interest revenue	30,000
Administration costs	5,000
Carrying amount of bonds payable	1,025,000

What amount should Fall report in its December 31, Year 2 balance sheet related to its noncurrent investment for bond sinking fund requirements?

a. $585,000
b. $580,000
c. $575,000
d. $540,000 (5/93, PI, #16, amended, 4058)

32. On March 1, Year 1, a company established a sinking fund in connection with an issue of bonds due in year 8. At December 31, Year 5, the independent trustee held cash in the sinking fund account representing the annual deposits to the fund and the interest earned on those deposits. How should the sinking fund be reported in the company's balance sheet at December 31, Year 5?

a. The cash in the sinking fund should appear as a current asset.
b. Only the accumulated deposits should appear as a noncurrent asset.
c. The entire balance in the sinking fund account should appear as a current asset.
d. The entire balance in the sinking fund account should appear as a noncurrent asset.

(11/93, Theory, #43, amended, 4548)

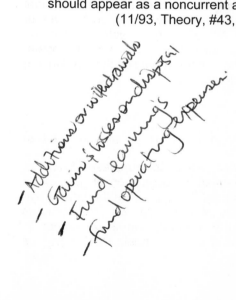

- Additions or withdrawals
- Gains & losses on disposal
- Fund earnings
- Fund operating expenses

Problem 5-2 ADDITIONAL MULTIPLE CHOICE QUESTIONS (22 to 28 minutes)

33. Malden Inc. has two patents that have allegedly been infringed by competitors. After investigation, legal counsel informed Malden that it had a weak case on patent A34 and a strong case in regard to patent B19. Malden incurred additional legal fees to stop infringement on B19. Both patents have a remaining legal life of 8 years. How should Malden account for these legal costs incurred relating to the two patents?
a. Expense costs for A34 and capitalize costs for B19
b. Expense costs for both A34 and B19
c. Capitalize costs for both A34 and B19
d. Capitalize costs for A34 and expense costs for B19 (11/92, Theory, #29, 3462)

34. On January 2, Rafa Co. purchased a franchise with a useful life of ten years for $50,000. An additional franchise fee of 3% of franchise operation revenues must be paid each year to the franchisor. Revenues from franchise operations amounted to $400,000 during the year. In its December 31 balance sheet, what amount should Rafa report as an intangible asset-franchise?
a. $33,000
b. $43,800
c. $45,000
d. $50,000 (5/94, FAR, #20, amended, 4835)

35. During January, Yana Co. incurred landscaping costs of $120,000 to improve leased property. The estimated useful life of the landscaping is fifteen years. The remaining term of the lease is eight years, with an option to renew for an additional four years. However, Yana has not reached a decision with regard to the renewal option. In Yana's December 31 balance sheet, what should be the net carrying amount of landscaping costs?
a. $0
b. $105,000
c. $110,000
d. $112,000 (11/97, FAR, #8, amended, 6488)

36. On January 2, Paye Co. purchased Shef Co. at a cost that resulted in recognition of goodwill of $200,000. During the first quarter of the year, Paye spent an additional $80,000 on expenditures designed to maintain goodwill. In its December 31 balance sheet, what amount should Paye report as goodwill?
a. $ 80,000
b. $195,000
c. $200,000
d. $280,000 (11/94, FAR, #17, amended, 9015)

37. On January 2, Year 1, Ames Corp. signed an eight-year lease for office space. Ames has the option to renew the lease for an additional four-year period on or before January 2, Year 8. During January of year 1, Ames incurred the following costs:

- $120,000 for general improvements to the leased premises with an estimated useful life of ten years.
- $50,000 for office furniture and equipment with an estimated useful life of ten years.

At December 31, year 1, Ames' intentions as to exercise of the renewal option are uncertain. A full year's amortization of leasehold improvements is taken for calendar year 1. In Ames' December 31, Year 1 balance sheet, accumulated amortization should be
a. $10,000
b. $15,000
c. $17,000
d. $21,250 (5/90, PI, #18, amended, 1003)

38. During the current year, Orr Co. incurred the following costs:

Research and development services performed by Key Corp. for Orr	$150,000
Design, construction, and testing of preproduction prototypes and models	200,000
Testing in search for new products or process alternatives	175,000

In its current year income statement, what should Orr report as research and development expense?
a. $150,000
b. $200,000
c. $350,000
d. $525,000 (11/94, FAR, #44, amended, 5306)

39. On January 1 of the current year, Jambon purchased equipment for use in developing a new product. Jambon uses the straight-line depreciation method. The equipment could provide benefits over a 10-year period. However, the new product development is expected to take five years, and the equipment can be used only for this project. Jambon's current year expense equals
a. The total cost of the equipment
b. One-fifth of the cost of the equipment
c. One-tenth of the cost of the equipment
d. Zero (11/91, Theory, #32, amended, 2540)

40. West Inc. made the following expenditures relating to Product Y:

- Legal costs to file a patent on Product Y—$10,000. Production of the finished product would not have been undertaken without the patent.
- Special equipment to be used solely for development of Product Y—$60,000. The equipment has no other use and has an estimated useful life of four years.
- Labor and material costs incurred in producing a prototype model—$200,000.
- Cost of testing the m prototype—$80,000.

What is the total amount of costs that will be expensed when incurred?
a. $280,000
b. $295,000
c. $340,000
d. $350,000 (5/92, PI, #52, 2622)

41. On December 31, Year 1, Bit Co. had capitalized costs for a new computer software product with an economic life of five years. Sales for year 2 were 30 percent of expected total sales of the software. At December 31, Year 2, the software had a net realizable value equal to 90 percent of the capitalized cost. What percentage of the original capitalized cost should be reported as the net amount on Bit's December 31, Year 2 balance sheet?
a. 70%
b. 72%
c. 80%
d. 90% (5/92, Theory, #14, amended, 2707)

42. Under East Co.'s accounting system, all insurance premiums paid are debited to prepaid insurance. For interim financial reports, East makes monthly estimated charges to insurance expense with credits to prepaid insurance. Additional information for the year ended December 31, Year 2, is as follows:

Prepaid insurance at December 31, Year 1	$105,000
Charges to insurance expense during year 2 (including a year-end adjustment of $17,500)	437,500
Prepaid insurance at December 31, Year 2	122,500

What was the total amount of insurance premiums paid by East during Year 2?
a. $332,500
b. $420,000
c. $437,500
d. $455,000 (5/91, PI, #30, amended, 9017)

43. The premium on a three-year insurance policy expiring on December 31, Year 3, was paid in total on January 2, Year 1. If the company has a 6-month operating cycle, then on December 31, Year 1, the prepaid insurance reported as a current asset would be for
a. 6 months
b. 12 months
c. 18 months
d. 24 months (5/90, Theory, #6, amended, 1758)

SIMULATION

Problem 5-3 (15 to 25 minutes)

Essay | Research Task

Clonal Inc., a biotechnology company, developed and patented a diagnostic product called Trouver. Clonal purchased some research equipment to be used exclusively for Trouver and other research equipment to be used on Trouver and subsequent research projects. Clonal defeated a legal challenge to its Trouver patent, and began production and marketing operations for the product.

Corporate headquarters' costs were allocated to Clonal's research division as a percentage of the division's salaries.

a. How should the equipment purchased for Trouver be reported in Clonal's income statements and balance sheets?

b. 1. Describe the matching principle.

2. Describe the accounting treatment of research and development costs and consider whether this is consistent with the matching principle. What is the justification for the accounting treatment of research and development costs?

c. How should corporate headquarters' costs allocated to the research division be classified in Clonal's income statement? Why?

d. How should the legal expenses incurred in defending Trouver's patent be reported in Clonal's statement of cash flows (direct method)? (11/90, Theory, #4, 6190)

Essay | Research Task

Research Question: What is the first step of the goodwill impairment test used to identify potential impairment?

Paragraph Reference Answer: ________________

Solution 5-1 MULTIPLE CHOICE ANSWERS

Intangible Assets

1. (a) Legal costs incurred to successfully defend a patent are capitalized, regardless of whether the patent was externally acquired or internally developed. Legal fees and other direct costs of registering a patent are capitalized and amortized over the lesser of the economic useful life or legal life, if determinable. R&D costs incurred to develop a patent are expensed when incurred (SFAS 2).

2. (d) Costs of goodwill from a business combination accounted for as a purchase should be capitalized. However, costs of developing, maintaining, or restoring goodwill should be expensed when incurred. Thus, the goodwill of $125,000 from the acquisition of the net assets of Apex should be capitalized, while the additional costs of developing goodwill should be expensed as incurred.

Intangibles After Acquisition

3. (c) The patented product was withdrawn from sale under governmental order. Therefore, the unamortized cost of the patent at 12/31, year 4 should be charged to income.

Purchase price of patent	$ 90,000
Less: Amortization prior to year 4 ($90,000 × 3/10)	(27,000)
Unamortized cost of patent, year 4	$ 63,000

4. (b) The cost of a successful legal defense of an existing patent is capitalized because it offers probable future benefits.

Cost of patent (year 1)	$45,000
Amortization (3 yrs. × $45,000/15)	(9,000)
Carrying value 12/31, year 3	36,000
Capitalization of legal costs	15,000
Carrying value of patent (year 4)	$51,000

Proceeds from sale	$75,000
Carrying value of patent	(51,000)
Gain from sale	$24,000

5. (a) A franchise represents a special right to operate under the name and guidance of another enterprise over a limited geographic area. A franchise is always externally purchased; it cannot be internally developed. Capitalize all significant costs incurred to acquire the franchise (e.g., purchase price, legal fees, etc.). If the acquisition cost of the franchise requires future cash payments, these payments should be capitalized at their present value using an appropriate interest rate. On the other hand, periodic service fees charged as a percentage of revenues are not capitalized; these costs represent a current operating expense of the franchisee.

6. (b) Leasehold improvements are lessee improvements to leased property which are not separable from the leased property and revert to the lessor at the end of the lease term. Since Nobb intends to exercise the renewal option, the leasehold improvement is amortized over the lesser of the sum of the remaining term of the lease and the period covered by the renewal option [i.e., (12 – 2) + 8 = 18 years] or the estimated useful life of the leasehold improvement (i.e., 15 years). At 12/31, year 3, the carrying amount of the leasehold improvement is $504,000 [$540,000 – ($540,000 / 15)].

7. (c) Leasehold improvements are lessee improvements to leased property which are not separable from the leased property and revert to the lessor at the end of the lease term. Since the lease is nonrenewable, the leasehold improvements are amortized over the lesser of the remaining term of the lease (i.e., 6 years) or the estimated useful life of the leasehold improvements (i.e., 8 years). ($48,000 – [($48,000 / 6) × 6 months/12 months] = $44,000)

8. (a) The building constructed on the leased property in lieu of rent represents a leasehold improvement because the building will revert to the lessor at the end of the lease term. The $840,000 cost of the building is allocated equally over the remaining 20-year period of the lease, resulting in annual amortization of $42,000. Thus, the building's carrying amount at 12/31, year 2 is $798,000 ($840,000 cost minus $42,000 amortization to date).

9. (b) The new walls and offices are leasehold improvements since they are not separable from the leased property and revert to the lessor at the end of the lease term. They are amortized over the lease term. The prepayment of the last month's rent was made to secure the lease and should be reported as a leasehold within intangible assets.

Rent for December	$60,000
Amortization of leasehold improvements for December ($360,000 / 60)	6,000
Total expense relating to use of office space	$66,000

10. (c) The $500,000 acquisition cost of the trademark is amortized over the useful life, resulting in accumulated amortization of $10,000 at 12/31. The unamortized cost on Krug's books is irrelevant in determining Judd's acquisition cost.

11. (a) An intangible asset with an indefinite useful life is not amortized. If no legal, regulatory,

contractual, competitive, economic, or other factors limit the useful life, it is considered to be indefinite. The term indefinite does not mean infinite. Goodwill and intangible assets with indefinite useful lives are not amortized, but rather are tested at least annually for impairment.

R&D

12. (c) Quality control during commercial production including routine testing of products is an example of an activity typically excluded in research and development costs. Laboratory research aimed at discovery of new knowledge, testing in search for or evaluation of product or process alternatives design, construction, and testing of pre-production prototypes and models are examples of activities typically included in research and development costs.

13. (a) Research and development costs are expensed as incurred. Only the costs of acquiring a patent should be capitalized. Thus, only the cost of registering the patent, $34,000, is capitalized. The capitalized cost of an intangible asset is amortized over the asset's economic life. One-half year of amortization is $1,700 ($34,000 / 10 years × 1/2 year). [($34,000 – $1,700) = $32,300]

14. (b) Materials, equipment, facilities, or intangibles purchased for a particular R&D project and have no alternative use in other R&D projects or in normal operations are expensed in the period in which acquired. However, if alternative future uses are expected, these items are recorded as assets and amortized over their useful lives. Machine A can only be used in one research project and is expensed in the current year. Machine B has alternative future uses and a 10-year life; thus, the current R&D expense includes depreciation for one year.

Machine A	$250,000
Machine B ($250,000/10 years)	25,000
R&D expense	$275,000

15. (d) The design of tools, jigs, molds, and dies involving new technology ($125,000) and the modification of the formulation of a process ($160,000) typically would be included in R&D (SFAS 2, ¶9). Troubleshooting in connection with breakdowns during commercial production and the adaptation of an existing capability to a particular customer's need as part of a continuing commercial activity typically are excluded from R&D (¶10).

Computer Software

16. (b) All costs incurred to establish the technological feasibility of a computer software product should be charged to R&D expense when incurred (SFAS 86, ¶3). The technological feasibility of a computer software product is established only when the enterprise has completed all planning, designing, coding, and testing activities that are necessary to establish that the product can be produced (¶4). Thus, the cost of completion of the detail program design ($13,000) and the costs incurred for coding and testing to establish technological feasibility of the product ($10,000) are R&D expense. The costs incurred for duplicating the computer software document and training materials from the product masters and for physically packaging the product for distribution are capitalized as inventory (¶9).

17. (c) Costs of producing product masters incurred subsequent to establishing technological feasibility should be capitalized. These costs include coding and testing performed subsequent to establishing technological feasibility (SFAS 86, ¶3). Thus, the costs of producing product masters for training materials, the coding costs, and testing costs incurred after establishment of technological feasibility should be capitalized ($15,000 + $24,000 + $20,000 = $59,000).

18. (b) R & D costs incurred internally in creating a computer software product are charged to expense when incurred as research and development until technological feasibility has been established for the product. Technological feasibility is established only upon completion of a detailed program design or, in its absence, completion of a working model. All costs of planning, designing, coding, and testing activities that are necessary to establish technological feasibility are expensed as research and development when incurred.

The costs of producing product masters incurred subsequent to establishing technological feasibility are capitalized. Capitalization of computer software costs ceases when the product is available for general release to customers. Capitalized software production costs are reported at the lower of unamortized cost or net realizable value. Costs incurred for (1) duplicating the computer software and training materials from product masters and (2) physically packaging the product for distribution are capitalized as inventory. Capitalized inventory costs are expensed when the inventory is sold.

19. (b) The annual amortization of computer software costs is the greater of the amount computed using the percentage of revenue approach and

the straight-line method applied over the product's remaining estimated economic life. $600,000 – ($600,000 / 4) = $450,000. Capitalized computer software costs are carried at the lower of unamortized cost or net realizable value, so the answer could not be $480,000.

20. (d) Neither of the two activities identified is an example of an activity that typically is considered an R&D activity (SFAS 2, ¶9). Most costs in the application development stage of developing software for internal use are capitalized and not expensed as incurred. Market research activities relate to the selling and marketing operations, not R&D.

Prepaid Expenses

21. (b) The amount to be reported as prepaid expenses is comprised of (1) the $1,600 (i.e., $3,200 × 6/12) portion of the annual insurance premium payment made 7/1, year 2 that pertains to year 3 and (2) the $2,000 advance one-year rental payment for the lease which begins in year 3. The $1,500 opening balance of the prepaid expense account pertains to insurance coverage that expired during year 2.

22. (d) On September 1, Year 1, Dyur Co. would have credited two months of taxes from the seller to *Property Taxes Payable.* At the end of September and October, Dyur would have recorded one month of property taxes each month by a credit to *Property Taxes Payable.* When the payment was made for six months of taxes on November 1, year 1, the payment would be for the four months prior to that date that have already been accrued and for the two months that follow the payment date which should be recorded as Prepaid Property Taxes. Therefore, 2/3 of the payment should be allocated to a decrease in property taxes payable and 1/3 of the payment should be recorded as an increase in prepaid property taxes.

23. (b) The correct amount to be shown in the *Prepaid Insurance* account at March 31 is 35 months of premiums: $7,200 / 36 months = $200 per month; $200 per month × 35 months = $7,000.

Prepaid Insurance		
Unadjusted balance (given)	300	
Adjustment (forced)	6,700	
Ending bal. 3/31	7,000	

Insurance Expense		
Unadjusted balance (given)	7,200	
		6,700 Adjustment
Ending bal. 3/31	500	

Other Assets

24. (b) Royalties were prepaid equal to the sum of two year's minimum annual fees on the contract date. Only the minimum annual fees were incurred in the first year of the contract. Since the second year's minimum annual fees will be consumed in the upcoming year, half of the royalty prepayment should be reported as an expense and half should be reported as a current asset at the end of the first contract year.

25. (d)

Prepaid royalties, 1/1	$ 65,000
Royalty payment, 10/31	110,000
Less: Royalty exp. ($110,000 – $25,000)	(85,000)
Prepaid royalties, 12/31	$ 90,000

Life Insurance

26. (c) Premiums paid on this policy consist of an amount for life insurance and a balance which constitutes a form of savings. In this question, the cash surrender value of the policy increased by $21,000 (i.e., $108,000 – $87,000) in year 6. This amount, which includes the dividends of $6,000 applied to increase the cash surrender value of the policy, is subtracted from the premium paid to determine the life insurance expense for the year (i.e., $40,000 – $21,000 = $19,000).

27. (b) The annual premium on a whole-life insurance policy includes a portion to cash surrender value. The balance is reported as life insurance expense. Jann Co. paid a total of $16,000 in premiums from ($4,000 × 4 years). Of this amount, $12,800 was charged to life insurance expense, and the balance of $3,200 ($16,000 –$12,800) is reported as an investment in cash surrender value.

28. (b) The cash surrender value has been accounted for as an asset and has reduced insurance expense over the years the premium payments have been made. The receipt of life insurance proceeds is first applied to the cash surrender value to remove the asset and the balance is recorded as revenue.

29. (a) The amount that a company should recognize as insurance expense for a life insurance policy that it owns is the annual premium less (1) the increase in cash surrender value and (2) any dividends received.

Special Purpose Funds

30. (a) The sinking fund is affected by (1) additions or withdrawals to the fund, (2) fund earnings,

(3) gains or losses on the disposal of fund assets, and (4) fund operating expenses. The exchange of one asset for another within the fund (such as the exchange of cash for an investment) will not have any net effect on the fund balance.

31. (b) The bond sinking fund balance increases as a result of the additional investment and the income on the investments in the fund (i.e., the dividend and interest revenue). It decreases due to the expenses of the fund (i.e., the administrative costs incurred). The carrying amount of the bonds payable does not affect the bond sinking fund balance.

Bond sinking fund, 12/31, year 1	$450,000
Add: Additional investment, year 2	90,000
Dividends on investments	15,000
Interest revenue	30,000
Less: Administrative costs	(5,000)
Bond sinking fund, 12/31, year 2	$580,000

32. (d) Because the bond sinking fund is earmarked for the retirement of long-term debt, its entire balance (i.e., all contributions to the fund plus all interest accumulations added to the fund balance to date) should be reported as a noncurrent asset in the investments section of the balance sheet.

Solution 5-2 ADDITIONAL MULTIPLE CHOICE ANSWERS

Intangible Assets

33. (a) While the cost of a successful defense of a patent should be capitalized because it establishes the legal rights of the owner, other legal costs incurred for an existing patent should be expensed as incurred. Therefore, Malden should capitalize the cost of the successful defense of patent B19 and expense the legal costs incurred to determine that it had a weak case of patent infringement for patent A34.

34. (c) The 3% of revenues fee is expensed in the period incurred, not capitalized and amortized. The franchise is amortized over its determinable useful life of 10 years.

Franchise	$ 50,000
Amortization ($50,000 × 10%)	(5,000)
Intangible asset, 12/31	$ 45,000

35. (b) The landscaping costs are leasehold improvements and should be capitalized and amortized over the lesser of the estimated useful life or the remaining term of the lease, including renewal options. The remaining term of the lease, with or without the renewal option, is less than the estimated useful life of 15 years. Because Yana Co. has not reached a decision to exercise the option to renew for the additional four years, the landscaping costs should be amortized over the 8-year remaining term of the lease. At December 31, one year of amortization, $15,000 ($120,000 / 8 years) should be expensed. Cost of $120,000 less amortization of $15,000 equals a net carrying amount of $105,000.

Developed Goodwill

36. (c) The $200,000 of goodwill acquired in connection with the purchase of Shef should be capitalized. The $80,000 of expenditures to maintain the goodwill should be expensed when incurred because costs of developing, maintaining, or restoring goodwill should not be capitalized.

Intangibles After Acquisition

37. (b) Leasehold improvements are improvements made by the lessee to leased property. The improvements are not separable from the leased property and revert to the lessor at the end of the lease term. Of the items listed, only the general improvements made to the leased premises represent a leasehold improvement. As such, it should be amortized over the lesser of the lease term (i.e., 8 years) or the estimated useful life of the leasehold improvement (i.e., 10 years). The likelihood of lease renewal is too uncertain to warrant apportioning the cost over the sum of the remaining term of the lease and the period covered by the renewal option (i.e., 12 years). Therefore, the accumulated amortization to be reported in the 12/31, year 1 balance sheet is $15,000 ($120,000 / 8 years). The office furniture and equipment are not leasehold improvements since they are separable from the leased premises and do not revert to the lessor at the end of the lease term.

R&D

38. (d) SFAS 2, ¶9 and 10, provides examples of activities that are typically included in, and those excluded from, R&D. All three activities are examples of activities that typically are included in R&D.

39. (a) The costs of equipment or facilities that are acquired or constructed for R&D activities and have alternative future uses (in R&D or otherwise) should be capitalized when acquired or constructed. However, the cost of equipment or facilities that are acquired or constructed for a particular R&D project and have no alternative future uses (in other R&D

projects or otherwise) are expensed as R&D costs at the time the costs are incurred (SFAS 2, ¶11).

40. (c) The cost of equipment is expensed as R&D cost when incurred when the equipment can be used only in one particular R&D project (i.e., the equipment has no alternative future uses in other R&D projects or otherwise). In addition, costs incurred in the design, construction, and testing of preproduction prototypes and models are also expensed as R&D costs when incurred. Thus, the total amount of costs that will be expensed as R&D costs when incurred is $340,000 (i.e., $60,000 + $200,000 + $80,000). The cost of the legal work in connection with patent application is capitalized as part of the cost of the patent (SFAS 2, ¶9 - 11).

Computer Software

41. (a) The annual amortization of the capitalized software cost is the greater of: (1) the ratio of current revenues to current and future revenues (e.g., 30%) or (2) the straight-line method over the remaining useful life of the software including the period to be reported upon (e.g., 1 / 5 = 20%). Because the software has a net realizable value of 90% of the capitalized cost, it can be reported on the balance sheet at 70% (i.e., 1 - 30%) of its capitalized cost (SFAS 86, ¶8).

Prepaid Expenses

42. (d) The insurance premiums paid can be determined by the analysis of the *Prepaid Insurance* account (work backwards through the account).

Prepaid Insurance

Balance, 12/31, year 1 (given)	105,000		
Premiums paid (forced)	455,000		
Balance before charges to expense (subtotal)	560,000	437,500	Charge to expense in year 2 (given)
Balance, 12/31, year 2 (given)	122,500		

43. (b) The operating cycle of an enterprise is the average period of time between the expenditure of cash for goods and services and the date those goods and services are converted into cash. Thus, it is the average length of time from cash expenditure, to inventory, to sale, to accounts receivable, and back to cash. A 1-year time period is to be used as a basis for the segregation of current assets in cases where there are several operating cycles occurring within a year (ARB 43, Ch. 3, ¶5). Since the company in question has a six-month operating cycle, it has two operating cycles within a year. Thus, the 1-year (i.e., twelve month) time period should be used as the basis for determining the amount of prepaid insurance to be reported as a current asset.

PERFORMANCE BY SUBTOPIC

Each category below parallels a subtopic covered in Chapter 5. Record the number and percentage of questions you correctly answered in each subtopic area.

Intangible Assets

Question #	Correct √
1	
2	
# Questions	2
# Correct	______
% Correct	______

Intangibles After Acquisition

Question #	Correct √
3	
4	
5	
6	
7	
8	
9	
10	
11	
# Questions	9
# Correct	______
% Correct	______

R&D

Question #	Correct √
12	
13	
14	
15	
# Questions	4
# Correct	______
% Correct	______

Computer Software

Question #	Correct √
16	
17	
18	
19	
20	
# Questions	5
# Correct	______
% Correct	______

Prepaid Expenses

Question #	Correct √
21	
22	
23	
# Questions	3
# Correct	______
% Correct	______

Other Assets

Question #	Correct √
24	
25	
# Questions	2
# Correct	______
% Correct	______

Life Insurance

Question #	Correct √
26	
27	
28	
29	
# Questions	4
# Correct	______
% Correct	______

Special Purpose Funds

Question #	Correct √
30	
31	
32	
# Questions	3
# Correct	______
% Correct	______

SIMULATION SOLUTION

Solution 5-3

Essay—R&D Costs/Patent

a. The costs of research equipment used exclusively for Trouver would be reported as research and development **expenses in the period incurred.**

The costs of research equipment used on **both Trouver and future** research projects would be **capitalized** and shown as **equipment (less accumulated depreciation)** on the **balance sheet.** An appropriate method of depreciation should be used. **Depreciation** on capitalized research equipment should be reported as a **research and development expense.**

b. 1. Matching refers to the process of expense recognition by **associating costs with revenues** on a cause and effect basis.

2. Research and development costs are usually **expensed** in the **period incurred** and may **not** be **matched** with revenues. This accounting treatment is justified by the **high degree** of **uncertainty** regarding the **amount and timing of future benefits.** A **direct relationship** between research and development costs and future revenues generally **cannot be demonstrated.**

c. Corporate headquarters' costs allocated to research and development would be classified as **general and administrative expenses** in the **period incurred,** because they are **not clearly related** to research and development activities.

d. On Clonal's statement of cash flows, the legal expenses incurred in defending the patent should be reported under **investing activities** in the **period paid.**

Research

FAS 142, Par. 19

19. The first step of the goodwill impairment test, used to identify potential impairment, compares the fair value of a reporting unit with its carrying amount, including goodwill. The guidance in paragraphs 23-25 shall be used to determine the fair value of a reporting unit. If the fair value of a reporting unit exceeds its carrying amount, goodwill of the reporting unit is considered not impaired, thus the second step of the impairment test is unnecessary. If the carrying amount of a reporting unit exceeds its fair value, the second step of the goodwill impairment test shall be performed to measure the amount of impairment loss, if any.

CHAPTER 6

BONDS

I. **Long-Term Investments** ... 6-2
- A. Overview ... 6-2
- B. Acquisition ... 6-2
- C. Premium or Discount ... 6-3
- D. Interest Accrual ... 6-4
- E. Sale of Bond Investments ... 6-5

II. **Bonds Payable** ... 6-5
- A. Overview ... 6-5
- B. Disclosures ... 6-5
- C. Bond Issuance ... 6-5
- D. Bond Selling Price ... 6-6
- E. Bond Issue Costs ... 6-6
- F. Bond Retirement ... 6-6

III. **Premium & Discount Amortization by Debtor** ... 6-8
- A. Straight-Line Method ... 6-8
- B. Effective Interest Method ... 6-8
- C. Amortization Effects ... 6-9
- D. Interest & Year-End Dates Differ ... 6-9
- E. Issuance Between Interest Dates ... 6-9

IV. **Bonds With Additional Features** ... 6-10
- A. Serial Bonds ... 6-10
- B. Convertible Bonds ... 6-10
- C. Debt Issued With Detachable Stock Warrants ... 6-11

V. **Comparison of Borrower & Investor Journal Entries** ... 6-12
- A. Premiums & Discounts ... 6-12
- B. Midperiod Issue ... 6-14
- C. Convertible Bonds ... 6-15
- D. Warrants ... 6-16

EXAM COVERAGE: Historically, exam coverage of the topics in Chapter 6 has been 5 to 10 percent of the FAR section. More information regarding exam coverage is included in Appendix B, *Practical Advice.*

CHAPTER 6

BONDS

I. Long-Term Investments

A. Overview

Bonds are contractual agreements wherein the issuer (borrower) promises to pay the purchaser (lender) a principal amount at a designated future date. In addition, the issuer makes periodic interest payments based on the face amount of the bond and the stated rate of interest.

1. **Held-to-Maturity Securities** Under SFAS 115, held-to-maturity (HTM) securities are defined as debt securities that the enterprise has the intent and the ability to hold to maturity. HTM securities are accounted for under the **amortized cost** method discussed here. Trading and available-for-sale securities are not accounted for under the amortized cost method. Temporary fluctuations in the market value of bonds classified as held-to-maturity are not recognized in the accounts. HTM securities, including other than temporary market value declines, are discussed in Chapter 2.

2. **Serial and Term Bonds** Bonds providing for repayment of principal in a series of installments are called *serial* bonds; bonds maturing at a specified date are called *term* bonds.

3. **Debenture Bonds** Debenture bonds are unsecured bonds; they are not supported by a lien or mortgage on specific assets.

4. **Callable Bonds** Callable bonds may be retired at the issuer's option.

5. **Convertible Bonds** Bonds may be converted to stock at the bondholder's option.

B. Acquisition

Initial recording will be at an amount equal to the purchase price of the bond plus other direct costs of acquisition (e.g., broker's fees). The market price of a bond is determined based on the "market interest rate" that takes into consideration the stated (face) interest rate of the bonds, the credit worthiness of the debtor, the maturity date of the bonds, and other factors. The market price of the bond is equal to the present value of the bond's interest and principal payments, discounted using the market interest rate for that type of bond. If bonds are bought between interest dates, the purchaser will have to pay an additional amount for the interest accrued on the bond since the last interest date (or the bond date, if before the first interest date). This additional amount is **not** part of the cost of the bond investment, but must be recorded separately as purchased interest (i.e., interest receivable).

Example 1 ▸ Acquisition of Bond & Interest Payment

X buys at par on September 1 a 10%, $1,000 bond issued on June 1 of the same year. Interest dates are June 1 and December 1.

Investment in Bonds	1,000	
Interest Receivable (10% × $1,000 × 3 months/12 months)	25	
Cash		1,025
To record the purchase of bonds on September 1.		
Cash (10% × $1,000 × 6/12)	50	
Interest Receivable		25
Interest Income		25
To record receipt of the interest proceeds on December 1.		

C. Premium or Discount

A premium or discount on bonds arises when the stated interest rate of the bonds is higher or lower, respectively, than the current market interest rate for similar securities. Bond premium or discount generally is **not** separately recorded by the investor (i.e., the bond investment is recorded at a net amount). Premiums or discounts on bonds held as a long-term investment must be amortized from date of acquisition to maturity date. APB 21, specifies that the interest method should be used to amortize these differences. Other methods of amortization (straight-line), may be used if the effects are not material. The premium amortization decreases both the bond investment and investment income, while the discount amortization increases these accounts.

Example 2 ▸ Bonds Acquired at a Discount

On June 30, Year 1, ABC Corp. purchased 100 new bonds issued by XYZ Inc., with a total face amount of $100,000 and a 10% stated interest rate. The bonds mature in ten years and pay interest semiannually, on June 30 and December 31 (20 semiannual payments). The effective yield for similar securities is 12% annually and is reflected in the $88,530 purchase price paid by ABC Corp.

Required: Show how the appropriate purchase price of $88,530 for the $100,000 face amount of bonds is determined using the appropriate present value (PV) tables in Appendix D. In addition, prepare the journal entry to record the acquisition of the bonds.

Solution:

Maturity (face) amount to be received	$ 100,000	
PV factor for a single amount (6%, 20 periods)—Table 2	× 0.311805	
Present value of the maturity amount		$31,180.50
Semiannual interest payment to be received ($100,000 × 10% × 6/12)	5,000	
PV factor for an ordinary annuity (6%, 20 periods)—Table 4	× 11.469921	
Present value of future interest payments		57,349.60
Present value of the bonds		$88,530.10

Bond Investment	88,530	
Cash		88,530

Example 3 ▸ Interest Income & Discount Amortization

Required: Refer to Example 2. Provide ABC Corporation's entries to record interest income and discount amortization for the year ending December 31, Year 1, assuming (1) straight-line and (2) effective interest methods of discount amortization.

Solution:

(1) *Straight-Line Method:*

Cash ($100,000 × 0.05)	5,000	
Bond Investment [($100,000 – $88,530) / 20]	574*	
Interest Income		5,574

(2) *Effective Interest Method:*

Cash ($100,000 × 0.05)	5,000	
Bond Investment (balancing amount)	312*	
Interest Income ($88,530 × .06)		5,312

* **NOTE:** The total amortization of the bond investment discount will be the same over the 10-year life of the bonds under either the straight-line or the interest method. As noted earlier, the amortization of the bond investment discount increases the bond *Investment* and *Interest Income* accounts. The amortization of a bond investment premium would decrease these accounts.

Exhibit 1 ▸ Bond Premiums and Discounts

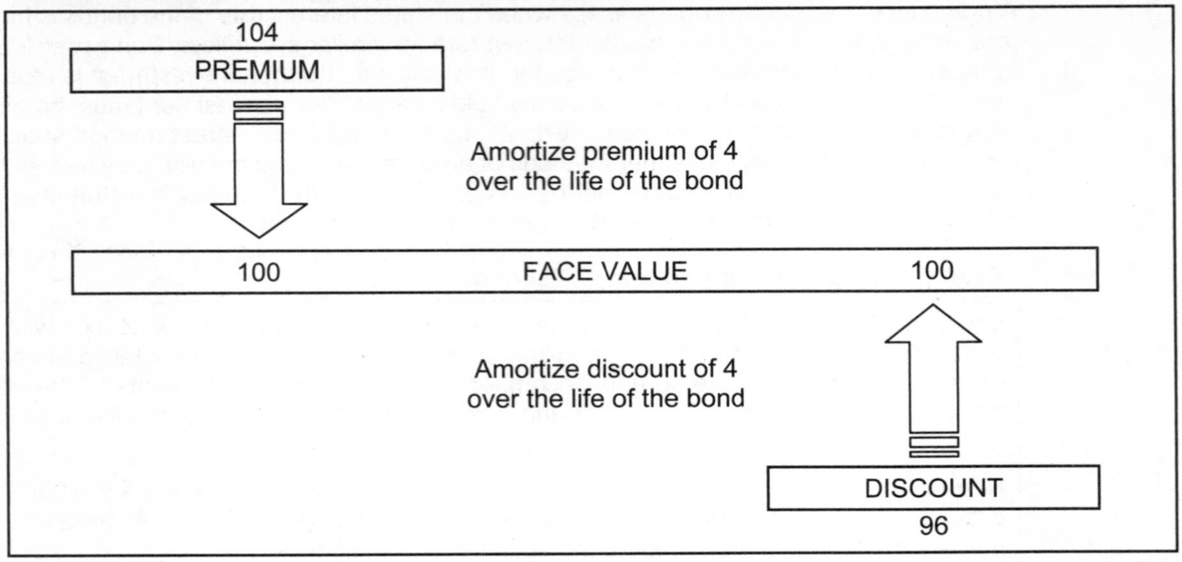

Exhibit 2 ▸ Effective Interest Method

Bond issued at:	Effective interest rate	×	Carrying value	=	Amount of interest income/expense
Discount	Constant		Increasing		Increasing
Premium	Constant		Decreasing		Decreasing

D. Interest Accrual

The bond interest payment date and the investor's year-end may not coincide. In this case, the investor must accrue the interest income earned through year-end, including the required amortization of premium or discount.

Example 4 ▸ Different Year-End and Payment Dates

Refer to Example 2, except that ABC's year-end is March 31.

Required: Provide ABC's journal entries on March 31, Year 2, to record interest and discount amortization under both the straight-line and the interest methods.

Solution:

(1)	*Straight-Line Method:*		
	Accrued Interest Receivable ($100,000 × 0.05 × 3/6)	2,500	
	Bond Investment ($574 × 3/6)*	287	
	Interest Income		2,787
(2)	*Interest Method:*		
	Accrued Interest Receivable	2,500	
	Bond Investment (balancing amount)	165	
	Interest Income [($88,530 + $312) × 0.06 × 3/6]		2,665

* On March 31, Year 2, ABC records interest income for 3 months of the six month payment. The 10% rate is an annual rate.

E. Sale of Bond Investments

The sale of bonds held for investment results in a gain or loss equal to the difference between the carrying amount of the bonds and the proceeds received on their disposal. This gain or loss is **not** an extraordinary item.

1. **Carrying Amount** In determining the carrying amount of the bonds, adjustment must be made for premium or discount amortization to date of sale.

2. **Bonds Sold Between Interest Dates** If the bonds are sold between interest dates, part of the proceeds must be assigned to the interest accrued since the last interest date.

Example 5 ▸ Sale of Bond Investment

Refer to the facts of Example 2. On August 31, Year 5, ABC sold the 100 bonds to LMN Inc. for $92,000, which included interest accrued on the bonds. ABC amortized the original discount on the bonds under the straight-line method.

Required: Determine the gain (or loss) to be recognized by ABC on the sale of the bonds.

Solution:

Proceeds received	$92,000
Less: Amount attributable to accrued interest, $100,000 × 0.05 × 2/6	(1,667)
Sale price of bonds	90,333
Carrying amount*	93,313
Gain (loss) on sale of bonds	$ (2,980)

Computations:

*Original purchase price, June 30, Year 1	$88,530
Plus discount amortization:	
Through June 30, Year 5 ($574 × 8)	4,592
July 1 to August 31, Year 5 ($574 / 3)	191
Carrying amount of the bonds	$93,313

II. Bonds Payable

A. Overview

Bonds payable represent a contractual obligation to make periodic interest payments on the amount borrowed and to repay the principal upon maturity. Therefore, when a company sells a bond issue it is in effect selling two cash flows.

1. **Principal** The receipt of the bond principal at its maturity

2. **Interest** The receipt of the periodic interest payments. The bonds' stated interest rate and face amount determine the amount of periodic interest payments.

B. Disclosures

SFAS 47 requires that the combined aggregate amount of maturities and sinking fund requirements for all long-term borrowings be disclosed for each of the five years following the date of the latest balance sheet presented.

C. Bond Issuance

When bonds are issued, only the face amount of the bonds is recorded in the *Bonds Payable* account. The bond discount or premium, if any, is recorded in a separate account and reported in the balance sheet as a direct deduction from or addition to the face amount of the bond.

Example 6 ▸ Bond Issuance

On January 1, Year 1, Maple Company issued five-year bonds with a face amount of $200,000 and a stated interest rate of 8%, payable semiannually on June 30 and December 31. The bonds were priced to yield 6%. The present value factor for the present value of $1 for 10 periods at 3% is 0.74409; the factor for the present value of an ordinary annuity of $1 for 10 periods at 3% is 8.53020.

Required: Determine the total issue price of the bonds. Record their issuance.

Solution:

Present value of principal payment [$200,000 × 0.74409 (PV of $1 for 10 periods at 3%)]	$148,818
Present value of periodic interest payments [($200,000 × 8% / 2) × 8.53020]	68,242
Amount received from the issuance of the bonds	$217,060

The stated rate of interest (8%) is above the market rate (6%). Therefore, these bonds were sold at a premium. The following entry is made to record the bond issuance.

Cash	217,060	
Bonds Payable		200,000
Bond Premium (difference)		17,060

D. **Bond Selling Price**
To estimate the proceeds to be received from the issuance of bonds payable (ignoring bond issue costs), the present values of the bond principal and interest payments must be determined. The prevailing market (yield) rate is used to discount the cash flows to arrive at their present value.

1. **Premium** A bond will sell at a **premium** (more than par) when the stated interest rate is *greater* than the market rate for similar debt.

2. **Discount** A bond will sell at a **discount** (less than par) when the stated interest rate is *less* than the market rate.

3. **Par** A bond will sell at **par** when the stated interest rate *equals* the market rate.

E. **Bond Issue Costs**
Bond issue costs include legal fees, accounting fees, underwriting commissions, registration, printing and engraving, and other such costs incurred in preparing and selling a bond issue.

1. **Classification** According to APB 21, *Interest on Receivables and Payables,* bond issue costs should be classified as a deferred charge (i.e., asset) and amortized over the life of the bonds as an increase to interest expense. (Alternately, under the Statements of Financial Accounting Concepts, issuance costs could be accounted for either as an expense in the period incurred or as a reduction of the noncurrent debt liability, and accounted for the same as debt discount.)

2. **Amortization** The amortization of bond issue costs is affected when a bond issue is sold between interest dates because the issue costs should be amortized over the period from the date of sale (not the date of the bond) to the maturity date.

F. **Bond Retirement**

1. **Debt Extinguishment** A debtor considers debt to be extinguished for financial reporting purposes in the following situations.

   a. **Payment** The debtor pays the creditor and is relieved of all its obligations with respect to the debt, including the debtor's reacquisition of its outstanding debt securities through cancellation or holding as treasury bonds.

b. **Legal Release** The debtor legally is released from being the primary obligor under the debt, either judicially or by the creditor.

2. **Extinguishment vs. Refunding** Extinguishment includes the reacquisition of debt securities regardless of whether the securities are canceled or held as so-called treasury bonds. Refunding refers to achieving the reacquisition by the use of proceeds from issuing other securities.

3. **Principal and Related Amounts** When all or part of a bond issue is retired before maturity, it is necessary to write off both the principal and the pro rata portion of the unamortized premium or discount on the retired bonds. If bond issue costs were incurred and recorded as an asset (i.e., as a deferred charge), it is also necessary to write off a pro rata portion of the bond issue costs (when a bond issue is retired before maturity). The amount of such write-off increases any loss or reduces any gain recognized on the retirement.

4. **Extraordinary Item** SFAS 145 removes the assumption that gains and losses from the early extinguishment of debt are extraordinary items. Entities must evaluate whether early debt extinguishment is extraordinary using the same criteria as other events.

Example 7 ▸ Extraordinary Item

On January 1, Year 1, Ben Corporation issued $600,000 of 5% ten-year bonds at 103. Ben records amortization using the straight-line method (i.e., the amount is considered immaterial). On December 31, Year 5, when the fair value of the bonds was 97, Ben repurchased $300,000 of the bonds in the open market at 97. Ben has an effective income tax rate of 30%. Ben has recorded interest and amortization for Year 5. Ben should record this retirement as follows:

Bonds Payable ($600,000 × 0.50)	300,000	
Bond Premium ($9,000 × 0.50)	4,500	
Taxes Payable ($13,500 × 0.30)		4,050*
Cash ($300,000 × 0.97)		291,000
Gain on Bond Retirement		9,450*

***Computations:**

Original carrying amount ($600,000 × 103%)		$618,000
Premium to be amortized ($618,000 – $600,000)	$18,000	
Amortization [($18,000 / 10) × 5 yrs.]	9,000	9,000
Carrying amount of bonds, 12/31, Year 5		609,000
Portion of bonds retired		× 50%
Carrying amount of bonds retired		304,500
Purchase price ($300,000 × 97%)		291,000
Gain on bond retirement, before income taxes		$ 13,500

NOTE: The gain, net of the related income tax effects, is $9,450 [$13,500 × (1 – 30%)]. This gain would be considered extraordinary only when it meets the criteria of being both unusual and infrequent considering the environment in which the company operates.

Example 8 ▸ Write-Off of Bond Issue Costs

If bond issue costs of $10,000 were recorded as an asset in the issuance of the bonds in Example 7, the gain on retirement before income taxes would be $11,000 [$13,500 – ($10,000 × 5/10 × 50%)].

III. Premium & Discount Amortization by Debtor

A. Straight-Line Method

Straight-line amortization calls for the amortization of an equal amount of premium or discount each period over the life of the bonds. The straight-line method is acceptable only when the premium or discount is immaterial, because it fails to determine the periodic interest expense in terms of the effective rate of interest.

Example 9 ▶ Straight-Line Amortization

To amortize the premium in Example 6 using the straight-line method, divide the premium by the number of interest periods: $17,060 / 10 = $1,706.

B. Effective Interest Method

The effective interest method of amortization calls for recognizing interest expense at the effective interest rate at which the bonds were sold. Thus, this interest method overcomes the criticism of the straight-line method because it offers a more accurate measurement of interest expense. Use of the effective interest method results in a constant rate of interest when applied to the carrying amount of the bonds at the beginning of the period. As with long-term notes payable, other amortization methods may be used when the results do not differ materially from those obtained with the effective interest method.

Example 10 ▶ Effective Interest Method Amortization

To amortize the premium in Example 6 using the effective interest method, multiply the carrying amount of the bond issue ($217,060) by the effective yield (3%). This equals interest expense for the period ($6,512). The difference between the cash interest payment and the interest expense equals the amount of premium amortization for the period ($8,000 – $6,512 = $1,488). This procedure is followed each period until the maturity date when the premium (or discount) will be fully amortized.

Example 11 ▶ Interest Payments

Required: Record the first four interest payments for the bonds illustrated in Example 6, rounding amounts to the nearest dollar.

Solution:

6/30, Year 1:	Interest Expense [($200,000 + 17,060) × 0.03]	6,512	
	Bond Premium (to balance)	1,488	
	Cash ($200,000 × 0.04)		8,000
12/31, Year 1:	Interest Expense [($200,000 + 15,572*) × 0.03]	6,467	
	Bond Premium (to balance)	1,533	
	Cash ($200,000 × 0.04)		8,000
6/30, Year 2:	Interest Expense [($200,000 + 14,039*) × 0.03]	6,421	
	Bond Premium (to balance)	1,579	
	Cash ($200,000 × 0.04)		8,000
12/31, Year 2:	Interest Expense [($200,000 + 12,460*) × 0.03]	6,374	
	Bond Premium (to balance)	1,626	
	Cash ($200,000 × 0.04)		8,000

* 12/31, Year 1: $17,060 – $1,488 = $15,572; 6/30/X2, $15,572 – $1,533; 12/31/X2, $14,039 – $1,579

Exhibit 3 ▸ Bond Premium Amortization Table

(1) Period	(2) Cash interest payments	(3) 3% × Prior (6) interest expense	(4) (2) – (3) Premium amortization	(5) Prior (5) – (4) unamortized premium	(6) $200,000 + (5) Carrying amount
0	--	--	--	$17,060.00	$217,060.00
1	$8,000	$6,511.80	$1,488.20	15,571.80	215,571.80
2	8,000	6,467.15	1,532.85	14,038.95	214,038.95
3	8,000	6,421.17	1,578.83	12,460.12	212,460.12
4	8,000	6,373.80	1,626.20	10,833.92	210,833.92
5	8,000	6,325.02	1,674.98	9,158.94	209,158.94
6	8,000	6,274.77	1,725.23	7,433.71	207,433.71
7	8,000	6,223.01	1,776.99	5,656.72	205,656.72
8	8,000	6,169.70	1,830.30	3,826.42	203,826.42
9	8,000	6,114.79	1,885.21	1,941.21	201,941.21
10	8,000	6,058.79*	1,941.21	0	200,000.00

* $0.55 difference due to rounding

C. Amortization Effects

Amortization of a bond premium decreases interest expense and the carrying amount of the bond for the issuer, while the amortization of a bond discount increases the issuer's interest expense and the carrying amount of the bond.

D. Interest & Year-End Dates Differ

An adjusting entry is required when interest dates do not coincide with the end of the accounting period, to record accrued interest expense and bond premium or discount amortization.

Example 12 ▸ Interest and Year-End Dates Differ

In Example 6, assume the end of the accounting period comes 3 months after the bonds are issued. The required entry at 3/31, Year 1 would be the following.

Interest Expense ($6,512 × 3/6)	3,256	
Bond Premium ($1,488 × 3/6)	744	
Accrued Interest Payable ($8,000 × 3/6)		4,000

E. Issuance Between Interest Dates

Bonds payable are often sold between interest dates. If bond issue costs or a bond premium or discount is involved, it must be amortized over the period the bonds are outstanding.

Example 13 ▸ Issuance Between Interest Dates

On March 1 of the current year, Trisha Company issued 12% ten-year bonds with a face amount of $1,000. The bonds are dated January 1 of this year, and interest is payable semiannually on January 1 and July 1. The bonds were sold at par and accrued interest.

Required: Provide journal entries to record the bond issuance and the first interest payment.

Solution:

The issuance of the bonds would be recorded as follows.

Cash	1,020	
Bonds Payable (face amount)		1,000
Accrued Interest Payable ($1,000 × 0.12 × 2/12)		20

The payment of interest on July 1 would be recorded as follows.

Interest Expense (to balance)	40	
Accrued Interest Payable (from above)	20	
Cash ($1,000 × 0.12 × 6/12)		60

IV. Bonds With Additional Features

A. Serial Bonds

Bonds providing for a series of installments for repayment of principal.

1. **Present Values** To determine the selling price of serial bonds, compute the present value of the principal and interest payments for each series separately, then total the present value of each series.

2. **Declining Principal** The amortization of bond premium or discount on serial bonds requires the recognition of a declining debt principal. Successive bond years cannot be charged with equal amounts of premium or discount because of a shrinking debt and successively smaller interest payments.

3. **Amortization of Premium/Discount** Bond premium or discount, if material, should be amortized using the effective interest method prescribed by APB 21.

B. Convertible Bonds

Convertible bonds provide the bond holder the option of converting the bond to capital stock, typically common stock. According to APB 14, *Accounting for Convertible Debt and Debt Issued With Stock Purchase Warrants,* no proceeds from the debt issue are to be assigned to the conversion feature (even though the convertible bonds may sell for substantially more than similar nonconvertible bonds). The reason for no allocation to equity is that the debt cannot be separated from the conversion feature, as would be the case with detachable stock warrants.

1. **Book Value Method** The conversion of the bonds into common stock is generally recorded by crediting the paid-in capital accounts for the carrying amount of the debt at the date of the conversion; thus, no gain or loss is recognized upon conversion. Costs associated with the conversion are **not** recognized as an expense. The paid-in capital accounts are credited for the carrying amount of the debt converted, **less** any costs associated with the conversion.

2. **Market Value Method** Alternately, the market value method recognizes a gain or loss on retirement equal to the difference between the carrying amount of the debt at the date of the conversion and the fair value of the shares issued upon conversion.

Example 14 ▸ Bond Conversion

Bonds with a face amount of $10,000 and a carrying amount of $10,400 are converted into 100 shares of $50 par common stock with $90 fair value.

Required: Record the conversion of the bonds in the books of the issuer under (a) the book value method, and (b) the market value method.

Solution:

(a)	*Book Value Method:*		
	Bonds Payable	10,000	
	Bond Premium	400	
	Common Stock (100 × $50 PV)		5,000
	Add'l. Paid-In Capital (to balance)		5,400
(b)	*Market Value Method:*		
	Bonds Payable	10,000	
	Bond Premium	400	
	Common Stock (100 × $50 PV)		5,000
	Add'l. Paid-In Capital [100 × ($90 FV – $50 PV)]		4,000
	Gain on Conversion ($10,400 – $9,000)		1,400

3. **Induced Conversions (SFAS 84)** APB 26 generally requires gain or loss recognition on the *retirement* of debt, including certain convertible debt. APB 26, however, does not apply to debt that is *converted* to equity securities of the debtor pursuant to conversion privileges provided in the terms of the debt at issuance. As illustrated in Example 14, the conversion of convertible debt securities to stock may or may not result in gain recognition, depending on whether the book value or the market value method is used. (However, the same method must be consistently applied.)

   a. **Applicability** SFAS 84, *Induced Conversions of Convertible Debt,* applies to a specific situation in which a debtor attempts to induce prompt conversion of convertible debt to equity securities.

      (1) To achieve this, the debtor may offer debt holders a higher conversion ratio, payment of additional consideration, or other favorable changes to the original terms of conversion. Induced conversions that meet certain specified criteria are excluded from the scope of APB 26 and are accounted for instead under the guidance of SFAS 84. These criteria are as follows.

         (a) The conversion occurs pursuant to changed conversion privileges that are exercisable only for a limited period of time.

         (b) The changed terms are applicable to the issuance of all of the equity securities issuable pursuant to the original conversion privileges for each debt instrument that is converted.

      (2) The changed terms may involve reduction of the original conversion price, thereby resulting in the issuance of additional shares of stock, issuance of warrants or other securities not provided for in the original conversion terms, or payment of cash or other consideration to those debt holders who convert during the specified time period.

   b. **Expense Recognition** When convertible debt is converted to equity securities of the debtor pursuant to an inducement offer described in a., above, the debtor enterprise should recognize an expense equal to the fair value of all securities and other consideration transferred in excess of the fair value of securities issuable pursuant to the original conversion terms.

      (1) This expense should **not** be reported as an extraordinary item.

      (2) The fair value of the securities or other consideration should be measured as of the date the inducement offer is accepted by the convertible debt holder. Normally this will be the date the debt holder converts the convertible debt into equity securities or enters into a binding agreement to do so.

   c. **Exclusions** SFAS 84 does not apply to conversions pursuant to other changes in conversion privileges or to changes in terms of convertible debt instruments that are different from those described above.

C. Debt Issued With Detachable Stock Warrants

When bonds are issued with detachable stock warrants, APB 14, *Accounting for Convertible Debt and Debt Issued With Stock Purchase Warrants,* requires allocation of the proceeds between the warrants and the debt security based on relative fair values. If the FV of one security is not determinable, the proceeds are assigned based on the FV of the other security. The rationale behind this allocation is that, even if the warrants are exercised, the debt will still remain. There are two separate elements, the debt and the warrants. The warrants are accounted for as paid-in capital.

Example 15 ▶ Detachable Stock Warrants

On November 1, Year 1, two hundred $1,000, 8% bonds due October 31, Year 5, were sold at 103 with one detachable stock purchase warrant attached to each bond. The fair value of the bonds without the stock warrants is 98. The fair value of the warrants has not been determined. Each warrant entitles the holder to purchase ten shares of common stock (par $10) at $30 per share.

Borrower			Investor (net)		
Cash	206,000		Bond Investment	196,000	
Bond Discount	4,000		Stock Warrants	10,000	
Bond Payable		200,000	Cash		206,000
APIC-Stock Warrants		10,000			

Computations:

Cash proceeds [(200 × $1,000) × 103%]	$206,000
Proceeds allocated to bonds (200 × $1,000 × 98%)	196,000
Proceeds allocated to warrants (remainder)	$ 10,000
Bond discount ($200,000 – $196,000)	$ 4,000

If 100 of the 200 stock purchase warrants are exercised:

Borrower			Investor (net)		
Cash (100 × 10 × $30)	30,000		Inv. in Common Stock		
APIC-Stock Warrants			(1,000 × $35)	35,000	
($10,000 × 100/200)	5,000		Stock Warrants		
Common Stock			($10,000 × 100/200)		5,000
(1,000 × $10 PV)		10,000	Cash (100 × 10 × $30)		30,000
APIC-Common St. (to bal.)		25,000			

V. Comparison of Borrower & Investor Journal Entries

A. Premiums & Discounts

Example 16 ▶ Straight-Line Premium Amortization

On January 1, Year 1, a $1,000 face value, two-year bond, with a 10% coupon rate of interest is sold for 104. The effective yield is 7.8%. Interest is paid semi-annually on June 30 and December 31. Use the straight-line method to amortize the premium.

Borrower			Investor		
January 1, Year 1					
Cash	1,040		Invest. in Bond	1,040	
Bond Payable		1,000	Cash		1,040
Premium		40			
June 30, Year 1					
Interest Expense	40		Cash	50	
Premium	10		Invest. in Bond		10
Cash		50	Interest Income		40
Same journal entries for next 3 periods.			Same journal entries for next 3 periods.		
December 31, Year 2					
Bond Payable	1,000		Cash	1,000	
Cash		1,000	Invest. in Bond		1,000

Example 17 ▸ Straight-Line Discount Amortization

Same as Example 16, except that the bond is sold for 96 and the effective interest rate is 12.3%.

Borrower			Investor		
January 1, Year 1					
Cash	960		Invest. in Bond	960	
Discount	40		Cash		960
Bond Payable		1,000			
June 30, Year 1					
Interest Expense	60		Cash	50	
Cash		50	Invest. in Bond	10	
Discount		10	Interest Income		60
Same journal entries for next 3 periods.			Same journal entries for next 3 periods.		
December 31, Year 2					
Bond Payable	1,000		Cash	1,000	
Cash		1,000	Invest. in Bond		1,000

Example 18 ▸ Effective Interest Method of Premium Amortization

Same as Example 16, except use the effective interest method to amortize the premium.

Borrower			Investor		
January 1, Year 1					
Cash	1,040.00				
Bond Payable		1,000.00	Invest. in Bond	1,040.00	
Premium		40.00	Cash		1,040.00
June 30, Year 1					
Interest Expense			Cash	50.00	
[($1,000 + $40) × 3.9%]	40.56		Invest. in Bond		9.44
Premium	9.44		Interest Income		40.56
Cash		50.00			
December 31, Year 1					
Interest Expense			Cash	50.00	
[($1,000 + 30.56) × 3.9%]	40.19		Invest. in Bond		9.81
Premium	9.81		Interest Income		40.19
Cash		50.00			
June 30, Year 2					
Interest Expense			Cash	50.00	
[(1,000 + 20.75) × 3.9%]	39.81		Invest. in Bond		10.19
Premium	10.19		Interest Income		39.81
Cash		50.00			
December 31, Year 2					
Interest Expense			Cash	50.00	
[(1,000 + 10.56) × 3.9%]	39.41		Invest. in Bond		10.59
Premium	10.59		Interest Income		39.41
Cash		50.00			
Bond Payable	1,000.00		Cash	1,000.00	
Cash		1,000.00	Invest. in Bond		1,000.00

(Amortization of Premium: 9.44 + 9.81 + 10.19 + 10.59 = 40.03 **NOTE:** Difference due to rounding.)

Example 19 ▸ Effective Interest Method of Discount Amortization

Same as Example 17, except use the effective interest method to amortize the discount.

Borrower			Investor		
January 1, Year 1					
Cash	960.00		Invest. in Bond	960.00	
Discount	40.00		Cash		960.00
Bond Payable		1,000.00			
June 30, Year 1					
Interest Expense			Cash	50.00	
[(1,000 – 40) × 6.15%]	59.04		Invest. in Bond	9.04	
Cash		50.00	Interest Income		59.04
Discount		9.04			
December 31, Year 1					
Interest Expense			Cash	50.00	
[($1,000 – 30.96) × 6.15%]	59.60		Invest. in Bond	9.60	
Cash		50.00	Interest Income		59.60
Discount		9.60			
June 30, Year 2					
Interest Expense			Cash	50.00	
[(1,000 – 21.36) × 6.15%]	60.19		Invest. in Bond	10.19	
Cash		50.00	Interest Income		60.19
Discount		10.19			
December 31, Year 2					
Interest Expense			Cash	50.00	
[(1,000 – 11.18) × 6.15%]	60.81		Invest. in Bond	10.81	
Cash		50.00	Interest Income		60.81
Discount		10.81			

(Amortization of discount: 9.04 + 9.60 + 10.19 + 10.81 = 39.63 **NOTE:** Difference due to rounding.)

B. Midperiod Issue

Example 20 ▸ Issuance Between Interest Dates

$1,000 face value, 2-year bond with a 10% coupon rate of interest is sold on April 1 of the current year at par. Interest is paid semi-annually on June 30 and December 31.

Borrower			Investor		
April 1					
Cash	1,025		Invest. in Bond	1,000	
Bond Payable		1,000	Interest Receivable	25	
Interest Payable		25	Cash		1,025
June 30					
Interest Expense	25		Cash	50	
Interest Payable	25		Interest Income		25
Cash		50	Interest Receivable		25

C. Convertible Bonds

Example 21 ▸ Convertible Bonds, Book Value Method

On January 1 of the current year, 100 bonds with $1,000 face values and each with 20 nondetachable stock warrants (100 × 20 = 2,000) are sold at 105. Twenty warrants, one bond, and $800 may be converted into one share of $200 par value common stock. 50% of the bonds are converted on June 30, and the book value method is used to record the conversion.

Borrower

January 1		
Cash	105,000	
Bond Payable		100,000
Premium		5,000
June 30		
Cash	40,000	
Bond Payable	50,000	
Premium	2,500	
Common Stock		10,000
APIC		82,500

Investor

Invest. in Bond	105,000	
Cash		105,000
Invest. in Stock	92,500	
Cash		40,000
Invest. in Bond		52,500

Computations:

Bond	$1,000 × 50 =	$ 50,000
Premium	$5,000 × 50% =	2,500
Cash	$ 800 × 50 =	40,000
		92,500
Common stock	$200 par × 50 =	(10,000)
APIC		$ 82,500

Example 22 ▸ Convertible Bonds, Market Value Method

On January 1 of the current year, 100 bonds with $1,000 face values and each with 20 nondetachable stock warrants (100 × 20 = 2,000) are sold at 105. Twenty warrants, one bond, and $800 may be converted into one share of $200 par value common stock. All of the bonds are converted on June 30. The market value method is used to record the conversion and the fair value of the stock on the date of conversion is $2,000.

Borrower

January 1		
Cash	105,000	
Bond Payable		100,000
Premium		5,000
June 30		
Cash	80,000	
Bond Payable	100,000	
Premium	5,000	
Loss on Conversion	15,000	
Common Stock		20,000
APIC		180,000

Investor

Invest. in Bond	105,000	
Cash		105,000
Invest. in Stock	200,000	
Cash		80,000
Invest. in Bond		105,000
Gain on Conversion		15,000

Computations:

Bond	$1,000 × 100 =	$100,000
Cash	$ 800 × 100 =	80,000
Common stock	$200 par × 100 =	20,000
APIC	($2,000 – 200)× 100 =	180,000

Common stock	$ 20,000	
APIC	180,000	
		$200,000
Bond	100,000	
Premium	5,000	
Cash	80,000	
		(185,000)
Gain		$ 15,000

D. Warrants

Example 23 ▸ Detachable Warrants

On January 1 of the current year, 100 bonds with $1,000 face values and each with 20 detachable stock warrants (100 × 20 = 2,000) are sold at 105. Twenty warrants and $800 may be converted into one share of $200 par value common stock. The warrants have a fair value of $12,000 and expire on July 1. One half of the warrants are exercised on June 30 and the other half expire on July 1.

Borrower			Investor		
January 1					
Cash	105,000		Invest. in Bond	93,000	
Discount	7,000		Warrants	12,000	
Bond Payable		100,000	Cash		105,000
APIC—Warrants		12,000			
June 30					
Cash	40,000		Invest. in Stock	46,000	
APIC—Warrant	6,000		Cash		40,000
Common Stock		10,000	Warrants		6,000
APIC		36,000			
July 1					
APIC—Warrant	6,000		Loss on Investment	6,000	
APIC		6,000	Warrants		6,000

Computations:

Warrant	$12,000 × 50% =	$ 6,000
Cash	$ 800 × 50 =	40,000
		46,000
Common stock	$200 par × 50 =	(10,000)
APIC		$ 36,000

CHAPTER 6—BONDS

Problem 6-1 MULTIPLE CHOICE QUESTIONS (78 to 98 minutes)

1. Kale purchased bonds at a discount on the open market as an investment and intends to hold these bonds to maturity. Kale should account for these bonds at
a. Cost
b. Amortized cost
c. Fair value
d. Lower of cost or market
(11/94, FAR, #10, amended, 5275)

2. On June 1 of the current year, Cross Corp. issued $300,000 of 8% bonds payable at par with interest payment dates of April 1 and October 1. In its income statement for the current year ended December 31, what amount of interest expense should Cross report?
a. $ 6,000
b. $ 8,000
c. $12,000
d. $14,000 (R/05, FAR, 0211F, #4, amended, 7748)

3. An investor purchased a bond classified as a long-term investment between interest dates at a discount. At the purchase date, the carrying amount of the bond is more than the

	Cash paid to seller	*Face amount of bond*
a.	No	Yes
b.	No	No
c.	Yes	No
d.	Yes	Yes

(5/91, Theory, #4, 1781)

4. On July 1 of the current year, York Co. purchased as a long-term investment $1,000,000 of Park Inc.'s 8% bonds for $946,000, including accrued interest of $40,000. The bonds were purchased to yield 10% interest. The bonds mature on January 1 seven years from now and pay interest annually on January 1. York uses the effective interest method of amortization. In its December 31 current year balance sheet, what amount should York report as investment in bonds?
a. $911,300
b. $916,600
c. $953,300
d. $960,600 (5/93, PI, #15, amended, 4057)

5. On July 1, Cody Co. paid $1,198,000 for 10%, 20-year bonds with a face amount of $1,000,000. Interest is paid on December 31 and June 30. The bonds were purchased to yield 8%. Cody uses the effective interest rate method to recognize interest income from this investment. What should be reported as the carrying amount of the bonds in Cody's December 31 balance sheet?
a. $1,207,900
b. $1,198,000
c. $1,195,920
d. $1,193,050 (5/92, PI, #12, amended, 2579)

6. On October 1, year 2, Park Co. purchased 200 of the $1,000 face amount, 10% bonds of Ott, Inc., for $220,000, including accrued interest of $5,000. The bonds, which mature on January 1, year 9, pay interest semiannually on January 1 and July 1. Park used the straight-line method of amortization and appropriately recorded the bonds as a long-term investment. On Park's December 31, year 3 balance sheet, the bonds should be reported at
a. $215,000
b. $214,400
c. $214,200
d. $212,000 (11/90, PI, #4, amended, 0971)

7. In the previous year, Lee Co. acquired, at a premium, Enfield Inc. 10-year bonds as a long-term investment. At December 31 of the current year, Enfield's bonds were quoted at a small discount. Which of the following situations is the most likely cause of the decline in the bonds' market value?
a. Enfield issued a stock dividend.
b. Enfield is expected to call the bonds at a premium, which is less than Lee's carrying amount.
c. Interest rates have declined since Lee purchased the bonds.
d. Interest rates have increased since Lee purchased the bonds.
(5/93, Theory, #11, amended, 4199)

8. A bond issued on June 1 of the current year, has interest payment dates of April 1 and October 1. Bond interest expense for the current year ended December 31, is for a period of
a. Three months
b. Four months
c. Six months
d. Seven months
(5/94, FAR, #46, amended, 4861)

9. On July 1, East Co. purchased as a long-term investment $500,000 face amount, 8% bonds of Rand Corp. for $461,500 to yield 10% per year. The bonds pay interest semiannually on January 1 and July 1. In its December 31 balance sheet, East should report interest receivable of

a. $18,460
b. $20,000
c. $23,075
d. $25,000 (11/88, PI, #18, amended, 9018)

10. Jent Corp. purchased bonds at a discount of $10,000. Subsequently, Jent sold these bonds at a premium of $14,000. During the period that Jent held this investment, amortization of the discount amounted to $2,000. What amount should Jent report as gain on the sale of bonds?

a. $12,000
b. $22,000
c. $24,000
d. $26,000 (5/94, FAR, #43, 4858)

11. Album Co. issued 10-year $200,000 debenture bonds on January 2. The bonds pay interest semiannually. Album uses the effective interest method to amortize bond premiums and discounts. The carrying value of the bonds on January 2 was $185,953. A journal entry was recorded for the first interest payment on June 30, debiting interest expense for $13,016 and crediting cash for $12,000. What is the annual stated interest rate for the debenture bonds?

a. 6%
b. 7%
c. 12%
d. 14% (R/05, FAR, 1199F, #27, 7771)

12. During the year, Lake Co. issued 3,000 of its 9%, $1,000 face value bonds at 101½. In connection with the sale of these bonds, Lake paid the following expenses:

Promotion costs	$ 20,000
Engraving and printing	25,000
Underwriters' commissions	200,000

What amount should Lake record as bond issue costs to be amortized over the term of the bonds?

a. $0
b. $220,000
c. $225,000
d. $245,000 (11/92, PI, amended, #37, 3270)

13. On January 1, year 2, Oak Co. issued 400 of its 8%, $1,000 bonds at 97 plus accrued interest. The bonds are dated October 1, year 1, and mature in fifteen years October 1. Interest is payable semiannually on April 1 and October 1. Accrued interest for the period October 1, year 1, to January 1, year 2, amounted to $8,000. On January 1, year 2, what amount should Oak report as bonds payable, net of discount?

a. $380,300
b. $388,000
c. $388,300
d. $392,000 (5/94, FAR, #29, amended, 4844)

14. The market price of a bond issued at a premium is equal to the present value of its principal amount

a. Only, at the stated interest rate.
b. And the present value of all future interest payments, at the stated interest rate.
c. Only, at the market (effective) interest rate.
d. And the present value of all future interest payments, at the market (effective) interest rate.

(11/97, FAR, #9, 6489)

15. Perk, Inc. issued $500,000, 10% bonds to yield 8%. Bond issuance costs were $10,000. How should Perk calculate the net proceeds to be received from the issuance?

a. Discount the bonds at the stated rate of interest.
b. Discount the bonds at the market rate of interest.
c. Discount the bonds at the stated rate of interest and deduct bond issuance costs.
d. Discount the bonds at the market rate of interest and deduct bond issuance costs.

(R/99, FAR, #9, 6778)

16. On January 2 of year 2, Gill Co. issued $2,000,000 of 10-year, 8% bonds at par. The bonds, dated January 1, year 2, pay interest semiannually on January 1 and July 1. Bond issue costs were $250,000. What amount of bond issue costs are unamortized at June 30, year 3?

a. $237,500
b. $225,000
c. $220,800
d. $212,500 (11/93, PI, #34, amended, 4403)

17. Dixon Co. incurred costs of $3,300 when it issued, on August 31 of the current year, 5-year debenture bonds dated April 1 of the current year. What amount of bond issue expense should Dixon report in its income statement for the current year ended December 31?

a. $ 220
b. $ 240
c. $ 495
d. $3,300 (5/92, PI, #29, amended, 2598)

18. A 15-year bond was issued in year 1 at a discount. During year 11, a 10-year bond was issued at face amount with the proceeds used to retire the 15-year bond at its face amount. The net effect of the year 11 bond transactions was to increase long-term liabilities by the excess of the 10-year bond's face amount over the 15-year bond's

a. Face amount
b. Carrying amount
c. Face amount less the deferred loss on bond retirement
d. Carrying amount less the deferred loss on bond retirement (5/91, Theory, #5, amended, 1782)

19. On July 31 of the current year, Dome Co. issued $1,000,000 of 10%, 15-year bonds at par and used a portion of the proceeds to call its 600 outstanding 11%, $1,000 face value bonds, due in ten years on July 31, at 102. On that date, unamortized bond premium relating to the 11% bonds was $65,000. In its year-end income statement, what amount should Dome report as gain or loss, before income taxes, from retirement of bonds?

a. $ 53,000 gain
b. $0
c. $ (65,000) loss
d. $ (77,000) loss

(11/94, FAR, #42, amended, 5304)

20. Weald Co. took advantage of market conditions to refund debt. This was the fifth refunding operation carried out by Weald within the last four years. The excess of the carrying amount of the old debt over the amount paid to extinguish it should be reported as a(an)

a. Deferred credit to be amortized over life of new debt
b. Part of continuing operations
c. Extraordinary gain, net of income taxes
d. Extraordinary loss, net of income taxes

(5/93, Theory, #18, amended, 9023)

21. On January 1, year 13, Hart Inc., redeemed its 15-year bonds of $500,000 face amount for 102. Hart's bond redemption meets the criteria of an extraordinary event. They were originally issued on January 1, year 1 at 98 with a maturity date of January 1, year 16. The bond issue costs relating to this transaction were $20,000. Hart amortizes discounts, premiums, and bond issue costs using the straight-line method. What amount of extraordinary loss should Hart recognize on the redemption of these bonds?

a. $16,000
b. $12,000
c. $10,000
d. $0 (11/90, PI, #50, amended, 1040)

22. On January 2, year 1, Nast Co. issued 8% bonds with a face amount of $1,000,000 that mature on January 2, year 7. The bonds were issued to yield 12%, resulting in a discount of $150,000. Nast incorrectly used the straight-line method instead of the effective interest method to amortize the discount. How is the carrying amount of the bonds affected by the error?

	At December 31, year 1	*At January 2, year 7*
a.	Overstated	Understated
b.	Overstated	No effect
c.	Understated	Overstated
d.	Understated	No effect

(5/95, FAR, #20, amended, 5556)

23. A company issued ten-year term bonds at a discount in year 1. Bond issue costs were incurred at that time. The company uses the effective interest method to amortize bond issue costs. Reporting the bond issue costs as a deferred charge would result in

a. More of a reduction in net income in year 2 than reporting the bond issue costs as a reduction of the related debt liability
b. The same reduction in net income in year 2 as reporting the bond issue costs as a reduction of the related debt liability
c. Less of a reduction in net income in year 2 than reporting the bond issue costs as a reduction of the related debt liability
d. No reduction in net income in year 2

(11/88, Theory, #15, amended, 9019)

24. Webb Co. has outstanding a 7%, 10-year $100,000 face-value bond. The bond was originally sold to yield 6% annual interest. Webb uses the effective interest rate method to amortize bond premium. On June 30, year 2, the carrying amount of the outstanding bond was $105,000. What amount of unamortized premium on bond should Webb report in its June 30, year 3 balance sheet?

a. $1,050
b. $3,950
c. $4,300
d. $4,500 (11/93, PI, #36, amended, 4405)

25. On January 2 of the current year, West Co. issued 9% bonds in the amount of $500,000, which mature in ten years. The bonds were issued for $469,500 to yield 10%. Interest is payable annually on December 31. West uses the interest method of amortizing bond discount. In its June 30 current year balance sheet, what amount should West report as bonds payable?

a. $469,500
b. $470,475
c. $471,025
d. $500,000 (11/94, FAR, #24, amended, 5288)

26. How would the amortization of discount on bonds payable affect each of the following?

	Carrying amount of bond	Net income
a.	Increase	Decrease
b.	Increase	Increase
c.	Decrease	Decrease
d.	Decrease	Increase

(11/84, Theory, #25, 1890)

27. A five-year term bond was issued by a company on January 1, year 1, at a premium. The carrying amount of the bond at December 31, year 2, would be

a. The same as the carrying amount at January 1, year 1
b. Higher than the carrying amount at December 31, year 1
c. Lower than the carrying amount at December 31, year 3
d. Lower than the carrying amount at December 31, year 1

(5/87, Theory, #17, amended, 1861)

28. On July 1 of the current year, Eagle Corp. issued 600 of its 10%, $1,000 bonds at 99 plus accrued interest. The bonds are dated April 1 of the current year, and mature in 10 years. Interest is payable semiannually on April 1 and October 1. What amount did Eagle receive from the bond issuance?

a. $579,000
b. $594,000
c. $600,000
d. $609,000 (5/95, FAR, #19, amended, 5555)

29. On November 1 of the current year, Mason Corp. issued $800,000 of its 10-year, 8% term bonds dated October 1 of the current year. The bonds were sold to yield 10%, with total proceeds of $700,000 plus accrued interest. Interest is paid every April 1 and October 1. What amount should Mason report for interest payable in its December 31 current year balance sheet?

a. $17,500
b. $16,000
c. $11,667
d. $10,667 (11/92, PI, #23, amended, 3256)

30. Blue Corp.'s December 31, year 1 balance sheet contained the following items in the long-term liabilities section:

9-3/4% registered debentures, callable in year 12, due in year 17	$700,000
9-1/2% collateral trust bonds, convertible into common stock beginning in year 10, due in year 20	600,000
10% subordinated debentures ($30,000 maturing annually beginning in year 7)	300,000

What is the total amount of Blue's term bonds?

a. $ 600,000
b. $ 700,000
c. $1,000,000
d. $1,300,000 (11/92, PI, #39, amended, 3272)

31. Hancock Co.'s December 31, year 1 balance sheet contained the following items in the long-term liabilities section:

Unsecured	
9.375% registered bonds ($25,000 maturing annually beginning in year 5)	$275,000
11.5% convertible bonds, callable beginning in year 10, due year 21	125,000
Secured	
9.875% guaranty security bonds, due 2020	$250,000
10.0% commodity backed bonds ($50,000 maturing annually beginning in year 6)	200,000

What are the total amounts of serial bonds and debenture bonds?

	Serial bonds	Debenture bonds
a.	$475,000	$400,000
b	$475,000	$125,000
c.	$450,000	$400,000
d.	$200,000	$650,000

(5/91, PI, #47, amended, 9024)

32. On March 31, Ashley Inc.'s bondholders exchanged their convertible bonds for common stock. The carrying amount of these bonds on Ashley's books was less than the market value but greater than the par value of the common stock issued. If Ashley used the book value method of accounting for the conversion, which of the following statements correctly states an effect of this conversion?

a. Stockholders' equity is increased.
b. Additional paid-in capital is decreased.
c. Retained earnings is increased.
d. An extraordinary loss is recognized.

(5/93, Theory, #12, amended, 4200)

33. Clay Corp. had $600,000 convertible 8% bonds outstanding at June 30. Each $1,000 bond was convertible into 10 shares of Clay's $50 par value common stock. On July 1, the interest was paid to bondholders, and the bonds were converted into common stock, which had a fair market value of $75 per share. The unamortized premium on these bonds was $12,000 at the date of conversion. Under the book value method, this conversion increased the following elements of the stockholders' equity section by

	Common stock	*Additional paid-in capital*
a.	$300,000	$312,000
b.	$306,000	$306,000
c.	$450,000	$162,000
d.	$600,000	$ 12,000

(11/91, PI, #37, amended, 2425)

Items 34 and 35 are based on the following:

On January 2, year 1, Chard Co. issued 10-year convertible bonds at 105. During year 4, these bonds were converted into common stock having an aggregate par value equal to the total face amount of the bonds. At conversion, the market price of Chard's common stock was 50 percent above its par value.

34. On January 2, year 1, cash proceeds from the issuance of the convertible bonds should be reported as

a. Contributed capital for the entire proceeds
b. Contributed capital for the portion of the proceeds attributable to the conversion feature and as a liability for the balance
c. A liability for the face amount of the bonds and contributed capital for the premium over the face amount
d. A liability for the entire proceeds

(11/90, Theory, #29, amended, 1799)

35. Depending on whether the book value method or the market value method was used, Chard would recognize gains or losses on conversion when using the

	Book value method	*Market value method*
a.	Either gain or loss	Gain
b.	Either gain or loss	Loss
c.	Neither gain nor loss	Loss
d.	Neither gain nor loss	Gain

(11/90, Theory, #30, 9025)

36. On December 31 of the current year, Moss Co. issued $1,000,000 of 11% bonds at 109. Each $1,000 bond was issued with 50 detachable stock warrants, each of which entitled the bondholder to purchase one share of $5 par common stock for $25. Immediately after issuance, the market value of each warrant was $4. On December 31, what amount should Moss record as discount or premium on issuance of bonds?

a. $ 40,000 premium
b. $ 90,000 premium
c. $110,000 discount
d. $200,000 discount

(5/94, FAR, #34, amended, 4849)

37. On March 1 of the current year, Evan Corp. issued $500,000 of 10% nonconvertible bonds at 103, due in ten years on February 28. Each $1,000 bond was issued with 30 detachable stock warrants, each of which entitled the holder to purchase, for $50, one share of Evan's $25 par common stock. On March 1, the market price of each warrant was $4. By what amount should the bond issue proceeds increase stockholders' equity?

a. $0
b. $15,000
c. $45,000
d. $60,000 (5/93, PI, #32, amended, 4073)

38. Bonds with detachable stock warrants were issued by Flack Co. Immediately after issue, the aggregate market value of the bonds and the warrants exceeds the proceeds. Is the portion of the proceeds allocated to the warrants less than their market value, and is that amount recorded as contributed capital?

	Less than warrants' market value	*Contributed capital*
a.	No	Yes
b.	Yes	No
c.	Yes	Yes
d.	No	No

(11/91, Theory, #37, 2545)

39. Main Co. issued bonds with detachable common stock warrants. Only the warrants had a known market value. The sum of the fair value of the warrants and the face amount of the bonds exceeds the cash proceeds. This excess is reported as

a. Discount on bonds payable
b. Premium on bonds payable
c. Common stock subscribed
d. Contributed capital in excess of par-stock warrants (11/90, Theory, #31, 1800)

Problem 6-2 ADDITIONAL MULTIPLE CHOICE QUESTIONS (22 to 28 minutes)

40. For a bond issue which sells for less than its face amount, the market rate of interest is
a. Dependent on rate stated on the bond
b. Equal to rate stated on the bond
c. Less than rate stated on the bond
d. Higher than rate stated on the bond
(11/86, Theory, #17, 1870)

41. How would the amortization of premium on bonds payable affect each of the following?

	Carrying amount of bond	*Net income*
a.	Increase	Decrease
b.	Increase	Increase
c.	Decrease	Decrease
d.	Decrease	Increase

(11/83, Theory, #15, 9020)

42. On January 1, year 1, Fox Corp. issued 1,000 of its 10%, $1,000 bonds for $1,040,000. These bonds were to mature on January 1, year 11, but were callable at 101 any time after December 31, year 4. Interest was payable semiannually on July 1 and January 1. On July 1, year 6, Fox called all of the bonds and retired them. Bond premium was amortized on a straight-line basis. Before income taxes, Fox's gain or loss in year 6 on this early extinguishment of debt was
a. $30,000 gain
b. $12,000 gain
c. $10,000 loss
d. $ 8,000 gain (5/90, PI, #40, amended, 9022)

43. On July 1, year 1, Pell Co. purchased Green Corp. ten-year, 8% bonds with a face amount of $500,000 for $420,000. The bonds mature on June 30, year 9 and pay interest semiannually on June 30 and December 31. Using the interest method, Pell recorded bond discount amortization of $1,800 for the six months ended December 31, year 1. From this long-term investment, Pell should report year 1 revenue of
a. $16,800
b. $18,200
c. $20,000
d. $21,800 (5/90, PI, #46, amended, 0976)

44. Which of the following could be accounted for as a deferred charge, a reduction of the related debt liability, or an expense of the period of borrowing?
a. Discount on bonds payable
b. Premium on bonds payable
c. Bond issue costs
d. Loss on extinguishment of debt
(11/84, Theory, #24, amended, 1889)

45. On June 30, Huff Corp. issued at 99, one thousand of its 8%, $1,000 bonds. The bonds were issued through an underwriter to whom Huff paid bond issue costs of $35,000. On June 30, Huff should report the bond liability at
a. $ 955,000
b. $ 990,000
c. $1,000,000
d. $1,025,000 (11/90, PI, #24, amended, 1031)

46. On June 30, year 1, King Co. had outstanding 9%, $5,000,000 face value bonds maturing on June 30, year 6. Interest was payable semiannually every June 30 and December 31. On June 30, year 1, after amortization was recorded for the period, the unamortized bond premium and bond issue costs were $30,000 and $50,000, respectively. On that date, King acquired all its outstanding bonds on the open market at 98 and retired them. At June 30, year 1, what amount should King recognize as gain before income taxes on redemption of bonds?
a. $ 20,000
b. $ 80,000
c. $120,000
d. $180,000 (11/92, PI, #47, amended, 3280)

47. On May 1, Bolt Corp. issued 11% bonds in the face amount of $1,000,000 that mature in ten years. The bonds were issued to yield 10%, resulting in bond premium of $62,000. Bolt uses the effective interest method of amortizing bond premium. Interest is payable semiannually on November 1 and May 1. In its October 31 balance sheet, what amount should Bolt report as unamortized bond premium?
a. $62,000
b. $60,100
c. $58,900
d. $58,590 (11/92, PI, #38, amended, 3271)

48. On July 1, year 1, Cobb Inc. issued 9% bonds in the face amount of $1,000,000, which mature in ten years. The bonds were issued for $939,000 to yield 10%, resulting in a bond discount of $61,000. Cobb uses the interest method of amortizing bond discount. Interest is payable annually on June 30. At June 30, year 3, Cobb's unamortized bond discount should be
a. $52,810
b. $51,000
c. $48,800
d. $43,000 (5/89, PI, #46, amended, 1064)

49. On December 30 of the current year, Fort Inc. issued 1,000 of its 8%, 10-year, $1,000 face value bonds with detachable stock warrants at par. Each bond carried a detachable warrant for one share of Fort's common stock at a specified option price of $25 per share. Immediately after issuance, the market value of the bonds without the warrants was $1,080,000 and the market value of the warrants was $120,000. In its December 31 balance sheet, what amount should Fort report as bonds payable?

a. $1,000,000
b. $ 975,000
c. $ 900,000
d. $ 880,000 (11/93, PI, #33, amended, 4402)

50. Ray Corp. issued bonds with a face amount of $200,000. Each $1,000 bond contained 100 detachable stock warrants for shares of Ray's common stock. Total proceeds from the issue amounted to $240,000. The market value of each warrant was $2, and the market value of the bonds without the warrants was $196,000. The bonds were issued at a discount of

a. $0
b. $ 678
c. $ 4,000
d. $33,898 (5/91, PI, #5, amended, 1023)

SIMULATIONS

Problem 6-3 (15 to 25 minutes)

Scenario	Responses	Research Task

On January 2 of the current year, North Co. issued bonds payable with a face value of $480,000 at a discount. The bonds are due in 10 years and interest is payable semiannually every June 30 and December 31.

On June 30, and on December 31, North made the semiannual interest payments due and recorded interest expense and amortization of bond discount.

Scenario	Responses	Research Task

For each item numbered 1 through 7, select and place the correct response into the partially-completed amortization table below.

Date	Cash	Interest Expense	Amortization	Discount	Carrying Amount
1/2					(3) ______
6/30	(2) ______	18,000	3,600	(1) ______	363,600
12/31	$14,400	(6) ______	(7) ______		

Annual Interest Rates: Stated (4)______ Effective (5)______

Selections may be made from the list below. Any choice may be used once, more than once, or not at all.

Rates		*Amounts*					
A.	3.0%	G.	$ 3,420	M.	$ 18,000	S.	$123,600
B.	4.5%	H.	$ 3,600	N.	$ 18,180	T.	$360,000
C.	5.0%	I.	$ 3,780	O.	$ 18,360	U.	$363,600
D.	6.0%	J.	$ 3,960	P.	$ 21,600	V.	$367,200
E.	9.0%	K.	$14,400	Q.	$116,400	W.	$467,400
F.	10.0%	L.	$17,820	R.	$120,000	X.	$480,000

(11/95, FAR, #71-77, 9911)

Scenario	Responses	Research Task

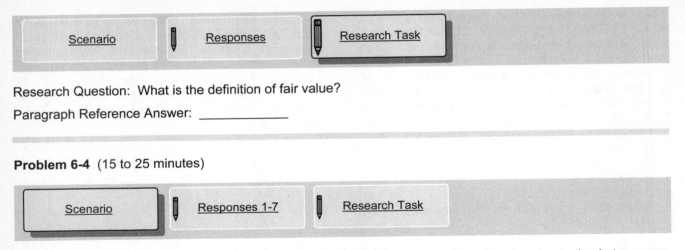

Research Question: What is the definition of fair value?

Paragraph Reference Answer: ____________

Problem 6-4 (15 to 25 minutes)

Scenario	Responses 1-7	Research Task

On July 1, year 1, Ring Co. issued $250,000, 14% bonds payable at a premium. The bonds are due in ten years. Interest is payable semiannually every June 30 and December 31. On December 31, year 1, and June 30, year 2, Ring made the semiannual interest payments due and recorded interest expense and amortization of bond premium. With the proceeds of the bond issuance, Ring retired other debt. Ring recorded a gain on the early extinguishment of the other debt.

Scenario	Responses 1-7	Research Task

Items 1 through 7, contained in the partially-completed amortization table below, represent formulas used to calculate information needed to complete the table. Select your answers from the list in the choices tab. Select the **best** answer for each item. Each formula may be selected once, more than once, or not at all. "Stated interest rate" and "effective interest rate" are stated on an annual basis. Place the correct letter response beside the item number in the boxes of the amortization table below.

	Cash paid	Interest expense	*Amortization*	Carrying amount	Unamortized premium
7/1, year 1				(1) ________	
12/31, year 1	(2) ________	$14,100	(3) ________	$349,100	(4) ________
6/30, year 2	$17,500	(5) ________	$3,536	(6) ________	

Effective Annual Interest Rate: (7) ________

Formulas	
A.	Face amount × stated interest rate
B.	Face amount × effective interest rate
C.	Carrying amount × stated interest rate
D.	Carrying amount × effective interest rate
E.	Present value of face amount + present value of all future payments at date of issuance
F.	Carrying amount of bonds in the previous period – amortization for the current period
G.	Carrying amount of bonds in the previous period + amortization for the current period
H.	Cash paid – interest expense

I.	Cash paid + interest expense
J.	(Face amount × stated interest rate) × ½
K.	(Face amount × effective interest rate) × ½
L.	(Carrying amount at the beginning of the period × stated interest rate) × ½
M.	(Carrying amount at the beginning of the period × effective interest rate) × ½
N.	Carrying amount – face amount
O.	(Interest expense/carrying amount at the beginning of the period) × 2
P.	(Cash paid/carrying amount) × 2
Q.	Face amount – unamortized premium

(11/98, FAR, #17, amended, 6739)

Scenario | Responses 1-7 | Research Task

Research Question: What is the Board's opinion of the interest method of amortization of debt discount and expense or premium?

Paragraph Reference Answer: ____________

Problem 6-5 (45-55 minutes)

Scenario | Responses | Research Task

Hamnoff Inc.'s $50 par value common stock has always traded above par. During the year, Hamnoff had several transactions that affected the following balance sheet accounts:

Bond discount
Bond premium
Bond payable
Common stock
Additional paid-in capital
Retained earnings

For items 1 through 5 determine whether the transaction increased (I), decreased (D), or had no effect (N) on each of the balances in the above accounts.

1. Hamnoff issued bonds payable with a nominal rate of interest that was less than the market rate of interest.
2. Hamnoff issued convertible bonds, which are common stock equivalents, for an amount in excess of the bonds' face amount.
3. Hamnoff issued common stock when the convertible bonds described in item 2 were submitted for conversion. Each $1,000 bond was converted into 20 common shares. The book value method was used for the early conversion.
4. Hamnoff issued bonds, with detachable stock warrants, for an amount equal to the face amount of the bonds. The stock warrants have a determinable value.
5. Hamnoff declared and issued a 2% stock dividend.

Determine whether the transaction increased (I), decreased (D), or had no effect (N) on each of the balances in the accounts. Place your response in the appropriate box.

Scenario | Responses | Research Task

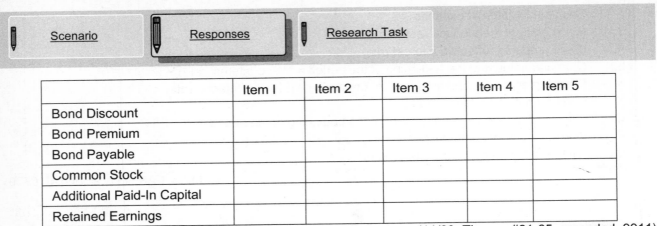

	Item I	Item 2	Item 3	Item 4	Item 5
Bond Discount					
Bond Premium					
Bond Payable					
Common Stock					
Additional Paid-In Capital					
Retained Earnings					

(11/93, Theory, #61-65, amended, 9911)

Scenario | Responses | Research Task

Research Question: When debt securities are issued with detachable stock purchase warrants, how is the portion of the proceeds allocable to the warrants accounted for?

Paragraph Reference Answer: ____________

Problem 6-6 (15 to 25 minutes)

Essay

On January 2, year 1, Company issued 9% term bonds dated January 2, year 1, at an effective annual interest rate (yield) of 10%. Drew uses the effective interest method of amortization. On July 1, year 3, the bonds were extinguished early when Drew acquired them in the open market for a price greater than face amount.

On September 1, year 3, Drew issued for cash 7% nonconvertible bonds dated September 1, year 3, with detachable stock purchase warrants. Immediately after issuance, both the bonds and the warrants had separately determined market values.

a. 1. Were the 9% term bonds issued at face amount, at a discount, or at a premium? Why?
   2. Would the amount of interest expense for the 9% term bonds using the effective interest method of amortization be higher in the first or second year of the life of the bond issue? Why?

b. 1. How should gain or loss on early extinguishment of debt be determined? Does the early extinguishment of the 9% term bonds result in a gain or loss? Why?
   2. How should Drew report the early extinguishment of the 9% term bonds on the year 3 income statement?

c. How should Drew account for the issuance of the 7% nonconvertible bonds with detachable stock purchase warrants? (5/90, Theory, #3, amended, 6191)

Solution 6-1 MULTIPLE CHOICE ANSWERS

Long-Term Investments

1. (b) Debt securities that the enterprise has the positive intent and ability to hold to maturity are classified as held-to-maturity securities and reported at amortized cost (SFAS 115, ¶7). Only securities classified as either trading securities or available-for-sale securities are reported at fair value (par. 12). Debt and equity securities should not be reported at cost or lower-of-cost-or-market if they are accounted for under SFAS 115.

2. (d) Interest expense from June 1 to December 31 is for 7 months.

$300,000	$ 2,000
× 8%	× 7 months
$ 24,000	$14,000
÷ 12 months	
$ 2,000 per month	

3. (b) A bond issued between interest payment dates requires the investor to pay the seller for accrued interest in addition to the price of the bond. A bond issued at a discount is a bond issued at a price below the bond's face amount. Hence, at the date of purchase, the carrying amount of a bond purchased at a discount between interest payment dates is less than the cash paid to the seller and is also less than the face amount of the bond.

4. (a) The carrying amount of the bond investment is the amortization of the bond discount from the purchase date plus the cost of the bond investment ($906,000 + $5,300 = $911,300).

Bond investment cost ($946,000 – $40,000)	$906,000
Times: Effective interest rate (10% / 2)	× 5%
Interest income, 7/1 - 12/31	45,300
Portion of annual interest payment applicable to 7/1 - 12/31 [($1,000,000 × 8%) / 2]	(40,000)
Amortization of bond discount to 12/31	$ 5,300

5. (c) $1,198,000 – $2,080 = $1,195,920

Bond investment carrying amount, 7/1	$1,198,000
Times: Effective interest rate (8% / 2)	× 4%
Interest income, 7/1 - 12/31	47,920
Semiannual interest payment [$1,000,000 × (10% / 2)]	(50,000)
Amortization of bond premium to 12/31	$ (2,080)

6. (d) The carrying amount of the bonds is determined by subtracting the amortization of the bond premium from the date of purchase from the cost of the bond investment.

Bond cost, 10/1, year 2 ($220,000 – $5,000)		$215,000
Bond investment cost, 10/1, year 2	$ 215,000	
Less: Face amount of bonds (200 × $1,000)	(200,000)	
Bond premium	$ 15,000	
Divided by: Months to maturity (10/1, year 2 to 1/1, year 9)	÷ 75	
Monthly premium amortization	$ 200	
Times: Months from issue	× 15	
Less amortization of premium to 12/31		(3,000)
Bond carrying amount, 12/31, year 3		$212,000

Valuation Factors

7. (d) The purchaser of a bond acquires the right to receive two cash flows: a lump sum paid at maturity for the face amount of the bond, and an annuity consisting of periodic interest payments over the life of the bond. The price the market is willing to pay for the bond is equal to the present value of these two cash flows, discounted at the prevailing market interest rate for bonds having the same maturity and perceived degree of risk. When interest rates increase, the present value of the two cash flows decreases, causing the market value of the bonds to decline. The issuance of a stock dividend should not cause a decline in the market value of the bonds. If the bonds currently are quoted at a small discount and the bonds are expected to be called at a premium (i.e., above face amount), this situation would most likely have the effect of causing a rise in the market value of the bonds. A decline in interest rates would cause a rise in the bond's market value.

8. (d) When the interest date does not coincide with the end of the accounting period, the issuer must accrue interest expense through year-end. Therefore, bond interest expense for the year ended December 31, is for a period of seven months—from the date of issuance of June 1 to year-end of December 31.

9. (b) The bonds pay interest semiannually on January 1 and July 1. The interest to be received on 1/1 the following year should be reported as bond interest receivable at 12/31 of the current year.

Face amount of bond investment	$500,000
Times: Semiannual stated interest rate (8% / 2)	× 4%
Semiannual interest payment	$ 20,000

10. (b) Since the bond was purchased at a discount, the initial carrying value of the bond investment is $10,000 less than the face amount. The amortization of the discount increases the bond investment and so, on the date of sale the bond investment is carried on Jent Corp.'s books at $8,000 less (i.e., $10,000 – 2,000) than the face amount. Therefore, the sale of the bond at a premium (i.e., at

$14,000 more than the face amount of the bond) results in recognition of a gain (i.e., $8,000 + $14,000).

Bond Issuance

11. (c) The bonds' stated interest rate and face amount determine the amount of periodic interest payments. The interest payment recorded on June 2 was for 6 months. To arrive at the annual rate multiply the interest payment by 2 and divide by the face amount of the bond.

$ 12,000
× 2
24,000
/ 200,000
12%

14% is the annual effective rate.
6% is the semi-annual stated interest rate.
7% is the semi-annual effective rate.

12. (d) Engraving and printing costs, accounting and legal fees, commissions paid to underwriters, promotion costs, and other similar charges are incurred when bonds are issued. According to generally accepted accounting principles (i.e., APB 21, *Interest on Receivables and Payables*), bond issue costs should be recorded as a deferred charge and amortized over the life of the debt, in a manner similar to that used for discount on bonds. Therefore, $245,000 (i.e., $20,000 + $25,000 + $200,000) should be recorded as bond issue costs to be amortized over the term of the bonds.

13. (b) 400 bonds × (1,000 × 97%) = $388,000 bonds payable.

14. (d) The market price of a bond is equal to the present value of the bond's interest and principal payments, discounted using the market interest rate for that type of bond.

15. (d) The net proceeds of a bond issuance is determined by calculating the present value of the projected cash flows of the bonds at the yield rate (market rate) of interest and then deducting bond issuance costs. The stated rate of interest is used to determine the amount of cash to be paid at each payment date, but the market rate is the rate used to discount the cash flows to present values.

16. (d) $250,000 – $37,500 = $212,500

Bond issue costs, 1/2, year 2	$250,000
Divide by: Number of semi-annual interest dates (10 × 2)	/ 20
Semiannual amortization of bond issue costs	12,500
Times: Number of interest dates from 1/2, year 2 to 6/30, year 3	× 3
Amortization, 1/2, year 2 to 6/30, year 3	(37,500)

17. (b) The bond issue was sold between interest dates (i.e., the bonds are dated April 1 but were issued five months later on August 31). The amortization of bond issue costs is affected when a bond issue is sold between interest dates because the issue costs should be amortized over the period from the date of sale (not the date of the bond) to the maturity date.

Bond issue costs	$3,300
Months from date of sale to maturity date [(5 × 12) – 5]	/ 55
Monthly bond issue cost amortization	60
Months bonds were outstanding during the year	× 4
Bond issue cost amortization for the year	$ 240

Bond Redemption

18. (b) The new 10-year bond was issued at its face amount which, from the facts, either equals or exceeds the face amount of the 15-year bond which exceeds the carrying amount of the 15-year bond because the 15-year bond was issued at a discount (a price less than the face amount). The excess of the retirement price (face amount) of the 15-year bond over its carrying amount will be recorded as a loss at retirement. Therefore, the issuance of the new bond and the retirement of the old bond will have the net effect of increasing the total of long-term liabilities by the excess of the new bond's face amount over the old bond's carrying amount.

19. (a) A gain is recognized because the cost to redeem the bonds is less than the carrying amount of the bonds.

Face amount of bonds retired (600 × $1,000)	$ 600,000
Add: Unamortized bond premium	65,000
Bond carrying amount at retirement date	665,000
Less: Cost to retire ($600,000 × 102%)	(612,000)
Pretax gain on retirement of bonds	$ 53,000

20. (b) Since the carrying amount of the old debt is greater than the amount paid to extinguish the old debt, the transaction results in a gain. To be classified as an extraordinary item, a transaction or event must be unusual in nature and infrequent in occurrence, given the environment in which the entity operates. Refunding operations are not infrequent for Weald. SFAS 145 requires that gains and losses from bond redemptions meet the same criteria as other events to be considered extraordinary.

21. (a) A loss is recognized on the redemption because the cost to redeem the bonds exceeds the carrying amount of the bonds. Information given in the question states that this bond redemption meets the criteria of an extraordinary event, so this redemption is considered an extraordinary loss.

Face amount of bonds		$ 500,000
Discount at issuance [$500,000 – ($500,000 × 98%)]	$10,000	
Amortization to extinguishment date ($10,000 × 12/15*)	(8,000)	
Less unamortized discount at extinguishment		(2,000)
Bond issue costs incurred	20,000	
Amortization to date of extinguishment ($20,000 × 12/15*)	(16,000)	
Less unamortized bond issue costs at extinguishment		(4,000)
Bond carrying amount at extinguishment		494,000
Cost to redeem ($500,000 × 102%)		(510,000)
Pretax extraordinary loss on early debt extinguishment		$ (16,000)

* The interest on the 15-year (i.e., 1/1, year 1 to 1/1, year 16) bonds was payable annually. Thus, there were 15 interest dates over the life of the bonds. The discount and bond issue costs must be amortized up to the extinguishment date (i.e., 1/1, year 12—the twelfth interest date).

Premium & Discount Amortization

22. (b) Using the straight-line method instead of the effective interest method to amortize the discount in the year of issue results in larger amortization of the discount, thus understating the discount and overstating the carrying amount of the bonds. The discount will be fully amortized by the maturity date using either method so there would be no effect on the carrying amount of the bonds at the maturity date for using an incorrect method.

Bonds payable		$1,000,000
Original discount	$150,000	
Amortization ($150,000 / 6 years)	(25,000)	
Less: Discount		(125,000)
Carrying value, SL method, 12/31, year 1		$ 875,000
Face amount of bonds		$1,000,000
Less: Discount on sale		(150,000)
Net cash realized		850,000
Effective interest rate		× 12%
Interest expense, 12/31, year 1		102,000
Less: Interest payment ($1,000,000 × 8%)		(80,000)
Amortization of discount, 12/31, year 1		$ 22,000
Bonds payable		$1,000,000
Original discount	$150,000	
Amortization	(22,000)	
Less: Discount, 12/31, year 1		(128,000)
Carrying value, effective interest method		$ 872,000

23. (b) The reporting of the bond issue costs as a deferred charge or as a reduction of the related debt liability does not affect the amortization of the bond issue costs. Interest expense is increased by an identical amount of bond issue cost amortization under both reporting alternatives.

24. (c)

Unamortized bond premium, 6/30, year 2 ($105,000 – $100,000)		$5,000
Bonds payable carrying amount, 6/30, year 2	$105,000	
Times: Annual effective interest rate	× 6%	
Interest expense, 6/30, year 2 - 6/30, year 3	6,300	
Annual interest payment ($100,000 × 7%)	(7,000)	
Bond premium amortization, 6/30, year 2 - 6/30, year 3		(700)
Unamortized bond premium, 6/30, year 3		$4,300

25. (b) $469,500 + $975 = $470,475

Bonds payable carrying amount, 1/2	$469,500
Effective interest rate (10% × 6/12)	× 5%
Interest expense, 1/2 - 6/30	23,475
Interest payment [$500,000 × (9% × 6/12)]	(22,500)
Amortization of discount, 1/2 - 6/30	$ 975

26. (a) When bonds are issued at a discount, the *Discount on Bonds Payable* account is a contra-liability account to *Bonds Payable,* i.e., it reduces the carrying amount of the bonds. Thus, as the bond discount is amortized, the carrying amount of the bonds increases. The bond discount amortization increases the interest expense on the bonds, and so net income decreases.

27. (d) When bonds are issued at a premium, the *Premium on Bonds Payable* account is added to the *Bonds Payable* account to determine the initial carrying amount of the bonds. As the bond premium is amortized, the carrying amount of the bond decreases.

28. (d)

Bond Price ($1,000 × 99% × 600 bonds)	$594,000
Plus: Accrued interest at stated interest rate (10% × $1,000 × 600 bonds × 3/12)	15,000
Proceeds from bond issuance	$609,000

29. (b) Interest payable is the cash interest accumulated that is not yet paid at the balance sheet date. The bonds have a semiannual interest payment of $32,000 [i.e., $800,000 × (8% / 2)]. Since the bonds are dated 10/1, Mason should report three months of interest payable, or $16,000 (i.e., $32,000 × 3/6), at 12/31.

Serial Bonds

30. (d) Bond issues maturing on a single date are called term bonds. Bond issues maturing in installments are called serial bonds. Since the debentures due in year 17 and the bonds due in year 20 each mature on a single date, the total amount of term bonds is $1,300,000 (i.e., $700,000 + $600,000). The total amount of serial bonds is $300,000.

31. (a) Bond issues maturing on a single date are called term bonds, whereas bond issues maturing in installments are called serial bonds. Since the registered bonds and the commodity-backed bonds both mature in installments, the total amount of serial bonds is $475,000 (i.e., $275,000 + $200,000). Debenture bonds are unsecured bonds; they are not supported by a lien or mortgage on specific assets. Since the registered bonds and the convertible bonds are unsecured, the total amount of debenture bonds is $400,000 (i.e., $275,000 + $125,000).

Convertible Bonds

32. (a) Ashley used the book value method to account for the conversion of the bonds to common stock. Under this method, paid-in capital (PIC) accounts are credited for the carrying amount of the debt and no gain or loss is recognized on the conversion. Therefore, Ashley's stockholders' equity is increased as a result of the conversion. Additional paid-in capital will be increased because the carrying amount of these bonds exceeds the par value of the common stock issued. Because PIC accounts are credited for the carrying amount of the debt under the book value method, retained earnings is unaffected.

33. (a) Under the book value method, the paid-in capital accounts are credited for the carrying amount of the debt; no gain or loss is recognized on the conversion. The market price per common share is irrelevant under this method.

Bonds Payable	600,000	
Bond Premium	12,000	
Common Stock		
[($600,000 / 1,000) × 10 shs. × $50 PV]		300,000
Additional Paid-In Capital (to balance)		312,000

34. (d) APB 14, ¶12 specifies that no portion of the proceeds from the issuance of convertible debt should be accounted for as attributable to the conversion feature; all of the proceeds should be recorded in debt accounts. The justification for this rule is that the conversion feature and the debt instrument are inseparable.

35. (c) A major characteristic of the book value method is that neither a gain nor a loss is recognized on the conversion of bonds to stock; the carrying amount of debt is taken out of the debt accounts and recorded in stockholders' equity accounts. The market value method may result in a gain or loss because the stock is to be recorded at the market value of the stock (or bonds) and the carrying amount of the debt is to be removed from liability accounts. A difference between the market value of the stock and the carrying amount of the debt is to be recorded as a gain or loss, whichever is appropriate. Because of the relationships of amounts involved, it is evident that the market value of the stock exceeds the carrying amount of the debt; therefore, a loss will be recorded on the conversion. Those relationships are as follows: (1) the aggregate par value of the stock was equal to the total face amount (par value) of the bonds, (2) the market value of the stock is 50% above its par, and (3) the carrying amount of the debt is less than 5% above its par (the bonds were issued in a prior year at a 5% premium and at least 30% of that premium had been amortized prior to year 4). (Also see Chapter 10.)

Detachable Stock Warrants

36. (c) Since the fair market value of the bonds is not determinable, the incremental method is used to determine the value of the bonds and warrants. That is, the market value is used for the warrants and the remainder of the purchase price is allocated to the bonds.

Purchase price (1,000 bonds × $1,000 × 109%)	$1,090,000
Fair value of the warrants (1,000 × 50 × $4)	(200,000)
Portion allocated to bonds	$ 890,000

Face value of bonds	$1,000,000
Portion allocated to bonds	(890,000)
Discount on bonds	$ 110,000

37. (d) APB 14 requires allocation of the proceeds between the bonds and the detachable stock purchase warrants based on their relative fair values at the date of issue. If both fair values are not known, then the fair value of either security is used. The question provides the fair value of the warrants, but not the fair value of the bonds without the warrants; therefore, the fair value of the warrants is used to allocate the proceeds for the two securities. A stockholders' equity account, *Paid-In Capital—Stock Purchase Warrants,* is increased by the $60,000 [i.e., ($500,000 / 1,000) × 30 × $4] fair value of the warrants. The remaining proceeds of $455,000 [i.e., ($500,000 × 103%) – $60,000] would be allocated to the bonds, which would result in the recording of a $45,000 (i.e., $500,000 – $455,000) discount on the bonds.

38. (c) The proceeds from the issuance of bonds with detachable stock purchase warrants should be allocated to the two securities based on the relative market values of the securities involved. The amount allocated to the warrants is reported as paid-in capital (i.e., contributed capital). Since the aggregate market value of the bonds and the warrants exceeds the proceeds, the amount of proceeds allocated to the bonds and the amount of proceeds allocated to the warrants will be less than the market values of the respective securities.

39. (a) The proceeds from the issuance of debt with detachable warrants is to be allocated to paid-in capital (the warrants) and to debt (the bonds) based on the relative fair values of the two securities at the time of issuance (APB 14, ¶16). When only the market value of the warrants is known, it is used to record the paid-in capital attributable to the issuance of the warrants. The remainder of the proceeds is recorded in debt accounts. A journal entry approach will be helpful in thinking through the rest of the question. *Paid-In Capital* is to be credited for the market value of the warrants. *Bonds Payable* is to be credited for the face amount of the bonds. *Cash* is to be debited for the cash proceeds. Because the question says that the fair value of the warrants and the face amount of the bonds exceed the cash proceeds, the entry needs a debit to balance. That debit has to relate to the bonds, so it must be to *Discount on Bonds Payable*. Thus, the amount of proceeds allocated to debt is less than the face amount of the bonds so the bonds were issued at a discount.

Solution 6-2 ADDITIONAL MULTIPLE CHOICE ANSWERS

Long-Term Investments

40. (d) A bond issue will sell for less than its face amount (i.e., at a discount) when the nominal or stated interest rate is less than the market rate [or, as indicated in answer (d), when the market rate of interest is higher than the nominal rate].

41. (d) The carrying amount of the bonds is the sum of their face amount and the unamortized premium. Therefore, premium amortization will reduce the carrying amount of the bonds. Bond premium amortization will increase income because it will reduce the interest expense associated with the bonds.

42. (d)

Face amount of bonds (1,000 × $1,000)		$ 1,000,000
Premium at issuance ($1,040,000 – $1,000,000)	$ 40,000	
Amortized to extinguishment date ($40,000 × 11/20*)	(22,000)	
Add unamortized premium at extinguishment		18,000
Bond carrying amount at extinguishment		1,018,000
Cost to reacquire ($1,000,000 × 101%)		(1,010,000)
Pretax gain on early extinguishment of debt		$ 8,000

* The interest on the 10-year (i.e., 1/1, year 1 - 1/1, year 11) bonds was payable semiannually. Therefore, there were 20 (i.e., 10 × 2) interest dates over the life of the bonds. The premium must be amortized up to the date of retirement (i.e., 7/1, year 6—the eleventh interest date).

Valuation Factors

43. (d) Bonds purchased at a discount are purchased at less than their face amount. The subsequent amortization of the discount increases the carrying amount of the bond investment and the amount of interest income recognized.

Simple interest, 7/1, year 1 - 12/31, year 1 [$500,000 × (8% / 2)]	$20,000
Amortization of discount on bond investment (given)	1,800
Interest revenue recognized in year 1	$21,800

Bond Issuance

44. (c) Bond issue costs is the only item that could theoretically be accounted for in any of the three manners listed. Because the borrower obtains the use of the proceeds received over the life of the bonds, it is argued that the bond issue costs benefit the borrower over this entire period and thus should be recorded as a deferred charge and amortized over the life of the bonds (APB 21, ¶16). Alternatively, the issue costs could be considered a reduction of the related debt liability, since these costs reduce the amount actually received by the borrower (and thus it also increases the effective interest rate on the obligation). This is the position taken by SFAC 3. Finally, it can be argued that since the expenditure for bond issue costs is not an asset, it should not be capitalized at all, but rather fully expensed in the year incurred.

45. (b) The $35,000 of bond issue costs should be reported as a deferred charge (i.e., an asset) and amortized over the term of the bonds (APB 21, ¶16). The bond liability should be reported at the sum of the face amount of the bonds less the related discount.

Face amount of bonds ($1,000 × 1,000)	$1,000,000
Discount on bonds [$1,000,000 – ($1,000,000 × 99%)]	(10,000)
Amount to be reported as bond liability, 6/30/X0	$ 990,000

Bond Redemption

46. (b) A gain is recognized because the cost to redeem the bonds is less than the carrying amount of the bonds.

Face amount of bonds	$ 5,000,000
Add: Unamortized bond premium	30,000
Less: Unamortized bond issue costs	(50,000)
Bond carrying amount at redemption date	4,980,000
Cost to redeem ($5,000,000 × 98%)	(4,900,000)
Pretax gain on redemption of bonds	$ 80,000

Premium & Discount Amortization

47. (b) $62,000 – $1,900 = $60,100

Bonds payable carrying amount, 5/1 ($1,000,000 + $62,000)	$1,062,000
Semiannual effective interest rate (10% / 2)	× 5%
Interest expense, 5/1 - 10/31	53,100
Semiannual interest payment due 11/1 [$1,000,000 × (11% / 2)]	(55,000)
Bond premium amortization, 5/1 - 10/31	$ (1,900)

48. (a)

Unamortized bond discount, 7/1, year 1		$61,000
Amortization for 7/1, year 1 - 6/30, year 2:		
Bonds payable carrying amount, 7/1, year 1	$939,000	
Effective interest rate	× 10%	
Interest expense, 7/1, year 1 - 6/30, year 2	93,900	
Interest payment ($1,000,000 × 9%)	(90,000)	
Bond discount amortization, 7/1, year 1 – 6/30, year 3		(3,900)
Bonds payable carrying amount, 7/1, year 2 ($939,000 + $3,900)	942,900	
Effective interest rate	× 10%	
Interest expense, 7/1, year 2 - 6/30, year 3	94,290	
Interest payment ($1,000,000 × 9%)	(90,000)	
Amortization for 7/1, year 2 - 6/30, year 3		(4,290)
Unamortized bond discount, 6/30, year 3		$52,810

Detachable Stock Warrants

49. (c) To compute the amount at which the bonds payable should be reported, the proceeds from the bonds and the detachable stock warrants must be allocated between the two securities based on their aggregate relative fair values at the date of issue. Since the bonds are allocated $900,000 of the proceeds received, they were issued at a discount of $100,000 (i.e., $1,000,000 – $900,000). The bonds should be reported in the balance sheet at face amount less unamortized discount.

	Relative aggregate fair value	FMV%	Proceeds to be allocated	Proceeds allocated to each
Bonds payable	$1,080,000	90%	$ 1,000,000	$ 900,000
Stock warrants	120,000	10%	1,000,000	100,000
	$1,200,000	100%		$1,000,000

50. (b) To determine the amount of the discount to be recorded for the bonds issued, the proceeds from the bonds and the detachable stock purchase warrants must be allocated between the securities based on their relative fair market values at the date of issue. Since the bonds are allocated $199,322 of the proceeds received, they were issued at a discount of $678 ($200,000 – $199,322).

	Relative aggregate fair value	FMV%	Proceeds to be allocated	Proceeds allocated to each
Bonds payable	$196,000	83.051%	$240,000	$199,322
Stock warrants	40,000	16.949%	240,000	40,678
	$236,000	100%		$240,000

* [($200,000 / $1,000) × 100 × $2]

PERFORMANCE BY SUBTOPICS

Each category below parallels a subtopic covered in Chapter 6. Record the number and percentage of questions you correctly answered in each subtopic area.

Long-Term Investments

Question #	Correct √
1	
2	
3	
4	
5	
6	
# Questions	6
# Correct	______
% Correct	______

Valuation Factors

Question #	Correct √
7	
8	
9	
10	
# Questions	4
# Correct	______
% Correct	______

Bond Issuance

Question #	Correct √
11	
12	
13	
14	
15	
16	
17	
# Questions	7
# Correct	______
% Correct	______

Bond Redemption

Question #	Correct √
18	
19	
20	
21	
# Questions	4
# Correct	______
% Correct	______

Premium & Discount Amortization

Question #	Correct √
22	
23	
24	
25	
26	
27	
28	
29	
# Questions	8
# Correct	______
% Correct	______

Serial Bonds

Question #	Correct √
30	
31	
# Questions	2
# Correct	______
% Correct	______

Convertible Bonds

Question #	Correct √
32	
33	
34	
35	
# Questions	4
# Correct	______
% Correct	______

Detachable Stock Warrants

Question #	Correct √
36	
37	
38	
39	
# Questions	4
# Correct	______
% Correct	______

SIMULATION SOLUTIONS

Solution 6-3

Table With Explanations—Bonds Payable

	Cash	Interest Expense	Amortization	Discount	Carrying Amount
1/2					(3) T $360,000
6/30	(2) K $14,400	18,000	3,600	(1) Q $116,400	363,600
12/31	$14,400	(6) N $18,180	(7) I $3,780		

Annual Interest Rates: Stated (4) D 6%
Effective (5) F 10%

1. Q The amount of the unamortized discount on 6/30 is the difference between the face value and the carrying amount on 6/30. ($480,000 – $363,600 = $116,400)

2. K The cash paid to bondholders is the same each semiannual payment; thus, the 6/30 cash paid is the same amount as the 12/31 cash paid, which is given in the problem, of $14,400. (The cash paid to bondholders is the stated rate applied to the face amount of $480,000, for 1/2 year.) In addition, the cash paid to bondholders when the bonds are issued at a discount is the difference between the interest expense and the amortization for the interest period. ($18,000 – $3,600 = $14,400)

3. T The difference between the face value of $480,000 and the discount at issuance equals the carrying amount at 1/2. Adding back the amortization at 6/3 of $3,600 to the discount at 6/30 of $116,400, the discount at issuance is equal to $120,000. Thus, $480,000 – $120,000 = $360,000. Another way to calculate the carrying amount at issuance from the information given is to subtract the 6/30 amortization of $3,600 from the carrying amount at 6/30 of $363,600.

4. D The stated interest rate is equal to double the semi-annual interest paid divided by the face value of the bonds. [($14,400 × 2) / $480,000 = 0.06]

5. F The effective interest rate is double the interest expense for the first six months divided by the actual cash received for the bond issue. [($18,000 × 2) / $360,000 = 0.10]

6. N The interest expense for the second six month period is the carrying amount as of 6/30 times half (6 months / 12 months) of the effective interest rate. ($363,600 × 0.10 × 6/12 = $18,180)

7. I The amortization for the second six month period is the interest expense for that period minus the cash paid. ($18,180 – $14,400 = $3,780)

Research

FASB 107, Par. 5

5. For purposes of this Statement, the fair value of a financial instrument is the amount at which the instrument could be exchanged in a current transaction between willing parties, other than in a forced or liquidation sale. If a quoted market price is available for an instrument, the fair value to be disclosed for that instrument is the product of the number of trading units of the instrument times that market price.

Solution 6-4

Table With Explanations—Bonds Payable

	Cash paid	*Interest expense*	*Amortization*	*Carrying amount*	*Unamortized premium*
7/1, year 1				**(1) E**	
12/31, year 1	**(2) J**	$14,100	**(3) H**	$349,100	**(4) N**
6/30, year 2	$17,500	**(5) M**	$3,536	**(6) F**	

Effective Annual Interest Rate: **(7) O**

1. E The market price, or carrying value, of a bond is equal to the present value of the interest and principal (face) payments. In this problem, the original carrying amount can easily be calculated once the first period's premium amortization is calculated, by adding the premium amortization to the carrying amount at the end of the payment period. ($349,100 + $3,400 = $352,500)

2. J The cash paid on each interest date is the face amount times the stated rate times the portion of the year included in the payment period. ($250,000 × 14% × ½ year = $17,500)

3. H Amortization of the bond premium is the amount of cash paid less the interest expense for the payment period. ($17,500 – $14,100 = $3,400)

4. N The unamortized premium is the current carrying amount less the face amount. ($349,100 – $250,000 = $99,100)

5. M The interest expense is the carrying amount at the beginning of the period times the effective interest rate times the portion of the year in the payment period. ($349,100 × 8% × ½ = $13,964)

In this problem, the interest expense can easily be derived by subtracting the premium amortization amount for the payment period from the cash paid. ($17,500 – $3,536 = $13,964)

6. F The carrying amount at the end of the period is the carrying amount at the beginning of the period less the premium amortization for the current period. ($349,100 – $3,536 = $345,564)

7. O The effective annual interest rate is the interest expense for the year divided by the carrying amount at the beginning of the period. Because the interest expense amount on the table is only for ½ year, it must be doubled. ($14,100/$352,500 × 2 = 8%); ($13,964/$349,100 × 2 = 8%)

Research

APB 12, Par. 17

In the Board's opinion, the interest method of amortization is theoretically sound and an acceptable method.

Solution 6-5

Chart With Explanations—Bond Issuance

	Item I	Item 2	Item 3	Item 4	Item 5
Bond Discount	I	N	N	I	N
Bond Premium	N	I	D	N	N
Bond Payable	I	I	D	I	N
Common Stock	N	N	I	N	I
Additional Paid-In Capital	N	N	I	I	I
Retained Earnings	N	N	N	N	D

1. I, N, I, N, N, N

A bond issue with a nominal rate of interest that is less than the market rate of interest will sell for less than its face amount (i.e., the bond will be sold at a discount). The entry to record bonds payable sold at a discount increases the *Bond Discount* and *Bonds Payable* accounts but has no effect on the *Bond Premium, Common Stock, Additional Paid-In Capital,* and *Retained Earnings* accounts.

Cash	XX	
Bond Discount	XX	
Bonds Payable		XX

2. N, I, I, N, N, N

APB 14, ¶12, specifies that no portion of proceeds from convertible debt should be accounted for as attributed to the conversion feature; all of the proceeds should be recorded in debt accounts. The justification for this rule is that the conversion feature and the debt feature are inseparable. The entry to record convertible bonds sold for an amount in excess of the bond's face amount (i.e., at a premium) increases the *Bond Premium and Bonds Payable* accounts but has no effect on the *Bond Discount, Common Stock, Additional Paid-In Capital, and Retained Earnings* accounts.

Cash	XX	
Bond Premium		XX
Bonds Payable		XX

3. N, D, D, I, I, N

Under the book value method, no gain or loss is recognized on the conversion of bonds payable to common stock. To record the conversion, paid-in capital accounts are credited for the carrying amount of the debt converted. The entry to record the conversion decreases the *Bond Payable* account and increases the *Common Stock* account by equal amounts because each bond has a $1,000 face amount and is convertible into 20 shares of $50 par value common stock (i.e., 20 × $50 = $1,000). Since the convertible bonds were issued at a premium, and the conversion entry decreases the *Bonds Payable* account and increases the *Common Stock* account by equal amounts, the conversion entry also decreases the *Bond Premium* account and increases the *Additional Paid-In Capital* accounts by the unamortized amount of the *Bond Premium.* The conversion entry has no effect on the *Bond Discount* or *Retained Earnings* accounts.

Bonds Payable	XX	
Bond Premium	XX	
Common Stock		XX
Additional Paid-In Capital		XX

4. I, N, I, N, I, N

Proceeds from the issuance of bonds with detachable stock warrants should be allocated between the bonds and warrants on the basis of their relative market values at time of issuance. The amount of proceeds allocable to the warrants increases

Additional Paid-In Capital. Bonds Payable increases by the face amount of the bonds issued. The question states that the bonds and warrants are issued for an amount equal to the face amount of the bonds. Since a portion of the proceeds is allocable to the warrants, the amount of proceeds allocable to the bonds is less than the face at a discount, thereby increasing the *Bond Discount* account. The issuance of the bonds with detachable stock purchase warrants has no effect on the *Bond Premium* and *Retained Earnings* accounts.

5. N, N, N, I, I, D

Since the 2% stock dividend is less than 20 to 25% of the number of shares outstanding, it is considered to be a "small" stock dividend. Therefore, it should be recorded by capitalizing a portion of *Retained Earnings* equal to the fair value of the shares issued. Thus, as a result of the "small" stock dividend, *Retained Earnings* will decrease by the fair value of the shares issued, Common stock will increase by the par value of the shares issued, and *Additional Paid-In Capital* will increase by the excess of the fair value over the par value of the shares issued. *Bond Discount, Bond Premium,* and *Bonds Payable* are not affected by the issuance of a stock dividend.

Research

C08.104

.104 The portion of the proceeds of debt securities issued with detachable stock purchase warrants that is allocable to the warrants shall be accounted for as additional paid-in capital.

Solution 6-6

Essay—Bonds Payable

a. 1. The 9% bonds were issued at a **discount** (less than face amount). Although the bonds provide for payment of interest of 9% of face amount, this rate was **less than** the **prevailing or market rate** for bonds of similar quality at the time the bonds were issued. Thus, the issue price of the bonds, which is the present value of the principal and interest payments discounted at 10%, is less than the face amount.

2. The amount of interest expense would be **higher in the second year** of the life of the bond issue than in the first year of the life of the bond issue. According to the effective interest method of amortization, the 10% effective interest rate is applied to the bond carrying amount. In a discount situation, the **bond carrying amount increases each year,** and this results in a greater interest expense in each successive year.

b. 1. Gain or loss on early extinguishment of debt should be determined by **comparing the carrying amount** of the bonds at the **date of extinguishment** with the **acquisition price.** If the carrying amount **exceeds** the acquisition price, a **gain** results. If the carrying amount is **less** than the acquisition price, a **loss** results. In this case, a **loss** results. The term bonds were **issued at a discount.** Therefore, the **carrying amount** of the bonds at the date of extinguishment must be **less than** the **face amount,** which is **less than** the **acquisition price.**

2. Drew should report the loss from early extinguishment of debt in its year 3 income statement as **income from continuing operations,** unless the early extinguishment of debt is an extraordinary event, in which case it is reported as an **extraordinary item, net of income taxes.** Extraordinary items are **infrequent** in occurrence and **unusual** in nature, considering the entity's operating **environment.**

c. The proceeds from the issuance of the 7% nonconvertible bonds with detachable stock purchase warrants should be recorded as an **increase in cash.** These proceeds should be **allocated between** the **bonds and the warrants** on the **basis of their relative market values.** The portion of the proceeds allocable to the bonds should be accounted for as **long-term debt,** while the portion allocable to the warrants should be accounted for as **paid-in capital.**

Wondering how you can prepare for simulations?

Some candidates who are otherwise confident about the exam are overwhelmed by simulations. The following tips are designed to help you increase your confidence when presented with these lengthy questions.

As you progress through your study plan, work simulations from each major topic; waiting until the last month leaves you little time to prepare for this question type. The more uncomfortable that you are with simulations, the more important this becomes. You might not realize that you are uncomfortable with simulations if you don't try working some of them.

After working a simulation (using the suggested time limit) and checking your answers, reflect on the questions. If you had trouble with some aspect, evaluate whether you need to review the material, refine your answering technique, or merely gain confidence with this format.

- Did you feel pressured for time? If you in fact didn't have enough time, this may indicate you need to review the text again. As you become more familiar with the material, your speed will increase. A shortage of time may also indicate a need to consider techniques to work simulations. Specific information about techniques to solve simulations is in the **Practical Advice** appendix.

- If you felt pressured for time, but actually had time to finish the question, work several more simulations using the suggested time limit. This experience will help you learn not to be intimidated by this format.

Once you know the content, you will be able to prepare a response regardless of the question format. Exam time is limited and you don't want the pressure of time considerations to distract you from providing your best answer to questions. To reduce the pressure, remember that you must earn 75 points to pass—the answer format that you use to earn those 75 points doesn't matter. Practice more simulations that cover topics that have high point value; be prepared to answer simulations in any topic area.

Remember, with the techniques and information in your material,

A passing score is well within reach!

CHAPTER 7

LIABILITIES

I. **Current Liabilities** 7-2
- A. Definition 7-2
- B. Valuation 7-2
- C. Definitely Determinable Liabilities 7-2
- D. Liabilities Dependent on Operating Results 7-4
- E. Estimated Liabilities 7-5
- F. Contingent Liabilities (SFAS 5) 7-8

II. **Long-Term Liabilities** 7-10
- A. Definition 7-10
- B. Disclosures 7-10
- C. Notes Payable 7-10
- D. Refinancing of Short-Term Obligations (SFAS 6) 7-12
- E. Asset Retirement Obligations (SFAS 143) 7-13

III. **Debt Extinguishment (SFAS 140)** 7-13
- A. Conditions 7-13
- B. In-Substance Defeasance Not Extinguishment 7-14
- C. Extinguishment vs. Refunding 7-14
- D. Extraordinary Item 7-14

IV. **Troubled Debt Restructurings (SFAS 15, 114, 118)** 7-14
- A. Definition 7-14
- B. Debt Restructuring vs. Troubled Debt Restructuring 7-14
- C. Types of Troubled Debt Restructurings 7-14
- D. Modification of Terms—Debtor Accounting 7-15

V. **Highlights of Federal Bankruptcy Law** 7-16
- A. Chapter 7 Bankruptcy 7-16
- B. Priority of Claims 7-16
- C. Distribution Rules 7-16

1- A/P
2- Notes payable
3- Dividends payable
4- Advances & returnable deposits
5- Accrued expenses

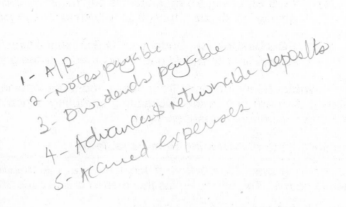

EXAM COVERAGE: Historically, exam coverage of the topics in Chapter 7 has been 5 to 15 percent of the FAR section. More information regarding exam coverage is included in Appendix B, *Practical Advice.*

CHAPTER 7

LIABILITIES

I. Current Liabilities

A. Definition

Liabilities are obligations, based on past transactions, to convey assets or perform services in the future. The definition of *current* liabilities is logically correlated with the definition of current assets. Current assets are economic benefits owned by a firm that are reasonably expected to be converted into cash or consumed during the entity's operating cycle or one year, whichever is longer. The term current liabilities is used principally to designate obligations whose liquidation is reasonably expected to require the use of existing resources properly classifiable as current assets, or the creation of other current liabilities (ARB 43). Accounting for, and classification of, current liabilities is affected by the degree of certainty attached to the future payments.

B. Valuation

Ideally, liabilities should be recorded based on the present value of the future outlays involved. In the case of current liabilities, the difference between the present value and the amount to be paid is not likely to be material; therefore, APB 21, *Interest on Receivables and Payables,* sanctions the reporting of current liabilities at their face amount.

C. Definitely Determinable Liabilities

The amounts and due dates of definitely determinable liabilities are established with considerable certainty. This certainty may be established by statutory law, contractual provision, or trade custom.

1. **Accounts Payable** Liabilities incurred in obtaining goods and services from vendors in the entity's ordinary course of business.

   a. **Unsecured** Generally, accounts payable are not secured by collateral and do not require the periodic payment of interest.

   b. **Proper Cutoff** Accounts payable should reflect the cost of those goods and services that have been appropriately included in inventory (or other asset account) or expensed.

      (1) **FOB Shipping Point** Materials purchased, F.O.B. shipping point, are inventoriable when shipped; thus, a liability should be recorded at that time.

      (2) **FOB Destination** Under an F.O.B. destination point contract, the goods and the related liability should not be recorded until the goods are received.

2. **Notes Payable** Loans obtained from banks and other lending institutions represent current liabilities if they are due in the succeeding operating period. These notes may be either *interest-bearing* or *noninterest-bearing.*

Example 1 ▸ Interest-Bearing Note Payable

ABC Inc. borrowed $5,000 from a local bank at the market rate of interest of 8% on June 30, year 1. The principal plus the interest is due June 30, year 2.

Required: Provide ABC's journal entries.

Solution:

6/30, year 1	Cash	5,000	
	Notes Payable, Short-Term		5,000
12/31, year 1	Interest Expense ($5,000 × 0.08 × 6/12)	200	
	Accrued Interest Payable		200
6/30, year 2	Notes Payable, Short-Term	5,000	
	Accrued Interest Payable	200	
	Interest Expense	200	
	Cash		5,400

Example 2 ▸ Noninterest-Bearing Note Payable

ABC borrowed $5,000 on June 30, year 1 and signed an 8% noninterest-bearing note due in one year.

Required: Provide ABC's journal entries.

Solution:

6/30, year 1	Cash (face amount less discount)	4,600	
	Discount on Notes Payable ($5,000 × 0.08)	400	
	Notes Payable, Short-Term		5,000
12/31, year 1	Interest Expense ($400 × 6/12)	200	
	Discount on Notes Payable		200
6/30, year 2	Notes Payable, Short-Term	5,000	
	Interest Expense ($400 × 6/12)	200	
	Discount on Notes Payable		200
	Cash		5,000

NOTE: The effective interest rate on the discounted note is approximately 8.7% ($400 / $4,600) since less cash is received than the amount on which the interest rate is computed.

3. **Dividends Payable** When declared, cash and property dividends represent legal obligations due within one year and are reported as current liabilities. Stock dividends and undeclared dividends on cumulative preferred stock are not reported as liabilities; however, cumulative preferred stock dividends in arrears must be disclosed in the notes to the statements.

4. **Advances & Returnable Deposits** Advanced payments received from customers and others are liabilities until the transaction is completed; returnable deposits are liabilities until the relationship with the third party is terminated.

5. **Accrued Liabilities (Expenses)** An accrued expense is an expense incurred, but not yet paid in cash.

Exhibit 1 ▸ Accrued Expenses Journal Entry

Expense	XX	
Payable or Accrued Liability		XX

a. An example of an accrued expense is salaries incurred for the last week of the accounting period that are not payable until the subsequent accounting period. Accrued payroll liabilities include social security taxes and federal unemployment taxes borne by the employer.

b. Federal income taxes withheld from employees and the employees' share of social security taxes are **not** classified as accrued payroll expenses by the employer.

6. **Deferred Revenues** Deferred revenue is revenue collected in cash, but not yet earned. An example of deferred revenue is rent collected in advance by a lessor in the last month of the accounting period, which represents the rent for the first month of the subsequent accounting period. Other examples include subscriptions collected in advance and gift certificates issued but not yet redeemed. When gift certificates are issued, a deferred revenue account should be increased by the face amount of the gift certificates. This deferred revenue account is decreased when the gift certificates are redeemed or lapse.

Exhibit 2 ▸ Deferred Revenues Journal Entry

Cash	XX	
Unearned Revenues (a liability account)		XX

Exhibit 3 ▸ Formerly Deferred Revenues Now Earned Journal Entry

Unearned Revenues	XX	
Revenue		XX

7. **Current Maturities of Long-Term Debt** The portion of long-term debt due within the next fiscal period is classified as a current liability if payment is expected to require the use of current assets or the creation of other current liabilities. The liability is not classified as current if the maturing portion will be paid from the proceeds of a new bond issue or noncurrent assets (e.g., a bond sinking fund).

D. Liabilities Dependent on Operating Results

1. **Income Tax Liability** In accordance with federal and state tax laws, a corporation computes income taxes payable based on operating results for the period.

   a. **Payable** Income taxes payable within the next period or operating cycle, whichever is longer, are classified as current liabilities.

   b. **Deferred** Taxable income and pretax accounting income may differ and, therefore, income tax payable (based on taxable income) and income tax expense (based on pretax accounting income) may differ substantially. This gives rise to deferred taxes. Deferred taxes should be netted out in their current and noncurrent portions for balance sheet presentation.

2. **Employee Bonuses** Bonus agreements based on profits usually fall into one of two classes: (1) the bonus is based on net income after income taxes, but before deducting the bonus, **or** (2) the bonus is based on net income after deducting both income taxes and the bonus. The amount of the bonus is determined by solving simultaneous equations that describe the terms of the bonus agreement.

Exhibit 4 ▸ Bonuses Based on Profits

B = Bonus
Br = Bonus rate
I = Income before income taxes and bonus
T = Tax
Tr = Tax rate

1. Bonus computed on net income after income taxes but before deducting the bonus; solve these simultaneous equations:

   a. $B = Br(I - T)$
   b. $T = Tr(I - B)$

2. Bonus computed on net income after deducting both income taxes and the bonus; solve these simultaneous equations:

   a. $B = Br(I - T - B)$
   b. $T = Tr(I - B)$

Example 3 ▸ Employee Bonus

Generous Corp. provides a bonus to its employees equal to 10% of net income (i.e., after deducting taxes and bonus). Income from operations for the year was $90,000. Assume a 40% tax rate.

Required: Compute the employee bonus liability for Generous Corp.

Solution:

Step 1: Substitute the value of T, as given in Exhibit 4, equation 2.b., into equation 2.a.

$B = Br(I - T - B)$ $B = Br[I - Tr\ (I - B) - B]$

Step 2: Substitute the known values and solve for B.

$B = 0.10\ [\$90{,}000 - 0.4\ (\$90{,}000 - B) - B]$
$B = 0.10\ [\$90{,}000 - \$36{,}000 + 0.4B - B]$
$B = \$9{,}000 - \$3{,}600 + 0.04B - 0.1B = \$5{,}400 - 0.06B$
$1.06B = \$5{,}400$
$B = \underline{\underline{\$5{,}094}}$

E. **Estimated Liabilities**
Estimated liabilities are known liabilities whose amount is uncertain at the end of the accounting period. Derivative instruments that represent obligations that meet the definition of liabilities are measured at fair value and reported as liabilities in the financial statements in accordance with SFAS 133.

1. **Product Warranties & Guarantees** A warranty or guarantee is a promise made by the seller to the buyer to make good certain deficiencies in the product during a specified period of time after the sale. Product guarantees and warranties create a liability for the seller from the date of the sale to the end of the warranty period. Recording of the liability may take place either at the point of sale or at the end of the accounting period.

   a. **Recording** When the liability is recorded at the end of the accounting period, no entry is made at the date of sale, and any direct costs for servicing customer claims are debited to warranty expense and credited to cash or other assets.

Exhibit 5 ▸ Warranties

Warranty Expense	XX	
Estimated Warranty Liability		XX
To record estimated warranty expense at point of sale.		
Estimated Warranty Liability	XX	
Cash or Other Assets		XX
To record actual warranty expenditures as incurred.		

   b. **Year-End Adjustment** At the end of the accounting period, an estimate of the year's warranty liability is made based on past experience and current estimates. Any difference between the estimate and the actual amounts already charged to warranty expense is recorded as follows (assuming the estimated liability exceeds the amounts actually charged).

Exhibit 6 ▸ Warranty Adjustment

Warranty Expense	XX	
Estimated Warranty Liability		XX

Example 4 ▸ Product Warranty

A new product introduced by Shoddy Corporation carries a two-year warranty against defects. The estimated warranty costs related to dollar sales are 3% in the year of sale and 5% in the year after sale.

Year	Sales	Actual Warranty Expenditures
1	$400,000	$10,000
2	500,000	35,000

Required: Determine Shoddy's estimated warranty liability as of December 31, year 2, and its warranty expense for year 2.

Solution:

Sales (year 1 and year 2)	$900,000
Estimated warranty cost percentage (3% and 5%)	× 8%
Estimated warranty costs for year 1 and year 2 sales	72,000
Warranty expenditures to date ($10,000 + $35,000)	(45,000)
Estimated warranty liability, 12/31, year 2	$ 27,000

The warranty expense recognized in year 2 is $40,000 [$500,000 × (3% + 5%)].

2. **Premiums** In order to increase sales and promote certain products, companies may offer premiums to those customers who return boxtops, coupons, labels, wrappers, etc., as proof of purchase. The cost of these premiums represents an expense that should be matched against revenue from the sales benefited. At the end of the accounting period, an expense account should be debited and a liability account credited for the cost of outstanding premiums *expected* to be redeemed in subsequent periods.

Example 5 ▸ Premiums

The Whole Grain Cereal Company offers a T-shirt to those customers who present 10 cereal boxtops. Whole Grain purchases 2,000 T-shirts at a unit cost of $2.50. Between the time the premiums were offered and the end of the accounting period, 25,000 boxes of cereal were sold. Whole Grain expects that 80% of the boxtops will be returned. A total of 2,000 boxtops had been received as of the end of the accounting period.

Required: Provide journal entries for Whole Grain to account for the premiums.

Solution:

	Debit	Credit
Premium Merchandise Inventory	5,000	
Cash (2,000 × $2.50)		5,000
To record the purchase of 2,000 T-shirts		
Premium Expense [(2,000* / 10) × $2.50]	500	
Premium Merchandise Inventory		500
To record the redemption of 2,000 boxtops for 200 shirts		
Premium Expense	4,500	
Estimated Premium Liability [(2,000* – 200) × $2.50]		4,500
To record the estimated premium liability at year-end		
Estimated Premium Liability [(4,000 / 10) × $2.50]	1,000	
Premium Merchandise Inventory		1,000
To record the redemption of 4,000 boxtops in the subsequent period		

* (25,000 × 0.80) / 10

3. **Compensated Absences (SFAS 43) and Postemployment Benefits (SFAS 112)** SFAS 43 and 112 do not apply to postemployment benefits provided through a pension or postretirement benefit plan, individual deferred compensation arrangements, or special or contractual termination benefits covered in SFAS 88 and 106.

   a. **Accrual** A liability is accrued at year-end for the estimated cost of material compensated absences and postemployment benefits.

      (1) **Compensated Absences** Compensated absences include vacation, occasional sick days, and holidays. The substance of the employer's sick leave policy takes precedence over its form. An employer generally is not required to accrue a liability for nonvesting accumulating rights to receive sick pay benefits. However, future compensation for sick leave is accrued if employees customarily are paid or allowed compensated absences for accumulated, nonvesting sick leave days, even though employees are not actually absent as a result of illness.

      (2) **Postemployment Benefits** Postemployment benefits to be provided to former or inactive employees prior to retirement include salary continuation, severance benefits, continuation of other fringe benefits such as insurance, job training, and disability related benefits such as workers' compensation.

   b. **Conditions** A liability for employees' compensation for future absences and postemployment benefits should be accrued if **all** the following conditions are met. If the first three conditions are met, but no amount is accrued due to inability to estimate future payments for compensated absences or postemployment benefits, this fact must be disclosed. Postemployment benefits that do not meet the conditions of SFAS 43 and 112 are accounted for in accordance with SFAS 5, *Accounting for Contingencies.*

      (1) The obligation is for employee services **already** rendered.

      (2) The obligation relates to employee rights that **vest or accumulate.** Vested rights are those for which the employer is obligated to pay to the employee, regardless of termination of employment. Accumulated rights are those that may be carried forward to one or more future periods, even though there might be a limitation on the amounts carried forward.

      (3) Payment of the compensation is **probable.**

      (4) The amount can be reasonably **estimated.**

Exhibit 7 ▸ Compensated Absences

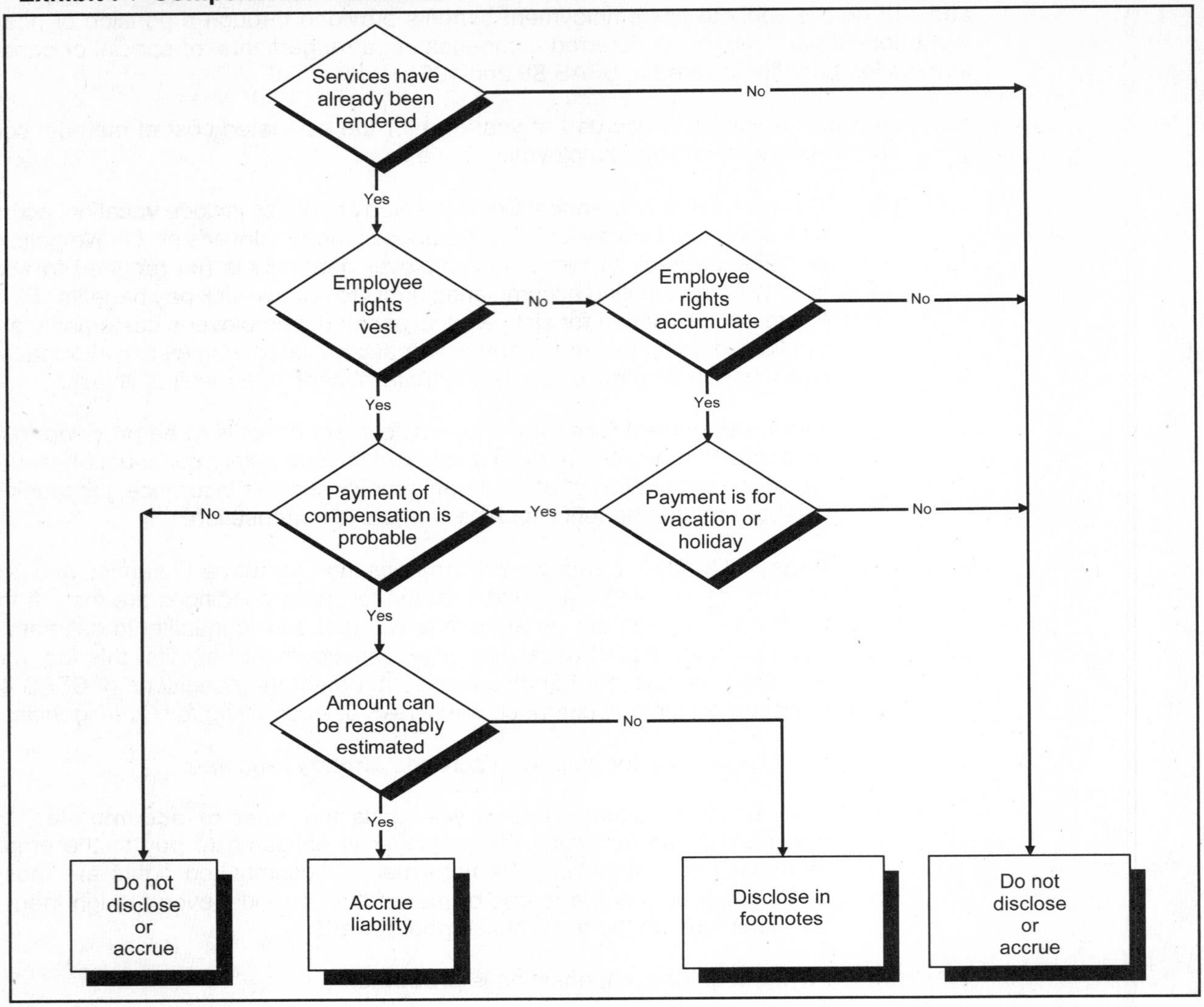

F. Contingent Liabilities (SFAS 5)

Contingent liabilities arise from events or circumstances occurring before the balance sheet date, the resolution of which is contingent upon a future event or circumstance. The distinction between contingencies and other liabilities hinges on the uncertainty as to the existence of the liability and **not** on the uncertainty as to the amount of the liability.

1. **Examples** Examples of contingent liabilities include (a) obligations related to product warranties, (b) obligations related to product coupons and premiums, (c) obligations related to product defects, (d) pending or threatened litigation, and (e) actual or possible claims and assessments.

2. **Classification** Accounting treatment depends on the likelihood that future events will confirm the contingent loss **and** whether the amount can be reasonably estimated.

   a. **Probable** Likely to occur. Where the likelihood of confirmation of a loss is considered probable and the loss can be reasonably estimated, the estimated loss should be accrued by a charge to income and the nature of the contingency should be disclosed. If, however, only a range of possible loss can be estimated—and no amount in the range is a better estimate than the others—the minimum amount in the range should be accrued. In addition, the nature of the contingency and the additional exposure to loss should be disclosed (FASB Interp. 14).

b. **Reasonably Possible** More than remote, but less than probable. Where the loss is considered reasonably possible, no charge should be made to income **but** the nature of the contingency should be disclosed. This treatment also applies to probable losses that cannot be reasonably estimated.

c. **Remote** Slight chance of occurring. Where likelihood of loss is considered remote, disclosure normally is **not** required. Exceptions include guarantees of indebtedness of others, banks' standby letters of credit, and guarantees to repurchase receivables.

3. **No Disclosure**

a. **Certain Unasserted Claims** No disclosure is required for a loss contingency concerning an unasserted claim or assessment when no claimant has shown an awareness of such unless it is considered probable that the claim will be asserted, **and** there is a reasonable possibility of an unfavorable result.

b. **Unspecified Business Risks** General, unspecified business risks are not loss contingencies; no accrual or disclosure is required.

4. **Gain Contingencies** Gain Contingencies should be disclosed but not recognized as income. Care should be taken to avoid misleading implications as to the likelihood of realization.

5. **Postemployment Benefits** Postemployment Benefits that do not meet the conditions for accrual stated in SFAS 43, *Accounting for Compensated Absences,* should be accounted for as a probable or reasonably possible contingency.

6. **Environmental Remediation Liabilities (SOP 96-1)** The accrual of an environmental liability is required if information available prior to issuance of the financial statements indicates that it is *probable* that a liability has been incurred at the date of the financial statements and the amount of the loss can be *reasonably estimated.*

a. **Condition Probable** If a claim has been asserted and an entity can be held responsible for it, then condition probable is met. If an entity has been notified by the EPA or a relevant state agency, for example, that the entity is a potentially responsible party (PRP) and the entity had some involvement, then it is probable that the entity will incur some costs.

b. **Estimate of Liability & Loss** A variety of factors should be considered in making the estimate, including pre-cleanup activities, such as testing, engineering studies, and feasibility studies, conducted to define the extent of the damage; remedial activities to clean up the environmental damage; government oversight and enforcement costs, which includes fines and penalties; and operation and maintenance activities, including post-remediation monitoring.

c. **Related Assets** An entity's balance sheet may include several assets that relate to an environmental remediation obligation, including receivables from other PRPs that are not providing initial funding, anticipated recoveries from insurers, and anticipated recoveries from prior owners.

Exhibit 8 ▸ Contingencies

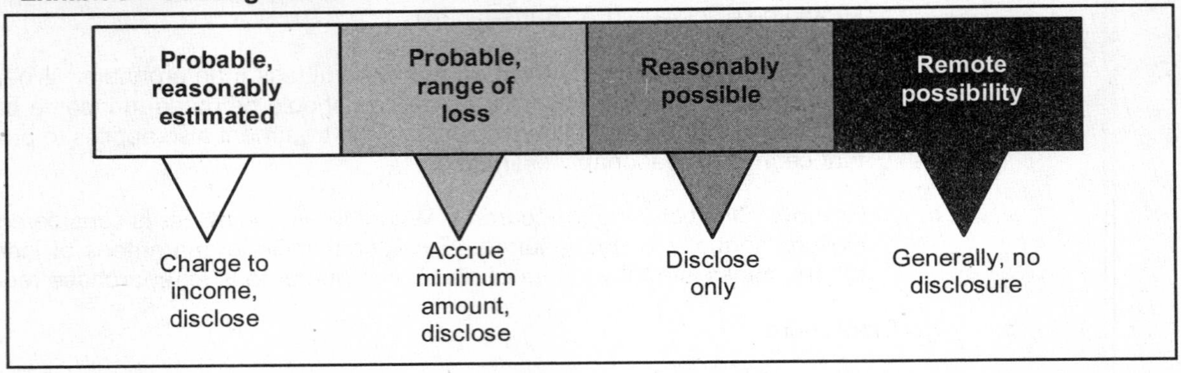

II. Long-Term Liabilities

A. Definition

Long-term liabilities are all obligations not expected to be liquidated by the use of existing current assets or by the creation of current liabilities. Examples include: (1) long-term notes payable, (2) refinancing of short-term obligations, and (3) bonds payable. As bonds payable are discussed in a separate chapter, they are not discussed here.

B. Disclosures

SFAS 47 requires that the combined aggregate amount of maturities and sinking fund requirements for all long-term borrowings be disclosed for each of the five years following the date of the latest balance sheet period.

C. Notes Payable

1. **Note Issued for Cash** APB 21, *Interest on Receivables and Payables,* specifies, when a note is issued solely for cash, it is generally presumed to have a present value at issuance equal to the cash proceeds exchanged. If special rights or privileges are included in the transaction, they must be measured separately.

2. **Note Exchanged for Property, Goods, or Services** When a note is exchanged for property, goods, or services, it is assumed that the rate of interest stipulated by the note is fair and adequate compensation. Therefore, unless the interest rate is not stated or is unreasonable, the note should be recorded at its face amount because this amount would approximate the note's present value.

3. **Interest Rate Not Stated or Unreasonable**

   a. **Fair Value** Record the note at the fair value of the property, goods, or services exchanged or at the amount that approximates the market value of the note, whichever is more clearly determinable. The difference between that amount and the face amount of the note is recorded as a discount or premium.

   b. **Present Value** In the absence of established exchange prices for the related property, goods, or services or evidence of the market value of the note, the note is recorded at its present value by discounting all future payments on the note using an imputed interest rate—the market rate of interest for the level of risk involved. The difference between the present value and the face amount of the note is recorded as a discount or premium.

   c. **Imputed Interest Rate** The imputed interest rate is determined by considering the debtor's credit standing, prevailing rates for similar debt, and rates at which the debtor can obtain funds.

d. **Discount or Premium Amortization** The discount or premium is amortized as interest expense over the life of the note in such a way as to result in a constant rate of interest when applied to the carrying amount of the note at the beginning of any given period. APB 21 allows the use of amortization methods other than the effective interest method (e.g., straight-line) if the results do not differ materially from those obtained with the effective interest method.

Example 6 ▸ Unstated Interest Rate

XYZ Company acquires a patent on January 1, year 1, in exchange for a three-year noninterest-bearing note of $100,000. There was no established exchange price for the patent and the note has no ready market. The prevailing rate of interest for a note of this type is 8% at the date of the exchange. (The imputed interest rate is the prevailing interest rate of 8%.) The PV interest factor for an amount in three years discounted at 8% is 0.79383 (see Appendix D, Table 2).

Required: Provide the journal entries to record the patent and the note, the interest expense at year-ends, and the payment of the note.

Solution:

To record the patent and the note.

1/1, year 1	Patent ($100,000 × .79383)	79,383	
	Discount on Note Payable ($100,000 – $79,383)	20,617	
	Note Payable		100,000

To record interest expense at year-ends.

Year 1:	Interest Expense [($100,000 – $20,617) × 0.08]	6,351	
	Discount on Note Payable		6,351
Year 2:	Interest Expense [($100,000 – $14,266*) × 0.08]	6,859	
	Discount on Note Payable		6,859
Year 3:	Interest Expense [($100,000 – $7,407**) × 0.08]	7,407	
	Discount on Note Payable		7,407

To record the payment of the note.

	Note Payable	100,000	
	Cash		100,000

* $20,617 – $6,351.
** $14,266 – $6,859.

Example 7 ▸ Unreasonable Interest Rate

The same as Example 6, except that the note specifies annual interest payments of 5% on December 31. This rate is considered unreasonably low based on the current market rate of 8%. The interest factor for a three-year annuity at 8% is 2.57710 (see Appendix D, Table 4).

Required: Provide the related journal entries.

Solution:

To record the asset and the note:

1/1, year 1	Patent	92,268	
	Discount on Note Payable ($100,000 – 92,268)	7,732	
	Note Payable		100,000

Present value of principal ($100,000 × 0.79383)	$ 79,383
Present value of interest payments ($5,000 × 2.57710)	12,885
Present value of note	$ 92,268

To record interest expense at year-ends:

Year 1:	Interest Expense [($100,000 – $7,732) × 0.08]	7,381	
	Cash ($100,000 × 0.05)		5,000
	Discount on Note Payable (to balance)		2,381
Year 2:	Interest Expense [($100,000 – $5,351*) × 0.08]	7,572	
	Cash ($100,000 × 0.05)		5,000
	Discount on Note Payable (to balance)		2,572
Year 3:	Interest Expense [($100,000 – $2,779**) × 0.08]	7,778	
	Cash ($100,000 × 0.05)		5,000
	Discount on Note Payable (to balance)		2,778

To record the repayment of the note:

12/31, year 3	Note Payable	100,000	
	Cash		100,000

* $7,732 – $2,381.
** $5,351 – $2,572.

D. **Refinancing of Short-Term Obligations (SFAS 6)**
SFAS 6 provides guidelines for the classification of short-term obligations that are expected to be refinanced on a long-term basis.

1. **Reclassification to Noncurrent Liabilities** Short-term obligations are those scheduled to mature within one year or operating cycle, whichever is longer. Generally, short-term obligations are classified as current liabilities, since they will require the use of working capital during the ensuing period. However, if they are to be refinanced on a long-term basis, they will not require the use of working capital; in this case, short-term obligations will be appropriately classified as noncurrent liabilities.

2. **Refinancing Defined** Refinancing a short-term obligation on a long-term basis means either of the following.

   a. Replacing it with long-term obligations or equity securities.

   b. Renewing, extending, or replacing it with short-term obligations for an uninterrupted period greater than one year (or operating cycle) from the balance sheet date.

3. **Reclassification Requirements** Exclusion from current liabilities requires that two conditions be met:

   a. **Intention** The enterprise must intend to refinance the obligation on a long-term basis.

   b. **Ability** The enterprise must have the ability to consummate the refinancing. Evidence of the ability to consummate the refinancing is provided by either of the following.

(1) A refinancing that occurs after the balance sheet date but before the balance sheet is issued.

(2) A financing agreement before the balance sheet is issued that permits the refinancing and extends beyond one year or operating cycle. If any violation of the agreement has occurred, a waiver from the lender must be obtained. Further, the lender must be expected to be financially capable of honoring the agreement.

4. **Portions of Past Obligations Not Refinanced** If post-balance sheet refinancing of a short-term obligation has taken place, any portion **not** refinanced must be shown as a current liability.

5. **Limitations on Exclusions From Current Liabilities** If a financing agreement provides evidence of the ability to refinance, the amount excluded from current liabilities is limited to the amount available for refinancing under the agreement. Limitations on the amount excluded arise from the following.

Example 8 ▸ Exclusions From Current Liabilities

The First National Bank agrees to lend ABC Corporation, on a revolving credit basis, an amount equal to 75% of the Company's receivables. ABC plans to continue the revolving credit. During the year the receivables are expected to range between a low of $500,000 in the first quarter to a high of $2,000,000 in the fourth quarter. The minimum amount available for refinancing of short-term liabilities is $375,000 based on the expected low for trade receivables of $500,000. For balance sheet presentation, the maximum amount that can be excluded from current liabilities is $375,000.

a. Obligations in excess of the amount available for refinancing under the agreement.

b. Restrictions imposed by other agreements on the use of funds obtained under the refinancing arrangement.

c. Agreements that do not specify that a fixed amount of funds will be available. In this case, only an amount equal to the minimum sum expected to be available at any date during the period can be excluded. If the minimum sum cannot be reasonably estimated, the obligation must be shown as a current liability.

6. **Repaid From Current Assets** FASB Interp. 8, *Classification of a Short-Term Obligation Repaid Prior to Being Replaced by a Long-Term Security,* indicates that short-term obligations repaid after the balance sheet date and subsequently refinanced before the issuance of the balance sheet must be classified as current liabilities as of the balance sheet date because current assets were used for the repayment.

E. Asset Retirement Obligations (SFAS 143)

SFAS 143 addresses accounting for costs and liabilities related to tangible long-term asset retirement. Asset retirement obligation must be recognized as a liability (not a contra-asset) at fair value in the period in which it is incurred, if it is subject to reasonable estimation. The liability is discounted and accretion expense is recognized using the credit-adjusted risk-free interest rate in effect at initial recognition. **Note:** The editors expect CPA exam coverage on SFAS 143 to be light.

III. Debt Extinguishment (SFAS 140)

A. Conditions

A liability should not be removed from the financial statements until it has been extinguished, which occurs if either of the following conditions are met.

1. **Payment** The debtor pays the creditor and is relieved of its obligation for the liability. This may include delivering cash, other financial assets, goods, or services, or reacquiring outstanding debt securities; or

2. **Release** The debtor is legally released from being the primary obligor on the liability, either by the creditor or the courts, such as in the case of bankruptcy.

B. In-Substance Defeasance Not Extinguishment

In-substance defeasance is no longer accounted for as an extinguishment of debt. In-substance defeasance is a situation where a debt remains outstanding, but the debtor places risk-free monetary assets, such as U.S. government securities, in a trust that restricts the use of the assets to meeting all of the cash flow requirements on the debt. Previously, this was allowed to be accounted for as an extinguishment of debt; the liability was removed from the balance sheet and the trust was not recognized as an asset on the balance sheet. SFAS 140 requires that this type of transaction be accounted for as a separate asset and liability.

C. Extinguishment vs. Refunding

Extinguishment includes the reacquisition of debt securities regardless of whether the securities are canceled or held as so-called treasury bonds. Refunding refers to achieving the reacquisition by the use of proceeds from issuing other securities.

D. Extraordinary Item

APB 26, *Early Extinguishment of Debt,* as amended by SFAS 140, indicates that all extinguishments are fundamentally alike. Therefore, the extinguishment of debt, irrespective of the method used (except certain conversions of convertible bonds into stock or extinguishment through a troubled debt restructuring) should involve recognition of a gain or loss in the period in which the extinguishment took place. The gain or loss is the difference between the reacquisition price and the net carrying amount of the extinguished debt. (Further discussion in Chapter 6.)

- SFAS 145 removes the assumption that gains and losses from the early extinguishment of debt are extraordinary items. Entities must evaluate whether early debt extinguishment is extraordinary considering their environments. SFAS 145 superseded SFAS 4, as amended.

IV. Troubled Debt Restructurings (SFAS 15, 114, 118)

A. Definition

A troubled debt restructuring occurs when a creditor, for economic or legal reasons related to the debtor's financial difficulties, grants a concession to the debtor that the creditor would not otherwise consider. This concession may take either of two forms: (1) *transfer of assets or an equity interest* in the debtor in satisfaction of the debt (C., below), or (2) a *modification of the terms* of the obligation, including a reduction of the interest rate, extension of the maturity date, or reduction of the face amount of the debt and accrued interest (D., below). Troubled debt restructurings are covered in SFAS 15 and amended by SFAS 114 and SFAS 118.

B. Debt Restructuring vs. Troubled Debt Restructuring

Generally, a debtor who can obtain funds from other than the existing creditor at an interest rate near the current rate for nontroubled debt is **not** involved with a troubled debt restructuring, even though the debtor may be experiencing difficulty. In a troubled debt restructuring, the creditor is granting the concession in order to protect as much of the investment as possible.

C. Types of Troubled Debt Restructurings

A troubled debt restructuring may involve the transfer of assets by the debtor to the creditor in partial or full settlement of the obligation. Alternatively, the agreement may call for the granting of an equity interest in the debtor to the creditor, or a combination of both. In either case, in a *troubled* debt restructuring the total fair value of the consideration given to discharge the obligation will be **less** than the recorded amount (i.e., principal and accrued interest) of the debt. (If the fair value of the consideration received by the creditor equals or exceeds the amount of the debt, the transaction will not be classified as a troubled debt restructuring, by definition.)

Example 9 ▸ Troubled Debt Restructuring

On January 1, year 2, Risky Developers Inc. borrowed $100,000 from Easymoney Corp. The promissory note calls for 10% interest, payable annually on Dec. 31, and matures on Dec. 31, year 4. Risky made the first interest payment on time, but defaulted on the payment due Dec. 31, year 3. On July 1, year 4, Risky and Easymoney reached an agreement whereby the entire obligation would be discharged by the transfer of a parcel of land valued at $40,000 and Risky preferred stock with a par and fair value of $35,000. The land had been purchased by Risky in year 1 for $50,000.

Required: Provide the journal entries for both the debtor and creditor.

Solution:

Debtor:

Note Payable, Including Accrued Interest		
[$100,000 + 10% ($100,000) + 10% ($110,000) (6/12)]	115,500	
Loss on Disposal of Land, Ordinary	10,000	
Land		50,000
Preferred Stock		35,000
Gain on Debt Restructuring		
[$115,500 – ($40,000 + $35,000)]		40,500

Creditor:

Land	40,000	
Investment in Risky Preferred Stock	35,000	
Loss on Settlement of Receivable (ordinary)	40,500	
Notes Receivable, Including Accrued Interest		115,500

1. **Debtors** The debtor recognizes a gain on the retirement of debt, equal to the difference between the carrying amount of the obligation settled and the fair value of the assets and/or equity interest transferred to the creditor.

   a. **Gain** The debtor records gain equal to the difference between the carrying amount of the payable (including accrued interest) and the aggregate future payments required under the new terms.

   b. **Ordinary Gain or Loss** To the extent assets are transferred pursuant to the restructuring, the debtor will recognize an ordinary gain or loss equal to the difference between the fair value and the carrying amount of the assets transferred (i.e., the same as if the assets had been sold at their fair value for cash).

2. **Creditors** The creditor recognizes a loss equal to the difference between the fair value of the assets and/or equity interest received and the recorded amount of the receivable (including accrued interest). This loss, to the extent not offset against an allowance for uncollectibles or other valuation account, will be recognized in full in the period the restructuring takes place.

   a. **Ordinary Loss** Generally, the loss recognized by the creditor will be ordinary.

   b. **Record at Fair Value** The creditor will record the assets and/or equity securities received at their fair value.

D. **Modification of Terms—Debtor Accounting**
A troubled debt restructuring may involve a reduction of interest rate, a partial forgiveness of principal and interest payments, and/or extension of maturity date. Accounting for debtors is determined by whether the sum of the cash payments under the new terms (not discounted to present value) equal or exceed the amount of the obligation.

1. **Payments Less Than Obligation** When the aggregate payments under new terms are **less** than the amount of the obligation, the debtor reduces the carrying amount of the payable to the aggregate future cash payments.

   a. **Gain** The debtor records gain equal to the difference between the carrying amount of the payable (including accrued interest) and the aggregate future payments required under the new terms.

   b. **Payments Reduce Principal** Future payments are recorded as a reduction of principal, and no interest expenses are recognized.

2. **Payments Equal To or More Than Obligation** When the aggregate payments under new terms are equal to or more than the amount of the obligation, the debtor

   a. **No Gain or Loss** Does not change the amount of the obligation, nor is any gain or loss recorded.

   b. **Payments To Principal and Interest** Allocates subsequent payments between interest and principal on the basis of a constant rate of interest (i.e., the interest method of APB 21).

3. **Debtor & Creditor Accounting Differ** Note that the debtor and creditor account for the modification differently. The debtor uses the aggregate of future cash payments and the creditor uses the present value of future cash payments. Creditor accounting of impaired loans is detailed in Chapter 2.

V. Highlights of Federal Bankruptcy Law

A. Chapter 7 Bankruptcy

The Bankruptcy Abuse Prevention and Consumer Protection Act of 2005 (BAPCPA-2005) amended the Federal Bankruptcy Code in many areas, but did not change the priority assigned to claims nor the distribution rules from Chapter 7 Bankruptcy. Bankruptcy law is tested primarily in the Regulation portion of the CPA exam. However, exams have frequently included a multiple choice question on this topic, generally concerning the rules of priority and distribution. These rules are summarized here for straight bankruptcies, or liquidations. Chapter 7 of the *Federal Bankruptcy Code* covers straight bankruptcies or liquidations. It involves the collection of the debtor's nonexempt property, the liquidation or sale of such property, and the distribution of the proceeds to the creditors by the trustee as provided by the Code. After distribution of the proceeds, the debtor is relieved from having to satisfy any personal liability concerning any of the discharged debts.

B. Priority of Claims

Claims filed by the creditors against the bankrupt debtor are classified according to their *priority,* that is, the order in which they will receive any of the liquidation proceeds that are ultimately distributed.

1. **Secured Claims** Claims secured by a lien on property are entitled to first priority, but only on the distribution of the proceeds from the liquidation of their collateral, and only to the extent the loan is secured. If the value of the collateral is **less** than the amount of the claim, the excess amount of the claim is unsecured.

2. **Unsecured Claims** Claims not secured by a lien on any property of the debtor. There are many different classes of unsecured claims and their priority depends upon the nature of the claim.

C. Distribution Rules

Under a Chapter 7 case, claims of a higher priority are satisfied before those of a next priority class. If the assets are insufficient to satisfy all the claims within a particular class, they will be satisfied pro rata for that class. Any liquidation proceeds and/or other assets remaining after satisfying **all** claims are returned to the debtor.

Example 10 ▸ Bankruptcy Distribution

ABC Company filed a petition for a bankruptcy under Chapter 7. Creditors have secured claims of $300,000 and unsecured claims of $625,000. The following list of assets has been obtained.

	Amount secured	Amount received upon liquidation
Asset #1	$100,000	$100,000
Asset #2	75,000	50,000
Asset #3	125,000	150,000
Assets without security interests	--	300,000
	$300,000	$600,000

Required: Determine the distribution of the proceeds received from liquidation.

Solution: Claims secured by Asset #1 and Asset #3 are fully secured and will be satisfied in full ($100,000 and $125,000, respectively). The excess $25,000 of proceeds received over the amount of the secured claim for Asset #3 will go towards satisfying unsecured claims. As for Asset #2, its secured creditor is only partially secured, since the amount received for the asset is less than the amount of the claim; therefore, this creditor is now an unsecured creditor in the amount of $25,000. There is ultimately $325,000 [$600,000 – ($100,000 + $50,000 + $125,000)] left to be distributed to the unsecured claims. Since the unsecured claims total $650,000 ($625,000 of original unsecured claims plus $25,000 unsecured claim from creditor of Asset #2), the unsecured creditors will each receive one-half of their claims. Therefore, Asset #2's secured creditor will receive <u>$62,500</u> [$50,000 + ($25,000 x 50%)].

Select Hot•Spots™ Video Description

CPA 2090 Bonds & Other Liabilities

This lecture examines bonds from both the issuer's and investor's perspectives. Learn about bond discounts and premiums, and both the straight-line and effective interest methods of amortizing the discounts and premiums. Journal entry examples are provided and term, serial, convertible, and debenture bonds are covered. Included in other liabilities are troubled debt restructuring, contingencies, warranty and coupon liabilities, and compensated absences. Actual questions from past exams are used by CPA Review expert Bob Monette to reinforce the material needed for the CPA exam.

Another Helpful Video

How to Pass the CPA Exam

Watching this video program, CPA candidates will gain insight about the CPA exam in general and computer-based testing in particular. Robert Monette discusses when to take the exam and the new content specifications. He explains the good and bad news about computer-based testing. Bob interprets what the AICPA examiners mean by on-demand exam and adaptive testing. Bob delineates the different question types and explores exam-taking, exam-scheduling, and study strategies. Approximately 30 minutes.

Complimentary copies of this valuable video are available for a limited time to qualified candidates.

Call our customer representatives toll-free at 1 (800) 874-7877 for more details about videos.

Subject to Change Without Notice

CHAPTER 7—LIABILITIES

Problem 7-1 MULTIPLE CHOICE QUESTIONS (100 to 125 minutes)

1. Brite Corp. had the following liabilities at December 31 of the current year:

Accounts payable	$ 55,000
Unsecured notes, 8%, due 7/1 next year	400,000
Accrued expenses	35,000
Contingent liability	450,000
Deferred income tax liability	25,000
Senior bonds, 7%, due 3/31 next year	1,000,000

The contingent liability is an accrual for possible losses on a $1,000,000 lawsuit filed against Brite. Brite's legal counsel expects the suit to be settled in 2 years, and has estimated that Brite will be liable for damages in the range of $450,000 to $750,000.

The deferred income tax liability is not related to an asset for financial reporting and is expected to reverse in 2 years.

What amount should Brite report in its current year December 31 balance sheet for current liabilities?

a. $ 515,000
b. $ 940,000
c. $1,490,000
d. $1,515,000 (5/94, FAR, #11, amended, 4826)

2. Wilk Co. reported the following liabilities at December 31 of the current year:

Accounts payable-trade	$ 750,000
Short-term borrowings	400,000
Bank loan, current portion $100,000	3,500,000
Other bank loan, matures June 30 next year	1,000,000

The bank loan of $3,500,000 was in violation of the loan agreement. The creditor had not waived the rights for the loan. What amount should Wilk report as current liabilities at December 31 this year?

a. $1,250,000
b. $2,150,000
c. $2,250,000
d. $5,650,000 (R/02, FAR, #6, amended, 7061)

3. Lyle Inc. is preparing its financial statements for the prior year ended December 31. Accounts payable amounted to $360,000 before any necessary year-end adjustment related to the following:

- At December 31, Lyle has a $50,000 debit balance in its accounts payable to Ross, a supplier, resulting from a $50,000 advance payment for goods to be manufactured to Lyle's specifications.
- Checks in the amount of $100,000 were written to vendors and recorded on December 29. The checks were mailed on January 5 of this year.

What amount should Lyle report as accounts payable in its prior year's December 31 balance sheet?

a. $510,000
b. $410,000
c. $310,000
d. $210,000 (11/93, PI, #30, amended, 4399)

4. Rabb Co. records its purchases at gross amounts but wishes to change to recording purchases net of purchase discounts. Discounts available on purchases recorded from last October 1 to this September 30 totaled $2,000. Of this amount, $200 is still available in the accounts payable balance. The balances in Rabb's accounts as of and for the current year ended September 30 before conversion are:

Purchases	$100,000
Purchase discounts taken	800
Accounts payable	30,000

What is Rabb's current year accounts payable balance as of September 30 after the conversion?

a. $29,800
b. $29,200
c. $28,800
d. $28,200 (11/92, PI, #21, amended, 3254)

5. As of December 15 of the current year, Aviator had dividends in arrears of $200,000 on its cumulative preferred stock. Dividends for this year of $100,000 have not yet been declared. The board of directors plan to declare cash dividends on its preferred and common stock on January 16 of next year. Aviator paid an annual bonus to its CEO based on the company's annual profits. The bonus for this year was $50,000, and it will be paid on February 10 of next year. What amount should Aviator report as current liabilities on its current year balance sheet at December 31.

a. $ 50,000
b. $150,000
c. $200,000
d. $350,000

(R/05, FAR, 1742F, #35, amended, 7779)

6. Which of the following is reported as interest expense?

a. Pension cost interest
b. Postretirement healthcare benefits interest
c. Imputed interest on noninterest-bearing note
d. Interest incurred to finance construction of machinery for own use

(11/93, Theory, #33, 4538)

7. On December 31, Roth Co. issued a $10,000 face value note payable to Wake Co. in exchange for services rendered to Roth. The note, made at usual trade terms, is due in nine months and bears interest, payable at maturity, at the annual rate of 3%. The market interest rate is 8%. The compound interest factor of $1 due in nine months at 8% is .944. At what amount should the note payable be reported in Roth's December 31 balance sheet?

a. $10,300
b. $10,000
c. $ 9,652
d. $ 9,440

(11/93, PI, #27, amended, 4396)

8. On March 1 of the prior year, Fine Co. borrowed $10,000 and signed a two-year note bearing interest at 12% per annum compounded annually. Interest is payable in full at maturity on February 28 of next year. What amount should Fine report as a liability for accrued interest at December 31 of the current year?

a. $0
b. $1,000
c. $1,200
d. $2,320

(11/95, FAR, #16, amended, 6098)

9. House Publishers offered a contest in which the winner would receive $1,000,000, payable over 20 years. On December 31 of the prior year, House announced the winner of the contest and signed a note payable to the winner for $1,000,000, payable in $50,000 installments every January 2. Also on that December 31, House purchased an annuity for $418,250 to provide the $950,000 prize monies remaining after the first $50,000 installment, which was paid on January 2 of this year. In its prior year December 31 balance sheet, what amount should House report as note payable-contest winner, net of current portion?

a. $368,250
b. $418,250
c. $900,000
d. $950,000

(11/94, FAR, #22, amended, 5286)

10. Barnel Corp. owns and manages 19 apartment complexes. On signing a lease, each tenant must pay the first and last months' rent and a $500 refundable security deposit. The security deposits are rarely refunded in total, because cleaning costs of $150 per apartment are almost always deducted. About 30% of the time, the tenants are also charged for damages to the apartment, which typically cost $100 to repair. If a one-year lease is signed on a $900 per month apartment, what amount would Barnel report as refundable security deposit?

a. $1,400
b. $ 500
c. $ 350
d. $ 320

(11/92, PI, #26, 3259)

11. Black Co. requires advance payments with special orders for machinery constructed to customer specifications. These advances are nonrefundable. Information for the current year is as follows:

Customer advances—prior year balance 12/31	$118,000
Advances received with orders in the current year	184,000
Advances applied to orders shipped in the current year	164,000
Advances applicable to orders canceled in the current year	50,000

In Black's current year December 31 balance sheet, what amount should be reported as a current liability for advances from customer?

a. $0
b. $ 88,000
c. $138,000
d. $148,000

(11/94, FAR, #25, amended, 9027)

12. Under state law, Acme may pay 3% of eligible gross wages or it may reimburse the state directly for actual unemployment claims. Acme believes that actual unemployment claims will be 2% of eligible gross wages and has chosen to reimburse the state. Eligible gross wages are defined as the first $10,000 of gross wages paid to each employee. Acme had five employees, each of whom earned $20,000 during the year. In its December 31 balance sheet, what amount should Acme report as accrued liability for unemployment claims?
a. $1,000
b. $1,500
c. $2,000
d. $3,000 (5/94, FAR, #22, amended, 4837)

13. Ross Co. pays all salaried employees on a Monday for the five-day workweek ended the previous Friday. The last payroll recorded for the year ended December 31, year 2, was for the week ended December 25, year 2. The payroll for the week ended January 1, year 3, included regular weekly salaries of $80,000 and vacation pay of $25,000 for vacation time earned in year 2 not taken by December 31, year 2. Ross had accrued a liability of $20,000 for vacation pay at December 31, year 1. In its December 31, year 2 balance sheet, what amount should Ross report as accrued salary and vacation pay?
a. $64,000
b. $68,000
c. $69,000
d. $89,000 (11/93, PI, #28, amended, 4397)

14. On July 1, Ran County issued realty tax assessments for its fiscal year ended next June 30. On September 1, Day Co. purchased a warehouse in Ran County. The purchase price was reduced by a credit for accrued realty taxes. Day did not record the entire year's real estate tax obligation, but instead records tax expenses at the end of each month by adjusting prepaid real estate taxes or real estate taxes payable, as appropriate. On November 1, Day paid the first of two equal installments of $12,000 for realty taxes. What amount of this payment should Day record as a debit to real estate taxes payable?
a. $ 4,000
b. $ 8,000
c. $10,000
d. $12,000 (11/94, FAR, #19, amended, 5283)

15. Dunne Co. sells equipment service contracts that cover a two-year period. The sale price of each contract is $600. Dunne's past experience is that, of the total dollars spent for repairs on service contracts, 40% is incurred evenly during the first contract year and 60% evenly during the second contract year. Dunne sold 1,000 contracts evenly throughout the year. In its current year December 31 balance sheet, what amount should Dunne report as deferred service contract revenue?
a. $540,000
b. $480,000
c. $360,000
d. $300,000 (11/93, PI, #38, amended, 4407)

16. For $50 a month, Rawl Co. visits its customers' premises and performs insect control services. If customers experience problems between regularly scheduled visits, Rawl makes service calls at no additional charge. Instead of paying monthly, customers may pay an annual fee of $540 in advance. For a customer who pays the annual fee in advance, Rawl should recognize the related revenue
a. When the cash is collected
b. At the end of the fiscal year
c. At the end of the contract year after all of the services have been performed
d. Evenly over the contract year as the services are performed (11/94, FAR, #21, 5285)

17. Regal Department Store sells gift certificates, redeemable for store merchandise, that expire one year after their issuance. Regal has the following information pertaining to its gift certificates sales and redemptions:

Unredeemed at 12/31 of prior year	$ 75,000
Current year sales	250,000
Redemptions of prior year sales	25,000
Redemptions of current year sales	175,000

Regal's experience indicates that 10% of gift certificates sold will not be redeemed. In its current year December 31 balance sheet, what amount should Regal report as unearned revenue?
a. $125,000
b. $112,500
c. $100,000
d. $ 50,000 (11/92, PI, #30, amended, 3263)

18. Able Inc. had the following amounts of long-term debt outstanding at December 31 of the current year:

14-1/2% term note, due next year	$ 3,000
11-1/8% term note, due in four years	107,000
8% note, due in 11 equal annual principal payments, plus interest beginning December 31 of next year	110,000
7% guaranteed debentures, due in five years	100,000
Total	$320,000

Able's annual sinking-fund requirement on the guaranteed debentures is $4,000 per year. What amount should Able report as current maturities of long-term debt in its current year December 31 balance sheet?

a. $ 4,000
b. $ 7,000
c. $10,000
d. $13,000 (11/92, PI, #5, amended, 3238)

19. Ivy Co. operates a retail store. All items are sold subject to a 6% state sales tax, which Ivy collects and records as sales revenue. Ivy files quarterly sales tax returns when due, by the 20th day following the end of the sales quarter. However, in accordance with state requirements, Ivy remits sales tax collected by the 20th day of the month following any month such collections exceed $500. Ivy takes these payments as credits on the quarterly sales tax return. The sales taxes paid by Ivy are charged against sales revenue. Following is a monthly summary appearing in Ivy's first quarter sales revenue account:

	Debit	Credit
January	$ --	$10,600
February	600	7,420
March	--	8,480
	$600	$26,500

In its March 31 balance sheet, what amount should Ivy report as sales taxes payable?

a. $ 600
b. $ 900
c. $1,500
d. $1,590 (5/95, FAR, #15, amended, 5551)

20. Pine Corp. is required to contribute, to an employee stock ownership plan (ESOP), 10% of its income after deduction for this contribution but before income tax. Pine's income before charges for the contribution and income tax was $75,000. The income tax rate is 30%. What amount should be accrued as a contribution to the ESOP?

a. $7,500
b. $6,818
c. $5,250
d. $4,773 (5/91, PI, #36, 1016)

21. For the week ended June 30, Free Co. paid gross wages of $20,000, from which federal income taxes of $2,500 and FICA were withheld. All wages paid were subject to FICA tax rates of 7% each for employer and employee. Free makes all payroll-related disbursements from a special payroll checking account. What amount should Free have deposited in the payroll checking account to cover net payroll and related payroll taxes for the week ended June 30?

a. $21,400
b. $22,800
c. $23,900
d. $25,300 (R/00, FAR, #6, amended, 6901)

22. Oak Co. offers a three-year warranty on its products. Oak previously estimated warranty costs to be 2% of sales. Due to a technological advance in production at the beginning of the current year, Oak now believes 1% of sales to be a better estimate of warranty costs. Warranty costs of $80,000 and $96,000 were reported in the two prior years. Sales for the year were $5,000,000. What amount should be disclosed in Oak's current year financial statements as warranty expense?

a. $ 50,000
b. $ 88,000
c. $100,000
d. $138,000 (11/95, FAR, #44, amended, 6126)

23. Dunn Trading Stamp Co. records stamp service revenue and provides for the cost of redemptions in the year stamps are sold to licensees. Dunn's past experience indicates that only 80% of the stamps sold to licensees will be redeemed. Dunn's liability for stamp redemptions was $6,000,000 at December 31 of the prior year. Additional information for the current year is as follows:

Stamp service revenue from stamps sold to licensees	$4,000,000
Cost of redemptions (stamps sold prior to 1/1 of the current year)	2,750,000

If all the stamps sold in the current year were presented for redemption in next year, the redemption cost would be $2,250,000. What amount should Dunn report as a liability for stamp redemptions at December 31 of the current year?

a. $7,250,000
b. $5,500,000
c. $5,050,000
d. $3,250,000 (11/90, PI, #28, amended, 1035)

24. During the prior year, Gum Co. introduced a new product carrying a two-year warranty against defects. The estimated warranty costs related to dollar sales are 2% within 12 months following the sale and 4% in the second 12 months following the sale. Sales and actual warranty expenditures for the prior and current year ended December 31, are as follows:

	Sales	Actual warranty expenditures
Prior year	$150,000	$2,250
Current year	250,000	7,500
	$400,000	$9,750

What amount should Gum report as estimated warranty liability in its current year December 31 balance sheet?
a. $ 2,500
b. $ 4,250
c. $11,250
d. $14,250 (5/92, PI, #35, amended, 2606)

25. In December, Mill Co. began including one coupon in each package of candy that it sells and offering a toy in exchange for 50 cents and five coupons. The toys cost Mill 80 cents each. Eventually 60% of the coupons will be redeemed. During December, Mill sold 110,000 packages of candy and no coupons were redeemed. In its December 31 balance sheet, what amount should Mill report as estimated liability for coupons?
a. $ 3,960
b. $10,560
c. $19,800
d. $52,800 (5/95, FAR, #21, amended, 5557)

26. At December 31 of the current year, Taos Co. estimates that its employees have earned vacation pay of $100,000. Employees will receive their vacation pay next year. Should Taos accrue a liability at December 31 if the rights to this compensation accumulated over time or if the rights are vested?

	Accumulated	*Vested*
a.	Yes	No
b.	No	No
c.	Yes	Yes
d.	No	Yes

(11/92, Theory, #25, amended, 3458)

27. The following information pertains to Rik Co.'s two employees:

Name	Weekly salary	Number of weeks worked during the year	Vacation rights vest or accumulate
Ryan	$800	52	Yes
Todd	600	52	No

Neither Ryan nor Todd took the usual two-week vacation during the year. In Rik's December 31 financial statements, what amount of vacation expense and liability should be reported?
a. $2,800
b. $1,600
c. $1,400
d. $0 (5/92, PII, #15, amended, 2647)

28. Invern Inc. has a self-insurance plan. Each year, retained earnings is appropriated for contingencies in an amount equal to insurance premiums saved less recognized losses from lawsuits and other claims. As a result of an accident this year, Invern is a defendant in a lawsuit in which it will probably have to pay damages of $190,000. What are the effects of this lawsuit's probable outcome on Invern's current year financial statements?
a. An increase in expenses and no effect on liabilities
b. An increase in both expenses and liabilities
c. No effect on expenses and an increase in liabilities
d. No effect on either expenses or liabilities
(11/92, Theory, #17, amended, 3450)

29. During the prior year, Manfred Corp. guaranteed a supplier's $500,000 loan from a bank. On October 1 of the current year, Manfred was notified that the supplier had defaulted on the loan and filed for bankruptcy protection. Counsel believes Manfred will probably have to pay between $250,000 and $450,000 under its guarantee. As a result of the supplier's bankruptcy, Manfred entered into a contract in December to retool its machines so that Manfred could accept parts from other suppliers. Retooling costs are estimated to be $300,000. What amount should Manfred report as a liability in its current year December 31 balance sheet?
a. $250,000
b. $450,000
c. $550,000
d. $750,000 (11/92, PI, #31, amended, 3264)

30. During the prior year, Haft Co. became involved in a tax dispute with the IRS. At December 31 of the prior year, Haft's tax advisor believed that an unfavorable outcome was probable. A reasonable estimate of additional taxes was $200,000, but could be as much as $300,000. After the prior year financial statements were issued, Haft received and accepted an IRS settlement offer of $275,000. What amount of accrued liability should Haft have reported in its prior year December 31 balance sheet?

a. $200,000
b. $250,000
c. $275,000
d. $300,000 (5/95, FAR, #22, amended, 5558)

31. Bell Co. is a defendant in a lawsuit that could result in a large payment to the plaintiff. Bell's attorney believes that there is a 90% chance that Bell will lose the suit, and estimates that the loss will be anywhere from $5,000,000 to $20,000,000 and possibly as much as $30,000,000. None of the estimates are better than the others. What amount of liability should Bell report on its balance sheet related to the lawsuit?

a. $0
b. $ 5,000,000
c. $20,000,000
d. $30,000,000 (R/05, FAR, 1743F, #36, 7780)

32. Management can estimate the amount of loss that will occur if a foreign government expropriates some company assets. If expropriation is reasonably possible, a loss contingency should be

a. Disclosed but not accrued as a liability
b. Disclosed and accrued as a liability
c. Accrued as a liability but not disclosed
d. Neither accrued as a liability nor disclosed (11/94, FAR, #26, 5289)

33. Ace Co. settled litigation on February 1 of the current year for an event that occurred during the prior year. An estimated liability was determined as of December 31 of the prior year. This estimate was significantly less than the final settlement. The transaction is considered to be material. The financial statements for prior year-end have not been issued. How should the settlement be reported in Ace's prior year-end financial statements?

a. Disclosure only of the settlement
b. Only an accrual of the settlement
c. Neither a disclosure nor an accrual
d. Both a disclosure and an accrual (R/02, FAR, #10, amended, 7065)

34. On January 17 of the current year, an explosion occurred at a Sims Co. plant causing extensive property damage to area buildings. Although no claims had yet been asserted against Sims by March 10, Sims' management and counsel concluded that it is likely that claims will be asserted and that it is reasonably possible Sims will be responsible for damages. Sims' management believed that $1,250,000 would be a reasonable estimate of its liability. Sims' $5,000,000 comprehensive public liability policy has a $250,000 deductible clause. In Sims' prior year December 31 financial statements, which were issued on March 25 of the current year, how should this item be reported?

a. As an accrued liability of $250,000
b. As a footnote disclosure indicating the possible loss of $250,000
c. As a footnote disclosure indicating the possible loss of $1,250,000
d. No footnote disclosure or accrual is necessary (5/92, PI, #36, amended, 2607)

35. What is the underlying concept governing the generally accepted accounting principles pertaining to recording gain contingencies?

a. Conservatism
b. Relevance
c. Consistency
d. Reliability (11/95, FAR, #3, 6085)

36. During the prior year, Smith Co. filed suit against West Inc. seeking damages for patent infringement. At December 31 of the prior year, Smith's legal counsel believed that it was probable that Smith would be successful against West for an estimated amount in the range of $75,000 to $150,000, with all amounts in the range considered equally likely. In March of the current year, Smith was awarded $100,000 and received full payment thereof. In its prior year financial statements, issued in February of the current year, how should this award be reported?

a. As a receivable and revenue of $100,000
b. As a receivable and deferred revenue of $100,000
c. As a disclosure of a contingent gain of $100,000
d. As a disclosure of a contingent gain of an undetermined amount in the range of $75,000 to $150,000 (5/94, FAR, #57, amended, 4872)

37. On December 30, of the current year Bart Inc. purchased a machine from Fell Corp. in exchange for a noninterest-bearing note requiring eight payments of $20,000. The first payment was made on December 30, and the others are due annually on December 30. At date of issuance, the prevailing rate of interest for this type of note was 11%. Present value factors are as follows:

Period	Present value of ordinary annuity of 1 at 11%	Present value of annuity in advance of 1 at 11%
7	4.712	5.231
8	5.146	5.712

On Bart's current year December 31 balance sheet, the note payable to Fell was
a. $ 94,240.
b. $102,920.
c. $104,620.
d. $114,240. (5/90, PI, #29, amended, 1045)

Items 38 and 39 are based on the following:

On October 1 of the prior year, Fleur Retailers signed a 4-month, 16% note payable to finance the purchase of holiday merchandise. At that date, there was no direct method of pricing the merchandise, and the note's market rate of interest was 11%. Fleur recorded the purchase at the note's face amount. All of the merchandise was sold by December 1 of the prior year Fleur's prior year financial statements reported interest payable and interest expense on the note for three months at 16%. All amounts due on the note were paid February 1 of the current year.

38. Fleur's prior year cost of goods sold for the holiday merchandise was
a. Overstated by the difference between the note's face amount and the note's October 1 present value
b. Overstated by the difference between the note's face amount and the note's October 1 present value plus 11% interest for two months
c. Understated by the difference between the note's face amount and the note's October 1 present value
d. Understated by the difference between the note's face amount and the note's October 1 present value plus 16% interest for two months
(5/92, Theory, #18, amended, 2711)

39. As a result of Fleur's accounting treatment of the note, interest, and merchandise, which of the following items was reported correctly?

	Prior year 12/31 retained earnings	*Prior year 12/31 interest payable*
a.	Yes	Yes
b.	No	No
c.	Yes	No
d.	No	Yes

(5/92, Theory, #19, amended, 2712)

40. Cali Inc. had a $4,000,000 note payable due on March 15 of the current year. On January 28 of the current year, before the issuance of its prior year financial statements, Cali issued long-term bonds in the amount of $4,500,000. Proceeds from the bonds were used to repay the note when it came due. How should Cali classify the note in its prior year December 31 financial statements?
a. As a current liability, with separate disclosure of the note refinancing
b. As a current liability, with no separate disclosure required
c. As a noncurrent liability, with separate disclosure of the note refinancing
d. As a noncurrent liability, with no separate disclosure required (5/95, FAR, #5, amended, 5541)

41. Included in Lee Corp.'s liability account balances at December 31, year 3, were the following:

14% note payable issued October 1, year 3, maturing September 30, year 4	$125,000
16% note payable issued April 1, year 1, payable in six equal annual installments of $50,000 beginning April 1, year 2	200,000

Lee's December 31, year 3 financial statements were issued on March 31, year 4. On January 15, year 4, the entire $200,000 balance of the 16% note was refinanced by issuance of a long-term obligation payable in a lump sum. In addition, on March 10, year 4, Lee consummated a noncancelable agreement with the lender to refinance the 14%, $125,000 note on a long-term basis, on readily determinable terms that have not yet been implemented. Both parties are financially capable of honoring the agreement, and there have been no violations of the agreement's provisions. On the December 31, year 3 balance sheet, the amount of the notes payable that Lee should classify as short-term obligations is
a. $175,000
b. $125,000
c. $ 50,000
d. $0 (11/90, PI, #11, amended, 1026)

42. At December 31 of the prior year, Cain Inc. owed notes payable of $1,750,000, due on May 15, of the current year. Cain expects to retire this debt with proceeds from the sale of 100,000 shares of its common stock. The stock was sold for $15 per share on March 10 of the current year, prior to the issuance of the year-end financial statements. In Cain's prior year December 31 balance sheet, what amount of the notes payable should be excluded from current liabilities?

a. $0
b. $ 250,000
c. $1,500,000
d. $1,750,000 (11/91, PI, #21, amended, 2409)

43. Verona Co. had $500,000 in short-term liabilities at the end of the current year. Verona issued $400,000 of common stock subsequent to the end of the year, but before the financial statements were issued. The proceeds from the stock issue were intended to be used to pay the short-term debt. What amount should Verona report as a short-term liability on its balance sheet at the end of the current year?

a. $0
b. $100,000
c. $400,000
d. $500,000 (R/05, FAR, 1676F, #33, 7777)

44. Nu Corp. agreed to give Rand Co. a machine in full settlement of a note payable to Rand. The machine's original cost was $140,000. The note's face amount was $110,000. On the date of the agreement:

- The note's carrying amount was $105,000, and its present value was $96,000.
- The machine's carrying amount was $109,000, and its fair value was $96,000.

What amount of gains (losses) should Nu recognize, and how should these be classified in its income statement?

	Extraordinary	*Other*
a.	$(4,000)	$0
b.	$0	$(4,000)
c.	$ 5,000	$(4,000)
d.	$ 9,000	$(13,000)

(5/92, PI, #53, amended, 2624)

45. On October 15, year 1, Kam Corp. informed Finn Co. that Kam would be unable to repay its $100,000 note due on October 31 to Finn. Finn agreed to accept title to Kam's computer equipment in full settlement of the note. The equipment's carrying value was $80,000 and its fair value was $75,000. Kam's tax rate is 30%. What amounts should Kam report as ordinary gain (loss) and extraordinary gain for the year ended September 30, year 2?

	Ordinary gain (loss)	*Extraordinary gain*
a.	$(5,000)	$17,500
b.	$0	$20,000
c.	$0	$14,000
d.	$20,000	$0

(11/92, PI, #59, amended, 3290)

46. Ace Corp. entered into a troubled debt restructuring agreement with National Bank. National agreed to accept land with a carrying amount of $75,000 and a fair value of $100,000 in exchange for a note with a carrying amount of $150,000. Disregarding income taxes, what amount should Ace report as extraordinary gain in its income statement?

a. $0
b. $25,000
c. $50,000
d. $75,000 (R/00, FAR, #10, amended, 6905)

47. In year 2, May Corp. acquired land by paying $75,000 down and signing a note with a maturity value of $1,000,000. On the note's due date, December 31, year 7, May owed $40,000 of accrued interest and $1,000,000 principal on the note. May was in financial difficulty and was unable to make any payments. May and the bank agreed to amend the note as follows:

- The $40,000 of interest due on December 31, year 7, was forgiven.
- The principal of the note was reduced from $1,000,000 to $950,000 and the maturity date extended 1 year to December 31, year 8.
- May would be required to make one interest payment totaling $30,000 on December 31, year 8.

As a result of the troubled debt restructuring, May should report a gain, before taxes, in its year 7 income statement of

a. $40,000
b. $50,000
c. $60,000
d. $90,000 (11/91, PI, #52, amended, 9030)

48. For a troubled debt restructuring involving only a modification of terms, which of the following items specified by the new terms would be compared to the carrying amount of the debt to determine if the debtor should report a gain on restructuring?
a. The total future cash payments
b. The present value of the debt at the original interest rate
c. The present value of the debt at the modified interest rate
d. The amount of future cash payments designated as principal repayments (R/01, FAR, #9, 6984)

49. Kamy Corp. is in liquidation under Chapter 7 of the Federal Bankruptcy Code. The bankruptcy trustee has established a new set of books for the bankruptcy estate. After assuming custody of the estate, the trustee discovered an unrecorded invoice of $1,000 for machinery repairs performed before the bankruptcy filing. In addition, a truck with a carrying amount of $20,000 was sold for $12,000 cash. This truck was bought and paid for in the year before the bankruptcy. What amount should be debited to estate equity as a result of these transactions?
a. $0
b. $1,000
c. $8,000
d. $9,000 (5/92, PII, #10, 2642)

50. Kent Co. filed a voluntary bankruptcy petition, and the statement of affairs reflected the following amounts:

	Book value	Estimated current value
Assets:		
Assets pledged with fully secured creditors	$ 300,000	$ 370,000
Assets pledged with partially secured creditors	180,000	120,000
Free assets	420,000	320,000
	$ 900,000	$ 810,000
Liabilities (book value):		
Liabilities with priority	$ 70,000	
Fully secured creditors	260,000	
Partially secured creditors	200,000	
Unsecured creditors	540,000	
	$1,070,000	

Assume that the assets are converted to cash at the estimated current values and the business is liquidated. What amount of cash will be available to pay unsecured nonpriority claims?
a. $240,000
b. $280,000
c. $320,000
d. $360,000 (11/90, PI, #31, amended, 1037)

Problem 7-2 ADDITIONAL MULTIPLE CHOICE QUESTIONS (46 to 58 minutes)

51. Mill Co.'s trial balance included the following account balances at December 31 of the current year:

Accounts payable	$15,000
Bonds payable, due next year	25,000
Discount on bonds payable, due next year	3,000
Dividends payable 1/31 next year	8,000
Notes payable, due in two years	20,000

What amount should be included in the current liability section of Mill's current year December 31 balance sheet?
a. $45,000
b. $51,000
c. $65,000
d. $78,000 (11/93, PI, #1, amended, 4370)

52. On August 1 of the current year, Vann Corp.'s $500,000, one-year, noninterest-bearing note due July 31 of next year, was discounted at Homestead Bank at 10.8%. Vann uses the straight-line method of amortizing bond discount. What amount should Vann report for notes payable in its current year December 31 balance sheet?
a. $500,000
b. $477,500
c. $468,500
d. $446,000 (11/92, PI, #22, amended, 3255)

53. Kew Co.'s accounts payable balance at December 31 of the prior year was $2,200,000 before considering the following data:

- Goods shipped to Kew F.O.B. shipping point on December 22 of the prior year were lost in transit. The invoice cost of $40,000 was not recorded by Kew. On January 7 of the current year, Kew filed a $40,000 claim against the common carrier.
- On December 27 of the prior year, a vendor authorized Kew to return, for full credit, goods shipped and billed at $70,000 on December 3 of the prior year. The returned goods were shipped by Kew on December 28 of the prior year. A $70,000 credit memo was received and recorded by Kew on January 5 of the current year.
- Goods shipped to Kew F.O.B. destination on December 20 of the prior year, were received on January 6 of the current year. The invoice cost was $50,000.

What amount should Kew report as accounts payable in its prior year December 31 balance sheet?
a. $2,170,000
b. $2,180,000
c. $2,230,000
d. $2,280,000 (5/91, PI, #34, amended, 1015)

54. A company issued a short-term note payable with a stated 12% rate of interest to a bank. The bank charged a .5% loan origination fee and remitted the balance to the company. The effective interest rate paid by the company in this transaction would be
a. Equal to 12.5%.
b. More than 12.5%.
c. Less than 12.5%.
d. Independent of 12.5%. (5/90, Theory, #8, 9026)

55. Cado Co.'s payroll for the month ended January 31 is summarized as follows:

Total wages	$100,000
Wages subject to payroll taxes:	
FICA	80,000
Unemployment	20,000
Payroll tax rates:	
FICA for employer and employee	7% each
Unemployment	3%

In its January 31 balance sheet, what amount should Cado accrue as its share of payroll taxes?
a. $ 6,200
b. $10,000
c. $11,800
d. $17,000 (R/03, FAR, #4, 7606)

56. Kent Co., a division of National Realty Inc., maintains escrow accounts and pays real estate taxes for National's mortgage customers. Escrow funds are kept in interest-bearing accounts. Interest, less a 10% service fee, is credited to the mortgagee's account and used to reduce future escrow payments. Additional information follows:

Escrow accounts liability, 1/1	$ 700,000
Escrow payments received during the year	1,580,000
Real estate taxes paid during the year	1,720,000
Interest on escrow funds during the year	50,000

What amount should Kent report as escrow accounts liability in its December 31 balance sheet?
a. $510,000
b. $515,000
c. $605,000
d. $610,000 (11/93, PI, #32, amended, 4401)

57. Lime Co.'s payroll for the month ended January 31 is summarized as follows:

Total wages	$10,000
Federal income tax withheld	1,200

All wages paid were subject to FICA. FICA tax rates were 7% each for employee and employer. Lime remits payroll taxes on the 15th of the following month. In its financial statements for the month ended January 31, what amounts should Lime report as total payroll tax liability and as payroll tax expense?

	Liability	*Expense*
a.	$1,200	$1,400
b.	$1,900	$1,400
c.	$1,900	$ 700
d.	$2,600	$ 700

(11/95, FAR, #13, amended, 6095)

58. In its current year financial statements, Cris Co. reported interest expense of $85,000 in its income statement and cash paid for interest of $68,000 in its cash flow statement. There was no prepaid interest or interest capitalization either at the beginning or end of the current year. Accrued interest at December 31 of the prior year was $15,000. What amount should Cris report as accrued interest payable in its current year December 31 balance sheet?
a. $ 2,000
b. $15,000
c. $17,000
d. $32,000 (11/94, FAR, #18, amended, 5282)

59. Todd Care Co. offers three payment plans on its 12-month contracts. Information on the three plans and the number of children enrolled in each plan for the September 1, year 1, through August 31, year 2, contract year follows:

Plan	Initial payment per child	Monthly fees per child	Number of children
#1	$500	$ --	15
#2	200	30	12
#3	--	50	9
			36

Todd received $9,900 of initial payments on September 1, year 1, and $3,240 of monthly fees during the period September 1 through December 31, year 1. In its December 31, year 1 balance sheet, what amount should Todd report as deferred revenues?

a. $3,300
b. $4,380
c. $6,600
d. $9,900 (11/92, PI, #29, amended, 3262)

60. Winn Co. sells subscriptions to a specialized directory that is published semiannually and shipped to subscribers on April 15 and October 15. Subscriptions received after the March 31 and September 30 cutoff dates are held for the next publication. Cash from subscribers is received evenly during the year and is credited to deferred subscription revenue. Data relating to the current year are as follows:

Deferred subscription revenue 1/1	$ 750,000
Cash receipts from subscribers	3,600,000

In its current year December 31 balance sheet, Winn should report deferred subscription revenue of

a. $2,700,000
b. $1,800,000
c. $1,650,000
d. $ 900,000 (11/91, PI, #29, amended, 2417)

61. KLU Broadcast Co. entered into an agreement to exchange unsold advertising time for travel and lodging services with Hotel Co. As of June 30, travel and lodging services of $10,000 were used by KLU. However, the advertising service had not been provided. How should KLU account for travel and lodging in its June 30 financial statements?

a. Revenue and expense is recognized when the agreement is complete.
b. An asset and revenue for $10,000 is recognized.
c. An expense and liability of $10,000 is recognized.
d. Not reported (R/03, FAR, #20, 7622)

62. In June, Northan Retailers sold refundable merchandise coupons. Northan received $10 for each coupon redeemable from July 1 to December 31 for merchandise with a retail price of $11. At June 30, how should Northan report these coupon transactions?

a. Unearned revenues at the merchandise's retail price
b. Unearned revenues at the cash received amount
c. Revenues at the merchandise's retail price
d. Revenues at the cash received amount

(11/92, Theory, #7, amended, 3440)

63. Case Cereal Co. frequently distributes coupons to promote new products. On October 1, Case mailed 1,000,000 coupons for $.45 off each box of cereal purchased. Case expects 120,000 of these coupons to be redeemed before the December 31 expiration date. It takes 30 days from the redemption date for Case to receive the coupons from the retailers. Case reimburses the retailers an additional $.05 for each coupon redeemed. As of December 31, Case had paid retailers $25,000 related to these coupons and had 50,000 coupons on hand that had not been processed for payment. What amount should Case report as a liability for coupons in its December 31 balance sheet?

a. $35,000
b. $29,000
c. $25,000
d. $22,500 (11/92, PI, #24, amended, 3257)

64. Gavin Co. grants all employees two weeks of paid vacation for each full year of employment. Unused vacation time can be accumulated and carried forward to succeeding years and will be paid at the salaries in effect when vacations are taken or when employment is terminated. There was no employee turnover in the current year. Additional information relating to the current year ended December 31 is as follows:

Liability for accumulated vacations at 12/31 of the prior year	$35,000
Pre-current year accrued vacations taken from 1/1 to 9/30 of the current year (the authorized period for vacations)	20,000
Vacations earned for work in the current year (adjusted to current rates)	30,000

Gavin granted a 10% salary increase to all employees on October 1 of the current year, its annual salary increase date. For the current year ended December 31, Gavin should report vacation pay increase of

a. $45,000
b. $33,500
c. $31,500
d. $30,000 (5/90, PII, #53, amended, 9028)

65. Vadis Co. sells appliances that include a three-year warranty. Service calls under the warranty are performed by an independent mechanic under a contract with Vadis. Based on experience, warranty costs are estimated at $30 for each machine sold. When should Vadis recognize these warranty costs?
a. Evenly over the life of the warranty
b. When the service calls are performed
c. When payments are made to the mechanic
d. When the machines are sold
(11/94, FAR, #27, 5290)

66. Wyatt Co. has a probable loss that can only be reasonably estimated within a range of outcomes. No single amount within the range is a better estimate than any other amount. The loss accrual should be
a. Zero
b. The maximum of the range
c. The mean of the range
d. The minimum of the range
(11/90, Theory, #35, 1801)

67. Eagle Co. has cosigned the mortgage note on the home of its president, guaranteeing the indebtedness in the event that the president should default. Eagle considers the likelihood of default to be remote. How should the guarantee be treated in Eagle's financial statements?
a. Disclosed only
b. Accrued only
c. Accrued and disclosed
d. Neither accrued nor disclosed
(11/95, FAR, #17, 6099)

68. During January of the current year, Haze Corp. won a litigation award for $15,000 which was tripled to $45,000 to include punitive damages. The defendant, who is financially stable, has appealed only the $30,000 punitive damages. Haze was awarded $50,000 in an unrelated suit it filed, which is being appealed by the defendant. Counsel is unable to estimate the outcome of these appeals. In its current year financial statements, Haze should report what amount of pretax gain?
a. $15,000
b. $45,000
c. $50,000
d. $95,000 (11/92, PII, #53, amended, 3387)

69. At December 31 of the current year, Date Co. awaits judgment on a lawsuit for a competitor's infringement of Date's patent. Legal counsel believes it is probable that Date will win the suit and indicated the most likely award together with a range of possible awards. How should the lawsuit be reported in Date's current year financial statements?
a. In note disclosure only
b. By accrual for the most likely award
c. By accrual for the lowest amount of the range of possible awards
d. Neither in note disclosure nor by accrual
(11/93, Theory, #21, amended, 4526)

70. Ames Inc. has $500,000 of notes payable due June 15 of the current year. Ames signed an agreement on December 1 of the prior year, to borrow up to $500,000 to refinance the notes payable on a long-term basis with no payments due for two years. The financing agreement stipulated that borrowings may not exceed 80% of the value of the collateral Ames was providing. At the date of issuance of the prior year December 31 financial statements, the value of the collateral was $600,000 and is not expected to fall below this amount during the current year. In Ames' prior year December 31 balance sheet, the obligation for these notes payable should be classified as

	Short-term	*Long-term*
a.	$500,000	$0
b.	$100,000	$400,000
c.	$ 20,000	$480,000
d.	$0	$500,000

(5/91, PI, #35, amended, 9029)

Items 71 and 72 are based on the following:

The following information pertains to the transfer of real estate pursuant to a troubled debt restructuring by Knob Co. to Mene Corp. in full liquidation of Knob's liability to Mene.

Carrying amount of liability liquidated	$150,000
Carrying amount of real estate transferred	100,000
Fair value of real estate transferred	90,000

71. What amount should Knob report as a pretax extraordinary gain (loss) on restructuring of payables?
a. $(10,000)
b. $0
c. $ 50,000
d. $ 60,000 (11/93, PI, #57, amended, 4426)

72. What amount should Knob report as ordinary gain (loss) on transfer of real estate?
a. $(10,000)
b. $0
c. $ 50,000
d. $ 60,000 (11/93, PI, #58, amended, 4427)

73. Seco Corp. was forced into bankruptcy and is in the process of liquidating assets and paying claims. Unsecured claims will be paid at the rate of forty cents on the dollar. Hale holds a $30,000 noninterest-bearing note receivable from Seco collateralized by an asset with a book value of $35,000 and a liquidation value of $5,000. The amount to be realized by Hale on this note is
a. $ 5,000
b. $12,000
c. $15,000
d. $17,000 (5/91, PII, #14, 1024)

SIMULATIONS

Problem 7-3 (15 to 25 minutes)

Scenario & Choices | Responses | Research Task

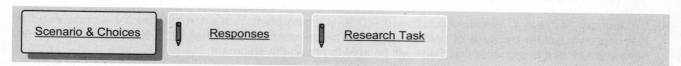

Edge Co., a toy manufacturer, is in the process of preparing its financial statements for the year ended December 31, year 3. Edge expects to issue its year 3 financial statements on March 1, year 4.

Items 1 through 12 represent various information that has not been reflected in the financial statements. For each item, the following two responses are required:

a. Determine if an adjustment is required and select the appropriate amount, if any, from the choices below.

Adjustment amounts

A.	No adjustment is required.
B.	$100,000
C.	$150,000
D.	$250,000
E.	$400,000
F.	$500,000

b. Determine (Yes/No) if additional disclosure is required, either on the face of the financial statements or in the notes to the financial statements.

1. Edge owns a small warehouse located on the banks of a river in which it stores inventory worth approximately $500,000. Edge is not insured against flood losses. The river last overflowed its banks twenty years ago.

2. During year 3, Edge began offering certain health care benefits to its eligible retired employees. Edge's actuaries have determined that the discounted expected cost of these benefits for current employees is $150,000.

3. Edge offers an unconditional warranty on its toys. Based on past experience, Edge estimates its warranty expense to be 1% of sales. Sales during year 3 were $10,000,000.

4. On October 30, year 3, a safety hazard related to one of Edge's toy products was discovered. It is considered probable that Edge will be liable for an amount in the range of $100,000 to $500,000.

5. On November 22, year 3, Edge initiated a lawsuit seeking $250,000 in damages from patent infringement.

6. On December 17, year 3, a former employee filed a lawsuit seeking $100,000 for unlawful dismissal. Edge's attorneys believe the suit is without merit. No court date has been set.

7. On December 15, year 3, Edge guaranteed a bank loan of $100,000 for its president's personal use.

8. On December 31, year 3, Edge's board of directors voted to discontinue the operations of its computer games division and sell all the assets of the division. The division was sold on February 15, year 4. On December 31, year 3, Edge estimated that losses from operations, net of tax, for the period January 1, year 4, through February 15, year 4, would be $400,000 and that the gain from the sale of the division's assets, net of tax, would be $250,000. These estimates were materially correct. The year 3 division loss was $500,000.

9. On January 5, year 4, a warehouse containing a substantial portion of Edge's inventory was destroyed by fire. Edge expects to recover the entire loss, except for a $250,000 deductible, from insurance.

10. On January 24, year 4, inventory purchased F.O.B. shipping point from a foreign country was detained at that country's border because of political unrest. The shipment is valued at $150,000. Edge's attorneys have stated that it is probable that Edge will be able to obtain the shipment.

11. On January 30, year 4, Edge issued $10,000,000 bonds at a premium of $500,000.

12. On February 4, year 4, the IRS assessed Edge an additional $400,000 for the year 2 tax year. Edge's tax attorneys and tax accountants have stated that it is likely that the IRS will agree to a $100,000 settlement.

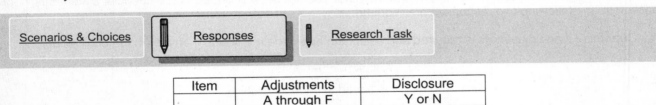

Scenarios & Choices | Responses | Research Task

Item	Adjustments	Disclosure
	A through F	Y or N
1.		
2.		
3.		
4.		
5.		
6.		
7.		
8.		
9.		
10.		
11.		
12.		

Scenarios & Choices | Responses | Research Task

Research Question: How is a contingency defined?

Paragraph Reference Answer: ____________

Problem 7-4 (7 to 13 minutes)

Scenario & Responses | Research Task

Items 1 through 6 represent various commitments and contingencies of Town, Inc. at December 31, year 4, and events subsequent to December 31, year 4, but prior to the issuance of the year 4 financial statements. Town, Inc. is preparing its financial statements for the year ended December 31, year 4. For each item, select the reporting requirement from the choices below. Place the letter in the space provided.

Reporting Requirement Choices	
A. Accrual only	D. Disclosure only
B. Both accrual and disclosure	N. Neither accrual nor disclosure

A choice may be selected once, more than once, or not at all.

1. _____ On December 1, year 4, Town was awarded damages of $75,000 in a patent infringement suit it brought against a competitor. The defendant did not appeal the verdict, and payment was received in January, year 5.

2. _____ A former employee of Town has brought a wrongful-dismissal suit against Town. Town's lawyers believe the suit to be without merit.

3. _____ At December 31, year 4, Town had outstanding purchase orders in the ordinary course of business for purchase of a raw material to be used in its manufacturing process. The market price is currently higher than the purchase price and is not anticipated to change within the next year.

4. _____ A government contract completed during year 4 is subject to renegotiation. Although Town estimates that it is reasonably possible that a refund of approximately $200,000-$300,000 may be required by the government, it does not wish to publicize this possibility.

5. _____ Town has been notified by a governmental agency that it will be held responsible for the cleanup of toxic materials at a site where Town formerly conducted operations. Town estimates that it is probable that its share of remedial action will be approximately $500,000.

6. _____ On January 5, year 5, Town redeemed its outstanding bonds and issued new bonds with a lower rate of interest. The reacquisition price was in excess of the carrying amount of the bonds.

(11/95, FAR, #78-83, amended, 6152)

Scenario & Responses | Research Task

Research Question: An estimated loss from a loss contingency shall be accrued by a charge to income if both of what conditions are met?

Paragraph Reference Answer: ______________

Essay 7-5 (15 to 20 minutes)

Essay | Research Task

Deck Co. has just hired a new president, Palmer, and is reviewing its employee benefit plans with the new employee. For current employees, Deck offers a compensation plan for future vacations. Deck also provides post-employment benefits to former or inactive employees.

On the date of Palmer's hire, Palmer entered into a deferred compensation contract with Deck. Palmer is expected to retire in ten years. The contract calls for a payment of $150,000 upon termination of employment following a minimum three-year service period. The contract also provides that interest of 10% compounded annually, be credited on the amount due each year after the third year.

a. Give an example of post-employment benefits. State the conditions under which Deck is required to accrue liabilities for compensated absences and post-employment benefits. State Deck's disclosure requirements if these conditions, in full or in part, are not met.

b. Describe the general accrual period for amounts to be paid under a deferred compensation contract. State the theoretical rationale for requiring accrual of these liabilities and related expenses.

(5/96, FAR, #16, 6289)

Essay | Research Task

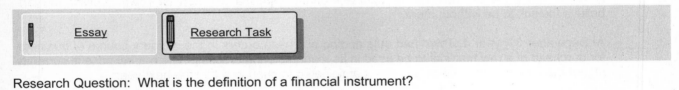

Research Question: What is the definition of a financial instrument?

Paragraph Reference Answer: ____________

Problem 7-6 (40 to 50 minutes)

Scenario | Requirements | Response A | Response B

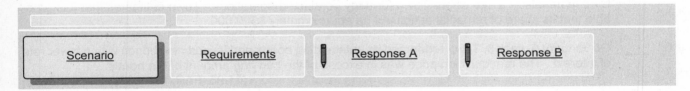

The following is the long-term liabilities section of Tempo Co.'s December 31, year 1 balance sheet:

Long-term liabilities:		
Note payable—bank; 15 principal payments of $5,000, plus 10% interest due annually on September 30	$ 75,000	
Less: Current portion	(5,000)	$ 70,000
Capital lease obligation—16 payments of $9,000 due annually on January 1	76,600	
Less: Current portion	(1,340)	75,260
Deferred income tax liability		15,750
Total long-term liabilities		$161,010

- Tempo's incremental borrowing rate on the date of the lease was 11% and the lessor's implicit rate, which was known by Tempo, was 10%.

- The only difference between Tempo's taxable income and pretax accounting income is depreciation on a machine acquired on January 1, year 1, for $250,000. The machine's estimated useful life is five years, with no salvage value. Depreciation is computed using the straight-line method for financial reporting purposes and the MACRS method for tax purposes. Depreciation expense for tax and financial reporting purposes for year 2 through year 5 is as follows:

Year	Tax depreciation	Financial depreciation	Tax depr'n over (under) financial depr'n
2	$80,000	$50,000	$30,000
3	40,000	50,000	(10,000)
4	35,000	50,000	(15,000)
5	30,000	50,000	(20,000)

The enacted federal income tax rates are 30% for years 1 and 2, and 35% for years 3 through 5.

- Included in Tempo's December year 1 balance sheet was a deferred tax asset of $9,000.
- For the year ended December 31, year 2, Tempo's income before income taxes was $430,000.
- On July 1, year 2, Tempo received proceeds of $459,725 from a $500,000 bond issuance. The bonds mature in 30 years and interest of 11% is payable each January 1 through July 1. The bonds were issued at a price to yield the investors 12%. Tempo uses the effective interest method to amortize the bond discount.

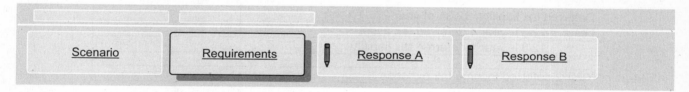

Scenario | Requirements | Response A | Response B

a. Prepare a schedule showing Tempo's income before income taxes, current income tax expense, deferred income tax expense, and net income. Show supporting calculations for current and deferred income tax amounts.

b. Prepare a schedule showing the calculation of Tempo's interest expense for the year ended December 31, year 2.

c. Prepare the long-term liabilities section of Tempo's December 31, year 2 balance sheet. Show supporting calculations.

Scenario | Requirements | Response A | Response B

Tempo Co.
Income Tax Expense and Net Income
For the Year Ended December 31, Year 2

Income before income taxes		
Income tax expense:		
Current		
Deferred [from computation below]		
Net income		
Computation:		
Deferred income tax expense		
Temporary difference—depreciation:		
Year 3	10,000	
Year 4	15,000	
Year 5	20,000	
Temporary difference—depreciation		
Effective tax rate for years 3 through 5		35%
Deferred tax liability, 12/31 of year 2		
Less: 12/31, year 1 deferred tax asset		
12/31, year 1 deferred tax liability		
Year 2 deferred income tax expense		

Scenario | Requirements | Response A | Response B

Tempo Co.
Calculation of Interest Expense
For the Year Ended December 31, Year 2

Note payable—bank 1/1 to 9/30		
10/1 to 12/31		
Capital lease obligation		
1/1 to 12/31		
Bonds payable 7/1 to 12/31		

Response C | Research Task

Tempo Co.
Long-Term Liabilities Section of
Balance Sheet
December 31, Year 2

Long-term liabilities:		
Note payable–bank		
Less current portion		
Capital lease obligation		
Less current portion		
11% bonds payable due June 30, year 22, less unamortized discount		
Deferred income tax liability		
Total long-term liabilities		

(5/92, P1, #5, amended, 6192)

Response C | Research Task

Research Question: When does an exception to the general rule of determining the present value of the minimum lease payments for recording the asset and obligation under a capital lease occur?

Paragraph Reference Answer: ______________

Solution 7-1 MULTIPLE CHOICE ANSWERS

Current Liabilities

1. (c)

Accounts payable	$ 55,000
Unsecured notes, due July 1	400,000
Accrued expenses	35,000
Senior bonds, due March 31	1,000,000
Current liabilities	$1,490,000

2. (d) Current liabilities are obligations whose liquidation is expected to require the use of existing current assets or the creation of other current liabilities. Current assets are assets that are reasonably expected to be converted into cash or used during the normal operating cycle of the business or one year, whichever is longer. Therefore, current liabilities are expected to be liquidated within the normal operating cycle of the business or one year whichever is longer.

Accounts Payable

3. (a) The $360,000 accounts payable balance should be increased for (1) the $50,000 debit balance for the advance to the supplier because Lyle should report this amount as an asset, and (2) the $100,000 of checks written to vendors recorded in the prior year but not mailed until after the financial statement date ($360,000 + $50,000 + $100,000 = $510,000).

4. (a) After the conversion, the accounts payable balance will be reported net of purchase discounts. The gross balance of the accounts payable of $30,000 is reduced by the $200 of discounts still available in the accounts payable balance to arrive at the net amount of $29,800.

Dividends Payable

5. (a) When declared, cash and property dividends represent legal obligations due within one year and are reported as current liabilities. Stock dividends and undeclared dividends on cumulative preferred stock are not reported as liabilities. The dividends for the current year have not yet been declared, and are not reported as liabilities. Cumulative preferred stock dividends in arrears must be disclosed in the notes to the statements, and are not reported as liabilities. The only amount that should be reported as a current liability is the bonus.

Notes Payable

6. (c) The note should not be recorded at its face amount because it is noninterest-bearing. APB 21 requires that noninterest-bearing notes be recorded at the fair value of the property, goods, or services exchanged, or at an amount which approximates the market value of the note, whichever is the more clearly determinable. If neither of these amounts can be determined, the note should be recorded at its present value, computed by discounting all future payments of the note at the prevailing rate of interest for similar notes. The difference between the face amount of the noninterest-bearing note payable and the amount at which it is recorded is amortized as interest expense over the life of the note by the effective interest method. Pension cost interest is a component of net periodic pension cost (SFAS 87, ¶20). Postretirement healthcare benefits interest is a component of net periodic postretirement healthcare benefits cost (SFAS 106, ¶46). Interest cost incurred to finance construction of machinery for a company's own use is capitalized as part of the cost of the machinery (SFAS 34, ¶9).

7. (b) The note payable arose from a transaction with a vendor in the normal course of business and is due in customary trade terms not exceeding one year; therefore, the note can be reported at its face amount of $10,000, despite the fact that the 3% stated interest rate of the note does not approximate the prevailing market interest rate of 8% for similar notes at the date of the transaction.

8. (d)

March 1, prior year to Feb. 28, current year ($10,000 @ 12% × 12/12)	$1,200
March 1 to Dec. 31, current year [12% ($10,000 + $1,200) × 10/12]	1,120
Total accrued interest, December 31 of the current year	$2,320

9. (b) The amount that should be reported as the noncurrent portion of *Note Payable to Contest Winner* at 12/31 of the prior year is $418,250, the cost of the annuity purchased to provide for the $950,000 of prize monies to be paid after 12/31 of the current year. This is the most objective available evidence of the present value of the prize money due.

Advances & Deposits

10. (b) The lessor should report the full amount of the $500 refundable security deposit as a liability until the lessor has earned a portion of it by cleaning or repairing vacated apartments. Revenue is not recognized until it has been earned. Deferred revenue is reported as a liability.

11. (b)

Customer Deposits

		118,000	Balance, 01/01
Advances applied to orders shipped	164,000	184,000	Advances received with orders
Advances applicable to orders canceled	50,000		
		88,000	Balance, 12/31

Accrued Liabilities

12. (a) 2% of $10,000 × 5 employees = $1,000. Acme has chosen to reimburse the state for actual claims instead of using the 3% of eligible gross wages rate. The liability is computed using eligible gross wages, not total wages, for each employee. The actual unemployment claim is accrued, not the state rate times actual wages.

13. (d)

Accrued salary, 12/31, year 2 ($80,000 × 4/5*)	$64,000
Accrued vacation time earned in year 2	25,000
Accrued salary and vacation time, 12/31, year 2	$89,000

* Four days of the 5-day workweek ended 1/1 pertain to year 2.

14. (b) On September 1, Day would have collected two months of real estate taxes from the seller and credited the amount to *Real Estate Taxes Payable.* At the end of September and October, Day would have recorded one month of real estate taxes each month by a credit to *Real Estate Taxes Payable.* When the payment was made for six months of real estate taxes, on November 1, the $12,000 payment would be for the four months prior to that date that would have already been accrued and for the two months that follow the payment date. Therefore, $8,000 (i.e., $12,000 × 4/6) of the payment should be recorded as a decrease in *Real Estate Taxes Payable* and $4,000 (i.e., $12,000 × 2/6) of the

payment should be recorded as an increase in *Prepaid Real Estate Taxes.*

Deferred Revenue

15. (b) Sales of service contracts in the current year are $600 × 1,000 contracts, for a total of $600,000. A portion of this revenue is earned and recognized in the current year and the rest is deferred. The 60% earned evenly during the second contract year is all deferred at the end of the year. The portion of the 40% that is earned in the first year is recognized as revenue and the balance is deferred. Because both the contract sales and the repairs expense are made evenly throughout the year, an average can be used; i.e., half of the 40% is recognized as revenue and half is deferred.

Second contract year ($600,000 × 60%)	$360,000
First contract year [($0 + $600,000)/2 × 40%]	120,000
Total deferred service contract revenue, 12/31	$480,000

16. (d) Accrual accounting recognizes revenue in the period(s) it is earned. Therefore, the revenue should be recognized evenly over the contract year as the services are performed.

17. (d) Of the $250,000 of gift certificates sold in the current year, only $225,000 [i.e., $250,000 × (100% – 10%)] are expected to be redeemed. Since $175,000 of the gift certificates sold in the current year were redeemed in the current year, $50,000 should be reported as unearned revenue at 12/31 of the current year. (At 12/31 there is no liability for unredeemed gift certificates sold in the prior year because the certificates expire one year after their issuance.)

Current Maturities of Long-Term Debt

18. (d) The principal payments on the long-term debt that are due in the next year are reported as current maturities of long-term debt at 12/31 of the current year.

14½% term note, due next year	$ 3,000
8% note, principal due 12/31 next year ($110,000 / 11)	10,000
Current maturities of long-term debt, 12/31	$13,000

Operating Result Liabilities

19. (b) Ivy Co. should report sales taxes based on February and March sales as sales taxes payable in its March 31 balance sheet. The taxes based on January sales were paid in February because they exceeded $500 ($10,600 sales / 1.06 = sales of $10,000; $10,600 – $10,000 = $600 in sales taxes). This is the $600 debit in February.

	(a) Total credits to sales revenue account	(b) Sales without taxes (a / 1.06)	(a–b) Sales taxes
March	$7,420	$7,000	$420
February	8,480	8,000	480
Total sales taxes payable, March 31			$900

20. (b) Where C = contribution:

$$C = 0.10\ (\$75{,}000 - C);\ C = \$7{,}500 - 0.10C$$
$$1.10\ C = \$7{,}500$$
$$C = \underline{\$6{,}818}$$

21. (a)

Net pay to employees	$16,100
Federal income taxes	2,500
FICA (employer's and employees' shares)	2,800
Total deposit to payroll checking account	$21,400

Estimated Liabilities

22. (a) As Oak believes 1% of sales to be the best estimate of warranty costs, warranty expense should be accrued accordingly. ($5,000,000 × 1% = $50,000). The technological advance applied only to current year sales; thus, in this case, the estimates of warranty costs reported in the two prior years are not changed.

23. (c)

Stamp redemption liability, 12/31 prior year	$ 6,000,000
Less: Cost of redemptions	(2,750,000)
Add: Est. redemption cost of current year stamps ($2,250,000 × 80%)	1,800,000
Stamp redemption liability, 12/31 current year	$ 5,050,000

24. (d)

Sales (both years)	$400,000
Estimated warranty cost percentage (2% + 4%)	× 6%
Estimated warranty cost for both years sales	24,000
Warranty expenditures to date	(9,750)
Estimated warranty liability, 12/31 current year	$ 14,250

25. (a)

Cost of toys to Mill Co., each	$ 0.80
Less: Cash to be received with redemption	(0.50)
Net cost to Mill Co. for each toy	$ 0.30

Total packages of candy sold in December	$110,000
Times: Anticipated redemption rate	× 60%
Total coupons anticipated to be redeemed	66,000
Divided by: Number of coupons required for each toy	/ 5
Anticipated number of toys needed	13,200
Times: Net cost to Mill Co. for each toy (above)	× $0.30
Total estimated coupon liability, 12/31	$ 3,960

Compensated Absences

26. (c) An employer must accrue a liability for employees' rights to receive vacation pay benefits if the four conditions identified in SFAS 43, ¶6, are met. Three of these conditions are met in the question data. These are: (1) the obligation is attributable to employees' services already rendered, (2) payment of the compensation is probable, and (3) the amount can be reasonably estimated (i.e., the employees have earned vacation pay of $100,000 that they will receive next year). The fourth condition necessary for accrual is that the employees' rights to receive the vacation pay benefits vest or accumulate.

27. (b) The employer should accrue a liability of $1,600 (i.e., $800 × 2) for Ryan's two weeks of vacation pay because the four conditions for accrual are met: (1) the obligation is attributable to employees' services already rendered, (2) the obligation relates to rights that vest or accumulate, (3) payment of the compensation is probable, and (4) the amount can be reasonably estimated (SFAS 43, ¶6). The employer should not accrue a liability for Todd's two weeks of vacation pay because Todd's vacation rights do not vest or accumulate.

Contingency Classification

28. (b) The potential loss for damages that may be paid should be reported by accruing a loss in the income statement and a liability in the balance sheet. Accrual is required because both of the following conditions are met: (1) it is considered probable that a liability has been incurred, and (2) the amount of the loss can be reasonably estimated (SFAS 5, ¶8). In addition, the nature of the lawsuit should be separately disclosed in the notes to the financial statements (¶9). The loss should not be charged to the appropriation of retained earnings for contingencies (¶15).

29. (a) To accrue a contingent liability, SFAS 5 requires that the likelihood of the loss be probable and the amount be reasonably estimable. It is probable that Manfred will have to pay between $250,000 to $450,000 under its guarantee of the supplier's loan. Since no indication is given that any amount in the range is a better estimate than the others, the lower limit of the range, $250,000, is accrued as a contingent liability. On the other hand, the contract Manfred entered into to retool its machines involves a commitment but not a liability because no performance has been made by the other party to the contract. Thus, there is no asset or liability to be reported for the contract.

30. (a) A loss from a contingent liability, arising from events or circumstances occurring before the balance sheet date and the resolution of which is contingent upon a future event or circumstance, of which an unfavorable outcome is probable, should be accrued (SFAS 5). The amount should be estimated and the minimum amount in the range of estimates, unless one amount is a better estimate than the others, should be accrued.

31. (b) Where the likelihood of confirmation of a loss is considered probable and the loss can be reasonably estimated, the estimated loss should be accrued by a charge to income and the nature of the contingency should be disclosed. If, however, only a range of possible loss can be estimated—and no amount in the range is a better estimate than the others—the minimum amount in the range should be accrued. In addition, the nature of the contingency and the additional exposure to loss should be disclosed.

Contingency Disclosure

32. (a) Since the contingent loss from the expropriation of assets is judged to be reasonably possible, it should be disclosed in the footnotes, but not accrued. A contingent loss is accrued only in situations where the loss is probable and estimable.

33. (d) SFAS 5, ¶8, provides that an estimated loss from a loss contingency shall be accrued by a charge to income if both of the following conditions are met: (1) it is probable that an asset has been impaired or a liability has been incurred, and (2) the amount of the loss can be reasonably estimated. When the amount of loss is known, as with a settlement after the balance sheet date but before issuance of the financial statements, that amount should be accrued and disclosed in the financial statements.

34. (b) To accrue a contingent liability, SFAS 5 requires that the likelihood of the loss be probable and the amount be reasonably subject to estimation. Since the likelihood of the loss contingency in question is only reasonably possible, the loss contingency should not be accrued; it should only be disclosed. The disclosure should indicate the nature of the contingency and the amount of the possible loss of $250,000, the deductible clause of the policy.

Gain Contingencies

35. (a) Gain contingencies should be disclosed in the financial statements in a footnote rather than being reflected in income because doing so could result in recognizing income prior to its realization. This treatment reflects the principle of conservatism which means that accountants who are selecting

between two possible alternatives should choose the accounting alternative which is least likely to overstate assets and income.

36. (d) Contingencies that might result in gains usually are not reflected in the accounts since to do so might be to recognize revenue prior to its realization (SFAS 5). Adequate disclosure is made of contingencies that might result in gains, but care is exercised to avoid misleading implications as to the likelihood of realization. Smith Co. may disclose the range of the contingent gain in the financial statement notes.

Long-Term Notes Payable

37. (a) The factor for the present value of an annuity in advance is used because the first payment of the note was made immediately (i.e., 12/30).

Periodic annual payments	$ 20,000
Times: Present value of an annuity in advance of $1 at 11% for 8 periods	× 5.712
Present value of all cash flows	114,240
Less: Payment, 12/30	(20,000)
Carrying amount of note, 12/31	$ 94,240

38. (c) The note should not be recorded at its face amount because its stated interest rate of 16% does not approximate the market rate of interest of 11% for similar notes. APB 21 requires that when a note which does not bear the market rate of interest is exchanged for property, goods, or services, the note is to be recorded at the fair value of the property, goods, or services or the fair value of the note, whichever is more clearly determinable. Since neither of these amounts are determinable for the note in question, the note should be recorded at its present value. The interest rate to be used in the discounting process is the borrower's incremental borrowing rate (market rate) at the date the note is issued (11% in this case). Because the market rate of 11% is less than the stated rate of the note of 16%, the present value of the note is greater than the face amount of the note. Therefore, the correct journal entry at the date the note was issued would involve a debit to *Purchases* for the present value of the note, a credit to *Note Payable* for the face amount of the note, and a credit to *Premium on Note Payable* for the excess of the note's present value over its face amount. Fleur recorded the purchase at the note's face amount which understated the cost of the merchandise which was subsequently sold in the prior year. Therefore, prior year cost of goods sold is understated by the amount of the unrecorded premium on the note (i.e., the excess of the note's present value over its face amount).

39. (d) The four-month note was issued on October 1 of the prior year. Fleur reported three months of interest payable at December 31 of the prior year, computed using the stated rate of the note. Therefore, interest payable is correctly reported at December 31 of the prior year. On the other hand, retained earnings is overstated at December 31 of the prior year, because (1) the prior year cost of goods sold was understated by the full amount of the unrecorded note premium, and (2) interest expense reported for the note for the prior year was overstated by 3/4 of the amount of the note premium (i.e., the amount of the note premium that should have been amortized for the three months the note was outstanding during the prior year).

Refinancing of Short-Term Obligations

40. (c) The portion of long-term debt due within the next fiscal period is classified as a current liability if payment is expected to require the use of current assets or the creation of other current liabilities. Short-term debt expected to be refinanced on a long-term basis is to be excluded from current liabilities when the enterprise has the intent and ability to refinance the obligation on a long-term basis (SFAS 6). One way intent and ability are demonstrated is by post-balance-sheet-date issuance of a long-term obligation or equity securities. Separate disclosure of such refinancing is required.

41. (d) The entire $200,000 balance of the 16% note is properly excluded from short-term obligations because before the balance sheet was issued, Lee refinanced the note by issuance of a long-term obligation. The $125,000, 14% note is also properly excluded from short-term obligations because before the balance sheet was issued, Lee entered into a financing agreement that clearly permits Lee to refinance the short-term obligation on a long-term basis on terms that are readily determinable, and all of the following conditions are met: (1) the agreement is noncancelable as to all parties and extends beyond one year; (2) at the balance sheet date, and at the date of its issuance, Witt is not in violation of the agreement; and (3) the lender is financially capable of honoring the agreement.

42. (c) Since after the date of the enterprise's balance sheet but before the balance sheet was issued, $1,500,000 (100,000 × $15) of common stock was issued for the purpose of refinancing the note payable on a long-term basis, $1,500,000 of the note payable should be excluded from current liabilities at the balance sheet date.

43. (b) If post-balance sheet refinancing of a short-term obligation has taken place, any portion not

refinanced must be shown as a current liability. The amount eliminated by the stock issue and the portion covered by the stock issue would not be reported as short-term liabilities.

Debt Extinguishment

44. (b) Under SFAS 4, Nu Corp. would have recognized an extraordinary gain on the early extinguishment of debt equal to the excess of the carrying amount of the obligation settled over the fair value of the asset transferred. SFAS 4 is superseded by SFAS 145 which classifies this gain as ordinary income unless evidence exists that it is infrequent in occurrence and unusual in nature. Nu Corp. also recognizes an ordinary loss equal to the excess of the carrying amount over the fair value of the asset transferred, which is reported in income from continuing operations. [$9,000 + ($13,000) = ($4,000)]

Carrying amount of obligation at extinguishment date	$105,000
Fair value of asset transferred	(96,000)
Ordinary gain on early debt extinguishment	$ 9,000

Carrying amount of asset transferred	$109,000
Fair value of asset transferred	(96,000)
Loss on transfer of asset	$ 13,000

Troubled Debt Restructurings

45. (d) The debtor recognizes an ordinary loss equal to the excess of the carrying amount over the fair value of the computer equipment transferred (i.e., $80,000 – $75,000 = $5,000). The loss is reported in income from continuing operations. Under SFAS 4, the debtor would have recognized an extraordinary gain on troubled debt restructuring equal to the difference between the carrying amount of the obligation settled and the fair value of the asset transferred. SFAS 145 superseded SFAS 4. Now, early debt extinguishment is extraordinary only if it meets the same criteria as other events (see Chapter 11). No evidence exists that the event meets these criteria. [($5,000) + $25,000 = $20,000]

Carrying amount of obligation at restructure date	$100,000
Less: Fair value of computer equipment transferred	(75,000)
Ordinary gain recognized on restructuring	$ 25,000

46. (a) Under SFAS 4, the debtor (Ace) would have recognized an extraordinary gain on the retirement of debt, equal to the difference between the carrying amount of the obligation settled and the fair value of the assets and/or equity interest transferred to the creditor. SFAS 4 is superseded by SFAS 145. This gain is ordinary income unless evidence exists that it is infrequent in occurrence and unusual in nature. The ordinary gain is $75,000.

Carrying amount of Ace Corp.'s note	$ 150,000
Less: Fair value of transferred land	(100,000)
Gain due to early debt extinguishment	$ 50,000

Fair value of transferred land	$ 100,000
Less: Carrying value of transferred land	(75,000)
Gain on land sale	$ 25,000

47. (c) When the aggregate payments under new terms of an impaired loan are less than the amount of the obligation, the debtor records a gain equal to the difference between the carrying amount of the payable, including accrued interest, and the aggregate future cash payments required under the new terms. May Corp. is the debtor and owes $1,000,000 principal plus $40,000 of accrued interest. Under the new terms, May is required to pay future cash payments of $950,000 plus $30,000. The gain, before taxes, is $1,040,000 – $980,000 = $60,000. Note that the creditor (in this case, the bank) would use the present value, not the aggregate, of the future cash payments in its accounting for this loan.

48. (a) Accounting for debtors when the restructuring is a modification of terms is determined by whether the sum of the cash payments under the new terms (not discounted to present value) equal or exceed the amount of the obligation.

Bankruptcy

49. (d) A trustee in a bankruptcy case takes over the assets of the debtor corporation and is accountable for those assets until released by the bankruptcy court. In liquidation (Chapter 7) cases, the trustee often establishes a new set of books for the bankruptcy estate. The assets are recorded at carrying amounts rather than at expected realizable values because of subjectivity in estimating realizable amounts at the time of filing. The trustee records gains and losses and liquidation expenses directly in the *Estate Equity* account. Any unrecorded assets or liabilities that are discovered by the trustee are also entered in the *Estate Equity* account. Therefore, $9,000 [i.e., $1,000 + ($20,000 – $12,000)] should be debited to *Estate Equity* as a result of the discovery of the unrecorded invoice and the sale of the truck.

50. (d) Secured creditors are paid first with the proceeds from the sale of specific assets upon which they have liens. Any excess proceeds from such sales are first applied against the liabilities with priority, and then to the unsecured creditors. If the claims of partially secured creditors exceed the proceeds from the sale of the assets pledged with such creditors, such excess constitutes an unsecured claim.

Total cash available		$ 810,000
Payments to fully secured creditors	$260,000	
Payments to partially secured creditors	120,000	
Payments to creditors with priority	70,000	(450,000)
Cash for unsecured nonpriority claims		$ 360,000

Problem 7-2 ADDITIONAL MULTIPLE CHOICE ANSWERS

Current Liabilities

51. (a) Current liabilities are obligations which are due within one year of the balance sheet date. The notes payable are due in two years; therefore, they are reported in the long-term liabilities section of the balance sheet at 12/31 of the current year.

Accounts payable		$15,000
Bonds payable, due next year	$25,000	
Discount on bonds payable	3,000	22,000
Dividends payable in next year		8,000
Current liabilities, 12/31 current year		$45,000

Notes Payable

52. (c) $500,000 – $31,500 = $468,500

Face amount of note	$500,000
Times: Discount rate	× 10.8%
Bank discount	54,000
Less: Amortization, Aug. 1- Dec. 31 ($54,000 × 5/12)	(22,500)
Unamortized discount, 12/31	$ 31,500

53. (a) The cost of goods should be included in accounts payable when legal title passes from the seller to the purchaser. Kew should include the $40,000 cost of the goods lost in transit in accounts payable at 12/31 of the prior year. The goods were shipped F.O.B. shipping point, and the title of these goods passed to Kew when the vendor delivered the goods to the common carrier on 12/22. Since the vendor authorized Kew to return goods for full credit before year-end, and Kew shipped the goods before year-end, the 12/31 accounts payable balance should be reduced by $70,000, the cost of the goods returned. The $50,000 cost of the goods that were shipped from a vendor F.O.B. destination on 12/20 should not be included in accounts payable at 12/31. Title of these goods did not pass to Kew until Kew received the goods on 1/6 of the current year. Thus, accounts payable should be reported at $2,170,000 ($2,200,000 + $40,000 – $70,000).

54. (b) The note's 12% rate of interest and the bank's 0.5% loan origination fee are based upon the face amount of the note. The cash received by the note holder is the face amount of the note *less* the loan origination fee. Since less cash is received than the amount on which the interest rate and loan origination fee is computed, the effective interest rate is more than 12.5%.

Accrued Liabilities

55. (a) ($80,000 × .07) + ($20,000 × .03) = ($5,600 + $600) = $6,200

56. (c)

Escrow liability, 1/1	$ 700,000
Add: Escrow payments received during year	1,580,000
Add: Interest on escrow funds during year	50,000
Less: 10% service fee ($50,000 × 10%)	(5,000)
Less: Real estate taxes paid	(1,720,000)
Escrow liability, 12/31	$ 605,000

57. (d)

	Liability	Expense
FIT withheld	$1,200	
FICA employee portion ($10,000 @ 7%)	700	
FICA employer portion ($10,000 @ 7%)	700	$700
Totals	$2,600	$700

58. (d)

Interest expense	$ 85,000
Cash paid for interest	(68,000)
Increase in accrued interest payable	17,000
Accrued interest payable, 12/31 prior year	15,000
Accrued interest payable, 12/31 current year	$ 32,000

Deferred Revenue

59. (c) Todd received $9,900 [i.e., ($500 × 15) + ($200 × 12)] of initial payments on its 12-month contracts for the 9/1, year 1 through 8/31, year 2 contract year. Since four months of the initial payments on the contracts have been earned as of 12/31, year 1, eight months of the initial payments on the contracts should be reported as deferred revenue at that date (i.e., $9,900 × 8/12 = $6,600).

60. (d) Because the deferred subscription revenues at 12/31 of the prior year were earned in the current year, they do not affect the computation of deferred subscription revenue at 12/31 of the current year.

Cash receipts from customers	$3,600,000
Portion received after 9/30 cutoff, to be earned in future	× 3/12
Deferred subscription revenue at 12/31 current year	$ 900,000

Estimated Liabilities

61. (c) Advanced payments received from customers and others are liabilities until the transaction is completed. The travel and lodging services that were used by KLU is a liability because use of the services indicated a payment in advance for the advertising time to be provided at a later date. Use of the services is an expense.

62. (b) When the refundable merchandise coupons are sold, the sales price collected represents unearned revenue. Earned revenue will be recognized later when the coupons are redeemed.

63. (a) The coupon liability at 12/31 is not reduced by the 50,000 coupons on hand because the coupons had not been processed for payment at 12/31.

Coupons expected to be redeemed	120,000
Times: Payment for redeemed coupon ($0.45 + $0.05)	× $0.50
Estimated total coupon liability	60,000
Less: Payments to retailers as of 12/31	(25,000)
Remaining coupon liability, 12/31	$ 35,000

64. (c) The amount of expense recognized is the increase in the cost of the pre-current year accrued vacations and the cost of vacations earned for work performed in the current year.

Liability for accrued vacations, 12/31 prior year	$ 35,000
Less: Accrued vacations taken 1/1 to 9/30 current year	(20,000)
Liability for pre-current year vacations at salary increase, 10/1	15,000
Times: 10% salary increase	× 10%
Additional cost of pre-current year vacations	1,500
Cost of vacations earned for work in the year	30,000
Vacation pay expense	$ 31,500

65. (d) If it is probable that customers will make claims under warranties relating to goods or services that have been sold, and a reasonable estimate of the costs involved can be made, the warranty costs should be charged to operating expense in the year of sale.

Contingency Classification

66. (d) SFAS 5, ¶8, provides that an estimated loss from a loss contingency shall be accrued by a charge to income if both of the following conditions are met: (1) it is probable that an asset has been impaired or a liability has been incurred, and (2) the amount of the loss can be reasonably estimated. FIN 14, ¶3 states that when the reasonable estimate of loss is a range and some amount within the range appears at the time to be a better estimate than any other amount within the range, that amount shall be accrued. "When no amount within the range is a better estimate than any other amount, however, the minimum amount in the range shall be accrued."

Contingency Disclosure

67. (a) Contingent liabilities that are considered to have a remote possibility of loss normally do not require disclosure. Exceptions include the guarantees of indebtedness of others, in which case disclosure, but not accrual, is required.

Gain Contingencies

68. (a) Haze should report a pretax gain of $15,000 (i.e., $45,000 – $30,000) for the amount of litigation award from the financially stable defendant that is not being appealed. The portion of the litigation awards that are being appealed (i.e., $30,000 and $50,000) represent gain contingencies and, thus, should not be accrued before realization; however, they should be disclosed in the financial statement notes.

69. (a) SFAS 5 requires that gain contingencies not be accrued before realization; however, the gain contingency should be disclosed in the financial statement notes.

Refinancing of Short-Term Obligations

70. (c) SFAS 6 provides that short-term obligations refinanced on a long-term basis should be reported as long-term obligations. The amount that may be classified as long-term obligations is limited to the amount available under the refinancing agreement. The refinancing agreement limits the amount available to the lesser of $500,000 or 80% of the value of the collateral provided. Thus, $480,000 [($600,000 × 80%) < $500,000] should be classified as long-term obligations and the remaining $20,000 should be classified as short-term obligations.

Troubled Debt Restructurings

71. (b) Under SFAS 4, the debtor would have recognized a pretax extraordinary gain on troubled debt restructuring equal to the excess of the carrying

amount of the obligation over the fair value of the asset transferred at the date of the restructuring. SFAS 145 supersedes SFAS 4. This gain is ordinary income unless evidence exists that it is infrequent in occurrence and unusual in nature.

72. (c) Knob reports a $10,000 (i.e., $100,000 – $90,000) ordinary loss equal to the excess of the carrying amount over the fair value of the real estate transferred, and also a $60,000 ($150,000 liability liquidated – $90,000 fair value) gain on the debt restructuring. The net gain reported in income from continuing operations. [($10,000) + $60,000 = $50,000]

Bankruptcy

73. (c)

Liquidation value of asset		$ 5,000
Face amount of note	$30,000	
Less: Liquidation value of asset	(5,000)	
Unsecured portion of note	25,000	
Times: Percentage for unsecured claims	× 40%	
Amount realized on unsecured portion of note		10,000
Amount realized on note receivable		$15,000

PERFORMANCE BY SUBTOPICS

Each category below parallels a subtopic covered in Chapter 7. Record the number and percentage of questions you correctly answered in each subtopic area.

Current Liabilities

Question #	Correct √
1	
2	

Questions 2

Correct ______
% Correct ______

Accounts Payable

Question #	Correct √
3	
4	

Questions 2

Correct ______
% Correct ______

Dividends Payable

Question #	Correct √
5	

Questions 1

Correct ______
% Correct ______

Notes Payable

Question #	Correct √
6	
7	
8	
9	

Questions 4

Correct ______
% Correct ______

Advances & Deposits

Question #	Correct √
10	
11	

Questions 2

Correct ______
% Correct ______

Accrued Liabilities

Question #	Correct √
12	
13	
14	

Questions 3

Correct ______
% Correct ______

Deferred Revenue

Question #	Correct √
15	
16	
17	

Questions 3

Correct ______
% Correct ______

Current Maturities of Long-Term Debt

Question #	Correct √
18	

Questions 1

Correct ______
% Correct ______

Operating Result Liabilities

Question #	Correct √
19	
20	
21	

Questions 3

Correct ______
% Correct ______

Estimated Liabilities

Question #	Correct √
22	
23	
24	
25	

Questions 4

Correct ______
% Correct ______

Compensated Absences

Question #	Correct √
26	
27	

Questions 2

Correct ______
% Correct ______

Contingency Classification

Question #	Correct √
28	
29	
30	
31	

Questions 4

Correct ______
% Correct ______

Contingency Disclosure

Question #	Correct √
32	
33	
34	

Questions 3

Correct ______
% Correct ______

Gain Contingencies

Question #	Correct √
35	
36	

Questions 2

Correct ______
% Correct ______

Long-Term Notes Payable

Question #	Correct √
37	
38	
39	

Questions 3

Correct ______
% Correct ______

Refinancing of Short-Term Obligations

Question #	Correct √
40	
41	
42	
43	

Questions 4

Correct ______
% Correct ______

Debt Extinguishment

Question #	Correct √
44	

Questions 1

Correct ______
% Correct ______

Troubled Debt Restructurings

Question #	Correct √
45	
46	
47	
48	

Questions 4

Correct ______
% Correct ______

Bankruptcy

Question #	Correct √
49	
50	

Questions 2

Correct ______
% Correct ______

SIMULATION SOLUTIONS

Solution 7-3

Responses 1-12—Estimated & Contingent Liabilities

1. A, N General, unspecified business risks, including the practice of self-insurance of catastrophes, are not considered loss contingencies. Therefore, no accrual or disclosure is required.

2. C, Y SFAS 112 requires accrual of the liability for postemployment benefits to be provided to former or inactive employees prior to retirement. Therefore, the $150,000 of expected costs to Edge for benefits for current employees must be accrued in the financial statements. Additional information relating to the postemployment benefit plan, including a description of the plan, must be disclosed in the notes to the financial statements.

3. B, N Based on past experience, it is probable that customers will make claims under Edge's unconditional warranty and a reasonable estimate of the costs can be made. Therefore, an accrual of the warranty expense and the related liability must be made for $100,000 (i.e., $10,000,000 × 1%). No additional disclosures are required for the warranty.

4. B, Y Where the likelihood of confirmation of a loss is considered probable and the loss can be reasonably estimated, the estimated loss should be accrued by a charge to income. If only a range of possible loss can be estimated, the minimum amount in the range should be accrued. In addition, the nature of the contingency and the additional exposure to loss should be disclosed. Therefore, Edge should accrue the $100,000 minimum loss with an additional disclosure describing the contingency and the potential additional $400,000 loss.

5. A, Y The lawsuit initiated by Edge represents a gain contingency. Gain contingencies should be disclosed but not recognized as income. In addition, care should be taken to avoid misleading implications as to the likelihood of realization. **NOTE:** In the *AICPA Unofficial Answers to Exam Questions,* the answer is listed as A, N. The Editors believe this is erroneous, as it contradicts SFAS 5.

6. A, N Where the likelihood of loss is considered remote (i.e., the suit is believed to be without Merit by Edge's attorneys), no accrual or disclosure normally is required.

7. A, Y Certain types of loss contingencies must be disclosed regardless of the probability of loss. These exceptions include guarantees of indebtedness of others, banks' standby letters of credit, and guarantees to repurchase receivables. Therefore, the guarantee of the president's loan must be disclosed by Edge in the financial statements.

8. F, Y An estimated loss on the sale of the component is indication of an impairment, and this devaluation is included in discontinued operations in the fiscal period incurred. A gain is not recognized until the sale period. Edge will report a $500,000 loss from discontinued operations in its December 31, year 3 financial statements. In addition, the financial statement notes must disclose the following information: (1) the circumstances leading to the disposal; (2) any impairment loss; (3) if applicable, revenue amounts and pretax profit or loss; (4) if applicable, the segment in which the long-lived asset (or disposal group) is reported under SFAS 131 guidance.

9. A, Y Subsequent events that arose after the balance sheet date do not result in adjustments to the account balances of the previous period. However, some events, including the purchase of a business, the loss of inventories or plant assets due to a casualty, and the sale of a bond or capital stock issue, must be disclosed in order to prevent the financial statements from being misleading. Thus, the loss must be disclosed by Edge in the financial statements.

10. A, N Subsequent events that arose after the balance sheet date do not result in adjustments to the account balances of the previous period. In addition, these events normally do not require disclosure in the financial statements.

11. A, Y Subsequent events that arose after the balance sheet date do not result in adjustments to the account balances of the previous period. However, some events, including the purchase of a business, the loss of inventories or plant assets due to a casualty, and the sale of a bond or capital stock issue, must be disclosed in order to prevent the financial statements from being misleading. Thus, the bond issue must be disclosed by Edge in the financial statements.

12. B, Y Where the likelihood of confirmation of a loss is considered probable and the loss can be reasonably estimated, the estimated loss should be accrued by a charge to income and the nature of the contingency should be disclosed. Since Edge's lawyers believe it is likely (i.e., probable) that the IRS will agree to a $100,000 settlement, an estimated

loss of $100,000 should be accrued in Edge's December 31, year 3 financial statements with an additional disclosure describing the nature of the contingency.

Research

FAS 5, Par. 1

1. For the purpose of this Statement, a contingency is defined as an existing condition, situation, or set of circumstances involving uncertainty as to possible gain (hereinafter a "gain contingency") or loss 1 (hereinafter a "loss contingency") to an enterprise that will ultimately be resolved when one or more future events occur or fail to occur. Resolution of the uncertainty may confirm the acquisition of an asset or the reduction of a liability or the loss or impairment of an asset or the incurrence of a liability.

Solution 7-4

Responses 1-6—Contingencies

1. B Because the damages were awarded prior to the balance sheet date and were received prior to issuance of the financial statements, the award should be both accrued and disclosed in the financial statements.

2. N Two conditions must be met for a loss contingency to be accrued as a charge to income as of the date of the financial statements. It must be probable that as of the date of the financial statements an asset has been impaired or a liability incurred, and the amount of the loss must be reasonably estimated. In this case the loss would not be accrued as the possibility of loss has been judged remote by Town's lawyers. If one or both of the conditions for loss accrual are not met and the loss contingency is classified as probable or reasonably possible, financial statement disclosure is required. In this case, the loss contingency is remote, therefore disclosure is not required.

3. N Because the outstanding purchase orders occurred in the ordinary course of business and the raw materials have not yet been received, the purchase is not required to be accrued. Because the price difference is only a market price difference occurring in the ordinary course of business, disclosure it not required.

4. D Two conditions must be met for a loss contingency to be accrued as a charge to income as of the date of the financial statements. It must be probable that as of the date of the financial statements an asset has been impaired or a liability incurred, and the amount of the loss must be reasonably estimated. In this case, an asset has not been impaired, nor a liability incurred, so no accrual is required. If one or both of the conditions for loss accrual are not met and the loss contingency is classified as probable or reasonably possible, financial statement disclosure is required, therefore disclosure is required in this case.

5. B Two conditions must be met for a loss contingency to be accrued as a charge to income as of the date of the financial statements. It must be probable that as of the date of the financial statements an asset has been impaired or a liability incurred, and the amount of the loss must be reasonably estimated. In this case, a liability has been incurred and the amount is reasonably estimated, so accrual is required. If the loss contingency is classified as probable or reasonably possible, financial statement disclosure is required, therefore disclosure is required in this case.

6. D Events that did not exist at the balance sheet date but arose subsequent to that date should not result in adjustment to the financial statements. Some of these events, however, may require disclosure in order to prevent the financial statements from being misleading. Examples of events that require disclosure include sale of bonds or capital stock and the redemption of outstanding bonds.

Research

FAS 5, Par. 8

8. An estimated loss from a loss contingency (as defined in paragraph 1) shall be accrued by a charge to income if both of the following conditions are met:

a. Information available prior to issuance of the financial statements indicates that it is probable that an asset had been impaired or a liability had been incurred at the date of the financial statements 4 It is implicit in this condition that it must be probable that one or more future events will occur confirming the fact of the loss.

b. The amount of loss can be reasonably estimated.

Solution 7-5

Essay—Employee Benefits

a. An example of post-employment benefits offered by employers is continuation of health care benefits. Deck is required to accrue liabilities for compensated absences and post-employment benefits if all of the following conditions are met:

- The obligation is attributable to employees' **services already rendered,**
- The employees' **rights accumulate or vest,**
- Payment is **probable,** and
- The amount of the benefits can be **reasonably estimated.**

If an obligation cannot be accrued solely because the amount cannot be reasonably estimated, the financial statements should **disclose** that fact.

b. Estimated amounts to be paid under a deferred compensation contract should be **accrued** over the period of an employee's active employment from the time the **contract is signed to the employee's full eligibility date.** The theoretical rationale for accrual of these obligations to be paid in the future is that accrual **matches the cost of the benefits to the period in which services are rendered,** and results in recognition of a measurable liability.

Research

FAS 107, Par. 3

3. A financial instrument is defined as cash, evidence of an ownership interest in an entity, or a contract that both:

a. Imposes on one entity a contractual obligation 1 (1) to deliver cash or another financial instrument to a second entity or (2) to exchange other financial instruments on potentially unfavorable terms with the second entity

b. Conveys to that second entity a contractual right (1) to receive cash or another financial instrument from the first entity or (2) to exchange other financial instruments on potentially favorable terms with the first entity.

Solution 7-6

Response A

Tempo Co.
Income Tax Expense and Net Income
For the Year Ended December 31, Year 2

Income before income taxes			$430,000	a
Income tax expense:				
Current [30% × (430,000 – 30,000)]	$120,000	b		
Deferred [see computation below]	9,000	c		
Income tax expense			(129,000)	d
Net income			$301,000	e
Computation:				
Deferred income tax expense				
Temporary difference—depreciation:				
Year 3	$ 10,000			
Year 4	15,000			
Year 5	20,000			
Temporary difference—depreciation			$ 45,000	f
Effective tax rate for years 3 through 5			35%	
Deferred tax liability, 12/31 of year 2			$ 15,750	g
Less: 12/31, year 1 deferred tax asset	9,000	h		
12/31, year 1 deferred tax liability	(15,750)	i		
Deferred tax liability			(6,750)	j
Year 2 deferred income tax expense			$ 9,000	k

Response B

Tempo Co.
Calculation of Interest Expense
For the Year Ended December 31, Year 2

Note payable—bank 1/1 to 9/30				
—$75,000 × 10% × 9/12	$5,625	l		
10/1 to 12/31				
—$70,000 × 10% × 3/12	1,750	m		
			$ 7,375	n
Capital lease obligation				
1/1 to 12/31				
—$75,260 × 10%			7,526	o
Bonds payable 7/1 to 12/31			27,584	p
—$459,725 × 12% × 6/12			$42,485	q

Response C

Tempo Co.
Long-Term Liabilities Section of Balance Sheet
December 31, Year 2

Long-term liabilities:				
Note payable–bank; 14 principal				
payments of $5,000 plus 10% interest				
due annually on September 30	70,000	r		
Less current portion	(5,000)	s		
Note payable–bank			$ 65,000	t
Capital lease obligation—15 payments				
of $9,000 due annually on January 1	75,260	u		
Less current portion	(1,474)	v		
Capital lease obligation			73,786	w
11% bonds payable due June 30, year 22,				
less unamortized discount of $40,191			459,809	x
Deferred income tax liability				
[($15,000 + $20,000) × .35]			12,250	y
Total long-term liabilities			$610,845	z

a. Income before taxes is given in scenario information

b. Year 2 income before taxes less depreciation temporary difference × enacted federal income tax rate for year 2 [($430,000 – $30,000) × .30]

c. Year 2 deferred income tax expense—for calculations, see step k

d. Income tax expense = current tax (step b) plus deferred tax expense (step c)

e. Net income = Income before taxes less income tax expense (step d)

f. Future tax differences for year 3 through year 5 given in scenario information ($10,000 + $15,000 + $20,000)

g. Future tax differences for year 3 through year 5 × applicable tax rate of 35% ($45,000 × .35)

h. Year 1 deferred tax asset given in scenario information

i. Year 1 deferred tax liability given in scenario information

j. Year 1 net deferred tax liability ($9,000 – $15,750)

k. Year 2 deferred tax liability less year 1 net deferred tax liability ($15,750 – $6,750)

l. $75,000 × 10% × 9/12

m. $70,000 × 10% × 3/12

n. The sum of step l and step m

o. $75,206 × 10%

p. $459,725 × 12% × 6/12

q. Sum of step n through step p

r. 14 principal payments of $5,000 (14 × $5,000). Discounted present value of payments plus interest equals the total payment amount without interest.

s. Current portion is given in the scenario information

t. 14 payments less the current portion ($70,000 – $5,000)

u. Discounted present value of 15 payments at $9,000 given in the scenario information

v. Payment less interest equals current portion [$9,000 – ($75,260 × .10)]

w. Capital lease obligation (1/1/X1) less current portion – step u less step v ($75,260 – $1,474)

x. Face amount of bonds less proceeds received equals unamortized discount ($500,000 – $459,725) divided by number of years to maturity ($40,275 / 30)

y. Deferred income tax liability (long term) × the applicable rate [($15,000 + $20,0000) × .35]

z. Sum of steps t, w, x, and y ($65,000 + $73,786 + $459,809 + $12,250)

Research

FAS 13: Accounting for Leases

An exception to that general rule occurs when (a) it is practicable for the lessee to ascertain the implicit rate computed by the lessor and (b) that rate is less than the lessee's incremental borrowing rate; if both of those conditions are met, the lessee shall use the implicit rate. However, if the present value of the minimum lease payments, using the appropriate rate, exceeds the fair value of the leased property at the inception of the lease, the amount recorded as the asset and obligation shall be the fair value. A number of respondents pointed out that in many instances, the lessee does not know the implicit rate as computed by the lessor.

CHAPTER 8

LEASES

I. **Overview** 8-2
- A. Definitions 8-2
- B. Minimum Lease Payments 8-2
- C. Executory Costs 8-3
- D. Present Value Discount Rates 8-3
- E. Residual Value 8-3
- F. Termination 8-3

II. **Classification Criteria** 8-4
- A. Lessee 8-4
- B. Lessor 8-4

III. **Operating Leases** 8-6
- A. Definition 8-6
- B. Payments 8-6
- C. Lessor 8-6
- D. Lessee 8-6

IV. **Lessee's Capital Leases** 8-7
- A. Initial Recording 8-7
- B. Amortization 8-7
- C. Impairment Loss Recognition 8-9

V. **Lessor's Capital Leases** 8-10
- A. Sales-Type Leases 8-10
- B. Direct Financing Leases 8-12

VI. **Sale-Leaseback Transactions** 8-14
- A. Definition 8-14
- B. Seller-Lessee 8-14
- C. Purchaser-Lessor 8-15

VII. **Disclosures** 8-16
- A. Lessee 8-16
- B. Lessor 8-16

EXAM COVERAGE: Historically, exam coverage of the topics in Chapter 8 has been 1 to 4 percent of the FAR section. More information regarding exam coverage is included in Appendix B, *Practical Advice*.

CHAPTER 8

LEASES

I. Overview

A. Definitions

A lease is an agreement conveying the right to use property, plant or equipment (land and/or depreciable assets) usually for a stated period of time. SFAS 13, *Accounting for Leases,* as amended and clarified by subsequent pronouncements, is the primary source of promulgated GAAP concerning leases. A lease that transfers substantially all of the benefits and risks incidental to the ownership of property should be accounted for as an acquisition of an asset and the incurrence of a liability by the lessee, and as a sale or financing agreement by the lessor. All other leases should be accounted for as operating leases.

1. **Lessor/Lessee** The lessor leases the asset to the lessee. Lease payments are made by the lessee to the lessor.

2. **Lease Term** The fixed noncancelable term of the lease **plus** the following.

   a. All periods, if any, covered by bargain renewal options.

   b. All periods for which failure to renew the lease imposes a penalty on the lessee in an amount such as to make renewal reasonably assured.

   c. All periods preceding the date that a bargain purchase option becomes exercisable.

   d. All periods representing renewals or extensions of the lease term at the lessor's option.

   In no case, however, should the lease term extend beyond the date at which a bargain purchase option becomes exercisable.

B. Minimum Lease Payments

The definition of minimum lease payments (MLP) parallels that of the lease term, above. If the lease contains a bargain purchase option, **only** the minimum rental payments over the lease term up to the date at which the bargain purchase option becomes exercisable **and** the payment called for by the bargain purchase option are included in the MLP. Otherwise, MLP includes the following.

1. Minimum rental payments called for by the lease over the lease term.

2. Any guarantee by the lessee, or a third party related to the lessee, of a residual value of the leased asset at the end of the lease.

3. Any penalty that the lessee may be required to pay upon failure to renew the lease. However, if the penalty is such that renewal has been assumed and the lease term accordingly extended (see 2.b.), the amount of the penalty should **not** be included in the MLP.

4. For lessors, in addition to the above amounts, minimum lease payments also include any guarantee of the residual value by a third party unrelated to either the lessor or lessee if the third party is financially capable of discharging its obligations.

5. Minimum lease payments do **not** include executory costs paid by either the lessor or the lessee, nor do they include any contingent rentals.

C. **Executory Costs**

Executory costs are expenditures such as insurance, maintenance and taxes required to be paid on the asset during the asset's economic life. They are considered period costs which should be expensed when paid or accrued by either the lessor or lessee.

1. If the **lessor** retains the responsibility to pay, the portion of the minimum lease payments representing these executory costs should be removed from the lessee's minimum lease payments (if the portion is unknown, it should be estimated).

2. If the **lessee** retains the responsibility to pay, executory costs are **not** included in minimum lease payments. Rather they are charged to an appropriate expense account (e.g., insurance expense, property taxes, repairs and maintenance, etc.).

D. **Present Value Discount Rates**

1. The **lessee** uses the **incremental borrowing rate** (discount rate lessee would pay in the lending market to purchase the asset leased) in computing the present value of the minimum lease payments, **unless both** of the following requirements are satisfied.

   a. The lessee knows or can practicably discover the **lessor's implicit interest rate** used in the lease.

   b. That implicit interest rate is **lower** than the lessee's incremental borrowing rate.

2. If both requirements are satisfied, the lessor's interest rate implicit in the lease is used in computing the present value of the minimum lease payments for asset and liability recording, instead of the lessee's incremental borrowing rate. The **lessor's** interest rate implicit in the lease is the interest rate that will discount the minimum lease payments **plus** unguaranteed residual value to the fair value of the leased property at the lease inception date.

E. **Residual Value**

The estimated fair value of the leased property at the end of the lease term.

1. **Guaranteed** The guaranteed residual value is a specifically determinable amount payable at termination of the lease.

   a. The payment may constitute a purchase payment for the leased property, or it may be made to satisfy a deficiency below a "stated amount" which the lessee guarantees the lessor on realization of the property. The "stated amount" would be the guaranteed residual value.

   b. The guaranteed residual value is **included** in the minimum lease payments for both lessors and lessees.

2. **Unguaranteed** The unguaranteed residual value is not guaranteed by the lessee or by a third party related to the lessee.

   a. The unguaranteed residual value is **not** included in MLP by either lessor or lessee.

   b. The lessor's gross investment in the lease is equal to the sum of MLP plus the unguaranteed residual value of the leased property.

F. **Termination**

Previous guidance called for recognizing lease termination costs in the period of commitment to an exit or disposal plan. SFAS 146 supercedes the previous guidance, effective for exit or disposal activities initiated on or after December 31, 2002. SFAS 146 requires recognizing lease termination costs related with exit or disposal activities in periods when obligations to others exist, not necessarily in the period of commitment to a plan.

II. Classification Criteria

A. Lessee

1. **Capital Lease** Classify and account for the lease as a capital lease if at the date of the lease agreement (date of lease inception), the lease satisfies **at least one** of the following four criteria. However, if the beginning of the lease term falls within the last 25% of the total estimated economic life of the leased asset, then criteria c. and d. are inapplicable. The lease then should be classified as a capital lease **only** if it meets a. or b.

Exhibit 1 ▸ Lessee Criteria

Lessee must meet just **ONE** condition to capitalize.

TO	Transfers Ownership at end of lease (upon final payment or required buyout)
BOP	Bargain Purchase Option
75	75% of asset economic life is committed in lease term
90	90% of leased property FMV $\leq$ PV of future lease payments

a. The lease transfers ownership of the property to the lessee by the end of the lease.

b. The lease contains a bargain purchase option.

c. The lease term is equal to 75% or more of the estimated economic life of the leased property (as determined at the inception of the lease).

d. The present value of the minimum lease payments (excluding executory costs) **equals or exceeds** 90% of the fair value of the leased property at lease inception.

2. **Operating Lease** If a lease does **not** satisfy at least one of the four criteria for a capital lease, then the lessee must classify and account for the lease as an operating lease.

B. Lessor

1. **Types of Leases** Lessor classifies leases meeting all the following criteria as either **sales-type** or **direct financing type** leases.

a. The lease is a capital lease for the lessee. It is important to note that the lessor always uses the interest rate implicit in the lease in calculating the present value of the minimum lease payments.

b. Collectibility of the minimum lease payments is reasonably predictable.

c. No important uncertainties exist regarding the unreimbursable costs yet to be incurred by the lessor under the lease.

2. **Sales-Type Leases** Sales-type leases are, in substance, sales of assets on an installment basis.

a. Sales-type leases contain a manufacturer's or dealer's profit (or loss). This profit (or loss) is the difference between the cost or carrying amount of the asset and its fair value. A second type of profit, interest income, is also recognized in a sales-type lease.

b. Manufacturer's or dealer's profit should be recognized in full at the lease's inception while interest income should be recognized over the period of the lease using the interest method.

Exhibit 2 ▸ Capital Lease Criteria

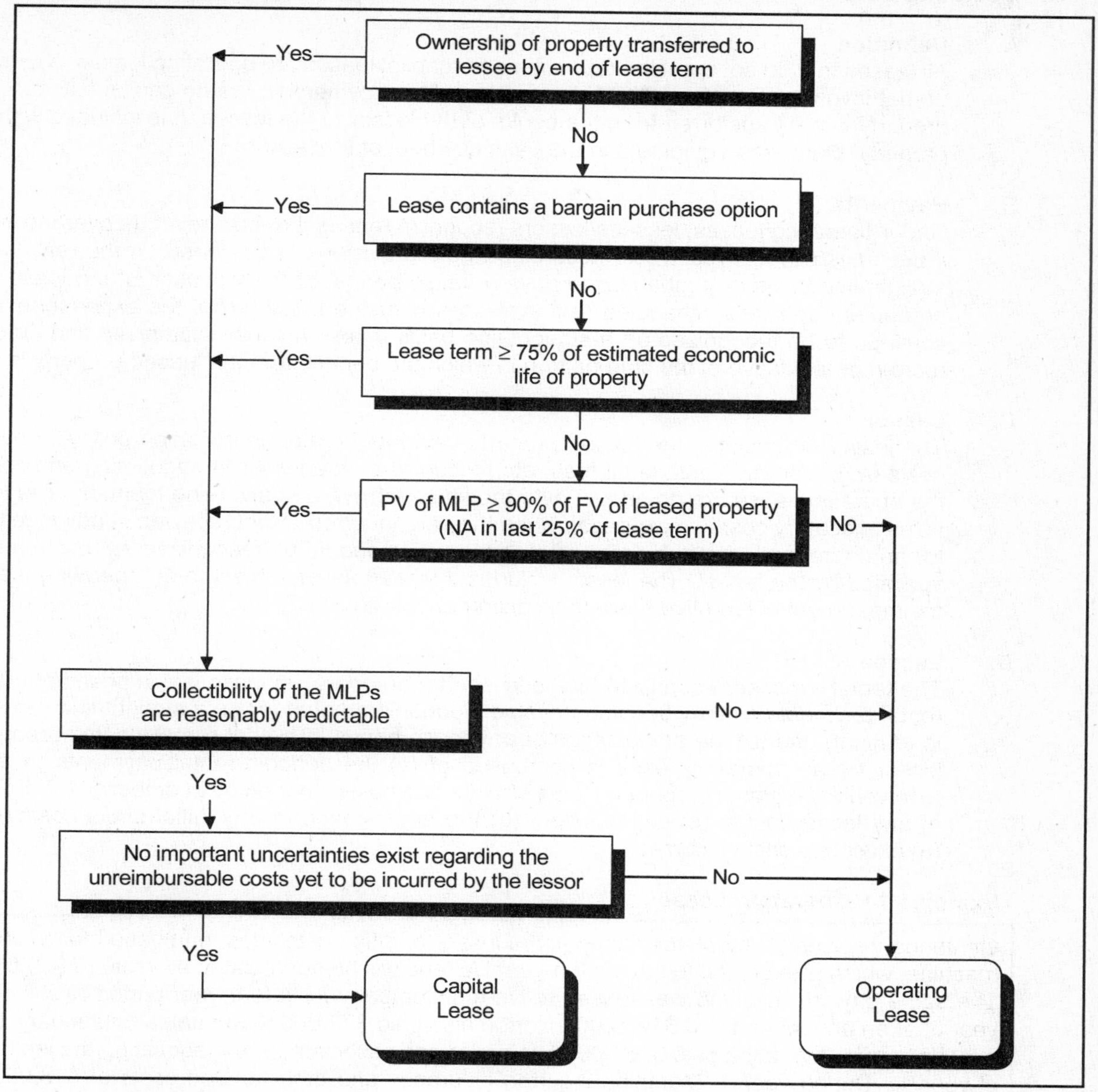

3. **Direct Financing** Direct financing leases differ from sales-type leases in that only interest income arises. Thus, no manufacturer's or dealer's profit results from a direct financing lease.

   a. Unearned interest income represents the difference between the lessor's gross investment in the lease (lessor's minimum lease payments plus unguaranteed residual value) and the cost or carrying amount of the leased asset (plus initial direct costs). The unearned interest income should also be recognized over the period of the lease by the interest method. Interest + unearned Revenue = Gross Invest [MLP + unguaranteed RV] + CA

   b. The lessor's net investment in the capital lease is equal to the present value of the gross investment in the lease (i.e., the gross investment less the unearned interest income).

4. **Operating Leases** Leases that do not meet all the criteria for sales-type or direct financing leases are operating leases.

III. Operating Leases

A. Definition

All leases that do not meet the four criteria for capital leases are operating leases. Operating leases do not involve a transfer of the risks and benefits of ownership (as do capital leases). The leased property is not transferred from the books of the lessor to the lessee; it is included with or near the property, plant, and equipment in the balance sheet of the lessor.

B. Payments

Under operating leases, lessees/lessors recognize rent as expense/revenue over the lease term as it becomes payable/receivable according to the provisions of the lease. If the rentals vary from a straight-line basis (e.g., the lessee pays a "lease bonus" at the inception of the lease or the lease agreement specifies scheduled rent increases over the lease term), the expense/revenue should continue to be recognized on a straight-line basis unless another systematic and rational basis is more representative of the time pattern in which the benefit from the leased property is diminished.

C. Lessor

The lessor depreciates the leased property using its normal depreciation policy. Any initial direct costs (e.g., commissions, legal fees, etc.) incurred by the lessor in negotiating and consummating the operating lease are amortized over the lease term in a straight-line manner. The lessor recognizes executory costs as expenses when they are incurred. Rent received in advance by the lessor for an operating lease is a deferred revenue which should be recognized as revenue in the period specified by the lease. The lessor includes a leased asset subject to an operating lease in testing for impairment of long-lived assets, in accordance with SFAS 144.

D. Lessee

The rental expense recognized by the lessee for an operating lease is comprised of (a) the periodic rental payments as they become payable if equal in amount (or on a straight-line basis if not equal in amount) and (b) the amortization of any lease bonus. The net rental income recognized by the lessor for an operating lease is comprised of (a) the periodic rental payments as they become receivable if equal in amount (or on a straight-line basis if not equal in amount), (b) the amortization of any lease bonus, (c) depreciation, (d) the amortization of any initial direct costs incurred, and (e) executory costs incurred.

Example 1 ▸ Operating Lease

On January 1, year 1, Montalba Company, a lessor of office machines, purchased for $700,000 a new machine, which is expected to have a ten-year life, and will be depreciated at a rate of $70,000 per year. The same day the machine was leased to Norton Company for a four-year period expiring January 1, year 5, at an annual rental of $120,000. Norton also paid $72,000 to Montalba on January 1, year 1, as a lease bonus. Montalba paid $16,000 of commissions associated with negotiating the lease in January of year 1. During year 1, Montalba incurred insurance and other related costs of $18,000 under the lease. There is no provision for the renewal of the lease or purchase of the machine by Norton at the expiration of the lease term.

Required:

a. Compute Norton Company's rental expense for the year ended December 31, year 1.

b. Compute Montalba Company's operating profit for this leased asset for the year ended December 31, year 1.

Solution: Both Norton and Montalba account for the lease as an operating lease because it fails to meet capital lease criteria.

a.	Equal annual rental payment		$120,000
	Amortization of lease bonus ($72,000 / 4 years)		18,000
	Rental expense, year 1		$138,000
b.	Equal annual rental payment		$120,000
	Amortization of lease bonus ($72,000 / 4 years)		18,000
	Rental revenue		138,000
	Less: Depreciation	$70,000	
	Amortization of initial direct costs ($16,000 / 4 years)	4,000	
	Executory costs	18,000	(92,000)
	Operating profit on leased asset, year 1		$ 46,000

IV. Lessee's Capital Leases

A. Initial Recording

Lessee must record a capital lease in an amount equal to (a) the fair value of the leased property at the inception date or, (b) the present value of the minimum lease payments (using the present value discount rate), whichever is **lower.** The same amount is recorded on the lessee's books both as an asset, "Leased Asset Under Capital Leases" and as a liability, "Obligations Under Capital Leases."

1. **Interest Factors** Where the annual rental is payable at the **beginning** of each lease year, the factor for the present value of annuity in **advance** (also referred to as an annuity **due**) is to be used to determine the present value of the minimum lease payments. If, however, the annual rental is payable at the **end** of each lease year, the factor for the present value of **ordinary** annuity (also referred to as an annuity **in arrears**) should be used.

2. **Bargain Purchase Options** The payment called for by a bargain purchase option should be capitalized at its present value. A purchase option is considered to be a bargain purchase option when the lessee can purchase the leased property for significantly less than the expected fair value of the property at the date the option becomes exercisable.

3. **Guarantee of Residual Value** Any guarantee of the residual value of the leased property by the **lessee** or a third party **related** to the lessee should be capitalized at its present value. A guarantee of the residual value of the leased property by a third party **unrelated** to the lessee should **not** be capitalized.

4. **Balance Sheet Classification** The obligation under capital lease is classified as both current and noncurrent, with the current portion being that amount that will be paid on the principal during the next year.

B. Amortization

1. **Leased Asset** Amortization should be consistent with the lessee's normal depreciation policy for similar owned assets.

   a. **Amortize Over Remaining Estimated Economic Life** If the lease qualifies as a capital lease because it satisfies **either** the first two lease classification criteria (i.e., the lease agreement transfers ownership of the asset by the end of the lease term **or** contains a bargain purchase option), the lessee must amortize the leased asset over the remaining **estimated economic life of the asset.**

   b. **Amortize Over Lease Term** If the lease is classified as a capital lease because it satisfies criteria other than the first two lease classification criteria, the lessee will amortize the leased asset over the **lease term** (rather than the life of the asset).

c. **Amortize to Expected Residual Value** For capital leases where there is a transfer of ownership (i.e., there is a title transfer or the lease contains a bargain purchase option), the leased asset is amortized to its expected residual value, if any, to the lessee at the end of the lease term.

2. **Lease Liability**

a. **Effective Interest Method** The effective interest method is used to amortize the lease liability.

b. **Allocation of Lease Payments** Each lease payment made by the lessee is allocated between interest expense and the reduction of the lease obligation; it is **not** recorded as rent expense. Under this method, each successive uniform payment is comprised of a **decreasing** amount of interest expense and an **increasing** amount of reduction of the lease obligation.

c. **Amortization Rate** Although the asset and liability balances at the inception of the lease are the same present value amount (or fair value if lower at lease inception), each balance will be amortized at different rates during the asset life or lease term.

Example 2 ▸ Lessee's Accounting for Capital Leases

Lessor and Lessee enter into a lease for a computer on January 1, year 1. The lease duration is 3 years, noncancelable, with 2 renewal options of 1 year each. The lease provides for a termination penalty assuring renewal of the lease for 2 years after the 3-year regular term ends. The leased equipment consists of a computer which has a cost and fair value to lessor at lease inception of $100,000. The estimated economic life of the asset is 6 years. The asset has no residual value. The lease rental is $27,991/year, which includes executory costs, payable at the beginning of each year. Lessor pays executory costs of $4,800/year, at beginning of each year. The lessee's incremental rate is 10%. The lessor's implicit rate is 8% and is known to the lessee.

Required: Record in lessee's books all entries related to the lease during the first year. Show supporting computations.

Solution: The lease is a capital lease because its term (5 years) exceeds 75% of the computer's estimated economic life (6 years). Additionally, the present value of the minimum lease payments ($100,000) exceeds 90% of the fair value of the computer ($100,000). See Schedule 3, below, for computation of PV of MLP.

01/01, year 1	Leased Equipment Under Capital Leases	100,000	
	Obligation Under Capital Leases		100,000
	To record capitalized lease. See Schedule 3.		
	Executory Expenses (detailed)	4,800	
	Obligation Under Capital Leases	23,191	
	Cash		27,991
	To record first year's minimum lease payment and executory costs. See Schedule 2.		
12/31, year 1	Amortization Expense on Leased Equipment	20,000	
	Accumulated Amortization of Leased Equipment Under Capital Leases		20,000
	To record the amortization of the asset based on the straight-line depreciation method (method normally used by lessee for other owned assets) over the lease term (no transfer of ownership; no bargain purchase option). Computation: $100,000 / 5 = $20,000. See Schedule 1 for lease term determination.		
12/31, year 1	Interest Expense	6,145	
	Accrued Interest Payable		6,145
	To record interest expense on lease obligation. See Schedule 4.		

01/01, year 2	Executory Expenses (detailed)	4,800	
	Accrued Interest Payable	6,145	
	Obligation Under Capital Leases	17,046	
	Cash		27,991

To record second-year's minimum lease payment and executory costs. See Schedule 4.

12/31, year 2 The entries to record depreciation and interest expense would be similar to the prior year's. The depreciation amount remains constant; the interest amount is from Schedule 4.

Schedule 1: Lease Term

Noncancelable term	3 years
Additional period for which termination penalty assures renewal	2 years
Total lease term	5 years

Schedule 2: Minimum Lease Payments

Yearly lease payments including yearly executory costs	$ 27,991
Yearly executory costs	(4,800)
Net yearly lease payments	23,191
Lease term (years)	× 5
Total lessee MLP	$115,955

Schedule 3: Present Value of Minimum Lease Payments

Since the lease payments are payable in advance, the present value factor is derived as follows: Choose from Appendix D the appropriate factor for the present value of an ordinary annuity of $1 per period for 4 periods at 8% (3.3121). To this 4-period factor add 1.000 (3.3121 + 1.000 = 4.3121) in order to find the present value of an annuity in advance payable in 5 years at 8%.

Minimum lease payments net of executory costs	$ 23,191
Factor for annuity in advance at 8%	× 4.3121
PV of MLP ($1.91 difference due to rounding)	$100,000

Since the lessor's implicit interest rate was known and was lower than the lessee's incremental borrowing rate of 10%, the lessor's implicit rate of 8% was used to calculate the present value of the asset and the liability on the lessee's books.

Schedule 4: Lease Payments and Interest Accruals (Lessee)

Date	Description	8% Interest expense	Lease payment amount	Interest	Amortization of principal	Balance of lease obligation
01/01, year 1	Initial bal.					$100,000
01/01, year 1	Payment		$23,191		$23,191	76,809
12/31, year 1	Int. accr.	$6,145				76,809
01/01, year 2	Payment		23,191	$6,145	17,046	59,763
12/31, year 2	Int. accr.	4,781				59,763
01/01, year 3	Payment		23,191	4,781	18,410	41,353
12/31, year 3	Int. accr.	3,308				41,353
01/01, year 4	Payment		23,191	3,308	19,883	21,470
12/31, year 4	Int. accr.	1,718				21,470
01/01, year 5	Payment		23,191	1,718	21,470	0*

* All calculations and balances rounded to balance.

C. Impairment Loss Recognition

In accordance with SFAS 144, assets subject to capital leases should be reviewed by the lessee whenever circumstances indicate that the carrying amount of the asset may not be recoverable. The review consists of estimating the future net cash flows; and, without discounting or considering interest charges, if the future cash flows is less than the carrying amount of the asset, impairment loss is recognized. Impairment loss recognized is the amount by which the carrying amount of the asset exceeds the **fair value** of the asset.

V. Lessor's Capital Leases

A. Sales-Type Leases

The lessor accounts for a sales-type lease by recording the following.

1. **Gross Investment in Lease** The lessor's gross investment in the lease is equal to the sum of the following:

   a. **Lessor's Minimum Lease Payments (MLP)**

      (1) **Guaranteed** residual value is included in the minimum lease payments of **both parties.**

      (2) Residual value or rental payments beyond the lease, guaranteed by a financially capable third party **unrelated** to either lessee or lessor, are also included in the **lessor's minimum lease payments.**

   b. **Unguaranteed Residual Value Accruing to Lessor** Estimated fair value of the leased property at the end of the lease term, exclusive of any portion guaranteed by the lessee or a third party unrelated to the lessor.

2. **Net Investment in the Lease** Present value of lessor's gross investment in the lease. In equation form: Net investment in lease = PV of (MLP + Unguaranteed residual value).

3. **Unearned Interest Income** Difference between the gross investment in the lease and the present value of its two components (i.e., the MLP and the unguaranteed residual value). Unearned interest income is reported as a contra-asset to gross investment in the lease. It is amortized as interest income by the "interest method" over the lease term.

4. **Sales Price in the Lease** Equal to the present value of the lessor's minimum lease payments (MLP)

   a. Present value computed using the lessor's implicit interest rate.

   b. Unguaranteed residual value is **not** included in the lessor's minimum lease payments.

   c. Since the lessor's implicit interest rate is used, the present value of the lessor's minimum lease payments will equal the fair value of the leased asset less the present value of any unguaranteed residual value accruing to the lessor.

5. **Cost of Sales** Book value or carrying amount of asset leased out reduced by the present value of the unguaranteed residual value accruing to the lessor. In equation form

   Cost of sales = Book value – PV of unguaranteed residual value

6. **Initial Direct Costs** Costs incurred by the lessor that are directly associated with negotiating and consummating **completed** leasing transactions. Examples include commissions, legal fees, cost of preparing documents and the applicable portion of the compensation of employees directly involved with completed leasing transactions.

   a. Does **not** include administrative expenses or expenses of negotiating leases that are not consummated.

   b. Does **not** include **executory costs.**

7. **Manufacturer's or Dealer's Profit** Equal to the present value of the minimum lease payments reduced by the cost of sales and by the initial direct costs. In equation form

Manufacturer's or dealer's profit = PV of MLP – (Cost of sales + Initial direct costs)

Example 3 ▸ Sales-Type Lease

Lessor and lessee sign a lease on January 1, year 1 containing the following terms:
Lease duration: 5 years beginning January 1, year 1.
Leased asset's estimated economic life: 6 years
Estimated residual value: $14,000, unguaranteed.
Lease payments: $50,000/year, payable at year-end.
Leased asset's manufacturing cost: $150,000
Lease closing costs: $2,000 (initial direct costs)
Lease provisions: Lease does not contain a bargain renewal or a bargain purchase option.
Implicit lease interest rate: 10%

Lessor has determined that the collectibility of lease payments is reasonably predictable and there are no important uncertainties regarding costs yet to be incurred by the lessor.

Required:

a. Is this an operating, sales-type, or direct financing lease? Support your answer.

b. Provide lessor's journal entries during the first year of the lease.

c. Provide lessor's journal entry at the end of the lease.

Solution:

a. Lease Classification—The lease satisfies the tests for classification as a sales-type lease.

Test 1: The lease term exceeds 75% of the estimated economic life of the leased property. Furthermore, the lease does not begin during the last 25% of the asset's total economic life. (5-year lease / 6-year economic life = 83%)

Test 2: Collectibility of lease rentals is reasonably assured, and there are no important uncertainties regarding lessor costs yet to be incurred.

Test 3: Sales-Type Test—The present value of the minimum lease payments (as determined in Schedule 1, below) exceeds the cost of the asset to the lessor, less the present value of the unguaranteed residual value accruing to the lessor, resulting in a manufacturer's or dealer's profit.

b. Journal entries to record lease during first year

01/01, year 1	Gross Investment in Lease (Schedule 1)	264,000	
	Cost of Goods Leased (Schedule 2)	141,307	
	Selling Expenses (Schedule 2)	2,000	
	Sales Revenue (Schedule 2)		189,540
	Equipment		150,000
	Unearned Interest Income (Schedule 1)		65,767
	Cash		2,000
	To record sale of property under lease to lessee.		
12/31, year 1	Cash	50,000	
	Gross Investment in Lease		50,000
	Unearned Interest Income	19,823	
	Interest Income (Schedule 3)		19,823
	To record first year's lease payment and interest income earned.		

c. Journal entry at end of the lease

12/31, year 5	Equipment	14,000	
	Gross Investment in Lease		14,000
	To record receipt of the leased asset by lessor at the end of lease term and removal of lease receivable from books.		

Schedule 1: Lessor's Gross Investment in the Lease, PV, and Unearned Interest Income

Annual lease payment		$ 50,000
Lease term (years)		× 5
Summation of MLP		250,000
Add: Unguaranteed residual value		14,000
Gross investment in lease		$ 264,000
PV of MLP, $50,000 × PVA (n=5, i=10%); $50,000 × 3.7908	$189,540	
PV of unguaranteed residual value, $14,000 × PV (n=5, i=10%); $14,000 × 0.6209	8,693	
PV of investment in lease		(198,233)
Unearned interest income		$ 65,767

Schedule 2: Lessor's Cost of Sales and Manufacturer's or Dealer's Profit

Sales price (i.e., PV of MLP)		$ 189,540
Manufacturing cost of asset	$150,000	
Less: PV of unguaranteed residual accruing to lessor	(8,693)	
Cost of goods leased		(141,307)
Gross margin		48,233*
Less: Initial direct costs		(2,000)
Manufacturer's or dealer's profit		$ 46,233*

* Not required for this problem, shown for illustrative purposes.

Schedule 3: Lease Payments and Interest Accruals

Date	Lease payment	Interest income on net investment in lease (10%)	Reduction of investment in lease	Net investment in lease
01/01, year 1				$198,233
12/31, year 1	$50,000	$19,823	$30,177	168,056
12/31, year 2	50,000	16,806	33,194	134,862
12/31, year 3	50,000	13,486	36,514	98,348
12/31, year 4	50,000	9,835	40,165	58,183
12/31, year 5	50,000	5,818	44,182	14,000*

* This balance remaining in the net investment account represents the estimated residual value of the leased asset at the end of the term ($1 difference due to rounding).

B. Direct Financing Leases

A direct financing lease is a lease that meets the same criteria as a sales-type lease **except** it does **not** give rise to a manufacturer's or dealer's profit (i.e., the cost or carrying amount of the asset is equal to its fair value). The only income that arises from this type of lease is interest income.

1. **Gross Investment in Lease** The sum of MLP (net of lessor-paid executory costs) and unguaranteed residual value should be recorded as gross investment in the lease.

2. **Unearned Income** The difference between gross investment in the lease and cost or carrying amount of the leased property should be recorded as unearned income.

3. **Initial Direct Costs** Initial direct costs should be added to the net investment in a direct financing lease and amortized over the life of the lease. It is not acceptable to recognize a portion of the unearned income at inception of the lease to offset initial direct costs.

4. **Net Investment in Lease** The net investment in the lease is the gross investment in the lease plus any unamortized initial direct costs less the unearned income.

5. **Amortization** The unearned income and any initial direct costs should be amortized over the lease term using the "interest" method.

Example 4 ▶ Direct Financing Lease

Lessor and lessee sign a lease on January 1, year 1. The lease contains the following terms:

Lease duration: 3 years beginning January 1, year 1
Estimated economic life: 4 years
Unguaranteed residual value: $5,200 at the end of year 3
Annual lease payments: (payable at year-end) $19,277
Leased asset cost (same as FV): $50,000
Lessor implicit rate: 12%
Lessee incremental borrowing rate: 12.5%
Present value of minimum lease payments: $50,000 [($19,277 × 2.4018) + ($5,200 × 0.7117)]

Required:

a. Classify the lease from the viewpoint of the lessor. Support your answer.

b. Provide lessor's entries to account for the lease during the lease term. Show supporting computations.

Solution:

a. One or more of the various criteria for classification as a capital lease are met because the lease term equals 75% of the equipment's estimated economic life and the present value of the minimum lease payments exceeds 90% of the fair value of the leased property at lease inception date. The cost and fair value of the property are identical; therefore, no manufacturer's or dealer's profit exists. The second test for direct financing lease classification is also satisfied because the lease in this example is assumed to be one in which (a) the collectibility of the minimum lease payments is reasonably assured and (b) there are no further unreimbursable costs yet to be incurred by the lessor.

b. Journal entries to record the lease during each of the three years of the lease term.

01/01, year 1	Gross Investment in Lease (Schedule 1)	63,031	
	Equipment		50,000
	Unearned Interest Income		13,031
	To record the lease at inception.		
12/31, year 1	Cash (Schedule 2)	19,277	
	Gross Investment in Lease		19,277
	Unearned Interest Income (Schedule 2)	6,000	
	Interest Income		6,000
	To record receipt of MLP and recognition of interest income.		
12/31, year 2	Cash (Schedule 2)	19,277	
	Gross Investment in Lease		19,277
	Unearned Interest Income (Schedule 2)	4,407	
	Interest Income		4,407
	To record the second year's receipt of MLP and recognition of interest income.		
12/31, year 3	Cash (Schedule 2)	19,277	
	Gross Investment in Lease		19,277
	Unearned Interest Income (Schedule 2)	2,622	
	Interest Income		2,622
	To record the third year's receipt of MLP and recognition of interest income.		
12/31, year 4	Equipment (Schedule 2)	5,200	
	Gross Investment in Lease		5,200
	To record the return of the equipment.		

Schedule 1: Gross Investment in Lease, Book Value, and Unearned Interest Income

Annual lease payment	$ 19,277
Lease term (years)	× 3
Summation of MLP	57,831
Add: Unguaranteed residual value	5,200
Gross investment in lease	63,031
Book value of the equipment (equal to its FV)	(50,000)
Unearned interest income	$ 13,031

Schedule 2: Lease Payments and Interest Income Recognized

Date	Lease Payment	Interest on Net Investment (12%)	Reduction of Net Investment in Lease	Balance of Net Investment
01/01, year 1				$50,000
12/31, year 1	$19,277	$6,000	$13,277	36,723
12/31, year 2	19,277	4,407	14,870	21,853
12/31, year 3	19,277	2,622	16,655	5,200*

* Balance remaining represents the estimated residual value of the leased asset (rounded).

VI. Sale-Leaseback Transactions

A. Definition

Sale-leaseback transactions involve the sale of property to a purchaser-lessor and a lease of the same property back to the seller-lessee. The economic purpose of this type of transaction is that the seller-lessee obtains financing for the use of the property and the purchaser-lessor (usually a financial institution or investor) obtains interest income. Tax considerations may also play an important role in sale-leaseback transactions. SFAS 145 requires sale-leaseback accounting for specified lease amendments with economic effects similar to sale-leaseback transactions

B. Seller-Lessee

If the lease meets any of the four criteria for classification as a capital lease, the lessee accounts for it as a capital lease. Otherwise, the lease is treated as an operating lease.

1. **Gains and Losses** A gain or loss on the sale of the asset generally will be deferred and amortized.

   a. **Capital Lease** If a capital lease, the gain or loss will be deferred and amortized in proportion to the amortization of the leased asset. For instance, in a capital lease where there is no ownership transfer and the asset is amortized in a straight-line manner, the deferred gain or loss will be amortized in a straight-line manner over the term of the lease. If ownership transfers, the gain or loss will be amortized over the estimated life of the asset. If the leased asset is amortized under another method, such as DDB or SYD, the same method should be used to amortize the deferred gain or loss. At the time of sale, the deferred gain or loss should be reported as an asset valuation allowance.

   b. **Operating Lease** If an operating lease, the gain or loss will be deferred and amortized in proportion to the related gross rentals charged to expense during the period. This usually will result in straight-line amortization. At the time of sale, a deferred gain should be reported as a deferred credit.

Example 5 ▶ Sale-Leaseback Capital Lease

On January 1 of the current year, ABC Co. sold equipment to XYZ Inc., having a $100,000 BV and $130,000 FV. Simultaneously, ABC agreed to lease back the equipment for five years, at an annual rental of $34,295, due at year-end (implicit interest rate of 10%). The estimated useful life of the equipment was 5 years, with no residual value. ABC Co. depreciates similar assets on a straight-line basis. ABC Co. would record the first year's entries as follows.

01/01	Cash	130,000	
	Equipment (net)		100,000
	Deferred Gain		30,000
	Leased Equipment Under Capital Lease	130,000	
	Obligation Under Capital Lease		130,000
12/31	Interest Expense (10% × 130,000)	13,000	
	Obligation Under Capital Lease ($34,295 – $13,000)	21,295	
	Cash		34,295
	Amortization Expense on Leased Equipment	26,000	
	Accumulated Amortization ($130,000 / 5)		26,000
	Deferred Gain ($30,000 / 5)	6,000	
	Amortization Expense on Leased Equipment		6,000

2. **Deferment Requirement Exceptions**

a. **Minor Portion Retained** If the seller-lessee retains only a **minor** portion of the remaining use of the property sold, the sale and leaseback are recorded as two separate transactions (i.e., the **entire** gain or loss is **recognized at the point of sale**). Professional judgment is required for determining whether the portion of remaining use retained by the seller-lessee is "minor." In general, if the PV of the rental payments under the leaseback agreement is **less than 10%** of the FV of the property sold, the seller-lessee will be deemed to retain a "minor" portion.

b. **Excess Gains** If the seller-lessee retains more than a minor portion of the leased asset but **less** than substantially all of its remaining use **and** realizes a gain on the sale, the excess gain (if any) is recognized at the date of sale, as follows.

(1) **Operating Lease** Gain in excess of the PV of MLP should be recognized at the date of sale. The remaining portion of the gain should be deferred and amortized. PV of MLP is determined using the smaller of lessee's incremental borrowing rate or interest rate implicit in the lease.

(2) **Capital Lease** The excess gain over the recorded amount of the leased asset should be recognized at the date of sale. The remaining portion of the gain should be deferred and amortized.

c. **Economic Losses** If the fair value of the property at the time of the transaction is less than its undepreciated cost, a **loss** should be recognized immediately up to the amount of the difference between undepreciated cost and fair value.

C. **Purchaser-Lessor**

A lessor will account for a sale-leaseback transaction in the same manner as for other leases, that is, as if the property had been purchased from and leased to two separate parties.

Example 6 ▸ Loss on Sale-Leaseback

Equipment with a book value of $15,000 is sold for $10,000 and simultaneously leased back by the seller. The fair market value and the present value of the lease payments is $13,000.

Required: Determine the amount of loss to be recognized at the date of sale and the amount to be deferred.

Solution: Of the loss of $5,000, the $2,000 difference between book value and fair value is a real (economic) loss and should be recognized immediately. The remaining amount of $3,000 is deferred and amortized.

Equipment book value	$ 15,000	
Sales price	(10,000)	
Total loss		$5,000
Equipment book value	15,000	
Fair value	(13,000)	
Loss recognized at date of sale		2,000
Loss deferred		$3,000

VII. Disclosures

A. Lessee

1. **Capital Leases** The lessee is required to disclose:

   a. The gross amount of assets recorded under capital leases as of the date of each balance sheet presented by major classes according to nature or function.

   b. The present value of future minimum lease payments as of the date of the latest balance sheet presented, in the aggregate and for each of the five succeeding fiscal years.

2. **Operating Leases With Initial or Remaining Noncancelable Term in Excess of 1 Year** The lessee is required to disclose the future minimum rental payments required, in aggregate, and for each of next 5 years and a general description of leasing arrangements.

B. Lessor

1. **Sales-Type and Direct Financing Leases** The lessor must disclose the net investment components, including future MLP, unguaranteed residual value, unearned income, and the future MLP to be received in each of the succeeding 5 years.

2. **Operating Leases** The lessor must disclose the cost and carrying amount, if different, of property leased or held for leasing, by major class and total accumulated depreciation; the minimum future rentals on noncancelable leases, in aggregate, for each of the next 5 years; and a general description of leasing arrangements.

CHAPTER 8—LEASES

Problem 8-1 MULTIPLE CHOICE QUESTIONS (72 to 90 minutes)

1. One criterion for a capital lease is that the term of the lease must equal a minimum percentage of the leased property's estimated economic life at the inception of the lease. What is this minimum percentage?
a. 51%
b. 75%
c. 80%
d. 90% (5/94, FAR, #26, 4841)

2. Crane Mfg. leases a machine from Frank Leasing. Ownership of the machine returns to Frank after the 15-year lease expires. The machine is expected to have an economic life of 17 years. At this time, Frank is unable to predict the collectibility of the lease payments to be received from Crane. The present value of the minimum lease payments exceeds 90% of the fair value of the machine. What is the appropriate classification of this lease for Crane?
a. Operating
b. Leveraged
c. Capital
d. Installment (R/03, FAR, #3, 7605)

3. On January 1, year 1, JCK Co. signed a contract for an 8-year lease of its equipment with a 10-year life. The present value of the 16 equal semi-annual payments in advance equaled 85% of the equipment's fair value. The contract had no provision for JCK, the lessor, to give up legal ownership of the equipment. Should JCK recognize rent or interest revenue in year 3, and should the revenue recognized in year 3 be the same or smaller than the revenue recognized in year 2?

	Year 3 revenues recognized	*Year 3 amount recognized compared to year 2*
a.	Rent	The same
b.	Rent	Smaller
c.	Interest	The same
d.	Interest	Smaller

(5/93, Theory, #38, amended, 4226)

4. A 20-year property lease, classified as an operating lease, provides for a 10% increase in annual payments every five years. In the sixth year compared to the fifth year, the lease will cause the following expenses to increase

	Rent	*Interest*
a.	No	Yes
b.	Yes	No
c.	Yes	Yes
d.	No	No

(5/90, Theory, #24, 2065)

5. As an inducement to enter a lease, Graf Co., a lessor, granted Zep Inc., a lessee, twelve months of free rent under a 5-year operating lease. The lease was effective on January 1, year 1, and provides for monthly rental payments to begin January 1, year 2. Zep made the first rental payment on December 30, year 1. In its year 1 income statement, Graf should report rental revenue in an amount equal to
a. Zero
b. Cash received during year 1
c. One-fourth of the total cash to be received over the life of the lease
d. One-fifth of the total cash to be received over the life of the lease

(11/94, FAR, #41, amended, 5303)

6. On January 1 of the current year, Wren Co. leased a building to Brill under an operating lease for ten years at $50,000 per year, payable the first day of each lease year. Wren paid $15,000 to a real estate broker as a finder's fee. The building is depreciated $12,000 per year. For the year, Wren incurred insurance and property tax expense totaling $9,000. Wren's net rental income for the year should be
a. $27,500
b. $29,000
c. $35,000
d. $36,500 (11/90, PI, #37, amended, 1194)

7. When should a lessor recognize in income a nonrefundable lease bonus paid by a lessee on signing an operating lease?
a. When received
b. At the inception of the lease
c. At the expiration of the lease
d. Over the life of the lease

(11/95, FAR, #34, 6116)

8. For a capital lease, the amount recorded initially by the lessee as a liability should
a. Equal the total of the minimum lease payments during the lease term
b. Exceed the total of the minimum lease payments during the lease term
c. Not exceed the fair value of the leased property at the inception of the lease
d. Exceed the present value at the beginning of the lease term of minimum lease payments during the lease term (11/87, Theory, #11, 2073)

9. On December 30 of the current year, Haber Co. leased a new machine from Gregg Corp. The following data relate to the lease transaction at the inception of the lease:

Lease term	10 years
Annual rental payable at the end of each lease year	$100,000
Estimated life of machine	12 years
Implicit interest rate	10%
Present value of an annuity of $1 in advance for 10 periods at 10%	6.76
Present value of an annuity of $1 in arrears for 10 periods at 10%	6.15
Fair value of the machine	$700,000

The lease has no renewal option, and the possession of the machine reverts to Gregg when the lease terminates. At the inception of the lease, Haber should record a lease liability of
a. $0
b. $615,000
c. $630,000
d. $676,000 (11/89, PI, #27, amended, 1203)

10. In the long-term liabilities section of its balance sheet at December 31, year 1, Mene Co. reported a capital lease obligation of $75,000, net of current portion of $1,364. Payments of $9,000 were made on both January 2, year 2, and January 2, year 3. Mene's incremental borrowing rate on the date of the lease was 11% and the lessor's implicit rate, which was known to Mene, was 10%. In its December 31, year 2 balance sheet, what amount should Mene report as capital lease obligation, net of current portion?
a. $66,000
b. $73,500
c. $73,636
d. $74,250 (5/94, FAR, #25, amended, 4840)

11. Cott, Inc. prepared an interest amortization table for a five-year lease payable with a bargain purchase option of $2,000, exercisable at the end of the lease. At the end of the five years, the balance in the leases payable column of the spreadsheet was zero. Cott has asked Grant, CPA, to review the spreadsheet to determine the error. Only one error was made on the spreadsheet. Which of the following statements represents the best explanation for this error?
a. The beginning present value of the lease did **not** include the present value of the bargain purchase option.
b. Cott subtracted the annual interest amount from the lease payable balance instead of adding it.
c. The present value of the bargain purchase option was subtracted from the present value of the annual payments.
d. Cott discounted the annual payments as an ordinary annuity, when the payments actually occurred at the beginning of each period. (R/99, FAR, #19, 6788)

12. East Company leased a new machine from North Company on May 1 under a lease with the following information:

Lease term	10 years
Annual rental payable at beginning of each lease year	$40,000
Estimated life of machine	12 years
Implicit interest rate	14%
Present value of an annuity of $1 in advance for 10 periods at 14%	5.95
Present value of $1 for 10 periods at 14%	0.27

East has the option to purchase the machine at the end of the lease by paying $50,000, which approximates the expected fair value of the machine on the option exercise date. On May 1, East should record a capitalized leased asset of
a. $251,500
b. $238,000
c. $224,500
d. $198,000 (5/86, PI, #20, amended, 1216)

13. At the inception of a capital lease, the guaranteed residual value should be
a. Included as part of minimum lease payments at present value
b. Included as part of minimum lease payments at future value
c. Included as part of minimum lease payments only to the extent that guaranteed residual value is expected to exceed estimated residual value
d. Excluded from minimum lease payments (11/94, FAR, #20, 5284)

14. On January 1 of the current year, Day Corp. entered into a 10-year lease agreement with Ward Inc. for industrial equipment. Annual lease payments of $10,000 are payable at the end of each year. Day knows that the lessor expects a 10% return on the lease. Day has a 12% incremental borrowing rate. The equipment is expected to have an estimated life of 10 years. In addition, a third party has guaranteed to pay Ward a residual value of $5,000 at the end of the lease.

The present value of an ordinary annuity of $1 at:
12% for 10 years is 5.6502
10% for 10 years is 6.1446
The present value of $1 at:
12% for 10 years is .3220
10% for 10 years is .3855

In Day's December 31 current year balance sheet, the principal amount of the lease obligation was
a. $63,374
b. $61,446
c. $58,112
d. $56,502 (5/90, PI, #35, amended, 1198)

15. A lessee had a 10-year capital lease requiring equal annual payments. The reduction of the lease liability in the third year should equal
a. The current liability shown for the lease at the end of the second year
b. The current liability shown for the lease at the end of the third year
c. The reduction of the lease obligation in the second year
d. One-tenth of the original lease liability (5/90, Theory, #11, amended, 2063)

16. On December 30, year 1, Rafferty Corp. leased equipment under a capital lease. Annual lease payments of $20,000 are due December 31 for 10 years. The equipment's estimated life is 10 years, and the interest rate implicit in the lease is 10%. The capital lease obligation was recorded on December 30, year 1, at $135,000, and the first lease payment was made on that date. What amount should Rafferty include in current liabilities for this capital lease in its December 31, year 1 balance sheet?
a. $ 6,500
b. $ 8,500
c. $11,500
d. $20,000 (11/92, PI, #4, amended, 3237)

17. On January 1 of the current year, Nori Mining Co. (lessee) entered into a 5-year lease for drilling equipment. Nori accounted for the acquisition as a capital lease for $240,000, which includes a $10,000 bargain purchase option. At the end of the lease, Nori expects to exercise the bargain purchase option. Nori estimates that the equipment's fair value will be $20,000 at the end of its 8-year life. Nori regularly uses straight-line depreciation on similar equipment. For the current year ended December 31, what amount should Nori recognize as depreciation expense on the leased asset?
a. $48,000
b. $46,000
c. $30,000
d. $27,500 (11/93, PI, #55, amended, 4424)

18. On January 1 of the current year, Tell Co. leased equipment from Swill Co. under a nine-year sales-type lease. The equipment had a cost of $400,000, and an estimated useful life of 15 years. Semiannual lease payments of $44,000 are due every January 1 and July 1. The present value of lease payments at 12% was $505,000, which equals the sales price of the equipment. Using the straight-line method, what amount should Tell recognize as depreciation expense on the equipment in the current year?
a. $26,667
b. $33,667
c. $44,444
d. $56,111 (R/05, FAR, 1173F, #24, 7768)

19. Oak Co. leased equipment for its entire 9-year estimated life, agreeing to pay $50,000 at the start of the lease term on December 31, year 1, and $50,000 annually on each December 31 for the next eight years. The present value on December 31, year 1, of the nine lease payments over the lease term, using the rate implicit in the lease which Oak knows to be 10%, was $316,500. The December 31, year 1 present value of the lease payments using Oak's incremental borrowing rate of 12% was $298,500. Oak made a timely second lease payment. What amount should Oak report as capital lease liability in its December 31, year 2 balance sheet?
a. $350,000
b. $243,150
c. $228,320
d. $0 (11/93, PI, #35, amended, 4404)

20. On January 1 of the current year, Marx Co. as lessee signed a 5-year noncancelable equipment lease with annual payments of $200,000 beginning December 31. Marx treated this transaction as a capital lease. The five lease payments have a present value of $758,000 at January 1, based on interest of 10%. What amount should Marx report as interest expense for the current year ended December 31?

a. $0
b. $48,400
c. $55,800
d. $75,800 (5/96, FAR, #4, amended, 6277)

21. A lease is recorded as a sales-type lease by the lessor. The difference between the gross investment in the lease and the sum of the present values of the two components of the gross investment (the net receivable) should be

a. Amortized over the period of the lease as interest revenue using the interest method
b. Amortized over the period of the lease as interest revenue using the straight-line method
c. Recognized in full as interest revenue at the lease's inception
d. Recognized in full as manufacturer's or dealer's profit at the lease's inception

(5/87, Theory, #27, 9033)

22. Peg Co. leased equipment from Howe Corp. on July 1 of the current year for an 8-year period. Equal payments under the lease are $600,000 and are due on July 1 of each year. The first payment was made on July 1 of the current year. The rate of interest contemplated by Peg and Howe is 10%. The cash selling price of the equipment is $3,520,000, and the cost of the equipment on Howe's accounting records is $2,800,000. The lease is appropriately recorded as a sales-type lease. What is the amount of profit on the sale and interest revenue that Howe should record for the current year ended December 31?

	Profit on sale	Interest revenue
a.	$720,000	$176,000
b.	$720,000	$146,000
c.	$ 45,000	$176,000
d.	$ 45,000	$146,000

(11/89, PI, #34, amended, 1204)

23. Farm Co. leased equipment to Union Co. on July 1 of the current year and properly recorded the sales-type lease at $135,000, the present value of the lease payments discounted at 10%. The first of eight annual lease payments of $20,000 due at the beginning of each year was received and recorded on July 3, this year. Farm had purchased the equipment for $110,000. What amount of interest revenue from the lease should Farm report in its current year income statement?

a. $0
b. $5,500
c. $5,750
d. $6,750 (5/95, FAR, #28, amended, 5564)

24. Howe Co. leased equipment to Kew Corp. on January 2, year 1, for an 8-year period expiring December 31, year 8. Equal payments under the lease are $600,000 and are due annually on January 2. The first payment was made on January 2, year 1. The list selling price of the equipment is $3,520,000 and its carrying cost on Howe's books is $2,800,000. The lease is appropriately accounted for as a sales-type lease. The present value of the lease payments at an imputed interest rate of 12% (Howe's incremental borrowing rate) is $3,300,000. What amount of profit on the sale should Howe report for the year ended December 31, year 1?

a. $720,000
b. $500,000
c. $ 90,000
d. $0 (11/93, PI, #44, amended, 4413)

25. Winn Co. manufactures equipment that is sold or leased. On December 31 of the current year, Winn leased equipment to Bart for a 5-year period ending December 31, in five years, at which date ownership of the leased asset will be transferred to Bart. Equal payments under the lease are $22,000 (including $2,000 executory costs) and are due on December 31 of each year. The first payment was made on December 31 of the current year. Collectibility of the remaining lease payments is reasonably assured, and Winn has no material cost uncertainties. The normal sales price of the equipment is $77,000, and cost is $60,000. For the current year ended December 31, what amount of income should Winn realize from the lease transaction?

a. $17,000
b. $22,000
c. $23,000
d. $33,000 (11/90, PI, #33, amended, 1193)

26. On August 1 of the current year, Kern Company leased a machine to Day Company for a 6-year period requiring payments of $10,000 at the beginning of each year. The machine cost $48,000, which is the fair value at the lease date, and has an estimated life of eight years with no residual value. Kern's implicit interest rate is 10% and present value factors are as follows:

Present value of an annuity due of $1 at 10% for 6 periods	4.791
Present value of an annuity due of $1 at 10% for 8 periods	5.868

Kern appropriately recorded the lease as a direct financing lease. At the inception of the lease, the gross lease receivables account balance should be

a. $60,000
b. $58,680
c. $48,000
d. $47,910 (5/85, PI, #6, amended, 9034)

27. Glade Co. leases computer equipment to customers under direct-financing leases. The equipment has no residual value at the end of the lease, and the leases do not contain bargain purchase options. Glade wishes to earn 8% interest on a 5-year lease of equipment with a fair value of $323,400. The present value of an annuity due of $1 at 8% for five years is 4.312. What is the total amount of interest revenue that Glade will earn over the life of the lease?

a. $ 51,600
b. $ 75,000
c. $129,360
d. $139,450 (11/95, FAR, #29, 6111)

28. The following information pertains to a sale and leaseback of equipment by Mega Co. on December 31 of the current year:

Sales price	$400,000
Carrying amount	$300,000
Monthly lease payment	$ 3,250
Present value of lease payments	$ 36,900
Estimated remaining life	25 years
Lease term	1 year
Implicit rate	12%

What amount of deferred gain on the sale should Mega report at December 31 of the current year?

a. $0
b. $ 36,900
c. $ 63,100
d. $100,000 5/92, PI, #31, amended, 2600)

29. In a sale-leaseback transaction, the seller-lessee retains the right to substantially all of the remaining use of the equipment sold. The profit on the sale should be deferred and subsequently amortized by the lessee when the lease is classified as a(an)

	Capital lease	*Operating lease*
a.	No	Yes
b.	No	No
c.	Yes	No
d.	Yes	Yes

(11/87, Theory, #10, 2072)

30. In a sale-leaseback transaction, a gain resulting from the sale should be deferred at the time of the sale-leaseback and subsequently amortized when

I. The seller-lessee has transferred substantially all the risks of ownership.
II. The seller-lessee retains the right to substantially all of the remaining use of the property.

a. I only
b. II only
c. Both I and II
d. Neither I nor II (11/95, FAR, #11, 6093)

31. On December 31 of the current year, Parke Corp. sold Edlow Corp. an airplane with an estimated remaining life of ten years. At the same time, Parke leased back the airplane for three years. Additional information is as follows:

Sales price	$600,000
Carrying amount of airplane at sale date	$100,000
Monthly rental under lease	$ 6,330
Interest rate implicit in the lease as computed by Edlow and known by Parke (this rate is lower than the lessee's incremental borrowing rate)	12%
Present value of operating lease rentals ($6,330 for 36 months @12%)	$190,581

The leaseback is considered an operating lease. In Parke's December 31 current year balance sheet, what amount should be included as deferred revenue on this transaction?

a. $0
b. $190,581
c. $309,419
d. $500,000 (11/88, PI, #21, amended, 9035)

32. Able sold its headquarters building at a gain, and simultaneously leased back the building. The lease was reported as a capital lease. At the time of sale, the gain should be reported as

a. Operating income
b. An extraordinary item, net of income tax
c. An item of other comprehensive income
d. An asset valuation allowance

(11/90, Theory, #24, amended, 2060)

33. On June 30 of the current year, Lang Co. sold equipment with an estimated useful life of eleven years and immediately leased it back for ten years. The equipment's carrying amount was $450,000; the sales price was $430,000; and the present value of the lease payments, which is equal to the fair value of the equipment, was $465,000. In its June 30 current year balance sheet, what amount should Lang report as deferred loss?

a. $35,000
b. $20,000
c. $15,000
d. $0

(11/92, PI, #35, amended, 3268)

34. Rig Co. sold its factory at a gain, and simultaneously leased it back for 10 years. The factory's remaining economic life is 20 years. The lease was reported as an operating lease. At the time of sale, Rig should report the gain as

a. An extraordinary item, net of income tax
b. An asset valuation allowance
c. An item of other comprehensive income
d. A deferred credit

(5/92, Theory, #32, amended, 2725)

35. On January 1, year 1, West Co. entered into a 10-year lease for a manufacturing plant. The annual minimum lease payments are $100,000. In the notes to the December 31, year 2 financial statements, what amounts of subsequent years' lease payments should be disclosed?

	Amount for appropriate required period	*Aggregate amount for the period thereafter*
a.	$100,000	$0
b.	$300,000	$500,000
c.	$500,000	$300,000
d.	$500,000	$0

(11/89, PI, #53, amended, 9038)

36. On July 1, year 1, South Co. entered into a 10-year operating lease for a warehouse facility. The annual minimum lease payments are $100,000. In addition to the base rent, South pays a monthly allocation of the building's operating expenses, which amounted to $20,000 for the year ended June 30, year 2. In the notes to South's June 30, year 2 financial statements, what amounts of subsequent years' lease payments should be disclosed?

a. $100,000 per annum for each of the next five years and $500,000 in the aggregate
b. $120,000 per annum for each of the next five years and $600,000 in the aggregate
c. $100,000 per annum for each of the next five years and $900,000 in the aggregate
d. $120,000 per annum for each of the next five years and $1,080,000 in the aggregate

(11/93, PI, #42, amended, 4411)

Problem 8-2 ADDITIONAL MULTIPLE CHOICE QUESTIONS (28 to 35 minutes)

37. Lease M does not contain a bargain purchase option, but the lease term is equal to 90% of the estimated economic life of the leased property. Lease P does not transfer ownership of the property to the lessee at the end of the lease term, but the lease term is equal to 75% of the estimated economic life of the leased property. How should the lessee classify these leases?

	Lease M	*Lease P*
a.	Capital lease	Operating lease
b.	Capital lease	Capital lease
c.	Operating lease	Capital lease
d.	Operating lease	Operating lease

(11/92, Theory, #27, 3460)

38. Clay Company leased a new machine from Saxe Corp. The following data relate to the lease transaction at the inception of the lease:

Lease term	10 years
Annual rental payable at beginning of each lease year	$50,000
Estimated life of machine	15 years
Implicit interest rate	10%
Present value of an annuity of $1 in advance for 10 periods at 10%	6.76
Present value of annuity of $1 in arrears for 10 periods at 10%	6.15
Fair value of the machine	$400,000

The lease has no renewal option, and the possession of the machine reverts to Saxe when the lease terminates. At the inception of the lease, Clay should record a lease liability of

a. $400,000
b. $338,000
c. $307,500
d. $0 (5/88, PI, #35, amended, 1207)

39. On January 1 of the current year, Mollat Co. signed a 7-year lease for equipment having a 10-year economic life. The present value of the monthly lease payments equaled 80% of the equipment's fair value. The lease agreement provides for neither a transfer of title to Mollat, nor a bargain purchase option. In its current year income statement, Mollat should report

a. Rent expense equal to the current year lease payments
b. Rent expense equal to the current year lease payments less interest expense
c. Lease amortization equal to one-tenth of the equipment's fair value
d. Lease amortization equal to one-seventh of 80% of the equipment's fair value

(5/92, Theory, #34, amended, 2727)

40. Wall Co. leased office premises to Fox Inc. for a 5-year term beginning January 1 of the current year. Under the terms of the operating lease, rent for the first year is $8,000 and rent for years 2 through 5 is $12,500 per annum. However, as an inducement to enter the lease, Wall granted Fox the first six months of the lease rent-free. In its current year December 31 income statement, what amount should Wall report as rental income?

a. $12,000
b. $11,600
c. $10,800
d. $ 8,000 (11/93, PI, #50, amended, 4419)

41. Conn Corp. owns an office building and normally charges tenants $30 per square foot per year for office space. Because the occupancy rate is low, Conn agreed to lease 10,000 square feet to Hanson Co. at $12 per square foot for the first year of a 3-year operating lease. Rent for remaining years will be at the $30 rate. Hanson moved into the building on January 1 of the current year, and paid the first year's rent in advance. What amount of rental revenue should Conn report from Hanson in its current year income statement for the year ended September 30?

a. $ 90,000
b. $120,000
c. $180,000
d. $240,000 (11/92, PI, #45, amended, 3278)

42. On January 1 of the current year, Park Co. signed a 10-year operating lease for office space at $96,000 per year. The lease included a provision for additional rent of 5% of annual company sales in excess of $500,000. Park's sales for the year ended December 31 were $600,000. Upon execution of the lease, Park paid $24,000 as a bonus for the lease. Park's rent expense for the current year ended December 31 is

a. $ 98,400
b. $101,000
c. $103,400
d. $125,000 (5/90, PI, #56, amended, 1200)

43. Robbins Inc. leased a machine from Ready Leasing Co. The lease qualifies as a capital lease and requires 10 annual payments of $10,000 beginning immediately. The lease specifies an interest rate of 12% and a purchase option of $10,000 at the end of the tenth year, even though the machine's estimated value on that date is $20,000. Robbins' incremental borrowing rate is 14%.

The present value of an annuity due of $1 at:
12% for 10 years is 6.328
14% for 10 years is 5.946

The present value of $1 at:
12% for 10 years is .322
14% for 10 years is .270

What amount should Robbins record as lease liability at the beginning of the lease term?

a. $62,160
b. $64,860
c. $66,500
d. $69,720 (5/92, PI, #34, 2605)

44. On December 31, year 1, Roe Co. leased a machine from Colt for a 5-year period. Equal annual payments under the lease are $105,000 (including $5,000 annual executory costs) and are due on December 31 of each year. The first payment was made on December 31, year 1, and the second payment was made on December 31, year 2. The five lease payments are discounted at 10% over the lease term. The present value of minimum lease payments at the inception of the lease and before the first annual payment was $417,000. The lease is appropriately accounted for as a capital lease by Roe. In its December 31, year 2 balance sheet, Roe should report a lease liability of
a. $317,000
b. $315,000
c. $285,300
d. $248,700 (11/90, PI, #22, amended, 1192)

45. On December 29 of the current year, Action Corp. signed a 7-year capital lease for an airplane to transport its sports team around the country. The airplane's fair value was $841,500. Action made the first annual lease payment of $153,000 on December 31 this year. Action's incremental borrowing rate was 12%, and the interest rate implicit in the lease, which was known by Action, was 9%. The following are the rounded present value factors for an annuity due:

9% for 7 years 5.5
12% for 7 years 5.1

What amount should Action report as capital lease liability in its current year December 31 balance sheet?
a. $841,500
b. $780,300
c. $688,500
d. $627,300 (11/92, PI, #33, amended, 3266)

46. On January 1 of the current year, Vick Company as lessee signed a 10-year noncancelable lease for a machine stipulating annual payments of $20,000. The first payment was made on January 1 this year. Vick appropriately treated this transaction as a capital lease. The ten lease payments have a present value of $135,000 at January 1 of the current year, based on implicit interest of 10%. For the current year ended December 31, Vick should record interest expense of
a. $0
b. $ 6,500
c. $11,500
d. $13,500 (11/86, PI, #45, amended, 1215)

47. Neal Corp. entered into a 9-year capital lease on a warehouse on December 31, year 1. Lease payments of $52,000, which include real estate taxes of $2,000, are due annually, beginning on December 31, year 2, and every December 31 thereafter. Neal does not know the interest rate implicit in the lease; Neal's incremental borrowing rate is 9%. The rounded present value of an ordinary annuity for nine years at 9% is 5.6. What amount should Neal report as capitalized lease liability at December 31, year 1?
a. $280,000
b. $291,200
c. $450,000
d. $468,000 (11/93, PI, #39, amended, 4408)

48. On January 2 of the current year, Cole Co. signed an 8-year noncancelable lease for a new machine, requiring $15,000 annual payments at the beginning of each year. The machine has an estimated life of 12 years, with no salvage value. Title passes to Cole at the lease expiration date. Cole used straight-line depreciation for all of its plant assets. Aggregate lease payments have a present value on January 2 of $108,000, based on an appropriate rate of interest. For the current year, Cole should record depreciation (amortization) expense for the leased machine at
a. $0
b. $ 9,000
c. $13,500
d. $15,000 (11/92, PI, #55, amended, 3287)

49. A 6-year capital lease specifies equal minimum annual lease payments. Part of this payment represents interest and part represents a reduction in the net lease liability. The portion of the minimum lease payment in the fourth year applicable to the reduction of the net lease liability should be
a. The same as in the third year
b. Less than in the third year
c. Less than in the fifth year
d. More than in the fifth year
(5/87, Theory, #13, 9032)

50. A 6-year capital lease entered into on December 31 of the current year specified equal minimum annual lease payments due on December 31 of each year. The first minimum annual lease payment, paid on December 31 this year, consists of which of the following?

	Interest expense	Lease liability
a.	Yes	Yes
b.	Yes	No
c.	No	Yes
d.	No	No

(11/95, FAR, #12, amended, 6094)

SIMULATIONS

Problem 8-3 (12 to 18 minutes)

Essay | Research Task

On December 31, year 1, Port Co. sold 6-month old equipment at fair value and leased it back. There was a loss on the sale. Port pays all insurance, maintenance, and taxes on the equipment. The lease provides for eight equal annual payments, beginning December 31, year 2, with a present value equal to 85% of the equipment's fair value and sales price. The lease's term is equal to 80% of the equipment's estimated life. There is no provision for Port to reacquire ownership of the equipment at the end of the lease term.

a. 1. Why is it important to compare an equipment's fair value to its lease payments' present value and its estimated life to the lease term?

2. Evaluate Port's leaseback of the equipment in terms of each of the four criteria for determination of a capital lease.

b. How should Port account for the sale portion of the sale-leaseback transaction at December 31, year 1?

c. How should Port report the leaseback portion of the sale-leaseback transaction on its December 31, year 2 balance sheet?

(5/91, Theory, #4, amended, 6193)

Essay | Research Task

Research Question: "What is the definition of a minor leaseback?"

Paragraph Reference Answer: ______________

Problem 8-4 (40 to 50 minutes)

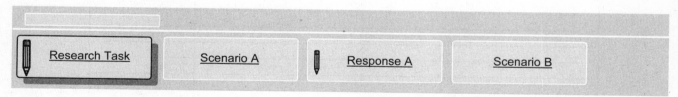

Research Task | Scenario A | Response A | Scenario B

Research Question: When accounting for Leases, how does the lessor account for indirect costs associated with a lease?

Paragraph Reference Answer: ______________

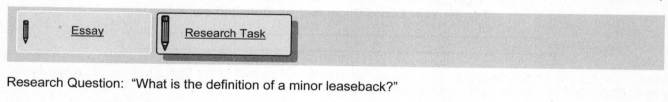

Research Task	Scenario A	Response A	Scenario B

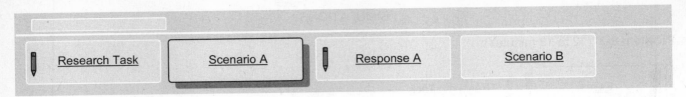

On February 20 of the current year, Riley Inc. purchased a machine for $1,200,000 for the purpose of leasing it. The machine is expected to have a 10-year life, no residual value, and will be depreciated on the straight-line basis. The machine was leased to Sutter Company on March 1 this year for a 4-year period at a monthly rental of $18,000. There is no provision for the renewal of the lease or purchase of the machine by the lessee at the expiration of the lease term. Riley paid $60,000 of commissions associated with negotiating the lease in February of this year.

Research Task	Scenario A	Response A	Scenario B

What expense should Sutter record as a result of the facts given for the current year ended December 31? Show supporting computations in good form.

Sutter Company
Computation of Expense on Operating Lease
For the Year Ended December 31, Current Year

What income or loss before income taxes should Riley record as a result of the facts given for the current year ended December 31? Show supporting computations in good form.

Riley Inc.
Computation of Income Before Income Taxes on Operating Lease
For the Year Ended December 31, Current Year

Research Task	Scenario A	Response A	Scenario B

Dumont Corporation, a lessor of office machines, purchased a new machine for $500,000 on December 31, year 1, which was delivered the same day (by prior arrangement) to Finley Company, the lessee. The following information relating to the lease transaction is available:

- The leased asset has an estimated useful life of seven years which coincides with the lease term.
- At the end of the lease term, the machine will revert to Dumont, at which time it is expected to have a residual value of $60,000 (none of which is guaranteed by Finley).
- Dumont's implicit interest rate is 12%, which is known by Finley.
- Finley's incremental borrowing rate is 14% at December 31, year 1.
- Lease rentals consist of seven equal annual payments, the first of which was paid on December 31, year 1.
- The lease is appropriately accounted for as a direct financing lease by Dumont and as a capital lease by Finley. Both lessor and lessee are calendar year corporations and depreciate all fixed assets on the straight-line basis.

Information of present value factors is as follows:

Present value of $1 for seven periods at 12%	0.452
Present value of $1 for seven periods at 14%	0.400
Present value of an annuity of $1 in advance for seven periods at 12%	5.111
Present value of an annuity of $1 in advance for seven periods at 14%	4.889

(5/81, P1, #5, amended, 9922)

Response B

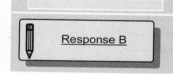

1. Compute the annual rental under the lease. Show all computations in good form, and round all amounts to the nearest dollar.

Dumont Corporation
Computation of Annual Rental Under Direct Financing Lease
Dated December 31, Year 1

2. Compute the amounts of the gross lease rentals receivable and the unearned interest revenue that Dumont should disclose at the inception of the lease on December 31, year 1. Show computations in good form, and round all amounts to the nearest dollar.

Dumont Corporation
Computation of Gross Lease Rentals
Receivable and Unearned Interest
Revenue at Inception of Direct
Financing Lease
Dated December 31, Year 1

3. What expense should Finley record for the year ended December 31, year 2? Show supporting computations in good form, and round all amounts to the nearest dollar.

Finley Company
Computation of Expense on Lease Recorded as a Capital Lease
For the Year Ended December 31, Year 2

SCHEDULE 1
Interest Expense
Year Ended December 31, Year 2

Solution 8-1 MULTIPLE CHOICE ANSWERS

Classification

1. (b) The lease term must be equal to 75% or more of the estimated economic life of the leased property for a capital lease.

2. (c) The question states that the present value of the minimum lease payments exceeds 90% of the fair value of the machine, and also give information that the lease term is equal to or greater than 75% of the estimated life of the asset (15/17 = 88%). The criteria to classify and account for the lease as a capital lease is that at the date of the lease agreement (date of lease inception), the lease must satisfy at least one of the following four criteria: The lease transfers ownership of the property to the lessee by the end of the lease; the lease contains a bargain purchase option; the lease term is equal to 75% or more of the estimated economic life of the leased property (as determined at the inception of the lease); or the present value of the minimum lease payments (excluding executory costs) equals or exceeds 90% of the fair value of the leased property at lease inception. Even though there is no transfer of ownership, the lease meets two of the four criteria to be classified as a capital lease.

3. (d) The lease meets one of the capital lease criteria since the term is equal to 75 percent or more (i.e., 8 / 10 = 80%) of the estimated economic life of the leased equipment. Since there is no indication that the collectibility of the minimum lease

payments is not reasonably assured or that important uncertainties surround the amount of unreimbursable costs yet to be incurred, the lessor apparently has entered into a sales-type or direct financing lease. Therefore, the lessor would recognize interest—not rent—revenue in year 3. In the lessor's balance sheet, an asset entitled "net investment in sales-type (or direct financing) lease" is reported, the balance of which decreases over the lease term. The interest revenue that the lessor recognizes in a period is calculated by multiplying the net lease investment by the implicit lease interest rate. Since the balance of the net lease investment decreases over the lease term and the rate is constant, the interest revenue recognized each period decreases over the lease term. Therefore, the lessor recognizes a smaller amount of interest revenue in year 3 compared to year 2.

Operating Leases

4. (d) Certain operating lease agreements schedule rent increases over the lease term. The effects of scheduled rent increases, which are included in minimum lease payments, should be recognized by lessors and lessees on a straight-line basis over the lease term, unless another systematic and rational allocation basis is more representative of the time pattern in which the leased property is employed physically (SFAS 13). Using factors such as the time value of money, anticipated inflation, or expected future revenues is inappropriate, because these factors do not relate to the time pattern of physical usage of the property. The annual rent expense for this lease is constant over the 20-year term of the lease. Since the lease is an operating lease, the lessee does not report any interest expense as a result of the lease.

5. (d) Revenue from an operating lease is recognized on a straight-line basis, even if the payments vary. Therefore, the total amount of rental revenue from the operating lease is allocated ratably over the 5-year lease term (SFAS 13).

6. (a)

Annual rental payment		$ 50,000
Less: Depreciation	$12,000	
Executory costs (insurance and property taxes)	9,000	
Amortization of initial direct costs ($15,000 / 10 years)	1,500	(22,500)
Net rental income		$ 27,500

7. (d) If rental payments vary from a straight-line basis (e.g., the lessee pays a "lease bonus" at the lease inception or the lease agreement schedules rent increases over the lease term), the expense for the lessee and the revenue for the lessor are recognized on a straight-line basis unless another systematic and rational basis is more representative of the time pattern in which the benefit derives from the leased property.

Lessee's Capital Lease

8. (c) SFAS 13, ¶10 states, "The lessee shall record a capital lease as an asset and an obligation at an amount equal to the present value at the beginning of the lease term of minimum lease payments during the lease term, excluding that portion of payments representing executory costs such as insurance, maintenance, and taxes to be paid by the lessor, together with any profit thereon. However, if the amount so determined exceeds the fair value of the leased property at the inception of the lease, the amount recorded as the asset and obligation shall be the fair value."

9. (b) The lease is a capital lease because the lease term is equal to 75% or more (10 / 12 = 83.3%) of the estimated useful life of the leased property. Therefore, the lessee, at the lease inception, records the asset and the corresponding lease liability at the lesser of the present value (PV) of the minimum lease payments (MLP) or the fair value of the lease property. Because the annual rental is payable at the *end* of each lease year, the PV factor for an annuity in *arrears* is to be used (i.e., the PV factor for an annuity in advance can only be used when the first annual rental payment is made immediately). The capital lease obligation is recorded at the PV of the MLP ($100,000 × 6.15 = $615,000) because it is less than the fair value of the machine ($700,000).

10. (b) The capital lease obligation must be reduced by only the principal portion of the $9,000 payment. The $75,000 already is net of the $1,364 payment made on January 2, year 2, and must be further reduced by the amount of amortization of the lease obligation for year 2. The lessor's implicit rate of interest is known to the lessee and it is less than the lessee's incremental borrowing rate, thus the lessee must use the lessor's implicit rate.

Noncurrent capital lease obligation, 12/31, yr 2	$75,000
Less: Current portion [$9,000 – ($75,000 × 10%)]	(1,500)
Noncurrent capital lease obligation, 12/31, yr 3	$73,500

11. (a) If the bargain purchase option (BPO) had been included in the capitalized lease amount, the final balance would have equaled the amount of the BPO. Since the balance was zero, the BPO must have been excluded. Subtracting the annual interest amount from the lease payable balance would have

resulted in a negative balance, rather than zero. Subtracting the present value of the BPO from the present value of the annual payments would have caused the beginning lease payable balance to be understated and a negative balance before the lease end. Discounting the annual payments as an ordinary (paid in arrears, rather than in advance) annuity, would have resulted in an understated beginning lease payable balance and a negative balance before the lease end.

12. (b) The lease qualifies as a capital lease because the lease term (10 years) equals or exceeds 75% of the machine's estimated life (12 years). The amount to be capitalized is the present value of the minimum lease payments (MLP), which does *not* include the $50,000 purchase option (only *bargain* purchase options are included in MLP).

Annual lease payment	$ 40,000
PV annuity in advance factor, i = 14%, n = 10	× 5.95
Capitalized lease amount	$238,000

13. (a) A capital lease refers to a capitalized lease from a lessee's viewpoint. Any guarantee by the lessee of the residual value at the lease term expiration is included in minimum lease payments (MLP). When the lessee agrees to make up any deficiency below a stated amount in the lessor's realization of the residual value, the guarantee to be included in the MLP shall be the stated amount, rather than an estimate of the deficiency. The lessee records the MLP at present value (SFAS 13).

14. (b) The lease is a capital lease because the lease term is equal to 75% or more (10 / 10 = 100%) of the property's estimated economic life. At the lease inception, Day records the asset and corresponding lease liability at the lesser of the fair value of the leased property (not provided) or the present value of the minimum lease payments (MLP). The implicit 10% interest rate of the lease is used to capitalize the lease liability because it is known by Day and it is lower than Day's incremental 12% rate. A guarantee by a third party related to the lessee of the residual value at the expiration of the lease term is considered to be a MLP. However, there is no indication that the third party that has guaranteed to pay Ward a residual value of $5,000 is related to the lessee. Therefore, the guarantee of the residual value by the apparently unrelated third party is not used to determine the capitalized lease liability.

Annual minimum lease payments	$ 10,000
Factor for 10% interest rate	× 6.1446
Balance of capitalized lease liability, 12/31	$61,446

15. (a) At the inception of a capital lease, the lessee records an asset and a liability. This liability is both current and noncurrent, with the current portion being the principal paid during the next year. Therefore, the reduction of the lease liability in the current year equals the current lease liability at the end of the previous year.

16. (b) At a capital lease inception, the lessee records an asset and a liability. This liability is both current and noncurrent, with the current portion being the next year's principal payment.

Minimum lease payment (MLP), 12/31, year 2		$ 20,000
Balance of capital lease obligation (CLO) before payment, 12/30, year 1	$135,000	
Less: MLP, 12/31, year 1	(20,000)	
Balance of CLO, 12/31, year 1	115,000	
Times: Implicit interest rate	× 10%	
Less interest portion of 12/31, year 2 MLP		(11,500)
Portion of 12/31, year 2 MLP allocable to principal reduction		$ 8,500

Capital Lease Amortization

17. (d) If a lease qualifies as a capital lease because it contains a bargain purchase option (BPO), then the lessee depreciates the leased asset over its estimated economic life (SFAS 13). The leased asset is recorded on the books at $240,000 and is depreciated over its estimated economic life of 8 years, since the lessee expects to exercise the BPO. The lessee amortizes the leased asset in the same manner as owned assets. The equipment's salvage value is its estimated fair value at the end of its estimated life. The annual depreciation expense Nori recognizes on the equipment is <u>$27,500</u> [i.e., ($240,000 – $20,000) / 8].

18. (d) If the lease is classified as a capital lease because it satisfies criteria other than the first two lease classification criteria (transfer of ownership or bargain purchase option), the lessee will amortize the leased asset over the lease term (rather than the life of the asset). Depreciation is calculated on the present value of the minimum lease payments because that amount equaled the fair value of the leased property at inception. ($505,000 / 9 years = 56,111)

19. (b)

Balance before payment, 12/31, year 1		$316,500
Less: Minimum lease payment, 12/31, year 1		(50,000)
Balance after MLP, 12/31, year 1		266,500
MLP, 12/31, year 2	$50,000	
Less: Portion allocable to interest ($266,500 × 10%)	(26,650)	
Less principal reduction from 12/31, year 2 MLP		(23,350)
Balance after MLP, 12/31, year 2		$243,150

20. (d) Lessee's accounting for a capital lease requires the use of the effective interest method. The present value of the lease payments is recorded as the lease liability. Interest expense is based on this amount. The balance of the $200,000 lease payment is applied to principal, reducing the lease liability. Interest expense in each subsequent year is based upon the lease liability as reduced by previous reductions in principal.

Lease liability	$758,000
Interest rate	× 10%
Interest expense	$ 75,800

Sales-Type Leases

21. (a) In a sales-type lease, the lessor recognizes two types of income: (1) manufacturer's or dealer's profit, and (2) interest income. The profit is the excess of the fair value of the leased property over the cost at the lease inception, and it is recognized fully at lease inception. The difference between the gross investment in the lease and the sum of the present values of the two components of the gross investment is unearned income. The unearned income is amortized over the lease term as interest revenue using the interest method.

22. (b) The interest revenue is determined by applying the interest rate implicit in the lease to the lessor's net receivable. The excess of the fair value of leased property at the lease inception over its cost or carrying amount is dealer's profit from a sales-type lease and recognized fully at lease inception.

Cash selling price of equipment	$ 3,520,000
Equipment cost	(2,800,000)
Profit on sale	$ 720,000

Gross investment before receipt, 7/1 ($600,000 × 8)	$ 4,800,000
Less: Receipt, 7/1	(600,000)
Gross investment after receipt, 7/1	4,200,000
Less: Unearned interest revenue ($4,800,000 – $3,520,000)	(1,280,000)
Net receivable, 7/1	2,920,000
Times: Implicit interest rate (10% / 2)	× 5%
Interest revenue	$ 146,000

23. (c)

Net investment in lease (PV), 7/1	$135,000
Less: Payment received, 7/3	(20,000)
Net investment in lease after 7/3 payment	115,000
Interest rate	10%
Whole year interest revenue	11,500
July through December, 1/2 year	0.5
Interest revenue	$ 5,750

24. (b) The fair value of the leased property at the lease inception is the present value of the minimum lease payments at the lessor's incremental borrowing rate. The excess of the fair value of leased property at the lease inception over its cost or carrying amount is the dealer's profit from a sales-type lease and recognized fully at lease inception.

FV of leased property at lease inception	$ 3,300,000
Less: Carrying amount of equipment	(2,800,000)
Dealer's profit recognized at inception	$ 500,000

25. (a) The lease qualifies as a sales-type lease because (1) the lease transfers ownership of the property to the lessee by the end of the lease term, (2) collectibility of the minimum lease payments is reasonably assured, and (3) no important uncertainties surround the amount of unreimbursable costs yet to be incurred by the lessor under the lease. In the current year, the lessor should recognize a manufacturer's profit of the excess of the normal sales price of the equipment over its cost ($77,000 – $60,000 = $17,000). The lessor does not recognize any interest income from this lease in the current year because the lease term began on December 31.

Direct Financing Leases

26. (a) The gross lease receivable under a direct financing lease is the sum of the minimum lease payments (net of executory costs) plus the unguaranteed residual value accruing to the lessor (SFAS 13). In this question, there is no unguaranteed residual involved; therefore, the receivable is calculated as 6 annual payments of $10,000, or $60,000.

27. (a) The unearned interest income is the difference between the lessor's gross investment in the lease and the fair value of the leased asset. The fair value of the equipment is divided by the present value of an annuity due at 8% to get the annual payment. The annual payment times the number of payments is the gross investment. [$323,400 / 4.312 = $75,000; $75,000 × 5 = $375,000; $375,000 – $323,400 = $51,600]

Sale-Leaseback Transaction

28. (a) Gains and losses on sale-leaseback transactions generally are deferred and amortized over the term of the lease. There are two exceptions to this general rule: (1) where the seller-lessee retains only a *minor* portion of the use of the property, or (2) where the seller-lessee retains more than a minor portion but less than substantially all of the use of the property. The seller-lessee is deemed to have retained a *minor* portion of the use of the property if the present value of the minimum lease payments is less than 10% of the fair value of the property. In this case, the sale and leaseback are accounted for as two separate transactions and the full amount of the gain or loss realized on the sale of the property is recognized at the date of sale. In this question, the present value of the minimum lease payments is less than 10% of the fair value of the property [i.e., $36,900 < ($400,000 × 10%)]. Therefore, the seller-lessee recognizes the full $100,000 (i.e., $400,000 sales price – $300,000 carrying amount) profit from the equipment sale at the sale date. No portion of the profit from the sale would be reported as deferred revenue.

29. (d) In this sale-leaseback transaction, the seller-lessee retains the right to substantially all of the remaining life of the equipment. If the lease meets one of the criteria for a capital lease, any profit on the sale is deferred and amortized in proportion to the amortization of the leased asset. If the seller-lessee accounts for the lease as an operating lease, any profit on the sale is deferred and amortized in proportion to the related gross rental charged to expense over the lease term.

30. (b) A sale-leaseback transaction in which the seller-lessee has transferred substantially all the risks of ownership is in substance a sale and should be accounted for on the separate terms of the sale and of the leaseback, unless the rentals called for by the leaseback are unreasonable in relation to current market conditions (SFAS 28). Thus, a gain on the sale is recognized at the point of sale and is not deferred. A sale-leaseback transaction in which the seller-lessee retains the right to substantially all of the remaining use of the property is in substance a financing transaction and the gain should be deferred and amortized (SFAS 28).

31. (b) This situation is a sale-leaseback transaction. SFAS 28 requires that when the seller-lessee retains *more than a minor part but less than substantially all* of the use of the property through the leaseback, any gain is recognized immediately to the extent that it exceeds the present value of the minimum lease payments. The remainder of the gain is deferred and recognized over the lease term as a reduction of reported rent expense. ($190,581 / $600,000 = 31.8%). Of the $500,000 ($600,000 – $100,000) gain realized on the sale of the airplane, <u>$190,581</u> (the present value of the lease rentals) should be reported as deferred revenue. The seller-lessee is deemed to have retained a *minor* part of the use of the property if the present value of the lease payments is less than 10% of the fair value of the property. On the other hand, *substantially all* means that the present value of the lease payments exceeds 90% of the fair value of the property.

32. (d) The gain on the sale of an asset in a sale-leaseback is deferred and amortized in proportion to the amortization of the leased asset, if the lease is a capital lease (SFAS 28, ¶3). The building is reported net of the unamortized deferred profit on the seller-lessee's balance sheet.

33. (b) Since the fair value of the asset sold is more than its carrying amount (i.e., $465,000 > $450,000), the $20,000 (i.e., $450,000 – $430,000) indicated loss on the sale is in substance a prepayment of rent. Thus, the $20,000 indicated loss should be deferred and amortized as prepaid rent.

34. (d) This situation is a sale-leaseback transaction. SFAS 28, 3 states that any profit or loss on the sale should be deferred and amortized in proportion to the related gross rental charged to expense over the lease term, if an operating lease (or in proportion to the amortization of the leased asset, if a capital lease). Thus, at the time of sale, the gain on the factory sale is reported as a deferred credit. Gains or losses on sale-leaseback transactions are not reported as extraordinary items or as items of other comprehensive income. Since the seller-lessee does not report an asset for the leased property under an operating lease, the gain on the sale-leaseback cannot be reported as an asset valuation allowance. The gain on the sale-leaseback is reported as a deferred credit in the liabilities section of the balance sheet.

Disclosure

35. (c) West discloses the minimum lease payments (MLP) of <u>$500,000</u> ($100,000 × 5) pertaining to the next five succeeding fiscal years *and* the <u>$300,000</u> [$100,000 × (10 – 2 – 5)] of MLP pertaining to the fiscal years after this 5-year period.

36. (c) For operating leases having initial or remaining noncancelable lease terms in excess of one year, the lessee should disclose future minimum lease payments (MLP) required as of the latest balance sheet date for *each of the five succeeding fiscal years and in the aggregate.* Since South is required

to make annual MLP of $100,000 over the remaining noncancelable 9-year (i.e., 10 – 1) lease term, South should disclose $100,000 per annum for each of the next five years and $900,000 (i.e., $100,000 × 9) in the aggregate for the subsequent years' lease payments in the financial statement notes.

Problem 8-2 ADDITIONAL MULTIPLE CHOICE ANSWERS

Classification

37. (b) SFAS 13, ¶7 states that a lease shall be classified as a capital lease by the lessee if at inception the lease meets one of four criteria: (1) the lease transfers ownership of the property to the lessee by the end of the lease term, (2) the lease contains a bargain purchase option, (3) the lease term is equal to 75% or more of the property's estimated economic life, (4) the present value of the minimum lease payment (excluding executory costs) equals or exceeds 90% of the fair value of the leased property. Since both leases meet the third criterion, both leases are capital leases.

38. (d) Clay should not record a lease liability at the lease inception as none of the following criteria of a capital lease are met: (1) The lease does *not* transfer ownership of the property to the lessee by the end of the lease term. (The possession of the machine reverts to the lessor when the lease terminates.) (2) The lease does *not* contain a bargain purchase option. (3) The lease term is *less than* 75 percent (10 / 15 = 66.7%) of the estimated economic life of the leased property. (4) The present value (PV) of the minimum lease payments (MLP) at the beginning of the lease term is *less than* 90% [($50,000 × 6.76) / $400,000 = 84.5%] of the fair value of the leased property at the inception of the lease. (The PV of the MLP in question is computed using the PV of annuity of $1 in advance because the rental payments are to be made at the *beginning* of each lease year.)

Operating Leases

39. (a) The lessee has entered into an operating lease because none of the capital lease criteria are met. The lease does not transfer ownership of the equipment to the lessee by the end of the lease term nor does it contain a bargain purchase option. The lease term is *less than* 75% (i.e., 7 / 10 = 70%) of the estimated economic life of the equipment and the present value of the minimum lease payments at the beginning of the lease term is *less than* 90% (i.e., 80% < 90%) of the fair value of the equipment. The lessee records neither an asset nor an obligation for an operating lease; instead, the lessee records its lease payments as rent expense.

40. (c) Accrual accounting recognizes revenue in the period(s) earned, rather than only when the related cash is received. Total rent revenue to be received is allocated ratably over the lease term.

Rental receipts during year 1 ($8,000 × 6/12)	$ 4,000
Rental receipts during years 2 - 5 ($12,500 × 4)	50,000
Rental receipts over lease term	54,000
Divide by: Years in lease term	/ 5
Annual rental revenue recognized	$ 10,800

41. (c) Accrual accounting generally recognizes revenues in the periods earned, rather than when the related cash is received. The rental revenue is allocated ratably over the lease term.

Receipts during 1st year (10,000 × $12)	$120,000
Receipts during 2nd & 3rd years (10,000 × $30 × 2)	600,000
Total rental revenue over lease term	720,000
Divide by: Months in lease term (3 × 12)	/ 36
Monthly rental revenue	20,000
Times: Months rented during period	× 9
Rental revenue, year ended 9/30	$180,000

42. (c) Accrual accounting recognizes expense in the period incurred, rather than only when the related cash is paid. The lease bonus is allocated ratably over the lease term as part of rent expense.

Equal annual rental payment	$ 96,000
Amortization of lease bonus ($24,000 / 10)	2,400
High sales premium [($600,000 – $500,000) × 5%]	5,000
Rental expense	$103,400

Lessee's Capital Lease

43. (c) The lessee records a capital lease as an asset and an obligation at an amount equal to the lesser of the fair value of the leased property (not provided) or the present value (PV) of the minimum lease payments (MLP). The MLP include the minimum rental payments called for by the lease over the lease term and payment called for by the bargain purchase option (BPO). The purchase option

qualifies as a BPO because the lessee is permitted to purchase the leased property for a price which is significantly lower than the expected fair value of the property at the option's exercise date (i.e., $10,000 < $20,000). Since the annual rental payment is payable at the *beginning* of each lease year, the PV factor for an *annuity due* is used. The PV of the MLP is computed using the lessor's implicit interest rate of 12%, since it is both known to the lessee (i.e., it was specified in the lease) and lower than the lessee's incremental borrowing rate.

PV of annual payments ($10,000 × 6.328)	$63,280
PV of bargain purchase option ($10,000 × 0.322)	3,220
Capital lease liability at beginning of lease term	$66,500

44. (d) Roe's annual MLP is $100,000 (i.e., $105,000 – $5,000). The lessor's obligation to pay executory costs (such as insurance, maintenance, and taxes in connection with leased property) is excluded from the MLP.

Balance before payment, 12/31, year 1		$ 417,000
Less: MLP, 12/31, year 1		(100,000)
Balance after MLP, 12/31, year 1		317,000
MLP, 12/31, year 2	$100,000	
Interest expense ($317,000 × 10%)	(31,700)	
Less principal reduction		(68,300)
Balance after MLP, 12/31, year 2		$ 248,700

45. (c) The lessee records a capital lease as an asset and an obligation at an amount equal to the lesser of the present value (PV) of the minimum lease payments (MLP) or the fair value of the leased property. The PV of MLP is computed using the lessor's implicit rate in the lease of 9%, since it is known to the lessee and lower than the lessee's incremental borrowing rate. Since the annual rental payment is payable at the *beginning* of each lease year, the PV factor for an *annuity due* is used. The capital lease obligation is recorded at the PV of the MLP ($153,000 × 5.5 = $841,500) on 12/29 because this amount does not exceed the fair value of the leased property (i.e., $841,500). The capital lease liability in the 12/31 current year balance sheet reflects the first annual rental payment made 12/29 ($841,500 – $153,000 = $688,500).

46. (c) Vick records interest expense based on the lease obligation outstanding during the year.

PV of lease obligation, January 1	$135,000
January 1 payment	(20,000)
Lease obligation outstanding	115,000
Implicit interest rate	× 10%
Interest expense	$ 11,500

47. (a) At a capital lease inception, the lessee records an asset and corresponding lease liability at the lesser of the fair value of the leased property (not provided in this problem) or the present value of the minimum lease payments (MLP). The lessee's incremental borrowing rate of 9% is used because the lessee does not know the rate implicit in the lease. The lessee's obligation to pay executory costs (such as insurance, maintenance, and taxes) are excluded from the amount of the annual MLP, thus the amount of Neal's MLP is $50,000 (i.e., $52,000 – $2,000). Neal's first MLP is not due until 12/31, year 2. Thus, in its 12/31, year 1 balance sheet, Neal should report a capitalized lease liability of $280,000 (i.e., $50,000 × 5.6).

48. (b) If a lease qualifies as a capital lease because it transfers ownership of the leased asset by the lease end or contains a bargain purchase option, then the lessee depreciates the leased asset over its estimated economic life (SFAS 13). The leased asset is recorded at $108,000 (given) and depreciated over its estimated economic life of 12 years, since title passes at the lease expiration. [($108,000 – $0) / 12 = $9,000]

49. (c) Obligations under capital leases are amortized using the interest method. Under this method, uniform payments are comprised of (1) interest expense and (2) principal reduction. Since part of each payment reduces the principal balance, the interest portion of the next payment is based on a smaller principal balance, and less interest is recognized. Each successive uniform payment is comprised of a decreasing amount of interest and an increasing amount of principal.

50. (c) When the first annual lease payment is paid at the inception of a capital lease, the whole payment reduces the lease liability (no time has passed for interest to accrue). Subsequent payments are allocated between interest expense and lease obligation reduction.

PERFORMANCE BY SUBTOPICS

Each category below parallels a subtopic covered in Chapter 8. Record the number and percentage of questions you correctly answered in each subtopic area.

Classification

Question #	Correct √
1	
2	
3	
# Questions	3
# Correct	
% Correct	

Operating Leases

Question #	Correct √
4	
5	
6	
7	
# Questions	4
# Correct	
% Correct	

Lessee's Capital Lease

Question #	Correct √
8	
9	
10	
11	
12	
13	
14	
15	
16	
# Questions	9
# Correct	
% Correct	

Capital Lease Amortization

Question #	Correct √
17	
18	
19	
20	
# Questions	4
# Correct	
% Correct	

Sales-Type Leases

Question #	Correct √
21	
22	
23	
24	
25	
# Questions	5
# Correct	
% Correct	

Direct Financing Leases

Question #	Correct √
26	
27	
# Questions	2
# Correct	
% Correct	

Sale-Leaseback Transaction

Question #	Correct √
28	
29	
30	
31	
32	
33	
34	
# Questions	7
# Correct	
% Correct	

Disclosure

Question #	Correct √
35	
36	
# Questions	2
# Correct	
% Correct	

SIMULATION SOLUTIONS

Solution 8-3

Essay—Sale-Leaseback Transactions

a. 1. Comparisons of an equipment's fair value to its lease payments' present value, and of its estimated life to the lease term, are used to determine whether the lease is equivalent to an **installment sale,** and therefore is a **capital lease.**

2. A lease is categorized as a capital lease, if, at the date of the lease agreement, it meets any one of four criteria. As the lease has no provision for Port to reacquire ownership of the equipment, it **fails** the two criteria of **transfer of ownership at the end of the lease** and a **bargain purchase option.** Port's lease payments, with a present value equaling 85% of the equipment's fair value, **fail** the criterion for a **present value equaling or exceeding 90% of the equipment's fair value.** However, the lease would be **classified as a capital lease,** because its term of 80% of the equipment's estimated life **exceeds the criterion** of being **at least 75% of the equipment's estimated life.**

b. Port should account for the sale portion of the sale-leaseback transaction at December 31, year 1, by **increasing cash** for the **sale price, decreasing equipment** by the **carrying amount,** and **recognizing a loss** for the excess of the equipment's carrying amount over its sale price.

c. On the December 31, year 2 balance sheet, the equipment should be included as a **fixed asset,** at the **lease payment's present value** at **December 31, year 1, less year 2 amortization.**

On the December 31, year 2 balance sheet, the **lease obligation** will equal the **lease payments' present value** at December 31, year 1, **less principal repaid** December 31, year 2. This amount will be reported in **current liabilities** for the principal to be **repaid in year 3,** and the balance in **noncurrent liabilities.**

Research

FAS 28, Par. 12

12. Footnote+ indicates that a test based on the 90 percent criterion of FASB Statement No. 13 could be used as a guideline to distinguish a "minor" leaseback. In that context, if the present value of the leaseback based on reasonable rentals is 10 percent or less of the fair value of the asset sold, the leaseback could be presumed to be minor. Some

respondents suggested that "minor" be defined using a test based on the 75 percent of economic life criterion of Statement No. 13. In that context, if the leaseback encompassed less than 25 percent of the remaining economic life of the asset sold, the leaseback could be presumed to be minor.

Solution 8-4

Research

FAS 13, Par. 19

c. Initial direct costs shall be deferred and allocated over the lease term in proportion to the recognition of rental income. However, initial direct costs may be charged to expense as incurred if the effect is not materially different from that which would have resulted from the use of the method prescribed in the preceding sentence.

Response A

Rental expense ($18,000 × 10 months)		$180,000

Rental income ($18,000 × 10 months)		$ 180,000
Deduct:		
Depreciation [($1,200,000 / 10) × 10/12]	$100,000	
Amortization of commission for negotiating lease ($60,000 × 10/48)	$ 12,500	(112,500)
Income from operating lease		$ 67,500

Response B

1.

Cost of leased machine	$500,000
Deduct present value of estimated residual value [$60,000 × 0.452] (present value of $1 at 12% for 7 periods)	(27,120)
Net investment to be recovered	472,880
Present value of an annuity of $1 in advance for 7 periods at 12%	/ 5.111
Annual rental	$ 92,522

2.

Gross lease rentals receivable ($92,522 × 7)		$ 647,654
Deduct recovery of net investment in machine on capital lease		
Cost of machine	$500,000	
Residual value of machine	(60,000)	(440,000)
Unearned interest revenue		$ 207,654

3.

Depreciation [$472,880 / 7]	$ 67,554
Interest expense	45,643
Total expense on lease	$ 113,197

SCHEDULE 1

Liability under capital lease (initial value) [$92,522 × 5.111] (present value of an annuity of $1 in advance for 7 periods at 12%*)	$ 472,880
Deduct lease payment on December 31, year 1	(92,522)
Balance December 31, year 1 (after initial payment)	380,358
Interest rate	× 12%*
Interest expense year ended December 31, year 2	$ 45,643

*Finley Company must use Dumont Corporation's (Lessor's) implicit rate of 12% (which is known to it), since it is lower than Finley's incremental borrowing rate+ of 14%.

What is eligible to be tested?

From the AICPA's *Uniform CPA Examination Candidate Bulletin*:

"Accounting and auditing pronouncements are eligible to be tested on the Uniform CPA Examination in the window beginning six months after a pronouncement's *effective* date, unless early application is permitted. When early application is permitted, the new pronouncement is eligible to be tested in the window beginning six months after the *issuance* date. In this case, both the old and new pronouncements may be tested until the old pronouncement is superseded.

For the federal taxation area, the Internal Revenue Code and federal tax regulations in effect six months before the beginning of the current window may be tested on the Uniform CPA Examination.

For all other materials covered in the Regulation and Business Environment and Concepts sections, material eligible to be tested includes federal laws in the window beginning six months after their *effective* date and uniform acts in the window beginning one year after their adoption by a simple majority of the jurisdictions."

See the **Practical Advice** section of this volume for additional information.

CHANGE ALERTS

SFAS 158, Employers' Accounting for Defined Benefit Pension and Other Postretirement Plans — an amendment of FASB Statements No. 87, 88, 106, and 132(R) (Issued 9/06)

In September 2006, the FASB issued Statement of Financial Accounting Standard No. 158, *Employers' Accounting for Defined Benefit Pension and Other Postretirement Plans.* This statement is an amendment of FASB Statements No. 87, 88, 106, and 132(R).

The objective of this statement is to improve the reporting of employers' obligations for pensions and other postretirement benefits by recognizing the overfunded or underfunded status of defined benefit postretirement plans as an asset or a liability in the statement of financial position. Specifically, this means that a sponsoring entity would recognize all previously unrecognized items (such as unrecognized actuarial gains and losses) even when the plan is fully funded.

This Statement is effective for a public entity with its fiscal year ending after December 15, 2006. The effective date for a nonpublic entity would be the fiscal year ending after June 15, 2007. (Chapter 9)

Editor's Note: Accounting and auditing pronouncements are eligible to be tested on the Uniform CPA Examination in the testing window beginning six months after an announcement's effective date, unless early application is permitted. The editors expect these new changes to be tested beginning in the July/August 2007 test cycle.

CHAPTER 9

POSTEMPLOYMENT BENEFITS

I. **Overview** 9-2
   A. Introduction 9-2
   B. Amendment (SFAS 158) 9-2
   C. Disclosures 9-3
   D. Defined Contribution Plans 9-5

II. **Single-Employer Defined Benefit Pension Plans** 9-5
   A. Overview 9-5
   B. Net Periodic Pension Cost 9-7
   C. Recognition of Liabilities & Assets Prior to SFAS 158 9-11
   D. Recognition of Liabilities & Assets Following Adoption of SFAS 158 9-13

III. **Benefit Settlement & Curtailment (SFAS 88)** 9-14
   A. Settlements 9-14
   B. Curtailments 9-14
   C. Settlements vs. Curtailments 9-14
   D. Termination Benefits 9-15
   E. Segment Disposal 9-15

IV. **Other Postretirement Benefits** 9-15
   A. Attribution Method 9-15
   B. Net Postretirement Benefit Cost 9-15
   C. Recognition of Liabilities & Assets 9-16

EXAM COVERAGE: Historically, exam coverage of the topics in Chapter 9 has been 1 to 5 percent of the FAR section. These questions tend to concentrate on defined benefit pension plans. More information regarding exam coverage is included in Appendix B, *Practical Advice*.

CHAPTER 9

POSTEMPLOYMENT BENEFITS

I. Overview

A. Introduction

There are many similarities in accounting for pensions and accounting for other postretirement benefits. SFAS 87, *Employers' Accounting for Pensions,* provides guidance on pensions. SFAS 106, *Employers' Accounting for Postretirement Benefits Other Than Pensions,* provides guidance on postretirement benefits. SFAS 132(R), *Employers' Disclosures About Pensions and Other Postretirement Benefits,* requires uniform disclosures about pension and nonpension benefit plans to provide information to financial statement users about benefit plans sponsored by employers. SFAS 158, *Employers' Accounting for Defined Benefit Pension and Other Postretirement Plans,* amends each of these statements. This chapter illustrates accounting for pensions in detail and then highlights the differences in accounting for postretirement benefits.

B. Amendment (SFAS 158)

SFAS 158 was issued in September 2006 by the Financial Accounting Standards Board (FASB). This statement is an amendment of FASB Statements No. 87, 88, 106, and 132(R). The objective of this statement is to improve the reporting of employers' obligations for pensions and other postretirement benefits by recognizing the overfunded or underfunded status of defined benefit postretirement plans as an asset or a liability in the statement of financial position.

1. **Effective** This statement is effective for a public entity with its fiscal year ending after December 15, 2006. The effective date for a nonpublic entity would be the fiscal year ending after June 15, 2007.

2. **CPA Examination** Accounting and auditing pronouncements are eligible to be tested on the Uniform CPA Examination in the testing window beginning six months after an announcement's effective date. Defined benefit pension and other postretirement plan changes in this statement will be eligible to be tested in the July/August 2007 test cycle.

3. **Fundamentals** This statement does not change the basic approach to measuring plan assets, benefit obligations, or net periodic benefit cost. It does result in the following requirements.

    a. **Recognition** An employer that is a business entity must recognize the following:

        (1) In its statement of financial position, the overfunded or underfunded status of a defined benefit postretirement plan measured as the difference between the fair value of plan assets and the benefit obligation. For a pension plan, the benefit obligation would be the projected benefit obligation; for any other retirement benefit plan, such as a retiree health care plan, the benefit obligation would be the accumulated postretirement benefit obligation.

        (2) As a component of other comprehensive income, net of tax, the actuarial gains and losses and the prior service costs and credits that arise during the period that are not recognized as components of net periodic benefit costs. Also, any transition asset or obligation remaining from the initial application of SFAS 87 or SFAS 106 would be recognized as a component of comprehensive income. Amounts recognized in accumulated other comprehensive income would be adjusted as they are subsequently recognized as components of net periodic benefit cost pursuant to the recognition and amortization provisions of SFAS 87 and SFAS 106.

b. **Measurement Date** The measurement of plan assets and benefit obligations will be the date of the employer's statement of financial position, effective for fiscal years ending after December 15, 2008. Currently entities can use a measurement date up to three months prior to their statement of financial position.

c. **Presentation** The excess of the fair value of plan assets over the benefit obligation should be classified as a noncurrent asset. A liability will be recognized if the obligation exceeds the fair value of plan assets. Each underfunded plan could be a current liability, a noncurrent liability, or a combination of both. The current portion of a net postretirement liability represents the amount of benefit payments expected to be paid in the next 12 months (or operating cycle, if longer) that cannot be funded from existing plan assets (measured as the excess benefits payments expected to be paid in the next 12 months, or operating cycle if longer, over the fair value of plan assets).

4. **Summary** SFAS 158 produces changes in recognition, measurement date, presentation, and disclosures of defined benefit pension and other post retirement plans. The primary change is that now the overfunded or underfunded status of defined benefit postretirement plans will be recognized as an asset or a liability in the statement of financial position. Another major change is that wherever the concept of unrecognized gain or loss from previous periods is used, it is now replaced with gain or loss recognized in accumulated other comprehensive income.

C. Disclosures

SFAS 132(R) requires disclosures about the assets, obligations, cash flows, and net periodic benefit cost of defined benefit pension plans and other defined benefit postretirement plans. In addition, it requires disclosure of significant events occurring during the period that are not otherwise apparent in the disclosures. The required information should be provided separately for pension plans and for other postretirement benefit plans.

1. **Requirements** SFAS 132(R) requires the following:

a. A reconciliation of beginning and ending balances of the benefit obligation showing separately the effects during the period of the following components: service cost, interest cost, contributions by plan participants, actuarial gains and losses, foreign currency exchange rate changes, benefits paid, plan amendments, business combinations, divestitures, curtailments, settlements, and special termination benefits.

b. A reconciliation of beginning and ending balances of the fair value of plan assets showing separately the effects during the period attributable to the following: actual return on plan assets, foreign currency exchange rate changes, contributions by the employer, contributions by employees or retirees, benefits paid, business combinations, divestitures, curtailments, and settlements.

c. The funded status of the plans, the amounts not recognized in the balance sheet, and the amounts recognized in the balance sheet including:

(1) The amount of any unamortized prior service cost.

(2) The amount of any unrecognized net gain or loss including asset gains and losses not yet reflected in the market-related value.

(3) The amount of any remaining unamortized transition amount from initially applying SFAS 87 or SFAS 106.

(4) The net pension and other postretirement benefit prepaid assets or accrued liabilities.

(5) Any intangible asset or accumulated element of other comprehensive income recognized under SFAS 87 because of an underfunded pension obligation (the minimum liability computation of SFAS 87).

Note: This disclosure was amended by SFAS 158 to read: "The funded status of the plans and the amounts recognized in the balance sheet showing separately the assets and the current and noncurrent liabilities recognized."

d. The amount of net periodic benefit cost recognized showing separately the following components: service cost, interest cost, expected return on plan assets, gain or loss, prior service cost or credit, and gain or loss recognized due to settlements or curtailments. (as slightly modified by SFAS 158)

e. Amount included in other comprehensive income (OCI) for the period because of a change in the additional minimum pension liability.

Note: This disclosure was amended by SFAS 158 to read: "Separately the net gain or loss and net prior service cost or credit recognized in other comprehensive income for the period pursuant to paragraphs 25 and 29 of Statement 87 and paragraphs 52 and 56 of Statement 106, as amended, and reclassification adjustments of other comprehensive income for the period, as those amounts, including amortization of the net transition asset or obligation, are recognized as components of net periodic benefit cost."

f. Key assumptions used in the computations including the weighted-average discount rate, the weighted-average rate of compensation increase, the weighted-average expected long-term rate of return on plan assets.

g. Assumed health care cost trend rate(s) for the next year and a general description of the direction and pattern of change as well as the ultimate trend rate(s) and when the rate is expected to occur.

h. The effect of a one-percentage-point increase and the effect of a one-percentage-point decrease in the assumed health care costs trend rates on:

(1) The aggregate of the service and interest cost; and

(2) The accumulated postretirement benefit obligations for health care benefits.

i. The amounts and types of securities of the employer and related parties included in plan assets, the approximate amount of future annual benefits of plan participants covered by insurance contracts issued by the employer or related parties and the plan during the period.

j. Any alternative amortization method used to amortize prior service amounts or unrecognized actuarial gains and losses.

k. Any substantive commitment, such as a past practice or history of regular benefit increases, used as the basis for accounting for the benefit obligation.

l. The cost of providing special or contractual termination benefits recognized during the period and a description of the nature of the event.

m. An explanation of any significant change in the benefit obligation or plan assets not readily apparent from the other disclosures.

2. **New Additional Requirements** In addition to amending some disclosures in SFAS 132(R), SFAS 158 requires the following additional disclosures:

a. The amounts in accumulated other comprehensive income that have not yet been recognized as components of net periodic benefit cost, showing separately the net gain or loss, net prior service cost or credit, and net transition asset or obligation.

b. The amounts in accumulated other comprehensive income expected to be recognized as components of net periodic benefit cost over the fiscal year that follows the most recent annual statement of financial position presented, showing separately the net gain or loss, net prior service cost or credit, and net transition asset or obligation.

c. The amount and timing of any plan assets expected to be returned to the employer during the 12-month period, or operating cycle if longer, that follows the most recent annual statement of financial position presented.

D. Defined Contribution Plans

Defined contribution plans are plans in which the terms specify how **contributions** to the individual participants' accounts are to be determined (**not** the benefits to be received). These plans provide an individual account for each participant. SFAS 87 establishes standards for an employer who offers pension benefits to employees, either a single-employer, defined **benefit** pension plan or a defined **contribution** plan. SFAS 88 expands standards for pensions. SFAS 158 amended SFAS 87 and 88 requiring employers to recognize the funded status of pensions and other retirement benefit plans on their balance sheets.

1. **Benefits** Participant benefits are determined by: the amounts contributed to the participants' account(s); returns earned on investments of contributions; and allocations of forfeitures of other participants' benefits.

2. **Net Pension Cost** The net pension cost is the contribution called for by the plan for the period in which the individual renders services. If the plan calls for contributions for periods after the individual has rendered services (e.g., after retirement), the cost should be accrued during the employee's service period.

II. Single-Employer Defined Benefit Pension Plans

A. Overview

A defined benefit pension plan is a plan that defines an amount of pension **benefit** to be provided, usually as a function of one or more factors such as age, years of service, or compensation. The fundamental objective in defined benefit plan reporting is to provide a measure of pension cost that reflects the terms of the underlying plan and recognizes the compensation cost of an employee's pension benefits over the employee's approximate service period. The following definitions apply specifically to accounting for pensions. Most of these terms apply also to accounting for postretirement benefits, with minor modification.

1. **Accumulated Benefit Obligation** The actuarial present value of benefits (whether vested or nonvested) attributed by the pension benefit formula to employee services rendered before a specified date and based on employee services and compensation (if applicable) prior to that date.

2. **Actuarial Present Value** The value, as of a specified date, of an amount or series of amounts payable or receivable thereafter, with each amount adjusted to reflect (a) the time value of money (through discounts for interest), and (b) the probability of payment (by means of decrements for events such as death, disability, withdrawal, or retirement) between the specified date and the expected date of payment.

3. **Amortization** In pension accounting, amortization is also used to refer to the systematic recognition in net pension cost over several periods of amounts previously recognized in other comprehensive income, that is, prior service costs or credits, gains or losses, and the transition asset or obligation existing at the date of initial application of these standards.

4. **Annuity Contract** A contract in which an insurance company unconditionally undertakes a legal obligation to provide specified pension benefits to specific individuals in return for a fixed consideration or premium.

5. **Assumptions** Estimates of the occurrence of future events affecting pension costs, such as mortality, withdrawal, disablement and retirement, changes in compensation and national pension benefits and discount rates to reflect the time value of money.

6. **Attribution** The process of assigning benefits or costs to periods of employee service.

7. **Contributory Plan** A pension plan under which employees contribute part of the cost. In some contributory plans, employees wishing to be covered must contribute; in other contributory plans, participants' contributions result in increased benefits.

8. **Expected Return on Plan Assets** An amount calculated as a basis for determining the extent of delayed recognition of the effects of changes in the fair value of assets. The expected return on plan assets is determined based on the expected long-term rate of return on plan assets and the market-related value of plan assets.

9. **Funding Policy** The program regarding the amounts and timing of contributions by the employer(s), participants, and any other sources to provide the benefits a plan specifies.

10. **Gain or Loss** A change in the value of either the projected benefit obligation or the plan assets resulting from **experience** different from that assumed or from a change in an actuarial assumption.

11. **Market-Related Value of Plan Assets** A balance used to calculate the expected return on plan assets. Market-related value can be either fair value or a calculated value that recognizes changes in fair value in a systematic and rational manner over not more than five years.

12. **Pension Benefit Formula** The basis for determining payments to which participants may be entitled under a pension plan. Pension benefit formulas usually refer to the employee's service or compensation or both.

13. **Plan Assets** Assets (usually stocks, bonds, and other investments) that have been segregated and restricted (usually in a trust) to provide benefits. Plan assets include amounts contributed by the employer (and by employees for a contributory plan) and amounts earned from investing the contributions, less benefits paid.

14. **Prior Service Cost** The cost of retroactive benefits granted in a plan amendment (or initiation of a new plan).

15. **Projected Benefit Obligation** The actuarial present value as of a date of all benefits attributed by the pension benefit formula to employee service rendered prior to that date. The projected benefit obligation is measured using assumptions as to future compensation levels if the pension benefit formula is based on those future compensation levels (pay-related, final-pay, final-average-pay, or career-average-pay plans).

16. **Retroactive Benefits** Benefits granted in a plan amendment (or initiation) that are attributed by the pension benefit formula to employee services rendered in periods prior to the amendment. The cost of the retroactive benefits is referred to as prior service cost.

17. **Unfunded Projected Benefit Obligation** The excess of the projected benefit obligation over the fair value of plan assets.

18. **Vested Benefit Obligation** The actuarial present value of vested benefits (benefits for which the employee's right to receive a present or future pension benefit is no longer contingent on remaining in the service of the employer).

B. Net Periodic Pension Cost

The amount recognized in an employer's financial statements as the cost of a pension plan for a period. Originally under SFAS 87 the components of net periodic pension cost are service cost, interest cost, actual return on plan assets, gain or loss, amortization of unrecognized prior service cost, and amortization of the unrecognized net obligation or asset existing at the date of initial application of SFAS 87. SFAS 158 amends this slightly in that the prior service cost or credit and transition asset or obligation will no longer be unrecognized; they will be included in accumulated other comprehensive income. Net periodic pension cost is the recognized cost of the plan for the period. Note that pension cost may be an expense for the period (e.g., pension cost related to administrative or marketing personnel) or it may be inventoriable as manufacturing overhead (e.g., pension cost related to factory personnel). Pension cost consists of six components.

Exhibit 1 ▸ Net Periodic Pension Cost Components

S	**S**ERVICE COST (+)
I	**I**NTEREST COST (+)
P	**P**LAN ASSET ACTUAL RETURN (–)
P	**P**RIOR SVC COST (+) OR CREDIT (–) AMORTIZATION
A	**A**CTUARIAL GAINS (–) OR LOSSES (+)
FASB	TRANSITION ASSET (–) OR OBLIGATION (+) AMORTIZATION
	NET PENSION EXPENSE

1. **Service Cost** The service cost component is the actuarial present value of benefits attributed by the pension benefit formula to the employee's service during the period (i.e., the benefits earned during the period).

   a. **Actuarial Assumptions** Service costs are based on actuarial assumptions (reflecting time value of money, mortality, turnover, early retirement, etc.).

   b. **Future Compensation** Service costs reflect future compensation levels to the extent that the pension benefit formula defines pension benefits as a function of future compensation levels.

2. **Interest Cost** This component is the increase in the projected benefit obligation (PBO) due to the passage of time. The interest rate to be used in the calculation is the rate at which the pension benefit could be effectively settled (i.e., the assumed discount rate). This same assumed discount rate is used in the measurement of the projected, accumulated, and vested benefit obligations, and the service cost component of net periodic pension cost.

3. **Plan Asset Actual Return** This component of net periodic pension cost reduces the pension cost for the period. It is based on the fair value of plan assets at the beginning and end of the period, adjusted for contributions and benefit payments.

Example 1 ▸ Plan Asset Actual Return

The following facts pertain to the ABC Co. pension plan for year 7.

Expected return on plan assets	15%
FV of plan assets, on 1/1, year 7	$100,000
on 12/31, year 7	$130,000
Contributions to pension plan	$ 14,000
Benefits paid to retired employees	$ 8,000

> **Required:** Determine the actual return on plan assets (ARPA) component of net pension cost for year 7. Assume contribution and benefit payments were made at year-end.
>
> **Solution:** ARPA = $130,000 – $100,000 – $14,000 + $8,000 = $24,000

a. Algebraically, ARPA = End FV – Beg. FV – C + B

Where:

ARPA	=	Actual return on plan assets
End FV	=	FV of plan assets at end of period
Beg. FV	=	FV of plan assets at beginning of period
C	=	Contributions to the plan during the period
B	=	Benefits paid during the period

b. For purposes of presenting the net periodic pension cost, SFAS 87 requires the disclosure of the actual return on plan assets, as indicated here. However, net periodic pension cost is subsequently adjusted for the difference between actual return and expected return. The net effect of this is that net pension cost for any given period reflects the expected return for that period. The difference between the expected and actual return is deferred and subject to amortization in future periods. Prior to adopting SFAS 158 this deferred amount was unrecognized; with SFAS 158 it will be included in accumulated other comprehensive income.

4. **Prior Service Cost Amortization** This is the spreading of the cost of retroactive benefits generated by a plan amendment that granted increased benefits based on service rendered in prior periods.

a. **Increase in Retroactive Benefits** The cost of retroactively increasing benefits is the increase in the projected benefit obligation at the date of the amendment. With SFAS 158, the cost shall be recognized as a charge to other comprehensive income. These costs are to be amortized as a component of net periodic pension cost by assigning an equal amount to each year of future service of each employee active at the date of the amendment who is expected to receive benefits under the plan. Prior service cost is incurred with the expectation that the employer will realize economic benefits in future periods. Plan amendments can reduce projected benefit obligations. These reductions reduce any other prior service costs and any excess is amortized. With SFAS 158, other comprehensive income is adjusted each period as prior service cost is amortized.

b. **Alternative Approaches** Since the amortization of prior service costs, as described in a., above, can be quite complex, SFAS 87 permits the use of alternative approaches that would amortize the cost over a shorter period of time. For example, a straight-line method that amortizes the cost over the average remaining service life of the active participants is acceptable.

c. **Retroactive Reduction in Benefits** Retroactively reducing benefits decreases the projected benefit obligation and shall be recognized as a prior service credit. This credit will be used to first reduce any prior service cost with any remaining credit amortized on the same basis as a cost would. With implementation of SFAS 158 these period costs or credits are included in accumulated other comprehensive income.

Exhibit 2 ▸ Prior Service Cost

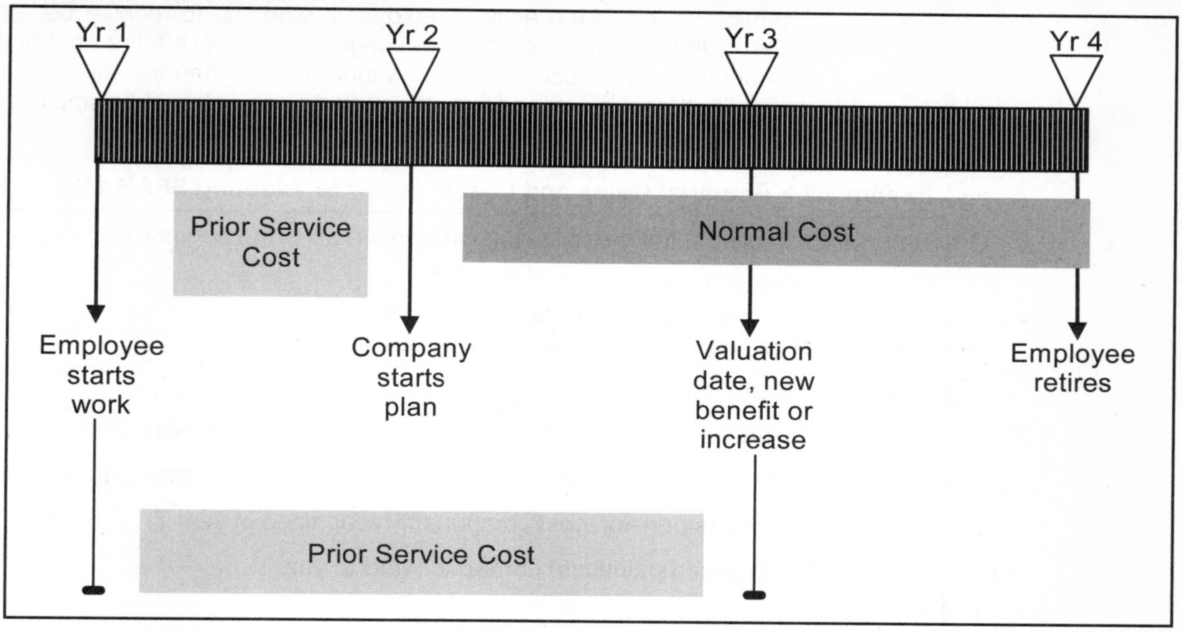

5. **Actuarial Gains and Losses** This refers to changes in the amount of either the projected benefit obligation or plan assets resulting from experience different from that assumed, and also changes in assumptions. It includes both realized and unrealized gains and losses. The gain or loss component of net periodic pension cost consists of (1) the difference between the actual return on plan assets and the expected return on plan assets, and (2) the amortization of the unrecognized net gain or loss from previous periods or with the implementation of SFAS 158, the net gain or loss included in accumulated other comprehensive income. Also, with SFAS 158, gains and losses that are not recognized immediately as a component of net periodic pension cost shall be recognized as increases or decreases in other comprehensive income as they arise.

   a. **Gain or Loss on Plan Assets** As far as plan assets are concerned, the gain or loss is the difference between the **actual** return on assets during the period and the **expected** return on assets for the period. The expected return is determined by using the expected long-term rate of return and the market-related value of plan assets.

      (1) The **expected long-term rate of return** is the average rate of earnings expected on the funds invested and includes the return expected to be available for reinvestment.

      (2) The **market-related value** of plan assets can be either the fair value of the assets or a calculated value that recognizes changes in fair value in a systematic and rational manner over not more than five years (e.g., a moving average of plan asset values over the last five years).

   b. **Amortization of Unrecognized Gains or Losses** SFAS 87 does **not** require the recognition of gains or losses as a component of net periodic pension cost in the period in which they arise. However, in some cases it does require, as a minimum, amortization of any unrecognized net gain or loss, or the net gain or loss recognized in accumulated other comprehensive income under SFAS 158, to be included as a component of net periodic pension cost.

      (1) This will be required if, as of the beginning of the year, the net gain or loss exceeds **10 percent** of the **greater** of the projected benefit obligation or the market-related value of plan assets.

(2) The excess must be amortized, at a minimum, over the average remaining service period of the active employees expected to receive benefits under the plan. Other methods of amortization may be used, but the amortization amount computed under such methods cannot be **less** than the minimum amortization described above. In addition, the method used should be applied consistently, applied similarly to both gains and losses, and disclosed.

Example 2 ▸ Actuarial Gains and Losses (prior to adopting SFAS 158)

Refer to Example 1, plus the following information as of the beginning of year 7.

Projected benefit obligation	$135,000
Unrecognized gain (loss) from previous periods	$ 20,000
Average remaining service period of active employees	20 years

Required: Determine

a. The difference between the actual and expected return on plan assets for year 7.

b. The amortization of the unrecognized net gain or loss from previous periods.

c. The gain or loss pension cost component recognized in year 7.

d. The unrecognized gain(loss) carried forward to year 8.

Solution:

a. Difference between actual and expected returns on plan assets, year 7:

Actual return on plan assets (determined in Example 1)	$ 24,000
Expected return on plan assets ($100,000 FV on 1/1, year 7 × 15%)	(15,000)
Difference between the actual and expected returns on assets	$ 9,000

b. Amortization of the unrecognized net gain(loss) from previous periods:

Unrecognized gain (loss)	$ 20,000
10% of the greater of projected benefit obligation ($135,000) or market-related value of assets on January 1 ($100,000)	(13,500)
Unrecognized net gain(loss) subject to amortization	6,500
Divided by average remaining service period of employees	/ 20
Amortization of unrecognized gain	$ 325

c. Gains and losses to the extent recognized, year 7:

Excess actual return on plan assets over expected return, deferred (a)	$ 9,000
Less: Amortization of unrecognized gain (loss) from previous periods (b)	(325)
Gain recognized	$ 8,675

d. Unrecognized gain (loss) carried forward to year 8:

Unrecognized gain (loss), 1/1, year 7	$ 20,000
Less amortization to date	(325)
Plus difference between actual and expected returns on plan assets during year 7 (a)	9,000
Unrecognized gain	$ 28,675

NOTE 1: The actual return ($24,000) is a reduction in net pension expense and the gain ($8,675) increases net pension expense. The net amount ($15,325) represents the expected return ($15,000) and the amortization of unrecognized gains ($325).

NOTE 2: The actual figures would be the same under SFAS 158, just that instead of unrecognized gains or losses, the gains or losses would be recognized as part of accumulated other comprehensive income.

6. **FASB 87 Adjustment** The plan sponsor must determine, as of the measurement date for the beginning of the fiscal year in which SFAS 87 is first applied, the amount of (a) the projected benefit obligation, and (b) the fair value of plan assets plus previously recognized unfunded accrued pension cost, or less previously recognized prepaid pension cost. The difference between these two amounts, whether it represents an unrecognized net obligation (and loss or cost) or an unrecognized net asset (and gain), should be amortized on a straight-line basis over the average remaining service period of employees expected to receive benefits under the plan. However, if the average remaining service period is less than 15 years, the employer may elect to use a 15-year period.

Exhibit 3 ▸ Elements of Pension Cost

Decreases Pension Cost	Increases Pension Cost
Plan Asset Actual Return	Service Cost
Actuarial Gain Amortized	Interest Cost
Actuarial Loss Deferred	Prior Service Cost Amortization
FASB 87 Adjustment	Actuarial Loss Amortized
Amortization of Unrecognized Net Asset	Actuarial Gain Deferred
	FASB 87 Adjustment
	Amortization of Unrecognized Net Obligation

C. **Recognition of Liabilities & Assets Prior to SFAS 158**
The recognition of a liability (unfunded accrued pension cost) is required when the net periodic pension cost exceeds the amount the employer has contributed to the plan. An asset (prepaid pension cost) is recognized when the amount contributed to the plan by the employer exceeds the net periodic pension cost recognized. In addition to the accrued or prepaid pension cost, if the accumulated benefit obligation exceeds the fair value of plan assets, a minimum liability must be recognized for the difference (i.e., the unfunded accumulated benefit obligation).

Example 3 ▸ Accrued/Prepaid Pension Cost

Taylor Co. implemented a defined-benefit pension plan for its employees on January 2, year 7 and contributed $185,000 to the plan during year 7. The net periodic pension cost for the year was determined to be $200,000.

Required: Determine the amount accrued/prepaid pension cost, as of 12/31, year 7.

Solution:

Net periodic pension cost, year 7	$ 200,000
Less: Contributions, year 7	(185,000)
Accrued pension cost, 12/31, year 7	$ 15,000

1. **Adjustment** The amount of the adjustment (i.e., the additional liability) considers any existing balance of accrued or prepaid pension cost. An existing balance in the *Accrued Pension Cost* account reduces the amount of the adjustment. An existing balance in the *Prepaid Pension Cost* account increases the amount of the adjustment.

2. **Intangible Asset Recognition** If an additional liability is recognized because of unfunded accumulated benefit obligations, an equal amount will be recognized as an intangible asset. However, this asset may not exceed the amount of unrecognized prior service cost.

3. **Recognition of Excess** If any excess does occur, it must be reported, net of any related income tax effect, in other comprehensive income.

Example 4 ▸ Minimum Liability

Refer to the facts of Example 3. In addition, as of 12/31, year 7, Taylor Co.'s accumulated benefit obligation was $225,000, the fair value of plan assets was $190,000, and the unrecognized prior service cost was $15,000.

Required: Determine as of 12/31, year 7, Taylor Co.'s year 7 (a) minimum liability required, (b) the additional liability, if any, required, (c) the amount, if any, of intangible asset to be recognized, and (d) the amount, if any, of minimum liability adjustments to be reported in other comprehensive income (ignore income taxes).

Solution:

	Accumulated benefit obligation	$ 225,000
	Less: FV of plan assets	(190,000)
(a)	Unfunded accumulated benefit obligation (minimum liability)	$ 35,000
	Minimum liability required (a)	$ 35,000
	Less: Accrued pension cost (Example 3)	(15,000)
(b)	Additional liability required	$ 20,000
(c)	Intangible asset: Additional liability of $20,000 is greater than the unrecognized prior service costs of $15,000; thus the intangible asset recognized is limited to $15,000.	
	Additional liability required (determined in b)	$ 20,000
	Less: Unrecognized prior service costs	(15,000)
(d)	Minimum liability adjustment to be reported in OCI	$ 5,000

Example 5 ▸ Comprehensive Defined Benefit Pension Plan

XYZ Corp. has an employee who is estimated to be retiring in 4 years (on 12/31, year 4). This employee is entered into a defined benefit pension plan at 1/1, year 1. The plan pays a lump sum upon retirement of $1,000 for each year of service after the date of entry into the plan. Assume an appropriate discount rate (from an actuary) of 10%, and an expected and actual return on plan assets of 10%. Additionally, assume funding by XYZ Corp. of $800 at 12/31, year 1 and $800 at 12/31, year 2. On 1/1, year 3, XYZ Corp. amended the plan to pay $1,500 for each year of service upon retirement, retroactive for one year of prior service. Funding at 12/31, year 3 was $1,800 and at 12/31, year 4 was $1,487.20.

NOTE: This example accounts for one employee enrolled in a pension plan. The example could easily be extended to combined groups of similar employees to account for all participants of a plan. Additionally, although pensions would usually pay participants on a periodic basis after retirement, these payments could be transformed into an equivalent lump-sum distribution at the date of retirement.

Required: Show the calculation of the projected benefit obligation and the net periodic pension cost and the necessary journal entries at 12/31 of years 1, 2, 3 and 4.

Solution:

12/31/Yr 1	Projected benefit obligation (P.V. at 10% of $1,000 in 3 years = 0.751315 × $1,000)	$ 751.31
	Service cost (0.751315 × $1,000)	$ 751.31
	Interest on projected benefit obligation	0
	Expected return on plan assets	0
	Prior service cost	0
	Gains and losses	0
	Net periodic pension cost	$ 751.31

12/31/Yr 1	Pension Expense	751.31	
	Prepaid/Accrued Pension Cost	48.69	
	Cash		800.00
	To record year 1 pension expense and funding.		

12/31/Yr 2	Projected benefit obligation (P.V. at 10% of $2,000 in 2 years = 0.826446 × $2,000)		$1,652.89
	Service cost (0.826446 × $1,000)		$ 826.45
	Interest on (beginning) projected benefit obligation (10% × $751.31)		75.13
	Actual return on plan assets (10% × $800)		(80.00)
	Prior service costs		0
	Gains and losses		0
	Net periodic pension cost		$ 821.58
12/31/Yr 2	Pension Expense	821.58	
	Prepaid/Accrued Pension Cost		21.58
	Cash		800.00
	To record year 2 pension expense and funding.		
12/31/Yr 3	Projected benefit obligation [P.V. at 10% in 1 year = 0.909091 × ($1,000 + $1,500 + $1,500)]		$3,636.36
	Service cost (0.909091 × $1,500)		$1,363.64
	Interest on projected benefit obligation (10% × 2,066.11*)		206.61
	Actual return on plan assets [10% × ($800 + $800 + 80)]		(168.00)
	Amortization of prior service costs ($413.22** / 2)		206.61
	Gains and losses		0
	Net periodic pension cost		$1,608.86

* Prior year's adjusted projected benefit obligation (0.826446 × $2,500 = $2,066.11)
** Prior service costs = P.V. of $500 = 0.826446 × $500 = $413.22

12/31/Yr 3	Pension Expense	1,608.86	
	Prepaid/Accrued Pension Cost	191.14	
	Cash		1,800.00
	To record year 3 pension expense and funding.		
12/31/Yr 4	Projected benefit obligation (P.V. at 10% of $5,500 in 0 years)		$5,500.00
	Service cost		$1,500.00
	Interest on projected benefit obligation (10% × $3,636.36)		363.64
	ARPA [10% ($800 + $800 + $80 + $1,800 + $168)]		(364.80)
	Amortization of prior service costs ($413.22 / 2)		206.61
	Gains and losses		0
	Net periodic pension cost		$1,705.45
12/31/Yr 4	Pension Expense	1,705.45	
	Prepaid/Accrued Pension Cost		218.25
	Cash		1,487.20
	To record year 4 pension expense and funding.		
Summary:	Total pension expense ($751.31 + $821.58 + $1,608.86 + $1,705.45)		$4,887.20
	Total return on plan assets ($0 + $80 + $168 + $364.80)		$ 612.80
	Total funding (cash) payments ($800 + $800 + $1,800 + $1,487.20)		4,887.20
	Amount due to retiring employee		$5,500.00

D. Recognition of Liabilities & Assets Following Adoption of SFAS 158

The recognition of a liability, or asset, is required if the projected benefit obligation differs from the fair value of the plan assets. A liability is required if the projected benefit obligation exceeds the fair value of the plan assets. This liability amount equals the unfunded projected benefit obligation. An asset is recognized if the fair value of the plan assets exceeds the projected benefit obligation. The asset amount equals the overfunded project benefit obligation.

1. **Presentation on the Balance Sheet** The aggregate amount of all overfunded plans shall be listed as an asset and separately the aggregate amount of all underfunded plans shall be listed as a liability. In a classified balance sheet the liability for underfunded plans will be classified as a current liability, a noncurrent liability, or a combination of both. The asset for an overfunded plan shall be classified as a noncurrent asset.

2. **Tax Effects** The asset or liability may result in a temporary difference for tax consequences. The deferred tax effects of any temporary differences shall be recognized in income tax expense for the year and allocated to various financial components, including other comprehensive income, pursuant to FASB 109.

3. **New Determination** When there is a new determination of the funded status of a plan as an asset or liability, or when net gains or losses, prior service costs or credits, or the net transition asset or obligation are amortized as components of net periodic pension cost, the related balances for those net gains or losses, prior service costs or credits, and transition asset or obligation in accumulated other comprehensive income shall be adjusted as necessary and reported in other comprehensive income.

III. Benefit Settlement & Curtailment (SFAS 88)

A. Settlements

Settlement is an irrevocable action that relieves the employer or plan of primary responsibility for a benefit obligation and eliminates significant risks related to the obligation and the assets used to effect the settlement. A gain or loss must be recognized in earnings when a pension obligation is settled. The amount of the gain or loss is limited to the unrecognized net gain or loss (or in adopting SFAS 158, the net gain or loss remaining in accumulated other comprehensive income plus any transition asset remaining) from realized or unrealized changes in the amount of either projected benefit obligation or plan assets resulting from experience different from that assumed or from changes in assumptions. In simple language, either all or a pro rata share of this gain or loss is recognized when a plan is settled. If full settlement takes place, all these net gains or losses are recognized. If only a portion of the plan is settled, a pro rata share of these net gains or losses is recognized.

B. Curtailments

Curtailment is an event that significantly reduces the expected years of future service of present employees or eliminates, for a significant number of employees, the accrual of defined benefits for some or all of their future services. The prior service cost, unrecognized or recognized in accumulated other comprehensive income per SFAS 158, associated with years of service no longer expected to be rendered as the result of the curtailment is a loss. This prior service cost includes any remaining net obligation existing at the date of initial application of SFAS 87. Note, in the case of a curtailment, the projected benefit obligation may also be decreased (a gain) or increased (a loss).

C. Settlements vs. Curtailments

1. **Purchase Annuity Contracts** If an employer purchases nonparticipating annuity contracts for vested benefits and continues to provide defined benefits for future service, either in the same plan or in a successor plan, a settlement has occurred, but **not** a curtailment.

2. **Benefits Reduced** If benefits to be accumulated in future periods are reduced (for example, because half of a work force is dismissed or a plant is closed), but the plan remains in existence and continues to pay benefits, to invest assets, and to receive contributions, a curtailment has occurred, but **not** a settlement.

3. **Plan Terminated** If a plan is terminated (that is, the obligation is settled and the plan ceases to exist) and not replaced by a successor defined benefit plan, **both** a settlement and a curtailment have occurred (whether or not the employees continue to work for the employer).

D. Termination Benefits

Termination benefits may be either special termination benefits offered only for a short period of time or contractual termination benefits required by the terms of a plan only if a specific event, such as a plant closing, occurs. When an employer offers special termination benefits to an employee, the employer must recognize a liability and a loss when the employee accepts the offer and the amount can be reasonably estimated. If the employer offers a contractual termination benefit, the employer must recognize a liability and a loss when it is probable that employees will be entitled to benefits and the amount can reasonably be estimated. The cost of termination benefits recognized as a liability and a loss includes the amount of any lump-sum payments and the present value of any expected future payments.

E. Segment Disposal

If the gain or loss from a settlement or curtailment is directly related to a disposal of a segment of a business, it should be included in determining the gain or loss associated with that event and recognized pursuant to SFAS 146. SFAS 146 requires recognizing lease termination costs and specified employee severance plan costs related with exit or disposal activities in periods when obligations to others exists, not necessarily in the period of commitment to a plan.

IV. Other Postretirement Benefits

A. Attribution Method

SFAS 106, *Employers' Accounting for Postretirement Benefits Other Than Pensions,* essentially represents an extension of the measurement principles related to defined benefit pension plans (modified for different fact circumstances) to postretirement benefits other than pensions. SFAS 106 focuses primarily on postretirement health care benefits. Both accounting for pensions (SFAS 87) and accounting for postretirement benefits other than pensions (SFAS 106) assign benefit costs on a years-of-service approach.

1. **Required** An employer's obligation for postretirement benefits expected to be provided to or for an employee is to be fully accrued by the date that employee attains full eligibility for all of the benefits expected to be received by that employee (the full eligibility date), even if the employee is expected to render additional service beyond that date.

2. **Attribution Period** The beginning of the attribution (accrual) period is the employee's date of hire, unless the plan only grants credit for service from a later date. An equal amount of the postretirement benefit obligation is attributed to each year of service in the attribution period unless the plan attributes a disproportionate share of the expected benefits to employees' early years of service.

B. Net Postretirement Benefit Cost

The components of the calculation of net benefit cost for postretirement benefits are essentially the same as the components for the calculation of net period pension cost, with some differences. There are some modifications in terminology due to the different benefit agreements being measured and differences in the treatment of transition amounts.

1. **Amortization Over 20 Years** In accounting for postretirement benefits other than pensions, amortization of the unrecognized net obligation (and loss or cost) or unrecognized net asset (and gain) existing at the date of the initial application of SFAS 106, *Employers' Accounting for Postretirement Benefits Other Than Pensions,* is amortized on a straight-line basis over the employees' average remaining service period. However, if the average remaining service period is less than 20 years, the employer may elect to use a 20-year period. (Under SFAS 87, *Employers' Accounting for Pensions,* the average remaining service period is less than 15 years, the employer may elect to use a 15-year period.)

2. **Option of Immediate Recognition** The transition amounts for postretirement benefits other than pensions may be recognized immediately in net income as a change in accounting principle, as an alternative to amortization. This option is not available in accounting for pension costs.

Exhibit 4 ▸ Components of Benefit Cost Under SFAS 106 vs. SFAS 87

	SFAS 106	SFAS 87
1. Service Cost	Actuarial present value of **postretirement** benefit obligation attributed to current period.	Actuarial present value of **pension** benefit obligation attributed to current period.
2. Interest Cost	Increase in the Accumulated Benefit Obligation to recognize the effects of the passage of time (uses assumed discount rates).	Increase in the Projected Benefit Obligation to recognize the effects of the passage of time (uses assumed discount rates).
3. Actual Return on Plan Assets	Change in fair value of plan assets during the period after adjusting for contributions and benefit payments.	Change in fair value of plan assets during the period after adjusting for contributions and benefit payments.
4. Prior Service Cost	Change in Accumulated Benefit Obligation for new or amended benefits granted to plan participants.	Change in Accumulated Benefit Obligation for new or amended benefits granted to plan participants.
5. Gains and Losses	Change in Accumulated Benefit Obligation and plan assets from experience different from that assumed or from changes in assumptions. May be recognized immediately or delayed with minimum amortization required.	Change in Accumulated Benefit Obligation and plan assets from experience different from that assumed or from changes in assumptions. May be recognized immediately or delayed with minimum amortization required.
6. Transition Amounts	Overfunded or underfunded Accumulated Benefit Obligation at transition to implementing SFAS 106. **May delay or immediately recognize** amounts. If delay, amortize over service lives with option for **20-year amortization** period when service lives are less than 20 years. **If immediate, recognize in net income as a change in accounting principle.**	Overfunded or underfunded Accumulated Benefit Obligation at transition to implementing SFAS 87. **Must delay recognition** and amortize over service lives with option for **15-year amortization** period when service lives are less than 15 years.
= Net Cost	Net **Postretirement Benefit** Cost	Net **Period Pension** Cost

C. Recognition of Liabilities & Assets

A liability or an asset is recognized for a postretirement benefit plan, much in the same manner as for a pension plan. The primary difference being that the accumulated postretirement benefit obligation, instead of the projected benefit obligation, is used for comparison to the fair value of plan assets in deciding whether the plan is underfunded or overfunded. The exception, prior to adopting SFAS 158, is that there is **no** minimum liability requirement in SFAS 106 and thus no intangible asset requirement.

CHAPTER 9—POSTEMPLOYMENT BENEFITS

Problem 9-1 MULTIPLE CHOICE QUESTIONS (70 to 88 minutes)

1. A company with a defined benefit pension plan must disclose in the notes to its financial statements a reconciliation of
a. The vested and nonvested benefit obligation of its pension plan with the accumulated benefit obligation
b. The accrued or prepaid pension cost reported in its balance sheet with the pension expense reported in its income statement
c. The accumulated benefit obligation of its pension plan with its projected benefit obligation
d. The funded status of its pension plan with the accrued or prepaid pension cost reported in its balance sheet (5/95, FAR, #57, 5593)

2. Which of the following information should be included in disclosures by a company providing health care benefits to its retirees?

I. The assumed health care cost trend rate used to measure the expected cost of benefits covered by the plan
II. The accumulated post-retirement benefit obligation

a. I and II
b. I only
c. II only
d. Neither I nor II

(5/93, Theory, #30, amended, 4218)

3. Which of the following disclosures is not required of companies with a defined benefit pension plan?
a. A description of the plan
b. The amount of pension expense by component
c. The weighted average discount rate
d. The estimates of future contributions (R/01, FAR, #8, 6983)

4. The following information pertains to Gali Co.'s defined benefit pension plan for the current year:

Fair value of plan assets at 1/1	$350,000
Fair value of plan assets at 12/31	525,000
Employer contributions	110,000
Benefits paid	85,000

In computing pension expense, what amount should Gali use as actual return on plan assets?
a. $ 65,000
b. $150,000
c. $175,000
d. $260,000 (5/95, FAR, #39, amended, 5575)

5. The following information pertains to Seda Co.'s pension plan for the current year:

Actuarial estimate of projected benefit obligation at 1/1	$72,000
Assumed discount rate	10%
Service costs for the year	18,000
Pension benefits paid during the year	15,000

If no change in actuarial estimates occurred during the year, Seda's projected benefit obligation at December 31 of the current year was
a. $64,200
b. $75,000
c. $79,200
d. $82,200 (11/90, FAR, #16, amended, 1223)

6. The following information pertains to Lee Corp.'s defined benefit pension plan for the current year:

Service cost	$160,000
Actual and expected gain on plan assets	35,000
Unexpected loss on plan assets related to a disposal of a subsidiary	40,000
Amortization of prior service cost (unrecognized or included in other comprehensive income)	5,000
Annual interest on pension obligation	50,000

What amount should Lee report as pension expense in its current year-end income statement?
a. $250,000
b. $220,000
c. $210,000
d. $180,000 (5/92, PII, #14, amended, 2646)

7. The following information pertains to the current year activity of Ral Corp.'s defined benefit pension plan:

Service cost	$300,000
Return on plan assets	80,000
Interest cost on pension benefit obligation	164,000
Amortization of actuarial loss	30,000
Amortization of remaining net obligation	70,000

Ral's current year pension cost was
a. $316,000
b. $484,000
c. $574,000
d. $644,000 (5/91, PII, #17, amended, 1221)

8. Visor Co. maintains a defined benefit pension plan for its employees. The service cost component of Visor's net periodic pension cost is measured using the
a. Unfunded accumulated benefit obligation
b. Unfunded vested benefit obligation
c. Projected benefit obligation
d. Expected return on plan assets
(11/93, Theory, #30, 4535)

9. Effective January 1 of the previous year, Flood Co. established a defined benefit pension plan with no retroactive benefits. The first of the required equal annual contributions was paid on December 31 of that previous year. A 10% discount rate was used to calculate service cost and a 10% rate of return was assumed for plan assets. All information on covered employees for the previous and current year is the same. Flood has not yet adopted SFAS 158. How should the service cost for the current year compare with the previous year, and should the previous year balance sheet report an accrued or a prepaid pension cost?

	Service cost for current year compared to the previous year	*Pension cost reported on the previous year balance sheet*
a.	Equal to	Accrued
b.	Equal to	Prepaid
c.	Greater than	Accrued
d.	Greater than	Prepaid

(11/90, Theory, #21, amended, 2059)

10. Interest cost included in the net pension cost recognized by an employer sponsoring a defined benefit pension plan represents the
a. Amortization of the discount on prior service cost
b. Increase in the fair value of plan assets due to the passage of time
c. Increase in the projected benefit obligation due to the passage of time
d. Shortage between the expected and actual returns on plan assets
(5/92, Theory, #20, amended, 2713)

11. For a defined benefit pension plan, the discount rate used to calculate the projected benefit obligation is determined by the

	Expected return on plan assets	*Actual return on plan assets*
a.	Yes	Yes
b.	No	No
c.	Yes	No
d.	No	Yes

(5/91, Theory, #37, 2057)

12. Jan Corp. amended its defined benefit pension plan, granting a total credit of $100,000 to four employees for services rendered prior to the plan's adoption. The employees, A, B, C, and D, are expected to retire from the company as follows:

"A" will retire after three years.
"B" and "C" will retire after five years.
"D" will retire after seven years.

What is the amount of prior service cost amortization in the first year?
a. $0
b. $ 5,000
c. $20,000
d. $25,000 (R/99, FAR, #13, 6782)

13. As of December 31 of the previous year, the projected benefit obligation and plan assets of a noncontributory defined benefit plan sponsored by Reed Inc., were:

Projected benefit obligation	$ 780,000
Plan assets at fair value	(600,000)
Initial unfunded obligation	$ 180,000

Reed elected to apply the provisions of SFAS 87 in its financial statements for the current year ended December 31. At December 31 of the previous year, all amounts accrued as net periodic pension cost had been contributed to the plan. The average remaining service period of active plan participants expected to receive benefits was estimated to be 10 years at the date of transition. Some participants' estimated service periods are 20 and 25 years. To minimize an accrual for pension cost, what amount of unrecognized or remaining net obligation should Reed amortize?
a. $ 7,200
b. $ 9,000
c. $12,000
d. $18,000 (5/89, PI, #35, amended, 1226)

14. Which of the following components should be included in net pension cost by an employer sponsoring a defined benefit pension plan?

	Amortization of prior service cost	*Fair value of plan assets*
a.	Yes	No
b.	Yes	Yes
c.	No	Yes
d.	No	No

(5/89, Theory, #20, 2069)

15. On July 31 of the current year, Tern Co. amended its single employee defined benefit pension plan by granting increased benefits for services provided prior to the current year. This prior service cost will be reflected in the financial statement(s) for
a. Years before the current year only
b. The current year only
c. The current year, and years before and following the current year
d. The current year and following years only
(11/92, Theory, #26, amended, 3459)

16. On January 2, year 2, Loch Co., who has not yet adopted SFAS 158, established a noncontributory defined benefit plan covering all employees and contributed $1,000,000 to the plan. At December 31, year 2, Loch determined that the service and interest costs on the plan were $620,000 for the year. The expected and the actual rate of return on plan assets for the year was 10%. There are no other components of Loch's pension expense. What amount should Loch report in its December 31, year 2 balance sheet as prepaid pension cost?
a. $280,000
b. $380,000
c. $480,000
d. $620,000 (11/93, PI, #26, amended, 4395)

17. On January 2, year 5, Loch Co., who has not yet adopted SFAS 158, established a noncontributory defined benefit pension plan covering all employees and contributed $400,000 to the plan. At December 31, year 5, Loch determined that the service and interest costs on the plan were $720,000 for the year. The expected and the actual rate of return on plan assets for the year was 10%. There are no other components of Loch's pension expense. What amount should Loch report as accrued pension cost in its December 31, year 5 balance sheet?
a. $280,000
b. $320,000
c. $360,000
d. $720,000 (R/00, FAR, #7, amended, 6902)

18. Prior to adopting SFAS 158, a company that maintains a defined benefit pension plan for its employees reports an unfunded accrued pension cost. This cost represents the amount that the
a. Cumulative net pension cost accrued exceeds contributions to the plan
b. Cumulative net pension cost accrued exceeds the vested benefit obligation
c. Vested benefit obligation exceeds plan assets
d. Vested benefit obligation exceeds contributions to the plan (11/93, Theory, #29, 4534)

19. Webb Co. implemented a defined benefit pension plan for its employees on January 1, year 5. During years 5 and 6, Webb's contributions fully funded the plan. The following data are provided:

	Year 8 Estimated	Year 7 Actual
Projected benefit obligation, December 31	$750,000	$700,000
Accumulated benefit obligation, December 31	520,000	500,000
Plan assets at fair value, December 31	675,000	600,000
Projected benefit obligation in excess of plan assets	75,000	100,000
Pension expense	90,000	75,000
Employer's contribution	?	50,000

What amount should Webb contribute in order to report an accrued pension liability of $15,000 in its December 31, year 8 balance sheet?
a. $ 50,000
b. $ 60,000
c. $ 75,000
d. $100,000 (5/92, PI, #25, amended, 2593)

20. The following information pertains to Kane Co.'s defined benefit pension plan for the year:

Prepaid pension cost, January 1	$ 2,000
Service cost	19,000
Interest cost	38,000
Actual return on plan assets	22,000
Amortization of unrecognized prior service cost	52,000
Employer contributions	40,000

The fair value of plan assets exceeds the accumulated benefit obligation. Prior to SFAS 158, in its December 31 balance sheet, what amount should Kane report as unfunded accrued pension cost?
a. $45,000
b. $49,000
c. $67,000
d. $87,000 (5/95, FAR, #18, amended, 5554)

21. On January 2, East Corp., who has not yet adopted SFAS 158, established a defined benefit pension plan. The plan's service cost of $150,000 was fully funded at the end of the year. In the year, prior service cost was funded by a contribution of $60,000 and amortization of prior service cost was $24,000. At December 31, what amount should East report as prepaid pension cost?
a. $90,000
b. $84,000
c. $60,000
d. $36,000 (5/93, PI, #28, amended, 4070)

22. At December 31, year 9, the following information was provided by the Kerr Corp. pension plan administrator:

Fair value of plan assets	$3,450,000
Accumulated benefit obligation	4,300,000
Projected benefit obligation	5,700,000

Kerr has not yet adopted SFAS 158. What is the amount of the pension liability that should be shown on Kerr's December 31, year 9, balance sheet?

a. $5,700,000
b. $2,250,000
c. $1,400,000
d. $ 850,000 (11/90, PI, #15, amended, 1222)

23. Cey Company has a defined benefit pension plan and has not yet adopted SFAS 158. Cey's policy is to fund net periodic pension cost annually, payment to an independent trustee being made two months after the end of each year. Data relating to the pension plan for the year are as follows:

Net pension cost for the year	$190,000
Unrecognized prior service cost, 12/31	150,000
Accumulated benefit obligation, 12/31	480,000
Fair value of plan assets, 12/31	500,000

How much should appear on Cey's balance sheet at December 31 for pension liability?

	Current	*Noncurrent*
a.	$0	$480,000
b.	$0	$330,000
c.	$190,000	$150,000
d.	$190,000	$0

(5/87, PI, #15, amended, 1228)

24. Dell Co. established a defined benefit pension plan on January 1, year 1, and has not yet adopted SFAS 158. Dell amortizes the prior service cost over 16 years and funds prior service cost by making equal payments to the fund trustee at the end of each of the first ten years. The service (normal) cost is fully funded at the end of each year. The following data are available for year 1:

Service (normal) cost for the year	$220,000
Prior service cost:	
Amortized	83,400
Funded	114,400

Dell's prepaid pension cost at December 31 is

a. $114,400
b. $ 83,400
c. $ 31,000
d. $0 (5/91, PI, #32, amended, 1220)

25. Payne Inc., implemented a defined benefit pension plan for its employees on January 2, year 3. The following data are provided for the year, as of December 31, year 3:

Accumulated benefit obligation	$103,000
Plan assets at fair value	78,000
Net periodic pension cost	90,000
Employer's contribution	70,000

What amount should Payne record as additional minimum pension liability at December 31, year 3?

a. $0
b. $ 5,000
c. $20,000
d. $45,000 (5/94, FAR, #28, amended, 4843)

26. Mercer Inc., maintains a defined benefit pension plan for its employees and has not yet adopted SFAS 158. As of December 31, year 7, the market value of the plan assets is less than the accumulated benefit obligation, and less than the projected benefit obligation. The projected benefit obligation exceeds the accumulated benefit obligation. In its balance sheet as of December 31, year 7, Mercer should report a minimum liability in the amount of the

a. Excess of the projected benefit obligation over the fair value of the plan assets
b. Excess of the accumulated benefit obligation over the fair value of the plan assets
c. Projected benefit obligation
d. Accumulated benefit obligation

(11/90, Theory, #20, amended, 2058)

27. An employer sponsoring a defined benefit pension plan is subject to the minimum pension liability recognition requirement. An additional liability must be recorded equal to the unfunded

a. Accumulated benefit obligation plus the previously recognized accrued pension cost
b. Accumulated benefit obligation less the previously recognized accrued pension cost
c. Projected benefit obligation plus the previously recognized accrued pension cost
d. Projected benefit obligation less the previously recognized accrued pension cost

(11/91, Theory, #31, 2539)

28. Barrett Co. maintains a defined benefit pension plan for its employees and has not yet adopted SFAS 158. At the balance sheet date, Barrett should report a minimum liability at least equal to the

a. Accumulated benefit obligation
b. Projected benefit obligation
c. Unfunded accumulated benefit obligation
d. Unfunded projected benefit obligation

(5/90, Theory, #37, 2066)

29. Nome Co. sponsors a defined benefit plan covering all employees and has not yet adopted SFAS 158. Benefits are based on years of service and compensation levels at the time of retirement. Nome determined that, as of September 30, year 2, its accumulated benefit obligation was $380,000, and its plan assets had a $290,000 fair value. Nome's September 30, year 2, trial balance showed prepaid pension cost of $20,000. In its September 30, year 2, balance sheet, what amount should Nome report as additional pension liability?
a. $110,000
b. $360,000
c. $380,000
d. $400,000 (11/92, PI, #25, amended, 3258)

30. On June 1, year 5, Ward Corp. established a defined benefit pension plan for its employees. The following information was available at May 31, year 7:

Projected benefit obligation	$14,500,000
Accumulated benefit obligation	12,000,000
Unfunded accrued pension cost	200,000
Plan assets at fair market value	7,000,000
Unrecognized prior service cost	2,550,000

Ward has not yet adopted SFAS 158. To report the proper pension liability in Ward's May 31, year 7 balance sheet, what is the amount of the adjustment required?
a. $2,250,000
b. $4,750,000
c. $4,800,000
d. $7,300,000 (11/91, PI, #23, amended, 2411)

Items 31 and 32 are based on the following:

The following information pertains to Hall Co.'s defined benefit pension plan at December 31, year 4:

Unfunded accumulated benefit obligation	$25,000
Unrecognized prior service cost	12,000
Net periodic pension cost	8,000

Hall made no contributions to the pension plan during the year and has not yet adopted SFAS 158.

31. At December 31, year 4, what amount should Hall record as additional pension liability?
a. $ 5,000
b. $13,000
c. $17,000
d. $25,000 (11/95, FAR, #14, amended, 6096)

32. In its December 31, year 4, other comprehensive income, what amount should Hall report as excess of additional pension liability over unrecognized prior service cost?
a. $ 5,000
b. $13,000
c. $17,000
d. $25,000 (11/95, FAR, #15, amended, 6097)

33. The following data relates to Nola Co.'s defined benefit pension plan as of December 31, year 3:

Unfunded accumulated benefit obligation	$140,000
Unrecognized prior service cost	45,000
Accrued pension cost	80,000

Nola has not yet adopted SFAS 158. What amount should Nola report as excess of additional pension liability over unrecognized prior service cost in other comprehensive income?
a. $ 15,000
b. $ 35,000
c. $ 95,000
d. $175,000 (11/94, FAR, #34, amended, 5296)

34. Bounty Co. provides postretirement health care benefits to employees who have completed at least 10 years service and are aged 55 years or older when retiring. Employees retiring from Bounty have a median age of 62, and no one has worked beyond age 65. Fletcher is hired at 48 years old. The attribution period for accruing Bounty's expected postretirement health care benefit obligation to Fletcher is during the period when Fletcher is age
a. 48 to 65
b. 48 to 58
c. 55 to 65
d. 55 to 62 (11/93, Theory, #27, 4532)

35. An employer's obligation for postretirement health benefits that are expected to be provided to or for an employee must be fully accrued by the date the
a. Employee is fully eligible for benefits
b. Employee retires
c. Benefits are utilized
d. Benefits are paid (5/94, FAR, #27, 4842)

SIMULATIONS

Problem 9-2 (40 to 50 minutes)

Scenario	Responses	Research Task

The following information pertains to Sparta Co.'s defined benefit pension plan and Sparta has not yet adopted SFAS 158.

Discount rate	8%
Expected rate of return	10%
Average service life	12 years
At January 1, year 2:	
Projected benefit obligation	$600,000
Fair value of pension plan assets	720,000
Unrecognized prior service cost	240,000
Unamortized prior pension gain	96,000
At December 31, year 2:	
Projected benefit obligation	$910,000
Fair value of pension plan assets	825,000

Service cost for the current year was $90,000. There were no contributions made or benefits paid during the year. Sparta's unfunded accrued pension liability was $8,000 at January 1, year 2. Sparta uses the straight-line method of amortization over the maximum period permitted.

Scenario	Responses	Research Task

For items 1 through 5, calculate the amounts to be recognized as components of Sparta's unfunded accrued pension liability at December 31, year 2:

1. __________ Interest cost.
2. __________ Expected return on plan assets.
3. __________ Actual return on plan assets.
4. __________ Amortization of prior service costs.
5. __________ Minimum amortization of unrecognized pension gain.

For items 6 through 10, determine whether the component increases (I) or decreases (D) Sparta's unfunded accrued pension liability.

6. __________ Service cost.
7. __________ Deferral of gain on pension plan assets.
8. __________ Actual return on plan assets.
9. __________ Amortization of prior service costs.
10. __________ Amortization of unrecognized pension gain. (5/93, P1, #4(61-70), amended, 4100)

Scenario | Responses | **Research Task**

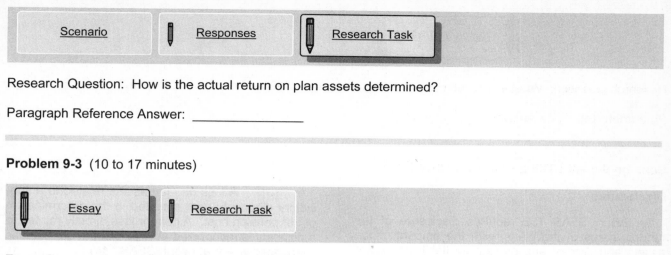

Research Question: How is the actual return on plan assets determined?

Paragraph Reference Answer: ______________

Problem 9-3 (10 to 17 minutes)

Essay | Research Task

Essex Company has a single-employer defined benefit pension plan for its employees.

a. Define the interest cost component of net pension cost for a period. How should Essex determine its interest cost component of net pension cost for a period?

b. Define prior service cost. How should Essex account for prior service cost? Why?

(11/89, Theory, #4a, b, 3572)

Essay | **Research Task**

Research Question: What are fundamental to the measurements of net periodic pension cost and pension obligations required in accounting for pensions?

Paragraph Reference Answer: ______________

Problem 9-4 (15 to 25 minutes)

Essay | Research Task

At December 31, year 1, as a result of its single employer-defined benefit pension plan, Bighorn Co. had an unrecognized net loss and an unfunded accrued pension cost. Bighorn's pension plan and its actuarial assumptions have not changed since it began operations fourteen years ago. Bighorn has made annual contributions to the plan and has not yet adopted SFAS 158.

a. Identify the components of net pension cost that should be recognized in Bighorn's year 1 financial statements.

b. What circumstances caused Bighorn's

1. Unrecognized net loss?
2. Unfunded accrued pension cost?

c. How should Bighorn compute its minimum pension liability and any additional pension liability?

(5/92, Theory, amended, #5, 9911)

Essay	Research Task

Research Question: What is the definition of a single-employer defined benefit pension plan?

Paragraph Reference Answer: ______________

Solution 9-1 MULTIPLE CHOICE ANSWERS

Disclosures

1. (d) SFAS 132 requires disclosure of the funded status of the plans, with the amount of the assets and current and noncurrent liabilities shown separately in the statement of financial position.

2. (a) An employer sponsoring a benefit plan should disclose, among other things, the assumed health care cost trend rate(s) for the next year and a general description of the direction and pattern of change as well as the ultimate trend rate(s) and when the rate is expected to occur. The employer must also disclose the accumulated post-retirement benefit obligation. (SFAS 132)

3. (d) Required pension disclosures include a plan description; the amount of net periodic benefit cost, by component; and several key assumptions, including the weighted average discount rate. Estimates of future contributions need not be disclosed.

Net Periodic Pension Cost

4. (b)

Increase in fair value of plan assets ($525,000 – $350,000)	$ 175,000
Less: Increase due to employer contributions	(110,000)
Add: Decrease due to benefit payments	85,000
Actual return on plan assets	$ 150,000

5. (d) Interest cost represents the increase in the projected benefit obligation due to the passage of time, and is computed by multiplying the projected benefit obligation at 1/1 by the assumed discount (settlement) rate. The projected benefit obligation is increased by the interest costs and service costs for the year and decreased by any pension benefits paid during the year.

Projected benefit obligation at 1/1	$ 72,000
Interest cost for the year ($72,000 × 10%)	7,200
Service costs for the year	18,000
Pension benefits paid during the year	(15,000)
Projected benefit obligation, 12/31	$ 82,200

6. (d) A loss on plan assets related to a subsidiary disposal is not included in the determination of net pension cost. A gain or loss directly related to a disposal is recognized as a part of the gain or loss associated with that event (SFAS 144).

Service cost	$160,000
Annual interest on pension obligation	50,000
Actual and expected gain on plan assets	(35,000)
Amortization of prior service cost	5,000
Net pension cost	$180,000

7. (b)

Service cost	$300,000
Return on plan assets	(80,000)
Interest cost on projected benefit obligation	164,000
Amortization of actuarial loss	30,000
Amortization of remaining net obligation	70,000
Pension cost	$484,000

8. (c) The service cost component of net periodic pension cost is a portion of the projected benefit obligation. Therefore, it is measured using the projected benefit obligation.

9. (d) Service cost for a period is the increase in the projected benefit obligation due to services rendered by employees during that period. All information on covered employees for the previous and current year is the same, and the current year is one year closer to the payment of retirement benefits. Therefore, service cost will be greater in the current year as compared to the previous year because the present value computation will be greater due to one less year of discounting. The plan requires equal annual contributions, but service costs are less in the beginning and more later. Therefore, the contribution in the previous year will exceed the previous year service costs, resulting in prepaid pension cost to be reported on the previous year balance sheet. **Note:** Had Flood adopted SFAS 158, the asset or liability would be based on the difference between the projected benefit obligation and the fair value of plan assets, not the difference between the previous year's contribution amount and service costs.

10. (c) Interest cost included in net pension cost is the increase in the projected benefit obligation due to the passage of time (SFAS 87, ¶22).

11. (b) The projected benefit obligation is determined using the settlement rate and not the expected or actual return on plan assets (SFAS 87, ¶44). These two rates, however, do have an impact on the determination of net periodic pension cost.

12. (c) The cost of retroactive benefits generated by a plan amendment is amortized by assigning an equal amount to each year of future service for each employee active at the date of the amendment expected to receive benefits under the plan. SFAS 87 permits the use of simplified methods, including the use of the straight-line method that amortizes the cost over the average remaining service life of the active participants. The average remaining service life is 5 years, calculated by adding the expected remaining years of service of the participants (3 + 5 + 5 + 7 = 20 years) and dividing by the number of participants (4). The total credit of $100,000 would thus be amortized over 5 years, at $20,000 per year. If instead the amortization is calculated by prorating for each year over the next 7 years, during the first year 4 participants remain in active service; 4/20 × ($100,000) = $20,000. In this problem, during each of the first three years the amortization is the same under either method.

13. (c) The $180,000 of unrecognized or remaining net obligation at the beginning of the current year is computed as the excess at that date of the projected benefit obligation over the fair value of plan assets ($780,000 – $600,000 = $180,000), since at that date all amounts accrued as net periodic pension cost had been contributed to the plan. Typically, the net obligation should be amortized on a straight-line basis over the average remaining service period of employees expected to receive benefits under the plan. However, because the average remaining service period is less than 15 years (10 < 15), Reed may elect to use a 15-year period. Therefore, the amount of net obligation that Reed should amortize to minimize its accrual for pension cost is <u>$12,000</u> ($180,000 / 15).

14. (a) The following components are included in net pension cost: (1) service cost, (2) interest cost, (3) actual return on plan assets, (4) amortization of prior service cost unrecognized or included in accumulated other comprehensive income, (5) gain or loss (including the effects of changes in assumptions) to the extent recognized, and (6) amortization of the unrecognized or remaining net obligation (and loss or cost) or unrecognized or remaining net asset (and gain) existing at the date of initial application of SFAS 87. The fair value of plan assets should *not* be included in net pension cost.

15. (d) The plan amendment granted increased benefits for services provided prior to the current year. Because the plan amendment was granted with the expectation that Tern will realize economic benefits in future periods, the cost of providing the retroactive benefits should not be included in pension cost entirely in the year of amendment. Instead, the prior service cost should be recognized during the future service periods of those employees active at the date of the amendment who are expected to receive benefits under the plan (i.e., in current and following years).

Recognition of Liabilities & Assets

16. (c) Loch contributed $1,000,000 to the plan. Therefore, in its 12/31, year 2 balance sheet, Loch should report prepaid pension cost an asset of <u>$480,000</u> (i.e., $1,000,000 – $520,000).

Service and interest cost	$ 620,000
Return on plan assets ($1,000,000 × 10%)	(100,000)
Pension cost	$ 520,000

Note: Following adoption of SFAS 158, the asset recognized on the balance sheet is the amount the fair value of plan assets exceeds the projected benefit obligation.

17. (a)

Service and interest costs	$ 720,000
Less: Contributions	(400,000)
Less: Actual return on plan assets (10% of $400,000)	(40,000)
Accrued pension cost	$ 280,000

Note: Following adoption of SFAS 158, the liability recognized on the balance sheet is the amount the projected benefit obligation exceeds the fair value of plan assets.

18. (a) Prior to adopting SFAS 158, a liability (unfunded accrued pension cost) is recognized for the amount that cumulative net periodic pension cost exceeds contributions to the plan. Following adoption of SFAS 158, the liability recognized is for the amount the projected benefit obligation exceeds the fair value of plan assets.

19. (d) During years 7 and 8, Webb expects to accrue pension cost of $165,000 (i.e., $75,000 + $90,000). In order to report an accrued pension liability of $15,000 in its 12/31, year 8 balance sheet, Webb must make funding payments of $150,000 (i.e., $165,000 – $15,000) during years 7 and 8.

Since Webb made a funding payment of $50,000 in year 7, it will have to make a funding payment of $100,000 (i.e., $150,000 – $50,000) in year 8. **Note:** If Webb had adopted SFAS 158, the pension liability, recognized would be the amount the projected benefit obligation exceeded the fair value of plan assets. The answer would be c, $75,000 (i.e., $750,000 – $675,000) in year 8.

20. (a) Unfunded accrued pension costs, a liability, consists of the net periodic pension cost adjusted for employer contributions and previous prepaid costs or accrued costs.

Service cost		$19,000
Interest cost		38,000
Amortization of prior service cost		52,000
Less: Actual return on plan assets		(22,000)
Net periodic pension cost		87,000
Less: Prepaid pension cost, 1/1	$ 2,000	
Employer contributions	40,000	(42,000)
Unfunded accrued pension cost 12/31		$45,000

Note: Following adoption of SFAS 158, the liability recognized on the balance sheet is the amount the projected benefit obligation exceeds the fair value of plan assets.

21. (d) In the current year, East accrued pension cost of $174,000 (i.e., $150,000 service cost + $24,000 prior service cost amortization) and made funding payments of $210,000 (i.e., $150,000 for service cost + $60,000 for prior service cost). The amount of East's prepaid pension cost at 12/31 is $36,000 (i.e., $210,000 funding payments – $174,000 accrued pension cost). **Note:** Following adoption of SFAS 158, the asset recognized on the balance sheet is the amount the fair value of plan assets exceeds the projected benefit obligation.

22. (d) Prior to SFAS 158, the amount of the pension liability that should be reported was the amount of the unfunded accumulated benefit obligation (i.e., the excess of the accumulated benefit obligation over the fair value of plan assets).

Accumulated benefit obligation	$ 4,300,000
Fair value of plan assets	(3,450,000)
Unfunded accumulated benefit obligation	$ 850,000

Note: Following adoption of SFAS 158, the liability recognized on the balance sheet is the amount the projected benefit obligation exceeds the fair value of plan assets. Under SFAS 158, the correct answer would be b, $2,250,000.

23. (d) The $190,000 net pension cost for the current year is to be funded two months after the financial statement date, and thus is reported as a current liability at December 31 of the current year. A liability is reported when the accumulated benefit obligation exceeds the fair value of plan assets. Since the fair value of plan assets ($500,000) exceeds the accumulated benefit obligation ($480,000) at December 31, no additional pension liability is reported. **Note:** Following adoption of SFAS 158, the liability recognized on the balance sheet is the amount the projected benefit obligation exceeds the fair value of plan assets. Under SFAS 158, the answer would not be able to be computed because no projected benefit obligation is given in this example.

24. (c) During the year, Dell accrued pension cost of $303,400 ($220,000 + $83,400) and made funding payments of $334,400 ($220,000 + $114,400). At 12/31, Dell's prepaid pension cost is $31,000 ($334,400 – $303,400). **Note:** Following adoption of SFAS 158, the asset recognized on the balance sheet is the amount the fair value of plan assets exceeds the projected benefit obligation.

Minimum Liability

25. (b) The additional minimum pension liability is $25,000 – $20,000 = $5,000.

Accumulated benefit obligation	$103,000
Less: Plan assets at fair value	(78,000)
Unfunded accumulated benefit obligation	$ 25,000

Net periodic pension cost	$ 90,000
Less: Employer's contribution	(70,000)
Accrued pension cost	$ 20,000

Note: SFAS 158 eliminated the need for any additional minimum liability. The amount of the liability to be recognized equals the unfunded projected benefit obligation.

26. (b) Prior to SFAS 158, SFAS 87, ¶36 stated, "If the accumulated benefit obligation exceeds the fair value of the plan assets, the employer shall recognize in the statement of financial position a liability (including unfunded accrued pension cost) that is at least equal to the unfunded accumulated benefit obligation." **Note:** SFAS 158 eliminated the need for any additional minimum liability. Under SFAS 158, the liability to be reported would be answer a, excess of the projected obligation over the fair value of the plan assets.

27. (b) Prior to SFAS 158, SFAS 87, ¶36 stated, "If the accumulated benefit obligation exceeds the fair value of plan assets, the employer shall recognize in the statement of financial position a liability (including unfunded accrued pension cost) that is at least equal to the unfunded accumulated

benefit obligation." Thus, if a liability for accrued pension cost is already reported, the additional liability to be recorded is the amount by which the minimum liability (unfunded accumulated benefit) exceeds the accrued pension cost. **Note:** The employer must not have adopted SFAS 158 yet because it eliminates the need for any additional minimum liability.

28. (c) Prior to SFAS 158, the amount to be reported as the minimum liability relating to the pension plan is the amount of the unfunded accumulated benefit obligation (i.e., the excess of the accumulated benefit obligation over the fair value of the plan assets). **Note:** SFAS 158 eliminated the need for any additional minimum liability. Under SFAS 158, the liability to be reported would be answer d, unfunded projected benefit obligation.

29. (a) This is a poorly worded question. It is included so candidates learn to handle such questions. Prior to SFAS 158, the excess of the accumulated benefit obligation over the fair value of plan assets (i.e., $90,000) is the amount of the pension liability to be reported in the 9/30 balance sheet. The prepaid pension cost of $20,000 and the additional liability of $110,000 are netted into one amount and reported as pension liability in the amount of $90,000.

Accumulated benefit obligation	$ 380,000
Less: Fair value of plan assets	(290,000)
Unfunded accumulated benefit obligation	90,000
Add: Prepaid pension cost	20,000
Additional liability to be recorded	$ 110,000

Note: SFAS 158 eliminated the need for any additional minimum liability. Under SFAS 158, the amount of the liability to be reported equals the unfunded projected benefit obligation.

30. (c) Prior to SFAS 158, the excess of the accumulated benefit obligation over the fair value of the plan assets is the amount of the pension liability to be reported in the balance sheet. Because there is accrued pension cost of $200,000, recognition of an additional pension liability of $4,800,000 is required. The accrued pension cost of $200,000 and the additional liability required of $4,800,000 are combined into one amount and reported as accrued pension cost or pension liability in the amount of $5,000,000.

Accumulated benefit obligation	$12,000,000
Less: Fair value of plan assets	(7,000,000)
Unfunded accumulated benefit obligation	5,000,000
Less: Accrued pension cost	(200,000)
Adjustment	$ 4,800,000

Note: Under SFAS 158, the amount of liability to be reported equals the unfunded projected benefit obligation of $7,500,000 ($14,500,000 – $7,000,000). Answer d would be the correct answer.

31. (c) The net periodic pension cost of $8,000 for the year exceeded the $0 cash contributions to the pension plan during the year by $8,000.

Unfunded accumulated benefit obligation	$25,000
Less: Accrued pension liability	(8,000)
Additional pension liability	$17,000

Note: SFAS 158 eliminated the need for any additional minimum liability. The amount to be reported would equal the unfunded projected benefit obligation.

OCI

32. (a)

Additional pension liability	$ 17,000
Less: Unrecognized prior service cost	(12,000)
Excess of additional pension liability, 12/31	$ 5,000

Note: SFAS 158 eliminated the need for any additional minimum liability.

33. (a) Nola has an unfunded accumulated benefit obligation of $140,000. Therefore, Nola reports a minimum pension liability for this amount. Because Nola has $80,000 of accrued pension cost, an additional pension liability is recognized for $60,000 (i.e., $140,000 – $80,000). In recording the additional pension liability, an intangible asset (i.e., deferred pension cost) can only be recorded for $45,000 because the recognition of the intangible asset is limited to the amount of unrecognized prior service cost. The $15,000 ($60,000 – $45,000) excess of the additional pension liability required to be recognized over the unrecognized prior service cost represents a net loss not yet recognized as net periodic pension cost and should be reported in other comprehensive income (SFAS 130). **Note:** SFAS 158 eliminated the need for any additional minimum liability.

Postretirement Benefits

34. (b) The attribution period for accruing the expected postretirement health care benefit obligation begins with the date of hire and ends at the full eligibility date (SFAS 106, ¶44). Bounty provides postretirement health care benefits to employees who have completed at least 10 years of service and are aged 55 years or older when retiring. Fletcher is hired at 48 years old. Therefore, the attribution period for accruing Bounty's expected postretirement health

care benefit obligation to Fletcher is during the period when Fletcher is aged 48 to 58, because at age 58, Fletcher will have completed 10 years of service and be 55 years or older.

35. (a) The postretirement benefit cost is accrued over the attribution period, which is defined as the period of service during which the employee earns the benefits under the terms of the plan. Generally, the attribution begins when an employee is hired and ends on the date the employee is eligible to receive the benefits and ceases to earn additional benefits.

PERFORMANCE BY SUBTOPICS

Each category below parallels a subtopic covered in Chapter 9. Record the number and percentage of questions you correctly answered in each subtopic area.

Disclosures

Question #	Correct √
1	
2	
3	
# Questions	3
# Correct	______
% Correct	______

Net Periodic Pension Cost

Question #	Correct √
4	
5	
6	
7	
8	
9	
10	
11	
12	
13	
14	
15	
# Questions	12
# Correct	______
% Correct	______

Recognition of Liabilities & Assets

Question #	Correct √
16	
17	
18	
19	
20	
21	
22	
23	
24	
# Questions	9
# Correct	______
% Correct	______

Minimum Liability

Question #	Correct √
25	
26	
27	
28	
29	
30	
31	
# Questions	7
# Correct	______
% Correct	______

OCI

Question #	Correct √
32	
33	
# Questions	2
# Correct	______
% Correct	______

Postretirement Benefits

Question #	Correct √
34	
35	
# Questions	2
# Correct	______
% Correct	______

SIMULATION SOLUTIONS

Solution 9-2

Responses 1-10

1. $48,000

Interest cost included in net pension cost is determined as the increase in the projected benefit obligation due to the passage of time (SFAS 87, ¶22).

Projected benefit obligation, 1/1	$600,000
Times: Discount rate at which pension benefits could be effectively settled	× 8%
Interest cost for the year	$ 48,000

2. $72,000

The expected return on plan assets is determined based on the expected long-term rate of return on plan assets and the market-related value of plan assets. The market-related value of plan assets is either fair value or a calculated value that recognizes changes in fair value in a systematic and rational manner over not more than five years (SFAS 87, ¶30).

Fair value of plan assets, 1/1	$720,000
Times: Expected rate of return	× 10%
Expected return on plan assets	$ 72,000

3. $105,000

For a funded plan, the actual return on plan assets is determined based on the fair value of plan assets at the beginning and the end of the period, adjusted for contributions and benefit payments (SFAS 87,¶23). Therefore, since there were no contributions made or benefits paid during the year, the actual return on Sparta's plan assets is $105,000 (i.e., $825,000 – $720,000), the increase in the fair value of plan assets in the year.

4. $20,000

Prior service cost is the increase in the projected benefit obligation at the date of a plan amendment (or initiation of a plan). Prior service cost is amortized during the future service periods of those employees active at the date of the amendment (or initiation) who are expected to receive benefits under the plan. Since the amortization of prior service cost can be quite complex, a straight-line method that amortizes the cost over the average remaining service life of the active participants is acceptable. Therefore, the amount of prior service cost that Sparta should include in the calculation of 20X2 net pension cost is $20,000 (i.e., $240,000 ÷ 12).

5. $2,000

The minimum amortization of unrecognized pension gain that Sparta should include in the calculation of net pension cost is determined, as of the beginning of the year, as the amount by which the unrecognized pension gain exceeds 10% of the greater of the projected benefit obligation or the market-related value of plan assets, divided by the average remaining service period of active employees expected to receive benefits under the plan.

Unrecognized pension gain, 1/1	$ 96,000
Less: 10% of fair value of plan assets (i.e., the market-related value of plan assets), 1/1 ($720,000* × 10%)	(72,000)
Excess of unrecognized pension gain over 10% of the greater of the projected benefit obligation or the market-related value of plan assets at 1/1	$ 24,000
Divide by: Average service life	/ 12
Minimum amortization of unrecognized pension gain	$ 2,000

* At 1/1, the fair value of plan assets exceeds the projected benefit obligation (i.e., $720,000 > $600,000).

6. I Service cost is the actuarial present value of benefits attributed by the pension benefit formula to employee service during that period (SFAS 87, ¶21). Since service cost increases net pension cost, it also increases the unfunded accrued pension liability.

7. I Since the deferral of the gain on pension plan assets increases net pension cost, it also increases the unfunded pension liability.

8. D Since the actual return on plan assets decreases net pension cost, it also decreases the unfunded accrued pension liability.

9. I Since the amortization of prior service costs increases net pension cost, it also increases the unfunded accrued pension liability.

10. D Since the amortization of unrecognized pension gain decreases net pension cost, it also decreases the unfunded accrued pension liability.

Research

FAS 87, Par. 23

23. For a funded plan, the actual return on plan assets shall be determined on the fair value of plan assets at the beginning and the end of the period, adjusted for contributions and benefit payments.

Solution 9-3

Essay—Interest & Prior Service Cost

a. The interest cost component of the net pension cost for a period is the **increase** in the **projected benefit obligation** due to the **passage of time.** Essex would determine its interest cost component by applying an **assumed discount rate** to the **beginning** projected benefit obligation.

b. Prior service cost is the cost of **retroactive benefits** (increased benefits based on services rendered in prior periods) granted at the **date of adoption or amendment** of a pension plan. Prior service cost should be included in **net pension cost** during the **future service periods** of those **employees active** at the date of the pension plan adoption or amendment, as appropriate, who are expected to **receive benefits** under the pension plan. Prior service cost is incurred with the expectation that the **employer** will **realize economic benefits** in **future periods.**

Research

FAS 87, Par. 15

15. The assumptions and the attribution of cost to periods of employee service are fundamental to the measurements of net periodic pension cost and pension obligations required by this Statement. The basic elements of pension accounting are described in paragraphs 16-19; they are the foundation of the accounting and reporting requirements set forth in this Statement.

Solution 9-4

Essay—Comprehensive Illustration

a. The components of Bighorn's net pension cost calculation are:

- **Service cost.**
- **Interest cost.**
- **Actual return on plan assets.**
- **Gain or loss.**
- **The difference between the actual and expected return on plan assets.**
- **Any amortization of the unrecognized gain or loss from previous periods.**

b. 1. Bighorn's unrecognized net loss results from differences between actuarial assumptions and experiences for both its projected benefit obligation and returns on plan assets.

2. Bighorn's unfunded accrued pension cost occurs because **cumulative net pension cost exceeds cash contributed** to the pension fund.

c. Bighorn's minimum pension liability equals the **excess** of the **accumulated benefit obligation** over the **fair value of plan assets.** Bighorn's additional pension liability would equal any **excess** of this **minimum pension liability** over the **unfunded accrued pension cost. Note:** Under SFAS 158, there would be no unrecognized gain or loss. This amount would be recognized in accumulated other comprehensive income. Also, there would be no additional minimum liability. The amount of the liability to be recognized would equal the unfunded projected benefit obligation. Conversely, an asset is recognized for an overfunded projected benefit obligation.

Research

FAS 87, Par. 11

11. The most significant parts of this Statement involve an employer's accounting for a single-employer defined benefit pension plan. For purposes of this Statement, a defined benefit pension plan is one that defines an amount of pension benefit to be provided, usually as a function of one or more factors such as age, years of service, or compensation.

CHAPTER 10

OWNERS' EQUITY

I. **Overview** 10-3
- A. Owners' Equity 10-3
- B. Capital 10-3
- C. Capital Stock Values 10-4
- D. Common Stock 10-4
- E. Preferred Stock 10-4
- F. Securities 10-5
- G. Participation Rights 10-5
- H. Stock Rights 10-5
- I. Disclosures (SFAS 129) 10-6

II. **Capital Stock Issues** 10-6
- A. Cash Consideration 10-6
- B. Subscription 10-6
- C. Property Other Than Cash 10-7
- D. Going Concern Incorporation 10-7
- E. Lump-Sum Purchase Price 10-8

III. **Retained Earnings** 10-8
- A. Classification 10-8
- B. Statement of Changes in Retained Earnings 10-8
- C. Quasi-Reorganization 10-9
- D. Effect of Various Transactions 10-9

IV. **Dividends** 10-10
- A. Definition 10-10
- B. Significant Dates 10-10
- C. Property Dividends 10-11
- D. Liquidating Dividends 10-11
- E. Stock Dividends 10-11
- F. Stock Splits 10-12

V. **Treasury Stock** 10-13
- A. Overview 10-13
- B. Cost Method 10-13
- C. Par Value Method 10-14
- D. Retirement 10-14

VI. **Equity Reclassification** 10-15
- A. Overview 10-15
- B. Applicability 10-15
- C. Exempt 10-15
- D. Impact on Private Companies 10-16

VII. **Employees & Stock** 10-16
- A. Stock Option Plans 10-16
- B. Noncompensatory Plans 10-16
- C. Compensatory Plans 10-17
- D. Disclosure 10-19

VIII. Partnership Formation ... 10-20
- A. Revised Uniform Partnership Act ... 10-20
- B. Identifiable Assets Contributed ... 10-20
- C. Unidentifiable Assets Contributed ... 10-20
- D. Owners' Equity Accounts ... 10-21
- E. Profit & Loss Division ... 10-21

IX. New Partner Admission ... 10-22
- A. Overview ... 10-22
- B. Purchase ... 10-22
- C. Additional Asset Investment ... 10-23

X. Partner Withdrawal ... 10-25
- A. Overview ... 10-25
- B. Bonus Method ... 10-25
- C. Goodwill Method ... 10-26

XI. Partnership Liquidation ... 10-27
- A. Overview ... 10-27
- B. Lump-Sum Distribution ... 10-27
- C. Installment Distributions ... 10-28

EXAM COVERAGE: Historically, exam coverage of the topics in Chapter 10 has been 1 to 3 percent of the FAR section. More information regarding exam coverage is included in Appendix B, Practical Advice.

CHAPTER 10

OWNERS' EQUITY

I. Overview

A. Owners' Equity

SFAC 6 defines owners' equity as the residual interest in the assets of an entity after deducting its liabilities. In a business enterprise, the equity is the ownership interest. In other words, it is the combined total of contributed capital and all other increments in capital from profitable operations or other sources. Owners' equity may take several forms, depending on the type of ownership involved.

1. A sole proprietorship's equity consists of a single proprietor's equity account, *Owner's Equity* or *Net Worth.* This is the sum of the beginning capital balance, plus additional investments during the period, plus net income (or minus net loss) minus withdrawals. Because of the simplicity of this concept, we will not review it any further.

2. A partnership's equity consists of one capital account for each partner. A partner's investments and allocations of income and withdrawals are recorded in her/his individual capital account.

3. A corporation's equity consists of three main components: (a) contributed capital, which includes capital stock and additional paid-in capital; (b) retained earnings; and (c) the accumulated balance of other comprehensive income, or OCI, (SFAS 130). OCI is reported separately from the capital and retained earnings accounts, in the following classifications.

   a. Foreign currency items

   b. Minimum pension liability adjustments

   c. Unrealized gains and losses on certain investments in debt and equity securities

   d. Gains and losses on certain hedging activities

B. Capital

1. **Contributed Capital** Contributed capital represents injections of capital by stockholders.

   a. **Capital Stock** The par or stated value of the stock purchased by owners.

   b. **Additional Paid-In Capital (APIC)** Paid-in capital in excess of par or stated value.

2. **Legal Capital** The portion of contributed capital required by statute to be retained in the business for the protection of creditors is called legal capital. Legal or stated capital is usually valued as the total par or stated value of all shares issued. If stock is issued without a par or stated value, the total amount received for the stock is used. The following limitations are placed upon the corporation by law to safeguard its legal capital.

   a. Legal capital may not be used as a basis for dividends.

   b. Acquisition of treasury stock is limited to the amount of retained earnings.

   c. The amount of legal capital cannot be reduced arbitrarily by the corporation.

C. Capital Stock Values

1. **Par Value** Stock with a specified par value per share printed on the certificate. Generally, the stockholder's maximum liability to creditors in the case of insolvency is par value. The par value of all shares issued and subscribed will normally represent the legal or stated capital.

2. **No-Par Value** Stock with no specific par value assigned to it. No-par stock avoids the contingent liability involved with the issuance of par value stock at a price below par (discount). Additionally, the stated or assigned consideration received for all no-par value shares generally represents the legal or stated capital of the corporation.

3. **No-Par With Stated Value** Essentially treated in the same manner as par value stock.

D. Common Stock

Common stock represents the residual ownership interest in the corporation. Distributions on common stock are generally subordinate to the rights of other securities. Thus, holders of common stock usually bear the greatest financial risks, but may also enjoy the greatest potential rewards. The four basic rights of a common stockholder are:

1. Voting rights.

2. Dividend rights.

3. Preemptive rights to purchase stock issued by the corporation.

4. Rights to share in the distribution of assets if the corporation is liquidated.

E. Preferred Stock

Preferred stock is a security that has certain preferences or priorities not found in common stock: preference as to assets in the event of a liquidating distribution; generally, absence of voting rights (must be prohibited specifically in the charter); and preference as to dividends at a stated percentage of par or, if no-par, at a stated dollar amount and paid before dividends on common stock.

1. **Features**

   a. **Redeemable** Shareholders may redeem shares, at their option, at a specified price per share.

   b. **Convertible** Shareholders may exchange shares, at their option, for common stock.

Exhibit 1 ▸ Conversion

Preferred Stock	(shs. × par)	
Add'l. PIC—Preferred	(if any)	
Common Stock		(shs. × par)
Add'l. PIC—Common		(to balance)

   c. **Callable** The corporation may, at its option, purchase preferred stock for the purpose of canceling it.

Exhibit 2 ▸ Cancellation

Preferred Stock	(par)	
Add'l. PIC—Preferred	(if any)	
Retained Earnings	("loss")	
Cash		(call price)
Add'l. PIC—Retirement of PS		("gain")

2. **Preferred Stock Dividends**

a. **Cumulative** If all or part of the stated dividend on cumulative preferred stock is not paid in a given year, the unpaid portion accumulates (i.e., dividends in arrears). No dividends can be paid on common stock until the accumulated dividends are paid on the preferred stock. Dividends in arrears are not a liability; however, they should be disclosed parenthetically or in the footnotes to the financial statements.

b. **Noncumulative** If a dividend on noncumulative preferred stock is not paid in a given year, the dividend is lost forever.

c. **Fully Participating** Entitled to share excess dividends on a pro rata basis (based on par or stated value) with common stock. For instance, 4% fully participating preferred stock will earn not only a 4% return, but also, if amounts paid on common stock exceed 4%, then dividends will be shared ratably with the common stockholders.

d. **Partially Participating** Limited in its participation with common stock to some additional percentage of par or stated value or a specified dollar amount per share as stated on the stock certificate. For instance, the stock certificate may specify that 6% preferred will participate up to a maximum of 9% of par value, or 6% preferred will participate only in distributions in excess of a 10% rate on common stock.

e. **Nonparticipating** Limited to receiving dividends at the preferential rate.

F. **Securities**
Securities are the evidence of debt or ownership or a related right. The term securities generally includes options and warrants as well as debt and stock.

G. **Participation Rights**
Participation rights are contractual rights of security holders to receive dividends or returns from the security issuer's profits, cash flows, or returns on investments.

H. **Stock Rights**
Represents privileges extended by corporations to acquire additional shares of capital stock under prescribed conditions within a stated time period. Corporations often issue stock rights to existing common stockholders if additional common shares are to be issued to give them the opportunity to purchase a proportionate number of shares of the new offering.

1. **Issuance** No entry is required when stock rights are issued to existing stockholders (other than a memorandum entry); therefore, common stock, additional paid-in capital, and retained earnings are **not** affected when stock rights are issued. With respect to stock rights, only common stock and additional paid-in capital increase when stock rights are exercised. Retained earnings is not affected when stock rights are exercised.

2. **Exercise** An entry is required only when stock rights are exercised. Cash is debited for the number of common shares acquired times the exercise price of the shares. Common stock is credited for the par or stated value of the shares issued. Additional paid-in capital is credited for the excess of the cash received over the par or stated value of the shares.

Exhibit 3 ▸ Stock Rights

Cash (shares × exercise price)	XX	
Common Stock (shares × par/stated value)		XX
Additional Paid-In Capital (to balance)		XX

3. **Lapse** No entry is required when stock rights are issued to existing stockholders (other than a memorandum entry); therefore, no entry is required when stock rights expire. Common stock, additional paid-in capital, and retained earnings are **not** affected when stock rights lapse.

4. **Stock Warrants** Physical evidence of stock rights. The warrants specify the number of rights conveyed, the number of shares to which the rightholders are entitled, the price at which the rightholders may purchase the additional shares, and the life of the rights (i.e., the time period over which the rights may be exercised).

I. Disclosures (SFAS 129)

1. **Rights and Privileges of Securities Outstanding** An entity is required to disclose in the financial statements, in summary form, the pertinent rights and privileges of the various securities outstanding. Examples include, dividend and liquidation preferences, participation rights, call prices and dates, conversion or exercise prices or rates and pertinent dates, sinking-fund requirements, unusual voting rights, and significant terms of contracts to issue additional shares.

2. **Number of Shares Issued** An entity is required to disclose the number of shares issued upon conversion, exercise, or satisfaction of required conditions during at least the most recent annual fiscal period and any subsequent.interim period presented.

3. **Liquidation Preference of Preferred Stock**

   a. If an entity issues preferred stock or other senior stock that has a preference in involuntary liquidation considerably in excess of the par or stated value of the shares, the entity is required to disclose this information in the equity section of the statement of financial position. The disclosure may be made parenthetically or "in short", but not on a per-share basis or in the notes.

   b. In addition, the entity is required to disclose, either on the statement of financial position or in the notes, the aggregate or per-share amounts at which preferred stock may be called or is subject to redemption through sinking-fund operations, and the aggregate or per share amounts of arrearages in cumulative preferred dividends.

4. **Redeemable Stock** The amount of redemption requirements related to redeemable stock must be disclosed for all issues of capital stock that are redeemable at fixed or determinable prices on fixed or determinable dates in each of the five years following the date of the latest statement of financial position presented.

II. Capital Stock Issues

A. Cash Consideration

The issuance of stock is generally recorded by debiting cash or the appropriate asset accounts for the fair value of the consideration received. *Capital Stock* is credited for the par or stated value of the shares issued, and the balancing figure is credited to *Additional Paid-In Capital.* A shareholder who acquires stock from the corporation at less than par value incurs a contingent liability to the corporation's creditors for the difference between the par value and the issue price. The issuance of stock at a discount is illegal in most states today.

Example 1 ▸ Stock Issue

500 shares of $10 par value common stock are sold for $30 per share.

Cash (500 shares × $30)	15,000	
Common Stock (500 shares × $10 par value)		5,000
APIC—Common (to balance)		10,000

B. Subscription

A subscription is a contract to purchase one or more shares of stock in the future. Usually, shares of stock are not issued until the full subscription price is paid. If a subscriber defaults on a subscription contract, amounts paid to the corporation may be: returned in full; retained by the corporation, and an equivalent number of shares issued; or retained to cover any losses on resale and the balance, if any, returned.

Example 2 ▸ Subscription Issue

ABC Corp. received subscriptions for 20,000 shares of $50 par value common stock at $75 per share. ABC required an initial payment of 25% of the subscription price.

<u>Date of subscription contract</u>		
Cash (20,000 × $75 × 25%)	375,000	
Subscriptions Receivable (20,000 × $75 × 75%)	1,125,000	
Common Stock Subscribed (20,000 × $50)		1,000,000
PIC—Common Stock (20,000 × $25)		500,000
<u>Cash receipt and issuance of stock</u>		
Cash	1,125,000	
Subscriptions Receivable		1,125,000
Common Stock Subscribed	1,000,000	
Common Stock		1,000,000

C. **Property Other Than Cash**

Where stock is issued for noncash consideration, the property received and the amount of contributed capital should be recorded at the fair value of the property received or the market value of the stock, whichever is more objectively determinable. If fair values are not determinable, then appraised values or values set by the board of directors may be used.

Exhibit 4 ▸ Stock Exchanged for Property

Assets	(FV)	
Common Stock		(par or stated value)
PIC—Common Stock		(to balance)

D. **Going Concern Incorporation**

An unincorporated firm (i.e., a sole proprietorship or a partnership) may decide to adopt the corporate form. To achieve this, the new corporation issues stock (and possibly debt securities) in exchange for the assets of the going concern. The newly created corporation does **not** recognize gain or loss on the issuance of securities in exchange for the business' assets.

1. The acquired assets are recorded at their fair values. Current liabilities assumed generally are recorded at face amount and long-term liabilities at their present value.

2. The issued stock is recorded at par or stated value. Any excess of net assets acquired over par or stated value of the capital stock is credited to *Additional Paid-in Capital.*

Example 3 ▸ Going Concern Incorporation

On January 1, year 2, Kyle Fleming decided to incorporate his automobile repair and restoration business, Fleming Automotive. To this effect, he transferred the assets and liabilities of his business to a new corporation, Auto Concepts, Inc., receiving in exchange all 1,000 shares of its $10 par value stock.

Fleming Automotive
Balance Sheet, as of December 31, Year 3

Current assets (fair value, $25,000)	$ 20,000
Equipment (appraised value, $130,000)	150,000
Less, accumulated depreciation	(60,000)
Total assets	$110,000
Liabilities	$ 30,000
Kyle Fleming, Capital	80,000
Total liabilities and equity	$110,000

Required: Provide the journal entry to record the incorporation of the business.

Solution:

Current Assets	25,000	
Equipment	130,000	
Liabilities		30,000
Common Stock, $10 Par		10,000
Add'l. Paid-in Capital (balancing figure)		115,000

E. Lump-Sum Purchase Price

When a corporation sells two or more classes of stock for a lump sum, the proceeds are allocated among several classes of stock by one of two methods.

1. **Proportional Method** Allocation of the lump sum between the classes of stock in accordance with their relative fair values.

2. **Incremental Method** Allocation of the lump sum based on the known fair value of one security with the remainder of the lump sum being allocated to the other security.

III. Retained Earnings = ACC. NI – DIV – APIC

A. Classification

The *Retained Earnings* account is the final terminus for all profit and loss accounts. The balance represents the accumulated income of the corporation, less dividends declared and amounts transferred to paid-in capital accounts. Retained earnings should not include the following: gains from treasury stock transactions; gifts of property; additions to owners' equity attributable to reappraisals of property; or accumulated balance of other comprehensive income.

1. **Appropriated Retained Earnings** The portion unavailable for dividends. Some reasons for appropriation are to create a reserve for plant expansion, to satisfy legal requirements of a bond indenture, or to provide a cushion for expected future losses. Owing to the application of most state corporate laws, retained earnings is often appropriated in the amount of the cost of treasury stock acquired under either the cost or par value methods.

Exhibit 5 ▸ Appropriation of Retained Earnings

Retained Earnings	XX	
Appropriated RE—Plant Construction		XX

Costs associated with the construction of the plant are not charged to the appropriation. When the appropriation is no longer needed, the entry is reversed.

2. **Unappropriated Retained Earnings** That portion of retained earnings available for dividend distribution.

B. Statement of Changes in Retained Earnings

APB 12 states, "disclosure of changes in the separate accounts comprising stockholders' equity (in addition to retained earnings) is required to make the financial statements sufficiently informative. Disclosure...may take the form of separate statements or may be made in the basic financial statements or notes thereto."

Exhibit 6 ▸ Statement of Changes in Retained Earnings

Retained earnings, Jan. 1, year 1, as reported	XXX
+/– Cumulative effect of retroactive changes in accounting principles	XXX
+/– Prior period adjustments	XXX
Retained earnings, Jan. 1, year 1, as adjusted	XXX
+ Net income (– Net loss)	XXX
– Dividends declared	(XXX)
Retained earnings, Dec. 31, year 1	XXX

C. Quasi-Reorganization

A reorganization or revision of the capital structure, which is permitted in some states. This procedure eliminates an accumulated deficit as if the company had been legally reorganized without much of the cost and difficulty of a legal reorganization. Thus, the corporation will be able to pay dividends again. It involves the following steps.

1. Assets are revalued at net realizable value, but there is no net asset increase. (Any loss on revaluation increases the deficit.)

2. A minimum of the amount of the adjusted deficit must be available in paid-in capital (PIC). This might be created by donation of stock from shareholders or reduction of the par value.

3. The deficit is charged against PIC and thus is eliminated.

D. Effect of Various Transactions

Frequently, CPA exam questions ask about the effect of common transactions.

1. **Increases** In general, retained earnings (RE) is increased only as a result of net income generated by the firm. In addition, retained earnings may increase as a result of a prior period adjustment (e.g., the correction of an error) or certain special changes in accounting principle (e.g., change from the completed contract to the percentage of completion method of accounting for long-term construction contracts).

2. **Decreases** Retained earnings decreases as a result of dividends (cash, property, or stock) and net losses suffered by the firm. In addition, treasury stock transactions, certain stock splits, prior period adjustments, and certain special changes in accounting principle may also reduce retained earnings.

Exhibit 7 ▸ Transactions Affecting Retained Earnings

Transactions	Effect on RE	Amount
Operations—gains and losses	Increase **or** decrease	Net income or net loss
Dividends—cash or property	Decrease	Amount of cash or FV of property distributed (Note that gain or loss is also recognized on declaration of property dividends.)
Stock dividends:		
1. Small (≤ 20 to 25%)	Decrease	FV of stock distributed
2. Large (> 25%)	Decrease	Par value of stock distributed
Stock splits:		
1. Par reduced proportionally	No change	-0-
2. Par not reduced	Decrease	Par value of new shares

Acquisition of treasury stock:		
1. Cost method	No change	-0-
2. Par value method	No change **or** decrease	-0- [if cost ≤ (par + APIC)] Purchase price in excess of par and pro rata APIC
Sale of treasury stock:		
1. Cost method	No change **or** decrease	-0- (if sale price > cost) Excess of cost over sale price, but offset first to APIC on TS transactions
2. Par value method	No change	-0-
Prior period adjustments	Increase **or** decrease	Amount of adjustment, net of income tax
Certain changes in accounting principle	Increase **or** decrease	Amount of adjustment, net of income tax

IV. Dividends

A. Definition

Dividends represent the distribution to stockholders of a proportionate share of retained earnings or, as in the case of liquidating dividends, a return of capital. Dividends (except stock dividends) reduce stockholders' equity through the distribution of assets or the incurrence of a liability.

B. Significant Dates

1. **Declaration** The date of declaration is the date on which dividends are formally declared by the board of directors and the declared dividends (except stock dividends) become a liability.

Exhibit 8 ▸ Recording Dividend Liability

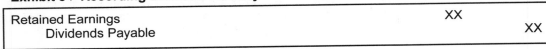

Retained Earnings	XX	
Dividends Payable		XX

2. **Record** The date of record is the date used to establish those stockholders who will receive the declared dividends. No journal entry is required unless the number of shares outstanding have changed from the date of declaration.

3. **Payment** The distribution of assets is made on the date of payment.

Exhibit 9 ▸ Dividend Payment

Dividends Payable	XX	
Cash or Other Property		XX

Exhibit 10 ▸ Cash Dividend

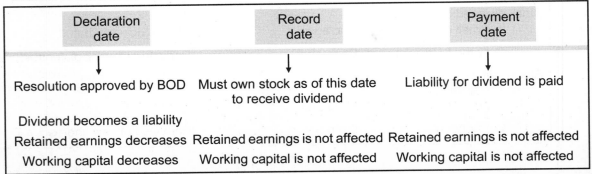

Declaration date	Record date	Payment date
↓	↓	↓
Resolution approved by BOD	Must own stock as of this date to receive dividend	Liability for dividend is paid
Dividend becomes a liability		
Retained earnings decreases	Retained earnings is not affected	Retained earnings is not affected
Working capital decreases	Working capital is not affected	Working capital is not affected

C. Property Dividends

At the date of declaration, property dividends are recorded at the fair value of assets given up, and any difference between fair value and carrying amount of the asset is recorded as a gain or loss as a component of income from continuing operations.

Example 4 ▸ Property Dividend

ABC Company transfers marketable debt securities that cost $1,500 to shareholders by declaring a property dividend. The fair value of the securities was $2,000 at the date of declaration.

Date of declaration		
Retained Earnings	2,000	
Property Dividends Payable		2,000
Investment in Marketable Securities	500	
Gain on Investment in Marketable Securities		500
Date of payment		
Property Dividends Payable	2,000	
Investment in Marketable Securities		2,000

NOTE: Any change in the fair value of the asset to be distributed between the date of declaration and date of payment is ignored.

D. Liquidating Dividends

Liquidating dividends are distributions in excess of retained earnings and, therefore, represent a return of investment rather than a share in profits.

Exhibit 11 ▸ Liquidating Dividend

Date of declaration		
Retained Earnings (nonliquidating portion)	XX	
Paid-In Capital in Excess of Par (liquidating portion)	XX	
Dividends Payable		XX
Date of payment		
Dividends Payable	XX	
Cash		XX

E. Stock Dividends

Issuance by a corporation of its own common shares to its common shareholders in proportion to their existing holdings (ARB 43).

1. **Effect on Shareholder Income** The shareholder has no income as a result of the stock dividend because the stock dividend (or stock split) is not a distribution division or severance of the corporate assets. The cost of the shares held *before* the stock dividend is allocated to all of the shares held *after* the receipt of the dividend (or split).

2. **Recording** Stock dividends operate to transfer a part of the retained earnings to contributed capital (capitalization of retained earnings). In recording the stock dividend, a charge is made to retained earnings (thereby making a portion of retained earnings no longer available for distribution) and credits are made to paid-in capital accounts. Because the declaration and issuance of a stock dividend decreases retained earnings and increases paid-in capital by equal amounts, total stockholders' equity is **not** affected. The amount of retained earnings capitalized depends on the size of the stock dividend and the apparent effect which the dividend has on the market value of the shares.

Exhibit 12 ▸ Stock Dividend

Small Stock Dividend Declaration & Issuance		
Retained Earnings	(FV)	
Common Stock		(Par)
Add'l. PIC—CS		(Balance)
Large Stock Dividend Declaration & Issuance		
Retained Earnings	(Par)	
Common Stock		(Par)

a. **Small** When the stock dividend is relatively small (not in excess of 20 to 25 percent of outstanding stock) the fair value (at the date of declaration) of the additional shares should be transferred from retained earnings to paid-in capital.

b. **Large** When the stock dividend is large (greater than 25% of the outstanding shares) only the *par or stated value* of the additional shares is to be capitalized.

F. Stock Splits

Increase the number of shares outstanding and proportionately decrease the par or stated value of the stock. There is no change in the dollar amount of capital stock, additional paid-in capital, retained earnings, or total stockholders' equity. Stock splits are issued mainly to reduce the unit market price per share of the stock, in order to obtain a wider distribution. *Reverse stock splits* simply decrease shares outstanding and proportionately increase the par or stated value of the stock (ARB 43).

Example 5 ▸ Stock Split

ABC Corp. declares a 3-for-1 stock split on common stock in order to increase trading of the stock on the open market. Prior to the split, the corporation had 300,000 shares of $12 par value common stock issued and outstanding. The journal entry to record the stock split would be the following.

Common Stock (par $12; 300,000 shares outstanding)	3,600,000	
Common Stock (par $4; 900,000 shares outstanding)		3,600,000

NOTE: The corporation may elect to record the stock split in a memorandum entry.

Exhibit 13 ▸ Total Stockholders' Equity

	RETAINED EARNINGS	PAR VALUE PER SHARE	TOTAL PAR VALUE	ADD'L. PAID-IN CAPITAL	# OF SHARES OUTST.	TOTAL S.H. EQUITY
Small stock dividend	⇓ by FV of shares issued	**x**	⇑	⇑	⇑	**x**
Large stock dividend	⇓ by par value of shares issued	**x**	⇑	**x**	⇑	**x**
Stock split	**x**	⇓	**x**	**x**	⇑	**x**

⇑ = increase; ⇓ = decrease; **x** = no change

V. Treasury Stock

A. Overview

Treasury stock is the corporation's common or preferred stock that has been reacquired by purchase, by settlement of an obligation to the corporation, or through donation. Acquisition of treasury stock reduces assets and total stockholders' equity (unless donated) while the reissuance of treasury stock increases assets and total stockholders' equity. There are two basic methods to account for treasury stock: the cost method and the par value method (ARB 43). The cost method is used more commonly.

1. Treasury stock is not an asset.
2. No gains or losses are recognized on treasury stock transactions.
3. Retained earnings may be decreased, but never increased, by treasury stock transactions.
4. Total stockholders' equity is the same under both the cost and par value methods. Total stockholders' equity decreases by the cost of treasury shares acquired and increases by the proceeds received from the reissuance of treasury stock, regardless of whether the treasury stock is accounted for by the cost or the par value method.
5. In many states, retained earnings must be appropriated in the amount of the cost of treasury stock.

B. Cost Method

The cost method views the purchase and subsequent disposition of stock as one transaction. The treasury stock is recorded (debited), carried, and reissued at the acquisition cost.

1. **Reissued in Excess of Acquisition Cost** If the stock is reissued at a price in *excess* of the acquisition cost, the excess is credited to an appropriately titled paid-in capital account (e.g., *Additional Paid-In Capital From Treasury Stock Transactions*).
2. **Reissued at Less Than Acquisition Cost** If the stock is reissued at **less** than the acquisition cost, the deficit is first charged against any existing balance in the *Additional Paid-In Capital From Treasury Stock Transactions* account. The excess, if any, is then charged against *Retained Earnings.*
3. **Balance Sheet Presentation** Under the cost method, treasury stock is presented on the balance sheet as an unallocated reduction of total stockholders' equity (i.e., contributed capital and retained earnings).

Example 6 ▸ Treasury Stock Transactions Comparison

Cost Method			Par Value Method		
Original Issue of 1,000 shares of $10 par value common stock at $15 per share:					
Cash (1,000 shares @ $15)	15,000		Cash	15,000	
Common Stock			Common Stock		10,000
(1,000 sh. @ $10)		10,000			
APIC—CS (1,000 sh. @ $5)		5,000	APIC—CS		5,000
Acquisition of 100 shares at $18 per share:					
Treasury Stock	1,800		Treasury Stock (100 sh. @ $10)	1,000	
Cash (100 sh. @ $18)		1,800	APIC—CS (100 sh. @ $5)	500	
			Retained Earnings (to balance)	300	
			Cash		1,800
Acquisition of 50 shares at $9 per share:					
Treasury Stock	450		Treasury Stock (50 sh. @ $10)	500	
Cash (50 sh. @ $9)		450	APIC—CS (50 sh. @ $5)	250	
			Cash (50 sh. @ $9)		450
			APIC—TS (to balance)		300

Reissuance of 50 shares at $20 per share (FIFO):					
Cash (50 sh. @ $20)	1,000		Cash (50 sh. @ $20)	1,000	
Treasury Stock (50 sh. @ $18)		900	Treasury Stock (50 sh. @ $10)		500
APIC—TS (to balance)		100	APIC—TS (to balance)		500
Reissuance of 50 shares at $9 per share (FIFO):					
Cash (50 sh. @ $9)	450		Cash (50 sh. @ $9)	450	
APIC—TS (up to existing bal.)	100		APIC—TS (to balance)	50	
Retained Earnings (to balance)	350		Treasury Stock (50 sh. @ $10)		500
Treasury Stock (50 sh. @ $18)		900			

C. **Par Value Method**

The par value method views the purchase and subsequent disposition of stock as two distinct transactions. Under this method, the acquisition of the treasury shares is viewed as a constructive retirement of the stock. Since capital stock is carried on the balance sheet at par (or stated value), the acquisition of treasury stock is also recorded at par (or stated value), by debiting *Treasury Stock*. Likewise, *Additional Paid-In Capital—Common Stock* is charged with a pro rata amount of any excess over par or stated value recorded on the original issuance of the stock. Note that the effect of these two entries is to remove the treasury stock from the accounts, i.e., as if it had been retired.

1. If the acquisition cost of the treasury stock is less than the price at which the stock was originally issued, the difference is credited to *APIC From Treasury Stock.*

2. On the other hand, if the acquisition price exceeds the stock's original issue price, then the excess is debited to *APIC From Treasury Stock,* but only to the extent of any existing balance (i.e., from prior treasury stock transactions). The excess, if any, is debited to *Retained Earnings.*

3. The reissuance of treasury stock under the par value method is accounted for in the same manner as an original stock issuance. However, any reissuances of treasury stock at less than par value will reduce (debit) *Additional Paid-In Capital From Treasury Stock* until that balance is exhausted, then debit *Retained Earnings* for any excess.

D. **Retirement**

A corporation may decide to retire some or all of its treasury stock. Retired stock is classified as authorized and unissued (i.e., as if it had never been issued). Accounting for the retirement of treasury stock depends on the method used initially to record it, i.e., cost or par value method.

Example 7 ▶ Retirement of Treasury Stock

Olde Company retires 20 shares of $100 par value stock originally issued at $105 per share.

Cost Method			Par Value Method		
Reacquisition of 20 shares at $110 per share:					
Common Stock (20 sh. @ $100)	2,000		Common Stock (20 sh. @ $100)	2,000	
APIC—CS (20 sh. @ $5)	100		Treasury Stock		2,000
Retained Earnings (to balance)	100				
Treasury Stock (20 sh. @ $110)		2,200			
Reacquisition of 20 shares at $98 per share:					
Common Stock	2,000		Common Stock	2,000	
APIC—CS	100		Treasury Stock		2,000
APIC—Retirement of CS (to bal.)		140			
Treasury Stock (20 sh. @ $98)		1,960			

VI. Equity Reclassification

A. Overview

SFAS 150 requires certain instruments previously classified as equity to be classified as liabilities, even though this classification is inconsistent with the current definition of a liability. SFAS 150 was issued in anticipation of a revision to the definition of liabilities encompassing certain obligations that a reporting entity can or must settle by issuing its own equity shares. It addresses questions about the classification of certain financial instruments that embody obligations to issue equity shares.

B. Applicability

SFAS 150 applies to issuer's classification and measurement of freestanding financial instruments, including those that comprise more than one option or forward contract. The following instruments are required to be reclassified as liabilities: A financial instrument

1. That is mandatorily redeemable, issued in the form of shares—that embodies an unconditional redemption obligation requiring a transfer of assets

   a. At a specified or determinable date(s) or

   b. Upon an event that is certain to occur.

2. Other than outstanding shares, that, at inception,

   a. Embodies an obligation to repurchase the issuer's equity shares, or

   b. Is indexed to an obligation to repurchase the issuer's equity shares, and

   c. Requires or may require settlement of the obligation by the transfer of assets.

3. That embodies an unconditional obligation that the issuer must or may settle by issuing a variable number of its equity shares, whether or not it is an outstanding share, if, at inception, the monetary value of the obligation is based solely or predominantly on any of the following:

   a. A fixed monetary amount known at inception.

   b. Variations in something other than the fair value of the issuer's equity shares.

   c. Variations inversely related to changes in the fair value of the issuer's equity shares.

C. Exempt

1. Features embedded in a financial instrument that is not a derivative in its entirety, such as conversion or conditional redemption features.

2. Classification or measurement of convertible bonds, puttable stock or other outstanding shares that are conditionally redeemable

3. Certain financial instruments indexed partly to the issuer's equity shares and partly, but not predominantly, to something else.

4. Nonsubstantive or minimal features are to be disregarded.

5. Forward contracts to repurchase an issuer's equity shares that require physical settlement in exchange for cash are initially measured at the fair value of the shares at inception, adjusted for any consideration or unstated rights or privileges, which is the same as the amount that would be paid under the conditions specified in the contract if settlement occurred immediately. Disclosures are required about the terms of the instruments and settlement alternatives.

D. **Impact on Private Companies**

1. Many privately-held businesses (including partnerships) require shares be sold back to the company upon termination of the agreement or death of the owner.

2. Events certain to occur (termination of the agreement or death of a shareholder) require classification of mandatorily redeemable shares of stock as liabilities, thus eliminating the equity of many privately-held businesses.

3. Publicly traded companies generally do not have these types of agreements.

Example 8 ▸ Equity Reclassification

Balance Sheet

Total Assets	$2,000,000
Liabilities other than shares	$1,400,000
Shares subject to mandatory redemption	600,000
Total Liabilities	$2,000,000

Note: The balance of the equity section is zero. "Shares subject to mandatory redemption" includes the value of common stock plus retained earnings as described in the notes to the financial statements.

Notes to the Financial Statements

Shares, all subject to mandatory redemption upon death of the holders, consist of:

Common stock, $100 par value, 10,000 shares authorized, 4,000 shares issued	$ 400,000
Retained earnings attributable to those shares	200,000
Total subject to mandatory redemption	$ 600,000

VII. Employees & Stock

A. **Stock Option Plans**
Basically, the appropriate accounting treatment for stock option plans is determined by whether the plan is compensatory or noncompensatory. Corporations often adopt plans whereby employees may obtain shares of stock under specified conditions. The reasons for establishing such plans include to raise additional equity capital, to enhance employees' loyalty to the company through widespread employee ownership of stock, and to provide additional compensation to key personnel.

B. **Noncompensatory Plans**
Noncompensatory plans (stock purchase plans) pose no unique accounting problems. These plans are adopted primarily to raise capital and induce widespread stock ownership among a company's employees. When the stock is issued, it is accounted for as an ordinary issue of stock.

1. **APB 25** Four criteria are essential to classify a plan as a noncompensatory plan under APB 25.

   a. Substantially all full-time employees may participate.

   b. Stock is offered to employees equally or based on a uniform percentage of salary.

   c. The time permitted for exercise is limited to a reasonable period.

   d. The discount from market price of the stock is no greater than would be reasonable in an offer to stockholders or others.

2. **SFAS 123** The SFAS 123 conditions to be met for an employee stock purchase plan to be considered noncompensatory, are more restrictive than the criteria under APB 25.

a. The plan contains no options features except that employees may be permitted to enroll in the plan during a short period, not more than 31 days, after the purchase price has been established. The purchase price may be based on the market price at the purchase date. The employees may be permitted to cancel participation before the purchase date and obtain a refund of amounts previously paid.

b. The discount from the market price does not exceed the greater of (1) a per-share discount that would be reasonable in a recurring offer of stock to shareholders or others, or (2) the per-share amount of stock issue costs avoided by not having to raise capital through a public offering. A 5% or smaller discount will automatically meet this condition. Larger discounts will require justification by the company.

c. Substantially all full-time employees that meet limited employment qualifications may participate on an equitable basis.

C. Compensatory Plans

Compensatory plans are those that do not meet the criteria for noncompensatory plans. If the employee pays less than the quoted market price of the stock at the measurement date, compensation expense must be measured and allocated to the appropriate periods of the employee's services. If the plan is deemed to be compensatory, then compensation cost will need to be recognized using the fair value method of option pricing.

1. **Employee** The definition of an employee includes elected outside members of the company's board of directors. An individual is considered an employee if the company granting the options has sufficient control over the individual as to establish an employer-employee relationship.

2. **Measurement Date** The measurement date is the date of the grant. When the measurement date occurs subsequent to the grant date, compensation expense is recorded and accrued at the end of each period based on the quoted market price at the end of the period, the estimated number of shares earned, and the option price.

3. **Intrinsic Value Method (APB 25)** SFAS 123 (revised 2004) superceded APB 25, and no longer allows the use of the Intrinsic Value Method.

4. **Fair Value Based Method (SFAS 12—Revised 2004)** SFAS 123 requires entities to adopt a **fair value based** method of accounting for stock-based compensation plans.

   a. **Fair Value** Fair value is defined as the amount at which willing parties in a current transaction would buy or sell an asset, other than in a forced or liquidation sale. The fair value based method calls for recognizing compensation cost of stock-based compensation based on the grant-date fair value of the award (with limited exceptions).

   b. **Valuation Models** SFAS 123 (Revised 2004) requires the use of a valuation model to estimate the value of the stock-based compensation granted. SFAS 123 (Revised 2004) suggests the use of the Black-Scholes, binomial, or similar pricing model which takes into account the following information as of the grant date: (1) the exercise price, (2) the expected life of the option, (3) the current price of the stock, (4) the expected volatility of the stock, (5) the expected dividends on the stock, and (6) the risk-free interest rate for the expected term of the option.

Exhibit 14 ▸ Black-Scholes Pricing Model

D	—	Dividends expected on the stock
E	—	Exercise price
V	—	Volatility of the stock
I	—	Interest rate (risk free rate) for the expected term of the option
L	—	Life of the option
S	—	Stock current price

c. **Exchanges With Nonemployees** When options or other equity instruments are exchanged for goods or services with a nonemployee, the transaction will need to be reflected at fair value. In such a case, the value received may be more readily determinable than the value of the options given.

5. **Future Services** If the stock or options are granted as compensation for future services, *Deferred Compensation Cost* is debited and the amount is recognized as compensation expense in the appropriate period. *Deferred Compensation Expense* is a contra-equity account.

6. **Previously Rendered Service** Where the employee works for several periods before the stock is issued, the employer accrues a portion of the compensation expense from the stock issuance.

Example 9 ▶ Compensatory Plan

An option is granted on January 1, year 1, to a key executive to purchase 5,000 shares of $20 par common stock at $40 per share when the market price is $46 per share. The key executive is awarded the option based on services to be rendered equally over four years. The options are worth $160,000.

Required: Make journal entries to record: (1) compensation cost on the measurement date, (2) annual compensation expense, and (3) issuance of the stock if the option is exercised at the end of 20X8.

Solution: On the balance sheet, deferred compensation cost is recorded as a deduction from stock options outstanding; it is not an asset. The "net" of these two accounts represents the compensation that the employee has earned to date.

(1)	*January 1, year 1*		
	Deferred Comp. Cost (value of options at date of grant)	160,000	
	Stock Options Outstanding		160,000
(2)	*December 31, year 1, year 2, year 3, and year 4*		
	Compensation Expense ($160,000 / 4)	40,000	
	Deferred Compensation Cost		40,000
(3)	*December 31, year 4*		
	Cash (5,000 shares × $40)	200,000	
	Stock Options Outstanding	160,000	
	Common Stock (5,000 × $20)		100,000
	Add'l. Paid-In Cap., Common (to balance)		260,000

7. **Unearned Stock Compensation** Where the stock is issued before some or all of the services are performed, the compensation that is unearned is shown as a separate reduction to shareholder equity, and is recognized as an expense over the years in which services are performed.

8. **Unexercised Stock Options for Nonvested Employees** If a stock option is *not exercised* because an employee fails to fulfill an obligation under the option agreement, the estimate of compensation expense recorded in previous periods should be adjusted by decreasing compensation expense in the year of forfeiture.

9. **Expired Stock Options of Vested Employees** Previously recognized compensation cost is not reversed if a vested employee's stock option expires unexercised.

10. **Adjustments to Compensation Expense** Adjustments to compensation expense in subsequent periods may be necessary as new estimates are determined.

11. **Repriced Options** When a company directly or indirectly reprices options, it has changed the terms of the plan, which would convert the award from a fixed to a variable award as of the date of the repricing. Accounting for variable awards under APB 25 includes an element of compensation expense.

12. **Employee Stock Ownership Plans (ESOP)**

Example 10 ▸ ESOP

On May 1 of the current year, Harrell Corporation established an employee stock ownership plan and contributed $20,000 cash and 1,000 shares of its $10 par value common stock to the ESOP. On this date the market price of the stock was $23 a share.

Required: Determine the amount of compensation expense that Harrell should report in its current year income statement.

Solution:

Cash contributed	$20,000
Fair value of common stock contributed (1,000 shares × $23)	23,000
Compensation expense recognized in the year	$43,000

a. **Valuation** The compensation expense that an entity recognizes for an ESOP is the amount contributed (or committed to be contributed) for the period. When a noncash asset or the entity's stock is contributed to the plan, the fair value of the asset or stock is used to measure compensation expense.

b. **Presentation** When an obligation of an ESOP is covered by an employer's guarantee or a commitment by the employer to make future contributions to the plan sufficient to meet debt service requirements, the obligation is presented as a liability in the employer's balance sheet. When the employer's liability is recorded, an offsetting debit is recorded that is reported as a reduction of stockholders' equity. Therefore, an employer reports a reduction of stockholders' equity equal to the obligation reported for the plan.

D. **Disclosure**

SFAS 148, *Accounting for Stock-Based Compensation,* amended the disclosure requirements of Statement 123 to require prominent disclosures in both annual and interim financial statements about the method of accounting for stock-based employee compensation and the effect of the method used on the reported results. The following information must be disclosed regardless of the method used.

1. The number and weighted-average exercise prices of options: (a) for those outstanding at the beginning of the year, (b) for those outstanding at the end of the year, (c) for those exercisable at the end of the year, (d) for those granted during the year, (e) for those exercised during the year, (f) for those forfeited during the year, and (g) for those expired during the year.

2. The weighted-average grant-date fair value of options granted during the year.

3. The number and weighted-average grant-date fair value of equity instruments other than options.

4. A description of the method and significant assumptions used during the year to estimate the fair values of options.

5. Total compensation cost recognized in income for stock-based employee compensation awards.

6. The terms of significant modifications of outstanding awards.

7. The method of reporting the change in accounting principles when a change to the fair value based method is adopted.

VIII. Partnership Formation

A. Revised Uniform Partnership Act

A majority of states have adopted the **Revised Uniform Partnership Act** (RUPA) which defines a partnership as an association of two or more persons to carry on, as co-owners, a business for profit. In addition to setting forth the legal rights and liabilities of the partners, the RUPA has some impact on accounting for partnership transactions. Accounting for partnerships must comply with the legal requirements as set forth by the RUPA (e.g., liquidation payments to partnership creditors before any distribution to partners) or other applicable state laws, as well as complying with the partnership agreement itself.

B. Identifiable Assets Contributed

All identifiable assets (e.g., cash, inventory, land, patents, etc.) contributed to the partnership are recorded by the partnership at their **fair values** (i.e., book values are ignored). All liabilities that the partnership assumes are recorded at their present values. If a partner contributes a noncash asset to the partnership (e.g., land or equipment) subject to a mortgage, the contributing partner's capital account is credited for the **fair value** of the noncash asset **less the mortgage assumed by the partnership.**

Example 11 ▸ Identifiable Assets Contributed

Alice and Brenda form a partnership: Alice contributes cash of $60,000; Brenda contributes a building with a fair value of $90,000 subject to a mortgage loan of $30,000.

Required: Provide the journal entry to record the partnership formation.

Solution:

Cash	60,000	
Building	90,000	
Mortgage Loan on Building		30,000
Alice, Capital		60,000
Brenda, Capital ($90,000 – $30,000)		60,000

C. Unidentifiable Assets Contributed

In the formation of a partnership, one or more of the partners may contribute an unidentifiable asset (e.g., managerial expertise or personal business reputation). Unidentifiable assets can be as valuable to the partnership as identifiable assets, such as cash, inventory, patents, and equipment. When one or more partners contribute unidentifiable assets, the formation of the partnership may be recorded under the **bonus** method or the **goodwill** method.

1. **Bonus Method** The bonus method assumes that unidentifiable assets contributed to the partnership do **not** constitute a partnership asset with a measurable cost. Under this approach, only identifiable assets contributed to the partnership, such as cash, inventory, patents, and equipment are recognized by the partnership. The bonus method allocates invested capital, equal to the fair value of the identifiable net assets contributed to the partnership, to the partners according to a specified ratio.

Example 12 ▸ Bonus Method

Alice and Brenda form a partnership. Alice contributes cash of $40,000 and her considerable managerial expertise; Brenda contributes a building with a fair value of $90,000 subject to a mortgage loan of $30,000. Alice and Brenda are to be given equal capital balances using the bonus method.

Required: Provide the journal entry to record the partnership formation.

Solution:

Cash	40,000	
Building	90,000	
Mortgage Loan on Building		30,000
Alice, Capital		50,000
Brenda, Capital		50,000

The bonus method does not consider Alice's managerial expertise to be a partnership asset with a measurable cost. The bonus method allocates the $100,000 [i.e., ($40,000 + $90,000) – $30,000] of invested capital to Brenda and Alice equally. Alice is receiving a capital bonus of $10,000 from Brenda because she is given a capital balance of $50,000, although she has only contributed identifiable assets of $40,000 to the partnership.

2. **Goodwill Method** The goodwill method assumes that unidentifiable assets contributed to the partnership constitute a partnership asset with a measurable cost. Under this approach, all assets contributed to the partnership, such as cash, inventory, patents, equipment, and managerial expertise are recognized by the partnership. The goodwill method credits the contributing partner's capital account for the fair value of the identifiable and unidentifiable assets contributed to the partnership, less the amount of any liabilities assumed by the partnership.

Example 13 ▸ Goodwill Method

Same situation as in Example 11, except that the goodwill method is to be used.

Required: Provide the journal entry to record the partnership formation.

Solution:

Cash	40,000	
Building	90,000	
Goodwill	20,000	
Mortgage Loan on Building		30,000
Alice, Capital		60,000
Brenda, Capital		60,000

The goodwill method considers Alice's managerial expertise to be a partnership asset with a measurable cost. Since Alice is to be given a $60,000 capital balance while only contributing identifiable assets with a fair value of $40,000, an implied value of $20,000 can be assigned to her managerial expertise. The goodwill method capitalizes the apparent value of Alice's contribution. Brenda is given a $60,000 capital balance, equal to the fair value of the building she contributed to the partnership less the mortgage assumed by the partnership (i.e., $90,000 – $30,000).

D. Owners' Equity Accounts

The **capital** account is an equity account used to account for permanent withdrawals, additional contributions and net income or loss. Other important accounts include the **drawing** account and **loans to or from partners.** The **drawing** account is used to account for normal withdrawals. It is closed at the end of the period into the capital account. **Loan accounts** are established for amounts intended as loans, rather than as additional capital investments. In liquidation proceedings, a loan to or from a partner is in essence treated as a decrease or increase to the partner's capital account, respectively.

E. Profit & Loss Division

The method of division to be used in any given situation generally is the method specified in the partnership agreement. This agreement must always be consulted first, since it is legally binding on the partners. The profit and loss sharing ratio may be entirely independent of the partners' ownership interests. For instance, two partners may share profits and losses equally, although they have ownership interests of 60% and 40%.

1. **No Arrangement Specified** If no profit and loss sharing arrangement is specified in the partnership agreement, RUPA requires that profits and losses be shared equally.

2. **No Arrangement for Losses** If the agreement specifies how profits are to be shared, but is silent as to losses, losses are to be shared in the same manner as profits. Conversely, if the agreement specifies the sharing of losses, but is silent as to profits, profits are shared in the same manner as losses.

3. **Equally or Specified Ratio** Equally or in accordance with a specified ratio set forth in the partnership agreement

4. **Capital Balance** According to the ratio of partners' capital balances as of a particular date or according to their weighted-average capital balances for the period

5. **Salary Bonus** According to the portions to be consumed as salaries or bonuses (guaranteed payments)

Example 14 ▸ Division of Profits

Foreman, Cramer, and Ramsey are partners in a going concern with capital accounts at the beginning of the period of $40,000, $24,000, and $28,000, respectively. Partnership income was $25,000. Foreman, Cramer, and Ramsey had drawings of $2,000, $1,000, and $2,000 respectively. The partnership agreement provides that:

a. All partners are to receive interest of 6% on beginning capital balances.
b. Cramer is to receive a $4,000 annual salary and Ramsey a $5,000 annual salary.
c. The remaining income is to be divided 30% to Foreman; 25% to Cramer; and 45% to Ramsey.

Required: Compute the ending capital balances of each partner.

Solution:

	Foreman	Cramer	Ramsey	Total
Beginning capital balances	$40,000	$24,000	$28,000	$ 92,000
6% interest on beginning capital balances	2,400	1,440	1,680	5,520
Guaranteed payments		4,000	5,000	9,000
Division of remaining income ($25,000 – $5,520 – $9,000)	3,144	2,620	4,716	10,480
Capital balances before drawings	45,544	32,060	39,396	117,000
Drawings	(2,000)	(1,000)	(2,000)	(5,000)
Ending capital balances	$43,544	$31,060	$37,396	$112,000

IX. New Partner Admission

A. Overview

A new partner may be admitted to the partnership by purchasing the interest of one or more of the existing partners or by contributing cash or other assets (i.e., investment of additional capital).

B. Purchase

When a new partner enters the partnership by purchasing some or all of the interest of an existing partner, the price paid for that interest is irrelevant to the partnership accounting records because it is a private transaction between the buyer and seller. The assets and liabilities of the partnership are not affected. The capital account of the new partner is recorded by merely relabeling the capital account of the old partner.

Example 15 ▸ Partnership Interest Purchase

Henry and Gerald are partners with capital accounts of $40,000 and $60,000, respectively. Rocky purchases Henry's interest for $50,000.

Required: Provide the journal entry to record this transaction.

Solution: After Rocky's purchase, total partnership capital continues to equal $100,000 (i.e., $40,000 + $60,000).

Henry, Capital	40,000	
Rocky, Capital		40,000

C. **Additional Asset Investment**
A new partner may be granted an interest in the partnership in exchange for contributed identifiable assets and/or goodwill (e.g., business expertise, an established clientele, etc.). The admission of the new partner and contribution of assets may be recorded on the basis of the **bonus** method or the **goodwill** method.

1. **Bonus Method** The bonus method assumes that unidentifiable assets contributed do not constitute a partnership asset with a measurable cost. Admittance of a new partner involves debiting cash or other identifiable assets for the fair value of the assets contributed and crediting the new partner's capital for the agreed (i.e., purchased) percentage of total capital. Total capital equals the **carrying amount** of the net assets prior to admittance of the new partner, plus the fair value of the identifiable assets contributed by the new partner. A difference between the fair value of the identifiable assets contributed and the interest granted to the new partner results in the recognition of a **bonus.**

Example 16 ▸ Bonus Method

Henry and Gerald are partners with capital accounts of $40,000 and $60,000, respectively; income and losses are shared equally (50%). The partnership records admissions of new partners under the bonus method. Rocky invests additional assets for a 1/3 ownership interest.

Required: Provide the journal entries to record Rocky's admission, if (a) Rocky invests $50,000; (b) Rocky invests $56,000; and (c) Rocky invests $44,000.

Solution:

(a) **No Bonus Recognized** Following the admittance of Rocky, the identifiable net assets of the partnership will have a carrying amount of $150,000 ($40,000 + $60,000 + $50,000). One-third of this amount, or $50,000, is assigned to Rocky's capital account. Since this is equal to the fair value of the identifiable assets contributed by Rocky ($50,000), no bonus results.

Cash (or other identifiable assets, as appropriate)	50,000	
Rocky, Capital (1/3 × $150,000)		50,000

After Rocky's admission, total partnership capital equals the carrying amount of the identifiable net assets of the partnership (i.e., $40,000 + $60,000 + $50,000 = $150,000).

(b) **Bonus to Old Partners** The total capital of the new partnership equals $156,000. Rocky's 1/3 interest of this new total is $52,000. The $4,000 excess of identifiable assets contributed by Rocky over his initial capital balance is divided among the old partners as a bonus on the basis of their profit and loss sharing ratio.

Cash	56,000	
Henry, Capital ($4,000 × 50%)		2,000
Gerald, Capital ($4,000 × 50%)		2,000
Rocky, Capital		52,000

After Rocky's admission, Henry's and Gerald's capital balances are $42,000 (i.e., $40,000 + $2,000) and $62,000 (i.e., $60,000 + $2,000), respectively, and total partnership capital equals the recorded amount of the identifiable net assets of the partnership (i.e., $42,000 + $62,000 + $52,000 = $156,000).

(c) **Bonus to New Partner** Since Rocky contributes $44,000, the total net assets of the new partnership will be $144,000. Rocky's 1/3 share of this is $48,000. The $4,000 difference between the fair value of the identifiable assets contributed by Rocky ($44,000) and the amount to be credited to him ($48,000) is allocated among the old partners in accordance with their profit and loss sharing ratio.

Cash	44,000	
Henry, Capital ($4,000 × 50%)	2,000	
Gerald, Capital ($4,000 × 50%)	2,000	
Rocky, Capital		48,000

After Rocky's admission, Henry's and Gerald's capital balances are $38,000 (i.e., $40,000 – $2,000) and $58,000 (i.e., $60,000 – $2,000), respectively, and total partnership capital equals the recorded amount of the identifiable net assets of the partnership (i.e., $38,000 + $58,000 + $48,000 = $144,000).

a. **No Bonus Recognized** When an incoming partner's capital account (ownership interest) is to be equal to the fair value of the identifiable assets contributed, the partnership books merely debit cash or other assets and credit capital for this amount.

b. **Bonus to Old Partners** When the fair value of the identifiable assets contributed by an incoming partner exceeds the amount of ownership interest to be credited to the capital account, the old partners recognize a bonus equal to this excess. This bonus is allocated on the basis of the same ratio used for income allocation (unless otherwise specified in the partnership agreement). Recording involves crediting the old partners' capital accounts for the allocated amounts of the bonus.

c. **Bonus Granted to New Partner** An incoming partner may contribute identifiable assets having a fair value less than the partnership interest granted to that new partner. Similarly, the new partner may not contribute any identifiable assets at all. The incoming partner is therefore presumed to contribute an unidentifiable asset, such as managerial expertise or personal business reputation. In this case, a bonus is granted to the new partner, and the capital accounts of the old partners are reduced on the basis of their profit and loss ratio.

2. **Goodwill Method** This method attempts to revalue the net worth of the partnership on the basis of the fair value of assets received in exchange for a percentage ownership interest. Following the admission of the new partner, the total capital (i.e., net worth) of the partnership is revalued to approximate its fair value. Existing identifiable assets must be revalued at their fair value; any excess valuation implied in the purchase price is recorded as goodwill.

Example 17 ▸ Goodwill Method

Same as Example 15, except the partnership records admissions of new partners under the goodwill method.

Required: Provide the journal entries to record Rocky's admission, as if (a) Rocky invests $56,000 and if (b) Rocky invests $44,000.

Solution:

(a) **Goodwill to Old Partners** As Rocky is to be credited with a 1/3 interest for $56,000, the implied capital (total fair value) of the partnership is $168,000 (i.e., $56,000 × 3). The $12,000 difference between the actual capital ($156,000) and the implied capital ($168,000) is recorded as goodwill attributable to the old partners in accordance with their profit and loss sharing ratio (50% each as stated above). The following journal entries are required:

Goodwill	12,000	
Henry, Capital		6,000
Gerald, Capital		6,000
Cash	56,000	
Rocky, Capital		56,000

After Rocky's admission, Henry's and Gerald's capital balances are $46,000 (i.e., $40,000 + $6,000) and $66,000 (i.e., $60,000 + $6,000), respectively, and total partnership capital equals the fair value of the net assets of the partnership (i.e., $46,000 + $66,000 + $56,000 = $168,000).

(b) **Goodwill to New Partner** As Rocky is to receive a 1/3 interest for $44,000, the old partners are to have a 2/3 interest. If 2/3X = $100,000 (old partners' capital), the implied value for 100% is $150,000 (100,000 / 2/3). Thus, Rocky's capital will be $50,000 consisting of $44,000 contributed and $6,000 goodwill. The journal entry is as follows:

Cash	44,000	
Goodwill	6,000	
Rocky, Capital		50,000

After Rocky's admission, Henry's and Gerald's capital balances are $40,000 and $60,000, respectively, and total partnership capital equals the fair value of the net assets of the partnership (i.e., $40,000 + $60,000 + $50,000 = $150,000).

a. **Goodwill Attributable to Old Partners** When a new partner's asset contribution is greater than the ownership interest s/he is to receive, the excess assets are accounted for as goodwill attributable to the old partners.

b. **Goodwill Attributable to New Partner** When a new partner's identifiable asset contribution is **less** than the ownership interest s/he is to receive, the excess capital allowed to the new partner is considered as goodwill attributable to her/him. This assumes that the recorded amounts of the old partners' capital accounts adequately reflect the fair value of the partnership's assets; otherwise, write off the excess carrying amount.

X. Partner Withdrawal

A. Overview

Admission of a new partner is not the only manner by which a partnership can undergo a change in composition. Over the life of any partnership, partners may leave the organization. Some method of equitably settling the withdrawing partner's interest in the business property is necessary. The withdrawal of a partner generally is recorded using either the **bonus** or the **goodwill** method.

B. Bonus Method

The difference between the balance of the withdrawing partner's capital account and the amount s/he is paid is the amount of the "bonus." The "bonus" is allocated among the remaining partners' capital accounts in accordance with their profit and loss ratios. Although the partnership's identifiable assets may be revalued to their fair value at the date of withdrawal, any goodwill implied by an excess payment to the retiring partner is **not** recorded.

Example 18 ▸ Bonus Method Withdrawal

On May 1, Able has decided to retire from the partnership. By mutual agreement, the assets are to be adjusted to their fair value of $260,000 at May 1, and the partnership would pay Able $60,000 for Able's partnership interest. No goodwill is to be recorded. On May 1, the balance sheet for the partnership of Able, Baker, and Cain, together with their respective profit and loss ratios, was as follows:

Assets, at cost	$200,000	Accounts Payable	$ 20,000
		Able, Capital (20%)	40,000
		Baker, Capital (20%)	50,000
		Cain, Capital (60%)	90,000
			$200,000

Required: Provide the journal entries to record this transaction and determine the balances of Baker's and Cain's capital accounts after Able's retirement.

Solution: The entry to adjust the partnership assets to their fair value is as follows.

Identifiable Assets ($260,000 – $200,000)	60,000	
Able, Capital ($60,000 × 20%)		12,000
Baker, Capital ($60,000 × 20%)		12,000
Cain, Capital ($60,000 × 60%)		36,000

After this entry, Able has a capital balance of $52,000 ($40,000 + $12,000).

Under the bonus method, the additional payment of $8,000 ($60,000 payment – $52,000 capital balance) made to Able is recorded as a decrease in the remaining partners' capital accounts. As Baker and Cain in the past have been receiving 20% and 60% of all profits and losses, respectively, 25% [0.2 / (0.2 + 0.6)] of this reduction is allocated to Baker and 75% [0.6 / (0.2 + 0.6)] to Cain:

Able, Capital	52,000	
Baker, Capital (25% × $8,000)	2,000	
Cain, Capital (75% × $8,000)	6,000	
Cash		60,000

After this entry, Baker's capital balance is $60,000 ($50,000 + $12,000 – $2,000) and Cain's capital balance is $120,000 ($90,000 + $36,000 – $6,000).

C. Goodwill Method

The partners may elect to record the implied goodwill in the partnership based on the payment to the withdrawing partner. The amount of the implied goodwill is allocated to all of the partners in accordance with their profit and loss ratios. After the allocation of the implied goodwill of the partnership, the balance in the withdrawing partner's capital account should equal the amount s/he is to receive in final settlement of her/his interest.

Example 19 ▸ Goodwill Method Withdrawal

Same as Example 17, except that goodwill is to be recorded in the transaction, as implied by the excess payment to Able.

Required: Provide the journal entries to record this transaction and determine the balances of Baker's and Cain's capital accounts after Able's retirement.

Solution: The entry to adjust the partnership assets to their fair value is the same.

Identifiable Assets ($260,000 – $200,000)	60,000	
Able, Capital ($60,000 × 20%)		12,000
Baker, Capital ($60,000 × 20%)		12,000
Cain, Capital ($60,000 × 60%)		36,000

After this entry, Able has a capital balance of $52,000 ($40,000 + $12,000).

Able's capital account must be increased by $8,000 to equal her $60,000 cash distribution. To accomplish this, goodwill is recognized for some amount, of which, $8,000 represents 20%, Able's profit and loss percentage. Therefore, the amount of goodwill to be recorded is $40,000 ($8,000 / 20%). The entries to record the implied goodwill of the partnership and the payment to Able in final settlement of her interest are as follows.

Goodwill	40,000	
Able, Capital ($40,000 × 20%)		8,000
Baker, Capital ($40,000 × 20%)		8,000
Cain, Capital ($40,000 × 60%)		24,000
Able, Capital ($52,000 + $8,000)	60,000	
Cash		60,000

After this entry, Baker's capital balance is $70,000 ($50,000 + $12,000 + $8,000) and Cain's capital balance is $150,000 ($90,000 + $36,000 + $24,000).

XI. Partnership Liquidation

A. Overview

Liquidation is the process of converting partnership assets into cash and distributing the cash to creditors and partners. Frequently, the sale of partnership assets will not provide sufficient cash to pay both creditors and partners. The creditors have priority on any distribution. The basic rule is that no distribution is made to any partner until all possible losses and liquidation expenses have been paid or provided for.

1. An individual prematurely distributing cash to a partner whose capital account later shows a deficit may be held personally liable if the insolvent partner is unable to repay such a distribution. The liquidation of a partnership may take place over a period of several months. The proceeds of a liquidation may be distributed in a lump sum after all assets have been sold and all creditors satisfied, or the proceeds may be distributed to partners in installments as excess cash becomes available.

2. In liquidation proceedings, a loan **to** a partner from the partnership is treated as a **decrease** to the partner's capital account. A loan **from** a partner to the partnership is treated as an **increase** to the partner's capital account.

B. Lump-Sum Distribution

The **first** step in the liquidation process is to sell all noncash assets and allocate the resulting gain or loss to the capital accounts of the partners in accordance with their profit and loss sharing ratio. The **second** step is to satisfy the liabilities owing to creditors other than partners. The **third** step is to satisfy liabilities owing to partners other than for capital and profits. The **final** step is to distribute any cash remaining to the partners for capital and finally for profits. Any deficiency (i.e., debit balance) in a solvent partner's capital will require that partner to contribute cash equal to the debit balance. If the deficient partner is insolvent, the debit balance must be absorbed by the remaining partners (usually in accordance with their profit and loss sharing ratio).

Example 20 ▸ Lump-Sum Distribution

XYZ Partnership is to be liquidated and excess cash, if any, is to be distributed to the partners in a lump sum. The balance sheet of the XYZ Partnership is shown with the profit-loss ratio indicated in parentheses next to each partner's capital account. A loss of $108,000 was realized on the sale of noncash assets.

XYZ Partnership
Balance Sheet

Cash	$ 22,000	Liabilities	$ 18,000
Other assets	128,000	Capital: (P/L ratio)	
		X (50%)	44,000
Total assets	$150,000	Y (30%)	44,000
		Z (20%)	44,000
		Total liabilities and capital	$150,000

Required: Provide a schedule showing the liquidation of assets and distribution of proceeds to creditors and partners.

Solution:

XYZ Partnership
Liquidation Statement

	Cash	Other Assets	Liabs.	Capital X(50%)	Capital Y(30%)	Capital Z(20%)
Balances before realization	$ 22,000	$ 128,000	$ 18,000	$ 44,000	$ 44,000	$ 44,000
Sale of assets at loss of $108,000	20,000	(128,000)		(54,000)	(32,400)	(21,600)
Balances after realization	42,000	$ 0	18,000	(10,000)	11,600	22,400
Payment of liabilities	(18,000)		(18,000)			
Balances	24,000		$ 0	(10,000)	11,600	22,000
Distribution of X's deficit	0			10,000	(6,000)	(4,000)
Balances	24,000			$ 0	5,600	18,400
Final distribution of cash	(24,000)				(5,600)	(18,400)
Balances	$ 0				$ 0	$ 0

C. **Installment Distributions**

Installment distributions may be made to partners on the basis of a **Schedule of Safe Payments**, in conjunction with a **Liquidation Schedule** similar to the one used for lump-sum liquidations. The Schedule of Safe Payments takes a conservative approach to the distribution by assuming that non-cash assets are worthless; thus no distribution may be made to partners on the basis of the value of partnership assets, until the assets are sold.

Example 21 ▸ Installment Distributions

Refer to Example 19. Liquidation of XYZ's partnership assets took place as per the schedule below. Disposal expenses to be incurred during the liquidation period were estimated at $5,000; this amount is to be held in escrow until the final liquidation.

XYZ Partnership
Liquidation of Assets

Date	Carrying Amount	Sale Price	(Loss)
June 24	$ 40,000	$ 5,000	$ (35,000)
July 7	60,000	13,000	(47,000)
August 3	28,000	2,000	(26,000)
	$128,000	$20,000	$(108,000)

Required: What is the safe amount of cash that may be distributed to each partner following each sale of partnership noncash assets? Show supporting schedule(s).

Solution:

XYZ Partnership
Liquidation Statement

	Cash	Other Assets	Liabs.	Capital X(50%)	Capital Y(30%)	Capital Z(20%)
Balances before realization	$ 22,000	$128,000	$ 18,000	$ 44,000	$ 44,000	$ 44,000
June 24 sale	5,000	(40,000)		(17,500)	(10,500)	(7,000)
Balance	27,000	88,000	18,000	26,500	33,500	37,000
Liabilities paid	(18,000)		(18,000)			
Balance	9,000	88,000	$ 0	26,500	33,500	37,000
Cash distribution*	(4,000)					(4,000)
Balance	5,000	88,000		26,500	33,500	33,000
July 7 sale	13,000	(60,000)		(23,500)	(14,100)	(9,400)
Balance	18,000	28,000		3,000	19,400	23,600
Cash distribution*	(13,000)				(1,400)	(11,600)
Balance	5,000	28,000		3,000	18,000	12,000
August 3 sale	2,000	(28,000)		(13,000)	(7,800)	(5,200)
Payment of liquidation costs	(5,000)			(2,500)	(1,500)	(1,000)
Balance	2,000	$ 0		(12,500)	8,700	5,800
Allocation of debit balance	0			12,500	(7,500)	(5,000)
Balance	2,000			$ 0	1,200	800
Cash distribution**	(2,000)				(1,200)	(800)
	$ 0				$ 0	$ 0

* See accompanying Schedule of Safe Cash Distribution.
** Note that final cash distribution may be made on the basis of balances shown in the partners' capital accounts, since all assets have been sold and liabilities paid.

XYZ Partnership
Schedule of Safe Cash Distribution

Date	Description	Capital Balances X(50%)	Capital Balances Y(30%)	Capital Balances Z(20%)	Total(100%)
June 25	Acct. bal. following sale of assets & pmt. of liabilities**	$ 26,500	$ 33,500	$ 37,000	$ 97,000
	Estimated cost of disposal	(2,500)	(1,500)	(1,000)	(5,000)
	Balance	24,000	32,000	36,000	92,000
	Maximum loss possible	(44,000)	(26,400)	(17,600)	(88,000)
	Balance	(20,000)	5,600	18,400	4,000
	Allocation of debit balance	20,000	(12,000)	(8,000)	
	Balance	$ 0	(6,400)	10,400	4,000
	Allocation of debit balance		6,400	(6,400)	
	Safe cash distribution*		$ 0	$ 4,000	$ 4,000
July 7	Acct. bal. following sale of fixed assets**	$ 3,000	$ 19,400	$ 23,600	$ 46,000
	Max. loss possible including $5,000 est. expense)	(16,500)	(9,900)	(6,600)	(33,000)
		(13,500)	9,500	17,000	13,000
	Allocation of debit balance	13,500	(8,100)	(5,400)	
	Safe cash distribution*	$ 0	$ 1,400	$ 11,600	$ 13,000

* To Liquidation Statement.
** From Liquidation Statement.

Don't forget the helpful hints in the material at the front and back of this text!

Now that you have had a chance to become familiar with the text format, you may want to skim the **Getting Started**, **Practical Advice,** and **Writing Skills** sections of the book again. These provide:

- Information on how to integrate materials so they work best for you
- Helpful information on answering all question types
- Information on the heavily tested topics on exams
- Information on how to use your time wisely
- Exam-taking techniques that will earn extra points on the exam

Remember, with the techniques and information in your material,

A passing score is well within reach!

CHAPTER 10—OWNERS' EQUITY

Problem 10-1 MULTIPLE CHOICE QUESTIONS (126 to 158 minutes)

cumulative preferred stock } Disclose in F/S notes

1. Rice Co. was incorporated on January 1 of the current year with $500,000 from the issuance of stock and borrowed funds of $75,000. During this first year of operations, net income was $25,000. On December 15, Rice paid a $2,000 cash dividend. No additional activities affected owners' equity in the year. At December 31, Rice's liabilities had increased to $94,000. In Rice's December 31 balance sheet, total assets should be reported at

a. $598,000
b. $600,000
c. $617,000
d. $692,000 (11/92, PI, #6, amended, 3239)

2. Zinc Co.'s adjusted trial balance at December 31 includes the following account balances:

Common stock, $3 par	$600,000
Additional paid-in capital	800,000
Treasury stock, at cost	50,000
Net unrealized loss on AFS marketable equity securities	20,000
Retained earnings: Appropriated for uninsured earthquake losses	150,000
Retained earnings: Unappropriated	200,000

What amount should Zinc report as total stockholders' equity in its December 31 balance sheet?

a. $1,680,000
b. $1,720,000
c. $1,780,000
d. $1,820,000 (5/92, PI, #5, amended, 2572)

3. On April 1 of the current year, Hyde Corp., a newly formed company, had the following stock issued and outstanding:

- Common stock, no par, $1 stated value, 20,000 shares originally issued for $30 per share.
- Preferred stock, $10 par value, 6,000 shares originally issued for $50 per share.

Hyde's April 1 statement of stockholders' equity should report

	Common stock	Preferred stock	Additional paid-in capital
a.	$ 20,000	$ 60,000	$820,000
b.	$ 20,000	$300,000	$580,000
c.	$600,000	$300,000	$0
d.	$600,000	$ 60,000	$240,000

(5/93, PI, #6, amended, 4048)

4. At December 31 of year 2 and year 3, Apex Co. had 3,000 shares of $100 par, 5% cumulative preferred stock outstanding. No dividends were in arrears as of December 31, year 1. Apex did not declare a dividend during year 2. During year 3, Apex paid a cash dividend of $10,000 on its preferred stock. Apex should report dividends in arrears in its year 3 financial statements as a (an)

a. Accrued liability of $15,000
b. Disclosure of $15,000
c. Accrued liability of $20,000
d. Disclosure of $20,000

(5/94, FAR, #8, amended, 4823)

5. During the previous year, Brad Co. issued 5,000 shares of $100 par convertible preferred stock for $110 per share. One share of preferred stock can be converted into three shares of Brad's $25 par common stock at the option of the preferred shareholder. On December 31 of the current year, when the market value of the common stock was $40 per share, all of the preferred stock was converted. What amount should Brad credit to Common Stock and to Additional Paid-In Capital—Common Stock as a result of the conversion?

	Common stock	Additional paid-in capital
a.	$375,000	$175,000
b.	$375,000	$225,000
c.	$500,000	$ 50,000
d.	$600,000	$0

(11/94, FAR, #29, amended, 5292)

6. At December 31 of year 1 and year 2, Carr Corp. had outstanding 4,000 shares of $100 par value 6% cumulative preferred stock and 20,000 shares of $10 par value common stock. At December 31, year 1, dividends in arrears on the preferred stock were $12,000. Cash dividends declared in year 2 totaled $44,000. Of the $44,000, what amounts were payable on each class of stock?

	Preferred stock	Common stock
a.	$44,000	$0
b.	$36,000	$ 8,000
c.	$32,000	$12,000
d.	$24,000	$20,000

(5/93, PII, #4, amended, 4113)

7. On November 2 of year 2, Fins Inc. issued warrants to its stockholders giving them the right to purchase additional $20 par value common shares at a price of $30. The stockholders exercised all warrants on March 1 of year 3. The shares had market prices of $33, $35, and $40 on November 2, year 2, December 31, year 2, and March 1, year 3, respectively. What were the effects of the warrants on Fins' additional paid-in capital and net income?

	Add'l paid-in capital	*Net income*
a.	Increased in year 3	No effect
b.	Increased in year 2	No effect
c.	Increased in year 3	Decreased in years 2 and 3
d.	Increased in year 2	Decreased in years 2 and 3

(11/93, Theory, #15, 4520)

8. Cricket Corp. issued, without consideration, rights allowing stockholders to subscribe for additional shares at an amount greater than par value but less than both market and book values. When the rights are exercised, how are the following accounts affected?

	Retained earnings	*Additional paid-in capital*
a.	Decreased	Not affected
b.	Not affected	Not affected
c.	Decreased	Increased
d.	Not affected	Increased

(5/91, Theory, #19, 1973)

9. In September of year 2, West Corp. made a dividend distribution of one right for each of its 120,000 shares of outstanding common stock. Each right was exercisable for the purchase of 1/100 of a share of West's $50 variable rate preferred stock at an exercise price of $80 per share. On March 20 of year 6, none of the rights had been exercised, and West redeemed them by paying each stockholder $0.10 per right. As a result of this redemption, West's stockholders' equity was reduced by

a. $ 120
b. $ 2,400
c. $12,000
d. $36,000 (11/95, FAR, #22, amended, 6104)

10. East Co. issued 1,000 shares of its $5 par common stock to Howe as compensation for 1,000 hours of legal services performed. Howe usually bills $160 per hour for legal services. On the date of issuance, the stock was trading on a public exchange at $140 per share. By what amount should the additional paid-in capital account increase as a result of this transaction?

a. $135,000
b. $140,000
c. $155,000
d. $160,000 (11/94, FAR, #28, 5291)

11. The condensed balance sheet of Adams & Gray, a partnership, at December 31, year 1, follows:

Current assets	$250,000
Equipment (net)	30,000
Total assets	$280,000
Liabilities	$ 20,000
Adams, capital	160,000
Gray, capital	100,000
Total liabilities and capital	$280,000

On December 31, year 1, the fair values of the assets and liabilities were appraised at $240,000 and $20,000, respectively, by an independent appraiser. On January 2 of year 2, the partnership was incorporated and 1,000 shares of $5 par value common stock were issued. Immediately after the incorporation, what amount should the new corporation report as additional paid-in capital?

a. $275,000
b. $260,000
c. $215,000
d. $0 (5/93, PII, #6, amended, 4115)

12. On March 1 of the current year, Rya Corp. issued 1,000 shares of its $20 par value common stock and 2,000 shares of its $20 par value convertible preferred stock for a total of $80,000. At this date, Rya's common stock was selling for $36 per share, and the convertible preferred stock was selling for $27 per share. What amount of the proceeds should be allocated to Rya's convertible preferred stock?

a. $60,000
b. $54,000
c. $48,000
d. $44,000 (5/92, PII, #1, amended, 2633)

13. The stockholders' equity section of Brown Co.'s December 31, year 1, balance sheet consisted of the following:

Common stock, $30 par, 10,000 shares authorized and outstanding	$ 300,000
Additional paid-in capital	150,000
Retained earnings (deficit)	(210,000)

On January 2, year 2, Brown put into effect a stockholder-approved quasi-reorganization by reducing the par value of the stock to $5 and eliminating the deficit against additional paid-in capital. Immediately after the quasi-reorganization, what amount should Brown report as additional paid-in capital?

a. $ (60,000)
b. $150,000
c. $190,000
d. $400,000 (11/95, FAR, #25, amended, 6107)

14. The following changes in Vel Corp.'s account balances occurred during the current year:

	Increase
Assets	$89,000
Liabilities	27,000
Capital stock	60,000
Additional paid-in capital	6,000

Except for a $13,000 dividend payment and the year's earnings, there were no changes in retained earnings for the year. What was Vel's net income for the year?
a. $ 4,000
b. $ 9,000
c. $13,000
d. $17,000 (5/93, PII, #3, amended, 4112)

15. At December 31, year 1, Eagle Corp. reported $1,750,000 of appropriated retained earnings for the construction of a new office building, which was completed in year 2 at a total cost of $1,500,000. In year 2, Eagle appropriated $1,200,000 of retained earnings for the construction of a new plant. Also, $2,000,000 of cash was restricted for the retirement of bonds due in year 3. In its year 2 balance sheet, Eagle should report what amount of appropriated retained earnings?
a. $1,200,000
b. $1,450,000
c. $2,950,000
d. $3,200,000 (5/93, PII, #5, amended, 4114)

16. On January 15 of the current year, Rico Co. declared its annual cash dividend on common stock for the current year ended January 31. The dividend was paid on February 9 of this year to stockholders of record as of January 28 of this year. On what date should Rico decrease retained earnings by the amount of the dividend?
a. January 15
b. January 31
c. January 28
d. February 9 (R/99, FAR, #10, 6779)

17. A company declared a cash dividend on its common stock on December 15 of the previous year, payable on January 12 of the current year. How would this dividend affect stockholders' equity on the following dates?

	December 15, previous year	*December 31, previous year*	*January 12, current year*
a.	Decrease	No effect	Decrease
b.	Decrease	No effect	No effect
c.	No effect	Decrease	No effect
d.	No effect	No effect	Decrease

(5/91, Theory, #17, amended, 1971)

18. In the current year, Bal Corp. declared a $25,000 cash dividend on May 8 to stockholders of record on May 23 and payable on June 3. As a result of this cash dividend, working capital
a. Was **not** affected
b. Decreased on June 3
c. Decreased on May 23
d. Decreased on May 8
(5/92, PII, #3, amended, 2635)

19. On June 27 of the current year, Brite Co. distributed to its common stockholders 100,000 outstanding common shares of its investment in Quik Inc., an unrelated party. The carrying amount on Brite's books of Quik's $1 par common stock was $2 per share. Immediately after the distribution, the market price of Quik's stock was $2.50 per share. In its income statement for the current year ended June 30, what amount should Brite report as gain before income taxes on disposal of the stock?
a. $250,000
b. $200,000
c. $ 50,000
d. $0 (5/93, PI, #45, amended, 4086)

20. East Corp., a calendar-year company, had sufficient retained earnings in year 1 as a basis for dividends, but was temporarily short of cash. East declared a dividend of $100,000 on April 1, year 1, and issued promissory notes to its stockholders in lieu of cash. The notes, which were dated April 1, year 1, had a maturity date of March 31, year 2, and a 10% interest rate. How should East account for the scrip dividend and related interest?
a. Debit retained earnings for $110,000 on April 1, year 1.
b. Debit retained earnings for $110,000 on March 31, year 2.
c. Debit retained earnings for $100,000 on April 1, year 1, and debit interest expense for $10,000 on March 31, year 2.
d. Debit retained earnings for $100,000 on April 1, year 1, and debit interest expense for $7,500 on December 31, year 1.
(5/94, FAR, #31, amended, 4846)

21. Instead of the usual cash dividend, Evie Corp. declared and distributed a property dividend from its overstocked merchandise. The excess of the merchandise's carrying amount over its market value should be
a. Ignored
b. Reported as a separately disclosed reduction of retained earnings
c. Reported as an extraordinary loss, net of income taxes
d. Reported as a reduction in income before extraordinary items (5/92, Theory, #36, 2729)

Loss in Income from Continuing operations

22. On January 2 of the current year, Lake Mining Co.'s board of directors declared a cash dividend of $400,000 to stockholders of record on January 18 and payable on February 10 of the current year. The dividend is permissible under law in Lake's state of incorporation. Selected data from Lake's previous year December 31 balance sheet are as follows:

Accumulated depletion	$100,000
Capital stock	500,000
Additional paid-in capital	150,000
Retained earnings	300,000

The $400,000 dividend includes a liquidating dividend of

a. $0
b. $100,000
c. $150,000
d. $300,000 (5/94, FAR, #32, amended, 4847)

23. Ole Corp. declared and paid a liquidating dividend of $100,000. This distribution resulted in a decrease in Ole's

	Paid-in capital	Retained earnings
a.	No	No
b.	Yes	Yes
c.	No	Yes
d.	Yes	No

(11/91, PII, #6, 2454)

24. A corporation declared a dividend, a portion of which was liquidating. How would this declaration affect each of the following?

	Additional paid-in capital	Retained earnings
a.	Decrease	No effect
b.	Decrease	Decrease
c.	No effect	Decrease
d.	No effect	No effect

(11/89, Theory, #21, 1987)

25. The following stock dividends were declared and distributed by Sol Corp.:

Percentage of common shares outstanding at declaration date	Fair value	Par value
10	$15,000	$10,000
28	40,000	30,800

What aggregate amounts should be debited to retained earnings for these stock dividends?

a. $40,800
b. $45,800
c. $50,000
d. $55,000 (5/91, PII, #12, 1093)

26. Plack Co. purchased 10,000 shares (2% ownership) of Ty Corp. on February 14 of the current year. Plack received a stock dividend of 2,000 shares on April 30 when the market value per share was $35. Ty paid a cash dividend of $2 per share on December 15. In its current year income statement, what amount should Plack report as dividend income?

a. $20,000
b. $24,000
c. $90,000
d. $94,000 (R/01, FAR, #5, 6980)

27. On May 18 of the current year, Sol Corp.'s board of directors declared a 10% stock dividend. The market price of Sol's 3,000 outstanding shares of $2 par value common stock was $9 per share on that date. The stock dividend was distributed on July 21 of this year, when the stock's market price was $10 per share. What amount should Sol credit to additional paid-in capital for this stock dividend?

a. $2,100
b. $2,400
c. $2,700
d. $3,000 (11/92, PII, #41, amended, 3375)

28. Universe Co. issued 500,000 shares of common stock in the current year. Universe declared a 30% stock dividend. The market value was $50 per share, the par value was $10, and the average issue price was $30 per share. By what amount will Universe decrease stockholders' equity for the dividend?

a. $0
b. $1,500,000
c. $4,500,000
d. $7,500,000 (R/05, FAR, 1481F, #30, 7774)

29. Long Co. had 100,000 shares of common stock issued and outstanding at January 1 of the current year. During the year, Long took the following actions:

March 15	— Declared a 2-for-1 stock split, when the fair value of the stock was $80 per share.
December 15	— Declared a $.50 per share cash dividend.

In Long's statement of stockholders' equity for the current year, what amount should Long report as dividends?

a. $ 50,000
b. $100,000
c. $850,000
d. $950,000 (11/94, FAR, #31, amended, 5294)

30. How would a stock split affect each of the following?

	Assets	Total stock-holders' equity	Additional paid-in capital
a.	Increase	Increase	No effect
b.	No effect	No effect	No effect
c.	No effect	No effect	Increase
d.	Decrease	Decrease	Decrease

(5/85, Theory, #17, 2012)

31. Nest Co. issued 100,000 shares of common stock. Of these, 5,000 were held as treasury stock at December 31 of year 3. During year 4, transactions involving Nest's common stock were as follows:

May 3 — 1,000 shares of treasury stock were sold.
August 6 — 10,000 shares of previously unissued stock were sold.
November 18 — A 2-for-1 stock split took effect.

Laws in Nest's state of incorporation protect treasury stock from dilution. At December 31 of year 4, how many shares of Nest's common stock were issued and outstanding?

	Shares	
	Issued	Outstanding
a.	220,000	212,000
b.	220,000	216,000
c.	222,000	214,000
d.	222,000	218,000

(11/95, FAR, #18, amended, 6100)

32. Murphy Co. had 200,000 shares outstanding of $10 par common stock on March 30 of the current year. Murphy reacquired 30,000 of those shares at a cost of $15 per share, and recorded the transaction using the cost method on April 15. Murphy reissued the 30,000 shares at $20 per share, and recognized a $50,000 gain on its income statement on May 20. Which of the following statements is correct?

a. Murphy's comprehensive income for the current year is correctly stated.
b. Murphy's net income for the current year is overstated.
c. Murphy's net income for the current year is understated.
d. Murphy should have recognized a $50,000 loss on its income statement for the current year.

(R/05, FAR, 1579F, #31, 7775)

33. Selected information from the accounts of Row Co. at December 31 follows:

Total income since incorporation	$420,000
Total cash dividends paid	130,000
Total value of property dividends distributed	30,000
Excess of proceeds over cost of treasury stock sold, accounted for using the cost method	110,000

In its December 31 financial statements, what amount should Row report as retained earnings?

a. $260,000
b. $290,000
c. $370,000
d. $400,000

(5/96, FAR, #1, amended, 6274)

34. On December 1 of the current year, Line Corp. received a donation of 2,000 shares of its $5 par value common stock from a stockholder. On that date, the stock's market value was $35 per share. The stock was originally issued for $25 per share. By what amount would this donation cause total stockholders' equity to decrease?

a. $70,000
b. $50,000
c. $20,000
d. $0

(5/93, PI, #11, amended, 4053)

35. If a corporation sells some of its treasury stock at a price that exceeds its cost, this excess should be

a. Reported as a gain in the income statement
b. Treated as a reduction in the carrying amount of remaining treasury stock
c. Credited to additional paid-in capital
d. Credited to retained earnings

(11/94, FAR, #32, 5295)

36. In the previous year, Seda Corp. acquired 6,000 shares of its $1 par value common stock at $36 per share. During the current year, Seda issued 3,000 of these shares at $50 per share. Seda uses the cost method to account for its treasury stock transactions. What accounts and amounts should Seda credit in the current year to record the issuance of the 3,000 shares?

	Treasury stock	Additional paid-in capital	Retained earnings	Common stock
a.		$102,000	$42,000	$6,000
b.		$144,000		$6,000
c.	$108,000	$ 42,000		
d.	$108,000		$42,000	

(11/91, PII, #7, amended, 2455)

37. At December 31 of the previous year, Rama Corp. had 20,000 shares of $1 par value treasury stock that had been acquired in that previous year at $12 per share. In May of the current year, Rama issued 15,000 of these treasury shares at $10 per share. The cost method is used to record treasury stock transactions. Rama is located in a state where laws relating to acquisition of treasury stock restrict the availability of retained earnings for declaration of dividends. At December 31 of the current year, what amount should Rama show in notes to financial statements as a restriction of retained earnings as a result of its treasury stock transactions?

a. $ 5,000
b. $10,000
c. $60,000
d. $90,000 (5/89, PII, #6, amended, 1103)

38. Treasury stock was acquired for cash at a price in excess of its original issue price. The treasury stock was subsequently reissued for cash at a price in excess of its acquisition price. Assuming that the par value method of accounting for treasury stock transactions is used, what is the effect on total stockholders' equity of each of the following events?

	Acquisition of treasury stock	*Reissuance of treasury stock*
a.	Decrease	No effect
b.	Decrease	Increase
c.	Increase	Decrease
d.	No effect	No effect

(5/90, Theory, #15, 1982)

39. Asp Co. was organized on January 2 with 30,000 authorized shares of $10 par common stock. During the year, the corporation had the following capital transactions:

January 5 — issued 20,000 shares at $15 per share.
July 14 — purchased 5,000 shares at $17 per share.
December 27 — reissued the 5,000 shares held in treasury at $20 per share.

Asp used the par value method to record the purchase and reissuance of the treasury shares. In its December 31 balance sheet, what amount should Asp report as additional paid-in capital in excess of par?

a. $100,000
b. $125,000
c. $140,000
d. $150,000 (11/95, FAR, #20, amended, 6102)

40. On incorporation, Dee Inc., issued common stock at a price in excess of its par value. No other stock transactions occurred except treasury stock was acquired for an amount exceeding this issue price. If Dee uses the par value method of accounting for treasury stock appropriate for retired stock, what is the effect of the acquisition on the following?

	Net common stock	*Additional paid-in capital*	*Retained earnings*
a.	No effect	Decrease	No effect
b.	Decrease	Decrease	Decrease
c.	Decrease	No effect	Decrease
d.	No effect	Decrease	Decrease

(5/91, Theory, #18, 1972)

41. The par-value method of accounting for treasury stock differs from the cost method in that

a. Any gain is recognized upon repurchase of stock but a loss is treated as an adjustment to retained earnings.
b. No gains or losses are recognized on the issuance of treasury stock using the par-value method.
c. It reverses the original entry to issue the common stock with any difference between carrying amount and purchase price adjusted through paid-in capital and/or retained earnings and treats a subsequent reissuance like a new issuance of common stock.
d. It reverses the original entry to issue the common stock with any difference between carrying amount and purchase price being shown as an ordinary gain or loss and does **not** recognize any gain or loss on a subsequent resale of the stock.

(5/89, Theory, #10, 1993)

42. On December 31 of the current year, Pack Corp.'s board of directors canceled 50,000 shares of $2.50 par value common stock held in treasury at an average cost of $13 per share. Before recording the cancellation of the treasury stock, Pack had the following balances in its stockholder's equity accounts:

Common Stock	$540,000
Additional paid-in capital	750,000
Retained earnings	900,000
Treasury stock, at cost	650,000

In its balance sheet at December 31, Pack should report common stock outstanding of

a. $0
b. $250,000
c. $415,000
d. $540,000 (11/92, PII, #50, amended, 3384)

43. Two years ago, Fogg Inc. issued $10 par value common stock for $25 per share. No other common stock transactions occurred until March 31 of the current year, when Fogg acquired some of the issued shares for $20 per share and retired them. Which of the following statements correctly states an effect of this acquisition and retirement?
a. Current year net income is decreased
b. Current year net income is increased
c. Additional paid-in capital is decreased
d. Retained earnings is increased
(5/93, Theory, #10, amended, 4198)

44. On January 2 of the current year, Kine Co. granted Morgan, its president, compensatory stock options to buy 1,000 shares of Kine's $10 par common stock. The options call for a price of $20 per share and are exercisable for 3 years following the grant date. The options are valued at $35,000 on the date of the grant. Morgan exercised the options on December 31 of the current year. The market price of the stock was $50 on January 2 and $70 on December 31. By what net amount should stockholders' equity increase as a result of the grant and exercise of the options?
a. $20,000
b. $30,000
c. $50,000
d. $70,000 (5/94, FAR, #33, amended, 4848)

45. On January 2, year 3, Farm Co. granted an employee an option valued at $32,000 to purchase 1,000 shares of Farm's $10 common stock at $40 per share. The option became exercisable on December 31, year 3, after the employee had completed one year of service, and was exercised on that date. The market prices of Farm's stock were as follows:

January 2, year 3	$50
December 31, year 3	65

What amount should Farm recognize as compensation expense for year 3?
a. $0
b. $30,000
c. $32,000
d. $60,000 (11/94, FAR, #33, amended, 9042)

46. In a compensatory stock option plan for which the grant, measurement, and exercise date are all different, the stock options outstanding account should be reduced at the
a. Date of grant
b. Measurement date
c. Beginning of the service period
d. Exercise date (5/93, Theory, #14, 4202)

47. On June 1 of the previous year, Oak Corp. granted stock options valued at $8,000 to certain key employees as additional compensation for the year. The options were for 1,000 shares of Oak's $2 par value common stock at an option price of $15 per share. Market price of this stock on June 1 of the previous year was $20 per share. The options were exercisable beginning January 2 of the current year and expire on December 31 of next year. On April 1 of the current year, when Oak's stock was trading at $21 per share, all the options were exercised. What amount of pretax compensation should Oak report in the previous year in connection with the options?
a. $8,000
b. $5,000
c. $2,500
d. $2,000 (11/92, PII, #56, amended, 3390)

48. Avers and Smith formed a partnership. Avers contributed cash of $50,000. Smith contributed property with a $36,000 carrying amount, a $40,000 original cost, and a fair value of $80,000. The partnership assumed the $35,000 mortgage attached to the property. What should Smith's capital account be on the partnership formation date?
a. $36,000
b. $40,000
c. $45,000
d. $80,000 (11/98, FAR, #9, amended, 6736)

49. Abel and Carr formed a partnership and agreed to divide initial capital equally, even though Abel contributed $100,000 and Carr contributed $84,000 in identifiable assets. Under the bonus approach to adjust the capital accounts, Carr's unidentifiable asset should be debited for
a. $46,000
b. $16,000
c. $ 8,000
d. $0 (5/91, PII, #1, 1300)

50. Cor-Eng Partnership was formed on January 2 of the current year. Under the partnership agreement, each partner has an equal initial capital balance accounted for under the goodwill method. Partnership net income or loss is allocated 60% to Cor and 40% to Eng. To form the partnership, Cor originally contributed assets costing $30,000 with a fair value of $60,000 on January 2 while Eng contributed $20,000 in cash. Eng's initial capital balance in Cor-Eng is
a. $20,000
b. $25,000
c. $40,000
d. $60,000 (11/92, PII, #48, amended, 3382)

51. The Low and Rhu partnership agreement provides special compensation to Low for managing the business. Low receives a bonus of 15 percent of partnership net income before salary and bonus, and also receives a salary of $45,000. Any remaining profit or loss is to be allocated equally. During the current year, the partnership had net income of $50,000 before the bonus and salary allowance. As a result of these distributions, Rhu's equity in the partnership would

a. Increase
b. Not change
c. Decrease the same as Low's
d. Decrease (5/89, Theory, #12, amended, 1994)

52. Red and White formed a partnership in the previous year. The partnership agreement provides for annual salary allowances of $55,000 for Red and $45,000 for White. The partners share profits equally and losses in a 60/40 ratio. The partnership had earnings of $80,000 for the current year before any allowance to partners. What amount of these earnings should be credited to each partner's capital account?

	Red	*White*
a.	$40,000	$40,000
b.	$43,000	$37,000
c.	$44,000	$36,000
d.	$45,000	$35,000

(5/94, FAR, #36, amended, 4851)

53. The Flat and Iron partnership agreement provides for Flat to receive a 20% bonus on profits before the bonus. Remaining profits and losses are divided between Flat and Iron in the ratio of 2 to 3, respectively. Which partner has a greater advantage when the partnership has a profit or when it has a loss?

	Profit	*Loss*
a.	Flat	Iron
b.	Flat	Flat
c.	Iron	Flat
d.	Iron	Iron

(11/91, Theory, #15, 2523)

54. In the Adel-Brick partnership, Adel and Brick had a capital ratio of 3:1 and a profit and loss ratio of 2:1, respectively. The bonus method was used to record Colter's admittance as a new partner. What ratio would be used to allocate, to Adel and Brick, the excess of Colter's contribution over the amount credited to Colter's capital account?

a. Adel and Brick's new relative capital ratio
b. Adel and Brick's new relative profit and loss ratio
c. Adel and Brick's old capital ratio
d. Adel and Brick's old profit and loss ratio

(5/92, Theory, #35, 2728)

55. Eagle and Falk are partners with capital balances of $45,000 and $25,000, respectively. They agree to admit Robb as a partner. After the assets of the partnership are revalued, Robb will have a 25% interest in capital and profits, for an investment of $30,000. What amount should be recorded as goodwill to the original partners?

a. $0
b $ 5,000
c. $ 7,500
d. $20,000 (5/98, FAR, #4, 6607)

56. Kern and Pate are partners with capital balances of $60,000 and $20,000, respectively. Profits and losses are divided in the ratio of 60:40. Kern and Pate decided to form a new partnership with Grant, who invested land valued at $15,000 for a 20% capital interest in the new partnership. Grant's cost of the land was $12,000. The partnership elected to use the bonus method to record the admission of Grant into the partnership. Grant's capital account should be credited for

a. $12,000
b. $15,000
c. $16,000
d. $19,000 (5/93, PII, #19, 4127)

57. Dunn and Grey are partners with capital account balances of $60,000 and $90,000, respectively. They agree to admit Zorn as a partner with a one-third interest in capital and profits, for an investment of $100,000, after revaluing the assets of Dunn and Grey. Goodwill to the original partners should be

a. $0
b. $33,333
c. $50,000
d. $66,667 (5/91, PII, #2, 1301)

Items 58 and 59 are based on the following:

On June 30 of the current year, the condensed balance sheet for the partnership of Eddy, Fox, and Grimm, together with their respective profit and loss sharing percentages, was as follows:

Assets, net of liabilities	$320,000	Eddy, capital (50%)	$160,000
		Fox, capital (30%)	96,000
		Grimm, capital (20%)	64,000
			$320,000

58. Hamm is admitted as a new partner with a 25% interest in the capital of the new partnership for a cash payment of $140,000. Total goodwill implicit in the transaction is to be recorded. Immediately after admission of Hamm, Eddy's capital account balance should be

a. $280,000
b. $210,000
c. $160,000
d. $140,000 (11/88, PI, #27, amended, 9063)

59. Assume instead that Hamm is not admitted as a new partner and that Eddy decided to retire from the partnership and by mutual agreement is to be paid $180,000 out of partnership funds for his interest. Total goodwill implicit in the agreement is to be recorded. After Eddy's retirement, what are the capital balances of the other partners?

	Fox	*Grimm*
a.	$ 84,000	$56,000
b.	$102,000	$68,000
c.	$108,000	$72,000
d.	$120,000	$80,000

(11/88, PI, #26, 9064)

60. Allen retired from the partnership of Allen, Beck, and Chale. Allen's cash settlement from the partnership was based on new goodwill determined at the date of retirement plus the carrying amount of the other net assets. As a consequence of the settlement, the capital accounts of Beck and Chale were decreased. In accounting for Allen's withdrawal, the partnership could have used the

	Bonus method	*Goodwill method*
a.	No	Yes
b.	No	No
c.	Yes	Yes
d.	Yes	No

(5/90, Theory, #17, 1984)

61. When Mill retired from the partnership of Mill, Yale, and Lear, the final settlement of Mill's interest exceeded Mill's capital balance. Under the bonus method, the excess

a. Was recorded as goodwill
b. Was recorded as an expense
c. Reduced the capital balances of Yale and Lear
d. Had **no** effect on the capital balances of Yale and Lear (11/94, FAR, #35, 5297)

62. The following condensed balance sheet is presented for the partnership of Smith and Jones, who share profits and losses in the ratio of 60:40, respectively:

Other assets	$ 450,000	Accounts payable	$ 120,000
Smith, loan	20,000	Smith, capital	195,000
	$ 470,000	Jones, capital	155,000
			$ 470,000

The partners have decided to liquidate the partnership. If the other assets are sold for $385,000, what amount of the available cash should be distributed to Smith?

a. $136,000
b. $156,000
c. $159,000
d. $195,000 (5/94, FAR, #37, 4852)

63. On January 1 of the current year, the partners of Cobb, Davis, and Eddy, who share profits and losses in the ratio of 5:3:2, respectively, decided to liquidate their partnership. On this date the partnership condensed balance sheet was as follows:

Cash	$ 50,000	Liabilities	$ 60,000
Other assets	250,000	Cobb, capital	80,000
	$300,000	Davis, capital	90,000
		Eddy, capital	70,000
			$ 300,000

On January 15 of the current year, the first cash sale of other assets with a carrying amount of $150,000 realized $120,000. Safe installment payments to the partners were made the same date. How much cash should be distributed to each partner?

	Cobb	*Davis*	*Eddy*
a.	$15,000	$51,000	$44,000
b.	$40,000	$45,000	$35,000
c.	$55,000	$33,000	$22,000
d.	$60,000	$36,000	$24,000

(5/87, PI, #33, amended, 1310)

Problem 10-2 ADDITIONAL MULTIPLE CHOICE QUESTIONS (66 to 83 minutes)

64. Which of the following would be reported in the income statement of a proprietorship?

	Proprietor's draw	*Depreciation*
a.	Yes	Yes
b.	Yes	No
c.	No	Yes
d.	No	No

(R/03, FAR, #13, 7615)

65. On January 2 of the current year, Smith purchased the net assets of Jones' Cleaning, a sole proprietorship, for $350,000, and commenced operations of Spiffy Cleaning, a sole proprietorship. The assets had a carrying amount of $375,000 and a market value of $360,000. In Spiffy's cash-basis financial statements for the current year ended December 31, Spiffy reported revenues in excess of expenses of $60,000. Smith's drawings during the year were $20,000. In Spiffy's financial statements, what amount should be reported as Capital—Smith?
a. $390,000
b. $400,000
c. $410,000
d. $415,000 (11/94, FAR, #36, amended, 5298)

66. Quoit Inc. issued preferred stock with detachable common stock warrants. The issue price exceeded the sum of the warrants' fair value and the preferred stocks' par value. The preferred stocks' fair value was not determinable. What amount should be assigned to the warrants outstanding?
a. Total proceeds
b. Excess of proceeds over the par value of the preferred stock
c. The proportion of the proceeds that the warrants' fair value bears to the preferred stocks' par value
d. The fair value of the warrants
(5/93, Theory, #13, 4201)

67. A company issued rights to its existing shareholders without consideration. The rights allowed the recipients to purchase unissued common stock for an amount in excess of par value. When the rights are issued, which of the following accounts will be increased?

	Common stock	*Additional paid-in capital*
a.	Yes	Yes
b.	Yes	No
c.	No	No
d.	No	Yes

(11/95, FAR, #21, 6103)

68. A company issued rights to its existing shareholders to purchase for $15 per share, 5,000 unissued shares of common stock with a par value of $10 per share. Common stock will be credited at
a. $15 per share when the rights are exercised
b. $15 per share when the rights are issued
c. $10 per share when the rights are exercised
d. $10 per share when the rights are issued
(5/84, Theory, #24, 9041)

69. On December 1 of the current year, shares of authorized common stock were issued on a subscription basis at a price in excess of par value. A total of 20% of the subscription price of each share was collected as a down payment on December 1 with the remaining 80% of the subscription price of each share due in the next year. Collectibility was reasonably assured. At December 31 the stockholders' equity section of the balance sheet would report additional paid-in capital for the excess of the subscription price over the par value of the shares of common stock subscribed and
a. Common stock issued for 20% of the par value of the shares of common stock subscribed
b. Common stock issued for the par value of the shares of common stock subscribed
c. Common stock subscribed for 80% of the par value of the shares of common stock subscribed
d. Common stock subscribed for the par value of the shares of common stock subscribed
(11/88, Theory, #17, amended, 1996)

70. Jay & Kay partnership's balance sheet at December 31, year 1, reported the following:

Total assets	$100,000
Total liabilities	20,000
Jay, capital	40,000
Kay, capital	40,000

On January 2, year 2, Jay and Kay dissolved their partnership and transferred all assets and liabilities to a newly formed corporation. At the date of incorporation, the fair value of the net assets was $12,000 more than the carrying amount on the partnership's books, of which $7,000 was assigned to tangible assets and $5,000 was assigned to goodwill. Jay and Kay were each issued 5,000 shares of the corporation's $1 par value common stock. Immediately following incorporation, additional paid-in capital in excess of par should be credited for
a. $68,000
b. $70,000
c. $77,000
d. $82,000 (11/91, PII, #8, amended, 2456)

71. On July 1 of the current year, Cove Corp., a closely held corporation, issued 6% bonds with a maturity value of $60,000, together with 1,000 shares of its $5 par value common stock, for a combined cash amount of $110,000. The market value of Cove's stock cannot be ascertained. If the bonds were issued separately, they would have sold for $40,000 on an 8% yield to maturity basis. What amount should Cove report for additional paid-in capital on the issuance of the stock?
a. $75,000
b. $65,000
c. $55,000
d. $45,000 (11/92, PII, #44, amended, 3378)

72. A retained earnings appropriation can be used to
a. Absorb a fire loss when a company is self-insured
b. Provide for a contingent loss that is probable and reasonable
c. Smooth periodic income
d. Restrict earnings available for dividends (5/92, Theory, #37, 2730)

73. The following information pertains to Meg Corp.:

- Dividends on its 1,000 shares of 6%, $10 par value cumulative preferred stock have not been declared or paid for 3 years.
- Treasury stock that cost $15,000 was reissued for $8,000.

What amount of retained earnings should be appropriated as a result of these items?
a. $0
b. $1,800
c. $7,000
d. $8,800 (5/92, PII, #6, 2638)

74. The primary purpose of a quasi-reorganization is to give a corporation the opportunity to
a. Obtain relief from its creditors
b. Revalue understated assets to their fair values
c. Eliminate a deficit in retained earnings
d. Distribute the stock of a newly-created subsidiary to its stockholders in exchange for part of their stock in the corporation (11/94, FAR, #37, 5299)

75. In the current year, on December 1, Nilo Corp. declared a property dividend of marketable securities to be distributed on December 31 to stockholders of record on December 15. On December 1 the marketable securities had a carrying amount of $60,000 and a fair value of $78,000. What is the effect of this property dividend on Nilo's current year retained earnings, after all nominal accounts are closed?
a. $0
b. $18,000 increase
c. $60,000 decrease
d. $78,000 decrease (5/92, PII, #4, amended, 2636)

76. Bain Corp. owned 20,000 common shares of Tell Corp. purchased several years ago for $180,000. On December 15 of the previous year, Bain declared a property dividend of all of its Tell Corp. shares on the basis of one share of Tell for every 10 shares of Bain common stock held by its stockholders. The property dividend was distributed on January 15 of the current year. On the declaration date, the aggregate market price of the Tell shares held by Bain was $300,000. The entry to record the declaration of the dividend would include a debit to retained earnings (or property dividends declared) of
a. $0
b. $120,000
c. $180,000
d. $300,000 (11/88, PI, #60, amended, 9040)

77. Stock dividends on common stock should be recorded at their fair market value by the investor when the related investment is accounted for under which of the following methods?

	Cost	*Equity*
a.	Yes	Yes
b.	Yes	No
c.	No	Yes
d.	No	No

(11/94, FAR, #39, 5301)

Items 78 and 79 are based on the following:

The following format was used by Gee Inc. for its current year statement of owners' equity:

	Common stock, $1 par	Additional paid-in capital	Retained earnings
Balance at 1/1	$90,000	$ 800,000	$ 175,000
Additions and deductions:			
100% stock dividend			
5% stock dividend			
Balance at 12/31			

When both the 100% and the 5% stock dividends were declared, Gee's common stock was selling for more than its $1 par value.

78. How would the 100% stock dividend affect the additional paid-in capital and retained earnings amounts reported in Gee's year-end statement of owners' equity?

	Additional paid-in capital	Retained earnings
a.	Increase	Increase
b.	Increase	Decrease
c.	No change	Increase
d.	No change	Decrease

(5/92, PI, #2, amended, 2569)

79. How would the 5% stock dividend affect the additional paid-in capital and retained earnings amounts reported in Gee's year-end statement of owners' equity?

	Additional paid-in capital	Retained earnings
a.	Increase	Decrease
b.	Increase	Increase
c.	No change	Decrease
d.	No change	Increase

(5/92, PI, #3, amended, 2570)

80. Beck Corp. issued 200,000 shares of common stock when it began operations two years ago and issued an additional 100,000 shares in the past year. Beck also issued preferred stock convertible to 100,000 shares of common stock. In the current year Beck purchased 75,000 shares of its common stock and held it in Treasury. At December 31 of the current year, how many shares of Beck's common stock were outstanding?

a. 400,000
b. 325,000
c. 300,000
d. 225,000 (5/93, PII, #2, amended, 4111)

81. Rudd Corp. had 700,000 shares of common stock authorized and 300,000 shares outstanding at December 31 of the previous year. The following events occurred during the current year:

January 31	Declared 10% stock dividend
June 30	Purchased 100,000 shares
August 1	Reissued 50,000 shares
November 30	Declared 2-for-1 stock split

At December 31 of the current year, how many shares of common stock did Rudd have outstanding?

a. 560,000
b. 600,000
c. 630,000
d. 660,000 (5/93, PII, #1, amended, 4110)

82. When preparing a draft of its year-end balance sheet, Mont Inc., reported net assets totaling $875,000. Included in the asset section of the balance sheet were the following:

Treasury stock of Mont Inc., at cost, which approximates market value on December 31	$24,000
Idle machinery	11,200
Cash surrender value of life insurance on corporate executives	13,700
Allowance for decline in market value of available-for-sale equity investments	8,400

At what amount should Mont's net assets be reported in the December 31 year-end balance sheet?

a. $851,000
b. $850,100
c. $842,600
d. $834,500 (5/91, PI, #1, amended, 1084)

83. Cyan Corp. issued 20,000 shares of $5 par common stock at $10 per share. On December 31 of the previous year, Cyan's retained earnings were $300,000. In March of the current year, Cyan reacquired 5,000 shares of its common stock at $20 per share. In June of the current year, Cyan sold 1,000 of these shares to its corporate officers for $25 per share. Cyan uses the cost method to record treasury stock. Net income for the current year ended December 31 was $60,000. At December 31 of the current year, what amount should Cyan report as retained earnings?

a. $360,000
b. $365,000
c. $375,000
d. $380,000 (11/95, FAR, #19, amended, 6101)

84. Grid Corp. acquired some of its own common shares at a price greater than both their par value and original issue price but less than their book value. Grid uses the cost method of accounting for treasury stock. What is the impact of this acquisition on total stockholders' equity and the book value per common share?

	Total stockholders' equity	Book value per share
a.	Increase	Increase
b.	Increase	Decrease
c.	Decrease	Increase
d.	Decrease	Decrease

(11/91, Theory, #40, 2548)

85. Posy Corp. acquired treasury shares at an amount greater than their par value, but less than their original issue price. Compared to the cost method of accounting for treasury stock, does the par value method report a greater amount for additional paid-in capital and a greater amount for retained earnings?

	Additional paid-in capital	Retained earnings
a.	Yes	Yes
b.	Yes	No
c.	No	No
d.	No	Yes

(11/91, Theory, #39, 2547)

86. Several years ago, Rona Corp. issued 5,000 shares of $10 par value common stock for $100 per share. In the current year, Rona reacquired 2,000 of its shares at $150 per share from the estate of one of its deceased officers and immediately canceled these 2,000 shares. Rona uses the cost method in accounting for its treasury stock transactions. In connection with the retirement of these 2,000 shares, Rona should debit

	Additional paid-in capital	Retained earnings
a.	$ 20,000	$280,000
b.	$100,000	$180,000
c.	$180,000	$100,000
d.	$280,000	$0

(11/89, PII, #12, amended, 1096)

87. Park Corp.'s stockholders' equity accounts at December 31 of the previous year were as follows:

Common stock, $20 par	$8,000,000
Additional paid-in capital	2,550,000
Retained earnings	1,275,000

All shares of common stock outstanding at December 31 of the previous year were issued originally for $26 a share. On January 4 of the current year, Park reacquired 20,000 shares of its common stock at $24 a share and retired them. Immediately after the shares were retired, the balance in additional paid-in capital would be

a. $2,430,000
b. $2,470,000
c. $2,510,000
d. $2,590,000 (5/88, PI, #42, amended, 1106)

Items 88 and 89 are based on the following data:

On April 1 of the current year, Fay Corporation established an employee stock ownership plan (ESOP). Selected transactions relating to the ESOP during the year were as follows:

- On April 1, Fay contributed $30,000 cash and 3,000 shares of its $10 par common stock to the ESOP. On this date, the market price of the stock was $18 a share.
- On October 1, the ESOP borrowed $100,000 from Union National Bank and acquired 5,000 shares of Fay's common stock in the open market at $17 a share. The note is for one year, bears interest at 10%, and is guaranteed by Fay.
- On December 15, the ESOP distributed 6,000 shares of Fay common stock to employees of Fay in accordance with the plan formula.

88. In its year-end income statement, how much should Fay report as compensation expense relating to the ESOP?

a. $184,000
b. $120,000
c. $ 84,000
d. $ 60,000 (11/87, PI, #56, amended, 1108)

89. In Fay's December 31, year-end balance sheet, how much should be reported as a reduction of shareholders' equity and as an endorsed note payable in respect of the ESOP?

	Reduction of shareholders' equity	Endorsed note payable
a.	$0	$0
b.	$0	$100,000
c.	$100,000	$0
d.	$100,000	$100,000

(11/87, PI, #57, amended, 1109)

90. For a compensatory stock option plan for which the date of grant and the measurement date are different, compensation cost should be recognized in the income statement

a. At the later of grant or measurement date.
b. At the exercise date.
c. At the adoption date of the plan.
d. Of each period in which the services are rendered. (11/84, Theory, #35, 9043)

91. On May 1, Cobb and Mott formed a partnership and agreed to share profits and losses in the ratio of 3:7, respectively. Cobb contributed a parcel of land that cost him $10,000. Mott contributed $40,000 cash. The land was sold for $18,000 on that same date, immediately after formation of the partnership. What amount should be recorded in Cobb's capital account on formation of the partnership?

a. $18,000
b. $17,400
c. $15,000
d. $10,000 (5/89, PII, #9, amended, 1308)

92. During the current year, Young and Zinc maintained average capital balances in their partnership of $160,000 and $100,000, respectively. The partners receive 10% interest on average capital balances, and residual profit or loss is divided equally. Partnership profit before interest was $4,000. By what amount should Zinc's capital account change for the year?
a. $ 1,000 decrease
b. $ 2,000 increase
c. $11,000 decrease
d. $12,000 increase (11/95, FAR, #23, 6105)

93. The partnership agreement of Axel, Berg & Cobb provides for the year-end allocation of net income in the following order:

- First, Axel is to receive 10% of net income up to $100,000 and 20% over $100,000.
- Second, Berg and Cobb each are to receive 5% of the remaining income over $150,000.
- The balance of income is to be allocated equally among the three partners.

The partnership's net income was $250,000 before any allocations to partners. What amount should be allocated to Axel?
a. $101,000
b. $103,000
c. $108,000
d. $110,000 (11/91, PII, #11, amended, 2459)

94. Blau and Rubi are partners who share profits and losses in the ratio of 6:4, respectively. On May 1 of the current year, their respective capital accounts were as follows:

Blau	$60,000
Rubi	50,000

On that date, Lind was admitted as a partner with a one-third interest in capital and profits for an investment of $40,000. The new partnership began with total capital of $150,000. Immediately after Lind's admission, Blau's capital should be
a. $50,000
b. $54,000
c. $56,667
d. $60,000 (11/89, PII, #19, amended, 1307)

Items 95 and 96 are based on the following:

The following condensed balance sheet is presented for the partnership of Alfa and Beda, who share profits and losses in the ratio of 60:40, respectively:

Cash	$ 45,000	Accounts payable	$ 120,000
Other assets	625,000	Alfa, capital	348,000
Beda, loan	30,000	Beda, capital	232,000
	$ 700,000		$ 700,000

95. The assets and liabilities are fairly valued on the balance sheet. Alfa and Beda decide to admit Capp as a new partner with a 20% interest. No goodwill or bonus is to be recorded. What amount should Capp contribute in cash or other assets?
a. $110,000
b. $116,000
c. $140,000
d. $145,000 (5/95, FAR, #23, 5559)

96. Instead of admitting a new partner, Alfa and Beda decide to liquidate the partnership. If the other assets are sold for $500,000, what amount of the available cash should be distributed to Alfa?
a. $255,000
b. $273,000
c. $327,000
d. $348,000 (5/95, FAR, #24, 5560)

SIMULATIONS

Problem 10-3 (15 to 25 minutes)

Research Task	Scenario	Additional Information	Responses

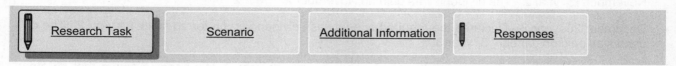

Research Question: According to the Accounting Principles Board, what should general accounting for non-monetary transactions (such as property dividends) be based on?

Paragraph Reference Answer: _______________

Research Task	Scenario	Additional Information	Responses

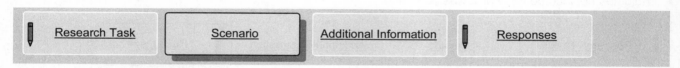

Min Co. is a publicly held company whose shares are traded in the over-the-counter market. The stockholders' equity accounts at December 31, year 1, had the following balances:

Preferred stock, $100 par value, 6% cumulative;	
5,000 shares authorized; 2,000 issued and outstanding	$ 200,000
Common stock, $1 par value, 150,000 shares authorized;	
100,000 issued and outstanding	100,000
Additional paid-in capital	800,000
Retained earnings	1,586,000
Total stockholders' equity	$2,686,000

(5/95, FAR, #2, amended, 5597)

Research Task	Scenario	Additional Information	Responses

Transactions during year 2 and other information relating to the stockholders' equity accounts were as follows:

- February 1, year 2—Issued 13,000 shares of common stock to Ram Co. in exchange for land. On the date issued, the stock had a market price of $11 per share. The land had a carrying value on Ram's books of $135,000, and an assessed value for property taxes of $90,000.
- March 1, year 2—Purchased 5,000 shares of its own common stock to be held as treasury stock for $14 per share. Min uses the cost method to account for treasury stock. Transactions in treasury stock are legal in Min's state of incorporation.
- May 10, year 2—Declared a property dividend of marketable securities held by Min to common shareholders. The securities had a carrying value of $600,000; fair value on relevant dates were:

Date of declaration 5/10	$720,000
Date of record 5/25	758,000
Date of distribution 6/1	736,000

- October 1, year 2—Reissued 2,000 shares of treasury stock for $16 per share.
- November 4, year 2—Declared a cash dividend of $1.50 per share to all common shareholders of record November 15, year 2. The dividend was paid on November 25, year 2.
- December 20, year 2—Declared the required annual cash dividend on preferred stock for year 2. The dividend was paid on January 5, year 3.
- January 16, year 3—Before closing the accounting records for year 2, Min became aware that no amortization had been recorded for year 1 for a patent purchased on July 1, year 1. The patent was properly capitalized at $320,000 and had an estimated useful life of eight years when purchased. Min's income tax rate is 30%. The appropriate correcting entry was recorded on the same day.
- Adjusted net income for year 2 was $838,000.

Research Task	Scenario	Additional Information	Responses

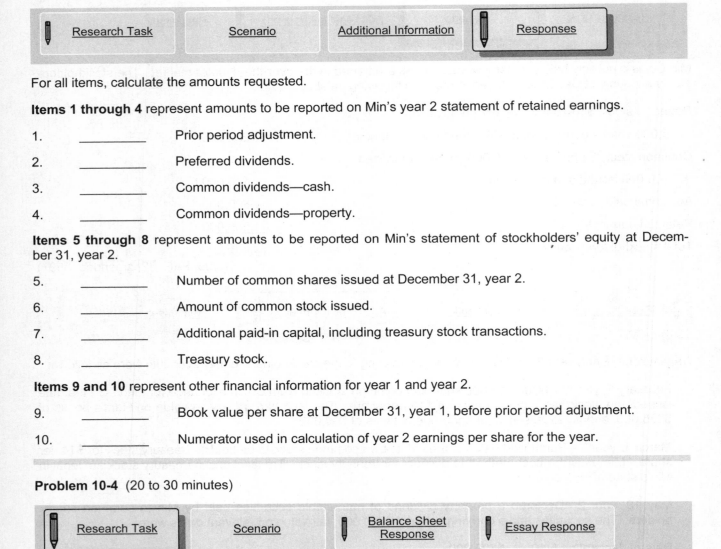

For all items, calculate the amounts requested.

Items 1 through 4 represent amounts to be reported on Min's year 2 statement of retained earnings.

1. ________ Prior period adjustment.
2. ________ Preferred dividends.
3. ________ Common dividends—cash.
4. ________ Common dividends—property.

Items 5 through 8 represent amounts to be reported on Min's statement of stockholders' equity at December 31, year 2.

5. ________ Number of common shares issued at December 31, year 2.
6. ________ Amount of common stock issued.
7. ________ Additional paid-in capital, including treasury stock transactions.
8. ________ Treasury stock.

Items 9 and 10 represent other financial information for year 1 and year 2.

9. ________ Book value per share at December 31, year 1, before prior period adjustment.
10. ________ Numerator used in calculation of year 2 earnings per share for the year.

Problem 10-4 (20 to 30 minutes)

Research Task	Scenario	Balance Sheet Response	Essay Response

Research Question: How should gains and losses on sales of treasury stock be accounted for?

Paragraph Reference Answer: ______________

Research Task | Scenario | Balance Sheet Response | Essay Response

Field Co.'s stockholders' equity account balances at December 31, year 2, were as follows:

Common stock	$ 800,000
Additional paid-in capital	1,600,000
Retained earnings	1,845,000

The following year 3 transactions and other information relate to the stockholders' equity accounts:

- Field had 400,000 authorized shares of $5 par common stock, of which 160,000 shares were issued and outstanding.
- On March 5, year 3, Field acquired 5,000 shares of its common stock for $10 per share to hold as treasury stock. The shares were originally issued at $15 per share. Field uses the cost method to account for treasury stock. Treasury stock is permitted in Field's state of incorporation.
- On July 15, year 3, Field declared and distributed a property dividend of inventory. The inventory had a $75,000 carrying value and a $60,000 fair market value.
- On January 2, year 1, Field granted stock options to employees to purchase 20,000 shares of Field's common stock at $16 per share, which was the market price on the grant date. The options are valued at $35,000 and may be exercised within a three-year period beginning January 2, year 3. On October 1, year 3, employees exercised all 20,000 options when the market value of the stock was $25 per share. Field issued new shares to settle the transaction.
- Field's net income for year 3 was $240,000.
- Field intends to issue new stock options to key employees in year 4. Field's management is aware that Statement of Financial Accounting Standards No. 123 revised, *Share Based Payment,* was issued in 2004. The "fair value" method of accounting for stock options is required by this statement.

a. Prepare the stockholders' equity section of Field's December 31, year 3, balance sheet. Support all computations.

b. In a brief memo to Field's management, explain how and when compensation cost is measured under the "fair value" method of accounting for stock options, and when the measured cost is recognized.

(11/97, FAR, #2, amended, 6502)

Research Task | Scenario | Balance Sheet Response | Essay Response

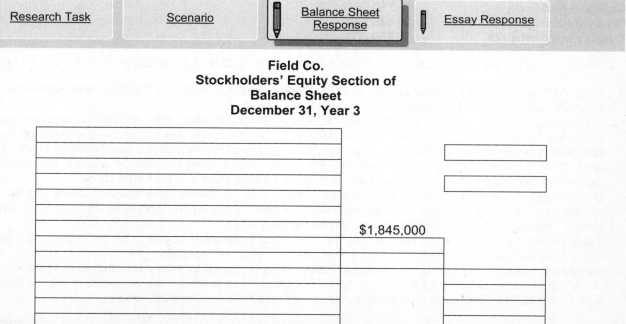

Field Co.
Stockholders' Equity Section of
Balance Sheet
December 31, Year 3

	$1,845,000	

Research Task | Scenario | Balance Sheet Response | Essay Response

In a brief memo to Field's management, explain how and when compensation cost is measured under the "fair value" method of accounting for stock options, and when the measured cost is recognized.

To:

Re:

Problem 10-5 (45 to 55 minutes)

Research Task | Scenario | Requirements | Statement of Retained Earnings

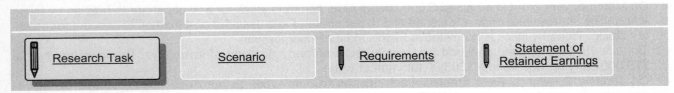

Research Question: What is the exception to the rule that paid-in capital "shall not be used to relieve income of the current or future years of charges which would otherwise be made against [income]"?

Paragraph Reference Answer: _______________

Research Task | Scenario | Requirements | Statement of Retained Earnings

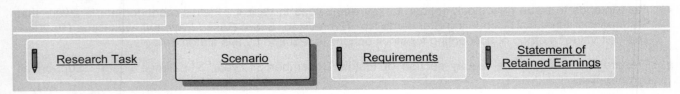

Trask Corp., a public company whose shares are traded in the over-the-counter market, had the following stockholders' equity account balances at December 31, year 5:

Common stock	$ 7,875,000
Additional paid-in capital	15,750,000
Retained earnings	16,445,000
Treasury common stock	750,000

Transactions during year 6, and other information relating to the stockholders' equity accounts, were as follows:

- Trask had 4,000,000 authorized shares of $5 par value common stock; 1,575,000 shares were issued, of which 75,000 were held in treasury.
- On January 21, year 6, Trask issued 50,000 shares of $100 par value, 6% cumulative preferred stock in exchange for all of Rover Co.'s assets and liabilities. On that date, the net carrying amount of Rover's assets and liabilities was $5,000,000. The carrying amounts of Rover's assets and liabilities equaled their fair values. On January 22, year 6, Rover distributed the Trask shares to its stockholders in complete liquidation and dissolution of Rover. Trask had 150,000 authorized shares of preferred stock.
- On February 17, year 6, Trask formally retired 25,000 of its 75,000 treasury common stock shares. The shares were originally issued at $15 per share and had been acquired on September 25, year 5, for $10 per share. Trask uses the cost method to account for treasury stock.
- Trask owned 15,000 shares of Harbor Inc. common stock purchased in year 5 for $600,000. The Harbor stock was included in Trask's short-term marketable securities portfolio. On March 5, year 6, Trask declared a property dividend of one share of Harbor common stock for every 100 shares of Trask common stock held by a stockholder of record on April 16, year 6. The market price of Harbor stock on March 5, year 6, was $60 per share. The property dividend was distributed on April 29, year 6.

- On January 2, year 4, Trask granted stock options valued at $75,000 to employees to purchase 150,000 shares of the company's common stock at $9 per share, which was also the market price on that date. The options are exercisable within a three-year period beginning January 2, year 6. On June 1, year 6, employees exercised all 150,000 options when the market value of the stock was $25 per share. Trask issued new shares to settle the transaction.
- On October 27, year 6, Trask declared a 2-for-1 stock split on its common stock and reduced the per share par value accordingly. Trask stockholders of record on August 2, year 6, received one additional share of Trask common stock for each share of Trask common stock held. The laws in Trask's state of incorporation protect treasury stock from dilution.
- On December 12, year 6, Trask declared the yearly cash dividend on preferred stock, payable on January 11, year 7, to stockholders of record on December 31, year 6.
- On January 16, year 7, before the accounting records were closed for year 6, Trask became aware that depreciation expense was understated by $350,000 for the year ended December 31, year 5. The after-tax effect on year 5 net income was $245,000. The appropriate correcting entry was recorded on the same day.
- Net income for year 6 was $2,400,000. (11/93, P1, #4, amended, 9911)

Research Task | Scenario | **Requirements** | Statement of Retained Earnings

a. Prepare Trask's statement of retained earnings for the year ended December 31, year 6. Assume that Trask prepares only single-period financial statements.

b. Prepare the stockholders' equity section of Trask's balance sheet at December 31, year 6.

c. Compute the book value per share of common stock at December 31, year 6.

Research Task | Scenario | Requirements | **Statement of Retained Earnings**

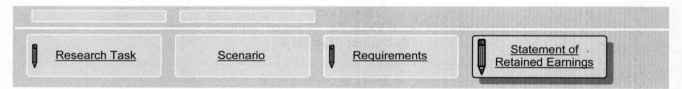

Trask Corp.
Statement of Retained Earnings
For the Year Ended December 31, Year 6

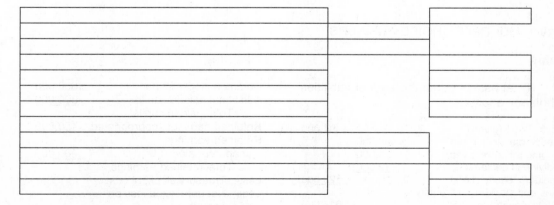

Stockholders' Equity | Book Value Per Share

Trask Corp.
Stockholders' Equity Section of
Balance Sheet
December 31, Year 6

Stockholders' Equity | Book Value Per Share

APIC is the excess of FV over the par value of the common stock

Trask Corp.
Computation of Book Value Per Share of Common Stock
December 31, Year 6

Solution 10-1 MULTIPLE CHOICE ANSWERS

Components

1. (c) Total assets equal the sum of liabilities and stockholders' equity.

Total liabilities, 12/31 (given)		$ 94,000
Proceeds from stock issue	$ 500,000	
Net income for current year	25,000	
Cash dividend declared	(2,000)	
Total stockholders' equity, 12/31		523,000
Total liabilities and stockholders' equity (and thus total assets) at 12/31		$617,000

2. (a)

Common stock, $3 par	$600,000	
Additional paid-in capital	800,000	
Total paid-in capital		$1,400,000
Retained earnings, appropriated	150,000	
Retained earnings, unappropriated	200,000	
Total retained earnings		350,000
Less: Treasury stock, at cost		(50,000)
Less: Net unrealized loss on AFS securities		(20,000)
Total stockholders' equity		$1,680,000

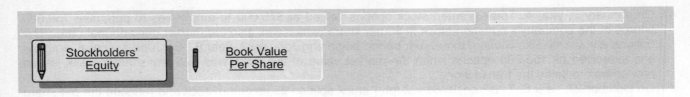

Decreases by the cost of treasury stock
Increases by issuance

3. (a) APIC = $580,000 + $240,000 = $820,000. If Hyde has only one APIC account, the issuance of the common and preferred stock would be recorded as follows.

Cash (20,000 × $30)	600,000	
Common Stock (20,000 × $1)		20,000
Additional Paid-In Capital (to balance)		580,000
Cash (6,000 × $50)	300,000	
Preferred Stock (6,000 × $10)		60,000
Additional Paid-In Capital (to balance)		240,000

Preferred Stock Dividends

4. (d) If a cumulative preferred stock dividend is not paid in any given year, it becomes a dividend in arrears. No liability exists until the board of directors declares a dividend; a dividend in arrears is not accrued, but is disclosed in the financial statement notes. No dividend was declared in year 2, resulting in a dividend in arrears of $15,000 ($100 × 5% × 3,000 shares). Therefore, in its year 3 financial statements, Apex reports dividends in arrears of $20,000 ($15,000 from year 2 + $5,000 from year 3).

Dividend amount ($100 × 5% × 3,000 shares)	$ 15,000
Less: Dividend paid, year 3	(10,000)
Dividend in arrears, year 3	$ 5,000

5. (a) *Common Stock* should be credited for $375,000 [i.e., (5,000 × 3) × $25], the par value of the common shares issued to effect the conversion. *Additional Paid-in Capital—Common Stock* should be credited for $175,000, the excess of the carrying amount of the preferred stock converted over the par value of common shares issued to effect the conversion [i.e., (5,000 × $110) – $375,000].

6. (b)

Cash dividends declared in year 2		$ 44,000
Dividends in arrears at 12/31, year 1	$12,000	
Dividend for year 2 (4,000 × $100 × 6%)	24,000	
Cash dividends payable to preferred stock		(36,000)
Cash dividends payable to common stock		$ 8,000

Stock Rights

7. (a) Stock rights have no impact on net income. No entry is required when stock rights are issued to existing stockholders (other than a memorandum entry); therefore, APIC was not affected when the stock rights were issued. Stock issued upon the exercise of stock rights is recorded the same as any other issuance; therefore, when the stock rights were exercised, APIC increased by the excess of the $30 exercise price over the $20 par value of the common stock.

8. (d) Stock issued upon the exercise of stock rights is recorded the same as any other issuance. Therefore, APIC will increase by the excess of the exercise price over par value and retained earnings will not be affected.

9. (c) No entry (other than a memorandum entry) is made when stock rights are issued to existing stockholders. However, the redemption of the rights resulted in an outflow of cash. As this did not increase a noncash asset or reduce liabilities, it must affect an equity account. 120,000 × $0.10 = $12,000.

Capital Stock Issues

10. (a) The acquisition of services by issuance of common stock is a nonmonetary exchange that should be recorded at the fair value of the stock issued or the services performed, whichever is more clearly evident. The fair value of the stock issued should be used to record this transaction because (1) on the date of issuance, the stock was trading on a public exchange and thus had the more clearly evident fair value, and (2) the fair value of the stock issued is less than the amount usually billed for the services received. Thus, the increase in *Additional Paid-in Capital* as a result of the transaction is the excess of the fair value over the par value of the common stock multiplied by the number of shares issued. ($140 – $5 = $135 × 1,000 = $135,000)

11. (c) *Additional Paid-In Capital* is credited for the difference between the fair value of the net assets contributed and the stock's par value.

Assets (at fair value)	240,000	
Liabilities (at fair value)		20,000
Common Stock (1,000 × $5)		5,000
Additional Paid-In Capital (to balance)		215,000

12. (c) The amount of the proceeds received that should be allocated to the preferred stock is $48,000 [i.e., ($54,000 / $90,000) × $80,000]. Since the fair value is available for each class of security, the lump sum received should be allocated to the two classes of securities by their relative fair value.

Fair value of common stock (1,000 × $36)	$36,000
Fair value of preferred stock (2,000 × $27)	54,000
	$90,000

Retained Earnings

13. (c) The balance in the APIC account after the quasi-reorganization is the beginning balance, plus the difference in the old and new par values, times the number of issued shares [($30 – $5) ×

10,000 = $250,000], less the retained earnings deficit. $150,000 + $250,000 – $210,000 = $190,000.

14. (b) During the current year, stockholders' equity increased by $62,000 (i.e., $89,000 – $27,000). Since paid-in capital increased by $66,000 (i.e., $60,000 + $6,000), retained earnings must have decreased by $4,000 (i.e., $66,000 – $62,000). Since the only charge to retained earnings was for a $13,000 dividend payment, net income for the year must have been $9,000.

15. (a) Since the new office building was completed in year 2, the retained earnings reported appropriated for that purpose at 12/31, year 1 should have been returned to unappropriated retained earnings in year 2. Restricted cash does not affect the amount of appropriated retained earnings.

Dividend Significant Dates

16. (a) The declaration date is the date on which dividends are declared by the board of directors. Declared cash dividends are a liability. The journal entry required at the date of declaration includes a debit (decrease) to *Retained Earnings.* Generally, no journal entry is required at the date of record. The journal entry on the payment date reduces *Cash* and the liability, but has no effect on *Retained Earnings.*

17. (b) A cash dividend is recorded when declared by a debit to *Retained Earnings* and a credit to *Cash Dividends Payable.* There is no adjusting entry at the end of the period. The entry at the payment date includes a debit to *Cash Dividends Payable* and a credit to *Cash.* Generally, the cash dividend reduces stockholders' equity only at the declaration date.

18. (d) On the declaration date, the liability for dividends payable is recorded by a debit to *Retained Earnings* and a credit to *Cash Dividends Payable.* Since the declaration of the cash dividend increases current liabilities without affecting current assets, working capital is decreased on this date. On May 23, the date of record, which stockholders will receive the cash dividend is determined. Assuming that the common shares outstanding did not change between the date of declaration and the date of record, no journal entry is made on the date of record and, thus, working capital is not affected on this date. On the payment date, the cash dividend is paid and is recorded by a debit to *Cash Dividends Payable* and a credit to *Cash.* Since current assets and current liabilities decrease by the same amount, working capital is not affected on this date.

Property Dividends

19. (c) Property dividends are recorded at the property's fair value at the declaration date. The excess of the fair value over the carrying amount of the property distributed is recognized as a gain by the distributing corporation at the declaration date.

Fair value of distributed shares (100,000 × $2.50)	$ 250,000
Less: Distributed share's carrying amount (100,000 × $2.00)	(200,000)
Pretax gain on distributed shares	$ 50,000

20. (d) At the end of the year, interest is accrued. At the date of declaration, April 1, year 1, the journal entry is as follows:

Retained Earnings	100,000	
Notes Payable to Stockholders		100,000
Interest Expense ($100,000 × 10% × 9/12)	7,500	
Interest Payable		7,500

The interest portion of the payment is not treated as part of the dividend. When the dividend is declared, it becomes a liability and is reported on the balance sheet. If the entry to accrue the interest expense is made on December 31, year 1, and is reversed on January 1, year 2, then interest expense would be debited for $10,000 on March 31, year 2. However, since answer (c) does not state this, assume that the reversing entry was not made.

21. (d) Evie records the property dividend at the merchandise's fair value at the declaration date. Since the merchandise's carrying amount exceeds its fair value at the declaration date, Evie recognizes the excess as a loss in income from continuing operations.

Liquidating Dividends

22. (b) Any dividend that does not come out of retained earnings is a reduction of corporate paid-in capital and, to that extent, is a liquidating dividend.

Dividend	$ 400,000
Retained earnings	(300,000)
Liquidating dividend	$ 100,000

23. (d) Any dividend not based on earnings must be a reduction of corporate paid-in capital and, to that extent, a liquidating dividend. Since no portion of the dividend is based on accumulated past earnings, paid-in capital decreases by the full dividend amount, while retained earnings is unaffected. The following journal entry illustrates the effects of the declaration of a $100,000 liquidating cash dividend.

Additional Paid-In Capital	100,000	
Cash Dividends Payable		100,000

24. (b) Any dividend not based on earnings must be a reduction of APIC and, to that extent, is a liquidating dividend.

Retained Earnings	XX	
Additional Paid-In Capital	XX	
Cash Dividends Payable		XX
To record a partially liquidating cash dividend.		

Stock Dividends

25. (b) The issuance of a "small" stock dividend (i.e., less than 20 to 25% of the number of shares outstanding) should be recorded by capitalizing a portion of retained earnings equal to the fair value of the shares issued. On the other hand, the issuance of a "large" stock dividend (i.e., more than 20 to 25% of the number of shares outstanding) should be recorded by capitalizing a portion of retained earnings equal to the par value of the shares issued. Thus, *Retained Earnings* should be debited for (1) the fair value of the 10% stock dividend ($15,000) and (2) the par value of the 28% stock dividend ($30,800).

26. (b) A stock dividend is not income under the cost or equity methods of accounting for equity investments, but it does impact the number of shares owned at the dividend declaration date. (10,000 + 2,000) × $2 = $24,000.

27. (a) The declaration of a "small" stock dividend (i.e., < 20-25% of the number of common shares outstanding) should be recorded by capitalizing a portion of retained earnings equal to the fair value of the shares to be issued. Fluctuations in the fair value of the shares between the declaration date and the issuance date are not recorded.

Retained Earnings [(3,000 × 10%) × $9 FMV]	2,700	
Common Stock Dividend Distributable [(3,000 × 10%) × $2 PV]		600
Additional Paid-In Capital (to balance)		2,100
To record the declaration of a 10% stock dividend.		

28. (a) Stock dividends operate to transfer a part of the retained earnings to contributed capital (capitalization of retained earnings). In recording the stock dividend, a charge is made to retained earnings (thereby making a portion of retained earnings no longer available for distribution) and credits are made to paid-in capital accounts. Because the declaration and issuance of a stock dividend decreases retained earnings and increases paid-in capital by equal amounts, total stockholders' equity is not affected.

Stock Splits

29. (b) The amount to be reported as dividends is determined as follows:

Common shares outstanding, 1/1	100,000
Adjustment for 2-for-1 stock split, 3/15	× 2
Common shares outstanding, declaration date	200,000
Times: Cash dividend per common share	× $0.50
Cash dividends declared during year	$100,000

30. (b) A stock split consists of a reduction in the par value per share, together with a proportional increase in the number of shares outstanding. For instance, in a 2-for-1 split, the par value per share is halved, while the number of shares outstanding is doubled. *Total* par value, additional paid-in capital, stockholders' equity, and total assets remain unchanged.

Treasury Stock Overview

31. (a)

	Issued	Outstanding
Beginning balance, shares	100,000	95,000
May 3, sale of treasury stock		1,000
Aug. 6, additional stock sold	10,000	10,000
Subtotal prior to stock split	110,000	106,000
Nov. 18, 2-for-1 stock split	× 2	× 2
Ending balance, shares	220,000	212,000

32. (b) The net income for the current year is overstated, because no gains or losses are recognized on treasury stock transactions.

33. (a) The excess of proceeds over cost of treasury stock sold, accounted for using the cost method, is credited to an appropriately titled paid-in capital account, such as *Additional Paid-In Capital From Treasury Stock Transactions.*

Income since incorporation	$ 420,000
Less: Cash dividends	(130,000)
Less: Property dividends	(30,000)
Retained earnings, 12/31	$ 260,000

34. (d) The question does not indicate whether the donated shares are accounted for as treasury stock under the cost or par value methods, or whether the donated shares were canceled and retired. Therefore, this question cannot be answered by constructing a journal entry to record the donation of the shares. Instead, the question can be answered by knowing that the donation of the common stock would be accounted for entirely within stockholders' equity accounts. Therefore, the amount reported for total stockholders' equity would be unchanged as a result of the donation of the stock.

Cost Method

35. (c) The answer to this question assumes that the cost method is used to account for the treasury stock. Under the cost method, if treasury stock is sold at a price that exceeds its cost, the excess should be credited to *Additional Paid-In Capital.* The excess is not reported as a gain in the income statement or as a credit to *Retained Earnings* under either the cost or par methods. *Retained Earnings* may be decreased, but never increased, by treasury stock transactions.

36. (c)

Treasury Stock (6,000 shares × $36)	216,000	
Cash		216,000
To record the acquisition of treasury stock.		
Cash (3,000 shares × $50)	150,000	
Treasury Stock (3,000 shares × $36)		108,000
Additional Paid-In Capital (to balance)		42,000
To record the issuance of treasury stock.		

37. (c) The amount that Rama discloses as a restriction of retained earnings as a result of treasury stock held is <u>$60,000</u> [(20,000 – 15,000) × $12 per share].

Par Value Method

38. (b) The effect on total stockholders' equity from either the acquisition or the reissuance of treasury stock is the same regardless of whether the shares are accounted for under the cost method or the par value method. Under both methods, the acquisition of treasury stock decreases assets and stockholders' equity by the acquisition cost of the shares. Under both methods, the reissuance of the treasury stock increases assets and stockholders' equity by the proceeds received for the shares. These answers are not affected by the relationships among the original issuance price of the stock, the cost of the treasury stock, and the reissuance price of the treasury stock.

39. (b) Under the par value method, the recording of the acquisition of treasury stock effectively removes the treasury stock from the accounts. The excess in acquisition price over the original issuance price ($17 – $15 = $2/share) is debited to *Additional Paid-In Capital From Treasury Stock,* but only to the extent of any existing balance from prior treasury stock transactions. The difference, if any, is debited to *Retained Earnings.*

20,000 shares @ $5/share over par, 1/5	$100,000
5,000 shares @ $5/share treasury stock, 7/14	(25,000)
5,000 shares @ ($20 – $10 par) = $10/per share, 12/27	50,000
APIC balance, 12/31	$125,000

40. (b) The entry to record the acquisition of the treasury stock in excess of its original issue price using the par value method will involve a debit to *Treasury Stock* for the par value of the stock, a debit to *APIC* for the amount of the premium on the original issuance, a debit to *Retained Earnings* for the excess of the cost of the treasury stock over the original issuance price, and a credit to *Cash* for the cost of the treasury shares. When the par value method is used, the balance of the *Treasury Stock* account is contra to the *Common Stock* account. Therefore, the use of the par value method will result in a decrease in net common stock, a decrease in APIC and a decrease in retained earnings.

Comparison Between Methods

41. (c) The theoretical justification for the par value method is that the purchase of treasury stock is in fact a constructive retirement of those shares; therefore, reacquired stock is recorded essentially by reversing the amounts at which the stock was originally issued and adjusting any difference to APIC or retained earnings. Reissuance of the stock is treated as if it were a new issue, i.e., the excess purchase price received over par is credited to APIC.

Treasury Stock Retirement

42. (c) Under the cost method, the cost of the treasury stock is reported as an unallocated reduction of the stockholders' equity. Under this method, the treasury stock did not reduce the *Common Stock* account prior to their cancellation.

Par value of common stock before recording cancellation of treasury stock	$ 540,000
Less: Par value of treasury stock canceled (50,000 shares × $2.50 par value)	(125,000)
Par value of common stock outstanding after cancellation of treasury stock	$ 415,000

43. (c) The effect of the acquisition and retirement of each common share is to decrease APIC by $10 (i.e., $15 – $5). A corporation cannot record a gain or loss on the acquisition and retirement of its own common stock. Retained earnings can be decreased, but never increased, as a result of the acquisition and retirement of its own common stock.

Common Stock	10	
APIC—Common Stock	15	
Cash		20
APIC—Retirement of Stock		5

To record the acquisition and retirement of one share of Fogg's own common stock.

Compensatory Plans

44. (a) Deferred compensation expense is a contra stockholders' equity account. Therefore, the net effect on stockholders' equity when the options are granted is zero. Stockholders' equity is increased $45,000 + $10,000 – $35,000 = $20,000.

January 2

Deferred Compensation Cost (value of options at date of grant)	35,000	
Stock Options Outstanding		35,000
To record the grant.		

Cash (1,000 shares × $20)	20,000	
Stock Options Outstanding	35,000	
Common Stock (1,000 × $10)		10,000
Add'l Paid-in Cap., Common Stock (to balance)		45,000
To record the exercise of options.		

45. (c) The cost of services received from employees in exchange for awards of share-based compensation generally shall be measured based on the grant-date fair value of the options. The account *Stock Options Outstanding* is increased on the grant date. The subsequent exercising, forfeiture, or lapsing of the stock options reduces this account.

January 2, Year 3

Deferred Compensation Cost (value of options at date of grant)	32,000	
Stock Options Outstanding		32,000

December 31, Year 3

Wages and Compensation Expense	30,000	
Deferred Compensation Cost		30,000

Cash (1,000 shares × $40)	40,000	
Stock Options Outstanding		30,000
Common Stock (1,000 × $10)		10,000
Add'l Paid-in Cap., Common Stock (to balance)		60,000

46. (d) The cost of services received from employees in exchange for awards of share-based compensation generally shall be measured based on the grant-date fair value of the options. The account *Stock Options Outstanding* is increased on the grant date. The subsequent exercising, forfeiture, or lapsing of the stock options reduces this account.

47. (a) The cost of services received from employees in exchange for awards of share-based compensation generally shall be measured based on the grant-date fair value of the options. The account *Stock Options Outstanding* is increased on the grant date. The subsequent exercising, forfeiture, or lapsing of the stock options reduces this account.

Deferred Compensation Cost (value of options at date of grant)	8,000	
Stock Options Outstanding		8,000
To record the grant.		

Partnership Formation

48. (c) All identifiable assets contributed to a partnership are recorded by the partnership at their fair values. All liabilities that the partnership assumes are recorded at their present values. The contributing partner's capital account is credited for the fair value of the property less the assumed mortgage. Smith's capital account would be the fair value of the property of $80,000 less the mortgage assumed by the partnership of $35,000, for a balance of $45,000.

49. (d) Carr must have made an intangible contribution to the partnership because Abel and Carr have agreed to divide initial capital equally, even though Carr contributed less in identifiable assets ($84,000 < $100,000). Because the bonus method is used to record the formation of the partnership, and the bonus method assumes that an intangible contribution does not constitute a partnership asset with a measurable cost, no unidentifiable asset (i.e., goodwill) is recognized by the partnership. The partnership formation adjusts the capital accounts of the two partners without recognizing goodwill.

Identifiable Assets ($100 + $84)	184,000	
Abel, Capital ($184,000 × 50%)		92,000
Carr, Capital ($184,000 × 50%)		92,000

50. (d) Under the partnership agreement, each partner has an equal initial capital balance accounted for under the goodwill method. Cor is given an initial capital balance of $60,000, equal to the fair value of the identifiable assets Cor contributed to the partnership. Eng is also given an initial capital balance of $60,000. Since Eng only contributed identifiable assets with a fair value of $20,000, Eng must have also contributed an unidentifiable asset (i.e., goodwill) with a fair value of $40,000.

Cash	20,000	
Identifiable Noncash Assets	60,000	
Goodwill	40,000	
Cor, Capital		60,000
Eng, Capital		60,000

Profit & Loss Division

51. (d)

Partnership profit prior to distributions	$ 50,000
Less: Bonus to Low (15% × $50,000)	(7,500)
Salary to Low	(45,000)
Residual partnership loss	(2,500)
Times: Rhu's loss percentage	× 50%
Decrease in Rhu's equity in partnership	$ (1,250)

52. (b) $20,000 × 60% = $12,000

	Partnership	Red	White
Partnership profit prior to salary allowances	$ 80,000		
Deduct salary allowances	(100,000)	$ 55,000	$45,000
Residual partnership loss	$ (20,000)	(12,000)	(8,000)
Credit to each partner's capital account		$ 43,000	$37,000

53. (b) When there is a profit, Flat receives 20% of the profits before the bonus and 40% of the remaining 80% (i.e., 32%), for a total of 52% of the profits. In loss situations, Flat receives only 40% of the loss. Thus Flat has a greater advantage whether the partnership has a profit or loss.

New Partner Admission

54. (d) Under the bonus method, the excess of the partner's contribution over the amount credited to the new partner's capital account is viewed as a bonus to the original partners. The bonus is allocated to the original partners based upon their old profit and loss ratio.

55. (d) In the goodwill method of recording the admission of a new partner, the assets are revalued at their fair values and any excess valuation implied in the purchase price is recorded as goodwill. Robb's 25% interest for an investment of $30,000 implies that total net assets are valued at $120,000 ($30,000/25%).

Net assets	$ 120,000
Less: Robb investment	(30,000)
Eagle capital	(45,000)
Falk capital	(25,000)
Goodwill	$ 20,000

56. (d) Under the bonus method, the total capital of the new partnership will equal the sum of the original partners' capital balances plus the fair value of the identifiable asset (i.e., land) contributed by the new partner. Immediately after admission, the balance of the new partner's capital account equals the total capital of the new partnership multiplied by the new partner's capital interest. After Grant's admission into the partnership, Kern's capital account balance would be $57,600 (i.e., $60,000 – $2,400), and Pate's capital account balance would be $38,400 (i.e., $40,000 – $1,600).

Original partnership capital ($60,000 + $20,000)	$80,000
Fair value of identifiable asset contributed by Grant	15,000
Total recorded capital of new partnership	95,000
Grant's capital interest	× 20%
Credit to Grant's capital account	$19,000

Land (fair value)	15,000	
Kern, Capital ($4,000 × 60%)	2,400	
Pate, Capital ($4,000 × 40%)	1,600	
Grant, Capital		19,000
To record Grant's admission into the partnership.		

57. (c) The goodwill method looks upon this transaction as an indication that the partnership possesses an actual value of $300,000 (i.e., $100,000 / 1/3) after Zorn's admission. Since, even with Zorn's investment, the partnership is reporting only $250,000 (i.e., $60,000 + $90,000 + $100,000) in net assets, a valuation adjustment of $50,000 is required. This adjustment is recorded as goodwill and would be allocated to Dunn and Grey, the original partners, by their respective profit and loss sharing percentages (not provided in this question).

58. (b) The goodwill method looks upon this transaction as an indication that the partnership possesses an actual value of $560,000 ($140,000 / 25%) after Hamm's admission. With Hamm's investment, the partnership is reporting $460,000 ($320,000 + $140,000) in net assets, so a valuation adjustment of $100,000 is required. This adjustment is recorded as goodwill and is allocated to the original partners—Eddy, Fox, and Grimm—by their respective profit and loss sharing percentages. Immediately after Hamm's admission, Eddy's capital account balance is $210,000 ($160,000 + $50,000).

Goodwill	100,000	
Eddy, Capital ($100,000 × 50%)		50,000
Fox, Capital ($100,000 × 30%)		30,000
Grimm, Capital ($100,000 × 20%)		20,000

Cash	140,000	
Hamm, Capital		140,000
To record Hamm's investment.		

Partner Withdrawal

59. (c) The goodwill method looks upon this transaction as an indication that the partnership possesses an actual value of $360,000 ($180,000 / 50%) prior to Eddy's retirement. The partnership is reporting $320,000 in net assets, so a $40,000 valuation adjustment of is required. This adjustment is recorded as goodwill and is allocated to Eddy, Fox,

and Grimm by their respective profit and loss sharing percentages. Immediately after Eddy's retirement, Fox's capital account balance is $108,000 ($96,000 + $12,000) and Grimm's capital account balance is $72,000 ($64,000 + $8,000).

Goodwill	40,000	
Eddy, Capital ($40,000 × 50%)		20,000
Fox, Capital ($40,000 × 30%)		12,000
Grimm, Capital ($40,000 × 20%)		8,000
Eddy, Capital ($160,000 + $20,000)	180,000	
Cash		180,000
To record the payment of $180,000 to Eddy.		

60. (d) Allen, the withdrawing partner, is to receive cash or other assets equal to his current capital balance plus his share of unrecorded goodwill. If the bonus method were to be used to account for this transaction, the payment made to Allen for his share of the unrecorded goodwill would be recorded as a *decrease* in the remaining partners' capital accounts. If the goodwill method were to be used to account for the withdrawal, a revaluation of partnership assets would be required. This adjustment would be recorded on the partnership's books as goodwill and allocated among the existing partners (i.e., Allen, Beck, and Chale) by their respective profit and loss sharing percentages, thereby *increasing* their respective capital accounts. Since the capital accounts of the remaining partners (i.e., Beck and Chale) decreased as a result of the settlement, the withdrawal could only have been recorded using the bonus method.

61. (c) The final settlement of Mill's interest exceeded his capital balance. The excess payment represents Mill's share of the unrecorded goodwill of the partnership. Under the bonus method, this excess payment would be recorded as a decrease in the remaining partners' capital accounts.

Liquidation

62. (a) Smith's capital balance of $195,000 is reduced by his $20,000 loan *from* the partnership ($195,000 – $20,000). (in 000's)

	Cash	Other assets	Liabs	Smith (60%)	Jones (40%)
Balances before realization	$ 0	$ 450	$ 120	$175	$155
Sale of other assets	385	(450)	0	(39)	(26)
Balances after realization	385	$ 0	120	136	129
Pay liabilities	(120)		(120)	0	0
Balances	$ 265		$ 0	$136	$129

63. (a) The maximum possible loss assumes that nothing will be received from the disposition of the remaining $100,000 of other assets. (in 000's)

				Capital		
	Cash	Other assets	Liabs.	Cobb 50%	Davis 30%	Eddy 20%
Balances before realization	$ 50	$ 250	$ 60	$ 80	$ 90	$ 70
1/15 sale	120	(150)		(15)	(9)	(6)
Balance	170	100	60	65	81	64
Liabs. paid	(60)		(60)			
Balance	110	100	0	65	81	64
Maximum loss		(100)		(50)	(30)	(20)
Safe cash distribution	$110	$ 0	$ 0	$ 15	$ 51	$ 44

Problem 10-2 ADDITIONAL MULTIPLE CHOICE ANSWERS

Components

64. (c) A sole proprietorship's equity consists of a single proprietor's equity account, *Owner's Equity* or *Net Worth.* This is the sum of the beginning capital balance, plus additional investments during the period, plus net income (or minus net loss) minus withdrawals. The proprietor's draw is not reported separately on the income statement, but rather is included in *Owner's Equity* or *Net Worth.* Depreciation is not included in the *Owner's Equity* or *Net Worth* account. It is reported on the income statement of a proprietorship.

65. (a)

Capital—Smith, 1/2 (i.e., cost of net assets contributed by owner at 1/2)	$ 350,000
Income of sole proprietorship	60,000
Less: Smith's drawings	(20,000)
Capital—Smith, 12/31	$ 390,000

Stock Rights

66. (d) The proceeds should be allocated between the preferred stock and the detachable stock purchase warrants based on their relative fair market values at date of issue. If the relative fair values are not known, then the fair value of either security is used. In this question, the fair value of the warrants is known, but the fair value of the preferred stock without the warrants is not. Therefore, the amount assigned to the warrants is the fair value of the warrants. The remaining amount of the proceeds is assigned to the preferred stock.

67. (c) No entry (other than a memorandum entry) is made when stock rights are issued to existing stockholders without consideration.

68. (c) A stock right issue generally is recorded by memorandum entry only (but must be disclosed in the financial statement notes). When the rights are

exercised, common stock is credited at its par value, regardless of the option price or the stock's FMV. The difference between the option price and the par value of the stock (i.e., $15 – $10 = $5) is credited to *Additional Paid-In Capital* when the stock is issued.

Capital Stock Issues

69. (d) The common stock's par value is recorded as *Common Stock Subscribed* and the excess of the subscription price over the common stock's par value is recorded as APIC.

Cash (20% down payment)	XX	
Subscriptions Receivable (balance due)	XX	
Common Stock Subscribed (shares × par value)		XX
Additional Paid-In Capital (to balance)		XX

70. (d)

Assets ($100,000 + $12,000)	112,000	
Liabilities (carrying amount = fair value)		20,000
Common Stock (5,000 × $1 × 2)		10,000
Additional Paid-In Capital (to balance)		82,000
To record the incorporation of the partnership.		

71. (b) Since the market value of both securities is not determinable, the incremental method should be used to allocate the cash proceeds between the two securities. Since the market value of the bonds is known, the cash proceeds in excess of this amount are allocated to the common stock. The excess of the proceeds allocated to the common stock over the par value is recorded as APIC.

Lump sum cash proceeds	$ 110,000
Less: Market value of bonds	(40,000)
Cash proceeds allocated to common stock	70,000
Less: Par value of common stock (1,000 × $5)	(5,000)
APIC on issuance of common stock	$ 65,000

Retained Earnings

72. (d) The purpose of a retained earnings appropriation is to restrict a portion of retained earnings as to availability for dividends. A retained earnings appropriation is not used to absorb a fire loss when a company is self-insured, provide for a contingent loss that is probable and reasonably estimable, or to smooth periodic income.

73. (a) Cumulative preferred stock dividends in arrears should be disclosed either on the face of the balance sheet or in a footnote to the financial statements (APB 15, ¶50). Most state corporate laws require retained earnings to be appropriated in the amount of the cost of treasury stock held; however, this treasury stock was reissued.

74. (c) The primary purpose of a quasi-reorganization is to eliminate an accumulated deficit (negative retained earnings balance) so that the corporation has a "fresh start" with a zero balance in retained earnings. Although the accounting procedures for a quasi-reorganization involve restating assets of the enterprise to their fair values, this is not the primary purpose. There should be no net asset write-up.

Property Dividends

75. (c) A transfer of a nonmonetary asset to a stockholder in a nonreciprocal transfer should be recorded at the fair value of the asset transferred, and a gain or loss should be recognized on the disposition of the asset equal to the difference between the fair value and carrying amount of the asset (APB 29, ¶18). After all nominal accounts (e.g., *Gain on Disposition of Investment*) are closed, the effect of this property dividend is to decrease *Retained Earnings* by $60,000 (i.e., $78,000 – $18,000). Nilo records the following entries at the declaration date.

Marketable Securities ($78,000 – $60,000)	18,000	
Gain on Disposition of Investment		18,000
Retained Earnings	78,000	
Property Dividend Payable		78,000

76. (d) A transfer of a nonmonetary asset to a stockholder in a nonreciprocal transfer should be recorded at the fair value of the asset transferred, and a gain or loss should be recognized on the disposition of the asset (APB 29, ¶18). Bain records the following entries at the declaration date.

Investment in Stock of Tell Corp. ($300,000 – $180,000)	120,000	
Gain on Disposal of Investment		120,000
Retained Earnings	300,000	
Property Dividend Payable		300,000

Stock Dividends

77. (d) Stock dividends received on common stock may be recorded only by memorandum entry, regardless of the method of accounting for the investment. Under the cost method, a new cost basis per share would be computed. Under the equity method, a new carrying amount per share would be computed.

78. (d) Since the 100% stock dividend exceeds 25% of the number of shares outstanding, it is considered a "large" stock dividend. Therefore, it should be recorded by capitalizing a portion of *Retained Earnings* equal to the par value of the shares issued.

As a result of the stock dividend, *Retained Earnings* will decrease and *Common Stock* will increase by the par value of the shares issued. *APIC* will not change as a result of the "large" stock dividend.

79. (a) Since the 5% stock dividend is less than 20 to 25% of the number of shares outstanding, it is considered to be a "small" stock dividend. Therefore, it should be recorded by capitalizing a portion of *Retained Earnings* equal to the fair value of the shares issued. As a result of the "small" stock dividend, *Retained Earnings* will decrease by the fair value of the shares issued, *Common Stock* will increase by the par value of the shares issued, and *APIC* will increase by the excess of the fair value over the par value of the shares issued.

Treasury Stock Overview

80. (d) The 225,000 common shares outstanding are computed by subtracting the 75,000 treasury shares from the 300,000 (i.e., 200,000 + 100,000) common shares issued. The number of common shares outstanding is not affected by the convertible preferred stock; there is no indication that any of the preferred stock was converted.

81. (a)

Common shares outstanding, previous 12/31	300,000
10% stock dividend, 1/31 (300,000 × 10%)	30,000
Treasury shares purchased, 6/30	(100,000)
Treasury shares reissued, 8/1	50,000
2-for-1 stock split, 11/30 (300,000 + 30,000 – 100,000 + 50,000)	280,000
Common shares outstanding, current 12/31	560,000

82. (a) The idle machinery, the cash surrender value of the life insurance on the corporate executives, and the contra account, *Allowance for Decline in Market Value of Noncurrent Equity Securities,* are all properly included in computing net assets.

Net assets, before adjustments	$ 875,000
Less: Cost of treasury stock	(24,000)
Net assets, 12/31	$ 851,000

Cost Method

83. (a) Under the cost method, treasury stock is recorded and carried at the acquisition cost ($20 per share). Cyan sold some of the shares for $5 per share more than the acquisition cost. This excess is credited to a *Paid-In Capital From Treasury Stock* account and *Retained Earnings* is not affected. If Cyan sold any of the shares for less than the acquisition cost, the deficit would first be charged to any existing balance in the *Paid-In Capital From Treasury Stock* account, and the excess, if any, would be charged against *Retained Earnings.*

Retained earnings, previous Dec. 31	$ 300,000
Net income, current year	60,000
Retained earnings, current Dec. 31	$ 360,000

84. (c) When treasury stock is acquired, total stockholders' equity decreases by the cost of the treasury shares, regardless of the method used to account for the treasury stock. The book value per common share is computed by dividing total stockholders' equity applicable to common stock by the number of common stock shares outstanding. The acquisition of treasury shares at a price less than their book value will reduce both the numerator and denominator of the book value ratio; however, the reduction of the numerator is less than the amount that was in there for these shares. The excess book value for those shares would now be spread over the remaining shares outstanding, resulting in an increase in the book value per common share.

85. (c) One way to analyze this question is by an example. Assume one share of $10 par stock was issued for $13 and reacquired at $12.

Treasury Stock	12	
Cash		12

To record a treasury stock acquisition under the cost method.

Treasury Stock	10	
Premium on Common Stock	3	
Cash		12
Paid-In Capital From Treasury Stock Transactions		1

To record a treasury stock acquisition under the par value method.

Both the *Premium on Common Stock* and *Paid-In Capital From Treasury Stock Transactions* accounts are APIC accounts. Because the par value method removes the effect of the original issuance price on APIC (the premium amount) from APIC and records the "gain" (excess of original issuance price over cost of treasury stock) as APIC, total APIC is reduced when the par value method is used in this scenario. APIC is not affected by the acquisition of treasury stock when the cost method is used. Retained earnings is not affected by either the cost method or the par value method in this situation. (Retained earnings would have been reduced in using the par value method if the cost of the treasury share had exceeded the original issuance price.)

Treasury Stock Retirement

86. (c) The *APIC* account decreases by the original increase to the *APIC* account when the 2,000 shares were issued. The *Retained Earnings* account decreases by the amount by which the cost of the 2,000 shares exceeds the proceeds from their issuance.

Common Stock (2,000 × $10 PV)	20,000	
Additional Paid-In Capital [2,000 × ($100 – $10 PV)]	180,000	
Retained Earnings [2,000 × ($150 – $100)]	100,000	
Cash (2,000 × $150)		300,000
To record retirement of common shares.		

87. (b) Immediately after the shares were retired, the APIC balance would be $2,470,000 ($2,550,000 – $80,000).

Common Stock (20,000 × $20 PV)	400,000	
Additional Paid-In Capital (to balance)	80,000	
Cash (20,000 × $24)		480,000
To record retirement of common stock.		

Compensatory Plans

88. (c)

Cash contributed	$30,000
Common stock contributed (3,000 shares × $18 fair value)	54,000
ESOP compensation expense	$84,000

89. (d) The $100,000 endorsed note payable pertaining to the ESOP appears both as a liability and a reduction of stockholders' equity.

90. (d) Compensation costs of a stock option plan should be recognized (i.e., expensed) in the period(s) in which the employee performs the services. Deferred compensation costs is recognized on the date of the grant.

Partnership Formation

91. (a) Using historical cost for assets such as inventory, land, or equipment would be inequitable to any partner investing appreciated property. Therefore, the contribution of noncash assets to a partnership should be recorded based on fair values.

Profit & Loss Division

92. (a) Young received $16,000 ($160,000 × 10%) and Zinc received $10,000 ($100,000 × 10%) for the interest on average capital balances. This makes the residual loss $22,000 ($4,000 – $16,000 – $10,000). As the residual loss is evenly divided between the two partners, Zinc gets $11,000 of loss. Zinc's interest allowance less Zinc's portion of the residual loss is the change in Zinc's capital balance. $10,000 – $11,000 = $1,000 decrease.

93. (c) $204,000 × 1/3 = $68,000

	Partnership profit	Allocation to Axel
Profit prior to distribution	$250,000	
Deduct bonus to Axel [($100 × 10%) + ($250 – 100) × 20%]	(40,000)	$ 40,000
Less: Bonuses to Berg & Cobb [$250 – ($150 + $40)] × 5% × 2]	(6,000)	
Residual profit	$204,000	68,000
Profit allocated to Axel		$108,000

New Partner Admission

94. (b) Because the total capital of the partners following the admission of Lind will be equal to the sum of the original partners' capital balances plus the cash contributed by Lind (i.e., $60,000 + $50,000 + $40,000 = $150,000), no goodwill is recognized.

Blau's capital balance, pre-admission		$60,000
Credit to Lind for 1/3 of new partnership capital ($150,000 × 1/3)	$50,000	
Less: Cash contributed by Lind	40,000	
Bonus to Lind from Blau and Rubi	10,000	
Times: Blau's share of bonus [60% / (60% + 40%)]	× 60%	
Decrease in Blau's capital account		(6,000)
Blau's capital balance, post-admission		$54,000

95. (d)

Total current capital ($348,000 + $232,000)	$ 580,000
Divided by: Percentage current capital is of new total capital (100% – Capp @ 20%)	/ 80%
Total new capital, including Capp	725,000
Less: Alfa & Beda Capital (current capital)	(580,000)
Capp's contribution for 20% interest	$ 145,000

96. (b)

Total Cash to Distribute:	
Cash	$ 45,000
Plus: Sale of other assets	500,000
Less: Accounts payable to settle	(120,000)
Total available cash	$ 425,000

Distribution of Available Cash:	Alfa (60%)	Beda (40%)
Beginning capital	$ 348,000	$ 232,000
Reduce Beda capital for loan		(30,000)
Allocate loss on sale of assets per profit and loss sharing ratio ($625,000 - $5000,000)	(75,000)	(50,000)
Distribution of cash	$ 273,000	$ 152,000

PERFORMANCE BY SUBTOPICS

Each category below parallels a subtopic covered in Chapter 10. Record the number and percentage of questions you correctly answered in each subtopic area.

Components

Question #	Correct √
1	
2	
3	
# Questions	3
# Correct	
% Correct	

Preferred Stock Dividends

Question #	Correct √
4	
5	
6	
# Questions	3
# Correct	
% Correct	

Stock Rights

Question #	Correct √
7	
8	
9	
# Questions	3
# Correct	
% Correct	

Capital Stock Issues

Question #	Correct √
10	
11	
12	
# Questions	3
# Correct	
% Correct	

Retained Earnings

Question #	Correct √
13	
14	
15	
# Questions	3
# Correct	
% Correct	

Dividend Significant Dates

Question #	Correct √
16	
17	
18	
# Questions	3
# Correct	
% Correct	

Property Dividends

Question #	Correct √
19	
20	
21	
# Questions	3
# Correct	
% Correct	

Liquidating Dividends

Question #	Correct √
22	
23	
24	
# Questions	3
# Correct	
% Correct	

Stock Dividends

Question #	Correct √
25	
26	
27	
28	
# Questions	4
# Correct	
% Correct	

Stock Splits

Question #	Correct √
29	
30	
# Questions	2
# Correct	
% Correct	

Treasury Stock Overview

Question #	Correct √
31	
32	
33	
34	
# Questions	4
# Correct	
% Correct	

Cost Method

Question #	Correct √
35	
36	
37	
# Questions	3
# Correct	
% Correct	

Par Value Method

Question #	Correct √
38	
39	
40	
# Questions	3
# Correct	
% Correct	

Comparison Between Methods

Question #	Correct √
41	
# Questions	1
# Correct	
% Correct	

Treasury Stock Retirement

Question #	Correct √
42	
43	
# Questions	2
# Correct	
% Correct	

Compensatory Plans

Question #	Correct √
44	
45	
46	
47	
# Questions	4
# Correct	
% Correct	

Partnership Formation

Question #	Correct √
48	
49	
50	
# Questions	3
# Correct	
% Correct	

Profit & Loss Division

Question #	Correct √
51	
52	
53	
# Questions	3
# Correct	
% Correct	

New Partner Admission

Question #	Correct √
54	
55	
56	
57	
58	
# Questions	5
# Correct	
% Correct	

Partner Withdrawal

Question #	Correct √
59	
60	
61	
# Questions	3
# Correct	
% Correct	

Liquidation

Question #	Correct √
62	
63	
# Questions	2
# Correct	
% Correct	

SIMULATION SOLUTIONS

Solution 10-3

Research

APB 29, Par. 18

18. The Board concludes that in general accounting for nonmonetary transactions should be based on the fair values of the assets (or services) involved which is the same basis as that used in monetary transactions. Thus, the cost of a nonmonetary asset acquired in exchange for another nonmonetary asset is the fair value of the asset surrendered to obtain it, and a gain or loss should be recognized on the exchange. The fair value of the asset received should be used to measure the cost if it is more clearly evident than the fair value of the asset surrendered. Similarly, a nonmonetary asset received in a nonreciprocal transfer should be recorded at the fair value of the asset received. A transfer of a nonmonetary asset to a stockholder or to another entity in a nonreciprocal transfer should be recorded at the fair value of the asset transferred, and a gain or loss should be recognized on the disposition of the asset. The fair value of an entity's own stock reacquired may be a more clearly evident measure of the fair value of the asset distributed in a nonreciprocal transfer if the transaction involves distribution of a nonmonetary asset to eliminate a disproportionate part of owners' interests (that is, to acquire stock for the treasury or for retirement).

Responses 1-10

1. $14,000

The correction of an error in financial statements of a prior period is a "prior period adjustment." Prior period adjustments should be reported in the current retained earnings statement as an adjustment of the opening balance, net of related income taxes (APB 9). The patent cost is properly amortized over its estimated useful life of 8 years and was owned for 6 months during year 1. Hake has a 30% tax rate. [($320,000 / 8) × 6/12 × (1–0.30) = $14,000.]

2. $12,000

The required cash dividend on preferred stock is calculated by multiplying the outstanding preferred stock by the par value and the earnings rate (2,000 shares × $100 par value × 6%). As there are no unpaid amounts from prior years, this is the only amount required to be paid this year.

3. $165,000

Cash dividends on common stock are calculated by multiplying the declared cash dividends per share times the number of outstanding common shares at the time of declaration (110,000 × $1.50). The outstanding shares on 11/4 are the original 100,000 shares + the 13,000 2/1 issue – the 5,000 treasury shares purchased 3/1 + 2,000 treasury shares reissued 10/1.

4. $720,000

Property dividends are recorded at the fair value of assets given up, and any difference between fair value and carrying amount of the asset is recorded as a gain or loss as a component of income from continuing operations. Any change in the fair value of the asset to be distributed between the date of declaration and date of payment is ignored.

5. 113,000

The number of common shares issued at 12/31 are the original 100,000 shares + the 13,000 2/1 issue. The treasury stock activity is irrelevant as none of these shares were retired. (Treasury stock is issued but not outstanding.)

6. $113,000

The number of common shares issued at 12/31 year 2, are the original 100,000 shares + the 13,000 2/1 issue. The treasury stock activity is irrelevant as none of these shares were retired. (Treasury stock is issued but not outstanding.) The par value of the stock is $1 per share (113,000 × $1 = $113,000).

7. $934,000

The additional paid-in capital (APIC) balance is the beginning balance of $800,000 adjusted for year 2 transactions. In issues of stock for property other than cash, the property received and the amount of contributed capital should be recorded at the fair value of the property received or the market value of the stock, whichever is more objectively determinable. The value of the land purchased on 2/1 is best determinable by the value of stock traded in the over-the-counter market. As the stock has a $1 par value, the remaining $10 per share goes to APIC ($10 × 13,000 = $130,000). Under the cost method of accounting for treasury stock, any reissuance at a price in excess of the acquisition cost, the excess is credited to an appropriate APIC account. [($16 – $14) × 2,000 shares = $4,000]; ($800,000 + $130,000 + $4,000 = $934,000).

8. $42,000

The treasury stock is recorded at cost under the cost method, so the Treasury Stock account is debited for $70,000 (5,000 × $14/shares) when the 5,000 treasury shares are purchased. Since 2,000 shares or 40% of the treasury shares are then resold, the Treasury Stock account is only credited for 40% of the $70,000, or $28,000. This leaves a balance of $42,000 in the Treasury Stock account at year end.

9. $24.86

The book value per share is computed by dividing the number of common shares outstanding at December 31, year 1 (100,000) into total stockholders' equity less the amount related to the preferred stock. ($2,686,000 – $200,000) ÷ 100,000 = $24.86

10. $826,000

The numerator to be used in calculating year 2 earnings per share is the adjusted net income for year 2 of $838,000 less the preferred dividends of $12,000, or $826,000.

Solution 10-4

Research

C23 Summary

If an enterprise acquires shares of its own capital stock, the cost if the acquired shares shall generally be shown as a deduction from capital. Dividends on such shares held in the enterprise's treasury (treasury stock) shall not be credited to income. Gains and losses on sales of treasury stock shall be accounted for as adjustments to capital and not as part of income.

Balance Sheet Solution

Field Co.
Stockholders' Equity Section of
Balance Sheet
December 31, Year 3

Common stock, $5 par value, 400,000 shares authorized, 180,000 shares issued, 175,000 shares outstanding		$ 900,000	[1]
Additional paid-in capital		1,860,000	[2]
Retained earnings:			
Beginning balance	$1,845,000	[given info]	
Add: Net income	240,000		[3]
Less: Property dividend distributed	(60,000)		[4]
Ending balance		2,025,000	[5]
		4,785,000	[6]
Less common stock in treasury, 5,000 shares at cost		(50,000)	[7]
Total stockholders' equity		$4,735,000	[8]

Explanations:

[1] Shares issued: 160,000 + 20,000 = 180,000 × $5 = $900,000

[2] Additional paid-in capital: 1,600,000 + 260,000 = 1,860,000

Cash (20,000 shares × $16)	325,000	
Stock Options Outstanding	35,000	
Common Stock (20,000 × $5)		100,000
Add'l Paid-in Cap., Common (to balance)		260,000

To record the exercise of options.

[3] Net income for year 3 increases retained earnings

[4] Property dividend distribution reduces retained earnings

[5] Ending balance of retained earnings: $1,845,000 + 240,000 – 60,000 = $2,025,000

[6] Common stock + Additional Paid in Capital + ending balance of retained earnings:

$900,000 + 1,860,000 + 2,025,000 = $4,785,000

[7] 5,000 shares of treasury stock @ $10.00 = $50,000 reduced stockholders equity when acquired.

[8] Total stockholders equity $4,785,000 – 50,000 = $4,735,000

Essay—Accounting for Stock Options

To: **Management, Field Co.**
Re: Accounting for Stock-Based Compensation

As you are aware, Statement of Financial Accounting Standards No. 123 Revised discusses the "fair value" method of accounting for stock options. The purpose of this memo is to inform you of when the company should record compensation cost associated with year 4 stock option issuances.

Under the **"fair value" method** of accounting for stock options meant to be salaries and wages, compensation cost is **measured at the grant date** based on the **value of the award.**

This value is computed using an **option-pricing model** such as the Black Scholes Pricing Model.

Compensation cost is **recognized over the service period,** which is usually the vesting period.

Solution 10-5

Research

A31.101

.101 Additional paid-in capital, however created, shall not be used to relieve income of the current or future years of charges which would otherwise be made against [income]. This rule might be subject to the exception that where, upon reorganization, a reorganized enterprise would be relieved of charges that would be made against income if the existing enterprise were continued, it might be regarded as permissible to accomplish the same result without reorganization provided the facts were as fully revealed to and the action as formally approved by the shareholders as in reorganization.

Statement of Retained Earnings

Trask Corp.
Statement of Retained Earnings
For the Year Ended December 31, Year 6

Balance, December 31, year 5		**$16,445,000**	
Less: Prior period adjustment from error understating depreciation	**$350,000**		
Reduced by: Income tax effect	**105,000**		
Total adjustments		**(245,000)**	
As restated (Beginning balance less adjustments)		16,200,000	
Net income		**2,400,000**	
(Restated amount plus Net Income)		18,600,000	
Deduct dividends			
Cash dividend on preferred stock	300,000		[1]
Dividend in kind on common stock	900,000		[2]
Total dividends (sum of dividends)		(1,200,000)	
Balance, December 31, year 6 (Net Income less dividends)		$17,400,000	

[1] Preferred stock dividend:

Par value of outstanding preferred shares	$5,000,000
Multiplied by: Dividend rate	× .06
Dividends paid on preferred stock	$ 300,000

[2] Dividend in kind on common stock:

Fair market value of Harbor stock distributed [15,000 shares @ $60]	$ 900,000

Stockholders' Equity

Trask Corp.
Stockholders' Equity Section of
Balance Sheet
December 31, Year 6

Preferred stock, $100 par value, 6% cumulative;		
150,000 shares authorized; 50,000 shares issued and outstanding (Given)	$ 5,000,000	
Common stock, $2.50 par value; 4,000,000 shares authorized; 3,400,000 shares issued	8,500,000	[3]
Additional paid-in capital	16,675,000	[4]
Retained earnings (See schedule A)	17,400,000	
	47,575,000	
Less: Common stock in treasury, 100,000 shares at cost [(75,000 + 25,000) × $5] (Information given in scenario)	(500,000)	
Total stockholders' equity (Preferred stock plus common stock)	$47,075,000	

[3] Number of common shares issued and outstanding:

Number of common shares issued, 12/31, year 5	1,575,000
Less: Common shares retired	(25,000)
Number of common shares issued, 6/1, year 6	150,000
	1,700,000
Two-for-one stock split, 10/27, year 6	× 2
Number of common shares issued after stock split	3,400,000
Less: Common shares held in treasury	(100,000)
Total number of common shares outstanding	**3,300,000**

Amount of common shares issued:

Amount of common shares issued, 12/31, year 5	$ 7,875,000
Less: Common shares retired at par value	(125,000)
Number of common shares issued, 6/1, year 6	750,000
Total amount of common shares issued	**$ 8,500,000**

[4] Amount of additional paid-in capital:

Amount at 12/31, year 5 (1,575,000 @ $10)	$15,750,000
Less: Treasury stock retired [25,000 shares @ $5 ($10 cost – $5 par value)]	(125,000)
APIC from exercise of stock options 6/1, year 6	1,050,000
	$16,675,000

Book Value Per Share

Trask Corp.
Computation of Book Value Per Share of Common Stock
December 31, Year 6

Total stockholders' equity	$47,075,000	[5]
Deduct allocation to preferred stock	(5,000,000)	[6]
Allocation to common stock	42,075,000	
Divided by number of common shares outstanding	/ 3,300,000	[7]
Book value per share of common stock	$ 12.75	

[5] Total stockholder equity from response B

[6] Common stock in treasury from Response B

[7] Number of common shares outstanding
[3,400,000 – 100,000]

Select Hot•Spots™ Video Descriptions

CPA 3246 Owners' Equity & Miscellaneous Topics
Learn about owners' equity, including stock issuance, retained earnings, and five types of dividends. Gary Waters discusses treasury stock transactions, and the treatment of stock options, warrants, and rights. He illustrates earnings per share calculations, partnership accounting, financial statement analysis, foreign currency translation, and price level accounting.

CPA 3220 Revenue Recognition & Income Statement Presentation
This program includes extensive coverage of the four income statement components, what is included in each component, and how components are presented in the financial statements. Learn about comprehensive income, what it includes, and how it is presented. Bob Monette provides in-depth coverage including accounting for long-term contracts, installment sales, discontinued operations, extraordinary items, prior period adjustments, changes in accounting principles, changes in estimates, changes in entities…and more!

Call our customer representatives toll-free at 1 (800) 874-7877 for more details about videos.

Subject to Change Without Notice

CHAPTER 11

REPORTING THE RESULTS OF OPERATIONS

I. **Overview** 11-2
- A. Concepts of Income 11-2
- B. Income Statement Format 11-2
- C. Definitions 11-4

II. **Income Statement Components** 11-5
- A. Continuing Operations 11-5
- B. Discontinued Operations 11-5
- C. Extraordinary Items 11-7

III. **Comprehensive Income (SFAS 130)** 11-8
- A. Overview 11-8
- B. Comprehensive Income 11-9
- C. Other Comprehensive Income (OCI) 11-9
- D. Accumulated Balance of OCI 11-10
- E. Reporting Related Income Tax 11-10
- F. Format Options 11-10

IV. **Additional Reporting Considerations** 11-12
- A. Changes in Accounting Principle 11-12
- B. Changes in Accounting Estimates 11-13
- C. Changes in Reporting Entity 11-14
- D. Correction of Errors (SFAS 154) 11-14
- E. Accounting Policies Disclosure (APB 22) 11-16
- F. Related Party Disclosures (SFAS 57) 11-16
- G. Development Stage Enterprises (SFAS 7) 11-17
- H. Accrual Accounting 11-18
- I. Other Comprehensive Basis of Accounting 11-19

V. **Interim Financial Reporting (APB 28)** 11-20
- A. Concepts 11-20
- B. Continuing Operations 11-20
- C. Discontinued Operations & Extraordinary Items 11-22
- D. Accounting Changes 11-22
- E. Minimum Disclosures 11-22

VI. **Segment Disclosures (SFAS 131)** 11-23
- A. Management Approach Method 11-23
- B. Aggregation Criteria 11-24
- C. Quantitative Thresholds 11-26
- D. Disclosures 11-27

EXAM COVERAGE: Historically, exam coverage of the topics in Chapters 11 and 12 has been about 20 to 25 percent of the FAR section. The income statement components and comprehensive income are tested heavily on almost every exam. More information regarding exam coverage is included in Appendix B, *Practical Advice*.

CHAPTER 11

REPORTING THE RESULTS OF OPERATIONS

I. Overview

A. Concepts of Income

The determination and presentation of various items on the income statement are influenced by two alternative concepts, the current operating concept and the all-inclusive concept. Proponents of the all-inclusive approach insist that the income statement should include unusual and nonrecurring items in order to measure the long-range operating performance of the enterprise. Proponents of the current operating concept emphasize the importance of normal recurring operations in evaluating the performance of the entity. They contend that the inclusion of unusual and nonrecurring items in the income statement distorts net income. The method required by APB 9, *Reporting the Results of Operations,* reflects a compromise between the all-inclusive and current-operating concepts.

1. All regular items of income and expense, including items that are unusual or infrequently occurring, are included in the determination of net income.

2. Income from discontinued operations and extraordinary items are reported separately from the results of continuing operations.

3. Prior period adjustments are presented as adjustments to the beginning balance of retained earnings.

B. Income Statement Format

1. **Single-Year Presentation** APB 30, *Reporting the Results of Operations,* indicates the following format for the presentation of the income statement for a single year.

Exhibit 1 ▸ Income Statement Presentation

Income from continuing operations before income taxes		$XXX
Provision for income taxes		XXX
Income (loss) from continuing operations (after income taxes)		XXX
Discontinued operations (Note X):		
Income (loss) from operations of discontinued Division A (including loss on disposal of $XXX)	$XXX	
Income taxes	XXX	
Income from discontinued operations		XXX
Income before extraordinary items		XXX
Extraordinary items (less applicable income taxes of $XXX)		XXX
Net income		$XXX

2. **Comparative Statements** The presentation of comparative financial statements enhances the usefulness of annual and other reports. Comparative statements project more relevant and meaningful information than do noncomparative statements. Moreover, comparative statements prepared on a consistent basis from one period to the next are especially valuable because they measure difference in operating results based on the same measurement criteria (ARB 43).

3. **Multiple-Step Format** The presentation of income from continuing operations in a *multiple step format* emphasizes a functional or object classification of each statement item, and sets forth various intermediate levels of income.

Exhibit 2 ▸ Multiple-Step Format

Sales			$ 950,000
Less sales returns and allowances			(16,500)
Net sales			933,500
Beginning inventory		$ 230,000	
Purchases	$590,000		
Less purchase returns and allowances	(19,300)		
Net purchases		570,700	
Freight-in		2,000	
Goods available for sale		802,700	
Less ending inventory		(220,000)	
Cost of goods sold			(582,700)
Gross margin			350,800
Selling		150,000	
General & administrative		72,000	
Operating expenses			(222,000)
Income from operations			128,800
Rent	2,500		
Interest and dividends	6,700		
Gain on sale of machinery	8,000		
Other revenues		17,200	
Interest	5,200		
Loss on sale of investments	6,000		
Other expenses		(11,200)	
			6,000
Income from continuing operations before income taxes			134,800
Provision for income taxes			(60,660)
Income from continuing operations			74,140
Extraordinary item:			
Loss due to earthquake, less tax saving of $3,150			(3,850)
Net income			$ 70,290

4. **Single-Step Format** Income from continuing operations may be presented in a *multiple step format* or a *single step format*. Presentation of income from continuing operations in a *single step format* is often used for publicly issued statements. Revenues are grouped under one classification while expenses are grouped under another classification.

Exhibit 3 ▸ Single-Step Format

Sales (less returns and allowances of $16,500)		$ 933,500
Rent		2,500
Interest and dividends		6,700
Gain on sale of machinery		8,000
Revenues		950,700
Cost of goods sold	$582,700	
Selling	150,000	
General & administrative	72,000	
Interest	5,200	
Loss on sale of investments	6,000	

Expenses	(815,900)
Income from continuing operations before income taxes	134,800
Provision for income taxes	(60,660)
Income from continuing operations	74,140
Extraordinary item: Loss due to earthquake, less tax saving of $3,150	(3,850)
Net income	$ 70,290

C. **Definitions**

1. **Accounting Change** A change in (a) an accounting principle, (b) an accounting estimate, or (c) the reporting entity. The correction of an error in previously issued financial statements is not an accounting change.

2. **Change in Accounting Principle** A change from one generally accepted accounting principle to another generally accepted accounting principle when there are two or more generally accepted accounting principles that apply or when the accounting principle formerly used is no longer generally accepted. A change in the method of applying an accounting principle also is considered a change in accounting principle.

3. **Change in Accounting Estimate** A change that has the effect of adjusting the carrying amount of an existing asset or liability or altering the subsequent accounting for existing or future assets or liabilities. Changes in accounting estimates result from new information. Examples of items for which estimates are necessary are uncollectible receivables, inventory obsolescence, service lives and salvage values of depreciable assets, and warranty obligations.

4. **Change in Accounting Estimate Effected by a Change in Accounting Principle** A change in accounting estimate that is inseparable from the effect of a related change in accounting principle. An example would be the change in the method of depreciation, amortization, or depletion for long-lived, nonfinancial assets.

5. **Change in Reporting Entity** A change that results in financial statements that, in effect, are those of a different reporting entity. A change in the reporting entity is limited mainly to (a) presenting consolidated or combined financial statements in place of financial statements of individual entities, (b) changing specific subsidiaries that make up the group of entities for which consolidated financial statements are presented, and (c) changing the entities included in combined financial statements.

6. **Direct Effects of a Change in Accounting Principle** Those recognized changes in assets or liabilities necessary to effect a change in accounting principle. An example is an adjustment to an inventory balance to effect a change in inventory valuation method. Related changes, such as an effect on deferred income tax assets or liabilities or an impairment adjustment resulting from applying the lower-of-cost-or-market test to the adjusted inventory balance, also are examples of direct effects of a change in accounting principle.

7. **Error in Previously Issued Financial Statements** An error in recognition, measurement, presentation, or disclosure in financial statements resulting from mathematical mistakes, mistakes in the application of GAAP, or oversight or misuse of facts that existed at the time the financial statements were prepared. A change from an accounting principle that is not generally accepted to one that is generally accepted is a correction of an error.

8. **Indirect Effects of a Change in Accounting Principle** Any changes to current or future cash flows of an entity that result from making a change in accounting principle that is applied retrospectively. An example of a indirect effect is a change in nondiscretionary profit sharing or royalty payment that is based on a reported amount such as revenue or net income.

9. **Restatement** The process of revising previously issued financial statements to reflect the correction of an error in those financial statements.

10. **Retrospective Application** The application of a different accounting principle to one or more previously issued financial statements, or to the statement of financial position at the beginning of the current period, as if that principle had always been used, or a change to financial statements of prior accounting periods to present the financial statement of a new reporting entity as if it had existed in those prior years. (Synonymous with the term retroactive restatement)

11. **Impracticable** After making every reasonable effort, an entity is unable to comply because needed information is unable to be substantiated.

II. Income Statement Components

A. Continuing Operations

1. **Revenues and Expenses** Revenue and expense items (and gains and losses) that are considered to be of a usual and recurring nature are reported in income from continuing operations.

2. **Unusual or Infrequent Items** Items that are considered to be *either* unusual in nature *or* infrequent in occurrence are reported as a *separate component* of income from continuing operations. The nature and financial effects of this type of item should be disclosed on the face of the income statement, or alternatively, in the notes to the financial statements. These items should not be reported net of income taxes or in any other manner that would imply that they are extraordinary items.

3. **Tax Provision** The provision for income taxes associated with income from continuing operations should be presented as a single line item.

B. Discontinued Operations

The results of discontinued operations are reported separately from continuing operations. *Discontinued operations* refers to the operations of a component of an entity that has been disposed of or is still operating, but is the subject of a formal plan for disposal. SFAS 144, *Accounting for Impairment or Disposal of Long-Lived Assets,* defines *component of an entity* as a segment, reporting unit, or asset group whose operations and cash flows are clearly distinguished from the rest of the entity, operationally as well as for financial reporting purposes.

Exhibit 4 ▸ Discontinued Operations: Component Vs. Non-Component Disposals

Component Disposals	Non-Component Disposals
Two companies manufacture and sell consumer products with several product groups, with different product lines and brands. For both companies, a product group is the lowest level at which operations and cash flows can be distinguished.	
Caring Pharmaceuticals plans to sell the beauty product group and its operations.	Nesbit Household Products discontinues cosmetic brands associated with losses.
Two companies operate nationwide restaurant chains, each with numerous company-owned sites. For both companies, a single restaurant is the lowest level at which operations and cash flows can be distinguished.	
Cluck-to-Go decides to exit its northeast region. It removes its name from the northeast restaurants and sells the buildings.	New Wave Coffee sells all restaurants in its west coast region to franchisees. New Wave will receive franchise fees, provide advertising, and supply select ingredients.

Two companies operate retail home appliance chains, each with numerous company-owned sites. For both companies, a single store is the lowest level at which operations and cash flows can be distinguished.	
Cheap Freddie's closes stores in areas with declining populations, selling the buildings and moving remaining inventory to stores in other regions.	Never-a-care, Inc., closes pairs of Never-a-care Appliances stores and opens Never-a-cloud Superstores, central to former locations, with an expanded range of products.
Two sporting goods producers have golf club divisions that design, manufacture, market, and distribute golf clubs. For both companies, a division is the lowest level at which operations and cash flows can be distinguished.	
Committed Sports, Inc., agrees to a plan to sell the golf club division to an independent conglomerate.	Never Say Die Manufacturers sells its golf club manufacturing plants. Never Say Die plans to outsource its golf club manufacturing.

1. **Non-Component Assets** Income from **continuing** operations includes gains or losses from an asset (or asset group) that is classified as held for sale, but that is below the level of a *component of the entity.* If disposal will not occur for more than 12 months, costs to sell are discounted to present value.

2. **Income Statement** SFAS 144 provides an illustration (incorporated into Exhibit 1) of the income statement presentation for reporting the results of discontinued operations. The results of operations of a component of an entity are reported as part of discontinued operations, for current and prior periods (in the periods in which they occur), provided that:

   a. **Operations** Operations and cash flows have been (or will be) removed from the entity's ongoing operations due to the disposal transaction.

   b. **Continuing Involvement** The entity ceases any significant continuing involvement in the component's operations after the disposal transaction.

3. **Balance Sheet** The component is valued at current fair value less cost to sell. Asset(s) that are classified as held for sale, and their related liabilities, are presented separately in the asset and liability sections of the balance sheet (not offset and presented as a single item).

   a. **Future Operating Losses** No liability for future operating losses is recognized. Expected future operating losses that other buyers and sellers would not recognize as part of the fair value less cost to sell are **not** indirectly recognized as part of an expected loss on the sale by reducing the book value of the asset (or asset group) to an amount less than its current fair value less cost to sell. This provision is designed to limit *big bath accounting* (the inclusion of losses with a questionable relation to the disposal, in order that profits in future periods appear more favorable).

   b. **Expenses** While classified as held for sale, the asset is not depreciated or amortized, although accrual of other related expenses, such as interest or rent, continue.

   c. **Future Liabilities** Previous guidance called for recognizing lease termination costs and specified employee severance plan costs in the period of commitment to an exit or disposal plan. SFAS 146 supercedes this previous guidance, effective for exit or disposal activities initiated on or after December 31, 2002. SFAS 146 requires recognizing lease termination costs and specified employee severance plan costs related with exit or disposal activities in periods when obligations to others exists, not necessarily in the period of commitment to a plan.

4. **Contingencies** Changes to the previously reported discontinued operations amounts are reported in current period statements as discontinued operations. Such adjustments may occur due to the resolution of contingencies regarding purchase price, purchaser

indemnification, environmental warranty obligations, product warranty obligations, and directly-related employee benefit plan obligations.

Example 1 ▸ Discontinued Operations

On April 30 Empire Corporation, whose fiscal year-end is September 30, adopted a plan to discontinue the operations of Bello Division on November 30. Bello contributed a major portion of Empire's sales volume. Empire estimated that Bello would sustain a loss of $460,000 from May 1 through September 30 and would sustain an additional loss of $220,000 from October 1 to November 30. Empire also estimated that it would realize a gain of $600,000 on the sale of Bello's assets. At September 30, Empire determined that Bello had actually lost $1,120,000 for the fiscal year, of which $420,000 represented the loss from May 1 to September 30. Empire's tax rate is 30%.

Required: Determine the amounts that should be reported in the discontinued operations section of Empire's income statement for the year ended September 30, for income from operations of the discontinued segment, and the gain or loss on disposal of the discontinued segment.

Solution:

Discontinued operations	
Loss from operations of discontinued Bello Division	$1,120,000
Income taxes	(336,000)
Loss from discontinued operations	$ 784,000

C. **Extraordinary Items**

An extraordinary item should be classified separately in the income statement if it is material in relation to income before extraordinary items or to the trend of annual earnings before extraordinary items, or is material by other appropriate criteria. Items should be considered individually and not in the aggregate in determining whether an extraordinary event or transaction is material. If the item is determined to be extraordinary, it should be presented separately on the income statement net of related income tax after discontinued operations of a segment of a business (see Exhibit 1).

1. **Criteria** Most events and transactions affecting the operations of an enterprise are of a normal, recurring nature. For an occurrence to be classified as extraordinary it must meet both of the following criteria (APB 30):

   a. **Unusual Nature** The underlying event or transaction should possess a high degree of abnormality and be of a type clearly unrelated to, or incidentally related to, the ordinary and typical activities of the entity, taking into account the environment in which the entity operates.

   b. **Infrequency of Occurrence** The underlying event or transaction should be of a type that would not reasonably be expected to recur in the foreseeable future, taking into account the environment in which the entity operates.

2. **Extinguishment of Debt** SFAS 145 removes the assumption that gains and losses from the early extinguishment of debt are extraordinary items. Entities must evaluate whether early debt extinguishment is extraordinary using the same criteria as other events.

3. **Non-Extraordinary Gains/Losses** The following gains and losses should **not** be reported as extraordinary items because they are usual in nature **or** may be expected to recur as a consequence of customary and continuing business activities. In certain circumstances, gains or losses such as a. and d., below, should be included in extraordinary items if they are the direct result of an event that meets the criteria for an extraordinary item.

a. Write-down or write-off of receivables, inventories, equipment leased to others, and intangible assets

b. Gains or losses from exchange or translation of foreign currencies, including those relating to major devaluations and revaluations

c. Gains or losses on disposal of a segment of a business

d. Other gains or losses from sale or abandonment of property, plant, or equipment used in the business

e. Effects of a strike, including strikes against competitors and major suppliers

f. Adjustments of accruals on long-term contracts

Exhibit 5 ▸ Summary of the Presentation of an Income Statement

Item	Criteria	Examples	Placement
Unusual or infrequent gains or losses	Unusual or infrequent but not both	Write-down or write-off of receivables, inventories, equipment leased to others, other gains or losses from the sale or abandonment or impairment of property, plant, or equipment used in the business	**C** D E
Changes in estimate	A revision of an accounting measurement	Changing the useful life of a depreciable asset from 5 to 7 years	**C** D E
Discontinued operations	The disposal of a component of the entity which represents separate operations and cash flows.	A component that has been sold, abandoned, or spun-off. The component's operations and cash flows must be clearly distinguished.	C **D** E
Extraordinary items	Both unusual and infrequent in nature	Casualty gains and losses	C D **E**

Exhibit 6 ▸ Income Statement Components Mnemonic

C	**C**ontinuing Operations
D	**D**iscontinued Operations
E	**E**xtraordinary Items

III. Comprehensive Income (SFAS 130)

A. Overview

SFAS 130 applies to all entities that report financial position, results of operations, and cash flows in a full set of financial statements. It does not apply to an entity that has no items of other comprehensive income in any period presented nor to not-for-profit organizations. SFAS 130 establishes standards on how to report and display comprehensive income and its components. It does not, however, specify when to recognize or how to measure the items that are included in comprehensive income. The recognition and measurement of comprehensive income is based upon current accounting standards (GAAP).

B. Comprehensive Income

Comprehensive income includes all changes in equity during a period except those resulting from investments by owners and distributions to owners. SFAS 130 divides comprehensive income into net income and other comprehensive income.

1. **Components and Total Reported** All components of comprehensive income must be reported in the financial statements in the period in which they are recognized. A total amount for comprehensive income must be displayed in the financial statement where the components of OCI are reported.

2. **Interim-Period Reporting** An entity must report a total for comprehensive income in condensed financial statements of interim periods.

C. Other Comprehensive Income (OCI)

Items that previously were included in the equity section as a separate component of owners' equity are required by SFAS 130 to be reported in other comprehensive income. These items continue to be determined in the same manner; GAAP has not changed regarding the nature of these items and how and when they are measured and reported. Other comprehensive income has no effect on direct adjustments to equity accounts, such as capital stock transactions and transactions related to retained earnings.

1. **Classification** An entity must classify items of other comprehensive income by their nature, in one of these classifications: foreign currency items, minimum pension liability adjustments, unrealized gains and losses on certain investments in debt and equity securities, and gains and losses on cash flow hedging derivative instruments. Additional classifications or additional items within current classifications may result from future accounting standards.

   a. **Foreign Currency Items** Included in this classification are foreign currency translation adjustments and gains and losses on foreign currency transactions that are designated as, and are effective as, economic hedges of a net investment in a foreign entity. Also included is the effective portion of gains and losses on hedging derivative instruments in a hedge of a forecasted foreign-currency-denominated transaction, and the effective portion of the gain or loss in the hedging derivative or nonderivative instrument in a hedge of a net investment in a foreign operation, in accordance with SFAS 133.

   b. **Minimum Pension Liability Adjustments** Where additional liability exceeds unamortized prior service cost, the excess is reported in other comprehensive income.

   c. **Unrealized Gains and Losses on Certain Investments** Unrealized gains and losses on certain investments in debt and equity securities, accounted for in accordance with SFAS 115, including

      (1) Unrealized holding gains and losses on available-for-sale (AFS) securities

      (2) Unrealized holding gains and losses that result from a debt security being transferred into the AFS category from the HTM category

      (3) Subsequent decreases or increases in the fair value of AFS securities previously written down as impaired

      (4) A change in the market value of a futures contract that qualifies as a hedge of an asset reported at fair value

   d. **Gains and Losses on Cash Flow Hedging Derivative Instruments** The effective portion of these gains and losses are reported as a component of OCI and reclassified into earnings when the hedged forecasted transaction affects earnings, in accordance with SFAS 133.

2. **Reclassification** Reclassification adjustments may be displayed on the face of the financial statement in which comprehensive income is reported. Alternatively, reclassification adjustments may be shown net on the face of the financial statement and the gross changes be disclosed in the notes to the financial statements.

   a. **Avoid Double Counting** Adjustments must be made to avoid double counting in comprehensive income items that are displayed as part of net income for a period that also had been included as part of OCI in that period or earlier periods.

   b. **Each Classification** Reclassification adjustments must be determined for each classification of OCI, except minimum pension liability adjustments. Minimum pension liability adjustments must be shown net.

D. Accumulated Balance of OCI

An entity is required to display the accumulated balance of OCI separately from retained earnings, capital stock, and additional paid-in capital in the equity section of a statement of financial position. A descriptive title such as *Accumulated Other Comprehensive Income* must be used. An entity must disclose accumulated balances for each classification in that separate component of equity on the face of the statement of financial position, in the statement of changes in equity, or in the notes to the financial statements. The classifications must correspond to classifications used elsewhere in the same set of statements for components of OCI.

E. Reporting Related Income Tax

An entity may display components of other comprehensive income in two alternative ways.

1. **Net-of-Tax Basis** Each of the components of comprehensive income may be reported on a net-of-tax basis.

2. **Summary Net-of-Tax Basis** Each of the other comprehensive income items may be reported before tax, with one line reporting the tax provision of all of those elements. If this alternative is used, the tax provision for each individual item must be shown within the notes to the financial statements.

F. Format Options

Comprehensive income must be displayed prominently within a financial statement in a full set of general-purpose financial statements. Comprehensive income must be shown on the face of one of the statements, not just in the notes to the financial statements. An entity may choose from several possible formats to report comprehensive income.

1. **One-Statement Approach** Since net income is a significant part of comprehensive income, the one-statement approach combines the statement of income and comprehensive income. The statement presents the various components of net income and then reports the elements of other comprehensive income. Although earnings per share may be shown for various income statement items, it is not required to be reported for comprehensive income.

2. **Two-Statement Approach** The income statement and the statement of comprehensive income are separate statements in the two-statement format. The statement of comprehensive income begins with net income and then includes the other items of comprehensive income.

3. **Statement-of-Changes-in-Equity Approach** Comprehensive income may be reported on the statement of changes in equity.

Exhibit 7 ▸ One-Statement Approach, With Tax Effect Shown Parenthetically

ABC Company
Statement of Income and Comprehensive Income
For the year ended December 31, Year 1

Revenues			$ 450,000
Expenses			(300,000)
Loss on sale of securities			(20,000)
Income from Continuing Operations, before taxes			130,000
Provision for taxes			(54,000)
Income from Continuing Operations			76,000
Discontinued Operations:			
Loss on operations of discontinued component		$(62,000)	
Income taxes		7,000	
Loss on Discontinued Operations			(55,000)
Income before Extraordinary Items			21,000
Extraordinary Gain, net of tax			18,000
Net Income			39,000
Other Comprehensive Income:			
Foreign currency adjustments, net of tax of $6,000		9,000	
Unrealized Loss on Marketable Securities:			
Unrealized holding loss arising during period, net of tax of $18,000	$(42,000)		
Less: reclassification adjustment, net of tax of $6,000, for loss included in net income	14,000	(28,000)	
Minimum pension liability adjustment, net of tax of $4,000		(6,000)	
Other Comprehensive Income			(25,000)
Comprehensive Income			$ 14,000

Exhibit 8 ▸ Statement-of-Changes-in-Equity Approach*

ABC Company
Statement of Changes in Equity
For the year ended December 31, Year 1

	Total	Comprehensive Income	Retained Earnings	Accumulated Other Comprehensive Income	Common Stock	Paid-in Capital
Beginning balance	$600,000		$200,000	$165,000	$ 50,000	$185,000
Comprehensive income						
Net income	39,000	$ 39,000	39,000			
Other comprehensive income, net of tax:						
Unrealized loss on marketable securities net of reclassification adjustment	(28,000)	(28,000)				
Foreign currency adjustment	9,000	9,000				
Minimum pension liability adjustment	(6,000)	(6,000)				
Other comprehensive income		(25,000)		(25,000)		
Comprehensive income		$ 14,000				
Common stock issued	50,000				20,000	30,000
Dividends declared on common stock	(20,000)		(20,000)			
Ending balance	$644,000		$219,000	$140,000	$ 70,000	$215,000

*Net-of-tax presentation with tax amounts reflected in notes

Exhibit 9 ▸ Two-Statement Approach, With Tax Effect Shown as a Single Amount*

ABC Company
Statement of Income
For the year ended December 31, Year 1

Revenues		$ 450,000
Expenses		(300,000)
Loss on sale of securities		(20,000)
Income from Continuing Operations, before taxes		130,000
Provision for taxes		(54,000)
Income from Continuing Operations		76,000
Discontinued Operations		
Loss on operations of discontinued segment	$(62,000)	
Income Tax	7,000	
Loss on discontinued operations		(55,000)
Income before Extraordinary Items		$ 21,000
Extraordinary Gain, net of tax		18,000
Net Income		$ 39,000

ABC Company
Statement of Comprehensive Income
For the year ended December 31, Year 1

Net Income			$ 39,000
Other Comprehensive Income:			
Foreign currency adjustments		$ 15,000	
Unrealized Loss on Marketable Securities:			
Unrealized holding loss arising during period	$(60,000)		
Less: reclassification adjustment for loss included in net income	20,000	(40,000)	
Minimum pension liability adjustment		(10,000)	
Other Comprehensive Income, before tax		(35,000)	
Income tax expense		10,000	
Other Comprehensive Income			(25,000)
Comprehensive Income			$ 14,000

*Tax effect reflected in notes

IV. Additional Reporting Considerations

A. Changes in Accounting Principle

A change in accounting principle results from the adoption of a generally accepted accounting principle (GAAP) different from the GAAP previously used for reporting purposes. The term "accounting principle" includes not only accounting principles but also the methods of applying them. Adoption of a principle to record transactions for the first time or to record the effects of transactions that were previously immaterial is **not** considered to be a change in accounting principle.

1. **Examples** Changes in accounting principle include the following.

   a. A change in the method of inventory pricing, such as from LIFO to FIFO

   b. A change in the method of accounting for long-term construction contracts, such as from the completed contract method to the percentage of completion method

2. **Justification** SFAS 154, *Accounting Changes and Error Corrections,* requires justification for a change in accounting principle. Promulgation of a new accounting principle by the FASB is considered sufficient justification for a change in accounting principle.

3. **Disclosures in the Fiscal Period in Which a Change in Accounting Principle is Made:**

   a. The nature and reason for the change in accounting principle and the method of applying the change.

   b. A description of the prior-period information that has been retrospectively adjusted, if any.

   c. The effect of the change on income before extraordinary items, net income, and the related per share amounts for all periods presented, either on the face of the income statement or in the notes thereto.

   d. The cumulative effect of the change on retained earnings or other components of equity or net assets in the statement of financial position as of the beginning of the earliest period presented.

   e. Presentation of the effect on financial statement subtotals and totals other than income from continuing operations and net income is not required.

B. Changes in Accounting Estimates

Changes in estimates used in accounting are necessary consequences of periodic presentations of financial statements. Preparing financial statements requires estimating the effects of future events. Future events and their effects cannot be perceived with certainty. Therefore, estimating requires the exercise of judgment. Accounting estimates change as new events occur, as more experience is acquired, or as additional information is obtained.

1. **Change in Estimate Inseparable From Change in Principle** In some cases, a change in accounting *estimate* and a change in accounting principle are inseparable. One example is a change in the method of depreciation affecting estimated future benefits. When the effects of the two changes cannot be separated, the change should be accounted for as a **change in estimate.**

2. **Examples of Changes in Estimates** Changes in the following items would usually require a change in accounting estimate.

   a. Useful lives and salvage values of depreciable assets

   b. Recovery periods benefited by a deferred cost

   c. Expected losses on receivables

   d. Warranty costs

3. **Period of Recognition** A change in accounting estimate should be accounted for in the period of change if the change only affects that period, or in the current and subsequent periods, if the change affects both, as a component of income from continuing operations. A change in estimate does **not** require restatement or retrospective adjustment to prior period financial statements. The effects of the change in estimate on income *before* extraordinary items, *net income,* and related *per share* amounts should be disclosed in the period of the change or in future periods if the change affects those periods.

4. **Disclosure** No disclosure is required for estimates made in the ordinary course of accounting if the effects are not material or long-term. An example is the bad debt estimate.

Example 2 ▸ Change in Estimate

Machinery with a cost of $450,000 is being depreciated over a 15-year life. After 10 years, information becomes available that indicates a useful life of 20 years for the machinery. Accounting for the change in depreciation estimate in the eleventh year would be as follows:

Historical cost	$ 450,000
Depreciation to date ($30,000 × 10)	(300,000)
Remaining balance	$ 150,000
Balance to be depreciated over remaining useful life ($150,000 / 10)	$ 15,000

To record depreciation expense in the year of the change:

Depreciation Expense	15,000	
Accumulated Depreciation		15,000

The notes to the income statement would include the following disclosure:

Note A: During the eleventh year, the estimated useful life of certain machinery was changed from 15 years to 20 years. The effect of the change was to increase net income by $15,000 (ignoring taxes). Earnings per share amounts increased $1.50.

The financial statements of prior periods presented would **not** be restated, nor would the pro forma effects of retroactive application be reported.

C. Changes in Reporting Entity
A change in accounting principle that results in financial statements of a different reporting entity (i.e., a different group of companies comprise the reporting entity after the change).

1. **Reporting the Change** Report by retrospectively applying the change to the financial statements of all prior periods presented to reflect the financial information for the new reporting entity for the periods. Do **not** report (1) the cumulative effect of the change on the amount of retained earnings at the beginning of the period in which the change is made or (2) pro forma effects on net income and earnings per share of retroactive application.

2. **Examples** Examples include (a) presenting consolidated or combined statements in place of statements of individual companies, (b) changing specific subsidiaries comprising the group of companies for which consolidated financial statements are presented, and (c) changing the companies included in combined financial statements.

D. Correction of Errors (SFAS 154)

1. **Overview** Errors in financial statements result from mathematical mistakes, mistakes in the application of accounting principles, or the oversight or misuse of facts that existed at the time the financial statements were prepared. Errors commonly found in financial statements include the following.

   a. Estimates based on unreasonable assumptions; for example, the use of an unrealistic depreciation rate.

   b. Recording erroneous amounts for assets and equities. For example, incorrect footing of inventory totals would cause inventories to be misstated on the balance sheet.

   c. Failure to record prepaid and accrued expenses.

   d. The improper classification of assets as expenses and vice versa. The purchase price of a plant asset may be incorrectly charged to expense rather than an asset account.

   e. In addition, the change from an accounting principle that is **not** generally accepted to one that **is** generally accepted is treated as the correction of an error; for example, a change from the direct write-off method to the allowance method of accounting for uncollectible accounts.

2. **Reported as Prior Period Adjustments**

   a. **Reporting Corrected Errors** SFAS 154, *Accounting Changes and Error Corrections,* states, "Any error in the financial statements of a prior period discovered subsequent to their issuance shall be reported as a prior-period adjustment by restating the prior period financial statements."

   b. **Restating Prior Periods** The cumulative effect of the error on periods prior to those presented shall be reflected in the carrying amounts of assets and liabilities as of the beginning of the first period presented. Any offsetting adjustment shall be made to the opening balance of retained earnings for that period. Financial statements for each individual prior period shall be adjusted to reflect correction of the period-specific effects of the error. APB 9, *Reporting the Results of Operation,* requires that statements of prior periods presented for comparative purposes be restated to reflect the retroactive application of the prior period adjustments.

   c. **Required Disclosures** SFAS 154 requires an entity to disclose as of the beginning of the earliest period presented that previously issued financial statements have been restated along with a description of the nature of the error, the effect of the correction on each financial statement and the per share amounts affected, the cumulative effect of the change on retained earnings and other components of equity or net assets. Financial statements of subsequent periods need not repeat the disclosures.

3. **Classification of Errors** Accounting errors may be classified by time of discovery or according to their effect on the balance sheet, income statement, or both.

   a. **Occurrence and Discovery in Different Periods** Errors that occur in one accounting period and are discovered in a subsequent accounting period are more involved: the cumulative effect of each error on periods prior to the period of discovery is calculated and recorded as a direct adjustment to the beginning balance of retained earnings.

   b. **Occurrence and Discovery in Same Period** Errors that occur and are discovered in the same accounting period may be corrected by reversing the incorrect entry and recording the correct one or by directly correcting the account balances with a single entry.

   c. **Effect on Balance Sheet** Only balance sheet accounts are affected, for instance, if the *Inventory* account is debited instead of the *Equipment* account or if *Notes Payable* is credited, instead of *Accounts Payable.* When the error is discovered, an entry is recorded to correct the account balances.

   d. **Effect on Income Statement** Revenue or expense classification errors will affect only the income statement for the period. If *Sales Revenue* is credited instead of *Rent Revenue* or *Interest Expense* is debited instead of *Wage Expense,* the amounts presented on the income statement for these accounts will be misstated. Net income for the period, however, will not be affected. If the error is discovered prior to the year-end closings, an entry can be recorded to correct the account balances. If the error is discovered *in a subsequent period,* no correction is necessary. However, the restatement of comparative financial statements is required.

   e. **Effect on Both Statements** Some errors affect both the balance sheet and the income statement, and may be classified in the following two ways:

      (1) **Counterbalancing Errors** Counterbalancing errors will "correct" themselves over two consecutive accounting periods. Generally, a counterbalancing error will cause a misstatement of net income and balance sheet accounts in one

period that will be offset by an equal misstatement in the following period. Balance sheet accounts and combined net income for both periods will be stated correctly at the end of the second period (ignoring tax effects).

Example 3 ▸ Counterbalancing Errors

A company neglects to record accrued wage expense at the end of a fiscal period. In the first year, the error would have the following effects:

Income Statement	Balance Sheet
Wage expense understated	Liabilities understated
Net income overstated	Retained earnings overstated

In the second year, the payment of accrued wage expense will be charged to wage expense of the current year causing the following effects:

Income Statement	Balance Sheet
Wage expense overstated	Accounts are correctly stated due to the counterbalancing effect on error.
Net income understated	

(2) **Non-Counterbalancing Errors** Errors that are **not** counterbalancing cause successive balance sheet amounts and net income to be incorrectly stated until the errors are discovered and corrected. For example, suppose that instead of capitalizing the cost of an asset, the cost is charged to expense. In the year the error occurs, expenses will be *overstated* and net income *understated*. During the life of the asset, net income will be overstated by the amount of unrecorded depreciation. Additionally, assets on the balance sheet will be understated throughout the service life of the unrecorded asset.

E. Accounting Policies Disclosure (APB 22)

All significant accounting policies followed by an enterprise should be disclosed in its financial statements. No specific disclosure format is required. APB 22 prefers a *separate* note, or a summary preceding the notes entitled *Summary of Significant Accounting Policies.* The accounting policy disclosures should identify and describe the principles and methods that materially affect the financial position and operations.

1. **Policy Choices** Disclosure should include policies involving a choice of alternative acceptable policies, policies peculiar to that particular industry, and unusual applications of acceptable principles.

2. **Examples** Examples of disclosure requirements include criteria for determining which investments are treated as cash equivalents, depreciation methods, methods of pricing inventory, methods of recognizing profit on long-term construction contracts, and basis of consolidation.

3. **No Duplication of Information** Financial statement disclosure of accounting policies should **not** duplicate details presented elsewhere as part of the financial statements, such as composition of inventories or plant assets, depreciation expense, and maturity dates of long-term debt.

F. Related Party Disclosures (SFAS 57)

Transactions between related parties include transactions among: (1) a parent company and its subsidiaries; (2) subsidiaries of a common parent; (3) an enterprise and its principal owners, management, or members of their immediate families; and (4) affiliates.

1. **Examples** Examples of related party transactions include

   a. Sales, purchases, and transfers of realty and personal property

b. Services received or furnished (e.g., accounting, management, engineering, and legal services)

c. Use of property and equipment by lease or otherwise

d. Borrowings, lendings, and guarantees

e. Intercompany billings based on allocations of common costs

f. Filings of consolidated tax returns

2. **Disclosures** Financial statements should include disclosures of material related party transactions, other than compensation arrangements, expense allowances, and other similar items in the ordinary course of business. However, disclosure of transactions that are eliminated in the preparation of consolidated or combined financial statements (e.g., intercompany sales) is not required. The disclosures should include the following:

a. The nature of the relationship(s) involved.

b. A description of the transactions, including transactions to which no amounts or nominal amounts were ascribed, for each of the periods for which income statements are presented, and such other information necessary to an understanding of the effects of the transactions on the financial statements.

c. The dollar amounts of transactions for each of the periods for which income statements are presented and the effects of any change in the method of establishing the terms from that used in the preceding period.

d. Amounts due from or to related parties as of the date of each balance sheet presented and, if not otherwise apparent, the terms and manner of settlement.

3. **Representations** Transactions involving related parties cannot be presumed to be carried out on an arm's-length basis, as the requisite conditions of competitive, free-market dealings may not exist. Representations about transactions with related parties, if made, should not imply that the related party transactions were consummated on terms equivalent to those that prevail in arm's length transactions unless such representations can be substantiated.

4. **Control Relationships** If the reporting enterprise and one or more other enterprises are under common ownership or management control and the existence of that control could result in operating results or financial position of the reporting enterprise significantly different from those that would have been obtained if the enterprises were autonomous, the nature of the control relationship should be disclosed even though there are no transactions between the enterprises.

G. Development Stage Enterprises (SFAS 7)

An enterprise is in the development stage if "substantially all" of its efforts are devoted to establishing a new business and either principal operations have not begun or principal operations have begun, but revenue produced is insignificant.

1. **Presentation** Financial statements issued by a development stage enterprise should be presented in conformity with generally accepted accounting principles (GAAP) applicable to established operating enterprises.

a. Special accounting practices that are based on a distinctive accounting for development stage enterprises are **not** acceptable.

b. Generally accepted accounting principles that apply to established operating enterprises govern the recognition of revenue by a development stage enterprise and determine whether a cost incurred by a development stage enterprise is to be charged to expense when incurred or is to be capitalized or deferred. Accordingly, capitalization or deferral of costs shall be subject to the same assessment of recoverability that would be applicable in an established operating enterprise.

c. Financial reporting by a development stage enterprise differs from financial reporting for an established operating enterprise in regard only to the additional information.

2. **Required Statements** The additional information to be included is as follows.

a. **Balance Sheet** Cumulative net losses are reported as part of stockholders' equity using terms such as "deficit accumulated during the development stage."

b. **Income Statement** Includes cumulative expenses and revenues from the inception of the development stage. Information on other comprehensive income, if any, may be combined with the income statement or presented separately.

c. **Statement of Cash Flows** Includes cumulative amounts from date of inception.

d. **Statement of Stockholders' Equity** Includes the following from the date of inception:

(1) Number of shares, warrants, etc., issued and date of issuance.

(2) Dollar amounts received for shares, etc., of each issuance. Noncash consideration received must be assigned a dollar value and must indicate the nature of the consideration and the valuation basis used.

3. **Disclosure** Financial statements of a development stage enterprise should be identified as such and the nature of activities disclosed.

H. Accrual Accounting

Accrual accounting recognizes and reports the effects of transactions and other events on the assets and liabilities of a business enterprise in the time periods to which they relate rather than only when cash is received or paid. Accrual accounting attempts to match revenues and the expenses associated with those revenues in order to determine net income for an accounting period.

1. **Revenue Recognition** Revenues are recognized when earned.

2. **Expense Recognition** Expenses are recognized and recorded as follows:

a. **Associating Cause and Effect** Some expenses are recognized and recorded on a presumed direct association with specific revenue.

b. **Systematic and Rational Allocation** In the absence of a direct association with specific revenue, some expenses are recognized and recorded by attempting to allocate expenses in a systematic and rational manner among the periods in which benefits are provided.

c. **Immediate Recognition** Some costs are associated with the current accounting period as expenses because (1) costs incurred during the period provide no discernible future benefits, (2) costs recorded as assets in prior periods no longer provide discernible benefits, or (3) allocating costs either on the basis of association with revenues or among several accounting periods is considered to serve no useful purpose.

3. **Accruals** An accrual represents a transaction that affects the determination of income for the period but has not yet been reflected in the cash accounts of that period.

a. **Accrued Revenue** Accrued revenue is revenue earned but not yet collected in cash. An example of accrued revenue is accrued interest revenue earned on bonds from the last interest payment date to the end of the accounting period.

b. **Accrued Expense** An accrued expense is an expense incurred but not yet paid in cash. An example of an accrued expense is salaries incurred for the last week of the accounting period that are not payable until the subsequent accounting period.

4. **Deferrals** A deferral represents a transaction that has been reflected in the cash accounts of the period but has not yet affected the determination of income for that period.

a. **Deferred Revenue** Deferred revenue is revenue collected or collectible in cash but not yet earned. An example of deferred revenue is rent collected in advance by a lessor in the last month of the accounting period, which represents the rent for the first month of the subsequent accounting period.

b. **Deferred/Prepaid Expense** A deferred (prepaid) expense is an expense paid or payable in cash but not yet incurred. An example of a deferred (prepaid) expense is an insurance premium paid in advance in the current accounting period, which represents insurance coverage for the subsequent accounting period.

Exhibit 10 ▸ Revenue and Expense Item Effects

Revenue or Expense Item	Plus or Minus Adjustments to Derive Accrual Basis	Illustrative Amounts
Collections from sales		$190
Adjustments:		
1. Increase in accounts receivable	+	7
2. Decrease in accounts receivable	–	
3. Uncollectible accounts written off	+	5
Sales revenue		$202
Collections from other revenues		$184
Adjustments:		
1. Increase in revenue receivable	+	
2. Decrease in revenue receivable	–	(4)
3. Increase in unearned revenue	–	(10)
4. Decrease in unearned revenue	+	
Revenue recognized		$170
Payments for purchases		$ 91
Adjustments:		
1. Increase in inventory	–	(7)
2. Decrease in inventory	+	
3. Increase in accounts payable	+	9
4. Decrease in accounts payable	–	
Cost of goods sold		$ 93
Payment for Expenses		$ 92
Adjustments:		
1. Increase in prepaid expenses	–	(9)
2. Decrease in prepaid expenses	+	
3. Increase in accrued expenses payable	+	8
4. Decrease in accrued expenses payable	–	
Expenses recognized		$ 91

NOTE: This exhibit is for revenue or expense item effects, **not** the effects to income.

I. Other Comprehensive Basis of Accounting

1. **Overview** An Other Comprehensive Basis of Accounting (OCBOA) is a basis of accounting **not** in conformity with generally accepted accounting principles, as follows:

a. A basis of accounting used to comply with regulatory requirements.

b. A basis of accounting used by an entity to file its tax return.

c. The cash receipts and disbursements basis of accounting.

d. A definite set of criteria having substantial support, such as the price-level basis of accounting.

2. **Cash Basis** In cash basis accounting, the effects of transactions and other events on the assets and liabilities of a business enterprise are recognized and reported only when cash is received or paid; while in accrual accounting, these effects are recognized and reported in the time periods to which they relate. Cash accounting does not attempt to match revenues and the expenses associated with those revenues. The conversion of various income statement amounts from the cash basis to the accrual basis is summarized in Exhibit 10.

3. **Income-Tax Basis** In income-tax basis accounting, the effects of events on a business enterprise are recognized when taxable income or deductible expense is recognized on the tax return. Nontaxable income and nondeductible expenses are still included in the determination of income.

V. Interim Financial Reporting (APB 28)

A. Concepts

In APB 28, the Board concluded that each interim period should be viewed as an *integral part of an annual period* and not as a separate, independent period. In order to maintain comparability between interim and annual financial statements, APB 28 states that the principles and practices used to prepare the latest annual financial statements also should be used to prepare the interim statements. However, certain procedures applied to the annual statements may require modification at the interim reporting dates so that the results for the interim period may better relate to the results of operations for the annual period. At the end of each interim period, the company should make its best estimate of the effective tax rate expected to be applicable for the full fiscal year. (FASB Interpretation 18) This estimated effective tax rate should be used to provide for income taxes on a current year-to-date basis. The effective tax rate should reflect foreign tax rates, percentage depletion, and other available tax planning alternatives.

1. **Estimated Effective Tax Rate** In arriving at the estimated full year tax rate, no effect should be included for the income tax related to significant unusual or extraordinary items that will be separately reported or reported net of their related income tax effects for the interim period or for the fiscal year.

2. **Nonordinary Items** Unusual or infrequently occurring items (nonordinary items) should be included in determining interim period income, but should be excluded in determining the full year effective income tax rate.

B. Continuing Operations

1. **Revenues** *Revenues* should be recognized as earned during an interim period on the same basis as followed for recognition of income for the full year. For example, revenues from long-term construction-type contracts accounted for under the percentage of completion method should be recognized in interim periods on the same basis as is followed for the full year. Losses from such contracts should be recognized in full during the interim period in which the existence of the losses becomes evident.

2. **Product Costs** *Costs* and *expenses* associated directly with products sold or services rendered for annual reporting purposes should be similarly treated for interim reporting purposes. Some exceptions are appropriate for valuing inventory at interim reporting dates.

a. **Inventory Estimation** Some companies use estimated gross profit rates to estimate ending inventory and cost of goods sold during interim periods or use other methods different from those used at annual inventory dates. These companies should disclose the methods used at the interim date and any significant adjustments that result from reconciliation with the annual physical inventory.

b. **LIFO and Liquidation of Base Period Inventories** Companies that use the *LIFO method* may encounter a liquidation of base period inventories at an interim date that is expected to be replaced by the end of the annual period. The inventory at the interim date should not give effect to the LIFO liquidation, and cost of sales for the interim reporting period should include the replacement cost of the liquidated LIFO base.

c. **Lower of Cost or Market** The use of *lower of cost or market* may result in inventory losses that should not be deferred beyond the interim period in which the decline occurs. Recoveries of these losses in subsequent periods should be recognized as gains, *but only to the extent* of losses recognized in previous interim periods of the same fiscal year. *Temporary* market declines need not be recognized at the interim date since no loss is expected to be incurred in the fiscal year.

d. **Standard Costs** Companies that use *standard costs* for valuing inventory at year-end should use the same procedures for valuing inventory at interim dates. Material and volume variances that are *planned* and expected to be absorbed by year-end should be deferred until the end of the year. *Unplanned* variances should be reported in the interim period in the same manner as year-end variances.

3. **Costs Other Than Product Costs** *Costs and expenses other than product costs* should be charged to income in interim periods as incurred, or be allocated among interim periods based on an estimate of time expired, benefit received, or activity associated with the periods. Procedures adopted for assigning specific cost and expense items to an interim period should be consistent with the bases followed by the company in reporting results of operations at annual reporting dates. However, when a specific cost or expense item charged to expense for annual reporting purposes benefits *more than one interim period,* the cost or expense item may be allocated to those interim periods.

a. **Not Identifiable to Specific Period** Some *costs and expenses* incurred in an interim period, however, cannot be readily identified with the activities or benefits of other interim periods and should be charged to the interim period in which incurred.

b. **No Arbitrary Assignment** *Arbitrary assignment* of the amount of such costs to an interim period should not be made.

c. **Gain & Loss Deferrals** *Gains and losses* that arise in any interim period similar to those that would not be deferred at year-end should not be deferred to later interim periods within the same fiscal year.

4. **Allocation of Indirect Cost Examples** The following examples from APB 28 may be helpful in applying the standards for allocation of costs and expenses not directly associated with revenues in interim financial statements.

a. When a cost that is expensed for annual reporting purposes clearly benefits two or more interim periods (e.g., annual major repairs), each interim period should be charged for an appropriate portion of the annual cost by the use of accruals or deferrals.

b. Property taxes (and similar costs such as insurance, interest, and rent) may be accrued or deferred at an annual reporting date to achieve a full year's charge of taxes to costs and expenses. Similar procedures should be adopted at each interim reporting date to provide an appropriate cost in each period.

c. Advertising costs may be deferred within a fiscal year if the benefits of an expenditure clearly extend beyond the interim period in which the expenditure is made.

5. **Financial Statements** Interim period financial statements should bear a reasonable portion of such year-end adjustments as inventory shrinkage, allowance for uncollectible accounts, and discretionary year-end bonuses.

6. **Seasonal Variations** Companies whose revenues and expenses are subject to material *seasonal variations* should disclose the seasonal nature of their activities, and consider supplementing their interim reports with information for twelve-month periods ended at the interim date for the current and preceding years.

C. Discontinued Operations & Extraordinary Items

Extraordinary items and the gain or loss from disposal of a component of an entity and their related income tax effects should be included in the determination of net income for the interim period in which they occur. An item should be classified as extraordinary in the interim period if it is material in relation to annual net income. Extraordinary items and the gain or loss from discontinued operations should **not** be prorated among interim periods.

D. Accounting Changes

Changes in accounting principle made in an interim period are to be reported by retrospective application in accordance with SFAS 154. The impracticability exception may not be applied to prior interim periods of the fiscal year in which the change is made.

1. **Cumulative Effect Change in Fourth Quarter** If a company regularly reports interim financial information, disclosure of the effects of the accounting change on interim-period results should be included in a separate fourth-quarter report or in its annual financial statements for the fiscal year the change was made.

2. **Disclosures** Disclosures of the following information are required in the period in which a change in accounting principle is made. Financial statements of subsequent periods need not repeat the required disclosures.

   a. The nature and reason for the change in accounting principle, including an explanation of why the newly adopted accounting principle is preferable.

   b. The method of applying the change.

   c. A description of the prior-period information that has been retrospectively adjusted.

   d. The effect of the change on income from continuing operations, net income, any other affected financial statement line item, and any affected per-share amounts for the current period and any prior periods retrospectively adjusted. Presentation of the effect on financial statement subtotals and totals other than income from continuing operations and net income is not required.

   e. The cumulative effect of the change on retained earnings or other components of equity or net assets as of the beginning of the earliest period presented.

   f. A description of the alternative method used to report the change if the retrospective application to all prior periods is impracticable.

   g. If indirect effects of the change are recognized, a description of the indirect effects including the amounts recognized in the current period and the related per-share amounts.

E. Minimum Disclosures

Disclosure requirements apply to reporting summarized financial data to security holders of **publicly** traded companies. When summarized financial data are regularly reported on a quarterly basis, information with respect to the current quarter and the current year-to-date or the last-twelve-months-to-date should be furnished together with comparable data for the preceding year.

1. Sales or gross revenues, provision for income taxes, extraordinary items, cumulative effect of a change in accounting principles, net income, and comprehensive income
2. Primary and fully diluted earnings per share data for each period presented
3. Seasonal revenue, costs or expenses
4. Significant changes in estimates or provisions for income taxes
5. Disposal of a segment of a business and extraordinary, unusual, or infrequently occurring items
6. Contingent items
7. Changes in accounting principles or estimates
8. Significant changes in financial position
9. Information about reportable operating segments, including revenues from external customers, intersegment revenues, a measure of segment profit or loss, material changes in total assets, a description of differences in segments or measurement of segment profit or loss, and a reconciliation of the total of segment profit or loss to consolidated income.

VI. Segment Disclosures (SFAS 131)

A. Management Approach Method

SFAS 131 requires that general-purpose financial statements include selected information reported on a single basis of segmentation using the management approach method. The management approach is based on the way that management organizes the segments within the enterprise for making operating decisions and assessing performance. The components are called *operating segments.* Consequently, the segments are evident from the structure of the enterprise's internal organization, and financial statement preparers should be able to provide the required information in a cost-effective and timely manner.

1. **Objectives** The objective of SFAS 131, *Disclosure about Segments of an Enterprise and Related Information,* is to provide information about an enterprise to help financial statement users better understand the enterprise's performance, better assess its prospects for future net cash flows, and make more informed judgments about the enterprise as a whole.

2. **Requirements** An enterprise is required to report a measure of segment profit or loss, segment assets and certain related items, but not segment cash flow or segment liabilities.

3. **Applicability** SFAS 131 applies to **public** business enterprises. It does not apply to non-public enterprises or not-for-profit organizations.

4. **Operating Segments** Operating segments have three characteristics. Not every part of an entity is necessarily part of an operating segment.

   a. **Revenue Producing** An operating segment is a component of an enterprise with revenue producing (even if no revenue is yet earned) and expense incurring activities.

   b. **Review by Decision Maker** The operating results of an operating segment are regularly reviewed by the entity's chief operating decision maker.

   c. **Availability of Financial Information** Discrete financial information is available for an operating segment.

5. **Chief Operating Decision Maker** The chief operating decision maker is identified by the function of allocating resources and assessing the performance of a segment, not necessarily by title. The chief operating decision maker may be, for example, the chief executive officer, the president, or the chief operating officer. It may be one person or it may be a group, such as the Chairman and the Board of Directors.

6. **Segment Manager** Generally, an operating segment has a segment manager directly accountable to the chief operating decision maker. The term segment manager is also identified by function, not necessarily by a specific title. The chief operating decision maker in some cases may also be the segment manager for an operating segment. The same person may be a segment manager for more than one operating segment.

7. **Reportable Segments** Reportable segments include operating segments that exceed the quantitative thresholds. A reportable segment may also result from aggregating two or more segments in accordance with the aggregation criteria. The quantitative thresholds and the aggregation criteria are outlined in the text that follows. Exhibit 11 summarizes identifying reportable operating segments.

B. Aggregation Criteria

Operating segments often exhibit similar long-term financial performance if they have similar economic characteristics. Two or more operating segments may be aggregated into a single operating segment if aggregation is consistent with the objective and basic principles of SFAS 131, if the segments have similar economic characteristics, and if the segments are similar in each of the following areas:

1. The nature of the products and services
2. The nature of the production processes
3. The type or class of customer for their products and services
4. The methods used to distribute their products or provide their services
5. The nature of the regulatory environment, if applicable; for example, banking, insurance, or public utilities

Exhibit 11 ▸ Diagram for Identifying Reportable Operating Segments

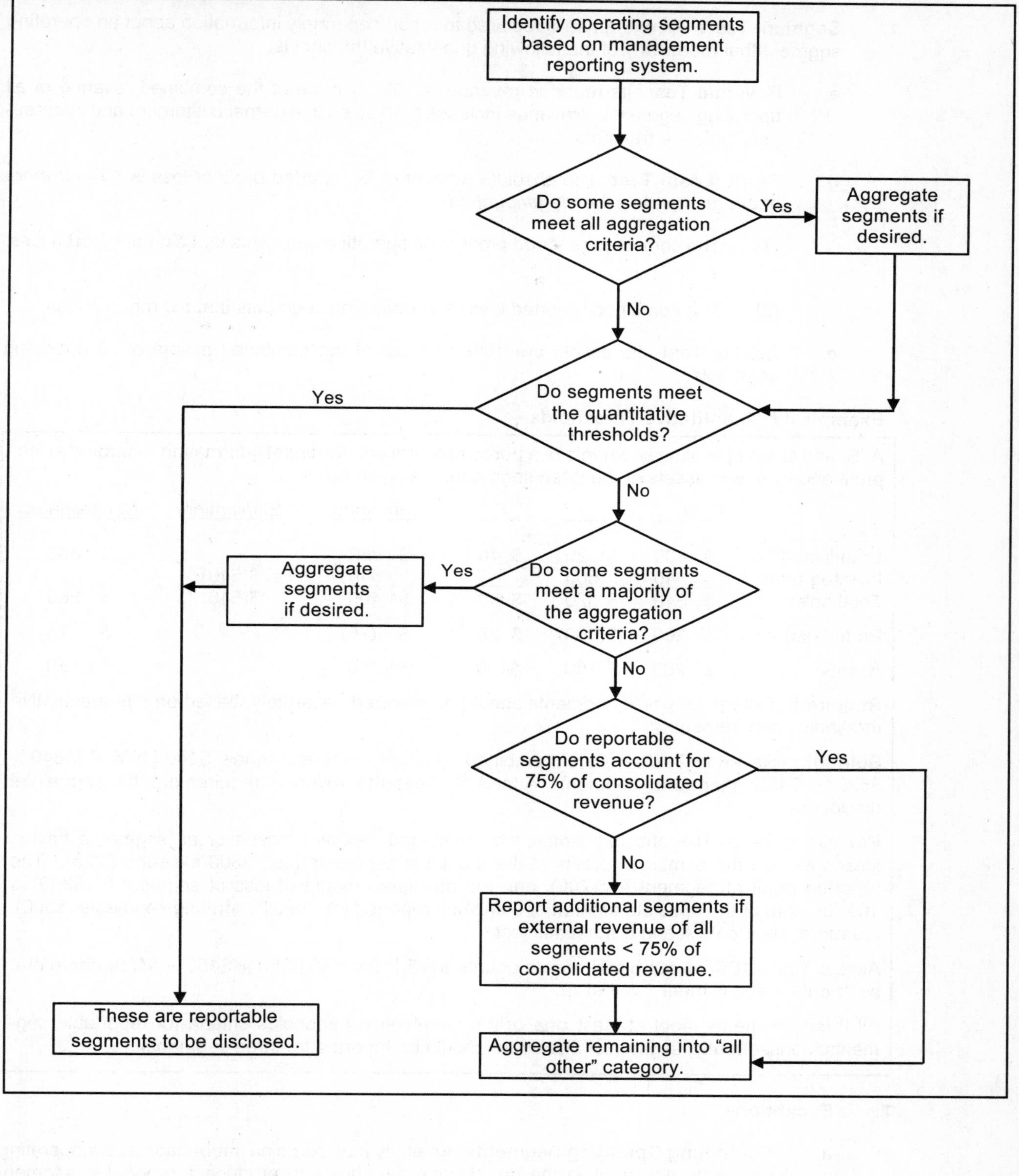

C. Quantitative Thresholds

1. **Segment Tests** An enterprise is required to report separately information about an operating segment that meets any of the following quantitative thresholds:

   a. **Revenue Test** Its reported revenue is 10% or more of the combined revenue of all operating segments. Revenue includes both sales to external customers and intersegment sales or transfers.

   b. **Profit (Loss) Test** The absolute amount of its reported profit or loss is *10% or more* of the *greater,* in *absolute amount,* of

      (1) The combined reported profit of all operating segments that did not report a loss, or

      (2) The combined reported loss of all operating segments that did report a loss.

   c. **Assets Test** Its assets are 10% or more of the combined assets of all operating segments.

Example 4 ▸ Quantitative Thresholds

A, B, and C are operating segments of a public corporation. Pertinent information regarding sales, profit and loss, and assets of the three segments are given below.

	A	B	C	Combined	Elimination	Consolidated
Sales:						
Unaffiliated	$ 800	$ 20	$ 40	$ 860		$ 860
Intersegment	40	500		540	$(540)	
Total sales	$ 840	$ 520	$ 40	$1,400	$(540)	$ 860
Profit(loss)	$ 200	$(300)	$ 25	$ (75)		$ (75)
Assets	$1,200	$ 150	$400	$1,750		$1,750

Required: Determine which segments should be reported separately, based on the quantitative thresholds requirements.

Solution: Revenue Test—10% of combined segment revenues equals $140 [10% × ($840 + $520 + $40)]; therefore, segments A and B meet the revenue requirement for segmental disclosure.

Profit(loss) Test—The absolute amount of combined reported losses of all segments having losses exceed the combined profits of the profitable segments (i.e., $300 exceeds $225). The reported profit of segment A ($200), and the absolute amount of loss of segment B ($300) is 10% or more of the absolute amount of combined reported loss of all operating segments ($300); therefore, segments A and B meet this test.

Assets Test—10% of combined assets equals $175 [10% × ($1,200 + $150 + $400]; therefore, segments A and C meet this test.

All three segments meet at least **one** of the quantitative thresholds criteria for reportable segments; consequently, segmental disclosure should be reported for three segments.

2. **Exceptions**

   a. **Combining Operating Segments** An entity may combine information about operating segments not meeting the quantitative thresholds to produce a reportable segment only if the operating segments share a majority of the aggregation criteria.

b. **Minimum Reportable Segments** If the total of external revenue reported by operating segments is less than 75% of total consolidated revenue, additional operating segments must be identified as reportable segments until at least 75% of total consolidated revenue is included in reportable segments.

c. **"All Other" Category** Non-reportable business activities and operating segments are required to be combined and disclosed in an "all other" category separate from other reconciling items in the reconciliations. The revenue sources must be described.

d. **Management Judgment** If management judges an operating segment to be of continuing significance even though it no longer meets the criteria for reportability, information about that segment should continue to be reported separately in the current period.

e. **Restatement of Prior-Period Information** Information from prior periods presented for comparative purposes must be restated to reflect the newly reportable segment as a separate segment, unless it is impracticable to do so, such as when the information is not available and the cost to develop the information would be excessive.

f. **Practical Limit Reached** There may be a practical limit to the number of reportable segments beyond which information may become overly detailed. No precise limit is set, but generally an enterprise should consider whether this limit has been reached as the number of reportable segments increases above 10.

D. Disclosures

1. **General** An enterprise must disclose the following general information.

   a. **Identification Factors** Factors used to identify reportable segments, such as differences in products and services, geographic areas, or regulatory environments.

   b. **Revenue Sources** Types of products and services from which each reportable segment derives its revenues.

2. **Basis of Measurement**

   a. **Profit/Loss and Total Assets** An enterprise shall report a measure of profit or loss and total assets for each reportable segment. These measures are generally based upon the measures as reported to, and used by, the chief operating decision maker, and may include revenues from external customers; revenues from transactions with other operating segments of the same enterprise; interest revenue; interest expense; depreciation, depletion, and amortization expense; unusual items; equity in the net income of investees accounted for by the equity method; income tax expense or benefit; extraordinary items; and significant other noncash items.

   b. **Interest Revenue and Interest Expense** An enterprise must report interest revenue separately from interest expense for each reportable segment unless a majority of the segment's revenues are from interest.

   c. **Investment in Equity Investees and Additions to Long-Lived Assets** If the specified amounts are included in the determination of segment assets reviewed by the chief operating decision maker, the enterprise is required to disclose the amount of investment in equity method investees, and total expenditures for additions to long-lived assets other than financial instruments, long-term customer relationships of a financial institution, mortgage and other servicing rights, deferred policy acquisition costs, and deferred tax assets.

   d. **Explanation of Measurements** An enterprise must provide an explanation of the measurements used, at a minimum:

(1) The basis of accounting for any transactions between reportable segments

(2) The nature of any differences between the measurements applied to the reportable segments and the consolidated statements

(3) The nature of any changes from prior periods in the measurement methods used

(4) The nature and effect of any asymmetrical allocations to segments. For example, an enterprise might allocate depreciation expense to a segment without allocating the related depreciable assets to that segment.

3. **Reconciliations** An enterprise is required to report reconciliations of the totals of segment revenues, reported profit or loss, assets, and other significant items to corresponding enterprise amounts. All significant reconciling items must be separately identified and described.

4. **Interim Period Reporting** An enterprise is required to disclose information about each reportable segment in condensed financial statements of interim periods, including revenues from external customers, intersegment revenues, measures of segment profit or loss, material changes in total assets, descriptions of differences in measurement or segmentation, and a reconciliation of segments profit or loss to consolidated income.

5. **Enterprise-Wide Disclosures** If the following information is not provided as part of the segment information disclosed, it must also be disclosed.

   a. Revenues from external customers for each product and service or group of similar products and services unless it is impracticable to do.

   b. Revenues from external customers based on geographic area, including domestic revenues and foreign revenue.

   c. Long-lived assets located in the enterprise's country of domicile, and located in foreign countries.

   d. Information about major customers. Enterprises must disclose the total amount of revenues from each single customer that amounts to 10% or more of the enterprise's revenues and identify the segment(s) reporting the revenues. The identity of the customer need not be disclosed.

CHAPTER 11—REPORTING THE RESULTS OF OPERATIONS

Problem 11-1 MULTIPLE CHOICE QUESTIONS (164 to 205 minutes)

Items 1 and 2 are based on the following:

Vane Co.'s trial balance of income statement accounts for the current year ended December 31, included the following:

	Debit	Credit
Sales		$575,000
Cost of sales	$240,000	
Administrative expenses	70,000	
Loss on sale of equipment	10,000	
Sales commissions	50,000	
Interest revenue		25,000
Freight out	15,000	
Loss on early retirement of LT debt	20,000	
Uncollectible accounts expense	15,000	
Totals	$420,000	$600,000

Other information:

Finished goods inventory:	
January 1	$400,000
December 31	360,000

Vane's income tax rate is 30%. In Vane's year-end multiple-step income statement,

1. What amount should Vane report as the cost of goods manufactured?
a. $200,000
b. $215,000
c. $280,000
d. $295,000 (5/94, FAR, #9, amended, 4824)

2. What amount should Vane report as income after income taxes from continuing operations?
a. $126,000
b. $129,500
c. $140,000
d. $147,000 (5/94, FAR, #10, 4825)

3. Which of the following should be included in general and administrative expenses?

	Interest	*Advertising*
a.	Yes	Yes
b.	Yes	No
c.	No	Yes
d.	No	No

(5/95, FAR, #34, 5570)

4. In Baer Food Co.'s current year single-step income statement, the section titled "Revenues" consisted of the following:

Net sales revenue		$187,000
Results from discontinued operations:		
Loss from operations of segment (net of $1,200 tax effect)	$ (2,400)	
Gain on disposal of segment (net of $7,200 tax effect)	14,400	12,000
Interest revenue		10,200
Gain on sale of equipment		4,700
Cumulative change in previous two years income due to change in depreciation method (net of $750 tax effect)		1,500
Total revenues		$215,400

In the revenues section of the income statement, Baer Food should have reported total revenues of
a. $216,300
b. $215,400
c. $203,700
d. $201,900 (5/91, PI, #3, amended, 1115)

5. A material loss should be presented separately as a component of income from continuing operations when it is
a. An extraordinary item
b. A cumulative-effect-type change in accounting principle
c. Unusual in nature and infrequent in occurrence
d. Not unusual in nature but infrequent in occurrence (5/95, FAR, #40, 5576)

6. On October 1, year 1, Acme Fuel Co. sold 100,000 gallons of heating oil to Karn Co. at $3 per gallon. Fifty thousand gallons were delivered on December 15, year 1, and the remaining 50,000 gallons were delivered on January 15, year 2. Payment terms were: 50% due on October 1, year 1, 25% due on first delivery, and the remaining 25% due on second delivery. What amount of revenue should Acme recognize from this sale during year 1?
a. $ 75,000
b. $150,000
c. $225,000
d. $300,000 (5/92, PI, #37, amended, 2608)

7. The following information pertained to Azur Co. for the year:

Purchases	$102,800
Purchase discounts	10,280
Freight-in	15,420
Freight-out	5,140
Beginning inventory	30,840
Ending inventory	20,560

What amount should Azur report as cost of goods sold for the year?

a. $102,800
b. $118,220
c. $123,360
d. $128,500 (R/99, FAR, #11, 6780)

8. The following information pertains to Deal Corp.'s current year cost of goods sold:

Inventory, 12/31 of the previous year	$ 90,000
Purchases	124,000
Write-off of obsolete inventory	34,000
Inventory, 12/31 of current year	30,000

The inventory written off became obsolete due to an unexpected and unusual technological advance by a competitor. In its year-end income statement, what amount should Deal report as cost of goods sold?

a. $218,000
b. $184,000
c. $150,000
d. $124,000 (5/93, PI, #48, amended, 4089)

9. On October 1, year 3, Wand Inc. committed itself to a formal plan to sell its Kam division's assets. Wand estimated that the loss from the disposal of assets in February of year 4 would be $25,000. Wand also estimated that Kam would incur operating losses of $100,000 for the period of October 1 through December 31, year 3, and $50,000 for the period January 1 through February 28, year 4. These estimates were materially correct. Disregarding income taxes, what should Wand report as loss from discontinued operations in its comparative year 3 and year 4 income statements?

	Year 3	*Year 4*
a.	$175,000	$0
b	$125,000	$ 50,000
c.	$100,000	$ 75,000
d.	$0	$175,000

(11/94, Theory, #52, amended, 5313)

10. A segment of Ace, Inc., was discontinued during the current year. In comparative financial statements for the previous year, Ace's loss on disposal should

a. Exclude comparative financial statements for contingent product warranty obligation costs
b. Include operating losses during the current fiscal year
c. Exclude additional pension costs associated with the decision to dispose
d. Include operating losses of the previous fiscal year up to the date a disposal plan was adopted (5/93, Theory, #37, amended, 4225)

Items 11 and 12 are based on the following:

On December 31 of the current year, the Board of Directors of Maxx Manufacturing Inc. committed to a plan to discontinue the operations of its Alpha division in the following year. Maxx estimated that Alpha's following year operating loss would be $500,000 and that Alpha's facilities would be sold for $300,000 less than their carrying amounts. Alpha's current year operating loss was $1,400,000, before any consideration of impairment loss. Maxx's effective tax rate is 30%. These estimates were accurate.

11. In its current year income statement, what amount should Maxx report as loss from discontinued operations?

a. $1,190,000
b. $1,400,000
c. $1,540,000
d. $2,200,000 (5/93, PI, #57, amended, 4096)

12. In its following year income statement, what amount should Maxx report as loss from discontinued operations?

a. $350,000
b. $500,000
c. $560,000
d. $800,000 (5/93, PI, #58, amended, 4097)

13. On February 2, Flint Corp.'s board of directors voted to discontinue operations of its frozen food division and to sell the division's assets on the open market as soon as possible. The division reported net operating losses of $20,000 in January and $30,000 in February. On February 26, sale of the division's assets resulted in a gain of $90,000. What amount of gain from disposal of a business segment should Flint recognize in its income statement for the three months ended March 31?

a. $0
b. $40,000
c. $60,000
d. $90,000 (R/00, FAR, #8, amended, 6903)

14. Ocean Corp.'s comprehensive insurance policy allows its assets to be replaced at current value. The policy has a $50,000 deductible clause. One of Ocean's waterfront warehouses was destroyed in a winter storm. Such storms occur approximately every four years. Ocean incurred $20,000 of costs in dismantling the warehouse and plans to replace it. The following data relate to the warehouse:

Current carrying amount	$ 300,000
Replacement cost	1,100,000

What amount of gain should Ocean report as a separate component of income before extraordinary items?
a. $1,030,000
b. $ 780,000
c. $ 730,000
d. $0 (5/92, PI, #46, 2617)

15. Hail damaged several of Toncan Co.'s vans. Hailstorms had frequently inflicted similar damage to Toncan's vans. Over the years, Toncan had saved money by not buying hail insurance and either paying for repairs, or selling damaged vans and then replacing them. The damaged vans were sold for less than their carrying amount. How should the hail damage cost be reported in Toncan's financial statements?
a. The actual hail damage loss as an extraordinary loss, net of income taxes
b. The actual hail damage loss in continuing operations, with **no** separate disclosure
c. The expected average hail damage loss in continuing operations, with **no** separate disclosure
d. The expected average hail damage loss in continuing operations, with separate disclosure (5/93, Theory, #35, amended, 4223)

16. In open market transactions, Gold Corp. simultaneously sold its long-term investment in Iron Corp. bonds and purchased its own outstanding bonds. The broker remitted the net cash from the two transactions. Gold's gain on the purchase of its own bonds exceeded its loss on the sale of the Iron bonds. Gold should report the
a. Net effect of the two transactions as an extraordinary gain
b. Net effect of the two transactions in income before extraordinary items
c. Effect of its own bond transaction gain in income before extraordinary items, and report the Iron bond transaction as an extraordinary loss
d. Effect of its own bond transaction as an extraordinary gain, and report the Iron bond transaction loss in income before extraordinary items (11/95, FAR, #41, amended, 6123)

17. Kent Co. incurred the following infrequent losses during the year:

- A $300,000 loss was incurred on disposal of one of four dissimilar factories.
- A major currency devaluation caused a $120,000 exchange loss on an amount remitted by a foreign customer.
- Inventory valued at $190,000 was made worthless by a competitor's unexpected product innovation.

In its year-end income statement, what amount should Kent report as losses that are **not** considered extraordinary?
a. $610,000
b. $490,000
c. $420,000
d. $310,000 (5/92, PI, #54, amended, 2625)

18. During the current year, both Raim Co. and Cane Co. suffered losses due to the flooding of the Mississippi River. Raim is located two miles from the river and sustains flood losses every two to three years. Cane, which has been located fifty miles from the river for the past twenty years, has never before had flood losses. How should the flood losses be reported in each company's year-end income statement?

	Raim	*Cane*
a.	As a component of income from continuing operations	As an extraordinary item
b.	As a component of income from continuing operations	As a component of income from continuing operations
c.	As an extraordinary item	As a component of income from continuing operations
d.	As an extraordinary item	As an extraordinary item

(11/95, FAR, #42, amended, 6124)

19. When a full set of general-purpose financial statements are presented, comprehensive income and its components should
a. Appear as a part of discontinued operations, extraordinary items, and cumulative effect of a change in accounting principle
b. Be reported net of related income tax effect, in total and individually
c. Appear in a supplemental schedule in the notes to the financial statements
d. Be displayed in a financial statement that has the same prominence as other financial statements (R/99, FAR, #1, 6770)

20. One of the elements of a financial statement is comprehensive income. Comprehensive income excludes changes in equity resulting from which of the following?
a. Loss from discontinued operations
b. Prior period error correction
c. Dividends paid to stockholders
d. Unrealized loss on investments in noncurrent marketable equity securities
(5/95, FAR, #2, 5538)

21. Rock Co.'s financial statements had the following balances at December 31:

Extraordinary gain	$ 50,000
Foreign currency translation gain	100,000
Net income	400,000
Unrealized gain on available-for-sale equity securities	20,000

What amount should Rock report as comprehensive income for the year ended December 31?
a. $400,000
b. $420,000
c. $520,000
d. $570,000 (R/02, FAR #1, 7056)

22. Under Statement of Financial Accounting Concepts No. 5, which of the following items would cause earnings to differ from comprehensive income for an enterprise in an industry **not** having specialized accounting principles?
a. Unrealized loss on investments in available-for-sale marketable equity securities
b. Unrealized loss on investments in trading marketable equity securities
c. Loss on exchange of similar assets
d. Loss on exchange of dissimilar assets
(5/91, Theory, #1, amended, 1750)

23. Which of the following describes how comprehensive income should be reported?
a. Must be reported in a separate statement, as part of a complete set of financial statements
b. Should not be reported in the financial statements but should only be disclosed in the footnotes
c. May be reported in a separate statement, in a combined statement of income and comprehensive income, or within a statement of stockholders' equity
d. May be reported in a combined statement of income and comprehensive income or disclosed within a statement of stockholders' equity; separate statements of comprehensive income are not permitted (R/05, FAR, C02129F, #47, 7791)

24. Which of the following items requires a prior period adjustment to retained earnings?
a. Purchases of inventory this year were overstated by $5 million.
b. Available-for-sale securities were improperly valued last year by $20 million.
c. Revenue of $5 million that should have been deferred was recorded in the previous year as earned.
d. The prior year's foreign currency translation gain of $2 million was **never** recorded.
(R/03, FAR, #1, 7603)

25. Milton Co. began operations on January 1, year 1. On January 1, year 3, Milton changed its inventory method from LIFO to FIFO for both financial and income tax reporting. If FIFO had been used in prior years, Milton's inventories would have been higher by $60,000 and $40,000 at December 31, year 3 and year 2, respectively. Milton has a 30% income tax rate. What amount should Milton report as the cumulative effect of this accounting change in its income statement for the year ended December 31, year 3?
a. $0
b. $14,000
c. $28,000
d. $42,000 (11/92, PI, #60, amended, 3291)

Items 26 and 27 are based on the following:

During the current year, Orca Corp. decided to change from the FIFO method of inventory valuation to the weighted-average method. Inventory balances under each method were as follows:

	FIFO	Weighted-average
January 1	$71,000	$77,000
December 31	79,000	83,000

Orca's income tax rate is 30%.

26. In its year-end financial statements, what amount should Orca report as the cumulative effect of this accounting change?
a. $2,800
b. $4,000
c. $4,200
d. $6,000 (5/95, FAR, #45, amended, 5581)

27. Orca should report the cumulative effect of this accounting change as a(an)
a. Prior period adjustment to the beginning balance of retained earnings
b. Component of income from continuing operations
c. Extraordinary item
d. Component of income after extraordinary items
(5/95, FAR, #46, 5582)

28. At December 31 of the current year, Off-Line Co. changed its method of accounting for demo costs from writing off the costs over two years to expensing the costs immediately. Off-Line made the change in recognition of an increasing number of demos placed with customers that did not result in sales. Off-Line had deferred demo costs of $500,000 at December 31 of the previous year, $300,000 of which were to be written off in the current year and the remainder in the following year. Off-Line's income tax rate is 30%. In its current year income statement, what amount should Off-Line report?
a. $140,000
b. $200,000
c. $350,000
d. $500,000 (R/99, FAR, #12, amended, 6781)

29. In the current year, Brighton Co. changed from the individual item approach to the aggregate approach in applying the lower of FIFO cost or market to inventories. The cumulative effect of this change should be reported in Brighton's financial statements as a(an)
a. Prior period adjustment, with separate disclosure
b. Component of income from continuing operations, with separate disclosure
c. Component of income from continuing operations, without separate disclosure
d. Adjustment to the beginning balance of retained earnings (11/91, Theory, #26, amended, 1943)

30. On January 1 of the current year, Poe Construction Inc., changed to the percentage of completion method of income recognition for financial statement reporting. Poe can justify this change in accounting principle. As of December 31 of the previous year, Poe compiled data showing that income under the completed contract method aggregated $700,000. If the percentage of completion method had been used, the accumulated income through December 31 of the previous year would have been $880,000. Assuming an income tax rate of 40% for all years, the cumulative effect of this accounting change should be reported by Poe in the current year
a. Retained earnings statement as a $180,000 credit adjustment to the beginning balance
b. Income statement as a $180,000 credit
c. Retained earnings statement as a $108,000 credit adjustment to the beginning balance
d. Income statement as a $108,000 credit (5/86, PI, #58, amended, 1160)

31. How should the effect of a change in accounting principle that is inseparable from the effect of a change in accounting estimate be reported?
a. As a component of income from continuing operations
b. By restating the financial statements of all prior periods presented
c. As a correction of an error
d. By footnote disclosure only (5/97, FAR, #4, 6476)

32. On January 2, year 3, to better reflect the variable use of its only machine, Holly Inc. elected to change its method of depreciation from the straight-line method to the units of production method. The original cost of the machine on January 2, year 1, was $50,000, and its estimated life was 10 years. Holly estimates that the machine's total life is 50,000 machine hours. Machine hours usage was 8,500 during year 2 and 3,500 during year 1. Holly's income tax rate is 30%. Holly should report the accounting change in its year 3 financial statements as a (an)
a. Cumulative effect of a change in accounting principle of $2,000 in its income statement
b. Adjustment to beginning retained earnings of $2,000
c. Current period transaction with no prior period adjustment
d. Adjustment to beginning retained earnings of $1,400 (11/93, PI, #4, amended, 4373)

33. For the previous year, Pac Co. estimated its two-year equipment warranty costs based on $100 per unit sold in the previous year. Experience during the current year indicated that the estimate should have been based on $110 per unit. The effect of this $10 difference from the estimate is reported
a. In current year income from continuing operations
b. As an accounting change, net of tax, below current year income from continuing operations
c. As an accounting change requiring the previous year financial statements to be restated
d. As a correction of an error requiring the previous year financial statements to be restated (11/93, Theory, #23, amended, 4528)

34. How should the effect of a change in accounting estimate be accounted for?
a. By restating amounts reported in financial statements of prior periods
b. By reporting pro forma amounts for prior periods
c. As a prior period adjustment to beginning retained earnings
d. In the period of change and future periods if the change affects both (11/94, Theory, #54, 5315)

35. On January 2, year 1, Union Co. purchased a machine for $264,000 and depreciated it by the straight-line method using an estimated useful life of eight years with no salvage value. On January 2, year 4, Union determined that the machine had a useful life of six years from the date of acquisition and will have a salvage value of $24,000. An accounting change was made in year 4 to reflect the additional data. The accumulated depreciation for this machine should have a balance at December 31, year 4, of

a. $176,000
b. $160,000
c. $154,000
d. $146,000 (11/93, PI, #60, amended, 4429)

36. Matt Co. included a foreign subsidiary in its current consolidated financial statements. The subsidiary was acquired six years ago and was excluded from previous consolidations. The change was caused by the elimination of foreign exchange controls. Including the subsidiary in the consolidated financial statements results in accounting change that should be reported

a. By footnote disclosure only
b. Currently and prospectively
c. Currently with footnote disclosure of pro forma effects of retroactive application
d. By retrospective application to the financial statements of all prior periods presented

(5/92, Theory, #40, amended, 2733)

37. Which of the following statements is correct regarding accounting changes that result in financial statements that are, in effect, the statements of a different reporting entity?

a. Cumulative-effect adjustments should be reported as separate items on the financial statements pertaining to the year of change.
b. No restatements or adjustments are required if the changes involve consolidated methods of accounting for subsidiaries.
c. No restatements or adjustments are required if the changes involve the cost or equity methods of accounting for investments.
d. The financial statements of all prior periods presented should be reported by retrospective application. (5/94, FAR, #39, amended, 4854)

38. Lore Co. changed from the cash basis of accounting to the accrual basis of accounting during the year. The cumulative effect of this change should be reported in Lore's financial statements as a

a. Correction of an error
b. Change in accounting principle
c. Component of income before extraordinary item
d. Component of income after extraordinary item

(11/95, FAR, #43, amended, 6125)

39. Conn Co. reported a retained earnings balance of $400,000 at December 31 of the previous year. In August of the current year, Conn determined that insurance premiums of $60,000 for the three-year period beginning January 1, last year had been paid and fully expensed in that year. Conn has a 30% income tax rate. What amount should Conn report as adjusted beginning retained earnings in its current year statement of retained earnings?

a. $420,000
b. $428,000
c. $440,000
d. $442,000 (11/93, PI, #10, amended, 4379)

40. In which of the following situations should a company report a prior-period adjustment?

a. A change in the estimated useful lives of fixed assets purchased in prior years
b. The correction of a mathematical error in the calculation of prior years' depreciation
c. A switch from the straight-line to double-declining balance method of depreciation
d. The scrapping of an asset prior to the end of its expected useful life

(R/05, FAR, A0480F, #43, 7787)

41. Pear Co.'s income statement for the current year ended December 31, as prepared by Pear's controller, reported income before taxes of $125,000. The auditor questioned the following amounts that had been included in income before taxes:

Equity in earnings of Cinn Co.	$ 40,000
Dividends received from Cinn	8,000
Adjustments to profits of prior years for arithmetical errors in depreciation	(35,000)

Pear owns 40% of Cinn's common stock. Pear's December 31 income statement should report income before taxes of

a. $ 85,000
b. $117,000
c. $120,000
d. $152,000 (5/93, PI, #5, amended, 4047)

42. Which of the following errors could result in an overstatement of both current assets and stockholders' equity?

a. An understatement of accrued sales expenses
b. Noncurrent note receivable principal is misclassified as a current asset.
c. Annual depreciation on manufacturing machinery is understated.
d. Holiday pay expense for administrative employees is misclassified as manufacturing overhead.

(5/93, Theory, #17, 4205)

43. Which of the following should be disclosed in a summary of significant accounting policies?

I. Management's intention to maintain or vary the dividend payout ratio
II. Criteria for determining which investments are treated as cash equivalents
III. Composition of the sales order backlog by segment

a. I only
b. I and III
c. II only
d. II and III (11/92, Theory, #37, 3470)

44. The summary of significant accounting policies should disclose the
a. Pro forma effect of retroactive application of an accounting change
b. Basis of profit recognition on long-term construction contracts
c. Adequacy of pension plan assets in relation to vested benefits
d. Future minimum lease payments in the aggregate and for each of the five succeeding fiscal years (5/91, Theory, #32, 1903)

45. Which of the following payments by a company should be disclosed in the notes to the financial statements as a related party transaction?

I. Royalties paid to a major stockholder as consideration for patents purchased from the shareholder
II. Officers' salaries

a. I only
b. II only
c. Both I and II
d. Neither I nor II (R/03, FAR, #14, 7616)

46. Dex Co. has entered into a joint venture with an affiliate to secure access to additional inventory. Under the joint venture agreement, Dex will purchase the output of the venture at prices negotiated on an arms'-length basis. Which of the following is(are) required to be disclosed about the related party transaction?

I. The amount due to the affiliate at the balance sheet date
II. The dollar amount of the purchases during the year

a. I only
b. II only
c. Both I and II
d. Neither I nor II (R/99, FAR, #20, 6789)

47. Lemu Co. and Young Co. are under the common management of Ego Co. Ego can significantly influence the operating results of both Lemu and Young. While Lemu had no transactions with Ego during the year, Young sold merchandise to Ego under the same terms given to unrelated parties. In the notes to their respective financial statements, should Lemu and Young disclose their relationship with Ego?

	Lemu	Young
a.	Yes	Yes
b.	Yes	No
c.	No	Yes
d.	No	No

(5/98, FAR, #6, 6609)

48. Dean Co. acquired 100% of Morey Corp. prior to the current year. During the current year, the individual companies included in their financial statements the following:

	Dean	Morey
Officers' salaries	$ 75,000	$50,000
Officers' expenses	20,000	10,000
Loans to officers	125,000	50,000
Intercompany sales	150,000	--

What amount should be reported as related party disclosures in the notes to Dean's year-end consolidated financial statements?
a. $150,000
b. $155,000
c. $175,000
d. $330,000 (11/90, PI, #53, amended, 1129)

49. For which type of material related-party transactions does Statement of Financial Accounting Standard No. 57, *Related-Party Disclosures,* require disclosure?
a. Only those not reported in the body of the financial statements
b. Only those that receive accounting recognition
c. Those that contain possible illegal acts
d. All those other than compensation arrangements, expense allowances, and other similar items in the ordinary course of business (11/95, FAR, #7, 6089)

50. Wind Co. incurred organization costs of $6,000 at the beginning of its first year of operations. How should Wind treat the organization costs in its financial statements in accordance with GAAP?
a. Never amortized
b. Amortized over 60 months
c. Amortized over 40 years
d. Expensed immediately (R/05, FAR, 1042F, #21, 7765)

51. Financial reporting by a development stage enterprise differs from financial reporting for an established operating enterprise in regard to footnote disclosures

a. Only
b. And expense recognition principles only
c. And revenue recognition principles only
d. And revenue and expense recognition principles

(5/92, Theory, #49, 2742)

52. Tanker Oil Co., a developmental stage enterprise, incurred the following costs during its first year of operations:

Legal fees for incorporation and other related matters	$55,000
Underwriters' fees for initial stock offering	40,000
Exploration costs and purchases of mineral rights	60,000

Tanker had no revenue during its first year of operation. What amount may Tanker capitalize as organizational costs?

a. $155,000
b. $ 95,000
c. $ 55,000
d. $0

(5/93, PII, #14, amended, 9049)

53. Deficits accumulated during the development stage of a company should be

a. Reported as organization costs
b. Reported as a part of stockholders' equity
c. Capitalized and written off in the first year of principal operations
d. Capitalized and amortized over a five-year period beginning when principal operations commence

(11/90, Theory, #8, 1908)

54. On April 1, Ivy began operating a service proprietorship with an initial cash investment of $1,000. The proprietorship provided $3,200 of services in April and received full payment in May. The proprietorship incurred expenses of $1,500 in April which were paid in June. During May, Ivy drew $500 against her capital account. What was the proprietorship's income for the two months ended May 31, under the following methods of accounting?

	Cash basis	*Accrual basis*
a.	$1,200	$1,200
b.	$1,700	$1,700
c.	$2,700	$1,200
d.	$3,200	$1,700

(11/93, PI, #43, amended, 4412)

55. Ward, a consultant, keeps her accounting records on a cash basis. During the current year, Ward collected $200,000 in fees from clients. At December 31 of the previous year, Ward had accounts receivable of $40,000. At December 31 of the current year, Ward had accounts receivable of $60,000, and unearned fees of $5,000. On an accrual basis, what was Ward's service revenue for the current year?

a. $175,000
b. $180,000
c. $215,000
d. $225,000

(5/95, FAR, #25, amended, 5561)

56. Compared to the accrual basis of accounting, the cash basis of accounting understates income by the net decrease during the accounting period of

	Accounts receivable	*Accrued expenses*
a.	Yes	Yes
b.	Yes	No
c.	No	No
d.	No	Yes

(5/94, FAR, #42, 4857)

57. During December of the previous year, Nile Co. incurred special insurance costs but did not record these costs until payment was made during the current year. These insurance costs related to inventory that had been sold by December 31 of the previous year. What is the effect of the omission on Nile's accrued liabilities and retained earnings at December 31 of the previous year?

	Accrued liabilities	*Retained earnings*
a.	No effect	No effect
b.	No effect	Overstated
c.	Understated	Overstated
d.	Understated	No effect

(R/03, FAR, #12, amended, 7614)

58. Fenn Stores Inc. had sales of $1,000,000 during December. Experience has shown that merchandise equaling 7% of sales will be returned within 30 days and an additional 3% will be returned within 90 days. Returned merchandise is readily resalable. In addition, merchandise equaling 15% of sales will be exchanged for merchandise of equal or greater value. What amount should Fenn report for net sales in its income statement for the month of December?

a. $900,000
b. $850,000
c. $780,000
d. $750,000

(5/93, PI, #37, amended, 4078)

59. Tara Co. owns an office building and leases the offices under a variety of rental agreements involving rent paid in advance monthly or annually. Not all tenants make timely payments of their rent. Tara's balance sheets contained the following data:

	Year 1	Year 2
Rentals receivable	$ 9,600	$12,400
Unearned rentals	32,000	24,000

During year 2, Tara received $80,000 cash from tenants. What amount of rental revenue should Tara record for year 2?

a. $90,800
b. $85,200
c. $74,800
d. $69,200 (5/91, PI, #53, amended, 1117)

60. UVW Broadcast Co. entered into a contract to exchange unsold advertising time for travel and lodging services with Hotel Co. As of June 30, advertising commercials of $10,000 were used. However, travel and lodging services were not provided. How should UVW account for advertising in its June 30 financial statements?

a. Revenue and expense is recognized when the agreement is complete.
b. An asset and revenue for $10,000 is recognized.
c. Both the revenue and expense of $10,000 are recognized.
d. Not reported (R/05, FAR, 1290F, #29, 7773)

61. On January 1, Brec Co. installed cabinets to display products in customers' stores. Brec expects to use these cabinets for five years. Brec's year-end multi-step income statement should include

a. One-fifth of the cabinet costs in cost of goods sold
b. One-fifth of the cabinet costs in selling, general, and administrative expenses
c. All of the cabinet costs in cost of goods sold
d. All of the cabinet costs in selling, general, and administrative expenses (5/92, Theory, #17, amended, 9044)

62. Ichor Co. reported equipment with an original cost of $379,000 and $344,000, and accumulated depreciation of $153,000 and $128,000, respectively, in its comparative financial statements for the years ended December 31, year 5, and year 4. During year 5, Ichor purchased equipment costing $50,000, and sold equipment with a carrying value of $9,000. What amount should Ichor report as depreciation expense for year 5?

a. $19,000
b. $25,000
c. $31,000
d. $34,000 (11/97, FAR, #10, amended, 6490)

63. Troop Co. frequently borrows from the bank to maintain sufficient operating cash. The following loans were at 12% interest rate, with interest payable at maturity. Troop repaid each loan on its scheduled maturity date.

Date of Loan	Amount	Maturity date	Term of loan
11/1, Yr 5	$10,000	10/31, Yr 6	1 year
2/1, Yr 6	30,000	7/31, Yr 6	6 months
5/1, Yr 6	16,000	1/31, Yr 7	9 months

Troop records interest expense when the loans are repaid. Accordingly, interest expense of $3,000 was recorded in year 6. If **no** correction is made, by what amount would year 6 interest expense be understated?

a. $1,080
b. $1,240
c. $1,280
d. $1,440 (5/97, FAR, #6, amended, 6478)

64. Zach Corp. pays commissions to its sales staff at the rate of 3% of net sales. Sales staff are not paid salaries but are given monthly advances of $15,000. Advances are charged to commission expense, and reconciliations against commissions are prepared quarterly. Net sales for the current year ended March 31 were $15,000,000. The unadjusted balance in the commissions expense account on March 31 was $400,000. March advances were paid on April 3. In its income statement for the current year ended March 31, what amount should Zach report as commission expense?

a. $465,000
b. $450,000
c. $415,000
d. $400,000 (5/93, PI, #49, amended, 4090)

65. House Publishers offered a contest in which the winner would receive $1,000,000, payable over 20 years. On December 31, year 1, House announced the winner of the contest and signed a note payable to the winner for $1,000,000, payable in $50,000 installments every January 2. Also on December 31, year 1, House purchased an annuity for $418,250 to provide the $950,000 prize monies remaining after the first $50,000 installment, which was paid on January 2, year 2. In its year 1 income statement, what should House report as contest prize expense?

a. $0
b. $ 418,250
c. $ 468,250
d. $1,000,000 (11/94, FAR, #23, amended, 5287)

66. Pak Co.'s professional fees expense account had a balance of $82,000 at December 31, year 1, before considering year-end adjustments relating to the following:

- Consultants were hired for a special project at a total fee not to exceed $65,000. Pak has recorded $55,000 of this fee based on billings for work performed in year 1.
- The attorney's letter requested by the auditors dated January 28, year 2, indicated that legal fees of $6,000 were billed on January 15, year 2, for work performed in November year 1, and unbilled fees for December year 1 were $7,000.

What amount should Pak report for professional fees expense for the year ended December 31, year 1?
a. $105,000
b. $ 95,000
c. $ 88,000
d. $ 82,000 (5/92, PI, #48, amended, 2619)

67. In financial statements prepared on the income-tax basis, how should the nondeductible portion of expenses, such as meals and entertainment, be reported?
a. Included in the expense category in the determination of income
b. Included in a separate category in the determination of income
c. Excluded from the determination of income but included in the determination of retained earnings
d. Excluded from the financial statements (11/95, FAR, #56, 6138)

68. On February 1, Tory began a service proprietorship with an initial cash investment of $2,000. The proprietorship provided $5,000 of services in February and received full payment in March. The proprietorship incurred expenses of $3,000 in February, which were paid in April. During March, Tory drew $1,000 against the capital account. In the proprietorship's financial statements for the two months ended March 31, prepared under the cash basis method of accounting, what amount should be reported as capital?
a. $1,000
b. $3,000
c. $6,000
d. $7,000 (11/95, FAR, #24, amended, 6106)

69. Hahn Co. prepared financial statements on the cash basis of accounting. The cash basis was modified so that an accrual of income taxes was reported. Are these financial statements in accordance with the modified cash basis of accounting?
a. Yes.
b. No, because the modifications are illogical.
c. No, because there is no substantial support for recording income taxes.
d. No, because the modifications result in financial statements equivalent to those prepared under the accrual basis of accounting. (R/02, FAR #5, 7060)

70. Which of the following is **not** a comprehensive basis of accounting other than generally accepted accounting principles?
a. Cash receipts and disbursements basis of accounting
b. Basis of accounting used by an entity to file its income tax return
c. Basis of accounting used by an entity to comply with the financial reporting requirements of a government regulatory agency
d. Basis of accounting used by an entity to comply with the financial reporting requirements of a lending institution. (11/98, FAR, #7, 6734)

71. APB Opinion No. 28, *Interim Financial Reporting,* concluded that interim financial reporting should be viewed primarily in which of the following ways?
a. As useful only if activity is spread evenly throughout the year
b. As if the interim period were an annual accounting period
c. As reporting for an integral part of an annual period
d. As reporting under a comprehensive basis of accounting other than GAAP (5/95, FAR, #3, 5539)

72. Wilson Corp. experienced a $50,000 decline in the market value of its inventory in the first quarter of its fiscal year. Wilson had expected this decline to reverse in the third quarter, and in fact, the third quarter recovery exceeded the previous decline by $10,000. Wilson's inventory did not experience any other declines in market value during the fiscal year. What amounts of loss and/or gain should Wilson report in its interim financial statements for the first and third quarters?

	First quarter	*Third quarter*
a.	$0	$0
b.	$0	$10,000 gain
c.	$50,000 loss	$50,000 gain
d.	$50,000 loss	$60,000 gain

(R/99, FAR, #18, 6787)

73. In general, an enterprise preparing interim financial statements should
a. Defer recognition of seasonal revenue
b. Disregard permanent decreases in the market value of its inventory
c. Allocate revenues and expenses evenly over the quarters, regardless of when they actually occurred
d. Use the same accounting principles followed in preparing its latest annual financial statements
(R/05, FAR, 0628F, #10, 7754)

74. Conceptually, interim financial statements can be described as emphasizing
a. Timeliness over reliability
b. Reliability over relevance
c. Relevance over comparability
d. Comparability over neutrality
(11/95, FAR, #6, 6088)

75. For interim financial reporting, a company's income tax provision for the second quarter should be determined using the
a. Effective tax rate expected to be applicable for the full year as estimated at the end of the first quarter
b. Effective tax rate expected to be applicable for the full year as estimated at the end of the second quarter
c. Effective tax rate expected to be applicable for the second quarter of the year
d. Statutory tax rate for the year
(11/93, Theory, #31, amended, 4536)

76. On March 15, Krol Co. paid property taxes of $90,000 on its office building for the calendar year. On April 1, Krol paid $150,000 for unanticipated repairs to its office equipment. The repairs will benefit operations for the remainder of the year. What is the total amount of these expenses that Krol should include in its quarterly income statement for the three months ended June 30?
a. $172,500
b. $ 97,500
c. $ 72,500
d. $ 37,500 (11/92, PII, #52, amended, 3386)

77. On June 30, Mill Corp. incurred a $100,000 net loss from disposal of a business component. Also, on June 30, Mill paid $40,000 for property taxes assessed for the calendar year. What amount of the foregoing items should be included in the determination of Mill's net income or loss for the six-month interim period ended June 30?
a. $140,000
b. $120,000
c. $ 90,000
d. $ 70,000 (5/92, PII, #12, amended, 2644)

78. Kell Corp.'s $95,000 net income for the quarter ended September 30, included the following after-tax items:

- A $60,000 extraordinary gain, realized on April 30, was allocated equally to the second, third, and fourth quarters of the year.
- A $16,000 cumulative-effect loss resulting from a change in inventory valuation method was recognized on August 2.

In addition, Kell paid $48,000 on February 1 for calendar-year property taxes. Of this amount, $12,000 was allocated to the third quarter of the year. For the quarter ended September 30, Kell should report net income of
a. $ 91,000
b. $103,000
c. $111,000
d. $115,000 (11/91, PII, #13, amended, 2461)

79. Which of the following qualifies as an operating segment?
a. Corporate headquarters, which oversees $1 billion in sales for the entire company
b. North American segment, whose assets are 12% of the company's assets of all segments, and management reports to the chief operating officer
c. South American segment, whose results of operations are reported directly to the chief operating officer, and has 5% of the company's assets, 9% of revenues, and 8% of the profits
d. Eastern Europe segment, which reports its results directly to the manager of the European division, and has 20% of the company's assets, 12% of revenues, and 11% of profits
(R/05, FAR, A0025F, #40, 7784)

80. Terra Co.'s total revenues from its three operating segments were as follows:

Segment	Sales to external Customers	Intersegment sales	Total revenues
Lion	$ 70,000	$ 30,000	$100,000
Monk	22,000	4,000	26,000
Nevi	8,000	16,000	24,000
Combined	100,000	50,000	150,000
Elimination	—	(50,000)	(50,000)
Consolidated	$100,000	$ —	$100,000

Which operating segment(s) is(are) deemed to be reportable segments?
a. None
b. Lion only
c. Lion and Monk only
d. Lion, Monk, and Nevi
(11/95, FAR, #8, amended, 6090)

81. Bean Co. included interest expense and transactions classified as extraordinary items in its determination of segment profit, which Bean's chief financial officer considered in determining the segment's operating budget. Bean is required to report the segment's financial data under SFAS No. 131, Disclosures about Segments of an Enterprise and Related Information. Which of the following items should Bean disclose in reporting segment data?

	Interest expense	Extraordinary items
a.	No	No
b.	No	Yes
c.	Yes	No
d.	Yes	Yes

(R/03, FAR, #19, 7621)

82. Opto Co. is a publicly-traded, consolidated enterprise reporting segment information. Which of the following items is a required enterprise-wide disclosure regarding external customers?

a. The fact that transactions with a particular external customer constitute more than 10% of the total enterprise revenues
b. The identity of any external customer providing 10% or more of a particular operating segment's revenue
c. The identity of any external customer considered to be "major" by management
d. Information on major customers is **not** required in segment reporting

(R/05, FAR, 0761F, #14, 7758)

Problem 11-2 ADDITIONAL MULTIPLE CHOICE QUESTIONS (68 to 85 minutes)

83. The following costs were incurred by Griff Co., a manufacturer, during the year:

Accounting and legal fees	$ 25,000
Freight-in	175,000
Freight-out	160,000
Officers' salaries	150,000
Insurance	85,000
Sales representatives' salaries	215,000

What amount of these costs should be reported as general and administrative expenses for the year?

a. $260,000
b. $550,000
c. $635,000
d. $810,000 (11/93, PI, #52, amended, 4421)

84. The effect of a material transaction that is infrequent in occurrence but **not** unusual in nature should be presented separately as a component of income from continuing operations when the transaction results in a

	Gain	Loss
a.	Yes	Yes
b.	Yes	No
c.	No	No
d.	No	Yes

(5/94, FAR, #40, 4855)

85. Kerr Company sold a parcel of land used as a plant site. The amount Kerr received was $100,000 in excess of the land's carrying amount. Kerr's income tax rate was 30%. In its income statement, Kerr should report a gain on sale of land of

a. $0
b. $ 30,000
c. $ 70,000
d. $100,000 (11/88, PI, #42, amended, 9045)

86. On October 1, year 4, Host Co. approved a plan to dispose of a segment of its business. Host expected that the sale would occur on April 1, year 5, at an estimated gain of $350,000. The segment had actual and estimated operating losses as follows:

1/1 to 9/30, year 4	$(300,000)
10/1 to 12/31, year 4	(200,000)
1/1 to 3/31, year 5	(400,000)

In its December 31, year 4, income statement, what should Host report as a loss from discontinued operations before income taxes?

a. $200,000
b. $250,000
c. $500,000
d. $600,000 (5/95, FAR, #44, amended, 5580)

87. During January of the previous year, Doe Corp. agreed to sell the assets and product line of its Hart division. The sale on January 15 of the current year resulted in a gain on disposal of $900,000. Not considering any impairment losses, Hart's operating losses were $600,000 for the previous year and $50,000 for the current year period January 1 through January 15. Disregarding income taxes, what amount of net gain(loss) should be reported in Doe's comparative current and previous years income statements?

	Current Year	Previous Year
a.	$0	$ 250,000
b.	$250,000	$0
c.	$850,000	$(600,000)
d.	$900,000	$(650,000)

(11/95, FAR, #39, amended, 6121)

88. On April 30, Deer approved a plan to dispose of a segment of its business. For the period January 1 through April 30, the segment had revenues of $500,000 and expenses of $800,000. The assets of the segment were sold on October 15, at a loss for which no tax benefit is available. In its income statement for the calendar year how should Deer report the segment's operations from January 1 to April 30?

a. $500,000 and $800,000 included with revenues and expenses, respectively, as part of continuing operations
b. $300,000 reported as a net loss, as part of continuing operations
c. $300,000 reported as an extraordinary loss
d. $300,000 reported as a loss from discontinued operations (11/95, FAR, #40, amended, 6122)

89. Midway Co. had the following transactions during the current year:

- $1,200,000 pretax loss on foreign currency exchange due to a major unexpected devaluation by the foreign government.
- $500,000 pretax loss from discontinued operations of a division.
- $800,000 pretax loss on equipment damaged by a hurricane. This was the first hurricane ever to strike in Midway's area. Midway also received $1,000,000 from its insurance company to replace a building, with a carrying value of $300,000, that had been destroyed by the hurricane.

What amount should Midway report in its year-end income statement as extraordinary loss before income taxes?

a. $ 100,000
b. $1,300,000
c. $1,800,000
d. $2,500,000 (5/93, PI, #59, amended, 4098)

90. A transaction that is unusual in nature and infrequent in occurrence should be reported separately as a component of income

a. After cumulative effect of accounting changes and before discontinued operations of a segment of a business.
b. After cumulative effect of accounting changes and after discontinued operations of a segment of a business.
c. Before cumulative effect of accounting changes and before discontinued operations of a segment of a business.
d. Before cumulative effect of accounting changes and after discontinued operations of a segment of a business. (11/94, Theory, #53, 5314)

91. In September, Koff Co.'s operating plant was destroyed by an earthquake. Earthquakes are rare in the area in which the plant was located. The portion of the resultant loss not covered by insurance was $700,000. Koff's income tax rate is 40%. In its year-end income statement, what amount should Koff report as extraordinary loss?

a. $0
b. $280,000
c. $420,000
d. $700,000 (5/97, FAR, #5, amended, 6477)

92. On August 31, Harvey Co. decided to change from the FIFO periodic inventory system to the weighted average periodic inventory system. Harvey is on a calendar year basis. The cumulative effect of the change is determined

a. As of January 1
b. As of August 31
c. During the eight months ending August 31, by a weighted average of the purchases
d. During the entire year by a weighted average of the purchases

(5/93, Theory, #20, amended, 4208)

Items 93 and 94 are based on the following:

On January 1 two years ago, Warren Co. purchased a $600,000 machine, with a five-year useful life and no salvage value. The machine was depreciated by an accelerated method for book and tax purposes. The machine's carrying amount was $240,000 on December 31 of last year. On January 1 of the current year, Warren changed retroactively to the straight-line method for financial statement purposes. Warren can justify the change. Warren's income tax rate is 30%.

93. In its current year income statement, what amount should Warren report as a prior period adjustment as a result of this change?

a. $120,000
b. $ 84,000
c. $ 36,000
d. $0 (5/93, PI, #53, amended, 4094)

94. On January 1 of the current year, what amount should Warren report as deferred income tax liability as a result of the change?

a. $120,000
b. $ 72,000
c. $ 36,000
d. $0 (5/93, PI, #54, amended, 4095)

95. When a company changes the expected service life of an asset because additional information has been obtained, which of the following should be reported?

	Pro forma effects of retroactive application	Cumulative effect of a change in accounting principle
a.	Yes	Yes
b.	No	Yes
c.	Yes	No
d.	No	No

(5/91, Theory, #27, 1901)

96. The cumulative effect of an accounting change on the amount of retained earnings at the beginning of the period in which the change is made should generally be included in net income for the period of the change for a

	Change in accounting principle	Change in accounting entity
a.	Yes	Yes
b.	Yes	No
c.	No	Yes
d.	No	No

(5/84, Theory, #32, 1959)

97. Frey Corp. failed to accrue warranty costs of $50,000 in its previous year December 31 financial statements. In addition, a change from straight-line to accelerated depreciation made at the beginning of the current year resulted in a cumulative effect of $30,000 on Frey's retained earnings. Both the $50,000 and the $30,000 are net of related income taxes. What amount should Frey report as a prior period adjustment in the current year?

a. $0
b. $30,000
c. $50,000
d. $80,000 (11/94, Theory, #55, amended, 5316)

98. On December 31 of the current year, Deal Inc. failed to accrue the December sales salaries that were payable on January 6 the following year. What is the effect of the failure to accrue sales salaries on working capital and cash flows from operating activities in Deal's current year financial statements?

	Working capital	Cash flows from operating activities
a.	Overstated	No effect
b.	Overstated	Overstated
c.	No effect	Overstated
d.	No effect	No effect

(11/92, Theory, #5, amended, 3438)

99. The correction of an error in the financial statements of a prior period should be reported

a. Net of applicable income taxes, in the current retained earnings statement after net income but before dividends
b. As a prior period adjustment by restating the prior-period financial statements
c. Net of applicable income taxes, in the current income statement after income from continuing operations and before extraordinary items
d. Net of applicable income taxes, in the current income statement after income from continuing operations and after extraordinary items

(11/93, Theory, #22, amended, 4527)

100. Which of the following information should be included in Melay Inc.'s summary of significant accounting policies?

a. Property, plant, and equipment is recorded at cost with depreciation computed principally by the straight-line method.
b. During the year, the Delay Segment was sold.
c. Operating segment sales for the year are Alay $1M, Belay $2M, and Celay $3M.
d. Future common share dividends are expected to approximate 60% of earnings.

(11/93, Theory, #19, amended, 4524)

101. Which of the following information should be disclosed in the summary of significant accounting policies?

a. Refinancing of debt subsequent to the balance sheet date
b. Guarantees of indebtedness of others
c. Criteria for determining which investments are treated as cash equivalents
d. Adequacy of pension plan assets relative to vested benefits (11/94, Theory, #59, 5319)

102. Which of the following related party transactions by a company should be disclosed in the notes to the financial statements?

I. Payment of per diem expenses to members of the board of directors
II. Consulting fees paid to a marketing research firm, one of whose partners is also a director of the company

a. I only
b. II only
c. Both I and II
d. Neither I nor II (11/96, FAR, #10, 6456)

103. A development stage enterprise should use the same generally accepted accounting principles that apply to established operating enterprises for

	Revenue recognition	*Deferral of expenses*
a.	Yes	Yes
b.	Yes	No
c.	No	No
d.	No	Yes

(11/95, FAR, #4, 6086)

104. Lex Corp. was a development stage enterprise from October 10, year 1 (inception), to December 31, year 2. The year ended December 31, year 3, is the first year in which Lex is an established operating enterprise. The following are among the costs incurred by Lex:

	For period 10/10 yr 1 to 12/31 yr 2	For year ended 12/31 yr 3
Leasehold improvements, equipment, and furniture	$1,000,000	$ 300,000
Security deposits	60,000	30,000
Research and development	750,000	900,000
Laboratory operations	175,000	550,000
General and administrative	225,000	685,000
Depreciation	25,000	115,000
	$2,235,000	$2,580,000

From its inception through the period ended December 31, year 3, what is the total amount of costs incurred by Lex that should be charged to operations?

a. $3,425,000
b. $2,250,000
c. $1,775,000
d. $1,350,000 (11/90, PI, #58, amended, 1131)

105. Lind Corp. was a development stage enterprise from its inception on October 10, year 1 to December 31, year 2. The following were among Lind's expenditures for this period:

Leasehold improvements, equipment, and furniture	$1,200,000
Research and development	850,000
Laboratory operations	175,000
General and administrative	275,000

The year ended December 31, year 3 was the first year in which Lind was an established operating enterprise. For the period ended December 31, year 2, what total amount of expenditures should Lind have capitalized?

a. $2,500,000
b. $2,225,000
c. $2,050,000
d. $1,200,000 (5/90, PII, #52, amended, 1139)

106. Compared to its current year cash basis net income, Potoma Co.'s current year accrual basis net income increased when it

a. Declared a cash dividend in the previous year that it paid in the current year
b. Wrote off more accounts receivable balances than it reported as uncollectible accounts expense in the current year
c. Had lower accrued expenses on December 31 than on January 1 of the current year
d. Sold used equipment for cash at a gain in the current year

(11/93, Theory, #40, amended, 4545)

107. Class Corp. maintains its accounting records on the cash basis but restates its financial statements to the accrual method of accounting. Class had $60,000 in cash basis pretax income for year 2. The following information pertains to Class's operations for the years ended December 31, year 2 and year 1:

	Year 2	Year 1
Accounts receivable	$40,000	$20,000
Accounts payable	15,000	30,000

Under the accrual method, what amount of income before taxes should Class report in its December 31, year 2 income statement?

a. $25,000
b. $55,000
c. $65,000
d. $95,000 (5/93, PI, #40, amended, 4081)

108. Clark Co.'s advertising expense account had a balance of $146,000 at December 31, year 1, before any necessary year-end adjustment relating to the following:

- Included in the $146,000 is the $15,000 cost of printing catalogs for a sales promotional campaign in January of year 2.
- Radio advertisements broadcast during December of year 1 were billed to Clark on January 2, year 2. Clark paid the $9,000 invoice on January 11, year 2.

What amount should Clark report as advertising expense in its income statement for the year ended December 31, year 1?

a. $122,000
b. $131,000
c. $140,000
d. $155,000 (11/94, Theory, #47, amended, 5308)

109. Able Co. provides an incentive compensation plan under which its president receives a bonus equal to 10% of the corporation's income before income tax but after deduction of the bonus. If the tax rate is 40% and net income after bonus and income tax was $360,000, what was the amount of the bonus?
a. $36,000
b. $60,000
c. $66,000
d. $90,000 (11/94, Theory, #48, 5309)

110. Income tax-basis financial statements differ from those prepared under GAAP in that income tax-basis financial statements
a. Do **not** include nontaxable revenues and non-deductible expenses in determining income.
b. Include detailed information about current and deferred income tax liabilities.
c. Contain **no** disclosures about capital and operating lease transactions.
d. Recognize certain revenues and expenses in different reporting periods. (R/99, FAR, #2, 6771)

111. The following information pertains to Eagle Co.'s sales for the year:

Cash sales	
Gross	$ 80,000
Returns and allowance	4,000
Credit sales	
Gross	120,000
Discounts	6,000

On January 1, customers owed Eagle $40,000. On December 31, customers owed Eagle $30,000. Eagle uses the direct write-off method for bad debts. No bad debts were recorded in the year. Under the cash basis of accounting, what amount of net revenue should Eagle report for the year?
a. $ 76,000
b. $170,000
c. $190,000
d. $200,000 (11/94, Theory, #58, amended, 5318)

112. During the first quarter of the current year, Tech Co. had income before taxes of $200,000, and its effective income tax rate was 15%. Tech's previous year effective annual income tax rate was 30%, but Tech expects its current year effective annual income tax rate to be 25%. In its first quarter interim income statement, what amount of income tax expense should Tech report?
a. $0
b. $30,000
c. $50,000
d. $60,000 (5/93, PII, #17, amended, 4125)

113. Due to a decline in market price in the second quarter, Petal Co. incurred an inventory loss. The market price is expected to return to previous levels by the end of the year. At the end of the year the decline had not reversed. When should the loss be reported in Petal's interim income statements?
a. Ratably over the second, third, and fourth quarters
b. Ratably over the third and fourth quarters
c. In the second quarter only
d. In the fourth quarter only
(5/93, Theory, #21, 9008)

114. An inventory loss from a permanent market decline of $360,000 occurred in May. Cox Co. appropriately recorded this loss in May after its March 31 quarterly report was issued. What amount of inventory loss should be reported in Cox's quarterly income statement for the three months ended June 30?
a. $0
b. $ 90,000
c. $180,000
d. $360,000 (5/90, PII, #43, amended, 1134)

115. For external reporting purposes, it is appropriate to use estimated gross profit rates to determine the cost of goods sold for

	Interim financial reporting	*Year-end financial reporting*
a.	Yes	Yes
b.	Yes	No
c.	No	Yes
d.	No	No

(11/83, Theory, #35, 1961)

116. Correy Corp. and its divisions are engaged solely in manufacturing operations. The following data (consistent with prior years' data) pertain to Correy's operating segments for the current year ended December 31:

Operating Segment	Total revenue	Operating profit	Identifiable assets at 12/31
A	$10,000,000	$1,750,000	$20,000,000
B	8,000,000	1,400,000	17,500,000
C	6,000,000	1,200,000	12,500,000
D	3,000,000	550,000	7,500,000
E	4,250,000	675,000	7,000,000
F	1,500,000	225,000	3,000,000
	$32,750,000	$5,800,000	$67,500,000

In its segment information for the current year, how many reportable segments does Correy have?
a. Three
b. Four
c. Five
d. Six (5/90, PII, #56, amended, 1141)

SIMULATIONS

Problem 11-3 (15 to 20 minutes)

Research Task	Scenario	Additional Information & Responses

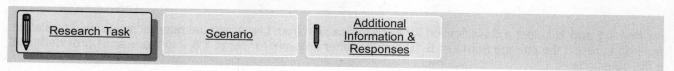

Research Question: What is the basic principle for the type of basis that should be used when accounting, in general, for nonmonetary transactions?

Paragraph Reference Answer: ________________

Research Task	Scenario	Additional Information & Responses

On January 2 of the current year, Falk Co. hired a new controller. During the year, the controller, working closely with Falk's president and outside accountants, made changes in existing accounting policies, instituted new accounting policies, and corrected several errors dating from prior to the current year.

Falk's financial statements for the current year ended December 31 will not be presented in comparative form with its previous year financial statements.

Items 1 through 4 represent Falk's transactions. Select the best answer for each item.

List A represents possible classifications of these transactions as a change in accounting principle, a change in accounting estimate, correction of an error in previously presented financial statements, or neither an accounting change nor an error correction.

List B represents the general accounting treatment required for these transactions. These treatments are:

- Cumulative effect approach—Include the cumulative effect of the adjustment resulting from the accounting change or error correction in the current year financial statements.
- Retroactive restatement approach—Adjust current year beginning retained earnings if the error or change affects a period prior to the current year.
- Prospective approach—Report current year and future financial statements on the new basis, but do not adjust beginning retained earnings or include the cumulative effect of the change in the current year income statements.

List A—Type of Change		List B—General Accounting Treatment	
A	Change in accounting principle.	X	Adjust beginning balance of retained earnings.
B	Change in accounting estimate.	Y	Retrospective restatement approach.
C	Correction of an error in previously presented financial statements.	Z	Prospective approach.
D	Neither an accounting change nor an error correction.		

(11/97, FAR, #2, amended, 6492-6501)

Research Task | Scenario | Additional Information & Responses

For **Items 1 and 2,** select a classification for each transaction from List A and the general accounting treatment required to report the change from List B. Place the letter answers for items 1 & 2 in the spaces provided next to the questions.

1. _____ _____ Falk manufactures customized equipment to customer specifications on a contract basis. Falk changed its method of accounting for these long-term contracts from the completed contract method to the percentage of completion method because Falk is now able to make reasonable estimates of future construction costs.

2. _____ _____ Based on improved collection procedures, Falk changed the percentage of credit sales used to determine the allowance for uncollectible accounts from 2% to 1%.

For **Items 3 and 4,** in addition to selecting a classification for each transaction from List A **and** the general accounting treatment required to report the change from List B, a third response is required. For these items, determine the amount, if any, of the cumulative change or prior period adjustment, ignoring income tax effects. Place the letter and numerical answers for items 3 & 4 in the spaces provided next to the questions.

3. _____ _____ $____ Effective January 1 of the current year, Falk changed from average cost to FIFO to account for its inventory. Cost of goods sold under each method was as follows:

Year	Average cost	FIFO
Years prior to last year	71,000	$77,000
Last year	9,000	82,000

4. _____ _____ $____ In January of the previous year, Falk purchased a machine with a five-year life and no salvage value for $40,000. The machine was depreciated using the straight-line method. On December 30 of the current year, Falk discovered that depreciation on the machine had been calculated using a 25% rate.

Problem 11-4 (15 to 25 minutes)

Research Task | Scenario | Information & Responses 1-4 | Information & Responses 5-6

Research Question: What is the criteria for extraordinary items?

Paragraph Reference Answer: _______________

Research Task | Scenario | Information & Responses 1-4 | Information & Responses 5-6

Hake Co. is in the process of preparing its financial statements for the year ended December 31, year 4.

Items 1 through 6 represent various transactions that occurred during year 4. The following **two** responses are required for each item:

- Compute the amount of gain, loss, or adjustment to be reported in Hake's year 4 financial statements. Disregard income taxes.
- Select from the list below the financial statement category in which the gain, loss, or adjustment should be presented. A category may be used once, more than once, or not at all.

Financial Statement Categories

A. Income from continuing operations
B. Extraordinary item
C. Prior period adjustment to beginning retained earnings
D. Other comprehensive income

(5/95, FAR, #3, amended, 5607)

Research Task | Scenario | Information & Responses 1-4 | Information & Responses 5-6

1. $_____ ____ On June 30, year 4, after paying the semiannual interest due and recording amortization of bond discount, Hake redeemed its 15-year, 8%, $1,000,000 par bonds at 102. The bonds, which had a carrying amount of $940,000 on January 1, year 4, had originally been issued to yield 10%. Hake uses the effective interest method of amortization, and had paid interest and recorded amortization on June 30. Compute the amount of gain or loss on redemption of the bonds and select the proper financial statement category.

2. $_____ ____ As of January 1, year 4, Hake decided to change the method of computing depreciation on its sole piece of equipment from the sum-of-the-years'-digits method to the straight-line method. The equipment, acquired in January of year 1 for $520,000, had an estimated life of five years and a salvage value of $20,000. Compute the amount of the accounting change and select the proper financial statement category.

3. $_____ ____ In October of year 4, Hake paid $375,000 to a former employee to settle a lawsuit out of court. The lawsuit had been filed in year 3, and at December 31, year 3, Hake had recorded a liability from lawsuit based on legal counsel's estimate that the loss from the lawsuit would be between $250,000 and $750,000. Compute the amount of gain or loss from settlement of the lawsuit and select the proper financial statement category.

4. $_____ ____ In November of year 4, Hake purchased two marketable equity securities, I and II, which it bought and held principally to sell in the near term, and in fact sold on February 28, year 5. Relevant data is as follows:

		Fair Value	
	Cost	12/31, yr 4	2/28, yr 5
I.	$125,000	$145,000	$155,000
II.	235,000	205,000	230,000

Compute the amount of holding gain or loss at December 31, year 4, and select the proper financial statement category.

Research Task	Scenario	Information & Responses 1-4	Information & Responses 5-6

5. $_____ ____ During year 4, Hake received $1,000,000 from its insurance company to cover losses suffered during a hurricane. This was the first hurricane ever to strike in Hake's area. The hurricane destroyed a warehouse with a carrying amount of $470,000, containing equipment with a carrying amount of $250,000 and inventory with a carrying amount of $535,000 and a fair value of $600,000. Compute the amount of gain or loss from the hurricane and select the proper financial statement category.

6. $_____ ____ At December 31, year 4, Hake prepared the following worksheet summarizing the translation of its wholly owned foreign subsidiary's financial statements into dollars. Hake had purchased the foreign subsidiary for $324,000 on January 2, year 4. On that date, the carrying amounts of the subsidiary's assets and liabilities equaled their fair values. Compute the amount of the foreign currency translation adjustment and select the proper financial statement category.

	Foreign currency amounts	Applicable exchange rates	Dollars
Net assets at			
January 2, year 4 (date of purchase)	720,000	$0.45	$324,000
Net income, year 4	250,000	0.42	105,000
Net assets at December 31, year 4	970,000		$429,000
Net assets at December 31, year 4	970,000	0.40	$388,000

Problem 11-5 (15 to 25 minutes)

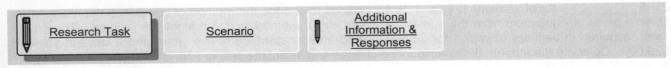

Research Task	Scenario	Additional Information & Responses

Research Question: What is the basic principle for the type of basis that should be used when accounting, in general, for nonmonetary transactions?

Paragraph Reference Answer: ______________

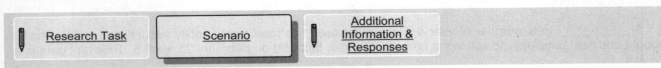

Research Task	Scenario	Additional Information & Responses

On January 2 of the current year, Quo Inc., hired Reed to be its controller. During the year, Reed, working closely with Quo's president and outside accountants, made changes in accounting policies, corrected several errors dating from the previous year and before, and instituted new accounting policies. Quo's current year financial statements will be presented in comparative form with its previous year financial statements.

Items 1 through 10 represent Quo's transactions.

List A represents possible classifications of these transactions as: a change in accounting principle, a change in accounting estimate, a correction of an error in previously presented financial statements, or neither an accounting change nor an accounting error.

List B represents the general accounting treatment required for these transactions. These treatments are:

- Cumulative effect approach—Include the cumulative effect of the adjustment resulting from the accounting change or error correction in the current year financial statements, and do **not** restate the previous year financial statements.
- Retrospective restatement approach—Restate the previous year financial statements and adjust previous year beginning retained earnings if the error or change affects a period prior to the previous year.
- Prospective approach—Report current year and future financial statements on the new basis, but do **not** restate previous year financial statements.

List A—Type of Change		List B—General Accounting Treatment	
A	Change in accounting principle.	X	Adjust beginning balance of retained earnings.
B	Change in accounting estimate.	Y	Retrospective restatement approach.
C	Correction of an error in previously presented financial statements.	Z	Prospective approach.
D	Neither an accounting change nor an error correction.		

Place the letter responses for each question in the spaces provided in front of the questions.
(11/96, FAR, #2, amended, 6492)

Research Task | Scenario | Additional Information & Responses

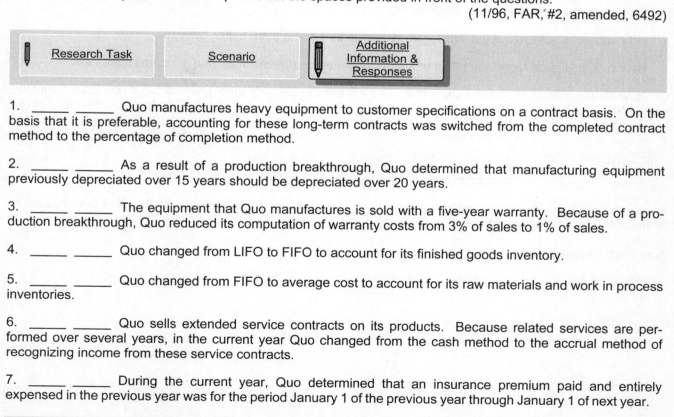

1. _____ _____ Quo manufactures heavy equipment to customer specifications on a contract basis. On the basis that it is preferable, accounting for these long-term contracts was switched from the completed contract method to the percentage of completion method.

2. _____ _____ As a result of a production breakthrough, Quo determined that manufacturing equipment previously depreciated over 15 years should be depreciated over 20 years.

3. _____ _____ The equipment that Quo manufactures is sold with a five-year warranty. Because of a production breakthrough, Quo reduced its computation of warranty costs from 3% of sales to 1% of sales.

4. _____ _____ Quo changed from LIFO to FIFO to account for its finished goods inventory.

5. _____ _____ Quo changed from FIFO to average cost to account for its raw materials and work in process inventories.

6. _____ _____ Quo sells extended service contracts on its products. Because related services are performed over several years, in the current year Quo changed from the cash method to the accrual method of recognizing income from these service contracts.

7. _____ _____ During the current year, Quo determined that an insurance premium paid and entirely expensed in the previous year was for the period January 1 of the previous year through January 1 of next year.

8. _____ _____ Quo changed its method of depreciating office equipment from an accelerated method to the straight-line method to more closely reflect costs in later years.

9. _____ _____ Quo instituted a pension plan for all employees in the current year and adopted Statement of Financial Accounting Standards No. 87, Employers' Accounting for Pensions. Quo had not previously had a pension plan.

10. _____ _____ During the current year, Quo increased its investment in Worth Inc. from a 10% interest, purchased in the previous year, to 30%, and acquired a seat on Worth's board of directors. As a result of its increased investment, Quo changed its method of accounting for investment in subsidiary from the cost method to the equity method.

Problem 11-6 (15 to 25 minutes)

Essay Information | Research Task

Hillside Company had a loss during the year ended December 31, year 1, that is properly reported as an extraordinary item.

On July 1, year 1, Hillside committed itself to a formal plan for sale of a business component. A loss is expected from the proposed sale. Segment operating losses were incurred continuously throughout year 1, and were expected to continue until final disposition in year 2. Costs were incurred in year 2 to relocate component employees.

Do not discuss earnings per share requirements.

a. How should Hillside report the extraordinary item in its income statement? Why?

b. How should Hillside report the effect of the discontinued operations in its year 1 income statement?

c. How should Hillside report the costs that were incurred to relocate employees of the discontinued component? Why?

(11/89, Theory, #5, amended, 3615)

Essay Information | Research Task

Research Question: When accounting for the impairment or disposal of long-lived assets, what term has been replaced by discontinued component?

Paragraph Reference Answer: ________________

Problem 11-7 (10 to 15 minutes)

Essay Information | Research Task

Barnet Co. is determining reporting of segments for operations. The company has separate financial information for several components of its operations and uses the information in various forms for decision making purposes. The components of operations are at sales and profitability levels ranging from 1%-35%.

a. What is the purpose of segment disclosures?

b. How should Barnet decide what segments to report?

(Editors, 9911)

Essay Information | Research Task

Research Question: How shall an entity measure changes in the liability for an asset retirement obligation due to passage of time?

Paragraph Reference Answer: ________________

Problem 11-8 (30 to 40 minutes)

Research Task | Scenario | Additional Information | Income Statement

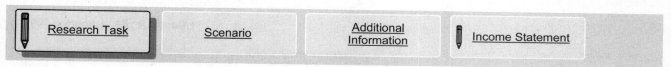

Research Question: What criteria should be met to classify an event or transaction as an extraordinary item?

Paragraph Reference Answer: ________________

Research Task | Scenario | Additional Information | Income Statement

The following condensed trial balance of Probe Co., a publicly held company, has been adjusted except for income tax expense.

→

Probe Co.
Condensed Trial Balance

	12/31 Yr 3 Balances Dr. (Cr.)	12/31 Yr 2 Balances Dr. (Cr.)	Net change Dr. (Cr.)
Cash	$ 473,000	$ 817,000	$(344,000)
Accounts receivable, net	670,000	610,000	60,000
Property, plant, and equipment	1,070,000	995,000	75,000
Accumulated depreciation	(345,000)	(280,000)	(65,000)
Dividends payable	(25,000)	(10,000)	(15,000)
Income taxes payable	35,000	(150,000)	185,000
Deferred income tax liability	(42,000)	(42,000)	--
Bonds Payable	(500,000)	(1,000,000)	500,000
Unamortized premium on bonds	(71,000)	(150,000)	79,000
Common stock	(350,000)	(150,000)	(200,000)
Additional paid-in capital	(430,000)	(375,000)	(55,000)
Retained earnings	(185,000)	(265,000)	80,000
Sales	(2,420,000)		
Cost of sales	1,863,000		
Selling and administrative expenses	220,000		
Interest income	(14,000)		
Interest expense	46,000		
Depreciation	88,000		
Loss on sale of equipment	7,000		
Gain on flood damage	(90,000)		
	$ 0	$ 0	$ 300,000

(11/94, FAR, #4, amended, 9911)

Research Task | Scenario | Additional Information | Income Statement

Additional information:

- During year 3, equipment with an original cost of $50,000 was sold for cash and equipment costing $125,000 was purchased.
- Insurance reimbursements exceeded the carrying amount of a warehouse and its contents destroyed in a year 3 flood. The flood was the first recorded flood at the warehouse's location.
- Probe's tax payments during year 3 were debited to *Income Taxes Payable*. For the year ended December 31, year 2, Probe recorded a deferred income tax liability of $42,000 based on temporary differences of $120,000 and an enacted tax rate of 35%. Probe's year 3 financial statement income before income taxes was greater than its year 3 taxable income, due entirely to temporary differences, by $60,000. Probe's cumulative net taxable temporary differences at December 31, year 3, were $180,000. Probe's enacted tax rate for the current and future years is 30%.
- 60,000 shares of common stock, $2.50 par, were outstanding on December 31, year 2. Probe issued an additional 80,000 shares on April 1, year 3.
- There were no changes to retained earnings other than dividends declared.

Prepare Probe Co.'s multiple-step income statement for the year ended December 31, year 3, with earnings per share information and supporting computations for current and deferred income tax expense.

Research Task | Scenario | Additional Information | Income Statement

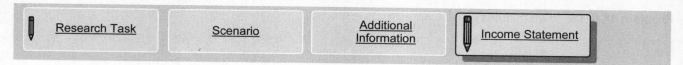

Probe Co.
Income Statement
For the Year Ended December 31, Year 3

Sales		
Cost of sales		
Gross profit		
Selling and administrative expenses		
Depreciation		
Operating income		
Other income (expenses):		
Interest income		
Interest expense		
Loss on sale of equipment		
Income before income tax and extraordinary item		
Income tax:		
Current		
Deferred		
Income before extraordinary item		
Extraordinary item:		
Gain on flood damage, net of income taxes of $27,000		
Net income		
Earnings per share:		
Earnings before extraordinary item		
Extraordinary item		
Net income		

Problem 11-9 (30 to 40 minutes)

Research Task	Scenario	Additional Information	Choices

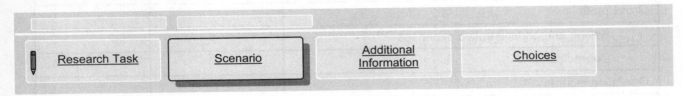

Research Question: When shall a reporting entity change an accounting principle?

Paragraph Reference Answer: ______________

Research Task	Scenario	Additional Information	Choices

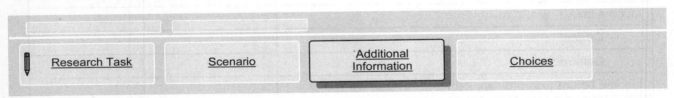

The following information pertains to Baron Flowers, a calendar-year sole proprietorship, which maintained its books on the cash basis during the year.

Baron has developed plans to expand into the wholesale flower market and is in the process of negotiating a bank loan to finance the expansion. The bank is requesting year 4 financial statements prepared on the accrual basis of accounting from Baron. During the course of a review engagement, Muir, Baron's accountant, obtained additional information. (11/95, FAR, #4, amended, 9911)

Research Task	Scenario	Additional Information	Choices

1. Amounts due from customers totaled $32,000 at December 31, year 4.
2. An analysis of the receivables in item 1 revealed that an allowance for uncollectible accounts of $3,800 should be provided.
3. Unpaid invoices for flower purchases totaled $30,500 and $17,000, at December 31, year 4, and December 31, year 3, respectively.
4. The inventory totaled $72,800 based on a physical count of the goods at December 31. The inventory was priced at cost, which approximates market value.
5. On May 1, year 4, Baron paid $8,700 to renew its comprehensive insurance coverage for one year. The premium on the previous policy, which expires on April 30, year 4, was $7,800.
6. On January 2, year 4, Baron entered into a 25-year operating lease for the vacant lot adjacent to Baron's retail store for use as a parking lot. As agreed in the lease, Baron paved and fenced in the lot at a cost of $45,000. The improvements were completed on April 1, year 4, and have an estimated useful life of fifteen years. No provision for depreciation or amortization has been recorded. Depreciation on furniture and fixtures was $12,000 for year 4.

→

7. Accrued expenses at December 31, year 3 and year 4, were as follows:

	Year 3	Year 4
Utilities	$ 900	$1,500
Payroll taxes	1,100	1,600
	$2,000	$3,100

8. Baron is being sued for $400,000. Coverage under the comprehensive insurance policy is limited to $250,000. Baron's attorney believes that an unfavorable outcome is probable and that a reasonable settlement estimate is $300,000.

9. The salaries account includes $4,000 per month paid to the proprietor. Baron also receives $250 per week for living expenses.

Please use the item numbers above to reference your answers in the spread sheet.

Research Task | Scenario | Additional Information | Choices

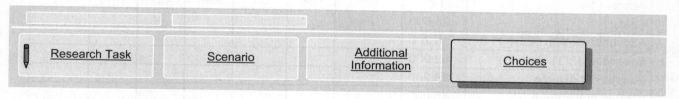

Reference (Ref) Choices			Amount Choices		
			300	12,000	50,000
			500	12,400	61,000
1	4	7	600	12,600	62,000
2	5	8	1,100	13,000	72,800
3	6	9	2,000	13,500	83,600
			2,600	14,250	118,200
			3,100	15,800	124,600
			2,900	16,200	174,000
			3,800	17,000	300,000
			8,700	45,000	305,100
			10,800	48,000	653,000

Title Choices for Additional Accounts		
Accrued expenses	Estimated liability from lawsuit	Lawsuit expenses
Allowance for uncollectible accounts	Estimated loss from lawsuit	Prepaid insurance
Bad debt expenses	Income summary—inventory	Unpaid expenses
Depreciation & amortization	Inventory adjustments	Uncollectible accounts

Any choice may be used once, more than once, or not at all.

Worksheet | Memo

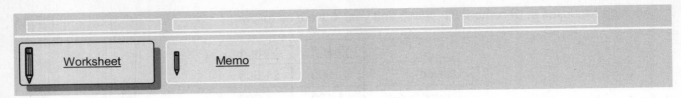

Using this worksheet, prepare the adjustments necessary to convert the trial balance of Baron Flowers to the accrual basis of accounting for the year ended December 31, year 4. Formal journal entries are not required to support your adjustments. The numbers given in the additional information (choices) section are to be placed in the Ref columns to cross-reference the postings placed in the adjustment columns.

Baron Flowers
Worksheet to Convert Trial Balance to Accrual Basis
December 31, Year 4

	Cash basis		Adjustments				Accrual Basis*	
Account title	Dr.	Cr.	Ref.	Dr.	Ref.	Cr.	Dr.*	Cr.*
Cash	25,600							
Accounts rec'ble, 12/31 Yr 3	16,200							
Inventory, 12/31 Yr 3	62,000							
Furniture & fixtures	118,200							
Land improvements	45,000							
Accumulated depreciation & amortization, 12/31 Yr 3		32,400						
Accounts payable, 12/31 Yr 3		17,000						
Baron, Drawings								
Baron, Capital, 12/31 Yr 3		124,600						
Saies		653,000						
Purchases	305,100							
Salaries	174,000							
Payroll taxes	12,400							
Insurance	8,700							
Rent	34,200							
Utilities	12,600							
Living expenses	13,000							
	827,000	827,000						

*Completion of these columns is not required but may be useful in checking your work.

(Duplicate worksheet provided at end of chapter.)

Worksheet | Memo

Write a brief memo to Baron explaining why the bank would require financial statements prepared on the accrual basis instead of the cash basis.

Solution 11-1 MULTIPLE CHOICE ANSWERS

Income Statement Format

1. (a) Freight out is classified as an operating expense, not as part of cost of goods sold.

Inventory, December 31	$ 360,000
Cost of sales	240,000
Goods available for sale	600,000
Less: Inventory, January 1	(400,000)
Cost of goods manufactured	$ 200,000

2. (a)

Sales		$ 575,000
Interest revenue		25,000
Cost of sales	$240,000	
Administrative expenses	70,000	
Sales commissions	50,000	
Interest revenue		25,000
Freight out	15,000	
Uncollectible accounts expense	15,000	
Loss on sale of equipment	10,000	
Loss on early retirement of debt	20,000	(420,000)
Income from continuing operations before taxes		180,000
Income taxes		(54,000)
Income from continuing op.		$ 126,000

3. (d) Neither expense should be included in general and administrative expenses. The advertising expense is a selling expense because it results from the company's efforts to make sales. The interest expense is a nonoperating expense because it results from secondary or auxiliary activities of the company.

Continuing Operations

4. (d) The results from discontinued operations and the cumulative effect of the change in depreciation method cannot be included in the revenues section of the single-step income statement. The change in depreciation method is reported as a separate component of income from continuing operations. The results from discontinued operations is reported separately below income from continuing operations.

Net sales revenue	$187,000
Interest revenue	10,200
Gain on sale of equipment	4,700
Total revenues reported in income from continuing operations	$201,900

5. (d) A transaction that is unusual in nature or infrequent in occurrence, but not both, is reported as a component of income from continuing operations (APB 30). A transaction must be *both* unusual in nature and infrequent in occurrence to be classified as an extraordinary item.

6. (b) Revenues are only considered earned when the entity has accomplished substantially what it must do to be entitled to the revenues (SFAC 5, ¶83). Although Acme has sold 100,000 gallons of heating oil to Karn during year 1, Acme has only delivered 50,000 of these gallons to Karn during year 1. Therefore, Acme should only recognize revenue of $150,000 (i.e., 50,000 gallons × $3) during year 1 from this sale.

7. (b) Freight-out is not included as part of cost of goods sold.

Beginning inventory		$ 30,840
Purchases	$102,800	
Purchase discount	(10,280)	
Freight-in	15,420	107,940
Available for sale		138,780
Ending inventory		(20,560)
Cost of goods sold		$118,220

8. (c) Because the amount of the write-off of obsolete inventory is material, it should be reported separately from cost of goods sold in income from continuing operations.

Inventory, 12/31 previous year		$ 90,000
Add: Purchases		124,000
Goods available for sale		214,000
Less: Inventory, 12/31 current year	$30,000	
Write-off of obsolete inventory	34,000	(64,000)
Cost of goods sold, current year		$150,000

Discontinued Operations

9. (b) SFAS 144, ¶43 states, "The income statement of a business enterprise for current and prior periods shall report the results of operations of the component...in discontinued operations...in the period(s) in which they occur." The impairment loss should be recognized in the period in which a sale at a loss is arranged; such a sale is evidence that the asset is impaired.

10. (d) SFAS 144, ¶43 states, "In the period in which a component of an entity either has been disposed of or is classified as held for sale, the income statement of a business enterprise for current and prior periods shall report the results of operations of the component...in discontinued operations...in the periods(s) in which they occur." SFAS 144, ¶44 lists amounts reported in discontinued operations, including, "the resolution of contingencies that arise from ...product warranty obligations...the settlement of employee benefit plan obligations (pension...and other post-employment benefits) provided that the settlement is directly related to the disposal transaction."

11. (a) Also see explanation #9.

Alpha's current year operating loss (before consideration of impairment)	$1,400,000
Impairment loss (recognized in current year)	300,000
Loss on discontinued operation, before taxes	1,700,000
Applicable income tax benefit ($1,700,000 × 0.30)	(510,000)
Loss on discontinued operation, net of taxes	$1,190,000

12. (a) Also see explanation #9.

Alpha's following year operating loss	$ 500,000
Applicable income tax benefit ($500,000 × 30%)	(150,000)
Loss on disposal, net of income tax	$ 350,000

13. (b) SFAS 144, ¶43 states, "In the period in which a component of an entity either has been disposed of or is classified as held for sale, the income statement of a business enterprise for current and prior periods shall report the results of operations of the component...in discontinued operations...in the periods(s) in which they occur."

Gain from sale of division assets on Feb 26	$ 90,000
Less: Operating loss during the fiscal year	(50,000)
Gain on discontinued operations, before tax	$ 40,000

Extraordinary Items

14. (c) FASB Interpretation 30 provides that a gain or loss on the involuntary conversion (e.g., casualty, condemnation, theft) of a nonmonetary asset is recognized in income even if the proceeds received as a result of the involuntary conversion are reinvested in a replacement nonmonetary asset. The warehouse was destroyed in a severe winter storm, which occur approximately every four years. Since the occurrence of such storms is not infrequent, the gain on the involuntary conversion is reported as a separate component of income from continuing operations.

Insurance proceeds ($1,100,000 – $50,000)		$1,050,000
Carrying amount at conversion date	$300,000	
Add: Dismantling cost	20,000	
Amount to determine gain		(320,000)
Gain recognized on involuntary conversion		$ 730,000

15. (b) To be classified as an extraordinary item, APB 30 requires that an event must be both unusual in nature and infrequent in occurrence, taking into account the environment in which the entity operates. The loss due to hailstorms is stated to occur frequently; therefore it should be reported in income from continuing operations. The full amount of a realized loss must be recognized in income when it occurs.

16. (b) SFAS 145 requires that an early extinguishment of debt meet the same criteria as other events to be deemed extraordinary. There is no indication that this event is extraordinary for Gold. (SFAS 145 supersedes SFAS 4. SFAS 4 deemed material aggregate gains and losses from debt extinguishment to be extraordinary items.) Gains or losses from the sale of long-term investments are reported as income from continuing operations.

17. (a) APB 30, ¶23, provides that (1) gains or losses from the sale of property, plant, or equipment used in the business; (2) gains or losses from exchange or translation of foreign currencies, including those relating to major devaluations and revaluations; and (3) the write-down or write-off of receivables, inventories, and intangible assets

should not be reported as extraordinary items. Thus, the amount of loss not considered extraordinary is $610,000 (i.e., $300,000 + $120,000 + $190,000).

18. (a) Generally, for an event to be classified as extraordinary, it must be both unusual in nature and infrequent of occurrence. As Raim sustains flood losses every two to three years, neither of these conditions is met. For Cane, the flood loss is both unusual and infrequent.

Comprehensive Income

19. (d) Comprehensive income and all items that are required to be recognized as components of comprehensive income should be reported in a financial statement that is displayed with the same prominence as other financial statements (SFAS 130). Discontinued operations, extraordinary items, and the cumulative effect of a change in accounting principle (other than the changes that require retroactive treatment) are components of the income statement, reported after income from continuing operations and before net income. If comprehensive income is reported in the same statement as net income, other comprehensive income (OCI) and comprehensive income are reported after net income. An entity may display components of OCI in either net-of-tax basis or summary net-of-tax basis. Comprehensive income must be shown on the face of one of the statements, not just in the notes to the financial statements.

20. (c) Comprehensive income includes all changes in equity during a period except those resulting from investments by owners and distributions to owners.

21. (c) Comprehensive income includes all changes in equity during a period except those resulting from investments by owners and distributions to owners. SFAS 130 divides comprehensive income into net income and other comprehensive income. An entity must classify items of other comprehensive income by their nature, in one of these classifications: foreign currency items, minimum pension liability adjustments, unrealized gains and losses on certain investments in debt and equity securities, and gains and losses on cash flow hedging derivative instruments. All regular items of income and expense, including unusual and infrequently occurring items, are included in the determination of net income. Extraordinary gain is already included in the net income amount that is given in this problem.

Translation adjustments and unrealized holding gains and losses are reported in other comprehensive income (OCI). They are excluded from current earnings and should **not** be included in the determination of net income.

22. (a) Under SFAC 5, unrealized loss on investments in available-for-sale marketable equity securities is a component of comprehensive income but is *not* a component of earnings. Unrealized loss on investment in trading securities, loss on exchange of similar assets, and loss on exchange of dissimilar assets are all items that are included in earnings (and therefore are *also* components of comprehensive income).

23. (c) An entity may choose from several possible formats to report comprehensive income. The income statement and the statement of comprehensive income are separate statements in the two-statement format. Comprehensive income may be reported on the statement of changes in equity. Comprehensive income must be displayed prominently within a financial statement in a full set of general-purpose financial statements. Comprehensive income must be shown on the face of one of the statements, not just in the notes to the financial statements.

24. (c) Errors in financial statements result from mathematical mistakes, mistakes in the application of accounting principles, or the oversight or misuse of facts that existed at the time the financial statements were prepared. Errors that occur in one accounting period and are discovered in a subsequent accounting period are more involved: the cumulative effect of each error on periods prior to the period of discovery is calculated and recorded as a direct adjustment to the beginning balance of retained earnings. Errors that occur and are discovered in the same accounting period may be corrected by reversing the incorrect entry and recording the correct one or by directly correcting the account balances with a single entry. Foreign currency gains and losses and available for sale securities are reported in other comprehensive income.

Changes in Principle

25. (a) A change from LIFO to another inventory method is a change in accounting principle that should be reported by retrospectively applying the new method to prior periods and adjusting the beginning balance of *retained earnings*. The cumulative effect of the accounting change is not reported in the income statement.

26. (c) A change from the FIFO method of inventory valuation to the weighted-average method is a change in accounting principle. The cumulative effect of the change in accounting principle is the

difference between the amount of retained earnings at the beginning of the period of change and the amount of retained earnings that would have been reported at that date if the new accounting principle had been applied retrospectively for all affected periods. Since the new (weighted-average) method results in a $6,000 higher inventory valuation than the old (FIFO) method at the beginning of the period of change, the amount of expense recognized as cost of goods sold in prior periods is reduced by $6,000. This has the effect of increasing the beginning balance of retained earnings. The beginning balance of retained earnings is not increased by the full $6,000, because the reduction in cost of goods sold would have increased the amount of income tax expense by $1,800 (i.e., $6,000 × 30%).

27. (a) A change in inventory valuation method is a change in accounting principle, and the cumulative effect of the change in accounting principle should be reported as an adjustment to the beginning balance of retained earnings in the period of change.

28. (d) SFAS 154 requires a change in accounting estimate affected by a change in accounting principle to be accounted for as a change in estimate. A change in accounting estimate shall be accounted for in (a) the period of change if the change affects that period only or (b) the period of change and future periods if the change affects both. A change in accounting estimate shall not be accounted for by restating or retrospectively adjusting amounts reported in financial statements of prior periods or by reporting pro forma amounts for prior periods. Because the change was made, the total of both the $300,000 and $200,000 would be recorded.

29. (d) Both the individual item approach and the aggregate approach are generally accepted methods of applying the lower-of-cost-or-market to inventory items. When an entity changes from one generally accepted method to another acceptable method, it has a change in accounting principle. In the period of change, the cumulative effect of the change on prior periods is adjusted to the beginning balance of retained earnings, and is not treated as a correction of an error.

30. (c) This type of change in accounting principle is accounted for as an adjustment to the beginning balance of retained earnings, net of its income tax effect.

Income under percentage of completion method	$ 880,000
Income under completed contract method	(700,000)
Increase in income under percentage of completion	180,000
Less: Income tax effect ($180,000 × 40%)	(72,000)
Credit to 1/1 current year retained earnings	$ 108,000

Changes in Estimates

31. (a) When a change in accounting estimate and a change in accounting principle are inseparable, the change should be accounted for as a change in estimate, which is a component of income from continuing operations. A change in estimate does not require the restatement of prior period financial statements. Corrections of errors are reported as prior-period adjustments and prior-period financial statements are restated. Material effects of a change in estimate on income before extraordinary items, net income, and related per share amounts should be disclosed. Footnote disclosure only is not proper accounting treatment of a change in estimate.

32. (c) SFAS 154 requires a change in depreciation method to be accounted for as a change in estimate. A change in accounting estimate shall be accounted for in (a) the period of change if the change affects that period only or (b) the period of change and future periods if the change affects both. A change in accounting estimate shall not be accounted for by restating or retrospectively adjusting amounts reported in financial statements of prior periods or by reporting pro forma amounts for prior periods.

33. (a) Per SFAS 154, a change in estimated warranty costs is an example of a change in accounting estimate. The effect of a change in accounting estimate should be accounted for as a component of income from continuing operations entirely in the period of change if it affects that period only. Therefore, the effect of the additional $10 of estimated warranty costs for the previous and current years should be reported in current year income from continuing operations since the change in accounting estimate affected only the current year.

34. (d) SFAS 154, ¶19 states, "A change in accounting estimate should be accounted for in (a) the period of change if the change affects that period only, or (b) the period of change and future periods if the change affects both. A change in accounting estimate should not be accounted for by restating or retrospectively adjusting amounts reported in financial statements of prior periods or by reporting pro forma amounts for prior periods."

35. (d) The change in the estimated useful life of the machine is a change in accounting estimate. SFAS 154 requires that the effect of the change in accounting estimate be accounted for prospectively in the period of change and future periods, because both are affected.

Accumulated depreciation, 1/1 year 4 [($264,000 – $0) / 8] × 3 years		$ 99,000
Cost of machine	$264,000	
Accumulated depreciation, 1/1 year 4	(99,000)	
Carrying amount of machine, 1/1 year 4	165,000	
Less: Estimated salvage value	(24,000)	
Depreciable base of machine, 1/1 year 4	141,000	
Divide by: Estimated remaining useful life (6 – 3)	/ 3	
Depreciation for year 4		47,000
Accumulated depreciation, 12/31 year 4		$146,000

Changes in Reporting Entity

36. (d) Since the subsidiary was excluded from previous consolidations, its inclusion in the current year's consolidated financial statements results in a change in accounting principle in which the financial statements, in effect, are those of a different reporting entity. The change in the reporting entity should be reported by retrospective application to the financial statements of all prior periods presented to reflect the new reporting entity. (SFAS 154, ¶23 and B27).

37. (d) An accounting change that results in a change of entity should be reported by retrospective application to the financial statements of all prior periods presented to show the financial information for the new reporting entity for all periods.

Error Correction

38. (a) The change from the cash basis of accounting (not GAAP) to the accrual basis of accounting (GAAP) is a correction of an error. The correction of an error in prior-period income is reported as a prior-period adjustment by restating prior-period financial statements.

39. (b) The recognition of the effect of fully expensing the premiums for the three-year insurance policy represents the correction of an error of a prior period. The correction of the error should be reported as a prior-period adjustment by restating the prior-period financial statements. The correction results in $40,000 (i.e., $60,000 × 2/3) less insurance expense recognized in the previous year. This increases the balance of retained earnings as corrected by the retrospective application. However, the balance of retained earnings cannot be increased by the full $40,000, because the reduction in insurance expense would have increased the amount of income tax expense previously recognized by $12,000 (i.e., $40,000 × 30%). Thus, the balance of retained earnings corrected by the retrospective application is increased by $28,000

(i.e., $40,000 – $12,000). Therefore, the amount to be reported as the balance of retained earnings as corrected by the retrospective application is $428,000 (i.e., $400,000 + $28,000).

40. (b) Errors in financial statements result from mathematical mistakes, mistakes in the application of accounting principles, or the oversight or misuse of facts that existed at the time the financial statements were prepared. SFAS 16, *Prior Period Adjustments,* specifies that for an item to be classified as a prior period adjustment, it must be an item of profit or loss related to the correction of an error in the financial statements of a prior period. SFAS 154, *Accounting Changes and Error Corrections,* states that any error in the financial statements of a prior period discovered subsequent to their issuance shall be reported as a prior period adjustment by restating the prior period financial statements. Prior period adjustments bypass the income statement. They are instead reported net of their income tax effect in the statement of retained earnings as an adjustment to the beginning balance of retained earnings. A change in accounting estimate should be accounted for in the period of change if the change only affects that period, or in the current and subsequent periods, if the change affects both, as a component of income from continuing operations. A change in estimate does not require the presentation of pro forma effects of retroactive application or restatement of prior period financial statements. A change in accounting principle results from the adoption of a generally accepted accounting principle (GAAP) different from the GAAP previously used for reporting purposes. The term "accounting principle" includes not only accounting principles but also the methods of applying them. Most changes in accounting principle should be recognized by including the cumulative effect of the change in the net income of the period of the change.

41. (d) Since Pear owns 40% of Cinn's common stock, Pear has the ability to exercise significant influence over Cinn by virtue of its investment and should account for its investment in Cinn by the equity method. Therefore, Pear's $40,000 equity in Cinn's earnings is properly included in Pear's current year income before taxes. Under the equity method, the dividends received from Cinn reduce the carrying amount of the investment; they do not affect the

amount of investment income that Pear recognizes. Therefore, the $8,000 of dividends received from Cinn erroneously included in the current year income before taxes are subtracted to correct that figure. The arithmetical errors in depreciation of prior years represents a correction of errors of prior periods. The correction of the errors should be reported as a prior-period adjustment by restating the prior-period financial statements. Therefore, the $35,000 of arithmetical errors in depreciation of prior years that Pear had inadvertently subtracted from current year income before taxes are added back to correct that figure.

Income before taxes, before adjustment	$ 125,000
Less: Dividends received from equity method investee	(8,000)
Add: Arithmetical errors in depreciation of prior years	35,000
Corrected income before taxes	$ 152,000

42. (d) Since holiday pay for administrative employees is a period cost, it should have been expensed when incurred. Instead, it was misclassified and inventoried as manufacturing overhead. This error overstates both inventory and net income, thus overstating both current assets and stockholders' equity. The understatement of an accrued expense overstates net income and stockholders' equity and understates current liabilities. Misclassifying noncurrent note receivable principal as a current asset overstates current assets and understates noncurrent assets but does not affect stockholders' equity. The understatement of depreciation expense overstates noncurrent assets, net income, and stockholders' equity.

Accounting Policy Disclosures

43. (c) The Summary of Significant Accounting Policies should identify and describe the accounting principles followed by the reporting entity and the methods of applying those principles (APB 22, ¶12). Examples of disclosures by a business enterprise commonly required with respect to accounting policies include those relating to basis of consolidation, depreciation methods, amortization of intangibles, inventory pricing, recognition of profit on long-term construction type contracts, and criteria for determining which investments are treated as cash equivalents. Items (I) and (III) are examples of disclosures that are not accounting policies.

44. (b) The Summary of Significant Accounting Policies should identify and describe the accounting principles followed by the reporting entity and the methods of applying those principles (APB 22, ¶12). Examples of disclosures by a business enterprise commonly required with respect to accounting policies include those relating to basis of consolidation, depreciation methods, amortization of intangibles, inventory pricing, and recognition of profit on long-term construction-type contracts (¶13). Financial statement disclosure of accounting policies should not duplicate details (for example, composition of inventories or of plant assets) presented elsewhere as part of the financial statements (¶14). Answers (a), (c), and (d) are examples of disclosures that are not accounting policies.

Related Party Disclosures

45. (a) Financial statements should include disclosures of material related party transactions, other than compensation arrangements, expense allowances, and other similar items in the ordinary course of business. Officers' salaries are compensation arrangements in the ordinary course of business. Transactions (such as the sale of the patent, and the resulting royalties) involving related parties cannot be presumed to be carried out on an arm's-length basis, as the requisite conditions of competitive, free market dealings may not exist.

46. (c) Financial statements should include disclosures of material related party transactions, including the nature of the relationships involved, a description of the transactions, the dollar amounts of transactions for each of the periods for which income statements are presented, and the amounts due from or to related parties as of the date of each balance sheet presented.

47. (a) If the reporting enterprise and one or more other enterprises are under common ownership or management control and the existence of that control could result in operating results or financial position of the reporting enterprise significantly different from those that would have been obtained if the enterprises were autonomous, the nature of the control relationship should be disclosed even though there are no transactions between the enterprises. Therefore, both Lemo and Young should disclose their relationship with Ego.

48. (c) Financial statements should include disclosures of material-related party transactions other than (1) compensation arrangements, (2) expense allowances, (3) other similar items in the ordinary course of business, and (4) transactions that are eliminated in the preparation of consolidated or combined financial statements. Thus, Dean should report related party disclosures totaling $175,000 ($125,000 + $50,000), the amount of the loans to officers. The amounts for officers' salaries, officers' expenses,

and intercompany sales should not be disclosed as related party transactions.

49. (d) SFAS 57 requires that all material related-party transactions that are not eliminated in consolidated or combined financial statements be disclosed. However, according to SFAS 57, the following related-party transactions do not have to be disclosed: compensation arrangements, expense allowances, and similar items incurred in the ordinary course of business.

Developmental Stage Enterprises

50. (d) Generally accepted accounting principles that apply to established operating enterprises govern the recognition of revenue by a development stage enterprise and determine whether a cost incurred by a development stage enterprise is to be charged to expense when incurred or is to be capitalized or deferred. Accordingly, capitalization or deferral of costs shall be subject to the same assessment of recoverability that would be applicable in an established operating enterprise. Amortization is a component of the tax treatment for organization costs; it is not an option for financial accounting purposes. Organization costs are written off over 60 months for tax purposes, not for financial accounting purposes. Organization costs should be expensed as incurred.

51. (a) Financial reporting by a development stage enterprise differs from financial reporting for an established operating enterprise in regard to footnote disclosures only (e.g., a development stage enterprise should disclose, from the date of its inception, cumulative revenues and expenses in regards to the income statement and cumulative amounts with respect to the statement of cash flows as certain additional information). Otherwise, no special accounting standards apply to development stage enterprises. Generally accepted accounting principles that apply to established operating enterprises govern the recognition of revenue by a development stage enterprise and determine whether a cost incurred by such an enterprise should be charged to expense when incurred or should be capitalized or deferred (SFAS 7, ¶10 - 12).

52. (d) Financial statements issued by a development stage enterprise should be presented in conformity with generally accepted accounting principles that apply to established operating enterprises. These accounting principles determine whether a cost incurred by a development stage enterprise should be charged to expense when incurred or should be capitalized or deferred. Organization costs include (1) accounting services incidental to organization, (2) legal services for drafting the corporate charter and bylaws, (3) state incorporation filing fees, and (4) costs of temporary directors and of organizational meetings. Organization costs should be expensed as incurred.

53. (b) The balance sheet of a development stage enterprise should include any cumulative net losses reported with a caption such as "deficit accumulated during the development stage" in the stockholders' equity section [SFAS 7, ¶11(a)]. It is never acceptable to capitalize a deficit. A deficit is a debit item that belongs in the equity section of the balance sheet, not in the asset section.

Accrual Accounting

54. (d) The sole proprietor's drawing of $500 is recorded as a reduction of her capital account under both the cash basis and accrual basis methods of accounting.

	Cash	Accrual
Revenue for services provided in April, payment received May	$3,200	$ 3,200
April expenses, paid June	--	(1,500)
Proprietorship's income for two months ended May 31	$3,200	$ 1,700

55. (c)

Collection of fees in current year	$ 200,000
Less: Accounts receivable, Jan. 1	(40,000)
Plus: Accounts receivable, Dec. 31	60,000
Less: Unearned revenue, Dec. 31	(5,000)
Service revenue for current year	$ 215,000

56. (d) When accounts receivable decrease during a period, revenues on a cash basis are more than revenues on an accrual basis because cash collections are more than revenues reported on an accrual basis. Thus, compared to the accrual basis of accounting, the cash basis of accounting overstates income by the net decrease in A/R. When accrued expenses decrease during a period, expenses on a cash basis are more than expenses on an accrual basis because cash payments are more than expenses reported on an accrual basis. Thus, compared to the accrual basis of accounting, the cash basis *understates* income by the net decrease in the accrued expenses.

57. (c) Accrual accounting recognized and reports the effects of transactions and other events on the assets and liabilities of a business enterprise in the time periods to which they relate rather than only when cash is received of paid. Accrual accounting attempts to match revenues and the expenses associated with those revenues in order to determine

net income for an accounting period. The insurance costs were not recorded during the period to which they relate, so the accrued liabilities is understated. Because the expense was not included in the inventory that was sold, the COGS was less than it should have been, and as a result, the retained earnings were overstated.

Revenue Recognition

58. (a) The amount reported for net sales should not be reduced for the portion of the sales equaling merchandise that is estimated to be exchanged for merchandise of equal or greater value.

Sales, December	$1,000,000
Less: Estimated sales that will be returned [$1,000,000 × (7% + 3%)]	(100,000)
Net sales, December	$ 900,000

59. (a) The $2,800 increase in rentals receivable represents rental revenue earned but not yet received in cash. The $8,000 decrease in unearned rentals represents rental revenue earned that had been received in cash in a prior period.

Cash (given)	80,000	
Rentals Receivable ($12,400 – $9,600)	2,800	
Unearned Rentals ($32,000 – $24,000)	8,000	
Rental Revenue (to balance)		90,800

60. (b) Accrual accounting recognizes and reports the effects of transactions and other events on the assets and liabilities of a business enterprise in the time periods to which they relate rather than only when cash is received or paid. Revenues are recognized when earned. A deferred (prepaid) expense is an expense paid or payable in cash but not yet incurred. A prepaid expense is reported in the financial statements as an asset.

Expense Recognition

61. (b) The cabinets are expected to provide benefits over five years; hence, they meet the definition of an asset (probable future economic benefits). The cabinets are used in the selling function; therefore, the expired portion of the cabinet costs should be classified as a selling expense and not as part of cost of goods sold.

62. (c)

Equipment cost, 12/31 year 4	$ 344,000
Cost of year 5 purchase	50,000
Equipment cost without sale	394,000
Equipment cost, 12/31 year 5	(379,000)
Cost of equipment sold	15,000
Carrying value of equipment sold	(9,000)
Accumulated depreciation of equipment sold	$ 6,000

Accumulated depreciation, 12/31 year 4	$ 128,000
Accumulated depreciation of equipment sold	(6,000)
Balance without year 5 depreciation	122,000
Accumulated depreciation, 12/31 year 5	(153,000)
Depreciation expense, year 5	$ 31,000

63. (a) Interest expense should be accrued in the period in which it is earned, rather than the period in which it is paid. In year 6, total interest expense of $4,080 should be reported, as shown below. If only $3,000 interest expense is recorded, the understatement is $1,080.

Loan Dates	Amount	Monthly Interest	Months in Year 6	Year 6 Interest
11/01 year 5 to 10/31 year 6	$10,000	$100	10	$ 1,000
02/01 year 6 to 07/31 year 6	30,000	300	6	1,800
05/01 year 6 to 01/31 year 7	16,000	160	8	1,280
Total interest				4,080
Less interest expense recorded				(3,000)
Understated interest				$ 1,080

64. (b) Accrual accounting recognizes expenses in the period they are incurred rather than when paid. Zach pays commissions to its sales staff at the rate of 3% of net sales. For the year ended 3/31, Zach should report commission expense of $450,000 ($15,000,000 × 3%).

65. (c) On 12/31 year 1, House announced the contest winner and signed a note payable to the winner.

First installment of note payable, due 1/2 year 2	$ 50,000
Cost of annuity purchased on 12/31 year 1 to provide prize monies remaining after first installment	418,250
Contest prize expense for year 1	$468,250

66. (b) The $55,000 consultants' fee for work performed in year 1 had already been recorded; therefore, no adjustment is necessary for this item.

Professional fee expense, before adjustment	$82,000
Legal fees for year 1 work, unbilled as of 12/31 year 1	13,000
Professional fee expense, year 1	$95,000

OCBOA

67. (a) In financial statements prepared on the income-tax basis, the nondeductible portion of expenses is included in the expense category in the determination of income, according to the AICPA Technical Information for Practitioners Series #1,

entitled, "Other Comprehensive Basis of Accounting," Section 11,500, ¶4. (Editorial note: This is an infrequently tested topic.)

68. (c) The balance in the capital account at March 31 is the beginning balance plus the service revenues received less the owner's draw. The expenses incurred in February and paid in April are not included in the calculation, as Tory has a cash basis of accounting. $2,000 + $5,000 – $1,000 = $6,000.

69. (a) According to SAS 62, a comprehensive basis of accounting other than generally accepted accounting principles is one of the following: (1) a basis of accounting used to comply with regulatory requirements; (2) a basis used for tax purposes; (3) a cash basis; (4) a definite set of criteria having substantial support, such as the price-level basis of accounting.

Cash basis does not attempt to match revenues and the expenses associated with those revenues, therefore conversion of income statement amounts from the cash basis to the accrual basis would be in accordance with the modified cash basis of accounting.

70. (d) According to SAS 62, a comprehensive basis of accounting other than generally accepted accounting principles is one of the following: (1) a basis of accounting used to comply with regulatory requirements; (2) a basis used for tax purposes; (3) a cash basis; (4) a definite set of criteria having substantial support, such as the price-level basis of accounting. A basis of accounting used by an entity to comply with the financial reporting requirements of a lending institution does not fit any of the categories.

Interim Reporting

71. (c) In APB 28, the Board concluded that each interim period should be viewed as an integral part of an annual period. In order to maintain comparability, the principles and practices used to prepare the latest annual statements should also be used to prepare the interim statements.

72. (a) The use of lower of cost or market may result in inventory losses that should not be deferred beyond the interim period in which the decline occurs. Recoveries of these losses in subsequent periods should be recognized as gains, but only to the extent of losses recognized in previous interim periods of the same fiscal year. Temporary market declines, however, need not be recognized at the interim dates since no loss is expected to be incurred in the fiscal year. Because Wilson expected the decline to reverse within the fiscal year, no loss should be recorded for the first quarter. Even though the recovery exceeded the previous decline by $10,000, gains are recognized only to the extent of losses recognized in previous interim periods of the same fiscal year.

73. (d) In APB 28, the Board concluded that each interim period should be viewed as an integral part of an annual period and not as s separate, independent period. In order to maintain comparability between interim and annual financial statements, APB 28 states that the principles and practices used to prepare the latest annual financial statements also be used to prepare the interim statements. Revenue should be recognized as earned during an interim period on the same basis as followed for recognition of income for the full year. Costs and expenses associated directly with products sold or services rendered for annual reporting purposes generally should be similarly treated for interim reporting purposes.

74. (a) Interim reporting requirements arose because annual financial statements are frequently not timely enough for decision makers. Because interim financial statements are annualized based on estimates, they may not be as reliable as annual financial statements.

75. (b) Per APB 28, ¶23, "At the end of each interim period, a company should make its best estimate of the effective tax rate expected to be applicable for the full fiscal year. The rate so determined should be used in providing for income taxes on a current year-to-date basis."

76. (c) Annual property taxes should be accrued or deferred at each interim reporting date to provide an appropriate cost in each period and allocated ratably to each interim period of the year [APB 28, ¶(c)]. Because the unanticipated repairs to the office equipment benefit the last three quarters of the year, each of these periods should be charged with an appropriate portion of the cost by the use of accruals or deferrals [¶(a)].

Annual property taxes ($90,000 / 4)	$22,500
Unanticipated repairs incurred in April ($150,000 / 3)	50,000
Expense reported in 6/30 income statement	$72,500

77. (b) The effects of discontinued operations should be included in the determination of net income for the interim period in which they occur (APB 28, ¶21). Annual property taxes may be accrued or deferred at each interim reporting date to provide an

appropriate cost in each period and thus are allocated ratably to each interim period of the year [¶16(c)].

Net loss on business component disposal	$100,000
Annual property taxes ($40,000 / 2)	20,000
Interim period inclusions	$120,000

78. (a) Kell reports all of the extraordinary gain realized in the second quarter in the second quarter's income statement. Extraordinary items should not be prorated over the balance of the fiscal year (APB 28, ¶22). The cumulative-effect-type accounting change made in the third quarter should be accounted for as if it occurred in the first quarter; no cumulative effect of the change should be included in net income of the third quarter (SFAS 3, ¶10). The $12,000 of calendar-year property taxes are allocated to the third quarter; annual property taxes should be accrued or deferred at each interim reporting date to provide an appropriate cost in each period and thus are allocated ratably to each interim period of the year [APB 28, ¶16(c)].

Net income for the quarter, as reported	$ 95,000
Less: Second quarter extraordinary gain allocated to third quarter ($60,000 / 3)	(20,000)
Add: Cumulative-effect loss resulting from change in accounting principle included in third quarter	16,000
Corrected net income for third quarter	$ 91,000

Segment Reporting

79. (b) Operating segments have three characteristics. The description in answer a contains no characteristics that would qualify it as an operating segment. The description in answer b meets all three characteristics of an operating segment as well as the quantitative thresholds criteria. Even though the description in answer c meets the characteristics of an operating segment, it does not meet the quantitative thresholds criteria. The description in answer d meets the quantitative thresholds criteria but does not meet all three characteristics of an operating segment.

80. (d) An operating segment is deemed to be a reportable segment if it meets one or more of the revenue, profit(loss), and assets tests. If an operating segment's revenue, including both sales to external customers and intersegment sales and transfers, is 10% or more of the combined revenue of all operating segments, it meets the revenue test. Lion, Monk, and Nevi each have more than 10% of combined revenues and are deemed to be reportable segments.

81. (d) An enterprise shall report a measure of profit or loss and total assets for each reportable segment. These measures are generally based upon the measures as reported to, and used by, the chief operating decision maker, and may include revenues from external customers; revenues from transactions with other operating segments of the same enterprise; interest revenue; interest expense; depreciation, depletion, and amortization expense; unusual items; equity in the net income of investees accounted for by the equity method; income tax expense or benefit; extraordinary items; and significant other noncash items.

82. (a) Information about major customers is required in an enterprise-wide disclosure. Enterprises must disclose the total amount of revenues from each single customer that amounts to 10% or more of the enterprise's revenues and identify the segment(s) reporting the revenues. Identity of the customer need not be disclosed.

Problem 11-2 ADDITIONAL MULTIPLE CHOICE ANSWERS

Income Concepts

83. (a) The freight-in cost is an inventoriable cost. The freight-out cost and the sales representatives' salaries should both be reported as selling expenses in the year.

Accounting and legal fees	$ 25,000
Officers' salaries	150,000
Insurance	85,000
General and administrative expenses	$260,000

84. (a) When a transaction is either infrequent or unusual, but not both, it is presented separately as a component of income from continuing operations. This is true regardless of whether the transaction results in a gain or loss.

85. (d) APB 30 provides that gains and losses from sale or abandonment of property, plant, or equipment used in the business should **not** be reported as extraordinary items. APB 30 goes on to provide that a material event or transaction that is unusual in nature or occurs infrequently but not both and, therefore, does not meet the criteria for classification as an extraordinary item, should be reported as a separate component of income from continuing operations. Such an item should **not** be reported on

the face of the income statement net of income taxes or in any other manner that may imply that it is extraordinary. Therefore, the gain on the sale of the parcel of land used as a plant site is reported at $100,000; it is **not** reported net of its related income tax effect.

Discontinued Operations

86. (c) SFAS 144, ¶43 states, "The income statement of a business enterprise for current and prior periods shall report the results of operations of the component...in discontinued operations...in the period(s) in which they occur."

87. (c) SFAS 144, ¶43 states, "The income statement of a business enterprise for current and prior periods shall report the results of operations of the component...in discontinued operations...in the period(s) in which they occur."

88. (d) The operating results of a discontinued component are reported separately from results of continuing operations. Results of the discontinued operations are reported as discontinued operations in the period in which they occur.

Extraordinary Items

89. (a) APB 30 provides that (1) gains or losses on disposal of a segment of a business and (2) gains or losses from exchange or translation of foreign currencies, including those relating to major devaluations and revaluations should not be reported as extraordinary items. To be classified as an extraordinary item, APB 30 requires that the item must be both unusual in nature and infrequent in occurrence, taking into account the environment in which the entity operates. The loss due to hurricane damage should be reported as an extraordinary item since the hurricane was the first ever to strike in Midway's area. Since the loss realized on the damage to the equipment and the gain realized on the destruction of the building are a direct result of the hurricane, they are considered to be extraordinary.

Pretax loss on damaged equipment		$ 800,000
Proceeds from insurance company	$1,000,000	
Carrying amount of building	(300,000)	
Less: Pretax gain on destroyed building		(700,000)
Extraordinary loss before income taxes		$ 100,000

90. (d) A gain or loss from a transaction that is unusual in nature and infrequent in occurrence should be reported as an extraordinary item (APB 30, ¶20). Extraordinary items should be reported separately as a component of income *before* the cumulative effect of accounting changes and *after* discontinued operations.

91. (c) The loss due to the earthquake qualifies as an extraordinary item because it is **both** unusual in nature and infrequent in occurrence. An extraordinary item should be presented separately on the income statement, net of related income tax.

Loss not covered by insurance	$ 700,000
Less: Tax benefit ($700,000 × 0.40)	(280,000)
Extraordinary item, net of tax	$ 420,000

Changes in Principle

92. (a) A change from the FIFO periodic inventory system to the weighted average periodic inventory system is a change in accounting principle. The cumulative effect of the change is the difference between the amount of retained earnings at the beginning of the period of change and the amount of retained earnings that would have been reported at that date if the new accounting principle had been retrospectively applied for all affected periods. Since Harvey is on a calendar year basis, the cumulative effect of the change in accounting principle should be determined as of January 1.

Changes in Estimates

93. (d) A change in depreciation method, such as from the accelerated to the straight-line method is a change in accounting principle that is inseparable from a change in accounting estimate. When the effects of the two changes cannot be separated, the change should be treated as a change in estimate. A change in accounting estimate should be accounted for in the period of change if the change only effects that period, or in the current and subsequent periods, if the change effects both, as a component of income from continuing operations. No prior period adjustment is made.

94. (c) Changing from an accelerated method to straight line for financial statement purposes results in a temporary difference of $120,000 in future taxable amounts (accumulated depreciation using the accelerated method of $360,000 less $240,000 using the straight-line method). The amount of tax effect for the taxable amounts is calculated by applying the enacted tax rate for future years of 30%, resulting in a $36,000 (i.e., $120,000 × 30%) deferred tax liability to be recorded as a result of the change.

95. (d) A change in the expected service life of an asset because additional information has been

obtained is an example of a change in an accounting estimate. According to SFAS 154, a change in estimate should be accounted for prospectively. Therefore, no cumulative effect of the change is reported and no pro forma effects of retroactive application are disclosed.

Changes in Reporting Entity

96. (b) Changes in accounting principle generally are accounted for as a prior-period adjustment to the beginning balance of retained earnings. A change in the accounting entity, on the other hand, is presented by retrospectively applying the change to the financial statements for all periods presented.

Error Correction

97. (c) The recognition of the effect in the current year of the failure to accrue $50,000 of warranty costs in the previous year is the correction of an error of a prior period. The correction of the error should be reported as a prior-period adjustment by restating the prior-period financial statements. The change from straight-line to accelerated depreciation represents a change in accounting estimate effected by a change in accounting principle. A change in accounting estimate should only be accounted for in the period of change if the change only effects that period, or in the current and subsequent periods, if the change effects both, as a component of income from continuing operations.

98. (a) The company failed to record an accrued expense at the end of the current year. This error understates current liabilities at the end of the current year, thus overstating working capital at the balance sheet date. The failure to accrue the expense has no effect on the cash account, and therefore no effect on cash flows from operating activities for the current year.

99. (b) The correction of an error in financial statements of a prior period is reported as a prior-period adjustment by restating the prior-period financial statements. (FASB 154, ¶25).

Accounting Policy Disclosures

100. (a) The Summary of Significant Accounting Policies should identify and describe the accounting policies followed by the reporting entity and the methods of applying those principles (APB 22, ¶12). Examples of disclosures by a business enterprise commonly required with respect to accounting policies include those relating to basis of consolidation, depreciation methods, amortization of intangibles, inventory pricing, recognition of profit on long-term construction-type contracts, and criteria for determining which investments are treated as cash equivalents. Answers (b), (c), and (d) are examples of disclosures that are not accounting policies.

101. (c) The Summary of Significant Accounting Policies should identify and describe the accounting principles, followed by the reporting entity and the methods of applying those principles (APB 22, ¶12). Examples of disclosures by a business enterprise commonly required with respect to accounting policies include those relating to the basis of consolidation, depreciation methods, amortization of intangibles, inventory pricing, recognition of profit on long-term construction-type contracts, and criteria for determining which investments are treated as cash equivalents. Answers (a), (b), and (d) are examples of disclosures that are not accounting policies.

Related Party Disclosures

102. (b) Financial statements should include disclosures of material related party transactions, other than compensation arrangements, expense allowances, and other similar items in the ordinary course of business. Therefore, the consulting fees paid to a director must be disclosed in the notes to the financial statements. The per diem expenses would be included in expense allowances and would not need to be disclosed.

Developmental Stage Enterprises

103. (a) Financial statements issued by a development stage enterprise should be presented in conformity with GAAP applicable to established operating enterprises. Special accounting practices that are based on a distinctive accounting for development stage enterprises are not acceptable. Financial reporting by a development stage enterprise differs from financial reporting for an established operating enterprise in regard only to required additional information.

104. (a) Financial statements issued by a development stage enterprise should be presented in conformity with GAAP that apply to established operating enterprises. These accounting principles determine whether a cost incurred by a development stage enterprise should be charged to expense when incurred or should be capitalized or deferred. Lex should capitalize both the cost of the leasehold improvements, equipment, and furniture, and the cost of the security deposits.

Research and development ($750,000 + $900,000)	$1,650,000
Laboratory operations ($175,000 + $550,000)	725,000
General and administrative ($225,000 + $685,000)	910,000
Depreciation ($25,000 + $115,000)	140,000
Total amount of costs charged to operations	$3,425,000

105. (d) Generally accepted accounting principles that apply to established operating enterprises determine whether a cost incurred by a development stage enterprise should be charged to expense when incurred or should be capitalized or deferred. Therefore, only the $1,200,000 cost of the leasehold improvements, equipment, and furniture should have been capitalized by Lind. The research and development costs, laboratory operations costs, and the general and administrative costs should have been expensed when incurred.

Accrual Accounting

106. (c) Potoma's accrued expenses decreased during the current year. Hence, Potoma's current year payments for expenses exceeded the amount of expense recognized on the accrual basis in the current year. The increased amount of expenses recognized in the current year under the cash basis increases Potoma's current year accrual basis net income as compared to its current year cash basis net income. The declaration or payment of a cash dividend does not affect net income computed under either the cash or accrual basis. Compared to its current year cash basis net income, Potoma's current year accrual basis net income decreased when it recognized uncollectible accounts expense in the current year. Potoma's current year cash basis net income is not affected by either the accounts receivable balances written off in the current year or the uncollectible account expense recognized in the current year. The sale of the used equipment at a gain increases net income under both the cash and accrual basis by equal amounts.

107. (d) Accrual accounting (1) recognizes revenue in the period it is earned rather than when the related cash is received and (2) recognizes expenses in the period incurred rather than when the related cash is paid.

Cash basis pretax income, year 2	$60,000
Add: Increase in accounts receivable—revenues earned but not yet collected in cash ($40,000 – $20,000)	20,000
Decrease in accounts payable—payments made not representing current year expenses ($30,000 – $15,000)	15,000
Accrual basis pretax income, year 2	$95,000

108. (c)

Advertising expense, before adjustment	$146,000
Add: December year 1 costs paid in year 2	9,000
Less: Prepayment for January year 2 campaign	(15,000)
Advertising expense, year 1	$140,000

109. (b) Net income after bonus and income taxes is $360,000. The income tax rate is 40%. Therefore, income after bonus but before income taxes is $600,000 [i.e., $360,000 / (100% – 40%)]. The bonus is equal to 10% of the corporation's income after bonus but before income taxes. Therefore, the amount of the bonus is $60,000 (i.e., $600,000 × 10%).

OCBOA

110. (d) Tax-basis financial statements recognize certain revenues and expenses in different reporting periods than GAAP financial statements. Nontaxable income and nondeductible expenses are still included in the determination of income in tax-basis statements. Detailed information about current and deferred income tax liabilities is included in GAAP financial statements. Income tax-basis financial statements may include disclosures about capital and operating lease transactions.

111. (d) The decrease in accounts receivable represents collections in the current period of credit sales of a prior period.

Gross cash sales	$ 80,000	
Less: Returns and allowances	(4,000)	
Receipts from cash sales		$ 76,000
Gross credit sales	120,000	
Less: Discounts	(6,000)	
Net credit sales	114,000	
Add: Decrease in accounts receivable ($40,000 – $30,000)	10,000	
Receipts from credit sales		124,000
Receipts from cash and credit sales		$200,000

Interim Reporting

112. (c) Per APB 28, ¶23, "At the end of each interim period, a company should make its best estimate of the effective tax rate expected to be applicable for the full fiscal year. The rate so determined should be used in providing for income taxes on a current year-to-date basis." Therefore, the amount of income tax expense that Tech should report in its current year first quarter interim income statement is $50,000—Tech's current year first quarter's income before taxes of $200,000 multiplied by the 25% effective annual income tax rate Tech expects for the current year.

113. (d) Petal incurred an inventory loss from a decline in market price in the second quarter which it expected to be restored by the end of the fiscal year. Per APB 28, ¶14(c), inventory losses from market declines, which can reasonably be expected to be restored in the fiscal year, need not be recognized at the interim date since no loss is expected to be incurred in the fiscal year. Therefore, since Petal expected the market price to return to previous levels by the end of the year, Petal would not have recognized the inventory loss until the fourth quarter, when the decline had not reversed.

114. (d) APB 28, ¶14(b), states, "Inventory losses from market declines should not be deferred beyond the interim period in which the decline occurs." Therefore, Cox recognizes the full amount of the inventory loss from the permanent market decline that occurred in May in the quarterly income statement for the three months ended June 30.

115. (b) APB 28 generally requires a company to use for interim financial reporting purposes the same principles and practices used for annual reporting. For the sake of expediency, however, certain practical deviations are permitted where the results of using a different practice are likely to be immaterial. Thus, APB 28 allows the use of gross profit rates for determining the cost of goods sold for interim period statements. The use of gross profit rates for estimating ending inventory is not acceptable for annual financial statements.

Segment Reporting

116. (c) An operating segment is identified as a reportable segment if it meets one or more of the three tests: revenue, profit(loss), and assets. (1) Revenue test—Its revenue (including both sales to external customers and intersegment sales and transfers) is 10% or more of the combined revenue of all operating segments. (2) Profit(loss) test—Its profit or loss is 10% or more of the greater of the following two absolute amounts: Combined profits of all segments that did not report losses, or the sum of all losses for all segments reporting losses. (3) Assets test—Its assets are 10% or more of the combined assets of all operating segments. Segments A, B, C, and E have revenue greater than $3,275,000, which is 10% of the combined revenue. They also have profits greater than $580,000, which is 10% of the combined profits (no segments reported losses). Segments A, B, C, D, and E all have assets greater than $6,750,000, which is 10% of the combined assets. Only segment F does not meet at least one of the three tests. Therefore, Correy has five reportable segments.

PERFORMANCE BY SUBTOPICS

Each category below parallels a subtopic covered in Chapter 11. Record the number and percentage of questions you correctly answered in each subtopic area.

Income Statement Format

Question #	Correct √
1	
2	
3	
# Questions	3
# Correct	______
% Correct	______

Continuing Operations

Question #	Correct √
4	
5	
6	
7	
8	
# Questions	5
# Correct	______
% Correct	______

Discontinued Operations

Question #	Correct √
9	
10	
11	
12	
13	
# Questions	5
# Correct	______
% Correct	______

Extraordinary Items

Question #	Correct √
14	
15	
16	
17	
18	
# Questions	5
# Correct	______
% Correct	______

Comprehensive Income

Question #	Correct √
19	
20	
21	
22	
23	
24	
# Questions	6
# Correct	______
% Correct	______

Change in Principles

Question #	Correct √
25	
26	
27	
28	
29	
30	
# Questions	6
# Correct	______
% Correct	______

Change in Estimate

Question #	Correct √
31	
32	
33	
34	
35	
# Questions	5
# Correct	______
% Correct	______

Change in Reporting Entity

Question #	Correct √
36	
37	
# Questions	2
# Correct	______
% Correct	______

Error Correction

Question #	Correct √
38	
39	
40	
41	
42	
# Questions	5
# Correct	
% Correct	

Accounting Policy Disclosures

Question #	Correct √
43	
44	
# Questions	2
# Correct	
% Correct	

Related Party Disclosures

Question #	Correct √
45	
46	
47	
48	
49	
# Questions	5
# Correct	
% Correct	

Developmental Stage Enterprises

Question #	Correct √
50	
51	
52	
53	
# Questions	4
# Correct	
% Correct	

Accrual Accounting

Question #	Correct √
54	
55	
56	
57	
# Questions	4
# Correct	
% Correct	

Revenue Recognition

Question #	Correct √
58	
59	
60	
# Questions	3
# Correct	
% Correct	

Expense Recognition

Question #	Correct √
61	
62	
63	
64	
65	
66	
# Questions	6
# Correct	
% Correct	

OCBOA

Question #	Correct √
67	
68	
69	
70	
# Questions	4
# Correct	
% Correct	

Interim Reporting

Question #	Correct √
71	
72	
73	
74	
75	
76	
77	
78	
# Questions	8
# Correct	
% Correct	

Segment Reporting

Question #	Correct √
79	
80	
81	
82	
# Questions	4
# Correct	
% Correct	

SIMULATION SOLUTIONS

Solution 11-3

Research

APB 29, Par. 18

18. The Board concludes that in general accounting for nonmonetary transactions should be based on the fair values of the assets (or services) involved which is the same basis as that used in monetary transactions. Thus, the cost of a nonmonetary asset acquired in exchange for another nonmonetary asset is the fair value of the asset surrendered to obtain it, and a gain or loss should be recognized on the exchange. The fair value of the asset received should be used to measure the cost if it is more clearly evident than the fair value of the asset surrendered. Similarly, a nonmonetary asset received in a nonreciprocal transfer should be recorded at the fair value of the asset received. A transfer of a nonmonetary asset to a stockholder or to another entity in a nonreciprocal transfer should be recorded at the fair value of the asset transferred, and a gain or loss should be recognized on the disposition of the asset. The fair value of an entity's own stock reacquired may be a more clearly evident measure of the fair value of the asset distributed in a nonreciprocal transfer if the transaction involves distribution of a nonmonetary asset to eliminate a disproportionate part of owners' interests (that is, to acquire stock for the treasury or for retirement).

Responses 1-4

1. A, X Changing from the completed contract method to the percentage of completion method of accounting for long term contracts is a change in accounting principle that should be reported as an adjustment to the beginning balance of retained earnings.

2. B, Z Changing the percentage of credit sales used to determine the allowance for uncollectible accounts from 2% to 1% is a change in accounting estimate and requires using the prospective approach. The allowance for uncollectible accounts and the related expense for current and future financial statements should be reported on the new basis, and beginning retained earnings should not be adjusted.

3. A, X, $9,000

Changing from the average cost to FIFO methods of inventory is a change in accounting principle requiring an adjustment to the beginning balance of retained earnings. The cumulative effect is the difference between the amount of retained earnings at the beginning of the period of a change and the amount of retained earnings that would have been reported at that date if the new accounting principle had been applied retroactively for all prior periods that would have been affected.

	FIFO	Average Cost	Difference
Prior to last year	$77,000	$71,000	$6,000
Last year	82,000	79,000	3,000
Cumulative effect prior to 1/1 of current year			$9,000

4. C, Y, $2,000

The error in the calculation of depreciation resulted in the need for a correction of the error in previously presented financial statements, requiring the retrospective restatement approach.

Incorrect depreciation calculation ($40,000 × 25%)	$10,000
Less: Correct depreciation calculation ($40,000 × 20%)	(8,000)
Adjustment to beginning retained earnings	$ 2,000

Solution 11-4

Research

APB 30, Par. 20

20. Extraordinary items are events and transactions that are distinguished by their unusual nature and by the infrequency of their occurrence. Thus, both of the following criteria should be met to classify an event or transaction as an extraordinary item:

a. Unusual nature—the underlying event or transaction should possess a high degree of abnormality and be of a type clearly unrelated to, or only incidentally related to, the ordinary and typical activities of the entity, taking into account the environment in which the entity operates. (See discussion in paragraph 21.)

b. Infrequency of occurrence—the underlying event or transaction should be of a type that would not reasonably be expected to recur in the foreseeable future, taking into account the environment in which the entity operates. (See discussion in paragraph 22.)

Responses 1-4

1. $73,000, A

Gains or losses on the extinguishment of debt are reported as components of continuing operations. The bonds are redeemed for $1,020,000 ($1,000,000 × 1.02). The amortization of the bond discount at June 30, year 4 must be added to the carrying amount of the bonds on January 1, year 5 before the gain or loss on extinguishment may be computed.

$ 940,000 × 0.10 × 6/12	$ 47,000
$1,000,000 × 0.08 × 6/12	(40,000)
Amortization of discount	$ 7,000

The carrying value at the time of redemption was $947,000 ($940,000 + $7,000). The excess of the price paid to redeem the bonds ($1,020,000) over the carrying value ($947,000) is the loss on the bond redemption of $73,000.

2. $100,000, A

	Straight-line	SYD
Year 1	$100,000	$166,667
Year 2	100,000	133,333
Year 3	100,000	100,000
Total	$300,000	$400,000

The annual straight-line depreciation is ($520,000 – $20,000) / 5 = $100,000. The SYD depreciation is computed as follows.

Year 1	($520,000 – $20,000) × 5/15	$166,667
Year 2	($520,000 – $20,000) × 4/15	$133,333
Year 3	($520,000 – $20,000) × 3/15	$100,000

The difference between the two totals ($100,000) is a change in estimate and is reported as part of continuing operations in the period of the change.

3. $125,000 loss, A

In year 3, the loss was probable according to the attorney with an estimated loss between $250,000 and $750,000. Since no amount within the range is more probable than any other amount, the lowest amount of the loss in the estimated range should be recorded. Therefore, $250,000 would have been accrued in the year 3 financial statements. When the actual loss realized was $375,000 in year 4, the accrued liability of $250,000 would be debited, a current period loss (reported in income from continuing operations) for $125,000 would be debited, and a credit would be made to cash for $375,000.

4. $10,000 loss, A

The holding loss to be reported in income from continuing operations at December 31, year 4 is $10,000. The cost of securities I and II is $360,000 ($125,000 + $235,000), while the fair value at December 31, year 4 is $350,000 ($145,000 + $205,000). The difference between the two is the holding loss. The securities are classified as trading because they were bought and held to sell in the near term. Since the securities are trading securities, the holding loss is reported in income from continuing operations.

Responses 5-6

5. $255,000 loss, B

Book value of the warehouse	$ 470,000
Book value of the equipment	250,000
Book value of the inventory	535,000
Total loss	1,255,000
Less: Insurance proceeds	(1,000,000)
Extraordinary loss	$ 255,000

The loss is extraordinary because of the unusual and infrequent (this is the first hurricane ever to hit this area) nature of the event causing the loss. The book value of the inventory is used in the computation of the loss.

6. $41,000 loss, D

The adjustment due to translation is the difference between the net assets at December 31, year 4 after the remeasurement ($429,000) and the net assets at December 31, year 4 translated for the exchange rate at the balance sheet date ($388,000), or $41,000. The foreign currency translation adjustment should be reported in other comprehensive income. Any gain or loss on the *remeasurement* of the financial statements should be reflected in the income statement. (See Ch. 17)

Solution 11-5

Research

APB 29, Par. 18

18. The Board concludes that in general accounting for nonmonetary transactions should be based on the fair values of the assets (or services) involved which is the same basis as that used in monetary transactions. Thus, the cost of a nonmonetary asset acquired in exchange for another nonmonetary asset is the fair value of the asset surrendered to obtain it, and a gain or loss should be recognized on the exchange. The fair value of the asset received should be used to measure the cost if it is more clearly evident than the fair value of the asset surrendered. Similarly, a nonmonetary asset received in a nonreciprocal transfer should be recorded at the fair value of the asset received. A transfer of a nonmonetary asset to a stockholder or to another entity in a nonreciprocal transfer should be recorded at the fair value of the asset transferred, and a gain or loss should be recognized on the disposition of the asset. The fair value of an entity's own stock reacquired may be a more clearly evident measure of the fair value of the asset distributed in a nonreciprocal transfer if the transaction involves distribution of a nonmonetary asset to eliminate a disproportionate part of owners' interests (that is, to acquire stock for the treasury or for retirement).

Responses 1-10

1. A, X SFAS 154 describes a change in accounting principle as "a change from one generally accepted accounting principle to another generally accepted accounting principle when there are two or more generally accepted accounting principles that apply or when the accounting principle formerly used is no longer generally accepted. A change in the *method* of applying an accounting principle also is considered a change in accounting principle."

SFAS 154 ¶7 says "An entity shall report a change in accounting principle through retrospective application of the new accounting principle to all prior periods, unless it is impracticable to do so. Retrospective application requires the following: (a) The cumulative effect of the change to the new accounting principle on periods prior to those presented shall be reflected in the carrying amounts of assets and liabilities as of the beginning of the first period presented; (b) an offsetting adjustment, if any, shall be made to the opening balance of retained earnings for that period; and (c) financial statements for each individual prior period presented shall be adjusted to reflect the period-specific effects of applying the new accounting principle."

2. B, Z Changes in service lives of depreciable assets are changes in estimate. Changes in estimate are to be reflected prospectively.

3. B, Z Warranty costs are also examples of changes in estimate which are to be handled prospectively.

4. A, X A change in the method of inventory pricing is a change in principle and should be should be accounted for by an adjustment to the beginning balance of retained earnings in the period of the change. (Also see answer to response 1)

5. A, X A change in the method applying a generally accepted accounting principle is considered a change in principle and should be should be accounted for by an adjustment to the beginning balance of retained earnings in the period of the change. (Also see answer to response 1)

6. C, Y A change from an accounting principle that is not generally accepted (e.g., the cash method) to one that is generally accepted (the accrual method) is a correction of an error. SFAS 154 requires that "The cumulative effect of the error on periods prior to those presented shall be reflected in the carrying amounts of assets and liabilities as of the beginning of the first period presented. An offsetting adjustment, if any, shall be made to the opening balance of retained earnings for that period. Financial statements for each individual prior period presented shall be adjusted to reflect correction of the period-specific effects of the error.

7. C, Y See solution to question #6.

8. B, Z When a new depreciation method is adopted in partial or complete recognition of a change in the estimated future benefits inherent in the asset, the effect of the change in accounting principle, or the method of applying it, may be inseparable from the effect of the change in accounting estimate. For this reason SFAS 154 requires that a change in depreciation methods should be accounted for as a change in estimate which is reported as part of continuing operations in the period of the change.

9. D, Z The initial adoption of an accounting principle in recognition of events or transactions occurring for the first time is not a change in principle.

10. D, Y A change in accounting principle is changing from one generally accepted accounting principles to another generally accepted accounting principle for the same events or transactions. Modification of an accounting principle necessitated by transactions or events that are clearly different in substance from those previously occurring is not a change in accounting principles. With a 30% interest in Worth, Inc., and a member on Worth's board of directors, Quo is in a different position than it was before. The cost method may have been appropriate then but would not be acceptable now, assuming Quo has considerable influence over the investee. Therefore, there is no change in accounting principle from one that is acceptable to one that is also acceptable. Only the equity method would be acceptable. Hence D., APB 18, ¶19(m), indicates that when "an investment qualifies for use of the equity method, the investor should adopt the equity method of accounting. The investment, results of operations (current and prior periods presented), and retained earnings of the investor should be adjusted retroactively in a manner consistent with the accounting for a step-by-step acquisition of a subsidiary.

Solution 11-6

Essay—Extraordinary Items/Discontinued Operations

a. Hillside should report the extraordinary item **separately, net of applicable income taxes, below** the **continuing operations** section in the income statement. Exclusion of extraordinary items from the results of continuing operations is intended to produce a measure of income from continuing operations that is useful in **projecting future operating cash flows.**

b. Hillside should report the discontinued operations **separately** in the year 1 income statement immediately **below income from continuing operations.** Discontinued operations should be reported **net of income taxes in the period in which they occur.**

c. Hillside should include the costs incurred to relocate employees in the **loss from discontinued operations** in its year 2 income statement. These costs are a **direct result** of the **commitment to dispose of its component** and are incurred in year 2.

Research

FAS 144, Par. C19

C19. FASB Interpretation No. 18, Accounting for Income Taxes in Interim Periods, is amended as follows:

a. Footnote 1 to paragraph 5 is replaced by the following:

The terms used in this definition are described in APB Opinion No. 20, Accounting Changes, in APB Opinion No. 30, Reporting the Results of Operations —Reporting the Effects of Disposal of a Segment of a Business, and Extraordinary, Unusual and Infrequently Occurring Events and Transactions, and in FASB Statement No. 144, Accounting for the Impairment or Disposal of Long-Lived Assets. See paragraph 10 of Opinion 30 for extraordinary items and paragraph 26 for unusual items and infrequently occurring items. See paragraph 20 of Opinion 20 for cumulative effects of changes in accounting principles. See paragraphs 41-44 of Statement 144 for discontinued operations.

b. Paragraph 19 is amended as follows:

(1) All references to measurement date are replaced by date on which the criteria in paragraph 30 of Statement 144 are met.

(2) In the first sentence, both (a) and (b) the gain (or loss) on disposal of discontinued operations (including any provision for operating loss subsequent to the measurement date) are deleted.

(3) All references to discontinued segment are replaced by discontinued component.

(4) Footnote 20 is replaced by the following:

The term discontinued component refers to the disposal of a component of an entity as described in paragraph 41 of Statement 144.

c. In paragraph 35, the references to segment of a business are replaced by component of an entity.

d. In paragraph 71, under Discontinued operations, Division is replaced by Component and Income (loss) on disposal of Division X, including provision of $XXXX for operating losses during phase-out period (less applicable income taxes of $XXXX) is deleted.

Solution 11-7

Essay—Segment Reporting

a. The objective of disclosures about segments of an enterprise is to provide information about the **different types of business activities** in which the enterprise engages and the **different economic environments** in which it operates. These objectives include helping stakeholders better **understand the enterprise's performance,** better **assess its prospects** for future net cash flows, and make **more informed judgments** about the enterprise as a whole.

b. Barnet should use the **management approach** in determining what segments to report. This approach is based on the way that management organizes the segments within the enterprise for **making operating decisions and assessing performance.**

The structure of the enterprise, within materiality limits, should be considered. Operating segments that provide **10% or more of combined revenue,** internal and external, or **10% or more of combined operating profits** for segments not reporting a loss, or **10% or more of combined reported losses** for segments that reported a loss should be included.

Research

FAS 143, Par. 14

14. An entity shall measure changes in the liability for an asset retirement obligation due to passage of time by applying an interest method of allocation to the amount of the liability at the beginning of the period. 12 The interest rate used to measure that change shall be the credit-adjusted risk-free rate that existed when the liability, or portion thereof, was initially measured. That amount shall be recognized as an increase in the carrying amount of the liability and as an expense classified as an operating item in the statement of income, hereinafter referred to as accretion expense. 13 Accretion expense shall not be considered to be interest cost for purposes of applying FASB Statement No. 34, Capitalization of Interest Cost.

Solution 11-8

Research

APB 30, par 20

20. Extraordinary items are events and transactions that are distinguished by their unusual nature and by the infrequency of their occurrence. Thus, both of the following criteria should be met to classify an event or transaction as an extraordinary item:

a. Unusual nature—the underlying event or transaction should possess a high degree of abnormality and be of a type clearly unrelated to, or only incidentally related to, the ordinary and typical activities of the entity, taking into account the environment in which the entity operates. (See discussion in paragraph 21.)

b. Infrequency of occurrence—the underlying event or transaction should be of a type that would not reasonably be expected to recur in the foreseeable future, taking into account the environment in which the entity operates.

Multiple-Step Income Statement

Probe Co.
Income Statement
For the Year Ended December 31, Year 3

	A	B	
Sales		**$2,420,000**	1
Cost of sales		**1,863,000**	2
Gross profit		557,000	3
Selling and administrative expenses	**$220,000**		4
Depreciation	**88,000**	308,000	5
Operating income		249,000	6
Other income (expenses):			
Interest income	**14,000**		7
Interest expense	**(46,000)**		8
Loss on sale of equipment	**(7,000)**	(39,000)	9
Income before income tax and extraordinary item		210,000	10
Income tax:			
Current	**45,000**		11
Deferred	**12,000**	57,000	12
Income before extraordinary item		153,000	13
Extraordinary item:			
Gain on flood damage, net of income taxes of $27,000		**63,000**	14
Net income		$ 216,000	15
Earnings per share:			
Earnings before extraordinary item		$ **1.275**	16
Extraordinary item		**.525**	17
Net income		$ 1.800	18

Explanations

1B. Sales given in scenario information.

2B. Cost of sales given in scenario information.

3B. Sales less cost of sales ($,420,000 – $1,863,000).

4A. Selling and administrative expenses given in scenario information.

5A. Depreciation given in scenario information.

5B. Total selling & administrative expenses plus depreciation ($220,000 + $88,000).

6B. Gross profit less expenses ($557,000 – $308,000).

7A. Interest income given in scenario information.

8A. Interest expense given in scenario information.

9A. Loss on sale of equipment given in scenario information.

9B. Total other income less expenses ($14,000 – $46,000 – $7,000).

10B. Sum of operating income and other income (expenses) ($249,000 – $39,000).

11A. Current income tax.

Income before income tax and extraordinary item	$210,000
Differences between financial statement and taxable income	(60,000)
Income subject to tax	150,000
Income tax rate	× 30%
Income tax excluding extraordinary item (current income tax expense)	$ 45,000

12A. Deferred income tax.

Cumulative temporary differences—12/31 year 3	$180,000
Income tax rate	× 30%
Deferred tax liability—12/31 year 3	54,000
Deferred tax liability—12/31 year 2	(42,000)
Deferred income tax expense for year 3	$ 12,000

12B. Total income taxes (current plus deferred) ($45,000 + $12,000).

13B. Income less taxes ($210,000 – $57,000).

14B. Gain on flood damage less taxes ($90,000 × .7).

15B. Income adjusted for extraordinary items ($153,000 + $63,000).

16B. Earnings per share before extraordinary item.

Earnings per share:	
January thru March	
60,000 × 3 months	180,000
April thru December	
140,000 × 9 months	1,260,000
Total	1,440,000
	/ 12
Weighted average number of shares outstanding for year 3	120,000
Income before extraordinary item	$ 153,000
Earnings per share ($153,000 / 120,000)	$ 1.275

17B. Extraordinary item per share: Extraordinary item divided by weighted average number of shares outstanding for year 3 ($63,000 / 120,000).

18B. Net income per share: Net income divided by weighted average number of shares outstanding for year 3 ($216,000 / 120,000)

Solution 11-9

Research

FAS 154, Par. 5

5. Neither (a) initial adoption of an accounting principle in recognition of events or transactions occurring for the first time or that previously were immaterial in their effect nor (b) adoption or modification of an accounting principle necessitated by transactions or events that are clearly different in substance from those previously occurring is a change in accounting principle. A reporting entity shall change an accounting principle only if (a) the change is required by a newly issued accounting pronouncement or (b) the entity can justify the use of an allowable alternative accounting principle on the basis that it is preferable.

Essay—Accrual Basis Financial Statements

To: Baron Flowers

From: Muir

Re: Accrual basis financial statements

You have asked me to explain why the bank would require financial statements prepared on the accrual basis instead of the cash basis. The bank is concerned about your **ability to repay the loan.** To **assess** that **ability,** it wants information about your **earnings** for the **period, total assets,** and all **claims** on those assets. This information about your enterprise's performance and financial position is provided **more completely** by accrual basis financial statements than by cash basis financial statements.

Under the cash basis, **revenues are recognized when received** and **expenses when paid.** Earnings can be **manipulated by the timing of cash receipts and disbursements.** Accrual basis accounting, while grounded in cash flows, reports transactions and other events with cash consequences at the time the transactions and events occur. Revenues and expenses are reported in the **accounting period benefited** and reflect receivables and payables, not just what the enterprise was able to collect or chose to pay.

Worksheet—Cash Basis to Accrual Basis

Baron Flowers
Worksheet to Convert Trial Balance to Accrual Basis
December 31, Year 4

	Cash basis		Adjustments				Accrual Basis*	
Account title	Dr.	Cr.	Ref	Dr.	Ref	Cr.	Dr.*	Cr.*
Cash	25,600						25,600	
Accounts receivable, 12/31 year 3	16,200		1	**15,800**			32,000	
Inventory, 12/31 year 3	62,000		4	**10,800**			72,800	
Furniture & fixtures	118,200						118,200	
Land improvements	45,000						45,000	
Accumulated depreciation & amortization, 12/31 year 3		32,400			6	**14,250**		46,650
Accounts payable, 12/31 year 3		17,000			3	**13,500**		30,500
Baron, Drawings			9	**61,000**			61,000	
Baron, Capital, 12/31 year 3		124,600	7	**2,000**	5	**2,600**		125,200
Allowance for uncollectible accounts					2	**3,800**		3,800
Prepaid insurance			5	**2,900**			2,900	
Accrued expenses					7	**3,100**		3,100
Est. liability from lawsuit					8	**50,000**		50,000
Sales		653,000			1	**15,800**		668,800
Purchases	305,100		3	**13,500**			318,600	
Salaries	174,000				9	**48,000**	126,000	
Payroll taxes	12,400		7	**500**			12,900	
Insurance	8,700				5	**300**	8,400	
Rent	34,200						34,200	
Utilities	12,600		7	**600**			13,200	
Living expenses	13,000				9	**13,000**		
Income summary—inventory			4	**62,000**	4	**72,800**		10,800
Uncollectible accounts			2	**3,800**			3,800	
Depreciation & amortization			6	**14,250**			14,250	
Estimated loss from lawsuit			8	**50,000**			50,000	
	827,000	827,000		237,150		237,150	938,850	938,850

These explanation reference numbers correspond with the entries on the lines with the same number.

[1] To convert year 4 sales to accrual basis.

Accounts receivable balances:	
December 31, year 4	$ 32,000
December 31, year 3	(16,200)
Increase in sales	$ 15,800

[2] To record provision for uncollectible accounts.

[3] To convert year 4 purchases to accrual basis.

Accounts payable balances:	
December 31, year 4	$ 30,500
December 31, year 3	(17,000)
Increase in purchases	$ 13,500

[4] To record increase in inventory from 12/31 year 3 to 12/31 year 4

Inventory balances:	
December 31, year 4	$ 72,800
December 31, year 3	(62,000)
Increase in inventory	$ 10,800

[5] To adjust prepaid insurance.

Prepaid balances:	
December 31, year 4 ($8,700 × 4/12)	$ 2,900
December 31, year 3 ($7,800 × 4/12)	(2,600)
Decrease in insurance expense	$ 300

[6] To record year 4 depreciation and amortization expense.

Cost of leasehold improvement	$45,000
Estimated life – 15 years	
Amortization ($45,000 × 1/15 × 9/12)	2,250
Depreciation expense on fixtures and equipment	12,000
	$14,250

[7] To convert expenses to accrual basis.

	Balances December 31, Year 4	Balances December 31, Year 3	Increase in expenses
Utilities	$1,500	$ 900	$ 600
Payroll taxes	1,600	1,100	500
	$3,100	$2,000	$1,100

[8] To record lawsuit liability at 12/31 year 4.

Attorney's estimate of probable loss	$ 300,000
Amount covered by insurance	(250,000)
Baron's estimated liability	$ 50,000

[9] To record Baron's drawings for year 4.

Salary ($4,000 × 12)	$ 48,000
Living expenses	13,000
	$ 61,000

Duplicate Worksheet for Problem 11-9

Using this worksheet, prepare the adjustments necessary to convert the trial balance of Baron Flowers to the accrual basis of accounting for the year ended December 31, year 4. Formal journal entries are not required to support your adjustments. The numbers given in the additional information (choices) section are to be placed in the Ref columns to cross-reference the postings placed in the adjustment columns.

Baron Flowers
Worksheet to Convert Trial Balance to Accrual Basis
December 31, Year 4

	Cash basis		Adjustments				Accrual Basis*	
Account title	Dr.	Cr.	Ref.	Dr.	Ref.	Cr.	Dr.*	Cr.*
Cash	25,600							
Accounts receivable, 12/31 year 3	16,200							
Inventory, 12/31 year 3	62,000							
Furniture & fixtures	118,200							
Land improvements	45,000							
Accumulated depreciation & amortization, 12/31 year 3		32,400						
Accounts payable, 12/31 year 3		17,000						
Baron, Drawings								
Baron, Capital, 12/31 year 3		124,600						
Sales		653,000						
Purchases	305,100							
Salaries	174,000							
Payroll taxes	12,400							
Insurance	8,700							
Rent	34,200							
Utilities	12,600							
Living expenses	13,000							
	827,000	827,000						

* Completion of these columns is not required but may be useful in checking your work.

CHAPTER 12

REPORTING: SPECIAL AREAS

I. **Alternative Revenue Recognition Methods** 12-2
- A. Installment 12-2
- B. Cost Recovery 12-3
- C. Completion of Production 12-3

II. ***Revenue Recognition When Right of Return Exists* (SFAS 48)** 12-4
- A. Time of Sale 12-4
- B. Deferral 12-4
- C. Costs or Losses 12-4

III. **Long-Term Construction Contracts (ARB 45)** 12-4
- A. Recommendation 12-4
- B. Completed Contract Method 12-4
- C. Percentage of Completion Method 12-5

IV. **Consignments** 12-8
- A. Overview 12-8
- B. Computation 12-8

V. **Franchise Fee Income (SFAS 45)** 12-8
- A. Revenue 12-8
- B. Costs 12-9

VI. **Royalties** 12-9
- A. Accrual Basis 12-9
- B. Computation 12-9

VII. **Changing Prices** 12-10
- A. Optional 12-10
- B. Monetary & Nonmonetary Items 12-11
- C. Presentation 12-12
- D. Inventory and PP&E 12-13
- E. Recoverable Amount 12-14
- F. Change in Current Costs of Inventory and PP&E, Net of Inflation 12-14
- G. Income From Continuing Operations 12-15
- H. Restatement of Current Cost Information Into Units of Constant Purchasing Power 12-16
- I. Purchasing Power Gain or Loss on Net Monetary Items 12-16
- J. Holding Gains & Losses on Nonmonetary Assets 12-17

EXAM COVERAGE: Historically, exam coverage of the topics in Chapters 11 and 12 has been about 25 percent of the FAR section. Long-term construction contracts and, to a lesser extent, alternative revenue recognition are tested on almost every exam. More information regarding exam coverage is included in Appendix B, *Practical Advice*.

CHAPTER 12

REPORTING: SPECIAL AREAS

I. Alternative Revenue Recognition Methods

A. Installment

Under GAAP, revenues are usually recognized when two conditions are met: (a) the earnings process is complete or virtually complete, and (b) an exchange has taken place. Thus, revenues generally are recognized at the point of sale. There are several exceptions to this rule. The installment method is an exception to this because it allows revenue to be deferred and recognized each year in proportion to the receivables collected during that year.

Example 1 ▸ Installment Method

The Thomas Equipment Company reports income using the installment method of accounting and uses a perpetual inventory system. Installment sales during year 3 amounted to $400,000.

Year of sale	Gross profit percentage	Installment receivables on Jan. 1, year 3	Collected during Year 3	Installment receivables on Dec. 31, year 3
1	46%	$ 60,000	$ 60,000	--
2	42%	100,000	68,000	$ 32,000
3	40%	--	120,000	280,000

Required: Determine

1. The realized gross profit on installment sales during year 3 from all sales.
2. The balance in the deferred gross profit account at December 31, year 3.

Solution:

1. The realized gross profit on installment sales is $104,160.

Year of sale	Gross profit percentage		Year 3 collections		Realized gross profit
1	46%	×	$ 60,000	=	$ 27,600
2	42%	×	68,000	=	28,560
3	40%	×	120,000	=	48,000
					$104,160

2. The balance in the deferred gross profit account is $125,440.

Year of sale	Gross profit percentage		Installment receivables on Dec. 31, year 3		Deferred gross profit
2	42%	×	$ 32,000	=	$ 13,440
3	40%	×	280,000	=	112,000
					$125,440

1. **Applicability** APB 10, par. 12, states that the installment method of accounting for sales is **not** acceptable unless circumstances exist such that collection of the sales price is "not reasonably assured." APB 10 also permits use of the installment method when receivables are collected over an extended period of time and when there is no reasonable basis for estimating the degree of collectibility.

2. **Computation** Income recognized using the installment method of accounting generally equals cash collected multiplied by the gross profit percentage applicable to those sales. Selling and administrative expenses are not used to compute the gross profit rate. Receivable accounts and deferred profit accounts must be kept separately for each year because the

gross profit rate will often vary from year to year. Where an installment receivable extends beyond one year, it should be recorded at the present value of the payments discounted at the market interest rate. At any time after the sale, the installment receivables' balance will be the present value of the remaining monthly payments discounted at the market interest rate at the time of the exchange.

B. Cost Recovery

Like the installment method, the cost recovery method of revenue recognition is **not** generally accepted; however, the cost recovery method may be used where (1) collectibility of proceeds is doubtful, (2) where an investment is very speculative in nature, and/or (3) where the final sale price is to be determined by future events.

Example 2 ▸ Cost Recovery Method

On January 2, year 2, Old Mine Co. sold a gold mine that had become unprofitable to Golddiggers, Inc., a newly incorporated venture that hoped to wring additional profits from the mine by use of a revolutionary—but yet unproven—method of extraction. At the time of the sale, the gold mine had a carrying amount of $450,000 in Old Mine's books. The sales agreement called for a $100,000 down payment and two notes of $200,000 bearing interest of 10% with one note payable, including accrued interest, due on January 2, year 3 and one note payable, including accrued interest, due on January 2, year 4. Because of the extreme uncertainty concerning the eventual collection of the notes' proceeds, Old Mine appropriately accounted for this transaction under the cost recovery method. The notes were paid when due, including interest and principal.

Required: Determine Old Mine's income from this transaction for the years ending December 31, year 2, year 3, and year 4. Provide appropriate journal entries.

Solution:

Year	Amount collected	Unrecovered cost (Year 1: $450,000)	Deferred profit Dr. (Cr.)	Recognized profit (Cr.)
2	$100,000	$350,000	($50,000)	$ 0
3	220,000	130,000	(20,000)	0
4	242,000	0	70,000	(112,000)

Year 2: Cash	100,000	
Notes Receivable	400,000	
Gold Mine (net)		450,000
Deferred Profit		50,000
Year 3: Cash [$200,000 + ($200,000 × 10%)]	220,000	
Notes Receivable		200,000
Deferred Profit		20,000
Year 4: Cash [$220,000 + ($220,000 × 10%)]	242,000	
Deferred Profit	70,000	
Recognized Profit		112,000
Notes Receivable		200,000

1. The cost recovery method is the most conservative revenue recognition method. This method is used when the uncertainty of collection is so great that use of the installment method is precluded.

2. All amounts collected are treated as a recoupment of the cost of the item sold, until the entire cost associated with the transaction has been recovered. Only at this point is profit recognized.

C. Completion of Production

Revenue sometimes is recognized at completion of the production activity. The three necessary conditions rarely are present except in the case of certain precious metals and agricultural products.

The recognition of revenue at completion of production is justified **only** if certain conditions are present.

1. There must be a relatively stable market for the product.

2. Marketing costs must be nominal.

3. The units must be homogeneous.

II. *Revenue Recognition When Right of Return Exists* (SFAS 48)

A. Time of Sale

Revenue from sales when the buyer has the right to return the product should be recognized at the time of sale only if all the following conditions are met.

1. The seller's price to the buyer is substantially fixed or determinable at the date of sale.

2. The buyer has paid the seller, or the buyer is obligated to pay the seller, and the obligation is not contingent on resale of the product.

3. The buyer's obligation to the seller would not be changed in the event of theft, physical destruction, or damage of the product.

4. The buyer acquiring the product for resale has economic substance apart from that provided by the seller.

5. The seller does not have significant obligations for future performance to directly bring about resale of the product by the buyer.

6. The amount of future returns can be reasonably estimated.

B. Deferral

If these conditions are **not** met, revenue (and cost of sales) must be recognized when the return privilege has substantially expired or when these conditions are subsequently met, whichever occurs first.

C. Costs or Losses

Any costs or losses that may be expected in connection with sales revenue recognized at the time of sale, must be accrued (see also SFAS 5, *Accounting for Contingencies*).

III. Long-Term Construction Contracts (ARB 45)

A. Recommendation

Due to the length of time implicit in long-term construction contracts, significant problems often arise concerning the measurement and timing of income recognition. The two methods most commonly used in these types of contracts are the completed contract method and the percentage of completion method. The use of the percentage of completion method is recommended when costs to complete and extent of progress can be reasonably estimated. If no dependable estimates can be made or inherent hazards are present, the completed contract method is preferable.

B. Completed Contract Method

No income is recognized on the contract until it is completed or substantially completed and the work accepted. However, if at any point expected contract costs exceed the contract price, losses are recognized immediately and in full in the current period.

1. **Balance Sheet Presentation** Excess of accumulated costs over related progress billings should be shown as a current asset on the balance sheet, while an excess of accumulated progress billings over related costs should be shown as a current liability. Contracts should be separated to accurately segregate asset and liability contracts.

2. **Advantage** The principal advantage of the completed contract method is that it is based on results as finally determined rather than on estimates for unperformed work which may involve unforeseen costs and possible losses.

3. **Disadvantage** The principal disadvantage is it does not reflect current performance when the life of the contract extends over several periods and thus diminishes the interperiod comparability of the financial statements.

C. **Percentage of Completion Method**
Income may be recognized as work on the contract progresses. The amount of income recognized in the period is added to Construction in Progress.

1. **Income Recognition** Income should be recognized on the basis of either of the following:

a. The percentage derived from incurred costs to date over total expected costs; or

$$\left(\frac{\textit{Actual cost to date}}{\textit{Estimated total cost}} \times \textit{Total estimated contract income}\right) - \textit{Income previously recognized} = \textit{Income to be recognized}$$

b. Some other measure of progress toward completion as may be appropriate under the circumstances. Thus, the percentage of completion method may be based on estimates of completion to date developed by architects or engineers.

2. **Progress Billings** Progress billings and collections on progress billings are **not** generally accepted as a method of recognizing income because they often do not bear a meaningful relationship to the work performed on the contract. Typically, billings may be accelerated in the early stages of the contract to provide the contractor with the working capital needed to begin performance. If income were recognized on progress billings, it would be possible for a contractor to materially distort income merely by rendering progress billings without regard to any degree of progress on the contract. *Progress Billings* is a contra account to *Construction in Progress.*

3. **Loss Recognition** When current estimates of total contract costs indicate a loss, the loss should be recognized immediately and in full in the current period.

4. **Current Assets/Liabilities** Each contract may give rise to a current asset or liability.

a. An excess of costs incurred and income recognized over progress billings should be reported as a current asset.

b. An excess of progress billings over related costs and income recognized constitutes a current liability.

c. Current assets and current liabilities pertaining to two or more contracts should not be netted out for financial statement presentation.

5. **Advantages** The principal advantages of the percentage of completion method are the following:

a. Periodic recognition of income as work is performed thus enhancing the interperiod comparability of the financial statements; and

b. Reflection of the status of uncompleted contracts provided through current estimates of completion costs.

6. **Disadvantage** The principal disadvantage is the necessity of relying on estimates of ultimate contract costs and of consequently accruing income based upon those estimates.

Example 3 ▸ Percentage of Completion vs. Completed Contract

On January 1, year 1, Estimator, Inc. entered into two $1,800,000 fixed-price contracts to construct office buildings. The estimated time for both projects was three years.

	Year 1	Year 2	Year 3
Contract A			
Incurred costs to date	$ 250,000	$ 320,000	$1,530,000
Est. costs to complete	1,250,000	1,280,000	0
Total estimated costs	1,500,000	1,600,000	1,530,000
Billed during year	220,000	1,130,000	450,000
Collected during year	180,000	1,040,000	580,000
Contract B			
Incurred costs to date	$ 250,000	$ 320,000	$1,810,000
Est. costs to complete	1,250,000	1,490,000	0
Total estimated costs	1,500,000	1,810,000	1,810,000
Billed during year	220,000	1,130,000	450,000
Collected during year	180,000	1,040,000	580,000

Required: Prepare the journal entries and determine income (loss) recognized in all three years for both contracts under the percentage of completion method and the completed contract method (in 1,000s).

Solution:

Percentage of Completion Entries
1. To record the costs of construction.
2. To record progress billings.
3. To record collections.
4. To recognize revenue and gross profit.
5. To record the completion of the contract.

Contract A		Year 1		Year 2		Year 3	
1.	Construction in Progress	250		70		1,210	
	Cash (or Accounts Payable)		250		70		1,210
2.	Accounts Receivable	220		1,130		450	
	Progress Billings		220		1,130		450
3.	Cash	180		1,040		580	
	Accounts Receivable		180		1,040		580
4.	Construction Expenses	250					
	Construction in Progress	50 [1]					
	Revenue from LT Contracts		300				
4.	Construction Expenses			70			
	Construction in Progress				10 [2]		
	Revenue from LT Contracts				60		
4.	Construction Expenses					1,210	
	Construction in Progress					230 [3]	
	Revenue from LT Contracts						1,440
5.	Progress Billings					1,800	
	Construction in Progress						1,800 [4]

[1] (250 / 1,500) × [1,800 – (250 + 1,250)] – 0 = 50
[2] (320 / 1,600) × [1,800 – (320 + 1,280)] – 50 = –10
[3] (1,530 / 1,530) × [1,800 – 1,530] – (50 – 10) = 230
[4] 250 + 50 + 70 – 10 + 230 + 1,210 = 1,800

Contract B

1.	Construction in Progress	250		70		1,490	
	Cash (or Accounts Payable)		250		70		1,490
2.	Accounts Receivable	220		1,130		450	
	Progress Billings		220		1,130		450
3.	Cash	180		1,040		580	
	Accounts Receivable		180		1,040		580
4.	Construction Expenses	250					
	Construction in Progress	50 [1]					
	Revenue from LT Contracts		300				
4.	Construction Expenses			70			
	Construction in Progress				60 [2]		
	Revenue from LT Contracts				10		
4.	Construction Expenses					1,490	
	Revenue from LT Contracts						1,490
5.	Progress Billings					1,800	
	Construction in Progress						1,800 [3]

[1] (250 / 1,500) × [1,800 – (250 + 1,250)] – 0 = 50
[2] Reverse recognized profit and recognize estimated loss in full. –50 + (1,800 – 1,810) = –60
[3] 250 + 50 + 70 – 60 + 1,490 = 1,800

Completed Contract Entries

1, 2, and 3. The entries to record the costs of construction, progress billings, and collections are the same as entries 1, 2, and 3 for the percentage of completion method for both contracts.
4. To record the contract loss first evident in year 2 on Contract B.
5. To recognize revenue and gross profit and record the completion of the contract.

		Year 1		Year 2		Year 3	
Contract A							
5.	Construction Expenses					1,530	
	Construction in Progress						1,530
	Progress Billings					1,800	
	Revenue from LT Contracts						1,800
Contract B							
4.	Loss From LT Contracts			10			
	Construction in Progress				10		
5.	Construction Expenses					1,800	
	Construction in Progress						1,800
	Progress Billings					1,800	
	Revenue from LT Contracts						1,800

Income (Loss) Recognized

Contract A	Year 1	Year 2	Year 3	Total
% of Completion	$50	($10)	$230	$270
Completed Contract	0	0	270	270
Contract B				
% of Completion	50	(60)	0	(10)
Completed Contract	0	(10)	0	(10)

NOTE: Contract A has a loss in year 2, but overall the contract is profitable. Contract B has an overall loss, which is recognized in year 2, the year the loss is evident.

IV. Consignments

A. Overview

A consignment is a transfer of goods from the owner (consignor) to another person (consignee) who acts as a sales agent for the owner in a principal-agent relationship. The transfer is **not** a sale and the consignee never has title to the goods. When the consignee sells the goods, title passes directly from the consignor to the third party buyer.

B. Computation

Consignment sales revenue is recognized at the time of the sale at the sales price. The commission paid to the consignee is reported as a selling expense; it is **not** netted against sales revenue.

Example 4 ▸ Consignment Sale

On October 10 of the current year, Dunn Co. consigned 50 freezers to Taylor Co. for sale at $1,000 each and paid $800 in transportation costs. On December 30, Taylor reported the sale of 20 freezers and remitted $18,000. The remittance was net of the agreed 10% commission.

Required: Determine the amount of consignment sales revenue for the year.

Solution: Consignment sales revenue is recognized at the time of the sale at the sales price. Thus, consignment sales revenue of $20,000 (20 freezers × $1,000 sales price) should be reported in the current year. The 10% commission should be reported as a selling expense; it should **not** be netted against sales revenue. The following journal entry would be used to record the consignment sale.

Cash	18,000	
Consignment Sales Commissions	2,000	
Consignment Sales Revenues		20,000

V. Franchise Fee Income (SFAS 45)

A. Revenue

Initial franchise fees from franchise sales ordinarily must be recognized (with provision for estimated uncollectible amounts) when all material services or conditions relating to the sale have been substantially performed or satisfied by the franchisor.

Example 5 ▸ Franchise Fee Revenue

Bigger Burger, Inc., sold a fast food restaurant franchise to Donald. The sale agreement, signed on January 2, year 1, called for a $30,000 down payment plus two $10,000 annual payments, due January 2, year 2 and January 2, year 3, representing the value of initial franchise services rendered by Bigger Burger. The agreement required the franchisee to pay 5% of its gross revenues to the franchisor; deemed sufficient to cover the cost and a reasonable profit margin on continuing franchise services to be performed by Bigger Burger. The restaurant opened early in year 1, and its sales for the year amounted to $500,000.

Required: Assuming a 10% interest rate, determine Bigger Burger's year 1 total revenue from the Donald franchise.

Solution:

Initial franchise fee:		
Down payment	$30,000	
P.V. of installments ($10,000 × 1.7355)	17,355	$47,355
5% of gross sales (.05 × $500,000)		25,000
Interest income ($17,355 × .10)		1,735
Year 1 Total Revenue		$74,090

1. **Substantial Performance** Services are considered to be substantially performed when

   a. The franchisor has no remaining obligation or intent to refund any cash received or forgive any unpaid notes or receivables.

   b. Substantially all *initial* services of the franchisor required by the franchise agreement have been performed.

   c. No other material conditions or obligations related to the determination of substantial performance exist.

2. **Installment and Cost Recovery Methods** Installment or cost recovery accounting methods may be used to account for franchise fee revenue only when revenue is collectible over an extended period and no reasonable basis exists for estimating collectibility.

3. **Deferred Income** If it is probable that continuing franchise fees will not cover the cost of the continuing services to be provided by the franchisor and also allow reasonable profit, then a portion of the original franchise fee should be deferred and amortized over the life of the franchise. The deferred amount should be enough to cover future costs and provide a reasonable profit on the continuing services. Report continuing franchise fees as revenue when the fees are earned and become receivable from the franchisee.

B. Costs

Costs related to continuing franchise fees should be expensed as incurred.

1. **Direct Costs** Direct incremental costs relating to franchise sales ordinarily are deferred until the related revenue is recognized; however, deferred costs must not exceed anticipated revenue less estimated additional related costs.

2. **Indirect Costs** Indirect costs of a regular and recurring nature irrespective of the level of sales should be expensed as incurred.

3. **Match Costs With Related Revenue** Costs yet to be incurred should be accrued and charged against income no later than the period in which the related revenue is recognized.

VI. Royalties

A. Accrual Basis

Royalty revenue and royalty expense are recognized under the rules of accrual accounting.

1. **Revenue** Royalty revenue is recognized in the period(s) the royalties are earned. Royalties received in advance are not recognized as revenue at the date of the royalty agreement.

2. **Expense** Royalty expense is recognized in the period the royalties are incurred. Royalties paid in advance are not recognized as an expense at the date of the royalty agreement.

B. Computation

In general, the amount of royalty revenue or expense to recognize during a period is computed by multiplying the period's sales applicable to the royalty agreement by the royalty percentage.

Example 6 ▸ Royalties

On January 2, year 1, Shaw Company sold the copyright to a book to Poe Publishers, Inc. for royalties of 20% of future sales. On the same date, Poe paid Shaw a royalty advance of $100,000 to be applied against royalties for year 2 sales. On September 30, year 1, Poe made a $42,000 royalty remittance to Shaw for sales in the six-month period ended June 30, year 1. In January year 2, before issuance of its year 1 financial statements, Shaw learned that Poe's sales of the book totaled $250,000 for the last half of year 1.

Required: Determine how much royalty revenue Shaw should report in year 1.

Solution: The $100,000 advance to be applied against royalties for year 2 sales is **not** used to compute royalty revenue. Neither royalty revenue nor royalty expense is recognized on the cash basis.

Royalties for Jan. 1 - June 30, year 1 (paid Sept. 30, year 1)	$42,000
Royalties for July 1 - Dec. 31, year 1 ($250,000 × 20%)	50,000
Royalty revenue for year 1	$92,000

VII. Changing Prices

A. Optional

A business enterprise that prepares its financial statements in U.S. dollars and in conformity with U.S. generally accepted accounting principles is encouraged, though not required, to disclose supplementary information on the effects of changing prices. SFAS 89, *Financial Reporting and Changing Prices,* defines the following terms.

1. **Current Cost/Constant Purchasing Power Accounting** A method of accounting based on measures of current cost or lower recoverable amount in units of currency, each of which has the same general purchasing power. For operations in which the dollar is the functional currency, the general purchasing power of the dollar is used, and the Consumer Price Index for All Urban Consumers (CPI-U) is the required measure of purchasing power.

2. **Current Market Value** The amount of cash, or its equivalent, expected to be derived from the sale of an asset, net of costs required to be incurred as a result of the sale.

3. **Historical Cost Accounting** The generally accepted method of accounting used in the primary financial statements that is based on measures of historical prices without restatement into units, each of which has the same general purchasing power.

4. **Historical Cost/Constant Purchasing Power Accounting** A method of accounting based on measures of historical prices in units of a currency, each of which has the same general purchasing power.

5. **Income From Continuing Operations** Income after applicable income taxes but excluding the results of discontinued operations, extraordinary items, the cumulative effect of accounting changes, purchasing power gains and losses on monetary items, and increases and decreases in the current cost or lower recoverable amount of nonmonetary assets and liabilities.

6. **Monetary Asset** Money or a claim to receive a sum of money, the amount of which is fixed or determinable without reference to future prices of specific goods or services.

7. **Monetary Liability** An obligation to pay a sum of money, the amount of which is fixed or determinable without reference to future prices of specific goods and services.

8. **Purchasing Power Gain or Loss on Net Monetary Items** The net gain or loss determined by restating in units of constant purchasing power the opening and closing balances of, and transactions in monetary assets and liabilities.

9. **Recoverable Amount** Current worth of the net amount of cash expected to be recoverable from the use or sale of an asset.

10. **Value in Use** The amount determined by discounting the future cash flows (including the ultimate proceeds of disposal) expected to be derived from the use of an asset at an appropriate rate that allows for the risk of the activities concerned.

B. **Monetary & Nonmonetary Items**

1. **Monetary Assets** Monetary assets are defined as money or a claim to receive a sum of money, the amount of which is fixed or determinable without reference to future prices of specific goods or services.

Exhibit 1 ▸ Monetary Assets

Time Deposits	Cash on hand and demand bank deposits
Bonds (other than convertible)	Foreign currency—on hand and claims to
Accounts and notes receivable	Preferred stock (nonconvertible and non-participating)
Loans to employees	Allowance for uncollectible accounts/notes receivable
Long-term receivables	Advances to unconsolidated subsidiaries
Refundable deposits	Cash surrender value of life insurance
Deferred tax assets	Advances to supplier—not on a fixed price contract

2. **Nonmonetary Assets**

a. Goods held primarily for resale or assets held primarily for direct use in providing services for the business of the enterprise.

b. Claims to cash in amounts dependent on future prices of specific goods or services.

c. Residual rights such as goodwill or equity interests.

Exhibit 2 ▸ Nonmonetary Assets

Investment in common stocks (in most circumstances)
Inventories (other than inventories used on contracts)
Property, plant, and equipment (PP&E)
Accumulated depreciation of PP&E
Purchase commitments—portion paid on fixed-price contracts
Patents, trademarks, licenses, and formulas
Goodwill
Other intangible assets and deferred charges

3. **Assets Requiring Individual Analysis**

a. **Preferred Stock (Convertible or Participating) and Convertible Bonds** If the market values the security primarily as a bond, it is monetary; if it values the security primarily as stock, it is nonmonetary.

b. **Inventories Used on Contracts** If the future cash receipts on the contracts will not vary due to future changes in specific prices, they are monetary. Goods used on contracts to be priced at market upon delivery are nonmonetary.

c. **Pension, Sinking, and Other Funds Under an Enterprise's Control** The specific assets in the fund should be classified as monetary or nonmonetary.

4. **Monetary Liabilities** Monetary liabilities are obligations to pay a sum of money, the amount of which is fixed or determinable without reference to future prices of specific goods or services.

Exhibit 3 ▸ Monetary Liabilities

Accounts and notes payable	Obligations payable in foreign currency
Accrued expenses payable	Customer advances—not on fixed price contracts
Cash dividends payable	Accrued losses on firm purchase commitments
Refundable deposits	Bonds payable and other long-terms debt
Convertible bonds payable	Unamortized premium or discount and prepaid interest on bonds or notes payable
Deferred tax	

5. **Nonmonetary Liabilities**

   a. Obligations to furnish goods or services in quantities that are fixed or determinable without reference to changes in prices.

   b. Obligations to pay cash in amounts dependent on future prices of specific goods or services.

Exhibit 4 ▸ Nonmonetary Liabilities

Sales commitments—portion collected on fixed-price contracts
Obligations under warranties
Deferred investment tax credits
Minority interests in consolidated subsidiaries

6. **Liabilities Requiring Special Analysis** Liabilities requiring special analysis include deferred revenue. If an obligation to furnish goods or services is involved, deferred revenue is nonmonetary.

7. **Stockholders' Equity—Preferred Stock** Capital stock of the enterprise or of its consolidated subsidiaries subject to mandatory redemption at fixed amounts is considered a monetary item. Therefore, preferred stock, which is fixed in terms of dollars to be paid in liquidation, is classified as a monetary item.

C. **Presentation**

1. **Five-Year Summary of Selected Financial Data** Enterprises are encouraged to provide information for each of the five most recent years for net sales and other operating revenues; income from continuing operations on a current cost basis; the purchasing power gain or loss on net monetary items; the increase or decrease in the current cost or lower recoverable amount of inventory and property, plant, and equipment, net of inflation; the aggregate foreign currency translation adjustment on a current cost basis, if applicable; net assets at year-end on a current cost basis; income per common share from continuing operations on a current cost basis; cash dividends declared per common share; and the market price per common share at year-end.

2. **Additional Current Year Disclosures** If income from continuing operations on a current cost/constant purchasing power basis would differ significantly from that reported in the primary financial statements, enterprises are encouraged to provide information about the current cost basis on the components, including the cost of goods sold, and the depreciation, depletion, and amortization expense. The information may be presented in a statement format or in a reconciliation format.

3. **Separate Disclosures** The enterprise is also encouraged to disclose separate amounts for the current cost of lower recoverable amount at the end of the current year of inventory and PPE; the increase or decrease in current cost or lower recoverable amount before and after adjusting for the effects of inflation of inventory and PPE for the current year; the principal types of information used to calculate the current cost of inventory, PPE, cost of goods sold, and depreciation depletion, and amortization expense; and any differences between the

depreciation methods, estimates of useful lives, and salvage values of assets used for calculations of current cost/constant purchasing power depreciation and the methods and estimates used for calculations of depreciation in the primary financial statements.

D. Inventory and PP&E

Current cost amounts of inventory and property, plant, and equipment (PP&E) are measured as follows.

1. **Inventory at Current Cost or Lower Recoverable Amount at Measurement Date** The current cost of inventory owned by an enterprise is the current cost of purchasing the goods concerned or the current cost of the resources required to produce the goods concerned (including an allowance for overhead), whichever would be applicable in the circumstances of the enterprise.

Example 7 ▸ Current Cost of Inventory

Rice Wholesaling Corporation accounts for inventory on a FIFO basis. There were 8,000 units in inventory on January 1 of the current year. Costs were incurred and goods purchased as follows during the year.

Period	Historical costs	Units purchased	Units sold
1st quarter	$ 410,000	7,000	7,500
2nd quarter	550,000	8,500	7,300
3rd quarter	425,000	6,500	8,200
4th quarter	630,000	9,000	7,000
	$2,015,000	31,000	30,000

Rice estimates that the current cost per unit of inventory was $57 at January 1, and $71 at December 31.

Required: Determine the amount of December 31 inventory to be reported in Rice's voluntary supplementary information restated into current cost.

Solution: 9,000 units × $71 / unit = $639,000

Units in inventory, 1/1	8,000
Units purchased during the year	31,000
Units available for sale	39,000
Units sold during the year	(30,000)
Units in inventory, 12/31	9,000

NOTE: The FIFO inventory cost flow method used for the primary financial statements is irrelevant to the computation of the current cost of the year-end inventory.

2. **PP&E at Current Cost or Lower Recoverable Amount of Assets, Remaining Service Potential at Measurement Date** The current cost of PP&E owned by an enterprise is the current cost of acquiring the same service potential as embodied by the asset owned; the information used to measure current cost reflects whatever method of acquisition would be currently appropriate in the circumstances of the enterprise. The current cost of a used asset may be calculated by measuring the current cost of:

   a. A new asset that has the same service potential as the used asset when it was new (the current cost of the asset as if it were new) and deducting an allowance for depreciation.

   b. A used asset of the same age and in the same condition as the asset owned.

   c. A new asset with a different service potential and adjusting that cost for the value of the difference in service potential due to differences in life, output capacity, nature of service, and operating costs.

Example 8 ▸ Current Cost of PP&E

Poe Corporation calculates depreciation at 10% per annum, using the straight-line method. A full year's depreciation is charged in the year of acquisition. There were no year 3 plant asset disposals. Details of Poe's plant assets at December 31, year 3, are as follows:

Year acquired	Percent depreciated	Historical cost	Estimated current cost
1	30	$200,000	$280,000
2	20	60,000	76,000
3	10	80,000	88,000

Required: Determine the net current cost (after accumulated depreciation) of the plant assets at December 31, year 3, to be reported in Poe's voluntary supplementary information restated into current cost.

Solution:

Year	Estimated current cost	Percent not depreciated	Net current cost
1	$280,000	70%	$196,000
2	76,000	80%	60,800
3	88,000	90%	79,200
Net current cost of plant assets at 12/31, year 3			$336,000

E. **Recoverable Amount**
Recoverable amount is the current worth of the net amount of cash expected to be recoverable from the use or sale of an asset.

1. **Measurement** It may be measured by considering the value in use or current market value of the asset concerned. Value in use is used to determine the recoverable amount of an asset if immediate sale of the asset is not intended. Current market value is used to determine the recoverable amount only if the asset is about to be sold.

2. **Asset Group** If the recoverable amount for a group of assets is judged to be materially and permanently lower than the current cost amount, the recoverable amount is used as a measure of the assets and of the expense associated with the use or sale of the assets. Decisions on the measurement of assets at their recoverable amount need not be made by considering assets individually unless they are used independently of other assets.

Example 9 ▸ Current Cost or Lower Recoverable Amount of Inventory and PP&E

At December 31 of the current year, Jannis Corp. owned two assets as follows:

	Equipment	Inventory
Current cost	$100,000	$80,000
Recoverable amount	95,000	90,000

Required: Determine the amount of total assets that Jannis should report in voluntarily disclosed supplementary information about current cost at December 31.

Solution:

Equipment	$ 95,000	(Recoverable amount lower than current cost)
Inventory	80,000	(Current cost lower than recoverable amount)
Total assets at 12/31	$175,000	

F. **Change in Current Costs of Inventory and PP&E, Net of Inflation**
The increase or decrease in the current cost amounts of inventory and PP&E represents the difference between the measures of the assets at their entry dates for the year and the measures of the assets at their exit dates for the year.

1. **Entry Date** Entry date is the beginning of the year or the acquisition date, whichever is applicable.

2. **Exit Date** Exit date is the end of the year or the date of use or sale, whichever is applicable.

3. **Inflation Component** The inflation component of the increase in current cost amount is the difference between the nominal dollar and constant dollar measures.

G. **Income From Continuing Operations**
An enterprise presenting the minimum information encouraged by SFAS 89 shall measure income from continuing operations on a current cost basis.

1. **Cost of Goods Sold** Cost of goods sold at current cost or lower recoverable amount at the date of sale. To compute cost of goods sold on a current cost basis, multiply the number of units sold by the average current cost of the units during the period. (Average current cost of the units during the period is the sum of the current cost of the units at the beginning and the end of the period, divided by two.)

Example 10 ▸ Current Cost of Cost of Goods Sold

Refer to Example 7 (Rice Wholesaling Corporation)

Required: Determine the cost of goods sold for the year restated into current cost.

Solution: The FIFO inventory cost flow method used for the primary financial statements is irrelevant to the current cost computation of the cost of goods sold for the year.

Average current cost per unit [($57 + $71) / 2]	$ 64
Units sold during the year	× 30,000
Cost of goods sold, average current cost	$1,920,000

2. **Cost Recovery Expense** Depreciation, depletion, and amortization expense on the basis of the *average* current cost of the assets, service potential or lower recoverable amount during the period of use. To compute depreciation on a current cost basis, divide the average current cost of the plant asset during the period by its estimated useful life. (Average current cost of the plant asset is the sum of the current cost of the plant asset at the beginning and the end of the period, divided by two.)

Example 11 ▸ Depreciation Expense Based on Average Current Cost

Kerr Company purchased a machine for $115,000 on January 1, the company's first day of operations. At the end of the year, the current cost of the machine was $125,000. The machine has no salvage value, a five-year life, and is depreciated by the straight-line method.

Required: Determine the amount of the current cost depreciation expense that would appear in voluntary supplementary current cost information for the first year ending December 31.

Solution:

Average current cost for the year ($115,000 + $125,000) / 2]	$120,000
Estimated useful life	/ 5
Current cost depreciation for the year	$ 24,000

3. **Other Revenues/Expenses and Gains/Losses** Other revenues, expenses, gains, and losses may be measured at the amounts included in the primary income statement.

H. Restatement of Current Cost Information Into Units of Constant Purchasing Power
Enterprises that do not have significant foreign operations are to use the CPI-U to restate current costs into units of constant purchasing power.

I. Purchasing Power Gain or Loss on Net Monetary Items
The purchasing power gain or loss on net monetary items is the net gain or loss determined by restating in units of constant purchasing power the opening and closing balances of, and transactions in, monetary assets and monetary liabilities.

1. **Economic Significance** The economic significance of monetary assets and liabilities depends heavily on the general purchasing power of money, although other factors may affect their significance. The economic significance of nonmonetary items depends heavily on the value of specific goods and services.

2. **Gains** Purchasing power gains result from holding:

   a. **Monetary Liabilities During Inflation** Monetary liabilities during a period of inflation because the obligations will be settled with dollars that have less purchasing power.

   b. **Monetary Assets During Deflation** Monetary assets during a period of deflation because a fixed amount of money will purchase more goods and services following a period of deflation.

3. **Losses** Purchasing power losses result from holding:

   a. **Monetary Assets During Inflation** Monetary assets during a period of *inflation* because the fixed amount of money will purchase *fewer* goods and services following a period of inflation.

Example 12 ▸ Purchasing Power Loss on Net Monetary Items

Lang Company's monetary assets exceeded monetary liabilities by $3,000 at the beginning of the current year and $4,000 at the end of the current year. On January 1, the general price level was 125. On December 31, the general price level was 150.

Required: Determine the amount of Lang's purchasing power gain or loss on net monetary items.

Solution:

	Nominal Dollars	Conversion Factor	Restated into year's Dollars
Net monetary assets, 1/1	$3,000	150/125	$ 3,600
Change in net monetary assets during the year	1,000	*	1,000
Balance in net monetary assets, 12/31	$4,000	150/150	(4,000)
Purchasing power loss on net monetary assets			$ 600

*Assumed to be in average year's dollars.

   b. **Monetary Liabilities During Deflation** Monetary liabilities during a period of *deflation* because the obligation will be settled with dollars that have *more* purchasing power.

Exhibit 5 ▸ Purchasing Power Gains and Losses

	DURING A PERIOD OF INFLATION	DURING A PERIOD OF DEFLATION
HOLDING MONETARY ASSETS	Purchasing Power Losses	Purchasing Power Gains
HOLDING MONETARY LIABILITIES	Purchasing Power Gains	Purchasing Power Losses

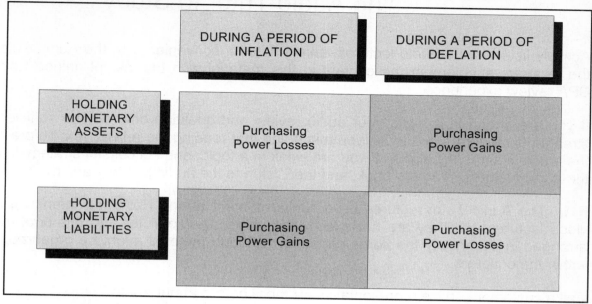

4. **Holding Nonmonetary Items** The holding of *nonmonetary* items during a period of changing prices does **not** give rise to purchasing power gains or losses.

J. **Holding Gains & Losses on Nonmonetary Assets**
Current cost financial statements measure and report both *realized* and *unrealized* holding gains and losses on *nonmonetary* assets.

1. **Realized Holding Gains/Losses** Realized holding gains and losses occur when the non-monetary asset has been *sold* or *consumed* in the earnings process. An increase in the current cost of inventory items sold is an example of a realized holding gain.

2. **Unrealized Holding Gains/Losses** Unrealized holding gains and losses occur when the nonmonetary asset is *held* from period to period. A decrease in the current cost of inventory items on hand is an example of an unrealized holding loss.

Using Audio Tutor to Study

Actively listen to the audio lectures, taking notes if convenient. In the Audio Tutor product, the lecturers supplement the content in this material with the insight gained from years of CPA review experience.

If you are strong in a topic, your audio review and question drill may be sufficient. If your strength is moderate in a topic, you might find that reading the related text before listening to the audio lectures is helpful. If you are weak in a topic, one successful strategy is to listen to the audio lectures, read the book, and then listen to the audio lectures again.

FYI: The Audio Tutor lectures have similar content as the Hot*Spot, Intensive, and online video lectures, but they are not exactly the same. Audio Tutor and this book have topics arranged in essentially the same chapters, although material might be organized differently within the chapters.

Call a customer service representative for more details about Audio Tutor.

CHAPTER 12—REPORTING: SPECIAL AREAS

Problem 12-1 MULTIPLE CHOICE QUESTIONS (120 to 150 minutes)

1. For financial statement purposes, the installment method of accounting may be used if the
a. Collection period extends over more than 12 months
b. Installments are due in different years
c. Ultimate amount collectible is indeterminate
d. Percentage of completion method is inappropriate (11/91, Theory, #6, 2514)

2. Luge Co., which began operations on January 1, appropriately uses the installment sales method of accounting. The following information is available for the year:

Installment accounts receivable, December 31	$800,000
Deferred gross profit, December 31 (before recognition of realized gross profit for the year)	560,000
Gross profit on sales	40%

For the year ended December 31, cash collections and realized gross profit on sales should be

	Cash collections	Realized gross profit
a.	$400,000	$320,000
b.	$400,000	$240,000
c.	$600,000	$320,000
d.	$600,000	$240,000

(11/93, PI, #16, amended, 4385)

3. Bear Co., which began operations on January 2, appropriately uses the installment sales method of accounting. The following information is available for the year:

Installment sales	$1,400,000
Realized gross profit on installment sales	240,000
Gross profit percentage on sales	40%

For the year ended December 31, what amounts should Bear report as accounts receivable and deferred gross profit?

	Accounts receivable	Deferred gross profit
a.	$600,000	$320,000
b.	$600,000	$360,000
c.	$800,000	$320,000
d.	$800,000	$560,000

(11/98, FAR, #8, amended, 6735)

4. Since there is no reasonable basis for estimating the degree of collectibility, Astor Co. uses the installment method of revenue recognition for the following sales:

	Year 2	Year 1
Sales	$900,000	$600,000
Collections from:		
Year 1 sales	100,000	200,000
Year 2 sales	300,000	--
Accounts written off:		
Year 1 sales	150,000	50,000
Year 2 sales	50,000	--
Gross profit percentage	40%	30%

What amount should Astor report as deferred gross profit in its December 31, year 2 balance sheet for the year 1 and year 2 sales?
a. $150,000
b. $160,000
c. $225,000
d. $250,000 (5/94, FAR, #23, amended, 4838)

5. On January 2, year 1, Blake Co. sold a used machine to Cooper Inc. for $900,000, resulting in a gain of $270,000. On that date, Cooper paid $150,000 cash and signed a $750,000 note bearing interest at 10%. The note was payable in three annual installments of $250,000 beginning January 2, year 2. Blake appropriately accounted for the sale under the installment method. Cooper made a timely payment of the first installment on January 2, year 2, of $325,000, which included accrued interest of $75,000. What amount of deferred gross profit should Blake report at December 31, year 2?
a. $150,000
b. $172,500
c. $180,000
d. $225,000 (11/93, PI, #45, amended, 4414)

6. Pie Co. uses the installment sales method to recognize revenue. Customers pay the installment notes in 24 equal monthly amounts, which include 12% interest. What is an installment note's receivable balance six months after the sale?
a. 75% of the original sales price
b. Less than 75% of the original sales price
c. The present value of the remaining monthly payments discounted at 12%
d. Less than the present value of the remaining monthly payments discounted at 12%
(11/92, Theory, #9, 3442)

7. On January 2 of the current year, Yardley Co. sold a plant to Ivory Inc. for $1,500,000. On that date, the plant's carrying cost was $1,000,000. Ivory gave Yardley $300,000 cash and a $1,200,000 note, payable in 4 annual installments of $300,000 plus 12% interest. Ivory made the first principal and interest payment of $444,000 on December 31. Yardley uses the installment method of revenue recognition. In its current year income statement, what amount of realized gross profit should Yardley report?
a. $344,000
b. $200,000
c. $148,000
d. $100,000 (5/93, PI, #42, amended, 4083)

8. Gant Co., which began operations on January 1, appropriately uses the installment method of accounting. The following information pertains to Gant's operations for the year:

Installment sales	$500,000
Regular sales	300,000
Cost of installment sales	250,000
Cost of regular sales	150,000
General and administrative expenses	50,000
Collections on installment sales	100,000

In its December 31 balance sheet, what amount should Gant report as deferred gross profit?
a. $250,000
b. $200,000
c. $160,000
d. $ 75,000 (11/92, PI, #28, amended, 3261)

9. Lang Co. uses the installment method of revenue recognition. The following data pertain to Lang's installment sales for the years ended December 31, year 1 and year 2:

	Year 1	Year 2
Installment receivables at year-end on year 1 sales	$60,000	$30,000
Installment receivables at year-end on year 2 sales	—	69,000
Installment sales	80,000	90,000
Cost of sales	40,000	60,000

What amount should Lang report as deferred gross profit in its December 31, year 2 balance sheet?
a. $23,000
b. $33,000
c. $38,000
d. $43,000 (11/95, FAR, #10, amended, 6092)

10. According to the installment method of accounting, gross profit on an installment sale is recognized in income
a. On the date of sale
b. On the date the final cash collection is received
c. In proportion to the cash collection
d. After cash collections equal to the cost of sales have been received (5/95, FAR, #27, 5563)

11. It is proper to recognize revenue prior to the sale of merchandise when

I. The revenue will be reported as an installment sale
II. The revenue will be reported under the cost recovery method

a. I only
b. II only
c. Both I and II
d. Neither I nor II (11/95, FAR, #31, 6113)

12. Wren Co. sells equipment on installment contracts. Which of the following statements best justifies Wren's use of the cost recovery method of revenue recognition to account for these installment sales?
a. The sales contract provides that title to the equipment only passes to the purchaser when all payments have been made.
b. No cash payments are due until one year from the date of sale.
c. Sales are subject to a high rate of return.
d. There is **no** reasonable basis for estimating collectibility. (5/94, FAR, #41, 4856)

13. The following information pertains to a sale of real estate by Ryan Co. to Sud Co. on December 31, year 1:

Carrying amount		$2,000,000
Sales price:		
Cash	$ 300,000	
Purchase money mortgage	2,700,000	3,000,000

The mortgage is payable in nine annual installments of $300,000 beginning December 31, year 2, plus interest of 10%. The December 31, year 2 installment was paid as scheduled, together with interest of $270,000. Ryan uses the cost recovery method to account for the sale. What amount of income should Ryan recognize in year 2 from the real estate sale and its financing?
a. $570,000
b. $370,000
c. $270,000
d. $0 (5/91, PI, #50, amended, 1317)

14. Drew Co. produces expensive equipment for sale on installment contracts. When there is doubt about eventual collectibility, the income recognition method **least** likely to overstate income is
a. At the time the equipment is completed
b. The installment method
c. The cost recovery method
d. At the time of delivery (5/91, Theory, #8, 1896)

15. Cash collection is a critical event for income recognition in the

	Cost recovery method	*Installment method*
a.	No	No
b.	Yes	Yes
c.	No	Yes
d.	Yes	No

(11/93, Theory, #39, 4544)

16. Several of Fox Inc.'s customers are having cash flow problems. Information pertaining to these customers for the years ended March 31, year 1 and year 2, follows:

	3/31, year 1	3/31, year 2
Sales	$10,000	$15,000
Cost of sales	8,000	9,000
Cash collections		
on year 1 sales	7,000	3,000
on year 2 sales	--	12,000

If the cost recovery method is used, what amount would Fox report as gross profit from sales to these customers for the year ended March 31, year 2?
a. $ 2,000
b. $ 3,000
c. $ 5,000
d. $15,000 (11/92, PI, #43, amended, 3276)

17. Amar Farms produced 300,000 pounds of cotton during the year 1 season. Amar sells all of its cotton to Brye Co., which has agreed to purchase Amar's entire production at the prevailing market price. Recent legislation assures that the market price will not fall below $.70 per pound during the next two years. Amar's costs of selling and distributing the cotton are immaterial and can be reasonably estimated. Amar reports its inventory at expected exit value. During year 1, Amar sold and delivered to Brye 200,000 pounds at the market price of $.70. Amar sold the remaining 100,000 pounds during year 2 at the market price of $.72. What amount of revenue should Amar recognize in year 1?
a. $140,000
b. $144,000
c. $210,000
d. $216,000 (11/90, PII, #6, amended, 1321)

18. On January 1, Dell Inc. contracted with the city of Little to provide custom built desks for the city schools. The contract made Dell the city's sole supplier and required Dell to supply no less than 4,000 desks and no more than 5,500 desks per year for two years. In turn, Little agreed to pay a fixed price of $110 per desk. During the year, Dell produced 5,000 desks for Little. At December 31, 500 of these desks were segregated from the regular inventory and were accepted and awaiting pickup by Little. Little paid Dell $450,000 during the year. What amount should Dell recognize as contract revenue in this year?
a. $450,000
b. $495,000
c. $550,000
d. $605,000 (11/91, PI, #31, amended, 2419)

19. Lin Co., a distributor of machinery, bought a machine from the manufacturer in November for $10,000. On December 30, Lin sold this machine to Zee Hardware for $15,000 under the following terms: 2% discount if paid within 30 days, 1% discount if paid after 30 days but within 60 days, or payable in full within 90 days if not paid within the discount periods. However, Zee had the right to return this machine to Lin if Zee was unable to resell the machine before expiration of the 90-day payment period, in which case Zee's obligation to Lin would be canceled. In Lin's net sales for the year ended December 31, how much should be included for the sale of this machine to Zee?
a. $0
b. $14,700
c. $14,850
d. $15,000 (5/87, PII, #20, amended, 9050)

20. During year 1, Mitchell Corp. started a construction job with a total contract price of $600,000. The job was completed on December 15, year 2. Additional data are as follows:

	Year 1	Year 2
Actual costs incurred	$225,000	$255,000
Estimated remaining costs	225,000	--
Billed to customer	240,000	360,000
Received from customer	200,000	400,000

Under the completed contract method, what amount should Mitchell recognize as gross profit for year 2?
a. $ 45,000
b. $ 72,000
c. $ 80,000
d. $120,000 (5/90, PII, #41, amended, 1325)

21. A company uses the completed contract method to account for a long-term construction contract. Revenue is recognized when recorded progress billings

	Are collected	*Exceed recorded costs*
a.	Yes	Yes
b.	No	No
c.	Yes	No
d.	No	Yes

(5/92, Theory, #44, 2737)

22. When should an anticipated loss on a long-term contract be recognized under the percentage of completion method and the completed contract method, respectively?

	Percentage of completion	*Completed contract*
a.	Over life of project	Contract complete
b.	Immediately	Contract complete
c.	Over life of project	Immediately
d.	Immediately	Immediately

(11/87, Theory, #16, 1850)

Items 23 and 24 are based on the following data pertaining to Pell Co.'s construction jobs, which commenced during the current year:

	Project 1	Project 2
Contract price	$420,000	$300,000
Costs incurred during the year	240,000	280,000
Estimated costs to complete	120,000	40,000
Billed to customers during the year	150,000	270,000
Received from customers during the year	90,000	250,000

23. If Pell used the completed contract method, what amount of gross profit (loss) would Pell report in its current year income statement?
a. $ (20,000)
b. $0
c. $340,000
d. $420,000 (5/93, PI, #38, amended, 4079)

24. If Pell used the percentage of completion method, what amount of gross profit (loss) would Pell report in its current year income statement?
a. $(20,000)
b. $ 20,000
c. $ 22,500
d. $ 40,000 (5/93, PI, #39, amended, 4080)

Items 25 and 26 are based on the following:

The following trial balance of Mint Corp. at December 31 of the current year has been adjusted except for income tax expense.

TRIAL BALANCE
December 31, YYYY

	Dr	Cr.
Cash	$ 600,000	
Accounts receivable, net	3,500,000	
Cost in excess of billings on long-term contracts	1,600,000	
Billings in excess of costs on long-term contracts		$ 700,000
Prepaid taxes	450,000	
Property, plant, and equipment, net	1,480,000	
Note payable—noncurrent		1,620,000
Common stock		750,000
Additional paid-in capital		2,000,000
Retained earnings—unappropriated		900,000
Retained earnings—restricted for note payable		160,000
Earnings from long-term contracts		6,680,000
Costs and expenses	5,180,000	
	$12,810,000	$12,810,000

Other financial data for the year ended December 31:

- Mint uses the percentage of completion method to account for long-term construction contracts for financial statement and income tax purposes. All receivables on these contracts are considered to be collectible within 12 months.
- During the year, estimated tax payments of $450,000 were charged to prepaid taxes. Mint has not recorded income tax expense. There were no temporary or permanent differences, and Mint's tax rate is 30%.

In Mint's December 31 current year balance sheet, what amount should be reported as:

25. Total noncurrent liabilities?
a. $1,620,000
b. $1,780,000
c. $2,320,000
d. $2,480,000 (11/92, PI, #2, amended, 3235)

26. Total current assets?
a. $5,000,000
b. $5,450,000
c. $5,700,000
d. $6,150,000 (11/92, PI, #3, amended, 3236)

27. State Co. recognizes construction revenue and expenses using the percentage of completion method. During year 1, a single long-term project was begun which continued through year 2. Information on the project follows:

	Year 1	Year 2
Accounts receivable from construction contract	$100,000	$300,000
Construction expenses	105,000	192,000
Construction in progress	122,000	364,000
Partial billings on contract	100,000	420,000

Profit recognized from the long-term construction contract in year 2 should be

a. $ 50,000
b. $108,000
c. $128,000
d. $228,000 (11/91, PI, #40, amended, 2428)

28. Barr Corp. started a long-term construction project in the current year. The following data relate to this project:

Contract price	$4,200,000
Costs incurred in the year	1,750,000
Estimated costs to complete	1,750,000
Progress billings	900,000
Collections on progress billings	800,000

The project is accounted for by the percentage of completion method of accounting. In Barr's current year income statement, what amount of gross profit should be reported for this project?

a. $350,000
b. $150,000
c. $133,333
d. $100,000 (5/91, PI, #49, amended, 1316)

29. Lake Construction Company has consistently used the percentage of completion method of recognizing income. During year 1, Lake entered into a fixed-price contract to construct an office building for $10,000,000. Information relating to the contract is as follows:

	At December 31,	
	Year 1	Year 2
Percentage of completion	20%	60%
Estimated total cost at completion	$7,500,000	$8,000,000
Income recognized (cumulative)	500,000	1,200,000

Contract costs incurred during year 2 were

a. $3,200,000
b. $3,300,000
c. $3,500,000
d. $4,800,000 (11/87, PI, #21, amended, 1329)

30. Haft Construction Co. has consistently used the percentage of completion method. On January 10, year 1, Haft began work on a $3,000,000 construction contract. At the inception date, the estimated cost of construction was $2,250,000. The following data relate to the progress of the contract:

Income recognized at 12/31, year 1	$ 300,000
Cost incurred 1/10, year 1 through 12/31, year 2	1,800,000
Estimated cost to complete at 12/31, year 2	600,000

In its income statement for the year ended December 31, year 2, what amount of gross profit should Haft report?

a. $450,000
b. $300,000
c. $262,500
d. $150,000 (5/93, PI, #41, amended, 4082)

31. A company used the percentage of completion method of accounting for a 5-year construction contract. Which of the following items will the company use to calculate the income recognized in the third year?

	Progress billings to date	*Income previously recognized*
a.	Yes	No
b.	No	Yes
c.	No	No
d.	Yes	Yes

(11/92, Theory, #8, 3441)

32. Which of the following is used in calculating the income recognized in the fourth and final year of a contract accounted for by the percentage of completion method?

	Actual total costs	*Income previously recognized*
a.	Yes	Yes
b.	Yes	No
c.	No	Yes
d.	No	No

(5/95, FAR, #26, 5562)

33. The calculation of the income recognized in the third year of a five-year construction contract accounted for using the percentage of completion method includes the ratio of

a. Costs incurred in year 3 to total billings
b. Costs incurred in year 3 to total estimated costs
c. Total costs incurred to date to total billings
d. Total costs incurred to date to total estimated costs (R/05, FAR, 0424F, #8, 7752)

34. In accounting for a long-term construction contract using the percentage of completion method, the progress billings on contracts account is a
a. Contra current asset account
b. Contra noncurrent asset account
c. Noncurrent liability account
d. Revenue account (11/85, Theory, #28, 1882)

35. On October 20 of the current year, Grimm Co. consigned 40 freezers to Holden Co. for sale at $1,000 each and paid $800 in transportation costs. On December 30, Holden reported the sale of 10 freezers and remitted $8,500. The remittance was net of the agreed 15% commission. What amount should Grimm recognize as consignment sales revenue for the current year?
a. $ 7,700
b. $ 8,500
c. $ 9,800
d. $10,000 (5/90, PI, #44, amended, 1323)

36. Garnett Co. shipped inventory on consignment to Hart Co. that originally cost $50,000. Hart paid $1,200 for advertising that was reimbursable from Garnett. At the end of the year, 40% of the inventory was sold for $32,000. The agreement stated that a commission of 10% will be provided to Hart for all sales. What amount should Garnett report as net income for the year?
a. $0
b. $ 7,600
c. $10,800
d. $12,000 (R/05, FAR, 1794F, #37, 7781)

37. On December 31, year 1, Rice Inc., authorized Graf to operate as a franchisee for an initial franchise fee of $150,000. Of this amount, $60,000 was received upon signing the agreement and the balance, represented by a note, is due in three annual payments of $30,000 each beginning December 31, year 2. The present value on December 31, year 1, of the three annual payments appropriately discounted is $72,000. According to the agreement, the nonrefundable down payment represents a fair measure of the services already performed by Rice; however, substantial future services are required of Rice. Collectibility of the note is reasonably certain. In Rice's December 31, year 1 balance sheet, unearned franchise fees from Graf's franchise should be reported as
a. $132,000
b. $100,000
c. $ 90,000
d. $ 72,000 (5/91, PI, #40, amended, 1315)

38. Each of Potter Pie Co.'s 21 new franchisees contracted to pay an initial franchise fee of $30,000. By December 31, year 1, each franchisee had paid a nonrefundable $10,000 fee and signed a note to pay $10,000 principal plus the market rate of interest on December 31, year 2, and December 31, year 3. Experience indicates that one franchise will default on the additional payments. Services for the initial fee will be performed in year 2. What amount of net unearned franchise fees would Potter report at December 31, year 1?
a. $400,000
b. $600,000
c. $610,000
d. $630,000 (11/91, PI, #27, amended, 2415)

39. Macklin Co. entered into a franchise agreement with Heath Co. for an initial fee of $50,000. Macklin received $10,000 when the agreement was signed. The balance was to be paid at a rate of $10,000 per year, starting the next year. All services were performed by Macklin and the refund period had expired. Operations started in the current year. What amount should Macklin recognize as revenue in the current year?
a. $0
b. $10,000
c. $20,000
d. $50,000 (R/05, FAR, 1184F, #26, 7770)

40. Baker Co. has a franchise restaurant business. On January 15 of the current year, Baker charged an investor a franchise fee of $65,000 for the right to operate as a franchisee of one of Baker's restaurants. A cash payment of $25,000 towards the fee was required to be paid to Baker during the current year. Four subsequent annual payments of $10,000 with a present value of $34,000 at the current market interest rate represent the balance of the fee which is expected to be collected in full. The initial cash payment is nonrefundable and no future services are required by Baker. What amount should Baker report as franchise revenue during the current year?
a. $0
b. $25,000
c. $59,000
d. $65,000 (R/05, FAR, 1705F, #34, 7778)

41. Under a royalty agreement with another company, Wand Co. will pay royalties for the assignment of a patent for three years. The royalties paid should be reported as expense
a. In the period paid.
b. In the period incurred.
c. At the date the royalty agreement began.
d. At the date the royalty agreement expired.
(5/95, FAR, #38, 5574)

42. On January 2 of the current year, Boulder Co. assigned its patent to Castle Co. for royalties of 10% of patent-related sales. The assignment is for the remaining four years of the patent's life. Castle guaranteed Boulder a minimum royalty of $100,000 over the life of the patent and paid Boulder $50,000 against future royalties during the year. Patent-related sales for the year were $300,000. In its current year income statement, what amount should Boulder report as royalty revenue?
a. $ 25,000
b. $ 30,000
c. $ 50,000
d. $100,000 (R/03, FAR, #11, 7613)

43. Wren Corp.'s trademark was licensed to Mont Co. for royalties of 15% of sales of the trademarked items. Royalties are payable semiannually on March 15 for sales in July through December of the prior year, and on September 15 for sales in January through June of the same year. Wren received the following royalties from Mont:

	March 15	September 15
Year 1	$10,000	$15,000
Year 2	12,000	17,000

Mont estimated that sales of the trademarked items would total $60,000 for July through December, year 2. In Wren's year 2 income statement, the royalty revenue should be
a. $26,000
b. $29,000
c. $38,000
d. $41,000 (11/94, Theory, #40, amended, 5302)

44. Rill Co. owns a 20% royalty interest in an oil well. Rill receives royalty payments on January 31 for the oil sold between the previous June 1 and November 30, and on July 31 for oil sold between the previous December 1 and May 31. Production reports show the following oil sales:

June 1, year 1—November 30, year 1	$300,000
December 1, year 1—December 31, year 1	50,000
December 1, year 1—May 31, year 2	400,000
June 1, year 2—November 30, year 2	325,000
December 1, year 2—December 31, year 2	70,000

What amount should Rill report as royalty revenue for year 2?
a. $140,000
b. $144,000
c. $149,000
d. $159,000 (11/95, FAR, #30, amended, 6112)

45. In year 1, Super Comics Corp. sold a comic strip to Fantasy Inc. and will receive royalties of 20% of future revenues associated with the comic strip. At December 31, year 2, Super reported royalties receivable of $75,000 from Fantasy. During year 3, Super received royalty payments of $200,000. Fantasy reported revenues of $1,500,000 in year 3 from the comic strip. In its year 3 income statement, what amount should Super report as royalty revenue?
a. $125,000
b. $175,000
c. $200,000
d $300,000 (5/93, PI, #44, amended, 4085)

46. Financial statements prepared under which of the following methods include adjustments for both specific price changes and general price-level changes?
a. Historical cost/nominal dollar
b. Current cost/nominal dollar
c. Current cost/constant dollar
d. Historical cost/constant dollar
(11/95, FAR, #57, 6139)

47. During a period of inflation, the specific price of a parcel of land increased at a lower rate than the consumer price index. The accounting method that would measure the land at the highest amount is
a. Historical cost/nominal dollar
b. Current cost/nominal dollar
c. Current cost/constant dollar
d. Historical cost/constant dollar
(5/90, Theory, #3, 1910)

48. DeeCee Co. adjusted its historical cost income statement by applying specific price indexes to its depreciation expense and cost of goods sold. DeeCee's adjusted income statement is prepared according to
a. Fair value accounting
b. General purchasing power accounting
c. Current cost accounting
d. Current cost/general purchasing power accounting (11/93, Theory, #2, 4507)

49. The following assets were among those that appeared on Baird Co.'s books at the end of the year:

Demand bank deposits	$650,000
Net long-term receivables	400,000
Patents and trademarks	150,000

In preparing constant dollar financial statements, how much should Baird classify as monetary assets?
a. $1,200,000
b. $1,050,000
c. $ 800,000
d. $ 650,000 (5/90, PII, #50, 1245)

50. The following items, among others, appeared on Rubi Co.'s books at the end of the current year:

Merchandise inventory	$600,000
Loans to employees	20,000

What amount should Rubi classify as monetary assets in preparing constant dollar financial statements?
a. $0
b. $ 20,000
c. $600,000
d. $620,000 (5/89, PII, #13, amended, 1247)

51. When computing purchasing power gain or loss on net monetary items, which of the following accounts is classified as nonmonetary?
a. Advances to unconsolidated subsidiaries
b. Allowance for uncollectible accounts
c. Unamortized premium on bonds payable
d. Accumulated depreciation of equipment
(11/93, Theory, #1, 4506)

52. A company that wishes to disclose information about the effect of changing prices in accordance with Statement of Financial Accounting Standards No. 89, *Financial Accounting and Changing Prices,* should report this information in
a. The body of the financial statements.
b. The notes to the financial statements.
c. Supplementary information to the financial statements.
d. Management's report to shareholders.
(11/94, FAR, #4, 5269)

53. Information with respect to Bruno Co.'s cost of goods sold for the current year is as follows:

	Historical cost	Units
Inventory, 1/1	$ 1,060,000	20,000
Production during year	5,580,000	90,000
	6,640,000	110,000
Inventory, 12/31	(2,520,000)	(40,000)
Cost of goods sold	$ 4,120,000	70,000

Bruno estimates that the current cost per unit of inventory was $58 at January 1, and $72 at December 31. In Bruno's supplementary information restated into average current cost, the cost of goods sold for the current year should be
a. $5,040,000
b. $4,550,000
c. $4,410,000
d. $4,060,000 (11/89, PI, #59, amended, 1246)

54. Manhof Co. prepares supplementary reports on income from continuing operations on a current cost basis in accordance with FASB Statement No. 89, *Financial Reporting and Changing Prices.* How should Manhof compute cost of goods sold on a current cost basis?
a. Number of units sold times average current cost of units during the year
b. Number of units sold times current cost of units at year end
c. Number of units sold times current cost of units at the beginning of the year
d. Beginning inventory at current cost plus cost of goods purchased less ending inventory at current cost (11/92, Theory, #40, 3473)

55. In its financial statements, Hila Co. discloses supplemental information on the effects of changing prices in accordance with Statement of Financial Accounting Standards No. 89, *Financial Reporting and Changing Prices.* Hila computed the increase in current cost of inventory as follows:

Increase in current cost (nominal dollars)	$15,000
Increase in current cost (constant dollars)	$12,000

What amount should Hila disclose as the inflation component of the increase in current cost of inventories?
a. $ 3,000
b. $12,000
c. $15,000
d. $27,000 (5/94, FAR, #58, 4873)

Items 56 and 57 are based on the following data:

In a period of rising general price levels, Pollard Corp. discloses income on a current cost basis in accordance with FASB Statement No. 89, *Financial Reporting and Changing Prices.*

56. Compared to historical cost income from continuing operations, which of the following conditions increases Pollard's current cost income from continuing operations?
a. Current cost of equipment is greater than historical cost.
b. Current cost of land is greater than historical cost.
c. Current cost of cost of goods sold is less than historical cost.
d. Ending net monetary assets are less than beginning net monetary assets.
(5/92, Theory, #4, 2696)

57. Which of the following contributes to Pollard's purchasing power loss on net monetary items?
a. Refundable deposits with suppliers
b. Equity investment in unconsolidated subsidiaries
c. Warranty obligations
d. Wages payable (5/92, Theory, #5, 2697)

58. During a period of inflation in which an asset account remains constant, which of the following occurs?
a. A purchasing power gain, if the item is a monetary asset
b. A purchasing power gain, if the item is a non-monetary asset
c. A purchasing power loss, if the item is a monetary asset
d. A purchasing power loss, if the item is a non-monetary asset (5/94, FAR, #59, 4874)

59. The following information pertains to each unit of merchandise purchased for resale by Vend Co.:

	March 1	December 31
Purchase price	$ 8	
Selling price	12	$ 15
Price level index	110	121
Replacement cost		10

Under current cost accounting, what is the amount of Vend's holding gain on each unit of this merchandise?
a. $0
b. $0.80
c. $1.20
d. $2.00 (5/92, PII, #13, amended, 2645)

60. Could current cost financial statements report holding gains for goods sold during the period and holding gains on inventory at the end of the period?

	Goods sold	*Inventory*
a.	Yes	Yes
b.	Yes	No
c.	No	Yes
d.	No	No

(5/91, Theory, #2, 1894)

SIMULATIONS

Problem 12-2 (15 to 25 minutes)

Research Task | Essay

Research Question: How and when are continuing franchise fees reported?

Paragraph Reference Answer: ______________

Research Task | Essay

At December 31 of the current year, Roko Co. has two fixed price construction contracts in progress. Both contracts have monthly billings supported by certified surveys of work completed. The contracts are:

- The Ski Park contract, which began in the previous year, is 80% complete, progressing according to bid estimates, and expected to be profitable.
- The Nassu Village contract, a project to construct 100 condominium units, was begun in this current year. Thirty-five units have been completed.

Work on the remaining units is delayed by conflicting recommendations on how to overcome unexpected subsoil problems. While the total cost of the project is uncertain, a loss is not anticipated.

a. Identify the alternatives available to account for long-term construction contracts, and specify the criteria used to determine which method is applicable to a given contract.

b. Identify the appropriate accounting method for each of Roko's two contracts, and describe each contract's effect on net income for the current year.

c. Indicate how the accounts related to the Ski Park contract should be reported on the current year balance sheet at December 31. (11/90, Theory, #3, amended, 3529)

Problem 12-3 (40 to 50 minutes)

Research Task	Scenario	Requirements	Response A

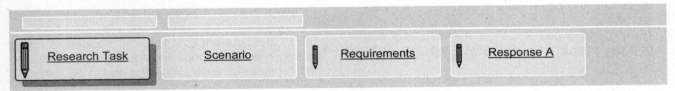

Research Question: What are the two accounting methods commonly followed by contractors?

Paragraph Reference Answer: ______________

Research Task	Scenario	Requirements	Response A

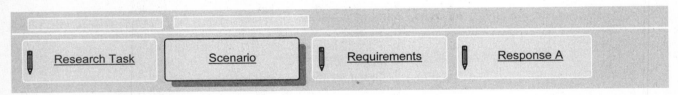

London Inc. began operation of its construction division on October 1, year 1, and entered into contracts for two separate projects. The Beta project contract price was $600,000 and provided for penalties of $10,000 per week for late completion. Although during year 2 the Beta project had been on schedule for timely completion, it was completed four weeks late in August year 3. The Gamma project's original contract price was $800,000. Change orders during year 3 added $40,000 to the original contract price.

The following data pertains to the separate long-term construction projects in progress:

	Beta	Gamma
As of September 30, year 2:		
Costs incurred to date	$360,000	$410,000
Estimated costs to complete	40,000	410,000
Billings	315,000	440,000
Cash collections	275,000	365,000
	Beta	Gamma
As of September 30, year 3:		
Costs incurred to date	$450,000	$720,000
Estimated costs to complete	--	180,000
Billings	560,000	710,000
Cash collections	560,000	625,000

- London accounts for its long-term construction contracts using the percentage of completion method for financial reporting purposes and the completed contract method for income tax purposes.
- Enacted tax rates are 25% for year 2 and 30% for future years.
- London's income before income taxes from all divisions, before considering revenues from long-term construction projects, was $300,000 for the year ended September 30, year 2. There were no other temporary or permanent differences.

Research Task | Scenario | Requirements | Response A

a. Prepare a schedule showing London's balances in the following accounts at September 30, 20X2, under the percentage of completion method:

- Accounts receivable
- Costs and estimated earnings in excess of billings
- Billings in excess of costs and estimated earnings

b. Prepare a schedule showing London's gross profit (loss) recognized for the years ended September 30, year 2 and year 3, under the percentage of completion method.

c. Prepare a schedule reconciling London's financial statement income and taxable income for the year ended September 30, year 2, and showing all components of taxes payable and current and deferred income tax expense for the year then ended. Do not consider estimated tax requirements.

Research Task | Scenario | Requirements | Response A

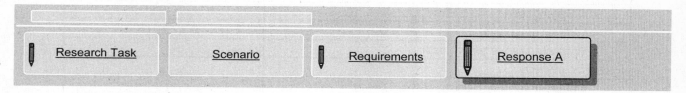

London Inc.
Schedule of Selected Balance Sheet Accounts
September 30, Year 2

Accounts receivable		
Costs and estimated earnings in excess of billings:		
Construction in progress		
Less: Billings		
Costs and estimated earnings in excess of billings		
Billings in excess of costs and estimated earnings		

Response B | Response C

London Inc.
Schedule of Gross Profit (Loss)

	Beta	Gamma
For the Year Ended September 30, Year 2:		
Estimated gross profit (loss):		
Contract price		
Less: Total costs		
Estimated gross profit (loss)		
Percent complete:		
Costs incurred to date		
Total costs	/	/
Percent complete		
Gross profit (loss) recognized		
For the Year Ended September 30, Year 3:		
Estimated gross profit (loss):		
Contract price		
Less: Total costs		
Estimated gross profit (loss)		
Percent complete:		
Costs incurred to date		
Total costs	/	/
Percent complete		
Gross profit (loss)		
Less: Gross (profit) loss recognized in prior year		
Gross profit (loss) recognized		

Response B

Response C

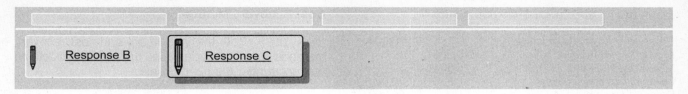

London Inc.
Schedule of Income Taxes Payable and Income Tax Expense
September 30, Year 2

Financial statement income:		
From other divisions		
From Beta project		
From Gamma project		
Total financial statement income		
Less temporary differences:		
Beta project income		
Gamma project loss		
Total taxable income		
Taxes payable ($300,000 × 25%)		
Deferred tax liability ($160,000 × 30%)		
Tax expense:		
Current		
Deferred		

(11/93, PI, #3, amended, 9911)

Solution 12-1 MULTIPLE CHOICE ANSWERS

Installment Method

1. (c) The installment method of accounting is a cash basis of accounting and, therefore, is usually not a generally accepted method. However, if the ultimate amount collectible is indeterminate, then the installment method is considered to be the appropriate method to apply and its use is acceptable in that circumstance (APB 10, ¶12).

2. (d)

Deferred gross profit at 12/31 before recognition of realized gross profit for the year	$ 560,000
Divide by: Gross profit rate on year's sales	/ 40%
Installment sales for the year	1,400,000
Less: Installment accounts receivable, 12/31	(800,000)
Cash collections on installment sales,	600,000
Times: Gross profit rate on year's sales	× 40%
Realized gross profit for the year	$ 240,000

3. (c) Deferred gross profit could also be calculated by multiplying accounts receivable of $800,000 by the gross profit percentage of 40%.

Installment sales		$ 1,400,000
Realized GP	$ 240,000	
Divided by GP%	/ 40%	
Less: Amount received		(600,000)
Accounts receivable		$ 800,000

Installment sales	$ 1,400,000
Times: GP%	× 40%
Total gross profit	560,000
Less: Realized gross profit	(240,000)
Deferred gross profit	$ 320,000

4. (d) $220,000 deferred gross profit (DGP) from year 2 sales + $30,000 DGP from year 1 sales = $250,000 DGP at December 31, year 2.

	Year 2	Year 1
Sales	$ 900,000	$ 600,000
Collections in 20X2	--	(200,000)
Collections in 20X3	(300,000)	(100,000)
Write-offs in 20X2	--	(50,000)
Write-offs in 20X3	(50,000)	(150,000)
	550,000	100,000
Gross profit percentage	× 40%	× 30%
Deferred gross profit	$ 220,000	$ 30,000

5. (a) $270,000 / $900,000 = 30%

Gross profit on sale of machine		$ 270,000
In year 1—$150,000 × 30%	$45,000	
In year 2—$250,000 × 30%	75,000	
Less: Gross profit realized		(120,000)
Deferred gross profit, 12/31, year 2		$ 150,000

6. (c) Since the installment notes extend beyond one year, they are recorded at the present value of the payments discounted at the market interest rate (assumed here to be 12%). At any time after the sale, the installment note's receivable balance will be the present value of the remaining monthly payments discounted at 12%.

7. (b) The gross profit on the sale of the plant is $500,000 (i.e., the $1,500,000 sales price minus the $1,000,000 cost). Thus, the gross profit margin ratio to be applied to the annual installment payments is 1/3 (i.e., $500,000 / $1,500,000). During the year, Yardley received (1) $300,000 at the time of sale, (2) the first annual installment on the note of $300,000, and (3) interest of $144,000 (i.e., $1,200,000 × 12%). The amount of realized gross profit that Yardley should recognize from the installment sale is the sum of the down payment and first installment on the note times the gross profit margin ratio [($300,000 + $300,000) × 1/3 = $200,000]. The $144,000 of interest received in the year is recognized separately as interest income.

8. (b) General and administrative expenses are not used to compute the deferred gross profit; they are expensed when incurred.

Installment sales	$ 500,000
Collections on installment sales	(100,000)
Installment accounts receivable, 12/31	400,000
Times: Gross profit on installment sales [($500,000 – $250,000) / $500,000]	× 50%
Deferred gross profit, 12/31	$ 200,000

9. (c)

Receivable on year 1 sales	$30,000	
@ GP% ($80,000 – $40,000)/$80,000	× 0.50	$15,000
Receivable on year 2 sales	69,000	
@ GP% ($90,000 – $60,000)/$90,000	× 0.33	23,000
Deferred gross profit, December 31, year 2		$38,000

10. (c) The installment method allows revenue to be deferred and recognized each year in proportion to the receivables collected during that year.

Cost Recovery Method

11. (d) Both the installment and cost recovery methods report revenue based upon cash collections that occur after the point of sale.

12. (d) The cost recovery method defers the recognition of all gross profit until cash collections of revenue are equal to the cost of the item sold. All remaining cash collections are recorded as profit. This method of revenue recognition is not generally accepted. However, the cost recovery method may be used where collectibility of proceeds is doubtful, where an investment is very speculative in nature, and/or where the final sale price is to be determined by future events. Therefore, Wren Co. would be justified in accounting for installment sales for which there is *no* reasonable basis for estimating collectibility under the cost recovery method.

13. (d) Under the cost recovery method, no profit is recognized until cash payments by the buyer exceed the seller's cost of sales. Therefore, Ryan should not recognize any income in year 2 from the real estate sale and its financing because the accumulated cash payments from the buyer are less than the carrying amount of the real estate [($300,000 + $270,000) < $2,000,000].

14. (c) The cost recovery method defers the recognition of all gross profit until cash collections of revenue are equal to the cost of the item sold. All remaining cash collections are recorded as profit. The recognition of income at the time the equipment is completed or at the time of delivery would provide for the recognition of profits before any or much of the cash is received. These methods are, therefore, not appropriate for situations where there is doubt about the collectibility of the sales price. The use of the installment method would allow for the recognition of profits in proportion to the amount of the revenue collected in cash. The cost recovery method is less likely to overstate income than the installment method because it defers the recognition of profits longer than the installment method.

15. (b) Cash collection is a critical event for income recognition under both the cost recovery and installment methods of accounting. Under the cost recovery method, recognition of all gross profit is deferred until cash collections of revenue are equal to the cost of the item sold. All remaining cash collections are recorded as profit. Gross profit recognized using the installment method is generally computed by multiplying cash collected during the period by the gross profit percentage applicable to those sales. Since both the cost recovery and installment methods of accounting use the cash

basis of accounting, neither is a generally accepted method.

16. (c) The cost recovery method defers the recognition of all gross profit until cash collections of revenue are equal to the cost of the item sold. All remaining cash collections are recorded as gross profit. No profit was recognized on the year 1 sales for the year ended 3/31, year 1 because the $7,000 collected in the period did not recover the $8,000 cost of sales. For the year ended 3/31, year 2 (1) collections to date on the year 1 sales were $10,000 (i.e., $7,000 + $3,000), permitting the recognition of $2,000 profit above the year 1 of sales of $8,000 and (2) collections on the year 2 sales were $12,000, permitting the recognition of $3,000 profit above the year 2 cost of sales of $9,000. Therefore, the amount of gross profit that Fox should recognize for the year ended 3/31, year 2 is $5,000 (i.e., $2,000 + $3,000).

Completion of Production Method

17. (c) Amar recognizes revenue of $210,000 (i.e., 300,000 lbs. × $0.70/lb.) in year 1 for the cotton produced in year 1. It is appropriate for Amar to recognize revenue when the cotton is produced because (1) there is a relatively stable market for the cotton, (2) Amar's costs of selling and distributing the cotton are immaterial and can be reasonably estimated, and (3) the units of cotton are homogeneous.

18. (c) Dell should recognize contract revenue of $550,000 (5,000 × $110). Dell properly recognizes the full amount of the contract revenue pertaining to the 5,000 desks produced because (1) the number of desks produced is within the parameters of the contract for the year, and (2) the earnings process is virtually complete.

Right of Return

19. (a) Zee has the right to return the machine to Lin if Zee is not able to resell the machine before expiration of the 90-day payment period. Per SFAS 48, if an enterprise sells its product but gives the buyer the right to return the product, revenue from the sales transaction is not recognized at the time of sale if the buyer is obligated to pay the seller and the obligation is contingent upon resale of the product.

Completed Contract Method

20. (d) Mitchell uses the completed contract method; thus, no portion of the estimated gross profit can be recognized in year 1. The full amount of the gross profit of the contract should be recognized in year 2, the final year of the contract.

Contract price		$ 600,000
Actual costs incurred	$225,000	
Estimated cost to complete	225,000	
Less: Estimated total costs		(450,000)
Estimated total gross profit, year 1		$ 150,000

Contract price	$ 600,000
Less: Actual cost incurred ($225,000 + $255,000)	(480,000)
Total gross profit of contract	$ 120,000

21. (b) Progress billings and collections on progress billings are not generally accepted as a method of recognizing income because they often do not bear a meaningful relationship to the work performed on the contract. If income were recognized on the basis of progress billings, it would be possible for a contractor to materially distort the contractor's income merely by rendering progress billings without regard to any degree of progress on the contract.

22. (d) The full amount of an anticipated loss on a long-term construction contract must be recognized immediately under both the percentage of completion and completed contract methods. The recognition of an anticipated loss cannot be deferred to future periods under either method.

23. (a) If the completed contract method is used, Pell recognizes a gross loss of $20,000 on the two projects because (1) no portion of the $60,000 estimated gross profit on Project 1 can be recognized in the current year since the project is not completed at 12/31, and (2) the full amount of the $20,000 anticipated loss on Project 2 must be recognized in the current year because the anticipated loss cannot be deferred to future periods.

	Project 1		Project 2	
Contract price		$ 420		$ 300
Cost incurred to date	$240		$280	
Less: Estimated costs to complete	120		40	
Less: Estimated total costs		(360)		(320)
Estimated total gross profit		$ 60		$ (20)

Percentage of Completion Method

24. (b) If the percentage of completion method is used, Pell recognizes a gross profit of $20,000 on the two projects combined because (1) $40,000 of the estimated gross profit on Project 1 is recognized in the current year, and (2) the full amount of the $20,000 anticipated loss on Project 2 is recognized in the current year because no portion of the anticipated loss can be deferred to future periods.

	Project 1		Project 2	
Contract price		$ 420		$ 300
Cost incurred to date	$240		$280	
Estimated costs to complete	120		40	
Less: Estimated total costs		(360)		(320)
Estimated total gross profit (loss)		60		$ (20)
Costs incurred to date	240			
Estimated total costs	/ 360			
Times: Percentage of completion		× 2/3		
Gross profit recognized		$ 40		

25. (a) Total noncurrent liabilities at 12/31 of the current year is comprised of the noncurrent note payable of $1,620,000. (The $700,000 of billings in excess of costs on long-term contracts is reported as a current liability. The $160,000 of retained earnings restricted for the note payable is reported as an element of retained earnings.)

26. (c) Under the completed contract method, cost in excess of related billings on long-term contracts is reported as a current asset, and billings in excess of related costs on long-term contracts is reported separately as a current liability. Current assets and current liabilities pertaining to two or more contracts should not be netted for financial statement purposes (ARB 45, ¶12). Mint does not report any prepaid taxes at 12/31 since the $450,000 of income tax expense recognized for the current year reduces the prior $450,000 balance in the Prepaid Taxes account to zero.

Cash	$ 600,000
Accounts receivable, net	3,500,000
Cost in excess of billings on LT contracts	1,600,000
Total current assets, 12/31	$5,700,000

27. (a) Under the percentage of completion method, an asset, *Construction in Progress,* is recorded for the actual costs incurred to date *plus* the profit recognized to date on the contract. Thus, the profit recognized from the contract in year 2 can be computed by subtracting the contract costs incurred in year 2 from the increase in the *Construction in Progress* account during year 2.

Construction in progress, 12/31, year 2	$ 364,000
Less: Construction in progress, 12/31, year 1	(122,000)
Increase during year 2 (contract costs incurred and profit recognized in year 2)	242,000
Less: Contract costs incurred in year 2	(192,000)
Profit recognized in year 2	$ 50,000

28. (a) Progress billings and collections on progress billings do not enter into the computation of the amount of gross profit recognized from the contract. Under the percentage of completion method, the gross profit recognized in the first year of the contract is determined by multiplying the estimated total gross profit of the contract by the estimated percentage of completion.

Contract price		$4,200,000
Costs incurred to date	$1,750,000	
Estimated costs to complete	1,750,000	
Less: Estimated total costs		(3,500,000)
Estimated total gross profit		700,000
Costs incurred to date	1,750,000	
Estimated total costs	/ 3,500,000	
Times: Estimated % of completion		× 50%
Gross profit recognized		$ 350,000

29. (b)

		Year 1		Year 2
Contract price		$10,000		$ 10,000
Estimated total cost at completion		(7,500)		(8,000)
Estimated gross profit		$ 2,500		$ 2,000
Estimated total cost at completion		$ 7,500		$ 8,000
GP recognized to date	$ 500		$1,200	
Estimated total GP	/2,500		/ 2,000	
Percentage of completion		× 20%		× 60%
Contract costs to date		1,500		4,800
Contract costs, prior years		(0)		(1,500)
Contract costs, current year		$ 1,500		$ 3,300

30. (d) Under the percentage of completion method, the gross profit recognized in the second year of the contract is determined by multiplying the estimated total gross profit of the contract by the estimated percentage of completion and then subtracting the gross profit recognized in the first year.

Contract price		$3,000,000
Costs incurred to date	$1,800,000	
Estimated costs to complete	600,000	
Less: Estimated total costs		(2,400,000)
Estimated total gross profit		600,000
Costs incurred to date	1,800,000	
Estimated total costs	/ 2,400,000	
Times: Estimated % of completion		× 75%
Gross profit recognizable to date		450,000
Less: Gross profit previously recognized		(300,000)
Gross profit to be recognized in year 2		$ 150,000

31. (b) Income previously recognized is used in the calculation, but progress billings to date are not. The formula used to determine the income recognized in a period under the percentage of completion method is as follows:

$$\text{Current Income} = \left(\frac{\text{Actual cost to date}}{\text{Estimated total cost}} \times \text{Total estimated income}\right) - \text{Income previously recognized}$$

32. (a) In the final year of a contract accounted for by the percentage of completion method, the final

income recognition would take place. The calculation would be the total revenue earned over the entire contract less the actual total costs incurred less the income previously recognized.

33. (d) The ratio used for the percentage of completion method is incurred costs to date over total expected costs. Progress billings are not generally accepted as a method of recognizing income because billings do not necessarily relate to work actually performed on a contract. Costs incurred in year 3 to total estimated costs are not part of the cost of completion ratio.

34. (a) The percentage of completion method requires that revenues and gross profit be recognized each period based upon the progress of completion. Construction costs plus gross profit earned to date are accumulated in an inventory account, *Construction in Progress,* and progress billings are accumulated in a contra inventory account (ARB 45, ¶12).

Consignments

35. (d) Consignment sales revenue is recognized at the time of the sale. Thus, consignment sales revenue of $10,000 (10 freezers × $1,000 sales price) is reported in the current year. The commission is a selling expense; it is **not** netted against sales revenue.

Cash	8,500	
Consignment Sales Commissions	1,500	
Consignment Sales Revenues		10,000
To record consignment sale		

36. (b) Consignment sales revenue is recognized at the time of the sale at the sales price. The commission paid to the consignee is reported as a selling expense; it is not netted against sales revenue. Net income would be sales revenue less commissions and other expenses.

Inventory sale	$32,000
Cost inventory sold ($50,000 × .4)	20,000
Gross income	12,000
Less: Commission	(3,200)
Less: Advertising	(1,200)
Net income	$ 7,600

Franchise Fee Income

37. (d) The $60,000 received in year 1 was for services already performed and is, therefore, recognized as income in year 1. The three payments of $30,000 have not yet been earned as of the signing of the agreement because Rice is required to perform substantial future services. Such payments may not be recognized as revenue until the services are performed. The annual payments should be discounted and reported as unearned franchise fees at their present value of $72,000 at 12/31, year 1.

38. (c) Services for the initial fee have not yet been performed and are expected to be performed in year 2. None of the initial fee, including the nonrefundable portion, should be recognized as revenue until year 2.

Initial franchise fee	$ 30,000
Times: New franchises contracted	× 21
Gross unearned franchise fees, 12/31, year 1	630,000
Less: Estimated defaults on additional payments	(20,000)
Net unearned franchise fees, 12/31, year 1	$610,000

39. (d) Initial franchise fees from franchise sales ordinarily must be recognized (with provision for estimated uncollectible amounts) when all material services or conditions relating to the sale have been substantially performed or satisfied by the franchisor.

40. (c) Initial franchise fees from franchise sales ordinarily must be recognized (with provision for estimated uncollectible amounts) when all material services or conditions relating to the sale have been substantially performed or satisfied by the franchisor. The balance is payable in 4 annual installments, and is expected to be collected in full, therefore the balance should be handled as a noninterest-bearing note. Accrual accounting treatment requires that the balance be reported at the present value of the future payments.

$ 25,000
+ 34,000
$ 59,000

Royalties

41. (b) Accrual accounting recognizes expenses in the period they are incurred, not paid. Royalties paid should not be recognized as an expense at the date the royalty agreement began or the date the royalty agreement expires.

42. (b) Revenue generally is recognized when both the earnings process is complete and an exchange has taken place. Deferred revenue is revenue collected, but not yet earned. Royalty revenue to Boulder would be $30,000 ($300,000 × .10). The remaining $20,000 balance of Castle's payment against future royalties is deferred revenue.

43. (a) Accrual accounting recognizes revenue in the period(s) it is earned, rather than when the related cash is received.

Royalties for 1/1 to 6/30, year 2 (received 9/15)	$17,000
Royalties for 7/1 to 12/31, year 2 ($60,000 × 15%)	9,000
Royalty revenue, year 2	$26,000

44. (c) Royalty revenue and expense are recognized in the period in which the royalties are earned.

Dec. 1, year 1, to May 31, year 2	$400,000
Less: Month of December year 1	(50,000)
June 1, year 2, to Nov. 30, year 2	325,000
Month of December year 2	70,000
Total royalty revenue	745,000
Times: Percentage of Rill's ownership	20%
Rill's royalty revenue	$149,000

45. (d) Accrual accounting recognizes revenue in the period it is earned rather than when the related cash is received. Under the royalty agreement, Super earns 20% of revenues associated with the comic strip. In year 3, Super should recognize royalty revenue of $300,000 ($1,500,000 × 20%).

Changing Prices Overview

46. (c) Financial statements prepared under the current cost/constant dollar method of accounting include adjustments for both specific price changes and general price-level changes. Historical cost/nominal dollar is the generally accepted method of accounting based on measures of historical prices without restatement. Current cost/nominal dollar is a method of accounting in which adjustments for specific price changes are made but not for general price-level changes. Historical cost/constant dollar is a method of accounting in which adjustments are not made for specific price changes but are made for general price-level changes.

47. (d) During a period of inflation, the specific rate of the parcel of land increased at a *lower rate* than the consumer price index. Therefore, the land would be reported at the highest amount under the historical cost/constant dollar method of accounting, since the land, a nonmonetary asset, would be reported at its historical cost measured in constant dollars. Under the historical cost/nominal dollar method of accounting, the land would be reported at its historical cost in the financial statements. The historical cost of the land would not be remeasured to reflect the change in the general purchasing power of the dollar that occurred during the period of inflation. The current cost/nominal dollar and current cost/constant dollar methods require that the land be reported at its current cost which is less than the amount that would be reported for the historical cost of the land measured in constant dollars because the specific price of the parcel of land increased at a *lower rate* than the consumer price index.

48. (c) DeeCee adjusts the depreciation and cost of goods sold reported in the historical cost income statement by applying specific price indexes to these amounts. Therefore, DeeCee's adjusted income statement is prepared using current cost accounting. The income statement is not prepared using fair value accounting because only depreciation expense and cost of goods sold are restated by applying specific price indexes. The income statement is not prepared using general purchasing power accounting because DeeCee's historical costs are not remeasured into units of a currency with the same general purchasing power. The income statement is not prepared using current cost/general purchasing power accounting because amounts are not remeasured into units of a currency with the same general purchasing power.

Monetary & Nonmonetary Items

49. (b) Monetary assets represent a claim to receive a fixed sum of money or an amount determinable without reference to future prices of specific goods and services. The demand bank deposits and net long-term receivables are monetary assets as they represent claims to receive a fixed sum of money, the amounts of which can be determined without reference to future prices of specific goods and services. All assets that are not monetary are nonmonetary. The patents and trademarks do not represent a claim to receive cash, and hence are classified as nonmonetary assets.

50. (b) Monetary assets represent a claim to receive a fixed sum of money or an amount determinable without reference to future prices of specific goods and services. All assets that are not monetary are nonmonetary. The merchandise inventory does not represent a claim to receive cash, and hence is classified as a nonmonetary asset. The loans to employees is a monetary asset as it does represent a claim to receive a fixed sum of money, the amount of which can be determined without reference to future prices of specific goods and services.

51. (d) In classifying balance sheet accounts as monetary or nonmonetary, a valuation account is classified the same as the account to which it relates. Accumulated depreciation on equipment is classified as nonmonetary because it is a valuation account to equipment, which is nonmonetary. Advances to unconsolidated subsidiaries is a receivable, and thus is monetary. Allowance for uncollectible accounts is a valuation allowance to accounts receivable, which is monetary. Premium on bonds payable is a valuation account to bonds payable, which is monetary.

Presentation

52. (c) A company disclosing voluntary information about the effect of changing prices should report this information in the supplementary information to the financial statements (SFAS 89, par. 3). This information should not be reported in the body of the financial statements, the notes to the financial statements, or management's report to shareholders.

Current Costs

53. (b)

Average current cost per unit [($58 + $72) / 2]	$	65
Times: Units sold during the year	×	70,000
Cost of goods sold, average current cost		$4,550,000

54. (a) To compute cost of goods sold on a current cost basis, multiply the number of units sold by the average current cost of the units during the year. (Average current cost of the units during the year is the sum of the current cost of the units at the beginning and the end of the year, divided by two.)

55. (a) Under SFAS 89, the "inflation component" of the increase in the current cost amount is defined as the difference between the nominal dollars and constant dollars measures.

56. (c) When current cost of goods sold is less than historical cost, current cost income from continuing operations will be greater than historical cost income from continuing operations. More depreciation expense will be included in current cost income from continuing operations than historical cost income from continuing operations when the current cost of equipment is greater than historical cost. Until the land is sold, the difference in its current cost and historical cost will not affect either current cost or historical cost income from continuing operations. A purchasing power loss occurs when ending net monetary assets are less than beginning net monetary assets for a period in which there were rising general price levels. Purchasing power gains and losses are not included in either current cost or historical cost income from continuing operations.

Purchasing Gains & Losses

57. (a) An entity suffers purchasing power losses in a period of rising general price levels from holding monetary assets. A monetary asset is money or a claim to receive a sum of money, the amount of which is fixed or determinable without reference to future prices of specific goods and services. A refundable deposit with a supplier is a monetary asset. An equity investment in unconsolidated subsidiaries is a nonmonetary asset. Warranty obligations are nonmonetary liabilities. Wages payable is a monetary liability. An entity would have purchasing power gains in a period of rising general price levels from holding monetary liabilities.

58. (c) Purchasing power *losses* result from holding monetary assets during a period of inflation because the fixed amount of money will purchase fewer goods and services following a period of inflation. The holding of nonmonetary items during a period of changing prices does not give rise to purchasing power gains or losses.

Holding Gains & Losses

59. (d) Under current cost accounting, the amount of holding gain on a unit of inventory is the increase in current cost from holding the inventory from period to period. The inventory in question was purchased at $8 per unit and has a replacement cost of $10 on December 31. Therefore, under current cost accounting, Vend has a holding gain of $2 ($10 – $8) on each unit of the inventory

60. (a) An increase in the current cost of inventory items sold is a realized holding gain. An increase in the current cost of inventory items on hand is an unrealized holding gain. Current cost financial statements will measure and report both realized and unrealized holding gains (SFAS 89, par. 34).

PERFORMANCE BY SUBTOPICS

Each category below parallels a subtopic covered in Chapter 12. Record the number and percentage of questions you correctly answered in each subtopic area.

Installment Method

Question #	Correct √
1	
2	
3	
4	
5	
6	
7	
8	
9	
10	
# Questions	10
# Correct	
% Correct	

Cost Recovery Method

Question #	Correct √
11	
12	
13	
14	
15	
16	
# Questions	6
# Correct	
% Correct	

Completion of Production Method

Question #	Correct √
17	
18	
# Questions	2
# Correct	
% Correct	

Right of Return

Question #	Correct √
19	
# Questions	1
# Correct	
% Correct	

Completed Contract Method

Question #	Correct √
20	
21	
22	
23	
# Questions	4
# Correct	
% Correct	

Percentage of Completion Method

Question #	Correct √
24	
25	
26	
27	
28	
29	
30	
31	
32	
33	
34	
# Questions	11
# Correct	
% Correct	

Consignments

Question #	Correct √
35	
36	
# Questions	2
# Correct	
% Correct	

Franchise Fee Income

Question #	Correct √
37	
38	
39	
40	
# Questions	4
# Correct	
% Correct	

Royalties

Question #	Correct √
41	
42	
43	
44	
45	
# Questions	5
# Correct	
% Correct	

Changing Prices Overview

Question #	Correct √
46	
47	
48	
# Questions	3
# Correct	
% Correct	

Monetary & Nonmonetary Items

Question #	Correct √
49	
50	
51	
# Questions	3
# Correct	
% Correct	

Presentation

Question #	Correct √
52	
# Questions	1
# Correct	
% Correct	

Current Costs

Question #	Correct √
53	
54	
55	
56	
# Questions	4
# Correct	
% Correct	

Purchasing Gains & Losses

Question #	Correct √
57	
58	
# Questions	2
# Correct	
% Correct	

Holding Gains & Losses

Question #	Correct √
59	
60	
# Questions	2
# Correct	
% Correct	

SIMULATION SOLUTIONS

Solution 12-2

Research

FAS 45, Par. 14

14. Continuing franchise fees shall be reported as revenue as the fees are earned and become receivable from the franchisee. Costs relating to continuing franchise fees shall be expensed as incurred. Although a portion of the continuing fee may be designated for a particular purpose, such as an advertising program, it shall not be recognized as revenue until the fee is earned and becomes receivable from the franchisee. An exception to the foregoing exists if the franchise constitutes an agency relationship under which a designated portion of the continuing fee is required to be segregated and used for a specified purpose. In that case, the designated amount shall be recorded as a liability against which the specified costs would be charged.

Essay—Long-Term Contracts

a. The **two** alternative accounting methods to account for long-term construction contracts are the **percentage of completion** method and the **completed contract** method. The **percentage of completion method must be used if both** of the following conditions are **met at the statement date:**

- Reasonable estimates of profitability at completion.
- Reliable measures of progress toward completion.

If one or both of these conditions are **not met** at the statement date, the **completed contract method must be used.**

b. The **Ski Park** contract must be accounted for by the **percentage of completion** method. **Eighty percent** of the **estimated total income** on the contract should be **recognized as of December 31 of the current year.** Therefore, the **current year income** to be **recognized** will equal **80%** of the **estimated total income less** the income reported under the contract **in the previous year.**

The **Nassu Village** contract must be accounted for by the **completed contract method.** Therefore, **no income or loss** is **recognized in the current year** under this contract.

c. The **receivable** on the Ski Park contract should be reported as a **current asset.** If **costs plus gross profit to date exceed billings,** the difference should be reported as a **current asset.** If **billings exceed cost plus gross profit to date,** the difference should be reported as a **current liability.**

Solution 12-3

Research

ARB 45, Par. 3.

Two accounting methods commonly followed by contractors are the percentage of completion method and the completed contract method.

Response A

London Inc.
Schedule of Selected Balance Sheet Accounts
September 30, Year 2

Accounts receivable			$115,000	1
Costs and estimated earnings in excess of billings:				
Construction in progress	$ 540,000	2		
Less: Billings	(315,000)	3		
Costs and estimated earnings in excess of billings			$225,000	4
Billings in excess of costs and estimated earnings			$ 50,000	5

Response B

London Inc.
Schedule of Gross Profit (Loss)

For the Year Ended September 30, Year 2:	Beta		Gamma	
Estimated gross profit (loss):				
Contract price	$ 600,000	6	$ 800,000	9
Less: Total costs	(400,000)	7	(820,000)	10
Estimated gross profit (loss)	$ 200,000	8	$ (20,000)	11
Percent complete:				
Costs incurred to date	$ 360,000	12	$ 410,000	16
Total costs	/ 400,000	13	/ 820,000	17
Percent complete	90%	14	50%	18
Gross profit (loss) recognized	$ 180,000	15	$ (20,000)	19
For the Year Ended September 30, Year 3:	Beta		Gamma	
Estimated gross profit (loss):				
Contract price	$ 560,000	20	$ 840,000	23
Less: Total costs	(450,000)	21	(900,000)	24
Estimated gross profit (loss)	$ 110,000	22	$ (60,000)	25
Percent complete:				
Costs incurred to date	$ 450,000	26	$ 720,000	29
Total costs	/ 450,000	27	/ 900,000	30
Percent complete	100%	28	80%	31
Gross profit (loss)	$ 110,000	32	$ (60,000)	35
Less: Gross (profit) loss recognized in prior year	(180,000)	33	20,000	36
Gross profit (loss) recognized	$ (70,000)	34	$ (40,000)	37

Response C

London Inc.
Schedule of Income Taxes Payable and Income Tax Expense
September 30, Year 2

Financial statement income:			
From other divisions		$ 300,000	38
From Beta project		180,000	39
From Gamma project		(20,000)	40
Total financial statement income		460,000	41
Less temporary differences:			
Beta project income		(180,000)	42
Gamma project loss		20,000	43
Total taxable income		$ 300,000	44
Taxes payable ($300,000 × 25%)		$ 75,000	45
Deferred tax liability ($160,000 × 30%)		48,000	46
		$ 123,000	47
Tax expense:			
Current	$ 75,000		48
Deferred	48,000		49
	$123,000		50

1. (Beta $315,000 – $275,000) + (Gamma $440,000 – $365,000) = $115,000.

2. [$360,000 / ($360,000 + $40,000)] $600,000 = $540,000. An excess of costs incurred and income recognized over progress billings in the Beta Project gave rise to a current asset.

3. Given in scenario information

4. Sum of 2 and 3

5. $410,000 costs incurred to date (Gamma) – $20,000 estimated loss = $390,000.

   Billings $440,000 – $390,000 = $50,000. An excess of progress billings over related costs and income in the Gamma Project gave rise to a current liability. The current asset and current liability should not be netted.

6. Given in scenario information

7. Year 2 costs incurred to date plus estimated costs to complete
   ($360,000 + $40,000)

8. Contract price less total costs
   ($600,000 – $400,000)

9. Given in scenario information

10. Year 2 costs incurred to date plus estimated costs to complete
    ($410,000 + $410,000)

11. Contract price less total costs
    ($800,000 – $820,000)

12. Given in scenario information

13. Year 2 costs incurred to date plus estimated costs to complete
    ($360,000 + $40,000)

14. Costs incurred to date divided by total costs
    ($360,000 / $400,000)

15. Percent completed × contract price
    (90% × $600,000)

16. Given in scenario information

17. Year 2 costs incurred to date plus estimated costs to complete
    ($410,000 + $410,000)

18. Costs incurred to date divided by total costs
    ($410,000 / $820,000)

19. Losses are recognized immediately and in full in the current period

20. Original contract price less penalties
    [$600,000 – (4 × $10,000)

21. Year 3 costs incurred to date plus estimated costs to complete
    ($450,000 + 0)

22. Contract price less total costs
    ($560,000 – $450,000)

23. Original contract price plus change orders
    ($800,000 + $40,000)

24. Year 3 costs incurred to date plus estimated costs to complete
    ($720,000 + $180,000)

25. Original contract price plus change orders and less total costs
    ($840,000 – $900,000)

26. Given in scenario information

27. Given in scenario information

28. Costs incurred to date divided by total costs
    ($450,000 / $450,000)

29. Given in scenario information

30. Year 2 costs incurred to date plus estimated costs to complete
    ($720,000 + $180,000)

31. Costs incurred to date divided by total costs
    ($720,000 / $900,000)

32. Contract price less total costs
    ($560,000 – $450,000)

33. Gross (profit) loss recognized in prior year

34. Current year gross profit (loss) less gross (profit) loss recognized in the prior year
    ($110,000 – $180,000)

35. Current year gross profit (loss)

36. Gross (profit) loss recognized in prior year

37. Current year gross profit (loss) less gross (profit) loss recognized in the prior year
    [($60,000) – $20,000]

38. Given in scenario information

39. Beta Division year 2 income arrived at in part b

40. Gamma Division year 2 income arrived at in part b

41. Total financial statement income from other divisions and long term construction projects
[$300,000 + $180,000 + (20,000)]

42. London uses the completed contract method for income tax purposes, therefore, income and loss on long term construction projects is not reported for income taxes until the projects are completed. The amount of this income or loss is a temporary difference.

43. London uses the completed contract method for income tax purposes, therefore, income or loss on long term construction projects is not reported for income taxes until the projects are completed. The amount of this income or loss is a temporary difference.

44. London uses the completed contract method for income tax purposes, therefore, income and loss on long term construction projects is not reported for income taxes until the projects are completed. Financial statement income is reduced by temporary differences to arrive at taxable income.
[$460,000 – $180,000 – (20,000)]

45. Taxable income × the enacted tax rate
($300,000 × .25)

46. Deferred tax liability × the enacted tax rate for future years
[$180,000 + (20,000) = $160,000 × 30%]

47. Taxes payable + deferred tax liability
($75,000 + $48,000)

48. Current taxable income × enacted tax rate = current tax expense
($300,000 × 25%)

49. Temporary differences × enacted tax rate for future years
($160,000 × 30%)

50. Current tax expense plus deferred tax liability
($75,000 + $48,000)

CHAPTER 13

ACCOUNTING FOR INCOME TAXES

I. **Basic Concepts** 13-2
- A. Pretax Financial Income 13-2
- B. Taxable Income 13-2
- C. Income Taxes Currently Payable (Refundable) 13-2
- D. Income Tax Expense (Benefit) 13-3
- E. Reconciliation of Pretax Financial Income & Taxable Income 13-4

II. **SFAS 109 Overview** 13-5
- A. Asset & Liability Method 13-5
- B. Basic Principles 13-6

III. **Differences** 13-6
- A. Temporary Differences 13-6
- B. Timing Sources 13-7
- C. Other Sources 13-9
- D. Not Linked to Particular Item 13-9
- E. Permanent Differences 13-10

IV. **Deferred Tax Liabilities & Assets** 13-13
- A. Recognition 13-13
- B. Computation 13-13
- C. Enacted Tax Rate 13-13
- D. Applicable Tax Rate 13-14
- E. Attributes of Asset & Liability Method 13-20

V. **Other Considerations** 13-21
- A. Valuation Allowance 13-21
- B. Enacted Change in Tax Laws or Rates 13-24
- C. Change in Enterprise Tax Status 13-25

VI. **Presentation & Disclosure** 13-26
- A. Balance Sheet 13-26
- B. Income Statement 13-27

VII. **Business Combinations & Investments in Common Stock** 13-29
- A. Combinations 13-29
- B. Cost Method Investments 13-29
- C. Equity Method Investments 13-29

EXAM COVERAGE: Historically, exam coverage of the topics in Chapter 13 has been 5 to 10 percent of the FAR section. More information regarding exam coverage is included in Appendix B, *Practical Advice*.

CHAPTER 13

ACCOUNTING FOR INCOME TAXES

I. Basic Concepts

A. Pretax Financial Income

Pretax financial income (often called pretax accounting income, and sometimes called book income, financial income, accounting income, or income for financial accounting purposes) is determined on the accrual basis. That is, expenses incurred for the period are deducted from revenues earned for the period to arrive at pretax financial income. Income tax expense (often called *provision for income taxes*) is then deducted from that subtotal to arrive at net income. An excess of expenses over revenues will cause a pretax financial loss. In situations where a loss situation results in a tax refund or tax savings, the provision is referred to as *income tax benefit.*

B. Taxable Income

Taxable income is determined by following the rules of the Internal Revenue Code. Deductions (called deductible amounts or tax deductible amounts or tax deductible expenses) allowed for the period and allowable exemptions are subtracted from income items (called taxable amounts or taxable revenues) for the period to arrive at taxable income (loss) for the period.

Exhibit 1 ▸ Financial vs Taxable Income

	Revenues earned		Taxable amounts
–	Expenses incurred	–	Deductible amounts
	Pretax financial income (loss)		Taxable income (loss)
–	Income tax expense (benefit)		
	Net income (loss)		

C. Income Taxes Currently Payable (Refundable)

Income taxes currently payable (refundable) is also called current tax expense (or benefit) and is determined by applying the provisions of the tax law to the taxable income or taxable loss figure for a period. The tax law provides that a net operating loss (NOL) may be carried back 2 years and forward 20 years.

Example 1 ▸ Income Taxes Currently Payable

Zanthe Corp. has taxable income for the year of $400,000 and a tax rate of 40%.

Required: Compute the amount of income taxes payable for the year.

Solution:

Taxable income	$400,000
Tax rate	× 40%
Income taxes currently payable	$160,000

Example 2 ▸ Income Taxes Currently Refundable

The Aspen Company has the following history of taxable income and taxes paid:

Year	Taxable income		Tax rate		Taxes paid
1	$ 60,000	×	50%	=	$30,000
2	50,000	×	45%	=	22,500
3	40,000	×	40%	=	16,000
4	80,000	×	35%	=	28,000

The tax rate for year 5 is 30%, and a 25% rate is enacted for year 6 and subsequent years. In year 5, Aspen reports a $200,000 excess of tax deductible expenses over taxable revenues on its tax return. This excess often is called a net operating loss (NOL).

Required: Compute the amount of taxes refundable due to a carryback of the year 5 NOL.

Solution: The $200,000 NOL in year 5 is first applied to year 3, which is the earliest of the two years prior to the loss year. The NOL exceeds the year 3 taxable income so the remaining NOL is then applied to the $80,000 taxable income of year 4 (in that order).

	Taxable income		Tax rate		Taxes paid
From year 3:	$ 40,000	×	40%	=	$ 16,000
From year 4:	80,000	×	35%	=	28,000
	$120,000				
Taxes refundable due to year 5 NOL					$ 44,000

NOTE: Because there was insufficient taxable income in the 2 years prior to year 5 to fully offset the NOL, there is an NOL carryforward for tax purposes of $80,000 (i.e., $200,000 – $120,000) at the end of year 5.

D. Income Tax Expense (Benefit) = Current tax expense + Deferred tax expense

Income tax expense (benefit) is the sum of *current* tax expense (benefit) and *deferred* tax expense (benefit). In the rare instances where taxable income is the same amount as pretax financial income, total income tax expense will equal income taxes currently payable. Income tax expense is often referred to as the *provision for income taxes.* Hence, there can be both a current portion and a deferred portion of the provision. A corporation often charges estimated tax payments to an account titled *Prepaid income taxes.* The balance of this account is used to offset the balance of the *Income taxes payable* account; the net amount is classified as a current asset if the prepaid account is larger or as a current liability if the payable account is larger.

Example 3 ▸ Current Income Tax Expense

Refer to Example 1. Pretax financial income for year 5 is also $400,000 (no differences in taxable income and pretax financial income).

Required: Prepare the journal entry to record year 5 income taxes.

Solution:

	Debit	Credit
Income Tax Expense—current	160,000	
Income Taxes Payable ($400,000 × 40%)		160,000

Discussion: Because there are no temporary differences, there are no deferred income taxes. There is only a current portion for the provision; hence, income tax expense (provision) is the same amount as income tax payable ($160,000). The expense account balance appears on the income statement and the payable account balance is reported as a current liability on the balance sheet.

Example 4 ▸ Deferred Income Tax Expense

Refer to Example 2. The pretax financial loss for year 5 was also $200,000 (no differences in taxable income and pretax financial income in any of the years affected). Aspen reports pretax financial income and taxable income of $92,000 for year 6 before consideration of the deduction for the NOL carryforward.

Required: Prepare the journal entry at the end of year 5 to record the benefits of the operating loss carryback and the expected future benefits of the $80,000 loss carryforward.

Solution:

Income Tax Refund Receivable	44,000	
Benefits of Loss Carryback (from Example 2)		44,000
Deferred Tax Asset ($80,000 × 25%)	20,000	
Benefits of Loss Carryforward		20,000

Discussion: The income tax refund receivable balance of $44,000 is classified as a current asset on the balance sheet. The deferred tax asset balance of $20,000 is classified as a current asset or a noncurrent asset, depending on whether the benefits of the NOL carryforward are expected to be realized in the year that immediately follows the balance sheet date (in which case, it would be classified as a current asset) or in a later year (noncurrent asset). The income statement for year 5 would report the following.

Operating loss before income taxes	$(200,000)
Benefits of loss carryback	44,000
Benefits of loss carryforward	20,000
Net loss, year 5	$(136,000)

The income taxes for year 6 are recorded as follows.

Income Tax Expense—current	3,000	
Income Tax Expense—deferred	20,000	
Income Taxes Payable [25% × ($92,000 – $80,000)]		3,000
Deferred Tax Asset (25% × $80,000)		20,000

The income statement for year 6 would report the following.

Income before income taxes		$ 92,000
Current tax expense	$ 3,000	
Deferred tax expense	20,000	
Total income tax expense		(23,000)
Net income		$ 69,000

E. Reconciliation of Pretax Financial Income & Taxable Income

Most revenues and most expenses are reported on the tax return in the same period that they are reported on the income statement. However, tax laws often differ from the recognition and measurement requirements of financial accounting standards, and it is common to find differences between the amount of pretax financial income (loss) and the amount of taxable income (loss) for a period. Some of the possible differences between the current period's pretax financial income and the current period's taxable income will not cause a difference between pretax financial income and taxable income in some *other* period (i.e., they will not turn around or reverse in some future year). Such differences were called *permanent differences* by APB 11, and many people continue to refer to them as permanent differences even though SFAS 109 does not use the term.

Exhibit 2 ▸ Income Reconciliation

Pretax financial income for the current period can be reconciled with taxable income for the current period by using the following format.

Pretax financial income (loss)	$X,XXX
Excess of taxable revenues over revenues per books	+ XXX
Excess of deductible amounts over expenses per books	(XXX)
Excess of revenues per books over taxable revenues	(XXX)
Excess of expenses per books over deductible amounts	+ XXX
Taxable income (loss)	$X,XXX

Example 5 ▸ Permanent Differences

Pretax financial income for the current year for Zippy Corporation is $300,000 including tax-exempt revenues of $40,000 and nondeductible expenses of $14,000. The tax rate for all years is 40%.

Required:

1. Compute the amount of taxable income for the year.
2. Prepare the journal entry to record income taxes for the year.
3. Show a condensed income statement for the year.

Solution:

1.

Pretax financial income	$ 300,000
Tax-exempt revenues	(40,000)
Nondeductible expenses	14,000
Taxable income	$ 274,000

2.

Income Tax Expense—current	109,600	
Income Taxes Payable ($274,000 × 40%)		109,600

3.

Income before income taxes	$ 300,000
Current income tax expense	(109,600)
Net income	$ 190,400

Discussion: Because differences between pretax financial income and taxable income in the year do not cause differences between pretax financial income and taxable income in any other period, there are no deferred taxes to compute and record. The amount due to the government is based on the amount of taxable income. Because there are no deferred taxes, the amount of income tax expense recorded is the same amount as income taxes payable. The effective tax rate ($109,600 / $300,000 = 36.53%) is less than the statutory rate due to an excess of tax-exempt revenues ($40,000) over nondeductible expenses ($14,000).

II. SFAS 109 Overview

A. Asset & Liability Method

SFAS 109 refers to some differences between (1) the amount of taxable income and pretax financial income for a year and (2) the tax bases of assets or liabilities and their reported amounts in financial statements as *temporary differences.* SFAS 109 requires that the *asset and liability method* be used in accounting and reporting for temporary differences.

1. **Recognition & Measurement** Under this method, a current or deferred tax liability or asset is recognized for the current or deferred tax consequences of all events that have been recognized in the financial statements, and the current or deferred tax consequences of an event are measured based on provisions of the enacted tax law to determine the amount of taxes payable or refundable currently or in future years.

2. **Comprehensive Allocation Approach** SFAS 109 also establishes accounting and reporting standards for the effects of operating losses and tax credit carrybacks and carryforwards. SFAS 109 requires a *comprehensive* (as opposed to a partial) *allocation* approach.

B. Basic Principles

1. **Objectives** The objectives of accounting for income taxes are to recognize (a) the amount of taxes payable or refundable for the current year and (b) deferred tax liabilities and assets for the future tax consequences of events that have been recognized in an enterprise's financial statements or tax returns. To implement the objectives, the following basic principles are applied in accounting for income taxes at the date of the financial statements:

   a. A current tax liability or asset is recognized for the estimated taxes payable or refundable on tax returns for the current year.

   b. A deferred tax liability or asset is recognized for the estimated future tax effects attributable to temporary differences and carryforwards.

   c. The measurement of current and deferred tax liabilities and assets is based on provisions of the *enacted tax law;* the effects of future changes in tax laws or rates are not anticipated.

   d. The measurement of deferred tax assets is reduced, if necessary, by the amount of any tax benefits that, based on available evidence, are not expected to be realized.

2. **Recognition of Deferred Tax Liabilities & Assets** Deferred tax liabilities or assets are recognized for the future tax consequences of the following:

   a. Revenues, expenses, gains, or losses that are included in taxable income of an earlier or later year than the year in which they are recognized in financial income

   b. Other events that create differences between the tax bases of assets and liabilities and their amounts for financial reporting

   c. Operating loss or tax credit carrybacks for refunds of taxes paid in prior years and carryforwards to reduce taxes payable in future years

III. Differences

A. Temporary Differences

A *temporary difference* is a difference between the tax basis of an asset or liability and its reported amount in the financial statements that will result in taxable or deductible amounts in future years when the reported amount of the asset is recovered or the liability is settled.

1. **Origin** The tax consequences of most events recognized in the current year's financial statements are included in determining income taxes currently payable. Because tax laws and financial accounting standards differ in their recognition and measurement of assets, liabilities, equity, revenues, expenses, gains, and losses, differences arise between the following.

   a. The amount of taxable income and pretax financial income for a year

   b. The tax basis of assets or liabilities and their reported amounts in financial statements

2. **Future Effects** Because it is assumed that the reported amounts of assets and liabilities will be recovered and settled, respectively, a difference between the tax basis of an asset or a liability and its reported amount in the balance sheet will result in a taxable or a deductible amount in some future year(s) when the reported amounts of assets are recovered and the reported amounts of liabilities are settled.

3. **Taxable & Deductible Temporary Differences** Temporary differences that will result in taxable amounts in future years when the related assets are recovered are often called *taxable* temporary differences. Likewise, temporary differences that will result in deductible amounts in future years when the related liabilities are settled are often called *deductible* temporary differences.

Example 6 ▸ Temporary Differences

Pretax financial income for the current year for Zippy Corporation is $400,000, including revenue of $50,000, which will not be taxable until a future period. Deductible amounts of $30,000 on the current year tax return will be expensed on a future income statement. The tax rate is 40% for all years. There is no existing balance in any deferred tax account at the beginning of the year.

Required:

1. Compute taxable income for the year.
2. Prepare the journal entry to record income taxes for the year.

Solution:

1.	Pretax financial income	$400,000
	Excess of revenues over taxable amounts	(50,000)
	Excess of deductible amounts over expenses	(30,000)
	Taxable income	$320,000

2.	Income Tax Expense—current	128,000	
	Income Tax Expense—deferred	32,000	
	Income Taxes Payable ($320,000 × 40%)		128,000
	Deferred Tax Liability [($50,000 + $30,000) × 40%]		32,000

Discussion: Because differences between pretax financial income and taxable income in the year do cause differences between pretax financial income and taxable income in some other period, there are deferred taxes to compute and record. The amount due to the government (income taxes payable) is based on the amount of taxable income. The deferred tax amount is computed in accordance with the asset and liability method, prescribed by SFAS 109.

Under the liability method, the deferred tax consequences of the $80,000 ($50,000 + $30,000) future taxable amounts are calculated using enacted future tax rates (40%). The total income tax expense (provision) figure ($160,000) is the amount needed to balance the entry [current tax expense (provision) of $128,000 plus deferred tax expense (provision) of $32,000].

B. Timing Sources

Differences between taxable income and pretax financial income that result from including revenues, expenses, gains, or losses in taxable income of an earlier or later year than the year in which they are recognized in financial income (referred to as "timing differences" by APB 11) create differences (sometimes accumulating over more than one year) between the tax basis of an asset or liability and its reported amount in the financial statements and, thus, are temporary differences.

Example 7 ▸ Taxable After Being Included in Financial Income

One example is the use of the accrual method for accounting for installment sales for computing financial income and the use of the installment (cash) method for tax purposes. This will cause an excess of the reported amount of an asset (receivable) over its tax basis that will result in a taxable amount in a future year(s) when the asset is recovered (when the cash is collected). This situation will result in future taxable amounts.

Example 8 ▸ Deductible After Being Included in Financial Income

Examples include accruals of items such as warranty expense and loss contingencies in computing financial income. Such items are deductible for tax purposes only when they are realized. This type of situation causes a reported amount of a liability to exceed its tax basis (zero) which will result in deductible amounts in a future year(s) when the liability is settled. This situation will result in future tax deductible amounts.

Example 9 ▸ Taxable Before Being Included in Financial Income

One example is accounting for revenue received in advance for rent or subscriptions. For tax purposes, the revenue is taxable in the period the related cash is received. The revenue is not included in the computation of financial income until the period in which it is earned. This situation causes a liability's reported amount on the balance sheet to exceed its tax basis (zero) which will result in future tax deductible amounts when the liability is settled. This case is said to result in future tax deductible amounts because of the future sacrifices required to provide goods or services or to provide refunds to those who cancel their orders. This situation will result in future tax deductible amounts.

Example 10 ▸ Deductible Before Being Included in Financial Income

These situations result in future taxable amounts. Typically, temporary differences of this type accumulate and then eliminate over several years. Future temporary differences for **existing** depreciable assets (in use at the balance sheet date) are considered in determining the future years in which existing temporary differences result in **net** taxable or deductible amounts.

a. **Prepaid Expense** One example is when a prepaid expense is deducted for tax purposes in the period it is paid, but deferred and deducted in the period the expense is incurred for purposes of computing financial (book) income.

b. **Depreciation Expense** The most commonly cited example is where a depreciable asset is depreciated faster for tax purposes than it is depreciated for book purposes. This will cause the asset's carrying amount to exceed its tax basis. Amounts received upon the future recovery of the asset's carrying amount (through use or sale) will exceed its tax basis and the excess will be a taxable amount when the asset is recovered.

Exhibit 3 ▸ Temporary Differences

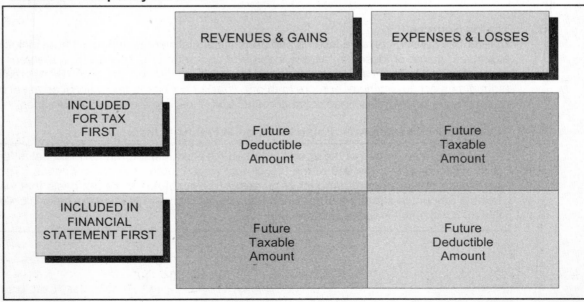

	REVENUES & GAINS	EXPENSES & LOSSES
INCLUDED FOR TAX FIRST	Future Deductible Amount	Future Taxable Amount
INCLUDED IN FINANCIAL STATEMENT FIRST	Future Taxable Amount	Future Deductible Amount

Example 11 ▸ Temporary Difference

An enterprise acquired a depreciable asset at the beginning of year 1. The asset has a cost of $60,000, no residual value, is being depreciated over six years using the straight-line method for financial reporting purposes, and is being depreciated over three years using the straight-line method and the one-half year convention for tax purposes.

Year	Depreciation for financial reporting	Depreciation for tax purposes	Difference
1	$10,000	$10,000	$ --
2	10,000	20,000	(10,000)
3	10,000	20,000	(10,000)
4	10,000	10,000	--
5	10,000	--	10,000
6	10,000	--	10,000
	$60,000	$60,000	$ --

Required: Determine the cumulative temporary difference at the end of each year and describe its impact on future tax returns.

Solution:

1. At the end of year 1 there is no temporary difference. The carrying amount of the asset is $50,000 and its tax basis is $50,000 (i.e., $60,000 – $10,000).
2. At the end of year 2 the cumulative temporary difference is $10,000 and will result in a net future taxable amount of $10,000. This amount will reverse in year 5.
3. At the end of year 3 the cumulative temporary difference is $20,000 and will result in a net future taxable amount of $20,000. This amount will reverse equally in year 5 and year 6.
4. At the end of year 4 the cumulative temporary difference is $20,000 and will result in a net future taxable amount of $20,000. This amount will reverse equally in year 5 and year 6.
5. At the end of year 5 the cumulative temporary difference is $10,000 and will result in a future taxable amount of $10,000. This amount will reverse in year 6.
6. At the end of year 6 there is no more temporary difference because the asset is fully depreciated both for financial statements and tax purposes.

C. Other Sources

Other situations that may cause temporary differences because of differences between the reported amount and the tax basis of an asset or liability are as follows.

1. **Tax Credits** A reduction in the tax basis of depreciable assets because of tax credits
2. **Investment Tax Credits** Investment tax credits accounted for by the deferred method
3. **Currency Issues** An increase in the tax basis of assets because of indexing whenever the local currency is the functional currency
4. **Business Combinations** Business combinations accounted for by the purchase method

D. Not Linked to Particular Item

Some temporary differences are deferred taxable income or tax deductions and have balances only on an income tax balance sheet and, therefore, cannot be identified with a particular asset or liability for financial reporting. There is no related, identifiable asset or liability for financial reporting, but there is a temporary difference that results from an event that has been recognized in the financial statements, and that difference will result in taxable or deductible amounts in future years. An example is a long-term contract that is accounted for by the percentage of completion method for financial reporting and by the completed contract method for tax purposes. The temporary difference (income on the contract) is deferred income for tax purposes that becomes taxable when the contract is completed.

E. Permanent Differences

Some events recognized in financial statements do not have tax consequences under the regular U.S. tax system. Certain revenues are exempt from taxation and certain expenses are not deductible. Events that do not have tax consequences do not give rise to temporary differences and, therefore, do not give rise to deferred tax assets or liabilities. These differences that will not have future tax consequences are often referred to as permanent differences.

1. **Revenue Examples** Permanent differences resulting from revenues that are included in the computation of financial income, but are not included in computing taxable income, include: (a) interest earned on state and municipal obligations; (b) life insurance proceeds received by an enterprise on one of its officers; and (c) dividends received by one U.S. corporation from another U.S. corporation that are excluded from taxable income due to the dividends-received deduction (70%, 80%, or 100%).

2. **Expense Examples** Permanent differences resulting from expenses that are included in the computation of financial income, but are not included in computing taxable income, include: (a) expenses incurred in generating tax-exempt income; (b) premiums paid for life insurance on officers when the enterprise is the beneficiary; and (c) fines, penalties, and other costs incurred from activities that are a violation of the law.

3. **Deduction Example** An example of a permanent difference resulting from deductions that are allowed in computing taxable income but are not allowed in computing financial income is excess of percentage depletion (statutory allowance) over cost of natural resources.

Example 12 ▸ Temporary & Permanent Differences

Tigger Corporation has pretax financial income of $100,000 for the current calendar year (first year of operations). The following differences exist between pretax financial income and taxable income.

1. Interest on investments in tax-exempt securities amounts to $22,000.
2. Fines and violations of the law amount to $3,000.
3. An excess of accrued warranty expense over amounts paid to satisfy warranties during the year is $18,000.
4. An excess of installment sales revenue over the cash received is $31,000 (accrual basis used for financial reporting and cash basis used for tax return).
5. Premiums paid for life insurance on officers is $6,000. Tigger Corp. is the beneficiary.
6. Depreciation for books is $70,000, whereas depreciation using an accelerated method for tax purposes is $90,000.
7. Losses accrued for financial accounting purposes for litigation contingencies amounts to $16,000.

Required:

a. Identify each difference between pretax financial income and taxable income as being either a permanent or temporary difference and reconcile pretax financial income with taxable income.

b. Compute the net future taxable (deductible) amounts due to temporary differences existing at the end of the year.

c. Assuming a tax rate for the current and future years of 40%, compute the amount of income taxes currently payable and the amount of deferred income taxes. Prepare the journal entry to record income taxes for the year.

Solution a:

Pretax financial income	$100,000
Permanent differences:	
Tax-exempt revenue [1]	(22,000)
Nondeductible fines [2]	3,000
Life insurance premiums [5]	6,000
Temporary differences originating:	
Excess of warranty expense per books [3]	18,000
Excess of installment revenue per books [4]	(31,000)
Excess of depreciation per tax return [6]	(20,000)
Excess of accrued losses per books [7]	16,000
Taxable income	$ 70,000

Solution b:

Future warranty deductions [3]	$ (18,000)
Future installment sale collections [4]	31,000
Excess of book depreciation over tax depreciation in future [6]	20,000
Future deductions for litigation [7]	(16,000)
Net future taxable amounts	$ 17,000

Solution c:

Taxable income	$70,000	Net future taxable amounts	$17,000
Current tax rate	× 40%	Enacted future tax rate	× 40%
Income taxes currently payable	$28,000	Deferred tax liability at 12/31	$ 6,800

NOTE: Because there is a flat tax rate for all future years, deferred taxes may be computed by one aggregate calculation; the future taxable and deductible amounts that will result from the elimination of existing temporary differences need not be scheduled for the individual future years affected.

NOTE: The temporary differences originating in the year that will cause future deductible amounts (accrual of warranty expense and loss contingency for book purposes) are added to pretax financial income to arrive at taxable income; temporary differences originating in the year that will cause future taxable amounts (installment sales method and accelerated depreciation for tax purposes) are deducted from pretax financial income to arrive at taxable income.

Income Tax Expense—current	28,000	
Income Tax Expense—deferred	6,800	
Income Taxes Payable ($70,000 × 40%)		28,000
Deferred Tax Liability ($6,800 – $0)		6,800

NOTE: The change required in the *Deferred Tax Liability* account is equal to its ending balance because there was a zero beginning balance.

Exhibit 4 ▸ Summary of Temporary & Permanent Differences

	GAAP Financial Statements	IRC Tax Return	TEMP	PERM	NONE
GROSS INCOME:					
Gross Sales	Income Now	Income Now			✓
Installment Sales	Income Now	Income (Later) When Rec'd	✓		
Dividends					
Equity Method	Income-Sub Earnings	Income is Dividends	✓		
100/80/70% Exclusion	No Exclusion	Excluded Forever		✓	
Rents & Royalties in Advance	Income When Earned	Income When Received	✓		
State & Muni Bond Interest	Income	Never Income		✓	
Life Insurance Proceeds	Income	Never Income		✓	
Gain/Loss Treasury Stock	Not Reported	Not Reported			✓
ORDINARY EXPENSES:					
Officers Compensation (Top)	Expense	$1,000,000 Limit			✓
Bad Debt	Allowance	Direct Write Off	✓		
Interest Expense					
Business Loan	Expense	Expense			✓
Tax Free Investment	Expense	Non Deductible		✓	
Taxable Investment	Expense	Up to Taxable Income			✓
Contributions	All Expensed	Limit to 10% of Inc.	✓		✓
Loss on Abandonment/Casualty	Expense	Expense			✓
Loss on Worthless Subsidiary	Expense	Expense			✓
Depreciation					
MACRS vs. S.L.	Slow Depreciation	Fast Depreciation	✓		
Bonus Depreciation (179, etc.)	Not Allowed, Must Depr.	$105,000 for '05; adjusted for inflation in subsequent years.	✓		
Diff. Basis of Asset	Use GAAP Basis	Use IRC Basis		✓	
Purchased Goodwill	Gain/Loss; Revalued each Year (Amortization no longer allowed)	Amortize S/L 15 Yrs.	✓	✓	✓
Depletion					
% vs. S.L.	Cost Over Years	% of Sales	✓		
% in Excess of Cost	Not Allowed	% of Sales		✓	
Life Insur. Exp. (Corp. Gets)	Expense	No Deduction		✓	
Profit & Pension Expense	Expense Accrued	No Deduction Until Paid	✓		
Accrued Exp. (50% owner/family)	Expense Accrued	No Deduction Until Paid	✓		
Net Capital Gain	Income	Income			✓
Research & Development	Expense	Exp. / Amortize / Capital.	✓	✓	✓
SPECIAL ITEMS:					
Net Capital Loss	Report as Loss	Not Deductible	✓		
Carryover (3 Yrs. & 5 Yrs.)	Not Applicable	Unused Loss Allowed	✓		
Shareholder Dealing	Report as Loss	Not Deductible		✓	
Penalties	Expense	Not Deductible		✓	
Est. Liab. Contingency/Warranty	Expense-Accrued	No Deduction Until Paid	✓		
Federal Income Taxes	Expense	Not Deductible		✓	
Bond Sinking Trust Fund	Inc. / Exp. / Gain / Loss	Inc. / Exp. / Gain / Loss	✓	✓	✓
Lobbying / Political	Expense	No Deduction		✓	

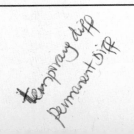

IV. Deferred Tax Liabilities & Assets

A. Recognition

An enterprise is to recognize a deferred tax liability or asset for all temporary differences and operating loss and tax credit carryforwards.

1. **Deferred Tax Expense or Benefit** Deferred tax expense or benefit is the change during the year in an enterprise's deferred tax liabilities and assets.

2. **Total Income Tax Expense or Benefit** Total income tax expense (provision) or benefit for the year is the sum of deferred tax expense or benefit and current tax expense or benefit (income taxes currently payable or refundable).

3. **Basis** The recognition and measurement of a deferred tax liability or asset is based on the future effects on income taxes, as measured by the provisions of enacted tax laws, resulting from temporary differences and operating loss and tax credit carryforwards at the end of the current year.

4. **Jurisdictions** A deferred tax liability or asset is separately computed for each tax jurisdiction (i.e., for each federal, state, local, and foreign taxing authority) because the tax attributes related to one taxing authority cannot be used to directly offset tax attributes related to a different taxing authority.

B. Computation

The steps in the annual computation of deferred tax liabilities and assets are as follows.

1. **Identification** Identify (a) the types and amounts of existing temporary differences and (b) the nature and amount of each type of operating loss and tax credit carryforward and the remaining length of the carryforward period;

2. **Measuring Deferred Tax Liability** Measure the total deferred tax liability for taxable temporary differences using the applicable tax rate;

3. **Measuring Deferred Tax Asset** Measure the total deferred tax asset for deductible temporary differences and operating loss carryforwards using the applicable tax rate;

4. **Tax Credit Carryforwards** Measure deferred tax assets for each type of tax credit carryforward; and

5. **Valuation Allowance** Reduce deferred tax assets by a valuation allowance if, based on the weight of available evidence, it is *more likely than not* (a likelihood of more than 50%) that some or all of the deferred tax assets will not be realized. The allowance must reduce the deferred tax asset to an amount that is more likely than not to be realized.

C. Enacted Tax Rate

The tax rate that is used to measure deferred tax liabilities and deferred tax assets is the enacted tax rate(s) expected to apply to taxable income in the years that the liability is expected to be settled or the asset recovered. Measurements are based on elections (for example, an election for loss carryforward instead of carryback) that are expected to be made for tax purposes in future years.

1. **Determining Applicable Tax Rate** Presently enacted changes in tax laws and rates that become effective for a particular future year or years must be considered when determining the tax rate to apply to temporary differences reversing in that year or years. Tax laws and rates for the current year are used if no changes have been enacted for future years.

2. **Measuring Asset or Liability** An asset for deductible temporary differences that are expected to be realized in future years through carryback of a future loss to the current or a prior year (or a liability for taxable temporary differences that are expected to reduce the refund claimed for the carryback of a future loss to the current or a prior year) is measured

using tax laws and rates for the current or a prior year, that is, the year for which a refund is expected to be realized based on loss carryback provisions of the tax law.

3. **Future Years** Therefore, if there are no new tax rates enacted for future years, the current rate(s) is (are) used to compute deferred taxes, and aggregate calculations are acceptable. However, if there are new tax rates enacted for future years, a scheduling of the individual future years affected by existing temporary differences is required.

   a. The schedule shows in which future years existing temporary differences cause taxable or deductible amounts.

   b. The appropriate enacted tax rate is applied to each future taxable and deductible amount.

4. **Assumptions About Future Taxable Income** In determining the appropriate tax rate, an assumption must be made about whether the entity will report taxable income or loss in the various individual future years expected to be affected by the reversal of existing temporary differences.

   a. If taxable income is expected in the year that a future taxable (or deductible) amount is scheduled, use the enacted rate for that future year to calculate the related deferred tax liability (or asset).

   b. If an NOL is expected in the year that a future taxable (or deductible) amount is scheduled, use the enacted rate of what will be the prior year the NOL will be carried back to or the enacted rate of the future year to which the carryforward will apply, whichever is appropriate, to calculate the related deferred tax liability (or asset).

D. Applicable Tax Rate

The objective is to measure a deferred tax liability or asset using the enacted tax rate(s) expected to apply to taxable income in the periods in which the deferred tax liability or asset is expected to be settled or realized.

1. **Flat Rate vs Graduated Rate** Under current U.S. federal tax law, if taxable income exceeds a specified amount, all taxable income is taxed, in substance, at a single flat tax rate. That tax rate is used for measurement of a deferred tax liability or asset by enterprises for which graduated tax rates are not a significant factor. Enterprises for which graduated tax rates are a significant factor measure a deferred tax liability or asset using the **average graduated tax rate** applicable to estimated annual taxable income in the periods in which the deferred tax liability or asset is estimated to be settled or realized.

2. **Other Tax Provisions** Other provisions of enacted tax laws are considered when determining the tax rate to apply to certain types of temporary differences and carryforwards (for example, the tax law may provide for different tax rates on ordinary income and capital gains). If there is a phased-in change in tax rates, determination of the applicable tax rate requires knowledge about when deferred tax liabilities and assets will be settled and realized.

Example 13 ▸ Annual Computation of Deferred Tax Liabilities & Assets

Bensen's first year of operations is year 1. For year 1, Bensen has pretax financial income of $150,000 and taxable income of $50,000. Taxable income is expected in all future years.

a. Tax rates enacted by the end of year 1 are as follows: year 1, 40%; year 2, 35%; years 3 through 6, 30%; and year 7, 25%.

b. Temporary differences and amounts existing at the end of year 1 are as follows.

Installment sale difference (taxable in year 2)	$ 30,000
Depreciation difference (see below)	90,000
Estimated expenses (deductible in year 7)	(20,000)
Net temporary difference	$100,000

c. The temporary difference related to depreciable assets will result in the following future taxable (deductible) amounts: for year 3, $50,000; for year 4, 40,000.

Solution:

Step 1: Identify the types and amounts of existing temporary differences and the nature and amount of each type of operating loss and tax credit carryforward and the remaining length of the carryforward period.

The installment sale causes a taxable temporary difference.

The estimated expenses accrued for accounting purposes and deferred for tax purposes cause a deductible temporary difference.

	Amount
Future taxable (deductible) types for temporary differences	
Installment sale	$ 30,000
Depreciation	90,000
Estimated expense	(20,000)

Step 2: Measure the total deferred tax liability for taxable temporary differences using the applicable tax rates.

	Amount	Rate	Deferred Tax Liab.
Future taxable types for temporary differences			
Installment sale	$30,000	35%	$ 10,500
Depreciation	90,000	30%	27,000
Total			$ 37,500

The enacted tax rate used to measure the deferred tax consequences of a future taxable amount is the rate at which the taxable amount will be taxed. The amount of temporary difference scheduled to reverse in year 2 and cause a taxable amount that year is tax effected at the 35% rate enacted for year 2. Similarly, the amount of temporary difference scheduled to reverse in year 3 ($50,000) and year 4 ($40,000) and result in a taxable amount those years is tax effected at the 30% tax rate already enacted for those years.

Step 3: Measure the total deferred tax asset for deductible temporary differences and operating loss carryforwards using the applicable tax rate.

	Amount	Rate	Deferred Tax Asset
Future deductible types for temporary differences			
Estimated expense	$(20,000)	25%	$ 5,000

The enacted tax rate used to measure the deferred tax consequences of a future deductible amount is the rate at which the deductible amount will provide tax benefits. Thus, the deductible amount scheduled for year 7 will provide tax benefits at a rate of 25%. (There are no operating loss carryforwards in this example.)

Step 4: Measure deferred tax assets for each type of tax credit carryforward. (There are no tax credit carryforwards in this example.)

Step 5: Reduce deferred tax assets by a valuation allowance if, based on the weight of available evidence, it is more likely than not (a likelihood of more than 50%) that some portion or all of the deferred tax assets will not be realized. The valuation allowance should be sufficient to reduce the deferred tax asset to the amount that is more likely than not to be realized. (There is no mention of any uncertainty regarding the future realization of the benefits associated with the deferred tax asset. Therefore, assume no valuation allowance is necessary.)

NOTE: Deferred tax liabilities and assets are not reported at discounted values.

Example 14 ▸ Income Tax Expense & Deferred Taxes

Refer to Example 13.

Required:

a. Prepare the journal entry to record income tax expense, deferred taxes, and income taxes payable for year 1.

b. Compute the total income tax expense for year 1. Indicate the portion that is current and the portion that is due to deferred tax expense or benefit. Draft the bottom portion of the income statement beginning with "Income before income taxes."

c. Indicate the proper classification(s) of deferred taxes for the December 31, year 1, balance sheet.

Solution a:

Income Tax Expense—current	20,000	
Income Tax Expense—deferred	32,500	
Deferred Tax Asset	5,000	
Income Taxes Payable ($50,000 × 40%)		20,000
Deferred Tax Liability		37,500
To record income taxes for year 1, in one compound entry.		

Balance of deferred tax liability, 12/31, year 1	$37,500*
Balance of deferred tax liability, 01/01, year 1	0
Increase in deferred tax liability	$37,500
Balance of deferred tax asset, 12/31, year 1	$ 5,000*
Balance of deferred tax asset, 01/01, year 1	0
Increase in deferred tax asset	$ 5,000

* These ending balances are the result of the annual computation of deferred tax liabilities and assets illustrated in Example 13. Beginning balances are the result of entries recorded in prior periods. There are no beginning balances because year 1 is Bensen's first year of operations.

Balance the entry by a debit or credit (whichever is appropriate) to *Income Tax Expense—Current* and *Income Tax Expense—Deferred.* In this situation, the net tax provision is $52,500. An alternative to the above entry is to record the amount of current income tax expense and the amount of deferred income taxes in separate entries.

Solution b: The effective tax rate is \$52,500 / \$150,000 = 35%.

Deferred tax liability, 12/31, year 1 (Example 13)	\$37,500
Deferred tax liability, 01/01, year 1	--
Deferred tax expense, year 1 (increase required in deferred tax liability account)	\$37,500
Deferred tax asset, 12/31, year 1 (Example 13)	\$ 5,000
Deferred tax asset, 01/01, year 1	--
Deferred tax benefit, year 1 (increase required in deferred tax asset account)	\$ 5,000
Deferred tax expense, year 1	\$37,500
Deferred tax benefit, year 1	(5,000)
Net deferred tax expense, year 1	32,500
Current tax expense, year 1 (\$50,000 × 40%)	20,000
Total income tax expense, year 1	\$52,500

Income before income taxes		\$150,000
Current tax expense	\$20,000	
Deferred tax expense	32,500	
Provision for income taxes		(52,500)
Net income		\$ 97,500

Solution c: Deferred income taxes should appear on the balance sheet at the end of year 1 in the following amounts and classifications.

Current liabilities:		Long-term liabilities:	
Deferred tax liability	\$10,500	Deferred tax liability	\$22,000

Explanation: The \$10,500 deferred tax liability caused by the installment sale is classified as a current liability because the installment receivable is classified as a current asset (for the temporary difference to reverse in year 2, the receivable will be collected in year 2). The \$27,000 net deferred tax liability related to the depreciation type temporary difference is classified as a noncurrent liability because the related assets (PP&E) are classified as noncurrent assets. The \$5,000 deferred tax asset resulting from the expenses accrued for accounting purposes is classified as a noncurrent asset because the related accrued liability is a noncurrent liability (for the temporary difference to reverse in year 7, the accrued liability is expected to be settled in year 7, which makes the liability noncurrent).

Type of difference	Temporary difference	Tax rate	Deferred taxes	Current or noncurrent
Installment sale	\$ 30,000	35%	\$10,500	Current
Depreciation	90,000	30%	27,000	Noncurrent
Accrued expenses	(20,000)	25%	(5,000)	Noncurrent

The net current amount is a liability of \$10,500. The net noncurrent amount is a liability of \$22,000.

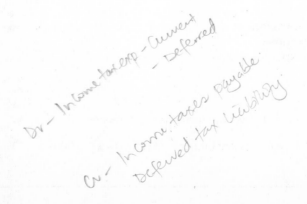

Dr - Income tax exp - Current
- Deferred

Cr - Income taxes payable
Deferred tax liability

Example 15 ▸ Deferred Tax Liabilities & Assets

The first year of operations for the Pandora Corporation was year 1. Taxable income for year 1 was $120,000. Pandora was subject to enacted U.S. tax rates of 40% in year 1 and 30% in year 2 and later years. Taxable income is expected in all future years. At the end of year 1, there was only one future taxable temporary difference of $140,000, related to depreciation.

Deferred taxes at the end of year 1 (using the liability method):

	Amount	Rate	Deferred Tax Liab.
Future taxable amounts for temporary differences			
Depreciation	$140,000	30%	$42,000

Income taxes for year 1 were properly recorded as follows.

Income Tax Expense—current	48,000	
Income Tax Expense—deferred	42,000	
Income Taxes Payable ($120,000 × 40%)		48,000
Deferred Tax Liability		42,000

Pandora has taxable income for year 2 of $110,000. Enacted tax rates have not changed so the rate for year 2 and future years is 30%. At the end of year 2, cumulative taxable temporary differences related to depreciation are $180,000.

Required:

a. Compute the amount of deferred taxes to be reported on the balance sheet at the end of year 2.

b. Prepare the journal entry to record income taxes for year 2.

c. Draft the section of the income statement for year 2 that relates to reporting income taxes.

Solution a:

	Amount	Rate	Deferred Tax Liab.
Future taxable amounts for temporary differences			
Depreciation	$180,000	30%	$54,000

Solution b:

Income Tax Expense—current	33,000	
Income Tax Expense—deferred	12,000	
Income Taxes Payable ($110,000 × 30%)		33,000
Deferred Tax Liability ($54,000 – $42,000)		12,000

Deferred tax liability, end of year 2	$ 54,000
Deferred tax liability, end of year 1	(42,000)
Deferred tax expense, year 2 (increase in deferred tax liability account)	12,000
Current tax expense, year 2	33,000
Total tax expense (provision), year 2	$ 45,000

Solution c:

Income before income taxes		$150,000
Current tax expense	$33,000	
Deferred tax expense	12,000	
Income tax expense		(45,000)
Net income		$105,000

Income before taxes is verified as follows (no permanent differences):

Pretax financial income	$ X
Increase in cumulative taxable temporary differences ($180,000 – $140,000)	(40,000)
Taxable income	$110,000

Solve for X: X = $150,000

Example 16 ▸ Deferred Tax Liabilities & Assets

Jersey Corporation uses different depreciation methods for accounting and tax purposes which result in a $60,000 cumulative temporary difference at December 31, year 4. This temporary difference will reverse equally over the next 5 years. Taxable income for year 4 is $46,000. Jersey's balance sheet at December 31, year 3, reported a net deferred tax liability of $8,000 (noncurrent deferred tax liability of $28,000 and a noncurrent deferred tax asset of $20,000). Jersey expects taxable income in all future years.

1. At December 31, year 4, Jersey has a $17,000 liability reported because of the accrual of estimated litigation claims. Jersey expects to pay the claims and have tax deductible amounts in year 8 of $15,000 and in year 9 of $2,000.

2. The enacted tax rates as of the beginning of year 3 are as follows: 50% in years 3 to 5; 40% in years 6 to 7; and 30% in year 8 and later years.

reverse equally over the next 5 yrs ⇒ 60,000/5 = 12000

Required:

a. Calculate the amount of net deferred taxes that should be reported on Jersey's balance sheet at December 31, year 4, and indicate whether that net amount is an asset or a liability.

b. Prepare the journal entry for Jersey to record income taxes for year 4.

Solution a: The $60,000 must be divided into three parts to account for the different tax rates.

	Amount	Rate	Deferred Tax Liab.
Future taxable amounts for temporary differences	$12,000	50%	$ 6,000
Depreciation—year 5	24,000	40%	9,600
Depreciation—years 6-7	24,000	30%	7,200
Depreciation—years 8-9	$60,000		$22,800

	Amount	Rate	Deferred Tax Asset
Future deductible amounts for temporary differences			
Litigation	$17,000	30%	$ 5,100

$22,800 + $(5,100) = $17,700 net deferred tax liability at December 31, year 4.

Solution b:

	Debit	Credit
Income Tax Expense—current	23,000	
Income Tax Expense—deferred ($14,900 – $5,200)	9,700	
Deferred Tax Liability ($28,000 – $22,800)	5,200	
Income Tax Payable ($46,000 × 50%)		23,000
Deferred Tax Asset ($20,000 – $5,100)		14,900

Deferred tax liability, 12/31, year 4—part (a)	$22,800
Deferred tax liability, 12/31, year 3	28,000
Deferred tax benefit, year 4 (decrease required in deferred tax liability account)	$ (5,200)
Deferred tax asset, 12/31, year 4—part (a)	$ 5,100
Deferred tax asset, 12/31, year 3	20,000
Deferred tax expense, year 4 (decrease required in deferred tax asset account)	$14,900
Deferred tax benefit, year 4	$ (5,200)
Deferred tax expense, year 4	14,900
Net deferred tax expense, year 4	9,700
Current tax expense, year 4	23,000
Total tax expense (provision) for year 4	$32,700

Example 17 ▸ Deferred Tax Liabilities & Assets

Jersey Corporation, from Example 16, expects taxable income in years 5 through 8 and an NOL in year 9, the benefits of which are expected to be realized by carryback.

Required:

a. Calculate the amount of net deferred taxes that should be reported on Jersey's balance sheet at December 31, year 4, and indicate whether that net amount is an asset or a liability.

b. Prepare the journal entry for Jersey to record income taxes for year 4.

Solution a: Because Jersey expects an NOL rather than taxable income in year 9, the tax rate to be used to tax effect the future taxable and deductible amounts scheduled for year 9 (due to temporary differences existing at the end of year 4) is the rate of the year to which the expected NOL of year 9 is to be carried back or forward. In this case, that would be year 7 (the data indicated an expected carryback and the provisions of the tax code require carryback to the earliest of two years prior to the loss year). Thus, the taxable amount of $12,000 scheduled for year 9 will reduce a tax refund computed at the rate of 40% and the deductible amount of $2,000 scheduled for year 9 will increase a tax refund computed at the rate of 40%.

	Amount	Rate	Deferred Tax Liab.
Future taxable amounts for temporary differences			
Depreciation—year 5	$12,000	50%	$ 6,000
Depreciation—years 6-7, 9	36,000	40%	14,400
Depreciation—years 8-9	12,000	30%	3,600
	$60,000		$24,000

NOTE: The $60,000 must be divided into three parts to account for the different tax rates.

	Amount	Rate	Deferred Tax Asset
Future deductible amounts for temporary differences			
Litigation—year 8	$15,000	30%	$ 4,500
Litigation—year 9	2,000	40%	800
	$17,000		$ 5,300

$24,000 + $(5,300) = $18,700 deferred tax liability at December 31, year 4.

Solution b:

Income Tax Expense—current	23,000	
Income Tax Expense—deferred ($14,700 – $4,000)	10,700	
Deferred Tax Liability ($28,000 – $24,000)	4,000	
Income Tax Payable ($46,000 × 50%)		23,000
Deferred Tax Asset ($20,000 – $5,300)		14,700

E. **Attributes of Asset & Liability Method**

1. **Balance Sheet Approach** There is an emphasis on the amount to be reported as deferred taxes on the balance sheet (hence, it is said to be a balance sheet approach or balance sheet-oriented).

2. **Balance of Deferred Tax Asset or Liability** The balance in a deferred tax liability or asset account on a balance sheet is the amount of taxes expected to be paid or refunded (or saved) in the future as a result of the turn-around (reversal) of temporary differences existing at the balance sheet date.

3. **Calculation** The amount to be reported for deferred taxes on a balance sheet is calculated by using *future tax rates* (i.e., rates that have already been *enacted* for the future) and applying them to cumulative temporary differences based on when and how the temporary differences are expected to affect the tax return in the future.

4. **Effect on Income Statement** A temporary difference originating in the current period that causes an increase in a deferred tax liability will also cause a debit (charge) to the provision for deferred taxes on the income statement; an increase in deferred tax asset will result in a credit to the provision for deferred taxes.

5. **Deferred Tax Expense or Benefit** Deferred tax expense (benefit) on the income statement is a "residual" amount because it merely reflects the change in the balance sheet deferred tax account(s) from the prior year. The amount of deferred tax expense (benefit) for a year is a by-product of the year's deferred tax calculation because it is the net change during the year in the net deferred tax liability or asset amount.

6. **Increase/Decrease in Deferred Tax Asset/Liability** An increase in a deferred tax liability or a decrease in a deferred tax asset on the balance sheet results in a *deferred tax expense* on the income statement; an increase in a deferred tax asset or a decrease in a deferred tax liability on the balance sheet will cause a *deferred tax benefit* on the income statement.

7. **Subsequent Changes** The balance sheet deferred tax account(s) is(are) to be adjusted for any subsequent changes in the tax rates or laws.

8. **Single Tax Rate vs Different Tax Rates** If a single tax rate applies to all future years, an aggregate computation is appropriate. However, if different tax rates apply to individual future years, a *scheduling* of future taxable and deductible amounts (due to existing temporary differences) with a separate computation for each future year affected is required.

V. Other Considerations

A. Valuation Allowance

1. **Deferred Tax Assets** Deferred tax assets are recorded for the future tax benefits of operating loss carryforwards, tax credit carryforwards, and deductible temporary differences existing at a balance sheet date. Deferred tax assets are to be reduced by a valuation allowance if, based on the weight of available evidence, it is more likely than not (a likelihood of more than 50%) that some portion or all of the deferred tax assets will not be realized. The valuation allowance should be sufficient to reduce the deferred tax asset to the amount that is more likely than not to be realized.

Example 18 ▸ Valuation Allowance

At December 31, year 1, at the end of XYZ's first year of operations, XYZ reports a net operating loss of $50,000 on its tax return. At December 31, year 1, XYZ has a temporary difference that will result in future deductible amounts of $80,000. The enacted tax rate for year 1 is 50%. The tax rate for year 2 and subsequent years is 40%. At the end of year 1, it is estimated that 30% of the company's deferred tax assets will not be realized in the future. In year 2, XYZ reports taxable income of $100,000 (before deduction of the NOL carryover and after deducting the $80,000 future deductible amount) and has no temporary differences at the end of year 2.

Required:

a. Prepare the journal entry(s) to record income taxes for year 1.

b. Draft the section of the year 1 income statement that reports income tax expense, beginning with the line "Income Before Income Taxes."

c. Prepare the appropriate journal entries to record income taxes and draft the section of the year 2 income statement that reports income tax expense.

Solution a:

Deferred Tax Asset	52,000	
Benefits of Loss Carryforward ($50,000 × 40%)		20,000
Income Tax Expense—deferred ($80,000 × 40%)		32,000
Benefits of Loss Carryforward ($20,000 × 30%)	6,000	
Income Tax Expense—deferred ($32,000 × 30%)	9,600	
Allowance to Reduce Deferred Tax Asset to Realizable Value		15,600

Solution b:

Operating loss before income taxes*		$(130,000)
Benefits of loss carryforward ($20,000 × 70%)	$14,000	
Deferred tax benefit ($32,000 × 70%)	22,400	
Income tax benefits		36,400
Net loss		$ (93,600)

* Pretax financial income	$ X	
Deductible temporary difference originating in Year 1	80,000	
Taxable loss	$(50,000)	Solve for X: X = $(130,000)

Solution c:

Income Tax Expense—current ($100,000 × 40%)	40,000	
Income Tax Expense—deferred ($32,000 – $9,600)	22,400	
Allowance to Reduce Deferred Tax Asset to Realizable Value (balance of account)	15,600	
Income Taxes Payable [($100,000 – $50,000) × 40%]		20,000
Deferred Tax Asset (balance of account)		52,000
Benefits of Loss Carryforward (income tax expense) ($20,000 × 30%)		6,000

Income Statement:

Income before income taxes**		$ 180,000
Current tax expense	$40,000	
Deferred tax expense	22,400	
Benefits of loss carryforward	(6,000)	
Total income tax expense		(56,400)
Net income		$ 123,600

** Pretax financial income	$ X	
Reversing temporary difference	(80,000)	
Taxable loss	$100,000	Solve for X: X = $180,000

The compound journal entry replaces the following three journal entries.

Income Tax Expense	40,000	
Income Tax Payable [($100,000 – $50,000) × 40%]		20,000
Benefit of Loss Carryforward		20,000

To record current income taxes.

Income Tax Expense—deferred	32,000	
Benefit of Loss Carryforward	20,000	
Deferred Tax Asset (balance of account)		52,000

To eliminate the deferred asset balance and to recognize deferred tax expense.

Allowance to Reduce Deferred Tax Asset to Realizable Value (balance of account)	15,600	
Benefits of Loss Carryforward ($20,000 × 30%)		6,000
Income Tax Expense—deferred (to balance)		9,600

To eliminate the allowance balance and to recognize the previously unrecognized benefits of the loss carryforward.

2. **Future Realization of Tax Benefit** Future realization of the tax benefit of an existing deductible temporary difference or carryforward ultimately depends on the existence of sufficient taxable income of the appropriate character (for example, ordinary income or capital gain) within the carryback, carryforward period available under the tax law. The following four possible sources of taxable income may be available under the tax law to realize a tax benefit for deductible temporary differences and carryforwards:

   a. Future reversals of existing taxable temporary differences

   b. Future taxable income exclusive of reversing temporary differences and carryforwards

   c. Taxable income in prior carryback year(s) if carryback is permitted under the tax law

   d. Tax-planning strategies that would, if necessary, be implemented to the following, for example:

      (1) Accelerate taxable amounts to utilize expiring carryforwards

      (2) Change the character of taxable or deductible amounts from ordinary income or loss to capital gain or loss

      (3) Switch from tax-exempt to taxable investments

3. **Tax-Planning Strategies** In some circumstances, there are actions (including elections for tax purposes) that (1) are prudent and feasible, (2) an enterprise ordinarily might not take, but would take to prevent an operating loss or tax credit carryforward from expiring unused, and (3) would result in realization of deferred tax assets. SFAS 109 refers to those actions as *tax-planning strategies.* An enterprise shall consider tax-planning strategies in determining the amount of valuation allowance required. Significant expenses to implement a tax-planning strategy or any significant losses that would be recognized if that strategy were implemented (net of any recognizable tax benefits associated with those expenses or losses) shall be included in the valuation allowance.

4. **Evidence to Determine Need for Valuation Allowance** All available evidence, both positive and negative, should be considered to determine whether, based on the weight of that evidence, a valuation allowance is needed. Information about an enterprise's current financial position and its results of operations for the current and preceding years ordinarily is readily available. That historical information is supplemented by all currently available information about future years. Sometimes, however, historical information may not be available (for example, start-up operations), or it may not be as relevant (for example, if there has been a significant, recent change in circumstances) and special attention is required.

5. **Negative Evidence** Forming a conclusion that a valuation allowance is not needed is difficult when there is negative evidence such as cumulative losses in recent years. Other examples of negative evidence include (but are not limited to) the following:

   a. A history of operating loss or tax credit carryforwards expiring unused

   b. Losses expected in early future years (by a presently profitable entity)

   c. Unsettled circumstances that, if unfavorably resolved, would adversely affect future operations and profit levels on a continuing basis in future years

   d. A carryback, carryforward period that is so brief that it would limit realization of tax benefits if (a) a significant deductible temporary difference is expected to reverse in a single year or (b) the enterprise operates in a traditionally cyclical business

6. **Positive Evidence Examples** Examples (not prerequisites) of positive evidence that might support a conclusion that a valuation allowance is not needed when there is negative evidence include (but are not limited to) the following:

   a. Existing contracts or firm sales backlog that will produce more than enough taxable income to realize the deferred tax asset based on existing sales prices and cost structures.

   b. An excess of appreciated asset value over the tax basis of the entity's net assets in an amount sufficient to realize the deferred tax asset.

   c. A strong earnings history exclusive of the loss that created the future deductible amount (tax loss carryforward or deductible temporary difference) coupled with evidence indicating that the loss (for example, an unusual, infrequent, or extraordinary item) is an aberration rather than a continuing condition.

7. **Weighing Evidence** An enterprise must use judgment in considering the relative impact of negative and positive evidence. The weight given to the potential effect of negative and positive evidence should be commensurate with the extent to which it can be objectively verified. The more negative evidence that exists the more positive evidence is necessary and the more difficult it is to support a conclusion that a valuation allowance is not needed for some portion or all of the deferred tax asset.

8. **Change in Valuation Allowance** The effect of a change in the beginning-of-the-year balance of a valuation allowance that results from a change in circumstances that causes a change in judgment about the realizability of the related deferred tax asset in future years ordinarily shall be included in income from continuing operations.

B. Enacted Change in Tax Laws or Rates

1. **Adjustment of Deferred Tax Liability or Asset** A deferred tax liability or asset is adjusted for the effect of a change in tax laws or rates. The deferred tax previously provided on items that will become taxable or deductible in any future year affected by the rate change is to be adjusted downward or upward to reflect the new rate. This cumulative effect is included in income from continuing operations for the period that includes the enactment date. Adjustments of a deferred tax liability or asset for enacted changes in tax laws or rates are a component of income tax expense attributable to continuing operations.

2. **Interim Period** If the date of enactment occurs during an interim period, APB 28 (as amended by SFAS 109) requires that the effect of the change on the existing balance of a deferred tax liability or asset be recognized in the interim period that includes the enactment date.

Example 19 ▸ Enacted Change in Tax Laws or Rates

Sean Corporation began operations in year 1. Taxable income for year 1 was $22,000. Pretax financial income for year 1 was $32,000. The tax rates enacted as of the beginning of year 1 were 50% for year 1 and 40% for year 2 and later years. At December 31, year 1, Sean Corporation had the following cumulative temporary differences.

1. The reported amount of installment receivables was in excess of the tax basis of those receivables which will result in future taxable amounts of $12,000 ($6,000 in each of years 3 and 4).

2. The reported amount of an estimated litigation liability was $2,000. There was no such liability for tax purposes (i.e., its tax basis was zero). The liability was expected to be paid (and then result in a tax deductible amount) in year 4.

The net deferred tax liability of $4,000 at the end of year 1 was calculated as follows.

	Amount	Rate	Deferred Tax Liability (Asset)
Future taxable amounts	$12,000	40%	$4,800
Future deductible amount	(2,000)	40%	(800)
Net deferred tax liability (asset)			$4,000

The journal entry to record income taxes for year 1 was as follows.

Income Tax Expense—current	11,000	
Income Tax Expense—deferred	4,000	
Deferred Tax Asset	800	
Income Taxes Payable ($22,000 × 50%)		11,000
Deferred Tax Liability		4,800

During year 2, a new tax rate of 30% was enacted for year 4. There were no new temporary differences originating in year 2, and none of the temporary differences existing at the beginning of year 2 reversed so the cumulative temporary differences existing at the end of year 2 were the same as those that existed at the end of year 1. Taxable income for year 2 amounted to $25,000. Pretax financial income was also $25,000.

Required: Record all journal entries related to income taxes for year 2.

Solution:

Income Tax Expense—current	10,000	
Deferred Tax Liability ($4,800 – $4,200)	600	
Income Tax Benefit—change in rates ($4,000 – $3,600)		400
Income Taxes Payable ($25,000 × 40%)		10,000
Deferred Tax Asset ($800 – $600)		200

Discussion: A change in an enacted tax rate causes an immediate cumulative effect on the income tax provision. The deferred tax previously provided on items that will become taxable or deductible in any future year affected by the rate change is to be adjusted to reflect the new rate. To determine the adjustment needed because of the change in the tax rate for year 4, prepare the scheduling process as it would have been prepared at the end of year 1, if the new rate for year 4 had been known at that point in time.

	Amount	Rate	Deferred Tax Liability (Asset)
Future taxable amounts			
Year 3	$ 6,000	40%	$2,400
Year 4	6,000	30%	1,800
Future deductible amount	(2,000)	30%	(600)
Net deferred tax liability (asset)			$3,600

Comparing this schedule with the schedule used in year 1, we find that the deferred tax liability account needs to decrease by $600 ($4,800 – $4,200) and the deferred tax asset account needs to decrease by $200 ($800 – $600). A comparative income statement would report the following.

	Year 1		Year 2	
Income before income taxes		$ 32,000		$25,000
Current	$11,000		$10,000	
Deferred	4,000			
Adjustment due to rate change			(400)	
Income tax expense		(15,000)		(9,600)
Net income		$ 17,000		$15,400

C. **Change in Enterprise Tax Status**

A deferred tax liability or asset is recognized for temporary differences at the date that a nontaxable enterprise becomes a taxable enterprise (e.g., partnership to corporation or S corporation to

C corporation). A deferred tax liability or asset should be eliminated at the date that an enterprise ceases to be a taxable enterprise (e.g., corporation to partnership or C corporation to S corporation). The effect of recognizing or eliminating a deferred tax liability or asset is included in income from continuing operations.

VI. Presentation & Disclosure

A. Balance Sheet

In a classified balance sheet, deferred tax assets and liabilities are separated and reported in a net current and a net noncurrent amount.

1. **Classification Based on Related Asset** Deferred tax assets and liabilities are classified as current or noncurrent based on the classification of the related asset or liability for financial reporting. A deferred tax liability or asset that is not related to an asset or liability for financial reporting, including deferred tax assets related to carryforwards, is classified according to the expected reversal date of the temporary difference (SFAS 37).

2. **Jurisdiction** The valuation allowance for a particular tax jurisdiction is to be allocated between current and noncurrent deferred tax assets for that jurisdiction on a pro rata basis. Deferred tax liabilities and assets attributable to different tax jurisdictions should not be offset.

Example 20 ▸ Balance Sheet Presentation of Deferred Taxes

Molly Corporation has a tax rate for all periods at 40% and the following temporary differences at December 31 of the current year:

1. Installment receivables appearing on their GAAP balance sheet have a zero tax basis. These receivables are to be collected equally over the next three years and will result in reporting $20,000 gross profit each year for tax purposes. Only one-third of the receivables are classified as a current asset.

2. An accrued payable of $45,000 appearing in the current liability section of the GAAP balance sheet has a zero tax basis.

3. Depreciable assets have an excess of carrying amount over tax basis of $50,000.

Required: Compute deferred taxes at December 31 and indicate how they should be classified on the balance sheet at that date.

Solution: $8,000 + $(18,000) = $(10,000) current; $16,000 + $20,000 = $36,000 noncurrent

Temporary difference	Future taxable (deductible) amount	Rate	Deferred tax liability (asset)	Current or noncurrent
Installment sales	$ 20,000	40%	$ 8,000	Current
Installment sales	40,000	40%	16,000	Noncurrent
Accrued expenses	(45,000)	40%	(18,000)	Current
Depreciation	50,000	40%	20,000	Noncurrent

Current assets:		Long-term liabilities:	
Deferred tax asset	$ 10,000	Deferred tax liability	$36,000

Discussion: The deferred tax liability related to the installment sales is one-third current and two-thirds noncurrent because of the classification of the related receivables. The deferred tax asset stemming from the accrual of expenses for books is a current asset because of the current classification of the related accrued payable. The deferred tax liability resulting from different depreciation policies for financial statements and tax returns is classified as noncurrent because the related plant assets have a noncurrent balance sheet classification.

The current deferred tax items are netted (liability of $8,000 and asset of $18,000) to arrive at an asset of $10,000; the noncurrent items (liabilities of $16,000 and $20,000) are netted to arrive at a liability of $36,000.

3. **Disclosures** The following are to be disclosed.

   a. Total of all deferred tax liabilities

   b. Total of all deferred tax assets

   c. Total valuation allowance recognized for deferred tax assets

   d. Net change during the year in the total valuation allowance

   e. Approximate tax effect of each type of temporary difference and carryforward that gives rise to a significant portion of deferred tax liabilities and deferred tax assets (before allocation of valuation allowances)

B. **Income Statement**

1. **Allocation** Income tax expense or benefit for the year is to be allocated among continuing operations, discontinued operations, extraordinary items, and items of other comprehensive income (e.g., foreign currency translation adjustments and market value adjustments attributable to available-for-sale marketable equity securities). The process of allocating income taxes to key components of the financial statements is called *intraperiod tax allocation.* Thus, items such as discontinued operations, extraordinary items, and prior period adjustments are reported *net of the related income tax effects.*

   a. **Continuing Operations** The amount allocated to continuing operations is the tax effect of the pretax income or loss from continuing operations that occurred during the year, plus or minus income tax effects of (1) changes in circumstances that cause a change in judgment about the realization of deferred tax assets in future years, (2) changes in tax laws or rates, and (3) changes in tax status. The remainder is allocated to items other than continuing operations.

   b. **Other Than Continuing Operations** If there is only one item other than continuing operations, the portion of income tax expense or benefit for the year that remains after the allocation to continuing operations is allocated to that item. If there are two or more items other than continuing operations, the amount that remains after the allocation to continuing operations shall be allocated among those other items in proportion to their individual effects on income tax expense or benefit for the year.

Example 21 ▸ Intraperiod Tax Allocation

Kelly Corporation's pretax financial income and taxable income are the same. Kelly's ordinary loss from continuing operations is $5,000. Kelly also has an extraordinary gain of $9,000 that is a capital gain for tax purposes. The tax rate is 40% on ordinary income and 30% on capital gains. Income taxes currently payable are $1,200 ($4,000 at 30%).

Required: Determine the amount of income tax expense (benefit) to allocate to continuing operations and the amount to allocate to the extraordinary item.

Solution:

Total income tax expense	$1,200
Tax benefit allocated to the loss from operations	1,500
Incremental tax expense allocated to the extraordinary gain	$2,700

The effect of the $5,000 loss from continuing operations was to offset an equal amount of capital gains that otherwise would be taxed at a 30% tax rate. Thus, $1,500 ($5,000 at 30%) of tax benefit is allocated to continuing operations. The $2,700 incremental effect of the extraordinary gain is the $1,200 of total tax expense and the $1,500 tax benefit from continuing operations.

c. **Reporting** The manner of reporting the tax benefit of an operating loss carryforward or carryback is determined by the source of income or loss of the current year that enabled its recognition. For example, if income from continuing operations in the current year permits recognition of an operating loss carryforward that arose from a discontinued operation of a prior year, the tax benefit attributable to that operating loss carryforward is allocated to income from continuing operations and not by (1) the source of the operating loss carryforward or taxes paid in a prior year or (2) the source of expected future income that will result in realization of a deferred tax asset for an operating loss carryforward from the current year. Thus, the benefit of an NOL carryback would be classified as a component of continuing operations if the income earned in the current year was due to continuing operations even though the NOL resulted from an extraordinary loss in a prior period. (There are a few exceptions to this guideline, including one that deals with business combinations and another involving quasi-reorganizations.)

d. **Stockholders' Equity** Stockholders' equity is charged or credited for the income tax effects of the following.

(1) Adjustments of the opening balance of retained earnings for certain changes in accounting principles or a correction of an error

(2) Gains and losses recognized in comprehensive income, but excluded from net income (e.g., foreign currency translation adjustments, market value adjustments attributable to certain investments in debt and equity securities, and minimum pension liability adjustments, per SFAS 130)

(3) An increase or decrease in contributed capital (e.g., expenditures reported as a reduction of the proceeds from issuing capital stock)

(4) Expenses for employee stock options recognized differently for financial reporting and tax purposes

2. **Components of Income Tax Expense** The significant components of income tax expense attributable to continuing operations for each year presented are disclosed in the financial statements or notes thereto. Those components would include the following.

a. Current tax expense or benefit

b. Deferred tax expense or benefit (exclusive of the effects of other components listed below)

c. Investment tax credits

d. Government grants (to the extent recognized as a reduction of income tax expense)

e. The benefits of operating loss carryforwards

f. Tax expense that results from allocating certain tax benefits either directly to contributed capital or to reduce other noncurrent intangible assets of an acquired entity

g. Adjustments of a deferred tax liability or asset for enacted changes in tax laws or rates or a change in the tax status of the enterprise

h. Adjustments of the beginning-of-the-year balance of a valuation allowance because of a change in circumstances that causes a change in judgment about the realizability of the related deferred tax asset in future years

3. **Reconciliation** A public enterprise discloses a reconciliation using percentages or dollar amounts of a reported amount of income tax expense attributable to continuing operations

for the year to an amount of income tax expense that would result from applying domestic federal statutory tax rates to pretax income from continuing operations.

4. **Losses & Carryforwards** The amounts and expiration dates of operating loss and tax credit carryforwards for tax purposes must be disclosed.

VII. Business Combinations & Investments in Common Stock

A. Combinations

1. **Goodwill** A deferred tax liability or asset is recognized for differences between the assigned values and the tax bases of the assets and liabilities recognized in a business purchase combination.

2. **Application of Tax Benefits** If a valuation allowance is recognized for the deferred tax asset for an acquired entity's deductible temporary differences or operating loss or tax credit carryforwards at the acquisition date, the tax benefits for those items that are first recognized (that is, by elimination of that valuation allowance) in financial statements after the acquisition date are applied (1) first to reduce to zero any goodwill related to the acquisition, (2) second to reduce to zero other noncurrent intangible assets related to the acquisition, and (3) third to reduce income tax expense.

B. Cost Method Investments

1. **No Temporary Differences** The basis for income recognition on investments accounted for by the cost method (i.e., the investor does not have the ability to exercise significant influence over the investee, less than 20% ownership) is dividends received, both for financial accounting and tax purposes. Thus, no temporary differences result from cost method investments.

2. **Dividends Received Deduction** Tax law has generally allowed corporate shareholders owning less than 20% of the stock of a qualifying domestic corporation to deduct 70% of the dividends received. That portion of the dividends received is an event recognized in the financial statements that does not have a tax consequence because it is exempt from taxation. Therefore, the financial accounting tax expense and the tax liability from cost-method investment income will be the same because no tax deferrals result.

Example 22 ▸ Cost Method Investments

Investments, Inc., owns a 10% interest in Goodbuy Co. In 20X1, Goodbuy reported net income of $500,000 and declared and paid dividends of $300,000.

Required: Assuming a 30% effective tax rate, determine Investments' tax expense and liability in connection with its ownership interest in Goodbuy.

Solution:

Dividends paid by Goodbuy	$300,000
Investments, Inc.'s ownership interest	× 10%
Dividends received	30,000
70% dividends received deduction	(21,000)
Taxable dividend income	9,000
Effective tax rate	× 30%
Tax expense **and** liability (no deferrals)	$ 2,700

C. Equity Method Investments

1. **GAAP Basis & Tax Basis Differ** When a company has investments accounted for under the "equity method" set forth in APB 18 (i.e., 20% to 50% ownership, "significant influence") investment income is recognized on a different basis for financial accounting and tax purposes.

2. **Dividends Received Deduction** Tax law has generally allowed corporate shareholders owning 20% or more, but less than 80% of the stock of a qualifying domestic corporation to deduct 80% of the dividends received. That portion of the dividends received that is excluded from taxable income is an event recognized in the financial statements that does not have a tax consequence because it is exempt from taxation.

3. **Income Taxes** Income taxes on income from equity method investments are accounted for under the assumption that the investor will eventually receive her/his share in the undistributed income of the equity-method investee.

   a. Therefore, an equity-method investee's undistributed income should be treated as a temporary difference.

   b. The tax effect of this temporary difference depends on whether the investor ultimately expects to receive the undistributed income as *dividends* or as a *realized gain* upon disposal of the investment (or as a combination of both).

      (1) If the undistributed income is expected to be received as dividends, the computation of temporary differences should allow for the dividends-received deduction.

      (2) If the undistributed income is expected to be received as a realized gain upon disposal of the investment, the computation of temporary differences should **not** include the dividends-received deduction.

Example 23 ▸ Equity Method Investments

Ivy, Inc., owns 30% of Goodbuy's common stock and no preferred stock. During the current year, Goodbuy reported income of $500,000 and paid $300,000 dividends on common stock and $50,000 on preferred stock. Ivy's tax rate is 30%, including federal and state taxes.

Required: Record Ivy's tax expense, liability and related deferrals, assuming no transactions occurred in the year other than those dealing with investments and that undistributed income is expected to be received as dividends.

Solution:

Tax Expense—current	5,400	
Tax Expense—deferred	2,700	
Taxes Payable ($18,000 [1] × 30%)		5,400
Deferred Tax Liability ($9,000 [2] × 30%)		2,700

[1]	Dividends paid to Ivy ($300,000 × 30%)	$ 90,000
	Less 80% deduction	(72,000)
	Dividends included in taxable income	$ 18,000
[2]	Ivy's equity in Goodbuy's income [($500,000 – $50,000) × 30%]	$135,000
	Dividends paid to Ivy ($300,000 × 30%)	(90,000)
	Undistributed income	45,000
	Less 80% deduction	(36,000)
	Temporary difference	$ 9,000

CHAPTER 13—ACCOUNTING FOR INCOME TAXES

Problem 13-1 MULTIPLE CHOICE QUESTIONS (82 to 103 minutes)

1. For the current year ended December 31, Tyre Co. reported pretax financial statement income of $750,000. Its taxable income was $650,000. The difference is due to accelerated depreciation for income tax purposes. Tyre's effective income tax rate is 30%, and Tyre made estimated tax payments during the year of $90,000. What amount should Tyre report as income tax expense for the year?
a. $105,000
b. $135,000
c. $195,000
d. $225,000 (5/95, FAR, #41, amended, 5577)

2. Mobe Co. reported the following operating income (loss) for its first three years of operations:

Year 1	$ 300,000
Year 2	(700,000)
Year 3	1,200,000

For each year, there were no deferred income taxes, and Mobe's effective income tax rate was 30%. In its year 2 income tax return, Mobe elected to carry back the maximum amount of loss possible. In its year 3 income statement, what amount should Mobe report as total income tax expense?
a. $120,000
b. $150,000
c. $240,000
d. $360,000 (5/95, FAR, #43, amended, 5579)

3. Dunn Co.'s current year income statement reported $90,000 income before provision for income taxes. To compute the provision for federal income taxes, the following data are provided:

Rent received in advance	$16,000
Income from exempt municipal bonds	20,000
Depreciation deducted for income tax purposes in excess of depreciation reported for financial statement purposes	10,000
Estimated tax payments	0
Enacted corporate income tax rate	30%

If the alternative minimum tax provisions are ignored, what amount of current federal income tax liability should be reported in Dunn's December 31 balance sheet?
a. $18,000
b. $22,800
c. $25,800
d. $28,800 (11/91, PI, #25, amended, 3310)

4. Pine Corp.'s books showed pretax income of $800,000 for the current year ended December 31. In the computation of federal income taxes, the following data were considered:

Gain on an involuntary conversion (Pine has elected to replace the property within the statutory period using total proceeds.)	$350,000
Depreciation deducted for tax purposes in excess of depreciation deducted for book purposes	50,000
Federal estimated tax payments	70,000
Enacted federal tax rates	30%

What amount should Pine report as its current federal income tax liability on its December 31 balance sheet?
a. $ 50,000
b. $ 65,000
c. $120,000
d. $135,000 (11/90, PI, #16, amended, 3311)

Items 5 and 6 are based on the following:

Zeff Co. prepared the following reconciliation of its pretax financial statement income to taxable income for the current year ended December 31, its first year of operations:

Pretax financial income	$160,000
Nontaxable interest received on municipal securities	(5,000)
Long-term loss accrual in excess of deductible amount	10,000
Depreciation in excess of financial statement amount	(25,000)
Taxable income	$140,000

Zeff's tax rate for the year is 40%.

5. In its income statement, what amount should Zeff report as income tax expense—current portion?
a. $52,000
b. $56,000
c. $62,000
d. $64,000 (11/95, FAR, #37, amended, 6119)

6. In its December 31 balance sheet, what should Zeff report as deferred income tax liability?
a. $2,000
b. $4,000
c. $6,000
d. $8,000 (11/95, FAR, #38, amended, 6120)

7. Ram Corp. prepared the following reconciliation of income per books with income per tax return for the current year ended December 31:

Book income before income taxes	$ 750,000
Add temporary difference:	
Construction contract revenue which will reverse in four years	100,000
Deduct temporary difference:	
Depreciation expense which will reverse in equal amounts in each of the next four years	(400,000)
Taxable income	$ 450,000

Ram's effective income tax rate for the year is 34%. What amount should Ram report in its current year income statement as the current provision for income taxes?

a. $ 34,000
b. $153,000
c. $255,000
d. $289,000 (11/90, PII, #7, amended, 3432)

8. Because Jab Co. uses different methods to depreciate equipment for financial statement and income tax purposes, Jab has temporary differences that will reverse during the next year and add to taxable income. Deferred income taxes that are based on these temporary differences should be classified in Jab's balance sheet as a

a. Contra account to current assets
b. Contra account to noncurrent assets
c. Current liability
d. Noncurrent liability (5/94, FAR, #24, 4839)

* 9. At the end of year 1, Cody Co. reported a profit on a partially completed construction contract by applying the percentage of completion method. By the end of year 2, the total estimated profit on the contract at completion in year 3 had been drastically reduced from the amount estimated at the end of year 1. Consequently, in year 2, a loss equal to one-half of the previous year profit was recognized. Cody used the completed contract method for income tax purposes and had no other contracts. The year 2 balance sheet should include a deferred tax

	Asset	*Liability*
a.	Yes	Yes
b.	No	Yes
c.	Yes	No
d.	No	No

(11/91, Theory, #4, amended, 9051)

10. Orleans Co., a cash basis taxpayer, prepares accrual basis financial statements. In its current year balance sheet, Orleans' deferred income tax liabilities increased compared to the previous year. Which of the following changes would cause this increase in deferred income tax liabilities?

I. An increase in prepaid insurance
II. An increase in rent receivable
III. An increase in warranty obligations

a. I only
b. I and II
c. II and III
d. III only (5/92, Theory, #9, amended, 3625)

11. Miro Co. began business on January 2, Year 1. Miro used the double-declining balance method of depreciation for financial statement purposes for its building, and the straight-line method for income taxes. On January 16, Year 3, Miro elected to switch to the straight-line method for both financial statement and tax purposes. The building cost $240,000 in year 1, which has an estimated useful life of 15 years and no salvage value. Data related to the building is as follows:

Year	Double-declining balance depreciation	Straight-line depreciation
1	$30,000	$16,000
2	20,000	16,000

Miro's tax rate is 40%. Which of the following statements is correct?

a. There should be **no** reduction in Miro's deferred tax liabilities or deferred tax assets in year 3.
b. Miro's deferred tax liability should be reduced by $7,200 in year 3.
c. Miro's deferred tax asset should be reduced by $7,200 in year 3.
d. Miro's deferred tax asset should be increased by $7,200 in year 3.

(R/05, FAR, 1632F, #32, amended, 7776)

12. In its current year income statement, Cere Co. reported income before income taxes of $300,000. Cere estimated that, because of permanent differences, taxable income would be $280,000. During the year Cere made estimated tax payments of $50,000, which were debited to income tax expense. Cere is subject to a 30% tax rate. What amount should Cere report as income tax expense?

a. $34,000
b. $50,000
c. $84,000
d. $90,000 (11/94, Theory, #51, amended, 5312)

13. Black Co., organized on January 2, year 1, had pretax financial statement income of $500,000 and taxable income of $800,000 for the year ended December 31, year 1. The only temporary differences are accrued product warranty costs, which Black expects to pay as follows:

Year 2	$100,000
Year 3	$ 50,000
Year 4	$ 50,000
Year 5	$100,000

The enacted income tax rates are 25% for year 1, 30% for years 2 through 4, and 35% for year 5. Black believes that future years' operations will produce profits. In its December 31, year 1, balance sheet, what amount should Black report as deferred tax asset?

a. $50,000
b. $75,000
c. $90,000
d. $95,000 (11/98, FAR, #10, amended, 6737)

14. Cory Inc. uses the accrual method of accounting for financial reporting purposes and appropriately uses the installment method of accounting for income tax purposes. Installment income of $250,000 will be collected in the following years when the enacted tax rates are:

Year	Collection of income	Enacted tax rates
2	$ 25,000	35%
3	50,000	30%
4	75,000	30%
5	100,000	25%

The installment income is Cory's only temporary difference. Taxable income is expected in all future years. What amount should be included in the deferred income tax liability in Cory's December 31, year 2 balance sheet?

a. $62,500
b. $71,250
c. $78,750
d. $87,500 (11/90, PI, #20, amended, 3301)

15. Rein Inc. reported deferred tax assets and deferred tax liabilities at the end of the previous year and at the end of the current year. For the current year ended, Rein should report deferred income tax expense or benefit equal to the

a. Decrease in the deferred tax assets
b. Increase in the deferred tax liabilities
c. Amount of the current tax liability plus the sum of the net changes in deferred tax assets and deferred tax liabilities
d. Sum of the net changes in deferred tax assets and deferred tax liabilities

(11/92, Theory, #41, amended, 3474)

16. Mill, which began operations on January 1, year 1, recognizes income from long-term construction contracts under the percentage of completion method in its financial statements and under the completed contract method for income tax reporting. Income under each method follows:

Year	Completed contract	Percentage of completion
1	$ --	$300,000
2	400,000	600,000
3	700,000	850,000

The income tax rate was 30% for years 1 through 3. For years after year 3, the enacted tax rate is 25%. There are no other temporary differences. Assuming Mill does not expect any tax losses in the near future, Mill should report in its December 31, year 3 balance sheet, a deferred income tax liability of

a. $ 87,500
b. $105,000
c. $162,500
d. $195,000 (11/91, PI, #38, amended, 3303)

17. West Corp. leased a building and received the $36,000 annual rental payment on June 15 of the current year. The beginning of the lease was July 1. Rental income is taxable when received. West's tax rates are 30% for the current year and 40% thereafter. West had no other permanent or temporary differences. West determined that no valuation allowance was needed. What amount of deferred tax asset should West report in its December 31 current year balance sheet?

a. $ 5,400
b. $ 7,200
c. $10,800
d. $14,400 (5/93, PI, #26, amended, 4068)

18. In year 1, Lobo Corp. reported for financial statement purposes the following revenue and expenses which were not included in taxable income:

Premiums on officers' life insurance under which the corporation is the beneficiary	$ 5,000
Interest revenue on qualified state or municipal bonds	10,000
Estimated future warranty costs to be paid in year 2 and year 3	60,000

Lobo's enacted tax rate for the current and future years is 30%. Lobo expects to operate profitably in the future. There were no temporary differences in prior years. The deferred tax benefit is

a. $18,000
b. $19,500
c. $21,000
d. $22,500 (5/90, PI, #41, amended, 3315)

19. On June 30 of the current year, Ank Corp. prepaid a $19,000 premium on an annual insurance policy. The premium payment was a tax deductible expense in Ank's cash basis tax return. The accrual basis income statement will report a $9,500 insurance expense in this year and next year. Ank's income tax rate is 30% in the current year and 25% thereafter. Taxable income is expected in all future years. In Ank's December 31 current year balance sheet, what amount related to the insurance should be reported as a deferred income tax liability?

a. $5,700
b. $4,750
c. $2,850
d. $2,375 (5/91, PI, #41, amended, 3305)

20. As a result of differences between depreciation for financial reporting purposes and tax purposes, the financial reporting basis of Noor Co.'s sole depreciable asset, acquired in the current year, exceeded its tax basis by $250,000 at December 31 of the current year. This difference will reverse in future years. The enacted tax rate is 30% for this year, and 40% for future years. Noor has no other temporary differences. In its December 31 current year balance sheet, how should Noor report the deferred tax effect of this difference?

a. As an asset of $75,000
b. As an asset of $100,000
c. As a liability of $75,000
d. As a liability of $100,000

(5/95, FAR, #16, amended, 5552)

21. In its year 1 income statement, Tow Inc. reported proceeds from an officer's life insurance policy of $90,000 and depreciation of $250,000. Tow was the owner and beneficiary of the life insurance on its officer. Tow deducted depreciation of $370,000 in its year 1 income tax return when the tax rate was 30%. Data related to the reversal of the excess tax deduction for depreciation follow:

Year	Reversal of excess tax deduction	Enacted tax rates
2	$50,000	35%
3	40,000	35%
4	20,000	25%
5	10,000	25%

There are no other temporary differences. Tow expects to report profits (rather than losses) for tax purposes for all future years. In its December 31, year 1 balance sheet, what amount should Tow report as a deferred income tax liability?

a. $36,000
b. $39,000
c. $63,000
d. $66,000 (11/91, PI, #35, amended, 3307)

22. For calendar year 1, Clark Corp. reported depreciation of $300,000 in its income statement. On its year 1 income tax return, Clark reported depreciation of $500,000. Clark's income statement also included $50,000 accrued warranty expense that will be deducted for tax purposes when paid. Clark's enacted tax rates are 30% for year 1 and year 2, and 25% for year 3 and year 4. Taxable income is expected in all future years. The depreciation difference and warranty expense will reverse over the next three years as follows:

Year	Depreciation difference	Warranty expense
2	$ 80,000	$10,000
3	70,000	15,000
4	50,000	25,000
	$200,000	$50,000

These were Clark's only temporary differences. In Clark's year 1 income statement, the deferred portion of its provision for income taxes should be

a. $67,000
b. $45,000
c. $41,000
d. $37,500 (11/90, PI, #48, amended, 3314)

23. Which of the following should be used to measure the deferred tax consequences of temporary differences that will result in taxable amounts in future years?

	Enacted changes in tax laws and rates scheduled for future years	*Anticipated change in tax laws and rates for future years*
a.	Yes	Yes
b.	Yes	No
c.	No	Yes
d.	No	No

(Editors, 3623)

24. Senlo Co., which uses a one-year operating cycle, recognized profits for both financial statement and tax purposes during its two years of operation. Depreciation for tax purposes exceeded depreciation for financial statement purposes in each year. These temporary differences are expected to reverse in years 3, 4, and 5. At the end of year 2, the deferred tax liability shown as a noncurrent liability is based on the

a. Enacted tax rates for years 3, 4, and 5
b. Enacted tax rates for years 4 and 5
c. Enacted tax rate for year 3
d. Tax rates for years 1 and 2

(11/90, Theory, #27, amended, 3633)

25. A deferred tax liability or asset should be adjusted for the effect of a change in

	Tax laws	Tax rates
a.	No	No
b.	No	Yes
c.	Yes	No
d.	Yes	Yes

(Editors, 3626)

26. For its first year of operations, Cable Corp. recorded a $100,000 expense in its tax return that will not be recorded in its accounting records until next year. There were no other differences between its taxable and financial statement income. Cable's effective tax rate for the current year is 45%, but a 40% rate has already been passed into law for next year. In its year-end balance sheet, what amount should Cable report as a deferred tax asset(liability)?
a. $40,000 asset
b. $40,000 liability
c. $45,000 asset
d. $45,000 liability (R/05, FAR, 0466F, #9, 7753)

27. On its current year December 31 balance sheet, Shin Co. had income taxes payable of $13,000 and a current deferred tax asset of $20,000 before determining the need for a valuation account. Shin had reported a current deferred tax asset of $15,000 at December 31 of the previous year. No estimated tax payments were made during the current year. At December 31, current year, Shin determined that it was more likely than not that 10% of the deferred tax asset would not be realized. In its current year income statement, what amount should Shin report as total income tax expense?
a. $ 8,000
b. $ 8,500
c. $10,000
d. $13,000 (11/95, FAR, #36, amended, 6118)

28. A deferred tax asset of $100,000 was recognized in the year 1 financial statements by the Chaise Company when a loss from discontinued segments was carried forward for tax purposes. A valuation allowance of $100,000 was also recognized in the year 1 statements because it was considered more likely than not that the deferred tax asset would not be realized. Chaise had no temporary differences. The tax benefit of the loss carried forward reduced current taxes payable on year 3 continuing operations. The year 3 income statement would include the tax benefit from the loss brought forward in
a. Income from continuing operations
b. Gain or loss from discontinued segments
c. Extraordinary gains
d. Cumulative effect of accounting changes
(5/90, Theory, #25, amended, 3632)

29. Dodd Corp. is preparing its December 31 current year financial statements and must determine the proper accounting treatment for the following situations:

- For the current year ended December 31, Dodd has a loss carryforward of $180,000 available to offset future taxable income. However, there are no temporary differences. Based on an analysis of both positive and negative evidence, Dodd has reason to believe it is more likely than not that the benefits of the entire loss carryforward will be realized within the carryforward period.

- On 12/31 of this year, Dodd received a $200,000 offer for its patent. Dodd's management is considering whether to sell the patent. The offer expires on 2/28 of next year. The patent has a carrying amount of $100,000 at 12/31.

Assume a current and future income tax rate of 30%. In its current year income statement, Dodd should recognize an increase in net income of
a. $0
b. $ 54,000
c. $ 70,000
d. $124,000 (5/90, PII, #60, amended, 3433)

30. At December 31, Dorr Inc. has a net operating loss carryforward of $90,000 available to offset future taxable income. At this date, Dorr has temporary differences that will result in taxable amounts of $60,000 during the operating loss carryforward period. The company has sufficient positive evidence to support an assumption that the benefits of the carryforward will be realized in the near future. Assuming a present and future enacted income tax rate of 30%, what amount of the tax benefit of the operating loss carryforward should be recognized in the income statement for the year ended December 31?
a. $0
b. $ 9,000
c. $18,000
d. $27,000 (Editors, 3318)

31. Hut Co. has temporary taxable differences that will reverse during the next year and add to taxable income. These differences relate to noncurrent assets. Deferred income taxes based on these temporary differences should be classified in Hut's balance sheet as a
a. Current asset
b. Noncurrent asset
c. Current liability
d. Noncurrent liability (11/97, FAR, #11, 6491)

32. At December 31, Bren Co. had the following deferred income tax items:

- A deferred income tax liability of $15,000 related to a noncurrent asset
- A deferred income tax asset of $3,000 related to a noncurrent liability
- A deferred income tax asset of $8,000 related to a current liability

Which of the following should Bren report in the noncurrent section of its December 31 balance sheet?

a. A noncurrent tax asset of $3,000 and a noncurrent liability of $15,000
b. A noncurrent tax liability of $12,000
c. A noncurrent tax asset of $11,000 and a noncurrent liability of $15,000
d. A noncurrent tax liability of $4,000

(5/95, FAR, #17, amended, 5553)

33. In year 1, Rand Inc. reported for financial statement purposes the following items, which were not included in taxable income:

Installment gain to be collected equally in years 2 through 4	$1,500,000
Estimated future warranty costs to be paid equally in years 2 through 4	2,100,000

Rand had the installment gain arise from the sale of an investment. There were no temporary differences in prior years. Rand expects taxable income in all future years. Rand's enacted tax rates are 25% for year 1 and 30% for years 2 through 4. In Rand's December 31, year 1 balance sheet, what amounts of the net deferred tax asset should be classified as current and noncurrent?

	Current	*Noncurrent*
a.	$60,000	$100,000
b.	$60,000	$120,000
c.	$50,000	$100,000
d.	$50,000	$120,000

(5/91, PI, #31, amended, 3319)

34. At the end of the year, the tax effects of temporary differences for Thorn Co. were as follows:

	Deferred tax assets (liabilities)	Related asset classification
Accelerated tax depreciation	$(75,000)	Noncurrent asset
Additional costs in inventory for tax purposes	25,000	Current asset
	$(50,000)	

A valuation allowance was not considered necessary. Thorn anticipates that $10,000 of the deferred tax liability will reverse in the next year. In Thorn's December 31 balance sheet, what amount should Thorn report as noncurrent deferred tax liability?

a. $40,000
b. $50,000
c. $65,000
d. $75,000

(11/94, Theory, #6, amended, 5271)

35. Rom Corp. began business in year 1 and reported taxable income of $50,000 on its year 1 tax return. Rom's enacted tax rate is 30% for year 1 and future years. The following is a schedule of Rom's December 31, year 1, temporary differences in thousands of dollars:

	Book basis over (under) tax basis 12/31 year 1	Future taxable (deductible) amounts Yr 2	Yr 3	Yr 4	Yr 5
Equipment	10	(5)	5	5	5
Warranty liability	(20)	(10)	(10)		
Deferred compensation liability	(15)		(5)		(10)
Installment receivables	30	10		20	
Totals	5	(5)	(10)	25	(5)

What amount should Rom report as current deferred tax assets in its December 31, year 1, balance sheet?

a. $0
b. $1,500
c. $4,500
d. $6,000

(5/92, PI, #24, amended, 2592)

36. Income tax expense or benefit for the year should be allocated among

	Discontinued operations	*Prior period adjustments*
a.	Yes	Yes
b.	Yes	No
c.	No	Yes
d.	No	No

(Editors, 3636)

37. Purl Corporation's income statement for the year ended December 31 shows the following:

Income before income tax and extraordinary item	$900,000
Gain on life insurance coverage—included in the above $900,000 income amount	100,000
Extraordinary item—loss due to earthquake damage	300,000

Purl's tax rate for the year is 30%. How much should be reported as the provision for income tax in Purl's income statement?
a. $150,000
b. $180,000
c. $240,000
d. $270,000 (Editors, 3321)

38. Generally, the manner of reporting the tax benefit of an operating loss carryforward or carryback is determined by the source of the

	Income or loss in the current year	*Operating loss carryforward or taxes paid in a prior year*
a.	Yes	Yes
b.	Yes	No
c.	No	Yes
d.	No	No

(Editors, 3631)

39. On January 1 of the current year, Lundy Corp. purchased 40% of the voting common stock of Glen Inc., and appropriately accounts for its investment by the equity method. During the year, Glen reported earnings of $225,000 and paid dividends of $75,000. Lundy assumes that all of Glen's undistributed earnings will be distributed as dividends in future periods when the enacted tax rate will be 30%. Ignore the dividends-received deduction. Lundy's current enacted income tax rate is 25%. Lundy uses the liability method to account for temporary differences and expects to have taxable income in all future periods. The increase in Lundy's deferred income tax liability for this temporary difference is
a. $45,000
b. $37,500
c. $27,000
d. $18,000 (5/89, PI, #40, amended, 3323)

40. Leer Corp.'s pretax income in the current year was $100,000. The temporary differences between amounts reported in the financial statements and the tax return are as follows:

- Depreciation in the financial statements was $8,000 more than tax depreciation.
- The equity method of accounting resulted in financial statement income of $35,000. A $25,000 dividend was received during the year, which is eligible for the 80% dividends received deduction.

Leer's effective income tax rate was 30%. In its current year income statement, Leer should report a current provision for income taxes of
a. $26,400
b. $23,400
c. $21,900
d. $18,600 (11/91, PI, #48, amended, 3312)

41. Taft Corp. uses the equity method to account for its 25% investment in Flame Inc. During the current year, Taft received dividends of $30,000 from Flame and recorded $180,000 as its equity in the earnings of Flame. Additional information follows:

- All the undistributed earnings of Flame will be distributed as dividends in future periods.
- The dividends received from Flame are eligible for the 80% dividends received deduction.
- There are no other temporary differences.
- Enacted income tax rates are 30% for this year and thereafter.

In its December 31 balance sheet, what amount should Taft report for deferred income tax liability?
a. $ 9,000
b. $10,800
c. $45,000
d. $54,000 (5/93, PI, #35, amended, 4076)

Problem 13-2 ADDITIONAL MULTIPLE CHOICE QUESTIONS (20 to 25 minutes)

42. On January 2, year 1, Ross Co. purchased a machine for $70,000. This machine has a 5-year useful life, a residual value of $10,000, and is depreciated using the straight-line method for financial statement purposes. For tax purposes, depreciation expense was $25,000 for year 1 and $20,000 for year 2. Ross' year 2 income, before income taxes and depreciation expense, was $100,000 and its tax rate was 30%. If Ross had made **no** estimated tax payments during year 2, what amount of current income tax liability would Ross report in its December 31, year 2 balance sheet?

a. $26,400
b. $25,800
c. $24,000
d. $22,500 (5/92, PI, #26, amended, 2595)

43. Busy Corp. prepared the following reconciliation between pretax accounting income and taxable income for the year ended December 31:

Pretax accounting income	$ 250,000
Taxable income	(150,000)
Difference	$ 100,000

Analysis of difference:	
Interest on municipal bonds	$ 25,000
Excess of tax over book depreciation	75,000
	$ 100,000

Busy's effective income tax rate for the year is 30%. The depreciation difference will reverse in equal amounts over the next three years at an enacted tax rate of 40%. In Busy's income statement, what amount should be reported as the current portion of its provision for income taxes?

a. $45,000
b. $67,500
c. $75,000
d. $82,500 (5/92, PI, #56, amended, 2628)

44. Under current generally accepted accounting principles, which approach is used to determine income tax expense?

a. Asset and liability approach
b. "With and without" approach
c. Net of tax approach
d. Periodic expense approach (R/99, FAR, #17, 6786)

45. Which of the following should be recognized for the amount of deferred tax consequences attributable to temporary differences that will result in taxable amounts in future years?

	Deferred tax asset	*Deferred tax liability*
a.	Yes	Yes
b.	Yes	No
c.	No	Yes
d.	No	No

(Editors, 3622)

46. Temporary differences arise when expenses are deductible for tax purposes

	After they are recognized in financial income	*Before they are recognized in financial income*
a.	No	No
b.	No	Yes
c.	Yes	Yes
d.	Yes	No

(11/89, Theory, #27, 3620)

47. Stone Co. began operations in the current year and reported $225,000 in income before income taxes for the year. Stone's tax depreciation exceeded its book depreciation by $25,000. Stone also had nondeductible book expenses of $10,000 related to permanent differences. Stone's tax rate for the current year was 40%, and the enacted rate for years after the current year is 35%. In its December 31 current year balance sheet, what amount of deferred income tax liability should Stone report?

a. $ 8,750
b. $10,000
c. $12,250
d. $14,000 (5/93, PI, #36, amended, 4077)

48. In its year 1 income statement, Noll Corp. reported depreciation of $400,000 and interest revenue on municipal obligations of $60,000. Noll reported depreciation of $550,000 on its year 1 income tax return. The difference in depreciation is the only temporary difference, and it will reverse equally over the next three years. Noll's enacted income tax rates are 35% for year 1, 30% for year 2 and 25% for year 3 and year 4. Assuming Noll expects to report taxable income in all future years, what amount should be included in the deferred income tax liability in Noll's December 31, year 1 balance sheet?

a. $40,000
b. $52,500
c. $63,000
d. $73,500 (11/90, PI, #19, amended, 3308)

49. Scott Corp. received cash of $20,000 that was included in revenues in its year 1 financial statements, of which $12,000 will not be taxable until year 2. Scott's enacted tax rate is 30% for year 1, and 25% for year 2. What amount should Scott report in its year 1 balance sheet for deferred income tax liability?
a. $2,000
b. $2,400
c. $3,000
d. $3,600 (5/92, PI, #33, amended, 2604)

50. Quinn Co. reported a net deferred tax asset of $9,000 in its December 31, year 1 balance sheet. For year 2, Quinn reported pretax financial statement income of $300,000. Temporary differences of $100,000 resulted in taxable income of $200,000 for year 2. At December 31, year 2, Quinn had cumulative taxable differences of $70,000. Quinn's effective income tax rate is 30%. In its December 31, year 2 income statement, what should Quinn report as deferred income tax expense?
a. $12,000
b. $21,000
c. $30,000
d. $60,000 (5/95, FAR, #42, amended, 5578)

51. Black Co., organized on January 2, year 1, had pretax accounting income of $500,000 and taxable income of $800,000 for the year ended December 31, year 1. The only temporary difference is accrued product warranty costs which are expected to be paid as follows:

Year 2	$100,000
Year 3	50,000
Year 4	50,000
Year 5	100,000

The enacted income tax rates are 35% for year 1, 30% for years 2 through 4, and 25% for year 5. Taxable income is expected in all future years. In Black's December 31, year 1 balance sheet, the deferred income tax asset should be
a. $ 75,000
b. $ 85,000
c. $ 90,000
d. $105,000 (5/90, PI, #21, amended, 3306)

SIMULATIONS

Problem 13-3 (15 to 25 minutes)

Scenario & Responses 1-4 | Scenario & Responses 5-8 | Research Task

Items 1 through 4 describe circumstances resulting in differences between financial statement income and taxable income. Select the **best** answer for each item. For each numbered item, determine whether the difference is:

List	
A.	A temporary difference resulting in a deferred tax asset
B.	A temporary difference resulting in a deferred tax liability
C.	A permanent difference

An answer may be selected once, more than once, or not at all.

1. ____ For plant assets, the depreciation expense deducted for tax purposes is in excess of the depreciation expense used for financial reporting purposes.

2. ____ A landlord collects some rents in advance. Rents received are taxable in the period in which they are received.

3. ____ Interest is received on an investment in tax-exempt municipal obligations.

4. ____ Costs of guarantees and warranties are estimated. (5/97, FAR, #1, amended, 6479)

Scenario & Responses 1-4	Scenario & Responses 5-8	Research Task

Items 5 through 8 represent amounts omitted from the following worksheet. For each item, determine the amount omitted from the worksheet. Select the amount from the following list. An answer may be used once, more than once, or not at all. The partially completed worksheet contains Lane Co.'s reconciliation between financial statement income and taxable income for the three years ended April 30, year 3, and additional information. The tax rate changes were enacted at the beginning of each tax year and were not known to Lane at the end of the prior year.

5. ____ Current tax expense for the year ended April 30, year 1.
6. ____ Cumulative temporary differences at April 30, year 2.
7. ____ Deferred tax expense for the year ended April 30, year 2.
8. ____ Deferred tax liability at April 30, year 3.

Amount

A.	$ 25,000	H.	$135,000
B.	$ 35,000	I.	$140,000
C.	$ 45,000	J.	$160,000
D.	$ 75,000	K.	$180,000
E.	$100,000	L.	$200,000
F.	$120,000	M.	$300,000
G.	$112,500	N.	$400,000

Lane Co.
Income Tax Worksheet
For the Three Years Ended April 30, Year 3

	April 30, Year 1	April 30, Year 2	April 30, Year 3
Pretax financial income	$900,000	$1,200,000	$1,000,000
Permanent differences	100,000	100,000	100,000
Temporary differences	200,000	100,000	150,000
Taxable income	$600,000	$ 800,000	$ 950,000
Cumulative temporary differences (future taxable amounts)	$200,000	$ **(6)**	$ 450,000
Tax rate	20%	25%	30%
Deferred tax liability	$ 40,000	$ 75,000	$ **(8)**
Deferred tax expense	$ —	$ **(7)**	$ —
Current tax expense	$ **(5)**	$ —	$ —

Scenario & Responses 1-4	Scenario & Responses 5-8	Research Task

Research Question: What are the objectives of accounting for income taxes?

Paragraph Reference Answer: ____________

Problem 13-4 (30 to 40 minutes)

Scenario	Schedule of Interest Expense	Essay	Research Task

Chris Green, CPA, is auditing Rayne Co.'s year 2 financial statements. The controller, Dunn, has provided Green with the following information:

- At December 31, year 1, Rayne had a note payable to Federal Bank with a balance of $90,000. The annual principal payment of $10,000, plus 8% interest on the unpaid balance, was paid when due on March 31, year 2.
- On January 2, year 2, Rayne leased two automobiles for executive use under a capital lease. Five annual lease payments of $15,000 are due beginning January 3, year 2. Rayne's incremental borrowing rate on the date of the lease was 11% and the lessor's implicit rate, which was known by Rayne, was 10%. The lease was properly recorded at $62,500, before the first payment was made.
- On July 1, year 2, Rayne received proceeds of $538,000 from a $500,000 bond issuance. The bonds mature in 15 years and interest of 11% is payable semiannually on June 30 and December 31. The bonds were issued at a price to yield investors 10%. Rayne uses the effective interest method to amortize bond premium.
- Dunn has prepared a schedule of all differences between financial statement and income tax return income. Dunn believes that as a result of pending legislation, the enacted tax rate at December 31, year 2, will be increased for year 3. Dunn is uncertain which differences to include and which rates to apply in computing deferred taxes under FASB 109, *Accounting for Income Taxes.* Dunn has requested an overview of FASB 109 from Green. (5/94, FAR, #5, amended, 4975)

Scenario	Schedule of Interest Expense	Essay	Research Task

Prepare a schedule of interest expense for the year ended December 31, year 2.

Rayne Co.
Schedule of Interest Expense
For the Year Ended December 31, Year 2

Note payable	
Capital lease obligation	
Bonds payable	
Total interest expense	

Scenario	Schedule of Interest Expense	Essay	Research Task

Prepare a brief memo to Dunn from Green:

- Identifying the objectives of accounting for income taxes,
- Defining temporary differences,
- Explaining how to measure deferred tax assets and liabilities, and
- Explaining how to measure deferred income tax expense or benefit.

Scenario	Schedule of Interest Expense	Essay	Research Task

Research Question: In which part of the income statement should deferred tax liabilities and assets be reported?

Paragraph Reference Answer: ____________

Problem 13-5 (40 to 50 minutes)

Scenario	Additional Information	Income Statement	Reconciliation Schedule

The following condensed trial balance of Powell Corp., a publicly owned company, has been adjusted except for income tax expense:

Powell Corp.
Condensed Trial Balance
June 30, Year 2

	Debit	Credit
Total assets	$25,080,000	
Total liabilities		$ 9,900,000
5% cumulative preferred stock		2,000,000
Common stock		10,000,000
Retained earnings		2,900,000
Machine sales		750,000
Service revenues		250,000
Interest revenues		10,000
Gain on sale of factory		250,000
Cost of sales—machines	425,000	
Cost of services	100,000	
Administrative exp.	300,000	
R & D expenses	110,000	
Interest expense	5,000	
Loss from asset disposal	40,000	
	$26,060,000	$26,060,000

a. Using the single-step format, prepare Powell's income statement for the year ended June 30, year 2.

b. Prepare a schedule reconciling Powell's financial statement net income to taxable income for the year ended June 30, year 2. (11/92, PI, #5, amended, 9911)

Scenario	Additional Information	Income Statement	Reconciliation Schedule

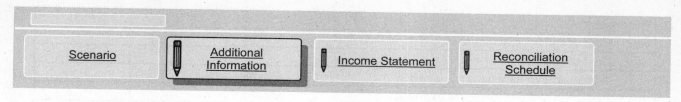

- The weighted average number of common shares outstanding during year 2 was 200,000. The potential dilution from the exercise of stock options held by Powell's officers and directors was not material.
- There were no dividends-in-arrears on Powell's preferred stock at July 1, year 1. On May 1, year 2, Powell's directors declared a 5% preferred stock dividend to be paid in August year 2.
- During year 2, one of Powell's foreign factories was expropriated by the foreign government, and Powell received a $900,000 payment from the foreign government in settlement. The carrying value of the plant was $650,000. Powell has never disposed of a factory.
- Administrative expenses includes a $5,000 premium payment for a $1,000,000 life insurance policy on Powell's president, of which the corporation is the beneficiary.
- Powell depreciates its assets using the straight-line method for financial reporting purposes and an accelerated method for tax purposes. There were no other temporary differences. The differences between book and tax depreciation are as follows:
- Powell's enacted tax rate for the current and future years is 30%.

June 30	Financial statements over (under) tax depreciation
Year 2	$(15,000)
Year 3	10,000
Year 4	5,000

- Powell's enacted tax rate for the current and future years is 30%.

Scenario	Additional Information	Income Statement	Reconciliation Schedule

Powell Corp.
Income Statement
For the Year Ended June 30, Year 2

Revenues:		
Machine sales		
Service revenues		
Interest revenue		
Total revenues		

Expenses:		
Cost of sales—machines		
Cost of services		
Administrative expenses		
Research and development expenses		
Interest expense		
Loss from asset disposal		
Current income tax expense		
Deferred income tax expense		
Total expenses and losses		
Income before extraordinary gain		
Extraordinary gain, net of income taxes of $75,000		
Net income		
Earnings (loss) per share:		
Income before extraordinary gain		
Net income		

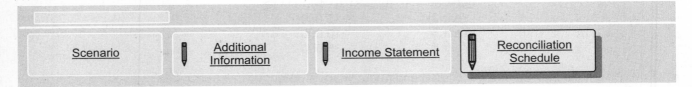

Scenario | Additional Information | Income Statement | Reconciliation Schedule

Powell Corp.
Reconciliation Schedule
For the Year Ended June 30, Year 2

Net income	
Add: Taxes on extraordinary gain	
Provision for income taxes	
Financial statement income before income taxes	
Permanent difference—officer's life insurance	
Temporary difference—excess of tax over financial statement depreciation	
Taxable income	

Research Task

Research Question: What is (are) the disclosure requirement(s) concerning a reconciliation of income tax expense?

Paragraph Reference Answer: ____________

Solution 13-1 MULTIPLE CHOICE ANSWERS

Tax Expense

1. (c) The amount to be reported as current tax expense is computed by multiplying the taxable income by the effective income tax rate ($650,000 × 30% = $195,000).

2. (c) The maximum Mobe could carry back to year 1 was $300,000. The remaining $400,000 of the operating loss ($700,000 – $300,000) would be carried forward to year 3, thereby reducing taxable operating income to $800,000 ($1,200,000 – $400,000)

Operating income for year 3	$1,200,000
Less: Operating loss carryforward	(400,000)
Net taxable income	800,000
Effective tax rate	× 30%
Current tax expense, year 3	$ 240,000

Income Reconciliation

3. (b) To determine Dunn's current federal income tax liability, Dunn's pretax financial income is adjusted to its taxable income; then, taxable income is multiplied by the current year's enacted corporate income tax rate.

Pretax financial income	$ 90,000
Rent received in advance	16,000
Income from municipal bonds, tax exempt	(20,000)
Depreciation deducted for income tax purposes in excess reported for book purposes	(10,000)
Taxable income	76,000
Enacted corporate income tax rate	× 30%
Current federal income tax liability	$ 22,800

4. (a) $120,000 – $70,000 = $50,000

Pretax financial income	$ 800,000
Gain on involuntary conversion deferred for tax purposes	(350,000)
Excess depreciation for tax purposes	(50,000)
Taxable income	400,000
Enacted tax rate	× 30%
Taxes payable	$ 120,000

5. (b) To determine the current portion of income tax expense, taxable income is multiplied by the current enacted corporate income tax rate. $140,000 × 40% = $56,000.

6. (c) Since both temporary items are noncurrent, the amount of the deferred tax liability to be reported is computed by considering the future tax effects of the cumulative net taxable type temporary differences. ($25,000 – $10,000) × 40% = $6,000. Being the first year of operations, the temporary differences originating in the current year are the cumulative temporary differences existing at the balance sheet date.

7. (b) The current portion of the provision for income taxes (which is the same as the amount of taxes due to the government for the current period) is computed by multiplying the taxable income figure by the statutory tax rate for the current period. The statutory tax rate is not given. However, because there are no permanent differences and because there are no temporary differences which are expected to reverse at tax rates different from the current statutory rate, the effective rate for the current year must be the same as the statutory tax rate. Thus, $450,000 × 34% = $153,000.

Differences

8. (d) The deferred tax liability is classified as noncurrent because it is related to the equipment, a noncurrent asset. Deferred tax accounts are reported on the balance sheet as assets and liabilities, not as contra accounts.

9. (b) At the end of year 1, a cumulative difference exists which is equal to the contract profit recognized on the income statement in the previous year. The cumulative difference will result in future taxable amounts, so a deferred tax liability is established for an amount equal to the cumulative temporary difference multiplied by the tax rate enacted for the year(s) in which the temporary difference is expected to reverse. In year 2, half of the cumulative temporary difference reverses because of the recognition of a loss to offset half of the profit reported in the previous year. With no change in enacted future tax rates, this reversal results in a decrease in the related deferred tax liability account. Therefore, at the end of year 2, Cody has a deferred tax liability balance equal to half of the balance that was in that account at the end of year 1.

10. (b) An increase in prepaid insurance can cause an increase in deferred tax liabilities because an expense deducted this period for tax purposes but deferred for financial accounting purposes will cause future taxable amounts. An increase in rent receivable can cause an increase in deferred tax liabilities because a revenue accrued for book purposes but not recognized for tax purposes until it is collected will give rise to future taxable amounts. A deferred tax liability represents the deferred tax consequences attributable to taxable temporary differences. An increase in cumulative temporary differences giving rise to future taxable amounts results

in an increase in deferred tax liabilities. An increase in warranty obligation can cause an increase in deferred tax assets rather than deferred tax liabilities. An expense accrued for book purposes, but deducted for tax purposes when paid, causes a temporary difference which gives rise to future deductible amounts. A deferred tax asset is the deferred tax consequences attributable to deductible temporary differences and carryforwards.

11. (c) Tax differences arise because the method used on the books is different than the method used on the tax returns. Micro has changed the method of accounting on the books to match the method used on the tax returns and will no longer be creating temporary differences. Using double-declining depreciation on the books and straight line depreciation on the tax return results in a deferred tax asset. The previous balance in the tax asset account will be reduced by the amount recovered in 2002.

Double declining method for year 1 and year 2	$ 50,000
Straight line method for year 1 and year 2	(32,000)
Previous balance in the tax asset account	18,000
Tax rate for year 3, 40%	× 40%
Reduction of deferred tax asset account	$ 7,200

12. (c) No temporary differences exist at the beginning or end of the year. Therefore, the amount to be reported as income tax expense is computed by multiplying Cere's taxable income for the year by the enacted tax rate for the year.

Deferred Tax Liabilities & Assets

13. (d) A deferred tax asset or liability is calculated by multiplying temporary differences by the enacted tax rate expected to apply to taxable income in the periods in which the deferred tax liability or asset is expected to be settled or realized.

Years 2 - 4	$200,000 × 30% =	$60,000
Year 5	100,000 × 35% =	35,000
Deferred tax asset		$95,000

14. (a) The deferred tax liability balance represents the amount of taxes expected to be paid in the future when installment receivables are collected. (The revenue from installment sales has already been included in the financial statements but will not be reported for tax purposes until the related receivables are collected.)

	Amount	Rate	Def. Tax Liab.
Years 3 and 4	$125,000	30%	$37,500
Year 5	100,000	25%	25,000
Deferred tax liability			$62,500

15. (d) Under SFAS 109, deferred income tax expense or benefit is calculated using the asset and liability method. Under this approach, deferred income tax expense or benefit is equal to sum of the net changes in deferred taxes assets and deferred tax liabilities on the balance sheet. Deferred income tax expense or benefit is equal to sum of the net changes in both deferred taxes assets and deferred tax liabilities. Answer (c) describes the amount of total income tax expense, assuming no estimated payments have been made.

16. (c) The $650,000 [($300,000 + $600,000 + $850,000) – ($400,000 + $700,000)] of contract income recognized in the financial statements in excess of that included in taxable income results in taxable amounts in future years. The enacted tax rate for later years is used to determine the deferred income tax liability ($650,000 × 25% = $162,500).

17. (b) While rental income is included in taxable income when received, it is recognized in computing financial income when earned. This causes the amount of a liability (i.e., unearned rental income) at the balance sheet date to exceed its tax basis (zero) which will result in *deductible amounts* in future years when the liability is settled. The $18,000 [i.e., $36,000 – ($36,000 × 6/12)] temporary difference as a result of the unearned rental income will reverse in the following year, and is multiplied by the enacted tax rate of 40% for the following year to arrive at a deferred tax asset of $7,200. The entire $7,200 can be reported as a deferred tax asset at 12/31 of the current year because no valuation allowance is needed.

18. (a) The amount of deferred tax benefit to be applied against current income tax expense is computed by considering the tax effects of the difference for accrued product warranty costs. Product warranty costs are accrued in computing financial income and deductible for tax purposes only when paid. This causes the product warranty liability to exceed its tax basis (zero), which will result in deductible amounts in years when the warranty liability is settled. A deferred tax asset (DTA) is recognized for the tax benefit of the future deductible amounts ($60,000 × 30% = $18,000). There is no apparent need for a valuation allowance against that DTA; Lobo expects to operate profitably in the future. Lobo had no temporary differences in prior years. Recognition of the DTA requires a debit to *Deferred Tax Asset* and a credit to *Income Tax Expense* for

$18,000. The credit to the expense account is called a deferred tax benefit of $18,000 to be applied against current income tax expense (current tax expense is computed by multiplying the taxable income figure by the current tax rate). The insurance premiums and interest revenue do not affect the recognition of the DTA because they are events recognized in financial statements that do not have tax consequences. The insurance premiums are not tax deductible, and the municipal bond interest is exempt from taxation.

19. (d) An expense deducted for tax purposes in a period prior to the period in which it is deducted for financial statement purposes will cause a temporary difference, resulting in a future taxable amount. The $9,500 difference will reverse and cause a taxable amount in the following year. The enacted tax rate of 25% for future years is multiplied by the $9,500 taxable amount to arrive at a current deferred tax liability of $2,375.

20. (d) Deferred tax effects are calculated using the rates in effect for the period of reversal (40% × $250,000 = $100,000). Because the financial reporting basis exceeded the tax basis, the $100,000 represents the amount of tax expected to be paid in future years as a result of the reversal of this difference. This is shown on the balance sheet as a deferred tax liability.

21. (b) The proceeds from the officer's life insurance policy is a tax-exempt revenue; therefore, no current or future tax consequences will result and no deferred taxes are to be recorded for this difference. The $120,000 ($370,000 – $250,000) difference due to depreciation is the only temporary difference existing at the balance sheet date. The tax rate that is used to measure the deferred tax consequences is the enacted tax rate(s) expected to apply to taxable income in the years that this difference reverses.

	Amount	Rate	Def. Tax Liab.
Depreciation			
Years 2 - 3	$90,000	35%	$31,500
Years 4 - 5	$30,000	25%	7,500
Deferred tax liability			$39,000

22. (c) The deferred portion of Clark's provision for income taxes (which means the deferred portion of income tax expense) is determined by the net change during the year in deferred tax accounts on the balance sheet. The temporary difference due to depreciation will result in taxable amounts in future years; the temporary difference due to accrued warranty expense will result in deductible amounts in future years.

	Amount	Rate	Deferred Tax Accounts
Future taxable amounts:			
Depreciation expense			
Year 2	$ 80,000	30%	$ 24,000
Years 3-4	120,000	25%	30,000
Deferred tax liability			$ 54,000

	Amount	Rate	Deferred Tax Accounts
Warranty expense			
Year 2	$ 10,000	30%	$ 3,000
Years 3-4	40,000	25%	10,000
Deferred tax asset			$ 13,000

Deferred tax liability	$ 54,000
Deferred tax asset	(13,000)
Tax expense—deferred	$ 41,000

The net deferred tax liability is $41,000 [i.e., $54,000 + $(13,000)]. There is no mention of a beginning balance of deferred taxes; therefore, the entry to record the $54,000 deferred tax liability and the $13,000 deferred tax asset will involve a credit to *Deferred Tax Liability* for $54,000, a debit to *Deferred Tax Asset* for $13,000, and a debit to *Income Tax Expense* for $41,000. This debit to expense represents deferred income tax expense, and it is referred to as the deferred portion of the provision for income taxes.

Tax Rates & Laws

23. (b) A deferred tax liability is computed at the date of the financial statements by applying tax law provisions to measure the deferred tax consequences of differences that will result in taxable amounts in each future year. *Enacted* changes in tax laws and rates that are scheduled for a particular future year (or years) are used to measure a liability for the deferred tax consequences of taxable amounts that will arise in that year (or years). Tax laws and rates for the current year are used if no changes have been enacted for future years.

24. (a) A difference caused by the excess of depreciation taken for tax purposes over the depreciation reported for financial statement purposes will result in taxable amounts in the periods that the difference reverses. The deferred tax liability related to this difference at the end of year 2 is calculated by scheduling the taxable amounts that are to occur in each future year because of the temporary difference and by applying enacted tax rates for those years to the amount of taxable amounts scheduled for those years. Deferred tax accounts are classified based on the classification of a related asset or liability. Depreciation relates to plant assets, which

are noncurrent assets. Hence, the entire related deferred tax liability is a noncurrent liability.

25. (d) SFAS 109, ¶27, states, "Deferred tax liabilities and assets shall be adjusted for the effect of a change in tax laws or rates. The effect shall be included in income from continuing operations for the period that includes the enactment date."

26. (b) The balance in a tax liability account is the amount of taxes expected to be paid in the future as a result of the turn-around (reversal) of the temporary difference(s). Because Cable deducted an expense from its income tax before it was reportable in the financial statements, the transaction results in a future tax liability. The amount of temporary difference is multiplied times the future tax rate(s) already enacted into law to arrive at the future tax asset or liability. ($100,000 × .40 = $40,000)

Valuation Allowance

27. (c)

Income taxes payable	$13,000
Plus: Deferred tax expense due to valuation allowance (10% × $20,000)	2,000
Less: Deferred tax benefit due to increase in deferred tax asset ($20,000 – $15,000)	(5,000)
Total income tax expense	$10,000

28. (a) Except for certain areas such as business combinations and quasi-reorganizations, the manner of reporting the tax benefits of an operating loss carryforward or carryback is determined by the source of income or loss in the current year and not by the source of the operating loss carryforward or taxes paid in a prior year (SFAS 109, ¶37). Therefore, the tax benefit of the operating loss in question reduces income tax expense from income from continuing operations because the realization of the tax benefit results from income from continuing operations. If realization of the tax benefit resulted from an extraordinary gain, the tax benefit would have been reported as an extraordinary item.

29. (b) A deferred tax asset (DTA) is recognized for the future benefits of a loss carryforward (SFAS 109). Therefore, Dodd will increase income by $54,000 ($180,000 × 30% future tax rate) when the benefits of the NOL carryforward are recorded by a debit to *Deferred Tax Asset* and a credit to *Benefits of Loss Carryforward* (a component of income tax expense on the income statement). No valuation allowance is required (which would reduce the DTA and the described impact on income) because the company expects the benefits of the loss carryforward to be realized in the future. In addition, the potential gain of $100,000 (i.e., $200,000 offer – $100,000 carrying amount) from the possible sale of the patent should *not* be recognized. Dodd Corp. has not sold the patent as of December 31; it is only considering whether to sell the patent. The excess of fair value over book value of the patent does serve, however, as some positive evidence in evaluating the realizability of the DTA related to the tax loss carryforward.

30. (d) A deferred tax asset is to be recognized for the future tax benefits of a loss carryforward ($90,000 × 30% future tax rate = $27,000). A valuation allowance is to be established only if it is more likely than not that a portion or all of the asset will not be realized. Dorr expects to realize the asset and does not need a valuation allowance.

Balance Sheet Presentation

31. (d) Deferred taxable temporary differences create deferred tax liabilities. SFAS 109 requires that deferred tax items are classified as current or noncurrent based on the related asset or liability. Since the related item is noncurrent, the deferred tax liability is noncurrent.

32. (b) In a classified balance sheet, deferred tax assets (DTA) and liabilities are reported in a net current and a net noncurrent amount. The classification of an individual deferred tax amount is based on the classification of the related asset or liability for financial reporting. The deferred tax liability of $15,000 related to a noncurrent asset is netted with the DTA of $3,000 related to a noncurrent liability for a noncurrent tax liability of $12,000. The DTA of $8,000 related to a current liability is a current tax asset.

33. (b) The classification of each deferred tax amount is based on the classification of the related asset or liability for financial reporting. The deferred tax liability arising from the installment sale is 1/3 current ($450,000 / 3 = $150,000) and 2/3 noncurrent because the related receivable is classified as 1/3 current and 2/3 noncurrent. The deferred tax asset arising from the accrual of warranty costs is 1/3 current ($630,000 / 3 = $210,000) and 2/3 noncurrent because the related warranty obligation is 1/3 current (one-third of the warranty liability comes due within one year of the balance sheet date). $150,000 + $(210,000) = $(60,000) current; $300,000 + $(420,000) = $(120,000) noncurrent

Temporary difference	Future taxable (deductible) amount	Tax rate	Deferred tax liability (asset)
Installment sale	$ 1,500,000	30%	$ 450,000
Accrued costs	(2,100,000)	30%	(630,000)

34. (d) Deferred tax liabilities and assets are classified as current or noncurrent, based on the classification of the related asset or liability (if any) for financial reporting and reported in a net current and a net noncurrent amount. The $75,000 deferred tax liability is reported as noncurrent because there is a related asset classified as noncurrent, and the $25,000 deferred tax asset is reported as current because there is a related asset classified as current.

35. (a) Deferred tax liabilities and assets are classified on the balance sheet as net current or net noncurrent based on the classification of the related asset or liability (SFAS 109). The deferred tax liability related to equipment is all noncurrent because equipment is noncurrent. The deferred tax asset (DTA) resulting from the warranty accrual is part current and part noncurrent because of the classification of the warranty obligation. The deferred compensation liability is all noncurrent, so the related DTA is all noncurrent. Apparently 1/3 of the total installment receivables are in a current classification, so 1/3 of the related deferred tax liability is current. The current amounts (– $3,000 + $3,000 = 0) and the noncurrent amounts are netted ($3,000 – $3,000 – $4,500 + $6,000 = $1,500).

Temporary difference	Future taxable (ded.) amounts	Tax rate	Deferred tax liab (asset)	Classification
Depreciation	$ 10	30%	$ 3	Noncurrent
Warranty accrual	(10)	30%	(3)	Current
Warranty accrual	(10)	30%	(3)	Noncurrent
Deferred comp.	(15)	30%	(4.5)	Noncurrent
Installment sales	10	30%	3	Current
Installment sales	20	30%	6	Noncurrent
Net (in 000's)	$ 5		$1.5	

Income Statement Presentation

36. (a) SFAS 109, ¶35, states, "Income tax expense or benefit for the year shall be allocated among continuing operations, discontinued operations, extraordinary items, and items charged or credited directly to shareholders' equity" such as prior period adjustments, certain changes in accounting principles, and changes in market values of investments in marketable equity securities classified as noncurrent assets.

37. (c)

Income before income taxes and extraordinary item	$ 900,000
Less: Nontaxable gain on life insurance coverage	(100,000)
Income before taxes and taxable extraordinary item	$ 800,000
Times: Applicable tax rate	× 30%
Provision for income taxes	$ 240,000

38. (b) Except for certain areas such as business combinations and quasi-reorganizations, the manner of reporting the tax benefits of an operating loss carryforward or carryback is determined by the source of the income or loss in the current year and *not* by the source of the operating loss carryforward or taxes paid in a prior year. Thus, for example, the tax benefit of an operating loss carryforward reduces income tax expense from continuing operations if realization of the tax benefit results from income from continuing operations; likewise, that tax benefit is reported as an extraordinary item if realization of the tax benefit results from an extraordinary gain.

Equity Method Investments

39. (d) The investor recognizes investment income for financial purposes based on its equity in the investee's earnings; for tax purposes, investment income is recognized on the cash basis when dividends are received. SFAS 109 requires that deferred taxes be recorded on this temporary difference. In this question, we are told to ignore the 80% dividends-received deduction (DRD).

Equity in investee's earnings, book ($225,000 × 40%)	$90,000
Less: Dividends received ($75,000 × 40%)	(30,000)
Temporary difference (without DRD)	60,000
Times: Enacted tax rate for future	× 30%
Increase in deferred tax liability	$18,000

40. (b) $78,000 × 30% = $23,400

Pretax financial income	$100,000
Less: Investment income (book) in excess of dividend income (tax) [$35,000 – ($25,000 × 20%)]	(30,000)
Add: Depreciation recorded in financial statements in excess of tax deduction	8,000
Taxable income	$ 78,000

41. (a) The investor recognizes investment income for financial purposes based on its equity in the investee's earnings; for income tax purposes, investment income is recognized when cash dividends are received. SFAS 109 requires that deferred

income taxes be recorded on this temporary difference which will result in a future taxable amount.

Equity in investee's earnings, book	$180,000
Less: Dividends received	(30,000)
Temporary difference before DRD consideration	150,000
Less: Dividends-received deduction applicable to temporary difference ($150,000 × 80%)	(120,000)
Taxable portion of temporary difference	30,000
Times: Enacted tax rate for future periods	× 30%
Deferred tax liability	$ 9,000

Solution 13-2 ADDITIONAL MULTIPLE CHOICE ANSWERS

Income Reconciliation

42. (c)

Pretax income before depreciation	$ 100,000
Depreciation for tax purposes	(20,000)
Taxable income	80,000
Tax rate expected	× 30%
Current income tax expense	24,000
Estimated tax payments	(0)
Current income tax liability	$ 24,000

43. (a)

Pretax financial income	$ 250,000
Permanent difference—interest	(25,000)
Temporary difference—excess tax depreciation	(75,000)
Taxable income	150,000
Tax rate	30%
Current provision	$ 45,000

Recognition & Measurement

44. (a) SFAS 109 requires that the assets and liability method be used in accounting and reporting for temporary differences between the amount of taxable income and pretax financial income and the tax bases of assets or liabilities and their reported amounts in financial statements. Under this method, a current or deferred tax liability or asset is recognized for the current or deferred tax consequences of all events that have been recognized in the financial statements.

Differences

45. (c) A deferred tax liability is recognized for the amount of deferred tax consequences attributable to temporary differences that will result in taxable amounts in future years. The liability is the amount of taxes that will be payable on those taxable amounts in future years based on the provisions of the tax law. On the other hand, a deferred tax asset is recognized for the amount of deferred tax consequences attributable to temporary differences that will result in tax deductions in future years which will reduce taxes payable in those future years.

46. (c) Expenses that are deductible before or after they are recognized in financial income create a difference between the tax basis of an asset or liability and its reported amount in the financial statements [SFAS 109, ¶11(b) and (d)]. These differences result in taxable or deductible amounts in a future period(s) when the reported amount of the related asset or liability is recovered or settled, respectively. Temporary differences include all existing differences that will result in taxable or deductible amounts in future years.

Deferred Tax Liabilities & Assets

47. (a) The amount of the deferred tax liability to be reported is computed by considering the future tax effects of the temporary difference for depreciation. Since tax depreciation exceeded book depreciation by $25,000, this causes the reported amount of an asset to exceed its tax basis by this amount, thereby resulting in $25,000 of taxable amounts in future years when the asset is recovered through use or sale. The tax effects of the taxable amounts are calculated by applying the presently enacted tax rate of 35% for later years, resulting in a current deferred tax liability of $8,750 (i.e., $25,000 × 35%). The $10,000 of nondeductible book expenses are related to permanent differences. Although the nondeductible book expenses are recognized in financial accounting income, they do not have tax consequences. Therefore, they do not give rise to temporary differences. Thus, the nondeductible book expenses do not affect the calculation of the deferred tax liability.

48. (a) Interest income on municipal obligations is a tax-exempt revenue; therefore, no current or future tax consequences will result and no deferred taxes are recorded for this difference. The $150,000 ($550,000 – $400,000) difference due to depreciation

is the only temporary difference existing at the balance sheet date. It will reverse equally over the next three years, resulting in future taxable amounts of $50,000 ($150,000 / 3). Noll expects to report taxable income in all future periods; therefore, the future taxable amounts are tax effected at the rates scheduled for individual future years.

	Amount	Rate	Def. Tax Liab.
Depreciation			
Year 2	$ 50,000	30%	$15,000
Years 3-4	100,000	25%	25,000
Deferred tax liability			$40,000

49. (c) The revenues recognized in financial income in year 1 that will not be included in taxable income until year 2 represent a future taxable amount. The deferred tax liability that should be reported at 12/31 of year 1 for the temporary difference is computed by multiplying the taxable amount scheduled for year 2 by the enacted tax rate for year 2 ($12,000 × 25% = $3,000).

50. (c) Deferred income tax expense reported for a period is determined by the net change during the year in the deferred tax accounts on the balance sheet. For Quinn, the elimination of the beginning $9,000 net deferred tax asset and the creation of the ending $21,000 ($70,000 cumulative taxable differences × 30% effective income tax rate) net deferred tax liability results in $30,000 of deferred income expense for year 2.

51. (b) The amount of the deferred tax asset is computed by considering the tax effects of the temporary difference for accrued product warranty costs. While product warranty costs are accrued in computing financial income, they are deductible for tax purposes only when they are paid. This causes the amount of a liability (i.e., product warranty liability) to exceed its tax basis (zero) which will result in deductible amounts in future years when the liability is settled. A deferred tax asset should be recognized for the expected tax benefits of the deductible amounts. Because taxable income is expected in all future years, the enacted tax rates for particular years are used to tax effect the individual deductible amounts scheduled to occur in each of those years. Black reports a deferred tax asset of $85,000 [30% ($100,000 + $50,000 + $50,000) + 25% ($100,000)].

PERFORMANCE BY SUBTOPICS

Each category below parallels a subtopic covered in Chapter 13. Record the number and percentage of questions you correctly answered in each subtopic area.

Tax Expense

Question #	Correct √
1	
2	
# Questions	2
# Correct	______
% Correct	______

Income Reconciliation

Question #	Correct √
3	
4	
5	
6	
7	
# Questions	5
# Correct	______
% Correct	______

Differences

Question #	Correct √
8	
9	
10	
11	
12	
# Questions	5
# Correct	______
% Correct	______

Deferred Tax Liabilities & Assets

Question #	Correct √
13	
14	
15	
16	
17	
18	
19	
20	
21	
22	
# Questions	10
# Correct	______
% Correct	______

Tax Rates & Laws

Question #	Correct √
23	
24	
25	
26	
# Questions	4
# Correct	______
% Correct	______

Valuation Allowance

Question #	Correct √
27	
28	
29	
30	
# Questions	4
# Correct	______
% Correct	______

Balance Sheet Presentation

Question #	Correct √
31	
32	
33	
34	
35	
# Questions	5
# Correct	______
% Correct	______

Income Statement Presentation

Question #	Correct √
36	
37	
38	
# Questions	3
# Correct	______
% Correct	______

Equity Method Investments

Question #	Correct √
39	
40	
41	
# Questions	3
# Correct	______
% Correct	______

SIMULATION SOLUTIONS

Solution 13-3

Research

FAS 109, Par. 6

The objectives of accounting for income taxes are to recognize (a) the amount of taxes payable or refundable for the current year and (b) deferred tax liabilities and assets for the future tax consequences of events that have been recognized in an enterprise's financial statements or tax returns.

Responses 1-4

1. B When an asset is depreciated faster for tax purposes than it is depreciated for financial accounting purposes, the temporary difference results in a deferred tax liability. In other words, the current amount due for taxes is less because of the larger depreciation deduction for tax purposes. Temporary differences of this type reverse themselves over time, and the entity has a deferred tax liability in the meantime.

2. A When revenue is received in advance, the temporary difference results in a deferred tax asset. For tax purposes, the revenue is taxable in the period the related cash is received. The revenue is not included in the computation of financial income until the period in which it is earned. In other words, a larger amount of taxes is due for the current period, and is similar to a prepaid expense.

3. C Interest received on an investment in tax-exempt securities is a permanent difference because tax-exempt income is recognized in the financial statements, but does not have tax consequences under the regular U.S. tax system. Therefore, this difference will not reverse in future tax periods.

4. A Costs of guarantees and warranties that are estimated and accrued for financial reporting create a temporary difference that results in a deferred tax asset. Such items will result in deductible amounts in future years for tax purposes when the liability is settled. This is similar to a prepaid expense in that both situations result in assets.

Responses 5-8

5. G

Taxable income	$600,000
Tax rate	× 20%
Current tax expense	$120,000

6. M

Temporary differences, year 1	$200,000
Temporary differences, year 2	100,000
Cumulative temporary differences	$300,000

7. B

Deferred tax liability, year 2	$ 75,000
Deferred tax liability, year 1	(40,000)
Deferred tax expense, year 2	$ 35,000

8. H

Cumulative temporary differences	$450,000
Tax rate	× 30%
Deferred tax liability, April 30, year 3	$135,000

Solution 13-4

Research

FAS 109, Par. 27

27. Deferred tax liabilities and assets shall be adjusted for the effect of a change in tax laws or rates. The effect shall be included in income from continuing operations for the period that includes the enactment date.

Schedule of Interest Expense

Rayne Co.
Schedule of Interest Expense
For the Year Ended December 31, Year 2

Note payable	**$ 6,600**	[1]
Capital lease obligation	**4,750**	[2]
Bonds payable	**26,900**	[3]
Total interest expense	*$38,250*	[4]

[1] 1,800 (90,000 × 8% × 3/12) + 4,800 (80,000 × 8% × 9/12) = $6,600

[2] 10% × 47,500 (62,500 – 15,000) = $4,750

[3] 538,000 × 10% × ½ = $26,900

[4] Sum of notes payable transactions (calculated amount).

Essay—Accounting for Income Taxes

To: Dunn

From: Green

Re: Accounting for income taxes

Below is a brief overview of accounting for income taxes in accordance with FASB 109.

The objectives of accounting for income taxes are to recognize (a) the **amount of taxes payable or refundable for the current year,** and (b) **deferred tax liabilities and assets** for the **estimated future tax consequences** of temporary differences and **carryforwards.** Temporary **differences are differences between the tax basis of assets or liabilities** and their reported **amounts in the financial statements** that will result in taxable or deductible amounts in future years.

Deferred tax assets and liabilities are measured based on the **provisions of enacted tax law;** the effects of future changes in the tax law or rates are not anticipated. The measurement of deferred tax assets is **reduced, if necessary, by a valuation allowance** to reflect the net asset amount that is more likely than not to be realized. Deferred income tax expense or benefit is measured as the **change during the year** in an enterprise's deferred tax liabilities and assets.

Solution 13-5

Research

FAS 109, Par. 47

47. A public enterprise shall disclose a reconciliation using percentages or dollar amounts of (a) the reported amount of income tax expense attributable to continuing operations for the year to (b) the amount of income tax expense that would result from applying domestic federal statutory tax rates to pretax income from continuing operations.

The "statutory" tax rates shall be the regular tax rates if there are alternative tax systems. The estimated amount and the nature of each significant reconciling item shall be disclosed. A nonpublic enterprise shall disclose the nature of significant reconciling items but may omit a numerical reconciliation. If not otherwise evident from the disclosures required by this paragraph and paragraphs 43-46, all enterprises shall disclose the nature and effect of any other significant matters affecting comparability of information for all periods presented.

Income Statement

Powell Corp.
Income Statement
For the Year Ended June 30, Year 2

Revenues:			
Machine sales	$750,000		1
Service revenues	250,000		2
Interest revenue	10,000		3
Total revenues		$1,010,000	4
Expenses:			
Cost of sales—machines	425,000		5
Cost of services	100,000		6
Administrative expenses	300,000		7
Research and development expenses	110,000		8
Interest expense	5,000		9
Loss from asset disposal	40,000		10
Current income tax expense [1]	6,000		11
Deferred income tax expense [2]	4,500		12
Total expenses and losses		(990,500)	13
Income before extraordinary gain		19,500	14
Extraordinary gain, net of income taxes of $75,000		175,000	15
Net income		$ 194,500	16
Earnings (loss) per share:			
Income before extraordinary gain [3]		$ (0.40)	17
Net income		$ 0.47	18

Reconciliation Schedule

Net income		$194,500	19
Add:	Taxes on extraordinary gain	75,000	20
	Provision for income taxes	10,500	21
Financial statement income before income taxes		280,000	22
Permanent difference—officer's life insurance		5,000	23
Temporary difference—excess of tax over financial statement depreciation		(15,000)	24
	Taxable income	$270,000	25

1. Machine sales given in scenario.
2. Service revenues given in scenario.
3. Interest revenue given in scenario.
4. Total revenues: Sum of all sales and revenues ($750,000 + $250,000 + $10,000).
5. Cost of sales given in scenario.
6. Cost of services given in scenario.
7. Administrative expense given in scenario.
8. Research and development expense given in scenario.
9. Interest expense given in scenario.
10. Loss from asset disposal given in scenario.
11. Current tax expense

    ($425,000 + $100,000 + $300,000 + $110,000 + $5,000 + 40,000 = $980,000)

    [($1,010,000 – $980,000 + $5,000 – $15,000) × .30 = $6,000]
12. ($15,000 × .30 = $4,500)
13. Total expenses and losses.
14. Income before extraordinary gain.
15. Extraordinary gain on sale of factory given in scenario net of taxes at 30% ($250,000 × .70)
16. Net income: Income before extraordinary gain plus extraordinary gain.
17. ($19,500 – $100,000) / 200,000 = ($0.40).
18. Net income less stock dividend divided by number of shares outstanding [($194,000 – $100,000) / 200,000].
19. Net income calculated in part A
20. ($250,000 × .30)
21. ($194,500 × .30)
22. Current income tax expense plus deferred income tax expense ($6,000 + $4,500)
23. Permanent difference given in scenario.
24. Temporary difference given in scenario.
25. Total taxable income.

CHAPTER 14

STATEMENT OF CASH FLOWS

I. **Overview** 14-2
   A. Purpose 14-2
   B. Focus 14-2
   C. Content & Form 14-3
   D. Non-Cash Investing & Financing Activities 14-4
   E. Per Share Information 14-4
   F. Preparation 14-4

II. **Receipt & Payment Classification** 14-5
   A. Operating Activities 14-5
   B. Investing Activities 14-6
   C. Financing Activities 14-7

III. **Illustrative Problem** 14-7
   A. Given Information for the Current Year 14-7
   B. Determination of Change in Cash & Cash Equivalents 14-9
   C. Determination of Net Cash Flow From Operating Activities 14-9
   D. Analysis of Nonoperating Accounts 14-11
   E. Direct Method 14-12
   F. Indirect Method 14-14

EXAM COVERAGE: Historically, exam coverage of the topics in Chapter 14 has been 5 to 10 percent of the FAR section. More information regarding exam coverage is included in Appendix B, *Practical Advice*.

CHAPTER 14

STATEMENT OF CASH FLOWS

I. Overview

A. Purpose

A business enterprise that provides a set of financial statements that reports both financial position and results of operations should also provide a statement of cash flows for each period for which results of operations are provided. The primary purpose of a statement of cash flows is to provide relevant information about the cash receipts and cash payments of an enterprise during a period.

1. **Information Use** The information provided in a statement of cash flows helps investors, creditors, and others to assess the following:

   a. The enterprise's ability to generate positive future net cash flows

   b. The enterprise's ability to meet its obligations, its ability to pay dividends, and its needs for external financing

   c. The reasons for differences between net income and associated cash receipts and payments

   d. The effects on an enterprise's financial position of both its cash and non-cash investing and financing transactions during the period

2. **Information to Report** To achieve its purpose of providing information to help investors, creditors, and others make these assessments, a statement of cash flows should report the cash effects during a period of an enterprise's operations, its investing transactions, and its financing transactions. Related disclosures should report the effects of investing and financing transactions that affect an enterprise's financial position, but do **not** directly affect cash flows during the period.

B. Focus

A statement of cash flows should explain the change during the period in cash and cash equivalents.

1. **Cash Equivalents** For purposes of SFAS 95, cash equivalents are short-term, highly liquid investments that are both (a) readily convertible into known amounts of cash and (b) so near their maturity that they present insignificant risk of changes in value because of changes in interest rates. Generally, only investments with original maturities to the entity holding the investment of **three months or less** qualify under this definition. Examples include Treasury bills, commercial paper, and money market funds.

2. **Investments** Cash purchases and sales of investments considered to be cash equivalents generally are part of the enterprise's cash management activities rather than part of its operating, investing, and financing activities, and details of those transactions need **not** be reported in a statement of cash flows.

3. **Policy** An enterprise should establish a policy concerning which short-term, highly liquid investments that satisfy the cash equivalents definition are treated as cash equivalents. An enterprise's policy for determining which items are treated as cash equivalents should be disclosed.

C. Content & Form

1. **Classification of Cash Receipts & Payments** A statement of cash flows should classify cash receipts and cash payments as resulting from investing, financing, or operating activities. A statement of cash flows should report the following:

   a. **Net Cash** Net cash provided or used by operating, investing, and financing activities

   b. **Net Effect** The net effect of those flows on cash and cash equivalents during the period in a manner that reconciles beginning and ending cash and cash equivalents

2. **Reporting Cash Flows From Operating Activities**

   a. **Direct Method** Under this method, enterprises are encouraged to report major classes of gross cash receipts and gross cash payments and their arithmetic sum—the net cash flow from operating activities.

      (1) At a minimum, the following classes of operating cash receipts and payments should be separately reported.

         (a) Cash collected from customers

         (b) Interest and dividends received

         (c) Other operating cash receipts, if any

         (d) Cash paid to employees and other suppliers of goods or services, including suppliers of insurance, advertising, and the like

         (e) Interest paid

         (f) Income taxes paid

         (g) Other operating cash payments, if any

      (2) Enterprises are encouraged to provide further breakdowns of operating cash receipts and payments that they consider meaningful and feasible; for example, a retailer or manufacturer might decide to further divide cash paid to employees and suppliers into payments for costs of inventory and payments for selling, general, and administrative expenses. If the direct method of reporting net cash flow from operating activities is used, a reconciliation of net income to net cash flow from operating activities should be provided in a separate schedule.

   b. **Indirect Method** Net cash flow from operating activities may also be reported under the indirect method by adjusting net income to reconcile it to net cash flow from operating activities. That requires adjusting net income to remove the effects of the following.

      (1) All deferrals of past operating cash receipts and payments, such as changes during the period in inventory and deferred income

      (2) All accruals of expected operating cash receipts and payments, such as changes during the period in receivables and payables

      (3) Items whose cash effects are investing cash flows, such as depreciation and gains and losses on sales of property, plant, and equipment and discontinued operations

      (4) Items whose cash effects are financing cash flows, such as gains and losses on extinguishment of debt

c. **Reconcile Net Income** The reconciliation of net income to net cash flow from operating activities should separately report all major classes of reconciling items. The reconciliation may be either reported within the statement of cash flows or provided in a separate schedule, with the statement of cash flows reporting only the net cash flow from operating activities. In addition, if the indirect method is used, amounts of interest paid (net of amounts capitalized) and income taxes paid during the period should be provided in related disclosures.

3. **Reporting Cash Flows From Investing and Financing Activities** Both investing cash inflows and outflows and financing cash inflows and outflows should be reported **separately** in a statement of cash flows. For example, outlays for acquisitions of property, plant, and equipment should be reported separately from proceeds from sale of property, plant, and equipment; proceeds of borrowings should be reported separately from repayments of debt; and proceeds from issuing stock should be reported separately from outlays to reacquire the enterprise's stock.

D. Non-Cash Investing & Financing Activities

Information about all investing and financing activities of an enterprise during a period that affects recognized assets or liabilities, but does **not** result in cash receipts or cash payments in the period, should be reported in related disclosures.

1. **Examples** Examples of non-cash investing and financing transactions are: converting debt to equity; acquiring assets by assuming *directly related liabilities,* such as purchasing a building by incurring a mortgage to the seller; obtaining an asset by entering into a capital lease; and exchanging non-cash assets or liabilities for other non-cash assets or liabilities.

2. **Cash Portion** If a transaction is part cash and part non-cash, only the cash portion should be reported in a statement of cash flows.

E. Per Share Information

Financial statements should not report an amount of cash flow per share.

F. Preparation

In simple situations, efficient preparation of the statement of cash flows may be accomplished by analysis of transactions and other events, the income statement, the statement of retained earnings, and comparative balance sheets. More complex problems may require a more systematic approach to the preparation of the statement, such as the T-account method or the worksheet method. However, these methods are merely aids in preparing the statement; no formal entries are made in the company's books. **NOTE:** Use of these methods is **not** required to solve CPA exam problems, but may be helpful.

1. **Cash and Cash Equivalents** Determine the change in cash and cash equivalents for the period.

2. **Operating Activities** Determine net cash flow from operating activities either by the direct method or the indirect method.

3. **Nonoperating Accounts** Analyze changes in the nonoperating accounts to determine the effect on cash. Investing and financing activities affecting cash are reported in the statement; significant non-cash investing and financing activities are reported in related disclosures.

4. **Presentation Guidelines**

   a. **Format** Present the above information using the following format for the statement of cash flows:

      (1) Net cash flow from operating activities—direct method or indirect method

      (2) Net cash flow from investing activities

(3) Net cash flow from financing activities

(4) Net increase (decrease) in cash and cash equivalents

(5) Cash and cash equivalents at beginning of year

(6) Cash and cash equivalents at end of year

b. **Disclosures** Report significant non-cash investing and financing activities in related disclosures. In addition, disclose the enterprise's policy for determining which items are treated as cash equivalents.

c. **Reconciliation of Net Income** If the direct method of reporting net cash flow from operating activities is used, provide a reconciliation of net income to net cash flow from operating activities in a separate schedule.

d. **Interest and Income Taxes** If the indirect method is used, amounts of interest paid (net of amounts capitalized) and income taxes paid during the period should be provided in related disclosures.

II. Receipt & Payment Classification

A. Operating Activities

producing delivering gds & svc

1. **Nature** Cash flows from operating activities are generally the cash effects of transactions and other events that enter into the determination of net income. Operating activities generally involve producing and delivering goods and providing services.

2. **Cash Inflows**

a. Cash receipts from sales of goods or services, including receipts from collection or sale of accounts receivable and both short- and long-term notes receivable from customers arising from those sales

b. Cash receipts from returns *on* loans, other debt instruments of other entities, and equity securities—interest and dividends

c. Cash receipts from sales and maturities of trading securities, in accordance with SFAS 115

d. All other cash receipts that do not stem from transactions defined as investing or financing activities, such as amounts received to settle lawsuits; proceeds of insurance settlements except for those that are directly related to investing or financing activities, such as from destruction of a building; and refunds from suppliers

3. **Cash Outflows**

a. Cash payments to acquire materials for manufacture or goods for resale, including principal payments on accounts and both short- and long-term notes payable to suppliers for those materials or goods

b. Cash payments to other suppliers and employees for other goods or services

c. Cash payments to governments for taxes

d. Cash payments to lenders and other creditors for interest

e. Cash payments for purchases of trading securities, per SFAS 115

f. All other cash payments that do not stem from transactions defined as investing or financing activities, such as payments to settle lawsuits, cash contributions to charities, and cash refunds to customers

B. Investing Activities

CASH FLOWS FROM INVESTING ACTIVITIES	
H	HELD TO MATURITY
A	AVAILABLE FOR SALE
P	PROPERTY
P	PLANT
E	EQUIPMENT

1. Nature

a. Making and collecting loans.

b. Acquiring and disposing of property, plant, and equipment, and other productive assets (assets held for or used in the production of goods or services by the enterprise other than materials that are part of the enterprise's inventory).

c. Purchases, sales, and maturities of debt and equity available-for-sale and held-to-maturity securities, in accordance with SFAS 115, and investments in equity securities not covered by SFAS 115. (SFAS 115 does not apply to investments accounted for under the equity method nor to consolidated subsidiaries.)

2. Cash Inflows Receipts from disposing of loans; debt or equity instruments; or property, plant, and equipment including directly related proceeds of insurance settlements, such as the proceeds of insurance on a building that is damaged or destroyed.

a. Receipts from collections or sales of loans made by the enterprise and of other entities' debt instruments (other than cash equivalents) that were purchased by the enterprise and held as available-for-sale or held-to-maturity securities.

b. Receipts from sales of equity instruments of other enterprises, held as available-for-sale securities or securities not covered by SFAS 115.

c. Receipts from sales of property, plant, and equipment, and other productive assets.

3. Cash Outflows

a. Disbursements for loans made by the enterprise.

b. Payments to acquire debt and equity instruments of other entities, to be held as available-for-sale or held-to-maturity securities, or securities not covered by SFAS 115.

c. Payments at the time of purchase, or soon before or after purchase, to acquire property, plant, and equipment, and other productive assets.

(1) Generally, only advance payments, the down payment, or other amounts paid at the time of purchase or soon before or after purchase of property, plant, and equipment and other productive assets are *investing cash outflows.*

(2) Generally, principal payments on seller-financed debt directly related to a purchase of property, plant, and equipment or other productive assets are *financing cash outflows.*

C. Financing Activities

CASH FLOWS FROM FINANCING ACTIVITIES	
PRINC	DEBT PRINCIPAL
DIV	PAY DIVIDENDS
I	ISSUE STOCK
TS	TREASURY STOCK

1. Nature

a. Obtaining resources from owners and providing them with a return on, and a return of, their investment.

b. Borrowing money and repaying amounts borrowed, or otherwise settling the obligation.

c. Obtaining and paying for other resources obtained from creditors on long-term credit.

d. FASB 149 requires cash flows from derivatives that contain a financing component and are accounted for as fair-value or cash-flow hedges, to be classified in the same cash flow category as the items being hedged. When a hedge of an identifiable transaction or event is discontinued, the subsequent cash flows are to be classified consistent with the nature of the instrument.

2. Cash Inflows

a. Proceeds from issuing equity instruments (e.g., common and preferred stock).

b. Proceeds from issuing bonds, mortgages, notes, and from other short- or long-term borrowing.

3. Cash Outflows

a. Payments of dividends or other distributions to owners, including outlays to reacquire the enterprise's equity instruments (e.g., treasury stock).

b. Repayments of amounts borrowed.

c. Other principal payments to creditors who have extended long-term credit.

III. Illustrative Problem

A. Given Information for the Current Year

1. On January 8, the company sold marketable equity securities for cash. These securities had a cost of $9,200.
2. On July 17, three acres of land were sold for cash of $32,000.
3. On September 3, the company purchased equipment for cash.
4. On November 10, bonds payable were issued by the company at par for cash.
5. On December 15, the company declared and paid an $8,000 dividend to common stockholders.
6. General and administrative expenses include $3,000 of bad debt expense.
7. No dividends were received during the year from the 30% owned investee.
8. The company's preferred stock is convertible into common stock at a rate of one share of preferred for two shares of common. The preferred stock and common stock have par values of $2 and $1, respectively.

9. For purposes of the statement of cash flows, the company considers all highly liquid debt instruments purchased with a maturity of three months or less to be cash equivalents.

10. **Required:** Prepare a statement of cash flows for the Wolverine Company.

Exhibit 1 ▸ Income Statement

Wolverine Company
Income Statement Data
For the Year Ended December 31, Current Year

Sales		$ 242,807
Gain on sale of available-for-sale securities		2,400
Equity in earnings of 30% owned company		5,880
Gain on sale of land		10,700
		261,787
Cost of sales	$138,407	
General and administrative expenses	25,010	
Depreciation	1,250	
Interest expense	1,150	
Income taxes	34,952	(200,769)
Net income		$ 61,018

Exhibit 2 ▸ Comparative Balance Sheet

Wolverine Company
Comparative Balance Sheet
December 31, Current Year

	Current Year	Previous Year	Change
Assets			
Cash	$ 46,400	$ 25,300	$ 21,100
Available-for-sale securities	7,300	16,500	(9,200)
Accounts receivable	50,320	25,320	25,000
Allowance for uncollectible accounts	(1,000)	(1,000)	--
Inventory	48,590	31,090	17,500
Investment in 30% owned company	67,100	61,220	5,880
Land	18,700	40,000	(21,300)
Building	79,100	79,100	--
Equipment	81,500	--	81,500
Less accumulated depreciation	(16,250)	(15,000)	(1,250)
Total Assets	$381,760	$262,530	$119,230
Liabilities			
Accounts payable	$ 17,330	$ 21,220	$ (3,890)
Income taxes payable	4,616	--	4,616
Bonds payable	115,000	50,000	65,000
Less unamortized discount	(2,150)	(2,300)	150
Deferred tax liability	846	510	336
Stockholders' Equity			
Preferred stock	--	30,000	(30,000)
Common stock	110,000	80,000	30,000
Retained earnings	136,118	83,100	53,018
Total Liabilities and Stockholders' Equity	$381,760	$262,530	$119,230

B. Determination of Change in Cash & Cash Equivalents
The increase in cash and cash equivalents is $21,100. The marketable equity securities are not considered to be cash equivalents. Cash equivalents are short-term, highly liquid investments, such as Treasury bills, commercial paper, and money market funds.

C. Determination of Net Cash Flow From Operating Activities
This amount is determined by using either the direct method or the indirect method.

1. **Direct Method** Under this method, enterprises report major classes of gross cash receipts and gross cash payments and their arithmetic sum—the net cash flow from operating activities. When the direct method is used, a reconciliation of net income to net cash flow from operating activities should be provided in a separate schedule. Presented below are the Wolverine Company's cash flows from operating activities for the current year ended December 31 using the direct method.

Example 1 ▸ Direct Method of Determining Net Cash From Operating Activities

Wolverine Company
Cash Flows From Operating Activities
For the Year Ended December 31, Current Year
Increase (Decrease) in Cash and Cash Equivalents

Cash flows from operating activities:	
Cash received from customers [1]	$ 214,807
Cash paid for inventory [2]	(159,797)
Cash paid for general and administrative expenses [3]	(22,010)
Interest paid [4]	(1,000)
Income taxes paid [5]	(30,000)
Net cash provided by operating activities	$ 2,000

[1] Cash received from customers is determined by subtracting the increase in accounts receivable (A/R) from sales; the increase in A/R represents sales that were not collected in cash. Under the direct method, the allowance for uncollectible accounts is used to determine cash collected from customers if write-offs occur during the period.

Sales	$ 242,807
Beginning balance of A/R	25,320
Write-offs	(3,000)
Ending balance of A/R	(50,320)
Cash from customers	$ 214,807

[2] The increase in inventory is added to cost of sales to determine inventory purchases. The decrease in accounts payable is added to inventory purchases to determine cash payments for inventory.

Cost of sales	$ 138,407
Add: Increase in inventory	17,500
Inventory purchases	155,907
Add: Decrease in accounts payable	3,890
Cash paid for inventory	$ 159,797

[3]

General & administrative expense	$ 25,010
Bad debt expense	(3,000)
Cash paid for G&A exp.	$ 22,010

[4] The bond discount amortization increased interest expense, but did not involve an outflow of cash; therefore, it is subtracted from interest expense to determine cash payments for interest.

Interest expense	$ 1,150
Less: Bond discount amortization	(150)
Interest paid	$ 1,000

[5] The increase in income taxes payable increased current income tax expense and the increase in the deferred tax liability caused the recognition of deferred income tax expense, but they did not involve an outflow of cash. Therefore, these increases are subtracted from income tax expense to determine cash used to pay income taxes.

Income tax expense	$ 34,952
Less: Increase in income taxes payable	(4,616)
Increase in deferred tax liability	(336)
Income taxes paid	$ 30,000

2. **Indirect Method** Net cash flow from operating activities is reported under this method by converting net income to net cash flow from operating activities. Presented below are the Wolverine Company's cash flows from operating activities for the current year ended December 31 using the indirect method.

Example 2 ▸ Indirect Method of Determining Net Cash From Operating Activities

Wolverine Company
Cash Flows From Operating Activities
For the Year Ended December 31, Current Year
Increase (Decrease) in Cash and Cash Equivalents

Net income		$ 61,018
Adjustments to reconcile net income to net cash provided by operating activities:		
Depreciation [1]	$ 1,250	
Bond discount amortization [1]	150	
Deferred income taxes [1]	336	
Gain on sale of available-for-sale securities [2]	(2,400)	
Gain on sale of land [2]	(10,700)	
Equity in earnings of equity method investee in excess of cash dividends [2]	(5,880)	
Increase in net accounts receivable [3]	(25,000)	
Increase in inventory [4]	(17,500)	
Decrease in accounts payable [5]	(3,890)	
Increase in income taxes payable [6]	4,616	
Total adjustments		(59,018)
Net cash provided by operating activities [7]		$ 2,000

[1] To convert net income to net cash flow from operating activities, non-cash charges to income for depreciation, bond discount amortization, and deferred income taxes are added back to net income because those items did not involve a cash outflow.

[2] The non-cash credits to income for the gain on sale of AFS securities, the gain on sale of land, and the equity in earnings of equity method investee in excess of cash dividends received must be deducted from net income for this conversion because those items did not produce an inflow of cash. The *Available-for-Sale Securities* account is not an operating asset; therefore, the net change in the account is not used to convert net income to net cash flow from operating activities.

[3] The $25,000 [i.e., ($50,320 – $1,000) – ($25,320 – $1,000)] increase in **net** accounts receivable represents sales that were not collected in cash. This amount must be deducted to convert net income to net cash flow from operating activities. Under the indirect method, the allowance for uncollectible accounts is used to determine the change in **net** accounts receivable during the period.

[4] The increase in inventories is an operating use of cash; the incremental investment in inventories reduced cash without increasing cost of sales. This amount must be deducted to convert net income to net cash flow from operating activities.

[5] The decrease in accounts payable is due to cash payments for inventory exceeding the amount of inventory purchases. This amount must be deducted to convert net income to net cash flow from operating activities.

[6] The increase in income taxes payable represents current income tax expense not paid out in cash. This amount must be added to convert net income to net cash flow from operating activities.

[7] When the indirect method is used, amounts of interest paid (net of amounts capitalized) and income taxes paid during the period are provided in related disclosures.

D. Analysis of Nonoperating Accounts

1. **Marketable Equity Securities** The proceeds from the sale resulted in an $11,600 cash inflow due to an investing activity. The $2,400 gain on the sale is a non-cash credit to income; therefore, it does not involve an inflow of cash. The gain on the sale is not used to determine net cash flow from operating activities under the direct method. If the indirect method is used, the gain is deducted from net income to determine net cash flow from operating activities.

Exhibit 3 ▸ Sale of Securities

Cash (to balance)	11,600	
Available-for-Sale Securities (cost from additional information)		9,200
Gain on Sale (from income statement)		2,400

2. **Equity Method Investment** The increase in the account of $5,880 represents Wolverine's equity in the investee's earnings for the year since no cash dividends were received from the investee during the year. This non-cash credit to income is not used to determine net cash flow from operating activities under the direct method. If the indirect method is used, this amount is deducted from net income to determine net cash flow from operating activities.

3. **Land** The decrease in the account is due to the sale of land. The proceeds from the sale resulted in a $32,000 cash inflow due to an investing activity. The $10,700 gain on the sale is a non-cash credit to income; therefore, it does not represent an inflow of cash. The gain on the sale is not used to determine net cash flow from operating activities under the direct method. If the indirect method is used, the gain is deducted from net income to determine net cash flow from operating activities.

4. **Equipment** The $81,500 ($81,500 – $0) purchase of equipment for cash is a cash outflow due to an investing activity.

5. **Accumulated Depreciation** There were no disposals of plant assets during the year; the $1,250 increase in the account is due to additional depreciation expense. Depreciation does not involve a cash outflow. Depreciation is not used to determine net cash flow from operating activities if the direct method is used. If the indirect method is used, depreciation is added to net income to determine net cash flow from operating activities.

6. **Bonds Payable** The $65,000 ($115,000 – $50,000) proceeds from the issuance of bonds payable is a cash inflow due to a financing activity.

7. **Unamortized Bond Discount** The bond discount amortization does not involve an outflow of cash. The bond discount amortization is not used to determine net cash flow from operating activities if the direct method is used. If the indirect method is used, the bond discount amortization is added to net income to determine net cash flow from operating activities.

Exhibit 4 ▸ Interest Expense

Interest Expense (from income statement)	1,150	
Bond Discount ($2,300 – $2,150)		150
Cash (to balance)		1,000

8. **Deferred Tax Liability** The $336 increase in the deferred tax liability resulted in recognition of $336 of deferred income tax expense. The deferred income tax expense do not involve an outflow of cash. The deferred income taxes not used to determine net cash flow from operating activities if the direct method is used. If the indirect method is used, the deferred income taxes are added to net income to determine net cash flow from operating activities.

9. **Preferred and Common Stock** The conversion of $30,000 of preferred stock into common stock is a non-cash financing transaction; therefore, it is reported in related disclosures to the statement.

10. **Retained Earnings** The $8,000 cash dividends paid during the year is a cash outflow due to a financing activity. If the dividends had been declared during the year, but not paid in the year, they would **not** have been reported in the statement of cash flows because their declaration would not have affected cash. Neither the declaration or issuance of a stock dividend nor the appropriation of retained earnings affects the enterprise's assets or liabilities; therefore, these transactions are not investing or financing transactions and need **not** be reported in related disclosures to the statement.

Exhibit 5 ▸ Explanation of Retained Earnings Increase

Retained earnings 1/1	$ 83,100
Add: Net income for the year	61,018
Less: Cash dividends declared in the year	(8,000)
Retained earnings, 12/31	$136,118

E. **Direct Method**

Presented below is the Wolverine Company's statement of cash flows for the current year ended December 31, using the direct method of reporting cash flows from operating activities. Note that the reconciliation of net income to net cash provided by operating activities on the direct-method statement is identical to the data reported in the statement under the heading "Cash Flow from Operating Activities" under the indirect method. (Compare the shaded areas.)

Beg R.E + NY - Div = End R.E

Exhibit 6 ▸ Direct Method Statement of Cash Flows

Wolverine Company
Statement of Cash Flows
For the Year Ended December 31, Current Year
Increase (Decrease) in Cash

Cash flows from operating activities:		
Cash received from customers	$ 214,807	
Cash paid for inventory	(159,797)	
Cash paid for general and administrative expenses	(22,010)	
Interest paid	(1,000)	
Income taxes paid	(30,000)	
Net cash provided by operating activities		$ 2,000
Cash flows from investing activities:		
Proceeds from sale of land	32,000	
Proceeds from sale of available-for-sale securities	11,600	
Purchase of equipment for cash	(81,500)	
Net cash used in investing activities		(37,900)
Cash flows from financing activities:		
Dividends paid	(8,000)	
Proceeds from issuance of bonds payable	65,000	
Net cash provided by financing activities		57,000
Net increase in cash		21,100
Cash at beginning of year		25,300
Cash at end of year		$ 46,400

Reconciliation of net income to net cash provided by operating activities:

Net income		$ 61,018
Adjustments to reconcile net income to net cash provided by operating activities:		
Depreciation	$ 1,250	
Bond discount amortization	150	
Deferred income taxes	336	
Gain on sale of available-for-sale securities	(2,400)	
Gain on sale of land	(10,700)	
Equity in earnings of equity method investee in excess of cash dividends	(5,880)	
Increase in net accounts receivable	(25,000)	
Increase in inventory	(17,500)	
Decrease in accounts payable	(3,890)	
Increase in income taxes payable	4,616	
Total adjustments		(59,018)
Net cash provided by operating activities		$ 2,000

Supplemental schedule of non-cash investing and financing activities:

Additional common stock was issued upon the conversion of $30,000 of preferred stock.

Disclosure of Accounting Policy—For purposes of the statement of cash flows, the Company considers all highly liquid debt instruments purchased with a maturity of three months or less to be cash equivalents.

F. **Indirect Method**

Presented below is the Wolverine Company's statement of cash flows for the current year ended December 31, using the indirect method of reporting cash flows from operating activities.

Exhibit 7 ▶ Indirect Method Statement of Cash Flows

Wolverine Company
Statement of Cash Flows
For the Year Ended December 31, Current Year
Increase (Decrease) in Cash

Cash flows from operating activities:		
Net income		$ 61,018
Adjustments to reconcile net income to net cash provided by operating activities:		
Depreciation	$ 1,250	
Bond discount amortization	150	
Deferred income taxes	336	
Gain on sale of available-for-sale securities	(2,400)	
Gain on sale of land	(10,700)	
Equity in earnings of equity method investee in excess of cash dividends	(5,880)	
Increase in net accounts receivable	(25,000)	
Increase in inventory	(17,500)	
Decrease in accounts payable	(3,890)	
Increase in income taxes payable	4,616	
Total adjustments		(59,018)
Net cash provided by operating activities		2,000
Cash flows from investing activities:		
Proceeds from sale of land	32,000	
Proceeds from sale of available-for-sale securities	11,600	
Purchase of equipment for cash	(81,500)	
Net cash used in investing activities		(37,900)
Cash flows from financing activities:		
Dividend paid	(8,000)	
Proceeds from issuance of bonds payable	65,000	
Net cash provided by financing activities		57,000
Net increase in cash		21,100
Cash at beginning of year		25,300
Cash at end of year		$ 46,400

Supplemental disclosures of cash flow information:

Cash paid during the year for:	
Interest (net of amount capitalized)	$ 1,000
Income taxes	$ 30,000

Supplemental schedule of non-cash investing and financing activities:

Additional common stock was issued upon the conversion of $30,000 of preferred stock.

Disclosure of Accounting Policy—For purposes of the statement of cash flows, the company considers all highly liquid debt instruments purchased with a maturity of three months or less to be cash equivalents.

CHAPTER 14—STATEMENT OF CASH FLOWS

Problem 14-1 MULTIPLE CHOICE QUESTIONS (86 to 108 minutes)

1. The primary purpose of a statement of cash flows is to provide relevant information about
   a. Differences between net income and associated cash receipts and disbursements
   b. An enterprise's ability to generate future positive net cash flows
   c. The cash receipts and cash disbursements of an enterprise during a period
   d. An enterprise's ability to meet cash operating needs (5/94, FAR, #5, 4820)

2. Which is the most appropriate financial statement to use to determine if a company obtained financing during a year by issuing debt or equity securities?
   a. Balance sheet
   b. Statement of cash flows
   c. Statement of changes in stockholders' equity
   d. Income statement (R/03, FAR, #18, 7620)

3. At December 31 of the current year, Kale Co. had the following balances in the accounts it maintains at First State Bank:

Checking account #101	$175,000
Checking account #201	(10,000)
Money market account	25,000
90-day certificate of deposit, due next 2/28	50,000
180-day certificate of deposit, due next 3/15	80,000

Kale classifies investments with original maturities of three months or less as cash equivalents. In its December 31 current year balance sheet, what amount should Kale report as cash and cash equivalents?
   a. $190,000
   b. $200,000
   c. $240,000
   d. $320,000 (5/94, FAR, #13, amended, 4828)

4. Mend Co. purchased a three-month U.S. Treasury bill. Mend's policy is to treat as cash equivalents all highly liquid investments with an original maturity of three months or less when purchased. How should this purchase be reported in Mend's statement of cash flows?
   a. As an outflow from operating activities
   b. As an outflow from investing activities
   c. As an outflow from financing activities
   d. Not reported (11/95, FAR, #47, 6129)

5. Inch Co. had the following balances at December 31, year 2:

Cash in checking account	$ 35,000
Cash in money market account	75,000
U.S. Treasury bill, purchased 12/1, year 2 maturing 2/28, year 3	200,000
U.S. Treasury bill, purchased 12/1, year 1 maturing 5/31, year 3	150,000

Inch's policy is to treat as cash equivalents all highly-liquid investments with a maturity of three months or less when purchased. What amount should Inch report as cash and cash equivalents in its December 31, year 2 balance sheet?
   a. $110,000
   b. $235,000
   c. $310,000
   d. $460,000 (R/00, FAR, #1, amended, 6896)

6. A company's accounts receivable decreased from the beginning to the end of the year. In the company's statement of cash flows (direct method), the cash collected from customers would be
   a. Sales revenues plus accounts receivable at the beginning of the year
   b. Sales revenues plus the decrease in accounts receivable from the beginning to the end of the year
   c. Sales revenues less the decrease in accounts receivable from the beginning to the end of the year
   d. The same as sales revenues (11/88, Theory, #34, 9054)

7. The following information was taken from the current year financial statements of Planet Corp.:

Accounts receivable, January 1	$ 21,600
Accounts receivable, December 31	30,400
Sales on account and cash sales	438,000
Uncollectible accounts	1,000

No accounts receivable were written off or recovered during the year. If the direct method is used in the current year statement of cash flows, Planet should report cash collected from customers as
   a. $447,800
   b. $446,800
   c. $429,200
   d. $428,200 (5/91, PI, #8, amended, 1234)

8. Which of the following is **not** disclosed on the statement of cash flows when prepared under the direct method, either on the face of the statement or in a separate schedule?
a. The major classes of gross cash receipts and gross cash payments
b. The amount of income taxes paid
c. A reconciliation of net income to net cash flow from operations
d. A reconciliation of ending retained earnings to net cash flow from operations
(11/95, FAR, #48, 6130)

9. Duke Co. reported cost of goods sold as $270,000 for the current year. Additional information is as follows:

	December 31	January 1
Inventory	$60,000	$45,000
Accounts payable	26,000	39,000

If Duke uses the direct method, what amount should Duke report as cash paid to suppliers in its current year statement of cash flows?
a. $242,000
b. $268,000
c. $272,000
d. $298,000 (11/93, PI, #9, amended, 4378)

10. Rory's Co.'s prepaid insurance was $50,000 at December 31, year 2, and $25,000 at December 31, year 1. Insurance expense was $20,000 for year 2 and $15,000 for year 1. What amount of cash disbursements for insurance would be reported in Rory's year 2 net cash flows from operating activities presented on a direct basis?
a. $55,000
b. $45,000
c. $30,000
d. $20,000 (11/90, PII, #17, amended, 1238)

11. In its current year income statement, Kilm Co. reported cost of goods sold of $450,000. Changes occurred in several balance sheet accounts as follows:

Inventory	$160,000 decrease
Accounts payable—suppliers	40,000 decrease

What amount should Kilm report as cash paid to suppliers in its current year cash flow statement, prepared under the direct method?
a. $250,000
b. $330,000
c. $570,000
d. $650,000 (5/97, FAR, #3, amended, 6475)

12. A company's wages payable increased from the beginning to the end of the year. In the company's statement of cash flows (direct method), the cash paid for wages would be
a. Salary expense plus wages payable at the beginning of the year
b. Salary expense plus the increase in wages payable from the beginning to the end of the year
c. Salary expense less the increase in wages payable from the beginning to the end of the year
d. The same as salary expense
(5/88, Theory, #31, 1935)

13. In a statement of cash flows, which of the following would increase reported cash flows from operating activities using the direct method? (Ignore income tax considerations.)
a. Dividends received from investments
b. Gain on sale of equipment
c. Gain on early retirement of bonds
d. Change from straight-line to accelerated depreciation (5/92, Theory, #7, 2699)

Items 14 through 18 are based on the following:

Flax Corp. uses the direct method to prepare its statement of cash flows. Flax's trial balances at December 31, year 2 and year 1, are as follows:

	December 31	
	Year 2	Year 1
Debits:		
Cash	$ 35,000	$ 32,000
Accounts receivable	33,000	30,000
Inventory	31,000	47,000
Property, plant, and equipment	100,000	95,000
Unamortized bond discount	4,500	5,000
Cost of goods sold	250,000	380,000
Selling expenses	141,500	172,000
General and administrative expenses	137,000	151,300
Interest expense	4,300	2,600
Income tax expense	20,400	61,200
	$756,700	$976,100
Credits:		
Allowance for uncollectible accounts	$ 1,300	$ 1,100
Accumulated depreciation	16,500	15,000
Trade accounts payable	25,000	17,500
Income taxes payable	21,000	27,100
Deferred income taxes	5,300	4,600
8% callable bonds payable	45,000	20,000
Common stock	50,000	40,000
Additional paid-in capital	9,100	7,500
Retained earnings	44,700	64,600
Sales	538,800	778,700
	$756,700	$976,100

- Flax purchased $5,000 in equipment during year 2.
- Flax allocated one-third of its depreciation expense to selling expenses and the remainder to general and administrative expenses.

What amounts should Flax report in its statement of cash flows for the year ended December 31, year 2, for the following:

14. Cash collected from customers?
a. $541,800
b. $541,600
c. $536,000
d. $535,800 (11/92, PI, #9, amended, 3242)

15. Cash paid for goods to be sold?
a. $258,500
b. $257,500
c. $242,500
d. $226,500 (11/92, PI, #10, amended, 3243)

16. Cash paid for interest?
a. $4,800
b. $4,300
c. $3,800
d. $1,700 (11/92, PI, #11, amended, 3244)

17. Cash paid for income taxes?
a. $25,800
b. $20,400
c. $19,700
d. $15,000 (11/92, PI, #12, amended, 3245)

18. Cash paid for selling expenses?
a. $142,000
b. $141,500
c. $141,000
d. $140,000 (11/92, PI, #13, amended, 3246)

19. Lino Co.'s worksheet for the preparation of its statement of cash flows included the following:

	December 31	January 1
Accounts receivable	$23,000	$29,000
Allowance for uncollectible accounts	1,000	800
Prepaid rent expense	8,200	12,400
Accounts payable	22,400	19,400

Lino's net income is $150,000. What amount should Lino include as net cash provided by operating activities in the statement of cash flows?
a. $151,400
b. $151,000
c. $148,600
d. $145,400 (11/93, PI, #5, amended, 4374)

20. Reed Co.'s current year statement of cash flows reported cash provided from operating activities of $400,000. For the year, depreciation of equipment was $190,000, impairment of goodwill was $5,000, and dividends paid on common stock were $100,000. In Reed's current year statement of cash flows, what amount was reported as net income?
a. $105,000
b. $205,000
c. $305,000
d. $595,000

(R/05, FAR, 0009F, #1, amended, 7745)

21. In its cash flow statement for the current year, Ness Co. reported cash paid for interest of $70,000. Ness did not capitalize any interest during the current year. Changes occurred in several balance sheet accounts as follows:

Accrued interest payable	$17,000 decrease
Prepaid interest	23,000 decrease

In its income statement for the current year, what amount should Ness report as interest expense?
a. $ 30,000
b. $ 64,000
c. $ 76,000
d. $110,000 (R/05, FAR, 0215F, #5, 7749)

22. Karr Inc. reported net income of $300,000 for the year. During the year, Karr sold equipment costing $25,000, with accumulated depreciation of $12,000, for a gain of $5,000. In December, Karr purchased equipment costing $50,000 with $20,000 cash and a 12% note payable of $30,000. Depreciation expense for the year was $52,000. Changes occurred in several balance sheet accounts as follows:

Equipment	$25,000 increase
Accumulated depreciation	40,000 increase
Note payable	30,000 increase

In Karr's statement of cash flows, net cash provided by operating activities should be
a. $340,000
b. $347,000
c. $352,000
d. $357,000 (11/93, PI, #6, amended, 4375)

23. In a statement of cash flows (indirect method), which of the following are subtracted from net income to determine net cash flow from operating activities?

	Increase in accrued interest payable	Depreciation expense
a.	Yes	Yes
b.	Yes	No
c.	No	Yes
d.	No	No

(Editors, 1966)

24. Would the following be added back to net income when reporting operating activities' cash flows by the indirect method?

	Excess of treasury stock acquisition cost over sales proceeds (cost method)	Bond discount amortization
a.	Yes	Yes
b.	No	No
c.	No	Yes
d.	Yes	No

(11/91, Theory, #21, 2529)

25. Which of the following information should be disclosed as supplemental information in the statement of cash flows?

	Cash flow per share	Conversion of debt to equity
a.	Yes	Yes
b.	Yes	No
c.	No	Yes
d.	No	No

(5/95, FAR, #49, 5585)

26. Deed Co. owns 2% of Beck Cosmetic Retailers. A property dividend by Beck consisted of merchandise with a fair value lower than the listed retail price. Deed in turn gave the merchandise to its employees as a holiday bonus. How should Deed report the receipt and distribution of the merchandise in its statement of cash flows?

a. As both an inflow and outflow for operating activities
b. As both an inflow and outflow for investing activities
c. As an inflow for investing activities and outflow for operating activities
d. As a noncash activity (11/92, Theory, #21, 3454)

Items 27 and 28 are based on the following:

A company acquired a building, paying a portion of the purchase price in cash and issuing a mortgage note payable to the seller for the balance.

27. In a statement of cash flows, what amount is included in investing activities for the above transaction?

a. Cash payment
b. Acquisition price
c. Zero
d. Mortgage amount (5/90, Theory, #27, 9052)

28. In a statement of cash flows, what amount is included in financing activities for the above transaction?

a. Cash payment
b. Acquisition price
c. Zero
d. Mortgage amount (5/90, Theory, #28, 9053)

Items 29 and 30 are based on the following:

In preparing its cash flow statement for the current year ended December 31, Reve Co. collected the following data:

Gain on sale of equipment	$ (6,000)
Proceeds from sale of equipment	10,000
Purchase of A.S. Inc. bonds (par value $200,000)	(180,000)
Amortization of bond discount	2,000
Dividends declared	(45,000)
Dividends paid	(38,000)
Proceeds from sale of treasury stock (carrying amount $65,000)	75,000

In its current year December 31 statement of cash flows,

29. What amount should Reve report as net cash used in investing activities?

a. $170,000
b. $176,000
c. $188,000
d. $194,000 (5/95, FAR, #47, amended, 5583)

30. What amount should Reve report as net cash provided by financing activities?

a. $20,000
b. $27,000
c. $30,000
d. $37,000 (5/95, FAR, #48, amended, 5584)

Items 31 through 33 are based on the following:

The differences in Beal Inc.'s balance sheet accounts at December 31, year 2 and year 1 are presented below:

Assets	Increase (Decrease)
Cash and cash equivalents	$ 120,000
Short-term, available-for-sale investments	300,000
Accounts receivable, net	--
Inventory	80,000
Long-term, available-for-sale investments	(100,000)
Plant assets	700,000
Accumulated depreciation	--
	$1,100,000

Liabilities and Stockholders' Equity	
Accounts payable and accrued liabilities	(5,000)
Dividends payable	160,000
Short-term bank debt	325,000
Long-term debt	110,000
Common stock, $10 par	100,000
Additional paid-in capital	120,000
Retained earnings	290,000
	$1,100,000

The following additional information relates to year 2:

- Net income was $790,000.
- Cash dividends of $500,000 were declared.
- Building costing $600,000 and having a carrying amount of $350,000 was sold for $350,000.
- Equipment costing $110,000 was acquired through issuance of long-term debt.
- A long-term investment was sold for $135,000. There were no other transactions affecting long-term investments.
- 10,000 shares of common stock were issued for $22 a share.

In Beal's year 2 statement of cash flows,

31. Net cash provided by operating activities was
a. $1,160,000
b. $1,040,000
c. $ 920,000
d. $ 705,000 (11/91, PI, #5, amended, 2393)

32. Net cash used in investing activities was
a. $1,005,000
b. $1,190,000
c. $1,275,000
d. $1,600,000 (11/91, PI, #6, amended, 2394)

33. Net cash provided by financing activities was
a. $ 20,000
b. $ 45,000
c. $150,000
d. $205,000 (11/91, PI, #7, amended, 2395)

34. Data regarding Ball Corp.'s investment in available-for-sale marketable equity securities follow:

	Cost	Fair Value
December 31, year 1	$150,000	$130,000
December 31, year 2	150,000	160,000

Differences between cost and fair values are considered temporary. The decline in fair value was considered temporary and was properly accounted for at December 31, year 1. Ball's year 2 statement of cash flows would report
a. The receipt of dividends as an investing activity
b. The receipt of dividends as a financing activity
c. Purchases of securities as an investing activity
d. The increase in value as an operating activity (5/91, PI, #18, amended, 0869)

35. Fara Co. reported bonds payable of $47,000 at December 31, year 1, and $50,000 at December 31, year 2. During year 2, Fara issued $20,000 of bonds payable in exchange for equipment. There was no amortization of bond premium or discount during the year. What amount should Fara report in its year 2 statement of cash flows for redemption of bonds payable?
a. $ 3,000
b. $17,000
c. $20,000
d. $23,000 (5/94, FAR, #50, amended, 4865)

36. During the current year, Beck Co. purchased equipment for cash of $47,000, and sold equipment with a $10,000 carrying value for a gain of $5,000. How should these transactions be reported in Beck's current year statement of cash flows?
a. Cash outflow of $32,000
b. Cash outflow of $42,000
c. Cash inflow of $5,000 and cash outflow of $47,000
d. Cash inflow of $15,000 and cash outflow of $47,000 (11/97, FAR, #7, amended, 6487)

37. Alp Inc. had the following activities during the year:

- Acquired 2,000 shares of stock in Maybel Inc. for $26,000
- Sold an investment in Rate Motors for $35,000 when the carrying amount was $33,000
- Acquired a $50,000, 4-year certificate of deposit from a bank (During the year, interest of $3,750 was paid to Alp.)
- Collected dividends of $1,200 on stock investments

In Alp's statement of cash flows, net cash used in investing activities should be
a. $37,250
b. $38,050
c. $39,800
d. $41,000 (5/91, PI, #11, amended, 1237)

38. Karr Inc. reported net income of $300,000 for the current year. During the year, Karr sold equipment costing $25,000, with accumulated depreciation of $12,000, for a gain of $5,000. In December, Karr purchased equipment costing $50,000 with $20,000 cash and a 12% note payable of $30,000. Depreciation expense for the year was $52,000. Changes occurred in several balance sheet accounts as follows:

Equipment	$25,000 increase
Accumulated depreciation	40,000 increase
Note payable	30,000 increase

In Karr's current year statement of cash flows, net cash used in investing activities should be
a. $ 2,000
b. $12,000
c. $22,000
d. $35,000 (11/93, PI, #7, amended, 4376)

39. In a statement of cash flows, if used equipment is sold at a gain, the amount shown as a cash inflow from investing activities equals the carrying amount of the equipment
a. Plus the gain
b. Plus the gain and less the amount of tax attributable to the gain
c. Plus both the gain and the amount of tax attributable to the gain
d. With **no** addition or subtraction
(11/93, Theory, #41, 4546)

40. On July 1, of the current year, Dewey Co. signed a 20-year building lease that it reported as a capital lease. Dewey paid the monthly lease payments when due. How should Dewey report the effect of the lease payments in the financing activities section of its current year statement of cash flows?
a. An inflow equal to the present value of future lease payments at July 1, less current year principal and interest payments
b. An outflow equal to the current year principal and interest payments on the lease
c. An outflow equal to the current year principal payments only
d. The lease payments should **not** be reported in the financing activities section
(11/93, Theory, #42, amended, 4547)

41. In a statement of cash flows, proceeds from issuing equity instruments should be classified as cash inflows from
a. Lending activities
b. Operating activities
c. Investing activities
d. Financing activities (11/89, Theory, #29, 1913)

42. During the current year, Xan Inc. had the following activities related to its financial operations:

Payment for the early retirement of long-term bonds payable (carrying amount $370,000)	$375,000
Distribution of cash dividend declared in previous year to preferred shareholders	31,000
Carrying amount of convertible preferred stock in Xan, converted into common shares	60,000
Proceeds from sale of treasury stock (carrying amount at cost, $43,000)	50,000

In Xan's current year statement of cash flows, net cash used in financing operations should be
a. $265,000
b. $296,000
c. $356,000
d. $358,000 (11/93, PI, #8, amended, 4377)

43. In a statement of cash flows, which of the following items is reported as a cash outflow from financing activities?

I. Payments to retire mortgage notes
II. Interest payments on mortgage notes
III. Dividend payments

a. I, II, and III
b. II and III
c. I only
d. I and III (5/91, Theory, #31, 1902)

SIMULATIONS

Problem 14-2 (25 to 30 minutes)

Research Task | Scenario | Responses

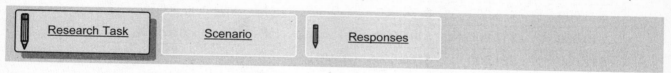

Research Question: What is the FASB guidance concerning reporting the reconciliation under the indirect method?

Paragraph Reference Answer: ______________

Research Task | Scenario | Responses

Following are selected balance sheet accounts of Zach Corp. at December 31, year 2 and year 1, and the increases or decreases in each account from year 1 to year 2. Also presented is selected income statement information for the year ended December 31, year 2, and additional information.

Selected balance sheet accounts	Year 2	Year 1	Increase (Decrease)
Assets:			
Accounts receivable	$ 34,000	$ 24,000	$ 10,000
Property, plant, and equipment	277,000	247,000	30,000
Accumulated depreciation	(178,000)	(167,000)	(11,000)
Liabilities and stockholder's equity:			
Bonds payable	49,000	46,000	3,000
Dividends payable	8,000	5,000	3,000
Common stock, $1 par	22,000	19,000	3,000
Additional paid-in capital	9,000	3,000	6,000
Retained earnings	104,000	91,000	13,000

Selected Information for year 2	
Sales revenue	$155,000
Depreciation	33,000
Gain on sale of equipment	13,000
Net income	28,000

- Accounts receivable relate to sales of merchandise.
- During year 2, equipment costing $40,000 was sold for cash.
- During year 2, $20,000 of bonds payable were issued in exchange for property, plant, and equipment. There was no amortization of bond discount or premium. (11/98, FAR, 00F #2, amended, 9914)

Research Task | Scenario | Responses

Items 1 through 5 represent activities that will be reported in Zach's statement of cash flows for the year ended December 31, year 2. The following two responses are required for each item.

- Determine the amount that should be reported in Zach's year 2 statement of cash flows.
- Using the lists below, determine the amount and category in which the amount should be reported in the statement of cash flows

→

Amount Choices		
$ 0	$13,000	$ 50,000
$ 3,000	$15,000	$ 70,000
$10,000	$17,000	$145,000
$12,000	$31,000	$165,000

Category Choices	
O.	Operating activity
I.	Investing activity
F.	Financing activity

1. $__________ ____ Cash collections from customers (direct method)
2. $__________ ____ Payments for purchase of property, plant, and equipment
3. $__________ ____ Proceeds from sale of equipment
4. $__________ ____ Cash dividends paid
5. $__________ ____ Redemption of bonds payable

Problem 14-3 (7 to 10 minutes)

Research Task | Scenario | Responses

Research Question: What is the primary purpose of the statement of cash flows?

Paragraph Reference Answer: ________________

Research Task | Scenario | Responses

On July 1, year 1, Ring Co. issued $250,000, 14% bonds payable at a premium. The bonds are due in ten years. Interest is payable semiannually every June 30 and December 31. On December 31, year 1 and June 30, year 2, Ring made the semiannual interest payments due and recorded interest expense and amortization of bond premium. With the proceeds of the bond issuance, Ring retired other debt. Ring recorded a gain on the early extinguishment of the other debt. (5/92, PI, #65, amended, 6746)

Research Task | Scenario | Responses

Items 1 through 4 describe amounts that will be reported in Ring's year 1 statement of cash flows prepared using the indirect method or disclosed in the related notes. For each item, select from the following list where the amount should be reported or disclosed. An answer may be selected once, more than once, or not at all. Select the **best** answer for each item.

1. _______ Proceeds received from sale of bonds
2. _______ Interest paid
3. _______ Amortization of bond premium
4. _______ Gain on early extinguishment of debt

O.	Operating Activities
I.	Investing Activities
F.	Financing activities
S.	Supplemental schedule

Problem 14-4 (25 to 30 minutes)

Research Task	Scenario	Additional Information	Responses

Research Question: Standards for cash flow reporting are established in which FASB Statement, and which APB Opinion does it supersede?

Paragraph Reference Answer: ______________

Research Task	Scenario	Additional Information	Responses

The condensed trial balance of Probe Co., a publicly held company, has been adjusted except for income tax expense.

Probe Co.
Condensed Trial Balance

	12/31, year 10 Balances Dr. (Cr.)	12/31, year 9 Balances Dr. (Cr.)	Net change Dr. (Cr.)
Cash	$ 473,000	$ 817,000	$ (344,000)
Accounts receivable, net	670,000	610,000	60,000
Property, plant, and equipment	1,070,000	995,000	75,000
Accumulated depreciation	(345,000)	(280,000)	(65,000)
Dividends payable	(25,000)	(10,000)	(15,000)
Income taxes payable	35,000	(150,000)	185,000
Deferred income tax liability	(42,000)	(42,000)	---
Bonds payable	(500,000)	(1,000,000)	500,000
Unamortized premium on bonds	(71,000)	(150,000)	79,000
Common stock	(350,000)	(150,000)	(200,000)
Additional paid in capital	(430,000)	(375,000)	(55,000)
Retained earnings	(185,000)	(265,000)	80,000
Sales	(2,420,000)		
Cost of sales	1,863,000		
Selling and administrative expenses	220,000		
Interest income	(14,000)		
Interest expense	46,000		
Depreciation	88,000		
Loss on sale of equipment	7,000		
Gain on extinguishment of bonds	(90,000)		
	$ 0	$ 0	$ 300,000

(11/94, FAR, #3, amended, 9911)

Research Task	Scenario	Additional Information	Responses

Additional information:

- During year 10 equipment with an original cost of $50,000 was sold for cash, and equipment costing $125,000 was purchased.
- On January 1, year 10, bonds with a par value of $500,000 and related premium of $75,000 were redeemed. The $1,000 face value, 10% par bonds had been issued on January 1, year 1, to yield 8%. Interest is payable annually every December 31 through year 20.
- Probe's tax payments during year 10 were debited to Income Taxes Payable. In year 9 Probe recorded a deferred income tax liability of $42,000 based on temporary differences of $120,000 and an enacted tax rate of 35%. Probe's year 10 financial statement income before income taxes was greater than its year 10 taxable income, due entirely to temporary differences, by $60,000. Probe's cumulative net taxable temporary differences at December 31, year 10, were $180,000. Probe's enacted tax rate for the current and future years is 30%
- 60,000 shares of common stock, $2.50 par, were outstanding on December 31, year 9. Probe issued an additional 80,000 shares on April 1, year 10. There were no changes to retained earnings other than dividends declared.

For each transaction in **items 1 through 6,** the following two responses are required:

- Determine the amount to be reported in Probe's year 10 statement of cash flows prepared using the indirect method.

Select from the list below where the specific item should be separately reported on the statement of cash flows prepared using the indirect method. Any choice may be used once, more than once, or not at all.

Research Task	Scenario	Additional Information	Responses

Calculation Choices	
$20,000	$115,000
$46,000	$185,000
$50,000	$145,000
$65,000	$255,000
$75,000	$485,000
$95,000	$665,000

Reporting Choices	
O.	Operating
I.	Investing
F.	Financing
S.	Supplementary information
N.	Not reported on Probe's statement of cash flows

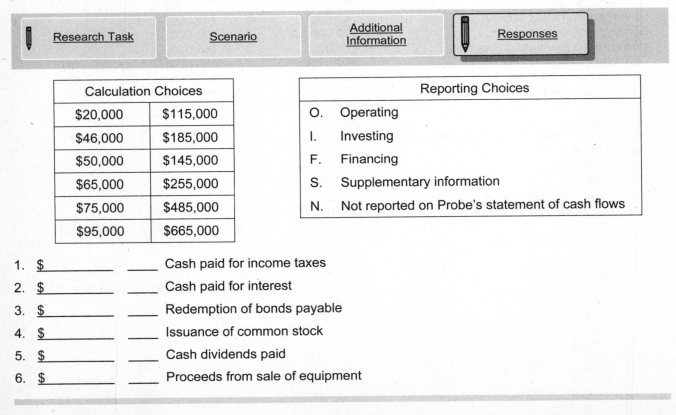

1. $________ ____ Cash paid for income taxes
2. $________ ____ Cash paid for interest
3. $________ ____ Redemption of bonds payable
4. $________ ____ Issuance of common stock
5. $________ ____ Cash dividends paid
6. $________ ____ Proceeds from sale of equipment

Problem 14-5 (40 to 50 minutes)

Research Task	Scenario	Additional Information	Statement of Cash Flows

Research Question: How does the statement of cash flows classify cash receipts and payments?

Paragraph Reference Answer: ______________

Research Task	Scenario	Additional Information	Statement of Cash Flows

Presented below are the balance sheet accounts of Kern Inc. as of December 31, year 4 and year 3, and their net changes.

Assets	Year 4	Year 3	Net change
Cash	$ 471,000	$ 307,000	$ 164,000
Marketable equity securities, at cost	150,000	250,000	(100,000)
Allowance to reduce marketable equity securities to market	(10,000)	(25,000)	15,000
Accounts receivable, net	550,000	515,000	35,000
Inventories	810,000	890,000	(80,000)
Investment in Word Corp., at equity	420,000	390,000	30,000
Property, plant, and equipment	1,145,000	1,070,000	75,000
Accumulated depreciation	(345,000)	(280,000)	(65,000)
Patent, net	109,000	118,000	(9,000)
Total assets	$3,300,000	$3,235,000	$ 65,000
Liabilities and Stockholders' Equity			
Accounts payable and accrued liabilities	$ 845,000	$ 960,000	$(115,000)
Note payable, long-term	600,000	900,000	(300,000)
Deferred tax liability	190,000	190,000	--
Common stock, $10 par value	850,000	650,000	200,000
Additional paid-in capital	230,000	170,000	60,000
Retained earnings	585,000	365,000	220,000
Total liabilities and stockholder's equity	$3,300,000	$3,235,000	$ 65,000

(11/89, PI, #5, amended, 3422)

Research Task	Scenario	Additional Information	Statement of Cash Flows

Additional information:

- On January 2, year 4, Kern sold equipment costing $45,000, with a carrying amount of $28,000, for $18,000 cash.
- On March 31, year 4, Kern sold one of its marketable equity security holdings for $119,000 cash. There were no other transactions involving marketable equity securities.
- On April 15, year 4, Kern issued 20,000 shares of its common stock for cash at $13 per share.

- On July 1, year 4, Kern purchased equipment for $120,000 cash.
- Kern's net income for year 4 is $305,000. Kern paid a cash dividend of $85,000 on October 26, year 4.
- Kern acquired a 20% interest in Word Corp.'s common stock during year 1. There was no goodwill attributable to the investment which is appropriately accounted for by the equity method. Word reported net income of $150,000 for the year ended December 31, year 4. No dividend was paid on Word's common stock during year 4.

Prepare a statement of cash flows for Kern Inc. for the year ended December 31, year 4, using the indirect method. A worksheet is not required.

Research Task	Scenario	Additional Information	Statement of Cash Flows

Kern Inc.
Statement of Cash Flows
For the Year Ended December 31, Year 4
Increase (Decrease) in Cash

Cash flows from operating activities:		
Net income		
Adjustments to reconcile net income to net cash provided by operating activities:		
Depreciation		
Amortization of patent		
Loss on sale of equipment		
Equity in income of Word Corp.		
Gain on sale of marketable equity securities		
Decrease in allowance to reduce marketable equity securities to market		
Increase in accounts receivable		
Decrease in inventories		
Decrease in accounts payable and accrued liabilities		
Net cash provided by operating activities		
Cash flows from investing activities:		
Sale of marketable equity securities		
Sale of equipment		
Purchase of equipment		
Net cash provided by investing activities		
Cash flows from financing activities:		
Issuance of common stock		
Cash dividend paid		
Payment on note payable		
Net cash used in financing activities		
Net increase in cash		
Cash at beginning of year		307,000
Cash at end of year		

Problem 14-6 (40 to 50 minutes)

Scenario	Additional Information	Statement of Cash Flows	Reconciliation of Net Income

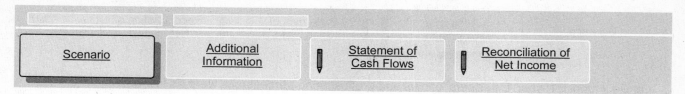

Presented below are the condensed statement of income for the year ended December 31, year 2, and the condensed statements of financial position of Linden Consulting Associates as of December 31, year 2 and year 1.

Linden Consulting Associates
Condensed Statement of Income
For the Year Ended December 31, Year 2

Fee revenue	$ 2,664,000
Operating expenses	(1,940,000)
Operating income	724,000
Equity in earnings of Zach, Inc.	
(net of $4,000 amortization of	
excess of cost over book value)	176,000
Net income	$ 900,000

Linden Consulting Associates
Condensed Statements of Financial Position
December 31, Year 2 and Year 1

Assets	Year 2	Year 1	Net change increase (decrease)
Cash	$ 652,000	$ 280,000	$372,000
Accounts receivable, net	446,000	368,000	78,000
Investment in Zach Inc., at equity	550,000	466,000	84,000
Property and equipment	1,270,000	1,100,000	170,000
Accumulated depreciation	(190,000)	(130,000)	(60,000)
Excess of cost over book value of investment in Zach Inc. (net)	152,000	156,000	(4,000)
Total assets	$2,880,000	$2,240,000	$640,000
Liabilities and Partners' Equity			
Accounts payable and accrued expenses	$ 320,000	$ 270,000	$ 50,000
Mortgage payable	250,000	270,000	(20,000)
Partners' equity	2,310,000	1,700,000	610,000
Total liabilities and partners' equity	$2,880,000	$2,240,000	$640,000

(11/90, PI, #5, amended, 9911)

a. Using the direct method, prepare Linden's statement of cash flows for the year ended December 31, year 2.

b. Prepare a reconciliation of net income to net cash provided by operating activities.

c. Prepare an analysis of changes in partners' capital accounts for the year ended December 31, year 2.

Scenario	Additional Information	Statement of Cash Flows	Reconciliation of Net Income

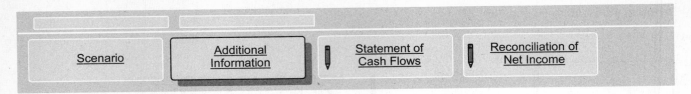

- On December 31, year 1, partners' capital and profit sharing percentages were as follows:

	Capital	Profit sharing %
Garr	$1,020,000	60%
Pat	680,000	40%
	$1,700,000	

- On January 1, year 2, Garr and Pat admitted Scott to the partnership for a cash payment of $340,000 to Linden Consulting Associates as the agreed amount of Scott's beginning capital account. In addition, Scott paid a $50,000 cash bonus directly to Garr and Pat. This amount was divided $30,000 to Garr and $20,000 to Pat. The new profit sharing arrangement is as follows:

Garr	50%
Pat	30%
Scott	20%

- On October 1, year 2, Linden purchased and paid for an office computer costing $170,000, including $15,000 for sales tax, delivery, and installation. There were no dispositions of property and equipment during year 2.
- Throughout year 2, Linden owned 25% of Zach Inc.'s, common stock. As a result of this ownership interest, Linden can exercise significant influence over Zach's operating and financial policies. During year 2, Zach paid dividends totaling $384,000 and reported net income of $720,000. Linden's year 2 amortization of excess of cost over book value in Zach was $4,000.
- Partners' drawings for year 2 were as follows:

Garr	$ 280,000
Pat	200,000
Scott	150,000
	$ 630,000

Scenario	Additional Information	Statement of Cash Flows	Reconciliation of Net Income

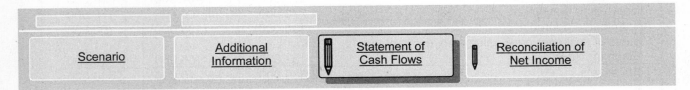

Linden Consulting Associates
Statement of Cash Flows
For the Year Ended December 31, Year 2
Increase (Decrease) in Cash

Cash flows from operating activities:		
Cash received from customers		
Cash paid to suppliers and employees		
Dividends received from affiliate		
Net cash provided by operating activities		
Cash flows from investing activities:		
Purchased property and equipment		

Cash flows from financing activities:		
Principal payment of mortgage payable		
Proceeds for admission of new partner		
Drawings against partners' capital accounts		
Net cash used in financing activities		
Net increase in cash		
Cash at beginning of year		
Cash at end of year		

Scenario | Additional Information | Statement of Cash Flows | Reconciliation of Net Income

Linden Consulting Associates
Reconciliation of Net Income to Net Cash Provided by Operating Activities
For the Year Ended December 31, Year 2

Net income		
Adjustments to reconcile net income to net cash provided by operating activities:		
Depreciation and amortization		
Undistributed earnings of affiliate		
Change in assets and liabilities:		
Increase in accounts receivable		
Increase in accounts payable and accrued expenses		
Total adjustments		
Net cash provided by operating activities		

Analysis of Partners' Changes | Research Task

Linden Consulting Associates
Analysis of Changes in Partners' Capital Accounts
For the Year Ended December 31, Year 2

	Total	Garr	Pat	Scott
Balance, December 31, Year 1				
Capital investment				
Allocation of net income				
Balance before drawings				
Drawings				
Balance, December 31, Year 2				

Analysis of Partners' Changes	Research Task

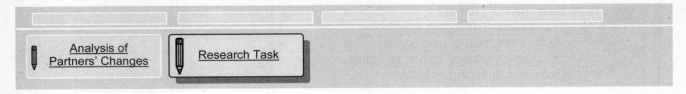

Research Question: What are the three things the information in a statement of cash flows should help investors, creditors, and others to assess?

Paragraph Reference Answer: ______________

Solution 14-1 MULTIPLE CHOICE ANSWERS

Purpose

1. (c) The primary purpose of a statement of cash flows is to provide relevant information about the cash receipts and cash disbursements of an enterprise during a period.

2. (b) The primary purpose of a statement of cash flows is to provide relevant information about the cash receipts and cash payments of an enterprise during a period. The information provided in a statement of cash flows helps investors, creditors, and others to assess the effects on an enterprise's financial position of both its cash and non-cash investing and financing transactions during the period. Related disclosures should report the effects of investing and financing transactions that affect an enterprise's financial position, but do **not** directly affect cash flows during the period. Neither the balance sheet nor the income statement would show changes in the balances of debt or equity accounts. The statement of changes in stockholders' equity would not indicate changes in debt accounts.

Cash Equivalents

3. (c)

Checking account #101	$175,000
Checking account #201	(10,000)
Money market account	25,000
90-day certificate of deposit	50,000
Cash and cash equivalents	$240,000

4. (d) The exchange of cash for a cash equivalent is not reported on the Statement of Cash Flows.

5. (c) Cash is by definition the most liquid asset of an enterprise; thus, it is usually the first item presented in the current assets section of the balance sheet. The U.S. Treasury bill purchased on 12/1, year 1, is not a cash equivalent because the maturity of the instrument was more than three months from the purchase date.

Cash in checking account	$ 35,000
Cash in money market account	75,000
U.S. Treasury Bill purchased 12/1, year 2	200,000
Total cash and cash equivalents on 12/31, year 2	$ 310,000

Direct Method

6. (b) Accounts receivable have decreased from the beginning to the end of the year, which means that cash collected from customers is greater than sales revenues reported on an accrual basis. The cash collected from customers is determined by adding the decrease in accounts receivable from the beginning to the end of the year to sales revenues.

7. (c) Accounts receivable have increased by $8,800 (i.e., $30,400 – $21,600) from the beginning to the end of the year, which means that cash collected from customers is less than the sales revenues reported on the accrual basis by this amount. Thus, the amount of cash collected from customers is $429,200 (i.e., $438,000 – $8,800). (It is important to note that since the direct method is used to determine cash flows from operating activities, the *Allowance for Uncollectible Accounts* is not used in determining cash collected from customers.)

8. (d) A reconciliation of ending retained earnings to net cash flow from operations is not disclosed on the Statement of Cash Flows under either method. The major classes of gross cash receipts and payments, the amount of income taxes paid, and a reconciliation of net income to net cash flow from operations all appear on the face of the Statement of Cash Flows or in a separate schedule when the direct method is used.

9. (d) Inventories have increased by $15,000 (i.e., $60,000 – $45,000) from the beginning to the end of the year, which means that inventory purchases were greater than cost of goods sold by this amount. Thus, the amount of inventory purchases is $285,000 (i.e., $270,000 + $15,000). Accounts payable have decreased by $13,000 (i.e., $39,000 –

$26,000) from the beginning to the end of the year, which means that cash payments for inventories were greater than inventory purchases by this amount. The amount of cash paid to suppliers for inventories is $298,000 (i.e., $285,000 + $13,000).

10. (b)

Insurance expense for year 2	$ 20,000
Increase in prepaid insurance ($50,000 – $25,000)	25,000
Cash disbursements for insurance in year 2	$ 45,000

11. (b)

Cost of sales	$ 450,000
Less: Decrease in inventory	(160,000)
Inventory purchases	290,000
Add: Decrease in accounts payable	40,000
Cash paid to suppliers	$ 330,000

12. (c) Wages payable have increased from the beginning to the end of the year, which means that a portion of the salaries has not been paid. Therefore, wages paid are less than salary expense reported on an accrual basis by the amount of the increase in wages payable from the beginning to the end of the year.

13. (a) Cash dividends received from investments produce a cash inflow due to operating activities so they increase the reported cash flow from operating activities using the direct method. The proceeds from the sale of equipment are to be classified as an inflow from investing activities; any associated gain on the sale will not impact the reported cash flows from operating activities using the direct method. The payment to retire bonds is a cash outflow due to financing activities; any associated gain will not impact the reported cash flows from operating activities using the direct method. A change from the straight-line method to an accelerated depreciation method does not affect cash nor does it impact the computation of net cash flows from operating activities using the direct method.

Content & Form

14. (d) Accounts receivable have increased by $3,000 (i.e., $33,000 – $30,000) from the beginning to the end of the year, which means that cash collected from customers is less than the sales revenues reported on the accrual basis by this amount. Thus, the amount of cash collected from customers is $535,800 (i.e., $538,800 – $3,000). (It is important to note that since the direct method is used to determine cash flows from operating activities, the *Allowance for Uncollectible Accounts* is not netted against *Accounts Receivable* in determining cash collected from customers.)

15. (d) Inventories have decreased by $16,000 (i.e., $47,000 – $31,000) from the beginning to the end of the year, which means that inventory purchases were less than cost of goods sold by this amount. Thus, the amount of inventory purchases is $234,000 (i.e., $250,000 – $16,000). Accounts payable have increased by $7,500 (i.e., $25,000 – $17,500) from the beginning to the end of the year, which means that cash payments for inventories were less than inventory purchases by this amount. Thus, the amount of cash paid for inventories is $226,500 (i.e., $234,000 – $7,500).

16. (c) Unamortized bond discount decreased by $500 (i.e., $5,000 – $4,500) from the beginning to the end of the year. The bond discount amortization decreases net income (because of the increase in interest expense) but has no affect on cash. Therefore, the amount of cash paid for interest is $3,800 (i.e., $4,300 – $500).

17. (a) Since income taxes payable decreased from the beginning to the end of the year, the amount of cash paid for income taxes is greater than income tax expense reported on an accrual basis by this amount. The increase in deferred income taxes is a noncash expense (i.e., it increases income tax expense but has no affect on cash), therefore it is subtracted from income tax expense to determine the amount of cash paid for income taxes.

Income tax expense	$ 20,400
Add: Decrease in income taxes payable ($27,100 – $21,000)	6,100
Less: Increase in deferred income taxes ($5,300 – $4,600)	(700)
Cash paid for income taxes	$ 25,800

18. (c)

Selling expenses	$ 141,500
Less: Allocated portion of depreciation expense [($16,500 – $15,000) / 3]	(500)
Cash paid for selling expenses	$ 141,000

Indirect Method

19. (a) The increase in net A/R represents sales that were not collected in cash; therefore, this amount must be subtracted from net income to compute net cash from operating activities. The decrease in prepaid rent expense represents expenses recognized that were not paid in cash, and thus must be added for the adjustment. The increase in A/P represents purchases that were not paid out in cash, and thus must be added for the adjustment.

Net income		$150,000
Increase in net accounts receivable ($29,000 – $1,000) – ($23,000 – $800)]	$ (5,800)	
Decrease in prepaid rent expense ($12,400 – $8,200)	4,200	
Increase in accounts payable ($22,400 – $19,400)	3,000	
Adjustments		1,400
Net cash provided by operating activities		$151,400

20. (b) Net cash provided by operating activities is adjusted to remove the effects of depreciation expense and goodwill impairment (see editor's note) expense. ($400,000 – $190,000 – $5,000 = $205,000) Dividends paid on common stock are not reported in operating activities.

21. (c) Prepaid expenses are expenses that have been paid, but not yet incurred. A decrease in the Prepaid Interest account indicates that Ness incurred interest expenses of $23,000 during the year. The journal entry would be a debit to Interest Expense $23,000 and a credit to Prepaid Interest $23,000, thus increasing interest expense for the year. It was not included in the $70,000 because no cash was paid out during the year.

Accrued Interest Payable is interest that has been incurred (previously Debited to Interest Expense), but has not been paid. A decrease in the Accrued Interest Payable account would indicate that cash was paid out during the year for the accrued interest. The journal entry would be a debit to Accrued Interest Payable and a credit to Cash. In the direct method of reporting cash flows, accrued interest payable was included in the $70,000 because cash was paid out, but should not be included in the current year's interest expense since it was expensed in a prior period.

$ 70,000
+ 23,000
– 17,000
$ 76,000

22. (b) Depreciation is a noncash expense; therefore, it is added back to net income to compute net cash provided by operating activities. The gain on the sale of equipment was added to determine net income, but it did not represent an inflow of cash. Therefore, the gain must be subtracted for the adjustment.

Net income		$ 300,000
Depreciation expense	$ 52,000	
Gain on sale of equipment	(5,000)	
Adjustments		47,000
Net cash provided by operating activities		$ 347,000

23. (d) When accrued interest payable increases during a period, interest expense on a cash basis is less than interest expense on an accrual basis, because cash interest payments are less than interest expense reported on an accrual basis. To convert net income to net cash flow from operating activities, the increase in accrued interest payable must be added. Depreciation is a noncash expense which was deducted in arriving at net income. Thus, it must be added back to net income to determine net cash flow from operating activities.

24. (c) When using the cost method, an excess of treasury stock acquisition cost over sales proceeds is recorded by a charge to an additional paid-in capital account or to the *Retained Earnings* account, **not** an income statement account. Therefore, this "loss" is **not** an adjustment in converting net income on an accrual basis to net cash provided by operating activities. The amortization of bond discount decreases net income (because of the increase in interest expense) but has no effect on cash. Thus, it is added to net income when using the indirect method of computing net cash provided by operating activities.

Non-Cash Investing & Financing Activities

25. (c) SFAS 95, ¶33, states, "Financial statements shall not report an amount of cash flow per share." The conversion of debt to equity is a noncash financing activity because the transaction affects the enterprise's liabilities but it does not result in cash receipts or payments during the period. The conversion of debt to equity should be disclosed as supplemental information in the statement of cash flows (*ibid.*, ¶32).

26. (d) The receipt and distribution of the merchandise affected recognized assets but did not result in cash receipts or cash payments in the period. Hence, it should be reported in the statement of cash flows as a noncash activity.

Classification

27. (a) To answer this question, reconstruct separate journal entries for the portion of the building acquired by issuing the mortgage note payable to the seller and the portion of the building acquired by paying cash.

Building	XX	
Mortgage Note Payable		XX
Building	XX	
Cash		XX

The portion of the building acquired by issuing the mortgage note payable to the seller (i.e., a seller-financed debt) is a noncash investing and financing activity. This portion of the transaction affects the enterprise's recognized assets and liabilities, but it does not result in cash receipts or payments. Therefore, this portion of the transaction should be reported in related disclosures and not in the body of the statement of cash flows. The portion of the building acquired by paying cash should be reported as a cash outflow due to an investing activity. Cash outflows for investing activities include payments at the time of purchase to acquire PP&E.

28. (c) The portion of the building acquired by paying cash should be reported as a cash outflow due to an investing activity. The portion of the building acquired by issuing the mortgage note payable to the seller (i.e., a seller-financed debt) is a noncash investing and financing activity. This portion of the transaction affects the enterprise's recognized assets and liabilities, but it does not result in cash receipts or payments. Therefore, this portion of the transaction should be reported in related disclosures and not in the statement body.

29. (a) If an exam question does not specify that a debt or equity investment is a cash equivalent or classed as a trading security, then the cash flows from the purchase, sale, or maturity should be classed as cash flows from investing activities.

Purchase of bond investment	$ 180,000
Proceeds from sale of equipment	(10,000)
Net cash used in investing activities	$ 170,000

30. (d)

Proceeds from sale of treasury stock	$ 75,000
Dividends paid	(38,000)
Net cash provided by financing activities	$ 37,000

31. (c) There was no change in the balance of the *Accumulated Depreciation* account in year 2. Therefore, year 2 depreciation expense equals the amount of accumulated depreciation removed from the account due to the sale of the building (i.e., $600,000 – $350,000 = $250,000).

Net income		$ 790,000
Depreciation expense	$ 250,000	
Gain on sale of long-term investment ($135,000 – $100,000)	(35,000)	
Increase in inventories	(80,000)	
Decrease in accounts payable	(5,000)	
Adjustments		130,000
Net cash provided by operating activities		$ 920,000

32. (a)

Net increase in plant assets during year 2 (given)	$ 700,000
Add: Cost of building sold during year 2	600,000
Less: Cost of equipment acquired through issuance of long-term debt (i.e., a noncash investing and financing transaction)	(110,000)
Purchases of plant assets for cash during year 2	$ 1,190,000

Purchase of short-term, available-for-sale investments	$ (300,000)
Proceeds from sale of long-term investment	135,000
Proceeds from sale of building	350,000
Purchase of plant assets (see above)	(1,190,000)
Net cash used in investing activities	$(1,005,000)

33. (d)

Cash dividends paid in year 2 ($500,000 – $160,000)	$(340,000)
Proceeds from common stock issue (10,000 × $22)	220,000
Proceeds from short-term bank debt	325,000
Net cash provided by financing activities	$ 205,000

34. (c) For available-for-sale securities, the cash flow statement shows purchasing activities as an investing activity. Receipt of dividends and interest is always reported as an operating activity. Purchases, sales, and maturities of trading securities are classified as operating activities.

Operating Activities

35. (b) The redemption amount can be determined by analysis of the *Bonds Payable* account.

Bonds Payable

		47,000	Balance, 1/1 (given)
Redemption	17,000	20,000	New bond issue (given)
		50,000	Balance, 12/31 (given)

Investing Activities

36. (d) The purchase of equipment is reported as a cash outflow of $47,000 and the receipt of $15,000 cash from the sale of equipment ($10,000 carrying value plus the gain of $5,000) is reported as a cash inflow of $15,000 in the investing activities section of the statement of cash flows. Investing cash inflows and outflows should be reported separately in a statement of cash flows.

37. (d) The cash receipts from interest ($3,750) and dividends ($1,200) are cash inflows from operating activities (SFAS 95, ¶27).

Payment to acquire 2,000 shares of Maybel stock	$ (26,000)
Proceeds from sale of investment in Rate Motors	35,000
Payment to acquire a certificate of deposit	(50,000)
Net cash used in investing activities	$ (41,000)

38. (a) In order to compute the net cash used in investing activities, the proceeds Karr received from the sale of the equipment must be computed. The carrying amount of the equipment sold was $13,000 (i.e., $25,000 cost minus $12,000 accumulated depreciation). Since the sale resulted in $5,000 gain, the proceeds Karr received from the sale were $18,000 (i.e., $13,000 carrying amount of equipment plus $5,000 gain recognized). Karr reports the $18,000 proceeds from the sale of the equipment as a cash inflow due to an investing activity in the statement of cash flows. In addition, Karr purchased equipment costing $50,000 with $20,000 cash and a 12% note payable of $30,000. Since this transaction is part cash and part noncash, only the cash portion is reported in the statement of cash flows. Karr reports the $20,000 paid at the time of purchase to acquire the equipment as a cash outflow due to an investing activity.

Cash paid for purchase of equipment	$ 20,000
Less: Proceeds from sale of equipment	(18,000)
Net cash used in investing activities	$ 2,000

39. (a) In the statement of cash flows, proceeds from the sale of used equipment should be reported as a cash inflow due to an investing activity. Since the equipment was sold at a gain, the amount of the proceeds would equal the equipment's carrying amount plus the gain recognized on disposal. The income tax effect of the gain on disposal does not affect the amount reported in the investing section because all income taxes are to be classified as an operating activity on a statement of cash flows (see SFAS 95, ¶91-92).

Financing Activities

40. (c) Capital lease payments are comprised of interest expense and a reduction of principal. Cash outflows for financing activities include principal payments to creditors who have extended long-term credit (SFAS 95, ¶20). Therefore, the amount of the capital lease payments that consist of principal payments is reported in the statement of cash flows as a cash outflow for financing activities. Cash outflows for operating activities include cash payments to lenders and other creditors for interest (¶23). Therefore, the amount of the capital lease payments that consist of interest payments should be reported as a cash outflow for operating activities in the statement of cash flows.

41. (d) Cash inflows from financing activities are (1) proceeds from issuing equity instruments and (2) proceeds from issuing bonds, mortgages, notes, and from other short- or long-term borrowing (SFAS 95, ¶19).

42. (c) Cash inflows from financing activities include proceeds from issuing equity securities (e.g., treasury stock). Cash outflows for financing activities include payments of dividends and repayments of amounts borrowed. Conversion of preferred stock into common stock is a *noncash* financing activity.

Payment for early retirement of bonds payable	$(375,000)
Payment of preferred stock dividend	(31,000)
Proceeds from sale of treasury stock	50,000
Net cash used in financing operations	$(356,000)

43. (d) Cash outflows from financing activities include payments of amounts borrowed and payments of dividends to owners. Interest payments, interest receipts, and dividends received are all operating activities.

PERFORMANCE BY SUBTOPICS

Each category below parallels a subtopic covered in Chapter 14. Record the number and percentage of questions you correctly answered in each subtopic area.

Purpose

Question #	Correct √
1	
2	
# Questions	2
# Correct	
% Correct	

Cash Equivalents

Question #	Correct √
3	
4	
5	
# Questions	3
# Correct	
% Correct	

Direct Method

Question #	Correct √
6	
7	
8	
9	
10	
11	
12	
13	
# Questions	8
# Correct	
% Correct	

Content & Form

Question #	Correct √
14	
15	
16	
17	
18	
# Questions	5
# Correct	
% Correct	

Indirect Method

Question #	Correct √
19	
20	
21	
22	
23	
24	
# Questions	6
# Correct	
% Correct	

Non-Cash Investing & Financing Activities

Question #	Correct √
25	
26	
# Questions	2
# Correct	
% Correct	

Classification

Question #	Correct √
27	
28	
29	
30	
31	
32	
33	
34	
# Questions	8
# Correct	
% Correct	

Operating Activities

Question #	Correct √
35	
# Questions	1
# Correct	
% Correct	

Investing Activities

Question #	Correct √
36	
37	
38	
39	
# Questions	4
# Correct	
% Correct	

Financing Activities

Question #	Correct √
40	
41	
42	
43	
# Questions	4
# Correct	
% Correct	

SIMULATION SOLUTIONS

Solution 14-2

Research

FAS 95, Par. 30

30. If the direct method of reporting net cash flow from operating activities is used, the reconciliation of net income to net cash flow from operating activities shall be provided in a separate schedule. If the indirect method is used, the reconciliation may be either reported within the statement of cash flows or provided in a separate schedule, with the statement of cash flows reporting only the net cash flow from operating activities. If the reconciliation is presented in the statement of cash flows, all adjustments to net income to determine net cash flow from operating activities shall be clearly identified as reconciling items.

Responses

1. $145,000, O

Accounts receivable have increased from the beginning to the end of the year, which means that cash collections from customers is less than sales revenues. The cash collections from customers is determined by subtracting the increase in accounts receivable from the beginning to the end of the year from sales revenues (i.e., $155,000 – $10,000 = $145,000). In the statement of cash flows, cash collections from customers are reported as cash inflows from *operating* activities.

2. $50,000, I

Payments for property, plant, and equipment are reported as cash outflows for *investing* activities.

Plant assets, 12/31, year 2		$277,000
Plant assets, 12/31, year 1	$247,000	
Less: Cost of equipment sold for cash	(40,000)	
Add: Plant assets acquired in exchange for bonds payable	20,000	
Less: Plant assets before consideration of year 2 purchases		227,000
Plant assets purchased for cash (forced)		$ 50,000

3. $31,000, I

Proceeds from the sale of equipment are reported as cash inflows from investing activities.

Depreciation	$ 33,000
Less: Net increase in accumulated depreciation	(11,000)
Accumulated depreciation on equipment sold	$ 22,000

Cost of equipment sold	$ 40,000
Less: Accumulated depreciation on equipment sold	(22,000)
Carrying amount of equipment sold	18,000
Gain on sale of equipment	13,000
Proceeds from sale of equipment	$ 31,000

4. $12,000, F

Cash dividends paid are reported as cash outflows for *financing* activities.

Net income	$ 28,000
Less: Increase in retained earnings	(13,000)
Dividends declared	15,000
Less: Increase in dividends payable	(3,000)
Cash dividends paid	$ 12,000

5. $17,000, F

Cash payments for the redemption of bonds payable are reported as cash outflows for *financing* activities.

B/P issued in exchange for plant assets	$20,000
Less: Increase in bonds payable (B/P)	(3,000)
Cash paid for bond redemption	$17,000

Solution 14-3

Research

FAS 95, Par. 4

4. The primary purpose of a statement of cash flows is to provide relevant information about the cash receipts and cash payments of an enterprise during a period.

Responses

1. F The proceeds received from the sale of bonds are reported in the financing section of the statement of cash flows.

2. S Under the indirect method, interest paid is provided in related disclosures. The net income amount shown in the operating section is net of interest paid and income taxes paid; so separate disclosure is needed for the statement to reflect this information.

3. O Under the indirect method, amortization of bond premium is shown in the statement of cash flows as an adjustment to net income in the operating section.

4. O Under the indirect method, items whose cash effects are financing cash flows, such as gain on early debt extinguishment, are shown in the statement of cash flows as adjustments to net income in the operating section.

Solution 14-4

Research

FAS 95, Par. 1

1. This Statement establishes standards for providing a statement of cash flows in general-purpose financial statements. This Statement supersedes APB Opinion No. 19, Reporting Changes in Financial Position, and requires a business enterprise to provide a statement of cash flows in place of a statement of changes in financial position. It also requires that specified information about noncash investing and financing transactions and other events be provided separately.

Responses

1. $185,000, S

The problem states that the accounts included in Probe's condensed trial balance have not yet been adjusted for income tax expense and that Probe's income tax payments during year 10 were debited to *Income Taxes Payable.* Therefore, the amount of cash paid for income taxes is the decrease in the *Income Taxes Payable* account. In the statement of cash flows prepared using the indirect method, amounts of payments for income taxes are reported in supplementary information.

2. $50,000, S

Decrease in premium on bonds payable (B/P)	$ 79,000
Decrease in premium on B/P due to extinguishment of B/P	(75,000)
Decrease in premium on B/P due to amortization of premium	4,000
Add: Interest expense recognized	46,000
Cash paid for interest	$ 50,000

Amortization of premium on bonds payable (B/P) decreases the amount of interest expense recognized. In the statement of cash flows prepared using the indirect method, amounts of payments for interest (net of amounts capitalized) are reported in supplementary information.

3. $485,000, F

Payments for bond redemption are reported as cash outflows for financing activities.

Face amount of bonds redeemed	$500,000
Premium on bonds redeemed	75,000
Carrying amount of bonds redeemed	$575,000
Pretax gain on early extinguishment	(90,000)
Cash paid for bond redemption	$485,000

4. $255,000, F

Proceeds from issuance of common stock are reported as cash inflows from financing activities.

Increase in Common Stock account (80,000 shares × $2.50 par value)	$200,000
Increase in Additional Paid-In Capital account	55,000
Proceeds from issuance of common stock	$255,000

5. $65,000, F

Since Probe's revenue and expense accounts are included in the condensed trial balance, they have not yet been closed to *Retained Earnings.* Therefore, the $80,000 decrease in *Retained Earnings* is due entirely to the declaration of cash dividends during year 10. Since the *Dividends Payable* account increased by $15,000 during year 10, the amount of cash dividends paid in year 10 is $65,000 (i.e., $80,000 – $15,000). Cash dividends payments are reported as cash outflows for financing activities.

6. $20,000, I

Proceeds from the sale of equipment are reported as cash inflows from investing activities.

Depreciation expense	$ 88,000
Less: Net increase in accumulated depreciation	(65,000)
Accumulated depreciation on equipment sold	$ 23,000

Cost of equipment sold	$ 50,000
Less: Related accumulated depreciation	(23,000)
Carrying amount of equipment sold	27,000
Less: Loss on sale of equipment	(7,000)
Proceeds from sale of equipment	$ 20,000

Solution 14-5

Statement of Cash Flows

Kern Inc.
Statement of Cash Flows
For the Year Ended December 31, Year 4
Increase (Decrease) in Cash

Cash flows from operating activities:			
Net income	$305,000		1
Adjustments to reconcile net income to net cash provided by operating activities:			
Depreciation	82,000		2
Amortization of patent	9,000		3
Loss on sale of equipment	10,000		4
Equity in income of Word Corp.	(30,000)		5
Gain on sale of marketable equity securities	(19,000)		6
Decrease in allowance to reduce marketable equity securities to market	(15,000)		7
Increase in accounts receivable	(35,000)		8
Decrease in inventories	80,000		9
Decrease in accounts payable and accrued liabilities	(115,000)		10
Net cash provided by operating activities		$ 272,000	11
Cash flows from investing activities:			
Sale of marketable equity securities	119,000		12
Sale of equipment	18,000		13
Purchase of equipment	(120,000)		14
Net cash provided by investing activities		17,000	15
Cash flows from financing activities:			
Issuance of common stock	260,000		16
Cash dividend paid	(85,000)		17
Payment on note payable	(300,000)		18
Net cash used in financing activities		(125,000)	19
Net increase in cash		164,000	20
Cash at beginning of year [Info given in worksheet – 0 points]		307,000	21
Cash at end of year		$ 471,000	22

1. Given in Additional Information.

2. Net increase in accumulated depreciation $65,000
   Accumulated depreciation on equipment sold 17,000
   Depreciation year $82,000

Net increase in accumulated depreciation	$65,000
Accumulated depreciation on equipment sold	17,000
Depreciation year	$82,000

3. Net change in patent given in scenario.

4.

Equipment sold for cash	$18,000
Carrying value of equipment	28,000
Loss on sale of equipment	$10,000

5.

Reported net income for Word Corp.	$150,000
Kern's ownership	× 20%
Equity in income of Word Corp.	$ 30,000

6.

Marketable equity securities balance 12/31, year 4	$ 150,000
Marketable equity securities balance 12/31, year 3	250,000
Change in marketable equity securities	(100,000)
Cash sale of marketable equity securities	119,000
Gain on sale of marketable equity securities	$ 19,000

7. Change in allowance to reduce marketable equity securities to market given in scenario.

8. Increase in accounts receivable given in scenario.

9. Decrease in inventories given in scenario.

10. Decrease in accounts payable and accrued liabilities given in scenario.

11. Sum of adjustments to reconcile net income to net cash provided by operating activities plus net income.

12. Sale of marketable equity securities given in additional information.

13. Sale of equipment given in additional information.

14. Purchase of equipment given in additional information.

15. Sum of cash flows from investing activities.

16. Issuance of common stock, 20,000 shares for cash at $13 per share $260,000

17. Cash dividend paid given in additional information.

18. Payment on note payable given in scenario.

19. Sum of cash used in financing activities.

20.

Net cash provided by operating activities	$ 272,000
Net cash provided by investing activities	17,000
Net cash used in financing activities	(125,000)
Net increase in cash	$ 164,000

21. Cash at beginning of year given in scenario.

22.

Net increase in cash	$164,000
Plus cash at beginning of year	307,000
Cash at end of year	$471,000

Research

FAS 95, Par. 14

14. A statement of cash flows shall classify cash receipts and cash payments as resulting from investing, financing, or operating activities. Generally, each cash receipt or payment is to be classified according to its nature without regard to whether it stems from an item intended as a hedge of another item. For example, the proceeds of a borrowing are a financing cash inflow even though the debt is intended as a hedge of an investment, and the purchase or sale of a futures contract is an investing activity even though the contract is intended as a hedge of a firm commitment to purchase inventory. However, cash flows from a derivative instrument that is accounted for as a fair value hedge or cash flow hedge may be classified in the same category as the cash flows from the items being hedged provided that the derivative instrument does not include an other-than-insignificant financing element at inception, other than a financing element inherently included in an at-the-market derivative instrument with no prepayments (that is, the forward points in an at-the-money forward contract) and that the accounting policy is disclosed. If the derivative instrument includes an other-than-insignificant financing element at inception, all cash inflows and outflows of the derivative instrument shall be considered cash flows from financing activities by the borrower. If for any reason hedge accounting for an instrument that hedges an identifiable transaction or event is discontinued, then any cash flows subsequent to the date of discontinuance shall be classified consistent with the nature of the instrument.

Solution 14-6

Statement of Cash Flows

Linden Consulting Associates
Statement of Cash Flows
For the Year Ended December 31, Year 2
Increase (Decrease) in Cash

Cash flows from operating activities:			
Cash received from customers	$2,586,000	1	
Cash paid to suppliers and employees	(1,830,000)	2	
Dividends received from affiliate	96,000	3	
Net cash provided by operating activities		4	$ 852,000
Cash flows from investing activities:			
Purchased property and equipment		5	(170,000)
Cash flows from financing activities:			
Principal payment of mortgage payable	(20,000)	6	
Proceeds for admission of new partner	340,000	7	
Drawings against partners' capital accounts	(630,000)	8	
Net cash used in financing activities		9	(310,000)
Net increase in cash		10	372,000
Cash at beginning of year		11	280,000
Cash at end of year		12	$ 652,000

1. Cash received from customers: Fee revenue less ending accounts receivable balance plus beginning accounts receivable balance ($2,664,000 – $446,000 + $368,000).

2. Cash paid to suppliers and employees: Operating expenses less depreciation less ending accounts payable balance plus beginning accounts payable balance ($1,940,000 – $60,000 – $320,000 + $270,000).

3. Dividends received from affiliate: Linden's share of dividends declared by Zach (25% × $384,000).

4. Sum of cash flows from operating activities ($2,586,000 – $1,830,000 + 96,000).

5. Net change in property plant and equipment given in scenario.

6. Change in mortgage payable given in scenario.

7. Proceeds from admission of new partner given in additional information.

8. Drawings against partners' capital accounts given in additional information.

9. Sum of cash flows from financing activities (–$20,000 + $340,000 – $630,000).

10. Net increase in cash: Sum of net cash flow provided by operating activities, investing activities and financing activities ($852,000 – $170,000 – $310,000).

11. Cash at beginning of year given in scenario information.

12. Cash at end of year: Sum of net increase in cash and cash at beginning of year ($372,000 + $280,000).

Reconciliation of Net Income

Reconciliation of net income to net cash provided by operating activities:

Net income		13	$900,000
Adjustments to reconcile net income to net cash provided by operating activities:			
Depreciation and amortization	$ 64,000	14	
Undistributed earnings of affiliate	(84,000)	15	
Change in assets and liabilities:			
Increase in accounts receivable	(78,000)	16	
Increase in accounts payable and accrued expenses	50,000	17	
Total adjustments		18	(48,000)
Net cash provided by operating activities		19	$852,000

13. Net income given in scenario information.

14. Sum of amortization and depreciation ($4,000 + 60,000).

15 Undistributed earnings of affiliate: Sum of Linden's share (25%) of Zach, Inc's reported net income ($720,000) and cash dividends paid ($384,000) for year 2 ($80,000 – $96,000).

16. Increase in accounts receivable given in scenario information.

17. Increase in accounts payable and accrued expenses given in scenario information.

18. Total adjustments: Sum of increase in accounts receivable and accounts payable (–$78,000 + $50,000).

19. Net cash provided by operating activities: Sum of net income and adjustments ($900,000 – $48,000).

Analysis of Partner's Changes

Linden Consulting Associates
Analysis of Changes in Partners' Capital Accounts
For the Year Ended December 31, Year 2

	Total	Garr	Pat	Scott	
Balance, December 31, Year 1	$1,700,000	$1,020,000	$680,000	$ --	20
Capital investment	340,000	--	--	340,000	21
Allocation of net income	900,000	450,000	270,000	180,000	22
Balance before drawings	2,940,000	1,470,000	950,000	520,000	23
Drawings	630,000	280,000	200,000	150,000	24
Balance, December 31, Year 2	$2,310,000	$1,190,000	$750,000	$370,000	25

20. Partners' balances as of 12/31, year 1 given in additional information.

21. Amount paid to admit new partner given in additional information. No entry needed for Garr and Pat.

22. Total allocation of net income given in scenario.

Information for Garr, Pat and Scott:

	Garr	Pat	Scott
$900,000 ×	50%	30%	20%
	450,000	270,000	180,000

23. Partners' balances before drawings: Sum of all capital account adjustments.

24. Partners' drawings given in additional information.

25. Partners' capital accounts balances as of 12/31, year 2.

Research

FAS 95, Par. 5

5. The information provided in a statement of cash flows, if used with related disclosures and information in the other financial statements, should help investors, credits, and others to (a) assess the enterprise's ability to generate positive future net cash flows; (b) assess the enterprise's ability to meet its obligations, its ability to pay dividends, and its needs for external financing; (c) assess the reasons for differences between net income and associated cash receipts and payments; and (d) assess the effects on an enterprise's financial position of both its cash and noncash investing and financing transactions during the period.

CHAPTER 15

FINANCIAL STATEMENT ANALYSIS

I. **Financial Analysis** 15-2
   A. Definition 15-2
   B. Purpose 15-2

II. **Ratio Analysis** 15-2
   A. Factors 15-2
   B. Evaluation of Solvency 15-2
   C. Operational Efficiency 15-4
   D. Profitability & Investment Analysis Ratios 15-5

III. **Earnings Per Share** 15-6
   A. Overview 15-6
   B. Basic EPS 15-7
   C. Diluted EPS 15-8
   D. Financial Statement Presentation 15-13

EXAM COVERAGE: Historically, exam coverage of the topics in Chapter 15 has been 1 to 3 percent of the FAR section. More information regarding exam coverage is included in Appendix B, *Practical Advice.*

CHAPTER 15

FINANCIAL STATEMENT ANALYSIS

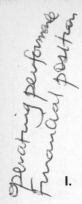

I. Financial Analysis

A. Definition

Financial statement analysis is an attempt to evaluate a business entity for financial and managerial decision-making purposes. In order to draw valid conclusions about the financial health of an entity, it is essential to analyze and compare specific types and sources of financial information. This analysis would include (1) a review of the firm's accounting policies, (2) an examination of recent auditors' reports, (3) analysis of footnotes and other supplemental information accompanying the financial statements, and (4) the examination of various relationships among items presented in financial statements (i.e., ratio analysis).

B. Purpose

Financial ratios measure elements of the firm's operating performance and financial position so that internal as well as industry-wide comparisons can be made on a consistent basis. Ratio analysis provides an indication of the firm's financial strengths and weaknesses and generally should be used in conjunction with other evaluation techniques. Ratio analysis is used primarily to draw conclusions about the solvency, operational efficiency, and profitability of a firm.

II. Ratio Analysis

A. Factors

When computing a ratio, consider the following:

1. Net or gross amounts (e.g., receivables)

2. Average for the period or year-end amounts (e.g., receivables, inventories, common shares outstanding)

3. Adjustments to income (e.g., interest, income taxes, preferred dividends)

B. Evaluation of Solvency

1. **Short-Term Solvency** Short-term solvency is the ability of a firm to meet its current obligations as they mature. The following ratios may be of primary interest to short-term creditors.

Exhibit 1 ▸ Working Capital

Current Assets – Current Liabilities

Comments: Represents the liquid portion of resources or enterprise capital. The greater the amount of working capital, the greater the cushion of protection available to short-term creditors, and the greater assurance that short-term debts will be paid when due.

Exhibit 2 ▸ Current Ratio

$$\frac{\textit{Current Assets}}{\textit{Current Liabilities}}$$

Comments: This is a primary test of the overall solvency of the enterprise and its ability to meet current obligations from current assets. When the current ratio exceeds 1.0 to 1.0, an equal increase in current assets and current liabilities decreases the ratio. When the current ratio is less than 1.0 to 1.0, an equal increase in current assets and current liabilities increases the ratio.

Exhibit 3 ▸ Acid-Test or Quick Ratio

$$\frac{\textit{Cash + Marketable Securities + Net Receivables}}{\textit{Current Liabilities}}$$

Comments: This ratio provides a more severe test of immediate solvency by eliminating inventories and prepaid expenses (current assets that are not quickly converted into cash).

Exhibit 4 ▸ Defensive-Interval Ratio

$$\frac{\textit{Cash + Marketable Securities + Net Receivables}}{\textit{Average Daily Cash Expenditures}}$$

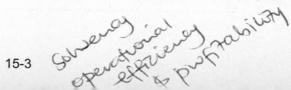

Comments: This ratio estimates the number of days that the company can meet its basic operational costs. The average daily cash expenditures can be approximated by reducing total expenses for the year by noncash charges (e.g., depreciation, amortization of intangibles) and dividing this amount by 365.

2. **Long-Term Solvency** Long-term solvency is the ability to meet interest payments, preferred dividends, and other fixed charges. Similarly, long-term solvency is a required precondition for the repayment of principal.

Exhibit 5 ▸ Debt to Equity

$$\frac{\textit{Total Liabilities}}{\textit{Owners' Equity}}$$

Comments: This ratio provides a measure of the relative amounts of resources provided by creditors and owners.

Exhibit 6 ▸ Times Interest Earned

$$\frac{\textit{Income Before Income Taxes and Interest Charges}}{\textit{Interest Charges}}$$

Comments: Measures the ability of the firm to meet its interest payments. Income taxes are *added* back to net income because the ability to pay interest is not dependent on the amount of income taxes to be paid, since interest is tax deductible.

Exhibit 7 ▸ Times Preferred Dividends Earned

$$\frac{\textit{Net Income}}{\textit{Annual Preferred Dividend Requirement}}$$

Comments: Measures the adequacy of current earnings for the payment of preferred dividends.

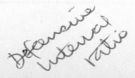

Defensive interval ratio

Solvency operational efficiency & profitability

C. Operational Efficiency

Operational efficiency is the ability of the business entity to generate income as well as its efficiency and effectiveness in using the assets employed.

Exhibit 8 ▸ Total Asset Turnover

$$\frac{\textit{Total Sales (Revenue)}}{\textit{Average Total Assets}}$$

Comments: This ratio is useful to determine the amount of sales that are generated from each dollar of assets. Average total assets is generally determined by adding the beginning and ending total assets and dividing by two.

Exhibit 9 ▸ Receivables Turnover

$$\frac{\textit{Net Credit Sales}}{\textit{Average Net Receivables}}$$

Comments: This ratio provides an indication of the efficiency of credit policies and collection procedures, and of the quality of the receivables. Average net receivables include trade notes receivable. Average net receivables is generally determined by adding the beginning and ending net receivables balances and dividing by two.

Exhibit 10 ▸ Number of Days' Sales in Average Receivables

$$\frac{\textit{360}}{\textit{Receivables Turnover}}$$

Comments: Tests the average number of days required to collect receivables. Some analysts prefer to use 365, 300, or 250 as the number of business days in the year.

Exhibit 11 ▸ Inventory Turnover

$$\frac{\textit{Cost of Goods Sold}}{\textit{Average Inventory}}$$

Comments: Indicates the number of times inventory was acquired and sold (or used in production) during the period. It can be used to detect inventory obsolescence or pricing problems. Average inventory is generally determined by adding the beginning and ending inventories and dividing by two.

Exhibit 12 ▸ Number of Days' Supply in Average Inventory

$$\frac{\textit{360}}{\textit{Inventory Turnover}} \quad \text{or} \quad \frac{\textit{Average (Ending) Inventory}}{\textit{Average Daily Cost of Goods Sold}}$$

Comments: Indicates the number of days inventory is held before it is sold. Some analysts prefer to use 365, 300, or 250 as the number of business days in the year. Average daily cost of goods sold is determined by dividing cost of goods sold by the number of business days.

Exhibit 13 ▸ Length of Operating Cycle

Number of days' sales in average receivables + *Number of days' supply in average inventory*

Comments: Measures the average length of time from the purchase of inventory to the collection of cash from its sale.

D. Profitability & Investment Analysis Ratios

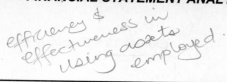

efficiency & effectiveness in using assets employed.

Exhibit 14 ▸ Book Value Per Common Share

$$\frac{\textit{Common Stockholders' Equity}}{\textit{Number of Common Shares Outstanding}}$$

To determine common stockholders' equity, preferred stock is subtracted from total stockholders' equity at the greater of its liquidation, par or stated value. Cumulative preferred stock dividends in *arrears* are also similarly subtracted. Treasury stock affects the denominator as the number of common shares outstanding is *reduced.*

Comments: This ratio measures the amount that common shareholders would receive if all assets were sold at their carrying amounts and if all creditors were paid. When balance sheet valuations do not approximate fair values, the importance of this ratio is diminished.

Exhibit 15 ▸ Book Value Per Preferred Share

$$\frac{\textit{Preferred Stockholders' Equity}}{\textit{Number of Preferred Shares Outstanding}}$$

Preferred stockholders' equity is comprised of (a) preferred stock at the greater of its liquidation, par or stated value and (b) cumulative preferred stock dividends in arrears.

Comments: This ratio measures the amount that preferred shareholders would receive if the company were liquidated on the basis of the amounts reported on the balance sheet.

Exhibit 16 ▸ Return on Total Assets

$$\frac{\textit{Net Income + Interest Expense (Net of Tax)}}{\textit{Average Total Assets}}$$

Comments: This ratio provides a measure of the degree of efficiency with which resources (total assets) are used to generate earnings.

Exhibit 17 ▸ Return on Common Stockholders' Equity

$$\frac{\textit{Net Income – Preferred Dividends}}{\textit{Average Common Stockholders' Equity}}$$

Comments: Measures the rate of earnings on resources provided by common stockholders. Common stockholders' equity is measured as indicated in Exhibit 13. Average common stockholders' equity is generally determined by adding beginning and ending common stockholders' equity and dividing by two.

Successful use of *leverage* is where a company earns more by the use of borrowed money than it costs to use the borrowed funds. When compared to the return on total assets, the return on common stockholders' equity measures the extent to which leverage is being employed for or against the common stockholders. When the return on common stockholders' equity is greater than the return on total assets, leverage is positive and common stockholders benefit.

Exhibit 18 ▸ Return on Stockholders' Equity

$$\frac{\textit{Net Income}}{\textit{Average Stockholders' Equity}}$$

Comments: Measures the rate of earnings on resources provided by all stockholders (i.e., common and preferred). Average stockholders' equity is generally determined by adding beginning and ending stockholders' equity and dividing by two.

Exhibit 19 ▸ Earnings Per Share (EPS)

$$\frac{\text{Net Income – Preferred Dividends}}{\text{Average Number of Common Shares Outstanding}}$$

Comments: Measures the ability to pay dividends to common stockholders by measuring profit earned per share of common stock. (EPS is discussed more thoroughly later in this chapter.)

Exhibit 20 ▸ Price Earnings Ratio

$$\frac{\text{Market Price Per Common Share}}{\text{Earnings Per Common Share}}$$

Comments: A measure of whether a stock is relatively cheap or relatively expensive based on its present earnings.

Exhibit 21 ▸ Dividend Payout Ratio

$$\frac{\text{Cash Dividend Per Common Share}}{\text{Earnings Per Common Share}}$$

Comments: This ratio represents the percentage of earnings per share distributed to common stockholders in cash dividends. A low ratio would probably indicate the reinvestment of profits by a growth-oriented firm.

Exhibit 22 ▸ Yield on Common Stock

$$\frac{\text{Dividend Per Common Share}}{\text{Market Price Per Common Share}}$$

Comments: Measures cash flow return on common stock investment.

III. Earnings Per Share

A. Overview

SFAS 128, *Earnings Per Share,* requires the presentation of basic and diluted earnings per share, and describes the calculations and how EPS data should be reported. Earnings per share data are required to be included in the financial statements of entities with publicly held common stock or potential common stock, if those securities trade in a public market. Potential common stock includes securities such as options, warrants, convertible securities, and contingent stock agreements.

1. **Earnings Per Share (EPS)** The amount of earnings attributable to each share of common stock. Note that EPS is computed for common stock only, **not** for preferred stock.

2. **Dilution (Dilutive)** Reduction in earnings per share due to the *assumed* conversion or exercise of certain securities into common stock.

3. **Antidilution (Antidilutive)** Increase in earnings per share or decrease in loss per share.

4. **Basic Earnings Per Share (Basic EPS)** The amount of earnings for the period available to each share of common stock outstanding during the reporting period.

5. **Diluted Earnings Per Share (Diluted EPS)** The amount of earnings for the period available to each share of common stock outstanding during the reporting period and to each share that would have been outstanding assuming the issuance of common shares for all dilutive potential common shares outstanding during the reporting period.

6. **Convertible Security** A security that is convertible into another security based on a conversion rate.

B. Basic EPS

1. **Formula** Basic EPS is computed by dividing income available to common stockholders (IAC) by the weighted-average number of shares outstanding during the period. Shares issued during the period and shares reacquired during the period are weighted for the portion of the period they were outstanding.

$$\text{Basic EPS} = \frac{\text{Income Available to Common Stockholders}}{\text{Weighted Average Number of Shares Outstanding}}$$

Example 1 ▶ Basic EPS

IAC is $100,000 and the weighted average number of shares of common stock outstanding is 250,000 shares.

Basic EPS is $100,000 / 250,000 shares = $0.40.

2. **Numerator** The numerator for basic EPS is fairly simple to determine. The income number used for basic EPS is *income from continuing operations* adjusted for the claims by senior securities. Senior security claims generally refer to preferred stock and are adjusted in the period earned.

   a. All preferred stock dividends declared reduce income to arrive at IAC.

   b. Cumulative preferred stock dividends of the current period, even though not declared, also reduce income to arrive at IAC.

   c. Dividends on common stock are **not** used in determining EPS.

Example 2 ▶ IAC—Noncumulative Preferred Stock

Corporation A has 10,000 shares of $100 par, noncumulative, 3% dividend, participating preferred stock. Net income has been $100,000 for each of the last four years. Dividends of $30,000 were paid in year 1, zero in year 2, $50,000 in year 3, and $60,000 in year 4. Income available to the common stockholders would be:

Year	Net Income	Preferred Dividends Earned	IAC
1	$100,000	$30,000	$ 70,000
2	$100,000	–	$100,000
3	$100,000	$50,000	$ 50,000
4	$100,000	$60,000	$ 40,000

Example 3 ▶ IAC—Cumulative Preferred Stock

Refer to Example 2, except that the preferred stock is cumulative. IAC would be:

Year	Net Income	Preferred Dividends Earned	IAC
1	$100,000	$30,000	$ 70,000
2	$100,000	$30,000*	$ 70,000
3	$100,000	$30,000**	$ 70,000
4	$100,000	$50,000***	$ 50,000

* The dividends in arrears are earned in year 2.

** The $50,000 declared in year 3 are $30,000 in arrears from year 2 and $20,000 of the $30,000 earned in year 3.

*** The $60,000 declared in year 4 are $10,000 in arrears from year 3, $30,000 earned in year 4, and $20,000 participation by the preferred stockholders in year 4.

3. **Denominator** The denominator is the weighted-average number of shares outstanding during the period. For basic EPS, this number will include shares outstanding the entire period, shares issued during the period, and shares where all of the conditions of issuance have been met.

   a. **Issue or Reacquire Stock** Issuance of stock and reacquisition of stock during the period changes the ownership structure and the shares only participate in earnings for the time that the stock is outstanding. For example, if a shareholder holds 10,000 shares the entire period and another shareholder purchases 10,000 in the middle of the year, you would not expect their EPS to be the same.

   b. **Stock Dividends and Stock Splits** Stock dividends, stock splits, and reverse stock splits change the total number of shares outstanding but not the proportionate shares outstanding. For example, an individual owning 10,000 shares of a company with 20,000 shares outstanding owns 50 percent of the stock. After a 2 for 1 stock split, ownership is 20,000 of 40,000 total shares, or still 50 percent. For this reason, stock dividends, stock splits, and reverse stock splits are reflected retroactively for all periods presented. Such changes occurring after the close of the accounting period but prior to the issuance of the financial statements are also reflected in the EPS for all periods presented.

   c. **Issue Stock in a Business Combination** When the purchase method is used, the weighted average is applied from the date of combination.

Example 4 ▸ Weighted Average Shares of Common Stock Outstanding

Date	Transaction	Change in Shares from Transaction	Total Shares Outstanding
1/1	Shares outstanding		10,000
4/1	Shares issued	8,000	18,000
6/1	Shares reacquired and held in treasury	(3,000)	15,000
7/1	Issued 10% stock dividend	1,500	16,500
8/1	Shares reacquired and held in treasury	(6,000)	10,500
9/1	Shares issued	12,000	22,500
12/1	Issued 2 for 1 stock split	22,500	45,000

Total Shares Outstanding		Months Outstanding		Stock Dividend		Stock Split		Weighted Average
10,000	×	3/12	×	1.10	×	2	=	5,500
18,000	×	2/12	×	1.10	×	2	=	6,600
15,000	×	1/12	×	1.10	×	2	=	2,750
16,500	×	1/12			×	2	=	2,750
10,500	×	1/12			×	2	=	1,750
22,500	×	3/12			×	2	=	11,250
45,000	×	1/12					=	3,750
Weighted average number of shares outstanding								34,350

Note: The stock dividend and stock split are applied retroactively to the beginning of the year from the date declared.

C. **Diluted EPS**

1. **Objective** The objective of reporting diluted EPS is to measure the performance of an entity over the reporting period while giving effect to all dilutive potential common shares that were outstanding during the period.

2. **Dilutive Security** With diluted EPS, the first step is to determine if a security is dilutive. A security is dilutive if the inclusion of the security in the computation of EPS results in a smaller EPS or increases the loss per share.

a. **Potentially Dilutive** Securities that are potentially dilutive include convertible preferred stock, convertible debt, options, warrants, participating securities, different classes of common stock, and agreements to issue these securities or shares of common stock in the future, referred to as contingently issuable shares.

b. **Anti-Dilutive Securities** Not all potential securities will be dilutive. When the per share effect of an individual security is greater than the total per share effect, the security is anti-dilutive. Anti-dilutive securities are excluded from diluted EPS. Thus it is necessary to calculate the per share effect of each potentially dilutive security and include only those which have a dilutive effect.

c. **Categories of Potentially Dilutive Securities**

(1) Convertible securities where the if-converted method is used

(2) Options, warrants, and their equivalents where the treasury stock method is used

(3) Contingently issuable shares

3. **If-Converted Method** Convertible securities may or may not be converted. If they are converted, they become common stock. The if-converted method assumes that they are converted; in other words, pretend that convertible securities are converted. The pretend conversion may impact the IAC and the weighted-average number of common shares outstanding.

a. **Numerator**

(1) **Convertible Debt** If the enterprise has convertible debt, the conversion would mean that the company does not have the interest expense for the debt and should be added back to income to arrive at IAC. The interest expense adjustment should be net of tax and increases income or decreases the loss for the period. If the tax amount impacts a nondiscretionary item such as bonuses, a further adjustment is necessary.

(2) **Convertible Preferred Stock** If convertible preferred stock is assumed to be exercised, the entity would not have the corresponding preferred dividends, and income from continuing operations would not be reduced for preferred dividends. These adjustments do not have nondiscretionary or tax effects.

b. **Denominator** Assuming convertible securities are converted to common stock increases the weighted average number of common shares outstanding.

Example 5 ▸ If-Converted Method

A company has IAC of $2,000,000 and weighted average common shares outstanding of 1,000,000. The company has a convertible bond that is convertible into 100,000 shares. This bond has been outstanding for the entire year, and the company reported $40,000 in related interest expense. The company has a profit-sharing plan of 10% of net income and a 40% tax rate. Additionally, the company has convertible preferred stock that is convertible into 50,000 common shares, and $125,000 of dividends were earned on this preferred stock during the period.

Basic EPS = $2,000,000 / 1,000,000	$ 2.00
Effect on IAC:	
Interest expense	$ 40,000
Increase in profit-sharing if converted	(4,000)
Effect before taxes	36,000
Tax effect ($36,000 × 40%)	(14,400)
Increase to IAC	21,600

Effect on weighted average common shares:	
Additional shares issued if converted; increases the weighted average	100,000
Per share effect of the convertible debt = $21,600 / 100,000	$ 0.216

The convertible debt has a dilutive effect since the per share effect is less than basic EPS.

Effect on IAC:	
Dividends on preferred stock added back to IAC	$125,000
Effect on weighted average common shares:	
Additional shares issued if converted; increases the weighted average	50,000
Per share effect of the convertible preferred stock = $125,000 / 50,000	$ 2.50

The convertible preferred stock is anti-dilutive since $2.50 is greater than $2.00.

Diluted EPS is calculated as follows: $\frac{\$2,000,000 + \$\ 21,600}{1,000,000 + \ 100,000} = \frac{2,021,600}{1,100,000}$ $ 1.838

Note: The adjustments for the convertible debt assumed converted are made because they are dilutive. No adjustments are made for the convertible preferred stock because they are anti-dilutive.

4. **Treasury Stock Method** Holders of options and warrants can exercise these securities for specified amounts of cash and receive common stock. The treasury stock method assumes that this cash is used to repurchase treasury stock at the average market price, and the net effect on the shares of common stock outstanding is the difference between the shares issued and the shares purchased.

   a. **Applied Separately** The treasury stock method is applied separately to each option and warrant to determine if the individual option or warrant is dilutive. Since the effect of options and warrants is only a denominator effect for the net additional shares that are issued, the per share effect of each option or warrant is $.00.

   b. **Dilutive vs. Anti-Dilutive** If the average market price is higher than the exercise price, the item is "in the money," and the options or warrants are dilutive. If the average market price is less than the exercise price, the options or warrants are anti-dilutive.

Example 6 ▸ Treasury Stock Method

A company has IAC of $100,000 and 250,000 weighted-average common stock outstanding for the period. The average market price of the common stock is $22 per share. The following options and warrants are outstanding:

	Options	Warrants Series A	Warrants Series B
Shares of Common Stock Issuable	10,000	5,000	7,000
Exercise price per share	$20	$15	$24

Step 1: Determine if the options and warrants are dilutive

Options: Market ($22) > Exercise ($20); Determination: Dilutive

Warrants, Series A: Market ($22) > Exercise ($15); Determination: Dilutive

Warrants, Series B: Market ($22) < Exercise ($24); Determination: Anti-Dilutive

Step 2: Determine the incremental shares for dilutive securities

Additional Shares of Common Stock		10,000
Proceeds (10,000 shares × $20)	$200,000	
Divided by market price	/ 22	
Less: Treasury Stock Purchased		(9,091)
Incremental Shares		909
Per Share Effect of Options (0 / 909)		$ .00
Additional Shares of Common Stock		5,000
Proceeds (5,000 shares × $15)	$ 75,000	
Divided by market price	/ 22	
Less: Treasury Stock Purchased		(3,409)
Incremental Shares		1,591
Per Share Effect of Warrants, Series A (0 / 1,591)		$ .00

Step 3: Calculate Basic and Diluted EPS

Item	IAC	Shares	EPS
Basic EPS	$100,000	250,000	$0.400
Warrants, Series A	0	1,591	
Subtotal	$100,000	251,591	$0.397
Options	0	909	
Diluted EPS	$100,000	252,500	$0.396

5. **Contingently Issuable Shares** Contingent issuances involve the meeting of specific conditions for the issuance of additional shares.

   a. **Passage of Time Contingency** If the contingency involves only the passage of time, the securities are assumed issued and are used in computing diluted EPS.

   b. **Contingency Not Met** If the contingency has not been met, the number of shares that would be issued if the contingency had been met at the end of the contingency period is used in computing diluted EPS.

   c. **Future Market Price Contingency** The number of shares contingently issuable may depend on the market price of the stock at a future date. In this case, computations of EPS should reflect the number of shares which would be issuable based on the market price at the close of the reporting period. For example, assume a company had a plan to issue 20,000 shares if the market price was $15 per share, 30,000 shares if the market price was $20 per share, and 50,000 shares if the market price was $30 per share. If the market price for the current period was $17 per share, EPS should show the 20,000 contingently issuable shares.

   d. **Earnings Contingency** If the contingency is contingent on attainment or maintenance of earnings at a certain level, the number of shares would be considered outstanding and used in computing diluted EPS if the earnings amount is currently being achieved.

6. **Calculation of Diluted EPS** Diluted EPS should reflect the maximum dilution of all potentially dilutive securities that have a dilutive effect. To accomplish this, the security with the smallest individual per share effect is first introduced into total EPS and additional securities are introduced until either all dilutive securities are included or further introduction would be anti-dilutive.

Example 7 ▸ Calculation of Diluted EPS

A company has the following earnings and securities. The tax rate is 30% and there are no non-discretionary items.

Net income for the period			$100,000
Weighted average common shares outstanding			75,000
Dividends on preferred stock earned			$ 5,000
Convertible Bonds	Series A	Series B	
Face amount and carrying value	$40,000	$60,000	
Interest rate	10%	12%	
Number of shares issuable	10,000	4,400	
Options			
Number of shares issuable			7,500
Exercise price			$ 25
Market price			$ 35
Warrants			
Number of shares issuable			2,500
Exercise price			$ 32

Step 1: Determine Basic EPS

Net income		$100,000
Preferred dividends earned		(5,000)
IAC		$ 95,000
IAC / Weighted-average shares outstanding = $95,000 / 75,000		$ 1.2667

Step 2: Determine the per share effect of each dilutive security

Interest expense		$ 4,000
Taxes		(1,200)
Adjustment to IAC (increase)		$ 2,800
Adjustment to weighted-average shares (increase): Number of shares issuable		10,000
Per share effect of Series A Convertible Bonds ($2,800 / 10,000)		$ 0.28
Interest expense		$ 7,200
Taxes		(2,160)
Adjustment to IAC (increase)		$ 5,040
Adjustment to weighted-average shares (increase): Number of shares issuable		4,400
Per share effect of Series B Convertible Bonds ($5,040 / 4,400)		$ 1.1455
Additional Shares of Common Stock		7,500
Proceeds (7,500 shares × $25)	$187,500	
Divided by market price	/ 35	
Less: Treasury Stock Purchased		(5,357)
Incremental Shares		2,143
Per Share Effect of Options (0 / 2,143)		$ 0.00
Additional Shares of Common Stock		2,500
Proceeds (2,500 shares × $32)	$ 80,000	
Divided by market price	/ 35	
Less: Treasury Stock Purchased		(2,286)
Incremental Shares		214
Per Share Effect of Warrants (0 / 214)		$ 0.00

Step 3: Begin with the most dilutive security and include all with a dilutive effect

Item	IAC	Shares	EPS
Basic EPS	$95,000	75,000	$ 1.2667
Options	0	2,143	
Subtotal	95,000	77,143	$ 1.2315
Warrants	0	214	
Subtotal	95,000	77,357	$ 1.2281
Series A Bonds	2,800	10,000	
Diluted EPS	$97,800	87,357	$ 1.1195

NOTE: The EPS number is adjusted for the most dilutive effect. Since the per share effect ($0.28) of the Series A Bonds is less than the previously calculated EPS number ($1.2281) the Series A Bonds are dilutive. However, the per share effect of the Series B Bonds ($1.1455) is greater than the previously calculated EPS number ($1.1195), and the security is excluded because it is anti-dilutive. The options are included first because they are more dilutive than the warrants.

D. Financial Statement Presentation

EPS data is required to be presented for all periods for which an income statement or summary of earnings is presented. If the capital structure is complex for any of the periods presented, dual presentation must be provided for all the periods presented.

1. Location

a. **Face** EPS is reported on the face of the income statement for income from continuing operations and net income.

b. **Face or Notes** An entity that reports a discontinued operation, an extraordinary item, or the cumulative effect of an accounting change in a period is required to present EPS amounts for those line items either on the face of the income statement or in the notes to the financial statements.

2. Simple Capital Structure An entity has a simple capital structure if it has only common stock outstanding and has no dilutive securities. An entity with a simple capital structure is required to present only basic EPS.

3. Complex Capital Structure EPS reporting is more involved if the reporting enterprise has a complex capital structure. An entity's capital structure is complex if it has dilutive securities. Dilutive securities dilute earnings per common share.

a. **Face** An entity with a complex capital structure is required to present both basic and diluted EPS for income from continuing operations and for net income on the face of the income statement with equal prominence.

b. **Face or Notes** For each component of income, including discontinued operations, extraordinary items, and cumulative effects of accounting changes, an entity must present per share information either on the income statement face or in the notes to the financial statements.

Example 8 ▸ Income Statement Presentation of EPS

Asp Company presents the following income statement information. Asp has 40,000 common shares outstanding. Asp has only convertible cumulative 8% preferred stock with a par value of $100,000, that would require 5,000 shares of common stock, if converted. Asp displays all EPS information on the face of the income statement.

Income from continuing operations	$100,000
Discontinued operations	(40,000)
Income before extraordinary item	60,000
Extraordinary item—gain on debt extinguishment	25,000
Net income	$ 85,000

Required: Determine earnings per share.

Basic EPS from continuing operations

Income from continuing operations	$100,000
Preferred dividends earned	(8,000)
IAC	$ 92,000
IAC / Weighted average common shares = $92,000 / 40,000	$ 2.30
Effect on IAC ($100,000 × 8%)	$ 8,000
Effect on weighted-average shares	5,000
Per share effect of Preferred Stock ($8,000 / 5,000)	$ 1.60

Diluted EPS

Item	IAC	Shares	EPS
Basic EPS	$ 92,000	40,000	$ 2.30
Preferred Stock	8,000	5,000	
	$100,000	45,000	$ 2.22

Basic EPS for other income items

Item	IAC	Shares	EPS
Basic EPS	$ 92,000	40,000	$ 2.30
Discontinued operations	(40,000)	0	
EPS for income before EI	52,000	40,000	$ 1.30
Extraordinary item	25,000	0	
EPS for net income	$ 77,000	40,000	$ 1.93

Diluted EPS for other income items

Item	IAC	Shares	EPS
Basic EPS	$ 92,000	40,000	$ 2.30
Preferred stock	8,000	5,000	
EPS for income from cont. op	100,000	45,000	$ 2.22
Discontinued operations	(40,000)	0	
EPS for income before EI	60,000	45,000	$ 1.33
Extraordinary item	25,000	0	
EPS for net income	$ 85,000	45,000	$ 1.89

EPS information would be presented as:

	Income	Basic EPS	Diluted EPS
Income from continuing operations	$100,000	$ 2.30	$ 2.22
Discontinued operations	(40,000)	(1.00)	(.89)
Income before extraordinary item	60,000	1.30	1.33
Extraordinary item—gain on debt extin.	25,000	.63	.56
Net income	$ 85,000	$ 1.93	$ 1.89

NOTE: The diluted EPS amount for income for extraordinary items is greater than the basic EPS. The effect of the convertible preferred stock is included in all computations if it is dilutive in computing EPS for continuing operations.

4. **Disclosures** SFAS 128 requires the following disclosures.

   a. A reconciliation of the numerators and the denominators of the basic and diluted per share computations for income from continuing operations. In this way, the financial statement reader can see the per share impact of each security.

   b. The effect that has been given to preferred dividends in determining the income available to common stockholders.

   c. Securities that could potentially dilute basic EPS in a future period, but that were antidilutive in the current period.

   d. A description of any transaction that occurs after the end of the period, but before the issuance of the financial statements that would have materially changed the number of common shares or potential common shares outstanding at the end of the period if the transaction had occurred before the end of the period. Examples would include issuance or acquisition of common shares, issuance or exercise/conversion of warrants, options, or convertible securities.

Using Videos to Study

Actively watch video classes, taking notes and answering questions as if it were a live class. If the lecturer recommends you to work an example as the video plays, write the information in the viewer guide, rather than merely following along. If the lecturer instructs you to stop the video to answer questions, stop the video. If the lecturer advises you to take notes, personalize your copy of the viewer guide. The lecturers provide these instructions with the insight gained from years of CPA review experience.

Each of the Hot•Spot™ videos concentrates on a few topics. Use them to help you study the areas that are most troubling for you. If you are strong in a topic, watching the video and answering the questions may be sufficient review. If your strength is moderate in a topic, you probably should read the related text before watching the video. If you are weak in a topic, one successful strategy is to watch the video (including following all of the lecturer's instructions), read the book, and then watch the video again.

Each of the Intensive videos is designed for a final, intensive review, after a candidate already has done considerable work. If time permits, use the Intensive videos at both the very beginning (for an overview) and set them aside until the final review in the last weeks before the exam. They contain concise, informative lectures, as well as CPA exam tips, tricks, and techniques that will help you to learn the material needed to pass the exam.

FYI: The Hot•Spot™ and Intensive video programs have similar content as the audio tutor and online video lectures, but they are not exactly the same.

For more information about video programs and passing the exam, contact a customer service representative about getting a copy of Bisk Education's video, *How to Pass the CPA Exam,* featuring Robert Monette, JD, CPA. Limited numbers of complimentary copies are available to qualified candidates.

CHAPTER 15—FINANCIAL STATEMENT ANALYSIS

Problem 15-1 MULTIPLE CHOICE QUESTIONS (80 to 100 minutes)

1. North Bank is analyzing Belle Corp.'s financial statements for a possible extension of credit. Belle's quick ratio is significantly better than the industry average. Which of the following factors should North consider as a possible limitation of using this ratio when evaluating Belle's creditworthiness?
a. Fluctuating market prices of short-term investments may adversely affect the ratio.
b. Increasing market prices for Belle's inventory may adversely affect the ratio.
c. Belle may need to sell its available-for-sale investments to meet its current obligations.
d. Belle may need to liquidate its inventory to meet its long-term obligations. (R/99, FAR, #4, 6773)

2. What effect would the sale of a company's trading securities at their carrying amounts for cash have on each of the following ratios?

	Current ratio	*Quick ratio*
a.	No effect	No effect
b.	Increase	Increase
c.	No effect	Increase
d.	Increase	No effect

(11/95, FAR, #58, 6140)

3. In analyzing a company's financial statements, which financial statement would a potential investor primarily use to assess the company's liquidity and financial flexibility?
a. Balance sheet
b. Income statement
c. Statement of retained earnings
d. Statement of cash flows (11/94, FAR, #5, 5270)

4. Are the following ratios useful in assessing the liquidity position of a company?

	Defensive-interval ratio	*Return on stockholders' equity*
a.	Yes	Yes
b.	Yes	No
c.	No	Yes
d.	No	No

(11/90, Theory, #10, 1755)

5. The following information pertains to Ali Corp. as of and for the current year ended December 31:

Liabilities	$ 60,000
Stockholders' equity	500,000
Shares of common stock issued and outstanding	10,000
Net income	30,000

During the year, Ali's officers exercised stock options for 1,000 shares of stock at an option price of $8 per share. What was the effect of exercising the stock options?
a. Debt-to-equity ratio decreased to 12%
b. Earnings per share increased by $0.33
c. Asset turnover increased to 5.4%
d. No ratios were affected

(5/92, PII, #17, amended, 2649)

Items 6 and 7 are based on the following data:

Apex Corporation
SELECTED FINANCIAL DATA
Year Ended December 31, Current Year

Operating income	$ 900,000
Interest expense	(100,000)
Income before income tax	800,000
Income tax expense	(320,000)
Net income	480,000
Preferred stock dividends	(200,000)
Net income available to common stockholders	$ 280,000

6. The times interest earned ratio is
a. 2.8 to 1
b. 4.8 to 1
c. 8.0 to 1
d. 9.0 to 1 (11/86, PI, #56, amended, 9056)

7. The times preferred dividend earned ratio is
a. 1.4 to 1
b. 1.7 to 1
c. 2.4 to 1
d. 4.0 to 1 (11/86, PI, #57, amended, 1263)

Items 8 and 9 are based on the following:

At December 31 of the current year, Curry Co. had the following balances in selected asset accounts:

	Current year	Increase over previous year
Cash	$ 300	$100
Accounts receivable, net	1,200	400
Inventory	500	200
Prepaid expenses	100	40
Other assets	400	150
Total assets	$2,500	$890

Curry also had current liabilities of $1,000 at December 31 and net credit sales of $7,200 for the year.

8. What is Curry's acid-test ratio at December 31 of the current year?
a. 1.5
b. 1.6
c. 2.0
d. 2.1 (5/93, PII, #15, amended, 4123)

9. What was the average number of days to collect Curry's accounts receivable during the year?
a. 30.4
b. 40.6
c. 50.7
d. 60.8 (5/93, PII, #16, amended, 4124)

10. Which of the following ratios should be used in evaluating the effectiveness with which the company uses its assets?

	Receivables turnover	*Dividend payout ratio*
a.	Yes	Yes
b.	No	No
c.	Yes	No
d.	No	Yes

(11/89, Theory, #37, 1762)

11. The following computations were made from Clay Co.'s current year end books:

Number of days' sales in inventory	61
Number of days' sales in trade accounts receivable	33

What was the number of days in Clay's current year operating cycle?
a. 33
b. 47
c. 61
d. 94 (5/92, PII, #16, amended, 2648)

12. The following financial ratios and calculations were based on information from Kohl Co.'s financial statements for the current year:

Accounts receivable turnover
Ten times during the year

Total assets turnover
Two times during the year

Average receivables during the year
$200,000

What was Kohl's average total assets for the year?
a. $2,000,000
b. $1,000,000
c. $ 400,000
d. $ 200,000 (R/05, FAR, 0942F, #16, 7760)

Items 13 through 15 are based on the following:

Selected data pertaining to Lore Co. for the calendar year is as follows:

Net cash sales	$ 3,000
Cost of goods sold	18,000
Inventory at beginning of year	6,000
Purchases	24,000
Accounts receivable at beginning of year	20,000
Accounts receivable at end of year	22,000

13. The accounts receivable turnover for the year was 5.0 times. What were Lore's net credit sales?
a. $105,000
b. $107,000
c. $110,000
d. $210,000 (5/95, FAR, #58, 5594)

14. What was the inventory turnover for the year?
a. 1.2 times
b. 1.5 times
c. 2.0 times
d. 3.0 times (5/95, FAR, #59, 5595)

15. Lore would use which of the following to determine the average days' sales in inventory?

	Numerator	*Denominator*
a.	365	Average inventory
b.	365	Inventory turnover
c.	Average inventory	Sales divided by 365
d.	Sales divided by 365	Inventory turnover

(5/95, FAR, #60, amended, 5596)

16. Kline Co. had the following sales and accounts receivable balances at the end of the current year:

Cash sales	$1,000,000
Net credit sales	3,000,000
Net accounts receivable, 1/1	100,000
Net accounts receivable, 12/31	400,000

What is Kline's average collection period for its accounts receivable?
a. 48.0 days
b. 30.0 days
c. 22.5 days
d. 12.0 days (R/02, FAR #3, 7058)

17. Frey Inc. was organized on January 2 of the current year with the following capital structure:

- 10% cumulative preferred stock, par value $100 and liquidation value $105; authorized, issued and outstanding 1,000 shares $100,000
- Common stock, par value $25; authorized 100,000 shares; issues and outstanding 10,000 shares 250,000

Frey's net income for the year ended December 31 was $450,000, but no dividends were declared. How much was Frey's book value per preferred share at December 31?
a. $100
b. $105
c. $110
d. $115 (5/85, PI, #14, amended, 1265)

18. The following data pertain to Cowl Inc. for the current year ended December 31:

Net sales	$ 600,000
Net income	150,000
Total assets, January 1	2,000,000
Total assets, December 31	3,000,000

What was Cowl's rate of return on assets?
a. 5%
b. 6%
c. 20%
d. 24% (11/95, FAR, #60, amended, 6142)

19. Successful use of leverage is evidenced by a
a. Rate of return on investment greater than the rate of return on stockholders' equity
b. Rate of return on investment greater than the cost of debt
c. Rate of return on sales greater than the rate of return on stockholders' equity
d. Rate of return on sales greater than the cost of debt (11/91, Theory, #17, 2525)

20. How are dividends per share for common stock used in the calculation of the following?

	Dividend per share payout ratio	*Earnings per share*
a.	Numerator	Numerator
b.	Numerator	Not used
c.	Denominator	Not used
d.	Denominator	Denominator

(5/87, Theory, #40, 9057)

21. The following data pertain to Thorne Corp. for the current calendar year:

Net income	$240,000
Dividends paid on common stock	120,000
Common stock outstanding (unchanged during year)	300,000 shares

The market price per share of Thorne's common stock at December 31 was $12. The price-earnings ratio at December 31 was
a. 9.6 to 1
b. 10.0 to 1
c. 15.0 to 1
d. 30.0 to 1 (11/89, PI, #57, amended, 1255)

22. Which of the following ratios are useful for evaluating the effectiveness with which the company uses its assets?

	Acid-test (quick) ratio	*Price-earnings ratio*
a.	Yes	Yes
b.	Yes	No
c.	No	No
d.	No	Yes

(5/88, Theory, #38, 1767)

le

23. Strauch Co. has one class of common stock outstanding and no other securities that are potentially convertible into common stock. During the previous year, 100,000 shares of common stock were outstanding. In the current year, two distributions of additional common shares occurred: On April 1, 20,000 shares of treasury stock were sold, and on July 1, a 2-for-1 stock split was issued. Net income was $410,000 in the current year and $350,000 in the previous year. What amounts should Strauch report as earnings per share in its current and previous year comparative income statements?

	Current Year	*Previous Year*
a.	$1.78	$3.50
b.	$1.78	$1.75
c.	$2.34	$1.75
d.	$2.34	$3.50

(11/91, PI, #60, amended, 2448)

24. Ute Co. had the following capital structure during the previous and current years:

Preferred stock, $10 par, 4% cumulative, 25,000 shares issued and outstanding	$ 250,000
Common stock, $5 par, 200,000 shares issued and outstanding	1,000,000

Ute reported net income of $500,000 for the current year ended December 31. Ute paid no preferred dividends during the previous year and paid $16,000 in preferred dividends during the current year. In its current year December 31 income statement, what amount should Ute report as earnings per share?

a. $2.42
b. $2.45
c. $2.48
d. $2.50 (11/95, FAR, #45, amended, 6127)

25. The following information pertains to Jet Corp.'s outstanding stock for the current year:

<u>Common stock, $5 par value</u>	
Shares outstanding 1/1	20,000
2-for-1 stock split 4/1	20,000
Shares issued 7/1	10,000
<u>Preferred stock, $10 par value, 5% cumulative</u>	
Shares outstanding 1/1	4,000

What are the number of shares Jet should use to calculate earnings per share?

a. 40,000
b. 45,000
c. 50,000
d. 54,000 (5/93, PI, #60, amended, 4099)

26. Deck Co. had 120,000 shares of common stock outstanding at January 1 of the current year. On July 1, it issued 40,000 additional shares of common stock. Outstanding all year were 10,000 shares of nonconvertible cumulative preferred stock. What is the number of shares that Deck should use to calculate earnings per share?

a. 140,000
b. 150,000
c. 160,000
d. 170,000 (R/00, FAR, #9, amended, 6904)

27. In computing the weighted-average number of shares outstanding during the year, which of the following midyear events must be treated as if it had occurred at the beginning of the year?

a. Declaration and distribution of stock dividend
b. Purchase of treasury stock
c. Sale of additional common stock
d. Sale of preferred convertible stock

(5/98, FAR, #5, 6608)

28. On June 30, of the previous year, Lomond, Inc. issued twenty $10,000, 7% bonds at par. Each bond was convertible into 200 shares of common stock. On January 1 of the current year, 10,000 shares of common stock were outstanding. The bondholders converted all the bonds on July 1 of the current year. The following amounts were reported in Lomond's income statement for the current year ended December 31:

Revenues	$ 977,000
Operating expenses	(920,000)
Interest on bonds	(7,000)
Income before income tax	50,000
Income tax at 30%	(15,000)
Net income	$ 35,000

What amount should Lomond report as its current year basic earnings per share?

a. $2.50
b. $2.85
c. $2.92
d. $3.50 (5/92, PI, #60, amended, 2632)

29. On January 31, year 2, Pack, Inc. split its common stock 2 for 1, and Young, Inc. issued a 5% stock dividend. Both companies issued their December 31, year 1, financial statements on March 1, year 2. Should Pack's year 1 earnings per share (EPS) take into consideration the stock split, and should Young's year 1 EPS take into consideration the stock dividend?

	Pack's year 1 EPS	*Young's year 1 EPS*
a.	Yes	No
b.	No	No
c.	Yes	Yes
d.	No	Yes

(11/92, Theory, #23, amended, 3456)

30. During the current year, Comma Co. had outstanding: 25,000 shares of common stock, 8,000 shares of $20 par, 10% cumulative preferred stock, and 3,000 bonds that are $1,000 par and 9% convertible. The bonds were originally issued at par, and each bond was convertible into 30 shares of common stock. During the year, net income was $200,000, no dividends were declared, and the tax rate was 30%. What amount was Comma's basic earnings per share for the current year?

a. $3.38
b. $7.36
c. $7.55
d. $8.00 (R/05, FAR, C02300F, #48, 7792)

Items 31 and 32 are based on the following information relating to the capital structure of Parke Corporation:

	December 31	
	Year 1	Year 2
Outstanding shares of:		
Common stock	90,000	90,000
Preferred stock, convertible into shares of common	30,000	30,000
10% convertible bonds, convertible into 20,000 shares of common	$1,000,000	$1,000,000

During year 2, Parke paid $45,000 dividends on the preferred stock, which was earned in year 2. Parke's net income for year 2 was $980,000 and the income tax rate was 40%.

31. For calendar year 2, basic EPS is
a. $10.89
b. $10.39
c. $ 8.17
d. $ 7.79 (11/85, PI, #54, amended, 1294)

32. For calendar year 2, diluted EPS is
a. $9.82
b. $8.29
c. $7.71
d. $7.43 (11/85, PI, #55, amended, 1295)

33. Dilutive stock options would generally be used in the calculation of

	Basic earnings per share	*Diluted earnings per share*
a.	No	No
b.	No	Yes
c.	Yes	Yes
d.	Yes	No

(11/88, Theory, #33, amended, 9062)

34. Cox Corporation had 1,200,000 shares of common stock outstanding on January 1, and December 31, year 2. In connection with the acquisition of a subsidiary company in June of year 1, Cox is required to issue 50,000 additional shares of its common stock on July 1, of year 3, to the former owners of the subsidiary. Cox paid $200,000 in preferred stock dividends in year 2, and reported net income of $3,400,000 for the year. Cox's diluted earnings per share for year 2 should be
a. $2.83
b. $2.72
c. $2.67
d. $2.56 (5/84, PI, #49, amended, 1299)

35. West Co. had earnings per share of $15.00 for the current year, before considering the effects of any convertible securities. No conversion or exercise of convertible securities occurred during the year. However, possible conversion of convertible bonds would have reduced earnings per share by $0.75. The effect of possible exercise of common stock options would have increased earnings per share by $0.10. What amount should West report as diluted earnings per share for the year?
a. $14.25
b. $14.35
c. $15.00
d. $15.10 (11/95, FAR, #46, amended, 6128)

36. Dunn, Inc. had 200,000 shares of $20 par common stock and 20,000 shares of $100 par, 6%, cumulative, convertible preferred stock outstanding for the entire current year ended December 31. Each preferred share is convertible into five shares of common stock. Dunn's net income for the year was $840,000. For the current year ended December 31, the diluted earnings per share is
a. $2.40
b. $2.80
c. $3.60
d. $4.20 (5/87, PI, #58, amended, 1289)

37. In determining earnings per share, interest expense, net of applicable income taxes, on convertible debt that is dilutive should be
a. Added back to net income for basic EPS, and ignored for diluted EPS
b. Ignored for basic EPS, and added back to net income for diluted EPS
c. Deducted from net income for basic EPS, and ignored for fully diluted EPS
d. Deducted from net income for both basic EPS and diluted EPS

(5/91, Theory, #29, amended, 1974)

38. The if-converted method of computing earnings per share data assumes conversion of convertible securities as of the
a. Beginning of the earliest period reported (or at time of issuance, if later)
b. Beginning of the earliest period reported (regardless of time of issuance)
c. Middle of the earliest period reported (regardless of time of issuance)
d. Ending of the earliest period reported (regardless of time of issuance)

(11/87, Theory, #33, 2006)

39. When computing diluted earnings per share, convertible securities are
a. Ignored
b. Recognized whether they are dilutive or anti-dilutive
c. Recognized only if they are anti-dilutive
d. Recognized only if they are dilutive
(11/93, Theory, #16, amended, 4521)

40. Earnings per share data should be reported in the financial statements for

	Cumulative effect of a change in accounting principle	An extraordinary item
a.	Yes	No
b.	Yes	Yes
c.	No	Yes
d.	No	No

(11/91, Theory, #16, amended, 2524)

Problem 15-2 ADDITIONAL MULTIPLE CHOICE QUESTIONS (24 to 30 minutes)

41. At December 30 of the current year, Vida Co. had cash of $200,000, a current ratio of 1.5:1 and a quick ratio of .5:1. On December 31, all cash was used to reduce accounts payable. How did these cash payments affect the ratios?

	Current ratio	Quick ratio
a.	Increased	Decreased
b.	Increased	No effect
c.	Decreased	Increased
d.	Decreased	No effect

(5/94, FAR, #60, amended, 4875)

42. Gil Corp. has current assets of $90,000 and current liabilities of $180,000. Which of the following transactions would improve Gil's current ratio?
a. Refinancing a $30,000 long-term mortgage with a short-term note
b. Purchasing $50,000 of merchandise inventory with a short-term account payable
c. Paying $20,000 of short-term accounts payable
d. Collecting $10,000 of short-term accounts receivable (11/91, PII, #19, 2467)

43. Barr Co. has total debt of $420,000 and stockholders' equity of $700,000. Barr is seeking capital to fund an expansion. Barr is planning to issue an additional $300,000 in common stock and is negotiating with a bank to borrow additional funds. The bank is requiring a debt-to-equity ratio of .75. What is the maximum additional amount Barr will be able to borrow?
a. $225,000
b. $330,000
c. $525,000
d. $750,000 (11/95, FAR, #59, 6141)

44. Which of the following ratios is(are) useful in assessing a company's ability to meet currently maturing or short-term obligations?

	Acid-test ratio	Debt-to-equity ratio
a.	No	No
b.	No	Yes
c.	Yes	Yes
d.	Yes	No

(5/89, Theory, #37, 9055)

45. Heath Co.'s current ratio is 4:1. Which of the following transactions would normally increase its current ratio?
a. Purchasing inventory on account
b. Selling inventory on account
c. Collecting an account receivable
d. Purchasing machinery for cash
(11/92, Theory, #38, 3471)

46. Zenk Co. wrote off obsolete inventory of $100,000 during the year. What was the effect of this write-off on Zenk's ratio analysis?
a. Decrease in current ratio but **not** in quick ratio
b. Decrease in quick ratio but **not** in current ratio
c. Increase in current ratio but **not** in quick ratio
d. Increase in quick ratio but **not** in current ratio
(5/92, PII, #18, amended, 2650)

47. On December 31 of the current year, Northpark Co. collected a receivable due from a major customer. Which of the following ratios would be increased by this transaction?
a. Inventory turnover ratio
b. Receivable turnover ratio
c. Current ratio
d. Quick ratio (5/92, Theory, #48, amended, 2741)

48. During the current year, Rand Co. purchased $960,000 of inventory. The cost of goods sold for the year was $900,000, and the ending inventory at December 31 was $180,000. What was the inventory turnover for the year?
a. 6.4
b. 6.0
c. 5.3
d. 5.0 (11/90, PI, #57, amended, 1253)

49. Selected information from the accounting records of Dalton Manufacturing Company is as follows:

Net sales for the current year	$1,800,000
Cost of goods sold for the current year	1,200,000
Inventories at December 31, previous year	336,000
Inventories at December 31, current year	288,000

Assuming there are 300 working days per year, what is the number of days' sales in average inventories for the current year?
a. 78
b. 72
c. 52
d. 48 (11/83, PI, #18, amended, 1267)

50. Hoyt Corp.'s current balance sheet reports the following stockholders' equity:

• 5% cumulative preferred stock, par value $100 per share; 2,500 shares issued and outstanding	$250,000
• Common stock, par value $3.50 per share; 100,000 shares issued and outstanding	350,000
• Additional paid-in capital in excess of par value of common stock	125,000
• Retained earnings	300,000

Dividends in arrears on the preferred stock amount to $25,000. If Hoyt were to be liquidated, the preferred stockholders would receive par value plus a premium of $50,000. The book value per share of common stock is
a. $7.75
b. $7.50
c. $7.25
d. $7.00 (11/91, PII, #3, 2451)

Items 51 and 52 are based on the following:

Mann, Inc. had 300,000 shares of common stock issued and outstanding at December 31 of the previous year. On July 1 of the current year, an additional 50,000 shares of common stock were issued for cash. Mann also had unexercised stock options to purchase 40,000 shares of common stock at $15 per share outstanding at the beginning and end of the year. The average market price of Mann's common stock was $20 during the year.

51. What is the number of shares that should be used in computing basic earnings per share for the current year ended December 31?
a. 325,000
b. 335,000
c. 360,000
d. 365,000 (5/85, PI, #51, amended, 1296a)

52. What is the number of shares that should be used in computing diluted earnings per share for the current year ended December 31?
a. 325,000
b. 335,000
c. 360,000
d. 365,000 (5/85, PI, #51, amended, 1296b)

SIMULATIONS

Problem 15-3 (15 to 25 minutes)

Research Task | Scenario & Responses

Research Question: If an impairment loss is recognized, what will be its new cost basis?

Paragraph Reference Answer: ________________

Research Task | Scenario & Responses

Daley Inc. is consistently profitable. Daley's normal financial statement relationships are as follows:

I.	Current ratio	3 to 1
II.	Inventory turnover	4 times
III.	Total debt/total assets ratio	0.5 to 1

For items 1 through 6, determine whether each transaction or event (I) increased, (D) decreased, or had (N) no effect on each of the ratios for the year. For each ratio choose only one of the three alternatives.

Current Ratio	Inventory Turn-over	Total debt/ Total assets	Transactions & Events to Analyze
I, D, or N	I, D, or N	I, D, or N	
			1. Daley issued a stock dividend.
			2. Daley declared, but did not pay, a cash dividend.
			3. Customers returned invoiced goods for which they had not paid.
			4. Accounts payable were paid on December 31.
			5. Daley recorded both a receivable from an insurance company and a loss from fire damage to a factory building.
			6. Early in the year, Daley increased the selling price of one of its products that had a demand in excess of capacity. The number of units sold was the same as the previous year.

(5/93, Theory, #61, amended, 9911)

Problem 15-4 (35 to 45 minutes)

Research Task	Scenario	Responses A&B	Response C

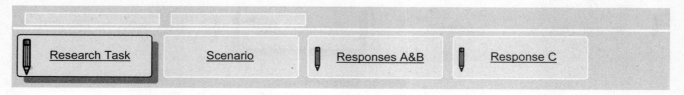

Research Question: Can the same convertible securities be dilutive and antidilutive at the same time?

Paragraph Reference Answer: _______________

Research Task	Scenario	Responses A&B	Response C

Mason Corporation's capital structure is as follows:

	December 31	
	Year 3	Year 2
Outstanding shares of:		
Common stock	336,000	300,000
Nonconvertible preferred stock	10,000	10,000
8% convertible bonds	$1,000,000	$1,000,000

- On September 1, year 3, Mason sold 36,000 additional shares of common stock.
- Net income for the year ended December 31, year 3, was $750,000.
- During year 3, Mason paid dividends of $3.00 per share on its nonconvertible preferred stock.
- The 8% convertible bonds are convertible into 40 shares of common stock for each $1,000 bond.
- Unexercised stock options to purchase 30,000 shares of common stock at $22.50 per share were outstanding at the beginning and end of year 3. The average market price of Mason's common stock was $36 per share during year 3. The market price was $33 per share at December 31, year 3.
- Warrants to purchase 20,000 shares of common stock at $38 per share were attached to the preferred stock at the time of issuance. The warrants, which expire on December 31, year 7, were outstanding at December 31, year 3.
- Mason's effective income tax rate was 40% for year 2 and year 3.

a. Compute* the number of shares which should be used for the computation of basic earnings per share for the year ended December 31, year 3.

b. Compute* the basic earnings per share for the year ended December 31, year 3.

c. Compute* the number of shares which should be used for the computation of diluted earnings per share for the year ended December 31, year 3.

d. Compute* the diluted earnings per share for the year ended December 31, year 3.

(11/81, PI, #5b, amended, 9911)

* Round earnings per share to the nearest penny

Research Task | Scenario | Responses A&B | Response C

Mason Corporation
Number of Shares for Computation of Basic Earnings Per Share
For Year Ended December 31, Year 3

Dates	Shares	Months outstanding	Weighted shares
Jan. 1 - Aug. 31		×	
Sept. 1, sold additional shares		×	
Weighted average number of shares outstanding			

Mason Corporation
Computation of Basic Earnings Per Share
For Year Ended December 31, Year 3

Income:	
Net income	
Deduct dividends paid on preferred stock	
Net income, adjusted	
Number of shares	
Basic earnings per share	

Research Task | Scenario | Responses A&B | Response C

Mason Corporation
Number of Shares for Computation
of Diluted Earnings Per Share
For Year Ended December 31, Year 3

Weighted average number of shares outstanding		
Common stock equivalents from stock options—dilutive*		
Shares assumed to be issued upon conversion of convertible bonds		
Total number of shares for diluted EPS computation		

*Calculations:		
Shares that would be issued upon exercise of options		
Cash proceeds that would be realized upon exercise		
Treasury shares that could be purchased		
Dilutive common stock equivalents		

Response D Essay

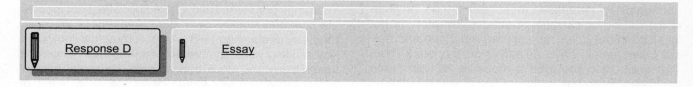

Mason Corporation
Computation of Diluted Earnings Per Share
For Year Ended December 31, Year 3

Income:	
Net income	
Deduct dividends paid on preferred stock	
Add interest expense (net of income tax effect) on convertible bonds	
Net income, adjusted	
Number of shares	
Diluted earnings per share	

Response D Essay

(15 to 25 minutes)

Columbine Co. issued 10-year convertible bonds on October 1, year 1. Each $1,000 bond is convertible, at the holder's option, into 20 shares of Columbine's $25 par value common stock. The bonds were issued at a premium when the common stock traded at $45 per share. After payment of interest on October 1, year 3, 30% of the bonds were tendered for conversion when the common stock was trading at $57 per share. Columbine used the book value method to account for the conversion.

- How should Columbine determine whether to include the convertible bonds in computing year 1 diluted earnings per share?
- How does the inclusion of convertible bonds affect the computation of year 1 diluted earnings per share?

(5/92, Theory, #3b, amended, 6186)

Solution 15-1 MULTIPLE CHOICE ANSWERS

Solvency

1. (a) The quick ratio is calculated by dividing the total of cash, marketable securities, and net receivables by current liabilities. Fluctuating market prices may cause the marketable securities in the numerator to decrease, thus creating an adverse effect on the quick ratio. Because inventory is not included in the quick ratio, increasing inventory market prices would have no effect on the quick ratio. The quick ratio provides a measure to help North evaluate if Belle has sufficient liquid assets, such as available-for-sale investments, to meet its current obligations. The quick ratio does not include inventory or long-term obligations.

2. (a) The sale of a company's trading securities at their carrying amounts for cash has no effect on either ratio. Both the trading securities and cash are current assets, thus the current asset amount does not change in the current ratio (current assets divided by current liabilities). The numerator of the quick ratio is cash plus marketable securities plus net receivables; so cash increases for the same amount that marketable securities decreases.

3. (a) The balance sheet is the financial statement that should be primarily used to assess a company's liquidity and financial flexibility (SFAC 5, ¶24). The balance sheet, however, provides an incomplete picture of either a company's liquidity or financial flexibility, unless it is used in conjunction with at least a cash flow statement (*ibid*).

4. (b) The defensive-interval ratio is a liquidity ratio and the return on stockholders' equity is a profitability (performance) ratio. The defensive-interval ratio is computed by dividing defensive assets (cash, marketable securities, and net receivables) by projected daily expenditures from operations. Projected daily expenditures are computed by dividing cost of goods sold plus selling and administrative expenses and other ordinary cash expenses by 365 days. This ratio measures the time span a firm can operate on present liquid assets without resorting to revenues from a future period.

5. (a) During the year the exercise of the stock options increased Ali's total assets and total stockholders' equity by $8,000 (i.e., 1,000 × $8). The debt to equity ratio is computed by dividing total liabilities by total stockholders' equity. Therefore, the exercise of the stock options decreased the debt to equity ratio to 12% (i.e., $60,000 / $500,000) because it increased total stockholders' equity, the denominator of the ratio, but did not affect total liabilities, the numerator of the ratio. Earnings per share (EPS) is computed by dividing net income to common stockholders by the weighted average number of common shares outstanding. The exercise of the stock options increased the weighted average number of common shares outstanding, the denominator of the earnings per share ratio, but did not affect net income to common stockholders, the numerator of the ratio, thereby decreasing EPS. Asset turnover is computed by dividing sales by average total assets. Since the exercise of the stock options increased total assets, Ali's asset turnover would decrease as a result of the exercise of the stock options.

6. (d) The times-interest-earned (TIE) ratio measures an entity's ability to meet its interest payments. Note that income taxes are not subtracted from operating income because interest is tax deductible.

$$\text{TIE Ratio} = \frac{\text{Income before interest \& taxes}}{\text{Interest expense}} = \frac{\$900{,}000}{\$100{,}000} = \mathbf{9.0 \text{ to } 1}$$

7. (c) The times-preferred-dividend-earned (TPDE) ratio measures an entity's ability to meet preferred dividend payments. Because dividends are not tax deductible, this ratio is computed on the basis of net income (i.e., after income taxes).

$$\text{TPDE Ratio} = \frac{\text{Net income}}{\text{Preferred dividends}} = \frac{\$480{,}000}{\$200{,}000} = \mathbf{2.4 \text{ to } 1}$$

8. (a) The acid-test ratio is computed by dividing cash, short-term marketable securities, and net receivables by current liabilities.

$$\text{Acid-test ratio} = \frac{\text{Cash + Marketable securities + Net receivables}}{\text{Current liabilities}}$$

$$= (\$300 + \$0 + \$1{,}200) / \$1{,}000 = \mathbf{1.5}$$

Operational Efficiency

9. (c) To compute the average number of days to collect accounts receivable, the number of days in the year is divided by the accounts receivable turnover ratio for the year.

$$\text{Accounts receivable turnover ratio} = \frac{\text{Net credit sales}}{\text{Average net accounts receivable}}$$

$$= \frac{\$7{,}200}{[(\$1{,}200 - \$400) + \$1{,}200] / 2}$$

$$= 7.2 \text{ times}$$

Average number of days to collect accounts receivable = *Number of days in year* / *Accounts receivable turnover ratio*

= 365 / 7.2 = **50.7 days**

10. (c) The receivables turnover is computed by dividing net credit sales by net average receivables. This calculation provides information related to how effectively an enterprise uses its assets because it provides a measure of how many times the receivables have been turned into cash during the year. The dividend payout ratio is computed by dividing dividends per common share by earnings per share. This ratio is an index showing whether an enterprise pays out most of its earnings in dividends or reinvests the earnings internally; it provides no information related to how effectively the enterprise uses its assets.

11. (d) The operating cycle is the average length of time that it takes to sell an inventory item and to collect the cash from the sale.

Number of days' sales in inventory	61
Number of days' sales in accounts receivable	33
Number of days in Clay's operating cycle	94

12. (b)

Net credit sales / average net receivables = accounts receivable turnover
Net credit sales / $200,000 = 10
Net credit sales = $2,000,000
Total assets turnover = total sales (net credit sales in this case) / average total assets
2 = 2,000,000 / average total assets
Average total assets = $2,000,000 / 2
Average total assets = $1,000,000

13. (a) Cash sales are not used to compute the accounts receivable turnover. The accounts receivable turnover ratio is computed by dividing net credit sales by average accounts receivable.

Average accounts receivable, [($20,000 + $22,000) / 2]	$ 21,000
Accounts receivable turnover	× 5.0
Net credit sales	$105,000

14. (c) To compute the inventory turnover for the year, the inventory at the end of the year must first be determined. Inventory turnover equals cost of goods sold divided by average inventory.

Inventory, 1/1	$ 6,000
Plus: Purchases	24,000
Goods available for sale	30,000
Less: Cost of goods sold	(18,000)
Inventory, 12/31	$ 12,000

Inventory turnover = $18,000 / (($6,000 + $12,000) / 2) = **2.0 times**

15. (b) The average days' sales in inventory is computed by dividing the number of days in the year (numerator) by the inventory turnover ratio (denominator).

16. (b) Receivables Turnover:

Net Credit Sales / Average Net Receivables

$3,000,000 / (($100,000 + $400,000) / 2) = 12

Number of Day's Sales in Average Receivables:

360 / Receivables Turnover

360 / 12 = 30 days

Profitability

17. (d) The book value per preferred share is the portion of stockholders' equity distributable to preferred stockholders in the event of liquidation (Liquidation value + Dividends in arrears), divided by the number of preferred shares outstanding. [($105 × 1,000 sh.) + (10% × $100,000)] / 1,000 shares = $115 share.

18. (b) Rate of Return on Assets = Net Income / Average Total Assets

$150,000 / (($2,000,000 + $3,000,000) / 2) = $150,000 / $2,500,000 = **6%**

19. (b) Successful use of leverage is where you can earn more by the use of borrowed money than it costs to use the borrowed funds. This is evidenced by a rate of return on investment that is greater than the cost of debt. The rate of return on stockholders' equity is less than the rate of return on investment when the cost of borrowing exceeds the rate of return on investment (unsuccessful use of leverage). Answers (c) and (d) are not measures of successful use of leverage.

20. (b) Dividends per share for common stock are used in the numerator of the dividend per share payout ratio, but are not used in computing earnings per share.

Dividend per share payout ratio = *Cash dividends per common share* / *Earnings per s*

$$\text{Earnings per share} = \frac{\text{Net income to common stockholders}}{\text{Weighted average common shares outstanding}}$$

21. (c) To determine the price-earnings ratio on common stock, the earnings per share must first be computed.

$$\text{Earnings per share} = \frac{\text{Net income} - \text{Preferred dividend requirement}}{\text{Weighted average common shares}}$$

$$= \frac{\$240{,}000 - \$0}{300{,}000}$$

$$\text{Price earnings ratio} = \frac{\text{Market price per share}}{\text{Earnings per share}} = \frac{\$12.00}{\$0.80} = \textbf{15.0 to 1}$$

22. (c) Neither ratio is useful for evaluating the effectiveness with which the company uses its assets. The acid-test (quick) ratio is a measure for assessing short-term liquidity risk; it measures a company's ability to meet its short-term obligations. The price-earnings ratio measures the relationship between the market price of a share of stock and the stock's current earnings per share.

Basic EPS

23. (b) Earnings per share for the previous and current year is $1.78 ($410,000 / 230,000 shares) and $1.75 ($350,000 / 200,000 shares), respectively. Stock dividends, stock splits, and reverse splits are given retroactive recognition in the computation of EPS for all periods presented. To compute EPS, the weighted average number of common shares outstanding must be computed for each year.

	Current year	Previous year
Common shares outstanding at 1/1	100,000	100,000
Sale of additional shares, 4/1 (20,000 × 9/12)		15,000
2-for-1 stock split, 7/1		
(Previous year: 100,000 × 100%)		100,000
(Current year: 115,000 × 100%)	115,000	
Weighted average common shares outstanding	230,000	200,000

24. (b) Basic EPS, with a simple capital structure, is equal to net income minus the preferred dividends declared or the dividend preference on cumulative preferred stock for the current period (even though not declared) divided by the number of shares of common stock and common stock equivalents outstanding. ($500,000 – $10,000) / 200,000 = $2.45. The cumulative preferred's $10,000 dividend preference for the previous year that was paid in the current year is not included in the calculation. The preferred dividends for the current year are included in the calculation, regardless of whether they have been paid.

25. (b) Stock splits are given retroactive recognition in the computation of EPS. Shares issued must be weighted averaged according to the length of time they are outstanding. Since the preferred stock is nonconvertible, it does not affect the number of shares used to calculate EPS. The weighted average number of common shares outstanding during the year, determined as follows, should be used to calculate earnings per share.

1/1 Common shares outstanding	20,000
4/1 Common shares issued due to 2-for-1 stock split	20,000
7/1 Common shares issued for cash (10,000 × 6/12)	5,000
Weighted average common shares, 12/31	45,000

26. (a) For EPS, the denominator is the weighted-average number of common shares outstanding during the period. This number will include common shares outstanding the entire period, shares issued during the period, and shares where all of the conditions of issuance have been met. In this case, there is no need for a diluted EPS adjustment because the preferred stock is not convertible.

Common shares outstanding on January 1		120,000
Common shares issued on July 1	$40,000	
Times: Weight factor for shares issued in July (1/2 year)	× 50%	20,000
Weighted-average number of shares outstanding		140,000

27. (a) In computing the weighted-average number of shares outstanding, stock dividends, stock splits, and reverse stock splits are reflected retroactively, because they change the total number of shares outstanding but not the proportionate shares outstanding. The purchase of treasury stock, the sale of additional common stock and preferred convertible stock affect the total number of shares and the proportionate shares outstanding. These shares participate in earnings for only the time the stock is outstanding.

28. (c) To reflect the actual conversion on July 1, 4,000 additional common shares are added to the 10,000 common shares outstanding since the beginning of the year, resulting in 12,000 weighted average common shares outstanding. Basic EPS = $35,000 / 12,000 = $2.92 per share.

10,000 × 12/12	10,000
4,000 × 6/12	2,000
Weighted average common shares o/s	12,000

29. (c) Stock dividends, stock splits, and reverse splits consummated after the close of the period but before completion of the financial report are given retroactive recognition in the computation of EPS. The per share computations are based on the new number of shares because the reader's primary interest is presumed to be related to the current capital structure.

30. (b) To arrive at basic EPS, the income available to common stock holders is divided by the number of common shares outstanding. Income available to common stockholders is net income less dividends on preferred stock (not net of tax).

Net income	$200,000
Less: Dividends on preferred stock [(8,000 × $20) × 10%]	(16,000)
Income available to common s/h	184,000
Divide: Common shares outstanding	/ 25,000
Basic EPS	$ 7.36

$3.38 would be the diluted EPS if the bonds had been converted.
$7.55 would be the EPS if dividends on preferred stock was added net of tax to net income for the year.
EPS of $8 does not adjust for dividends paid on the cumulative preferred stock.

31. (b) Basic earnings per share (EPS) is computed by dividing net income less preferred stock dividends by the weighted average common shares of stock outstanding. ($980,000 – $45,000) / 90,000 shares = $10.39/share.

Diluted EPS

32. (d) Diluted EPS is computed in the same manner as basic EPS, except that all convertible securities are assumed to be converted (if dilutive) and the numerator is adjusted accordingly.

$$\frac{\$980{,}000 \text{ NI} + [\$100{,}000\ (\textit{interest}) - \$40{,}000\ (\text{tax})]}{90{,}000\ (\text{common}) + 30{,}000\ (\textit{convertible preferred}) + 20{,}000\ (\textit{convertible bonds})} = \mathbf{\$7.43}$$

33. (b) Stock options should be used in the calculation of diluted EPS if the effect is dilutive (their inclusion has the effect of decreasing the EPS amount or increasing the loss per share amount otherwise computed).

34. (d) If shares are to be issued in the future upon the mere passage of time, they should be considered as outstanding for the computation of EPS.

$$\frac{\textit{NI} - \textit{Preferred Dividend}}{\textit{Outstanding Shares} + \textit{Contingent Shares}} = \text{EPS}$$

$$\frac{\$3{,}400{,}000 - \$200{,}000}{1{,}200{,}000 + 50{,}000} = \$2.56$$

35. (a) Dilutive securities are included in the calculation of diluted EPS; thus, the convertible bonds would be included, reducing EPS of $15.00 by $0.75. Antidulitive securities are excluded from dilutive EPS; thus, the options are not included.

36. (b) Earnings per share (EPS) is computed by dividing net income less preferred stock dividends by the weighted average shares of common stock outstanding. Diluted EPS adjusts this calculation to reflect all potentially dilutive securities. The convertible preferred stock is assumed converted at the beginning of the year. The preferred stock dividend of $120,000 (20,000 × $100 × 6%) is added back to the numerator (canceling out its original subtraction) and the 100,000 (20,000 × 5) shares of converted common stock are added to the denominator.

$$\frac{\$840{,}000\ \textit{Net income}}{200{,}000\ \textit{Common} + 100{,}000\ \textit{Convertible preferred}} = \mathbf{\$2.80}$$

37. (b) Convertible debt is not included in the calculations of basic EPS. The interest expense is added back to net income in determining dilutive EPS.

38. (a) Dilutive convertible securities are included in EPS computations under the if-converted method. Under that method, the security is assumed to have been converted at the beginning of the earliest period reported (or at time of issuance, if later).

39. (d) Convertible securities are only included in the computation of diluted EPS for any period for which their effect is dilutive.

Financial Statement Presentation

40. (b) Earnings per share amounts should be reported on the face of the income statement or in the notes to the financial statements for a discontinued operation, an extraordinary item, and the cumulative effect of an accounting change.

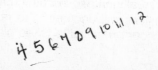

4 5 6 7 8 9 10 11 12

Problem 15-2 ADDITIONAL MULTIPLE CHOICE ANSWERS

Solvency

41. (a) When the current ratio is greater than 1:1, any decrease in current liabilities, even when accompanied by a decrease in current assets by an equal amount, will cause an increase in the current ratio. When the quick ratio is less than 1:1, any decrease in quick assets, even when accompanied by a decrease in current liabilities by an equal amount, will cause a decrease in the quick ratio.

42. (b) The purchase of the merchandise inventory with a short-term account payable increases both current assets and current liabilities by $50,000. Since Gil's current ratio before this transaction was less than 1.0 (i.e., $90,000 / $180,000 = 0.5 to 1), increasing both current assets and current liabilities by the same amount increases the current ratio [i.e., ($90,000 + $50,000) / ($180,000 + $50,000) = 0.61 to 1].

$$\textit{Current ratio} = \frac{\textit{Current assets}}{\textit{Current liabilities}}$$

43. (b)

Current stockholders' equity	$ 700,000
Anticipated sales of stock	300,000
Total projected stockholders' equity	$1,000,000

Maximum debt-to-equity ratio: MD/$1,000,000 = .75

Maximum debt ($1,000,000 × .75)	$ 750,000
Less: Current debt	(420,000)
Additional maximum Barr may borrow	$ 330,000

44. (d) The acid-test (quick) ratio is a measure for assessing short-term liquidity risk; it measures a company's ability to meet its currently maturing or short-term obligations. On the other hand, the debt-to-equity ratio is a measure for assessing long-term liquidity risk; it measures the portion of assets being provided by creditors and the portion of assets being provided by the stockholders of a firm.

45. (b) Current assets increase when inventory is sold on account at a profit because the increase in accounts receivable exceeds the related decrease in the inventory account. Since the current ratio is computed by dividing current assets by current liabilities, selling inventory on account at a profit would increase the current ratio. The purchase of inventory on account increases both current assets and current liabilities by equal amounts. When the current ratio is greater than 1:1, an equal increase in both current assets and current liabilities will decrease the ratio. The collection of an account receivable takes place entirely within current assets. Therefore, the total amounts of current assets and current liabilities do not change as a result of the collection. Purchasing machinery for cash decreases current assets. Thus, the current ratio decreases as a result of this transaction.

46. (a) The current ratio is computed by dividing current assets by current liabilities. The write-off of the inventory reduces current assets, the numerator of the current ratio, thereby decreasing the ratio. The quick ratio is computed by dividing cash, short-term marketable securities, and net receivables by current liabilities. Since inventory is not used in the calculation of the quick ratio, the ratio is not effected by the write-off of the inventory.

Operational Efficiency

47. (b) The collection of the receivable due from a major customer reduces net average receivables, the denominator of the ratio, thereby increasing the ratio. Neither cash nor accounts receivables are used in computing the inventory turnover ratio. Although the collection of an account receivable affects the composition of current assets, the numerator of the current ratio, the total amount of current assets is unchanged. The collection of an account receivable increases cash and decreases accounts receivable; thus, the total amount of the numerator of the quick ratio (i.e., cash + marketable securities + net receivables) is unchanged.

$$\textit{Receivable turnover} = \frac{\textit{Net credit sales}}{\textit{Net average receivables}}$$

48. (b) To determine the inventory turnover for the year, the beginning inventory at January 1 must first be determined by working backwards through the cost of goods sold schedule. The inventory turnover for the year can then be computed.

Cost of goods sold for the year	$ 900,000
Add: Ending inventory, 12/31	180,000
Goods available for sale	1,080,000
Less: Purchases for the year	(960,000)
Beginning inventory, 1/1	$ 120,000

$$\textit{Inventory turnover} = \frac{\textit{Cost of goods sold}}{\textit{Average inventory}}$$

$$\frac{\$900{,}000}{\$120{,}000 + \$180{,}000)\ /\ 2}$$

49. (a) Number of days sales in average inventories = average inventory / cost of goods sold / 300 business days.

$$\frac{(\$336{,}000 + \$288{,}000) / 2}{\$1{,}200{,}000 / 300} = \frac{\$312{,}000}{\$4{,}000} = \textbf{78 days}$$

Profitability

50. (d) The book value per common share is calculated as total stockholders' equity less preferred stockholders' equity, divided by the number of common shares outstanding. The liquidating value of the preferred stock of $300,000 ($250,000 par value + $50,000 premium) is used to determine preferred stockholders' equity because that amount exceeds the par value of the preferred stock. The cumulative preferred stock dividends in arrears of $25,000 is also used in determining preferred stockholders' equity because they must be paid before any dividends can be paid on the common shares.

$$\textit{Book value per common share} = \frac{\textit{Stockholders' equity} - \textit{Preferred stockholders' equity}}{\textit{Common shares outstanding}}$$

$$= \frac{\$1{,}025{,}000^{*} - (\$300{,}000 + \$25{,}000)}{100{,}000} = \textbf{\$7.00}$$

* $250,000 + $350,000 + $125,000 + $300,000

Basic EPS

51. (a)

Common shares outstanding throughout period	300,000
Additional shares issued 7/1 (50,000 × 6/12)	25,000
Weighted CS o/s for basic EPS	325,000

Diluted EPS

52. (b)

Weighted CS o/s for basic EPS	325,000
Options pretended exercised	40,000
Less treasury stock pretended purchased (40,000 × $15)/$20	(30,000)
Shares used in diluted EPS calculation	335,000

PERFORMANCE BY SUBTOPICS

Each category below parallels a subtopic covered in Chapter 15. Record the number and percentage of questions you correctly answered in each subtopic area.

Solvency

Question #	Correct √
1	
2	
3	
4	
5	
6	
7	
8	
# Questions	8
# Correct	
% Correct	

Operational Efficiency

Question #	Correct √
9	
10	
11	
12	
13	
14	
15	
16	
# Questions	8
# Correct	
% Correct	

Profitability

Question #	Correct √
17	
18	
19	
20	
21	
22	
# Questions	6
# Correct	
% Correct	

Basic EPS

Question #	Correct √
23	
24	
25	
26	
27	
28	
29	
30	
31	
# Questions	9
# Correct	
% Correct	

Diluted EPS

Question #	Correct √
32	
33	
34	
35	
36	
37	
38	
39	
# Questions	8
# Correct	
% Correct	

Financial Statement Presentation

Question #	Correct √
40	
# Questions	1
# Correct	
% Correct	

SIMULATION SOLUTIONS

Solution 15-3

Research

FAS 144, Par. 15

If an impairment loss is recognized, the adjusted carrying amount of a long-lived asset shall be its new cost basis. For a depreciable long-lived asset, the new cost basis shall be depreciated (amortized) over the remaining useful life of that asset. Restoration of a previously recognized impairment loss is prohibited.

Responses 1-6

1. N, N, N

- Current Ratio—The current ratio is computed by dividing current assets by current liabilities. Since the issuance of the stock dividend was recorded entirely within Daley's stockholders' equity accounts, it **had no effect** on the amount of Daley's current assets or current liabilities. Thus, it also had no effect on Daley's current ratio.
- Inventory Turnover—The inventory turnover ratio is computed by dividing cost of goods sold by average inventory. Since the issuance of the stock dividend was recorded entirely within Daley's stockholders' equity accounts, it had no effect on the amount of Daley's cost of goods sold or average inventory. Thus, it also **had no effect** on Daley's inventory turnover ratio.
- Total Debt/Total Assets Ratio—Since the issuance of the stock dividend was recorded entirely within Daley's stockholders' equity accounts, it had no effect on the amount of Daley's total assets or total liabilities. Thus, it also had no effect on Daley's total debt/total assets ratio.

2. D, N, I

- Current Ratio—The current ratio is computed by dividing current assets by current liabilities. The declaration of the cash dividend increased current liabilities, the denominator of the current ratio. Therefore, Daley's current ratio **decreased** as a result of the declaration of the cash dividend.
- Inventory Turnover—The inventory turnover ratio is computed by dividing cost of goods sold by average inventory. Since the declaration of the cash dividend had no effect on the amount of Daley's cost of goods sold or average inventory, it also **had no effect** on Daley's inventory turnover ratio.
- Total Debt/Total Assets Ratio—The declaration of the cash dividend increased total debt, the numerator of the ratio. Therefore, Daley's total debt/total assets ratio **increased** as a result of the declaration of the cash dividend.

3. D, D, I

- Current Ratio—The current ratio is computed by dividing current assets by current liabilities. Assuming that the goods had been sold at a profit, the customer returns decreased current assets—the numerator of the current ratio—because the amount of the decrease to accounts receivable exceeded the amount of the increase to merchandise inventory. Therefore, Daley's current ratio **decreased** as a result of the customer returns.
- Inventory Turnover—The inventory turnover ratio is computed by dividing cost of goods sold by average inventory. The customer returns decreased cost of goods sold (the numerator of the ratio) and increased average inventory (the denominator of the ratio). Therefore, Daley's inventory turnover ratio **decreased** as a result of the customer returns.
- Total Debt/Total Assets Ratio—Assuming that the goods had been sold at a profit, the customer returns decreased total assets—the denominator of the ratio—because the amount of the decrease to accounts receivable exceeded the amount of the increase to merchandise inventory. Therefore, Daley's total debt/total assets ratio **increased** as a result of the customer returns.

4. I, N, D

- Current Ratio—The current ratio is computed by dividing current assets by current liabilities. The payment of the accounts payable decreased current liabilities and current assets by an equal amount; therefore, since Daley's current ratio was greater than 1:1 (i.e., 3.0 to 1), Daley's current ratio **increased** as a result of the payment of the accounts payable.
- Inventory Turnover—The inventory turnover ratio is computed by dividing cost of goods sold by average inventory. Since the payment of the accounts payable had no effect on the amount of Daley's cost of good sold or average inventory, it also **had no effect** on Daley's inventory turnover ratio.
- Total Debt/Total Assets Ratio—The payment of the accounts payable decreased total debt and total assets by an equal amount; therefore, since

the total debt/total assets ratio was less than 1:1 (i.e., 0.5 to 1), the ratio decreased as a result of the payment of the accounts payable.

5. I, N, I

- Current Ratio—The current ratio is computed by dividing current assets by current liabilities. The recording of the receivable from the insurance company increased current assets, the numerator of the current ratio. Therefore, Daley's current ratio increased as a result of the recording of the receivable from the insurance company.
- Inventory Turnover—The inventory turnover ratio is computed by dividing cost of goods sold by average inventory. Since the recording of the receivable from the insurance company and the loss from fire damage to the factory building had no effect on the amount of Daley's cost of goods sold or average inventory, they also **had no effect** on Daley's inventory turnover ratio.
- Total Debt/Total Assets Ratio—Daley recorded a loss from the fire damage to the factory building. Therefore, the amount of the receivable recorded from the insurance company was less than the carrying amount of the building (or portion thereof) removed from the accounts. This decreased total assets, the denominator of the ratio. Therefore, Daley's total debt/total assets ratio **increased** as a result of these events.

6. I, N, D

- Current Ratio—The current ratio is computed by dividing current assets by current liabilities. Daley increased the selling price of a product that had a demand in excess of capacity. The number of units of the product sold in each year was the same. Therefore, Daley was more profitable in the current year than the previous. The increased profits increased retained earnings, which in turn increased total stockholders' equity; therefore, since the increase in the selling price of the product had no effect on total liabilities, total assets must have increased. Since noncurrent assets would not be affected by the increase in the product's selling price, current assets—the numerator of the current ratio—must have increased. Therefore, Daley's current ratio increased as a result of the increase in the selling price of the product.
- Inventory Turnover—The inventory turnover ratio is computed by dividing cost of goods sold by average inventory. Since the increase in the selling price of the product had no effect on the amount of Daley's cost of goods sold or average inventory, it also **had no effect** on Daley's inventory turnover ratio.
- Total Debt/Total Assets Ratio—Daley increased the selling price of one of its products that had a demand in excess of capacity. The number of units sold in the two years was the same. Therefore, Daley was more profitable in the current year than the previous. The increased profits increased retained earnings, which in turn increased total stockholders' equity. Since the increase in the selling price of the product increased total stockholders' equity while having no effect on total liabilities, it also increased total assets, the denominator of the ratio. Therefore, Daley's total debt/total assets ratio decreased as a result of the increase in the selling price of the product.

Solution 15-4

Research

FAS 128, Par. 14

14. Convertible securities may be dilutive on their own but antidilutive when included with other potential common shares in computing diluted EPS. To reflect maximum potential dilution, each issue or series of issues of potential common shares shall be considered in sequence from the most dilutive to the least dilutive. That is, dilutive potential common shares with the lowest "earnings per incremental share" shall be included in diluted EPS before those with a higher earnings per incremental share. Illustration 4 in Appendix C provides an example of that provision.

Responses A & B

Mason Corporation
Number of Shares for Computation of Basic Earnings Per Share
For Year Ended December 31, Year 3

	A	B	C	
		Months	Weighted	
Dates	Shares	outstanding	shares	
Jan. 1 - Aug. 31	300,000	× 8/12	200,000	[1]
Sept. 1, sold additional shares	336,000	× 4/12	112,000	[2]
Weighted average number of shares outstanding			*312,000*	[3]

1 A. Number of shares given in scenario

1 B. 1/1 through 8/31 = 8 months

1 C. 300,000 × 8/12 = 200,000

2 A. Number of shares given in scenario

2 B. 9/1 through 12/31 = 4 months

2 C. 336,000 × 4/12 = 112,000

3 C. Sum of weighted shares.

Mason Corporation
Computation of Basic Earnings Per Share
For Year Ended December 31, Year 3

Income:		
Net income	$750,000	[4]
Deduct dividends paid on preferred stock 10,000 shares × $3	(30,000)	[5]
Net income, adjusted	*$720,000*	[6]
Number of shares (from Part A.)	/ 312,000	[7]
Basic earnings per share	*$ 2.31*	[8]

4. Net income given in scenario.

5. 10,000 shares × $3 = $30,000

6. Total net income.

7. Number of shares from part A = 312,000

8. Net income divided by number of shares from part A.

Response C

Mason Corporation
Number of Shares for Computation
of Diluted Earnings Per Share
For Year Ended December 31, Year 3

Weighted average number of shares outstanding (from Part A.)	[9]	312,000
Common stock equivalents from stock options—dilutive*	[10]	11,250
Shares assumed to be issued upon conversion of convertible bonds $1,000,000 / $1,000 = 1,000 bonds × 40	[11]	40,000
Total number of shares for diluted EPS computation	[12]	*363,250*
*Calculations:		
Shares that would be issued upon exercise of options	[13]	30,000
Cash proceeds that would be realized upon exercise 30,000 shares possible × $22.50 (option price)	$675,000	[14]
Treasury shares that could be purchased option price / $36 (average market price)	[15]	(18,750)
Dilutive common stock equivalents	[16]	*11,250*

9. Number of shares from part A = 312,000
10. From calculations made below.
11. $1,000,000 / $1,000 = 1,000 bonds × 40 = $40,000
12. Sum of Weighted average number of shares outstanding plus Common stock equivalents from stock options plus shares assumed to be issued upon conversion (312,000 + 11,250 + 40,000)
13. Unexercised stock options given in scenario
14. 30,000 shares possible × $22.50 (option price) = $675,000
15. $22.50 (option price) / $36 (average market price) = $18,750
16. Unexercised options less number of shares of treasury stock that could be purchased (30,000 – 18,750)

Response D

Mason Corporation
Computation of Diluted Earnings Per Share
For Year Ended December 31, Year 3

Income:		
Net income	$750,000	[17]
Deduct dividends paid on preferred stock 10,000 shares × $3	(30,000)	[18]
Add interest expense (net of income tax effect) on convertible bonds $1,000,000 × 8% × (1.0 – .40 tax rate)	48,000	[19]
Net income, adjusted	$768,000	[20]
Number of shares (from Part C.)	/ 363,250	[21]
Diluted earnings per share	$ 2.11	[22]

17. Net income given in scenario.

18. 10,000 shares × $3 = $30,000

19. $1,000,000 × 8% × (1.0 – .40 tax rate) = $48,000

20. Sum of net income and adjustments ($750,000 – 30,000 + 48,000)

21. Total number of shares for diluted EPS computation from part C

22. Net income divided by number of shares ($768,000 / 363,250)

Essay—Convertible Bonds

- If the bonds are **dilutive,** they are **included** in computing Columbine's year 1 diluted earnings per share.
- Both **earnings and number of shares** are affected by including the convertible bonds in computing diluted earnings per share. **Interest expense** on convertible bonds, **net of income taxes,** is **added to net income.** The **number of shares outstanding** is **increased by** the number of shares **potentially issuable on conversion** (number of bonds times 20), **multiplied by** the **proportion of the year** that the **bonds were outstanding** (one-quarter).

CHAPTER 16

FOREIGN OPERATIONS

I. Translation of Foreign Currency Financial Statements 16-2
- A. Translation Objectives 16-2
- B. Functional Currency 16-2
- C. Computation 16-4
- D. Remeasurement Into Functional Currency 16-6
- E. Functional Currency Determination 16-8

II. Foreign Currency Transactions 16-9
- A. General Provisions 16-9
- B. Forward Exchange Contracts 16-10

III. Foreign Currency Hedges 16-11
- A. Hedge Designation 16-11
- B. Reporting Hedging Gains & Losses 16-11

IV. Income Tax Consequences of Rate Changes 16-12
- A. Foreign Currency Transactions 16-12
- B. Foreign Currency Financial Statement Translation Adjustments 16-12

EXAM COVERAGE: Historically, exam coverage of the topics in Chapter 16 has been 1 to 3 percent of the FAR section. Mo[...] information regarding exam coverage is included in Appendix B, *Practical Advice.*

CHAPTER 16

FOREIGN OPERATIONS

I. Translation of Foreign Currency Financial Statements

A. Translation Objectives

SFAS 52, *Foreign Currency Translation,* deals with two main subjects: (1) translation of foreign currency financial statements and (2) foreign currency transactions, which include foreign currency forward exchange contracts.

1. Provide information that is generally compatible with the expected economic effects of a rate change on an enterprise's cash flows and equity.

2. Reflect in consolidated statements the financial results and relationships of individual consolidated entities as measured in their **functional currencies** in conformity with U.S. generally accepted accounting principles (GAAP).

B. Functional Currency

The assets, liabilities, and operations of a foreign entity should be measured in its functional currency. An entity's functional currency is the currency of the primary economic environment in which the entity operates; normally, that is the currency of the environment in which an entity primarily generates and expends cash. An entity's functional currency is basically a matter of fact. In some cases, however, the nature of a foreign entity's operations is such that its functional currency is not clearly determinable.

Example 1 ▸ Functional Currency

Americana Inc., a U.S. company, owns 100% of the stock of Frenchie's, a self-contained subsidiary incorporated in the United Kingdom. Frenchie's records all its transactions in Pounds Sterling, even though the bulk of its operations are conducted in Germany (i.e., the Euro is the functional currency). In order to prepare its consolidated financial statements, Americana will first **remeasure** the Pound Sterling statements into Euros and then **translate** them into U.S. dollars.

1. **Determining Functional Currency** The functional currency of a foreign entity may be its **local currency**, the **U.S. dollar**, or **another foreign currency**.

    a. **Local Currency** Where a foreign operation is relatively self-contained (i.e., most activities are performed independently of the parent company) and integrated within one country, the entity's functional currency will be the local currency. In this case, **translation** of financial statements from the functional currency into the parent's reporting currency (e.g., the U.S. dollar) will be required.

    b. **U.S. Dollar** Where the foreign operation is, in essence, an extension of the parent's U.S. operations (e.g., a sales branch that purchases all its inventory from the U.S. home office, in U.S. dollars), the functional currency will be the U.S. dollar.

        (1) If the foreign entity's books are kept in the local currency, then **remeasurement** into U.S. dollars will be required. A gain or loss from remeasurement will be included in the foreign entity's **income from continuing operations.**

        (2) If the foreign entity keeps its books in U.S. dollars, then its trial balance can be directly incorporated into the reporting entity's financial statements. Transactions denominated in foreign currency will result in foreign currency gains and losses. The **net** gain or loss will be **the same** as the remeasurement gain or

loss. In other words, if the functional currency of the foreign entity is the U.S. dollar, the aggregate net gain or loss from exchange rate fluctuations will be the same whether the foreign entity keeps its books in the local currency or U.S. dollars.

c. **Another Foreign Currency** A foreign entity may keep its books in the local currency (i.e., "recording currency"), yet have another foreign currency as functional currency. In this case, remeasuring of the recording currency statements into functional currency will be required. Once the statements have been remeasured into the functional currency, then translation into U.S. dollars is required.

Exhibit 1 ▸ Functional Currency

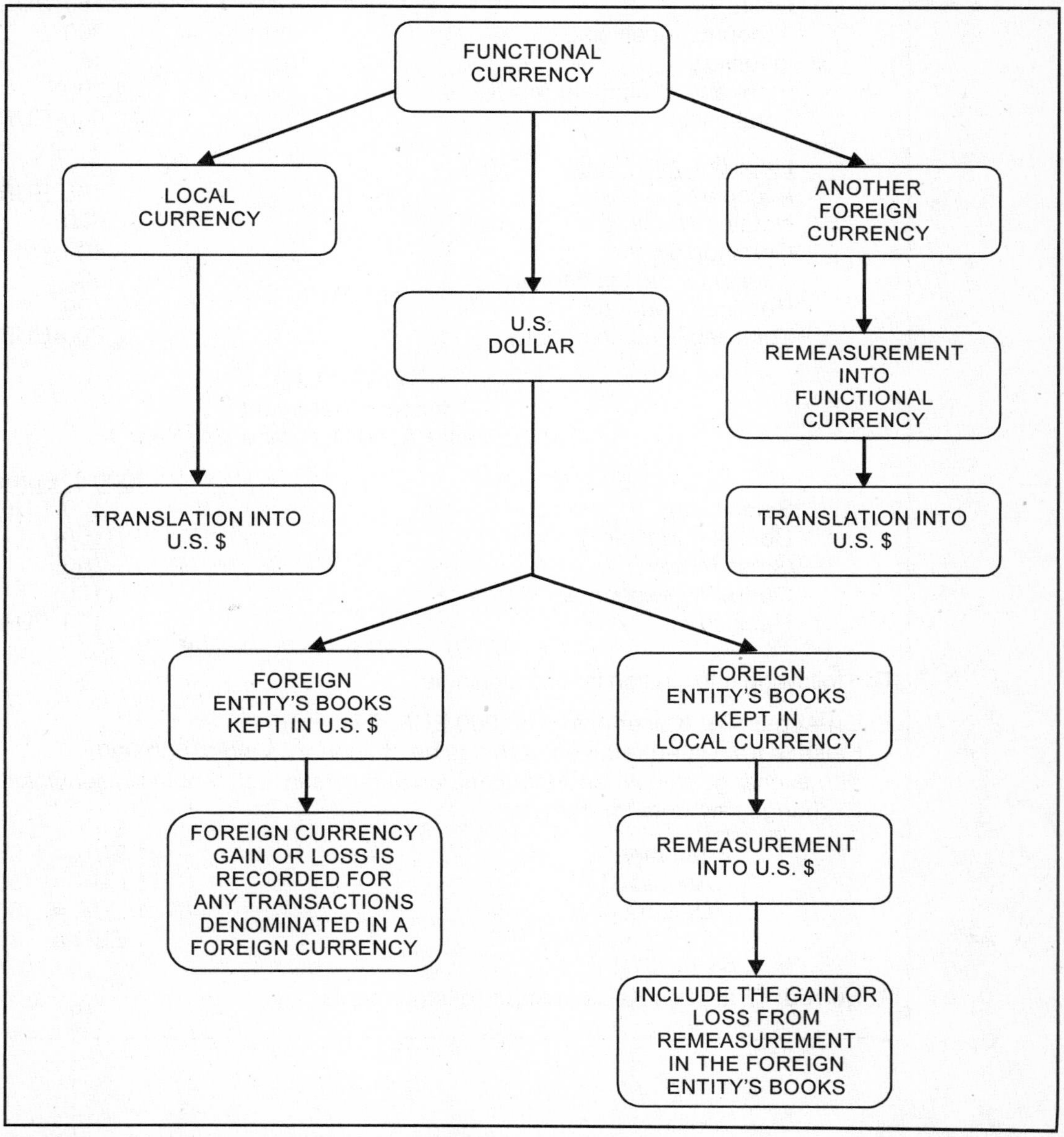

2. **Highly Inflationary Economies** Where a foreign country's cumulative inflation rate over the three-year period preceding the date of financial statements is approximately 100% or more, the local currency is not considered stable enough to be the functional currency. In this case, the reporting currency (e.g., the U.S. dollar) will be the functional currency, and **remeasurement** will be required.

C. Computation

Example 2 ▸ Computation

Americana Inc., a U.S. corporation, owns 100% of the outstanding common stock of Kaiser Ltd., a German company. Kaiser's financial statements for the year ending December 31 are reproduced below.

KAISER LTD.
Balance Sheet
December 31, Year 1

	(000's, Euros)
Assets	
Cash	150 EUR
Accounts receivable	200
Inventory	450
Plant and equipment (net)	1,200
Total assets	2,000 EUR
Liabilities and Equity	
Accounts payable	100 EUR
Notes payable	500
Common stock	400
Additional paid-in capital	300
Retained earnings	700
Total liabilities and equity	2,000 EUR

KAISER LTD.
Income Statement
For the Year Ended December 31, Year 1

	(000's, Euros)
Sales	400 EUR
Cost of goods sold	(150)
Gross margin	250
Operating expenses	(100)
Net income	150 EUR

The following information is also available:

- On August 31, Kaiser paid a 50,000 EUR dividend.
- Kaiser's translated retained earnings as of January 1 was $600,000.
- The exchange rate when Americana acquired its investment in Kaiser was 1 EUR = U.S. $1.
- Exchange rate data for the year:

January 1	1 EUR = $.95
August 31	1 EUR = .90
December 31	1 EUR = .80
Year's average	1 EUR = .85

Required: Translate Kaiser's financial statements.

translation adjustment is reported under OCI – Other Comprehensive Income

Income stat use here Year's average rate

Solution:

	Balance Sheet (000's)		
Assets	Euros	Rate	U.S. Dollars
Cash	150 EUR	$ .80/EUR	$ 120.0
Accounts receivable	200	.80/EUR	160.0
Inventory	450	.80/EUR	360.0
Plant and equipment (net)	1,200	.80/EUR	960.0
Total assets	2,000 EUR		$1,600.0
Liabilities and Equity			
Accounts payable	100 EUR	$ .80/EUR	$ 80.0
Notes payable	500	.80/EUR	400.0
Common stock	400	1.00/EUR	400.0
Additional paid-in capital	300	1.00/EUR	300.0
Retained earnings*	700		682.5
Translation adjustment (bal. fig.)**	--		(262.5)
Total liabs. and equity	2,000 EUR		$1,600.0

* Translated retained earnings (RE) equals beginning RE as previously translated, plus net income at a weighted average rate, less dividends, at the rate in effect when declared.

** The translation adjustment is reported in other comprehensive income.

Beginning RE (from information above)	$600,000
Net income (below)	127,500
Dividends (50,000 EUR × $.90/EUR)	(45,000)
Translated RE, Dec. 31	$682,500

	Income Statement (000's)		
	Euros	Rate	U.S. Dollars
Sales	400 EUR	$ .85/EUR	$ 340.0
Cost of goods sold	(150)	.85/EUR	(127.5)
Operating expenses	(100)	.85/EUR	(85.0)
Net income	150 EUR		$ 127.5

1. **U.S. GAAP** Prior to translation, the foreign currency statements must be conformed to U.S. GAAP and be measured in the functional currency of the foreign entity (otherwise, remeasurement into the functional currency is required).

2. **Rates** Foreign currency financial statements should be translated by means of the following rates:

   a. **All Assets and Liabilities** Current exchange rate at the balance sheet date.

   b. **Revenues and Expenses** Conceptually, the exchange rate at the time the revenue or expense was recognized. However, due to the impracticability of this where rates change frequently, a **weighted-average** exchange rate for the period may be used.

   c. **Contributed Capital** Historical exchange rate.

   d. **Retained Earnings** The translated amount of retained earnings for the prior period (i.e., beginning retained earnings), plus (less) net income (loss) at the weighted-average rate, less dividends declared during the period, at the exchange rate when declared.

3. **Reporting Translation Adjustments** Translation of foreign currency statements as indicated above will result in a **translation adjustment**. This translation adjustment is reported in other comprehensive income. It should not be included in the determination of net income.

4. **Sale or Disposal of Investment in Foreign Entity** The translation adjustments accumulated in other comprehensive income should be removed using a reclassification adjustment and reported as part of the gain or loss on the disposal of the investment.

D. Remeasurement Into Functional Currency

1. **Before Translation** If an entity does not maintain its books in its functional currency, **remeasuring** into the functional currency is required prior to **translation** into the reporting currency (i.e., the U.S. dollar). If the functional currency is the same as the reporting currency, remeasurement will eliminate the need for translation (i.e., the statements will be remeasured into U.S. dollars, and thus no translation will be required).

2. **Remeasurement Purpose** The remeasuring process should achieve the same result as if the books had been initially recorded in the functional currency.

   a. This requires the remeasuring of certain accounts (nonmonetary items) at **historical rates**. All other accounts are remeasured at **current rates**.

   b. The remeasuring process will result in exchange gains and losses. The net gain or loss from **remeasurement** should be recognized in **income from continuing operations** for the current period.

   c. The following items should be remeasured at historical rates:

      (1) Marketable securities carried at cost

      (2) Inventories carried at cost

      (3) Prepaid expenses such as insurance, advertising, and rent

      (4) Property, plant, and equipment

      (5) Accumulated depreciation on property, plant, and equipment

      (6) Patents, trademarks, licenses, formulas, goodwill, and other intangible assets

      (7) Common stock and preferred stock carried at issuance price

      (8) Revenues and expenses related to nonmonetary items; for example: (a) Cost of goods sold; (b) Depreciation of property, plant, and equipment; and (c) Amortization of certain intangible items such as patents

Example 3 ▸ Remeasurement Into Functional Currency

Figueras S.A. is a Spanish sales subsidiary formed on January 1 of the current year, and is 100 percent owned by Americana Inc. Management has determined that Figueras S.A. is, in fact, a foreign extension of Americana's operations, and thus, its functional currency is the U.S. dollar. The following additional information is available.

- No dividends were paid by Figueras S.A. during the year.
- Inventories are carried at weighted-average cost.
- Figueras' office is located in a building purchased on May 5.
- Figueras' trial balance (in Euros) is reproduced in column (1) of the trial balance.
- Exchange rate information for the year follows:

January 1	1 Euro	=	$1.00
May 5		=	.98
December 31		=	.90
Year's Average		=	.95

Based on the preceding information, Figueras' accounts have been **remeasured** as indicated in column (3) of the trial balance. The remeasured balance sheet and income statement are presented below.

FIGUERAS S.A.
Remeasured Balance Sheet (000's)

Assets		Liabilities	
Cash	$ 180	Accounts payable	$ 270
Inventory	475	Mortgage payable	540
Office building, net	784		810
		Equities	
		Common stock	350
		Retained earnings	279*
			629
Total assets	$1,439	Total liabilities & equity	$1,439

* Same as NI, since this was the first year of operations, and no dividends were paid.

FIGUERAS S.A.
Trial Balance (000's)
Dr. (Cr.)

	(1) Euros	(2) Rate	(3) U.S. Dollars
Assets			
Cash	200	$ .90/EUR	$ 180
Inventory (w. avg. cost)	500	.95/EUR	475
Office building (net)	800	.98/EUR	784
Total assets	1,500		1,439
Liabilities			
Accounts payable	(300)	$ .90/EUR	(270)
Mortgage payable	(600)	.90/EUR	(540)
Total liabilities	(900)		(810)
Equity			
Common stock	(350)	$1.00/EUR	(350)
Retained earnings	0	*	0*
Total equity	(350)		(350)
Operations			
Sales	(700)	$ .95/EUR	(665)
Cost of goods sold	350	.95/EUR	332.5
General and administrative	100	.95/EUR	95
Exchange gain (to balance)	--		(41.5)
Total debits and credits	0		$ 0

* Because this was the first year of operations, the beginning RE balance is zero. Had the company been in operation for more than a year, the RE balance as **remeasured at the end of the prior year** would have been the amount entered in column (3).

FIGUERAS S.A.
Remeasured Income Statement (000's)

Sales	$ 665.0
Cost of goods sold	(332.5)
General and administrative	(95.0)
Exchange gain (from trial balance)	41.5
Net income	$ 279.0

E. **Functional Currency Determination**

The functional currency is the foreign currency or parent's currency that most closely correlates with the following economic indicators.

1. **Cash Flow**

   a. **Foreign** Cash flows related to the foreign entity's assets and liabilities are primarily in the foreign currency and do not directly impact the parent company's cash flows.

   b. **Parent's** Cash flows related to the foreign entity's assets and liabilities directly impact the parent's cash flows on a current basis and are readily available for remittance to the parent company.

2. **Sales Price**

   a. **Foreign** Sales prices for the foreign entity's products are not primarily responsive on a short-term basis to changes in exchange rates but are determined more by local competition or local government regulation.

   b. **Parent's** Sales prices for the foreign entity's products are primarily responsive on a short-term basis to changes in exchange rates; for example, sales prices are determined more by worldwide competition or by international prices.

3. **Sales Market**

   a. **Foreign** There is an active local sales market for the foreign entity's products, although there also might be significant amounts of exports.

   b. **Parent's** The sales market is mostly in the parent's country or sales contracts are denominated in the parent's currency.

4. **Expense**

   a. **Foreign** Labor, materials, and other costs for the foreign entity's products or services are primarily local costs, even though there also might be imports from other countries.

   b. **Parent's** Labor, materials, and other costs for the foreign entity's products or services, on a continuing basis, are primarily costs for components obtained from the country in which the parent company is located.

5. **Financing**

   a. **Foreign** Financing is primarily denominated in foreign currency, and funds generated by the foreign entity's operations are sufficient to service existing and normally expected debt obligations.

   b. **Parent's** Financing is primarily from the parent or other dollar-denominated obligations, or funds generated by the foreign entity's operations are not sufficient to service existing and normally expected debt obligation without the infusion of additional funds from the parent company. Infusion of additional funds from the parent company for expansion is not a factor, provided funds generated by the foreign entity's expanded operations are expected to be sufficient to service that additional financing.

6. **Intercompany Transactions & Arrangements**

   a. **Foreign** There is a low volume of intercompany transactions, and there is not an extensive interrelationship between the operations of the foreign entity and the parent company. However, the foreign entity's operations may rely on the parent's or affiliates' competitive advantages, such as patents and trademarks.

b. **Parent's** There is a high volume of intercompany transactions and there is an extensive interrelationship between the operations of the foreign entity and the parent company. Additionally, the parent's currency generally would be the functional currency if the foreign entity is a device or shell corporation for holding investments, obligations, intangible assets, etc., that could readily be carried on the parent's or an affiliate's books.

II. Foreign Currency Transactions

A. General Provisions

Foreign currency transactions are transactions denominated in a currency other than the entity's functional currency. Foreign currency transactions may produce receivables or payables that are fixed in terms of the amount of foreign currency that will be received or paid.

1. **Fluctuations** A change in exchange rates between the functional currency and the currency in which a transaction is denominated increases or decreases the expected amount of functional currency cash flows upon settlement of the transaction.

   a. That increase or decrease in expected functional currency cash flows is a foreign currency transaction gain or loss that generally should be included as a component of income from continuing operations for the period in which the exchange rate changes.

   b. Likewise, a transaction gain or loss (measured from the transaction date or the most recent intervening balance sheet date, whichever is later) realized upon settlement of a foreign currency transaction generally should be included as a component of income from continuing operations for the period in which the transaction is settled.

2. **Exceptions** Forward exchange contracts involve exceptions to this requirement for inclusion in net income of transaction gains and losses.

3. **General Rule** For other than forward exchange contracts, the following should apply to all foreign currency transactions of an enterprise and its investees.

   a. At the date a transaction is recognized, each asset, liability, revenue, expense, gain, or loss arising from the transaction should be measured and recorded in the functional currency of the recording entity by use of the exchange rate in effect at that date.

   b. At each balance sheet date, recorded balances that are denominated in a currency other than the functional currency of the recording entity should be adjusted to reflect the current exchange rate. These adjustments should be currently recognized as transaction gains or losses and reported as a component of income from continuing operations.

Example 4 ▸ Exchange Rates

On November 1, year 1, Americana Inc. purchased equipment from an unrelated French company for 10,000 Euros, payable on January 30, year 6. The following exchange rate information is available:

November 1, year 1	1 Euro	=	$.90
December 31, year 1		=	.92
January 30, year 6		=	.93

Americana would account for this transaction as follows:

Nov. 1, year 1:		
Equipment	9,000	
Note Payable (10,000EUR × $.90/EUR)		9,000
Dec. 31, year 1:		
Exchange Loss [10,000EUR × ($.92/EUR – $.90/EUR)]	200	
Note Payable		200

The $200 transaction loss from November 1, year 1 to December 31, year 1 is included as a component of income from continuing operations for year 1.

Jan. 30, year 6:		
Note Payable ($9,000 + $200)	9,200	
Exchange Loss (to balance)	100	
Cash (10,000EUR × $.93/EUR)		9,300

The $100 transaction loss from December 31, year 1 to January 30, year 6 is included as a component of income from continuing operations for year 6.

NOTE: The recorded amount of the equipment is not affected by exchange rate fluctuations between the date of purchase and the date of payment.

B. Forward Exchange Contracts

A **forward exchange contract** (forward contract) is an agreement to exchange different currencies at a specified future date and at a specified rate (the **forward rate**). A forward contract is a foreign currency **transaction**.

1. **Nonspeculative** A gain or loss (whether or not deferred) on a forward contract, except a speculative forward contract, should be computed by multiplying the foreign currency amount of the forward contract by the difference between the **spot rate** at the **balance sheet date** and the **spot rate** at the **date of inception of the forward contract** (or the spot rate last used to measure a gain or loss on that contract for an earlier period). The **spot rate** is the exchange rate for immediate delivery of currencies exchanged.

2. **Speculative** A gain or loss on a **speculative forward contract** (that is, a contract that does not hedge an exposure) should be computed by multiplying the foreign currency amount of the forward contract by the difference between the forward rate available for the remaining maturity of the contract and the contracted forward rate (or the forward rate last used to measure a gain or loss on that contract for an earlier period). No separate accounting recognition is given to the discount or premium on a speculative forward contract.

3. **Discount or Premium** The **discount or premium on a forward contract** should be accounted for **separately** from the gain or loss on the contract and generally should be **amortized** over the **life of the forward contract**. The discount or premium on a forward contract is the foreign currency amount of the contract multiplied by the difference between the contracted forward rate and the spot rate at the date of inception of the contract.

Example 5 ▸ Discount or Premium on a Forward Contract

On November 1, year 1, Americana Inc. contracted with The Money Exchange Ltd. for the delivery of 10,000 Euros in 3 months, at a rate of .9015. At the date the contract was entered into, the exchange rate was 1 Euro = $.9. At the balance sheet date, the value of the Euro had risen to $.92. On January 30, year 2, the Euro was worth $.93. Americana would post the journal entries below. Note that all entries are posted in U.S. $ (e.g., the 9,000 debit posted on November 1 represents the translated value in U.S. $ of 10,000 Euros).

Nov. 1, year 1:		
Euros Due From Broker	9,000	
Deferred Forward Contract Cost	15	
Payable to Broker		9,015
Dec. 31, year 1:		
Euros Due From Broker	200	
Exchange Gain		200
Forward Contract Expenses ($15 × 60/90)	10	
Deferred Forward Contract Cost		10
Jan. 30, year 2:		
Payable to Broker	9,015	
Investment in Euros	9,300	
Euros Due From Broker		9,200
Cash		9,015
Exchange Gain		100
Forward Contract Expense	5	
Deferred Forward Contract Cost		5

NOTE: In this Example, the cumulative gain on the forward exchange contract (i.e., $300) would offset the **loss** recognized in Example 4. Thus by entering into the forward exchange contract Americana, in fact, protected itself from future exchange losses.

III. Foreign Currency Hedges

A. Hedge Designation

In accordance with SFAS 133, an entity may designate the following types of hedges of foreign currency exposure:

1. **Fair Value Hedge** A fair value hedge of an unrecognized firm commitment or an available-for-sale security.

2. **Cash Flow Hedge** A cash flow hedge of a forecasted foreign-currency-denominated transaction or a forecasted intercompany foreign-currency-denominated transaction.

3. **Hedge of a Net Investment in a Foreign Operation** A derivative instrument or a nonderivative financial instrument that may give rise to a foreign currency transaction gain or loss can be designated as hedging the foreign currency exposure of a net investment in a foreign operation.

B. Reporting Hedging Gains & Losses

1. **Foreign Currency Fair Value Hedge** The gain or loss on the hedging instrument designated as a fair value foreign currency hedge is recognized currently in earnings. The gain or loss on the hedged item adjusts the carrying amount of the hedged item and is recognized currently in earnings. If the hedged item is an available-for-sale security, the recognition of gain or loss in earnings rather than in other comprehensive income is an exception to the normal accounting treatment of gains and losses on available-for-sale securities, in order to offset the gain or loss on the hedging instrument that is reported in current earnings.

2. **Foreign Currency Cash Flow Hedge** The **effective portion** of the gain or loss on a derivative designated as a cash flow hedge is reported in **other comprehensive income,** and the ineffective portion is reported in earnings. Effectiveness is defined as the degree that the gain (loss) for the hedging instrument offsets the loss (gain) on the hedged item.

3. **Hedge of Net Investment in Foreign Operation** The gain or loss on a hedging derivative instrument, or the foreign currency transaction gain or loss on a nonderivative hedging instrument, that is designated as and is effective as an economic hedge, of the net investment in a foreign operation is reported in **other comprehensive income,** as part of the cumulative translation adjustment, to the extent it is effective as a hedge.

IV. Income Tax Consequences of Rate Changes

A. Foreign Currency Transactions

Exchange gains or losses from an entity's **foreign currency transactions** that are included in taxable income of an earlier or later year than the year in which they are recognized in financial income result in **temporary differences**.

B. Foreign Currency Financial Statement Translation Adjustments

These adjustments should be accounted for as **temporary differences** under the provisions of APB 23 and SFAS 109.

CHAPTER 16—FOREIGN OPERATIONS

Problem 16-1 MULTIPLE CHOICE QUESTIONS (58 to 72 minutes)

1. In preparing consolidated financial statements of a U.S. parent company with a foreign subsidiary, the foreign subsidiary's functional currency is the currency
a. In which the subsidiary maintains its accounting records.
b. Of the country in which the subsidiary is located.
c. Of the country in which the parent is located.
d. Of the environment in which the subsidiary primarily generates and expends cash.
(R/99, FAR, #16, 6785)

2. The following trial balance of Trey Co. at December 31 has been adjusted except for income tax expense:

	Dr.	Cr.
Cash	$ 550,000	
Accounts receivable, net	1,650,000	
Prepaid taxes	300,000	
Accounts payable		$ 120,000
Common stock		500,000
Additional paid-in capital		680,000
Retained earnings		630,000
Foreign currency translation adjustment	430,000	
Revenues		3,600,000
Expenses	2,600,000	
	$5,530,000	$5,530,000

Additional information:

- During the year, estimated tax payments of $300,000 were charged to prepaid taxes. Trey has not yet recorded income tax expense. There were no differences between financial statement and income tax income, and Trey's tax rate is 30%.
- Included in accounts receivable is $500,000 due from a customer. Special terms granted to this customer require payment in equal semi-annual installments of $125,000 every April 1 and October 1.

In Trey's December 31 balance sheet, what amount should be reported as total retained earnings?
a. $1,029,000
b. $1,200,000
c. $1,330,000
d. $1,630,000 (11/94, FAR, #9, amended, 5274)

3. Certain balance sheet accounts of a foreign subsidiary of Rowan Inc., at December 31, have been translated into U.S. dollars as follows:

	Translated at	
	Current Rates	Historical Rates
Note receivable, long-term	$240,000	$200,000
Prepaid rent	85,000	80,000
Patent	150,000	170,000
	$475,000	$450,000

The subsidiary's functional currency is the currency of the country in which it is located. What total amount should be included in Rowan's December 31 consolidated balance sheet for the above accounts?
a. $450,000
b. $455,000
c. $475,000
d. $495,000 (5/90, PII, #44, amended, 9059)

4. A foreign subsidiary's functional currency is its local currency, which has not experienced significant inflation. The weighted average exchange rate for the current year would be the appropriate exchange rate for translating

	Sales to customers	*Wages expense*
a.	No	No
b.	Yes	Yes
c.	No	Yes
d.	Yes	No

(5/92, Theory, #39, 2732)

5. Which of the following should be reported in accumulated other comprehensive income?
a. Discount on convertible bonds that are common stock equivalents
b. Premium on convertible bonds that are common stock equivalents
c. Cumulative foreign exchange translation loss
d. Organization costs
(11/93, Theory, #14, amended, 4519)

6. Gains resulting from the process of translating a foreign entity's financial statements from the functional currency, which has not experienced significant inflation, to U.S. dollars should be included as a(an)
a. Other comprehensive income item
b. Deferred credit
c. Component of income from continuing operations
d. Extraordinary item
(11/85, Theory, #21, amended, 9060)

7. When remeasuring foreign currency financial statements into the functional currency, which of the following items would be remeasured using historical exchange rates?
a. Inventories carried at cost
b. Marketable equity securities reported at market values
c. Bonds payable
d. Accrued liabilities (11/93, Theory, #36, 4541)

8. Park Co.'s wholly owned subsidiary, Schnell Corp., maintains its accounting records in euros. Because all of Schnell's branch offices are in Switzerland, its functional currency is the Swiss franc. Remeasurement of Schnell's current year financial statements resulted in a \$7,600 gain, and translation of its financial statements resulted in an \$8,100 gain. What amount should Park report as a foreign exchange gain in its income statement for the current year ended December 31?
a. \$0
b. \$ 7,600
c. \$ 8,100
d. \$15,700 (5/95, FAR, #31, amended, 5567)

9. A balance arising from the translation or remeasurement of a subsidiary's foreign currency financial statements is reported in the consolidated income statement when the subsidiary's functional currency is the

	Foreign currency	*U.S. dollar*
a.	No	No
b.	No	Yes
c.	Yes	No
d.	Yes	Yes

(5/90, Theory, #22, 2088)

10. Gains from remeasuring a foreign subsidiary's financial statements from the local currency, which is not the functional currency, into the parent company's currency should be reported as a(an)
a. Deferred foreign exchange gain
b. Other comprehensive income item
c. Extraordinary item, net of income taxes
d. Part of continuing operations
(11/90, Theory, #39, amended, 2087)

11. Fogg Co., a U.S. company, contracted to purchase foreign goods. Payment in foreign currency was due one month after the goods were received at Fogg's warehouse. Between the receipt of goods and the time of payment, the exchange rates changed in Fogg's favor. The resulting gain should be included in Fogg's financial statements as a(an)
a. Component of income from continuing operations
b. Extraordinary item
c. Deferred credit
d. Component of other comprehensive income
(11/95, FAR, #32, amended, 6114)

12. Hunt Co. purchased merchandise for £300,000 from a vendor in London on November 30 of the current year. Payment in British pounds is due on January 30 of the next year. The exchange rates to purchase one pound were as follows:

	Nov. 30	Dec. 31
Spot-rate	\$1.65	\$1.62
30-day rate	1.64	1.59
60-day rate	1.63	1.56

In its December 31, current year income statement, what amount should Hunt report as foreign exchange gain?
a. \$12,000
b. \$ 9,000
c. \$ 6,000
d. \$0 (11/93, PI, #49, amended, 4418)

13. On September 1 of the previous year, Cano & Co., a U.S. corporation, sold merchandise to a foreign firm for 25,000 euros. Terms of the sale require payment in euros on February 1 of the current year. On September 1 of the previous year, the spot exchange rate was \$2.00 per euro. At December 31 of the previous year, Cano's year-end, the spot rate was \$1.90, but the rate increased to \$2.20 by February 1 of the current year, when payment was received. How much should Cano report as foreign exchange gain or loss in its current year income statement?
a. \$0
b. \$2,500 loss
c. \$5,000 gain
d. \$7,500 gain (11/91, PI, #46, amended, 2434)

14. On October 1, Velec Co., a U.S. company, contracted to purchase foreign goods requiring payment in euros one month after their receipt at Velec's factory. Title to the goods passed on December 15. The goods were still in transit on December 31. Exchange rates were one dollar to 2.2 euros, 2.0 euros, and 2.1 euros on October 1, December 15, and December 31 respectively. Velec should account for the exchange rate fluctuation in the year as

a. A loss included in net income before extraordinary items
b. A gain included in net income before extraordinary items
c. An extraordinary gain
d. An extraordinary loss

(5/93, Theory, #34, amended, 4222)

15. On November 15, year 1, Celt Inc., a U.S. company, ordered merchandise F.O.B. shipping point from a German company for 100,000 euros. The merchandise was shipped and invoiced to Celt on December 10, year 1. Celt paid the invoice on January 10, year 2. The spot rates for euros on the respective dates are as follows:

November 15, year 1	\$.991
December 10, year 1	.975
December 31, year 1	.935
January 10, year 2	.895

In Celt's December 31, year 1 income statement, the foreign exchange gain is

a. \$9,600
b. \$8,000
c. \$4,000
d. \$1,600

(11/90, PI, #38, amended, 1334)

16. Shore Co. records its transactions in U.S. dollars. A sale of goods resulted in a receivable denominated in Japanese yen, and a purchase of goods resulted in a payable denominated in euros. Shore recorded a foreign exchange gain on collection of the receivable and an exchange loss on settlement of the payable. The exchange rates are expressed as so many units of foreign currency to one dollar. Did the number of foreign currency units exchangeable for a dollar increase or decrease between the contract and settlement dates?

	Yen exchangeable for \$1	*Euros exchangeable for \$1*
a.	Increase	Increase
b.	Decrease	Decrease
c.	Decrease	Increase
d.	Increase	Decrease

(11/91, Theory, #18, amended, 2526)

17. Ball Corp. had the following foreign currency transactions during the current year:

- Merchandise was purchased from a foreign supplier on January 20 for the U.S. dollar equivalent of \$90,000. The invoice was paid on March 20, at the U.S. dollar equivalent of \$96,000.
- On July 1, Ball borrowed the U.S. dollar equivalent of \$500,000 evidenced by a note that was payable in the lender's local currency on July 1, in two years. On December 31, the U.S. dollar equivalents of the principal amount and accrued interest were \$520,000 and \$26,000, respectively. Interest on the note is 10% per annum.

In Ball's year-end income statement, what amount should be included as foreign exchange loss?

a. \$0
b. \$ 6,000
c. \$21,000
d. \$27,000

(11/90, PI, #43, amended, 1335)

18. On September 22 of the previous year, Yumi Corp. purchased merchandise from an unaffiliated foreign company for 10,000 units of the foreign company's local currency. On that date, the spot rate was \$.55. Yumi paid the bill in full on March 20 of the current year, when the spot rate was \$.65. The spot rate was \$.70 on December 31 of the previous year. What amount should Yumi report as a foreign currency transaction loss in its income statement for the previous year ended December 31?

a. \$0
b. \$ 500
c. \$1,000
d. \$1,500

(5/95, FAR, #32, amended, 5568)

19. On July 1, year 1, Clark Company borrowed 1,680,000 local currency units (LCUs) from a foreign lender, evidenced by an interest bearing note due on July 1, year 2, which is denominated in the currency of the lender. The U.S. dollar equivalent of the note principal was as follows:

Date	Amount
7/1, year 1 (date borrowed)	\$210,000
12/31, year 1 (Clark's year end)	240,000
7/1, year 2 (date repaid)	280,000

In its income statement for year 2, what amount should Clark include as a foreign exchange gain or loss?

a. \$70,000 gain
b. \$70,000 loss
c. \$40,000 gain
d. \$40,000 loss

(5/86, PI, #56, amended, 1341)

20. Post Inc. had a credit translation adjustment of $30,000 for the current year ended December 31. The functional currency of Post's subsidiary is the currency of the country in which it is located. Additionally, Post had a receivable from a foreign customer payable in the local currency of the customer. On December 31 of the previous year, this receivable for 200,000 local currency units (LCUs) was correctly included in Post's balance sheet at $110,000. When the receivable was collected on this February 15, the United States dollar equivalent was $120,000. In Post's current year consolidated income statement, how much should be reported as foreign exchange gain?

a. $0
b. $10,000
c. $30,000
d. $40,000 (11/86, PI, #43, amended, 1340)

21. Fay Corp. had a realized foreign exchange loss of $15,000 for the current year ended December 31, and must also determine whether the following items will require year-end adjustment:

- Fay had an $8,000 loss resulting from the translation of the accounts of its wholly owned foreign subsidiary for the year ended December 31.
- Fay had an account payable to an unrelated foreign supplier payable in the supplier's local currency. The U.S. dollar equivalent of the payable was $64,000 on the October 31 invoice date, and it was $60,000 on December 31. The invoice is payable on January 30 of next year.

In Fay's current year consolidated income statement, what amount should be included as foreign exchange loss?

a. $11,000
b. $15,000
c. $19,000
d. $23,000 (5/90, PI, #52, amended, 1336)

22. On October 1 of the current year, Mild Co., a U.S. company, purchased machinery from Grund, a German company, with payment due on April 1 of next year. If Mild's current year operating income included no foreign exchange transaction gain or loss, then the transaction could have

a. Resulted in an extraordinary gain
b. Been denominated in U.S. dollars
c. Caused a foreign currency gain to be reported as a contra account against machinery
d. Caused a foreign currency translation gain to be reported in other comprehensive income (11/93, Theory, #35, amended, 4540)

23. Which of the following statements regarding foreign exchange gains and losses is correct?

a. An exchange gain occurs when the exchange rate increases between the date a payable is recorded and the date of cash payment.
b. An exchange gain occurs when the exchange rate increases between the date a receivable is recorded and the date of cash receipt.
c. An exchange loss occurs when the exchange rate decreases between the date a payable is recorded and the date of the cash payment.
d. An exchange loss occurs when the exchange rate increases between the date a receivable is recorded and the date of the cash receipt. (R/03, FAR, #2, 7604)

24. The following information pertains to Flint Co.'s sale of 10,000 foreign currency units under a forward contract dated November 1 of the current year for delivery on January 31 of the following year:

	11/1	12/31
Spot rates	$0.80	$0.83
30-day future rates	0.79	0.82
90-day future rates	0.78	0.81

Flint entered into the forward contract in order to speculate in the foreign currency. In Flint's income statement for the current year ended December 31, what amount of loss should be reported from this forward contract?

a. $400
b. $300
c. $200
d. $0 (5/92, PI, #52, amended, 2623)

25. On November 2, year 1, Platt Co. entered into a 90-day futures contract to purchase 50,000 Swiss francs when the contract quote was $0.70. The purchase was for speculation in price movement. The following exchange rates existed during the contract period:

	30-day futures	Spot rate
November 2, year 1	$0.62	$0.63
December 31, year 1	0.65	0.64
January 30, year 2	0.65	0.68

What amount should Platt report as foreign currency exchange loss in its income statement for the year ended December 31, year 1?

a. $2,500
b. $3,000
c. $3,500
d. $4,000 (R/02, FAR #4, 7059)

Items 26 through 28 are based on the following:

On December 12, year 1, Imp Co. entered into three forward exchange contracts, each to purchase 100,000 euros in 90 days. The relevant exchange rates are as follows:

	Spot rate	Forward rate (for 3/12, yr 2)
December 12, year 1	$1.86	$1.80
December 31, year 1	1.96	1.83

26. Imp entered into the first forward contract to hedge a purchase of inventory in November of year 1, payable in March of year 2. At December 31, year 1, what amount of foreign currency transaction gain should Imp include in income from this forward contract?
a. $0
b. $ 3,000
c. $ 5,000
d. $10,000 (11/92, PI, #48, amended, 3281)

27. Imp entered into the second forward contract to hedge a commitment to purchase equipment being manufactured to Imp's specifications. At December 31, year 1, what amount of foreign currency transaction gain should Imp include in income from this forward contract?
a. $0
b. $ 3,000
c. $ 5,000
d. $10,000 (11/92, PI, #49, amended, 3282)

28. Imp entered into the third forward contract for speculation. At December 31, year 1, what amount of foreign currency transaction gain should Imp include in income from this forward contract?
a. $0
b. $ 3,000
c. $ 5,000
d. $10,000 (11/92, PI, #50, amended, 3283)

29. The functional currency of Nash Inc.'s subsidiary is the euro. Nash borrowed euros as a partial hedge of its investment in the subsidiary. In preparing consolidated financial statements, Nash's translation loss on its investment in the subsidiary exceeded its exchange gain on the borrowing. How should the effects of the loss and gain be reported in Nash's consolidated financial statements?
a. The translation loss less the exchange gain is reported in other comprehensive income.
b. The translation loss less the exchange gain is reported in net income.
c. The translation loss is reported in other comprehensive income and the exchange gain is reported in net income.
d. The translation loss is reported in net income and the exchange gain is reported in other comprehensive income.
(5/92, Theory, #38, amended, 2731)

SIMULATION

Problem 16-2 (15 to 25 minutes)

Essay | Research Task

Jay Co.'s current year consolidated financial statements include two wholly owned subsidiaries, Jay Co. of Australia (Jay A) and Jay Co. of France (Jay F). Functional currencies are the U.S. dollar for Jay A and the euro for Jay F.

a. What are the objectives of translating a foreign subsidiary's financial statements?

b. How are gains and losses arising from translating or remeasuring of each subsidiary's financial statements measured and reported in Jay's consolidated financial statements?

c. FASB Statement No. 52 identifies several economic indicators that are to be considered both individually and collectively in determining the functional currency for a consolidated subsidiary. List three of those indicators.

d. What exchange rate is used to incorporate each subsidiary's equipment cost, accumulated depreciation, and depreciation expense in Jay's consolidated financial statements? (5/91, Theory, #5, amended, 3597)

Essay	Research Task

Research Question: The currency of the environment in which an entity primarily generates and expends cash is known by what term?

Paragraph Reference Answer: ______________

Solution 16-1 MULTIPLE CHOICE ANSWERS

Translation of Foreign Currency F/S

1. (d) An entity's functional currency is the currency of the primary economic environment in which the entity operates. Normally, that is the currency of the environment in which an entity primarily generates and expends cash. The functional currency of a foreign entity may be its local currency, the U.S. dollar, or another foreign currency. Where a foreign operation is relatively self-contained and integrated within one country, the entity's functional currency will be the local currency. Where the foreign operation is, in essence, an extension of the parent's U.S. operations, the functional currency will be the U.S. dollar. A foreign entity may keep its books in the local currency, yet have another foreign currency as functional currency; in which case remeasurement of the recording currency statements into functional currency will be required.

2. (c) Foreign currency translation adjustments are not included in determining net income. Instead, they are reported in other comprehensive income.

Revenues	$ 3,600,000
Less: Expenses	(2,600,000)
Income before income taxes	1,000,000
Less: Income taxes ($1,000,000 × 30%)	(300,000)
Net income	700,000
Add: Retained earnings, 1/1	630,000
Retained earnings, 12/31	$ 1,330,000

3. (c) Since the subsidiary's functional currency is the currency of the country in which it is located, all of its assets are translated at the current rate (i.e., the exchange rate in effect at the balance sheet date).

4. (b) Since the foreign subsidiary's functional currency is its local currency, which has not experienced significant inflation, it is appropriate to *translate* the amounts of its revenues, expenses, gains, and losses at a weighted average exchange rate for the period (SFAS 52, ¶11 and 12).

5. (c) If an entity's functional currency is a foreign currency which has not experienced significant inflation, translation adjustments result from the process of translating that entity's financial statements into the reporting currency (SFAS 52). Translation adjustments should not be included in determining net income but should be reported in OCI. A cumulative foreign exchange translation loss would be reported in accumulated OCI as a stockholders' equity contra account. A discount or premium on bonds payable should be reported as part of the related liability for bonds payable in the balance sheet. Organization costs should be expensed as incurred.

6. (a) If an entity's functional currency is the foreign currency, which has not experienced significant inflation, translation adjustments result from the process of **translating** that entity's financial statements into the reporting currency (SFAS 52). Translation adjustments (gains or losses) are not included in net income, but in other comprehensive income.

Remeasurement Into Functional Currency

7. (a) If an entity does not maintain its books in its functional currency, SFAS 52 requires remeasurement into the functional currency prior to translation into the reporting currency (i.e., the parent company's currency). In this process, nonmonetary balance sheet items are remeasured using historical exchange rates. Hence, inventories carried at cost should be remeasured using historical exchange rates because it is cited as an example of a nonmonetary balance sheet item in SFAS 52. Marketable equity securities, bonds payable, and accrued liabilities balance sheet items are remeasured using the current exchange rate.

8. (b) Park's foreign subsidiary does not maintain its accounting records in its functional currency (the Swiss franc). Therefore, the financial statements of the foreign subsidiary must be remeasured. The $7,600 remeasurement gain is reported in income

from continuing operations. The $8,100 translation gain is reported in other comprehensive income. Translation gains and losses are not reported in income.

9. (b) The functional currency of a foreign entity may be its local currency (i.e., the foreign currency) or the reporting currency (e.g., the U.S. dollar). If the functional currency is the foreign currency, the foreign currency financial statements must be translated into U.S. dollars. The translation adjustments which result from this process are not reported in the consolidated income statement but are reported in other comprehensive income. If the functional currency is the U.S. dollar, the foreign currency financial statements must be remeasured into U.S. dollars. The foreign exchange gains/losses which result from this process are reported in the consolidated income statement.

10. (d) If an entity does not maintain its books in its functional currency, remeasuring into the functional currency is required prior to translation into the reporting currency (i.e., the parent company's currency). Exchange gains and losses that result from the remeasuring process are recognized in income from continuing operations.

Foreign Currency Transactions

11. (a) A change in exchange rates between the functional currency and the currency in which the transaction is denominated increases or decreases the expected amount of functional currency cash flows upon a settlement of the transaction. That increase or decrease in expected functional currency cash flows is a foreign currency transaction gain or loss that generally should be included as a component of income from continuing operations for the period in which the transaction is settled.

12. (b) Whenever a transaction is denominated (i.e., payable) in a foreign currency, changes in the translation rate (i.e., the spot rate) of the foreign currency with respect to the entity's functional currency (i.e., the dollar in this case) will result in a gain or loss. The gain or loss should be recognized in income in the period(s) the rate changes, and the related asset or liability (i.e., accounts payable in this case) should be adjusted accordingly.

Initial obligation, 11/30, in $US (£300,000 × $1.65)	$ 495,000
Amount payable, 12/31, in $US (£300,000 × $1.62)	(486,000)
Foreign exchange gain recognized	$ 9,000

13. (d) Whenever a transaction is denominated (i.e., payable) in a foreign currency, changes in the translation rate of the foreign currency with respect to the entity's functional currency (i.e., the dollar in this case) will result in a transaction gain or loss. The gain or loss should be included in the determination of net income in the period(s) the rate changes, and the related asset or liability (i.e., accounts receivable in this case) should be adjusted accordingly. Likewise, if the transaction is finally settled at a rate different from that reflected in the related asset or liability, gain or loss should also be recognized.

Initial obligation, 9/1 of the previous year, in $US (25,000 euros × $2.00)	$ 50,000
Amount receivable, 12/31 of the previous year (25,000 euros × $1.90)	(47,500)
Foreign exchange loss recognized, previous year	$ 2,500

Amount receivable, 12/31 of the previous year	$ 47,500
Amount of settlement, 2/1 of the current year (25,000 euros × $2.20)	(55,000)
Foreign exchange gain recognized, current year	$ (7,500)

14. (b) The payable resulting from the merchandise purchased from the foreign supplier is denominated in a foreign currency. Therefore, changes in the relative value of the dollar and the foreign currency will result in exchange gains or losses which should be recognized in income from continuing operations in the period they occur. Velec should not have recorded the purchase, and the related payable, until 12/15, the date title to the goods passed to Velec. At that date, the exchange rate was one dollar to 2.0 euros. At 12/31, the exchange rate was one dollar to 2.1 euros. Since the exchange rate of euros to one U.S. dollar increased from the date the payable was recorded to the end of the year (i.e., each U.S. dollar could purchase 0.1 additional euro), Velec realized a foreign exchange gain in the year which should be included in income from continuing operations in the year.

15. (c) Whenever a **transaction** is denominated (i.e., payable) in a foreign currency, changes in the translation rate of the foreign currency with respect to the entity's functional currency (i.e., the dollar in this case) will result in a transaction gain or loss. The gain or loss should be recognized in income in the period(s) the rate changes, and the related asset or liability (i.e., accounts payable in this case) should be adjusted accordingly. Likewise, if the transaction is finally settled at a rate different from that reflected in the related asset or liability, gain or loss will also be recognized. The purchase and the related payable should not have been recorded until 12/10, year 1, because no liability had been incurred until the merchandise was shipped (i.e., the merchandise was ordered F.O.B. shipping point).

Initial obligation, 12/10, year 1, in $US (100,000 euros × $0.975)	$ 97,500
Amount payable, 12/31, year 1 (100,000 euros × $0.935)	(93,500)
Foreign exchange gain recognized, year 1	$ 4,000
Amount payable, 12/31, year 1 (above)	$ 93,500
Amount of settlement, 1/10, year 2 (100,000 euros × $0.895)	(89,500)
Foreign exchange gain recognized, year 2	$ 4,000

16. (b) To record a foreign exchange gain on collection of the receivable, the exchange rate of Japanese yen to one U.S. dollar must have decreased. For instance, assume a receivable for 1,000 yen and an exchange rate of 10 yen to 1 dollar at the contract date. If the exchange rate changed to 5 yen to 1 dollar, the 1,000 yen when collected could be converted into 200 U.S. dollars at the settlement date. This $200 is twice the $100 that could have been obtained from the conversion of currency at the contract date (1,000 / 10 = $100). To record an exchange loss on settlement of the payable, the exchange rate of euros to one dollar must have decreased. For example, assume a payable for 1,000 euros and an exchange rate of 4 euros to 1 dollar at the contract date. If the exchange rate changed to 2 euros to 1 dollar, the 1,000 euros paid at the settlement date required more US dollars than would have been required at the date of contract (1,000 / 2 = $500 at date of settlement versus 1,000 / 4 = $250 at date of contract).

17. (d) The payables resulting from the merchandise purchased from the foreign supplier and the borrowing are **transactions** denominated in a foreign currency. The payable from the merchandise purchased was recorded at $90,000 on 1/20. It was paid on 3/20 at the U.S. dollar equivalent of $96,000, resulting in a $6,000 foreign exchange loss. The payable from the borrowing was recorded at $500,000 at 7/1. Accrued interest on the borrowing was $25,000 (i.e., $500,000 × 10% × 6/12) at 12/31. At 12/31, the U.S. dollar equivalents of principal and accrued interest were $520,000 and $26,000, respectively, resulting in an additional $21,000 [i.e., ($520,000 + $26,000) – ($500,000 + $25,000)] foreign exchange loss. Thus, the foreign exchange loss recognized in the year-end income statement is $27,000 (i.e., $6,000 + $21,000).

18. (d) Whenever a transaction is denominated (i.e., payable) in a foreign currency, changes in the translation rate of the foreign currency with respect to the entity's functional currency (i.e., the dollar in this case) will result in a transaction gain or loss. The gain or loss should be included in the determination of net income in the period(s) the rate changes, and the related asset or liability (i.e., accounts payable in this case) should be adjusted accordingly.

Accounts payable, 12/31 of previous year, in $US (10,000 local currency units × $0.70)	$ 7,000
Initial obligation, 9/22 of previous year, in $US (10,000 local currency units × $0.55)	(5,500)
Foreign exchange loss recognized in the previous year	$ 1,500

19. (d) A transaction gain or loss (measured from the transaction date or most recent balance sheet date, whichever is later) is realized upon settlement of a foreign currency transaction. In year 2, a *loss* of $40,000 (i.e., $240,000 – $280,000) is recorded due to the additional amount that must be repaid since the last balance sheet date.

Transaction Gains & Losses

20. (b) Translation adjustments relating to foreign subsidiaries are **not** included in the determination of consolidated income. These adjustments are reported in other comprehensive income (OCI). Post's receivable from a foreign customer was denominated in a foreign currency; therefore, changes in the relative value of the dollar and the foreign currency results in exchange gains or losses, which are included in the determination of net income. The recorded amount of the receivable was $110,000 and it was settled for $120,000; thus, Post recognizes a $10,000 foreign exchange gain in this transaction.

21. (a) The payable to the unrelated foreign supplier is a **transaction** denominated in a foreign currency. The payable was initially recorded at $64,000. It was included in the December 31 balance sheet at $60,000. The decrease in the payable represents a $4,000 transaction gain which is recognized in income from continuing operations in the current year. On the other hand, the $8,000 loss resulting from the **translation** of the accounts of the foreign subsidiary is not recognized in the income statement. Translation gains and losses are reported in OCI.

Foreign exchange loss before adjustment	$15,000
Gain on transaction denominated in a foreign currency	(4,000)
Foreign exchange loss, current year	$11,000

22. (b) Foreign currency transactions are transactions denominated in a currency other than the entity's functional currency. Hence, no foreign currency transaction gain or loss would occur if the purchase of the machinery by the U.S. company is denominated in U.S. dollars. Foreign exchange

transaction gains and losses are recognized as a component of income from continuing operations in the period they occur.

23. (b) Receivable: Rate increase results in a gain (receive more at settlement), rate decrease results in a loss (receive less at settlement). Payable: Rate increase results in a loss (pay more at settlement), rate decrease results in a gain (pay less at settlement).

Forward Exchange Contract

24. (a) A forward exchange contract (forward contract) is an agreement to exchange different currencies at a specified future date and at a specified rate (the forward rate). A forward contract is a foreign currency **transaction.** Therefore, a gain or loss on a forward contract is included in determining net income in accordance with the requirements for other foreign currency transactions (subject to exceptions for certain intercompany transactions and certain hedges of net investments and foreign currency commitments, which are deferred). A gain or loss on a speculative forward contract (that is, a contract that does not hedge an exposure) is computed by multiplying the foreign currency amount of the contract by the difference between the forward rate available for the remaining maturity of the contract and the contracted forward rate (or the forward rate last used to measure a gain or loss on that contract for an earlier period).

Foreign currency units	10,000
Times: Excess of forward rate available for the remaining maturity of the contract and the contracted forward rate ($0.82 – $0.78)	× $0.04
Loss on forward contract	$ 400

25. (a) The **spot rate** is the exchange rate for immediate delivery of currencies exchanged.

A gain or loss on a **speculative forward contract** (that is, a contract that does not hedge an exposure) should be computed by multiplying the foreign currency amount of the forward contract by the difference between the forward rate available for the remaining maturity of the contract and the contract forward rate (or the forward rate last used to measure a gain or loss on that contract for an earlier period). No separate accounting recognition is given to the discount or premium on a speculative forward contract.

A gain or loss (whether or not deferred) on a forward contract, **except a speculative forward contract,** should be computed by multiplying the foreign currency amount of the forward contract by the difference between the spot rate at the balance sheet date and the spot rate at the date of inception of the forward contract (or the spot rate last used to measure a gain or loss on that contract for an earlier period).

$0.70
–0.65
$0.05 × $50,000 = $2,500

26. (d) A forward exchange contract is an agreement to exchange different currencies at a specified future date and at a specified rate (the forward rate). A forward contract is a foreign currency transaction. Therefore, a gain or loss on a forward contract is included in determining income from continuing operations in accordance with the requirements for other foreign currency transactions (subject to exceptions for certain intercompany transactions, certain hedges of net investments, and foreign currency commitments, which are deferred). The gain or loss realized on a forward exchange contract, other than a speculative forward contract, is computed by multiplying the foreign currency amount of the contract by the difference between the *spot* rate at the balance sheet date and the *spot* rate at the inception of the contract (or the spot rate last used to measure a gain or loss on that contract for an earlier period).

Foreign currency units to be purchased	100,000
Times: Excess of spot rate at the balance sheet date over the spot rate at the inception of the contract ($1.96 – $1.86)	× $0.10
Foreign currency transaction gain, year 1	$ 10,000

27. (d) Since the forward contract is not a speculative forward contract, the gain realized on the contract is computed by multiplying the foreign currency amount of the contract by the difference between the spot rate at the balance sheet date and the spot rate at the inception of the contract (or the spot rate last used to measure a gain or loss on that contract for an earlier period).

Foreign currency units to be purchased	100,000
Times: Excess of spot rate at the balance sheet date over the spot rate at the inception of the contract ($1.96 – $1.86)	× $0.10
Foreign currency transaction gain, year 1	$ 10,000

28. (b) A gain or loss on a speculative forward exchange contract is included in determining income from continuing operations in accordance with the requirements for other foreign currency transactions. A gain or loss on a speculative forward contract is computed by multiplying the foreign currency amount

of the contract by the difference between the forward rate available for the remaining maturity of the contract and the contracted forward rate (or the forward rate last used to measure a gain or loss on that contract for an earlier period).

Foreign currency units to be purchased	100,000
Times: Excess of forward rate available for remaining portion of contract and the contracted forward rate ($1.83 – $1.80)	× $0.03
Foreign currency transaction gain, year 1	$ 3,000

Hedging Gains & Losses

29. (a) **Translation** adjustments are not included in determining net income, but in OCI. Gains and losses on foreign currency transactions that are designated as, and are effective as, economic hedges of a net investment in a foreign entity are not included in determining net income, but are reported in the same manner as translation adjustments. Therefore, the net translation loss is reported in OCI in Nash's consolidated financial statements.

PERFORMANCE BY SUBTOPICS

Each category below parallels a subtopic covered in Chapter 16. Record the number and percentage of questions you correctly answered in each subtopic area.

Translation of Foreign Currency F/S

Question #	Correct √
1	
2	
3	
4	
5	
6	
# Questions	6
# Correct	______
% Correct	______

Remeasurement Into Functional Currency

Question #	Correct √
7	
8	
9	
10	
# Questions	4
# Correct	______
% Correct	______

Foreign Currency Transactions

Question #	Correct √
11	
12	
13	
14	
15	
16	
17	
18	
19	
# Questions	9
# Correct	______
% Correct	______

Transaction Gains & Losses

Question #	Correct √
20	
21	
22	
23	
# Questions	4
# Correct	______
% Correct	______

Forward Exchange Contract

Question #	Correct √
24	
25	
26	
27	
28	
# Questions	5
# Correct	______
% Correct	______

Hedging Gains & Losses

Question #	Correct √
29	
# Questions	1
# Correct	______
% Correct	______

SIMULATION SOLUTION

Solution 16-2

Essay—Foreign Currency

a. The objectives of translating a foreign subsidiary's financial statements are to:

Provide information that is generally compatible with the expected economic effects of a rate change on a subsidiary's cash flows and equity.

Reflect the subsidiary's financial results and relationships in **single currency consolidated financial statements,** as measured in its **functional currency** and in **conformity with GAAP.**

b. Applying different exchange rates to the various financial statement accounts causes the restated statements to be unbalanced. The **amount required to bring the restated statements into balance** is termed the gain or loss from the translation or remeasurement. The gain or loss arising from remeasuring Jay A's financial statements is reported in the **consolidated income statement.** The gain or loss arising from translating Jay F's financial statements is reported in **other comprehensive income.**

c. The functional currency is the foreign currency or parent's currency that most closely correlates with the following economic indicators:

- Cash flow indicators
- Sales price indicators
- Sales market indicators
- Expense indicators
- Financing indicators
- Intercompany transactions and arrangement indicators

d. All accounts relating to **Jay A's** equipment are remeasured by the **exchange rate prevailing** between the **U.S. and Australian dollars** at the **time equipment** was **purchased.**

All accounts relating to **Jay F's** equipment are translated by the **current exchange rates** prevailing between the **U.S. dollar and the euro.** For the **equipment cost** and **accumulated depreciation,** this is the current exchange rate at **December 31. Depreciation expense** is translated at the rate prevailing on the **date the depreciation expense** was **recognized** or an appropriate **weighted average** exchange rate **for the current year.**

Research

FAS 52, Par. 5

5. The assets, liabilities, and operations of a foreign entity shall be measured using the functional currency of that entity. An entity's functional currency is the currency of the primary economic environment in which the entity operates; normally, that is the currency of the environment in which an entity primarily generates and expends cash. Appendix A provides guidance for determination of the functional currency. The economic factors cited in Appendix A, and possibly others, should be considered both individually and collectively when determining the functional currency.

Post-Exam Diagnostics

The AICPA Board of Examiners' Advisory Grading Service will provide boards of accountancy with individual diagnostic reports for all candidates along with the candidates' grades. The diagnostic reports show the candidate's level of proficiency on each examination section. The boards of accountancy **may** mail the diagnostic reports to candidates along with their grades: candidates should contact the state board in their jurisdiction to find out its policy on this.

There no longer is a Uniform Grade Mailing date. The examination contains structured response questions that requires answers to be transmitted to the AICPA for scoring. The AICPA anticipates that a minimum of 2-4 weeks will be required to process grades/scores. Plans are to shorten and make the score reporting more predictable.

Remember, candidates are required to sign a statement of confidentiality in which they promise not to reveal questions or answers. Due to the nondisclosure requirements, Bisk Education's editors are no longer able to address questions about specific examination questions, although we continue to supply help with similar study problems and questions in our texts.

CHAPTER 17

CONSOLIDATED FINANCIAL STATEMENTS

I. **Business Combinations** 17-2
- A. Overview 17-2
- B. Purchase Method 17-2
- C. Pooling of Interests Method 17-2

II. **Immediately Following Acquisition** 17-3
- A. Acquisition 17-3
- B. Record Combination (Purchase Method) 17-3

III. **Subsequent to Acquisition** 17-8
- A. Consolidation Procedures 17-8
- B. Subsidiary Purchase 17-8
- C. Subsidiary Disposal 17-8
- D. Purchase Method Consolidations 17-8
- E. Disclosures 17-12

IV. **Transactions Between Affiliated Companies** 17-13
- A. Intercompany Receivables, Payables & Loans 17-13
- B. Intercompany Sales of Inventory 17-14
- C. Intercompany Sales of Fixed Assets 17-14
- D. Intercompany Bonds 17-15

V. **Subsidiary Entity Records** 17-20
- A. Traditional 17-20
- B. Push-Down Accounting 17-20

VI. **Combined Financial Statements** 17-20
- A. Use 17-20
- B. Procedures 17-20

EXAM COVERAGE: Historically, exam coverage of the topics in Chapter 17 has been 3 to 10 percent of the FAR section. The pooling of interests method is unlikely to be tested; it might appear as an incorrect response to a question. More information regarding exam coverage is included in Appendix B, *Practical Advice.*

CHAPTER 17

CONSOLIDATED FINANCIAL STATEMENTS

I. Business Combinations

A. Overview

Consolidated Financial Statements (ARB 51) states, "...consolidated statements are more meaningful than separate statements and are usually necessary for a fair presentation when one of the companies in the group directly or indirectly has a controlling financial interest in the other companies" (par. 1). All majority-owned subsidiaries—all companies in which a parent has a controlling financial interest through direct or indirect ownership of a **majority voting interest** (i.e., greater than 50 percent)—should be consolidated, unless specifically exempted.

1. **Definition** A business combination occurs when an entity acquires net assets or equity interests of one or more other businesses and obtains control over that entity or entities.

2. **Chain of Interests** On occasion, intercorporate stock ownership arrangements may indicate a chain of interests (e.g., A owns 80 percent of B, B owns 60 percent of C) the product of which (e.g., 80% × 60% = 48%) does not represent control of the lower level subsidiary, where control is defined in terms of the 50 percent stock ownership minimum. In this instance, the preparation on consolidated statements is warranted, notwithstanding the 48 percent indirect interest of A Company in C Company. The product of the percentages of stock ownership in the chain is not a determinant in establishing a minimal condition for preparation of consolidated financial statements.

3. **Exceptions** SFAS 94, *Consolidation of All Majority-Owned Subsidiaries,* as amended, provides that a majority-owned subsidiary should **not** be consolidated if control does **not** rest with the majority owner. For example, if the subsidiary is in legal reorganization or in bankruptcy or operates under foreign exchange restrictions, controls, or other governmentally imposed uncertainties so severe that they cast significant doubt on the parent's ability to control the subsidiary. Consolidation of majority-owned subsidiaries is required even if they have nonhomogeneous operations, a large minority interest, or a foreign location.

B. Purchase Method

SFAS 141, *Business Combinations,* requires business combinations initiated after June 30, 2001, to be accounted for under the purchase method.

1. **Net Identifiable Assets** The acquiring corporation records the net assets acquired at the sum of the fair value of the consideration given and direct costs incurred as a result of the purchase.

2. **Goodwill** Any excess of the purchase price over the fair value (FV) of the net identifiable assets is recorded as goodwill. SFAS 147, *Acquisitions of Certain Financial Institutions,* classifies long-term core deposit intangible assets (depositor and borrower relationships) as goodwill. Goodwill must be tested for impairment at least annually. Goodwill is impaired if carrying value exceeds the fair value.

C. Pooling of Interests Method

Business combinations initiated before June 30, 2001, that were exchanges of common stock for common stock and met several conditions, were allowed to be accounted for by the pooling of interests method. Even though new combinations must be accounted for under the purchase method, consolidated companies that have been accounted for under the pooling method will continue to be consolidated using the pooling method.

1. **Summary** The pooling method accounts for a combination of two firms as a union of the ownership interests of two previously separated groups of stockholders. No sale or purchase is deemed to have occurred and no new goodwill is recorded. The assets and liabilities of the combining firms continue to be carried at their recorded amounts. The income of the constituents are combined and restated for each period presented. Consolidated financial statements for the year the combination is effected should be presented as if the combination had taken place at the **beginning** of the period.

2. **Consolidation Procedures** Consolidation procedures are similar to those for purchase method subsidiaries for adjusting the carrying amount of the investment eliminating capital and investment accounts, and eliminating intercompany transactions. The assets and liabilities of the combining entities are carried at their recorded amounts. The income of the companies are combined and restated for each period presented.

II. Immediately Following Acquisition

A. Acquisition

The acquisition of a controlling interest in a company may be effected in different manners.

1. **Assets** The acquiring corporation may negotiate with management to obtain the assets (and assume the liabilities) of the company being acquired in exchange for cash, securities, or other consideration. Upon consummation, the acquired company ceases to exist as a separate economic, legal, and accounting entity. The surviving corporation records in its books the assets and liabilities of the acquired company. Note that this results in automatic consolidation for the current and subsequent periods, since the assets and liabilities of both companies are recorded in the same set of books.

2. **Equity Interests** An acquiring corporation may acquire ownership (or control) of a subsidiary by obtaining all (or a majority) of its outstanding common stock. The separate legal entity of the subsidiary is preserved and it continues to maintain its own separate set of books. For financial reporting purposes, the two companies may be viewed as a single reporting entity in accordance with ARB 51; this creates the need for consolidated financial statements.

B. Record Combination (Purchase Method)

Investment in the acquired corporation is recorded at the sum of the fair value of the consideration given or net assets received, whichever is more clearly determinable, and direct acquisition costs.

1. **Assign Amounts to Assets and Liabilities Acquired**

   a. **Marketable Securities** at fair values

   b. **Receivables** at present values of amounts to be received determined at appropriate current interest rates, less allowances for uncollectibility and collection costs

   c. **Inventories**

      (1) **Finished Goods & Merchandise** at estimated selling prices less the sum of the costs of disposal and a reasonable profit allowance for the selling effort of the acquiring entity

      (2) **Work in Process** at the costs noted above plus the costs to complete

      (3) **Raw Materials** at current replacement costs

   d. **Plant & Equipment**

      (1) **To Be Used** at current replacement cost for similar capacity

      (2) **To Be Sold** at fair value less cost to sell

e. **Intangible Assets**

Exhibit 1 ▸ Examples of Intangible Assets Recognized

1. Marketing-Related Intangible Assets—Trademarks, tradenames, service marks, collective marks, certification marks, trade dress (unique color, shape, or package design), newspaper mastheads, internet domain names, noncompetition agreements
2. Customer-Related Intangible Assets—Customer lists, order or production backlog, customer contracts and related customer relationships, noncontractual customer relationships
3. Artistic-Related Intangible Assets—Plays, operas, ballets, books, magazines, newspapers, other literary works, musical works such as compositions, song lyrics, advertising jingles, pictures, photographs, video and audiovisual material, including motion pictures, music videos, television programs
4. Contract-Based Intangible Assets—Licensing, royalty, and standstill agreements; advertising, construction, management, service or supply contracts; lease agreements; construction permits; franchise agreements; operating and broadcast rights; use rights such as drilling, water air, mineral, timber cutting, and route authorities; servicing contracts such as mortgage servicing contracts; employment contracts
5. Technology-Based Intangible Assets—Patented technology; computer software and mask works; unpatented technology; databases, including title plants; trade secrets, such as secret formulas, processes, recipes

(1) **Goodwill & Deferred Income Taxes Previously Recorded by Acquired Entity** not recognized by the acquiring entity

(2) **Arising From Contractual or Legal Rights** at estimated fair values

(3) **Other Intangibles Separable From Entity** at estimated fair values, apart from goodwill

(4) **Other Intangibles Not Separable** not recognized separately from goodwill

f. **Other Assets Such as Land, Natural Resources & Nonmarketable Securities** at appraised values

g. **Accounts & Notes Payable, and Long-Term Debt** at present values of amounts to be paid determined at appropriate current interest rates

h. **Liabilities & Accruals** at present values of amounts to be paid determined at appropriate current interest rates

i. **Preacquisition Contingencies** at fair value if the fair value can be determined during the allocation period. If not, the contingency is included if information available prior to the end of the allocation period indicates that it is probable that one or more future events will occur to confirm the existence of the asset, liability, or impairment; and the amount can be reasonably estimated.

2. **Purchase Price Exceeds FV** If the purchase price exceeds the net of the amounts assigned to assets acquired and liabilities assumed, the excess is recognized as goodwill.

3. **FV Exceeds Purchase Price** No "negative goodwill" is recognized.

   a. **Reduce Asset Amounts** If the purchase price is less than the net of the amounts assigned to assets acquired and liabilities assumed, the excess is allocated as a pro rata reduction of the acquired asset amounts, except financial assets other than investments accounted for by the equity method, assets to be disposed of by sale, deferred tax assets, prepaid assets relating to pension or other postretirement benefit plans, and any other current assets.

   b. **Extraordinary Gain** If any excess remains after reducing to zero the acquired asset amounts, the remaining excess shall be recognized as an extraordinary gain. This gain is recognized in the period in which the business combination is completed.

4. **Acquisition Costs** Direct acquisition costs incurred (e.g., fees of finders and consultants, cost of furnishing information to stockholders) must be capitalized as part of the total purchase price. Indirect and general expenses related to the acquisition are expensed as incurred.

5. **Equity Securities Issued** If the purchaser issues its own equity securities as part of the consideration, these must be credited to paid-in capital on the basis of their fair value. Costs of registering and issuing equity securities are a reduction of the otherwise determinable fair value of the securities (i.e., a reduction of additional paid-in capital).

6. **Purchase of Partial Interest** A purchase of less than 100 percent interest in a business at a price exceeding the book value of the proportionate interest acquired should **not** result in the recognition of "implied value" based on the purchase price and the percentage ownership acquired.

   a. Generally, identifiable assets are adjusted to FV only to the extent of the proportionate interest acquired.

   b. If the consideration paid exceeds the FV of identifiable net assets, identifiable assets would be presented in the consolidated balance sheet at an amount determined as follows: Original BV + [% ownership × (FV – BV)].

Example 1 ▸ Purchase Price Allocation

Purchaser Inc., acquired for cash the assets and liabilities of the Acquired Co. Acquired's balance sheet prior to its dissolution is reproduced below. Book values approximate fair values except where otherwise indicated.

	BV	FV (if different)
Cash	$ 3,000	
Accounts receivable	8,000	
Inventories	22,000	$20,000
Held-to-maturity securities	50,000	55,000
Property, plant, and equipment, net (PPE)	60,000	50,000
Land	20,000	28,000
Total assets	$163,000	
Current liabilities	$ 4,000	
Long-term liabilities	20,000	
C/S, $10 par	30,000	
APIC	50,000	
R/E	59,000	
Total liabilities and equity	$163,000	

Required: Determine the amounts assigned to the individual assets and liabilities acquired for a purchase price of: (a) $160,000; (b) $120,000; and (c) $60,000.

Solution:

		Assigned Cost		
Item, Dr. (Cr.)	FV	Case (a)	Case (b)	Case (c)
Cash	$ 3,000	$ 3,000	$ 3,000	$ 3,000
Accounts receivable	8,000	8,000	8,000	8,000
Inventories	20,000	20,000	20,000	20,000
Held-to-maturity securities	55,000	55,000	55,000	55,000
Current liabilities	(4,000)	(4,000)	(4,000)	(4,000)
Long-term liabilities	(20,000)	(20,000)	(20,000)	(20,000)
Total net FV, excluding PPE & land	$ 62,000			
Purchase price		160,000	120,000	60,000
Net FV above		(62,000)	(62,000)	(62,000)
Excess (deficit) purchase price		98,000	58,000	(2,000)
Allocate to noncurrent assets and/or goodwill:				
PPE, net*	$ 50,000	(50,000)	(37,179)	0
Land**	28,000	(28,000)	(20,821)	0
Goodwill (Extraordinary Income)		$ 20,000	$ 0	$ (2,000)

* PPE = $50,000 / ($50,000 + $28,000) × $58,000 = $37,179
** Land = $28,000 ($50,000 + $28,000) × $58,000 = $20,821

Example 2 ▸ Purchase of Partial Interest

Same as Example 1, except that the transaction involved the acquisition by Purchaser, Inc., of 80% of Acquired's common stock outstanding, in exchange for $128,000 cash.

Required:

a. Provide the journal entry to record the investment in Purchaser's books.
b. Determine the adjustments needed if the carrying amounts of individual assets are to reflect FV only to the extent of proportionate ownership acquired (proprietary theory).
c. Present a consolidation worksheet starting with the separate balance sheets of the two companies given in the first two columns of Solution c., below. Show eliminating entries and the consolidated balance sheet.

Solution:

a.

Investment in Sub	128,000	
Cash		128,000

b.

Item	80% × (FV – BV)				Adjustment
Assets					
Cash	80% × ($ 3,000	–	3,000)	=	$ 0
A/R	80% × (8,000	–	8,000)	=	0
Inventories*	80% × (20,000*	–	22,000)	=	(1,600)
HTM Securities	80% × (55,000	–	50,000)	=	4,000
PPE	80% × (50,000	–	60,000)	=	(8,000)
Land	80% × (28,000	–	20,000)	=	6,400
Subtotal					$ 800
Liabilities					
Current liabilities	80% × (4,000	–	4,000)	=	0
Long-term liabilities	80% × (20,000	–	20,000)	=	0
Net identifiable assets	80% × ($140,000	–	139,000)	=	$ 800

Purchase price		$ 128,000
FV of net assets	$140,000	
% ownership	× 80%	
FV of 80% net assets		(112,000)
Goodwill		$ 16,000

* For illustration purposes only; if inventories are overvalued by $2,000, a write-down for that **entire** amount should be recorded in Acquired's books.

c. [1] Entry to eliminate 80% of subsidiary's owners' equity account balances.
[2] Entry to adjust assets to FV and record purchased goodwill.

	Balance Sheets		Eliminations		Minority Interest	Consolidated Balance Sheet	
Assets	Purchaser*	Acquired	Dr.	Cr.	(20%)	Dr.	Cr.
Cash	$ 20,000	$ 3,000				$ 23,000	
A/R	35,000	8,000				43,000	
Inventories	32,000	22,000		[2] $ 1,600		52,400	
HTM securities	80,000	50,000	[2] $ 4,000			134,000	
PPE (net)	150,000	60,000		[2] 8,000		202,000	
Land	40,000	20,000	[2] 6,400			66,400	
Invest. in sub (80% int.)	128,000			[1] 111,200 [2] 16,800			
Goodwill			[2] 16,000			16,000	
Total	$485,000	$163,000					
Liab. & Equity							
Cur. liabs.	$ 25,000	$ 4,000					$ 29,000
Long-term liabs.	40,000	20,000					60,000
C/S, $3 par (P)	90,000						90,000
APIC (P)	160,000						160,000
R/E (P)	170,000						170,000
C/S, $10 par (S)		30,000	[1] 24,000		$ 6,000		
APIC (S)		50,000	[1] 40,000		10,000		
R/E (S)		59,000	[1] 47,200		11,800		
Minority interest					(27,800)		27,800
Total	$485,000	$163,000	$137,600	$137,600	$ 0	$536,800	$536,800

* All P's balance sheet amounts, except **Investment in Sub,** are arbitrary.

Example 3 ♦ Purchase of 100% Interest

Refer to the balance sheet and FV's provided for Acquired Co. in Example 1, except that the acquisition price consisted of the following: $100,000 cash, 5,000 shares of Purchaser, Inc. ($3 par, $10 FV), and $10,000 paid for legal fees and commissions directly related to the purchase.

Required: Provide the journal entry to record the transaction in Purchaser's books.

Solution:

	Dr.	Cr.
Investment in Sub (balancing figure)	160,000	
Cash ($100,000 + $10,000)		110,000
C/S, $3 Par (5,000 × $3)		15,000
APIC [(5,000 × $10) – $15,000 par]		35,000

NOTE: If the $10,000 paid was for registration fees, APIC would be recorded at $25,000 ($35,000 – $10,000) and the investment in subsidiary would be recorded at $150,000 (the balancing figure).

III. Subsequent to Acquisition

A. Consolidation Procedures

Subsequent to a business combination, the newly affiliated companies continue to maintain their separate accounting records. Furthermore, the eliminations and adjustments made as part of the consolidation procedures are **not** entered into the books of any of the companies; these adjustments are simply worksheet entries that are never formally journalized.

1. **Consolidated Financial Statements** Consolidated financial statements are required by ARB 51, Consolidated Financial Statements, when a company owns more than 50% of the voting stock of another firm, with few exceptions. SFAS 141, Business Combinations, provides accounting and reporting standards.

Exhibit 2 ▸ Accounting for Investments

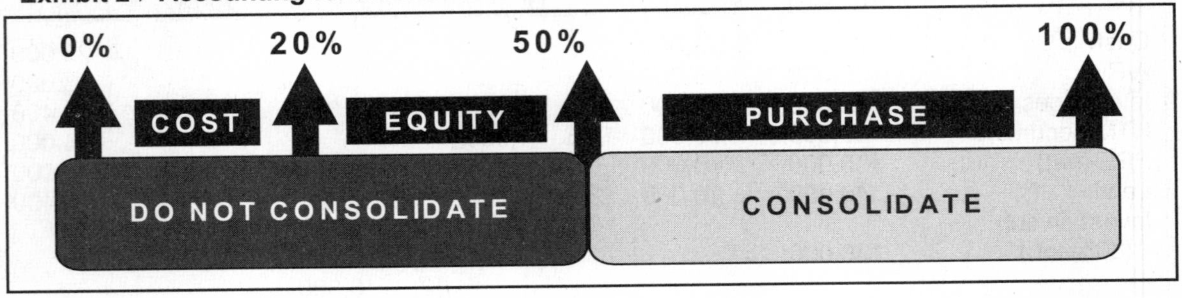

2. **Frequency** As a result, consolidation procedures must be performed every period in which financial statements are presented. Generally, the parent company carries its interest in a subsidiary in a single account, *Investment in Subsidiary.* This account is generally carried under one of two methods: the cost method or the equity method.

3. **Final Result** Consolidation procedures are partly determined by the consolidation method used. However, the final result, (the consolidated statements themselves) must be the same regardless of how the investment is carried on the parent's books.

B. Subsidiary Purchase

When a subsidiary is purchased during a year, there are alternative methods of dealing with the results of its operations in the consolidated income statement.

1. **Preferable Method** The preferable method is to include the subsidiary in the consolidation as though it had been acquired at the beginning of the period and then deduct near the bottom of the consolidated income statement the preacquisition portion of earnings applicable to each block of stock.

2. **Alternative Method** The alternative method is to include in the consolidated statement only the subsidiary's revenues and expenses subsequent to the date of acquisition.

C. Subsidiary Disposal

Where an investment in a subsidiary is disposed of during the year, it is preferable to omit from consolidated statements all details of the subsidiary's operations and to merely show the equity of the parent in the earnings of the subsidiary prior to disposal as a separate line in the income statement (equity method).

D. Purchase Method Consolidations

Consolidation procedures involve the following.

1. **Adjust the Carrying Amount of Investment** Entries to adjust the carrying amount of the investment to the equity method balance.

2. **Eliminate Capital and Investment Accounts** Entries to eliminate the subsidiary's capital accounts (except for minority interest, if any), and the parent's investment account.

3. **Adjust for Depreciation on Excess Purchase Price Over Book Value of Assets**

4. **Eliminate Intercompany Transactions** Entries to eliminate intercompany balances and unrealized intercompany gains and losses.

Example 4 ▸ Cost Method

The December 31, Year 3, trial balances of Purchasing Inc., (P) and Subsidiary Corporation (S) are reproduced in the first two columns of the worksheet in the solution, below. Purchasing acquired its 80% interest in the common stock of S on January 1, Year 1, for $150,000 cash. At the time of acquisition, the recorded amounts of all assets and liabilities of S were deemed to approximate their FV, except equipment, which was undervalued by $50,000 in S's books. The equipment has an estimated remaining useful life of 10 years, and it has been depreciated on the straight-line basis. S has not issued or retired stock since its incorporation. P carries its investment in S under the cost method.* Net income and dividend distributions for S have been as follows.

Year	Net Income	Dividends Declared
1	$15,000	$ 8,000
2	13,000	10,000
3	16,000	5,000
	$44,000	$23,000

* The **equity** method is generally required for **unconsolidated** investments exceeding 20% ownership; since the investment in S is to be consolidated, however, it is permissible for P to use the **cost method** for internal purposes.

Required: Provide elimination entries to consolidate the financial statements of P and S. Show all computations.

Solution: Three steps are recommended before attempting to complete the consolidation worksheet.

Step 1: Determine the net book value of S at the time of the 80% stock acquisition by P.

Beg. R/E + NI – Divids. = End R/E; Beg. R/E = End R/E – NI + Divids.

Beg. R/E [$79,000 – ($15,000 + $13,000) + ($8,000 + $10,000)]	$ 69,000
C/S (from trial balance)	20,000
Net BV Co. S, January 1, Year 1	$ 89,000

Step 2: Determine amount of excess cost over BV of identifiable assets and purchased goodwill, if any.

Purchase price	$150,000
Less: BV of net assets acquired [$89,000 (Step 1) × .80]	(71,200)
Excess cost over BV of net assets acquired	78,800
Attributable to equipment ($50,000 × .80)	(40,000)
Goodwill	$ 38,800

Step 3: Determine amount of depreciation on excess purchase price over book value.

Excess FV over BV, equipment (Step 2)	$ 40,000
Useful life (in years)	/ 10
Depreciation on excess, per year	$ 4,000

Consolidation Worksheet, 80% Ownership, Cost Method Investment

	Trial Balance Dr. (Cr.)		Eliminations		Consolidated Income Statement	Minority Interest	Controlling R/E	Consolidated Balance Sheet	
	P	S	Dr.	Cr.	Dr. (Cr.)	Dr. (Cr.)	Dr. (Cr.)	Dr.	Cr.
Current assets	50,000	15,000						65,000	
Equipment	200,000	120,000	[3] 40,000	[5] 12,000				348,000	
Investment in S	150,000		[4] 8,000	[2] 16,000					
				[2] 63,200					
				[3] 78,800					
Goodwill			[3] 38,800					38,800	
Liabilities	(70,000)	(25,000)							95,000
C/S, $1 par (P)	(100,000)								100,000
R/E, Jan. 1, Year 3 (P)	(131,000)		[5] 8,000	[4] 8,000			(131,000)		
C/S, $2 par (S)		(20,000)	[2] 16,000			(4,000)			
R/E, Jan. 1, Year 3 (S)		$(79,000)	[2] 63,200			(15,800)			
Revenues	$(255,000)	(71,000)			(326,000)				
Expenses	160,000	55,000	[5] 4,000		219,000				
Subsidiary dividend income	(4,000)		[1] 4,000						
Dividends declared		5,000		[1] 4,000		1,000			
	0	0	182,000	182,000					
Consolidated NI					(107,000)		(107,000)		
Minority NI, 20% × (71,000 – 55,000)						(3,200)	3,200		
Minority interest						(22,000)			22,000
R/E, controlling interest							(234,800)		234,800
								451,800	451,800

Worksheet entries:

[1] To eliminate current year dividends.
[2] To eliminate 80% of S equity balances.
[3] To record goodwill and excess valuation of equipment, as determined in Step 2.
[4] To adjust investment account and R/E for S income and dividends during Years 1 through 2. (80% × R/E) = 80% × ($79,000 – $69,000) = $8,000.
[5] To record accumulated depreciation (3 year) and current year expense.

Example 5 ▸ Equity Method

Same as Example 4, except that P maintains its investment in S under the **equity method** of accounting for investments. The trial balances of P and S are provided below. Note that while S's trial balance is the same as in Example 4, P's trial balance shows different amounts for the *Investment in S* account and *Subsidiary Income* account. This is the result of accounting for the investment in S under the equity method.

Required: Same as Example 4.

Solution: A basic understanding of the **equity** method of accounting for common stock investments is essential in solving this problem. Before attempting to work through the elimination entries required, you should carefully study the T-account analysis of P's *Investment in Sub, Investment Income,* and *Retained Earnings* accounts, as illustrated below. While this step is not necessary in solving the problem, it will facilitate the solution and increase your understanding.

Investment in S				Subsidiary Income				Retained Earnings			
(a)	150,000	18,400	(c)	(e)	4,000	12,800	(b)	(d)	8,000	22,400	(b)
(b)	35,200	8,000	(d)							116,600	(f)
		4,000	(e)								
bal.	154,800	12/31, Year 3			12/31, Year 3	8,800	bal.		1/1, Year 3	131,000	bal.

T-Account entries:

(a) To record acquisition cost of 80% interest in S (credit to cash for same amount not shown).

(b) To record P's share of S's cumulative NI for Year 1 through 3 (80% × $44,000). Note, the beginning (i.e., 1/1, Year 3) balance of R/E has been credited for P's portion of the earnings for Years 1 and 2 [80% × ($15,000 + $13,000)]. The portion of NI reported by S in Year 3 (80% × $16,000 = $12,800) has been credited to *Subsidiary Income,* but is properly not reflected in the beginning (1/1, Year 3) balance of R/E.

(c) This entry represents the reduction in the carrying amount of the investment due to dividends declared by S during Years 1 through 3. (80% × $23,000).

(d) These entries reduce the investment for the amount of depreciation of the excess cost over BV, for the Years 1 and 2. Note, debit to R/E for similar reasons as in (b), above.

(e) Current year additional depreciation—credit *Investment* account, as in (d), above, and charge *Subsidiary Income.*

(f) This is not an entry or a balancing figure. It represents P's balance in R/E not including the income recognized from S. This figure may be independently determined by an analysis of P's cost method R/E, $131,000 (see worksheet in Example 4, above). Under the cost method, R/E would have been increased by dividends received from S in prior years. Subtracting these dividends, we obtain $116,600 [$131,000 – 80% × ($8,000 + $10,000)]. NOTE: The R/E balance, $131,000 credit is the same as shown in the "Controlling Interest" column (i.e., after adjustments) of the cost-method worksheet (see Example 4).

Consolidation Worksheet, 80% Ownership, Equity Method

	Trial Balance Dr. (Cr.)		Eliminations		Consolidated Income Statement	Minority Interest	Controlling R/E	Consolidated Balance Sheet	
	P	S	Dr.	Cr.	Dr. (Cr.)	Dr. (Cr.)	Dr. Cr.)	Dr.	Cr.
Current assets	50,000	15,000						65,000	
Equipment	200,000	120,000	[3] 40,000	[4] 12,000				348,000	
Investment in S	154,800		[1] 4,000	[1] 12,800					
			[4] 12,000	[2] 16,000					
				[2] 63,200					
				[3] 78,800					
Goodwill			[3] 38,800					38,800	
Liabilities	(70,000)	(25,000)							95,000
C/S, $1 par (P)	(100,000)								100,000
R/E, Jan. 1, Year 3 (P)	(131,000)						(131,000)		
C/S, $2 par (S)		(20,000)	[2] 16,000			(4,000)			
R/E, Jan. 1, Year 3 (S)		(79,000)	[2] 63,200			(15,800)			
Revenues	(255,000)	(71,000)			(326,000)				
Expenses	160,000	55,000	[4] 4,000		219,000				
Subsidiary income	(8,800)		[1] 12,800	[4] 4,000					
Dividends declared		5,000		[1] 4,000		1,000			
	0	0	190,800	190,800					
Consolidated NI					(107,000)		(107,000)		
Minority NI, 20% × (71,000 – 55,000)						(3,200)	3,200		
Minority interest						(22,000)			22,000
R/E, controlling interest							(234,800)		234,800
								451,800	451,800

Worksheet entries:

[1] To reverse current year subsidiary income (80% × $16,000) and dividends (80% × $5,000).
[2] To eliminate 80% of S capital account balances.
[3] To record goodwill and write-up equipment to FV at time of acquisition.
[4] To record accumulated depreciation and current year expense.

4000 ×3 12000

E. **Disclosures**

The notes to the financial statements of a combined entity in the period in which a material business combination is completed should include the following information.

1. The name and brief description of the acquired entity and the percentage of voting equity interests acquired

2. The primary reasons for the acquisition and a description of the factors contributing to any recognition of goodwill

3. The period for which the results of operations of the acquired entity are included in the combined income statement

4. The cost of the acquired entity and, if applicable, the number and assigned value of shares of equity interests issued or issuable

5. A condensed balance sheet disclosing the amount assigned to each major asset and liability caption of the acquired entity at the acquisition date

6. Contingent payments, options or commitments and projected accounting treatment upon occurrence of the contingencies

7. The amount of purchased research and development assets acquired and written off in the period as having no alternative future use and the line item in the income statement that includes that amount

8. The description and reasons for any purchased price allocation, if any, that has not been finalized—in subsequent periods, the nature and amount of the adjustments must be disclosed

9. If the amounts assigned to goodwill or to other intangible assets acquired are significant in relation to the total purchase, the following must be disclosed:

   a. For intangible assets subject to amortization, the amount assigned, the amount of residual value, and the weighted-average amortization period must be disclosed.

   b. For intangible assets not subject to amortization, the total amount assigned and the amount assigned to any major intangible asset class must be disclosed.

   c. For goodwill, the total amount and the amount that is expected to be deductible for tax purposes must be disclosed. In addition, if the combined entity is required to disclose segment information, the amount of goodwill by reportable segment must be disclosed, unless not practicable.

10. If a series of individually immaterial business combinations completed during the period are material in the aggregate, the number and brief description of entities acquired and the aggregate costs and amounts involved must be disclosed.

11. If the combined entity is a public business enterprise, the following supplemental information of a pro forma basis must be included:

    a. Results of operations for the current period (and prior period if comparative statements are presented) as though the business combination had been completed at the beginning of the period (or prior period); and

    b. At a minimum, the information shall display revenue, income before extraordinary items and the cumulative effect of accounting changes, net income, and earnings per share.

IV. Transactions Between Affiliated Companies

A. Intercompany Receivables, Payables & Loans

1. **Receivables and Payables** Originate from intercompany transactions such as the sale of inventory and fixed assets or the rendering of services. These receivables and payables appear in the affiliated company's trial balance at the end of the period; note, however, that no asset or liability exists outside the consolidated group. Elimination of the receivable/payable simply involves a "worksheet entry" reversing the original recording.

2. **Intercompany Loans** These must also be eliminated from consolidated statements, in a manner similar to that used for receivables and payables. In addition, interest income and expense and interest accruals must be eliminated.

Example 6 ▸ Intercompany Loans

P Co. lent $10,000 on June 1, Year 1 to S Co., its 90% owned subsidiary. The note is to be repaid May 30, Year 2, along with 12% interest. The partial trial balances of P and S are reproduced below.

	P	S
Assets	$ XXX	$ XX
Note receivable—S	10,000	
Accrued interest on note	600	
Investment in S	XXX	
Liabilities	(XX)	(XX)
Note payable—P		(10,000)
Accrued interest on note		(600)
C/S	(XXXX)	(XXX)
R/E	(XXX)	(XX)
Sales revenue	(50,000)	(20,000)
Interest revenue	(600)	0
Expenses	36,000	17,000
Interest expense		600
	$ 0	$ 0

Required: Provide the elimination entries related to the intercompany note. Also, compute consolidated net income and allocate it to controlling and minority interest.

Solution: Note that whereas interest is not an expense for the consolidated entity, it is nevertheless a cost of doing business for S. It must be included in S's net income in order to determine the minority interest in S's net income.

	Dr.	Cr.
Notes Payable	10,000	
Accrued Interest Payable	600	
Notes Receivable		10,000
Accrued Interest Receivable		600
To eliminate intercompany receivable/payable and related accrued interest.		
Interest Income	600	
Interest Expense		600
To eliminate interest income and expense on intercompany notes.		

	P	S	Consolidated
Sales Revenue (CR)	$(50,000)	$(20,000)	$(70,000)
Expenses	36,000	17,000	53,000
Minority interest in NI, 10% × ($20,000 – $17,000 – $600)			240
Controlling interest in NI			$(16,760)

B. **Intercompany Sales of Inventory**
Intercompany sales of merchandise create three problems.

1. **Sales and Cost of Goods Sold** The sale and CGS are recorded twice: first, the seller records a sale and related CGS as the merchandise is "sold" to the affiliated buyer; secondly, the buyer resells the goods to outsiders, also recording a sale and CGS. For consolidated purposes, however, it is obvious that only one sale has occurred.

2. **Gross Profit** When one company sells merchandise to its affiliate at a price above cost, the ending inventory of the buyer contains an element of unrealized gross profit. The gross profit is not realized to the economic entity until it is sold to outsiders. The preparation of consolidated financial statements requires that unrealized gross profit be eliminated.

3. **Minority Interest** Minority interest in the subsidiary's income must be based on the sales and CGS originally reported by the subsidiary. As was the case in interaffiliate interest income and expense, the minority income should reflect the expense incurred (or revenues obtained) in intercompany transactions. The sale, however, may not be recognized until after the goods have been sold to an outside buyer.

Example 7 ▸ Intercompany Sales of Inventory

Parent sells merchandise to its 90% owned Sub at 25% above cost. The following chart summarizes the transactions in intercompany sales at year-end.

	Parent's sales price (= cost to Sub)	Cost	Parent's gross profit	
Beginning inventory 1/1	$ 50,000	$ 40,000	$ 10,000	(realized)
Sales	200,000	160,000	40,000	
Total	250,000	200,000	50,000	
Ending inventory 12/1	(75,000)	(60,000)	(15,000)	(unrealized)
Cost of goods sold	$175,000	$140,000	$ 35,000	

Required: Provide the consolidation elimination entries.

Solution:

		Dr.	Cr.
(1)	R/E	10,000	
	CGS		10,000
	To adjust beginning R/E and CGS for the overstated beginning inventory.		
(2)	Sales	200,000	
	Purchases		200,000
	To eliminate intercompany sales and purchases.		
(3)	CGS	15,000	
	Inventory		15,000
	To eliminate unrealized gross profit in ending inventory.		

C. **Intercompany Sales of Fixed Assets**
Sales of fixed assets between members of an affiliated group may result in the recognition of gain or loss by the seller, if the selling price differs from the carrying amount of the asset. Again, no gain or loss has taken place for the consolidated entity; assets have merely been transferred from one set of books to another. Additional complications result from the fact that the buyer of the asset will record it in its books at the agreed upon purchase price; subsequent depreciation charges will be based upon this purchase price, thus requiring adjustment. In summary, an interaffiliate sale of fixed assets involves the following.

1. **Carrying Amount** In the year of sale, restore the carrying amount of the asset to its original BV and eliminate the gain (loss) recorded by the seller.

2. **Depreciation** For each period, adjust depreciation expense and accumulated depreciation to reflect the original BV of the asset.

3. **Retained Earnings** For periods subsequent to the year of sale, R/E must be adjusted to eliminate the gain (loss) contained therein.

   a. If the parent is the seller, controlling interest R/E absorbs the entire adjustment.

   b. If a less than 100 percent owned subsidiary is the seller, the adjustment to R/E should be allocated to the controlling and minority interests on the basis of their ownership ratio.

Example 8 ▸ Intercompany Sale of Depreciable Assets

Parent sells machinery for $1,500 to its wholly owned subsidiary. The machinery cost Parent $2,000 and accumulated depreciation at date of sale was $1,000. Parent had been depreciating the machinery on the SL method over a 10-year life. Sub continues this depreciation method.

Required: Provide the elimination entries at the end of Years 1 and 2.

Solution: The debit to RE is $400 ($500 – $100). Thus, the yearly indirect increase in consolidated income (from decreasing depreciation expense) will cause the $500 gain to be fully recognized by the seller by the end of the fifth year, when the asset is fully depreciated.

Year 1	Gain on Intercompany Sale of Assets	500	
	Machinery	500	
	Accumulated Depreciation		1,000
	To eliminate gain and restore asset and accumulated depreciation accounts to their original balances.		
	Accumulated Depreciation	100*	
	Depreciation Expense ($500 / 5)		100*
	To adjust consolidated depreciation charges.		

* Gain / Life remaining to buyer = Depreciation elimination per year

Year 2	Retained Earnings	400	
	Machinery	500	
	Accumulated Depreciation		800
	Depreciation Expense		100

D. Intercompany Bonds

1. **Direct Sale & Purchase** A direct sale and purchase of bonds between affiliates poses problems similar to the interaffiliate lending and borrowing transactions already discussed. Intercompany receivables and payables (including accrued interest) must be eliminated, as well as interest income/expense. Note that in a direct acquisition of bonds, no gain or loss results to either party, even if a premium or discount is involved, since the net carrying amount of the bond liability on the issuer's books will always equal the bond investment amount on the purchaser's books.

Example 9 ▸ Direct Sale of Bonds

Parent purchases $100,000 bonds from Sub on December 31, Year 1. The bonds' stated interest rate is 10%. Parent pays $110,000 for the bonds. The effective interest rate of the bonds is 8%.

Required: Prepare the consolidation elimination entry at the date of the transaction and at December 31, Year 2.

Solution: On December 31, Year 1, the following journal entries were made on the books of the acquirer and the issuer.

Acquirer (Parent)			Issuer (Sub)		
Investment in Bonds	110,000		Cash	110,000	
Cash		110,000	Bonds Payable		100,000
			Premium on Bonds		10,000

The consolidation elimination entry required is

Bond Premium	10,000	
Bonds Payable	100,000	
Investment in Bonds		110,000

During Year 2, the following journal entries would be made to record income and expenses.

Acquirer			Issuer		
Cash	10,000		Interest Expense	8,800*	
Interest Income		8,800*	Bond Premium	1,200	
Bond Investment		1,200	Cash		10,000

* Interest income or expense = Effective interest rate x Net carrying amount (8% × $110,000).

The consolidation elimination entries required at the end of Year 2 are as follows.

Interest Income	8,800	
Interest Expense		8,800
Bonds Payable	100,000	
Bond Premium	8,800	
Investment in Bonds		108,800

2. **Third Party** A member of an affiliated group may issue its bonds to outsiders. These bonds may then be purchased from the outside parties by a second affiliate.

   a. For consolidated purposes, the bonds have been retired, since they are no longer held by outsiders.

   b. A gain or loss will typically result from the acquisition by the second affiliate, in the open market, of bonds originally issued by the first affiliate to outsiders. This occurs because the FV of the bonds at the time of reacquisition is likely to be different than the carrying amount of the bond obligation on the books of the issuer. No gain or loss is recorded by the individual affiliates, yet a gain or loss on retirement must be recognized at the consolidated level.

   c. This gain or loss will be periodically recognized by the issuer as the difference between interest expense to the issuer and interest income to the purchaser. Upon maturity of the bond issue, the entire consolidated gain (loss) realized at the time of reacquisition of the bond will have been amortized and no further adjustments will be necessary.

Example 10 ▸ Bonds Originally Issued to Third Parties (face amount)

P owns a 90% interest in S, which it acquired several years ago. P accounts for its investment in S under the equity method. No intercompany sales of fixed assets or inventories have taken place.

- On January 1, Year 1, S issued to outsiders $100,000, 8%, 10-year bonds at face amount. Interest is paid annually, on December 30.
- On January 1, Year 3, P bought the entire bond issue, when the prevailing interest rate for that type of bond was 12%.
- Operating income before interest charges and revenue was as follows.

	P	S
Year 3	$55,000	$33,000
Year 4	60,000	30,000

Required: Provide elimination entries and allocate consolidated income to the minority and controlling interest for (a) Year 3, and (b) Year 4. Ignore income taxes.

Solution: For consolidated purposes, the bonds have been retired. A gain is calculated and recognized as follows.

$100,000 × P (8, 12%)	$40,388	P(8, 12%) = PV of $1 in 8 years at 12%, 0.40388
$ 8,000 × P_A (8, 12%)	39,741	P_A(8, 12%) = PV of $1 annuity, 8 years at 12%, 4.96763
	$80,129	

Carrying amount of bonds in S books	$100,000
Less: Price paid by P to acquire bonds	(80,129)
Gain on retirement	$ 19,871

a. The following entries would have been made by P and S during Year 3

P			S		
Cash	8,000		Interest Expense	8,000	
Investment in S Bonds	1,615		Cash		8,000
Interest Income		9,615			

Elimination entries are illustrated by the following partial consolidation worksheet:

	P Dr. (Cr.)	S Dr. (Cr.)	Eliminations Dr.	Eliminations Cr.	Consolidated Income Statement Dr. (Cr.)
Invest. in S bonds ($80,129 + $1,615)	81,744			81,744	
Bonds payable		(100,000)	100,000		
Operating income (excluding interest)	(55,000)	(33,000)			(88,000)
Interest income	(9,615)		9,615		
Interest expense		8,000		8,000	
Gain on retirement of S bonds				19,871	(19,871)
			109,615	109,615	
Consolidated NI (Cr)					(107,871)
Minority interest, 10% ($33,000 – $8,000 – $1,615 + $19,871)*					$ 4,326
Controlling interest, $55,000 + $9,615 + (90% × $43,256)					103,545
					$107,871

* The entire gain on retirement is allocated to S, and interest expense is adjusted to reflect the current rate (12%). To understand the reasoning behind this, assume two transactions:

(1) S retires $100,000 BV bonds at a cost of $80,129, realizing a $19,871 gain.

(2) S reissues debt for $80,129 at face value. The interest rate on this debt is the prevailing rate, or 12%; therefore, interest expense for Year 3 is $8,000 + $1,615 = $9,615 (i.e., 12% × $80,129).

b. The following entries would have been made by P and S during Year 4.

P			S		
Cash	8,000		Interest Expense	8,000	
Bond Investment	1,809		Cash		8,000
Interest Income ($81,744 × 12%)		9,809			

	P	S	Eliminations		Consolidated Income Statement
	Dr. (Cr.)	Dr. (Cr.)	Dr.	Cr.	Dr.(Cr.)
Invest. in S bonds (81,744 + 1,809)	83,553			83,553	
Bonds payable		(100,000)	100,000		
Operating income (excluding interest)	(60,000)	(30,000)			(90,000)
Interest income	(9,809)		9,809		
Interest expense		8,000		8,000	
Retained earnings, P	(XXX)			16,430*	
Retained earnings, S		(XX)		1,826*	
			109,809	109,809	
Consolidated NI (Cr)					(90,000)
Minority interest, 10% × ($30,000 – $8,000 – $1,809)					$ 2,019
Controlling interest, $60,000 + $9,809 + (90% × $20,191)					87,981
					$ 90,000

* Consolidated R/E must include the gain on retirement of the bonds ($19,871) less the amount amortized prior to Year 4 ($1,615 additional interest expense charged to S in Year 3, see part a, above). The remaining adjustment to R/E of $18,256 is allocated to the controlling and minority interests in proportion to their ownership percentage.

Example 11 ▸ Bonds Originally Issued to Third Parties at Discount

On January 1, Year 1, S issued to outside parties $100,000, 8% bonds to yield 9% and due to mature on December 30, Year 4. The bonds were purchased by P on January 1, Year 3, when the prevailing interest rate for that type of bond was 12%. Operating income before interest charges and revenues was as follows.

Year	P	S
3	$80,000	$35,000
4	90,000	38,000

Required: Provide the consolidation worksheet entries to eliminate the intercompany bonds and allocate consolidated net income to the minority and controlling interests for (a) Year 3, and (b) Year 4. Ignore income taxes.

Solution:

$100,000 × P (n = 4, i = 9%; 0.70843)	$ 70,843
$ 8,000 × P_A (n = 4, i = 9%; 3.23975)	25,918
Bond issue price, January 1, Year 1	96,761
Face amount	100,000
Discount, January 1, Year 1	$ 3,239

Table 1—S Discount Amortization Schedule

Date	Cash payment	Interest expense	Amortization	Carrying amount
Jan. 1, Year 1				$ 96,761
Dec. 30, Year 1	$8,000	$8,707	$707	97,468
Dec. 30, Year 2	8,000	8,772	772	98,240
Dec. 30, Year 3	8,000	8,842	842	99,082
Dec. 30, Year 4	8,000	8,918*	918	100,000

*$1 difference due to rounding

$100,000 × P (n = 2, i = 12%; 0.79720)	$79,720
$ 8,000 × P_A (n = 2, i = 12%; 1.6900)	13,520
Retirement price	93,240
Carrying amount in S books (Table 1)	98,240
Consolidated gain on retirement	$ 5,000

Table 2—P Discount Amortization Schedule

Date	Cash payment	Interest expense	Amortization	Carrying amount
Jan. 1, Year 3				$ 93,240
Dec. 30, Year 3	$8,000	$11,189	$3,189	96,429
Dec. 30, Year 4	8,000	11,571	3,571	100,000

a. Year 3 Partial Consolidation Worksheet

	P Dr. (Cr.)	S Dr. (Cr.)	Eliminations Dr.	Eliminations Cr.	Consolidated Income Statement Dr.(Cr.)
Investment in S bonds (Table 2)	96,429			96,429	
Bonds payable		(100,000)	100,000		
Discount (Table 1)		918		918	
Operating income (Cr) (excluding interest)	(80,000)	(35,000)			(115,000)
Int. income (Table 2)	(11,189)		11,189		
Int. expense (Table 1)		8,842		8,842	
Gain on retirement				5,000	(5,000)
			111,189	111,189	
Consolidated NI (Cr)					(120,000)
Minority interest, 10% ($35,000 – $11,189* + $5,000)					$ 2,881
Controlling interest, $80,000 + $11,189 + 90% ($28,810)					117,119
					$ 120,000

* See note following consolidated worksheet in Example 10. Computed by applying effective rate at time of purchase by P to the net payable (i.e., 12% × $93,240 = $11,189).

b. Year 4 Partial Consolidation Worksheet

	P Dr. (Cr.)	S Dr. (Cr.)	Eliminations Dr.	Eliminations Cr.	Consolidated Income Statement Dr.(Cr.)
Investment in S bonds (Table 2)	100,000			100,000	
Bonds payable		(100,000)	100,000		
Operating income (Cr) (excluding interest)	(90,000)	(38,000)			(128,000)
Int. income (Table 2)	(11,570)		11,570		
Int. expense (Table 1)		8,917		8,917	
R/E, P	(XXXX)			2,388*	
R/E, S		(XX)		265*	
			111,570	111,570	
Consolidated NI (Cr)					(128,000)
Minority interest, 10% ($38,000 – $11,570)					$ 2,643
Controlling interest, $90,000 + $11,570 + 90% ($26,430)					125,357
					$ 128,000

* Gain on requirement of S bonds		$ 5,000
Interest income, P	$ 8,842	
Interest expense, S	(11,189)	
Less: Year 3 amortization:		(2,347)
Unamortized gain, adjust beginning R/E		$ 2,653
Minority interest, 10%		$ 265
Controlling interest, 90%		2,388
		$ 2,653

V. Subsidiary Entity Records

A. Traditional

Our review of business combinations has focused on (1) the recording by the parent company and (2) the required consolidation procedures. Historically, where separate incorporation is maintained, the subsidiary's financial records are not affected by either the acquisition or the consolidation.

B. Push-Down Accounting

Under push-down accounting, however, the subsidiary records purchase price allocations and subsequent amortization. The subsidiary records the allocations attributed to its identifiable net assets (e.g., inventory, land, building, equipment) and goodwill with a balancing entry to an *Additional Paid-In Capital* account. Every year thereafter, the subsidiary recognizes depreciation expense, as appropriate, on these various allocations.

1. **Simplicity** Because the allocations and amortization are already entered into the records of the subsidiary, the use of push-down accounting simplifies the consolidation process.

2. **Better Internal Reporting** In addition, push-down accounting provides better internal reporting. Since the subsidiary's separate figures may include additional depreciation expense resulting from the purchase, the net income reported by the subsidiary is a good representation of the impact that the acquisition has on the earnings of the business combination.

VI. Combined Financial Statements

A. Use

There are circumstances where combined financial statements (as distinguished from consolidated statements) of commonly controlled companies are likely to be more meaningful than their separate statements. Combined financial statements are often prepared for a group of related companies (e.g., a group of unconsolidated subsidiaries) or a group of commonly controlled companies (e.g., one individual owns a controlling interest in several corporations that are related in their operations). Consolidated statements are not appropriate if there is no investment by one affiliate in another to eliminate.

B. Procedures

Combined financial statements are prepared by combining the individual companies' financial statement classifications into one set of financial statements.

1. **Intercompany Issues** Intercompany transactions, balances, and profits or losses are eliminated in the same manner as in consolidated statements.

2. **Other Issues** If there are problems in connection with such matters as minority interests, foreign operations, different fiscal periods, or income taxes, they are treated in the same manner as in consolidated statements.

Investment at cost less FV of Net Assets = Gd will

CHAPTER 17—CONSOLIDATED FINANCIAL STATEMENTS

Problem 17-1 MULTIPLE CHOICE QUESTIONS (96 to 120 minutes)

1. Consolidated financial statements are typically prepared when one company has a controlling financial interest in another **unless**

a. The subsidiary operates under foreign exchange restrictions.
b. The fiscal year-ends of the two companies are more than three months apart.
c. Such control is likely to be temporary.
d. The two companies are in unrelated industries, such as manufacturing and real estate.

(5/94, FAR, #7, amended, 4822)

2. Penn, Inc., a manufacturing company, owns 75% of the common stock of Sell, Inc., an investment company. Sell owns 60% of the common stock of Vane, Inc., an insurance company. In Penn's consolidated financial statements, should consolidation accounting or equity method accounting be used for Sell and Vane?

a. Consolidation used for Sell and equity method used for Vane
b. Consolidation used for both Sell and Vane
c. Equity method used for Sell and consolidation used for Vane
d. Equity method used for both Sell and Vane

(11/92, Theory, #31, 3464)

3. On November 30, Parlor, Inc. purchased for cash at $15 per share all 250,000 shares of the outstanding common stock of Shaw Co. At November 30, Shaw's balance sheet showed a carrying amount of net assets of $3,000,000. At that date, the fair value of Shaw's property, plant, and equipment exceeded its carrying amount by $400,000. In its November 30 consolidated balance sheet, what amount should Parlor report as goodwill?

a. $750,000
b. $400,000
c. $350,000
d. $0

(5/93, PI, #25, amended, 4067)

4. In a business combination, how should long-term debt of the acquired company generally be reported under each of the following methods?

	Pooling of interest	*Purchase*
a.	Fair value	Carrying amount
b.	Fair value	Fair value
c.	Carrying amount	Fair value
d.	Carrying amount	Carrying amount

(11/95, FAR, #52, 6134)

5. In a business combination accounted for as a pooling

a. Income is combined only from date of combination, **not** for prior periods presented.
b. Income is combined for all periods presented.
c. After the combination, balance sheet amounts are carried at fair market value.
d. Direct acquisition costs are recorded as part of the cost of the investment.

(11/93, Theory, #12, 4517)

6. A business combination is accounted for as a purchase. Which of the following expenses related to the business combination should be included, in total, in the determination of net income of the combined corporation for the period in which the expenses are incurred?

	Fees of finders and consultants	*Registration fees for equity securities issued*
a.	Yes	Yes
b.	Yes	No
c.	No	Yes
d.	No	No

(R/01, FAR, #7, 6982)

7. A business combination is accounted for properly as a purchase. Direct costs of combination, other than registration and issuance costs of equity securities, should be

a. Capitalized as a deferred charge and amortized
b. Deducted directly from the retained earnings of the combined corporation
c. Deducted in determining the net income of the combined corporation for the period in which the costs were incurred
d. Included in the acquisition cost to be allocated to identifiable assets according to their fair values

(5/95, FAR, #53, 5589)

8. In a business combination accounted for as a purchase, the appraised values of the identifiable assets acquired exceeded the acquisition price. How should the excess appraised value be reported?

a. As negative goodwill
b. As extraordinary gain
c. As a reduction of the values assigned to non-current assets and extraordinary gain for any unallocated portion
d. As positive goodwill

(11/95, FAR, #53, amended, 6135)

9. PDX Corp. acquired 100% of the outstanding common stock of Sea Corp. in a purchase transaction. The cost of the acquisition exceeded the fair value of the identifiable assets and assumed liabilities. The general guidelines for assigning amounts to the inventories acquired provide for
a. Raw materials to be valued at original cost
b. Work in process to be valued at the estimated selling prices of finished goods, less both costs to complete and costs of disposal
c. Finished goods to be valued at replacement cost
d. Finished goods to be valued at estimated selling prices, less both costs of disposal and a reasonable profit allowance (5/93, Theory, #7, 4195)

10. Company J acquired all of the outstanding common stock of Company K in exchange for cash. The acquisition price exceeds the fair value of net assets acquired. How should Company J determine the amounts to be reported for the plant and equipment and long-term debt acquired from Company K?

	Plant and equipment	*Long-term debt*
a.	K's carrying amount	K's carrying amount
b.	K's carrying amount	Fair value
c.	Fair value	K's carrying amount
d.	Fair value	Fair value

(11/90, Theory, #4, 2019)

11. On December 31, Saxe Corporation was merged into Poe Corporation. In the business combination, Poe issued 200,000 shares of its $10 par common stock, with a market price of $18 a share, for all of Saxe's common stock. The stockholders' equity section of each company's balance sheet immediately before the combination was:

	Poe	Saxe
Common stock	$3,000,000	$1,500,000
Additional paid-in capital	1,300,000	150,000
Retained earnings	2,500,000	850,000
	$6,800,000	$2,500,000

In the December 31 consolidated balance sheet, additional paid-in capital should be reported at
a. $ 950,000
b. $1,300,000
c. $1,450,000
d. $2,900,000 (11/89, PI, #10, amended, 1275)

12. On June 30, Year 2, Pane Corp. exchanged 150,000 shares of its $20 par value common stock for all of Sky Corp.'s common stock. At that date, the fair value of Pane's common stock issued was equal to the book value of Sky's net assets. Both corporations continued to operate as separate businesses, maintaining accounting records with years ending December 31. Information from separate company operations follows:

	Pane	Sky
Retained earnings—12/31, year 1	$3,200,000	$925,000
Net income—six months ended 6/30, year 2	800,000	275,000
Dividends paid—3/25, year 2	750,000	--

What amount of retained earnings would Pane report in its June 30, Year 2, consolidated balance sheet?
a. $5,200,000
b. $4,450,000
c. $3,525,000
d. $3,250,000 (5/93, PI, #8, amended, 4050)

13. Sun Co. is a wholly owned subsidiary of Star Co. Both companies have separate general ledgers, and prepare separate financial statements. Sun requires stand-alone financial statements. Which of the following statements is correct?
a. Consolidated financial statements should be prepared for both Star and Sun.
b. Consolidated financial statements should only be prepared by Star and **not** by Sun.
c. After consolidation, the accounts of both Star and Sun should be changed to reflect the consolidated totals for future ease in reporting.
d. After consolidation, the accounts of both Star and Sun should be combined together into one general-ledger accounting system for future ease in reporting. (R/05, FAR, C02893F, #49, 7793)

14. A 70%-owned subsidiary company declares and pays a cash dividend. Under the purchase method, what effect does the dividend have on the retained earnings and minority interest balances in the parent company's consolidated balance sheet?
a. No effect on either retained earnings or minority interest
b. No effect on retained earnings and a decrease in minority interest
c. Decreases in both retained earnings and minority interest
d. A decrease in retained earnings and **no** effect on minority interest

(11/92, Theory, #34, amended, 3467)

Items 15 through 18 are based on the following:

The separate condensed balance sheets and income statements of Purl Corp. and its wholly owned subsidiary, Scott Corp., are as follows:

BALANCE SHEETS
December 31, Year 2

Assets	Purl	Scott
Current assets	$ 310,000	$135,000
Property, plant, and equipment (net)	625,000	280,000
Investment in Scott (equity method)	400,000	--
Total assets	$1,335,000	$415,000
Liabilities and Stockholders' Equity		
Current liabilities	$ 270,000	$125,000
Stockholders' equity		
Common stock ($10 par)	300,000	50,000
Additional paid-in capital	--	10,000
Retained earnings	765,000	230,000
Total stockholders' equity	1,065,000	290,000
Total liabilities and stockholders' equity	$1,335,000	$415,000

INCOME STATEMENTS
For the Year Ended December 31, Year 2

	Purl	Scott
Sales	$2,000,000	$750,000
Cost of goods sold	1,540,000	500,000
Gross margin	460,000	250,000
Operating expenses	260,000	150,000
Operating income	200,000	100,000
Equity in earnings of Scott	70,000	--
Income before income taxes	270,000	100,000
Provision for income taxes	60,000	30,000
Net income	$ 210,000	$ 70,000

Additional information:

- On January 1, Year 2, Purl purchased for $360,000 all of Scott's $10 par, voting common stock. On January 1, Year 2, the fair value of Scott's assets and liabilities equaled their carrying amount of $410,000 and $160,000, respectively, except that the fair values of certain items identifiable in Scott's inventory were $10,000 more than their carrying amounts. These items were still on hand at December 31, Year 2.
- During year 2, Purl and Scott paid cash dividends of $100,000 and $30,000, respectively. For tax purposes, Purl receives the 100% exclusion for dividends received from Scott.
- There were no intercompany transactions, except for Purl's receipt of dividends from Scott and Purl's recording of its share of Scott's earnings.
- Both Purl and Scott paid income taxes at the rate of 30%.

In the December 31, Year 2 consolidated financial statements of Purl and its subsidiary:

15. Total current assets should be
a. $455,000
b. $445,000
c. $310,000
d. $135,000 (5/91, PI, #13, amended, 9073)

16. Total assets should be
a. $1,750,000
b. $1,460,000
c. $1,350,000
d. $1,325,000 (5/91, PI, #14, amended, 9074)

17. Total retained earnings should be
a. $985,000
b. $825,000
c. $795,000
d. $765,000 (5/91, PI, #15, amended, 9075)

18. Net income should be
a. $270,000
b. $210,000
c. $190,000
d. $170,000 (5/91, PI, #16, amended, 9076)

Items 19 through 21 are based on the following:

On January 2, Year 3, Pare Co. purchased 75% of Kidd Co.'s outstanding common stock. Selected balance sheet data at December 31, Year 3, is as follows:

	Pare	Kidd
Total assets	$420,000	$180,000
Liabilities	$120,000	$ 60,000
Common stock	100,000	50,000
Retained earnings	200,000	70,000
	$420,000	$180,000

During year 3, Pare and Kidd paid cash dividends of $25,000 and $5,000, respectively, to their shareholders. There were no other intercompany transactions.

19. In its December 31, Year 3, consolidated statement of retained earnings, what amount should Pare report as dividends paid?
a. $ 5,000
b. $25,000
c. $26,250
d. $30,000 (11/95, FAR, #49, amended, 6131)

20. In Pare's December 31, Year 3, consolidated balance sheet, what amount should be reported as minority interest in net assets?
a. $0
b. $ 30,000
c. $ 45,000
d. $105,000 (11/95, FAR, #50, amended, 6132)

21. In its December 31, Year 3, consolidated balance sheet, what amount should Pare report as common stock?
a. $ 50,000
b. $100,000
c. $137,500
d. $150,000 (11/95, FAR, #51, amended, 6133)

Items 22 and 23 are based on the following:

On January 1, Dallas, Inc. purchased 80% of Style, Inc.'s outstanding common stock for $120,000. On that date, the carrying amounts of Style's assets and liabilities approximated their fair values. During the year, Style paid $5,000 cash dividends to its stockholders. Summarized balance sheet information for the two companies follows:

	Dallas	Style	
	12/31	12/31	01/01
Investment in Style (equity method)	$132,000		
Other assets	138,000	$115,000	$100,000
	$270,000	$115,000	$100,000
Common stock	$ 50,000	$ 20,000	$ 20,000
Additional paid-in capital	80,250	44,000	44,000
Retained earnings	139,750	51,000	36,000
	$270,000	$115,000	$100,000

22. What amount should Dallas report as earnings from subsidiary in its year-end income statement?
a. $12,000
b. $15,000
c. $16,000
d. $20,000 (5/92, PI, #6, amended, 2573)

23. What amount of total stockholders' equity should be reported in Dallas' December 31 consolidated balance sheet?
a. $270,000
b. $286,000
c. $362,000
d. $385,000 (5/92, PI, #7, amended, 2574)

24. Sun, Inc. is a wholly owned subsidiary of Patton, Inc. On June 1 of the current year, Patton declared and paid a $1 per share cash dividend to stockholders of record on May 15. On May 1 of this year Sun bought 10,000 shares of Patton's common stock for $700,000 on the open market, when the book value per share was $30. What amount of gain should Patton report from this transaction in its consolidated income statement for the current year ended December 31?
a. $0
b. $390,000
c. $400,000
d. $410,000 (11/94, FAR, #56, amended, 5317)

25. In its financial statements, Pare, Inc. uses the cost method of accounting for its 15% ownership of Sabe Co. At December 31, Pare has a receivable from Sabe. How should the receivable be reported in Pare's December 31 balance sheet?
a. The total receivable should be reported separately.
b. The total receivable should be included as part of the investment in Sabe, without separate disclosure.
c. Eighty-five percent of the receivable should be reported separately, with the balance offset against Sabe's payable to Pare.
d. The total receivable should be offset against Sabe's payable to Pare, without separate disclosure. (5/94, FAR, #16, amended, 4831)

26. Wright Corp. has several subsidiaries that are included in its consolidated financial statements. In its December 31 trial balance, Wright had the following intercompany balances before eliminations:

	Debit	Credit
Current receivable due from Main Co.	$ 32,000	
Noncurrent receivable from Main	114,000	
Cash advance to Corn Corp.	6,000	
Cash advance from King Co.		$ 15,000
Intercompany payable to King		101,000

In its December 31 consolidated balance sheet, what amount should Wright report as intercompany receivables?
a. $152,000
b. $146,000
c. $ 36,000
d. $0 (5/93, PI, #14, amended, 4056)

Items 27 through 29 are based on the following:

Selected information from the separate and consolidated balance sheets and income statements of Pare, Inc. and its subsidiary, Shel Co., as of December 31, and for the current year ended is as follows:

Balance sheet accts	Pare	Shel	Consolidated
Accounts receivable	$ 52,000	$ 38,000	$ 78,000
Inventory	60,000	50,000	104,000
Income statement accts			
Revenues	$ 400,000	$ 280,000	$ 616,000
Cost of goods sold	(300,000)	(220,000)	(462,000)
Gross profit	$ 100,000	$ 60,000	$ 154,000

During the year, Pare sold goods to Shel at the same markup on cost that Pare uses for all sales.

27. At December 31, what was the amount of Shel's payable to Pare for Intercompany sales?
a. $ 6,000
b. $12,000
c. $58,000
d. $64,000 (5/95, FAR, #51, amended, 5587)

28. What was the amount of intercompany sales from Pare to Shel during the year?
a. $ 6,000
b. $12,000
c. $58,000
d. $64,000 (5/95, FAR, #50, amended, 5586)

29. In Pare's consolidating worksheet, what amount of unrealized intercompany profit was eliminated?
a. $ 6,000
b. $12,000
c. $58,000
d. $64,000 (5/95, FAR, #52, amended, 5588)

30. Perez, Inc. owns 80% of Senior, Inc. During the current year, Perez sold goods with a 40% gross profit to Senior. Senior sold all of these goods in this year. For year-end consolidated financial statements, how should the summation of Perez and Senior income statement items be adjusted?
a. Sales and cost of goods sold should be reduced by the intercompany sales.
b. Sales and cost of goods sold should be reduced by 80% of the intercompany sales.
c. Net income should be reduced by 80% of the gross profit on intercompany sales.
d. No adjustment is necessary.
(11/93, Theory, #11, amended, 4516)

31. During the current year, Pard Corp. sold goods to its 80%-owned subsidiary, Seed Corp. At December 31, one-half of these goods were included in Seed's ending inventory. Reported selling expenses were $1,100,000 and $400,000 for Pard and Seed, respectively. Pard's selling expenses included $50,000 in freight-out costs for goods sold to Seed. What amount of selling expenses should be reported in Pard's year-end consolidated income statement?
a. $1,500,000
b. $1,480,000
c. $1,475,000
d. $1,450,000 (11/91, PI, #53, amended, 2441)

32. Clark Co. had the following transactions with affiliated parties during the current year:

- Sales of $60,000 to Dean, Inc., with $20,000 gross profit. Dean had $15,000 of this inventory on hand at year end. Clark owns a 15% interest in Dean and does not exert significant influence.
- Purchases of raw materials totaling $240,000 from Kent Corp., a wholly owned subsidiary. Kent's gross profit on the sale was $48,000. Clark had $60,000 of this inventory remaining on December 31.

Before eliminating entries, Clark had consolidated current assets of $320,000. What amount should Clark report in its December 31 consolidated balance sheet for current assets?
a. $320,000
b. $317,000
c. $308,000
d. $303,000 (5/93, PI, #9, amended, 4051)

33. Parker Corp. owns 80% of Smith, Inc.'s common stock. During the current year, Parker sold Smith $250,000 of inventory on the same terms as sales made to third parties. Smith sold all of the inventory purchased from Parker in this year. The following information pertains to Smith and Parker's sales for the year:

	Parker	Smith
Sales	$1,000,000	$ 700,000
Cost of sales	(400,000)	(350,000)
	$ 600,000	$ 350,000

What amount should Parker report as cost of sales in its year-end consolidated income statement?
a. $750,000
b. $680,000
c. $500,000
d. $430,000 (5/92, PI, #11, amended, 2578)

Items 34 and 35 are based on the following:

Scroll, Inc., a wholly owned subsidiary of Pirn, Inc., began operations on January 1 of the current year. The following information is from the condensed year-end income statements of Pirn and Scroll:

	Pirn	Scroll
Sales to Scroll	$ 100,000	$ --
Sales to others	400,000	300,000
	500,000	300,000
Cost of goods sold:		
Acquired from Pirn	--	(80,000)
Acquired from others	(350,000)	(190,000)
Gross profit	150,000	30,000
Depreciation	(40,000)	(10,000)
Other expenses	(60,000)	(15,000)
Income from operations	50,000	5,000
Gain on sale of equipment to Scroll	(12,000)	--
Income before income taxes	$ 38,000	$ 5,000

- Sales by Pirn to Scroll are made on the same terms as those made to third parties.
- Equipment purchased by Scroll from Pirn for $36,000 on January 1 is depreciated using the straight-line method over four years.

34. In Pirn's December 31 consolidating worksheet, how much intercompany profit should be eliminated from Scroll's inventory?
a. $30,000
b. $20,000
c. $10,000
d. $ 6,000 (5/92, PI, #8, amended, 2575)

35. What amount should be reported as depreciation expense in Pirn's year-end consolidated income statement?
a. $50,000
b. $47,000
c. $44,000
d. $41,000 (5/92, PI, #9, amended, 2576)

36. Water Co. owns 80% of the outstanding common stock of Fire Co. On December 31, Fire sold equipment to Water at a price in excess of Fire's carrying amount, but less than its original cost. On a consolidated balance sheet at December 31, the carrying amount of the equipment should be reported at
a. Water's original cost
b. Fire's original cost
c. Water's original cost less Fire's recorded gain
d. Water's original cost less 80% of Fire's recorded gain (11/90, Theory, #2, amended, 2017)

37. Port, Inc. owns 100% of Salem, Inc. On January 1 of the current year, Port sold Salem delivery equipment at a gain. Port had owned the equipment for two years and used a five-year straight-line depreciation rate with no residual value. Salem is using a three-year straight-line depreciation rate with no residual value for the equipment. In the consolidated income statement, Salem's recorded depreciation expense on the equipment for the year will be decreased by
a. 20% of the gain on sale
b. 33-1/3% of the gain on sale
c. 50% of the gain on sale
d. 100% of the gain on sale
(5/93, Theory, #4, amended, 4192)

38. On January 1 of the current year, Poe Corp. sold a machine for $900,000 to Saxe Corp., its wholly owned subsidiary. Poe paid $1,100,000 for this machine, which had accumulated depreciation of $250,000. Poe estimated a $100,000 salvage value and depreciated the machine on the straight-line method over 20 years, a policy which Saxe continued. In Poe's December 31 consolidated balance sheet, this machine should be included in cost and accumulated depreciation as

	Cost	*Accumulated depreciation*
a.	$1,100,000	$300,000
b.	$1,100,000	$290,000
c.	$ 900,000	$ 40,000
d.	$ 850,000	$ 42,500

(5/91, PI, #7, amended, 1268)

39. P Co. purchased term bonds at a premium on the open market. These bonds represented 20 percent of the outstanding class of bonds issued at a discount by S Co., P's wholly owned subsidiary. P intends to hold the bonds until maturity. In a consolidated balance sheet, the difference between the bond carrying amounts in the two companies would be
a. Included as a decrease to retained earnings
b. Included as an increase to retained earnings
c. Reported as a deferred debit to be amortized over the remaining life of the bonds
d. Reported as a deferred credit to be amortized over the remaining life of the bonds
(5/90, Theory, #2, 2021)

40. Wagner, a holder of a $1,000,000 Palmer, Inc. bond, collected the interest due on March 31 of the current year, and then sold the bond to Seal, Inc. for $975,000. On that date, Palmer, a 75% owner of Seal, had a $1,075,000 carrying amount for this bond. What was the effect of Seal's purchase of Palmer's bond on the retained earnings and minority interest amounts reported in Palmer's March 31 consolidated balance sheet?

	Retained earnings	*Minority interest*
a.	$100,000 increase	$0
b.	$ 75,000 increase	$ 25,000 increase
c.	$0	$ 25,000 increase
d.	$0	$100,000 increase

(5/92, PI, #4, amended, 2571)

41. Combined statements may be used to present the results of operations of

	Companies under common management	*Commonly controlled companies*
a.	No	Yes
b.	Yes	No
c.	No	No
d.	Yes	Yes

(5/93, Theory, #8, 4196)

42. For which of the following reporting units is the preparation of combined financial statements most appropriate?
a. A corporation and a majority-owned subsidiary with nonhomogeneous operations
b. A corporation and a foreign subsidiary with non-integrated homogeneous operations
c. Several corporations with related operations with some common individual owners
d. Several corporations with related operations owned by one individual

(11/91, Theory, #8, 2516)

43. Which of the following items should be treated in the same manner in both combined financial statements and consolidated statements?

	Different fiscal periods	*Foreign operations*	*Minority interest*
a.	No	No	No
b.	No	Yes	Yes
c.	Yes	Yes	Yes
d.	Yes	No	No

(11/89, Theory, #40, amended, 2026)

44. The following information pertains to shipments of merchandise from Home Office to Branch during the current year:

Home Office's cost of merchandise	$160,000
Intracompany billing	200,000
Sales by Branch	250,000
Unsold merchandise at Branch on December 31	20,000

In the combined income statement of Home Office and Branch for the year ended December 31, what amount of the above transactions should be included in sales?
a. $250,000
b. $230,000
c. $200,000
d. $180,000 (11/92, PII, #60, amended, 3394)

45. Ahm Corp. owns 90% of Bee Corp.'s common stock and 80% of Cee Corp.'s common stock. The remaining common shares of Bee and Cee are owned by their respective employees. Bee sells exclusively to Cee, Cee buys exclusively from Bee, and Cee sells exclusively to unrelated companies. Selected information for Bee and Cee follows:

Current Year	Bee Corp.	Cee Corp.
Sales	$130,000	$91,000
Cost of sales	100,000	65,000
Beginning inventory	None	None
Ending inventory	None	65,000

What amount should be reported as gross profit in Bee and Cee's combined income statement for the current year ended December 31?
a. $26,000
b. $41,000
c. $47,800
d. $56,000 (5/92, PII, #20, amended, 2652)

46. Mr. Cord owns four corporations. Combined financial statements are being prepared for these corporations, which have intercompany loans of $200,000 and intercompany profits of $500,000.

What amount of these intercompany loans and profits should be included in the combined financial statements?

	Intercompany Loans	*Intercompany Profits*
a.	$200,000	$0
b.	$200,000	$500,000
c.	$0	$0
d.	$0	$500,000

(11/90, PI, #60, 1273)

Items 47 and 48 are based on the following:

Nolan owns 100% of the capital stock of both Twill Corp. and Webb Corp. Twill purchases merchandise inventory from Webb at 140% of Webb's cost. During the current year, merchandise that cost Webb $40,000 was sold to Twill. Twill sold all of this merchandise to unrelated customers for $81,200 during this year. In preparing combined financial statements for the year, Nolan's bookkeeper disregarded the common ownership of Twill and Webb.

47. By what amount was unadjusted revenue overstated in the combined income statement for the year?
a. $16,000
b. $40,000
c. $56,000
d. $81,200 (5/91, PII, #19, amended, 1270)

48. What amount should be eliminated from cost of goods sold in the combined income statement for the year?
a. $56,000
b. $40,000
c. $24,000
d. $16,000 (5/91, PII, #20, amended, 1271)

Problem 17-2 ADDITIONAL MULTIPLE CHOICE QUESTIONS (18 to 23 minutes)

49. Pride, Inc. owns 80% of Simba, Inc.'s outstanding common stock. Simba, in turn, owns 10% of Pride's outstanding common stock. What percentage of the common stock cash dividends declared by the individual companies should be reported as dividends declared in the consolidated financial statements?

	Dividends declared by Pride	*Dividends declared by Simba*
a.	90%	0%
b.	90%	20%
c.	100%	0%
d.	100%	20%

(11/91, Theory, #9, 2517)

50. When a parent-subsidiary relationship exists, consolidated financial statements are prepared in recognition of the accounting concept of
a. Reliability
b. Materiality
c. Legal entity
d. Economic entity (5/93, Theory, #5, 4193)

51. A subsidiary, acquired for cash in a business combination, owned inventories with a market value different than the carrying amount as of the date of combination. A consolidated balance sheet prepared immediately after the acquisition would include this difference as part of
a. Deferred credits
b. Goodwill
c. Inventories
d. Retained earnings (11/86, Theory, #3, 2034)

52. Penn Corp. paid $300,000 for the outstanding common stock of Star Co. At that time, Star had the following condensed balance sheet:

	Carrying amounts
Current assets	$ 40,000
Plant and equipment, net	380,000
Liabilities	200,000
Stockholders' equity	220,000

The fair value of the plant and equipment was $60,000 more than its recorded carrying amount. The fair values and carrying amounts were equal for all other assets and liabilities. What amount of goodwill, related to Star's acquisition, should Penn report in its consolidated balance sheet?
a. $20,000
b. $40,000
c. $60,000
d. $80,000 (5/93, PII, #8, 4117)

53. On August 31, Wood Corp. issued 100,000 shares of its $20 par value common stock for the net assets of Pine, Inc., in a business combination accounted for by the purchase method. The market value of Wood's common stock on August 31 was $36 per share. Wood paid a fee of $160,000 to the consultant who arranged this acquisition. Costs of registering and issuing the equity securities amounted to $80,000. No goodwill was involved in the purchase. What amount should Wood capitalize as the cost of acquiring Pine's net assets?

a. $3,600,000
b. $3,680,000
c. $3,760,000
d. $3,840,000 (5/91, PII, #13, amended, 1269)

54. On September 29, Wall Co. paid $860,000 for all the issued and outstanding common stock of Hart Corp. On that date, the carrying amounts of Hart's recorded assets and liabilities were $800,000 and $180,000, respectively. Hart's recorded assets and liabilities had fair values of $840,000 and $140,000, respectively. In Wall's September 30 balance sheet, what amount should be reported as goodwill?

a. $ 20,000
b. $160,000
c. $180,000
d. $240,000 (R/00, FAR, #5, amended, 6900)

55. On September 1, year 1, Phillips, Inc. issued common stock in exchange for 20% of Sago, Inc.'s outstanding common stock. On July 1, year 3, Phillips issued common stock for an additional 75% of Sago's outstanding common stock. Sago continues in existence as Phillips' subsidiary. Phillips uses the purchase method in this consolidation. How much of Sago's year 3 net income should be reported as accruing to Phillips?

a. 20% of Sago's net income to June 30 and all of Sago's net income from July 1 to December 31
b. 20% of Sago's net income to June 30 and 95% of Sago's net income from July 1 to December 31
c. 95% of Sago's net income
d. All of Sago's net income

(5/93, Theory, #6, amended, 4194)

Items 56 and 57 are based on the following:

On January 1 of the current year, Owen Corp. purchased all of Sharp Corp.'s common stock for $1,200,000. On that date, the fair values of Sharp's assets and liabilities equaled their carrying amounts of $1,320,000 and $320,000, respectively. During the year, Sharp paid cash dividends of $20,000. Selected information from the separate balance sheets and income statements of Owen and Sharp as of December 31, and for the current year ended follows:

	Owen	Sharp
Balance sheet accounts		
Investment in subsidiary	$1,300,000	--
Retained earnings	1,240,000	560,000
Total stockholders' equity	2,620,000	1,120,000
Income statement accounts		
Operating income	420,000	200,000
Equity in earnings of Sharp	120,000	--
Net income	400,000	140,000

56. In Owen's year-end consolidated income statement, what amount should be reported for amortization of goodwill?

a. $0
b. $12,000
c. $18,000
d. $20,000 (5/94, FAR, #55, amended, 4870)

57. In Owen's December 31 consolidated balance sheet, what amount should be reported as total retained earnings?

a. $1,240,000
b. $1,360,000
c. $1,380,000
d. $1,800,000 (5/94, FAR, #56, amended, 4871)

SIMULATIONS

Problem 17-3 (45 to 55 minutes)

Research Task	Selected Amounts	Scenario 1 - 4	Responses 1 - 4

Research Question: What is the purpose of consolidated statements?

Paragraph Reference Answer: ______________

Research Task	Selected Amounts	Scenario 1 - 4	Responses 1 - 4

Presented below are selected amounts from the separate unconsolidated financial statements of Poe Corp. and its 90%-owned subsidiary, Shaw Co., at December 31 of the current year. Additional information follows.

	Poe	Shaw
Selected income statement amounts		
Sales	$ 710,000	$ 530,000
Cost of goods sold	490,000	370,000
Gain on sale of equipment	--	21,000
Earnings from investment in subsidiary	63,000	--
Interest expense	--	16,000
Depreciation	25,000	20,000
Selected balance sheet amounts		
Cash	$ 50,000	$ 15,000
Inventories	229,000	150,000
Equipment	440,000	360,000
Accumulated depreciation	(200,000)	(120,000)
Investment in Shaw	191,000	--
Investment in bonds	100,000	--
Discount on bonds	(9,000)	--
Bonds payable	--	(200,000)
Common stock	(100,000)	(10,000)
Additional paid-in capital	(250,000)	(40,000)
Retained earnings	(402,000)	(140,000)
Selected statement of retained earnings amounts		
Beginning balance, December 31, previous year	$ 272,000	$ 100,000
Net income	210,000	70,000
Dividends paid	80,000	30,000

Research Task | Selected Amounts | Scenario 1 - 4 | Responses 1 - 4

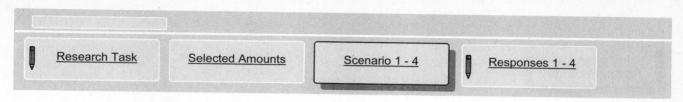

- On January 2, Poe, Inc. purchased 90% of Shaw Co.'s 100,000 outstanding common stock for cash of $155,000. On that date, Shaw's stockholders' equity equaled $150,000 and the fair values of Shaw's assets and liabilities equaled their carrying amounts.
- On September 4, Shaw paid cash dividends of $30,000.
- On December 31, Poe recorded its equity in Shaw's earnings.

Research Task | Selected Amounts | Scenario 1 - 4 | Responses 1 - 4

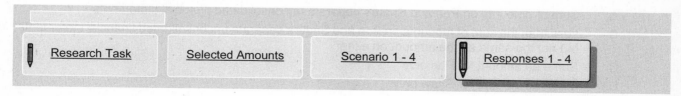

Items 1 through 4 represent transactions between Poe and Shaw during the year. Using the table of selected information from the consolidated and unconsolidated financial statements, determine the dollar amount effect of the consolidating adjustment on consolidated income before considering minority interest. Ignore income tax considerations. State if the change is an increase, decrease, or not considered.

1. $________ __________ On January 3, Shaw sold equipment with an original cost of $30,000 and a carrying value of $15,000 to Poe for $36,000. The equipment had a remaining life of three years and was depreciated using the straight-line method by both companies.

2. $________ __________ During the year, Shaw sold merchandise to Poe for $60,000, which included a profit of $20,000. At December 31, half of this merchandise remained in Poe's inventory.

3. $________ __________ On December 31, Poe paid $91,000 to purchase 50% of the outstanding bonds issued by Shaw. The bonds mature in six years, on December 31, and were originally issued at par. The bonds pay interest annually on December 31 of each year, and the interest was paid to the prior investor immediately before Poe's purchase of the bonds.

4. $________ __________ Determine the amount recorded by Poe as amortization of goodwill for the year.

Choices

Increase	$ 0	$14,000
Decrease	$ 2,000	$21,000
Not Considered	$ 9,000	$30,000
Not Calculated	$10,000	$91,000

Choices & Responses 5 - 16

Items 5 through 16 refer to accounts that may or may not be included in Poe and Shaw's consolidated financial statements. The list of responses refers to the various possibilities of those amounts to be reported in Poe's consolidated financial statements for the current year ended December 31. Consider all transactions stated in items 5 through 16 in determining your answer. Ignore income tax considerations. Any choice may be used once, more than once or not at all.

A. Sum of amounts on Poe and Shaw's separate unconsolidated financial statements
B. Less than the sum of amounts on Poe and Shaw's separate unconsolidated financial statements but not the same as the amount on either
C. Same as amount for Poe only
D. Same as amount for Shaw only
E. Eliminated entirely in consolidation
F. Shown in consolidated financial statements but not in separate unconsolidated financial statements
G. Neither in consolidated nor in separate unconsolidated financial statements.

5. ______ Cash
6. ______ Equipment
7. ______ Investment in subsidiary
8. ______ Bonds payable
9. ______ Minority interest
10. ______ Common stock
11. ______ Beginning retained earnings
12. ______ Dividends paid
13. ______ Gain on retirement of bonds
14. ______ Cost of goods sold
15. ______ Interest expense
16. ______ Depreciation expense

(11/93, P11, #5, amended, 4502-4504)

Problem 17-4 (45 to 55 minutes)

Research Task | Scenario | Worksheet

Research Question: What is the purpose of consolidated statements?

Paragraph Reference Answer: ______________

Research Task | Scenario | Worksheet

The December 31, current year condensed balance sheets of Pym Corp. and its 90% owned subsidiary, Sy Corp., are presented in the worksheet provided. Additional current year information follows.

- Pym's investment in Sy was purchased for $1,200,000 cash on January 1 and is accounted for by the equity method.
- At January 1, Sy's retained earnings amounted to $600,000, and its common stock amounted to $200,000.
- Sy declared a $1,000 cash dividend in December, payable in January of next year.
- As of December 31, Pym had not recorded any portion of Sy's net income or dividend declaration for the year.
- Sy borrowed $100,000 from Pym on June 30, with the note maturing on June 30 of next year at 10% interest. Correct accruals have been recorded by both companies.
- During the year, Pym sold merchandise to Sy at an aggregate invoice price of $300,000, which included a profit of $60,000. At December 31, Sy had not paid Pym for $90,000 of these purchases and 5% of the total merchandise purchased from Pym still remained in Sy's inventory.
- Pym's excess cost over book value of Pym's investment in Sy has appropriately been identified as goodwill

Complete the worksheet provided for Pym Corp. and its subsidiary, Sy Corp., at December 31. A formal consolidated balance sheet and journal entries are not required. (11/87, P11, #5, amended, 9911

Research Task | Scenario | Worksheet

Pym Corp. and Subsidiary
Consolidated Balance Sheet Worksheet
December 31, Current Year

			Adjustment and Eliminations		
	Pym Corp.	Sy Corp.	Debit	Credit	Consolidated
Assets					
Cash	75,000	15,000			
Accounts and other current receivables	410,000	120,000			
Merchandise inventory	920,000	670,000			
Plant and equipment (net)	1,000,000	400,000			
Investment in Sy Corp.	1,200,000				
Goodwill					
Totals	3,605,000	1,205,000			
Liabilities and Stockholders' Equity					
Accounts payable and other current liabilities	140,000	305,000			
Common stock ($10 par)	500,000	200,000			
Retained earnings	2,965,000	700,000			
Minority interest, 10%					
Totals	3,605,000	1,205,000			

Problem 17-5 (60 to 70 minutes)

Research Task	Scenario	Additional Information	Worksheet

Research Question: What is the purpose of consolidated statements?

Paragraph Reference Answer: ______________

Research Task	Scenario	Additional Information	Worksheet

On April 1 of the current year, Jared, Inc., purchased 100% of the common stock of Munson Manufacturing Company for $5,850,000 and 20% of its preferred stock for $150,000. At the date of purchase the book and fair values of Munson's assets and liabilities were as follows:

	Book Value	Fair Value
Cash	$ 200,000	$ 200,000
Notes receivable	85,000	85,000
Accounts receivable, net	980,000	980,000
Inventories	828,000	700,000
Land	1,560,000	2,100,000
Machinery and equipment	7,850,000	10,600,000
Accumulated depreciation	(3,250,000)	(4,000,000)
Other assets	140,000	50,000
	$ 8,393,000	$10,715,000
Notes payable	$ 115,000	$ 115,000
Accounts payable	400,000	400,000
Subordinated 7% debentures	5,000,000	5,000,000
Preferred stock; noncumulative, nonparticipating, par value $5 per share; authorized, issued, and out standing 150,000 shares	750,000	--
Common stock; par value $10 per share; authorized, issued, and outstanding 100,000 shares	1,000,000	--
Additional paid-in capital (common stock)	122,000	--
Retained earnings	1,006,000	--
	$ 8,393,000	

(5/74, P11, #5, amended, 9911)

Research Task | Scenario | **Additional Information** | Worksheet

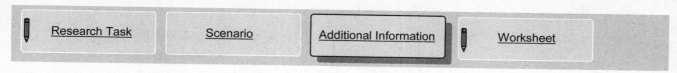

By the year-end, December 31, the following transactions had occurred during the year:

- The balance of Munson's net accounts receivable at April 1, had been collected.
- The inventory on hand at April 1, had been charged to cost of sales. Munson used a perpetual inventory system in accounting for inventories.
- Prior to this year, Jared had purchased at face value $1,500,000 of Munson's 7% subordinated debentures. These debentures mature in seven years on October 31, with interest payable annually on October 31.
- As of April 1, the machinery and equipment had an estimated remaining life of six years. Munson uses the straight-line method of depreciation. Munson's depreciation expense calculation for the nine months ended December 31, was based upon the old depreciation rates.
- The other assets consist entirely of long-term investments made by Munson and do **not** include any investment in Jared.
- During the last nine months of the year, the following intercompany transactions occurred between Jared and Munson:

Intercompany sales:

	Jared to Munson	Munson to Jared
Net sales	$158,000	$230,000
Included in purchaser's inventory at December 31	36,000	12,000
Balance unpaid at December 31	16,800	22,000

Jared sells merchandise to Munson at cost. Munson sells merchandise to Jared at regular selling price including a normal gross profit margin of 35 percent. There were no intercompany sales between the two companies prior to April 1.

Accrued interest on intercompany debt is recorded by both companies in their respective accounts receivable and accounts payable accounts.

- The account, "Investment in Munson Manufacturing Company," includes Jared's investment in Munson's debentures and its investment in the common and preferred stock of Munson.

Complete the worksheet to prepare the consolidated trial balance for Jared, Inc., and its subsidiary, Munson Manufacturing Company, at December 31.

Jared's revenue and expense figures are for the twelve-month period while Munson's are for the last nine months of the year. You may assume that both companies made all the adjusting entries required for separate financial statements unless stated to the contrary. Round all computations to the nearest dollar. Ignore income taxes.

Research Task | Scenario | Additional Information | Worksheet

Jared, Inc., and Subsidiary
Worksheet to Prepare Consolidated Trial Balance
December 31, Current Year

	Jared, Inc.	Munson Mfg. Co.	Adjustment and Eliminations		Consolidated Balances
Assets	Dr.(Cr.)	Dr.(Cr.)	Debit	Credit	Dr.(Cr.)
Cash	$ 822,000	$ 530,000			
Notes receivable	--	85,000			
Accounts receivable, net	2,758,000	1,368,400			
Inventories	3,204,000	1,182,000			
Land	4,000,000	1,560,000			
Machinery and equipment	15,875,000	7,850,000			
Acc. depr.—mach. and equip.	(6,301,000)	(3,838,750)			
Buildings	1,286,000	--			
Acc. depr.—buildings	(372,000)	--			
Investment in Munson Mfg. Co.	7,500,000	--			
Other assets	263,000	140,000			
Excess of cost over FV of net assets acquired					
Notes payable	--	(115,000)			
Accounts payable	(1,364,000)	(204,000)			
Long-term debt	(10,000,000)	--			
Subordinated debentures—7%	--	(5,000,000)			
Preferred stock	--	(750,000)			
Common stock	(2,400,000)	(1,000,000)			
Additional paid-in capital	(240,000)	(122,000)			
Retained earnings	(12,683,500)	--			
Retained earnings	--	(1,006,000)			
Sales	(18,200,000)	(5,760,000)			
Cost of sales	10,600,000	3,160,000			
Selling, G&A expenses	3,448,500	1,063,900			
Depr. exp.—mach. and equip.	976,000	588,750			
Depr. exp.—buildings	127,000	--			
Interest revenue	(105,000)	(1,700)			
Interest expense	806,000	269,400			
	$ 0	$ 0			

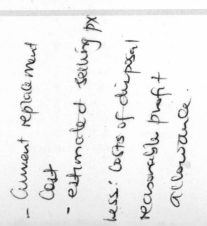

Solution 17-1 MULTIPLE CHOICE ANSWERS

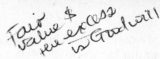

Business Combinations

1. (a) A majority-owned subsidiary should **not** be consolidated if control does not rest with the majority owner, for example, if the subsidiary is in legal reorganization or in bankruptcy or operates under foreign exchange restrictions, controls, or other governmentally imposed uncertainties so severe that they cast significant doubt on the parent's ability to control the subsidiary. Consolidation of majority-owned subsidiaries is required even if they have "nonhomogeneous" operations, a large minority interest, or a foreign location. SFAS 141 removes the former exception for temporary control.

2. (b) Penn should consolidate both Sell and Vane. Penn has a controlling financial interest in Sell through direct ownership of a majority voting interest (i.e., 75%). The intercorporate stock ownership arrangement with respect to Vane indicates a chain of interests, the product of which (i.e., 75% × 60% = 45%) does not represent control of the lower level subsidiary, where control is defined in terms of the 50% stock ownership minimum. Notwithstanding the 45% indirect interest of Penn in Vane, the preparation of consolidated statements is warranted in this instance. While the product of equities in the chain are factors in the determination of consolidated net income and consolidated retained earnings, it is not a determinant in establishing a minimal condition for preparation of consolidated financial statements. There is no evidence that control of Sell or Vane doesn't rest with Penn.

3. (c) Goodwill is the excess of the investment cost over the fair value of the identifiable net assets (INA) acquired.

Investment cost (250,000 × $15)		$ 3,750,000
Carrying amount of INA	$3,000,000	
Fair value of plant assets in excess of carrying amount	400,000	
Less: Fair value of INA acquired		(3,400,000)
Goodwill		$ 350,000

4. (c) In a business combination under the pooling of interest method, assets and liabilities of the acquired company generally are reported at their carrying amounts. In a business combination under the purchase method, the identifiable assets of the acquired company and the liabilities assumed are recorded at their fair values.

5. (b) Pooling of interests is no longer allowed for new business combinations in accordance with SFAS 141. Prior business combinations accounted for as pooling of interests continue to be accounted for as pooling of interests. In a business combination accounted for as a pooling of interests, income is combined for all periods presented. In a pooling of interests, the recorded assets and liabilities of the parties are carried forward at their recorded amounts. Direct costs related to effecting a business combination accounted for by the pooling-of-interests method should be deducted from the net income of the resulting combined corporation for the period in which the costs are incurred.

Record Combination

6. (d) The acquiring corporation records the net assets acquired at the sum of the fair value of the consideration given and direct costs incurred as a result of the purchase.

7. (d) The acquisition cost of a company acquired in a business combination accounted for by the purchase method includes direct costs of combination, other than registration and issuance costs of equity securities. The acquisition cost of the "purchased" company is allocated to the identifiable assets acquired according to their fair values.

8. (c) Under the purchase method, current assets and noncurrent marketable securities of the acquired company are always recorded at their fair values and all liabilities assumed are recorded at their fair value (present value). If the purchase price is less than the fair value of the identifiable net assets, any excess purchase price paid after recording the above items is allocated among the remaining noncurrent assets on the basis of their fair value. If the purchase price is less than the net fair value of said items, then extraordinary gain is recorded, and the remaining noncurrent assets are carried at a basis of zero.

9. (d) The general guidelines for assigning amounts to inventories acquired in a purchase method business combination provide for finished goods to be valued at estimated selling prices, less both costs of disposal and a reasonable profit allowance. The guidelines provide for raw materials to be valued at current replacement cost, and work in process to be valued at estimated selling prices, less (1) costs to complete, (2) costs of disposal, and (3) a reasonable profit allowance.

10. (d) The acquisition corporation allocates the cost of the acquired company to the assets acquired and the liabilities assumed. All identifiable assets acquired and liabilities assumed are assigned a portion of the cost, normally equal to their fair

Additional Paid in Capital

values at the date of acquisition. The excess of the acquisition price over the fair value of the net identifiable assets acquired is goodwill.

11. (d) The additional paid-in capital (APIC) to be reported in the consolidated balance sheet is equal to the parent's APIC at that date. The subsidiary's stockholders' equity accounts are eliminated through consolidation so that only the asset and liability accounts of the subsidiary remain to be combined with the parent company accounts.

Poe's APIC before merger	$1,300,000
Increase in APIC from common stock issued to effect the combination [200,000 × ($18 – $10)]	1,600,000
Consolidated APIC, after merger	$2,900,000

12. (d) At the date at which a purchase method business combination occurs, the balances reported for the consolidated stockholders' equity accounts equal the balances of the parent company's stockholders' equity accounts. The subsidiary's stockholders' equity accounts are eliminated through consolidation so that only the asset and liability accounts of the subsidiary remain to be combined with the parent company accounts. Therefore, consolidated retained earnings is $3,250,000 (i.e., $3,200,000 + $800,000 – $750,000), the retained earnings for Pane (i.e., the parent company) at that date.

Subsequent to Acquisition

13. (b) Consolidated statements are required when a company owns more than 50% of the voting stock in another company. Star owns more than 50% of Sun; Sun does not own more than 50% of Star, therefore, Star would prepare consolidated financial statements and Sun would not. Consolidating entries are prepared on a worksheet only and are not formally entered into the books of either company. Consolidating procedures must be preformed every period in which financial statements are presented.

14. (b) Under the purchase method, the amount of consolidated retained earnings is equal to the parent company's retained earnings because the subsidiary's stockholders' equity accounts are eliminated in the consolidation process. Thus, the cash dividend declared by the subsidiary has no effect on consolidated retained earnings. The minority interest balance reported in the consolidated statements is based upon the balances of the subsidiary's stockholders' equity accounts. Since the cash dividend declared by the subsidiary decreases the amount of the subsidiary's retained earnings, the minority interest balance reported in the consolidated balance sheet decreases.

15. (a) At the date of combination, Purl must allocate the cost of its investment in the subsidiary to the assets acquired and the liabilities assumed. Because there are no reciprocal or intercompany accounts at year end, the amount of consolidated current assets at that date is the sum of Purl's current assets at carrying amounts ($310,000) and Scott's current assets at fair values ($135,000 + $10,000 inventory adjustment) for a total of $455,000.

16. (b) Purl's *Investment in Subsidiary* account is not included in total consolidated assets because it is eliminated in the consolidation process.

Purchase price		$ 360,000
Fair value of identifiable assets ($410,000 + $10,000 inventory adjustment)	$420,000	
Fair value of liabilities	160,000	
Fair value of identifiable net assets (INA)	260,000	
Percentage acquired	× 100%	
Fair value of INA acquired		(260,000)
Goodwill		$ 100,000

Consolidated current assets (see MCQ# 17)	$ 455,000
Purl's plant assets at carrying amounts (net)	625,000
Scott's plant assets at fair values (net)	280,000
Goodwill	100,000
Total consolidated assets	$1,460,000

17. (d) The equity method accrues subsidiary earnings and recognizes the amortization associated with the acquisition cost in the exact manner as is effected by the consolidation process. Thus, total consolidated retained earnings will equal the retained earnings reported by the parent company (assuming no intercompany transactions).

18. (b) The equity method accrues subsidiary earnings and recognizes the amortization associated with the acquisition cost in the exact manner as is effected by the consolidation process. Thus, the consolidated reported net income will equal the reported net income reported by the parent company (assuming no intercompany transactions).

19. (b) The amount paid by Kidd to Pare (75% × $5,000) is eliminated on a consolidated statement of retained earnings and the amount paid to minority shareholders reduces the *Minority Interest* balance.

20. (b) Kidd's net assets are $180,000 – $60,000 = $120,000. $120,000 × 25% = $30,000.

21. (b) Pare reports the same amount of common stock as it did before the purchase. No new Pare common stock was issued for the purchase. Pare's Kidd common stock is not Pare common stock.

22. (c) During the year, the subsidiary's retained earnings increased by $15,000 (i.e., $51,000 – $36,000). Since the subsidiary declared and paid a $5,000 cash dividend, the subsidiary's net income was $20,000 (i.e., $15,000 + $5,000). Since at the date of the 80% purchase, the carrying amount of the subsidiary's assets and liabilities approximated their fair values, the parent company's earnings from the subsidiary is $16,000 (i.e., $20,000 × 80%).

23. (a) The equity method accrues subsidiary earnings in the exact manner as is effected by the consolidation process. Thus, total consolidated stockholders' equity will equal the total stockholders' equity reported by the parent company (assuming no intercompany transactions).

Intercompany Transactions

24. (a) When parent shares are obtained by a subsidiary, no gain or loss is reported from the transaction in the consolidated income statement. Any dividends paid to the subsidiary on this stock are eliminated in the consolidation process because they are considered intercompany cash transfers.

25. (a) The total receivable from Sabe should be separately reported in Pare's financial statements since Sabe is not a subsidiary of Pare (i.e., Pare has only a 15% interest in Sabe). Pare would have to own a majority voting interest (i.e., > 50%) in Sabe in order for Sabe to be considered a subsidiary.

26. (d) Consolidated financial statements should not include any intercompany payables, receivables, or advances pertaining to consolidated subsidiaries.

27. (b) Intercompany receivables and payables are eliminated in the preparation of consolidated financial statements. The amount of Shel's payable to Pare for intercompany sales can be computed by subtracting the amount reported for consolidated accounts receivable from the sum of the accounts receivable reported in the separate financial statements of Pare and Shel [i.e., ($52,000 + $38,000) – $78,000 = $12,000].

Intercompany Inventory

28. (d) Intercompany sales are eliminated in the preparation of consolidated financial statements. The amount of intercompany sales can be computed by subtracting consolidated revenues from the sum of the revenues reported in the separate financial statements of Pare and Shel [i.e., ($400,000 + $280,000) – $616,000 = $64,000].

29. (a) Unrealized profit on intercompany inventory transactions is eliminated in the preparation of consolidated financial statements. The amount of unrealized intercompany profit from inventory transactions is computed by subtracting the amount reported for consolidated inventory from the sum of inventory reported in the separate financial statements of Pare and Shel [i.e., ($60,000 + $50,000) – $104,000 = $6,000].

30. (a) The sale of inventory between two affiliates triggers the individual accounting systems for both companies. Revenue is recorded by the seller, while the purchase simultaneously is entered into the accounts of the acquiring company. However, from a consolidated perspective, neither a sale nor a purchase has occurred. Therefore, the amount reported as sales in the consolidated income statement is reduced by the full amount of the intercompany sale. In recording the inventory sale to the purchasing affiliate, the selling affiliate recognized cost of goods sold (CGS) based upon its acquisition cost. The purchasing affiliate later recognized cost of goods sold equal to the amount of the intercompany sale when it later resold all of these goods to unaffiliated customers. The CGS to unaffiliated customers should be based upon the CGS to the selling affiliate. Therefore, the amount reported as CGS sold in the consolidated income statement is reduced by the full amount of the intercompany sale because this is the amount of CGS recognized by the purchasing affiliate.

31. (d) No portion of the $50,000 of freight costs on the intercompany inventory transfer is reported as selling expense in the consolidated income statement. Although this expense is "freight-out" to Pard, for consolidated purposes, it is not freight-out to a buyer. It is part of the inventory cost and when the related goods are sold, the freight costs will increase the amount reported as cost of goods sold in the consolidated income statement.

32. (c) When one company sells merchandise to an affiliate at a price above cost, the ending inventory of the buyer contains an element of unrealized gross profit. The gross profit is not realized to the economic entity until the inventory is sold to an unaffiliated company. The preparation of the consolidated financial statements requires that the unrealized gross profit be eliminated from inventory. Dean is not an affiliate of Clark because Clark cannot exercise significant influence over Dean by virtue of its investment (i.e., Clark owns only a 15% interest in Dean). Therefore, no elimination entry should be made for the transaction with Dean.

Consolidated current assets before elimination entries	$ 320,000
Less: Unrealized gross profit on intercompany inventory transfer to wholly-owned subsidiary [($60,000 / $240,000) × $48,000]	(12,000)
Consolidated current assets to be reported in consolidated balance sheet	$ 308,000

33. (c) Parker, in recording the inventory sale to its subsidiary, Smith, recognized cost of goods sold of $100,000 [i.e., $250,000 × ($400,000 / $1,000,000)]. In recording the later sale of the same inventory to an unrelated customer, Smith recognized cost of goods sold of $250,000. However, from a consolidated perspective, the sale to Smith (the affiliated company) did not occur. Therefore, the amount to be reported as cost of goods sold in the consolidated income statement is $500,000 (i.e., $400,000 + $350,000 – $250,000).

34. (d) When one company sells merchandise to an affiliate at a price above cost, the ending inventory of the purchasing affiliate contains an element of unrealized gross profit. The gross profit is not realized to the economic entity until the inventory is sold to an unaffiliated company. The unrealized gross profit in inventory must be eliminated in the preparation of consolidated financial statements.

Scroll's ending inventory acquired from Pirn ($100,000 – $80,000)	$20,000
Times: Pirn's gross profit percentage [100% – ($350,000 / $500,000)]	× 30%
Unrealized intercompany profit in Scroll's ending inventory	$ 6,000

Intercompany Fixed Assets

35. (b) The cost of the equipment to the purchasing affiliate exceeds the carrying amount of the equipment to the consolidated entity by the gain recognized on the sale by the selling affiliate. Consolidated depreciation expense must be based upon the cost of the equipment to the consolidated entity. Therefore, consolidated depreciation expense must be reduced by the excess depreciation recorded by the purchasing affiliate [i.e., ($40,000 + $10,000) – ($12,000 / 4) = $47,000].

36. (c) Consolidated statements should not include gain or loss on transactions among the companies in the group. Any intercompany profit or loss on assets remaining within the group should be eliminated and is not affected by the existence of a minority interest. Therefore, the carrying amount of the equipment should be reported at the cost of the equipment to the purchasing affiliate (Water) less the entire gain recorded by the selling affiliate (Fire).

37. (b) In the consolidated balance sheet, the machine's cost and accumulated depreciation must be based upon the cost of the machine to the consolidated entity. Likewise, consolidated depreciation expense must be reduced by the excess depreciation recorded by the purchasing affiliate. Since the machine's useful life on the date of sale is 3 years, Salem's depreciation expense must be decreased by 1/3, or 33-1/3%, of the gain for consolidated purposes.

38. (a) In the consolidated balance sheet, the machine's cost and accumulated depreciation must be based upon the cost of the machine to the consolidated entity. Therefore, the machine is reported at its cost to the consolidated entity of $1,100,000, and thus, the balance of the machine's accumulated depreciation is $300,000 [$250,000 + ($1,100,000 – $100,000) / 20].

Intercompany Bonds

39. (a) To the consolidated entity, the acquisition of an affiliate's debt from an outside party is the equivalent of retiring the obligation. Therefore, the consolidated entity must immediately recognize any difference between the price paid and the carrying amount of the bonds as a gain or loss. The consolidated entity would recognize a loss from the acquisition because the price paid for the bonds exceeded their carrying amount on the affiliate's books (i.e., the bonds were originally issued at a discount and were purchased in the open market at a premium). The loss that the consolidated entity recognizes would be included in the consolidated balance sheet as a decrease to retained earnings. Answer (b) would be correct only if the consolidated entity recognized a gain from the purchase of the bonds. The consolidated entity must immediately recognize any difference between the price paid and the carrying amount of the bonds as a gain or loss; the gain or loss cannot be reported as a deferred credit or debit, respectively, to be amortized over the remaining life of the bonds.

40. (a) An investment by one member of a consolidated group of companies in the bonds of another member of that group is, in substance, the same thing as the purchase by a member of its own bonds. Although the bonds cannot physically be retired, since two separate entities are involved in the transaction, from a consolidated viewpoint, the transaction is treated as a constructive retirement of the bonds to the extent of the investment in the bonds. Thus, the consolidated financial statements will reflect any gain or loss on the retirement of bonds in the year of purchase. This is true despite the fact that the books of the affiliates involved in the transaction continue

to reflect the *Investment in Bonds* and *Bond Payable* accounts, respectively. Thus, the consolidated entity in question recognizes a gain of $100,000 (i.e., $1,075,000 carrying amount of bond – $975,000 cost to subsidiary) on the bond retirement. Gains and losses on the early retirement of bonds can only be reflected on the books of the issuer. Thus, Palmer, the parent company, is attributed the entire $100,000 gain on the retirement, thereby increasing consolidated *Retained Earnings* by the same amount. Since no portion of the gain on retirement is attributed to the subsidiary, the amount reported in the consolidated financial statements for the 25% minority interest in the subsidiary is unaffected by the intercompany bond transaction.

Combined Financial Statements

41. (d) Combined financial statements may be used to present the financial position and results of operations of commonly controlled companies, such as a group of unconsolidated subsidiaries. They might also be used to combine the financial statements of companies under common management.

42. (d) There are circumstances where combined financial statements (as distinguished from consolidated financial statements) of commonly controlled companies are likely to be more meaningful than their separate statements. Examples of such circumstances are: (1) where one individual owns a controlling interest in several corporations which are related in their operations, (2) to present the financial position and the results of operations of a group of unconsolidated subsidiaries, and (3) to combine the financial statements of companies under common management.

43. (c) In combined financial statements, if there are problems in connection with minority interests, foreign operations, different fiscal periods, or income taxes, they should be treated in the same manner as in consolidated statements.

44. (a) Any sale of inventory between a home office and a branch will trigger the individual accounting systems of both units. Revenue is recorded by the seller while the purchase simultaneously is entered into the acquirer's accounts. However, from a combined perspective, neither sale nor purchase has occurred. Thus, only the $250,000 of sales by Branch should be included in the combined income statement; the intracompany billing of $200,000 should be eliminated in preparing the combined statement.

45. (b) Because Bee sells exclusively to Cee, from a combined perspective, the only sales that have occurred are the sales of Cee to unrelated companies, which total $91,000. Of the $130,000 in intercompany "sales" from Bee to Cee, half (or $65,000) remained in Cee's ending inventory and the other half (or $65,000) were sold. However, from a combined perspective, the combined cost of the ending inventory and the cost of sales is only $100,000, not $130,000. The additional $30,000 represents intercompany profits, which are eliminated in combined statements. The $100,000, in the combined statements, is allocated half to cost of sales and half to ending inventory; based on the ratio of ending inventory and cost of sales of Cee.

Gross sales	$ 91,000
Cost of sales	(50,000)
Gross profit	$ 41,000

46. (c) Where combined statements are prepared for a group of related companies, such as a group of unconsolidated subsidiaries or a group of commonly controlled companies, intercompany transactions and profits or losses should be eliminated (ARB 51).

47. (c) Any sale of inventory made between two commonly controlled companies will trigger the individual accounting systems for both companies. Revenue is recorded by the seller while the purchase simultaneously is entered into the buyer's accounts. However, from a combined perspective, neither sale nor purchase has occurred. Thus, all intercompany sales are eliminated from the combined financial statements. Since the intercompany sale was not eliminated in preparing the combined financial statements, unadjusted revenue is overstated by $56,000 ($40,000 × 140%).

48. (a) In recording the sale of inventory to Twill, Webb recognized cost of goods sold of $40,000. In recording the later sale of this inventory to an unrelated customer, Twill recognized cost of goods sold of $56,000 ($40,000 × 140%). However, from a combined perspective, the sale to Twill did not occur, and thus the cost of the goods sold to the unaffiliated company is $40,000. Therefore, $56,000 is eliminated from cost of goods sold in the combined income statement.

Problem 17-2 ADDITIONAL MULTIPLE CHOICE ANSWERS

Business Combinations

49. (a) With regard to Simba's dividends, 80% are eliminated in the consolidation because of intra-company ownership and the other 20% are charged against the minority interest. Thus, 0% of the dividends declared by Simba are to be reported in the consolidated financial statements. Normally, 100% of Pride's dividends would appear as dividends declared in the consolidated financial statements. However, because Simba owns 10% of Pride's stock, Simba's dividend income will be eliminated against Pride's dividends declared in the consolidation process and only 90% of the dividends declared by Pride will be reported as dividends declared in the consolidated financial statements.

Acquisition

50. (d) Consolidated financial statements are prepared to present the financial position and operating results of the two separate organizations (i.e., parent company and subsidiary) as if only a single entity existed. Although the companies may be legally separate, the control of all decision making is now held by a single party, which indicates that only one economic entity exists. Reliability pertains to whether accounting information represents what it purports to represent, and is coupled with an assurance for the user that it involves the magnitude of an omission or misstatement of accounting information that, in light of the surrounding circumstances, makes it probable that the judgment of a reasonable person relying on the information would have been changed or influenced by the omission or misstatement.

Record Combination

51. (c) Under the purchase method, a consolidated balance sheet prepared immediately after the acquisition includes the assets of the subsidiary at their fair values.

52. (a) Goodwill is the excess of the investment cost over the fair value of the identifiable net assets (INA) acquired.

Purchase price		$ 300,000
Current assets	$ 40,000	
Plant and equipment, net ($380,000 + $60,000)	440,000	
Fair value of identifiable assets	480,000	
Less: Liabilities assumed	(200,000)	
Fair value of INA acquired		(280,000)
Goodwill		$ 20,000

53. (c) Wood's investment in Pine should be recorded at the fair value of the common shares issued to effect the combination. The bargained exchange price is $3,600,000 since the mode of payment by Wood will be 100,000 shares of its common stock having a fair value of $36 per share. In addition, Wood will pay a $160,000 finder's fee to a consultant who arranged the acquisition. Any direct costs of the combination, such as the finder's fee, are included, along with the bargained exchange price, in calculating the total acquisition cost because such costs are a necessary element in carrying out an acquisition. On the other hand, the $80,000 cost of registering and issuing the common stock is considered to be a cost of the securities rather than a cost of the acquisition. As such, the $80,000 should be accounted for as a reduction in the additional paid-in capital figure of the issued shares. ($3,600,000 + $160,000 = $3,760,000).

54. (b) Goodwill is recognized and recorded at an amount equal to the excess of the cost of the enterprise acquired over the fair value of the identifiable net assets (INA).

Purchase price of 100% of Hart O/S CS	$ 860,000
Less: Fair value Hart Corp.'s INA	(700,000)
Goodwill	$ 160,000

Subsequent to Acquisition

55. (b) When a business combination is accounted for as a purchase, the parent company accrues its equity in the subsidiary's earnings that occur subsequent to the date of the investment. Therefore, in year 3, Phillips should accrue 20% of Sago's net income from January 1 to June 30, and 95% of Sago's net income from July 1 to December 31.

56. (a) Goodwill is not amortized (SFAS 142).

57. (a) Under the purchase method, consolidated retained earnings are comprised solely of the *parent's* retained earnings at the balance sheet date since the subsidiary's owners' equity accounts are eliminated in the process of consolidation.

PERFORMANCE BY SUBTOPICS

Each category below parallels a subtopic covered in Chapter 17. Record the number and percentage of questions you correctly answered in each subtopic area.

Business Combinations

Question #	Correct √
1	
2	
3	
4	
5	
# Questions	5
# Correct	
% Correct	

Record Combination

Question #	Correct √
6	
7	
8	
9	
10	
11	
12	
# Questions	7
# Correct	
% Correct	

Subsequent to Acquisition

Question #	Correct √
13	
14	
15	
16	
17	
18	
19	
20	
21	
22	
23	
# Questions	11
# Correct	
% Correct	

Intercompany Transactions

Question #	Correct √
24	
25	
26	
27	
# Questions	4
# Correct	
% Correct	

Intercompany Inventory

Question #	Correct √
28	
29	
30	
31	
32	
33	
34	
# Questions	7
# Correct	
% Correct	

Intercompany Fixed Assets

Question #	Correct √
35	
36	
37	
38	
# Questions	4
# Correct	
% Correct	

Intercompany Bonds

Question #	Correct √
39	
40	
# Questions	2
# Correct	
% Correct	

Combined Financial Statements

Question #	Correct √
41	
42	
43	
44	
45	
46	
47	
48	
# Questions	8
# Correct	
% Correct	

SIMULATION SOLUTIONS

Solution 17-3

Research Task

C51.101

.101 The purpose of consolidated statements is to present, primarily for the benefit of the shareholders and creditors of the parent company, the results of operations and the financial position of a parent company and its subsidiaries essentially as if the group were a single enterprise with one or more branches or divisions. There is a presumption that consolidated statements are more meaningful than separate statements and that they are usually necessary for a fair presentation when one of the enterprises in the group directly or indirectly has a controlling financial interest in the other enterprises. [ARB 51, ¶1] If an enterprise has one or more subsidiaries, consolidated [statements] rather than parent-company financial statements are the appropriate general-purpose financial statements. [FAS 94, ¶61]

Responses 1-4

1. $14,000 decrease

The intercompany equipment sale resulted in an unrealized gain of $21,000 ($36,000 proceeds received – $15,000 carrying amount) to Shaw, that must be eliminated from consolidated net income. In addition, consolidated net income must be increased by $7,000 [($36,000 cost to Poe / 3) – ($15,000 carrying amount to Shaw / 3)] to eliminate the excess depreciation recorded by Poe, because consolidated depreciation expense must be based upon the equipment cost to the consolidated entity.

Unrealized gain recognized by Shaw from equipment sale	$21,000
Less: Excess depreciation recognized by Poe	(7,000)
Adjustment for intercompany equipment transfer	$14,000

2. $10,000 decrease

When one company sells merchandise to an affiliate at a price above cost, the ending inventory of the purchasing affiliate contains an element of unrealized gross profit. The gross profit is not realized to the economic entity until the inventory is sold to an unaffiliated company, and thus must be eliminated in the preparation of consolidated financial statements.

Poe's 12/31 inventory acquired from Shaw ($60,000 × 50%)	$30,000
Times: Shaw's gross profit percentage ($20,000 / $60,000)	× 1/3
Adjustment for unrealized inter-company profit in Poe's 12/31 inventory	$10,000

3. $9,000 increase

To the consolidated entity, the acquisition of an affiliate's debt from an outside party is the equivalent of retiring the obligation. Therefore, the consolidated entity must immediately recognize any difference between the price paid and the carrying amount of the bonds retired as a gain or loss.

Carrying amount of Shaw's bonds purchased by Poe	$100,000
Price Poe paid for bonds	(91,000)
Adjustment for gain recognized by consolidated entity on retirement of debt	$ 9,000

4. $0 Goodwill is not amortized (SFAS 142).

Responses 5-16

5. A No consolidating entry affects the *Cash* account. Therefore, the amount to be reported for cash in the consolidated financial statements is the sum of the amounts on Poe's and Shaw's separate unconsolidated financial statements.

6. B The amount reported for equipment in consolidated financial statements (CFS) must be based upon the equipment cost to the consolidated entity. Due to the intercompany equipment sale, the amount reported for equipment in the CFS must be decreased by $6,000, the excess of the equipment's $36,000 cost to Poe (the purchasing affiliate) over the equipment's cost of $30,000 to both Shaw and the consolidated entity. Thus, the amount to be reported for equipment in the CFS is $794,000 [i.e., ($440,000 – $6,000) + $360,000]. This amount is less than the sum of the amounts on Poe's and Shaw's separate unconsolidated financial statements but not the same as the amount on either [i.e., $794,000 < ($440,000 + $360,000)].

7. E The *Investment in Subsidiary* account is eliminated entirely in the consolidation process so that the subsidiary's individual assets and liabilities can be combined with the parent company accounts.

8. B To the consolidated entity, the acquisition of 50% of Shaw's outstanding bonds by Poe from an outside party is the equivalent of retiring the bonds. Thus, the amount to be reported for bonds payable in the consolidated financial statements is $100,000 [i.e., $0 + ($200,000 × 50%)]. This amount is less than the sum of the amounts on Poe's and Shaw's separate unconsolidated financial statements but not the same as the amount on either [i.e., $100,000 < ($0 + $200,000)].

9. F While no amount is reported for minority interest in the separate unconsolidated financial statements of Poe and Shaw, an amount for minority interest must be presented in the consolidated balance sheet because Poe did not acquire complete ownership of Shaw.

10. C The subsidiary's stockholders' equity accounts are eliminated through consolidation so that only the asset and liability accounts of the subsidiary remain to be combined with the parent company accounts. Therefore, the amount to be reported for common stock in the consolidated financial statements is the same as the amount as reported for Poe in its separate unconsolidated financial statements.

11. C The subsidiary's stockholders' equity accounts are eliminated through consolidation so that only the asset and liability accounts of the subsidiary remain to be combined with the parent company accounts. Therefore, the amount to be reported for beginning retained earnings in the consolidated financial statements is the same as the amount as reported for Poe in its separate unconsolidated financial statements.

12. C The subsidiary's stockholders' equity accounts are eliminated through consolidation so that only the asset and liability accounts of the subsidiary remain to be combined with the parent company accounts. Therefore, the amount to be reported for dividends paid in the consolidated financial statements is the same as the amount reported for Poe in its separate unconsolidated financial statements.

13. F To the consolidated entity, the acquisition of Shaw's bonds by Poe from an outside party is the equivalent of retiring the bonds. The consolidated entity includes the excess of the $100,000 carrying amount of the bonds over the $91,000 price paid by Poe as a $9,000 gain on the early extinguishment of debt in consolidated net income. The gain on the retirement of the bonds is reported in the consolidated financial statements, but not in the separate unconsolidated financial statements of Poe and Shaw.

14. B In recording the intercompany sale of the inventory to Poe, Shaw recognized cost of goods sold (CGS) of $40,000 (i.e., $60,000 – $20,000). From a consolidated perspective, the sale to Poe (the affiliated company) did not occur. Thus, consolidated cost of goods sold must be decreased by $40,000 as a result of the intercompany sale. In recording the later sale of half of the same inventory to an unaffiliated customer, Shaw recognized CGS of $30,000 (i.e., $60,000 × 50%). However, consolidated CGS is based upon the cost of the inventory to the consolidated entity (i.e., $40,000). Thus, the amount of consolidated CGS that should be recognized from the sale of half of the inventory to the unaffiliated customer is $20,000 (i.e., $40,000 × 50%). Thus, consolidated CGS must be decreased by $10,000 (i.e., $30,000 – $20,000), the excess of the amount of CGS recognized by Shaw on the sale to the unaffiliated customer over the amount that should be recognized by the consolidated entity. Therefore, consolidated CGS must be decreased by $50,000 (i.e., $40,000 + $10,000). Thus, the amount to be reported for CGS in the consolidated financial statements is $810,000 (i.e., $490,000 + $370,000 – $40,000 – $10,000). This amount is less than the sum of the amounts on Poe's and Shaw's separate unconsolidated financial statements, but not the same as the amount on either [i.e., $810,000 < ($490,000 + $370,000)].

15. D (A is also correct.) Poe purchased bonds issued by Shaw on 12/31. The bonds pay interest annually on December 31 of each year, and the interest was paid to the prior investor immediately before Poe's purchase of the bonds. Thus, no consolidating entry affects the *Interest Expense* account. Since Poe did not report any interest expense, the amount to be reported for interest expense in the consolidated financial statements is the same as the amount Shaw reports in its separate unconsolidated financial statements.

16. B Consolidated depreciation expense is based upon the cost of depreciable plant assets to the consolidated entity. Therefore, the expense must be decreased by $7,000 [i.e., ($36,000 cost to Poe / 3) – ($15,000 carrying amount to Shaw / 3)] to eliminate the excess depreciation recorded by Poe, the purchasing affiliate. Thus, the amount to be reported for depreciation expense in the consolidated financial statements is $38,000 [i.e., ($25,000 – $7,000) + $20,000]. This amount is less than the sum of the amounts on Poe's and Shaw's separate unconsolidated financial statements but not the same as the amount on either [i.e., $38,000 < ($25,000 + $20,000)].

Solution 17-4

Research

ARB 51, par. 41

1. The purpose of consolidated statements is to present, primarily for the benefit of the shareholders and creditors of the parent company, the results of operations and the financial position of a parent company and its subsidiaries essentially as if the group were a single company with one or more branches or divisions. There is a presumption that consolidated statements are more meaningful than separate statements and that they are usually necessary for a fair presentation when one of the companies in the group directly or indirectly has a controlling financial interest in the other companies.

Worksheet

Pym Corp. and Subsidiary
Consolidated Balance Sheet Worksheet
December 31, Current Year

			Adjustment and Eliminations		
	Pym Corp.	*Sy Corp.*	*Debit*	*Credit*	*Consolidated*
Assets					
Cash	75,000	15,000			*90,000*
Accounts and other current receivables	410,000	120,000	[b] **900**	[e] **900** [f] **5,000** [g] **100,000** [i] **90,000**	*335,000*
Merchandise inventory	920,000	670,000		[h] **3,000**	*1,587,000*
Plant and equipment (net)	1,000,000	400,000			*1,400,000*
Investment in Sy Corp.	1,200,000		[a] **90,900**	[b] **900** [c] **480,000** [d] **810,000**	
Goodwill			[c] **480,000**		*480,000*
Totals	3,605,000	1,205,000			*3,892,000*
Liabilities and Stockholders' Equity					
Accounts payable and other current liabilities	140,000	305,000	[e] **900** [f] **5,000** [g] **100,000** [i] **90,000**		*249,100*
Common stock ($10 par)	500,000	200,000	[d] **200,000**		*500,000*
Retained earnings	2,965,000	700,000	[d] **700,000** [h] **3,000**	[a] **90,900**	*3,052,900*
Minority interest, 10%				[d] **90,000**	*90,000*
Totals	3,605,000	1,205,000	*1,670,700*	*1,670,700*	*3,892,000*

Explanation of Adjustments & Eliminations:

[a] To record net income of Sy Corp. accruing to Pym Corp.

Sy Corp.'s retained earnings at 12/31	$ 700,000
Sy Corp.'s retained earnings at 1/1	(600,000)
Increase in retained earnings after dividend declaration	100,000
Add dividend declaration	1,000
Sy Corp.'s net income for the year ended 12/31	101,000
Pym Corp.'s share, 90%	0.90
Amount to be recorded	$ 90,900

[b] To record Pym Corp.'s share of dividend declared by Sy Corp.

Dividend declared by Sy Corp.	$ 1,000
Pym Corp.'s share, 90%	0.90
Amount to be recorded	$ 900

[c] To record goodwill.

Purchase price of 90% of Sy Corp.'s common stock		$1,200,000
Sy Corp.'s book value at 1/1:		
Common stock	$200,000	
Retained earnings	600,000	
Total	$800,000	
Pym Corp.'s share, 90%	0.90	
FV of Pym Corp's share of Sy Corp		(720,000)
Goodwill to be recorded		$ 480,000

[d] To eliminate 90% of Sy Corp.'s book value and record minority interest.

Common stock	$200,000
Retained earnings at 12/31	700,000
Total	$900,000
Pym Corp.'s share, 90%	$810,000
Minority interest, 10%	90,000
Total	$900,000

[e] To eliminate intercompany dividend receivable and payable.

Dividend	$1,000
Pym Corp.'s share, 90%	0.90
Total	$ 900

[f] To eliminate intercompany accrued interest.

Note maturing on June 30 of next year	$100,000
Interest, 10% rate for ½ year	0.05
$100,000 @ 10% × ½ year	$ 5,000

[g] To eliminate intercompany loan. $100,000

[h] To eliminate intercompany profit in Sy Corp.'s 12/31 inventory

Sales from Pym Corp. to Sy Corp.	$300,000
Percentage remaining in Sy Corp.'s 12/31 inventory, 5%	0.05
Total amount remaining	15,000
Multiply by 20% (60,000 profit / 300,000 inventory sold)	0.20
Amount to be eliminated	$ 3,000

[i] To eliminate intercompany trade A/R and A/P

The amount of purchases not yet paid for	$90,000

Solution 17-5

Research

ARB 51, par. 1

1. The purpose of consolidated statements is to present, primarily for the benefit of the shareholders and creditors of the parent company, the results of operations and the financial position of a parent company and its subsidiaries essentially as if the group were a single company with one or more branches or divisions. There is a presumption that consolidated statements are more meaningful than separate statements and that they are usually necessary for a fair presentation when one of the companies in the group directly or indirectly has a controlling financial interest in the other companies.

Worksheet

Jared, Inc., and Subsidiary
Worksheet to Prepare Consolidated Trial Balance
December 31, Current Year

	Jared, Inc.	Munson Mfg. Co.	Adjustment and Eliminations		Consolidated Balances
	Dr.(Cr.)	Dr.(Cr.)	Debit	Credit	Dr.(Cr.)
Cash	$ 822,000	$ 530,000			*$ 1,352,000*
Notes receivable	--	85,000			*85,000*
Accounts receivable, net	2,758,000	1,368,400		**$ 17,500** [6] **38,800** [7]	*4,070,100*
Inventories	3,204,000	1,182,000		**4,200** [8]	*4,381,800*
Land	4,000,000	1,560,000	**$ 540,000** [1]		*6,100,000*
Machinery and equipment	15,875,000	7,850,000	**2,750,000** [1]		*26,475,000*
Acc. depr.—mach. and equip.	(6,301,000)	(3,838,750)		**750,000** [1] **236,250** [5]	*(11,126,000)*
Buildings	1,286,000	--			*1,286,000*
Acc. depr.—buildings	(372,000)	--			*(372,000)*
Investment in Munson Mfg. Co.	7,500,000	--		**2,322,000** [1] **1,400,000** [3] **2,128,000** [2] **1,500,000** [6] **150,000** [4]	
Other assets	263,000	140,000		**90,000** [1]	*313,000*
Excess of cost over FV of net assets acquired			**1,400,000** [3]		*1,400,000*
Notes payable	--	(115,000)			*(115,000)*
Accounts payable	(1,364,000)	(204,000)	**17,500** [6] **38,800** [7]		*(1,511,700)*
Long-term debt	(10,000,000)	--			*(10,000,000)*
Subordinated debentures—7%	--	(5,000,000)	**1,500,000** [6]		*(3,500,000)*
Preferred stock	--	(750,000)	**150,000** [4]		*(600,000)*
Common stock	(2,400,000)	(1,000,000)	**1,000,000** [2]		*(2,400,000)*
Additional paid-in capital	(240,000)	(122,000)	**122,000** [2]		*(240,000)*
Retained earnings	(12,683,500)	--			*(12,683,500)*
Retained earnings	--	(1,006,000)	**1,006,000** [2]		
Sales	(18,200,000)	(5,760,000)	**388,000** [7]		*(23,572,000)*
Cost of sales	10,600,000	3,160,000	**4,200** [8]	**388,000** [7] **128,000** [1]	*13,248,200*
Selling, G&A expenses	3,448,500	1,063,900			*4,512,400*
Depr. exp.—mach. and equip.	976,000	588,750	**236,250** [5]		*1,801,000*
Depr. exp.—buildings	127,000	--			*127,000*
Interest revenue	(105,000)	(1,700)	**78,750** [9]		*(27,950)*
Interest expense	806,000	269,400		**78,750** [9]	*996,650*
	$ 0	*$ 0*	*$9,231,500*	*$ 9,231,500*	*$ 0*

			Debit	Credit
[1] Land			540,000	
Machinery and equipment			2,750,000	
Other assets				90,000
Accumulated depreciation—machinery & equipment				750,000
Investment in Munson Manufacturing Company				2,322,000
Cost of sales				128,000
To adjust Munson's assets to fair value at date of purchase.				
[2] Common Stock			1,000,000	
Additional Paid-in Capital (Common)			122,000	
Retained Earnings			1,006,000	
Investment in Munson Manufacturing Company				2,128,000
To eliminate Jared's investment in Munson's equity at date of purchase.				
[3] Excess of Cost Over FV of Net Assets Acquired			1,400,000	
Investment in Munson Manufacturing Company				1,400,000
To record excess of cost over fair value of Munson's net assets at date of purchase as follows:				
Computation				
Purchase price (common stock)		$ 5,850,000		
Less: Adj. of Munson's assets to FV (J/E No. 1)	$ 2,322,000			
Elimination of investment in Munson's equity (J/E No. 2)	2,128,000	(4,450,000)		
Excess		$ 1,400,000		
[4] Preferred Stock			150,000	
Investment in Munson Manufacturing Company				150,000
To eliminate Jared's investment in Munson's preferred stock at date of purchase.				
[5] Depr. exp.—Mach. and Equip.			236,250	
Acc. Depr.—Mach. And Equip.				236,250
To adjust to fair value at date of purchase.				
Computation				
Mach. and Equip.— $10,600,000 – 4,000,000 / 6 years =		$ 1,100,000		
Depr. exp. for nine months ($1,100,000 × 9/12)		$ 825,000		
Depreciation expense per books		(588,750)		
Adjustment		$ 236,250		
[6] Subordinated Debentures 7%			1,500,000	
Accounts Payable			17,500	
Investment in Munson Mfg. Co.				1,500,000
Accounts Rec. Net				17,500
To eliminate intercompany bonds and related accrued interest for two months.				
[7] Accounts Payable			38,800	
Sales			388,000	
Accounts Rec. Net				38,800
Cost of Sales				388,000
To eliminate intercompany sales and unpaid balances at December 31, 2007.				
[8] Cost of Sales			4,200	
Inventories				4,200
To eliminate intercompany profit (35%) in Jared's inventory at December 31, 2007 ($12,000 × 35% = $4,200).				
[9] Interest Revenue			78,750	
Interest Expense				78,750
To eliminate intercompany interest expense and revenue on debentures for nine months. ($105,000 × 9/12 = $78,750)				

Select Hot•Spots™ Video Descriptions

CPA 2035 FASB 109: Accounting for Income Taxes
Bob Monette provides comprehensive coverage of the temporary and permanent differences between financial and taxable income, current tax liability, current tax expense, deferred tax assets and liabilities, what to do when future tax rates differ from current tax rates, and how to report the various income tax-related accounts in the financial statements.

CPA 2033 FASB 95: Statement of Cash Flows
Bob Monette provides comprehensive coverage of both the direct and indirect methods of preparing the Statement of Cash Flows, with detailed explanations of the operating, investing, and financing sections of the statement and easy ways of remembering just what goes in each. In addition, learn when, where, and how to include non-cash transactions.

CPA 2020 Consolidations
This video program provides comprehensive coverage of the cost and equity methods of accounting for investments in subsidiaries and the purchase method of consolidation. Candidates will learn when to use each method and the accounting rules for each. Robert Monette details appropriate journal entries for consolidations, while discussing questions from past CPA exams. Your confidence will soar as you become comfortable with this complex subject.

Call our customer representatives toll-free at 1 (800) 874-7877 for more details about videos.

Subject to Change Without Notice

CHAPTER 18

GOVERNMENTAL OVERVIEW

I. **Governmental Accounting Environment** 18-2
- A. Nature of Governmental Entities 18-2
- B. Financial Reporting 18-2
- C. Definitions 18-5
- D. Funds 18-6
- E. Fund Accounting 18-7

II. **GASB 34 Reporting Model** 18-8
- A. Overview 18-8
- B. Management's Discussion & Analysis (MD&A) 18-10
- C. Government-Wide Financial Statements 18-11
- D. Fund Financial Statements 18-15
- E. Statement of Cash Flows 18-24
- F. Other Required Supplementary Information (RSI) 18-26
- G. Comprehensive Annual Financial Report 18-26

III. **Recognition of Specific Revenues & Liabilities** 18-28
- A. Nonexchange Transactions 18-28
- B. Certain Grants & Other Financial Assistance 18-29
- C. Capital Lease Obligations 18-29
- D. Municipal Solid Waste Landfills 18-31
- E. Escheat Property 18-31

IV. **Appendix: Limited Scope Topics** 18-32
- A. Governmental Colleges & Universities 18-32
- B. Postemployment Benefits 18-32
- C. Accounting for Termination Benefits 18-34
- D. Securities Lending Transactions 18-35
- E. Public Entity Risk Pools 18-35
- F. Investments 18-36
- G. Inventory Accounting Methods 18-38
- H. Service Efforts & Accomplishments (SEA) 18-38
- I. Component Unit Determination 18-38

V. **Appendix: Account Groups** 18-39
- A. Former Reporting Model 18-39
- B. GASB 34 Reporting Model 18-39

EXAM COVERAGE: The governmental accounting portion of the FAR section of the CPA exam is designated by the examiners to be 8 percent to 12 percent of the section's point value. Bear in mind that (1) the division of governmental topics into two chapters is somewhat arbitrary, and (2) a thorough grasp of the concepts of the first section of Chapter 18, *Governmental Accounting Environment,* is necessary to understand Chapter 19. Candidates with less than a semester course in fund accounting may need to repeat Chapters 18 and 19. A thorough understanding of the other topics in both governmental chapters should be gained before candidates pursue mastery of the appendix topics.

More information about the point value of various topics is included in the *Practical Advice* section of this volume.

CHAPTER 18

GOVERNMENTAL OVERVIEW

I. Governmental Accounting Environment

A. Nature of Governmental Entities

1. **Service** Governmental entities are established by the citizenry through the constitutional and charter process. The primary objective of governmental entities is to render services to those citizens.

2. **Lack of Profit Motive** In most cases, governmental entities do not seek to profit from the activities in which they engage. This general absence of profit motive is the primary distinguishing characteristic of governmental entities as compared to commercial enterprises.

3. **Dependence on Legislative Authorities** Governmental entities generally receive their authority to act directly from legislative authorities, which ultimately oversee and circumscribe governmental operations. Although the operation of commercial sector enterprises is also overseen to some extent by public authorities, this type of oversight is regulatory rather than proprietary in nature.

4. **Responsibility to Citizens** In financial reporting matters, governmental entities have the responsibility of demonstrating good stewardship over financial resources provided and entrusted to them by the citizenry. In contrast, commercial sector enterprises have a similar stewardship duty to their debt and equity owners.

5. **Taxes as Source of Revenue** The principal source of revenue for governmental entities is taxes levied on the citizenry. Commercial sector enterprises have no comparable source of revenue.

6. **Restrictions and Controls** In the absence of a profit motive, a net income bottom line, or other performance indicators, governments are subjected to a variety of restrictions and controls. The most important are overall restrictions on the use of resources (which leads to fund accounting) and exercise of expenditure control through the annual budget (which leads to budgetary accounting).

B. Financial Reporting

Financial reporting takes into consideration the influence of the governmental environment on reporting both governmental- and business-type activities, and the information needs of users. NCGA and GASB pronouncements primarily address annual financial statements.

1. **Accountability and Interperiod Equity** Governmental accountability requires governments to justify the raising of public resources and to disclose the purposes for which they are used. Accountability means that governments must ultimately answer to the citizenry through financial reporting, part of a government's duty in a democratic society. Accountability is the primary objective. Interperiod equity refers to the concept of paying for current-year services so as not to shift the burden to future-year taxpayers. Interperiod equity is an integral part of accountability. The primary objectives of financial reporting are to

   a. Provide assistance in fulfilling government's duty to be publicly accountable and enable users to assess that accountability.

   b. Assist users in assessing the operating results of the governmental entity for the year, the level of services that can be provided by the governmental entity, and its ability to meet its obligations as they become due.

2. **Users of Financial Reports**

   a. **Citizens** This group includes taxpayers, voters, service recipients, the media, advocate groups, and public finance researchers.

   b. **Legislative and Oversight Bodies** This group includes members of state legislatures, county commissions, city councils, boards of trustees, school boards, and executive branch officials with oversight responsibilities.

   c. **Investors and Creditors** This group includes individual and institutional investors and creditors, municipal security underwriters, bond rating agencies, bond insurers, and financial institutions.

   d. **Internal Users** Internal users are not considered primary users, although they have many uses for external financial reports.

3. **Characteristics of Financial Reporting Information**

   a. **Understandability** To be publicly accountable, financial reports must be understood by those who may not have detailed knowledge of accounting principles.

   b. **Reliability** Information in financial reports should be comprehensive, verifiable, free from bias, and representative of what it purports.

   c. **Relevance** Information must be reliable and bear a close logical relationship with the purpose for which it is needed.

   d. **Timeliness** Financial reports should be issued soon after the reported events to facilitate timely decisions.

   e. **Consistency** Financial reports should be consistent over time in regard to accounting principles, reporting and valuation methods, basis of accounting, and determination of the reporting entity. Changes occurring in these areas should be disclosed.

   f. **Comparability** Differences among financial reports should be due to substantive differences in the underlying transactions or structure rather than due to different alternatives in accounting practices or procedures.

   g. **Limitations of Financial Reporting** Users must understand limitations of the information to properly assess needs. Limitations are similar to those in commercial accounting.

4. **Governmental-Type Activities**

   a. **Accountability** The need for public accountability in financial reporting arises because of characteristics unique to governmental environments.

      (1) Resources are provided by essentially involuntary means, i.e., taxes. Accordingly, difficulties arise when attempting to measure optimal quantity or quality, because consumers cannot choose what or how much to purchase as is the case in the commercial arena.

      (2) There is no direct relationship between taxes collected and services rendered except in some instances when fees are charged for specific services. The only relationship that does exist in the governmental sector is a timing relationship, i.e., resources provided and services rendered occurring during the fiscal year.

      (3) Governments have monopolies on some services provided to the public. It is difficult to measure efficiency without the element of competition.

(4) Because there is no single overall performance measure, the users of governmental financial reports must assess accountability by means of a variety of measures that evaluate performance.

b. **Annual Budget** The annual budget is a plan for the coordination of revenues and expenditures. Legislative approval authorizes expenditures within the limits of the appropriations and any applicable laws. When developing the financial reporting objectives of the budget, the budget is an expression of

(1) **Public Policy** The budget is a result of not only the legislative process but also of the direct or indirect participation of the citizenry.

(2) **Financial Intent** A financial plan sets forth the proposed expenditures for the year and the means for financing them. The balanced-budget concept is important to many who expect governments not to exceed their means.

(3) **Control** A government should demonstrate that it is accountable from both the authorization and the limitation perspectives, because (a) budgetary allowances and authorizations are the direct result of competition for resources and (b) budget limitations cannot be legally exceeded.

(4) **Performance Evaluation** The budget may be a means of evaluating performance by comparing actual results to the legally adopted budget.

c. **Uses of Financial Reports**

(1) Assessing financial condition and the results of operations

(2) Determining compliance with finance-related laws and regulations

(3) Evaluating efficiency and effectiveness

d. **Capital Assets** Commitments to build and maintain infrastructure do not provide a direct return to governments.

5. **Business-Type Activities** Governmental activities resemble private-sector business activities when they provide the same services and/or are self-sufficient, operating as separate, legally constituted organizations.

a. **Exchange Relationship** There is often a direct relationship between charges and services rendered; for example, bus fares and tolls. Users of financial reports are able to measure costs and revenues and the differences between them. Further, users may determine the full cost of operating the activity and the financial implications of subsidies or grants. This information is useful for public policy decision-making.

b. **Annual Budget** The use of the budget and fund accounting is less common in business-type activities. The budget is often merely an internal management process. Similarly, fund accounting is not as common because the business-type activity often represents a single function only.

c. **Uses of Financial Reports** The primary difference in use for business-type activities is the emphasis on financial condition and results of operations, as opposed to the comparison of actual results with budgeted amounts. Uses include assessing reasonableness of user charges and assessing the potential need to subsidize activities with general governmental revenues.

d. **Capital Assets** Unlike many governmental-type activities, capital assets of business-type activities have a direct relationship to the entity's revenue-raising capabilities.

6. **Nonprofit Organizations** Some nonprofit organizations have strong ties to governments, making it difficult to determine which guidance applies. Along with public corporations and bodies corporate and politic, the following are governments:

   a. Entities that have one or more of the following traits:

      (1) Popular election of officers or approval (or appointment) of a controlling majority of the entity's governing board members by state or local government's officials

      (2) The possibility of unilateral dissolution by a government with the reversion of the entity's net assets to a government

      (3) The ability to enact and enforce a tax levy

   b. Entities that have the power to directly issue debt (as opposed to through a state or local authority) that pays interest exempt from federal taxation. Entities having only this trait may refute the presumption that the entity is a government if they provide compelling, relevant evidence.

7. **Governmental Reporting Entity** The governmental reporting entity often coincides with the legal unit (entity) as defined in law or by charter. However, some governments also control other governmental units, quasi-governmental units, or nonprofit corporations (that are in substance its departments or agencies) and must report them in their financial statements.

C. Definitions

Most governmental fund accounting systems use both budgetary accounts and regular accounts. Budgetary accounts are nominal accounts used to record approved budgetary estimates of revenues and expenditures (appropriations). Regular accounts are used to record the actual revenues, expenditures, and other transactions affecting the fund. Although terminology varies, the following accounts are usually employed in governmental funds:

1. **Estimated Revenues** Forecasts of asset inflows of estimated sources of fund working capital (except from other financing sources). The *Estimated Revenues Control* account is debited to record the revenue budget (and is closed at the end of the period with a credit).

2. **Appropriations** Forecasts of (and authorizations of) asset outflows of estimated uses of fund working capital (except for other financing uses). The *Appropriations Control* account is credited to record the budgeted expenditures (and is closed at the end of the period with a debit).

3. **Revenues** Additions to fund assets or decreases in fund liabilities (except from other financing sources) that increase the residual equity of the fund—inflows (sources) of fund working capital. Governmental fund revenues differ from the commercial concept of revenues in that they often are levied (e.g., taxes) rather than earned per se, and the related financial resources must be available working capital for revenue to be recognized. (Revenue recognition criteria for the various funds are discussed in D.)

4. **Other Financing Sources** Nonrevenue increases in fund net assets and residual equity (e.g., from certain interfund transfers and bond issue proceeds).

5. **Expenditures** Increases in fund liabilities or decreases in fund assets (except for other financing uses) that decrease the residual equity of the fund—outflows (uses) of fund working capital. Expenditures differ from expenses (as defined in commercial accounting) because expenditures include—in addition to current operating expenditures that benefit the current period—capital outlays for general fixed assets and repayment of general long-term debt principal.

6. **Other Financing Uses** Nonrevenue decreases in fund net assets and residual equity—e.g., for interfund transfers.

7. **Fund Balance** The fund residual equity account that balances the asset and liability accounts of a governmental fund (and trust funds), thus recording the amount available for expenditures. (The *Fund Balance* account is similar to the owners' equity account of a commercial enterprise only in this balancing feature; however, it does not purport to show any ownership in a fund's assets.)

8. **Fund Balance Reserves** When some of the assets of a governmental fund are not working capital available for expenditure—e.g., assets of one fund have been loaned to another fund for several years—a fund balance reserve is established (e.g., *Fund Balance Reserved for Interfund Advances* or simply *Reserve for Interfund Advances*) and the *Fund Balance* account should be retitled *Unreserved Fund Balance* (but may be called simply *Fund Balance*) and reduced accordingly.

D. **Funds**

1. **Governmental Funds** Governmental funds are used to finance general government activities such as police and fire protection, courts, inspection, and general administration. Most of their financial resources are subsequently budgeted (appropriated) for specific general government uses (expenditures) by the legislative body. Governmental funds are essentially working capital funds, and their operations are measured in terms of sources and uses of working capital, that is, changes in working capital. Capital assets and long-term general obligation debt are excluded from all governmental fund statements. The accounting equation of most governmental funds is as follows:

   Current Assets – Current Liabilities = Fund Balance

   a. General fund

   b. Special revenue fund

   c. Capital projects fund

   d. Debt service fund

   e. Permanent fund

2. **Proprietary Funds** Proprietary funds are used to finance a government's self-supporting business-type activities (for example, utilities). The accounting equation of proprietary funds is identical to that of a business corporation—it includes accounts for **all** related assets and liabilities, not just for current assets and current liabilities, as well as for contributed capital and retained earnings. Proprietary fund operations are measured in terms of revenues earned, expenses incurred, and net income or loss.

   a. Enterprise funds (for example, utilities)

   b. Internal service funds (for example, central repair shop)

3. **Fiduciary Funds** Fiduciary funds account for resources (and related liabilities) held by governments in a trustee capacity (trust funds) or as an agent for others (agency funds).

   a. Pension trust funds

   b. Investment trust funds

   c. Private-purpose trust funds

   d. Agency funds are purely custodial (assets equal liabilities).

Funds: Type and Government-Wide Statement Column

	Fund	Type	Activities Column
P	**P**ension trust fund	Fiduciary	not in GWS
I	**I**nvestment trust fund	Fiduciary	not in GWS
P / **P**	**P**rivate-**P**urpose trust fund	Fiduciary	not in GWS
A	**A**gency trust fund	Fiduciary	not in GWS
C	**C**apital projects fund	Governmental	Governmental
G	**G**eneral fund	Governmental	Governmental
R	Special **R**evenue fund	Governmental	Governmental
I	**I**nternal service fund	Proprietary	Governmental (typically)
P	**P**ermanent fund	Governmental	Governmental
E	**E**nterprise fund	Proprietary	Business-type
S	Debt **S**ervice fund	Governmental	Governmental

NOTE: All PIPPA funds are fiduciary and do not appear in the government-wide financial statements. Amounts from any C GRIPES funds appear in the government-wide statements (GWS). The vowels in C GRIPES indicate the proprietary funds; the consonants indicate the governmental funds.

E. Fund Accounting

A specific governmental unit is not accounted for through a single accounting entity. Instead, the accounts of a government are divided into several funds. A fund is a fiscal and accounting entity with a self-balancing set of accounts recording cash and other financial resources, together with all related liabilities and residual equities and balances, and changes therein, that are segregated for the purpose of carrying on specific activities or attaining certain objectives in accordance with special regulations, restrictions, or limitations. A government should have only one general fund. It may have one, none, or several of the other types of funds, depending on its activities. Governments should use the minimum number of funds consistent with their laws (and contracts) and sound financial management. Comparisons among the types of funds are common questions on the exam.

1. **Budgets** Annual budgets of estimated revenues and estimated expenditures are prepared for most governmental-type funds. The approved budgets of such funds are recorded in budgetary accounts in the accounting system to provide control over governmental fund revenues and expenditures. Proprietary and fiduciary funds—and most capital projects funds—are not dependent on annual budgets and legislative appropriations of resources, and thus budgets are not usually incorporated into their accounts. The balances of budget accounts are generally the **opposite** of the companion accounts. For instance, the *Revenues* account ordinarily has a credit balance, but *Estimated Revenues* is opened with a debit balance.

2. **Encumbrance System** The encumbrance system is used in governmental funds (General, special revenue, and capital projects funds) to prevent over-expenditure and to demonstrate compliance with legal requirements. When a purchase order is issued or a contract is approved, the estimated amount of the planned expenditure is encumbered (committed) by debiting *Encumbrances* and crediting *Reserve for Encumbrances.* When the related invoice is received, the encumbrance entry is reversed and the actual expenditure is recorded.

   a. The unencumbered balance of the *Appropriations* account is the amount of uncommitted appropriations funds available for expenditures.

$$\begin{matrix}\text{Unencumbered}\\\text{Appropriations}\end{matrix} = \text{Appropriations} - \left(\begin{matrix}\text{Outstanding}\\\text{Encumbrances}\end{matrix} + \begin{matrix}\text{Year-to-date}\\\text{Expenditures}\end{matrix}\right)$$

b. If funds are encumbered but not yet expended at the end of the period, the usual accounting treatment is to close the encumbrances account (i.e., credit *Encumbrances,* debit *Fund Balance*). This reduces the *Unreserved Fund Balance* account and causes the *Reserve for Encumbrances* account—which merely offsets the *Encumbrances* account during the year—to be a true fund balance reserve. The *Reserve for Encumbrances* account thus is not a liability, but a reservation of *Fund Balance* similar to the appropriated retained earnings of a business enterprise. At the beginning of the subsequent period, the encumbrances closing entry is reversed, returning the *Encumbrances* and *Reserve for Encumbrances* accounts to their usual offsetting relationship.

3. **Basis of Accounting** The basis of accounting used depends on the nature of the fund and the financial statement being presented.

Exhibit 1 ▸ Basis of Accounting

	Accrual	Modified Accrual
Revenues	Accrued as earned	Accrued when available and measurable
Expenses	Fixed assets are capitalized	Fixed assets are expenditures

a. The modified accrual basis is used in the governmental-type fund statements (general, special revenue, capital projects, and debt service funds), where revenues and **expenditures** are recorded.

b. The accrual basis is used in the government-wide statements for all amounts. The accrual basis is used in proprietary fund statements, where revenues and **expenses** are recorded and net income (loss) is reported. The accrual basis is also used in fiduciary fund statements, except for the recognition of certain liabilities of defined benefit pension plans (GASB 25) and certain postemployment healthcare plans (GASB 26).

II. GASB 34 Reporting Model

A. Overview

While legal restrictions generally mandate the continuation of fund segregation in accounting systems, many users want to see the government-wide information to assess the overall financial position of the government. Users are interested in both the short-term and the long-term view. The former reporting model provided incomplete information about the long-term perspective of the government's financial position and operations, particularly with regard to governmental funds.

1. **Objective** The objective for GASB 34, *Basic Financial Statements and Management's Discussion and Analysis for State and Local Governments,* is "to establish a basic financial reporting model that will result in greater accountability by state and local governments by providing more useful information to a wider range of users than the existing model."

a. Operational accountability is important to assess the government's ability to provide services. GASB 34 states that operational accountability "includes the periodic economic cost of the services provided. It also informs users about whether the government is raising sufficient revenues each period to cover that cost, or whether the government is deferring costs to the future or using up accumulated resources to provide current-period services." The government-wide statements (GWS) are designed to provide an economic long-term view of the government that cannot be seen with the presentation of a collection of funds.

b. The former reporting model included a liftable section termed the *general purpose financial statements.* GASB 34 shifts to the concept of *basic financial statements,* incorporating government-wide statements. The GASB hopes that the new formats will simplify the external reports and create a user-friendly environment. [The GASB encourages governments to issue a comprehensive annual financial report (CAFR).]

2. **Universities** GASB 34 originally excluded public colleges and universities from its scope. GASB 35 includes these institutions and permits those issuing separate financial statements to use the new reporting model guidance for special purpose governments.

3. **Effective Dates** The staggered implementation schedule was based on governments' revenues, with implementation required no later than fiscal years beginning after the implementation date for that size government. (There is additional time to implement the requirements for *retroactive* reporting of infrastructure assets. Early application is encouraged.) Institutions that are component units implemented the GASB 34 or GASB 35 reporting model at the same time as the primary government.

Exhibit 2 ▸ Effective Dates for GASB 34 and 35

Phase	Revenue Range (in millions)	General Implementation Date	Retroactive Infrastructure Implementation Date
1	> $100	June 15, 2001	June 15, 2005
2	> $10 and < $100	June 15, 2002	June 15, 2006
3	< $10	June 15, 2003	optional

4. **Basis of Accounting** All amounts in the government-wide statements, including from the governmental funds, are determined using the economic resources measurement focus and accrual basis of accounting. Governmental funds presented in the fund financial statements use current financial resources and modified accrual basis. Proprietary and fiduciary funds use the economic resources focus and accrual basis in the fund statements, with limited exceptions for some fiduciary funds.

5. **Basic Financial Statements** Basic financial statements (BFS) include both the government-wide statements and the fund statements, as well as the notes.

6. **Government-Wide Statements** Government-wide statements (GWS) aggregate information for all governmental and business-type activities. GASB 34 requires economic resources measurement focus and accrual basis of accounting for all amounts in the GWS. There are four required columns in the GWS, one each for: governmental activities, business-type activities, the primary government (sum of the previous two), and component units. Note that funds do not explicitly appear in GWS; the amounts in governmental fund, proprietary fund, and component unit statements match or are reconciled to GWS amounts. Most component units should be included in the financial reporting entity by discrete presentation (reported in columns separate from primary government).

7. **Fund Statements** Fund statements appear between the GWS and the notes. Fund types are retained by GASB 34, but reporting in the fund financial statements shifts to major fund reporting. Users indicated that specific fund information for significant funds is more important than the traditional fund type reporting. The combining statements report funds by type for the fiduciary funds and the combination of nonmajor funds.

   a. A reconciliation to government-wide statements appears on the face of the governmental fund financial statements, in a separate schedule, or in the notes.

   b. Cash flows statements appear only in the fund statements for proprietary funds. (The governmental funds pose significant problems for developing meaningful information for a government-wide cash flow statement.)

   c. Optional combining fund statements (for nonmajor funds) may be presented after the notes to the financial statements.

8. **Terminology**

a. **Fiduciary Funds** The fiduciary fund category includes only those funds used to report assets held in a trustee or agency capacity for others and that cannot be used to support the government's own programs. *Private-purpose trust funds* and *permanent funds* distinguish between resources held in a fiduciary capacity and those available to the government. Private purpose trusts are fiduciary funds; permanent funds are governmental funds, not fiduciary funds.

b. **Proprietary Funds** Enterprise and internal service funds are *proprietary funds.* If the sponsoring government is the predominant "customer" for the activity, the activities are reported in an internal service fund. Otherwise, an enterprise fund is used. GASB 34 establishes criteria that *require* the use of an enterprise fund in certain circumstances. Internal service fund activities are generally classified as governmental activities in the GWS.

c. **Capital Assets** The concept of *fixed assets* generally refers to land, building, and equipment, as well as improvements to those assets. GASB 34 uses the term *capital assets* to include easements, infrastructure, and all other tangible or intangible assets that are used in operations and that have initial useful lives extending beyond a single reporting period.

d. **Special & Extraordinary Items** Special and extraordinary items are nonoperating sources or uses. They are displayed separately on the statement of activities after the calculation of excess revenues. Special items are transactions or other events *within* the control of management that are *both* abnormally large in size and *either* unusual in nature *or* infrequent in occurrence. An event is presumed to be *within* management's control if management normally can influence the occurrence of that event. Extraordinary items are transactions or other events that are *both* unusual in nature *and* infrequent in occurrence.

e. **Eliminations & Reclassifications** Combined statements in the former reporting model do not reflect *eliminations* and *reclassifications* of interfund activities. GASB 34 includes provisions for these adjustments in the aggregated data presented in the government-wide statements. Eliminations deduct the duplication resulting from interfund transfers and internal service fund transactions. Interfund receivables and payables are eliminated, except for residual balances between governmental and business-type activities. Internal events that are essentially allocations of overhead expenses are also eliminated from the statement of activities. Interfund services provided and used between functional categories, such as sales of utilities, are not eliminated.

f. **Reciprocal Interfund Activity** The internal counterpart to exchange and exchange-like transactions, including loans or interfund services provided and used.

g. **Nonreciprocal Interfund Activity** Includes internal nonexchange transactions such as transfers or reimbursements.

B. **Management's Discussion & Analysis (MD&A)**
MD&A is required supplementary information (RSI) in the general purpose external financial report. Although MD&A is classified as RSI, it is presented before the financial statements. The GASB encourages entities not to duplicate information in the MD&A and the more subjective letter of transmittal. GASB 37 limits MD&A to eight categories.

- **Letter of Transmittal** Governments that participate in the Government Finance Officers Association (GFOA) Certificate of Achievement for Excellence in Financial Reporting include a *letter of transmittal* in the CAFR. The GASB does not require a transmittal letter or provide specific guidance for its contents, although the GASB recommends including a transmittal letter. The GFOA has revised some components of the transmittal letter to reflect the GASB requirement for an MD&A.

1. **Discussion** Brief discussion of the basic financial statements, including the relationship among them and the significant differences in the perspective that they provide.

2. **Comparison** Condensed financial information derived from government-wide statements comparing the current and prior year.

3. **Analysis of Overall Financial Position & Results of Operations** This should include reasons for significant changes from the prior year, including important economic factors.

4. **Analysis of Balances and Transactions of Individual Funds**

5. **Analysis of Significant Budget Changes** Analysis of differences between original and final budget amounts as well as final budget amounts and actual results for the general fund.

6. **Capital Asset & Long-Term Liability Activity Description**

7. **Infrastructure Discussion** (Only by governments using the modified approach.)

8. **Currently Known Facts, Decisions, or Conditions** that are expected to have significant effect on the government's financial condition

C. **Government-Wide Financial Statements**
The only required government-wide statements (GWS) are the Statement of Net Assets and the Statement of Activities. The entity reports net assets, not fund balances or fund equity.

1. **Fiduciary Activities** Fiduciary activities are not included in the GWS because the assets and liabilities cannot be used to support the government's own programs. (There are two required statements to report fiduciary activities in the fund statements.)

2. **Primary Government** Sum of governmental and business-type activities.

3. **Governmental Activities** This classification includes the amounts from the governmental funds (restated on the accrual basis of accounting) plus, typically, the amounts from the internal service funds. An exception applies if the internal service fund provides services primarily to enterprise funds; such a fund is included in business-type activities in the GWS.

4. **Business-Type Activities** This classification includes the amounts from the enterprise funds and exceptional internal service funds.

5. **Capital Assets & Long-Term Liabilities** Reporting capital assets and long-term liabilities is required in the GWS.

   a. Amounts are presented within the appropriate governmental activities, business-type activities, and component unit classification.

   b. Depreciation is not required if governments meet certain criteria for providing alternative information about the condition and financial impact of infrastructure assets and adopt the modified approach for reporting infrastructure. Retroactive reporting is required four years after the effective date on the basic provisions for all major general infrastructure assets that were acquired or significantly reconstructed, or that received significant improvements, in fiscal years ending after June 30, 1980. Infrastructure assets that are part of a network or subsystem of a network are not required to be depreciated as long as two requirements are met: (1) the government manages the eligible infrastructure assets using an asset management system that has the characteristics set forth below; and (2) the government documents that the eligible infrastructure assets are being preserved approximately at (or above) a condition level established and disclosed by the government.

(1) Have an up-to-date inventory of eligible infrastructure assets

(2) Perform condition assessments of the eligible infrastructure assets and summarize the results using a measurement scale

(3) Estimate each year the annual amount to maintain and preserve the eligible infrastructure assets at the condition level established and disclosed by the government.

c. Governments should capitalize works of art, historical treasures, and similar assets at their historical cost or fair value at date of donation whether they are held as individual items or in a collection. Capitalized collections or individual items that are exhaustible, such as exhibits whose useful lives are diminished by display or educational or research applications, should be depreciated over their estimated useful lives. Depreciation is not required for collections or individual items that are inexhaustible. Governments are encouraged, but not required, to capitalize a collection (and all additions to that collection) whether donated or purchased that meets all of the following. The collection is:

(1) Held for public exhibition, education, or research in furtherance of public service, rather than financial gain

(2) Protected, kept unencumbered, cared for, and preserved

(3) Subject to an organizational policy that requires the proceeds from sales of collection items to be used to acquire other items for collections

d. A capital asset generally should be considered impaired if both (a) the decline in service utility of the capital asset is large in magnitude and (b) the event or change in circumstance is outside the normal life cycle of the capital asset.

(1) If not otherwise apparent from the face of the financial statements, the description, amount, and financial statement classification of impairment losses should be disclosed in the notes to the financial statements.

(2) If evidence is available to demonstrate that the impairment will be temporary, the capital asset should not be written down. Impaired capital assets that are idle should be disclosed, regardless of whether the impairment is considered permanent or temporary.

e. An insurance recovery associated with events or changes in circumstances resulting in impairment of a capital asset should be netted with the impairment loss.

(1) Restoration or replacement of the capital asset using the insurance recovery should be reported as a separate transaction.

(2) Insurance recoveries should be disclosed if not apparent from the face of the financial statements. Insurance recoveries for circumstances other than impairment of capital assets should be reported in the same manner.

6. **Notes to the Financial Statements** The notes are considered part of the basic financial statements. Note disclosure requirements tend not to be heavily tested.

a. GASB 38 highlights the following required disclosures: descriptions of activities within major funds, internal service fund types, and fiduciary fund types; the time period defining "available" for revenue recognition; follow-up on significant finance-related legal or contractual violations; debt service requirements through debt maturity; separate identification of lease obligations, debt principal, and interest for five years subsequent to the financial statement date and in five year increments thereafter; schedule of short-term debt changes and purposes; details on interfund balances and transfers; terms of interest rate changes for variable rate debt; interest requirements using the year-end effective rate for variable rate debt; details about major components of receivables and payables, if obscured by aggregation; identification of long-term receivable balances.

b. GASB 40 highlights the following disclosure requirements: deposit and investment risk disclosures should be organized by investment type and contain a brief description of deposit or investment policies related to risks; credit quality ratings of investments in debt securities as of the date of the financial statements; custodial credit risk; concentration of credit risk by amount and issuer representing 5% or more of total investments; interest rate risk of debt investments and terms of investments with fair values; foreign currency risk stated in U.S. dollar balances and organized by currency denomination; obligations of, or guaranteed by, the U.S. government do not require disclosure of credit quality.

c. GASB 42 requires the following disclosures about the impairment of capital assets: A capital asset generally should be considered impaired if both (a) the decline in service utility of the capital asset is large in magnitude and (b) the event or change in circumstance is outside the normal life cycle of the capital asset. If not otherwise apparent from the face of the financial statements, the description, amount, and financial statement classification of impairment losses should be disclosed in the notes to the financial statements. If evidence is available to demonstrate that the impairment will be temporary, the capital asset should not be written down. Impaired capital assets that are idle should be disclosed, regardless of whether the impairment is considered permanent or temporary.

d. GASB 42 requires the following disclosures about insurance recoveries: An insurance recovery associated with events or changes in circumstances resulting in impairment of a capital asset should be netted with the impairment loss. Restoration or replacement of the capital asset using the insurance recovery should be reported as a separate transaction. Insurance recoveries should be disclosed if not apparent from the face of the financial statements. Insurance recoveries for circumstances other than impairment of capital assets should be reported in the same manner.

e. GASB 46 addresses restrictions of net assets resulting from enabling legislation, and amends GASB Statement No. 34, par. 34. Enabling legislation authorizes the government to assess, levy, charge, or otherwise mandate payment of resources (from external resource providers). GASB 46 clarifies that legal enforceability means that a government can be compelled by an external party (such as citizens, public interest groups, or the judiciary) to use resources created by enabling legislation only for the purposes specified by the legislation. At the end of the reporting period, the amount of the primary government's net assets restricted by enabling legislation should be disclosed in the notes to the financial statements.

Exhibit 3 ▸ Government-Wide Statement of Net Assets

Sample City
Statement of Net Assets
December 31, Year

	Primary Government			
	Governmental Activities	Business-Type Activities	Total	Component Units
ASSETS				
Cash and cash equivalents	$ 13,597,899	$ 10,279,143	$ 23,877,042	$ 303,935
Investments	27,365,221	—	27,365,221	7,428,952
Receivables (net)	12,833,132	3,609,615	16,442,747	4,042,290
Internal balances	175,000	(175,000)	—	—
Inventories	322,149	126,674	448,823	83,697
Capital assets, net	170,022,760	151,388,751	321,411,511	37,744,786
Total assets	224,316,161	165,229,183	389,545,344	49,603,660
LIABILITIES				
Accounts payable	6,783,310	751,430	7,534,740	1,803,332
Deferred revenue	1,435,599	—	1,435,599	38,911
Noncurrent liabilities:				
Due within one year	9,236,000	4,426,286	13,662,286	1,426,639
Due in more than one year	83,302,378	74,482,273	157,784,651	27,106,151
Total liabilities	100,757,287	79,659,989	180,417,276	30,375,033
NET ASSETS				
Invested in capital assets, net of related debt	103,711,386	73,088,574	176,799,960	15,906,392
Restricted for:				
Capital projects	11,705,864	—	11,705,864	492,445
Debt service	3,020,708	1,451,996	4,472,704	—
Community development projects	4,811,043	—	4,811,043	—
Other purposes	3,214,302	—	3,214,302	—
Unrestricted (deficit)	(2,904,429)	11,028,624	8,124,195	2,829,790
Total net assets	$123,558,874	$ 85,569,194	$209,128,068	$19,228,627

7. **Statement of Activities** Fund statements present the traditional revenue and expenditure format, but the net revenue (expense) format is required for the government-wide statement of activities. The net program cost format provides information about the cost of primary functions of the government and outlines how much each of those programs depends on general revenues of the government. This format also introduces the concept of matching program revenues and costs and allows governments to distribute administrative costs with indirect cost allocations.

Exhibit 4 ▸ Government-Wide Operating Statement

Sample City
Statement of Activities
For the Year Ended December 31, Year

		Program Revenues			Net (Expense) Revenue and Changes in Net Assets			
					Primary Government			
Functions/Programs	Expenses	Charges for Services	Operating Grants and Contributions	Capital Grants and Contributions	Governmental Activities	Business-type Activities	Total	Component Units
Primary government:								
Governmental activities:								
General government	$ 9,571,410	$ 3,146,915	$ 843,617	$ —	$ (5,580,878)	$ —	$ (5,580,878)	$ —
Public safety	34,844,749	1,198,855	1,307,693	62,300	(32,275,901)	—	(32,275,901)	—
Public works	10,128,538	850,000	—	2,252,615	(7,025,923)	—	(7,025,923)	—
Engineering services	1,299,645	704,793	—	—	(594,852)	—	(594,852)	—
Health and sanitation	6,738,672	5,612,267	575,000	—	(551,405)	—	(551,405)	—
Cemetery	735,866	212,496	—	—	(523,370)	—	(523,370)	—
Culture and recreation	11,532,350	3,995,199	2,450,000	—	(5,087,151)	—	(5,087,151)	—
Community development	2,994,389	—	—	2,580,000	(414,389)	—	(414,389)	—
Education (payment to school district)	21,893,273	—	—	—	(21,893,273)	—	(21,893,273)	—
Interest on long-term debt	6,068,121	—	—	—	(6,068,121)	—	(6,068,121)	—
Total governmental activities	105,807,013	15,720,525	5,176,310	4,894,915	(80,015,263)	—	(80,015,263)	—
Business-type activities:								
Water	3,595,733	4,159,350	—	1,159,909	—	1,723,526	1,723,526	—
Sewer	4,912,853	7,170,533	—	486,010	—	2,743,690	2,743,690	—
Parking facilities	2,796,283	1,344,087	—	—	—	(1,452,196)	(1,452,196)	—
Total business-type activities	11,304,869	12,673,970	—	1,645,919	—	3,015,020	3,015,020	—
Total primary government	$117,111,882	$28,394,495	$5,175,310	$6,540,834	(80,015,263)	3,015,020	(77,000,243)	—
Component units:								
Landfill	$ 3,382,157	$ 3,857,858	$ —	$ 11,397	—	—	—	487,098
Public school system	31,186,498	705,765	3,937,083	—	—	—	—	(26,543,650)
Total component units	$ 34,568,655	$ 4,563,623	$3,937,083	$ 11,397	—	—	—	(26,056,552)
General revenues:								
Taxes:								
Property taxes, levied for general purposes					51,693,573	—	51,693,573	—
Property taxes, levied for debt service					4,726,244	—	4,726,244	—
Franchise taxes					4,055,505	—	4,055,505	—
Public service taxes					8,969,887	—	8,969,887	—
Payment from Sample City					—	—	—	21,893,273
Grants and contributions not restricted to specific programs					1,457,820	—	1,457,820	6,461,708
Investment earnings					1,958,144	601,349	2,559,493	881,763
Miscellaneous					884,907	104,925	989,832	22,464
Special item—Gain on sale of park land					2,653,488	—	2,653,488	—
Transfers					501,409	(501,409)	—	—
Total general revenues, special items, and transfers					76,900,977	204,865	77,105,842	29,259,208
Change in net assets					(3,114,286)	3,219,885	105,599	3,202,656
Net assets—beginning					126,673,160	82,349,309	209,022,469	16,025,971
Net assets—ending					$ 123,558,874	$85,569,194	$209,128,068	$ 19,228,627

D. Fund Financial Statements

GASB 34 shifts to a fund reporting format that presents major fund financial statements to highlight the importance of individual funds and the relationship to the government-wide financial statements. Two statements are required for governmental funds: (1) balance sheet; and (2) statement of revenues, expenditures, and changes in fund balance. Basic fund financial statements will present a separate column for the General Fund, a separate column for each major fund and a single column to aggregate all nonmajor funds. Governmental and proprietary fund statements are segregated since the bases of accounting are different. (Fund information is reconciled in a summary format to the government-wide statements.)

1. **Reporting** Minimum reporting requirements for fund financial information in the basic financial statements include:

- Governmental Funds: (1) a Fund Balance Sheet and (2) a Statement of Revenues, Expenditures, and Changes in Fund Balances.
- Proprietary Funds: (1) a Statement of Fund Net Assets or Fund Balance Sheet; (2) a Statement of Revenues, Expenses, and Changes in Fund Equity or Fund Net Assets; and (3) a Statement of Cash Flows.
- Fiduciary Funds: (1) a Statement of Fiduciary Net Assets and (2) a Statement of Changes in Fiduciary Net Assets.

Exhibit 5 ▸ Governmental Funds Balance Sheet

Sample City
Balance Sheet
Governmental Funds
December 31, Year

	General	HUD Programs	Community Redevelopment	Route 7 Construction	Other Governmental Funds	Total Governmental Funds
ASSETS						
Cash and cash equivalents	$ 3,418,485	$1,236,523	—	$ —	$ 5,606,792	$ 10,261,800
Investments	—	—	$13,262,695	10,467,037	3,485,252	27,214,984
Receivables, net	3,644,561	2,953,438	33,340	11,000	10,221	6,972,560
Due from other funds	1,370,757	—	—	—	—	1,370,757
Receivables from other governments	—	119,059	—	—	1,596,038	1,715,097
Liens receivable	791,926	3,195,745	—	—	—	3,987,671
Inventories	182,821	—	—	—	—	182,821
Total assets	$9,408,550	$7,504,765	$13,616,035	$10,478,037	$10,689,303	$ 51,705,690
LIABILITIES AND FUND BALANCES						
Liabilities:						
Accounts payable	$3,408,680	$ 129,975	$ 190,548	$ 1,104,632	$ 1,074,831	$ 5,908,666
Due to other funds	—	25,369	—	—	—	25,369
Payable to other governments	94,074	—	—	—	—	94,074
Deferred revenue	4,250,430	6,273,045	250,000	11,000	—	10,784,475
Total liabilities	7,753,184	6,428,389	440,548	1,115,632	1,074,831	16,812,584
Fund balances:						
Reserved for:						
Inventories	182,821	—	—	—	—	182,821
Liens receivable	791,926	—	—	—	—	791,926
Encumbrances	40,292	41,034	119,314	5,792,586	1,814,122	7,807,349
Debt service	—	—	—	—	3,832,062	3,832,062
Other purposes	—	—	—	—	1,405,300	1,405,300
Unreserved, reported in:						
General fund	640,327	—	—	—	—	640,327
Special revenue funds	—	1,035,342	—	—	1,330,718	2,366,060
Capital projects funds	—	—	13,056,173	3,569,818	1,241,270	17,867,261
Total fund balances	1,655,366	1,076,376	13,175,487	9,362,405	9,623,472	34,893,106
Total liabilities and fund balances	$9,408,550	$7,504,765	$13,616,035	$10,478,037	$10,698,303	

Amounts reported for governmental activities in the statement of net assets (Exhibit 3) are different because (see Note 4, also):	
Capital assets used in governmental activities are not financial resources and therefore are not reported in the funds.	161,082,708
Other long-term assets are not available to pay for current-period expenditures and therefore are deferred in the funds.	9,348,876
Internal service funds are used by management to charge the costs of certain activities, such as insurance and telecommunications, to individual funds. The assets and liabilities of the internal service funds are included in governmental activities in the statement of net assets (Exhibit 3).	2,994,691
Long-term liabilities, including bonds payable, are not due and payable in the current period and therefore are not reported in the funds (see Note 4a).	(84,760,507)
Net assets of governmental activities	$123,558,874

Exhibit 6 ▸ Governmental Funds—Statement of Revenues, Expenditures, and Changes in Fund Balances

Sample City
Statement of Revenues, Expenditures, and Changes in Fund Balances
Governmental Funds
For the Year Ended December 31, Year

	General	HUD Programs	Community Redevelopment	Route 7 Construction	Other Governmental Funds	Total Governmental Funds
REVENUES						
Property taxes	$51,173,436	$ —	$ —	$ —	$ 4,680,192	$ 55,853,628
Franchise taxes	4,055,505	—	—	—	—	4,055,505
Public service taxes	8,969,887	—	—	—	—	8,969,887
Fees and fines	606,946	—	—	—	—	606,946
Licenses and permits	2,287,794	—	—	—	—	2,287,794
Intergovernmental	6,119,938	2,578,191	—	—	2,830,916	11,529,045
Charges for services	11,374,460	—	—	—	30,708	11,405,168
Investment earnings	552,325	87,106	549,489	270,161	364,330	1,823,411
Miscellaneous	881,874	66,176	—	2,939	94	951,083
Total revenues	86,022,165	2,731,473	549,489	273,100	7,906,240	97,482,467
EXPENDITURES						
Current						
General government	8,630,835	—	417,814	16,700	121,052	9,186,401
Public safety	33,729,623	—	—	—	—	33,729,623
Public works	497,775	—	—	—	3,721,542	8,697,317
Engineering services	1,299,645	—	—	—	—	1,299,645
Health and sanitation	6,070,032	—	—	—	—	6,070,032
Cemetery	706,305	—	—	—	—	706,305
Culture and recreation	11,411,685	—	—	—	—	11,411,685
Community development	—	2,954,389	—	—	—	2,954,389
Education—payment to school district	21,893,273	—	—	—	—	21,893,273
Debt service:						
Principal	—	—	—	—	3,450,000	3,450,000
Interest and other charges	—	—	—	—	5,215,151	5,215,151
Capital outlay	—	—	2,246,671	11,281,769	3,190,209	16,718,649
Total expenditures	88,717,173	2,954,389	2,664,485	11,298,469	15,697,954	121,332,470
Excess (deficiency) of revenues over expenditures	(2,695,008)	(222,916)	(2,114,996)	(11,025,369)	(7,791,714)	(23,850,003)
OTHER FINANCING SOURCES (USES)						
Proceeds of refunding bonds	—	—	—	—	38,045,000	38,045,000
Proceeds of long-term capital-related debt	—	—	17,529,560	—	1,300,000	18,829,560
Payment to bond refunding escrow agent	—	—	—	—	(37,284,144)	(37,284,144)
Transfers in	129,323	—	—	—	5,551,187	5,680,510
Transfers out	(2,163,759)	(348,046)	(2,273,187)	—	(219,076)	(5,004,068
Total other financing sources and uses	(2,034,436)	(348,046)	15,256,373	—	7,392,967	20,266,858
SPECIAL ITEM						
Proceeds from sale of park land	3,476,488	—	—	—	—	3,476,488
Net change in fund balances	(1,252,956)	(570,962)	13,141,377	(11,025,369)	(398,747)	(106,657)
Fund balances—beginning	2,908,322	1,647,338	34,110	20,387,774	10,022,219	34,999,763
Fund balances—ending	$ 1,655,366	$1,076,376	$13,175,487	$ 9,362,405	$ 9,623,472	$ 34,893,106

2. **Long-Term Debt & Capital Assets** These balances are not included in the governmental fund statements.

3. **Reconciliation** The link between government-wide and fund statements requires a reconciliation to convert the governmental funds to the economic resources measurement and accrual basis of accounting. Adjustments usually include moving transactions for general capital assets and general long-term liabilities from the operating statements to the balance sheet. Other reconciling items may include adjustments to deferred revenues or internal service fund net assets. If the entity presents summary information on the face of the financial statements, detailed schedules in the notes may be necessary.

4. **Major Funds** Major funds are reported (in both the governmental and the proprietary fund statements) to provide users with detailed fund information on significant activities of the government. The general fund is always major. There are two other criteria for determining major funds. (GASB 37 clarifies that major fund reporting requirements apply if the same element exceeds both the 10 and 5 percent criteria.) In addition to funds that meet the major-fund criteria, any other funds that the government's officials believe are particularly important to financial statement users are reported as major funds. Total assets, liabilities, revenues, or expenditures/expenses of major individual funds are both:

   a. At least 10% of the corresponding total for the relevant fund category (governmental or proprietary).

   b. At least 5% of the corresponding total for all governmental and proprietary funds combined.

5. **Presentation** The fund financial statements for major funds are presented before the notes to the financial statements. Combining statements for nonmajor funds are not required, but may be presented after the notes as supplementary information.

6. **Proprietary Fund** Financial statements should be prepared using the economic resources measurement focus and the accrual basis of accounting. Internal service funds also should be reported in the aggregate in a separate column on the proprietary fund statements. Enterprise fund financial statements consist of:

   a. Statement of net assets or balance sheet—net assets should be reported in the same categories required for the government-wide financial statements

   b. Statement of revenues, expenses, and changes in fund net assets—distinguish between: (1) current and noncurrent assets and liabilities; (2) operating and nonoperating revenues and expenses; (3) should display restricted assets; and (4) at the bottom of the statement, should report capital contributions, contributions to permanent and term endowments, special and extraordinary items, and transfers separately to arrive at the all-inclusive change in fund net assets.

   c. Statement of cash flows—should be prepared using the direct method

7. **Fiduciary Funds** Major fund reporting is not used in the fiduciary fund category. Statements should be prepared using the economic resources measurement focus and the accrual basis of accounting. Required statements for fiduciary funds: (1) statement of fiduciary net assets; and (2) statement of changes in fiduciary net assets. Fiduciary statements include separate columns for each fiduciary fund type used by the governmental entity. Financial statements for individual pension plans and investment trusts are presented in the notes to the financial statements of the primary government if separate, audited financial reports are not issued. The statement of fiduciary net assets and statement of changes in fiduciary net assets are included in the fund statements to report fiduciary activities. GASB 31 provides guidance for investment trust funds.

Exhibit 7 ▶ Proprietary Funds Balance Sheet

Sample City
Balance Sheet
Proprietary Funds
December 31, Year

	Business-type Activities— Enterprise Funds			Governmental Activities—
	Water and Sewer	Parking Facilities	Totals [2]	Internal Service Funds (Note 4)
ASSETS [1]				
Current assets:				
Cash and cash equivalents	$ 8,416,653	$ 369,168	$ 8,785,821	$ 3,336,099
Investments	—	—	—	150,237
Receivables, net	3,564,586	3,535	3,568,121	157,804
Due from other governments	41,494	—	41,494	—
Inventories	126,674	—	126,674	139,328
Total current assets	12,149,407	372,703	12,522,110	3,783,468
Noncurrent assets:				
Restricted cash and cash equivalents	—	1,493,322	1,493,322	—
Capital assets:				
Land	813,513	3,021,637	3,835,150	—
Distribution and collection systems	39,504,183	—	39,504,183	—
Buildings and equipment	106,135,666	23,029,166	129,164,832	14,721,786
Less accumulated depreciation	(15,328,911)	(5,786,503)	(21,115,414)	(5,781,734)
Total noncurrent assets	131,124,451	21,757,622	152,882,073	8,940,052
Total assets	143,273,858	22,130,325	165,404,183	12,723,520
LIABILITIES				
Current liabilities:				
Accounts payable	447,427	304,003	751,430	780,570
Due to other funds	175,000	—	175,000	1,170,388
Compensated absences	112,850	8,827	121,677	237,690
Claims and judgments	—	—	—	1,687,975
Bonds, notes, and loans payable	3,944,609	360,000	4,304,609	249,306
Total current liabilities	4,679,886	672,830	5,353,716	4,125,929
Noncurrent liabilities:				
Compensated absences	451,399	35,306	486,705	—
Claims and judgments	—	—	—	5,602,900
Bonds, notes and loans payable	54,451,549	19,544,019	73,995,568	—
Total noncurrent liabilities	54,902,948	19,579,325	74,482,273	5,602,900
Total liabilities	59,582,834	20,252,155	79,834,989	9,728,829
NET ASSETS				
Invested in capital assets, net of related debt	72,728,293	360,281	73,088,574	8,690,746
Restricted for debt service	—	1,451,996	1,451,996	—
Unrestricted	10,962,731	65,893	11,028,624	(5,696,055)
Total net assets	83,691,024	1,878,170	85,569,194	2,994,691
Total liabilities and net assets	$143,273,858	$22,130,325	$165,404,183	$12,723,520

[1] This statement illustrates the "balance sheet" format; the "net assets" format also is permitted. Classification of assets and liabilities is required in either case.

[2] Even though internal service funds (ISF) are classified as proprietary funds, the nature of the activity accounted for in them is generally governmental. By reporting ISFs separately from the proprietary funds that account for business-type activities, the information in the "Totals" column on this statement flows directly to the "Business-type Activities" column on the statement of net assets, and the need for a reconciliation on this statement is avoided.

Exhibit 8 ▸ Proprietary Funds Operating Statement

Sample City
Statement of Revenues, Expenses, and Changes in Fund Net Assets
Proprietary Funds
For the Year Ended December 31, Year

	Business-type Activities—Enterprise Funds			Governmental Activities—Internal Service Funds (Note 5)
	Water and Sewer	Parking Facilities	Totals [1]	
Operating revenues:				
Charges for services	$11,329,883	$ 1,340,261	$12,670,144	$15,256,164
Miscellaneous	—	3,826	3,826	1,066,761
Total operating revenues	11,329,883	1,344,087	12,673,970	16,322,925
Operating expenses:				
Personal services	3,400,559	762,348	4,162,907	4,157,156
Contractual services	344,422	96,032	440,454	584,396
Utilities	754,107	100,726	854,833	214,812
Repairs and maintenance	747,315	64,617	811,932	1,960,490
Other supplies and expenses	498,213	17,119	515,332	234,445
Insurance claims and expenses	—	—	—	800,286
Depreciation	1,163,140	542,049	1,705,189	1,707,872
Total operating expenses	6,907,756	1,582,891	8,490,647	16,863,457
Operating income (loss)	4,422,127	(238,804)	4,183,323	(540,532)
Nonoperating revenues (expenses):				
Interest and investment revenue	454,793	146,556	601,349	134,733
Miscellaneous revenue	—	104,925	104,925	20,855
Interest expense	(1,600,830)	(1,166,546)	(2,767,376)	(41,616)
Miscellaneous expense	—	(46,846)	(46,846)	(176,003)
Total nonoperating revenue (expenses)	(1,146,037)	(961,911)	(2,107,948)	(62,031)
Income (loss) before contributions and transfers	3,276,090	(1,200,715)	2,075,375	(602,563)
Capital contributions	1,645,919	—	1,645,919	18,788
Transfers out	(290,000)	(211,409)	(501,409)	(175,033)
Change in net assets	4,632,009	(1,412,124)	3,219,885	(758,808)
Total net assets—beginning	79,059,015	3,290,294	82,349,309	3,753,499
Total net assets—ending	$83,691,024	$ 1,878,170	$85,569,194	$ 2,994,691

[1] Even though internal service funds are classified as proprietary funds, the nature of the activity accounted for in them is generally *governmental.* By reporting internal service funds separately from the proprietary funds that account for business-type activities, the information in the "Totals" column on this statement flows directly to the "Business-type Activities" column on the statement of net assets, and the need for a reconciliation on this statement is avoided.

Exhibit 9 ▸ Proprietary Funds Cash Flows Statement

Sample City
Statement of Cash Flows
Proprietary Funds
For the Year Ended December 31, Year

	Business-type Activities—Enterprise Funds			Governmental Activities—Internal Service Funds (Note 5)
	Water and Sewer	Parking Facilities	Totals	
CASH FLOWS FROM OPERATING ACTIVITIES				
Receipts from customers	$11,400,200	$ 1,345,292	$12,745,492	$15,356,343
Payments to suppliers	(2,725,349)	(365,137)	(3,090,486)	(2,812,238)
Payments to employees	(3,360,055)	(750,828	(4,110,883)	(4,209,688)
Internal activity—payments to other funds	(1,296,768)	—	(1,296,768)	—
Claims paid	—	—	—	(8,482,451)
Other receipts (payments)	(2,325,483)	—	(2,325,483)	1,061,118
Net cash provided by operating activities	1,692,545	229,327	1,921,872	883,084
CASH FLOWS FROM NONCAPITAL FINANCING ACTIVITIES				
Operating subsidies and transfers to other funds	(290,000)	(211,409)	(501,409)	(175,033)
CASH FLOWS FROM CAPITAL AND RELATED FINANCING ACTIVITIES				
Proceeds from capital debt	4,041,322	8,660,779	12,702,100	—
Capital contributions	1,645,919	—	1,645,919	—
Purchases of capital assets	(4,194,035)	(144,716)	(4,338,751)	(400,086)
Principal paid on capital debt	(2,178,491)	(8,895,000)	(11,073,491)	(954,137)
Interest paid on capital debt	(1,479,708)	(1,166,546)	(2,646,254)	(41,616)
Other receipts (payments)	—	19,174	19,174	131,416
Net cash (used) by capital and related financing activities	(2,164,993)	(1,526,303)	(3,691,303)	(1,264,423)
CASH FLOWS FROM INVESTING ACTIVITIES				
Proceeds from sales and maturities of investments	—	—	—	15,684
Interest and dividends	454,793	143,747	598,540	129,550
Net cash provided by investing activities	454,793	143,747	598,540	145,234
Net (decrease) in cash and cash equivalents	(307,655)	(1,364,645)	(1,672,300)	(411,138)
Balances—beginning of the year	8,724,308	3,227,135	11,951,443	3,747,237
Balances—end of the year	$ 8,416,653	$ 1,862,490	$10,279,143	$ 3,336,099
Reconciliation of operating income (loss) to net cash provided (used) by operating activities				
Operating income (loss)	$ 4,422,127	$ (238,804)	$ 4,183,323	$ (540,532)
Adjustments to reconcile operating income to net cash provided (used) by operating activities:				
Depreciation expense	1,163,140	542,049	1,705,189	1,707,872
Change in assets and liabilities:				
Receivables, net	653,264	1,205	654,469	31,941
Inventories	2,829	—	2,829	39,790
Accounts and other payables	(297,446)	(86,643)	(384,089)	475,212
Accrued expenses	(4,251,369)	11,520	(4,239,849)	(831,199)
Net cash provided by operating activities	$ 1,692,545	$ 229,327	$ 1,921,872	$ 883,084

Note: Required information about noncash investing, capital, and financing activities is not illustrated.

Exhibit 10 ▸ Fiduciary Funds Balance Sheet

Sample City
Statement of Fiduciary Net Assets
Fiduciary Funds
December 31, Year

	Employee Retirement Plan	Private-Purpose Trusts	Agency Funds
ASSETS			
Cash and cash equivalents	$ 1,973	$ 1,250	$ 44,889
Receivables:			
Interest and dividends	508,475	760	—
Other receivables	6,826	—	183,161
Total receivables	515,301	760	183,161
Investments, at fair value:			
U.S. government obligations	13,056,037	80,000	—
Municipal bonds	6,528,019	—	—
Corporate bonds	16,320,047	—	—
Corporate stocks	26,112,075	—	—
Other investments	3,264,009	—	—
Total investments	65,280,187	80,000	—
Total assets	65,797,461	82,010	$228,050
LIABILITIES			
Accounts payable	—	1,234	—
Refunds payable and others	1,358	—	228,050
Total liabilities	1,358	1,234	$228,050
NET ASSETS			
Held in trust for pension benefits and other purposes	$65,796,103	$80,776	

Statements of individual pension plans and external investment pools are required to be presented in the notes to the financial statements if separate GAAP statements for those individual plans or pools are not available.

Exhibit 11 ▸ Fiduciary Funds Operating Statement

Sample City
Statement of Changes in Fiduciary Net Assets
Fiduciary Funds
For the Year Ended December 31, Year

	Employee Retirement Plan	Private-Purpose Trusts
ADDITIONS		
Contributions:		
Employer	$ 2,721,341	$ —
Plan members	1,421,233	—
Total contributions	4,142,574	—
Investment earnings:		
Net (decrease) in fair value of investments	(272,522)	—
Interest	2,460,871	4,560
Dividends	1,445,273	—
Total investment earnings	3,633,622	4,560
Less investment expense	216,428	—
Net investment earnings	3,417,194	4,560
Total additions	7,559,768	4,560
DEDUCTIONS		
Benefits	2,453,047	3,800
Refunds of contributions	464,691	—
Administrative expenses	87,532	678
Total deductions	3,005,270	4,478
Change in net assets	4,554,498	82
Net assets—beginning of the year	61,241,605	$80,694
Net assets—end of the year	$65,796,103	$80,776

Exhibit 12 ▸ Component Units Balance Sheet

Sample City
Statement of Net Assets
Component Units
For the Year Ended December 31, Year

	Sample City School District	Sample City Landfill	Total
ASSETS			
Cash and cash equivalents	$ 303,485	$ 450	$ 303,935
Investments	3,658,520	1,770,432	5,428,952
Receivables, net	3,717,026	325,264	4,042,290
Inventories	83,697	—	83,697
Restricted assets—landfill closure	—	2,000,000	2,000,000
Capital assets, net	34,759,986	2,984,800	37,744,786
Total assets	42,522,714	7,080,946	49,603,660
LIABILITIES			
Accounts payable	1,469,066	334,266	1,803,332
Deposits and deferred revenue	38,911	—	38,911
Long-term liabilities:			
Due within one year	1,426,639	—	1,426,639
Due in more than one year	22,437,349	4,668,802	27,106,151
Total liabilities	25,371,965	5,003,068	30,375,033
NET ASSETS			
Invested in capital assets, net of related debt	12,921,592	2,984,800	15,906,392
Restricted for capital projects	492,445	—	492,445
Unrestricted	3,736,712	(906,922)	2,829,790
Total net assets	$17,150,749	$2,077,878	$19,228,627

Nonmajor component units are aggregated into a single column. Combining statements of nonmajor components have the same status as combining statements for nonmajor funds (supplementary information).

Exhibit 13 ▸ Component Units Operating Statement

Sample City
Statement of Activities
Component Units
For the Year Ended December 31, Year

	Program Revenues				Net (Expense) Revenue and Changes in Net Assets		
	Expenses	Charges for Services	Operating Grants and Contributions	Capital Grants and Contributions	School District	Landfill	Totals
Sample City School District							
Instructional	$16,924,321	$ 147,739	$2,825,109	$ —	$(13,951,473)	$ —	$(13,951,473)
Support services	7,972,559	300	751,711	—	(7,220,548)	—	(7,220,548)
Operation of non-instructional services	1,523,340	557,726	359,092	—	(606,522)	—	(606,522)
Facilities acquisition and construction services	48,136	—	1,171	—	(46,965)	—	(46,965)
Interest on long-term debt	546,382	—	—	—	(546,382)	—	(546,382)
Unallocated depreciation	4,171,760	—	—	—	(4,171,760)	—	(4,171,760)
Total—Sample City School District	31,186,498	705,765	3,937,083	—	(26,543,650)	—	—
Sample City Landfill							
Landfill operations	3,382,157	3,857,858	—	11,397	—	487,098	487,098
Total component units	$34,568,655	$4,563,623	$3,937,083	$11,397			(26,056,552)
General revenues:							
Payment from Sample City					21,893,273	—	21,893,273
Grants, entitlements, and contributions not restricted to specific programs					6,461,708	—	6,461,708
Investment earnings					674,036	207,727	881,763
Miscellaneous					19,950	2,514	22,464
Total general revenues					29,048,967	210,241	29,259,208
Change in net assets					2,505,317	697,339	3,202,656
Net assets—beginning					14,645,432	1,380,539	16,025,971
Net assets—ending					$ 17,150,749	$2,077,878	$ 19,228,627

E. **Statement of Cash Flows**

The major differences between the GASB 9 statement and the SFAS 95 statement are that four categories are used for classifying cash flows instead of three and the operating category is more narrowly focused. This statement classifies cash receipts and payments of all proprietary funds as resulting from operating activities, noncapital financing, capital and related financing, or investing activities. Generally, only investments with a maturity date of three months or less at date of purchase are reported as cash or cash equivalents.

1. **Operating Activities** Cash inflows, receipts, and payments that do not result from transactions defined as capital and related financing, noncapital financing, or investing activities.

   a. **Cash Inflows** Include receipts from cash

      (1) Sales of goods or services, including receipts from collection of accounts receivable and both short- and long-term notes receivable from customers arising from those sales.

      (2) Quasi-external operating transactions with other funds.

      (3) Grants for specific activities that are considered to be operating activities of the grantor government. (A grant arrangement of this type is essentially the same as a contract for services.)

      (4) Other funds for reimbursement of operating transactions.

      (5) Loan programs that are made and collected as part of a governmental program such as student loans or low-income housing mortgages. Investment type loans would not be included in this category.

   b. **Cash Outflows** Include cash payments

      (1) To acquire materials for providing services and manufacturing goods for resale, including principal payments on accounts payable and both short- and long-term notes payable to suppliers for those materials or goods.

      (2) To other suppliers for other goods or services, including employees.

      (3) For grants to other governments or organizations for specific activities that are considered to be operating activities of the grantor government.

      (4) For taxes, duties, fines, and other fees or penalties.

      (5) For quasi-external operating transactions with other funds, including payments in lieu of taxes.

2. **Noncapital Financing Activities** Include borrowing for purposes other than to acquire, construct, or improve capital assets, as well as repaying borrowed amounts, including interest. This category includes proceeds from all borrowings (such as revenue anticipation notes) not clearly attributable to capital assets, regardless of the form of the borrowing. Also included are certain other interfund and intergovernmental receipts and payments.

   a. **Cash Inflows**

      (1) Proceeds from issuing bonds, notes, and other short- or long-term borrowing not clearly attributable to capital assets.

      (2) Receipts from grants or subsidies except those specifically restricted for capital purposes and those for specific activities that are considered to be operating activities of the grantor government.

(3) Receipts from other funds except those amounts that are clearly attributable to capital assets, quasi-external operating transactions, and reimbursement for operating transactions.

(4) Receipts from property and other taxes collected for the governmental enterprise and not specifically restricted for capital purposes.

b. **Cash Outflows**

(1) Repayments of amounts borrowed for purposes other than acquiring, constructing, or improving capital assets.

(2) Interest payments to lenders and other creditors on amounts borrowed or credit extended for purposes other than capital assets.

(3) Payments as grants or subsidies to other governments or organizations, except those for specific activities that are considered to be operating activities of the grantor government.

(4) Payments to other funds, except for quasi-external operating transactions.

3. **Capital and Related Financing Activities** Include acquiring and disposing of capital assets used in providing services or producing goods; borrowing money for acquiring, constructing, or improving capital assets and repaying the amounts borrowed, including interest; and paying for capital assets obtained from vendors on credit.

a. **Cash Inflows** Inflows from

(1) Issuing or refunding bonds, mortgages, notes, and other short- or long-term borrowing clearly attributable to capital assets.

(2) Capital grants awarded to the governmental enterprise.

(3) Contributions made by other funds, governments, and organizations or individuals for the specific purpose of defraying the cost of capital assets.

(4) Sales of capital assets; also, proceeds from insurance on capital assets that are stolen or destroyed.

(5) Special assessments or property and other taxes levied specifically to finance capital assets.

b. **Cash Outflows**

(1) Payments to acquire, construct, or improve capital assets.

(2) Repayments or refundings of amounts borrowed specifically to acquire, construct, or improve capital assets.

(3) Other principal payments to vendors who have extended credit directly to acquire, construct or improve capital assets.

(4) Payments to creditors for interest directly related to capital assets.

4. **Investing Activities** Investing activities include making and collecting loans (except program loans) and acquiring and disposing of debt or equity instruments.

a. **Cash Inflows** Include: (1) receipts from collections of loans (except program loans) made by the governmental enterprise and sales of other entities' debt instruments (other than cash equivalents) that were purchased by the governmental enterprise;

(2) interest and dividends received as returns on loans (except program loans), debt instruments of other entities, equity securities, and cash management or investment pools; and (3) withdrawals from investment pools that the governmental enterprise is not using as demand accounts.

b. **Cash Outflows** Disbursements for: (1) Loans (except program loans) made by the governmental enterprise and payments to acquire debt instruments of other entities (other than cash equivalents); and (2) deposits into investment pools that the governmental enterprise is not using as demand accounts.

F. **Other Required Supplementary Information (RSI)**
Required supplementary information is outside the scope of the auditor's opinion. Except for MD&A, RSI is presented after the financial statements.

1. **Budgetary Comparison Schedule (BCS)** is presented for the general fund and for each major special revenue fund that has a legally adopted annual budget, on the **budgetary** basis of accounting. The BCS presents both the original and final budget as well as actual inflows, outflows, and balances. It uses the same format, terminology, and classifications as either the budget document or a statement of revenues, expenditures, and changes in fund balances. The BCS is accompanied by a reconciliation (in either a separate schedule or RSI notes) of budgetary information to GAAP information. This reconciliation provides the link from the budgetary comparisons to the GAAP statements in the BFS. Significant budgetary perspective differences arise when a government does not adopt its legal budget using the general fund and major special revenue fund classifications. These governments should present budgetary comparison schedules as RSI based on the fund, organization or program structure used for their legally adopted budget.

2. **Infrastructure Schedules** (Only for assets reported using the modified approach.) These schedules include (1) information on the assessed condition (assessed at least every 3 years) for at least the 3 most recent assessments (i.e., this information could be from 9 years); and (2) the estimated annual amount to maintain the condition level established and disclosed by the government compared with amounts actually expensed for the past 5 reporting periods. The schedules are accompanied by (1) disclosures on the basis for the condition measurement and the measurement scale; (2) the condition level at which the government intends to preserve assets reported using the modified approach; and (3) factors that could effect trends in these schedules.

G. **Comprehensive Annual Financial Report**
NCGA Statement 1 requires every governmental entity to prepare and publish, as a matter of public record, a comprehensive annual financial report (CAFR) that encompasses all funds of the primary government (including its blended component units). The CAFR should also encompass all discretely presented component units of the reporting entity.

1. **Introduction Section**

a. Title Page and Table of Contents

b. Report of the Independent Auditor (if an audit has been performed)

c. Letter of Transmittal: Cites legal and policy requirements for report. Governments are encouraged not to duplicate information contained in MD&A in the Letter of Transmittal.

d. Other material deemed appropriate by management

2. **Financial Section**

a. **Management's Discussion & Analysis (MD&A)**

b. **Basic Financial Statements**

(1) **Government-Wide Financial Statements**

(a) Statement of net assets

(b) Statement of activities

(2) **Fund Financial Statements**

(a) Governmental Funds: Balance sheet; statement of revenues, expenditures, and changes in fund balances

(b) Proprietary Funds: Statement of net assets; statement of revenues, expenses, and changes in fund net assets; statement of cash flows

(c) Fiduciary Funds: Statement of fiduciary net assets; statement of changes in fiduciary net assets

(3) **Notes to the Financial Statements**

c. **Required Supplementary Information (RSI)**

(1) The budgetary comparison schedule should present both the original and the final appropriated budgets for the reporting period as well as actual inflows, outflows, and balances, stated on the government's budgetary basis.

(2) Governments adopting the modified approach for reporting infrastructure assets should include schedules presenting infrastructure asset condition, required asset preservation amounts, basis for the measurement of asset condition, and the established asset condition level

d. **Combining Statements** for nonmajor funds by fund type of the primary government and the nonmajor discretely presented component units.

e. **Individual Fund Statements & Schedules**

3. **Statistical Section** The objectives of statistical section information are to provide financial statement users with additional historical perspective, context, and detail to assist in using the information in the financial statements, notes to financial statements, and required supplementary information to understand and assess a government's economic condition (typically for the last ten fiscal years). Statistical section information should be presented in five categories:

a. **Financial trends information** assists users in understanding and assessing how a government's financial position has changed over time.

b. **Revenue capacity information** assists users in understanding and assessing the factors affecting a government's ability to generate its own-source revenues.

c. **Debt capacity information** assists users in understanding and assessing a government's debt burden and its ability to issue additional debt.

d. **Demographic and economic information** assists users in understanding the socioeconomic environment within which a government operates and provides information that facilitates comparisons of financial statement information over time and among governments.

e. **Operating information** provides contextual information about a government's operations and resources to assist readers in using financial statement information to understand and assess a government's economic condition.

4. **Financial Trends Information** GASB 44, *Economic Condition Reporting: The Statistical Section* requires that governments should present, at a minimum, two types of information in statistical section schedules—net assets and changes in net assets.

   a. The three components of net assets should be shown separately for governmental activities, business-type activities, and the total primary government.

      (1) Net assets invested in capital assets net of related debt

      (2) Net assets restricted

      (3) Net assets unrestricted

   b. At a minimum, governments should present the following information separately for governmental activities and business-type activities:

      (1) Expenses by function, program, or identifiable activity

      (2) Program revenues by category

      (3) Total net (expense) revenue

      (4) General revenues and other changes in net assets by type

      (5) Total change in net assets.

   c. Governments should also present individually their most significant charges for services revenue, categorized by function, program, or identifiable activity.

III. Recognition of Specific Revenues & Liabilities

A. Nonexchange Transactions

GASB 24 provides guidance for food stamps and on-behalf payments for fringe benefits and salaries. All other grants fall within the scope of GASB 33, Nonexchange Transactions, as amended by GASB 36. One of the basic principles of GASB 33 is symmetry between expense or expenditure recognition by a provider government and revenue recognition by the recipient government. Recipient governments do not apply the criteria for derived tax revenues or imposed nonexchange revenues on transactions involving provider governments. NCGA and GASB pronouncements require revenue recognition using the modified accrual basis of accounting for revenues from nonexchange transactions. Revenues should be recognized "in the accounting period when they become available and measurable."

1. **Applicability**

   a. Under the accrual basis of accounting, recipients of resources from nonexchange transactions report assets when the applicable recognition criterion is met or when resources are received, whichever occurs first. Revenues are recognized when the applicable revenue recognition criterion is met. Resources received in advance are recognized as deferred revenues (liabilities). Similar recognition criteria apply to providers.

   b. Under the modified accrual basis of accounting, revenues are not recognized unless resources are available.

2. **Derived Tax Revenues** Derived tax revenues are assessments imposed by governments on exchange transactions and generally include sales taxes, income taxes, motor fuel taxes, and similar taxes on earnings or consumption. Assets are recognized when the underlying exchange transaction occurs. Revenues generally are recognized in the period when the underlying exchange transaction has occurred and the resources are available.

3. **Imposed Nonexchange Transactions** Imposed nonexchange revenues represent assessments imposed on non-governmental entities and include property taxes and fines or forfeitures. Assets are recognized when the government has an enforceable legal claim to the resources. Recipients should recognize revenues when they are available and measurable. The term available means "collected within the current period or expected to be collected soon enough thereafter to be used to pay liabilities of the current period." Usually, such time shall not exceed 60 days.

4. **Government-Mandated Nonexchange Transactions** Government-mandated nonexchange transactions occur when a government at one level provides resources to a government at another level and requires that government to use the resources for a specific purpose. Intergovernmental grants fall into this category. Recipients recognize assets and revenues when all eligibility requirements have been met and the resources are available. Providers recognize liabilities and expenses using the same criteria. Eligibility requirements include time requirements. Purpose restrictions result in restricted assets until resources are used for the specified purpose. [Noncompliance with time criteria cancels the transaction. Neither the provider nor the recipient recognizes liabilities (or assets) or expenses (or revenues) until all eligibility requirements have been met.]

5. **Voluntary Nonexchange Transactions** Voluntary nonexchange transactions result from legislative or contractual agreements, but do not involve an exchange of equal value. Certain grants, entitlements, and donations are classified as voluntary nonexchange transactions. Both parties may or may not be governmental entities. Specific recognition criteria are the same as those for government-mandated nonexchange transactions.

6. **Continuing Appropriations** If distributions from a provider government are authorized by continuing appropriations (involving no further legislative action), the recipient governments can use any reasonable estimate to accrue revenues.

B. Certain Grants & Other Financial Assistance

GASB 24 requires that cash-conduit arrangements be included in the agency funds. Examples are pass-through grants, food stamps, and on-behalf payments for fringe benefits and salaries. If the recipient government monitors secondary recipients, determines eligibility, or has the ability to exercise discretion for allocating funds, the grant is **not** a cash conduit and should be reported in governmental, proprietary, or trust funds, as appropriate.

1. **State Governments** Required to recognize revenues and expenditures when benefits, such as food stamps, are distributed to individual recipients by the entity or its agents.

2. **State and Local Governments** The guidance for on-behalf payments for fringe benefits and salaries affects both state and local governments. If the employer is not legally liable for these benefits, the employer recognizes revenues and expenditures in equal amounts based on payments of the grantor. If the employer is legally liable for these payments, the expenditures are recognized based on the legal provisions associated with the salaries and the accounting standards that apply. Revenues are recognized based on third-party payments or amounts that meet criteria for receivables at year-end. There are required disclosure provisions for both the employer and payor government that are beyond the scope of this discussion.

C. Capital Lease Obligations

The criteria used to determine whether a lease is capital or operating is the same for governments and businesses.

1. **Capital Leases** If a lease meets any one of the following criteria, it is a capital lease.

   a. Ownership of the property transfers to the lessee by the end of the lease term.

   b. The lease contains an option to purchase the leased property at a bargain price.

c. The lease term is equal to or greater than 75 percent of the estimated economic life of the leased property.

d. The present value of the minimum lease payments equals or exceeds 90 percent of the fair value of the leased property at the inception of the lease.

2. Operating Leases If none of the criteria for a capital lease is met, the lessee classifies the lease as an operating lease. Payments for assets used by governmental funds are recorded by the using fund as expenditures. Payments for assets used by proprietary funds are recorded by the using fund as expenses.

3. Governmental Funds

a. Governmental-Type Fund The governmental fund records an expenditure and an Other Financing Source, just as if the general fixed asset had been constructed or acquired from debt issue proceeds. The amount to be recorded is the lesser of (1) the present value of the minimum lease payments or (2) the fair value of the leased property.

b. Debt Service Fund Commonly, governmental units use the Debt Service Fund (DSF) to record capital lease payments because the annual payments are installments of general long-term debt. Although part of each payment is interest at a constant rate on the unpaid balance of the lease obligation, and part is payment on the principal, the *Expenditures* account is debited in the DSF for the full amount of the lease payment. Only the detail records in the DSF show how much of the expenditure was for interest and how much was for principal.

Exhibit 14 ▸ Leased General Fixed Asset*

1. Lease Inception		
a. <u>Governmental Fund</u>		
Expenditures	XX	
Other Financing Sources—Capital Leases		XX
2. Lease Repayment		
a. <u>Debt Service Fund</u>		
Expenditures (principal and interest)	XX	
Cash		XX

*These entries may be more clear to candidates who are familiar with the material in Chapter 19.

4. Proprietary Funds Assets acquired under capital leases are depreciated by the proprietary fund. Capital leases are generally recorded as an asset and liability at the lesser of (a) the present value of the minimum lease payments or (b) the fair value of the leased property. Lease payments for capital leases are comprised of interest expense and principal reduction.

Exhibit 15 ▸ Leased Proprietary Fixed Asset (in the related proprietary fund)

1. Lease Inception		
Equipment	XX	
Capital Leases Payable		XX
2. Lease Repayment		
Expenses—Interest	XX	
Capital Leases Payable	XX	
Cash		XX

D. Municipal Solid Waste Landfills

Municipal solid waste landfills (MSWLFs) are required by the Environmental Protection Agency (EPA) to follow certain closure functions and postclosure monitoring and maintenance procedures in order to operate. Any state or local government that is required by federal, state, or local laws or regulations to incur MSWLF closure and postclosure care costs is subject to GASB 18.

1. **Estimated Total Current Cost** The estimated total current costs of closure and postclosure care should include those costs that result in disbursements near the date that the MSWLF stops accepting solid waste and during the postclosure period: equipment expected to be installed and facilities expected to be built; final cover (capping) costs; and monitoring and maintenance costs. These costs are based on laws or regulations enacted or approved as of the balance sheet date, regardless of their effective date. The estimated current cost is reevaluated annually to adjust for the effects of inflation, deflation, or other changes in estimated costs.

2. **Measurement and Recognition** The type of fund employed by the MSWLF determines the recognition method. Estimated total current costs should be based on MSWLF use, not the passage of time. The current year closure and post-closure cost recognition is the difference between the total costs to be recognized to date and the total costs recognized in prior periods. The total costs to be recognized to date are the total estimated costs times the cumulative used percentage of total capacity. (Costs and liabilities are recognized as the MSWLF accepts solid waste.)

    a. **Proprietary Fund** Capital assets should be fully depreciated by the date the MSWLF stops accepting solid waste or, in the case of a single cell, the date that cell is closed.

    b. **Governmental-Type Fund** The MSWLF recognizes expenditures using the modified accrual basis of accounting, with liability reported as with other general long-term debt. Expenditures are disclosed in the notes to the financial statements or appear as a parenthetical display on the statement of operations.

    c. **Governmental Colleges and Universities That Use the AICPA College Guide Model** Expenditures and liabilities should be calculated similarly to other governmental-type funds and be reported in an unrestricted current fund.

3. **Disclosure** The disclosure requirements include the nature of closure and postclosure care estimates, the reported liability at the balance sheet date, the estimated total closure and postclosure care cost remaining to be recognized, the percentage of MSWLF capacity used to date, and the estimated remaining MSWLF life in years. Disclosure of how closure and postclosure care financial assurance requirements are being met is also required.

E. Escheat Property

Escheat property is property that reverts to a governmental entity in the absence of legal claimants or heirs. GASB 37 specifies that escheat property is to be reported in either a private-purpose trust fund or the fund to which the property ultimately escheats.

1. **Reporting Revenue** Revenue from escheat property should be reduced and a fund liability reported to the probable extent that the property will be reclaimed and paid to claimants. These payments reduce the liability. The total liability represents an estimate of the amount expected to be reclaimed and paid to claimants.

2. **Interfund Transfers** When a trust fund is the initial reporting vehicle, amounts that are transferred to the ultimate fund should be reported as an operating transfer. The difference resulting from the transfer when the remaining assets of the trust are less than the liabilities should be reported as an "advance to" in the trust fund and an "advance from" in the ultimate fund. When the assets exceed the liabilities in the trust fund, the difference is reported as fund balance.

IV. Appendix: Limited Scope Topics

A. Governmental Colleges & Universities

GASB 19 provides guidance on reporting for all **governmental** colleges and universities.

1. **Pell Grants** Pell grants are scholarships granted to students requesting financial assistance who meet the federal government criteria for aid. Pell grants must be reported in a restricted current fund.

2. **Risk-Taking Activities** If a single fund is used to account for risk financing activities, it must be reported as an unrestricted current fund.

B. Postemployment Benefits

1. **Defined Benefit Pension Plans and Defined Contribution Plans** GASB 25 establishes standards for defined benefit pension plans and defined contribution plans. It does not address healthcare benefits, any plans not providing postretirement income, or the measurement of employer costs.

   a. **Defined Contribution Plans** Disclosures must include a brief plan description, a summary of significant accounting policies (including the fair value of plan assets), and information about contributions and investment concentrations.

   b. **Defined Benefit Pension Plans** Plans may elect to report one or more years of the required information in an additional financial statement or in the notes to the financial statements. A plan and its participating employer(s) must use the same methods and assumptions for financial reporting.

      (1) A statement of plan net assets provides information about the fair value and composition of plan assets, liabilities, and net assets.

      (2) A statement of changes in plan net assets provides information about the year-to-year changes in plan net assets, for a minimum of six years.

      (3) Notes to the financial statements include a short plan description; a summary of significant accounting policies; and information about contributions, legally required reserves, and investment concentrations.

      (4) Required supplementary information includes two schedules of historical trend information for a minimum of six years. Disclosures related to these schedules include the actuarial methods and significant assumptions used for financial reporting. The **schedule of funding progress** reports the actuarial value of assets, the actuarial accrued liability, and the relationship between the two over time. The **schedule of employer contributions** provides information about the employer's annual required contributions (ARC) and the percentage of the ARC recognized by the plan as contributed.

2. **Other Postemployment Benefit Plans** GASB 43, *Financial Reporting for Postemployment Benefit Plans Other Than Pension Plans,* supersedes GASB 26 and establishes uniform financial reporting standards for other postemployment benefit (OPEB) plans administered by defined benefit pension plans. GASB 45, *Accounting and Financial Reporting by Employers for Postemployment Benefits other Than Pensions,* requires systematic, accrual-based measurement and recognition of OPEB costs (expenses) and requires reporting of information about actuarial accrued liabilities.

   a. OPEB includes postemployment healthcare and other forms of postemployment benefits, such as life insurance, when provided separately from a pension plan.

   b. Plans that administer OPEB plans **must** present:

(1) A statement of plan net assets

(2) A statement of changes in plan net assets

(3) Notes to the financial statements

(a) Brief plan description

(b) A summary of significant accounting policies

(c) Information about contributions and legally required reserves

(4) Two multiyear schedules—required supplementary information (RSI) providing long-term historical trend information immediately following the notes to financial statements:

(a) Funded status of the plan and sufficiency of assets to pay benefits when due

(b) Employer contributions to the plan

3. **Pensions** GASB 27 establishes standards for the measurement, recognition, and display of pension expenditures/expense and related liabilities, assets, disclosures, and required supplementary information. Pension trust funds included in the employer's financial statements are **not** subject to GASB 27. (They are subject to GASB 25.)

a. **Annual Costs** For single-employer or agent multiple-employer plans, annual pension costs are equal to the employer's annual required contributions (ARC).

b. **Multiple Plans** When an employer has more than one plan, all recognition requirements should be applied separately for each plan.

c. **Multiple Funds** If the contributions are made from more than one fund, the ARC should be allocated on a pro-rata share to the various funds. In addition, the interest and the adjustment to reverse the actuarial amortization should also be allocated on the fund's proportionate share of the beginning balance of the NPO.

d. **Multiple-Employer Plans** Employers participating in multiple-employer plans share costs regardless of individual employer member demographics. The actuary usually calculates a single contribution requirement for all participants. Employers recognize pension expenditures equal to this contractual requirement. The plan description in the employer financial statements should include a reference to any separate issuance of pension plan reports.

e. **Disclosures** Requirements are similar to pension plans' requirements. Single or agent employers have additional requirements to outline the annual pension cost, contributions, and NPOs for the current year and two previous years.

f. **Transfer of Obligation** If an insurance company unconditionally undertakes a legal obligation to pay employees' pension benefits, the employer recognizes pension expense equal to the insurance premiums. The notes disclose information about this transfer and describe the benefits provided in the event of the company's default.

g. **Defined Contribution Plans** The annual expense or expenditure is based on the amounts required by the plan. Benefits are based on accumulated contributions. Differences between required and actual contributions are accumulated as assets or liabilities, and future contributions do not reflect amortization of previous deficiencies. Note disclosures include identification of the plan, description of the plan provisions, contribution requirements, and actual member and employer contributions.

4. **Deferred Compensation Plans** Under GASB 32, as amended by GASB 34, an IRC §457 deferred compensation plan that meets the criteria in NCGA Statement No. 1 for inclusion in the fiduciary funds of a government is reported as a pension trust fund in the financial statements. The government must determine whether it has fiduciary accountability for IRC §457 plans and whether it holds the assets in a trustee capacity. NCGA guidance generally does not require the use of fiduciary funds when the assets are administered by a third party. The likely result of GASB 32 is that many government employers that formerly reported IRC §457 plan assets on their balance sheet will no longer do so.

C. Accounting for Termination Benefits

GASB 47 establishes accounting standards for termination benefits.

1. Recognition in Financial Statements Prepared on the Accrual Basis of Accounting

a. Involuntary Plans

(1) A *plan of involuntary termination* is defined as a plan that (a) identifies, at a minimum, the number of employees to be terminated, the job classifications or functions that will be affected and their locations, and when the terminations are expected to occur and (b) establishes the terms of the termination benefits in sufficient detail to enable employees to determine the type and amount of benefits they will receive if they are involuntarily terminated.

(2) Recognize a liability and expense for *involuntary* termination benefits (i.e., severance benefits) when a plan of termination has been approved, communicated to the employees, and the amount can be estimated

(3) If a plan of involuntary termination requires that employees render future service in order to receive benefits, the employer should recognize a liability and expense for the portion of involuntary termination benefits that will be provided after completion of future service ratably over the employees' future service period, beginning when the plan otherwise meets the recognition criteria.

b. **Voluntary Plans** Recognize a liability and expense for voluntary termination benefits (i.e., early-retirement incentives) when the offer is accepted and the amount can be estimated.

2. **Financial Statements Prepared on the Modified Accrual Basis of Accounting** Liabilities and expenditures for termination benefits should be recognized to the extent the liabilities are normally expected to be liquidated with expendable available financial resources

3. Measurement Requirements

a. Healthcare-related termination benefits that are part of a large-scale, age-related program (i.e., early-retirement incentive program affecting a significant portion of employees) should be measured at their discounted present values based on projected total claims costs (or age-adjusted premiums approximating claims costs) for terminated employees, with consideration given to the expected future healthcare cost trend rate.

b. Healthcare-related termination benefits that are not part of a large-scale, age-related termination program are permitted, but not required, to measure cost of termination benefits based on projected claims costs for terminated employees (the cost of termination benefits may be based on unadjusted premiums).

c. The cost of non-healthcare-related termination benefits for which the benefit terms establish an obligation to pay specific amounts on fixed or determinable dates should be measured at the discounted present value of expected future benefit payments (including an assumption regarding changes in future cost levels during the periods covered by the employer's commitment to provide the benefits).

d. If the benefit terms do not establish an obligation to pay specific amounts on fixed or determinable dates, the cost of non-healthcare-related benefits should be calculated as either (a) the discounted present value of expected future benefit payments or (b) the undiscounted total of estimated future benefit payments at current cost levels.

4. Exception for Termination Benefits Affecting Defined Benefit Pension or OPEB Obligations These should be accounted for and reported under the requirements of Statement No. 27 or Statement No. 45, as applicable.

5. Disclosure Requirements

a. Description of the termination benefit arrangement

b. Cost of the termination benefits

c. Significant methods and assumptions used to determine termination benefit liabilities

D. Securities Lending Transactions

Governments lend securities from their investment portfolios to enhance income opportunities. The securities are lent to brokers or financial institutions that need to cover "short" positions until they can purchase the specific securities. GASB 28 establishes standards for income recognition, reporting, and disclosures for securities lending transactions.

1. Balance Sheet The underlying securities loaned are reported as assets. Cash or securities received as collateral, and the obligation to return these assets is also reported on the balance sheet, unless the lender cannot pledge or sell the collateral. Transactions that are secured by letters of credit or securities that cannot be pledged or sold should not be reported as assets and the liabilities to return this collateral are not included in liabilities of the lending government.

2. Income Statement Costs of lending transactions (including borrower rebates, interest costs, or agent fees) are reported as expenditures or expenses, **not** netted against income.

3. Disclosures The notes include general information about the securities, collateral, terms and conditions of the agreements. Notes also describe the source of legal or contractual authorization for the use of securities lending transactions, any violations of legal restrictions, whether maturities of investments match the maturities of loans, and the credit risk associated with these transactions.

E. Public Entity Risk Pools

GASB 30, *Risk Financing Omnibus,* revises the method that public entity risk pools use for calculating a premium deficiency and expands disclosure requirements for reinsurance, gross, ceded, and net premium and claims costs in the 10 year historical tables.

1. Public Entity Risk Pools Capitalization contributions to public entity risk pools with transfer (or pooling) of risk are reported as deposits if it is probable that the contributions will be returned to the entity upon the dissolution of the pool or an approved withdrawal from the pool. Otherwise, they are reported as prepaid insurance. Contributions made without transfer or pooling of risk are reported as a deposit or a reduction of claims liabilities.

2. Entities Other Than Pools These entities must include specific incremental claim adjustment expenses, salvage, and subrogation in the determination of the liability for unpaid claims. Disclosures must reflect whether liabilities related to claims include these claim adjustment expenses.

F. Investments

Recent failures (e.g., Orange County) in the governmental sector related to investment performance raised public awareness of investments. GASB 31 requires revenue recognition for changes in the investments' fair value. Internal and external investment pools are required to report, as assets, the equity position of each fund and component unit of the reporting entity that sponsors the pools.

1. **Applicability** GASB 31 establishes standards for all investments held by external investment pools (EIPs). For most other governmental entities, it establishes fair value standards for investments in participating interest-earning investment contracts, external investment pools, open-end mutual funds, debt securities, and equity securities with readily determinable fair values. GASB 31 does **not** apply to securities that are accounted for under the equity method.

2. **Valuation** Fluctuations due to market changes are presented in the financial statements. Non-participating contracts may be valued using a cost-based measure. Participating interest-earning investment contracts include investments whose value is affected by market (interest rate) changes. They participate chiefly because they are negotiable, transferable, or their redemption value considers market rates. GASB 31 states that fair value is, "the amount at which a financial instrument could be exchanged in a current transaction between willing parties, other than in a forced or liquidation sale." Broader than *market value* (associated only with the price for an actively traded security), *fair value* includes active, inactive, primary, and secondary assessments based on negotiations between sellers and buyers.

   a. Entities other than EIPs may use amortized cost for money market investments with a remaining maturity of one year or less at the time of purchase.

   b. EIPs may report short-term debt investments with a remaining maturity of up to 90 days at the financial statement date at amortized cost, provided that the fair value of those investments is not significantly affected by market factors.

   c. Investments in open-end mutual funds and EIPs are valued using the fund's current share price. If the investments are in external pools that are not SEC registered, fair value is determined by the fair value per share of the pool's underlying portfolio.

   d. EIPs that are 2a7-like pools are permitted to report their investments at amortized cost. (This standard parallels an SEC rule that allows money market mutual funds to use amortized cost to report net assets. The pool must operate in a manner consistent with this SEC rule.)

3. **Reporting** The changes in the fair value of investments is included in revenues, captioned *net increase (decrease) in the fair value of investments.* Separate classification for realized and unrealized gains and losses is optional. EIPs can separately display realized gains and losses in their separate reports. Assets are reported in the funds and component units that hold the equity interests. Accounting for the allocations of income based on legal and contractual provisions can be based on those restrictions. For allocations based on management policies, the fund that holds the investment should report the income and record an operating transfer for the amounts transferred to other funds. Notes to the financial statements include:

   a. The methods and significant assumptions used to estimate the fair value of investments, when that fair value is based on other than quoted market prices.

   b. The policy for determining which investments, if any, are reported at amortized costs.

   c. Allocations, if any, of income from investments associated with one fund that is assigned to another fund.

d. If realized gains and losses are disclosed separately, the notes should also disclose that

(1) The calculation of realized gains and losses is independent of a calculation of the net change in the fair value of investments.

(2) Realized gains and losses on investments that had been held in more than one fiscal year and sold in the current year were included as a change in the fair value of investments reported in the prior year(s) and the current year.

4. **External Investment Pools** EIPs are organized to consolidate investment holdings for multiple governmental units and improve performance with the resulting larger holdings. As such, EIPs are likely to be more sensitive to investment performance fluctuations.

a. An investment trust fund reports the transactions and balances of the EIPs. The investment trust fund reports the external portion of each pool in the financial statements of the sponsoring government, using the accrual basis of accounting. The external portion of the EIP represents the equity interests of legally separate entities that are not part of the sponsoring government. Financial statements for the investment trust fund should include a statement of net assets and a statement of changes in net assets. The difference between EIP assets and liabilities should be captioned *net assets held in trust for pool participants.*

b. Disclosures in the financial statements of an EIP include: (1) a brief description of any regulatory oversight; (2) the frequency and purpose of determining the fair value of investments; (3) the method used to determine participants shares sold and redeemed and whether that method differs from the method used to report investments; (4) whether the pool sponsor has provided or obtained any legally binding guarantees during the period to support the value of shares; (5) the extent of involuntary participation in the pool, if any; (6) summary of the fair value, the carrying amount (if different from fair value), the number of shares or the principal amount, ranges of interest rates, and maturity dates of each major investment classification; and (7) the accounting policy for defining each of the income components, if the investment income is separated into interest, dividend, and other income versus the net increase or decrease in fair value of investments.

c. Disclosures for the sponsoring government are expanded if the pool does not issue separate financial statements. These additional disclosures include

(1) Disclosures required by GASB 31 for separate pool financial statements.

(2) Disclosures required by GASB 3 and GASB 28 should be presented separately for the external portion of each pool.

(3) Condensed statements of net assets and changes in net assets, for each pool. Pools with internal and external investors should present net assets in total and distinguish between internal and external portions of assets held in trust for pool participants.

d. The assets and liabilities arising from reverse repurchase and fixed coupon reverse repurchase agreements should not be netted on the balance sheet. These agreements should be reported as a fund liability and the underlying securities should be reported as investments. Income from repurchase and fixed coupon repurchase agreements should be shown as interest income. The interest cost of reverse repurchase and fixed coupon reverse repurchase agreements should be reported as interest expenditure/expense. The interest cost associated with reverse repurchase or fixed coupon reverse repurchase agreements should not be netted with interest earned on any related investments.

G. Inventory Accounting Methods

Three different means of accounting for inventories are commonly used. Only the consumption method is used in government-wide statements, as the purchases method is not full accrual.

Exhibit 16 ▸ Comparison of Inventory Accounting Methods

	Purchases Method *Periodic System*	Consumption Method *Periodic System*	Consumption Method *Perpetual System*
Reserve for Supply Inventory	Required	Optional	Optional
Interim Purchase	Expenditures 100 Vouchers Payable 100	Expenditures 100 Vouchers Payable 100	Supply Inventory 100 Vouchers Payable 100
Interim Issue/Use	No entry	No entry	Expenditures 80 Supply Inventory 80
Year-end (inventory increase)	Supply Inventory 20 OFS-Inventory Increase 20 Unreserved FB 20 Reserve for Supplies Inv. 20	Supply Inventory 20 Expenditures 20	No entry— unless there is an overage (decrease expenditures and increase inventory)
Year-end (inventory decrease)	OFS-Inventory Increase 15 Supply Inventory 15 Reserve for Supplies Inv. 15 Unreserved FB 15	Expenditures 15 Supply Inventory 15	No entry— unless there is a shortage (increase expenditures and decrease inventory)

H. Service Efforts & Accomplishments (SEA)

Financial reporting under both the old and new governmental reporting models is limited in scope. Currently, reporting SEA information is optional, but is under discussion by standard-setting bodies.

1. **Sample Measures** Proposed measures for elementary and secondary education include the following indicators. The number of student days indicates a general measure of workload. The number of students promoted or graduated indicates the degree to which educational requirements are fulfilled. The absenteeism and dropout rates indicate the degree of student participation and interest. The percentage of graduates employed or in college indicates the suitability of preparation for these pursuits.

2. **Difficulties** Implementation of mandatory SEA reporting is hindered by several challenges. Few performance indicators are readily or accurately measurable. By selecting readily measured indicators, there may be poor association of reported performance measures with goals. Actions that do not improve substantive value, but result in favorable measurements, manipulate SEA performance numbers. Because several indicators may be necessary for a well-rounded measurement of a single activity, there is a risk of information overload. Finally, apparently similar programs may have considerable substantive differences, compounding the difficulties of comparison among entities, or even different divisions of the same entity.

I. Component Unit Determination

GASB 39, *Determining Whether Certain Organizations Are Component Units—an Amendment of GASB Statement No. 14,* provides additional guidance to determine whether certain entities for which a primary government is not accountable financially must be reported as component units based on the nature and significance of their relationship with the primary government. Generally, it requires reporting, as a component unit, an entity that raises and holds economic resources for the direct benefit of a government.

1. **Criteria** Legally separate, tax-exempt entities that meet **all** three criteria must be presented discretely as component units.

a. **Direct Benefit** Economic resources received or held by the separate entity are totally—or nearly totally—for the direct benefit of the primary government, its component units, or its constituents.

b. **Majority** The primary government, or its component units, is entitled to—or has the ability to otherwise access—a majority of the economic resources received or held by the separate entity.

c. **Significance** The economic resources received or held by an individual entity that the specific primary government, or its component units, is entitled to, or has the ability to otherwise access, are significant to that primary government.

2. **Professional Judgment** GASB 14 continues to require the application of professional judgment in determining whether the relationship between a primary government and other organizations for which the primary government is not financially accountable and that do not meet these criteria is such that exclusion of the organization would render the financial statements of the reporting entity misleading or incomplete.

V. Appendix: Account Groups

A. Former Reporting Model

The focus of the former reporting model was on individual funds and fund types. The governmental funds and account groups, taken together, accounted for the general government. The two account groups were memorandum list and offset accounts that provided a record of general government fixed assets and long-term debt, as these were not recorded in the governmental funds. Both account groups used the modified accrual basis of accounting and didn't have any operating accounts. Depreciating fixed assets and reporting infrastructure were both optional and uncommon. If optional accumulated depreciation was reported, the corresponding debit reduced the related Investment in General Fixed Asset account, not an expenditure or expense account.

B. GASB 34 Reporting Model

The GASB 34 reporting model does not require the use of account groups to report capital assets or long-term debt of governmental funds. Though no longer used for external reporting, as a practical matter, entities may first account for assets and long-term debt within the account groups and then adjust the financial statements according to GASB No. 34.

Research Skills

Expect all simulations on the CPA Exam to include a research element. This type of element probably will be about 2% of the point value for an Exam section with simulations. (Initially, the BEC Exam section will not have simulations.)

If you can search the Internet using Boolean logic and the advanced search features of an Internet search engine such as www.google.com, you probably already have sufficient skills to earn the points related to the research elements of simulations on the CPA Exam. This is not to indicate that answers to the research elements of the simulations can be found on the internet; they cannot.

The AICPA has made a free six months subscription to the Financial Accounting Research System (FARS) database available to candidates who have received their notice to schedule (NTS). This subscription is accessible through the CPA Exam website (www.cpa-exam.org). We recommend that when you have access to the databases, you should continue to do searches until you feel comfortable using the database tool. This will alleviate the undue stress of facing an unknown program when you enter the test site.

The research element of the simulation requires a candidate to narrow the search down to a paragraph reference. The candidate doesn't provide commentary or conclusions. Be sure to follow directions for your particular Exam section as different sections of the Exam require responses in different formats. In some cases, the entire paragraph should be pasted into the response form, in others, only the paragraph reference is required. Candidates cannot avoid the research merely by answering the question; they must provide the reference to the authoritative literature that answers the question. The search can be made by using the table of contents feature or the search engine and Boolean operators.

A search using "accounting OR auditing" will find all documents containing either the word "accounting" or the word "auditing." All other things being equal, a search using OR typically will find the most documents. OR typically is used to search for terms that are used as synonyms, such as "management" and "client." As more terms are combined in an OR search, more documents are included in the results.

A search using "accounting AND auditing" will find all documents containing both the word "accounting" and the word "auditing." All other things being equal, a search using AND typically will find fewer documents than a search using OR, but more than a search using NOT. As more terms are combined in an AND search, fewer documents are included in the results.

A search using "accounting NOT auditing" will find all documents containing the word "accounting" except those that also contain the word "auditing." All other things being equal, a search using NOT typically will find the fewest documents. As more terms are combined in a NOT search, fewer documents are included in the results.

Boolean operators can be combined to refine searches. For example, the following parameters would find information on letters to a client's attorney inquiring about litigation, claims, and assessments: (attorney OR lawyer) AND (letter OR inquiry).

If you get too many or too few results from a search, refine your search parameters until you find what you need. The exam doesn't limit candidates from repeating searches with refined parameters.

Candidates should visit the AICPA's website (www.cpa-exam.org) and practice the free tutorial and sample exams presented there. For more information about simulations, also see the **Practical Advice** section of this volume.

CHAPTER 18—GOVERNMENTAL OVERVIEW

Problem 18-1 MULTIPLE CHOICE QUESTIONS (100 to 125 minutes)

1. Which of the following lead(s) to the use of fund accounting by a governmental organization?

	Financial control	*Legal restrictions*
a.	Yes	Yes
b.	Yes	No
c.	No	No
d.	No	Yes

(R/00, AR, #1, 6906)

2. A city taxes merchants for various central district improvements. Which of the following accounting methods assist(s) in assuring that these revenues are expended legally?

	Fund accounting	*Budgetary accounting*
a.	Yes	No
b.	No	Yes
c.	No	No
d.	Yes	Yes

(R/03, FAR, #7, 7609)

3. The primary authoritative body for determining the measurement focus and basis of accounting standards for governmental fund operating statements is the

a. Governmental Accounting Standards Board (GASB)
b. Financial Accounting Standards Board (FASB)
c. Government Accounting and Auditing Committee of the AICPA (GAAC)
d. National Council on Governmental Accounting (NCGA) (5/91, Theory, #51, amended, 2095)

4. What is the basic criterion used to determine the reporting entity for a governmental unit?

a. Special financing arrangement
b. Geographic boundaries
c. Scope of public services
d. Financial accountability (11/95, AR, #62, 5805)

5. Governmental financial reporting should provide information to assist users in which situation(s)?

I. Making social and political decisions.
II. Assessing whether current-year citizens received services but shifted part of the payment burden to future-year citizens.

a. I only
b. II only
c. Both I and II
d. Neither I nor II (5/95, AR, #52, 5470)

6. Which of the following statements is correct regarding comparability of governmental financial reports?

a. Comparability is **not** relevant in governmental financial reporting.
b. Similarly designated governments perform the same functions.
c. Selection of different alternatives in accounting procedures or practices account for the differences between financial reports.
d. Differences between financial reports should be due to substantive differences in underlying transactions or the governmental structure.

(11/94, AR, #2, 4979)

7. Which event(s) is(are) supportive of interperiod equity as a financial reporting objective of a governmental unit?

I. A balanced budget is adopted.
II. Residual equity transfers out equals residual equity transfers in.

a. I only
b. II only
c. Both I and II
d. Neither I nor II (11/95, AR, #59, 5802)

8. An unrestricted grant received from another government to support enterprise fund operations should be reported as

a. Contributed capital
b. Nonoperating revenues
c. Operating revenues
d. Revenues and expenditures

(R/03, FAR, #6, 7608)

9. Dayne County's general fund had the following disbursements during the year.

Payment of principal on long-term debt	$100,000
Payments to vendors	500,000
Purchase of a computer	300,000

What amount should Dayne County report as expenditures in its governmental funds statement of revenues, expenditures, and changes in fund balances?

a. $300,000
b. $500,000
c. $800,000
d. $900,000 (R/05, FAR, 1043G, #22, 7766)

10. Interperiod equity is an objective of financial reporting for governmental entities. According to the Governmental Accounting Standards Board, is interperiod equity fundamental to public administration and is it a component of accountability?

	Fundamental to public administration	*Component of accountability*
a.	Yes	No
b.	No	No
c.	No	Yes
d.	Yes	Yes

(11/92, Theory, #51, 3484)

11. Which of the following fund types used by a government most likely would have a Fund Balance Reserved for Inventory of Supplies?
a. General
b. Internal service
c. Nonexpendable trust
d. Capital projects (11/90, Theory, #52, 2105)

12. The measurement focus of governmental-type funds is on the determination of

	Flow of financial resources	*Financial position*
a.	Yes	No
b.	No	Yes
c.	No	No
d.	Yes	Yes

(5/96, AR, #4, 6201)

13. The modified accrual basis of accounting should be used for which of the following funds?
a. Capital projects fund
b. Enterprise fund
c. Pension trust fund
d. Proprietary fund (5/93, PII, #22, 4130)

14. Financial statements for which fund type generally report net assets?
a. Capital projects
b. Expendable pension trust
c. Special revenue
d. Enterprise (11/95, AR, #69, amended, 5812)

15. Which of the following fund types of a governmental unit has(have) income determination as a measurement focus?

	General funds	*Capital project funds*
a.	Yes	Yes
b.	Yes	No
c.	No	No
d.	No	Yes

(11/95, AR, #57, amended, 5800)

16. Lys City reports a compensated absences liability in its combined balance sheet. The salary rate used to calculate the liability should normally be the rate in effect
a. When the unpaid compensated absences were earned
b. When the compensated absences were earned or are to be paid, or at the balance sheet date, whichever results in the lowest amount
c. At the balance sheet date
d. When the compensated absences are to be paid (11/95, AR, #70, amended, 5813)

17. In governmental accounting, a fund is

I. The basic accounting unit
II. Used to assist in ensuring fiscal compliance

a. I only
b. II only
c. Both I and II
d. Neither I nor II (R/03, FAR, #8, 7610)

18. Sig City used the following funds for financial reporting purposes:

General fund	Capital projects fund
Internal service fund	Special revenue fund
Airport enterprise fund	Debt service fund
Pension trust fund	

How many of Sig's funds use the accrual basis of accounting?
a. Two
b. Three
c. Four
d. Five (R/05, FAR, 0693G, #12, 7756)

19. The statement of activities of the government-wide financial statements is designed primarily to provide information to assess which of the following?
a. Operational accountability
b. Financial accountability
c. Fiscal accountability
d. Functional accountability (R/02, AR, #9, 7074)

20. South City School District has a separate elected governing body that administers the public school system. The district's budget is subject to the approval of the city council. The district's financial activity should be reported in the City's financial statements by
a. Blending only
b. Discrete presentation
c. Inclusion as a footnote only
d. Either blending or inclusion as a footnote (11/97, AR, #13, 6541)

21. Marta City's school district is a legally separate entity but two of its seven board members are also city council members and the district is financially dependent on the city. The school district should be reported as a

a. Blended unit
b. Discrete presentation
c. Note disclosure
d. Primary government (11/97, AR, #14, 6542)

22. The statement of activities of the government-wide financial statements is designed primarily to provide information to assess which of the following?

a. Operational accountability
b. Financial accountability
c. Fiscal accountability
d. Functional accountability (R/01, AR, #8, 6993)

23. GASB Statement No. 34, *Basic Financial Statements—and Management's Discussion and Analysis—for State and Local Governments,* requires governments to include which of the following in management's discussion and analysis (MD&A)?

a. Analysis of significant budget variances
b. Comparisons of current year to prior year, based on government-wide information
c. Currently known facts, decisions, or conditions that are expected to have a significant effect on financial position or results of operations
d. All of the above (Editors, 6894)

24. Nox City reported a $25,000 net increase in the fund balances for total governmental funds. Nox also reported an increase in net assets for the following funds:

Motor pool internal service fund	$ 9,000
Water enterprise fund	12,000
Employee pension fund	7,000

The motor pool internal service fund provides service to the general fund departments. What amount should Nox report as the change in net assets for governmental activities?

a. $25,000
b. $34,000
c. $41,000
d. $46,000 (R/02, AR, #7, 7072)

25. Chase City uses an internal service fund for its central motor pool. The assets and liabilities account balances for this fund that are not eliminated normally should be reported in the government-wide statement of net assets as

a. Governmental activities
b. Business-type activities
c. Fiduciary activities
d. Note disclosures only (R/01, AR, #3, 6988)

26. Tree City reported a $1,500 net increase in fund balance for governmental funds. During the year, Tree purchased general capital assets of $9,000 and recorded depreciation expense of $3,000. What amount should Tree report as the change in net assets for governmental activities?

a. ($ 4,500)
b. $ 1,500
c. $ 7,500
d. $10,500 (R/02, AR, #3, 7068)

27. The portion of special assessment debt maturing in 5 years, to be repaid from general resources of the government, should be reported in the

a. General fund column
b. Governmental activities column
c. Agency fund column
d. Capital projects fund column (11/94, AR, #13, amended, 4990)

28. Berry Township has adopted GASB Statement No. 34, *Basic Financial Statements—and Management's Discussion and Analysis—for State and Local Governments.* Berry's eligible infrastructure assets are exempt from depreciation if the modified approach is used. Which of the following are requirements of the modified approach?

I. The entity performs condition assessments of eligible assets and summarizes the results using a measurement scale.
II. The entity annually estimates the amount to preserve the eligible assets at an established and disclosed condition level.
III. The entity assesses asset conditions in comparison to condition levels established by the National Association of Public Works Engineers or a comparable organization.

a. I
b. I and II
c. I and III
d. I, II, and III (Editors, 6888)

29. Palm City acquired, through forfeiture as a result of nonpayment of property taxes, a parcel of land that the city intends to use as a parking lot for general governmental purposes. The total amount of taxes, liens, and other costs incurred by Palm incidental to acquiring ownership and perfecting title was $20,000. The land's fair market value at the forfeiture date was $60,000. What amount should be reported in the governmental activities column of the government-wide financial statements for this land?

a. $0
b. $20,000
c. $60,000
d. $80,000 (11/93, PII, #15, amended, 4444)

30. The following are Boa City's long-term assets:

Fixed assets used in enterprise fund activities	$1,000,000
Infrastructure assets	9,000,000
All other general fixed assets	1,800,000

What aggregate amount should Boa report in the governmental activities column of the government-wide financial statements?
a. $ 9,000,000
b. $10,000,000
c. $10,800,000
d. $11,800,000 (5/92, PII, #33, amended, 2665)

31. Kingwood Town paid $22,000 cash for a flat-bed trailer to be used in the general operations of the town. The expected useful life of the trailer is 6 years with an estimated $7,000 salvage value. Which of the following amounts would be reported?
a. $15,000 increase in equipment in the general fund
b. $15,000 increase in the governmental activities column for fixed assets
c. $22,000 increase in the governmental activities column for fixed assets
d. $22,000 increase in equipment in the general fund (R/99, AR, #16, amended, 6805)

32. Where does GASB Statement No. 34, *Basic Financial Statements—and Management's Discussion and Analysis—for State and Local Governments,* require fund financial statements for major funds to be presented?
a. Before the notes to the financial statements
b. In the notes to the financial statements
c. After the notes to the financial statements, before other required supplementary information
d. After the notes to the financial statements and required supplementary information (RSI) (Editors, 6872)

33. For which of the following governmental entities that use proprietary fund accounting should a statement of cash flows be presented?

	Public benefit corporations	*Governmental utilities*
a.	No	No
b.	No	Yes
c.	Yes	Yes
d.	Yes	No

(5/94, AR, #52, 4657)

34. With regard to the statement of cash flows for a governmental unit's enterprise fund, items generally presented as cash equivalents are?

	2-month treasury bills	*3-month certificates of deposit*
a.	No	No
b.	No	Yes
c.	Yes	Yes
d.	Yes	No

(11/93, Theory, #58, 4563)

35. Hill City's water utility fund held the following investments in U.S. Treasury securities at June 30, year 5:

Investment	Date purchased	Maturity date	Carrying amount
3-month T-bill	5/31, Yr 5	7/31, Yr 5	$ 30,000
3-year T-note	6/15, Yr 5	8/31, Yr 5	50,000
5-year T-note	10/1, Yr 1	9/30, Yr 6	100,000

In the fund's balance sheet, what amount of these investments should be reported as cash and cash equivalents at June 30, year 5?
a. $0
b. $ 30,000
c. $ 80,000
d. $180,000 (11/93, PII, #19, amended, 4448)

36. Dogwood City's water enterprise fund received interest of $10,000 on long-term investments. How should this amount be reported on the Statement of Cash Flows?
a. Operating activities
b. Non-capital financing activities
c. Capital and related financing activities
d. Investing activities (R/01, AR, #5, 6990)

37. GASB Statement No. 34, *Basic Financial Statements—and Management's Discussion and Analysis—for State and Local Governments,* requires presentation of a budgetary comparison schedule in required supplementary information. Which of the following must this schedule include?

I. Actual inflows, outflows, and balances, stated on the basis in the government's budget, with a reconciliation between the budgetary and GAAP information
II. Original budget
III. A separate column to report the variances between the final budget and actual amounts

a. I only
b. I and II only
c. I and III only
d. I, II, and III (Editors, 6895)

38. According to GASB 34, *Basic Financial Statements and Management's Discussion and Analysis for State and Local Governments,* certain budgetary schedules are required supplementary information. What is the minimum budgetary information required to be reported in those schedules?

a. A schedule of unfavorable variances at the functional level
b. A schedule showing the final appropriations budget and actual expenditures on a budgetary basis
c. A schedule showing the original budget, the final appropriations budget, and actual inflows, outflows, and balances on a budgetary basis
d. A schedule showing the proposed budget, the approved budget, the final amended budget, actual inflows and outflows on a budgetary basis, and variances between budget and actual

(R/02, AR, #10, 7075)

39. Vale City adopts a cash budget under GASB Statement No. 34, *Basic Financial Statements—and Management's Discussion and Analysis—for State and Local Governments.* What basis should be used in Vale's budgetary comparison schedule?

a. Accrual
b. Cash
c. Modified accrual
d. Cash or modified accrual (Editors, 6893)

40. In which situation(s) should property taxes due to a governmental unit be recorded as deferred revenue?

I. Property taxes receivable are recognized in advance of the year for which they are levied.
II. Property taxes receivable are collected in advance of the year in which they are levied.

a. I only
b. Both I and II
c. II only
d. Neither I nor II (11/94, AR, #17, 4994)

41. Chase City imposes a 2% tax on hotel charges. Revenues from this tax will be used to promote tourism in the city. Chase should record this tax as what type of nonexchange transaction?

a. Derived tax revenue
b. Imposed nonexchange revenue
c. Government-mandated transaction
d. Voluntary nonexchange transaction

(R/02, AR, #4, 7069)

42. The following information pertains to property taxes levied by Oak City for the calendar year 1:

Collections during year 1	$500,000
Expected collections during the first 60 days of year 2	100,000
Expected collections during the balance of year 2	60,000
Expected collections during January of year 3	30,000
Estimated to be uncollectible	10,000
Total levy	$700,000

What amount should Oak report for year 1 net property tax revenues?

a. $700,000
b. $690,000
c. $600,000
d. $500,000 (11/93, PII, #10, amended, 4439)

43. Property taxes and fines represent which of the following classes of nonexchange transactions for governmental units?

a. Derived tax revenues
b. Imposed nonexchange revenues
c. Government-mandated nonexchange transactions
d. Voluntary nonexchange transactions

(R/01, AR, #4, 6989)

44. When a capital lease of a governmental unit represents the acquisition of a general fixed asset, the acquisition should be reflected as

a. An expenditure but **not** as an other financing source
b. An other financing source but **not** as an expenditure
c. Both an expenditure and an other financing source
d. Neither an expenditure nor an other financing source (11/94, AR, #10, 4987)

45. Cy City's Municipal Solid Waste Landfill Enterprise Fund was established when a new landfill was opened May 3, year 1. The landfill is expected to close December 31, year 20. Cy's year 1 expenses would include a portion of which of the year 21 expected disbursements?

I. Cost of a final cover to be applied to the landfill
II. Cost of equipment to be installed to monitor methane gas buildup

a. I only
b. II only
c. Both I and II
d. Neither I nor II (5/95, AR, #55, amended, 5473)

46. Polk County's solid waste landfill operation is accounted for in a governmental fund. Polk used available cash to purchase equipment that is included in the estimated current cost of closure and post-closure care of this operation. How would this purchase affect the long-term asset and the long-term liability amounts in Polk's general fund?

	Asset amount	Liability amount
a.	Increase	Decrease
b.	Increase	No effect
c.	No effect	Decrease
d.	No effect	No effect

(11/95, AR, #68, amended, 5811)

47. Which of the following statements meet the measurement and recognition criteria for landfill closure and postclosure costs?
a. Landfills should only be accounted for in the general fund.
b. Total landfill liabilities should be recognized in the general long-term debt account group.
c. Expense recognition should begin when waste is accepted and should continue through the post-closure period.
d. Equipment and facilities included in estimated total current cost of closure and postclosure care should not be reported as capital assets.
(R/99, AR, #19, 6808)

48. River City has a defined contribution pension plan. How should River report the pension plan in its financial statements?
a. Amortize any transition asset over the estimated number of years of current employees' service.
b. Disclose in the notes to the financial statements the amount of the pension benefit obligation and the net assets available for benefits.
c. Identify in the notes to financial statements the types of employees covered and the employer's and employees' obligations to contribute to the fund.
d. Accrue a liability for benefits earned but **not** paid to fund participants. (11/92, Theory, #58, 3491)

49. Which of the following statements is correct concerning disclosure of reverse repurchase and fixed coupon reverse repurchase agreements?
a. Related assets and liabilities should be netted.
b. Related interest cost and interest earned should be netted.
c. Credit risk related to the agreements need **not** be disclosed.
d. Underlying securities owned should be reported as "Investments." (11/94, AR, #6, 4983)

50. Which of the following characteristics of service efforts and accomplishments is the most difficult to report for a governmental entity?
a. Comparability
b. Timeliness
c. Consistency
d. Relevance (R/99, AR, #20, 6809)

Problem 18-2 ADDITIONAL MULTIPLE CHOICE QUESTIONS (42 to 53 minutes)

51. Under the modified accrual basis of accounting for a governmental unit, revenues should be recognized in the accounting period in which they
a. Are collected
b. Are earned and become measurable
c. Become available and measurable
d. Become available and earned (Editors, 2128)

52. Allen Town has adopted GASB Statement No. 34, *Basic Financial Statements—and Management's Discussion and Analysis—for State and Local Governments*. For which of the following funds does Allen use the modified accrual basis of accounting in the fund financial statements?
a. Capital projects fund
b. Enterprise fund
c. Investment trust fund
d. Pension trust fund (Editors, 6884)

53. Fund accounting is used by governmental units with resources that must be
a. Composed of cash or cash equivalents
b. Incorporated into combined or combining financial statements
c. Segregated for the purpose of carrying on specific activities or attaining certain objectives
d. Segregated physically according to various objectives (11/95, AR, #60, 5803)

54. According to GASB Statement No. 34, *Basic Financial Statements—and Management's Discussion and Analysis—for State and Local Governments,* what is the paramount objective of governmental financial reporting?
a. Accountability
b. Consistency
c. Understandability
d. Usefulness (Editors, 6871)

55. The basic financial statements of a state government that has adopted GASB Statement No. 34, *Basic Financial Statements—and Management's Discussion and Analysis—for State and Local Governments*

a. Are comprised of the government-wide financial statements and related notes
b. Are comprised of the primary government funds' financial statements and related notes
c. Contain more detailed information regarding the state government's finances than is contained in the comprehensive annual financial report
d. Do not include management's discussion and analysis (MD&A) (Editors, 6879)

56. Arbor City has adopted GASB Statement No. 34, *Basic Financial Statements—and Management's Discussion and Analysis—for State and Local Governments.* What basis of accounting does Arbor use to present the general fund in the financial statements?

I. Modified accrual basis in all financial statements
II. Accrual basis in the government-wide statement of activities and statement of net assets
III. Modified accrual basis in the fund financial statements with a reconciliation to the accrual basis

a. I only
b. II only
c. III only
d. Both II and III (Editors, 6877)

57. Which of the following is required by GASB No. 34, *Basic Financial Statements—and Management's Discussion and Analysis—for State and Local Governments?*

I. Governmental activities information using the economic resources measurement focus in the government-wide financial statements
II. Governmental fund information included in the statement of cash flows

a. I only
b. II only
c. Both I and II
d. Neither I nor II (Editors, 6816)

58. River City has adopted GASB Statement No.34, *Basic Financial Statements—and Management's Discussion and Analysis—for State and Local Governments.* River has a defined contribution pension plan. How should River report the pension plan in its financial statements?

a. Within the component units column of its government-wide financial statements
b. Within the fiduciary column of its government-wide financial statements
c. Within its fund financial statements
d. Within the governmental activities column of its government-wide financial statements

(Editors, 6876)

59. Where does GASB Statement No. 34, *Basic Financial Statements—and Management's Discussion and Analysis—for State and Local Governments,* require management's discussion and analysis (MD&A) to be presented?

a. Before the financial statements
b. Before the notes to the financial statements, but after the financial statements
c. In the notes to the financial statements
d. After the notes to the financial statements, before other required supplementary information

(Editors, 6873)

60. Dale Town has adopted GASB Statement No. 34, *Basic Financial Statements—and Management's Discussion and Analysis—for State and Local Governments.* Dale's public school system is administered by a separately elected board of education. The board of education is not organized as a separate legal entity and does not have the power to levy taxes or issue bonds. Dale's town council approves the school system's budget. Where should Dale report the public school system in its government-wide information?

a. Within the component units column
b. Within the governmental activities column
c. In the notes to the financial statements
d. In the required supplementary information

(Editors, 6875)

61. Which total columns does GASB Statement No. 34, *Basic Financial Statements—and Management's Discussion and Analysis—for State and Local Governments,* require governments to include in the government-wide financial statements?

	Primary government	Entity as a whole
a.	Yes	Yes
b.	Yes	No
c.	No	Yes
d.	No	No

(Editors, 6874)

62. Zebra Town has adopted GASB Statement No. 34, *Basic Financial Statements—and Management's Discussion and Analysis—for State and Local Governments.* Which of the following funds will Zebra rarely report within in the same activity column as the general fund in the government-wide financial statements?

a. Debt service fund
b. Enterprise fund
c. Internal service fund
d. Permanent fund (Editors, 6885)

63. Does GASB Statement No. 34, *Basic Financial Statements—and Management's Discussion and Analysis—for State and Local Governments,* allow estimates of general infrastructure assets historical cost based on current replacement cost for assets existing upon adoption of the Statement and does it allow the use of composite methods to calculate depreciation expense?

	Estimates	Composite depreciation
a.	Yes	Yes
b.	Yes	No
c.	No	Yes
d.	No	No

(Editors, 6891)

64. Kellick City has adopted GASB Statement No. 34, *Basic Financial Statements—and Management's Discussion and Analysis—for State and Local Governments.* It is inappropriate to record depreciation expense in the government-wide financial statements related to the assets in which of Kellick's funds?

a. Agency fund
b. Enterprise fund
c. General fund
d. Special revenue fund (Editors, 6881)

65. GASB Statement No. 34, *Basic Financial Statements—and Management's Discussion and Analysis—for State and Local Governments,* does **not** require depreciation of which of the following assets purchased after June 30, 1980?

I. Land and land improvements
II. Historical treasures and works of art that meet the conditions of an inexhaustible collection
III. Infrastructure assets that are part of a network or subsystem of a network, when the modified approach is used

a. I only
b. I and II only
c. I and III only
d. I, II, and III (Editors, 6889)

66. Farmer Township has adopted all provisions of GASB Statement No. 34, *Basic Financial Statements—and Management's Discussion and Analysis—for State and Local Governments.* In which financial statements does Farmer present its general-use capital assets?

	Fund	Government-wide
a.	Yes	Yes
b.	Yes	No
c.	No	Yes
d.	No	No

(Editors, 6890)

67. GASB Statement No. 34, *Basic Financial Statements—and Management's Discussion and Analysis—for State and Local Governments,* requires large governments (annual revenues in the range above $100 million) to

I. Report all fixed assets (land, buildings, and equipment).
II. In fiscal periods beginning after June 15, 2001, report all major general infrastructure asset acquisitions.
III. In fiscal periods beginning after June 15, 2005, retroactively report all major general infrastructure assets acquired in fiscal years ending after June 30, 1980, and before adoption of GASB Statement No. 34.

a. I only
b. I and II only
c. I and III only
d. I, II, and III (Editors, 6886)

68. GASB Statement No. 34, Basic Financial Statements—and Management's Discussion and Analysis—for State and Local Governments, requires small governments (revenues of less than $10 million) to

a. Report and depreciate all buildings, and equipment, except for infrastructure assets.
b. Report and depreciate all buildings, and equipment, and report all major general infrastructure assets.
c. Report and depreciate all buildings, equipment, and major general infrastructure assets.
d. Report and depreciate all buildings and equipment as well as all major general infrastructure assets acquired in fiscal periods beginning after June 15, 2003. (Editors, 6887)

69. Baker Town has adopted GASB Statement No. 34, *Basic Financial Statements—and Management's Discussion and Analysis—for State and Local Governments.* Baker accounts for construction of assets for general use in a single capital projects fund. Which event(s) should Baker include in a statement of cash flows?

I. Cash inflow from issuing bonds to finance city hall construction.
II. Cash outflow from a city utility representing payments in lieu of property taxes.

a. I only
b. II only
c. Both I and II
d. Neither I nor II (Editors, 6880)

70. Zephyr City has adopted GASB Statement No. 34, *Basic Financial Statements—and Management's Discussion and Analysis—for State and Local Governments.* Which activities and basis of accounting must appear in Zephyr's statement(s) of cash flows?

I. Business-type activities in the fund financial statements
II. Government-type activities in the fund financial statements
III. Business-type and government-type activities in the government-wide financial statements

a. I only
b. II only
c. III only
d. I and III only (Editors, 6878)

71. Property taxes levied in fiscal year 1 to finance the general fund budget of fiscal year 2 should be reported as general fund revenues in fiscal year 2
a. Regardless of the fiscal year in which collected
b. For the amount collected before the end of fiscal year 2 or shortly thereafter
c. For the amount collected before the end of fiscal year 2 only
d. For the amount collected in fiscal year 1 only (5/92, Theory, #58, amended, 2751)

Solution 18-1 MULTIPLE CHOICE ANSWERS

Governmental Environment

1. (a) In the absence of a profit motive, a net income bottom line, or other uniform object performance indicators, governments use fund accounting to demonstrate compliance with restrictions and controls.

2. (d) In the absence of a profit motive, a net income bottom line, or other performance indicators, governments are subjected to a variety of restrictions and controls. The most important are overall restrictions on the use of resources (which leads to fund accounting) and exercise of expenditure control through the annual budget (which leads to budgetary accounting)

Financial Reporting

3. (a) The GASB sets accounting and financial reporting standards for state and local governments. The FASB sets standards for financial reports published by business and nonprofit enterprises.

4. (d) GASB Codification §2100.108 focuses on the ability of a governmental unit to exercise oversight responsibility over an entity when considering that entity's inclusion in a governmental unit. Oversight responsibility includes "financial inter-dependency, selection of governing authority, designation of management, ability to significantly influence operations, [and] *accountability for fiscal matters.*"

5. (c) GASB §100.132 states that governmental financial reporting is used in making social and political decisions. Section 100.161 states that because interperiod equity is important, financial reporting should help users assess whether current-year revenues are sufficient to provide current services or whether future taxpayers are assuming the burden of previously provided services.

6. (d) According to GASB No. 1, financial reports should be comparable, which implies that differences between financial reports should be due to substance (actual events) rather than form (accounting policies).

7. (a) Interperiod equity is the idea of using the revenues from one period to pay for the expenditures of that same period and that period only. A balanced budget is a plan for this occurrence. Residual equity transfers are between funds, not between periods.

8. (b) Interest income, interest expense, gain or loss on sales of capital assets, grants to or from

other governments, operating transfers to or from other funds, and residual equity transfers are examples of transactions that are reported as nonoperating revenue.

9. (d) Expenditures differ from expenses (as defined in commercial accounting) because expenditures include—in addition to current operating expenditures that benefit the current period—capital outlays for general fixed assets and repayment of general long-term debt principal.

Payments of principal on long-term debt	$100,000
Payments to vendors	500,000
Purchase of a computer	300,000
Total expenditures	$900,000

10. (d) The GASB believes that interperiod equity is a significant component of accountability and is fundamental to public administration. It therefore needs to be considered when establishing financial reporting objectives. In short, financial reporting should help users assess whether current-year revenues are sufficient to pay for services provided that year and whether future taxpayers will be required to assume burdens for services previously provided (Cod. 100.161).

Funds & Fund Accounting

11. (a) The *Fund Balance Reserved for Inventory of Supplies* account is an equity balance indicating the presence of fund assets that are not available for expenditure. The account would most likely appear in the general fund because the general fund would be more likely to have a significant amount of supplies on hand at the end of the year and it reports a fund balance. Internal service and nonexpendable trust funds report retained earnings rather than fund balance. Capital projects funds report a fund balance, but it is not likely that they would have significant amounts of supplies on hand at year-end. FYI: Nonexpendable trust funds are used under the pre-GASB 34 reporting model.

12. (d) GASB §1300.102 states, "The governmental fund measurement focus is on determination of financial position and changes in financial position..., rather than on net income determination." GASB §C60.108 states, "In governmental funds, the primary emphasis is on the flow of financial resources...."

13. (a) The modified accrual basis of accounting for a governmental unit recognizes revenues in the period in which they become available and measurable. The modified accrual basis is the appropriate basis of accounting for governmental-type funds. Proprietary and fiduciary funds use the accrual basis of accounting. The accrual basis of accounting recognizes revenues in the period in which they become earned and measurable.

14. (d) Enterprise funds generally report net assets. Capital projects and special revenue funds are governmental-type funds, and thus report a fund balance. Expendable trust funds (under the outgoing reporting model) use fund balance accounts also.

15. (c) The general and capital project funds are governmental-type funds. All governmental-type funds have the fund flow measurement focus. GASB Codification §1300.102 places the measurement focus of both these funds on "determination of financial position and changes in financial position, rather than on net income determination."

16. (c) GASB Codification §C60.107 states, "Liabilities for compensated absences should be inventoried at the end of each accounting period and adjusted to current salary costs."

17. (c) A specific governmental unit is not accounted for through a single accounting entity. Instead, the accounts of a government are divided into several funds. A fund is a fiscal and accounting entity with a self-balancing set of accounts recording cash and other financial resources, together with all related liabilities and residual equities and balances, and changes therein, that are segregated for the purpose of carrying on specific activities or attaining certain objectives in accordance with special regulations, restrictions, or limitations.

18. (b) The three funds using the accrual basis of accounting are the (1) internal service fund, (2) airport enterprise fund, and (3) pension trust fund (fiduciary fund). The modified accrual basis of accounting is used by the general fund, capital projects fund, special revenue fund, and debt service fund.

Financial Statement Overview

19 (a) Operational accountability is important to assess the government's ability to provide services. GASB 34 states that operational accountability "includes the periodic economic cost of the services provided. It also informs users about whether the government is raising sufficient revenues each period to cover that cost, or whether the government is deferring costs to the future or using up accumulated resources to provide current-period services." The government-wide statements (GWS) are designed to provide an economic long-term view of the

government that cannot be seen with the presentation of a collection of funds.

20. (b) According to GASB No. 14, component units should be presented discretely unless either (a) the components unit's governing body is substantively the same as the governing body of the primary government, or (b) the component unit provides services almost entirely to the primary government, or almost exclusively benefits the primary government although it does not provide services directly to it.

21. (b) According to GASB No. 14, component units should be presented discretely unless either (a) the components unit's governing body is substantively the same as the governing body of the primary government, or (b) the component unit provides services almost entirely to the primary government, or almost exclusively benefits the primary government although it does not provide services directly to it.

22. (a) The government-wide statements, which include the statement of activities, are designed to provide operational accountability by showing an economic long-term view of a government's ability to provide services. Operational accountability includes the periodic economic cost of the services provided.

MD&A

23. (d) In the MD&A, GASB 34 requires comparisons of current to prior year results, based on government-wide information; a brief discussion of the basic financial statements, an analysis of the government's overall financial position and results of operations to assist users in assessing whether financial position has improved or deteriorated as a result of annual operations; an analysis of balances and transactions of individual funds; significant variances between original and final budget amounts, and between final budget and actual results; a description of significant capital asset and long-term debt activity; and currently known facts, decisions, or conditions that are expected to have a significant effect on financial position or results of operations. Governments that use the modified approach to report infrastructure assets must also discuss significant changes in the assessed condition of infrastructure assets from previous assessments; how the current condition compares with the established condition level; and any significant differences from the estimated annual amount to maintain or preserve infrastructure assets compared with the actual spending during the current period. (¶9, 11)

GWS

24. (b) The GWS governmental activities column includes the governmental funds plus most internal service funds and capital assets not specific to business-type activities or fiduciary funds. $25,000 + $9,000 = $34,000. The water enterprise fund is a business-type activity. The employee pension fund is a fiduciary fund; it doesn't appear anywhere in the GWS.

25. (a) Although internal service funds are proprietary funds, they appear in the government-wide statements as governmental activities in the new reporting model.

26. (c) The GWS governmental activities column includes the governmental funds plus most internal service funds and capital assets not specific to business-type activities or fiduciary funds. GWS show capital asset depreciation. $1,500 + $9,000 – $3,000 = $7,500.

27. (b) General government fixed assets and long-term debt, are *not* recorded in the governmental funds, but are shown in the governmental activities column of the government-wide financial statements. General long-term debt to be repaid from general resources of the government should not be reported in any fund.

Capital Assets

28. (b) Infrastructure assets that are part of a network or a sub-system of a network (eligible infrastructure assets) are not required to be depreciated, if the government: documents that eligible infrastructure assets are preserved approximately at (or above) a condition level established and disclosed by the government; has an up-to-date inventory of eligible infrastructure assets; consistently performs condition assessments of eligible assets at least triannually and summarizes the results using a measurement scale; and annually estimates the amount to preserve the eligible assets at a condition level established and disclosed by the government. (GASB 34, ¶23, 24)

29. (b) General fixed assets acquired by foreclosure are recorded at the lower of (1) the amount due for taxes, special assessments, penalties and interest, plus foreclosure costs or (2) appraised fair market value. Therefore, since the $20,000 Palm incurred for taxes, liens, and other costs incidental to acquiring ownership and perfecting title is less than the land's $60,000 fair market value at the forfeiture date, the land is reported in the government-wide statements at $20,000.

30. (c) The government-wide financial statements report all general capital assets (fixed assets plus infrastructure) in the governmental activity column. Usually internal service fund fixed assets also appear in this column. Enterprise fund fixed assets appear in a different column. Fiduciary funds do not appear in the GWS.

31. (c) Purchased assets are reported at cost. Long-term capital assets are not recorded in any governmental fund.

Fund Statements

32. (a) The major fund financial statements are presented before the notes to the financial statements, as part of the basic financial statements, not RSI (¶1, 2). GASB 34 (¶8) states, "The basic financial statements should be preceded by MD&A, which is required supplementary information." GASB 34 (¶6) states, "The basic financial statements should include…(1) the government-wide statements [that] …display information about the reporting government as a whole, except for its fiduciary activities… (2) Fund financial statements for the primary government's governmental, proprietary, and fiduciary funds should be presented after the government-wide statements…(3) Notes to the financial statements. Except for MD&A, required supplementary information, including the required budgetary comparison information, should be presented immediately following the notes to the financial statements."

Statement of Cash Flows

33. (c) A statement of cash flows is required for *all* proprietary funds, including public benefit corporations and governmental utilities.

34. (c) For purposes of preparing a statement of cash flows, cash equivalents are short-term, highly liquid investments that are both (1) readily convertible into known amounts of cash and (2) so near their maturity that they present insignificant risk of changes in value because of changes in interest rates. Generally, only investments with original maturities to the entity holding the investment of three months or less qualify under as cash equivalents. Examples of items that the GASB considers to be cash equivalents are Treasury bills, commercial paper, certificates of deposit, money market funds, and cash management pools. Therefore, both the 2-month Treasury bill and the 3-month certificate of deposit should be presented as a cash equivalent by the governmental unit.

35. (c) For purposes of preparing a statement of cash flows, cash equivalents are short-term, highly liquid investments that are both (1) readily convertible into known amounts of cash and (2) so near their maturity that they present insignificant risk of changes in value because of changes in interest rates. Generally, only investments with original maturities to the reporting entity of three months or less qualify as cash equivalents. Both a 3-month bill and a 3-year note purchased three months from maturity qualify as cash equivalents. However, a note purchased three years ago does not become a cash equivalent when its remaining maturity is three months. Therefore, the amount of the investments that Hill should report as cash and cash equivalents at 6/30 of year 5 is the sum of the 3-month bill and the 3-year note purchased less than three months from maturity. The note with an original maturity to Hill of five years (i.e., 10/1 of year 1 to 9/30 of year 6) will never be reported as a cash equivalent by Hill.

36. (d) For the statement of cash flows, investing activity cash inflows include interest and dividends received as returns on loans (except program loans), debt of other entities, equity securities, and cash management or investment pools.

Other RSI

37. (b) The budgetary comparison schedule includes the original and final budgets as well as actual inflows, outflows, and balances, stated on the government's budgetary basis of accounting, with a reconciliation between the budgetary and GAAP information (GASB 34, ¶130). The schedule may have the same format as the budget documents or the statement of revenues, expenditures, and changes in fund balances (¶131). A column reporting the variances between the final budget and actual amounts is encouraged, but not required (¶131).

38. (c) Budgetary Comparison Schedule (BCS) is presented for the general fund and for each major special revenue fund that has a legally adopted annual budget, on the **budgetary** basis of accounting. The BCS presents both the original and final budget as well as actual inflows, outflows, and balances. It uses the same format, terminology, and classifications as either the budget document or a statement of revenues, expenditures, and changes in fund balances.

39. (b) GASB 34 (¶130, 131) states "Budgetary comparison schedules should be presented as RSI for the general fund and for each major special revenue fund that has a legally adopted annual budget…. The budgetary comparison schedule should present both (a) the original and (b) the final…as well as (c) actual inflows, outflows, and balances, **stated on the government's budgetary**

basis.... Governments may present the budgetary comparison schedule using the same format, terminology, and classifications as the budget document, or using the format, terminology, and classifications in a statement of revenues, expenditures, and changes in fund balances. Regardless of the format used, the schedule should be accompanied by information (either in a separate schedule or in notes to RSI) that reconciles budgetary information to GAAP information...." This reconciliation provides the link from the budgetary comparisons to the GAAP operating statements in the basic financial statements.

Nonexchange Transactions

40. (b) Revenues are susceptible to accrual at the time they become measurable and available for use under NCGA Statement 1 modified accrual basis guidelines. Significant amounts received prior to the normal time of collection (i.e., early payment of property taxes) are recorded as *Deferred Revenues* (GASB §1600.116).

41. (a) Derived tax revenues are assessments imposed by governments on exchange transactions and generally include sales taxes, income taxes, motor fuel taxes, and similar taxes on earnings or consumption. Assets are recognized when the underlying exchange transaction occurs. Revenues generally are recognized at the same time. Imposed nonexchange revenues represent assessments imposed on non-governmental entities and include property taxes and fines or forfeitures. Government-mandated nonexchange transactions occur when a government at one level provides resources to a government at another level and requires that government to use the resources for a specific purpose. Voluntary nonexchange transactions result from legislative or contractual agreements, but do not involve an exchange of equal value.

42. (c) Governmental funds use the modified accrual basis of accounting, under which revenues susceptible to accrual (e.g., property taxes) are recognized when they become measurable and available for use. "Available for use" means that the revenues will be collected within the current period or collected early enough in the next period (i.e., within 60 days or so) to be used to pay for expenditures incurred in the current period. For year 1, Oak should report property tax revenues of $600,000, the sum of the property taxes levied and collected in year 1 and the expected property tax collections during the first 60 days of year 2.

43. (b) Imposed nonexchange revenues are assessments on non-governmental entities, and include property taxes and fines or forfeitures.

Capital Leases

44. (c) The acquisition of a general fixed asset is an expenditure, with the asset recorded in the GFAAG. A capital lease is an other financing source, recorded in the GLTDAG.

MSWLF

45. (c) GASB No. 18 establishes accounting standards for MSWLF costs. A portion of the estimated total current costs must be recognized as an expense and as a liability in each period during which the MSWLF accepts solid waste. The estimated total current costs of MSWLF closure and postclosure care should include those costs which result in disbursements near, or after, the date that the MSWLF stops accepting solid waste and during the post-closure period, including the cost of a final cover and monitoring equipment.

46. (d) A MSWLF accounted for in a governmental-type fund should recognize expenditures and fund liabilities on the modified accrual basis of accounting, with the long-term capital assets and liabilities reported in the government-wide financial statements, but not the governmental funds. GASB No. 18, ¶11, states, "Equipment, facilities, services, and final cover included in the estimated total current cost of closure and postclosure care should be reported as a reduction of the reported liability for closure and postclosure care when they are acquired." If the entity uses a GLTDAG, the following entry would be made in the GLTDAG:

DR:	MSWLF Payable	XX	
CR:	Amount to Be Provided for Payment of MSWLF Obligation		XX

47. (d) Proprietary funds may account for landfills. Liabilities are recognized in a proprietary fund when a proprietary fund accounts for the landfill. Expense recognition should be finished when the post-closure period begins. Capital assets should be fully depreciated by the date the MSWLF stops accepting solid waste.

Limited Scope Topics

48. (c) Governmental employers identify in the notes to the financial statements the types of employees covered under the defined contribution pension plan and the employer's and employees' obligations to contribute to the fund (GASB Cod. P20.137).

49. (d) The underlying securities owned with regard to reverse repurchase and fixed coupon reverse repurchase agreements should be reported as "Investments." Related assets and liabilities and interest cost and interest earned should not be netted. Credit risk related to such agreements must be disclosed.

50. (d) Comparability, consistency, and timeliness in SEA reporting are readily accomplished for a single governmental entity. Ensuring that reported performance yardsticks measure goals and desired effects is more complex.

Solution 18-2 ADDITIONAL MULTIPLE CHOICE ANSWERS

Funds & Fund Accounting

51. (c) The modified accrual basis of accounting for governments recognizes revenues in the period they become measurable and available to cover approved expenditures of the period.

52. (a) The modified accrual basis of accounting for a governmental unit recognizes revenues in the accounting period in which they become available and measurable. The modified accrual basis is the appropriate basis of accounting for governmental-type funds (i.e., general, special revenue, capital projects, debt service, and permanent funds). Proprietary and fiduciary funds use the accrual basis of accounting in all financial statements in the GASB 34 reporting model. The accrual basis of accounting recognizes revenues in the period in which they become earned and measurable.

53. (c) Fund accounting is used when there are legal separations between sources and uses of funds. Fund accounting may be used to account for assets aside from cash and cash equivalents. Combined or combining financial statements may be used with or without fund accounting. The resources may be physically in the same account or location.

Financial Statement Overview

54. (a) The objective of GASB 34 is "to enhance the understandability and usefulness of the general purpose external financial reports of state and local governments..."; however, GASB 34 reiterates Concepts Statement 1, stating, "accountability is the paramount objective of governmental financial reporting—the objective from which all other financial reporting objectives flow." (¶1, 2)

55. (d) The basic financial statements (BFS) consist of both government-wide and fund financial statements along with the accompanying notes (GASB 34, ¶6). Although it is presented before the BFS, MD&A is classified as required supplementary information, not BFS. The MD&A is a component of the *minimum* reporting requirements for state and local governments. A CAFR includes the BFS.

56. (d) GASB 34 requires that government-wide statements aggregate information for all governmental and business-type activities on the accrual basis of accounting (¶16). A reconciliation to the government-wide statement must appear on the face of the governmental-type fund financial statements or in a separate schedule (¶77).

57. (a) Only business-type activities appear in the statement of cash flows. (The governmental funds pose problems for developing meaningful information for a government-wide statement.) All funds use the economic resources measurement focus and accrual basis of accounting in the government-wide statements.

58. (c) GASB 34 (¶6) states, "The government-wide statements should display information about the reporting government as a whole, except for its fiduciary activities." A pension plan is a fiduciary activity, and thus a pension trust fund is reported in the fund financial statements, but not the government-wide statements. GASB 34 (¶6) states, "These statements display information about major funds individually and non-major funds in the aggregate for governmental and enterprise funds. Fiduciary statements should include financial information for fiduciary funds and similar component units. Each of the three fund categories should be reported using the measurement focus and basis of accounting required for that category."

MD&A

59. (a) GASB 34 (¶8) states, "The basic financial statements should be preceded by MD&A, which is required supplementary information. MD&A should provide an objective and easily readable analysis of the government's financial activities based on currently known facts...."

GWS

60. (b) GASB 34 (¶6) states, "The government-wide statements should display information about the reporting government as a whole, except for its fiduciary activities. The statements should include separate columns for the governmental and business type activities of the primary government as well as for its component units." GASB 34 (footnote 4) states, "The term *primary government* includes... blended component units, as defined in Statement 14." GASB 14 states, "The reporting entity's financial statements should present the... primary government (including its blended component units, which are, in substance, part of the primary government) and provide an overview of the discretely presented component units.... A primary government is also a special-purpose government (for example, a school district...) that meets all of the following criteria: a. It has a separately elected governing body. b. It is legally separate. c. It is fiscally independent.... A special-purpose government is fiscally independent if it has the authority to do all three of the following: a. determine its budget..., b. levy taxes... without approval..., c. issue bonded debt without approval by another government." This school district is a unit that is blended, not discretely presented. Thus, it is not reported in the component unit column, but rather the governmental activities column.

61. (b) GASB 34 (¶14) states, "The focus of the government-side financial statements should be on the primary government.... A total column should be presented for the primary government. A total column for the government as a whole may be presented, but is not required."

62. (b) The governmental-type funds and internal service funds usually appear in the government activities column in the government-wide financial statements. Enterprise funds generally appear in the business-type activities column in the government-wide financial statements (¶15). Note that GASB 34 (¶62) states, "Internal service fund assets and liability balances that are not eliminated in the statement of net assets should normally be reported in the governmental activities column. Although internal service funds are reported as proprietary funds, the activities accounted for in them...are usually more governmental than business-type in nature. If enterprise funds are the predominant...participants in an internal service fund, however, the governmental should report that internal service funds' residual assets and liabilities within the business-type activities column in the statement of net assets." Also see explanation 17.

Capital Assets

63. (a) GASB 34 (¶155) states that governments may use any approach that complies with the intent of GASB 34 (when actual historical cost data is not available) to **estimate the costs of existing** general infrastructure assets. Reporting of non-major networks is encouraged but not required (¶156). GASB 34 (¶158) states, "A government may estimate the historical cost of general infrastructure assets by calculating the current replacement cost of a similar asset and deflating this cost through the use of price-level indexes to the acquisition year (or estimated acquisition year if the actual year is unknown).... Accumulated depreciation would be calculated based on the deflated amount, except for general infrastructure assets reported according to the modified approach." GASB 34 (¶160) states, "Other information may provide sufficient support for establishing initial capitalization...include[ing] bond documents used to obtain financing for construction or acquisition of infrastructure assets, expenditures reported in capital project funds or capital outlays in governmental funds, and engineering documents." GASB 34 (¶161) states, "Governments may use any established depreciation method. Depreciation may be based on the estimated useful life of a class of assets, a network of assets, a subsystem of a network, or individual assets. For estimated useful lives, governments can use (a) general guidelines obtained from professional or industry organizations, (b) information for comparable assets of other governments, or (c) internal information. In determining estimated useful life, a government also should consider an asset's present condition and how long it is expected to meet service demands." GASB 34 (¶163) states, "Governments also may use **composite methods** to calculate depreciation expense. Composite methods refer to depreciating a grouping of similar assets (for example, all the interstate highways in a state) or dissimilar assets of the same class (for example, all the roads and bridges of a state) using the same depreciation rate."

64. (a) GASB 34 (¶73) states, "Agency funds should be used to report resources held by the reporting government in a purely custodial capacity (assets equal liabilities). Agency funds typically involve only the receipt, temporary investment, and remittance of fiduciary resources to individuals, private organizations, or other governments." Agency funds generally have neither capital assets nor expenses. Also see explanation 33.

65. (d) Unless held as a collection, works of art, historical treasures, and similar assets should be capitalized at historical cost or fair value at date of donation. GASB 34 merely encourages capitalization

of these assets when held as collections. Collections are held for public exhibition, education, or research in furtherance of public service rather than financial gain; protected, kept unencumbered, cared for, and preserved; and are subject to policies that require sales proceeds be used to acquire collection items. An exhaustible capitalized collection must be depreciated over its estimated useful life. Also see explanations 31, 62, and 63. (¶27, 29)

66. (c) GASB 34 (¶80) states, "General capital assets…are not specifically related to activities reported in proprietary or fiduciary funds. [They]…are associated with, and generally arise from, governmental activities…. They should **not** be reported as assets in governmental funds, but should be reported in the governmental activities column in the government-wide statement of net assets." (added emphasis)

67. (d) GASB 34 requires all governments to report all current fixed assets and new capital assets. Capital assets include assets formerly listed in the general fixed asset account group (land, buildings, and equipment) and infrastructure assets. The retroactive infrastructure asset reporting requirements are required for the largest two categories of governments and optional for small governments (annual revenues under $10 million). GASB 34 (¶149) states, "If determining the actual historical cost of general infrastructure assets is not practical because of inadequate records, governments should report the estimated historical cost for major general infrastructure assets that were acquired or significantly reconstructed, or that received significant improvements, in fiscal years ending after June 30, 1980." Capital assets should be depreciated over their estimated useful lives unless they are either inexhaustible or are eligible infrastructure assets reported using the modified approach (¶21); however, the modified approach (condition assessment) is not one of the answer options.

68. (d) GASB 34 requires all governments to report all new capital assets at historical cost (¶18). Capital assets include assets formerly listed in the general fixed asset account group (land, buildings, equipment) and infrastructure assets (¶19). Capital assets should be depreciated over their estimated useful lives unless they are either inexhaustible or are eligible infrastructure assets reported using the modified approach (¶21). The retroactive infrastructure reporting requirements are optional for small governments (¶148). Also see explanation 17.

Statement of Cash Flows

69. (b) A cash flows statement includes receipts and payments resulting only from the proprietary funds' activities (GASB 34, ¶78, 105, 106). Baker accounts for city hall construction in its capital projects fund, a governmental-type fund. The payments in lieu of property taxes are from an operating activity of an enterprise fund.

70. (a) Governmental-type funds pose problems for developing a meaningful government-wide cash flows statement. Only funds for business-type activities are required in the statement of cash flows (GASB 34, ¶16, 78, 91, 105).

Nonexchange Transactions

71. (b) Governmental funds use the modified accrual basis of accounting, under which, revenues are recognized when they become measurable and available for use. "Available for use" means that the revenues will be collected within the current period or collected early enough in the next period to be used to pay for expenditures incurred in the current period. The property taxes collected before the end of fiscal year 2 or shortly thereafter should be reported as revenues in fiscal year 2.

PERFORMANCE BY SUBTOPICS

Each category below parallels a subtopic covered in Chapter 18. Record the number and percentage of questions you correctly answered in each subtopic area.

Governmental Environment

Question #	Correct √
1	
2	
# Questions	2
# Correct	
% Correct	

Financial Reporting

Question #	Correct √
3	
4	
5	
6	
7	
8	
9	
10	
# Questions	8
# Correct	
% Correct	

Funds & Fund Accounting

Question #	Correct √
11	
12	
13	
14	
15	
16	
17	
18	
# Questions	8
# Correct	
% Correct	

Financial Statement Overview

Question #	Correct √
19	
20	
21	
22	
# Questions	4
# Correct	
% Correct	

MD&A

Question #	Correct √
23	
# Questions	1
# Correct	
% Correct	

GWS

Question #	Correct √
24	
25	
26	
27	
# Questions	4
# Correct	
% Correct	

Capital Assets

Question #	Correct √
28	
29	
30	
31	
# Questions	4
# Correct	
% Correct	

Fund Statements

Question #	Correct √
32	
# Questions	1
# Correct	
% Correct	

Statement of Cash Flows

Question #	Correct √
33	
34	
35	
36	
# Questions	4
# Correct	
% Correct	

Other RSI

Question #	Correct √
37	
38	
39	
# Questions	3
# Correct	
% Correct	

Nonexchange Transactions

Question #	Correct √
40	
41	
42	
43	
# Questions	4
# Correct	
% Correct	

Capital Leases

Question #	Correct √
44	
# Questions	1
# Correct	
% Correct	

MSWLF

Question #	Correct √
45	
46	
47	
# Questions	3
# Correct	
% Correct	

Limited Scope Topics

Question #	Correct √
48	
49	
50	
# Questions	3
# Correct	
% Correct	

Wondering how you can prepare for written communication questions?

Some candidates who are otherwise confident about the exam are overwhelmed by written communication questions. The following tips are designed to help you increase your confidence when presented with questions requiring free-form answers.

Review the **Writing Skills** appendix. This appendix has an example of what the AICPA labels as "ideal" and "good" solutions. Notice that the gap between "ideal" and "good" is larger than the gap between "good" and "poor." This works to your benefit.

As you progress through your study plan, answer a written communication question from each major topic; waiting until the last month leaves you little time to prepare for written communication questions. The more uncomfortable that you are with written communication questions, the more important this becomes. Bear in mind, you might not realize that you are uncomfortable with written communication questions, if you don't try answering some of them.

Once you grade your written communication question in comparison to the unofficial solution, reflect on the question. Assigning a point value is probably the least important part of answering the question. Any mistakes or omissions are solid learning opportunities. Additional information about written communication techniques is in the **Practical Advice** appendix.

Read through the written communication questions (with their related unofficial solutions) of written communication questions you will not be answering within the next few days. This provides a good review of the material you have just covered, as well as acquainting you with the types of questions and the length of the expected responses.

Once you know the content, you will be able to prepare a response regardless of the question format. However, exam time is limited, and you don't want the pressure of time considerations to distract you from providing your best answer to a question. To reduce the pressure, remember that you must earn 75 points to pass—it doesn't matter which format that you use to earn those 75 points. Practice more written communication questions that cover topics that have high point value; be prepared to answer a written communication question in any topic area.

Remember, with the techniques and information in your material,

A passing score is well within reach!

CHAPTER 19

GOVERNMENTAL FUNDS & TRANSACTIONS

I. **Governmental-Type Funds** 19-2
- A. Overview 19-2
- B. General Fund 19-4
- C. Special Revenue Funds 19-6
- D. Capital Projects Fund 19-7
- E. Debt Service Funds 19-8
- F. Permanent Funds 19-9

II. **Proprietary Funds** 19-10
- A. Overview 19-10
- B. Internal Service Funds 19-10
- C. Enterprise Funds 19-11

III. **Fiduciary Funds** 19-13
- A. Overview 19-13
- B. Pension Trust Funds 19-13
- C. Investment Trust Funds 19-13
- D. Private-Purpose Trust Funds 19-13
- E. Agency Funds 19-13

IV. **Interfund Transactions & Relationships** 19-15
- A. Overview 19-15
- B. Interfund Transactions 19-15

EXAM COVERAGE: The governmental accounting portion of the FAR section of the CPA exam is designated by the examiners to be 8 percent to 12 percent of the section's point value. More information about the point value of various topics is included in the *Practical Advice* section of this volume.

CHAPTER 19

GOVERNMENTAL FUNDS & TRANSACTIONS

I. Governmental-Type Funds

A. Overview

The governmental funds are used to account for the general government activities of a state or local government. The fund flow accounting for governmental funds is one of the **truly unique aspects** of state and municipal accounting, and it's a **heavily tested** topic on CPA exams. There are three types of journal entries: those to record (and close) the budget, those to record (and close) encumbrances, and those to record (and close) actual activity.

1. **Budget** Budgetary accounting is used by governmental-type funds.

   a. **Establish** The following entry is typical of the general fund's entry to record the budget at the beginning of the year.

Estimated Revenues Control	700	
Estimated Other Financing Sources	200	
Budgetary Fund Balance (DR or CR)		75
Estimated Other Financing Uses		300
Appropriations		525

   b. **Close** The following entry is typical of the general fund's entry to close the budget at the end of the year. (Note the same dollar amounts are used as the recording entry.)

Estimated Other Financing Uses	300	
Appropriations	525	
Budgetary Fund Balance (CR or DR)	75	
Estimated Revenues Control		700
Estimated Other Financing Sources		200

   c. **Transfers** Note that GASB §1700 states, "The appropriations constitute maximum expenditure authorization during the fiscal year." Thus estimated transfers (other financing sources and uses) are merely a specific kind of appropriation. Transfers (either budgeted or actual) are not netted.

2. **Encumbrances** Encumbrance accounting records obligations to spend (purchase orders) to prevent overspending of appropriations. Encumbrances are not liabilities.

   a. An encumbrance entry is made when an item is ordered in the amount of the estimated cost. Many amounts are controlled by another means and are frequently not encumbered. For example, salaries and wages are set by contract and controlled by established payroll procedures and are not encumbered.

   b. The reverse entry is made for the same dollar amount when the invoice arrives.

   c. Outstanding encumbrances at year end are carried forward as a reserve of fund balance with a corresponding deduction of unreserved fund balance.

   d. The spending of a prior year's outstanding encumbrances is a use of reserved fund balance, not a current year expenditure.

3. **Actual Activity** The emphasis on reporting activity is on cash flow, as opposed to profit and loss. The matching principle of accrual accounting is not applicable. NCGA Statement No. 1 offers the following **modified** accrual basis guidelines:

   a. **Revenues** Revenues are recorded as received in cash except for revenues susceptible to accrual and revenues of a material amount that have not been received at the normal time of receipt. Revenues are considered susceptible to accrual at the time they become **measurable** and **available** for use.

      (1) **Billed** Available means collected or collectible within the current period or early enough in the next period (e.g., within 60 days or so) to be used to pay for expenditures incurred in the current period (for example, property taxes). If revenue-related assets (e.g., taxes receivable) are **not** available, a *Deferred Revenue* account should be credited initially; when the assets become available, the *Deferred Revenue* account is debited and *Revenue* is credited.

      (2) **Received** GASB No. 22, *Accounting for Taxpayer-Assessed Tax Revenues in Governmental Funds,* guides revenue recognition. All governmental entities that report using governmental funds should recognize revenues from taxpayer-assessed taxes in the accounting period in which they become susceptible to accrual. In other words, these revenues are recognized when they become both **measurable** and **available** to finance expenditures of the fiscal period.

         (a) Personalty and realty property taxes.

         (b) Taxpayer-assessed sales and income taxes.

         (c) Sales taxes **collected** and held by one government agency for another at year-end should be accrued if they are remitted in time to be used as a resource for payment of obligations incurred during the preceding year. Remitted in time means collected during the year or within about 60 days after year-end.

      (3) **Restricted** Whereas *unrestricted* grants should be recognized immediately as revenue of governmental funds, if available, *restricted* grants should not be recognized as revenue until they are earned. A restricted grant must be expended for the specific purposes to be considered earned. Deferred grant revenue is recorded initially, and the grant revenue is recognized only when qualifying expenditures are incurred.

      (4) **Exception** Significant amounts received before the normal collection time (i.e., early property tax payments) are recorded as deferred revenues.

   b. **Expenditures** Expenditures (not expenses) are recorded when fund liabilities are incurred or assets are expended, except

      (1) Inventory items may be recorded as expenditures either (a) at the time of purchase or (b) at the time the items are used.

      (2) Expenditures normally are **not** allocated between years by the recording of prepaids (e.g., a two-year insurance policy). Prepaid **expenses** may be recorded as expenditures or may be allocated to periods (in funds using accrual accounting).

      (3) Interest on **general** long-term debt, usually accounted for in debt service funds, normally are recorded as an expenditure on its due date rather than being accrued prior to its due date.

   c. **Other Financing Sources/Uses** Transfers in/out or to/from are not netted. Transfers are reported after revenues and expenditures, as they affect operating results.

d. **Assets** Assets are treated as (capital outlay) expenditures and are not capitalized within the fund. Capital assets are not carried in governmental-type funds, but are included in government-wide financial statements. Fixed assets are rarely expected to contribute to revenues. Depreciation expense is **not** recorded in the governmental-type funds.

e. **Debt** Long-term debts are not carried in governmental-type funds, but are included in government-wide financial statements. Money is repaid through the debt service fund.

B. General Fund

This primary governmental fund is used to account for most routine operations of the governmental entity. All general government resources that are not required to be accounted for in another fund are accounted for in the general fund. General fund revenues primarily consist of taxes (property, sales, income, and excise), licenses, fines, and interest. General fund expenditures are budgeted (and appropriated for) by the legislative body.

1. **Purpose** The general fund finances other funds through capital contributions and operating subsidies. An example is found in the section of the chapter on interfund transactions.

2. **Operation** The general fund [C **G**RIPES] uses modified accrual accounting. Budgetary, encumbrance, and actual activity entries usually appear in the general fund.

Exhibit 1 ▸ Sample General Fund Entries

1. To record the budget:

Estimated Revenues Control	1,000	
Estimated Other Financing Sources	100	
Appropriations Control		625
Appropriations: Estimated Other Financing Uses		425
Budgetary Fund Balance [difference—the **planned** change in fund balance during year. May be Dr. or Cr.]		50

NOTE: Estimated operating transfers are recorded separately as *Estimated Other Financing Sources (Uses);* they are not included with *Estimated Revenues* or *Appropriations.*

NOTE: Some governments use the *Fund Balance* account for both actual and budgetary amounts. Their budgetary entry causes the *Fund Balance* account to be carried during the year at its planned end-of-year balance. Then, the year-end closing entries adjust the *Fund Balance* account from its planned year-end balance to its actual year-end balance. This combination of actual and budget amounts is theoretically less sound than the approach illustrated here.

2. To record actual revenues:

Cash or Receivables	600	
Allowance for Uncollectible Receivables		30
Revenues Control		570

NOTE: Governmental fund revenues are recorded net of estimated bad debts. That is, estimated uncollectible accounts are recorded as direct reductions from revenues rather than as expenditures. If all the revenues are collected in cash, there would not be a credit to the allowance account.

3. To record an encumbrance, in the form of a purchase order issued or contract commitment, for two shipments (one for $120, and one for $10 close to year end):

Encumbrances Control [expected cost]	130	
Reserve for Encumbrances		130

NOTE: Alternatively, the credited account may be titled *Budgetary Fund Balance Reserved for Encumbrances.*

4. To record expenditures (for slightly more than the purchase order total) upon receipt of an invoice for the first shipment:

Reserve for Encumbrances [reverse entry 3.]	120	
Encumbrances Control		120
Expenditures Control [actual cost]	125	
Vouchers Payable		125

5. To record unencumbered expenditures incurred:

Expenditures Control - Salaries	490	
Vouchers Payable		490

6. To record increase in supplies inventory on hand at year-end (supplies purchased were previously recorded as expenditures):

Supplies Inventory	20	
Fund Balance Reserved for Supplies Inventory [indicates that a portion of fund balance is not available]		20

NOTE: This customary entry compounds these two more proper entries:

a. Supplies Inventory	20	
Fund Balance		20
b. Fund Balance	20	
Fund Balance Reserved for Supplies Inventory		20

The entry(ies) would be reversed had the supplies inventory decreased. The increase (decrease) in supplies inventory is reported as an *Other Financing Source (Use)* in the governmental fund operating statement.

7. To record receipt of a grant from the state government and a bond issue:

Cash (or Receivable)	350	
Grant Revenues		100
Other Financing Sources: Bond Proceeds		250

8. To record payment of a grant to the school district:

Other Financing Uses	245	
Cash (or Payable)		245

9. To record closing entries at year-end:

Appropriations Control [budgeted]	625	
Appropriations: Estimated Other Financing Uses [budgeted]	425	
Budgetary Fund Balance [difference—debit or credit]	50	
Estimated Revenues Control [budgeted]		1,000
Estimated Other Financing Sources [budgeted]		100
Revenues Control [actual]	670	
Other Financing Sources [actual]	250	
Expenditures Control [actual]		615
Other Financing Uses [actual]		245
Fund Balance [difference—debit or credit]		60
Fund Balance	10	
Encumbrances Control [amount outstanding at year-end]		10

The third closing entry reduces the (Unreserved) Fund Balance account by the amount of the encumbrances outstanding and causes the Reserve for Encumbrances account—which is offset by the Encumbrances account during the year-to become a true fund balance reserve account at year-end. Alternatively, a compound closing entry may be made. The amount is the $10 shipment that has not been received ($130 – $120 = $10).

NOTE: Since closing the budgetary accounts (i.e., *Estimated Revenues, Appropriations, Estimated Other Financing Sources,* and *Estimated Other Financing Uses*) simply reverses the entry to record the budget, their closing has no effect on fund balance. It is the closing of the activity accounts (i.e., *Revenues, Other Financing Sources, Expenditures, Encumbrances*, and *Other Financing Uses*) that increases or decreases the fund balance.

10. To record encumbrance reversing entry—beginning of next year:

Encumbrances Control	10	
Fund Balance		10

NOTE: This entry reverses the encumbrance closing entry, restoring the *Encumbrances* and *Reserve for Encumbrances* accounts to their usual off-setting relationship.

NOTE: None of the exhibits in this chapter are related to the other exhibits.

C. Special Revenue Funds

Used to account for revenues that are externally restricted or designated by the legislative body for specific general government purposes other than capital projects.

Exhibit 2 ▸ Sample Special Revenue Fund Entries

1. To record endowment earnings that are restricted for library purposes:

Cash (or Due From Permanent Fund)	45	
Other Financing Sources: Library Permanent Fund		45

2. To record expenditures for library purposes:

Expenditures—Library Books	40	
Cash or Payable		40

3. To close the accounts at year-end:

Other Financing Sources: Library Permanent Fund	45	
Expenditures—Library Books		40
Fund Balance		5

1. **Use** The deciding factor for use of this fund as opposed to an enterprise fund is intent. If the intent is to recover less than 50 percent of expenses from user fees, then the activity is handled in a special revenue fund. The deciding factor for use of this fund as opposed to a private-purpose trust fund are the beneficiaries. If the beneficiaries are citizens or the reporting entity, then the activity is handled in a special revenue fund. If the beneficiaries are individuals, private organizations, or other governments, then the activity is handled in a private-purpose trust fund.

Exhibit 3 ▸ Examples of Special Revenues and Corresponding Uses

Source	*Use*
Hotel bed tax	Operate tourist center
Gasoline tax	Maintain streets
Parking fines	Operate traffic court
Library fines	Operate library
Donations	Purchase library books
Endowment income	Maintain public cemetery
State Juvenile Rehabilitation Grant	Operate youth programs

2. **Operation** The special revenue fund uses modified accrual accounting. Budgetary, encumbrance, and actual activity entries usually appear in special revenue funds. Accounting practices for special revenue funds [C G**R**IPES] parallel those for the general fund, so the only sample entries presented are related to a permanent fund endowment.

D. Capital Projects Fund

Used to account for the acquisition and use of financial resources to construct or otherwise acquire major long-lived general government capital facilities. Does not include assets used by trusts or proprietary funds. Most capital project(s) fund [**C** GRIPES] entries are similar to those illustrated earlier for the general fund.

1. **Use** Each capital project fund has a life limited to the construction period of the project. Alternatively, several overlapping capital projects may be accounted for in one capital projects fund, which exists as long as any one project is under construction. The acquisition of mobile property (for example, a car) need not be accounted for in a capital projects fund unless required by law or contractual agreement.

2. **Operation** Capital project(s) funds use modified accrual accounting. Encumbrance and actual activity entries usually appear in the capital projects fund. Budget entries are optional, and are usually used when accounting for more than one project in the same fund. Budget and encumbrance entries are similar to those in the general fund.

3. **Financial Resources** Typically are provided by bond issue proceeds, other funds, and interest earnings.

   a. Interfund transfers are classified as operating transfers (other financing sources) or residual equity transfers, as appropriate.

   b. Bond issue proceeds are classified as other financing sources. Premiums and discounts are recorded as other financing sources and uses, respectively. Debt issue costs paid out of proceeds are reported as expenditures. A net premium is usually transferred to the debt service fund.

4. **Interim Financing** Often needed during the early stages of the capital projects to pay for expenditures incurred before the bond issue proceeds or other resources are received.

   a. The interim financing may be obtained from funds of other governmental units, bond anticipation notes (BANs), or borrowings from local banks.

   b. Interim borrowing, if short-term, is a current liability of the capital projects fund and is credited to *Notes Payable or Due To (Fund).*

   c. Certain BANs are an exception to the above rule if (1) all legal steps have been taken to refinance the bond anticipation notes and (2) the intent is supported by an ability to consummate refinancing the short-term note on a long-term basis in accordance with the criteria set forth in SFAS 6, *Classification of Short-Term Obligations Expected to Be Refinanced.*

Exhibit 4 ▸ Sample Capital Project Fund Entries

1. To record deferred revenues and other financing received and accrued:

Due From Federal Grantor Agency	200	
Cash	300	
Deferred Grant Revenues [unearned until expended for project]		225
Bond Issue Proceeds [a nonrevenue other financing source]		275

2. To recognize grant revenue earned through expenditures having been incurred (recorded previously) for specified purposes:

Deferred Grant Revenues [project expenditures amount earned]	225	
Grant Revenues		225

NOTE: Other capital projects fund entries are illustrated in Interfund Transactions (Section IV).

E. Debt Service Funds

Used to account for the accumulation of resources for the periodic payment of interest on and principal of general obligation long-term debt. The debt service fund uses modified accrual accounting. Budgetary, encumbrance, and actual activity entries usually appear in the debt service fund.

Exhibit 5 ▸ Sample Debt Service Fund Entries

1. Debt service fund budgetary accounts **may** be used to record the estimated revenues (e.g., from taxes), estimated other financing sources (e.g., from interfund transfer from the general fund for retirement of debt principal and for payment of matured interest), and estimated income (e.g., from investments). To record the budget:

Estimated Other Financing Sources [e.g., from interfund transfers]	350	
Required Additions [estimated tax revenues]	250	
Required Earnings [estimated investment income]	150	
Appropriations [for debt service payments		700
Budgetary Fund Balance [planned change—debit or credit]		50

2. To record actual tax revenues and other financing sources (for example, loans):

Cash or Receivables	550	
Allowance for Uncollectible Taxes		10
Tax Revenues		240
Operating Transfer From General Fund		300

3. Debt service payments are recorded by debiting liability accounts (and crediting cash). To record expenditures for debt principal retirement (at maturity date) and interest (at due date):

Expenditures	700	
Bonds Payable (or Matured Bonds Payable)		50
Interest Payable (or Matured Interest Payable)		650

4. **Maturing** bond or other long-term debt principal and related interest and fiscal agent charges are recorded as debt service fund expenditures and liabilities when **due.** To record payment of matured debt and interest due:

Bonds Payable	50	
Interest Payable	650	
Cash		700

NOTE: Payment of matured debt and interest due is generally effected by transferring the required amount of cash to a bank or other fiscal agent, who then pays the creditors.

5. Any matured debt principal and interest that is **unpaid** at year-end (e.g., because bond interest coupons have not been presented to the fiscal agent for payment) should be recorded, as should the cash with fiscal agent, in the year-end adjusting entry process. To record unpaid liabilities and cash with fiscal agent at year-end:

Cash With Fiscal Agent	50	
Unredeemed Bonds Payable		30
Unredeemed Interest Coupons Payable		20

6. To record closing entries:

Appropriations	700	
Required Additions		250
Required Earnings		150
Estimated Other Financing Sources		350
Budgetary Fund Balance [difference—debit or credit]	50	

Tax Revenues	240	
Investment Revenues (entry to record revenue not shown)	210	
Operating Transfer From General Fund	300	
Expenditures		700
Fund Balance [difference—debit or credit]		50

F. **Permanent Funds**

Used to account for nonexpendable resources that may be used for the government's programs, in other words, to benefit the reporting entity or its citizens. The permanent funds [C GRI**P**ES] use modified accrual accounting. Budgetary and encumbrance entries usually aren't made in permanent funds. Accounting practices for permanent funds parallel those for the general fund, so few sample entries are presented.

Exhibit 6 ▶ Sample Permanent Fund Entries

1. To record receipt of a gift of an investment portfolio to establish an endowment; the principal including capital gains and losses, must be maintained intact, but the other earnings are to be transferred to a special revenue fund (SRF) to support the city library operations:

Cash	100	
Investments	1,000	
Contribution Revenues		1,100

NOTE: Donations are recorded as revenue at fair value, regardless of their cost to the donor, reported at fair value at statement dates, and closed to *Fund balance—Principal* at year-end.

2. To close revenue and expense accounts to determine earnings to transfer to the SRF:

Revenues—Investments	100	
Expenses—Commissions		30
Expenses—Administration		10
Expenses—Other		5
Fund Balance—Earnings		55

NOTE: Revenue and expense accounts, but not investment gains, are closed to *Fund balance—Earnings* to determine the earnings as defined by the donor. (The entries recording revenues, expenses, and gains are not illustrated.)

3. To record transfer of earnings, as defined, to a special revenue fund:

Other Financing Uses: Transfer to Library SRF	55	
Cash (or Due to Library SRF)		55

NOTE: A transfer does not necessarily indicate that cash has been disbursed, but may be accrued—and should be accrued if its necessity is indicated in a CPA exam question. Accounting for interfund transfers is discussed further in a later part of this chapter.

4. To close the remaining accounts:

Fund Balance—Earnings	55	
Other Financing Uses: Transfer to Library SRF		55
Gain on Sale of Investments	20	
Contribution Revenues	1,100	
Fund Balance—Principal		1,120

NOTE: The gains on sale of investments are closed to principal because the donor's restrictions specified that earnings are to be computed without regard to gains or losses on sale of investments.

II. Proprietary Funds

A. Overview

While the governmental funds account for the general government activities of a state or local government, its business type activities are accounted for in **proprietary** funds essentially as if they were private sector profit-seeking business enterprises. The proprietary fund accounting equation is the familiar business accounting equation.

Cur. Assets + *Fixed Assets* + *Other Assets* = *Cur. Liab.* + *Long-Term Debt* + *Net Assets*

1. **Business-Type Accounting** Revenues and **expenses** (not expenditures) are measured using the accrual basis of accounting, as in business accounting. Fixed assets and long-term debt are recorded in the fund as well as the associated depreciation and interest charges. Contributed capital is no longer separated from retained earnings in the balance sheet; both are labeled *Net Assets.*

2. **Not-for-Profit Accounting and Financial Reporting** GASB 29 allows the use of either the Nonprofit (or AICPA) model or the Governmental model for accounting and reporting by state or local governmental units that have previously applied the principles of SOP 78-10 or *Audits of Voluntary Health and Welfare Organizations.* However, proprietary funds that implement FASB pronouncements released after November 31, 1989, should only apply those pronouncements that are intended for business (as opposed to nonprofit) organizations.

3. **Refundings of Debt Reported by Proprietary Activities** GASB 23 provides standards of accounting and reporting for current refundings and advance refundings resulting in defeasance of debt reported by proprietary activities (proprietary funds and other governmental entities that use proprietary fund accounting). GASB 23 requires that the difference between the reacquisition price and the net carrying amount of the old debt be deferred and amortized as a component of interest expense over the remaining life of the old debt or the life of the new debt, whichever is shorter. The deferred amount is reported on the balance sheet as an addition to or a deduction from the new debt liability. Additionally, current refundings reported by proprietary activities are subject to the disclosure requirements of GASB 7, *Advance Refundings Resulting in Defeasance of Debt.*

   a. **Current Refundings** Involve the issuance of new debt, the proceeds of which are to be used immediately.

   b. **Advance Refundings** Involve the issuance of new debt that is placed in escrow to be used at a later date to pay principal and interest on the old debt.

B. Internal Service Funds

Internal service funds [C GRIPES] are used to account for *in-house* business enterprise activities; that is, to account for the financing of goods or services provided by **one** government department or agency to **other** departments or agencies of the government (and perhaps also to other governments) on a **cost reimbursement** basis. Common examples of internal service funds (ISF) are those used to account for government motor pools, central repair shops and garages, data processing departments, and photocopy and printing shops.

1. **Zero Profit** ISFs are supposed to break even annually and/or over a period of years. That is, the charges to other departments—that are accounted for as ISF revenues—are intended to **recoup** ISF **expenses.** ISF thus are, in essence, cost accounting and cost distribution (to other funds) accounting entities. They are accounted for in essentially the same manner as enterprise funds.

2. **Establishment** The initial capital to finance an ISF may come from the general fund, the issuance of general obligation bonds, transfers from other funds, or advances from other

governments. Permanent capital contributions (i.e., residual equity transfers) must be distinguished from loans and advances that are to be repaid.

3. **Differences Between Enterprise Fund and Internal Service Fund Accounting**

   a. Only the fixed assets that are expected to be replaced through the ISF are recorded therein and depreciated. Thus, the printing equipment for a central printing shop located in the basement of a county courthouse would be recorded in (and depreciated in) the print shop ISF. The courthouse is reported in the government-wide financial statements, a portion of the courthouse cost would **not** be recorded in the ISF.

   b. An account such as *Billings to Departments* serves as the ISF sales account rather than the usual *Revenues* account.

C. Enterprise Funds

Enterprise funds [C GRIP**ES**] **must** be used to account for a government's business-type operations that are financed and operated like private businesses—where the government's **intent** is that **all** costs (expenses, including depreciation) of providing goods or services to the general public on a continuing basis are to be financed or recovered primarily through user charges. Most government-owned public utilities (e.g., electricity, gas, water, and sewage systems) must be accounted for in enterprise funds under these mandatory criteria.

1. **Optional Use** NCGA Statement No. 1 also **permits** governments to account for virtually any type of self-contained business-type activity in enterprise funds if it prefers to do business-type accounting rather than general government accounting. City bus or other mass transit systems are examples of government activities that are often accounted for through enterprise funds under the NCGA's permissive criteria.

2. **Subfunds** If capital, debt service, trust, or agency funds related to an enterprise activity are required (e.g., by bond indentures, other contractual agreements, grant provisions, or laws), they are accounted for as enterprise fund subfunds rather than as separate funds.

   a. Assets and liabilities of such subfunds are accounted for by using separate asset and liability accounts (e.g., *Cash—Construction*, *Contracts Payable—Construction, Investments—Debt Service, Accrued Interest Payable—Debt Service,* and *Cash—Customer Deposits*) and need not balance, though all except agency subfunds may be balanced by net assets reserve accounts such as *Reserve for Construction* or *Reserve for Debt Service.*

   b. Revenues and expenses related to the subfunds are recorded as enterprise revenues and expenses, **not** in separate subfund revenue and expense accounts.

   c. Customers' security deposits that cannot be spent for normal operating purposes should be classified in the balance sheet of the enterprise funds as both a restricted asset and a liability.

Exhibit 7 ▸ Sample Enterprise Fund Entries

1.	To record operating revenues:		
	Cash or Receivables	850	
	Revenues—Sale of Electricity		725
	Revenues—Sale of Appliances		50
	Revenues—Other		75

2. To record federal grants for operating and capital purposes:

Cash or Receivables	100	
Cash—Construction	350	
Revenues—Federal Grants [operating grant]		100
Contributed Capital—Federal Grants [capital grant]		350

NOTE: If grants must be expended to be considered earned, they are initially credited to deferred revenues and deferred contributed capital accounts, then credited to revenue and contributed capital accounts when earned by being expended. Also, this entry (and entry 4) assumes that a capital projects subfund is required by federal grant and/or bond indenture provisions.

3. To record operating expenses:

Expenses—Cost of Electricity Purchased	400	
Expenses—Depreciation	100	
Expenses—Salaries and Wages	100	
Expenses—Other	50	
Accumulated Depreciation		100
Cash		500
Payables		50

4. To record issuance of enterprise revenue bonds to finance new electricity distribution lines and acquiring transmission equipment under capital lease:

Cash—Construction	450	
Bonds Payable		450
Transmission Equipment	200	
Capital Leases Payable		200

5. To record use of revenue bond issue proceeds to build new electricity distribution lines:

Transmission Lines	750	
Cash—Construction (or Payables—Construction)		750

6. To record payment of bond and capital lease principal and interest:

Bonds Payable	15	
Expenses—Interest [on bonds]	35	
Cash—Debt Service		50
Capital Leases Payable	10	
Expenses—Interest [on capital lease]	20	
Cash		30

NOTE: This entry assumes that a debt service subfund is used for bond debt service but that the capital lease is serviced from enterprise fund operating cash.

7. To close the accounts at year-end:

Revenues—Sale of Electricity	725	
Revenues—Sale of Appliances	50	
Revenues—Federal Grants [operating grant]	100	
Revenues—Other	75	
Expenses—Cost of Electricity Purchased		400
Expenses—Depreciation		100
Expenses—Salaries and Wages		100
Expenses—Interest ($20 + $35)		55
Expenses—Other		50
Net Assets [debit or credit]		245

NOTE: The revenue and expense accounts may be closed initially to a *Revenue and Expense Summary* account, which is then closed to *Net Assets*.

III. Fiduciary Funds

A. Overview

Fiduciary funds are used to account for a government's fiduciary or stewardship responsibilities as an agent (agency funds) or trustee (trust funds) for other governments, funds, organizations, and/or individuals.

1. **GASB 34 Reporting Model** All fiduciary funds [PIPPA] are accounted for on the accrual basis, in essentially the same manner as proprietary funds.

2. **Previous Reporting Model** Under the previous reporting model, both agency funds and expendable trust funds are accounted for on the **modified** accrual basis in essentially the same manner as governmental funds. Nonexpendable trust funds and pension trust funds are accounted for on the accrual basis, in essentially the same manner as proprietary funds. There are no private-purpose trust funds in the previous model.

3. **Transition** Both expendable and nonexpendable trust funds are eliminated by the GASB 34 reporting model. Former expendable trust funds that benefit the reporting entity or its citizens become special revenue funds [C G**R**IPES]. Former nonexpendable trust funds that benefit the reporting entity or its citizens become permanent funds [C GRI**P**ES]. Both expendable and nonexpendable trust funds that benefit other governments, funds, organizations, and/or individuals become private-purpose trust funds [PI**PP**A].

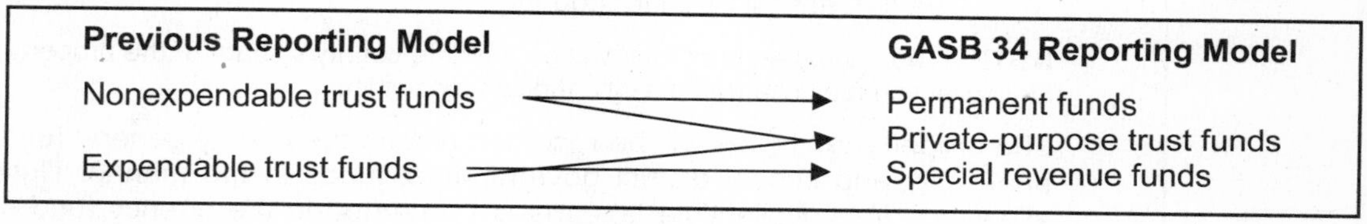

B. Pension Trust Funds

Used to account for a government's fiduciary responsibilities and activities in managing pension or retirement trust funds for its retired, active, and former employees and their beneficiaries.

1. **Use** Pension trust funds are needed only by governments that manage their own pension plans rather than participate in statewide plans or contract with an insurance or pension management company to manage the plans. (While relatively few businesses manage their own pension plans, many governments do so.)

2. **Basis of Accounting** Pension trust funds [**P**IPPA] are accounted for in essentially the same manner as proprietary funds. Accordingly, all contributions to and earnings of the plan are accounted for as revenues; and all benefit payments, refunds of contributions, and pension plan administrative costs are accounted for as **expenses.** Depreciation expense is recorded on depreciable fixed assets used in administering the pension plan. A unique series of fund balance reserve accounts is employed to account for the equities of the several types of plan participants.

C. Investment Trust Funds

Used to account for a government's fiduciary responsibilities and activities in managing an investment plan. [P**I**PPA] Further details are in Chapter 18 in the Limited Scope Topics Appendix.

D. Private-Purpose Trust Funds

Private-purpose trust funds [PI**PP**A] are used to account for fiduciary responsibilities and activities in managing all other trust arrangements that benefit individuals, private organizations, or other governments.

E. Agency Funds

Used to account for the custodial activities of a government serving as an agent for other governments, private organizations, or individuals. Agency funds [PIPP**A**] are purely custodial (assets equal liabilities). The government has no equity in agency funds. Further, agency funds do not have operating accounts (for instance, *Revenues*). No operating statement is prepared for agency funds.

1. **Accounting Equation**

Current Assets = Current Liabilities

2. **Common Types** The most common type of agency fund is the tax agency fund—used when one government collects property (or other) taxes for several governments, usually including the collecting government. Also, some governments use a payroll withholding agency fund to accumulate the payroll taxes, insurance premiums, etc., withheld in its several funds, then remit them to the proper governments, insurance companies, etc.

Exhibit 8 ▸ Sample Property Tax Agency Fund Entries

1. To record property taxes, levied by other governments (in this instance, the city and school district) and for other county funds, which are to be collected through the county's property tax agency fund:

Taxes Receivable—Other Funds and Units	2,000	
Due to City		250
Due to School District		250
Due to General Fund [of county]		1,500

NOTE: The county general fund will be paid the county's share of the property taxes collected plus any collection fees charged the city and school district.

The property tax levies will be recorded also in the county general fund and in the appropriate city and school district governmental funds in the manner illustrated earlier. An allowance for uncollectible taxes is not recorded in the agency fund since the county is responsible for collecting all taxes possible and returning the uncollected tax receivables to the city and school districts (and the county general fund) for further collection effort.

County's General Fund:

Taxes Receivable—Current	1,500	
Allowance for Uncollectible Taxes		75
Revenues—Property Taxes		1,425

2. To record tax collections:

Cash	1,975	
Taxes Receivable—Other Funds and Units		1,975

3. To record payment of tax collections to other units and to the county general fund:

Due to City [collections less any fee] ($245 – $5)	240	
Due to School District [collections less any fee] ($245 – $5)	240	
Due to General Fund [collections **plus** any fees] ($1,485 + $5 + $5)	1,495	
Cash		1,975

NOTE: Entries in the general funds would be the following:

County's General Fund:

Cash	1,495	
Taxes Receivable—Current		1,485
Revenues—Property Tax Collection Fees		10

City's and School District's General Funds:

Cash	240	
Expenditures—Property Tax Collection Fees	5	
Taxes Receivable—Current		245

IV. Interfund Transactions & Relationships

A. Overview

The preceding discussions and illustrations focus primarily on accounting for each of the several different types of funds. Interfund transactions and relationships are important aspects of governmental accounting. This part of the chapter focuses on interfund transactions (where one transaction affects two or more funds). These discussions and illustrations also review and expand upon the material covered earlier in this chapter.

B. Interfund Transactions

Interfund transactions simultaneously affect two or more funds of the government. Transfers are **nonreciprocal** shifts of resources among funds and are **not** intended to be repaid. GASB 34 details three types of interfund transactions in the GASB 34 reporting model. (NCGA Statement No. 1 previously provided specific guidance on accounting for four types of interfund transactions.)

1. **Quasi-External Transactions** These are transactions that would result in recognizing revenues and expenditures or expenses, as appropriate, if they were with organizations apart from the government. These transactions should also result in recognition of revenues and expenditures or expenses, as appropriate, when they occur between or among funds of the government. Examples include routine employer contributions to pension trust funds, enterprise and internal service fund billings to government departments, and enterprise fund payments in lieu of taxes to the general fund or other governmental funds.

Exhibit 9 ▸ Sample Quasi-External Transactions Entries

1. To record billings to departments financed by the general fund for services rendered through enterprise and internal service fund departments:

a.	*General Fund:*		
	Expenditures—Services	115	
	Due to Enterprise Fund		35
	Due to Internal Service Fund		80
b.	*Enterprise Fund:*		
	Due From General Fund	35	
	Revenues—Services		35
c.	*Internal Service Fund:*		
	Due From General Fund	80	
	Billings for Services		80

NOTE: Note that an account such as *Billings for Services* is used in internal service fund accounting instead of *Revenues*.

2. To record employer contributions from the general and enterprise funds to the pension trust fund:

a.	*General Fund:*		
	Expenditures—Pension Contribution	300	
	Due to Pension Trust Fund (or Cash)		300
b.	*Enterprise Fund:*		
	Expenses—Pension Contribution	100	
	Due to Pension Trust Fund (or Cash)		100
c.	*Pension Trust Fund:*		
	Due From General Fund (or Cash)	300	
	Due From Enterprise Fund (or Cash)	100	
	Revenues—Employer Contributions		400

NOTE: The cash account would be used if an actual cash transfer had occurred.

2. **Reimbursements** These are transactions that reimburse one fund for expenditures or expenses initially recorded there but properly attributable to another fund. Reimbursements are recorded as expenditures or expenses, as appropriate, in the reimbursing fund and as reductions of the recorded expenditures or expenses (**not** as revenues) in the fund that is reimbursed.

3. **Transfers** The difference between operating transfers and residual equity transfers (RETs) of the previous reporting model is not always easy to distinguish and practice varies widely. GASB 34 eliminated the **requirement** to distinguish between operating transfers and RETs. (The following illustrations distinguish between the two, as candidates may encounter this terminology.) GASB 34, ¶420 notes that all transfers must be reported as *Other Financing Sources* or *Other Financing Uses.* [See the sample financial statements. Note that transfers don't include quasi-external transactions and reimbursements.]

Exhibit 10 ▸ Sample Transfer Entries

1. To record transfers made from the general fund to establish a new internal service fund:

a.	*General Fund:*		
	OFU: Residual Equity Transfer to Internal Service Fund	500	
	Cash		500
b.	*Internal Service Fund:*		
	Cash	500	
	OFS: Residual Equity Transfer From General Fund		500

NOTE: This is a residual equity transfer. In internal service funds, the RET account(s) will be closed to a *Contribution From Municipality* (or similar contributed capital) account. The general fund RET accounts will be closed to *Fund Balance.*

2. To record routine transfers from the general fund to a debt service fund:

a.	*General Fund:*		
	OFU: Operating Transfer to Debt Service Fund	350	
	Cash		350
b.	*Debt Service Fund:*		
	Cash	350	
	OFS: Operating Transfer From General Fund		350

NOTE: All interfund transfers that are not RETs are operating transfers.

4. **Financial Statement Presentation** These three types of transactions all appear in the operating statements of the affected funds. Quasi-external transactions and reimbursements are buried in expenditures, expenses, and revenues account detail. Transfers (RETs and operating) appear in the *Other Financing Sources (Uses)* section.

5. **Interfund Loans** Amounts that are expected to be repaid appear in the balance sheets of affected funds. They have no impact on operating statements. Both short-term and noncurrent loans are indicated using *Receivable* and *Payable* accounts, appropriately classified in the balance sheets. Governments are encouraged, but not required, to present assets and liabilities in order of their relative liquidity. Liabilities whose average maturities are greater than one years should be reported in two components (a short-term component and a non-current component).

Exhibit 11 ▸ Other Sample Interfund Entries

1. To record reimbursement of the general fund for previously recorded operating expenditures that are properly attributable to special revenue and enterprise funds:

a. *General Fund:*

Cash	125	
Expenditures—Operating		125

b. *Special Revenue Fund:*

Expenditures—Operating	40	
Cash		40

c. *Enterprise Fund:*

Expenses—Operating	85	
Cash		85

NOTE: If cash was not involved, appropriate *Due From* and *Due to* accounts would be debited and credited rather than *Cash*.

2. To record four payments from an enterprise fund to the general fund—(1) a routine payment to subsidize general fund operations, (2) a payment in lieu of taxes, (3) a payment to reimburse the general fund for enterprise fund wages erroneously recorded in the general fund, and (4) a payment reducing the municipality's contributed capital investment in the enterprise fund:

a. *Enterprise Fund:*

Operating Transfer to General Fund	50	
Expenses—Payments in Lieu of Taxes	130	
Expenses—Wages	40	
Residual Equity Transfer to General Fund	350	
Cash		570

b. *General Fund:*

Cash	570	
Operating Transfer From Enterprise Fund		50
Revenues—Payments in Lieu of Taxes		130
Expenditures—Wages		40
Residual Equity Transfer From Enterprise Fund		350

NOTE: These entries demonstrate and review accounting for quasi-external transactions, reimbursements, residual equity transfers, and operating transfers.

3. To record a short-term loan from the general fund to a special revenue fund:

a. *General Fund:*

Due From Special Revenue Fund	100	
Cash		100

b. *Special Revenue Fund:*

Cash	100	
Due to General Fund		100

NOTE: In the previous reporting model, the *Due to* and *Due From* accounts indicate a short-term interfund loan that is expected to be repaid during the current year or early the next year. The GASB 34 reporting model uses an account title including the word *payable,* although governments may still use the old account titles internally. The GASB 34 reporting model shows the short-term and noncurrent payables separately.

4. To record a long-term loan from the general fund to an enterprise fund:

a. *General Fund:*

Advance to Enterprise Fund	200	
Cash		200
Fund Balance (or Unreserved Fund Balance)	200	
Reserve for Advance to Enterprise Fund		200

b. *Enterprise Fund:*

Cash	200	
Advance From General Fund		200

NOTE: (a) The terms *advance to* and *advance from* denote accounts for noncurrent or long-term interfund loans; and (b) since the amount loaned to the enterprise fund on a long-term basis does not now represent current assets available to finance general fund expenditures, an appropriate fund balance reserve must be established in the general fund. (The general fund reserve will be reduced when the advance becomes an available current asset—in full or in installments.)

5. To record closing of selected operating transfer and RET accounts in governmental (e.g., the general) and proprietary (e.g., enterprise and internal service) funds:

a. *General Fund:*

Operating Transfer From Enterprise Fund	XX	
Residual Equity Transfer From Enterprise Fund	XX	
Operating Transfer to Enterprise Fund		XX
Residual Equity Transfer to Internal Service Fund		XX
Fund Balance [difference—debit or credit]		XX

b. *Enterprise Fund:*

Operating Transfer From General Fund	XX	
Retained Earnings [difference—debit or credit]	XX	
Operating Transfer to General Fund		XX
Contributions From Municipality (or Contributed Capital)	XX	
Residual Equity Transfer to General Fund		XX

c. *Internal Service Fund:*

Residual Equity Transfer From General Fund	XX	
Contributions From Municipality (or Contributed Capital)		XX

NOTE: All transfers are closed to *Fund Balance* accounts of **governmental** funds. In **proprietary** funds: (a) operating transfers are closed to *Retained Earnings*, since they affect reported operating results, while (b) residual equity transfers are considered capital (**not** operating) transactions, and thus, are closed to the *Contributions From Municipality* (or similar contributed capital) account.

CHAPTER 19—GOVERNMENTAL FUNDS & TRANSACTIONS

Problem 19-1 MULTIPLE CHOICE QUESTIONS (120 to 150 minutes)

1. Expenditures of a governmental unit for insurance extending over more than one accounting period
a. Must be accounted for as expenditures of the period of acquisition
b. Must be accounted for as expenditures of the periods subsequent to acquisition
c. Must be allocated between or among accounting periods
d. May be allocated between or among accounting periods or may be accounted for as expenditures of the period of acquisition
(11/94, AR, #15, amended, 4992)

2. On January 2, City of Walton issued $500,000, 10-year, 7% general obligation bonds. Interest is payable annually, beginning January 2 of the following year. What amount of bond interest is Walton required to report in the statement of revenue, expenditures, and changes in fund balance of its governmental funds at the close of this fiscal year, September 30?
a. $0
b. $17,500
c. $26,250
d. $35,000 (R/05, FAR, 0749G, #13, 7757)

3. During the current year Knoxx County levied property taxes of $2,000,000, of which 1% is expected to be uncollectible. The following amounts were collected during the current year:

Prior year taxes collected within the 60 days of the current year	$ 50,000
Prior year taxes collected between 60 and 90 days into the current year	120,000
Current year taxes collected in the current year	1,800,000
Current year taxes collected within the first 60 days of the subsequent year	80,000

What amount of property tax revenue should Knoxx County report in its entity-wide statement of activities?
a. $1,800,000
b. $1,970,000
c. $1,980,000
d. $2,000,000 (R/05, FAR, 1031G, #19, 7763)

4. The revenues control account of a governmental unit is increased when
a. The encumbrances account is decreased
b. Appropriations are recorded
c. Property taxes are recorded
d. The budget is recorded (11/95, AR, #65, 5808)

5. Which of the following journal entries should a city use to record $250,000 for fire department salaries incurred during May?

		Debit	*Credit*
a.	Salaries expense	$250,000	
	Appropriations		$250,000
b.	Salaries expense	$250,000	
	Encumbrances		$250,000
c.	Encumbrances	$250,000	
	Salaries payable		$250,000
d.	Expenditures—salaries	$250,000	
	Salaries payable		$250,000

(11/96, AR, #12, amended, 6305)

6. During its fiscal year ended June 30, Cliff City issued purchase orders totaling $5,000,000 which were properly charged to encumbrances at that time. Cliff received goods and related invoices at the encumbered amounts totaling $4,500,000 before year end. The remaining goods of $500,000 were not received until after year end. Cliff paid $4,200,000 of the invoices received during the year. What amount of Cliff's encumbrances were outstanding at June 30?
a. $0
b. $300,000
c. $500,000
d. $800,000 (11/93, PII, #4, amended, 4433)

7. Elm City issued a purchase order for supplies with an estimated cost of $5,000. When the supplies were received, the accompanying invoice indicated an actual price of $4,950. What amount should Elm debit (credit) to the reserve for encumbrances after the supplies and invoice were received?
a. $(50)
b. $ 50
c. $4,950
d. $5,000 (11/93, PII, #5, 4434)

8. The estimated revenues control account of a governmental unit is debited when
a. Actual revenues are recorded
b. Actual revenues are collected
c. The budget is closed at the end of the year
d. The budget is recorded (11/95, AR, #72, 5815)

9. Which account should Spring Township credit when it issues a purchase order for supplies?
a. Appropriations control
b. Vouchers payable
c. Reserve for encumbrances
d. Encumbrance control (11/95, AR, #71, 5814)

10. The following information pertains to Spruce City's current year liability for claims and judgments:

Current liability at January 1	$100,000
Claims paid during the year	800,000
Current liability at December 31	140,000
Noncurrent liability at December 31	200,000

What amount should Spruce report for current year claims and judgments expenditures?
a. $1,040,000
b. $ 940,000
c. $ 840,000
d. $ 800,000 (11/93, PII, #7, amended, 4436)

11. The following information pertains to Pine City's general fund for the current year:

Appropriations	$6,500,000
Expenditures	5,000,000
Other financing sources	1,500,000
Other financing uses	2,000,000
Revenues	8,000,000

After Pine's general fund accounts were closed at the end of the year, the fund balance increased by
a. $3,000,000.
b. $2,500,000.
c. $1,500,000.
d. $1,000,000. (11/90, PII, #46, amended, 1350)

12. The budget of a governmental unit, for which the appropriations exceed the estimated revenues, was adopted and recorded in the general ledger at the beginning of the year. During the year, expenditures and encumbrances were less than appropriations; whereas revenues equaled estimated revenues. The budgetary fund balance account is
a. Credited at the beginning of the year and debited at the end of the year
b. Credited at the beginning of the year and **not** changed at the end of the year
c. Debited at the beginning of the year and credited at the end of the year
d. Debited at the beginning of the year and **not** changed at the end of the year
(5/91, Theory, #52, 2096)

13. When a purchase order is released, a commitment is made by a governmental unit to buy a computer to be manufactured to specifications for use in property tax administration. This commitment should be recorded in the general fund as a (an)
a. Appropriation
b. Encumbrance
c. Expenditure
d. Fixed asset (R/00, AR, #3, 6908)

14. For the budgetary year, Maple City's general fund expects the following inflows of resources:

Property taxes, licenses, and fines	$9,000,000
Proceeds of debt issue	5,000,000
Interfund transfers for debt service	1,000,000

In the budgetary entry, what amount should Maple record for estimated revenues?
a. $ 9,000,000
b. $10,000,000
c. $14,000,000
d. $15,000,000 (11/93, PI, #3, amended, 4432)

15. In the current year, New City issued purchase orders and contracts of $850,000 that were chargeable against current year budgeted appropriations of $1,000,000. The journal entry to record the issuance of the purchase orders and contracts should include a
a. Credit to vouchers payable of $1,000,000
b. Credit to reserve for encumbrances of $850,000
c. Debit to expenditures of $1,000,000
d. Debit to appropriations of $850,000
(11/94, AR, #18, amended, 4995)

16. The following information pertains to Park Township's general fund at December 31:

Total assets, including $200,000 of cash	$1,000,000
Total liabilities	600,000
Reserved for encumbrances	100,000

Appropriations do not lapse at year-end. At December 31, what amount should Park report as unreserved fund balance in its general fund balance sheet?
a. $200,000
b. $300,000
c. $400,000
d. $500,000 (11/93, PII, #20, amended, 4449)

17. Cal City maintains several major fund types. The following were among Cal's cash:

Unrestricted state grant	$1,000,000
Interest on bank accounts held for employees' pension plan	200,000

What amount of these cash receipts should be accounted for in Cal's general fund?
a. $1,200,000
b. $1,000,000
c. $ 200,000
d. $0 (11/93, PII, #8, amended, 4437)

18. A budgetary fund balance reserved for encumbrances in excess of a balance of encumbrances indicates
a. An excess of vouchers payable over encumbrances
b. An excess of purchase orders over invoices received
c. An excess of appropriations over encumbrances
d. A recording error (11/93, Theory, #52, 4557)

19. The following proceeds received by Arbor City are legally restricted to expenditure for specified purposes:

Expendable donation mandated by a benefactor to provide meals for the needy	$100,000
Sales taxes to finance the maintenance of tourist facilities in the shopping district	300,000

What amount should be accounted for in Arbor's special revenue funds?
a. $0
b. $100,000
c. $300,000
d. $400,000 (Editors, 1384)

20. The following information pertains to certain monies held by Blair County at December 31 that are legally restricted to expenditures for specified purposes:

Proceeds of short-term notes to be used for advances to permanent trust funds	$ 8,000
Proceeds of long-term debt to be used for a major capital project	90,000

What amount of these restricted monies should Blair account for in special revenue funds?
a. $0
b. $ 8,000
c. $90,000
d. $98,000 (11/93, PII, #18, amended, 4447)

21. Lake County received the following proceeds that are legally restricted to expenditure for specified purposes:

Levies on affected property owners to install sidewalks	$500,000
Gasoline taxes to finance road repairs	900,000

What amount should be accounted for in Lake's special revenue funds?
a. $1,400,000
b. $ 900,000
c. $ 500,000
d. $0 (5/92, PII, #27, 2659)

22. On December 31, Walk Township paid a contractor $3,000,000 for the total cost of a new police building built during the year. Financing was by means of a $2,000,000 general obligation bond issue sold at face amount on December 31, with the remaining $1,000,000 transferred from the general fund. What amount should Walk record as revenues in the capital projects fund in connection with the bond issue proceeds and the transfer?
a. $0
b. $1,000,000
c. $2,000,000
d. $3,000,000 (Editors, 1381)

23. In the current year, Mentor Town received $4,000,000 of bond proceeds to be used for capital projects. Of this amount, $1,000,000 was expended in this year. Expenditures for the $3,000,000 balance were expected to be incurred in the following year. These bonds proceeds should be recorded in capital projects funds for
a. $4,000,000 in the current year
b. $4,000,000 in the following year
c. $1,000,000 in the current year and $3,000,000 in the following year
d. $1,000,000 in the current year and in the general fund for $3,000,000 in the following year
(Editors, 9201)

24. Japes City issued $1,000,000 general obligation bonds at 101 to build a new city hall. As part of the bond issue, the city also paid a $500 underwriter fee and $2,000 in debt issue costs. What amount should Japes City report as other financing sources?
a. $1,010,000
b. $1,008,000
c. $1,007,500
d. $1,000,000 (R/01, AR, #9, 6994)

25. Financing for the renovation of Fir City's municipal park, begun and completed during the year, came from the following sources:

Grant from state government	$400,000
Proceeds from general obligation bond issue	500,000
Transfer from Fir's general fund	100,000

In its capital projects fund operating statement, Fir should report these amounts as

	Revenues	Other financing sources
a.	$1,000,000	$0
b.	$ 900,000	$ 100,000
c.	$ 400,000	$ 600,000
d.	$0	$1,000,000

(11/93, PII, #11, amended, 4440)

26. Grove Township issued $50,000 of bond anticipation notes at face amount in the current year and placed the proceeds into its capital projects fund. All legal steps were taken to refinance the notes, but Grove was unable to consummate refinancing. In the capital projects fund, what account should be credited to record the $50,000 proceeds?
a. Other Financing Sources Control
b. Revenues Control
c. Deferred Revenues
d. Bond Anticipation Notes Payable
(5/90, PII, #10, amended, 1373)

27. The debt service fund of a governmental unit is used to account for the accumulation of resources to pay, and the payment of, general long-term debt

	Principal	*Interest*
a.	Yes	Yes
b.	No	Yes
c.	No	No
d.	Yes	No

(Editors, 2145)

28. Oak County incurred the following expenditures in issuing long-term bonds:

Issue cost	$400,000
Debt insurance	90,000

When Oak establishes the accounting for operating debt service, what amount should be deferred and amortized over the life of the bonds?
a. $0
b. $ 90,000
c. $400,000
d. $490,000 (5/92, PII, #28, amended, 2660)

29. The following obligations were among those reported by Fern Village at December 31:

Vendor financing with a term of 10 months when incurred, in connection with a capital asset acquisition that is not part of a long-term financing plan	$ 150,000
Long-term bonds for financing of capital asset acquisition	3,000,000
Bond anticipation notes due in six months, issued as part of a long-term financing plan for capital purposes	400,000

What aggregate amount should Fern report as general long-term capital debt at December 31?
a. $3,000,000
b. $3,150,000
c. $3,400,000
d. $3,550,000 (5/92, PII, #34, amended, 2666)

30. Wood City, which is legally obligated to maintain a debt service fund, issued the following general obligation bonds on July 1:

Term debt	10 years
Face amount	$1,000,000
Issue price	101
Stated interest rate	6%

Interest is payable January 1 and July 1. What amount of bond premium should be amortized in Wood's debt service fund for the year ended December 31?
a. $1,000
b. $ 500
c. $ 250
d. $0 (11/93, PII, #6, amended, 4435)

31. The debt service fund of a governmental unit is used to account for the accumulation of resources for, and the payment of, principal and interest in connection with a

	Private-purpose trust fund	*Proprietary funds*
a.	No	No
b.	No	Yes
c.	Yes	Yes
d.	Yes	No

(11/94, AR, #12, 4989)

32. Tott City's serial bonds are serviced through a debt service fund with cash provided by the general fund. In a debt service fund's statements, how are cash receipts and cash payments reported?

	Cash receipts	*Cash payments*
a.	Revenues	Expenditures
b.	Revenues	Operating transfers
c.	Operating transfers	Expenditures
d.	Operating transfers	Operating transfers

(5/91, Theory, #54, 2098)

33. Arlen City's fiduciary funds contained the following cash balances at December 31:

Under the Forfeiture Act—cash confiscated from illegal activities; principal can be used only for law enforcement activities	$300,000
Sales taxes collected by Arlen to be distributed to other governmental units	500,000

What amount of cash should Arlen report in its permanent funds at December 31?
a. $0
b. $300,000
c. $500,000
d. $800,000 (11/93, PII, #14, amended, 4443)

34. The orientation of accounting and reporting for all proprietary funds of governmental units is
a. Income determination
b. Project
c. Flow of funds
d. Program (11/94, AR, #3, 4980)

35. The following equity balances are among those maintained by Cole City:

Enterprise funds	$1,000,000
Internal service funds	400,000

Cole's proprietary equity balances amount to
a. $1,400,000
b. $1,000,000
c. $ 400,000
d. $0 (11/93, PII, #12, 4441)

36. Which of the following bases of accounting should a government use for its proprietary funds in measuring financial position and operating results?

	Modified accrual basis	*Accrual basis*
a.	No	Yes
b.	No	No
c.	Yes	Yes
d.	Yes	No

(11/90, Theory, #51, 2104)

37. Which of the following does **not** affect an internal service fund's net income?
a. Depreciation expense on its fixed assets
b. Operating transfer sources
c. Residual equity transfers
d. Temporary transfers
(11/93, Theory, #55, amended, 4560)

38. The billings for transportation services provided to other governmental units are recorded by the internal service fund as
a. Transportation appropriations
b. Operating revenues
c. Interfund exchanges
d. Intergovernmental transfers
(11/95, AR, #73, 5816)

39. Gem City's internal service fund received a residual equity transfer of $50,000 cash from the general fund. This $50,000 transfer should be reported in Gem's internal service fund as a credit to
a. Revenues
b. Other Financing Sources
c. Accounts Payable
d. Contributed Capital (5/92, PII, #31, 2663)

40. Through an internal service fund, New County operates a centralized data processing center to provide services to New's other governmental units. This internal service fund billed New's parks and recreation fund $150,000 for data processing services. What account should New's internal service fund credit to record this $150,000 billing to the parks and recreation fund?
a. Data Processing Department Expenses
b. Intergovernmental Transfers
c. Interfund Exchanges
d. Operating Revenues Control
(11/93, PII, #13, amended, 4442)

41. Shared revenues received by an enterprise fund of a local government for operating purposes should be recorded as
a. Operating revenues
b. Nonoperating revenues
c. Other financing sources
d. Interfund transfers (5/94, AR, #56, 4661)

42. On January 2, Basketville City purchased equipment with a useful life of three years to be used by its water and sewer enterprise fund. Which of the following is the correct treatment for the asset?
a. Record the purchase of the equipment as an expenditure
b. Capitalize; depreciation is optional
c. Capitalize; depreciation is required
d. Capitalize; depreciation is **not** permitted
(R/05, FAR, 0688G, #11, 7755)

43. An enterprise fund would be used when the governing body requires that

I. Accounting for the financing of an agency's services to other government departments be on a cost-reimbursement basis
II. User charges cover the costs of general public services
III. Net income information be provided for an activity

a. I only
b. I and II
c. I and III
d. II and III (11/91, Theory, #55, 2562)

44. Cedar City issued $1,000,000, 6% revenue bonds at par on April 1, to build a new water line for the water enterprise fund. Interest is payable every six months. What amount of interest expense should be reported for the year ended December 31?
a. $0
b. $30,000
c. $45,000
d. $60,000 (R/01, AR, #6, 6991)

45. A state government had the following activities:

I.	State-operated lottery	$10,000,000
II.	State-operated hospital	3,000,000

Which of the above activities should be accounted for in an enterprise fund?
a. Neither I nor II
b. I only
c. II only
d. Both I and II (11/94, AR, #22, 4999)

46. The following fund types used by Ridge City had total assets at December 31 as follows:

Special revenue funds	$100,000
Agency funds	200,000
Pension funds	400,000

Total fiduciary fund assets amounted to
a. $300,000
b. $400,000
c. $600,000
d. $700,000 (Editors, 1388)

Items 47 and 48 are based on the following:

Elm City contributes to and administers a single-employer defined benefit pension plan on behalf of its covered employees. The plan is accounted for in a pension trust fund. Actuarially determined employer contribution requirements and contributions actually made for the past three years, along with the percentage of annual covered payroll, were as follows:

	Contribution made		Actuarial requirement	
	Amount	Percent	Amount	Percent
Year 3	$11,000	26	$11,000	26
Year 2	5,000	12	10,000	24
Year 1	None	None	8,000	20

47. What account should be credited in the pension trust fund to record the year 3 employer contribution of $11,000?
a. Revenues Control
b. Other Financing Sources Control
c. Due From Special Revenue Fund
d. Pension Benefit Obligation
(5/90, PII, #7, amended, 1370)

48. To record the year 3 pension contribution of $11,000, what debit is required in the governmental-type fund used with employer pension contributions?
a. Other Financing Uses Control
b. Expenditures Control
c. Expenses Control
d. Due to Pension Trust Fund
(5/90, PII, #8, amended, 1371)

49. Maple City's public employee retirement system (PERS) reported the following account balances at June 30:

Reserve for employer's contributions	$5,000,000
Actuarial deficiency in reserve for employer's contributions	300,000
Reserve for employees' contributions	9,000,000

Maple's PERS fund balance at June 30 should be
a. $ 5,000,000
b. $ 5,300,000
c. $14,000,000
d. $14,300,000 (5/92, PII, #22, amended, 2654)

50. Both Curry City and the state have a general sales tax on all merchandise. Curry City's tax rate is 2 percent and the state's rate is 4 percent. Merchants are required by law to remit all sales tax collected each month to the state by the 15th of the following month. By law, the state has 45 days to process the collections and to make disbursements to the various jurisdictions for which it acts as an agent. Sales tax collected by merchants in Curry total $450,000 in May and $600,000 in June. Both merchants and the state make remittances in accordance with statutes. What amount of sales tax revenue for May and June is included in the June 30 year-end financial statements of the state and Curry?

	State	*Curry*
a.	$1,050,000	$0
b.	$1,050,000	$350,000
c.	$ 700,000	$350,000
d.	$ 300,000	$150,000

(R/00, AR, #2, 6907)

51. Which of the following transactions is an expenditure of a governmental unit's general fund?
a. Contribution of enterprise fund capital by the general fund
b. Transfer from the general fund to a capital projects fund
c. Operating subsidy transfer from the general fund to an enterprise fund
d. Routine employer contributions from the general fund to a pension trust fund
(11/94, AR, #19, 4996)

52. For which of the following funds do operating transfers affect the results of operations?

	Governmental funds	*Proprietary funds*
a.	No	No
b.	No	Yes
c.	Yes	Yes
d.	Yes	No

(11/94, AR, #11, 4988)

53. In preparing combined financial statements for a governmental entity, interfund receivables and payables should be
a. Reported as reservations of fund balance
b. Reported as additions to or reductions from the unrestricted fund balance
c. Reported as amounts due to and due from other funds
d. Eliminated (5/95, AR, #53, 5471)

54. The following information pertains to Grove City's interfund receivables and payables at December 31:

Due to special revenue fund from general fund	$10,000
Due to agency fund from special revenue fund	4,000

In Grove's special revenue fund balance sheet at December 31, how should these interfund amounts be reported?
a. As an asset of $6,000
b. As a liability of $6,000
c. As an asset of $4,000 and a liability of $10,000
d. As an asset of $10,000 and a liability of $4,000
(11/93, PII, #9, amended, 4438)

55. Kew City received a $15,000,000 federal grant to finance the construction of a center for rehabilitation of drug addicts. The proceeds of this grant should be accounted for in the
a. Special revenue funds
b. General fund
c. Capital projects funds
d. Trust funds (11/90, PII, #47, 1351)

56. On March 2, year 1, Finch City issued 10-year general obligation bonds at face amount, with interest payable March 1 and September 1. The proceeds were to be used to finance the construction of a civic center over the period April 1, year 1 to March 31, year 2. During the fiscal year ended June 30, year 1, no resources had been provided to the debt service fund for the payment of principal and interest.

Proceeds from the general obligation bonds may be recorded in the
a. General fund
b. Capital projects fund
c. General long-term debt account group
d. Debt service fund
(11/90, Theory, #55, amended, 2108)

57. Central County received proceeds from various towns and cities for capital projects financed by Central's long-term debt. A special tax was assessed by each local government, and a portion of the tax was restricted to repay the long-term debt of Central's capital projects. Central should account for the restricted portion of the special tax in which of the following funds?
a. Internal service fund
b. Enterprise fund
c. Capital projects fund
d. Debt service fund (5/93, PII, #34, 4141)

58. Receipts from a special tax levy to retire and pay interest on general obligation bonds should be recorded in which fund?
a. General
b. Capital projects
c. Debt service
d. Special revenue (11/97, AR, #12, 6540)

59. The town of Hill operates municipal electric and water utilities. In which of the following funds should the operations of the utilities be accounted for?
a. Enterprise fund
b. Internal service fund
c. Agency fund
d. Special revenue fund (5/93, PII, #28, 4135)

60. Fish Road property owners in Sea County are responsible for special assessment debt that arose from a storm sewer project. If the property owners default, Sea has no obligation regarding debt service, although it does bill property owners for assessments and uses the monies it collects to pay debt holders. What fund type should Sea use to account for these collection and servicing activities?
a. Agency
b. Debt service
c. Expendable trust funds
d. Capital projects (11/95, AR, #64, 5807)

Problem 19-2 ADDITIONAL MULTIPLE CHOICE QUESTIONS (58 to 73 minutes)

61. The budgetary fund balance reserved for encumbrances account of a governmental-type fund is increased when
a. The budget is recorded
b. Appropriations are recorded
c. Supplies previously ordered are received
d. A purchase order is approved
(11/92, Theory, #53, 3486)

62. When Rolan County adopted its budget for the current year ending June 30, $20,000,000 was recorded for estimated revenues control. Actual revenues for the fiscal year amounted to $17,000,000. In closing the budgetary accounts at June 30,
a. Revenues Control should be debited for $3,000,000
b. Estimated Revenues control should be debited for $3,000,000
c. Revenues Control should be credited for $20,000,000
d. Estimated Revenues control should be credited for $20,000,000
(11/90, PII, #57, amended, 1360)

63. The encumbrance account of a governmental unit is debited when
a. The budget is recorded
b. A purchase order is approved
c. Goods are received
d. A voucher payable is recorded
(11/93, Theory, #51, 4556)

64. A county's balances in the general fund included the following:

Appropriations	$745,000
Encumbrances	37,250
Expenditures	298,000
Vouchers payable	55,875

What is the remaining amount available for use by the county?
a. $353,875
b. $391,125
c. $409,750
d. $447,000
(R/99, AR, #17, 6806)

65. When a snowplow purchased by a governmental unit is received, it should be recorded in the general fund as a(an)
a. Encumbrance
b. Expenditure
c. Fixed Asset
d. Appropriation
(11/94, AR, #9, 4986)

66. Which of the following amounts are included in a general fund's encumbrance account?

I. Outstanding vouchers payable amounts
II. Outstanding purchase order amounts
III. Excess of the amount of a purchase order over the actual expenditure for that order

a. I only
b. I and III
c. II only
d. II and III
(5/91, Theory, #53, 2097)

Items 67 through 69 are based on the following:

Park City uses encumbrance accounting and formally integrates its budget into the general fund's accounting records. For the current year ending July 31, the following budget was adopted:

Estimated revenues	$30,000,000
Appropriations	27,000,000
Estimated transfer to debt service fund	900,000

67. When Park's budget is adopted and recorded, Park's budgetary fund balance would be a
a. $3,000,000 credit balance
b. $3,000,000 debit balance
c. $2,100,000 credit balance
d. $2,100,000 debit balance
(5/92, PII, #23, amended, 2655)

68. Park should record budgeted appropriations by a
a. Credit to appropriations control, $27,000,000
b. Debit to estimated expenditures, $27,000,000
c. Credit to appropriations control, $27,900,000
d. Debit to estimated expenditures, $27,900,000
(5/92, PII, #24, amended, 2656)

69. Park incurred salaries and wages of $800,000 for the month of April. What account should Park debit to record this $800,000?
a. Encumbrances control
b. Salaries and wages expense control
c. Expenditures control
d. Operating funds control
(5/92, PII, #25, amended, 2657)

70. Which of the following accounts of a governmental unit is credited when taxpayers are billed for property taxes?
a. Appropriations
b. Taxes Receivable—Current
c. Estimated Revenues
d. Revenues
(11/93, Theory, #53, 4558)

71. Which of the following accounts of a governmental unit is credited when supplies previously ordered are received?
a. Expenditures Control
b. Encumbrances Control
c. Fund Balance Reserved for Encumbrances
d. Appropriations Control (Editors, 2157)

Items 72 through 77 are based on the following:

Cliff Township's fiscal year ends on July 31. Cliff uses encumbrance accounting. On October 2, year 1, an approved $5,000 purchase order was issued for supplies. Cliff received these supplies on November 2, year 1, and the $5,000 invoice was approved for payment by the general fund.

During the year ended July 31, year 2, Cliff received a state grant of $150,000 to finance the purchase of a senior citizens recreation bus, and an additional $15,000 grant to be used for bus operations during the year ended July 31, year 2. Only $125,000 of the capital grant was used during the year ended July 31, year 2 for the bus purchase, but the entire operating grant of $15,000 was disbursed during the year.

Cliff's governing body adopted its general fund budget for the year ending July 31, year 3, comprising estimated revenues of $50,000,000 and appropriations of $40,000,000. Cliff formally integrates its budget into the accounting records.

72. To record the $40,000,000 of budgeted appropriations, Cliff should
a. Debit estimated expenditures control
b. Credit estimated expenditures control
c. Debit appropriations control
d. Credit appropriations control (Editors, 9248)

73. When Cliff records budgeted revenues, estimated revenues control should be
a. Debited for $10,000,000
b. Credited for $10,000,000
c. Debited for $50,000,000
d. Credited for $50,000,000 (Editors, 9250)

74. The $10,000,000 budgeted excess of revenues over appropriations should be
a. Debited to budgetary fund balance—unreserved
b. Credited to budgetary fund balance—unreserved
c. Debited to estimated excess revenues control
d. Credited to estimated excess revenues control (Editors, 9249)

75. The senior citizens recreation bus program is accounted for as part of Cliff's general fund. What amount should Cliff report as grant revenues for the year ended July 31, year 1, in connection with the state grants?
a. $165,000
b. $150,000
c. $140,000
d. $125,000 (Editors, 9245)

76. What accounts should Cliff debit and credit on October 2, year 1, to record the approved $5,000 purchase order?

	Debit	*Credit*
a.	Encumbrances Control	Appropriations Control
b.	Appropriations Control	Encumbrances Control
c.	Encumbrances Control	Budgetary Fund Balance—Reserved for Encumbrances
d.	Budgetary Fund Balance—Reserved for Encumbrances	Encumbrances Control

(Editors, 9246)

77. What accounts should Cliff debit and credit on November 2, year 1, upon receipt of the supplies and approval of the $5,000 invoice?

	Debit	*Credit*
a.	Budgetary Fund Balance—Reserved for Encumbrances	Encumbrances Control
	Expenditures Control	Vouchers Payable
b.	Encumbrances Control	Budgetary Fund Balance—Reserved for Encumbrances
	Appropriations Control	Vouchers Payable
c.	Appropriations Control	Encumbrances Control
	Supplies Inventory	Vouchers Payable
d.	Encumbrances Control	Appropriations Control
	Expenditures Control	Vouchers Payable

(Editors, 9247)

78. On December 31, Hill City paid a contractor $5,000,000 for the total cost of a new municipal annex built during the year on city-owned land. Financing was provided by a $3,000,000 general obligation bond issue sold at face amount on December 31, with the remaining $2,000,000 transferred from the general fund. What account and amount should be reported in Hill's year-end financial statements for the general fund?
a. Other financing uses control, $2,000,000
b. Other financing sources control, $3,000,000
c. Expenditures control, $5,000,000
d. Other financing sources control, $5,000,000 (Editors, 9200)

79. In connection with Alma Township's long-term debt, the following cash accumulations are available to cover payment of principal and interest on

Bonds for financing of water treatment plant construction	$2,000,000
General long-term obligations	700,000

The amount of these cash accumulations that should be accounted for in Alma's debt service funds is
a. $0
b. $ 700,000
c. $2,000,000
d. $2,700,000 (Editors, 1385)

80. Dale City is accumulating financial resources that are legally restricted to payments of general long-term debt principal and interest maturing in future years. At December 31, $5,000,000 has been accumulated for principal payments and $300,000 has been accumulated for interest payments. These restricted funds should be accounted for in the

	Debt service fund	*General fund*
a.	$0	$5,300,000
b.	$ 300,000	$5,000,000
c.	$5,000,000	$ 300,000
d.	$5,300,000	$0

(5/92, PII, #36, amended, 2668)

Items 81 and 82 are based on the following events relating to the City of Arrow's debt service funds that occurred during the year ended December 31:

All principal and interest due in the year were paid on time.

Debt principal matured	$3,000,000
Unmatured (accrued) interest on outstanding debt at Jan. 1	45,000
Interest on matured debt	700,000
Unmatured (accrued) interest on outstanding debt at Dec. 31	93,000
Interest revenue from investments	800,000
Cash transferred from general fund for retirement of debt principal	2,000,000
Cash transferred from general fund for payment of matured interest	600,000

81. What is the total amount of expenditures that Arrow's debt service funds should record for the year?
a. $ 700,000
b. $ 745,000
c. $3,700,000
d. $3,745,000 (Editors, 1413)

82. How much revenue should Arrow's debt service funds record for the year?
a. $ 800,000
b. $2,600,000
c. $2,800,000
d. $3,400,000 (Editors, 1414)

83. A major exception to the general rule of expenditure accrual for governmental units relates to unmatured

	Principal of general long-term debt	*Interest on general long-term debt*
a.	Yes	Yes
b.	Yes	No
c.	No	Yes
d.	No	No

(11/94, AR, #14, 4991)

84. Fixed assets donated to a governmental unit should be recorded
a. At the donor's carrying amount
b. At estimated fair value when received
c. At the lower of the donor's carrying amount or estimated fair value when received
d. As a memorandum entry only
(11/95, AR, #58, 5801)

85. The following information for the year ended June 30 pertains to a proprietary fund established by Glen Village in connection with Glen's public parking facilities:

Receipts from users of parking facilities	$600,000
Expenditures	
Parking meters	410,000
Salaries and other cash expenses	96,000
Depreciation of parking meters	94,000

For the year ended June 30, this proprietary fund should report net income of
a. $0.
b. $ 94,000.
c. $ 96,000.
d. $410,000. (Editors, 9203)

86. How would customers' security deposits which can **not** be spent for normal operating purposes be classified in the balance sheet of the enterprise fund of a governmental unit?

	Restricted asset	*Liability*	*Fund equity*
a.	No	Yes	No
b.	Yes	Yes	No
c.	Yes	Yes	Yes
d.	Yes	No	Yes

(Editors, 2155)

87. A city's electric utility, which is operated as an enterprise fund, rendered billings for electricity supplied to the general fund. Which of the following accounts should be debited by the general fund?
a. Appropriations
b. Expenditures
c. Due to Electric Utility Enterprise Fund
d. Other Financing Uses—Operating Transfers Out (11/94, AR, #16, 4993)

88. Operating transfers received by a governmental-type fund should be reported in the Statement of Revenues, Expenditures, and Changes in Fund Balance as a(an)
a. Addition to contributed capital
b. Addition to retained earnings
c. Other financing source
d. Reimbursement (11/94, AR, #20, 4997)

89. Proceeds of General Obligation Bonds is an account of a governmental unit that would be included in the
a. Debt service fund
b. Internal service fund
c. Capital projects fund
d. Enterprise fund (Editors, 2163)

SIMULATIONS

Problem 19-3 (20 to 25 minutes)

Research Task	Scenario	Additional Information	Responses

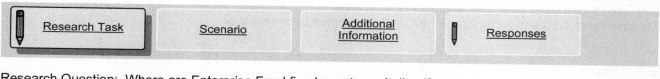

Research Question: Where are Enterprise Fund fixed assets capitalized?

Paragraph Reference Answer: ____________

Research Task	Scenario	Additional Information	Responses

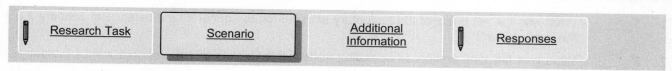

Jey City adopted GASB Statement No. 34. Jey requires its landfill to recover its cost through user fees. The following events affected the financial statements of Jey City during the current year:

Budgetary activities:

- Total general fund estimated revenues $8,000,000
- Total general fund budgeted expenditures 7,500,000
- Planned construction of a courthouse improvement expected to cost $1,500,000, and to be financed in the following manner: $250,000 from the general fund, $450,000 from state entitlements, and $800,000 from the proceeds of 20-year, 8% bonds dated and expected to be issued at par on June 30. Interest on the bonds is payable annually on July 1, together with one-twentieth of the bond principal from general fund revenues of the payment period.
- A budgeted general fund payment of $180,000 to subsidize operations of a solid waste landfill enterprise fund.

Actual results included the following:

- Jey recorded property tax revenues of $5,000,000 and a related allowance for uncollectibles—current of $60,000. On December 31, the remaining $56,000 balance of the allowance for uncollectibles—current was closed, and an adjusted allowance for uncollectibles—delinquent was recorded equal to the property tax receivables balance of $38,000. A police car with an original cost of $25,000 was sold for $7,000.

- Office equipment to be used by the city fire department was acquired through a capital lease. The lease required 10 equal annual payments of $10,000 beginning with the July 1 acquisition date. Using a 6% discount rate, the 10 payments had a present value of $78,000 at the acquisition date.

- The courthouse was improved and financed as budgeted except for a $27,000 cost overrun that was paid for by the general fund. Jey plans to transfer cash to the debt service fund during the following year to service the interest and principal payments called for in the bonds. (11/96, AR, #3, amended, 6317 - 6328)

Research Task	Scenario	Additional Information	Responses

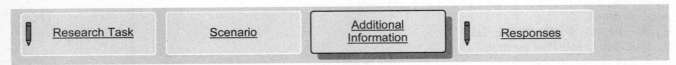

- Information related to the solid waste landfill at December 31.

Capacity	1,000,000 cubic yards
Usage prior to the current year	500,000 cubic yards
Usage in the current year	40,000 cubic yards
Estimated total life	20 years
Closure costs incurred to date	$ 300,000
Estimated future costs of closure and post-closure care	1,700,000
Expense for closure and post-closure care recognized prior to current year	973,000

Research Task	Scenario	Additional Information	Responses

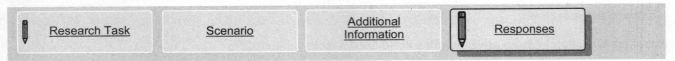

For Items 1 through 10, determine the amounts based solely on the above information.

1. $______ What was the net effect of the budgetary activities on the general fund balance at January 1 of the current year?

2. $______ What was the total amount of operating transfers out included in the general fund's budgetary accounts at January 1 of the current year?

3. $______ What amount of interest payable related to the 20-year bonds should be reported by the general fund at December 31 of the current year?

4. $______ What lease payment amount should be included in current year general fund expenditures?

5. $______ What amount was collected from current year property taxes in the current year?

6. $______ What was the total amount of the capital project fund's current year revenues?

7. $______ What amount should be reported as long-term liabilities in the government-wide statement of net assets in the governmental activities column at December 31 of the current year?

8. $______ What net increase in capital assets should be reported in the government-wide statement of net assets in the governmental activities column at December 31 of the current year?

9. $______ What current year closure and postclosure care expenses should be reported in the solid waste landfill enterprise fund?

10. $______ What should be the December 31 current year closure and post closure care liability reported in the solid waste landfill enterprise fund?

For Items 11 and 12, indicate the measurement focus of the Jey fund mentioned.

11. __________ Capital project fund
12. __________ Solid waste landfill enterprise fund

A. Subsidy restrictions
B. Bond restrictions
C. Expenditures
D. Financial resources
E. Capital maintenance/intergenerational equity

Problem 19-4 (8 to 15 minutes)

Research Task | Scenario | Choices & Responses

Research Question: What is the proper reporting of general capital assets not specifically related to other activities?

Paragraph Reference Answer: ______________

Research Task | Scenario | Choices & Responses

The following information relates to Dane City during its fiscal year ended December 31:

- On October 31, to finance the construction of a city hall annex, Dane issued 8% 10-year general obligation bonds at their face value of $600,000. Construction expenditures during the period equaled $364,000.
- Dane reported $109,000 from hotel room taxes, restricted for tourist promotion, in a special revenue fund. The fund paid $81,000 for general promotions and $22,000 for a motor vehicle.
- The general fund revenues of $104,500 were transferred to a debt service fund and used to repay $100,000 of 9% 15-year term bonds, and to pay $4,500 of interest. The bonds were used to acquire a citizens' center.
- At December 31, as a consequence of past services, city firefighters had accumulated entitlements to compensated absences valued at $86,000. General fund resources available at December 31 are expected to be used to settle $17,000 of this amount, and $69,000 is expected to be paid out of future general fund resources.
- At December 31, Dane was responsible for $83,000 of outstanding general fund encumbrances, including the $8,000 for supplies indicated below.
- Dane uses the purchases method to account for supplies. The following information relates to supplies:

Inventory—1/1	$ 39,000
12/31	42,000
Encumbrances outstanding—1/1	6,000
12/31	8,000
Purchase orders during the year	190,000
Amounts credited to vouchers payable during the year	181,000

(11/95, AR, #117 - 126, amended, 5860 - 5869)

Research Task	Scenario	Choices & Responses

For Items 1 through 10, determine the amounts based solely on the above information.

1. _______ What is the amount of general fund operating transfers out?
2. _______ How much should be reported as general fund liabilities from entitlements for compensated absences?
3. _______ What is the reserved amount of the general fund balance?
4. _______ What is the capital projects fund balance?
5. _______ What is the fund balance on the special revenue fund for tourist promotion?
6. _______ What is the amount of debt service fund expenditures?
7. _______ What amount should be included in the general fund for capital assets acquired in the year?
8. _______ What amount stemming from transactions and events decreased the long-term liabilities reported in the government activities column of the government-wide statements?
9. _______ Using the purchases method, what is the amount of supplies expenditures?
10. _______ What was the total amount of supplies encumbrances?

Amount Choices					
$ 0	$17,000	$ 86,000	$125,000	$ 181,000	$236,000
$4,500	$28,000	$100,000	$139,000	$1,872,000	$364,000
$6,000	$83,000	$104,500	$169,000	$ 190,000	$386,000

Problem 19-5 (45 to 55 minutes)

Research Task	Scenario & Responses 1-10	Responses 11-20

Research Question: What should be recorded as a deferred revenue?

Paragraph Reference Answer: _______________

Research Task	Scenario & Responses 1-10	Responses 11-20

Items 1 through 10 represent various transactions pertaining to a municipality that uses encumbrance accounting. For 1 through 10, select the appropriate recording of the transaction (A through L). A method of recording the transactions may be selected once, more than once, or not at all.

Transactions

1. _______ General obligation bonds were issued at par.
2. _______ Approved purchase orders were issued for supplies.
3. _______ The above-mentioned supplies were received and the related invoices were approved.
4. _______ General fund salaries and wages were incurred.

→

5. _______ The internal service fund had interfund billings.
6. _______ Revenues were earned from a previously awarded grant.
7. _______ Property taxes were collected in advance.
8. _______ Appropriations were recorded on adoption of the budget.
9. _______ Short-term financing was received from a bank, secured by the city's taxing power.
10. _______ There was an excess of estimated inflows over estimated outflows.

Recording of Transactions Choices		
A. Credit appropriations control.	E. Credit interfund revenues.	I. Debit appropriations control.
B. Credit budgetary fund balance—unreserved.	F. Credit tax anticipation notes payable.	J. Debit deferred revenues.
C. Credit expenditures control.	G. Credit other financing sources.	K. Debit encumbrances control.
D. Credit deferred revenues.	H. Credit other financing uses.	L. Debit expenditures control.

(11/92, P11, #4 (61 - 80), amended, 3395 - 3413)

Research Task | Scenario & Responses 1-10 | Responses 11-20

Items 11 through 20 represent the funds and accounts used by the municipality. For 11 through 20, select the appropriate method of accounting and reporting (M through V). An accounting and reporting method may be selected once, more than once, or not at all.

11. ______ Enterprise fund fixed assets.
12. ______ Capital projects fund.
13. ______ Internal service fund fixed assets.
14. ______ Private-purpose trust fund cash.
15. ______ Enterprise fund cash.
16. ______ General fund.
17. ______ Agency fund cash.
18. ______ Pension trust fund cash.
19. ______ Special revenue fund.
20. ______ Debt service fund.

Accounting and Reporting by Funds Choices	
M. Accounted for in a fiduciary fund.	R. Accounts for major construction activities.
N. Accounted for in a proprietary fund.	S. Accounts for property tax revenues.
O. Accounted for in a quasi-endowment fund.	T. Accounts for payment of interest and principal on tax supported debt.
P. Accounted for in a self-balancing account group.	U. Accounts for revenues from earmarked sources to finance designated activities.
Q. Accounted for in a special assessment fund.	V. Reporting is optional.

Problem 19-6 (5 to 10 minutes)

Research Task	Scenario	Choices & Responses

Research Question: A governmental accounting system must make it possible to do what two things?

Paragraph Reference Answer: ______________

Research Task	Scenario	Choices & Responses

Items 1 through 5 represent transactions by governmental-type funds based on the following selected information taken from Dease City's year-end financial records:

General fund	
Beginning fund balance	$ 700,000
Estimated revenues	10,000,000
Actual revenues	10,500,000
Appropriations	9,000,000
Expenditures	8,200,000
Ending encumbrances	500,000
Ending vouchers payable	300,000
Operating transfers in	100,000
The year's property tax levy	9,500,000
The year's property taxes estimated to be uncollectible when property tax levy for the year is recorded	100,000
The year's property taxes delinquent at end of the year	150,000
Capital projects fund	
Operating transfers in	100,000
Construction of new library wing started and completed in the year	
• Proceeds from bonds issued at 100	2,000,000
• Expenditures	2,100,000

(5/97, AR, #2, amended, 6355 - 6350)

Research Task	Scenario	Choices & Responses

For Items 1 through 5, determine the amounts solely on the above information.

1. $______ What was the net amount credited to the budgetary fund balance when the budget was approved?
2. $______ What was the amount of property taxes collected on the property tax levy for the year?
3. $______ What amount for the new library wing was included in the capital projects fund balance at the end of the year?
4. $______ What amount for the new library wing was reported in the government-wide statement of net assets in the governmental activities column at the end of the year?
5. $______ What amount for the new library wing bonds was reported in the government-wide statement of net assets in the governmental activities column at the end of the year?

Amount Choices	
$ 0	$ 9,000,000
$ 100,000	$ 9,250,000
$ 200,000	$ 9,350,000
$2,000,000	$ 9,500,000
$2,100,000	$10,000,000

Problem 19-7 (23 to 35 minutes)

Research Task | Scenario | Other Information | Responses 1-16

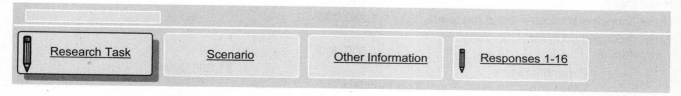

Research Question: Which governmental fund is used to account general long-term debt?

Paragraph Reference Answer: ______________

Research Task | Scenario | Other Information | Responses 1-16

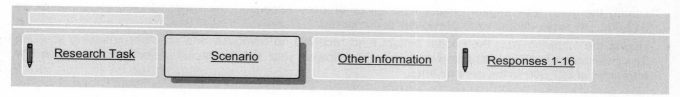

Bel City, whose first fiscal year ended December 31, has only the long-term debt specified in the information and only the funds necessitated by the information.

1. General fund:

- The following selected information is taken from Bel's general fund financial records:

	Budget	Actual
Property taxes	$5,000,000	$4,700,000
Other revenues	1,000,000	1,050,000
Total revenues	$6,000,000	$5,750,000
Total expenditures	$5,600,000	$5,700,000
Property taxes receivable—delinquent		$ 420,000
Less: Allowance for estimated uncollectible taxes—delinquent		50,000
		$ 370,000

- There were no amendments to the budget as originally adopted.
- No property taxes receivable have been written off, and the allowance for uncollectibles balance is unchanged from the initial entry at the time of the original tax levy.
- There were no encumbrances outstanding at December 31. (5/95, AR, #2 (61 - 84), amended, 5479 - 5502)

Research Task | Scenario | Other Information | Responses 1-16

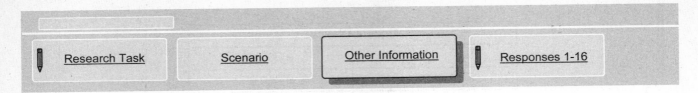

2. Capital project fund:

- Finances for Bel's new civic center were provided by a combination of general fund transfers, a state grant, and an issue of general obligation bonds. Any bond premium on issuance is to be used for the repayment of the bonds at their $1,200,000 par value. At December 31 the capital project fund for the civic center had the following closing entries:

Revenues	$ 800,000	
Other financing sources— bond proceeds	1,230,000	
Other financing sources—operating transfers in	500,000	
Expenditures		$1,080,000
Other financing uses—operating transfers out		30,000
Unreserved fund balance		1,420,000

- Also at December 31, capital project fund entries reflected Bel's intention to honor the $1,300,000 purchase orders and commitments outstanding for the center.
- During the year, total capital project fund encumbrances exceeded the corresponding expenditures by $42,000. All expenditures were previously encumbered.
- During the following year the capital project fund received no revenues and no other financing sources. The civic center building was completed early the following year and the capital project fund was closed by a transfer of $27,000 to the general fund.

3. Water utility enterprise fund:

- Bel issued $4,000,000 revenue bonds at par. These bonds, together with a $700,000 transfer from the general fund, were used to acquire a water utility. Water utility revenues are to be the sole source of funds to retire these bonds beginning in 8 years.

Research Task | Scenario | Other Information | Responses 1-16

For 1 through 16, indicate if the answer to each item is yes (**Y**) or no (**N**).

Items 1 through 8 relate to Bel's general fund.

1. _____ Did recording budgetary accounts at the beginning of the year increase the fund balance by $50,000?
2. _____ Should the budgetary accounts for the year include an entry for the expected transfer of funds from the general fund to the capital projects fund?
3. _____ Should the $700,000 payment from the general fund, which was used to help to establish the water utility fund, be reported as an "other financing use—operating transfers out"?
4. _____ Did the general fund receive the $30,000 bond premium from the capital projects fund?

5. _____ Should a payment from the general fund for water received for normal civic center operations be reported as an "other financing use—operating transfers out"?

6. _____ Does the net property taxes receivable of $370,000 include amounts expected to be collected after the following March 15?

7. _____ Would closing budgetary accounts cause the fund balance to increase by $400,000?

8. _____ Would the interaction between budgetary and actual amounts cause the fund balance to decrease by $350,000?

Items 9 through 16 relate to Bel's financial statements.

9. _____ In the government-wide statement of net assets, is there a total elimination of interfund transactions?

10. _____ In the government-wide statement of activities, are general revenues separated from program revenues?

11. _____ In the government-wide statement of net assets, is the internal service fund reported as a governmental activity?

12. _____ In the primary government's financial statements, is the general fund a nonmajor fund?

13. _____ In the government-wide statements of net assets, are fiduciary funds reported as business-type activities?

In which fund should Bel report capital and related financing activities in its statement of cash flows?

14. _____ Debt service fund.

15. _____ Capital project fund.

16. _____ Water utility enterprise fund.

Responses 17-22

For 17 through 22, determine the amount.

Items 17 and 18 relate to Bel's general fund.

17. $_______ What was the amount recorded in the opening entry for appropriations?

18. $_______ What was the total amount debited to property taxes receivable?

Items 19 through 22 relate to Bel's funds other than the general fund.

19. $_______ What was the completed cost of the civic center?

20. $_______ How much was the state capital grant for the civic center?

21. $_______ In the capital project fund, what was the amount of the total encumbrances recorded during the year?

22. $_______ In the capital project fund, what was the unreserved fund balance reported at December 31?

Problem 19-8 (20 to 30 minutes)

Research Task	Scenario	Responses 1-6	Responses 7-13

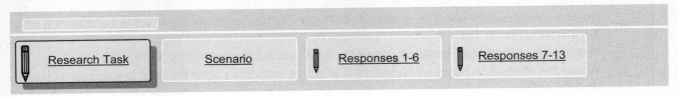

Research Question: What are the character classifications of expenditures?

Paragraph Reference Answer: ______________

Research Task	Scenario	Responses 1-6	Responses 7-13

The following selected information is taken from Shar City's general fund operating statement for the year ended December 31, year 2:

Revenues	
Property taxes—year 2	$825,000
Expenditures	
Current services	
Public safety	428,000
Capital outlay (police vehicles)	100,000
Debt service	74,000

Expenditures—year 2	$1,349,000
Expenditures—year 1	56,000
Expenditures	$1,405,000
Excess of revenues over expenditures	$ 153,000
Other financing uses	(125,000)
Excess of revenues over expenditures and other financing uses	28,000
Decrease in reserve for encumbrances during year 2	15,000
Residual equity transfers out	(190,000)
Decrease in unreserved fund balance during year 2	(147,000)
Unreserved fund balance January 1, year 2	304,000
Unreserved fund balance December 31, year 2	$ 157,000

The following selected information is taken from Shar's December 31, year 2, general fund balance sheet:

Property taxes receivable—delinquent—year 2	$ 34,000
Less: Allowance for estimated uncollectible taxes—delinquent	20,000
Vouchers payable	89,000
Fund balance—	
reserved for encumbrances—year 2	43,000
reserved for supplies inventory	38,000
unreserved	157,000

Additional Information:

- Debt service was for bonds used to finance a library building and included interest of $22,000.
- $8,000 of year 2 property taxes receivable were written-off; otherwise, the allowance for uncollectible taxes balance is unchanged from the initial entry at the time of the original tax levy at the beginning of the year.
- Shar reported supplies inventory of $21,000 at December 31, year 1.

(5/96, AR, #17 - 35, amended, 6214 - 6232)

Research Task | Scenario | Responses 1-6 | Responses 7-13

For items 1 through 3, indicate the type of classification used by Shar.

A. Character
B. Function
C. Object

1. _____ Expenditures—current services
2. _____ Expenditures—capital outlay
3. _____ Expenditures—health

For items 4 through 6, select the best answer.

4. _____ What recording method did Shar use for its general fund supplies inventory?
   A. Consumption
   B. Purchase
   C. Perpetual inventory

5. _____ How should fund equity be reported in Shar's electric utility enterprise fund?
   A. An amount described as fund balance
   B. An amount described as net assets
   C. Separately for amount due to general fund and retained income

6. _____ Shar's electric utility enterprise fund borrowed $1,000,000 subject to Shar's general guarantee. Where should the liability be reported in the government-wide statement of net assets?
   A. The business-type activities column
   B. The general long-term debt account group
   C. Both the business-type activities column and the general long-term debt account group

Research Task | Scenario | Responses 1-6 | Responses 7-13

For items 7 through 13, indicate the part of Shar's general fund statement of activities affected by the transaction. Any choice may be used once, more than once, or not at all.

A. Revenues
B. Expenditures
C. Other financing sources
D. Other financing uses
E. Statement of activities is **not** affected

7. _____ An unrestricted state grant is received.
8. _____ The general fund paid pension fund contributions that were recoverable from an internal service fund.
9. _____ The general fund paid $60,000 for electricity supplied by Shar's electric utility enterprise fund.
10. _____ General fund resources were used to subsidize Shar's swimming pool enterprise fund.
11. _____ $90,000 of general fund resources were loaned to an internal service fund.
12. _____ A motor pool internal service fund was established by a transfer of $80,000 from the general fund. This amount will not be repaid unless the motor pool is disbanded.
13. _____ General fund resources were used to pay amounts due on an operating lease.

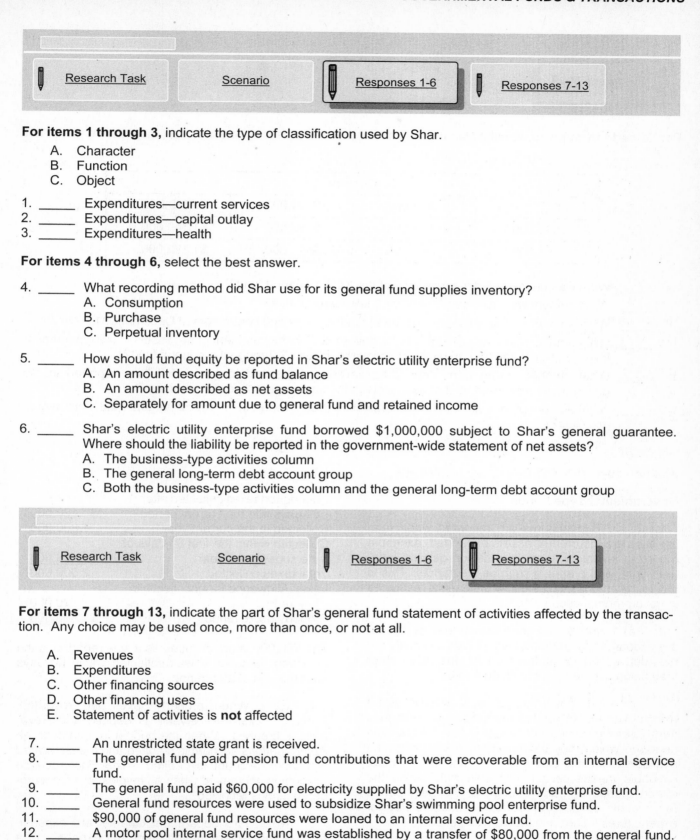

Responses 14-19

For items 14 through 19, calculate the numeric amount. Any choice may be used once, more than once, or not at all.

Choices			
$ 0	$79,000	$100,000	$ 819,000
$39,000	$89,000	$132,000	$1,349,000
$52,000	$96,000	$811,000	$1,392,000

14. _____ What was the reserved fund balance of the Year 1 general fund?
15. _____ What amount was collected from Year 2 tax assessments?
16. _____ What amount is Shar's liability to general fund vendors and contractors at December 31, Year 2?
17. _____ What amount should be included in the government-wide statement of net assets in the governmental activities column for capital assets acquired in Year 2 through the general fund?
18. _____ What amount arising from Year 2 transactions decreased long-term liabilities reported in the government-wide statement of net assets in the governmental activities column?
19. _____ What amount of total actual expenditures should Shar report in its Year 2 general fund statement of activities?

Solution 19-1 MULTIPLE CHOICE ANSWERS

Governmental-Type Funds

1. (d) Expenditures are recorded when fund liabilities are incurred or assets expended, except in regard to inventory items, interest on general long-term debt, and prepaids such as insurance. This is due to the emphasis on the flow of financial resources in governmental accounting.

2. (a) Interest on general long-term debt, usually accounted for in debt service funds, normally are recorded as an expenditure on its due date rather than being accrued prior to its due date.

3. (c) All governmental entities that report using governmental funds should recognize revenues from taxpayer-assessed taxes in the accounting period in which they become both measurable and available to finance expenditures of the fiscal period. Available means collected or collectible within the current period or early enough in the next period (e.g., within 60 days or so) to be used to pay for expenditures incurred in the current period.

Prior period taxes collected after 60 days into the current period	$ 120,000
Collected in the current year	1,800,000
Collected within the first 60 days of the subsequent year	80,000
Total taxes collected	2,000,000
Less: Allowance for uncollectible amounts	(20,000)
Property tax revenue	$1,980,000

The $50,000 is not included as it was reported in the prior year because it was collected within 60 days after the end of that period.

4. (c) When property taxes are recorded, *Property Taxes—Receivable* is debited and *Revenues* is credited. When the budget is recorded, the *Appropriations* account is credited and the *Estimated Revenues* account is debited. The *Encumbrance* account is decreased when an invoice for an encumbered item is received.

5. (d) Fire department salaries are *expenditures* of the general government, not *expenses* of a propriety fund. While goods and services committed for by purchase order or contract are encumbered in

governmental funds to avoid overspending appropriations, some expenditures are controlled by other means and need not be encumbered. Salaries are set by contract and controlled by established payroll procedures and are not encumbered.

6. (c) The amount of Cliff's encumbrances that were outstanding at June 30 is $500,000 (i.e., $5,000,000 – $4,500,000). When the purchase orders were issued, the following entry was made:

Encumbrances Control (estimated cost)	5,000,000	
Reserve for Encumbrances		5,000,000

Upon receipt of the goods and related invoices, the following entries were made:

Reserve for Encumbrances	4,500,000	
Encumbrances Control		4,500,000
(reverse original entry)		
Expenditures (actual cost)	4,200,000	
Vouchers Payable		4,200,000

7. (d) When the purchase order for the supplies was issued, the following entry was made:

Encumbrances Control (estimated cost)	5,000	
Reserve for Encumbrances		5,000

Upon receipt of the supplies and invoice, the following entries were made:

Reserve for Encumbrances		
(reverse original entry)	5,000	
Encumbrances Control		5,000
Expenditures (actual cost)	4,950	
Vouchers Payable		4,950

8. (d) The *Estimated Revenues* account is a budgetary account. Budgetary accounts are generally opened with balances opposite of the corresponding actual account.

9. (c) The *Appropriations* account is credited when the budget is recorded. The entry when a $100 purchase order is issued is as follows:

DR: Encumbrances	100	
CR: Reserve for Encumbrances		100

When a corresponding invoice is received for $105, the following two entries are made:

DR: Reserve for Encumbrances	100	
CR: Encumbrances		100

DR: Expenditures	105	
CR: Vouchers Payable		105

General Fund

10. (c) In governmental funds, the primary emphasis is on the flow of financial resources. Accordingly, the amount of claims and judgments recorded as expenditures (and liabilities) in governmental funds is the amount accrued during the year that would normally be liquidated with expendable available financial resources. Optionally, noncurrent claims and judgment liabilities are recorded initially in the GLTDAG. They only become governmental fund expenditures in the year in which they mature or become current liabilities.

Claims paid during the year	$ 800,000
Increase in current liability for claims and judgments during the year ($140,000 – $100,000)	40,000
Annual claims and judgment expenditures	$ 840,000

11. (b) *Appropriations* is a budgetary account which will be closed. However, since closing the budgetary accounts (which are not all given) simply reverses the entry to record the budget, their closing has no effect on fund balance. The closing entry for the activity accounts given would increase the fund balance, as follows:

Revenues	8,000,000	
Other Financing Sources	1,500,000	
Expenditures		5,000,000
Other Financing Uses		2,000,000
Fund Balance (difference)		2,500,000

12. (c) The *fund balance* account of the governmental unit is *debited* at the beginning of the year because appropriations *exceed* estimated revenues, shown in Entry (1). During the year, revenues *equaled* estimated revenues; therefore, the *fund balance* account is *not affected* by the revenue closing entry, as in Entry (2). During the year, expenditures and encumbrances were *less than* appropriations; therefore, the *fund balance* account is *credited* for the closing entry for the appropriations, expenditures, and encumbrances, as in Entry (3).

(1)	Estimated Revenues Control	XX	
	Fund Balance (to balance)	XX	
	Appropriations Control		XX
(2)	Revenues Control	XX	
	Estimated Revenues Control		XX
(3)	Appropriations Control	XX	
	Expenditures Control		XX
	Encumbrances Control		XX
	Fund Balance (to balance)		XX

13. (b) Commitments made by a government are encumbrances. Appropriations are amounts budgeted to be spent. Expenditures are amounts

that have been spent. A fixed assets account is not debited until the property is placed in service.

14. (a) The general fund records the expected $9,000,000 of inflows of resources for property taxes, licenses, and fines as estimated revenues in the entry to record the adoption of the budget. In this same entry, the expected inflows of resources from the proceeds of the debt issue and the interfund transfers for debt service are recorded as other financing sources.

15. (b) To record purchase orders issued or contract commitments, the *Encumbrances* account is debited and *Reserve for Encumbrances* is credited.

16. (b) Because Park's appropriations do not lapse at year-end, the *Fund Balance Reserved for Encumbrances* account is converted from an offsetting memorandum account in the general ledger to a true reservation of *Fund Balance* at year-end. The amount that Park should report as *Unreserved Fund Balance* in its general fund balance sheet is computed as follows:

Total assets	$ 1,000,000
Less: Total liabilities	600,000
Total fund balance	400,000
Less: Fund balance reserved for encumbrances	100,000
Unreserved fund balance, December 31	$ 300,000

17. (b) The $1,000,000 unrestricted grant received from the state should be accounted for as revenue in Cal City's general fund. The $200,000 of interest received on bank accounts held for employees' pension plans should be accounted for in Cal City's pension trust fund.

18. (d) The *Encumbrance* and *Budgetary Fund Balance Reserved for Encumbrances* (BFBRFE) accounts increase by equal amounts when a $200 purchase order is approved:

Encumbrances (estimated cost)	200	
Reserve for Encumbrances		200

The *Encumbrance* and BFBRFE accounts decrease by equal amounts when the receipt of the related goods for $203 and the vouchers payable are recorded:

Fund Balance Reserved for Encumbrances	200	
Encumbrances (estimated cost)		200
Expenditures (actual cost)	203	
Vouchers Payable		203

The *Encumbrance* and BFBRFE accounts will have identical balances unless a recording error was made.

Special Revenue Funds

19. (c) Special revenue funds are used to account for revenues that have been legally restricted as to expenditure. The NCGA provides several examples of revenues which would fall under this heading: (1) a state gasoline tax collected in order to maintain streets, (2) proceeds from parking meters which finance the local traffic court, and (3) state juvenile rehabilitation grants used to operate and maintain juvenile rehabilitation centers. In each of these cases, a service is being provided, but the funding comes from a specific source rather than from general revenues. The sales taxes collected to finance the maintenance of tourist facilities in the shopping district should be accounted for in a special revenue fund. The donation mandated to provide meals for the needy should be accounted for in a private-purpose trust fund. Special revenue funds are used to account for resources held in trust by a government for a specific purpose where both the principal and any earnings may be expended for government programs. Private-purpose trust funds are resources to be expended for the benefit of individuals, organizations, or other governments.

20. (a) Special revenue funds are used to account for financial resources that are restricted by law or by contractual agreement to specific purposes *other than for permanent funds or major capital projects.* Thus, neither the $8,000 of proceeds of the short-term notes to be used for advances to permanent fund nor the $90,000 of proceeds on long-term debt to be used for a major capital project should be accounted for in a special revenue fund.

21. (b) The $900,000 of gasoline taxes collected to finance road repairs should be accounted for in a Special Revenue Fund. Special Revenue Funds are used to account for revenues that have been legally restricted as to expenditure. The NCGA provides several examples of revenues which would fall under the heading: (1) a state gasoline tax collected in order to maintain streets, (2) proceeds from parking meters which finance the local traffic court, and (3) state juvenile rehabilitation grants used to operate and maintain juvenile rehabilitation centers. In each of these cases, a service is being provided, but the funding comes from a specific revenue source rather than from property taxes or any other general revenues.

Capital Projects Fund

22. (a) Capital projects fund inflows from intergovernmental grants and from interest on investments are considered *revenue.* On the other hand, capital projects fund inflows from bond or other

long-term general obligation debt issues and transfers from other funds should be reported as *other financing sources.* Therefore, Walk should report a total of $3,000,000 ($2,000,000 from the bond issue + $1,000,000 from the general fund) in the *Other Financing Sources Control* account, not in revenue.

23. (a) Debt proceeds should be recognized by a capital projects fund at the time the debt is incurred, rather than the time the debt is authorized or when the proceeds are expended. Debt proceeds should be reported in the capital projects fund as *Other Financing Sources* rather than as *Revenues.* The entry in the capital projects fund to record the issuance of the bonds is as follows:

Cash	4,000,000	
Other Financing Sources—Bond Proceeds		4,000,000

24. (a) GASB 34 requires long-term debt issued ($1,000,000) to be reported as an other financing source. Premiums ($10,000) and discounts are reported as other financing sources and uses, respectively. Debt issue costs paid out of proceeds are reported as expenditures. Therefore, the city should report the entire $1,010,000 as an other financing source, not net of expenditures.

25. (c) The capital projects fund reports unrestricted grants received from other governmental units as revenue. Therefore, the $400,000 grant from the state is reported as revenue in Fir's capital projects fund's operating statement. The capital projects fund reports long-term debt proceeds and operating transfers from other funds as other financing sources. Therefore, the $500,000 proceeds from the general obligation bond issue and the $100,000 transfer from Fir's general fund are reported as other financing sources of $600,000 in the capital project fund's operating statement.

26. (d) A governmental unit would issue bond anticipation notes to provide funds to defray costs expected to be incurred before the related bonds are issued. Such notes are treated as long-term debt, even if due within one year, if (1) they are to be repaid with the proceeds of the bond issue, (2) all legal steps have been taken to refinance the notes, and (3) the intent is supported by an ability to refinance the short-term notes on a long-term basis. Since all of these criteria are not met for the bond anticipation notes in question, they are reported as a liability of the capital projects fund.

27. (a) Debt service funds are used to account for the accumulation of resources for, and the payment of, general long-term debt principal and interest.

Debt Service Funds

28. (a) Neither the bond issue costs nor the debt insurance are deferred and amortized over the life of the bonds. The bond issue proceeds are recorded at the amount received net of any issue and insurance costs incurred.

29. (c) Fern should report $3,400,000 as long-term capital debt. This amount is comprised of (1) long-term bonds for financing of capital asset acquisition and (2) bond anticipation notes (BANs) due in six months that were issued as part of a long-term financing plan for capital purposes. Although the BANs are due in six months, the intent is to refinance the BANs on a long-term basis. The vendor financing is not reported as long-term capital debt because it is not part of a long-term financing plan.

30. (d) Governmental-type funds do not defer and amortize a bond premium or discount over the life of the bonds. Bond issue proceeds are recorded in the appropriate governmental fund at the amount received, net of any bond premium or discount.

31. (a) Only general obligation long-term debt should be serviced through debt service funds. Fiduciary and proprietary fund debt are rarely general government obligations.

32. (c) The debt service fund of a governmental unit is used to account for accumulation of resources for, and the payment of, general long-term debt principal and interest. The debt service fund reports cash receipts from the general fund as operating transfers. Cash payments for long-term debt principal and related interest are reported as expenditures in the fund.

Permanent Funds

33. (a) The cash, which can be used only for law enforcement activities, should be accounted for in special revenue fund because the Act does not require the preservation of fund principal and the principal may be used for Arlen's benefit. An agency fund is established to account for assets received by a government in its capacity as an agent for individuals, businesses, or other governments. Therefore, the sales taxes collected by Arlen to be distributed to other governments are accounted for in an agency fund.

Proprietary Funds

34. (a) Proprietary funds are accounted for essentially as if they were private sector, profit seeking business enterprises. Therefore, the orientation of these funds is income determination.

35. (a) The proprietary funds consist of the enterprise and internal service funds. Therefore, Cole's proprietary equity balances amount to $1,400,000 (i.e., $1,000,000 + $400,000).

36. (a) The appropriate basis of accounting for proprietary and fiduciary funds is the accrual basis, under which revenues are recognized in the accounting period in which they are earned and become measurable.

Internal Service Funds

37. (d) An internal service fund's net income is not affected by temporary transfers. Internal service funds report residual equity transfers in and out as other financing sources and other financing uses, respectively. An internal service fund's net income is affected by operating revenues and expenses, nonoperating revenues and expenses, and operating and residual equity transfers.

38. (b) Internal service funds are accounted for in a similar manner to enterprise funds. A *Revenues* or *Billings To Others* account is used for services provided to other departments or other governments. Appropriations accounts are budgetary accounts. Interfund exchanges would be between departments in the same government unit. Intergovernmental transfers are used when the same entity is doing the accounting for both governments.

39. (b) Residual equity transfers are as *Other Financing Sources* or *Other Financing Uses.*

40. (d) Billings for services provided to other governmental units are recorded by the internal service fund as operating revenues.

Enterprise Funds

41. (b) Grants, entitlements, and shared revenues received by proprietary funds should be reported as nonoperating revenues unless they are externally restricted to capital acquisitions.

42. (c) Depreciation of fixed assets is required and is not optional in an enterprise fund. Enterprise funds must be used to account for a government's business-type operations that are financed and operated like private businesses—where the government's intent is that all costs (expenses, including depreciation) of providing goods or services to the general public on a continuing basis are to be financed or recovered primarily through user charges. Fixed assets are not treated as expenditures in an enterprise fund.

43. (d) Enterprise funds should be used to account for operations (1) that are financed in a manner to private business enterprises—where the intent of the governing body is that the costs, including depreciation, of providing goods or services to the general public on a continuing basis be financed or recovered primarily through user charges or (2) where the governing body has decided that periodic determination of revenues earned, expenses incurred, and/or net income is appropriate for capital maintenance, public policy, management control, accountability, or other purposes. Internal service funds are used to account for the financing of goods or services provided by one department or agency to other departments or agencies of a government, or to other governments, on a cost reimbursement basis.

44. (c) Since this is an enterprise fund, accrual applies. Interest expense for the year includes the $30,000 ($1,000,000 × 6% × 1/2 year) paid on October 1 and the $15,000 ($1,000,000 × 6% × 1/4 year) accrued expense from October 1 through December 31.

45. (d) Where the government's intent is that all costs of providing goods or services to the general public are to be financed or recovered primarily through user charges, an enterprise fund must be used. The assumption that the lottery is not intended to be subsidized by the state is easily reached, since this is not an ordinary purpose of government. Those who are able to pay will likely be charged by the hospital, without contrary information stated in the question. The state likely has a separate program to pay for qualified indigents' healthcare, with reimbursement available to any qualified provider. In this case, the state hospital would be similar to a private facility in regard to reimbursement from state and federal indigents' healthcare programs. Thus, the hospital's costs are to be recovered *primarily* through user charges. Alternatively, the hospital may be heavily subsidized by the state, in which case it should *not* be accounted for in an enterprise fund.

Fiduciary Funds

46. (c) Fiduciary funds are used to account for assets held by a governmental unit acting as a trustee or agent for individuals, organizations, other governmental units, or other funds of the same government. Four distinct types of fiduciary funds exist: (1) pension trust funds, (2) investment trust funds,

(3) private-purpose trust funds, and (4) agency funds. Ridge City's total fiduciary fund assets amounted to $600,000 ($200,000 of agency fund assets and $400,000 of pension trust fund assets). The special revenue fund is a governmental, not a fiduciary, fund.

47. (a) All pension trust fund contributions and earnings are accounted for as fund revenues. The pension trust fund makes the following entry to record employer contributions:

Cash	11,000	
Revenues Control—Employer Contribution		11,000

48. (b) *Governmental-type funds* record contributions to the pension trust fund as *expenditures.* A governmental-type fund would make the following entry to record its contribution:

Expenditures Cntrl—Pension Contribution	11,000	
Cash		11,000

It is important to note that *proprietary-type funds* (i.e., enterprise and internal service funds) record contributions to the pension trust fund as *expenses.* The following entry would be recorded in a proprietary-type fund to reflect its contribution to the pension trust fund:

Expenses Control—Pension Contribution	XX	
Cash		XX

49. (d) The PERS should be accounted for in a pension trust fund. Under the traditional approach of accounting for pension trust funds under NCGA Statement 1, the $14,300,000 Fund Balance of the pension trust fund can be determined by adding the Reserve for Employee Contributions (i.e., $9,000,000), the Reserve for Employer Contributions (i.e., $5,000,000), and the Actuarial Deficiency in Reserve for Employer's Contributions (i.e., $300,000).

50. (c) Under the modified basis of accounting, governments accrue sales tax revenue when it is measurable and available for use. "Available for use" means that the revenues will be collected within the current period or early enough in the next period (i.e., within 60 days or so) to be used to pay for expenditures incurred in the current period. All of these revenues will be collected within 60 days. Curry City's portion of the total is not reported as revenues in the state's financial statements. Curry's portion is reported in the state's books in an agency fund (which does not have operating accounts) in an account such as *Due to City.*

Interfund Transactions

51. (d) NCGA Statement 1 provides specific guidance on accounting for four types of interfund transactions. This is a quasi-external transaction, or one that would result in recognizing revenues and expenditures or expenses, as appropriate, as if it was with an organization apart from the government. The transactions in the other answers would not occur with an independent organization.

52. (c) Operating transfers should be reported in *Other Financing Sources Uses* or *Other Financing* accounts and reported after revenues and expenditures or expenses, but before determining the results of operations in the operating statements.

53. (c) GASB Section 2200.903 illustrates interfund receivables and payables reported as amounts due to and due from other funds. They are not reported as reservations of fund balance or additions to or reductions from the unrestricted fund balance. Section 2200.108 allows the option of eliminating the interfund assets and liabilities, but requires that such eliminations be apparent from the headings, or be disclosed in the notes to the financial statements.

54. (d) The interfund receivables and payables of a governmental fund should not be netted. Therefore, the special revenue fund should report an asset of $10,000 for the amount *due from* the general fund and a liability of $4,000 for the amount *due to* the agency fund.

Determining Fund or Group

55. (c) Capital project funds are used to account for financial resources that are to be used to construct or otherwise acquire major long-lived "general government" capital facilities—such as buildings and infrastructure. Since the federal grant is restricted to construction of a center for rehabilitation of drug addicts, it should be accounted for in the capital project funds.

56. (b) Capital project funds are used to account for the acquisition and use of financial resources to construct or otherwise acquire long-lived general government fixed assets. Project resources, which include *proceeds* of general obligation bonds, are recorded in the capital project funds as received or accrued. Debt service funds account for the accumulation of resources for, and the payment of, general long-term debt principal and interest. Thus, a debt service fund would not account for the general obligation bond itself; rather it would maintain

resources that are then used to meet the general obligation bonds as they become due.

57. (d) Since it is a governmental fund, long-term debt of the capital projects fund is not reported in the fund. Debt service funds account for the accumulation of resources for, and the payment of, general long-term debt principal and interest. Therefore, the portion of the special tax that is restricted to repay the long-term debt of the capital projects fund should be accounted for in a debt service fund.

58. (c) The debt service fund is used to account for the accumulation of resources for the periodic payment of interest and principal of general obligation long-term debt. Special revenue funds are used when other governmental-type funds are not more appropriate.

59. (a) Enterprise funds are used to account for a government's "business-type" operations that are financed and operated like private businesses (i.e., where the government's intent is that all costs, including depreciation, of providing goods or services to the general public on a continuing basis are to be financed or recovered primarily through user charges). Most government-owned public utilities must be accounted for in the enterprise funds under these criteria. Internal service funds account for the financing of goods or services provided by one department or agency to other departments or agencies of a governmental unit, or to other governmental units, on a cost-reimbursement basis. Agency funds account for resources held by a government as an agent for individuals or other governmental units. Special revenue funds account for general government resources that are restricted by law or contract for specific purposes.

60. (a) The agency fund is used to account for the custodial activities of the governmental unit. The debt service fund is used to account for the repayment of the general long-term debt. The capital projects fund accounts for the project itself, not the repayment of debt.

Solution 19-2 ADDITIONAL MULTIPLE CHOICE ANSWERS

Governmental-Type Funds

61. (d) The *Budgetary Fund Balance Reserved for Encumbrances* is increased when a purchase order is approved. The *Budgetary Fund Balance Reserved for Encumbrances* is not affected when the budget (along with the related appropriations) is recorded. Upon the receipt of the item previously ordered, *Budgetary Fund Balance Reserved for Encumbrances* is decreased. The following entry is made when a purchase order is approved:

Encumbrances	XX	
Budgetary FB Reserved for Encumbrances		XX

62. (d) The *Estimated Revenues Control* account of a governmental fund type is a budgetary account (i.e., it is not used to record actual revenues). Its balance is eliminated when the budgetary accounts are closed. The entry to close the *Estimated Revenues Control* and *Revenues Control* accounts to *Fund* Balance is as follows:

Revenues Control	17,000,000	
Fund Balance (difference)	3,000,000	
Estimated Revenues Control		20,000,000

63. (b) The following entry is made when a purchase order for $50 is approved:

Encumbrances (estimated cost)	50	
Reserve for Encumbrances		50

The following entries would be made to record the receipt of the related goods for $55 and the vouchers payable:

Fund Balance Reserved for Encumbrances	50	
Encumbrances (estimated cost)		50
Expenditures (actual cost)	55	
Vouchers Payable		55

The *Encumbrances* account is not affected when the budget is recorded. The following entry would be made to record the budget:

Estimated Revenues	XX	
Estimated Other Financing Sources	XX	
Appropriations		XX
Estimated Other Financing Uses		XX
Fund Balance (difference—debit or credit)		XX

General Fund

64. (c) Appropriations are budgeted expenditures. Encumbrances are commitments for purchases that are not yet received. Expenditures are paid or accrued for purchases already received. \$745,000 – \$37,250 – \$298,000 = \$409,750

65. (b) Governmental fund types include the general fund and use the modified accrual basis of accounting. This basis of accounting follows the "flow of financial resources" concept, and the term "expenditure" means decreases in (uses of) fund financial resources. (GASB 1800.114) The acquisition of a general fund fixed asset is a use of financial resources or an expenditure. The asset has been received and not just ordered. The fixed asset may be recorded in the general fixed asset account group. Appropriations relate to a budgetary account that is only changed upon budget modification or closure.

66. (c) The encumbrance system is used by governmental funds to prevent overexpenditure and to demonstrate compliance with legal requirements. When a purchase order is issued, the estimated amount of the planned expenditure is **encumbered** by debiting *Encumbrances* and crediting *Fund Balance Reserved for Encumbrances.* When the related invoice is received, the encumbrance entry is reversed and the actual expenditure is recorded. Thus, the balance of the *Encumbrance* account will equal the outstanding purchase order amounts until the books are closed at year-end.

67. (c) Although authorized transfers to other fund entities may be viewed as appropriation expenditures from the point of view of the general fund entity, for purposes of financial reporting they are distinguished from expenditures. Control over authorized transfers to other fund entities is achieved by recording them as estimated other financing uses at the beginning of the period for which they are authorized (budgeted), rather than by including them in the budget entry for appropriations. The journal entry to record the adoption of the budget is as follows:

Estimated Revenues Control	30,000,000	
Appropriations Control		27,000,000
Estimated Other Financing Uses		900,000
Fund Balance (to balance)		2,100,000

68. (a) See the explanation to question #67.

69. (c) While goods and services committed for by purchase order or contract are encumbered in governmental funds to avoid overspending appropriations, some expenditures are controlled by other means and need not be encumbered. Salaries and wages are set by contract and controlled by established payroll procedures and are *not* encumbered. Salaries and wages should be recorded as follows:

Expenditures Control	800,000	
Vouchers Payable		800,000

70. (d) Taxes Receivable—Current is *debited* when taxpayers are billed for property taxes. *Appropriations* and *Estimated Revenues* accounts are affected when the budget is recorded. The following entry is made to record the assessment of property taxes:

Taxes Receivable—Current	XX	
Allowance for Uncollectible Taxes—Current		XX
Revenues—Property Taxes		XX

71. (b) When $100 of supplies are ordered, the following entry is made:

Encumbrances Control (expected cost)	100	
Reserve for Encumbrances		100

Upon receipt of the supplies and an invoice for $105, the following entries are made:

Reserve for Encumbrances (reverse prior entry)	100	
Encumbrances Control		100
Expenditures (actual cost)	105	
Vouchers Payable		105

72. (d) The journal entry to record the adoption of the budget is as follows:

Estimated Revenues Control	50,000,000	
Appropriations Control		40,000,000
Budgetary Fund Balance—Unreserved		10,000,000

73. (c) The journal entry to record the adoption of the budget is as follows:

Estimated Revenues Control	50,000,000	
Appropriations Control		40,000,000
Budgetary Fund Balance—Unreserved		10,000,000

74. (b) The journal entry to record the adoption of the budget is as follows:

Estimated Revenues Control	50,000,000	
Appropriations Control		40,000,000
Budgetary Fund Balance—Unreserved		10,000,000

75. (c) Grant revenues are recognized as being earned when expended. Prior to expenditure, they should be reported as deferred revenue. During the current fiscal year, Cliff spent $125,000 of the capital grant and $15,000 of the operating grant. Therefore, $140,000 should be reported as grant revenues for the period. The $25,000 not yet expended is reported as deferred revenue at the end of the period.

76. (c) When the purchase order was approved, the following journal entry was made:

Encumbrances Control	5,000	
Budgetary Fund Balance—Reserved for Encumbrances		5,000

77. (a) When the supplies are received, the encumbering entry is reversed, and the actual amounts are recorded.

Budgetary Fund Balance—Reserved for Encumbrances	5,000	
Encumbrances Control		5,000
Expenditures Control	5,000	
Vouchers Payable		5,000

78. (a) The $2,000,000 from the general fund was only "transferred" to the capital projects fund. The *Other Financing Uses Control* account should be used to report the interfund transfer in the financial statements for the general fund. The issuance of the $3,000,000 general obligation bond issue for capital outlay purposes is not recorded in the general fund and, thus, is not reported in its financial statements. (The issuance of the bond is recorded in the capital projects fund and optionally, in the general long-term debt account group.)

Debt Service Funds

79. (b) Debt service funds are used to account for the accumulation of resources for, and the payment of, general long-term debt principal and interest. Therefore, the cash accumulation of $700,000 pertaining to general long-term obligations should be accounted for in Alma's debt service fund. The proprietary funds (enterprise and internal service funds) record their own assets, liabilities, revenues, and expenses. Therefore, the cash accumulation related to the bonds issued to finance the construction of the water treatment plant should be accounted for in an enterprise fund—not in Alma's debt service fund.

80. (d) Debt service funds are used to account for the accumulation of resources for, and the payment of, general long-term debt principal and interest.

81. (c) **Mature** long-term debt principal and related interest are recorded as debt service fund expenditures when *due.* Debt service funds are used to account for resources for repayment of all general long-term debt and payment of related interest.

82. (a) Debt service fund budgetary accounts may be used to record estimated revenues from taxes or other financing sources, or estimated investment earnings. Actual amounts are then recorded as revenues. The operating transfer from the general fund is recorded as an other financing source, not revenue.

83. (a) GASB §1600.122 begins…"A major exception to the general rule of expenditure accrual relates to unmatured principal and interest on general long-term debt…." This question relates to the criterion related to the expenditure recognition on debt known as the "when due" criterion. Entities that budget cash outflows for debt when they legally become due include budget appropriations for debt in the year in which the cash outflow occurs. Because the financial flow of funds to make payment has not been budgeted for, interest and principal payments are not subject to accrual.

Permanent Funds

84. (b) GASB Codification §1400.113 states that fixed assets donated to a governmental unit are recorded at fair value when received.

Proprietary Funds

85. (d) Proprietary funds account for their fixed assets in the same manner as commercial enterprises; therefore, the expenditure for the parking meters should be recorded in the fund's fixed asset accounts. Enterprise funds and internal service funds are the two types of proprietary funds. The fund in question is an enterprise fund because it is a self-supporting fund which provides goods and/or services to the general public.

Receipts from users of parking facilities		$600,000
Less: Salaries and other cash expenses	$96,000	
Depreciation of parking meters	94,000	(190,000)
Net income		$410,000

Enterprise Funds

86. (b) The customers' security deposits cannot be spent for normal operating purposes. In the balance sheet of the enterprise fund, the cash received is classified as a restricted asset and a liability is created for the customer deposits payable.

Interfund Transactions

87. (b) NCGA Statement 1 provides specific guidance on accounting for interfund transactions. This is a quasi-external transaction, or one that would result in recognizing revenues and expenditures or expenses, as appropriate, as if it was with an organization apart from the government. The general fund expenditures account is debited when the general fund liabilities increase.

88. (c) Operating transfers should be recorded in distinctive Operating Transfers From (To) [Name of Fund] or Operating Transfers In (Out) accounts and reported after revenues and expenditures or expenses, but before determining the results of operations in the fund's operating statement.

Determining Fund

89. (c) Capital projects funds are used to account for the acquisition and use of financial resources to construct or otherwise acquire long-lived "general government" real property and equipment. Project resources, which include proceeds of general obligation bonds, are recorded as received or accrued.

PERFORMANCE BY SUBTOPICS

Each category below parallels a subtopic covered in Chapter 19. Record the number and percentage of questions you correctly answered in each subtopic area.

Governmental-Type Funds

Question #	Correct √
1	
2	
3	
4	
5	
6	
7	
8	
9	
# Questions	9
# Correct	______
% Correct	______

General Fund

Question #	Correct √
10	
11	
12	
13	
14	
15	
16	
17	
18	
# Questions	9
# Correct	______
% Correct	______

Special Revenue Funds

Question #	Correct √
19	
20	
21	
# Questions	3
# Correct	______
% Correct	______

Capital Projects Fund

Question #	Correct √
22	
23	
24	
25	
26	
# Questions	5
# Correct	______
% Correct	______

Debt Service Funds

Question #	Correct √
27	
28	
29	
30	
31	
32	
# Questions	6
# Correct	______
% Correct	______

Permanent Funds

Question #	Correct √
33	
# Questions	1
# Correct	______
% Correct	______

Proprietary Funds

Question #	Correct √
34	
35	
36	
# Questions	3
# Correct	______
% Correct	______

Internal Service Funds

Question #	Correct √
37	
38	
39	
40	
# Questions	4
# Correct	______
% Correct	______

Enterprise Funds

Question #	Correct √
41	
42	
43	
44	
45	
# Questions	5
# Correct	______
% Correct	______

Fiduciary Funds

Question #	Correct √
46	
47	
48	
49	
50	
# Questions	5
# Correct	______
% Correct	______

Interfund Transactions

Question #	Correct √
51	
52	
53	
54	
# Questions	4
# Correct	______
% Correct	______

Determining Fund or Group

Question #	Correct √
55	
56	
57	
58	
59	
60	
# Questions	6
# Correct	______
% Correct	______

SIMULATION SOLUTIONS

Solution 19-3

Research

NCGAS 1 Par. 35

35. Enterprise Fund fixed assets are capitalized in the fund accounts because the fixed assets are used in the production of the goods or services provided and sold. Depreciation of these fixed assets must be recorded to determine total expenses, net income, and changes in fund equity. Moreover, Enterprise Fund fixed assets may serve as security for debt issued to establish, acquire, or improve a public enterprise.

Responses 1-12

1. $70,000

The general fund budgetary entry is as follows:

DR: Estimated Revenues	8,000,000	
CR: Budgetary Fund Balance		70,000
CR: Appropriations		7,500,000
CR: Est. Other Financing Uses (capital proj.)		250,000
CR: Est. Other Financing Uses (enter. fund)		180,000

2. $430,000

($250,000 + $180,000 = $430,000) Also see the explanation to #1.

3. -0-

Interest is recorded when due.

4. $10,000

The full $10,000 lease payment amount should be included in general fund expenditures. In total, $78,000 would be debited in the general fund. The other $68,000 would be credited to Other Financing Sources—Capital Leases in the general fund.

5. $5,018,000

Because the December 31 balance of $56,000 was closed and a delinquent receivables account was established for only $38,000, $18,000 must have been collected. (The $4,000 difference between $60,000 and $56,000 was written off during the year.) The estimate for uncollectible taxes was not increased, so apparently the full $5,000,000 of the original entry was collected. ($5,000,000 + $56,000 – $38,000 = $5,018,000) The original entry to record property taxes is:

DR: Property tax receivable	5,060,000	
CR: Allowance for estimated uncollectible taxes		60,000
CR: Property tax revenue		5,000,000

6. $450,000

The state entitlements are revenues. The general fund money and debt proceeds are Other Financing Source, not revenue.

7. $868,000

The amount of the principal on the bonds ($800,000) plus the net present value of $68,000 for the capital lease (not counting the $10,000 payment already made) are included.

8. $1,580,000

The courthouse improvements ($1,527,000), police car retirement ($25,000), and office equipment acquisition ($78,000) all had an impact on the capital assets amount. The $7,000 paid for the car would not affect the capital assets.

9. $107,000

Usage to date (in cubic yards)	540,000
Divided by: Total capacity	1,000,000
Equals: Capacity used to date (percentage)	54%
Times: Est. closure & post-closure costs	$2,000,000
Total to be recognized to date	1,080,000
Total previously recognized	973,000
Current year recognition	$ 107,000

10. $780,000

Total to be recognized to date	$1,080,000
Total incurred to date	300,000
Closure & post-closure liability	$ 780,000

11. D The primary focus of a capital project is not exceeding available resources.

12. E The primary focus of an MSWLF fund is concerned with not allowing a shortfall of resources for future closure and post-closure costs.

Solution 19-4

Research

General Principles

1400.114

.114 General capital assets are capital assets of the government that are not specifically related to activities reported in proprietary or fiduciary funds. General capital assets are associated with and generally arise from governmental activities. Most often, they result from the expenditure of governmental fund financial resources. They should not be reported as assets in governmental funds but should be reported in the governmental activities column in the government-wide statement of net assets. Reporting general infrastructure assets at transition to GASB Statement No. 34, *Basic Financial Statements—and Management's Discussion and Analysis—for State and Local Governments,* is discussed beginning at paragraph .124. [GASBS 34, ¶80]

Responses 1-10

1. $104,500

The general fund operating transfers out (other financing uses) are composed of the $104,500 for bond principal and interest payment.

2. $17,000

Compensated absences are valued at the salary and wage rates in effect as of the balance sheet date. The liabilities in the general fund are the amounts expected to be settled with resources available at the balance sheet date. The remainder of $69,000 would appear in the government-wide statement of net assets as long-term liability but is not booked in the general fund.

3. $125,000

The reserved amount is the $83,000 for total encumbrances outstanding at December 31 and the $42,000 in ending supplies inventory. The reserve for supplies inventory indicates that a portion of fund balance is not available.

4. $236,000

Fund balance of the capital projects fund is $600,000 – $364,000 = $236,000.

5. $6,000

Fund balance of the special revenue fund is $109,000 – $81,000 – $22,000 = $6,000.

6. $104,500

The debt service fund expenditures for the year are the $100,000 of principal repaid and the $4,500 of interest paid.

7. $0

The cost of capital assets acquired in the year is $22,000 from the special revenue fund's purchase of a motor vehicle plus $364,000 from the capital projects fund. This appears in the government-wide financial statements in the governmental activities column, but is not booked in the general fund.

8. $100,000

The $100,000 repayment of debt decreased the reported long-term liabilities.

9. $181,000

Under the encumbrances method, the amount of supplies expenditures is the $181,000 credited to the *Vouchers Payable* account during the year less the $6,000 credited to *Vouchers Payable* account and debited to the *Fund Balance Reserved for Encumbrances* account for the encumbrances outstanding as of 1/1. Under the purchases method, the fund balance is not reserved for prior year encumbrances, and thus the amount for expenditures is the full $181,000.

10. $190,000

The $190,000 of purchase orders issued during the year is the total amount of supplies encumbrances.

Solution 19-5

Research

General Principles

1600.114

.114 Material revenues received prior to normal time of receipt should be recorded as deferred revenue. For example, property taxes or other revenues may be collected in advance of the fiscal year to which they apply. Such prepayments should be recorded as deferred revenues and recognized as revenue of the period to which they apply. [NCGAS 1, ¶66; 1974 ASLGU, p. 15]

Responses 1-10

1. G Proceeds of general obligation bonds should not be recorded as a credit to fund liabilities or revenues. Instead they should be recorded as a credit to other financing sources.

Cash	XX	
Other Financing Sources—Bond Proceeds		XX

2. K When a purchase order is approved, the following journal entry is made:

Encumbrances Control	XX	
Budgetary Fund Balance—Reserved for Encumbrances		XX

3. L When the supplies are received, the original encumbering entry is reversed, and the actual amounts are entered into the accounts as follows:

Budgetary Fund Balance—Reserved for Encumbrances	XX	
Encumbrances Control		XX
Expenditures Control	XX	
Vouchers Payable		XX

4. L The general fund salaries and wages incurred should be recorded as follows:

Expenditures Control	XX	
Vouchers Payable		XX

5. E The billings of the internal service fund is a "quasi-external" transaction. The internal service fund: (1) debits to receivable for the amount due, and (2) credits interfund revenues.

6. J Where revenues are not properly recognized at the time the grant is awarded, Entry (1) is appropriate. When the conditions of the previously awarded grant are met, the deferred revenue is recognized as revenue, as in Entry (2).

Due From Grantor	XX	
Deferred Revenues		XX
Deferred Revenues	XX	
Revenues		XX

7. D A deferred revenue account is credited if property taxes are collected prior to the year they apply.

8. A The appropriations control account is credited when the following entry is made to record the budget:

Estimated Revenues Control	XX	
Appropriations Control		XX
Budgetary Fund Balance—Unreserved (to balance)		XX

9. F Local banks customarily meet the working capital needs of a governmental unit by accepting a "tax anticipation note" from the unit. The journal entry to record the short-term financing received from the bank that is secured by the city's taxing power is as follows:

Cash	XX	
Tax Anticipation Notes Payable		XX

10. B If there is an excess of estimated inflows over estimated outflows at the adoption of the budget, the Budgetary Fund Balance—Unreserved account is increased (i.e., credited). This can be seen from the following journal entry to record the adoption of the budget in question:

Estimated Revenues Control	XX	
Estimated Other Financing Sources	XX	
Appropriations Control		XX
Estimated Other Financing Uses		XX
Budgetary Fund Balance—Unreserved (to balance)		XX

Responses 11-20

11. N The enterprise fund is a proprietary fund. Therefore, it records its own assets and liabilities, including fixed assets and long-term debt.

12. R Capital projects funds are used to account for financial resources that are to be used to construct or otherwise acquire major long-lived "general government" capital facilities—such as buildings, highways, storm sewer systems, and bridges.

13. N The internal service fund is a proprietary fund. (See the explanation to #11.)

14. M The private-purpose trust fund is a fiduciary fund. (See the explanation to #17.)

15. N The enterprise fund is a proprietary fund. Proprietary funds are used to account for a government's continuing business-type activities that are similar to private business enterprises.

16. S Property taxes usually are a major revenue source of local governments. Unless the property taxes are restricted for specific purposes or required to be accounted for in another fund, they are accounted for in the general fund.

17. M The agency fund is a fiduciary fund. Fiduciary funds are used to account for assets held by a government in a trustee or agency capacity.

18. M The pension fund is a fiduciary fund. (See the explanation to #17)

19. U Special revenue funds account for proceeds of specific revenue sources that are restricted by law or contract for specified purposes.

20. T Debt service funds account for the accumulation of resources for, and the payment of, general long-term debt principal and interest.

Solution 19-6

Research

General Principles

1100.101

.101 A governmental accounting system must make it possible both: (a) to present fairly and with full disclosure the funds and activities of the governmental unit in conformity with generally accepted accounting principles, and (b) to determine and demonstrate compliance with finance-related legal and contractual provisions.

Responses 1-5

1. $1,000,000

The budgetary entry is as follows:

DR: Estimated Revenues	10,000,000	
CR: Appropriations		9,000,000
CR: Budgetary Fund Balance		1,000,000

2. $9,350,000

There were no write-offs of current year property taxes. Therefore, the amount collected is the amount of the current year property tax levy ($9,500,000) less the current-year property taxes delinquent at the end of the year ($150,000).

3. -0-

$100,000 + $2,000,000 – $2,100,000 = -0- All the current year expenditures are transferred out of the capital projects fund upon completion of the project.

4. $2,100,000

The full cost of the library wing is reported.

5. $2,000,000

The full amount of the bond debt is reported.

Solution 19-7

Research

General Principles

1300.107

.107 Debt service funds—to account for the accumulation of resources for, and the payment of, general long-term debt principal and interest. Debt service funds are required if they are legally mandated and/or if financial resources are being accumulated for principal and interest payments maturing in future years.

Responses 1-8

1. N The following entry would be made to record the budget in the General Fund, based on budgeted amounts:

Estimated Revenues	5,000,000	
Estimated Other Financing Sources	1,000,000	
Appropriations		4,400,000 [2]
Estimated Other Financing Uses		1,200,000 [1]
Budgetary Fund Balance		400,000

<u>Explanation of Amounts</u>:

[1] Capital Projects Fund ($500,000) operating transfer plus

Water Utility Fund ($700,000) residual equity transfer.

[2] Total budgeted expenditures minus Other financing uses

($5,600,000 – $1,200,000 = <u>$4,400,000</u>).

2. Y Although authorized transfers to other fund entities may be viewed as appropriation expenditures from the point of view of the General Fund entity, for purposes of financial reporting they are distinguished from expenditures. Control over authorized transfers to other fund entities is achieved by recording them as estimated other financing uses at the beginning of the period for which they are authorized (budgeted), rather than by including them in the budget entry for appropriations.

3. N This nonrecurring transfer of equity between funds is recorded in a distinctive Residual Equity Transfers to Water Utility Enterprise Fund account and is reported after the results of operations in the general fund's operating statement. GASB Section 1800.106 distinguishes between two major types of interfund transfers (residual equity

and operating) and provides the specific example of the contribution of enterprise fund capital by the general fund as a residual equity transfer.

4. N Bond proceeds are classified as other financing sources and are recorded at the net amount received, including premiums and deducting discounts and issuance costs. A net premium is usually transferred to the Debt Service fund, which is used to account for the accumulation of resources for payment of general long-term debt principal and interest (GASB Section 1500.109).

5. N Quasi-external transactions are transactions that would result in recognizing revenues and expenditures or expenses, as appropriate, if they were with organizations apart from the government.

6. N GASB Section P70.103 states, "The revenue produced from any property tax assessment should be recognized in the fiscal period for which it was levied, provided the available criteria are met. Available means then due, or past due and receivable within the current period, and collected within the current period or expected to be collected soon enough thereafter to be used to pay liabilities of the current period. Such time thereafter shall not exceed 60 days." Since the fiscal year ends December 31, and March 1 is 60 days later, the net delinquent property taxes receivable should be expected to be collected before March 15.

7. N The entry to close budgetary accounts is the exact opposite of the one to record the budget. Thus, there is a credit of $400,000 to the *budgetary* fund balance. (Also see the explanation to #1.)

8. N The net budgetary effects are zero and the actual amount is a credit of $50,000, so the net impact on the year-end general fund balance is $50,000.

Responses 9-16

9. N Interfund transactions are partially eliminated in the government-wide statement of net assets.

10. Y General and program revenues are separated in the government-wide statement (GWS) of activities.

11. Y The ISF typically is reported in the GWS in the governmental activities column.

12. N The general fund is always a major fund.

13. N Fiduciary funds do not appear in the government-wide statements.

14. N Only proprietary funds report in the statement of cash flows. Governmental-type funds do not report a statement of cash flows.

15. N See the explanation to question #14.

16. Y Proprietary funds report in the statement of cash flows. Enterprise funds are proprietary funds.

Responses 17-22

17. $5,600,000

Per GASB Section 1700.105, "The appropriations constitute maximum expenditure authorizations during the fiscal year."

18. $4,750,000

The total amount debited to property taxes receivable is the actual amount of property taxes. The entry to record property taxes is:

Property taxes receivable	4,750,000	
Allowance for estimated uncollectible taxes		50,000
Property tax revenue		4,700,000

19. $2,473,000

The total cost of the project is calculated as follows:

Revenues	$ 800,000
Bond proceeds	1,230,000
Less: Transfer to debt service fund	(30,000)
Operating transfers in	500,000
Less: Transfer to general fund at close	(27,000)
Total cost of project	$2,473,000

20. $800,000

Grants from another government for a capital project are recorded as deferred revenues in the capital project fund until expended for the project and are then transferred to a revenue account for the remainder of the construction period. Since the state grant is the only grant involved in the project, the amount of the state grant must be the balance in the revenues account at the end of the project life.

21. $2,422,000

The total expenditures in the year were $1,080,000, and the related encumbrances were greater by $42,000. To calculate the total encumbrances, add to this sum the unpaid encumbrances of $1,300,000. [($1,080,000 + $42,000) + $1,300,000 = $2,422,000]

22. $120,000

The fund balance is affected by the opening and closing budget entries and the (actual) closing entries. The illustrated closing entry has a $1,420,000 credit entry to unreserved fund balance. Since there is no opening balance and the budget entries are equal in amount and opposite in direction, the combined closing entry amounts are also the ending balance. (**NOTE:** $1,420,000 – $1,300,000 = $120,000) The illustrated closing entry omits the following entry.

Fund Balance	1,300,000	
Encumbrances Control		1,300,000

Solution 19-8

Research

General Principles

1800.120

.120 Expenditures should be further classified by character, that is, on the basis of the fiscal period they are presumed to benefit. The major character classifications of expenditures are "Current Expenditures," which benefit the current fiscal period; "Capital Outlays," which are presumed to benefit both the present and future fiscal periods; and "Debt Service," which presumably benefits prior fiscal periods as well as current and future periods. "Intergovernmental," a fourth character classification, is appropriate where one governmental unit transfers resources to another, such as when states transfer "shared revenues" to local governments or act as an intermediary in federally financed programs. Character classification may be accomplished by grouping the object classifications, discussed below, which are subdivisions of the character classifications. [NCGAS 1, ¶115]

Responses 1-6

1. A GASB Section 1800.119 states, "Expenditures should be further classified by *character,* that is, on the basis of the fiscal period they are presumed to benefit. The major character classifications of expenditures are 'Current Expenditures,' which benefit the current fiscal period..."

GASB 1800.118 explains the *activity* classification as facilitating evaluation of the economy and efficiency of operations by providing information for figuring costs per unity of activity.

2. A GASB Section 1800.119 states, "Expenditures should be further classified by *character,* that is, on the basis of the fiscal period they are presumed to benefit. The major character classifications of expenditures are 'Current Expenditures,' which benefit the current fiscal period; 'Capital Outlays,' which are presumed to benefit both the present and future fiscal periods; and 'Debt Service,' which presumably benefits prior fiscal periods as well as current and future periods. 'Intergovernmental,' a fourth character classification, is appropriate where one governmental unit transfers resources to another.... Character classification may be accomplished by grouping the object classification..., which are subdivisions of the character classifications." GASB 1800.120 defines the classification *object classes* as the types of items purchased or services obtained (sales and wages).

3. B GASB Section 1900.115 explains that the *function* or *program* classification provides information on the overall purposes of expenditures.

4. B GASB Section 1600.122 states, "Other alternative expenditure recognition methods in governmental fund accounting, usually of a relatively minor nature, include: inventory items (for example, materials and supplies) may be considered expenditures either when purchased (purchases method) or when used (consumption method), but significant amounts of inventory should be reported in the balance sheet...." GASB Section 2200.903.b (a nonauthoritative discussion) states, "Under the *consumption* method (1) inventory acquisitions are recorded in inventory accounts initially and charged as expenditures when used, and (2) an equity reserve for inventories need not be established unless minimum amounts of inventory must be maintained and, thus, are not available for use (expenditure). Under the *purchases* method (1) inventories are recorded as expenditures on acquisition, and (2) significant inventories on hand at year-end are reflected in the *Assets* section of the balance sheet and are fully reserved in the equity section." These sections make no mention of perpetual inventory beyond what is mentioned for the consumption method. As no mention of minimum inventories is included in the given information, we must assume there is no such requirement. Because the reserve for inventory exists, Shar City must be using the purchase method.

5. B Proprietary funds account use the term net assets. Fund balances are appropriate in governmental-type funds. A debt is liability, not equity.

6. A Proprietary fund debt is reported in the business-type activity column. As a matter of convenience, the account groups may be used to account for long-term debt and capital assets, but they do not appear in the financial statements.

Responses 7-13

7. A Unrestricted grants are reported as revenues.

8. E The general fund has a receivable due from the internal service fund (ISF).

9. B The purchase of goods or services by a governmental-type fund from a proprietary fund are handled like purchases from other vendors.

10. D Operating transfers to internal service or enterprise funds are other financing uses.

11. E Loans to an internal service fund would be recorded in the general fund as follows:

DR: Receivable from Internal Service Fund	90,000	
CR: Cash		90,000
DR: Fund Balance (or Unreserved Fund Bal.)	90,000	
CR: Reserve for Advance to Int. Serv. Fund		90,000

12. D A transfer to establish a proprietary fund is a residual equity transfer, which is reported as an other financing use.

13. B General fund payments on operating leases are expenditures.

Responses 14-19

14. $79,000

The fund balance reserve for encumbrances for year 2 year-end is $43,000. The decrease in reserve for encumbrances is $15,000. Working back to year 1 year-end, the year 1 year-end fund balance reserve for encumbrances was $43,000 + $15,000 = $58,000. The reserve for supplies inventory at year 1 year-end was $21,000. ($58,000 + $21,000 = $79,000)

15. $811,000

As $8,000 was written-off, $845,000 remained to be collected. Of this, $34,000 was uncollected at year-end, meaning $811,000 was collected during the year. The initial property tax entry was as follows:

DR: Property Taxes Receivable	$853,000	
CR: Allow. Property Taxes Uncollectible		28,000
CR: Property Tax Revenues		825,000

16. $89,000

Vouchers payable is $89,000. Encumbrances are not liabilities until the goods or services are provided. Then they are removed from the encumbrances account and recorded in the payable account.

17. $100,000

The only capital outlay for governmental activities was the purchase of the police vehicles.

18. $52,000

The total debt service expenditure was $74,000. This amount included interest of $22,000; the rest reduced debt principal. ($74,000 – $22,000 = $52,000)

19. $1,392,000

Total actual expenditures for year 2 are the $1,349,000 made in year 2 and the $43,000 that will be made in year 3 for year 2 encumbrances.

CHAPTER 20

NONPROFIT ACCOUNTING

I. **Standard Nonprofit Accounting** 20-2
- A. Concepts 20-2
- B. Definitions 20-2
- C. Financial Statements 20-3
- D. Contributions 20-7
- E. Contributions for Others (SFAS 136) 20-8
- F. Investments 20-10
- G. Depreciation 20-10
- H. Related Organizations 20-11

II. **Unique Accounting Features** 20-12
- A. Health Care Entities 20-12
- B. Colleges & Universities 20-14
- C. Voluntary Health & Welfare Organizations (VHWO) 20-15
- D. Other Nonprofit Organizations (ONPO) 20-17

III. **Appendix: Health Care Entity Fund Accounting** 20-17
- A. Concepts 20-17
- B. Fund Types 20-17

IV. **Appendix: University Fund Accounting** 20-19
- A. Concepts 20-19
- B. Restricted vs. Unrestricted Current Funds 20-20
- C. Current Fund Unique Accounting Conventions 20-20
- D. Current Fund Budgetary Accounts 20-21
- E. Trust & Agency Funds 20-21
- F. Annuity & Life Income Funds 20-21
- G. Plant Funds 20-21
- H. Statement of Financial Position 20-22

V. **Appendix: VHWO Fund Accounting** 20-24
- A. Concepts 20-24
- B. Fund Types 20-24

EXAM COVERAGE: Exam coverage of the topics in Chapter 20 is projected to be 8 to 12 percent of the FAR section. It is heavily concentrated on the first section, *Standard Nonprofit Accounting,* and, to a lesser degree, the second section, *Unique Accounting Features.*

CHAPTER 20

NONPROFIT ACCOUNTING

I. Standard Nonprofit Accounting

A. Concepts

The fundamental presumption used by the FASB in developing financial reporting standards for (non-governmental) nonprofit organizations (NPO) is that the financial reporting practices of non-profit entities should be the same as those for commercial entities.

1. **Standards** Statement on Auditing Standards No. 69, *The Meaning of "Present Fairly in Conformity With Generally Accepted Accounting Principles" in the Independent Auditor's Report,* establishes a parallel hierarchy where non-governmental nonprofit entities are subject to the FASB rather than the GASB standards. In SFAS 117, the FASB requires nonprofit entities to provide financial statements on an entity-wide basis similar to the concept of consolidated statements for business entities.

2. **Fund Accounting** Disaggregated financial statements, common with fund accounting, are insufficient, by themselves, to meet the requirements of SFAS 117. Use of fund accounting for nonprofit organizations is allowed but not required by SFAS 117. This relegates fund statements to a supplementary role for external reporting purposes. Although fund accounting is redundant with the adoption of SFAS 117, fund accounting remains an option, and many entities may be slow to eliminate it. [Expect the majority of (nongovernmental) nonprofit accounting CPA exam points to be in areas other than fund accounting.] NPOs generally do not use budgetary and encumbrance accounting.

B. Definitions

1. **Board-Restricted** The governing board of an entity may earmark assets for specific purposes as long as these do not conflict with donor conditions. These assets may be designated board-restricted in the financial statements, but they remain in the unrestricted category.

2. **Endowment Fund** A fund of assets to provide support for the activities of a not-for-profit organization. Endowment funds are typically composed of donor-restricted gifts to provide a permanent source of support. However, use of the fund assets may also be temporarily restricted or unrestricted.

3. **Functional Classification** A manner of arranging costs by the activities for which the costs are attributable. Program services and supporting activities are the two main classifications.

4. **Natural Classification** A manner of arranging costs by the item or service obtained. For example, utilities and salaries.

5. **Permanent Restriction** A donor-imposed restriction. The principal of a permanent endowment may not be exhausted.

6. **Program Services** Activities that further the mission of the organization. For example, a university's program services might include instruction and research.

7. **Supporting Activities** Activities that are secondary to the mission of the organization. These include administration activities, general activities, fund-raising activities, and member development activities.

8. **Temporary Restriction** A donor-imposed restriction that will lapse upon occurrence of conditions specified by the donor. The principal of a temporary endowment or donation may be used after the conditions of the restriction are fulfilled. The allowable use of the income of a temporarily restricted asset may also be restricted by the terms of the donation.

9. **Unrestricted Assets** The assets from donations unrestricted by the donors, and assets formerly temporarily restricted by the donors that have since become unrestricted. Unrestricted assets include board-restricted assets.

C. Financial Statements

SFAS 117 requires that nonprofit organizations present at least three statements. The statements exhibited in this section are similar to those used by a commercial entity. Some entities may choose to also disclose the fund statements. Several formats are acceptable for nonprofit entities. However, in order to meet the requirements of SFAS 117, *aggregated* statements must be used.

Because terms such as operating income, operating profit, operating surplus, operating deficit, and results of operations are used with different meanings, if an intermediate measure of operations (for example, excess or deficit of operating revenues over expenses) is reported, it shall be in a financial statement that, at a minimum, reports the change in unrestricted net assets for the period. If an organization's use of the term operations is not apparent from the details provided on the face of the statement, a note to financial statements shall describe the nature of the reported measure of operations or the items excluded from operations. (SFAS 117 par. 23)

1. **Statement of Financial Position** Entities report assets, liabilities, and net assets in this statement. Entities are required to classify net assets based upon the existence or absence of donor-imposed restrictions. Thus, net assets are classified into at least three categories: permanently restricted, temporarily restricted, and unrestricted. Assets are arranged by relative liquidity. Assets restricted to a particular use assume the liquidity of that use. For instance, cash and marketable securities restricted for the purchase of property, plant, and equipment (PPE) are presented below inventories.

Exhibit 1 ▸ Statement of Financial Position

Name of Nonprofit Entity
Statement of Financial Position
December 31, Year 2

Assets:		Liabilities:	
Cash	$ 38	Accounts Payable	$ 1,285
Contributions Receivable	1,512	Grants Payable	438
Accounts Receivable	1,065	Annuity Obligation	842
Marketable Securities	700	Bonds Payable	2,750
Inventory	300	Total Liabilities	5,315
Prepaid Expenses	5	Net Assets	
Assets Restricted to Investment:		Unrestricted	57,614
PPE	2,605	Temporarily Restricted	12,171
Property, Plant, and Equipment	30,850		
Long-Term Investments	109,035	Permanently Restricted	71,010
Total Assets	$146,110	Total Net Assets	140,795
		Total Liabilities and Net Assets	$146,110

2. **Statement of Activities** This statement is similar to a for-profit entity's income statement. The change in the net assets is reported in the Statement of Activities. The revenues, expenses, gains, and losses are classified into the same three groups as in the statement of financial position (unrestricted, temporarily restricted, and permanently restricted).

a. **Subtotals** Subtotals for changes in classes of net assets are required to be reported before income from **C**ontinuing operations, income from **D**iscontinued operations, **E**xtraordinary items, and the e**F**fect of Accounting changes (CDEF).

b. **Sequence** The Statement of Activities is presented in the following sequence:

Revenues and Other Additions
Expenditures and Other Deductions
Transfers Among Funds
Net Increase (Decrease) in Net Assets
Net Assets—Beginning of Year
Net Assets—End of Year

c. **Change** Entities display the change in each of the three classes of net assets.

Exhibit 2 ▸ Statement of Activities

Name of Nonprofit Entity
Statement of Activities
Year Ending December 31, Year 2

	Total	Unrestricted	Temporarily Restricted	Permanently Restricted
Revenues and Gains:				
Contributions	$ 8,515	$ 4,320	$ 4,055	$ 140
Services Fees	2,700	2,700		
Investment Income	4,575	3,225	1,290	60
Net Unrealized and Realized Gains on Long-Term Investments	7,900	4,114	1,476	2,310
Other	75	75		
Net Assets Released From Restrictions:				
Expiration of Time Requirements		5,995	(5,995)	
Fulfilled Conditions of Equipment Acquisition		750	(750)	
Fulfilled Conditions of Program Services		625	(625)	
Total Revenues, Gains, and Other Support	$ 23,765	$21,804	$ (549)	$ 2,510
Expenses and Losses:				
Program Expenses	$ 13,700	$13,700		
Administration Expenses	1,210	1,210		
Fund-raising Expenses	1,075	1,075		
Loss on Sale of Equipment	40	40		
Actuarial Loss on Annuity Obligations	15		15	
Total Expenses and Losses	$ 16,040	$16,025	$ 15	
Change in Net Assets (or change in equity)	$ 7,725	$ 5,779	$ (564)	$ 2,510
Net Assets at December 31, Year 1	133,070	51,835	12,735	68,500
Net Assets at December 31, Year 2	$140,795	$57,614	$12,171	$71,010

3. **Alternative Two-Part Format** The statement of activities may be divided into two parts, as illustrated in Exhibits 3 and 4.

a. **Statement of Activities: Statement of Unrestricted Revenues, Expenses, and Other Changes in Unrestricted Net Assets** This alternative format divides the statement into two parts. The statements exhibited in this section are what an entity using optional fund accounting might present. The first part of the Statement of Activities is based on the operation of the General Funds. It may also be named Statement of Operations. Increases and decreases in donor-restricted funds are considered in the other part.

b. **Statement of Activities: Statement of Changes in Net Assets** This part summarizes the first part and reports the changes in restricted assets.

4. **Statement of Functional Expenses** The Statement of Functional Expenses is required only for Voluntary Health and Welfare Organizations (VHWO). This details the expenses on the Statement of Activities by functional and object (or natural) classification, as opposed to only the functional classification in the Statement of Activities. This statement is illustrated in Exhibit 12.

5. **Statement of Cash Flows** This statement reports the change in cash and cash equivalents similar to commercial enterprises. SFAS 117 amends SFAS 95, *Statement of Cash Flows,* to extend the provisions of SFAS 95 to nonprofit organizations. Furthermore, SFAS 117 expands the description of cash flows from financing activities to include certain donor-restricted cash that must be used for long-term purposes.

Exhibit 3 ▸ Health Care Entity Statement of Activities: Part 1

Name of Nonprofit Entity
Statement of Unrestricted Revenue, Expenses,
and Other Changes in Unrestricted Net Assets
Year Ending December 31, Year 2

Unrestricted Revenues and Gains:		
Contributions	$ 4,320	
Service Fees	2,700	
Investment Income	3,225	
Net Unrealized and Realized Gains on Long-Term Investments	4,114	
Investment Income	75	
Net Assets Released From Restrictions:		
Expiration of Time Requirements	5,995	
Fulfilled Conditions of Equipment Acquisition	750	
Fulfilled Conditions of Program Services	625	
Total Unrestricted Revenues, Gains, and Other Support		$ 21,804
Expenses and Losses:		
Program Expenses	13,700	
Administration Expenses	1,210	
Fund-raising Expenses	1,075	
Loss on Sale of Equipment	40	
Total Expenses and Losses		16,025
Change in Unrestricted Net Assets		$ 5,779

Exhibit 4 ▸ Statement of Activities: Part 2

Name of Nonprofit Entity
Statement of Changes in Net Assets
Year Ending December 31, Year 2

Unrestricted Net Assets		
Total Unrestricted Revenues and Gains	$ 14,434	
Net Assets Released From Restrictions	7,370	
Total Expenses and Losses	(16,025)	
Change in Unrestricted Net Assets		$ 5,779
Temporarily Restricted Net Assets		
Contributions	4,055	
Investment Income	1,290	
Net Unrealized and Realized Gains on Long-Term Investments	1,476	
Actuarial Loss on Annuity Obligations	(15)	
Net Assets Released From Restrictions	(7,370)	
Change in Temporarily Restricted Net Assets		(564)
Permanently Restricted Net Assets (Endowment Funds)		
Contributions	140	
Long-Term Investment Income	60	
Net Unrealized and Realized Gains on Long-Term Investments	2,310	
Change in Permanently Restricted Net Assets		2,510
Change in Net Assets		7,725
Net Assets at December 31, Year 1		133,070
Net Assets at December 31, Year 2		$ 140,795

Exhibit 5 ▸ Statement of Cash Flows

Name of Nonprofit Entity
Statement of Cash Flows
Year Ending December 31, Year 4

Cash Flows From Operating Activities:	
Cash Received From Service Recipients	$ 5,220
Cash Received From Contributors	8,030
Collections on Pledges	2,616
Interest and Dividends Received	8,570
Miscellaneous Receipts	150
Cash Paid to Vendors and Employees	(23,808)
Cash Paid for Interest	(382)
Cash Paid for Grants	(424)
Net Cash Used by Operating Activities	$ (28)
Cash Flows From Investing Activities:	
Cash Paid for Purchase of Investments	$ (74,900)
Cash Received from Sale of Investments	76,100
Cash Paid for Property, Plant, and Equipment	(1,500)
Cash Received from Sale of Property, Plant, and Equipment	250
Net Cash Used by Investing Activities	$ (50)
Cash Flows From Financing Activities:	
Proceeds from Contributions Restricted for:	
Investment in Endowment	$ 200
Investment in Term Endowment	70
Investment in Property, Plant, and Equipment	1,210
Investment Income Restricted for Reinvestment	200
Interest and Dividends Restricted for Reinvestment	300
Less: Payment of Annuity Obligations	(146)
Less: Payment of Notes Payable	(1,140)
Less: Payment on Bonds Payable	(1,000)
Net Cash Used by Financing Activities	$ (306)
Net Increase in Cash and Cash Equivalents	$ (384)
Cash and Cash Equivalents at December 31, Year 3	460
Cash and Cash Equivalents at December 31, Year 4	$ 76
Reconciliation of Change in Net Assets to Net Cash Used by Operating Activities	
Change in Net Assets	$ 15,450
Reconciling Adjustments:	
Plus: Depreciation	$ 3,200
Plus: Loss on Sale of Equipment	80
Plus: Actuarial Loss on Annuity Obligations	30
Less: Increase in Accounts and Interest Receivable	(460)
Less: Increase in Contributions Receivable	(324)
Plus: Decrease in Inventories and Prepaid Expenses	390
Less: Decrease in Refundable Advance	(650)
Less: Decrease in Grants Payable	(424)
Plus: Increase in Accounts Payable	1,520
Less: Contributions Restricted for Long-Term Investment	(2,740)
Less: Investment Income Restricted for Long-Term Investment	(300)
Less Net Unrealized and Realized Gains on Long-Term Investment	(15,800)
Net Cash Used by Operating Activities	$ (28)
Supplemental Data for Noncash Investing and Financing Activities:	
Gifts of Property, Plant, and Equipment	$ 140
Gifts of Paid-Up Life Insurance, Cash Surrender Value	80

6. **Disclosures** SFAS 136 requires an NPO that discloses in its financial statements a ratio of fundraising expenses to amounts raised, to also disclose how it computes that ratio.

D. Contributions

SFAS 116 governs contributions received and made for nonprofit entities. Contributions are unconditional donations, or gifts, of assets, including both property (either for general operating purposes or restricted for a specific purpose) and services (under certain limited circumstances).

Exhibit 6 ▸ Sample Donation Entries

1. To record gifts, bequests, and donations received:

Cash (or other assets)	XX	
Nonoperating Gains—(Unrestricted) Contributions		XX
Liabilities (if any are assumed)		XX
(Restricted) Revenue		XX

NOTE: Unrestricted gifts, bequests, and donations are recorded as nonoperating gains, generally. If restricted, they are recorded as permanently or temporarily restricted revenue in the appropriate donor-restricted fund.

2. To record donations (to a hospital) of pharmacy supplies and professional services:

Inventory of Pharmacy Supplies	XX	
Operating Expenses (functional expense accounts)	XX	
Contributions—Donated Pharmacy Supplies		XX
Contributions—Donated Professional Services		XX

NOTE: Report the contributions as operating gains or revenue or nonoperating gains depending on whether the donation constitutes the entity's major or central operations or are peripheral and incidental to the entity's operations.

1. **Assets** Donated assets are recorded as revenue at **fair value** as of the date of the gift.

   a. Donated assets other than property and equipment—If **unrestricted,** report as operating gains or revenue or nonoperating gains depending on whether the donations constitute the entity's ongoing major or central operations or are peripheral and incidental to the entity's operations. If **restricted,** report as restricted gain or revenue.

   b. Donations of property and equipment, or of assets to acquire property and equipment, may be initially reported as restricted gain or revenue. A transfer to the unrestricted net assets is reported when the donated property or equipment is placed in service, or when the donated assets are used to acquire property and equipment. If the entity recognizes an implicit restriction in the donation (to be used for the life of the asset, for instance), then the transfer is to the restricted net assets.

   c. A nonprofit organization has the option of not recognizing the contributions of artwork, antiques, and similar items if the donated property is added to a collection that meets three criteria: (1) held for research or exhibition for public service as opposed to monetary gain; (2) are preserved and kept unencumbered; and (3) proceeds from sales of collection components must be used to acquire other artwork or antiques for collections. Contributed collection assets are recognized as revenues if collections are capitalized and not recognized as revenues if collections are not capitalized.

2. **Services** Report the fair value of donated services (e.g., doctors, nurses) as both an expense and a revenue if (1) the services would otherwise be purchased; (2) the value of the services is measurable; and (3) the entity controls the employment and duties of the service donors (i.e., there is the equivalent of an employer-employee or hired contractor relationship).

   a. Contributions of services are recognized as revenues only if (1) nonfinancial assets are created or enhanced, and (2) special skills are required that would otherwise be purchased. The debit depends on the form of the benefit received.

b. Participation of volunteers in philanthropic activities generally does not meet the foregoing criteria because there is no effective employer-employee relationship.

3. **Classification** Contributions are classified as gains when they are peripheral or incidental to the activities of the entity. However, they are classified as revenue in those circumstances in which these sources are deemed to be ongoing major or central activities by which the provider attempts to fulfill its basic function. For example, donor's contributions are revenues if fund-raising is an ongoing major activity by which the provider attempts to fulfill its basic function. The same donations, however, would be a gain to a provider that does not actively seek contributions and receives them only occasionally.

4. **Pledges** Pledges are reported in the period in which they are made, net of an allowance for uncollectible amounts. Pledges are also called promises to give. Conditional pledges are not recorded until they become unconditional.

   a. Unrestricted pledges are reported in the statement of revenue and expenses. If part of the pledge is to be applied during some future period, that part is reported as restricted revenue. A pledge to give in the future has an **implied** restriction for future use.

   b. Restricted pledges are reported as restricted revenues.

5. **Intermediary Transactions** When a nonprofit organization (NPO) receives assets in a nonexchange transaction from a resource provider, with the proviso that the assets be redistributed to another specific organization (or ultimate recipient) chosen by the resource provider, the NPO intermediary is functioning as an agent. However, if the NPO has some discretion as the timing, manner, and recipient of the assets, the NPO intermediary may then be either an agent for the resource provider or a donee. The degree of discretion exercised by the NPO intermediary determines the classification of the event as a donation or as an agency transaction.

Exhibit 7 ▸ Some Guidelines for Separating Donations From Agency Transactions

Attribute	Donation Status	Agency Status
NPO's assertions when requesting donations.	Requests assets to provide for own activities.	Requests assets to provide for others or is not much involved in requesting assets.
Composition of assets	Changes while NPO holds assets (Land received, cash redistributed).	Assets redistributed in same composition. (Land received, land redistributed).
Legal title to assets.	NPO holds legal title.	NPO doesn't hold legal title.
Intent of transfer.	NPO commonly has programs that the assets are intended to support.	NPO doesn't commonly have programs that the assets are intended to support.
Donor awareness.	Providers unaware of ultimate recipient.	Providers are aware of ultimate recipient.
Type of NPO operation.	NPO has programs.	NPO exists to collect and redistribute assets.

E. Contributions for Others (SFAS 136)

SFAS 136, *Transfers of Assets to a Not-for-Profit Organization or Charitable Trust That Raises or Holds Contributions for Others,* applies to contributions for others and also to transactions that are not contributions because the transfers are revocable, repayable, or reciprocal.

1. Definitions

   a. **Recipient** A not-for profit entity or charitable trust that accepts assets from donors and agrees to use those assets on behalf of, or transfer those assets to, another entity specified by the donor. This transfer of assets includes the assets, the return on investment of those assets, or both.

b. **Financially Interrelated Organizations (Entities)** One entity has the ability to influence the operating and financial decisions of the other and one entity has an ongoing economic interest in the net assets of the other.

2. **Recipient** A recipient that accepts assets from a donor on behalf of a specified beneficiary recognizes the fair value of those assets as a liability concurrent with the recognition of the assets. If the donor explicitly gives the recipient variance power or if the recipient and the specified beneficiary are financially interrelated entities, the recipient instead recognizes the transaction as a contribution. Four circumstances exist in which a transfer of assets by a donor is recognized by the recipient as a liability and by the donor as an asset.

   a. **Donor May Redirect** The transfer is subject to the donor's unilateral right to redirect the use of the assets to another beneficiary.

   b. **Donor May Revoke** The transfer is accompanied by the donor's conditional promise to give or is otherwise revocable or repayable.

   c. **Donor Controls** The donor controls the recipient and specifies an unaffiliated beneficiary.

   d. **Donor Benefits** The donor specifies itself or its affiliate as the beneficiary and the transfer is not an equity transaction.

3. **Beneficiary** A specified beneficiary recognizes rights to assets held by a recipient as an asset (either an interest in the net assets of the recipient, a beneficial interest, or a receivable) unless the donor has explicitly granted variance power to the recipient.

   a. **Net Asset Interest** If the beneficiary and the recipient are financially interrelated entities, the beneficiary recognizes an interest in the net assets of the recipient, adjusting that interest for its share of the change in the recipient's net assets.

   b. **Beneficiary Interest** If the beneficiary has an unconditional right to specified cash flows from a charitable trust or other identifiable pool of assets, the beneficiary is required to recognize that beneficial interest, at fair value as of the transaction date and reporting dates.

   c. **Nonrecognition** If the recipient is explicitly granted variance power, the specified beneficiary doesn't recognize an asset.

   d. **Receivable** In all other circumstances, a beneficiary recognizes its rights as a receivable.

4. **Equity Transaction** If the transfer is an equity transaction and the donor specifies itself as beneficiary, the donor records an interest in the net assets of the recipient. If the donor specifies an affiliate as beneficiary, the donor records an equity transaction as a separate line item in its statement of activities, and the beneficiary records an interest in the net assets of the recipient entity. The recipient entity records an equity transaction as a separate line item in its statement of activities.

5. **Disclosures** If a NPO transfers assets to a recipient and specifies itself or an affiliate as beneficiary or if it includes a ratio of fundraising expenses to amount raised in its financial statements, the NPO must make the following disclosures for each period that it presents a statement of financial position: recipient identity; whether variance power was granted to the recipient and the terms of any variance power; the distribution conditions; and the classification (as a beneficial interest or an interest in the net assets of the recipient, etc.) and aggregate amount recognized in the statement of financial position for these transfers.

F. Investments

SFAS 124, *Accounting For Certain Investments Held by Not-for-Profit Organizations,* applies to all investments of all NPOs in debt securities and to investments in equity securities that have a readily determinable market value for all nonprofit organizations. Investments in equity securities accounted for under the equity method, or that are consolidated, are not within the scope of SFAS 124.

1. **Applicability** Fair value of equity securities is deemed to be readily determinable if any of the following conditions are met:

   a. Sales prices or bid-and-ask quotations are available on an exchange which is registered with the SEC or where over-the-counter quotations are reported by NASDAQ or the Pink Sheets LLC, formerly known as the National Quotation Bureau.

   b. For securities traded in a foreign market, the market must be of breadth and scope to make it comparable to a U.S. market which meets the condition just mentioned.

   c. For mutual funds, the fair value per share or unit is determined and published, and represents the basis for current transactions.

2. **Valuation** SFAS 124 requires that all applicable investments be measured at fair value. Gains and losses on the investments are included in the statement of activities as increases and decreases, respectively, in unrestricted net assets unless the use of the securities is temporarily or permanently restricted in accordance with the definitions found in SFAS 117.

3. **Investment Income** Any dividends, interest, or other investment income are to be included in the statement of activities as earned. Such amounts would be reported as adjustments to unrestricted net assets unless some restriction exists.

4. **Disclosures**

   a. Composition of the investment return including investment income, net realized gains or losses on investments reported at other than fair value, and net gains or losses on investments reported at fair value.

   b. A reconciliation of investment return to amounts reported in the statement of activities, if investment return is separated into operating and nonoperating amounts, together with a description of the policy used to determine the amount that is included in the measure of operations and a discussion of circumstances leading to a change in the policy.

   c. Aggregate carrying amount of the investment by major types.

   d. Basis for determining the carrying amount for investments, other than those to which SFAS 124 applies.

   e. Methods and significant assumptions used to estimate the fair values of investments other than financial instruments, if those other investments are reported at fair value.

   f. Aggregate amount of the deficiencies for all donor-restricted endowment funds for which the fair value of the assets at the reporting date is less than the level required by donor stipulations or law.

   g. The nature and carrying amount of each individual investment group which represents a significant concentration of market risk.

G. Depreciation

SFAS 93, *Recognition of Depreciation by Not-for-Profit Organizations,* requires all nonprofit organizations to recognize depreciation in general purpose external financial statements. SFAS 93 does not cover matters of financial statement display, recognition of assets, or measurement, such as the amount of depreciation to be recognized for a particular period.

1. **Required Disclosures**

   a. Depreciation expense for the period

   b. Depreciable asset balances, by nature or function of asset

   c. Total accumulated depreciation, or accumulated depreciation for the major classes of assets

   d. The depreciation method or methods used for each major class of assets

2. **Exception** Depreciation should not be recognized on individual pieces of artwork or antiquities. Artwork or antiquities shall be deemed to have those characteristics only if verifiable evidence exists that

   a. The asset has cultural, aesthetic, or historical value that is worth preserving perpetually.

   b. The holder has the technological and financial ability to protect and preserve, essentially undiminished, the service potential of the asset and is doing so.

H. Related Organizations

Reporting of Related Entities by Not-For-Profit Organizations (SOP 94-3) unifies guidance involving reporting related organizations.

1. **Required Conditions** A foundation, auxiliary, or guild is considered to be related to a nonprofit entity if one of the following conditions is met:

   a. The nonprofit entity **controls** the separate organization through contracts or other legal documents that provide the entity with the authority to direct the separate organization's activities, management, and policies.

   b. The nonprofit entity is considered to be the **sole beneficiary** of the organization because one of the three following circumstances exists:

      (1) The organization has solicited funds in the name of the nonprofit entity and substantially all of the funds were intended by the contributor to be transferred to or used by the nonprofit entity.

      (2) The nonprofit entity has transferred some of the resources to the organization, and substantially all of the organization's resources are held for the benefit of the entity.

      (3) The entity has assigned certain of its functions (e.g., the operation of a dormitory) to the organization, which is operating primarily for the benefit of the entity.

   c. The nonprofit entity, upon liquidation of the group, is **liable** for any deficit or due the net assets of the group.

2. **Disclosure** If the nonprofit entity both **controls** the separate organization and is considered to be its **sole beneficiary,** and if the financial statements of the entity and the related organization are not consolidated or combined in accordance with ARB 51, *Consolidated Financial Statements,* then the entity should disclose summarized financial information about the related organization (e.g., total assets, total liabilities, results of operations, and changes in net assets) and describe the nature of the relationship in a note to the nonprofit entity's financial statements.

II. Unique Accounting Features

A. Health Care Entities

All revenues (restricted and unrestricted) and expenses are recognized on the accrual basis. The basis and timing of the recognition of expenses for health care entities are generally the same as for other business organizations. Thus, **depreciation** and amortization is reported in conformity with commercial GAAP, as is the provision for **bad debts.**

1. **Unrestricted Revenues and Expenses** Mostly classified as **operating** because they arise from activities associated with the provision of health care services. Unrestricted revenues are further classified as *patient service revenue* or *other revenue.*

   a. The major classifications of **functional expenses** include nursing and other professional, general, fiscal, and administrative services; bad debts; depreciation; and interest.

   b. **Other revenues** include tuition from educational programs, cafeteria revenues, parking fees, fees for copies of medical records, gift shop revenues, and other activities somewhat related to the provision of patient service revenues.

2. **Patient Service Revenue** Patient service revenue (revenue from health care services) is recorded gross, at the provider's regularly established rates, regardless of collectibility. **Charity** care is **not** included in patient service revenues because these services were provided free of charge and, thus, were never expected to result in cash flows.

   a. **Deductions From Patient Service Revenues** Provisions for *contractual adjustments* (i.e., the difference between established rates and third-party payor payments) and *other adjustments* are recorded on the accrual basis and deducted from gross patient service revenue to determine *net patient service revenue.*

   b. **Bad Debts** The *provision for bad debts* is reported as an expense in accordance with GAAP. It is not acceptable to deduct an allowance for uncollectible accounts from gross patient service revenues in determining net patient service revenue.

3. **Other Revenue** Normally includes revenue from services other than health care provided to patients, as well as sales and services to nonpatients. Depending on the relation to the health care entity's operations, other revenue may include:

   a. Revenue from educational programs, including tuition from schools, such as nursing.

   b. Revenue from research and other gifts and grants, either unrestricted or for a specific purpose.

   c. Revenue such as gifts, grants, or endowment income restricted to finance charity care.

   d. Revenue from miscellaneous sources, such as (1) proceeds from sale of cafeteria meals and guest trays to employees, medical staff, and visitors; (2) proceeds from sales at gifts shops, snack bars, newsstands, parking lots, and vending machines; and (3) fees charged for copies of medical records.

Exhibit 8 ▸ Sample Health Care Entity Journal Entries

1. To record gross charges to patients at established rates:

Accounts Receivable	XX	
Patient Service Revenues		XX

NOTE: Charity care is not included in gross patient service revenues because the services are provided free of charge.

2. To record deductions from gross patient service revenues:

Contractual and Other Adjustments	XX	
Accounts Receivable		XX

NOTE: Contractual and other adjustments are recognized as deductions from patient service revenues rather than as operating expenses.

3. To record hospital operating expenses and other revenues (that is, operating revenues other than patient service revenues):

Operating Expenses (functional expense accounts)	XX	
Depreciation Expense	XX	
Cash or Payable		XX
Inventory		XX
Accumulated Depreciation		XX
Cash or Receivables	XX	
Other Revenues		XX

4. **Gains and Losses** Are generally classified as nonoperating because they generally result from transactions that are peripheral or incidental to the provision of health care services. However, a gain or loss closely related with the provision of health care services may be classified as operating. Therefore, depending on the relation of the transactions to the health care entity's ongoing or major operations, gains (losses) normally include:

   a. Contributions

   b. Returns on investments (i.e., interest, dividends, rents, and gains and losses resulting from increases and decreases in the value of investments). Investment income essential to the provision of health care services is reported as revenue (e.g., a provider with a large endowment that provides funds that are necessary for the provider to operate).

   c. Amounts from Endowment Funds that are available for general operating purposes, which include interest and dividends on Endowment Fund investments. Realized gains or losses on the sale of investments of Endowment Funds are recorded as restricted revenue or gains in the Endowment Fund principal unless such amounts are legally available for other use or are chargeable against other funds.

   d. Miscellaneous gains (losses) such as a gain or loss on the sale of the entity's properties.

5. **Receivables** Receivables for health care services do not include charges related to charity care. They are reported net of valuation allowances for uncollectibles and contractual and other adjustments.

6. **Other Health Care Entities**

   a. **Commercial** Financial statements of investor-owned health care entities are similar to those of other investor-owned entities.

b. **Governmental** The financial activities of a health care entity operated by a governmental unit should be accounted for as an enterprise fund when incorporated into the basic financial statements or CAFR of the governmental unit.

B. Colleges & Universities

Also see annuity and life income funds (in Section IV).

1. **Revenue** Where standard established tuition and fee charges are waived, whether partially or entirely, the full amounts of the standard tuition and fees are recognized as revenues and the amounts waived are recorded as expenditures. The amount of *tuition remissions* allowed to faculty members' families and *scholarships* are also recorded as both a revenue and an expenditure. The amount of *class cancellation refunds,* however, are not classified as either a revenue or an expenditure.

2. **Typical Operating Accounts** Revenues, expenditures, and transfers typically are recorded in accounts such as the following, which are adapted from NACUBO's *College and University Business Administration* (CUBA) chart of accounts:

- Tuition and Fees
- Appropriations [by source, e.g., state, local]
- Grants and Contracts [by source, e.g., federal]
- Private Gifts, Grants, and Contracts
- Endowment Income
- Sales and Service of Educational Activities [e.g., testing services]
- Auxiliary Enterprises [e.g., residence halls, food service, athletic programs, hospitals]
- Educational and General [subclassified—e.g., Instruction, Research, Public Services, Academic Support, Student Services, Institutional Support, Operation and Maintenance of Plant, Scholarships and Fellowships]
- Mandatory Transfers
- Nonmandatory Transfers
- Auxiliary Enterprises [e.g., as contra to the revenue account]
- Other

NOTE: Past CPA exam problems have required knowledge of the eight functional subclassifications within Educational and General.

3. **Statement of Activities** The university Statement of Activities is usually presented in a columnar format with one column for each fund group or major subdivision. (Exhibit 9)

Exhibit 9 ▸ University Statement of Activities Column Headings

Current Fund		Trust Funds			Plant Funds		
Unrestricted	Restricted	Loan funds	Endowment & similar funds	Annuity & life income funds	Unexpended	Renewals & replacements	Investment in plant

NOTE: These fund groups may be viewed in three categories: (1) current funds, (2) trust funds, and (3) plant funds—though the university accounting literature does not use the trust funds label as such. Agency funds are not included in this statement because agency funds are purely custodial—assets equal liabilities—and, thus, do not have net assets.

Exhibit 10 ▸ University Statement of Changes in Unrestricted Net Assets

(Heading)

	Current Funds			
	Unrestricted	Temporarily restricted	Permanently restricted	Total
Revenues:				
Educational and General [listed by major source]	XX			XX
State Appropriations	XX			XX
Federal Grants and Contracts		XX	XX	XX
Private Gifts, Grants, and Contracts	XX	XX	XX	XX
Endowment Income	XX	XX	XX	XX
Expired Term Endowment	XX	XX		XX
Interest Income	XX			XX
Auxiliary Enterprises	XX	XX	XX	XX
Total Revenues	XX	XX	XX	XX

Net Assets Released From Restrictions:				
Expiration of Time Requirements	XX	XX		
Fulfilled Conditions of Equipment Acquisition	XXX	XXX		
Fulfilled Conditions of Program Services	XX	XX		
Total Net Assets Released From Restrictions	XXX	XXX		
Expenditures and Mandatory Transfers:				
Educational and General Expenditures [listed by type]	XX		XX	XX
Total Educational and General Expenditures	XX		XX	XX
Mandatory Transfers for:				
Debt Service Principal and Interest	XX			XX
Loan Fund Equity	XX		XX	XX
Plant Expansion, Renewal, and Replacement	XX		—	XX
Total Mandatory Transfers	XX		XX	XX
Auxiliary Enterprises:				
Expenditures	XX		XX	XX
Mandatory Transfers	XX		XX	XX
Total Auxiliary Enterprises	XX		XX	XX
Total Expenditures and Mandatory Transfers	XX		XX	XX
Other Transfers and Additions (Deductions):				
Excess of Restricted Receipts and Accruals Over Amounts Reported as Revenues			XX	XX
Nonmandatory Transfers to Plant Funds	XX		—	—
Increase (Decrease) in Net Assets	XX	XX	XX	XX

C. **Voluntary Health & Welfare Organizations (VHWO)**

Voluntary health and welfare organizations (VHWOs) offer free or low cost services to the general public or to certain segments of society, and are supported primarily by public contributions. Examples include the United Way, the American Heart Association, Girl Scouts, Boy Scouts, the YMCA, and the YWCA. **Four** statements are required for VHWOs: the same statements required for all NPOs, plus a fourth, the Statement of Functional Expenses.

1. **Statement of Functional Expenses** The "extra" primary VHWO statement is in substance a schedule detailing expenses. SFAS 117 prescribes that the information in this statement be disclosed for VHWOs. One format of this statement is illustrated in Exhibit 12.

2. **Statement of Financial Position**

3. **Statement of Cash Flows**

4. **Statement of Activities (or Support, Revenue, and Expenses and Changes in Net Assets)** Many features of typical VHWO accounting and reporting are apparent in the primary VHWO operating statement, which may be presented in the format shown in Exhibit 11. Note that there is a distinct difference between support and revenue.

Exhibit 11 ▸ VHWO Statement of Activities

(Heading)

	Current Funds Unrestricted	Current Funds Restricted	Land, Building, and Equipment Fund	Endowment Fund	Total
PUBLIC SUPPORT AND REVENUE					
Public Support:					
Operating Contributions (net)	XX	XX			XX
Capital Contributions (net)			XX	XX	XX
Legacies and Bequests		XX	XX	XX	XX
Special Events (net of related costs)	XX	XX	XX		XX
United Way [or similar federated or nonfederated support organizations]	XX				XX
Total Public Support	XX	XX	XX	XX	XX
Revenue:					
Membership Dues	XX				XX
Investment Income	XX	XX	XX	XX	XX
Investment Gains	XX	XX	XX	XX	XX
Client Service Fees	XX				XX
Total Revenue	XX	XX	XX	XX	XX
EXPENSES					
Program Services:					
Research	XX	XX	XX		XX
Education	XX	XX	XX		XX
Community Services	XX		XX		XX
Total Program Services	XX	XX	XX		XX
Supporting Services:					
Management and General	XX		XX		XX
Fund-raising	XX		XX		XX
Total Supporting Services	XX	XX	XX		XX
OTHER CHANGES IN NET ASSETS					
Fixed Asset Acquisitions From Unrestricted Funds	(XX)		XX		
Transfer of Realized Endowment Appreciation	XX			(XX)	
Returned to Grantor or Donor		(XX)			(XX)
Net Assets, Beginning	XX	XX	XX	XX	XX
Net Assets, Ending	XX	XX	XX	XX	XX

Exhibit 12 ▸ VHWO Statement of Functional Expenses

(Heading)

	Program Services				Support Services			
	Research	Education	Community Services	Total	Management and General	Fund Raising	Total	Grand Total
Salaries	XX	XX	XX	XX	XX	XX	XX	XX
Employee Benefits	XX	XX	XX	XX	XX	XX	XX	XX
Payroll Taxes	XX	XX	XX	XX	XX	XX	XX	XX
.	.	.	.	.	.	.	.	.
.	.	.	.	.	.	.	.	.
.	.	.	.	.	.	.	.	.
Total	XX	XX	XX	XX	XX	XX	XX	XX
Professional Fees and Contractual Services	XX	XX	XX	XX	XX	XX	XX	XX
Supplies	XX	XX	XX	XX	XX	XX	XX	XX
Telephone	XX	XX	XX	XX	XX	XX	XX	XX
.	.	.	.	.	.	.	.	.
.	.	.	.	.	.	.	.	.
.	.	.	.	.	.	.	.	.
Miscellaneous	XX	XX	XX	XX	XX	XX	XX	XX
Total	XX	XX	XX	XX	XX	XX	XX	XX
Total Expenses Before Depreciation	XX	XX	XX	XX	XX	XX	XX	XX
Depreciation	XX	XX	XX	XX	XX	XX	XX	XX
Total Expenses	XX	XX	XX	XX	XX	XX	XX	XX

D. Other Nonprofit Organizations (ONPO)

Other nonprofit organizations include all nonbusiness organizations **except** (1) those covered by AICPA audit guides, and (2) entities that operate essentially as commercial businesses for the direct economic benefit of stockholders or members (for example, mutual insurance companies or farm cooperatives). Examples of the types of organizations classified as ONPOs are in Exhibit 13. ONPOs are required to present the standard three basic financial statements. The ONPO funds are similar to those of VHWOs.

Exhibit 13 ▸ Types of Organizations Classified as ONPO

Civic organizations	Social and country clubs	Performing arts organizations
Labor unions	Cemetery organizations	Private and community foundations
Political parties	Professional organizations	Private elementary and secondary schools
Trade associations	Fraternal organizations	Public broadcasting stations
Libraries	Religious organizations	Research and scientific organizations
Museums	Other cultural institutions	Zoological and botanical societies

III. Appendix: Health Care Entity Fund Accounting

A. Concepts

All (optional) fund formats are insufficient on their own, without the aggregate information required by SFAS 117. Nonprofit health care entities may use fund accounting to account for resources received from donors and grantors and to satisfy their fiduciary responsibilities. The fund accounting model and procedures used are closer to business accounting than to governmental fund accounting. For example, the entity's revenues, expenses, gains, and losses are accounted for and reported in a manner similar to businesses.

1. Except for the aggregate amount reported for revenues and gains in excess of expenses and losses, all other changes in the net assets of the General Fund reported in the Statement of Operations are not reported in the Statement of Revenues and Expenses of General Funds. For example, transfers to the General Fund from the Plant Replacement and Expansion Fund are treated as restricted revenues.

2. Note that investment income restricted for a specific operating purpose by donors and grantors is reported as restricted revenues in the appropriate donor-restricted fund. Unrestricted income of the donor-restricted funds is reported in the Statement of Revenues and Expenses of General Funds.

B. Fund Types

To facilitate reporting on the use of assets available for (the governing board's) use versus assets held under external restrictions, health care entities use two categories of funds—the General Funds and donor-restricted funds—each consisting of a self-balancing group of accounts composed of assets, liabilities, and net assets. All **unrestricted** resources and obligations are accounted for in the General Funds. Donor-restricted funds are used to account for financial resources that are *externally restricted* for specified operating or research, capital outlay, or endowment purposes. The fund structure of a health care entity is readily apparent in the format of its Statement of Financial Position, shown here in the pancake format with each fund reported separately.

Exhibit 14 ▸ Health Care Entity Statement of Financial Position, Fund Accounting

(Heading)

GENERAL FUNDS

Current assets: (e.g., cash, receivables, due from Specific-Purpose Funds)	XX	Current liabilities: (same as business entities)	XX
Assets whose use is limited	XX	Long-term debt: (same as business entities)	XX
Property and equipment, net of accumulated depreciation:	XX	Contingencies: (same as business entities)	XX
Other assets (e.g., investment in affiliated company)	XX		
	XX	Net assets: Unrestricted	XX

DONOR-RESTRICTED FUNDS

Specific-Purpose Funds

Cash	XX	Due to General Funds	XX
Investments	XX	Net Assets: Temp. Restricted	XX
Due From Endowment Funds	XX	Net Assets: Perm. Restricted	XX
	XX		XX

Plant Replacement and Expansion Funds

Cash	XX	Accounts payable	XX
Investments	XX	Contracts payable	XX
Due From Endowment Funds	XX	Net Assets (Temp. or Perm. Restricted)	XX
	XX		XX

Endowment Funds

Cash	XX	Due to Specific-Purpose Funds	XX
Investments	XX	Due to Plant Replacement and	
Pledges receivable, net	XX	Expansion Funds	XX
Property and Equipment, net	XX	Mortgage Assets (related)	XX
		Net Assets (Temp. or Perm. Restricted)	XX
	XX		XX

1. **General Funds** Account for all assets and liabilities that are not required to be accounted for in a donor-restricted fund, including assets whose use is limited, Agency Funds, and property and equipment related to the general operations of the entity. Assets and liabilities of General Funds are classified as current or noncurrent in conformity with GAAP.

   a. Assets whose use is limited include assets set aside by the governing board for identified purposes. The board retains control over the board-restricted assets and may, at its discretion, subsequently use them for other purposes.

   b. Agency funds are included in General Funds as both an asset and a liability. Transactions involving receipt and disbursement of agency funds are not included in the results of operations.

   c. Property and equipment used for general operations, and the related liabilities, are reported in General Funds. Property and equipment whose use is restricted (e.g., real estate investments of Endowment Funds) are reported in the appropriate donor-restricted fund.

2. **Donor-Restricted Funds** Account for resources whose use is restricted by donors or grantors and essentially act as holding funds until the resources are used. Donor-restricted funds may be temporarily or permanently restricted and include resources for specific operating purposes, additions to property and equipment, and endowments. Increases and decreases in the donor-restricted fund types are recorded as additions to and deductions from the appropriate fund net assets and are reported in the Statement of Activities (after original recognition as revenue).

Hospital Funds	
U	**U**nrestricted general
P	**P**lant replacement
S	**S**pecific purpose
E	**E**ndowment
T	**T**erm Endowment

a. Specific-Purpose Funds account for resources restricted by donors and grantors for specific operating purposes (e.g., research or education). They are recorded as restricted revenue (or gains) when received. Their expenditure (1) decreases the net assets of the Specific-Purpose Fund and (2) are generally recorded as expenses and net assets released from restrictions in the General Funds.

b. Plant Replacement and Expansion Funds account for resources restricted by donors and grantors for capital outlay purposes. They are recorded as restricted revenues (or gains) when received. Their expenditure (1) decreases the net assets of the Plant Replacement and Expansion Fund, and (2) increases property and equipment and the net assets of the General Funds. Neither the plant assets acquired nor any long-term debt issued for capital outlay purposes is accounted for in the Plant Replacement and Expansion Funds.

c. Endowment Funds include resources whose principal may not be expended (i.e., an Endowment Fund is generally a permanently restricted fund).

(1) The receipt of gifts and bequests restricted for endowments are reported as permanently restricted revenues of the Endowment Fund.

(2) Realized gains or losses on the sale of investments of Endowment Funds are reported as restricted revenues of the Endowment Fund unless such amounts are legally available for other use.

(3) Investment income of Endowment Funds is accounted for in accordance with the donor's instructions. If unrestricted, the income is generally reported as a (unrestricted) nonoperating gain in the General Funds. Investment income is reported as a temporarily or permanently restricted revenue (a) in the Specific Purpose Fund if restricted for a specified operating purposes (e.g., research or education), or (b) in the Plant Replacement and Expansion Fund if restricted for capital outlay purposes.

d. Term Endowment Funds account for resources whose principal may be expended after the donor-imposed restrictions are satisfied (e.g., for 15 years or until after the donor's death). Term endowments are accounted for as discussed above during the endowment term. When the term of the endowment ends, the assets are transferred to other funds, as specified by the donor. The transfer increases the net assets of the specific purpose fund or plant replacement and expansion fund, as appropriate, if restricted for specified operating or capital outlay purposes. If the assets are available for general operating purposes, the transfer is generally recorded as an increase in the unrestricted net assets in the general funds.

IV. Appendix: University Fund Accounting

A. Concepts

University (and college) fund accounting is both similar and different from that for governments and hospitals. Universities have only a few fund groups, as do hospitals, but divide these into major fund group subdivisions that resemble the municipal funds.

University Funds
Current Funds [Unrestricted Current Funds, Restricted Current Funds] **P**lant Funds **A**gency Funds **L**oan Funds **A**nnuity Fund **L**ife Income Fund **E**ndowment Fund [Endowment Funds (pure), Term Endowment Funds, Quasi-Endowment Funds (internally designated)]

1. **Transfers** Universities account for interfund quasi-external transactions, reimbursements, and transfers similarly to governments.

2. **Number of Fund Groups** Like hospitals, universities **may** use only one fund of each group for accounting purposes. Alternatively, they may use a separate fund for each major subdivision or may use many separate funds as do municipalities.

B. Restricted vs. Unrestricted Current Funds

Unrestricted Current Funds are used to account for all university financial resources (and related current liabilities) that are expendable for any legal and reasonable institutional purposes and that have **not** been (1) externally restricted by donors or grantors for specified purposes, or (2) designated by the governing board and, thus, accounted for as Net Assets—Unrestricted in another fund. Financial resources (and related current liabilities) that are externally restricted for current operating purposes of the university are accounted for in the *Restricted Current Funds.*

C. Current Fund Unique Accounting Conventions

Current Funds are accounted for on the accrual basis of accounting.

1. **Unrestricted Current Funds**

   a. Where the **full amount** of specific fees or other revenue sources is legally or contractually restricted for *debt service* or *capital outlay* purposes, the fees are recorded as restricted revenues of the appropriate plant funds rather than as current fund revenues.

   b. Where only **part** of specific fees or other revenue sources is legally or contractually restricted for *debt service* or *capital outlay* purposes, (1) the full amount is reported as unrestricted current fund revenue, and (2) the restricted amount is recorded as a mandatory transfer to the appropriate plant funds.

   c. Where the governing board has **designated** unrestricted resources for purposes usually financed in other funds, the revenues are reported in the unrestricted current fund, as is a *nonmandatory* transfer to the other fund(s). Likewise, returns of such sums are recorded as transfers to the unrestricted current fund rather than as revenues.

   d. Residual balances of endowment and similar funds and annuity and life income funds that become unrestricted at the end of their term are recorded in distinctively titled *Net Assets Released From Restrictions* (NARFR) accounts in the unrestricted current fund.

   e. Inventory may be accounted for on the consumption or use method whereby (a) inventory purchases are charged to *Expenses,* but (b) the change in inventories during the year is recorded as an adjustment to the *Expenses* account at year-end. (No inventory reserve is needed unless there is a base stock of inventories that is not available for use.)

2. **Restricted Current Funds**

   a. Financial resources restricted for operating purposes are recorded as assets and restricted revenues—in the restricted current funds.

   b. Restricted current fund expenditures are recorded in expenditures accounts of that fund—**not** of the unrestricted current funds.

D. **Current Fund Budgetary Accounts**
Universities may use budgetary accounts—particularly in the current funds—in a manner like that illustrated for a municipal general fund.

1. **Encumbrance Accounting** Generally used in budgeted university funds, parallel to that for municipal general and special revenue funds.

2. **Budgets** The university budgetary account entry usually varies somewhat from that for a municipal general fund. This entry follows a budgetary fund balance approach in that the *Unallocated (or Unassigned) Budget Balance* account is a balancing or offsetting account. The budgetary entry is reversed in the year-end closing entries.

E. **Trust & Agency Funds**
Accounting for university loan funds, endowment and similar funds, and agency funds parallels that for municipalities and/or hospitals.

F. **Annuity & Life Income Funds**
Annuity and life income funds are used to account for assets (and related liabilities) given to the university on the condition that the university either (1) make annuity payments of a fixed amount periodically to a named recipient(s) for a fixed or determinable period of time (annuity fund), or (2) pay the income earned by the fund to a named recipient(s) for a fixed or determinable period of time, often the donor's and/or the recipient's lifetime (life income fund).

1. **Fundamental Distinction** The annuity fund guarantees the recipient(s) a fixed dollar payment periodically during its term, while the life income fund involves no guarantees except that whatever income is earned will be paid to the recipient(s) during its term.

   a. **Initial Recording** No payable to the beneficiary is recorded at the inception of the Life Income Fund because there is no obligation to make fixed payments to the beneficiary. (The beneficiary is entitled only to receive the **income** from the fund's assets, if any.)

   b. **Closing Entries** Revenues are **not** credited for the income generated by the life income fund's assets, since the income is payable to the beneficiary. Therefore, life income fund income is credited to an *Income Payable to Beneficiary* account.

2. **Closing** At the end of their terms, the fund balances of both annuity funds and life income funds become expendable for unrestricted and/or specified restricted purposes and are transferred to the unrestricted current fund or to the appropriate restricted fund.

G. **Plant Funds**
The plant funds group is used to account for financial resources restricted and/or designated for university capital outlay and debt service, its fixed assets, and its long-term debt. All fixed assets and long-term debt that are not related to the university's trust funds are recorded in the plant funds. This is reasonable since most universities cannot incur long-term debt except for fixed asset acquisitions. The four plant fund subdivisions are closely related, and their accounting procedures are relatively simple.

U	**Unexpended** Plant Fund
R	Fund for **Renewals** and **Replacements**
R	Fund for **Retirement** of Indebtedness
I	**Investment** in Plant

1. **Unexpended Plant Funds** Used to account for financial resources restricted or designated for acquisition of **new** fixed assets, the current and long-term liabilities related to such unexpended financial resources, and the net amount available for expenditure for new fixed assets. The new fixed assets acquired consist of both new fixed assets and existing fixed assets newly acquired for university purposes—as opposed to renovating existing university fixed assets. The new fixed assets are capitalized in the *Investment in Plant* accounts.

2. **Plant Funds for Renewals and Replacements** Identical to unexpended plant funds except the financial resources are used to renovate or perhaps replace existing university fixed assets. Long-term debt is not often incurred for such purposes and most renovations, in particular, are not capitalized in the *Investment in Plant* accounts—though major betterment and replacements are capitalized in the *Investment in Plant* accounts.

   NOTE: Both unexpended plant funds and plant funds for renewals and replacements are similar to municipal capital projects funds, except that long-term debt may be accounted for temporarily in these plant fund subdivisions. Because of their similarity, it is acceptable to account for both of these plant fund subdivisions in one plant fund subdivision, provided that separate *Net Assets* accounts distinguish the net assets of the two subfunds.

3. **Plant Funds for Retirement of Indebtedness** Used to account for restricted and designated financial resources to be used for university debt service, related current liabilities for long-term debt principal and interest payable, and the net amount available for future debt service expenditures. The accounting procedures for plant funds for retirement of indebtedness parallel those for municipal debt service funds.

4. **Investment in Plant** An account group in a governmental accounting sense, which is used to record the university's general fixed assets, general long-term debt, and the difference between its fixed assets and long-term debt, referred to as net investment in plant. Thus, the investment in plant fund functions like a combination of the pre-GASB 34 municipal general fixed assets and general long-term debt account groups. Nongovernmental colleges and universities *must* report accumulated depreciation on these assets and the periodic depreciation provision *must* be reported in the Statement of Activities. Colleges and universities that are part of a government had the option of not reporting these amounts (prior to adoption of GASB No. 34) and, historically, have not done so.

H. Statement of Financial Position

The university fund group and major fund subdivisions structure is readily apparent in the format of the university Statement of Financial Position (balance sheet), when presented in the fund pancake format. (See Exhibit 15.)

1. **Unrestricted and Restricted Current Funds** Similar to municipal general and special revenue funds, respectively, and the restricted current fund is like a hospital specific purpose fund.

2. **Trust Funds** The loan fund, endowment funds, and annuity and life income funds are all trust funds. The loan fund is like one of the municipal nonexpendable trust funds. The annuity and life income funds are special types of trust funds.

3. **Agency Fund** Similar to the simpler municipal agency funds.

4. **Plant Funds** Like a combination of municipal (a) capital projects funds—the unexpended funds and fund for renewals and replacements; (b) debt service funds—the funds for

retirement of indebtedness; and (c) general fixed assets and general long-term debt account groups—the investment in plant fund. The distinction between the unexpended funds and the fund for renewals and replacements is that (a) the unexpended funds are used to account for resources (and related debt) to be expended for new construction (capitalized in the *Investment in Plant* accounts), while (b) the fund for renewals and replacements are used to account for financial resources to be expended for renovation of existing fixed assets (which are **not** usually capitalized in *Investment in Plant* accounts).

Exhibit 15 ▸ University Statement of Financial Position, Fund Accounting

(Heading)

Assets		Liabilities and Net Assets	
		CURRENT FUNDS	
Unrestricted		Unrestricted	
Current Assets [list]	XX	Current Liabilities [list]	XX
		Net Assets: Unrestricted	XX
	XX		XX
Restricted		Restricted	
Current Assets [list]	XX	Current Liabilities [list]	XX
		Net Assets: Temporarily Restricted	XX
		Net Assets: Permanently Restricted	XX
Total Current Funds	XX	Total Current Funds	XX
		LOAN FUNDS	
Current Assets [list]	XX	Net Assets:	
Loan Notes Receivable	XX	Unrestricted	XX
Long-Term Investments	XX	Temporarily Restricted	XX
		Permanently Restricted	XX
Total Loan Funds	XX	Total Loan Funds	XX
		ENDOWMENT AND SIMILAR FUNDS	
Current Assets [list]	XX	Current Liabilities [list]	XX
Long-Term Investments [list]	XX	Long-Term Liabilities [list]	XX
Fixed Assets [list, net of accumulated depreciation]	XX		XX
		Net Assets:	
		Perm. Restricted: Endowment	XX
		Temp. Restricted: Term Endowment	XX
		Unrestricted: Quasi-Endowment	XX
Total Endowment and Similar Funds	XX	Total Endowment and Similar Funds	XX
		ANNUITY AND LIFE INCOME FUNDS	
Current Assets [list]	XX	Annuities Payable	XX
Long-Term Investments	XX	Life Income Earnings Payable	XX
		Net Assets: Permanently Restricted	
		Annuity Funds	XX
		Life Income Funds	XX
Total Annuity and Life Income Funds	XX	Total Annuity and Life Income Funds	XX
		PLANT FUNDS	
Unexpended		Unexpended	
Current Assets [list]	XX	Current Liabilities [list]	XX
Long-Term Investments	XX	Notes Payable	XX
Construction in Process	XX		XX
		Net Assets:	
		Unrestricted	XX
		Temporarily Restricted	XX
		Permanently Restricted	XX
Total Unexpended Plant Funds	XX	Total Unexpended Plant Funds	XX

For Renewals and Replacements		For Renewals and Replacements	
Current Assets [list]	XX	Current Liabilities [list]	XX
Long-Term Investments	XX	Net Assets:	
		Unrestricted	XX
		Temporarily Restricted	XX
		Permanently Restricted	XX
Total for Renewals and Replacements	XX	Total for Renewals and Replacements	XX
For Retirement of Indebtedness		For Retirement of Indebtedness	
Current Assets [list]	XX	Net Assets:	
Long-Term Investments	XX	Restricted (Temp. or Perm)	XX
Sinking Fund—Bank Trustee	XX	Unrestricted	XX
Total for Retirement of Indebtedness	XX	Total for Retirement of Indebtedness	XX
Investment in Plant		Investment in Plant	
Fixed Assets [list]	XX	Long-Term Debt [list]	XX
		Net Investment in Plant	XX
Total Investment in Plant	XX	Total Investment in Plant	XX

V. Appendix: VHWO Fund Accounting

A. Concepts

The VHWO fund structure is similar to that used by universities; furthermore, VHWOs use only one fund of each fund type. Note that fund accounting is **not** required. Whereas hospital accounting records all revenues and expenses in a single unrestricted fund, VHWOs record revenues and expenses in **each** fund—summarizing them in the total column of a columnar Statement of Activities.

B. Fund Types

1. **Land, Buildings, and Equipment (or Plant) Fund** Used to account for (a) unexpended restricted resources to be used to acquire VHWO fixed assets, (b) the VHWO's general fixed assets, (c) long-term debt related to the VHWO's fixed assets, and (d) the net investment in VHWO general fixed assets. (This fund is identical to the university plant fund—although VHWOs may record debt service in the current unrestricted fund rather than in the plant fund.)

   a. VHWO general fixed assets and related general long-term debt are recorded in the land, buildings, and equipment (or plant) fund, while those related to endowments are recorded in the endowment fund.

   b. If fixed assets are donated to a VHWO to be sold and the proceeds used for operating purposes, the fixed assets are recorded in the current unrestricted fund or current restricted fund pending their sale, depending on whether the use of the sale proceeds is unrestricted or restricted.)

   c. Net Assets of the land, buildings, and equipment (or plant) fund are classified as between (1) expended and (2) unexpended, as well as between unrestricted and temporarily and permanently restricted.

2. **Custodian Fund** Used to account for resources held by the VHWO in an agency capacity for other organizations or individuals. (This fund is identical to the university agency fund and to simple municipal agency funds.)

3. **Restricted Current Fund** Used to account for available financial resources (and related current liabilities) that are expendable only for operating purposes specified by the donor or grantor. (This fund is identical to the university restricted current fund.)

4. **Unrestricted Current Fund** Used to account for all unrestricted resources (and related current liabilities) except those invested in fixed assets, which are accounted for in the land, buildings, and equipment (or plant) fund. (This fund is identical to the university unrestricted current fund.)

5. **Endowment Fund** Used to account for the principal (corpus) of gifts or bequests accepted with donor stipulations that (a) the principal is to be maintained intact—in perpetuity or for a fixed or determinable term of time, and (b) the earnings may be expended for unrestricted purposes and/or specified restricted purposes. (The VHWO endowment fund is identical to those of hospitals and universities and is like some municipal nonexpendable trust funds.)

6. **Loan and Annuity Fund** Used to account for resources restricted to making loans and/or annuity payments to specified recipients for a specified term—after which the VHWO is the remainderman beneficiary of the net assets, which may be unrestricted or restricted to use. (This fund is similar to the university annuity and life Income fund.)

A•CRUEL

Asset—Land, Building, and Equipment (or Plant) Fund

Custodian Fund
Restricted Current Fund
Unrestricted Current Fund
Endowment Fund
Loan and Annuity Fund

Select Hot•Spots™ Video Descriptions

CPA 2040 Governmental & Nonprofit Accounting
Following previous exam emphasis, this program concentrates on accounting for governments. Funds, their uses, and their presentation are examined. Encumbrance, budget, and modified accrual accounting are clarified. This program also covers accounting for health-care organizations, colleges & universities, and voluntary health & welfare organizations. Robert Monette explains two extensive examples, several multiple choice questions, and two problems as well as discussing problem-solving techniques and introducing proven mnemonics.

CHAPTER 20—NONPROFIT ACCOUNTING

Problem 20-1 MULTIPLE CHOICE QUESTIONS (98 to 122 minutes)

1. The Jones family lost its home in a fire. On December 25, of the previous year, a philanthropist sent money to the Amer Benevolent Society, a non-profit organization, to purchase furniture for the Jones family. During January of the current year, Amer purchased this furniture for the Jones family. How should Amer report the receipt of the money in its previous year-end financial statements?
a. As an unrestricted contribution
b. As a temporarily restricted contribution
c. As a permanently restricted contribution
d. As a liability (5/95, AR, #58, amended, 5476)

2. Functional expenses recorded in the general ledger of ABC, a nongovernmental not-for-profit organization, are as follows:

Soliciting prospective members	$45,000
Printing membership benefits brochures	30,000
Soliciting membership dues	25,000
Maintaining donor list	10,000

What amount should ABC report as fund raising expenses?
a. $ 10,000
b. $ 35,000
c. $ 70,000
d. $110,000 (R/99, AR, #2, 6811)

3. The expenditure element "salaries and wages" is an example of which type of classification?
a. Object
b. Program
c. Function
d. Activity (5/95, AR, #54, 5472)

4. During the current year, Mill Foundation, a nongovernmental not-for-profit organization, received $100,000 in unrestricted contributions from the general public. Mill's board of directors stipulated that $75,000 of these contributions would be used to create an endowment. At the end of the current year, how should Mill report the $75,000 in the net assets section of the statement of financial position?
a. Permanently restricted
b. Unrestricted
c. Temporarily restricted
d. Donor restricted (R/05, FAR, 1004G, #18, 7762)

5. Stanton College, a not-for-profit organization, received a building with no donor stipulations as to its use. Stanton does not have an accounting policy implying a time restriction on donated assets. What type of net assets should be increased when the building was received?

I. Unrestricted
II. Temporarily restricted
III. Permanently restricted

a. I only
b. II only
c. III only
d. II or III (R/01, AR, #1, 6986)

6. FASB Statement No. 117, Financial Statements of Not-for-Profit Organizations, focuses on
a. Basic information for the organization as a whole
b. Standardization of funds nomenclature
c. Inherent differences of not-for-profit organizations that impact reporting presentations
d. Distinctions between current fund and non-current fund presentations (11/94, AR, #30, 5007)

7. Which of the following classifications is required for reporting of expenses by all not-for-profit organizations?
a. Natural classification in the statement of activities or notes to the financial statements
b. Functional classification in the statement of activities or notes to the financial statements
c. Functional classification in the statement of activities and natural classification in a matrix format in a separate statement
d. Functional classification in the statement of activities and natural classification in the notes to the financial statements (11/97, AR, #17, 6545)

8. Pharm, a nongovernmental not-for-profit organization, is preparing its year-end financial statements. Which of the following statements is required?
a. Statement of changes in financial position
b. Statement of cash flows
c. Statement of changes in fund balance
d. Statement of revenue, expenses and changes in fund balance (R/01, AR, #10, 6995)

9. Forkin Manor, a nongovernmental not-for-profit organization, is interested in having its financial statements reformatted using terminology that is more readily associated with for-profit entities. The director believes that the term "operating profit" and the practice of segregating recurring and nonrecurring items more accurately depict the organization's activities. Under what condition will Forkin be allowed to use "operating profit" and to segregate its recurring items from its nonrecurring items in its statement of activities?

a. The organization reports the change in unrestricted net assets for the period.
b. A parenthetical disclosure in the notes implies that the not-for-profit organization is seeking for-profit entity status.
c. Forkin receives special authorization from the Internal Revenue Service that this wording is appropriate.
d. At a minimum, the organization reports the change in permanently restricted net assets for the period. (R/02, AR, #6, 7071)

10. In year 1, Gamma, a not-for-profit organization, deposited at a bank $1,000,000 given by a donor to purchase endowment securities. The securities were purchased January 2, year 2. At December 31, year 1, the bank recorded $2,000 interest on the deposit. In accordance with the bequest, this $2,000 was used to finance ongoing program expenses in March year 2. At December 31, year 1, what amount of the bank balance should be included as current assets in Gamma's classified balance sheet?

a. $0
b. $ 2,000
c. $1,000,000
d. $1,002,000 (11/96, AR, #11, amended, 6304)

11. On December 30, Leigh Museum, a not-for-profit organization, received a $7,000,000 donation of Day Co. shares with donor stipulated requirements as follows:

- Shares valued at $5,000,000 are to be sold with the proceeds used to erect a public viewing building.
- Shares valued at $2,000,000 are to be retained with the dividends used to support current operations.

As a consequence of the receipt of the Day shares, how much should Leigh report as temporarily restricted net assets on its statement of financial position?

a. $0
b. $2,000,000
c. $5,000,000
d. $7,000,000 (5/95, AR, #57, amended, 5475)

12. Cancer Educators, a not-for-profit organization, incurred costs of $10,000 when it combined program functions with fund raising functions. Which of the following cost allocations might Cancer report in its statement of activities?

	Program services	*Fund raising*	*General*
a.	$0	$0	$10,000
b.	$0	$6,000	$ 4,000
c.	$ 6,000	$4,000	$0
d.	$10,000	$0	$0

(11/94, AR, #26, 5003)

13. In its fiscal year ended June 30, year 1, Barr College, a private nonprofit institution, received $100,000 designated by the donor for scholarships for superior students. On July 26, year 1, Barr selected the students and awarded the scholarships. How should the July 26 transaction be reported in Barr's statement of activities for the year ended June 30, year 2?

a. As both an increase and a decrease of $100,000 in unrestricted net assets
b. As a decrease only in unrestricted net assets
c. By footnote disclosure only
d. Not reported (5/96, AR, #5, amended, 6202)

14. A large not-for-profit organization's statement of activities should report the net change for net assets that are

	Unrestricted	*Permanently restricted*
a.	Yes	Yes
b.	Yes	No
c.	No	No
d.	No	Yes

(11/95, AR, #74, 5817)

15. The Jackson Foundation, a not-for-profit organization, received contributions during the year as follows:

- Unrestricted cash contributions of $500,000.
- Cash contributions of $200,000 to be restricted to acquisition of property.

Jackson's statement of cash flows should include which of the following amounts?

	Operating activities	*Investing activities*	*Financing activities*
a.	$700,000	$0	$0
b.	$500,000	$200,000	$0
c.	$500,000	$0	$200,000
d.	$0	$500,000	$200,000

(11/97, AR, #18, 6546)

16. Famous, a nongovernmental not-for-profit art museum, has elected not to capitalize its permanent collections. In the previous year, a bronze statue was stolen. The statue was not recovered and insurance proceeds of $35,000 were paid to Famous in the current year. This transaction would be reported in

I. The statement of activities as permanently restricted revenues.
II. The statement of cash flows as cash flows from investing activities.

a. I only
b. II only
c. Both I and II
d. Neither I nor II (R/99, AR, #23, amended, 6812)

17. A not-for-profit voluntary health and welfare organization should report a contribution for the construction of a new building as cash flows from which of the following in the statement of cash flows?
a. Operating activities
b. Financing activities
c. Capital financing activities
d. Investing activities
(R/05, FAR, 1076G, #23, 7767)

18. Hunt Community Development Agency (HCDA), a financially independent authority, provides loans to commercial businesses operating in Hunt County. This year, HCDA made loans totaling $500,000. How should HCDA classify the disbursements of loans on the cash flow statement?
a. Operating activities
b. Noncapital financing activities
c. Capital and related financing activities
d. Investing activities (R/01, AR, #2, 6987)

19. An unrestricted cash contribution should be reported in a nongovernmental not-for-profit organization's statement of cash flows as an inflow from
a. Operating activities
b. Investing activities
c. Financing activities
d. Capital and related financing activities
(R/05, FAR, 0116G, #2, 7746)

20. On January 2, the Baker Fund, a nongovernmental not-for-profit corporation, received a $125,000 contribution restricted to youth activity programs. During the year, youth activities generated revenues of $89,000 and had program expenses of $95,000. What amount should Baker report as net assets released from restrictions for the year?
a. $0
b. $ 6,000
c. $ 95,000
d. $125,000 (R/00, AR, #5, amended, 6910)

21. In the current year, Jones Foundation received the following support:

- A cash contribution of $875,000 to be used at the board of directors' discretion
- A promise to contribute $500,000 in the following year from a supporter who has made similar contributions in prior periods
- Contributed legal services with a value of $100,000, which Jones would have otherwise purchased

At what amounts would Jones classify and record these transactions as revenue?

	Unrestricted	*Temporarily restricted*
a.	$1,375,000	$0
b.	$ 875,000	$500,000
c.	$ 975,000	$0
d.	$ 975,000	$500,000

(R/00, AR, #4, amended, 6909)

22. State University received two contributions during the year that must be used to provide scholarships. Contribution A for $10,000 was collected during the year, and $8,000 was spent on scholarships. Contribution B is a pledge for $30,000 to be received next fiscal year. What amount of contribution revenue should the university report in its statement of activities?
a. $ 8,000
b. $10,000
c. $38,000
d. $40,000 (R/02, AR, #2, 7067)

23. Pica, a nongovernmental not-for-profit organization, received unconditional promises of $100,000 expected to be collected within one year. Pica received $10,000 prior to year end. Pica anticipates collecting 90% of the contributions and has a June 30 fiscal year end. What amount should Pica record as contribution revenue as of June 30?
a. $ 10,000
b. $ 80,000
c. $ 90,000
d. $100,000 (R/02, AR, #5, 7070)

24. Oz, a nongovernmental not-for-profit organization, received $50,000 from Ame Company to sponsor a play given by Oz at the local theater. Oz gave Ame 25 tickets, which generally cost $100 each. Ame received no other benefits. What amount of ticket sales revenue should Oz record?
a. $0
b. $ 2,500
c. $47,500
d. $50,000 (R/02, AR, #1, 7066)

25. The Pel Museum, a nonprofit organization, received a contribution of historical artifacts. It need not recognize the contribution if the artifacts are to be sold and the proceeds used to
a. Support general museum activities
b. Acquire other items for collections
c. Repair existing collections
d. Purchase buildings to house collections
(5/95, AR, #59, amended, 5477)

26. Community Enhancers, a nongovernmental not-for-profit organization, received the following pledges:

Unrestricted	$400,000
Restricted for capital additions	300,000

All pledges are legally enforceable. However, Community's experience indicates that 5% of all pledges prove to be uncollectible. What amount should Community report as pledges receivable, net of any required allowance account?
a. $700,000
b. $665,000
c. $380,000
d. $285,000 (R/05, FAR, 0126G, #3, 7747)

27. Maple Church has cash available for investments in several different accounting funds. Maple's policy is to maximize its financial resources. How may Maple pool its investments?
a. Maple may **not** pool its investments.
b. Maple may pool all investments, but must equitably allocate realized and unrealized gains and losses among participating funds.
c. Maple may pool only unrestricted investments, but must equitably allocate realized and unrealized gains and losses among participating funds.
d. Maple may pool only restricted investments, but must equitably allocate realized and unrealized gains and losses among participating funds.
(5/93, PII, #40, 4146)

28. Midtown Church received a donation of marketable equity securities from a church member. The securities had appreciated in value after they were purchased by the donor, and they continued to appreciate through the end of Midtown's fiscal year. At what amount should Midtown report its investment in marketable equity securities in its year-end balance sheet?
a. Donor's cost
b. Market value at the date of receipt
c. Market value at the balance sheet date
d. Market value at either the date of receipt or the balance-sheet date (5/93, PII, #38, 4144)

29. In a statement of activities of the People's Environmental Protection Association, a voluntary community organization, depreciation expense should
a. Not be included
b. Be included as an element of support
c. Be included as an element of other changes in net assets
d. Be included as an element of expense
(11/94, AR, #29, amended, 5006)

30. On December 31 of the previous year, Dahlia, a nongovernmental not-for-profit organization, purchased a vehicle with $15,000 unrestricted cash and received a donated second vehicle having a fair value of $12,000. Dahlia expects each vehicle to provide it with equal service value over each of the next five years and then to have no residual value. Dahlia has an accounting policy implying a time restriction on gifts of long-lived assets. In Dahlia's current year statement of activities, what depreciation expense should be included under changes in unrestricted net assets?
a. $0
b. $2,400
c. $3,000
d. $5,400 (R/03, FAR, #5, 7607)

31. Unrestricted earnings on specific purpose fund investments that are part of a hospital's central operations are reported as
a. Specific purpose fund restricted revenues
b. Specific purpose fund unrestricted revenues
c. General fund deferred revenues
d. General fund unrestricted revenues
(5/92, Theory, #60, amended, 2753)

32. Which of the following normally would be included in other operating revenues of a hospital?

	Revenues from educational programs	*Unrestricted gifts*
a.	No	No
b.	No	Yes
c.	Yes	No
d.	Yes	Yes

(11/94, AR, #28, 5005)

33. Which of the following normally would be included in Other Revenue of a hospital?

	Revenue from grants, specified by the donor for research	*Revenue from a gift shop*
a.	No	No
b.	No	Yes
c.	Yes	No
d.	Yes	Yes

(Editors, 2171)

34. Valley's community hospital normally includes proceeds from sale of cafeteria meals in
a. Deductions from dietary service expenses
b. Ancillary service revenues
c. Patient service revenues
d. Other revenues (5/94, AR, #60, 4665)

35. Terry, an auditor, is performing test work for a not-for-profit hospital. Listed below are components of the statement of operations:

Revenue relating to charity care	$100,000
Bad debt expense	70,000
Net assets released from restrictions used for operations	50,000
Other revenue	80,000
Net patient service revenue (includes revenue related to charity care)	500,000

What amount would be reported as total revenues, gains, and other support on the statement of operations?
a. $460,000
b. $530,000
c. $580,000
d. $630,000 (R/05, FAR, A0015N, #39, 7783)

36. Hospital, Inc., a not-for-profit organization with no governmental affiliation, reported the following in its accounts for the current year ended December 31:

Gross patient services revenue from all services provided at the established billing rates of the hospital (note that this figure includes charity care of $25,000)	$775,000
Provisions for bad debts	15,000
Difference between established billing rates and fees negotiated with third-party payors (contractual adjustments)	70,000

What amount would the hospital report as net patient service revenue in its statement of operations for the current year ended December 31?
a. $680,000
b. $690,000
c. $705,000
d. $735,000 (R/05, FAR, C01648F, #46, 7790)

37. A not-for-profit hospital issued long-term tax exempt bonds for the hospital's benefit. The hospital is responsible for the liability. Which fund may the hospital use to account for this liability?
a. Enterprise
b. Specific purpose
c. General
d. General long-term debt account group (5/94, AR, #58, 4663)

38. Which of the following should normally be considered ongoing or central transactions for a not-for-profit hospital?

I. Room and board fees from patients
II. Recovery room fees

a. Neither I nor II
b. Both I and II
c. II only
d. I only (11/95, AR, #75, 5818)

39. For the fall semester, Ames University assessed its students $3,000,000 for tuition and fees. The net amount realized was only $2,500,000 because scholarships of $400,000 were granted to students, and tuition remissions of $100,000 were allowed to faculty members' children attending Ames. What amount should Ames report for the period as unrestricted current fund gross revenues from tuition and fees?
a. $2,500,000
b. $2,600,000
c. $2,900,000
d. $3,000,000 (5/93, PII, #33, amended, 4140)

40. The following expenditures were among those incurred by Hope University during the year:

Administrative data processing	$100,000
Fellowships	200,000
Operation and maintenance of physical plant	400,000

The amount to be included in the functional classification "Institutional Support" expenditures account is
a $100,000
b. $300,000
c. $500,000
d. $700,000 (Editors, 1408)

41. The following funds were among those held by State College at December 31:

Principal specified by the donor as nonexpendable	$500,000
Principal expendable after 10 years from present	300,000
Principal designated from current funds	100,000

What amount should State College classify as regular endowment funds?
a. $100,000
b. $300,000
c. $500,000
d. $900,000 (5/92, PII, #35, amended, 2667)

42. During the year, Smith University's board of trustees established a $100,000 fund to be retained and invested for scholarship grants. The fund earned $6,000 which had not been disbursed at December 31. What amount should Smith report in a quasi-endowment fund's net assets at December 31?
a. $0
b. $ 6,000
c. $100,000
d. $106,000 (11/93, PII, #17, amended, 4446)

43. Calvin College makes a discretionary transfer of $100,000 to its library fund. This transfer should be recorded by a debit to
a. Unrestricted current fund net assets.
b. Restricted current fund net assets.
c. General fund expenditures.
d. Library fund expenditures.
(5/92, PII, #37, amended, 2669)

44. A college's plant funds group includes which of the following subgroups?

I. Renewals and replacement funds
II. Retirement of indebtedness funds
III. Restricted current funds

a. I and II
b. I and III
c. II and III
d. I only (5/91, Theory, #58, 2102)

45. Which of the following accounts would appear in the plant fund of a not-for-profit private college?

	Fuel inventory for power plant	*Equipment*
a.	Yes	Yes
b.	No	Yes
c.	No	No
d.	Yes	No

(5/93, Theory, #57, 9209)

46. Community College had the following encumbrances at December 31:

Outstanding purchase orders	$12,000
Commitments for services not received	50,000

What amount of these encumbrances should be reported as liabilities in Community's balance sheet at December 31?
a. $62,000
b. $50,000
c. $12,000
d. $0 (5/92, PII, #38, amended, 2670)

47. Home Care, Inc., a nongovernmental voluntary health and welfare organization, received two contributions in the current year. One contribution of $250,000 was restricted for use as general support in the following year. The other contribution of $200,000 carried no donor restrictions. What amount should Home Care report as temporarily restricted contributions in its current year statement of activities?
a. $450,000
b. $250,000
c. $200,000
d. $0 (R/03, FAR, #9, 7611)

48. A not-for-profit voluntary health and welfare organization received a $500,000 permanent endowment. The donor stipulated that the income must be used for a mental health program. The endowment fund reported $60,000 net decrease in market value and $30,000 investment income. The organization spent $45,000 on the mental health program during the year. What amount of change in temporarily restricted net assets should the organization report?
a. $ 75,000 decrease
b. $ 15,000 decrease
c. $0
d. $425,000 increase (R/02, AR, #8, 7073)

49. In the previous year, Citizens' Health, a voluntary health and welfare organization, received a bequest of a $200,000 certificate of deposit maturing in the current year. The testator's only stipulations were that this certificate be held until maturity and that the interest revenue be used to finance salaries for a preschool program. Interest revenue for the current year was $16,000. When the certificate matured and was redeemed, the board of trustees adopted a formal resolution designating $40,000 of the proceeds for the future purchase of equipment for the preschool program. What amount should Citizen report in its current year-end current funds balance sheet as net assets designated for the preschool program?
a. $0
b. $16,000
c. $40,000
d. $56,000 (5/93, PII, #21, amended, 4129)

Problem 20-2 ADDITIONAL MULTIPLE CHOICE QUESTIONS (54 to 68 minutes)

50. In hospital accounting, restricted funds are
a. **Not** available unless the board of directors removes the restrictions
b. Restricted as to use only for board-designated purposes
c. **Not** available for current operating use; however, the income generated by the funds is available for current operating use
d. Restricted as to use by the donor, grantor, or other source of the resources

(5/93, PII, #29, 4136)

51. A labor union had the following receipts:

Per capita dues	$680,000
Initiation fees	90,000
Sales of organizational supplies	60,000
Nonexpendable gift restricted by donor for loan purposes for 10 years	30,000
Nonexpendable gift restricted by donor for loan purposes in perpetuity	25,000

The union's constitution provides that 10% of the per capita dues are designated for the Strike Insurance Fund to be distributed for strike relief at the discretion of the union's executive board. In the statement of activity, what amount should be reported as permanently restricted revenues?
a. $123,000
b. $ 93,000
c. $ 55,000
d. $ 25,000

(Editors, 1361)

52. A labor union had the following expenses:

Labor negotiations	500,000
Fund-raising	100,000
Membership development	50,000
Administrative and general	200,000

In the statement of activity, what amount should be reported under the classification of program services?
a. $850,000
b. $600,000
c. $550,000
d. $500,000

(Editors, 1362)

53. The Board of Trustees of Rose Foundation designated $200,000 for college scholarships. The foundation received a bequest of $400,000 from an estate of a benefactor who specified that the bequest was to be used for hiring teachers to tutor handicapped students. What amount should be accounted for as restricted resources?
a. $0
b. $200,000
c. $400,000
d. $600,000

(Editors, 1391)

54. A not-for-profit organization receives $150 from a donor. The donor receives two tickets to a theater show and an acknowledgment in the theater program. The tickets have a fair market value of $100. What amount is recorded as contribution revenue?
a. $0
b. $ 50
c. $100
d. $150

(11/97, AR, #16, 6544)

55. Land valued at $400,000 and subject to a $150,000 mortgage was donated to Beaty Hospital without restriction as to use. Which of the following entries should Beaty make to record this donation?

a.	Land	400,000	
	Mortgage Payable		150,000
	Permanently Restricted Revenues		250,000
b.	Land	400,000	
	Net Assets		150,000
	Contributions		250,000
c.	Land	400,000	
	Net Assets		150,000
	Temporarily Restricted Revenues		250,000
d.	Land	400,000	
	Mortgage Payable		150,000
	Unrestricted Revenues		250,000

(Editors, 4133)

56. Lori Hospital received a pure endowment grant. The pure endowment grant
a. May be expended by the governing board only to the extent of the principal since the income from this fund must be accumulated
b. Should generally be reported as a nonoperating gain when the full amount of principal is expended
c. Should be recorded as a memorandum entry only
d. Should be recorded as donor-restricted revenue upon receipt

(Editors, 1428)

57. Super Seniors is a not-for-profit organization that provides services to senior citizens. Super employs a full-time staff of 10 people at an annual cost of $150,000. In addition, two volunteers work as part-time secretaries replacing last years' full-time secretary who earned $10,000. Services performed by other volunteers for special events had an estimated value of $15,000. These volunteers were employees of local businesses and they received small-value items for their participation. What amount should Super report for salary and wage expenses related to the above items?
a. $150,000
b. $160,000
c. $165,000
d. $175,000 (5/93, PII, #30, 4137)

58. In May, Ross donated $200,000 cash to a church with the stipulation that the revenue generated from this gift be paid to Ross during Ross' lifetime. The conditions of this donation are that, after Ross dies, the principal may be used by the church for any purpose voted on by the church elders. The church received interest of $16,000 on the $200,000 for the year ended June 30, and the interest was remitted to Ross. In the church's June 30 annual financial statements
a. $200,000 should be reported as revenue.
b. $184,000 should be reported as revenue.
c. $16,000 should be reported under support and revenue.
d. The gift and its terms should be disclosed only in notes to the financial statements. (Editors, 4599)

59. Child Care Centers, Inc., a not-for-profit organization, receives revenue from various sources during the year to support its day-care centers. The following cash amounts were received in the year:

- $2,000 restricted by the donor to be used for meals for the children.
- $1,500 received for subscriptions to a monthly child-care magazine with a fair market value to subscribers of $1,000.
- $10,000 to be used only upon completion of a new playroom that was 75% complete at December 31.

What amount should Child Care Centers record as contribution revenue in its Statement of Activities?
a. $ 2,000
b. $ 2,500
c. $10,000
d. $11,000 (11/97, AR, #15, amended, 6543)

60. Lema Fund, a voluntary welfare organization funded by contributions from the general public, received unrestricted pledges of $200,000 during the current year. It was estimated that 10% of these pledges would be uncollectible. By the end of the year, $130,000 of the pledges had been collected. It was expected that $50,000 more would be collected in the following year and that the balance of $20,000 would be written off as uncollectible. What amount should Lema include under public support in the current year for net contributions?
a. $200,000
b. $180,000
c. $150,000
d. $130,000 (5/90, PII, #13, amended, 4601)

61. The League, a not-for-profit organization, received the following pledges:

Unrestricted	$200,000
Restricted for capital additions	150,000

All pledges are legally enforceable; however, the League's experience indicates that 10% of all pledges prove to be uncollectible. What amount should the League report as pledges receivable, net of any required allowance account?
a. $135,000
b. $180,000
c. $315,000
d. $350,000 (5/93, PII, #35, 4142)

62. A voluntary health and welfare organization received a cash donation in year 1 from a donor specifying that the amount donated be used in year 3. The cash donation should be accounted for as
a. Revenue in year 1
b. Revenue in year 1, year 2, and year 3, and as a deferred credit in the balance sheet at the end of year 1 and year 2
c. Revenue in year 3, and **no** deferred credit in the balance sheet at the end of year 1 and year 2
d. Revenue in year 3, and as a deferred credit in the balance sheet at the end of year 1 and year 2 (Editors, 4602)

63. Oz, a nongovernmental not-for-profit organization, received $50,000 from Ame Company to sponsor a play given by Oz at the local theater. Oz gave Ame 25 tickets, which generally cost $100 each. Ame received no other benefits. What amount of ticket sales revenue should Oz record?
a. $0
b. $ 2,500
c. $47,500
d. $50,000 (R/02, AR, 1, 7066)

64. Allan Rowe established a $100,000 endowment, the income from which is to be paid to Elm Hospital for general operating purposes. The present value of the income is estimated at $95,000. Elm does not control the endowment's principal. Rowe appointed West National Bank as trustee. What journal entry is required by Elm to record the establishment of the endowment?

		Debit	Credit
a.	Beneficiary Interest in Trust	$ 95,000	
	Nonexpendable Endowment: Net Assets		$ 95,000
b.	Beneficiary Investment in Trust	$ 95,000	
	Permanently Restricted Revenues: Contributions		$ 95,000
c.	Beneficiary Interest in Trust	$100,000	
	Permanently Restricted Revenues: Contributions		$100,000
d.	Memorandum entry only	--	--

(Editors, 1420)

Items 65 through 67 are based on the following:

Metro General is a municipally owned and operated hospital and a component unit of Metro City. The hospital received $7,000 in unrestricted gifts and $4,000 in unrestricted bequests. The hospital has $1,200,000 in fixed assets.

The hospital has transferred certain resources to a hospital guild. Substantially all of the guild's resources are held for the benefit of the hospital. The hospital controls the guild through contracts that provide it with the authority to direct the guild's activities, management, and policies. The hospital has also assigned certain of its functions to a hospital auxiliary, which operates primarily for the benefit of the hospital. The hospital does **not** have control over the auxiliary. The financial statements of the guild and the auxiliary are **not** consolidated with the hospital's financial statements. The guild and the auxiliary have total assets of $20,000 and $30,000, respectively.

Before the hospital's financial statements were combined with those of the city, the city's statements included data on one special revenue fund and one enterprise fund. The city's statements showed $500,000 in enterprise fund fixed assets and $6,000,000 in general fixed assets.

65. In the hospital's notes to financial statements, total assets of hospital-related organizations required to be disclosed amount to
a. $0
b. $20,000
c. $30,000
d. $50,000

(Editors, 1432)

66. What account or accounts should generally be credited for the $7,000 of unrestricted gifts and the $4,000 of unrestricted bequests?

a.	Other revenue	$11,000
b.	Nonoperating gains	$11,000
c.	Other revenue	$ 7,000
	Nonoperating gains	$ 4,000
d.	Nonoperating gains	$ 7,000
	Other revenue	$ 4,000

(Editors, 1430)

67. The hospital's fixed assets are reported in the city's government-wide statement of net assets as

a. Special revenue fund fixed assets of $1,200,000 in a separate discrete presentation hospital column
b. Part of $7,200,000 general fixed assets in the governmental activities column
c. Part of $1,700,000 enterprise fund type fixed assets in the business-type activities column
d. Part of $7,200,000 fixed assets in the general fixed assets account group column

(Editors, 1433)

68. Under Abbey Hospital's established rate structure, the hospital would have earned patient service revenue of $6,000,000 for the year. However, Abbey did not expect to collect this amount because of charity care of $1,000,000 and discounts of $500,000 to third-party payors. How much should Abbey record as patient service revenue for the year?
a. $6,000,000
b. $5,500,000
c. $5,000,000
d. $4,500,000

(Editors, 1422)

69. What describes a private nonprofit university's internally designated asset, the income from which will be used for a specified purpose?
a. Endowment
b. Term endowment
c. Quasi-endowment
d. Restricted

(Editors, 9204)

70. For the summer session, Unity University assessed its students $3,000,000 for tuition and fees. However, the net amount realized was only $2,900,000 because of the following reductions:

Tuition remissions granted to faculty members' families	$30,000
Class cancellation refunds	70,000

How much unrestricted current funds revenues from tuition and fees should Unity report for the period?
a. $2,900,000
b. $2,930,000
c. $2,970,000
d. $3,000,000

(Editors, 1406)

71. At the end of the year Cram University had $15,000,000 of unrestricted assets (including $300,000 restricted by the donors for use the next year for any board-designated purpose) and $9,000,000 of liabilities. What are Cram's unrestricted net assets?

a. $ 5,700,000
b. $ 6,000,000
c. $ 6,300,000
d. $15,000,000 (Editors, 4134)

72. The current funds group of a not-for-profit private university includes which of the following?

	Loan funds	*Plant funds*
a.	No	No
b.	No	Yes
c.	Yes	Yes
d.	Yes	No

(Editors, 2149)

73. Which basis of accounting should a voluntary health and welfare organization use?

a. Accrual basis for some resources and modified accrual basis for resources
b. Modified accrual basis
c. Accrual basis
d. Cash basis (Editors, 9205)

Items 74 and 75 are based on the following:

Burr Foundation is a voluntary welfare organization funded by contributions from the general public. Burr sold a computer for $36,000. Its cost was $42,000 and its book value was $30,000. Burr made the correct entry to record the gain on sale.

74. In addition to the entry recording the gain on sale of the computer, the other accounts that Burr should debit and credit in connection with this sale are

	Debit	*Credit*
a.	Current Unrestricted Funds	Net Assets—Undesignated
b.	Excess Revenues Control	Sale of Equipment
c.	Net Assets—Unexpended	Net Assets—Expended
d.	Net Assets—Expended	Net Assets—Unexpended

(Editors, 9211)

75. The amount that should be debited and credited for the additional entry in connection with the sale of the computer is

a. $ 6,000
b. $30,000
c. $36,000
d. $42,000 (Editors, 9212)

76. In a statement of activities of a voluntary health and welfare organization, contributions to the building fund should

a. Be included as an element of support
b. Be included as an element of revenue
c. Be included as an element of other changes in net assets
d. Not be included (Editors, 9210)

SIMULATIONS

Problem 20-3 (15 to 25 minutes)

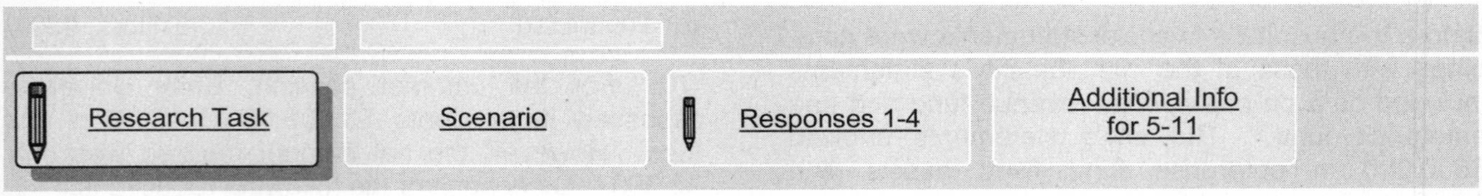

Research Question: What is the primary purpose of a statement of cash flows of a not-for-profit organization?

Paragraph Reference Answer: ______________

Research Task | Scenario | Responses 1-4 | Additional Info for 5-11

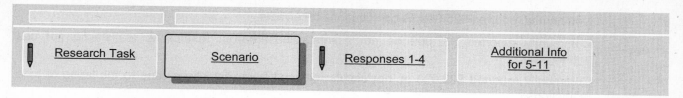

Community Service, Inc. is a nongovernmental not-for-profit voluntary health and welfare calendar-year organization that began operations on January 1, year 1. It performs voluntary services and derives its revenue primarily from voluntary contributions from the general public. Community implies a time restriction on all promises to contribute cash in future periods. However, no such policy exists with respect to gifts of long-lived assets.

Items 1 through 4 are based on the following selected transactions that occurred during Community's year 2 calendar year:

- Unrestricted written promises to contribute cash—year 1 and year 2
  - — year 1 promises (collected in year 2) $22,000
  - — year 2 promises (collected in year 2) 95,000
  - — year 2 promises (uncollected) 28,000
- Written promises to contribute cash restricted to use for community college scholarships
  - — year 1 and year 2
  - — year 1 promises (collected and expended in year 2) 10,000
  - — year 2 promises (collected and expended in year 2) 20,000
  - — year 2 promises (uncollected) 12,000
- Written promise to contribute if matching funds are raised for the capital campaign during year 2 $25,000
  - — Cash received in year 2 from contributor as a good faith advance 25,000
  - — Matching funds received in year 2 0
- Cash received in year 1 with donor's only stipulation that a bus be purchased
  - — Expenditure of full amount of donation July 1, year 2 37,000

(5198, AR, #3, amended, 6656, 6674)

Research Task | Scenario | Responses 1-4 | Additional Info for 5-11

Items 1 through 4 represent the year 2 amounts that Community reported for selected financial statement elements in its December 31, year 2, statement of financial position and year 2 statement of activities. For each item, indicate whether the amount was overstated, understated, or correctly stated.

List	
O.	Overstated.
U.	Understated.
C.	Correctly stated.

→

1. ______ Community reported $28,000 as contributions receivable.
2. ______ Community reported $37,000 as net assets released from restrictions (satisfaction of use restrictions).
3. ______ Community reported $22,000 as net assets released from restrictions (due to the lapse of time restrictions).
4. ______ Community reported $97,000 as contributions—temporarily restricted.

Research Task	Scenario	Responses 1-4	Additional Info for 5-11

Items 5 through 11 are based on the following selected transactions that occurred during Community's year 2 calendar year:

• Debt security endowment received in year 2 income to be used for community service		• Reading material donated to Community and distributed to the children in year 2	
— Face value	$90,000	— Fair market value	8,000
— Fair value at time of receipt	88,000	• Federal youth training fee for service grant	
— Fair value at December 31, year 2	87,000	— Cash received during year 2	30,000
— Interest earned in year 2	9,000	— Instructor salaries paid	26,000
• 10 concerned citizens volunteered to serve meals to the homeless (400 hrs. free; fair market value of services $5 per hr.)	2000	• Other cash operating expenses	
		— Business manager salary	60,000
		— General bookkeeper salary	40,000
		— Director of community activities salary	50,000
• Short-term investment in equity securities in year 2		— Space rental (75% for community activities, 25% for office activities)	20,000
— Cost	10,000	— Printing and mailing costs for pledge cards	2,000
— Fair value December 31, year 2	12,000		
— Dividend income	1,000		
• Music festival to raise funds for a local hospital		• Interest payment on short-term bank loan in year 2	1,000
— Admission fees	5,000	• Principal payment on short-term bank loan in year 2	20,000
— Sales of food and drinks	14,000		
— Expenses	4,000		

Choices & Responses 5-11 | Choices & Responses 12-19

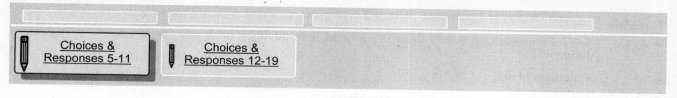

For Items 5 through 11, determine the amounts for the following financial statement elements in the year 2 statement of activities. Select your answer from the following list of amounts. An amount may be selected once, more than once, or not at all.

Choices					
A.	$0	F.	$ 9,000	K.	$87,000
B.	$2,000	G.	$14,000	L.	$88,000
C.	$3,000	H.	$16,000	M.	$90,000
D.	$5,000	I.	$26,000	N.	$94,000
E.	$8,000	J.	$50,000	O.	$99,000

5. _____ Contributions—permanently restricted
6. _____ Revenues—fees
7. _____ Investment income—debt securities
8. _____ Program expenses
9. _____ General fund-raising expenses (excludes special events)
10. _____ Income on long-term investments—unrestricted
11. _____ Contributed voluntary services

Choices & Responses 5-11 | Choices & Responses 12-19

Items 12 through 19 are based on the fact pattern and financial information found in **both Section 1 - 4, and Section 5 - 11.**

Items 12 through 19 represent Community's transactions reportable in the statement of cash flows. For each of the items listed, select the classification that best describes the item. A classification may be selected once, more than once, or not at all.

Classifications	
O.	Cash flows from operating activities.
I.	Cash flows from investing activities.
F.	Cash flows from financing activities.

12. _____ Unrestricted year 1 promises collected
13. _____ Cash received from a contributor as a good faith advance on a promise to contribute matching funds
14. _____ Purchase of bus
15. _____ Principal payment on short-term bank loan
16. _____ Purchase of equity securities
17. _____ Dividend income earned on equity securities
18. _____ Interest payment on short-term bank loan
19. _____ Interest earned on endowment

Problem 20-4 (5 to 10 minutes)

Research Task | Scenario, Choices & Responses

Research Question: What is the guidance on recognition of contributed services?

Paragraph Reference Answer: _______________

Research Task | Scenario, Choices & Responses

Alpha Hospital, a large not-for-profit organization, has adopted an accounting policy that does not imply a time restriction on gifts of long-lived assets.

For Items 1 through 6, indicate the manner in which the transaction affects Alpha's financial statements. Select the **best** answer for each item.

A. Increase in unrestricted revenues, gains, and other support
B. Decrease in an expense
C. Increase in temporarily restricted net assets
D. Increase in permanently restricted net assets
E. No required reportable event

1. _____ Alpha's board designates $1,000,000 to purchase investments whose income will be used for capital improvements.
2. _____ Income from investments in item 1, which was not previously accrued, is received.
3. _____ A benefactor provided funds for building expansion.
4. _____ The funds in item 3 are used to purchase a building in the fiscal period following the period the funds were received.
5. _____ An accounting firm prepared Alpha's annual financial statements without charge to Alpha.
6. _____ Alpha received investments subject to the donor's requirements that investment income be used to pay for outpatient services. (11/95, AR, #111-116, amended, 5854-5859)

Solution 20-1 MULTIPLE CHOICE ANSWERS

Definitions

1. (b) SFAS 116 requires that nonprofits' donations be recognized in income in the period of receipt and that donations be allocated among three classifications: unrestricted, temporarily restricted, and permanently restricted. This is a temporary restriction because, upon meeting the conditions of the donor, the donation may be disbursed.

2. (a) Maintaining a donor list is a fund raising activity. Soliciting prospective members, printing membership benefit brochures, and soliciting dues are member development activities.

3. (a) GASB Section 1800.120 defines the classification *object classes* as the types of items purchased or services obtained (salaries and wages). Section 1800.116 explains that the *function* or *program* classification provides information on the overall purposes of expenditures. Section 1800.118 explains the *activity* classification as facilitating evaluation of the economy and efficiency of operations by providing information for figuring costs per unit of activity.

4. (b) The governing board of an entity may earmark assets for specific purposes as long as these do not conflict with donor conditions. Assets may be designated board-restricted in the financial statements, but they remain in the unrestricted category. Donations are reported as unrestricted unless the restrictions are placed by a donor.

5. (a) Only a donor may impose temporary or permanent restrictions on assets. Otherwise, donated assets are unrestricted.

Financial Statements—General

6. (a) SFAS 117 focuses on basic information for the organization as a whole. Standardization of fund nomenclature is a secondary consideration. As this statement establishes standards for financial reporting applicable to all nonprofit organizations, it focuses on the similarities between different organizations or types of organizations. Distinctions between current and noncurrent presentations are also secondary.

7. (b) SFAS 117, para. 26 states, "...a statement of activities or notes to financial statements shall provide information about expenses reported by their functional classification such as major classes of program services and supporting activities. [VHWO]...shall report that information as well as information about expenses by their natural classification...in a separate financial statement. Other [NPO]...are encouraged, but not required, to provide information about expenses by their natural classification."

8. (b) SFAS 117 requires nonprofit organizations to present, at a minimum, a statement of financial position, a statement of activities, and a statement of cash flows.

9. (a) At minimum, nonprofit entities must report in the statement of activities four subtotals of income (from continuing operations, discontinued operations, extraordinary items, and the effect of accounting changes) showing the change of three (not one) classes of net assets: unrestricted, temporarily restricted, and permanently restricted. Any reporting format that meets these requirements is allowed. Disclosures should state clearly and accurately the entity's status; a change to for-profit status doesn't seem accurate, in this situation. The IRS doesn't authorize financial reporting standards.

Statement of Financial Position

10. (b) Assets restricted to a particular use assume the liquidity of that use. Endowment funds are typically long-term assets. (Endowment implies a permanent restriction.)

11. (c) SFAS 117 requires that net assets be allocated among three classifications for nonprofits: unrestricted, temporarily restricted, and permanently restricted. The $2,000,000 is permanently restricted because only the income may be used to support current operations. The $5,000,000 for the public viewing building is temporarily restricted because the terms of the donation will be met when the building is built.

Statement of Activities

12. (c) AICPA SOP 87-2, *Accounting for Joint Costs of Informational Materials and Activities of NFP Organizations that Include a Fund-Raising Appeal,* allows that all joint costs of informational materials or activities should be reported as fund-raising expense, unless it can be demonstrated that a program or management and general function has been conducted in conjunction with the appeal for funds. In this question, it appears that a program function and a fundraising appeal are joint costs. There is the alternative of no cost allocation and classifying all costs as fundraising costs, but this is not one of the options. Answers (a) and (b) are not

appropriate; no general service is mentioned as having been accomplished. Since no general services are mentioned, no allocation would be appropriate to this function. Only answer (c), which allows for joint allocation, might be appropriate. One must assume that the 60/40 allocation is appropriate under the circumstances—although no information is given to verify this assumption.

13. (a) When the terms of a gift are met, the assets and net assets are reclassified, increasing unrestricted net assets. With the concurrent use of the assets, unrestricted net assets decreases.

14. (a) SFAS 117 requires the statement of activities to report the net change for all three types of net assets: unrestricted, temporarily restricted, and permanently restricted.

Statement of Cash Flows

15. (c) SFAS 117 expands the description of cash flows from financing activities in SFAS 95 to include donor-restricted cash that must be used for long-term purposes. Unrestricted cash from contributors is included in operating activities. Investing activities includes the sale and purchase of investments and PP&E.

16. (b) Contributed collection assets are recognized as revenues if collections are capitalized. Revenues are not recognized if collections are not capitalized. Cash flows from operating activities are generally the cash effect of events that enter into the determination of income. Cash flows from financing activities include paying or incurring debt principal, paying dividends, or issuing or acquiring stock.

17. (b) SFAS 117 expands the description of cash flows from financing activities to include certain donor-restricted cash that must be used for long-term purposes. Contributions for construction of a capital asset would not be included in the operating or investing activities section. Not-for-profit organizations follow the FASB 95 format of statement of cash flows which does not include a capital financing activities section.

18. (a) Hunt Community Development Agency provides loans as its operating activity, not as financing or investing activities.

Contributions

19. (a) A nongovernmental not-for-profit organization reports its changes in cash and cash equivalents using the SFAS 95 model. Unrestricted cash contributions should be reported as an inflow in the operating activities section of the statement of cash flows unless there is a restriction that is donor imposed. Unrestricted cash contributions are not inflows from investing activities. Capital and related financing activities is not a section of the SFAS 95 model of the statement of cash flows.

20. (c) The $125,000 contribution is not restricted to the shortfall between youth activity program revenue and expenses; thus, the entire amount of program expenses satisfies the restriction on $95,000 of the contribution. (The youth activity program revenues are not restricted.)

21. (d) Contributions that may be used at the board of directors' discretion are unrestricted. Pledges are recognized in the period they are made, net of any appropriate allowance for uncollectible amounts. There is an implicit time restriction on the $500,000 donation, because it will not be made until the next year. The fair value of donated services is recognized as both a revenue and expense if the services (1) would otherwise be purchased, (2) the value of the services is measurable, and (3) there is the equivalent of an employer-employee or hired contractor relationship.

22. (d) Pledges are reported in the period in which they are made, net of an allowance for uncollectible amounts. The name implies that this may be a governmental university, and, if so, would then be under GASB guidance with the unexpended portion of the current year's contribution classed as deferred revenue. The title of the report prepared by the university will alert you whether it actually is a governmental university or a nonprofit university. A governmental university would prepare a statement of changes in fiduciary net assets; a nonprofit university would prepare a statement of activities.

23. (c) Pledges are reported in the period in which they are made, net of an allowance for uncollectible amounts. $100,000 × 90% = $90,000.

24. (b) SFAS 116 governs contributions received and made for nonprofit entities. Contributions are unconditional donations, or gifts of assets, including property and services. By definition, contributions are nonreciprocal and involve no delivery of services or transfer of ownership. Oz gave tickets with a fair market value (FMV) of $2,500 (25 × $100) to the donor, Acme, therefore, Oz should recognize ticket sales revenue for the FMV of the tickets.

25. (b) SFAS 116 has an exemption to the rule of recognizing donations of collections of historical artifacts if they are held as a collection or are sold and the proceeds used to acquire other items for collections.

26. (b)

Unrestricted	$400,000
Restricted for capital additions	300,000
Total pledges	700,000
Less: Uncollectible allowance of 5%	(35,000)
Pledges receivable net of allowance	$665,000

Investments

27. (b) The church is an other nonprofit organization (ONPO). ONPOs may establish investment pools. Such pools should be accounted for on a market value basis to ensure equitable allocations of realized and unrealized gains and losses among participating funds. An ONPO may pool both unrestricted and restricted investments.

28. (c) Investments of nonprofit organizations are recorded initially at cost, except that donated securities are recorded at their fair market value at date of receipt. Thereafter, marketable equity and debit securities are accounted for in accordance with SFAS 124 (fair market value at balance sheet date).

Depreciation

29. (d) SFAS 93 requires all (nongovernmental) nonprofit organizations to recognize depreciation in external financial statements.

30. (d) ($15,000 + $12,000 – $0) / 5 = $5,400)

Healthcare Entities

31. (d) Unrestricted earnings on specific purpose fund investments that are part of a hospital's central operations are reported as general fund unrestricted revenues. If, on the other hand, the investment earnings were restricted by donors or grantors for a specified operating purpose (e.g., research or education), they would be reported as restricted revenues in the specific purpose fund. Deferred revenue is no longer used in nongovernmental nonprofit accounting.

32. (c) Operating revenues include "Net Patient Revenue" and "Other Revenues." Other revenues of a hospital are defined as amounts generated from *activities that are major and central to ongoing operations other than patient services.* This classification includes activities from gift shops, cafeterias, education programs, snack bars, newsstands, parking lots, etc. However, unrestricted gifts are not included and are classified as "Nonoperating Gains," a separate and distinct section of the operating statement.

33. (d) Other Revenue of a healthcare entity is the usual day-to-day revenue that is not derived from patient care and services, and generally includes (1) revenue from grants for such specific purposes as research and education; (2) revenue from educational programs; and (3) revenues from miscellaneous sources, such as revenue from gift shops and parking lots. Additional sources of Other Revenue include rentals of hospital plant, sales of supplies to physicians, and fees charged for copies of documents.

34. (d) Other Revenue of a healthcare entity is the usual day-to-day revenue that is not derived from patient care and services, and generally includes (1) proceeds from the sale of cafeteria meals, (2) revenue from educational programs, and (3) revenues from miscellaneous sources, such as revenue from gift shops and parking lots. The proceeds from the sale of cafeteria meals do not offset dietary service expenses. Under the old AICPA *Hospital Audit Guide,* Ancillary Service Revenue represented a subcategory of Patient Service Revenue consisting of professional services such as lab fees, radiology fees, etc. Patient service revenues consist of revenue from routine services (e.g., room, board, general nursing and home health), other nursing services (e.g., operating room, recovery room, and delivery room), and professional services (e.g., physicians' care, laboratories, radiology, and pharmacy).

35. (b) Patient service revenue (revenue from health care services) is recorded gross, at the provider's regularly established rates, regardless of collectibility. Charity care is not included in patient service revenues because these services were provided free of charge and, thus, were never expected to result in cash flows.

Net patient service revenue	$ 500,000
Less: Revenue related to charity care	(100,000)
	400,000
Plus: Net assets released from restrictions	50,000
Plus: Other revenue	80,000
Total revenues, gains, and other support	$ 530,000

36. (a) Patient service revenue (revenue from health care services) is recorded gross, at the provider's regularly established rates, regardless of collectibility. Charity care is not included in patient service revenues because these services were provided free of charge and, thus, were never expected to result in cash flows. Provisions for *contractual adjustments* (i.e., the difference between established rates and third-party payor payments) and *other adjustments* are recorded on the accrual basis and

deducted from gross patient service revenue to determine *net patient service revenue.*

Gross patient services revenue	$775,000
Less: charity care include in gross revenue	(25,000)
Less: contractual adjustments	(70,000)
	$680,000

37. (c) Healthcare entities have only two categories of funds: (1) the general funds and (2) the donor-restricted funds. The general fund is used to account for all assets and liabilities that are not required to be accounted for in a donor-restricted fund. Since the bonds in question were issued for the hospital's benefit and are unrelated to any donor-restricted assets, they should be accounted for in the general fund. Both enterprise funds and the general long-term debt account group are utilized by state and local governments rather than by nonprofit healthcare entities. Specific-purpose funds are a type of donor-restricted funds that are used to account for resources restricted by donors and grantors for specific operating purposes.

38. (b) Room and board for patients and recovery room activities are both central to a hospital's services.

Colleges and Universities

39. (d) Tuition and fees are recorded as revenue at standard established rates, with amounts waived (such as scholarships or tuition remissions) recorded as expenditures. Therefore, Ames University should report $3,000,000 as unrestricted current fund revenues from tuition and fees.

40. (a) There are separate functional classifications for expenditures pertaining to "Institutional Support," "Scholarships and Fellowships," and "Operation and Maintenance of Plant." Therefore, the only expenditure in question that should be included in the functional classification "Institutional Support" expenditures account is the one for administrative data processing.

41. (c) The $500,000 donated for which a donor or external agency has specified that the principal remains intact in perpetuity should be accounted for in an Endowment Fund. The $300,000 of principal expendable after the year 2010 should be accounted for in a Term Endowment Fund because the principal may be expended after a specified period of time. The $100,000 of principal designated from Current Funds should be accounted for in a Quasi-Endowment Fund because the amount was set aside by the governing board of the institution to function as endowments.

42. (d) Quasi-Endowment Funds are used by colleges and universities to account for amounts set aside by the governing board to function as endowments. Smith University should report as quasi-endowment fund net assets at December 31, the sum of the $100,000 set aside by the governing board to be invested for scholarship grants and the $6,000 of fund earnings which had not been disbursed at December 31.

43. (a) The question implies that the library fund is separate from the current fund. Therefore, a discretionary transfer could only be made from the unrestricted portion of the current fund. Consequently, the transfer should be recorded by a debit to the unrestricted current fund net assets.

44. (a) The plant funds group for colleges and universities includes four subgroups: (1) unexpended plant funds, (2) funds for renewals and replacements, (3) funds for retirement of indebtedness, and (4) investment in plant. A college's plant funds group does not include a subgroup for restricted current funds.

45. (b) The asset accounts in the Investment in Plant subgroup of the Plant Funds group of a college contain the carrying amounts of the institution's fixed assets. Therefore, the equipment would be reported in the Investment in Plant subgroup of the Plant Funds group of the college. The fuel inventory for the college's power plant should be reported in the Unrestricted Current Funds under Inventory of Materials and Supplies.

46. (d) Outstanding encumbrances cannot be reported as liabilities. Any encumbrance outstanding should be reported as part of the equity section of the balance sheet.

VHWO Accounting

47. (b) Entities are required to classify net assets based upon the existence or absence of donor-imposed restrictions. Thus, net assets are classified into at least three categories: permanently restricted, temporarily restricted, and unrestricted. A temporary restriction is a donor-imposed restriction that will lapse upon occurrence of conditions specified by the donor. The allowable use of the income of a temporarily restricted asset may also be restricted by the terms of the donation.

48. (c) There are no temporarily restricted net assets in this question. The donor placed permanent restrictions on the use of the income as well as on the Endowment Funds. Endowment Funds are used to account for the principal (corpus) of gifts or bequests accepted with donor stipulations that (a) the

principal is to be maintained intact—in perpetuity or for a fixed or determinable term of time, and (b) the earnings may be expended for specified restricted purposes and/or unrestricted purposes. (The VHWO endowment fund is identical to those of hospitals and universities and is like some municipal nonexpendable trust funds.) Realized gains or losses on the sale of investments of Endowment Funds are reported as restricted (not temporarily restricted) revenues of the Endowment Fund unless such amounts are legally available for other use.

49. (c) The voluntary health and welfare organization (VHWO) used an endowment fund to account for the certificate of deposit because the testator stipulated that the certificate be held until maturity and that the interest revenue be restricted for a special purpose (i.e., to be used to finance salaries for a preschool program). In 2000, the restrictions on the endowment fund principal lapsed (i.e., the certificate of deposit matured). Since the testator did not place any restrictions on the principal of the certificate, that amount was transferred to the current unrestricted fund. The board of trustees then adopted a formal resolution designating $40,000 of the proceeds of the certificate of deposit for the future purchase of equipment for the preschool program. Therefore, $40,000 should be reported in the current funds balance sheet as net assets designated by the governing board for the preschool program. The interest revenue is restricted per testator specifications for a special purpose. Therefore, it cannot be reported in the current funds balance sheet as net assets designated by the governing board for the preschool program.

Solution 20-2 ADDITIONAL MULTIPLE CHOICE ANSWERS

Definitions

50. (d) In hospital accounting, restricted funds account for financial resources that are externally restricted by donors and grantors for specified operating or research, capital outlay, or endowment purposes. The board of directors of a hospital cannot remove restrictions on the use of financial resources imposed by donors and grantors. While unrestricted resources may be appropriated or designated by the governing board of a hospital for special uses, the board nevertheless has the authority to rescind such actions. Therefore, board-designated assets of a hospital are accounted for in the General Fund. The income generated by a restricted fund may or may not be available for current operating use, depending upon the restrictions imposed upon such income by the donor or grantor.

51. (d) Only donor restrictions create restricted revenue. Permanently restricted revenue is restricted in perpetuity. Restrictions that lapse are temporary.

52. (d) Expenses of nonprofit organizations are reported in two categories: program services and support services. Program services are related directly to the primary missions of the nonprofit organization. A labor union would report the cost of labor negotiations under the classification of program services. Support services do not relate to the primary missions of the nonprofit organization and include such costs as management and general administration, membership development, and fund-raising.

53. (c) The bequest of $400,000 received by the foundation from the estate of the benefactor who specified that the bequest was to be used for hiring teachers to tutor handicapped students is restricted. Restricted resources are financial resources that are *externally restricted* for specified purposes. On the other hand, the *board-designated* resources of $200,000 are unrestricted. Restrictions imposed by the Board of Trustees may be removed by the Board; they therefore do not impose restrictions as to when or how the resources may be used and should not be presented in the foundation's financial statements as restrictions.

Contributions

54. (b) By recording the full $150 as a contribution, the entity would overstate the amount of contributions. Only that portion exceeding the fair market value of a benefit to the contributor is included in contribution revenue.

55. (d) The land was donated to the hospital without restriction as to use; therefore, the hospital records the donation with a debit to Land, a credit to Mortgage Payable, and a credit to Unrestricted Revenues for the excess of the fair value of the land over the mortgage assumed by the hospital.

56. (d) SFAS 116 requires that donations be recognized in the period of receipt, not in the period of expenditure for the donor's specified purpose. The principal of a pure endowment may *not* be expended. The receipt of the pure endowment grant is recorded as permanently restricted revenues upon receipt.

57. (b) Other nonprofit organizations (ONPOs) should report donated services as revenue and expense if the following conditions are met: (1) the

services are a normal part of the program or supporting services and would otherwise be performed by salaried personnel, (2) the organization exercises control over the employment and duties of the donors of the services, (3) the ONPO has a clearly measurable basis for the amount, (4) the services are significant, and (5) the services of the ONPO are not primarily for the benefit of its members. Since all of the above conditions are met for the part-time secretaries, Super Seniors should report salary and wages expense of <u>$160,000</u>, comprised of the $150,000 annual cost of its full-time staff and the $10,000 estimated value of the donated secretarial services.

58. (a) The principal of life income gifts (where a specified person is to receive the income from the assets for life or another determinable period of time) should be reported as restricted support in the balance sheet of a nonprofit organization, until the terms of the life income gift have been met.

59. (b) By recording the full $1,500 as a contribution, the entity would overstate the amount of contributions. Only that portion exceeding the fair market value of a benefit received by the contributor should be included in contribution revenue. A donor-imposed restriction limits the use of contributed assets to a use more specific than broad limits resulting from the nature of the organization, etc. A donor-imposed restriction on a contributed assets considered revenue if it is an unconditional transfer or promise to transfer. In contrast, a donor-imposed condition specifies a future and uncertain event whose occurrence or failure to occur gives the promisor a right of return of transferred assets, or release a promisor form its obligation to transfer promised assets. [$2,000 + $1,500 – $1,000]

60. (b) SFAS 116 prescribes the accounting for contributions received and made. Pledges are reported in the period in which they are made, net of an allowance for uncollectible accounts.

61. (c) Since the League is an ONPO and all of its pledges are legally enforceable, the League should report <u>$315,000</u> [i.e., ($200,000 + $150,000) × (100% – 10%)] as pledges receivable, net of the allowance for uncollectible pledges.

62. (a) Contributions received in advance of the year the donor intends them to be used—even if usable then for unrestricted purposes—are initially recorded in a "restricted support" account. They should be accounted for as support in the year the unconditional promise to give is made. The term "deferred" is no longer applied to donations.

63. (b) SFAS 116 governs contributions received and made for nonprofit entities. Contributions are unconditional donations, or gifts of assets, including property and services. By definition, contributions are nonreciprocal and involve no delivery of services or transfer of ownership. Oz gave tickets with a fair market value (FMV) of $2,500 (25 x $100) to the donor, Acme, therefore, Oz should recognize ticket sales revenue for the FMV of the tickets.

Contributions for Others

64. (b) The establishment of an endowment requires a nonprofit organization (NPO) to recognize restricted contribution revenue. The NPO includes an asset in its balance sheet. When a beneficiary has an unconditional right to specific cash flows from a trust, the beneficiary interest is measured and subsequently remeasured at fair value, using a valuation technique such as the present value of estimated expected future cash flows. (SFAS 136, ¶15).

Healthcare Entities

65. (b) Metro General should disclose the assets of the guild (i.e., $20,000) in the notes to the financial statements because it controls the guild through contracts or other legal documents that provide Metro General with the authority to direct the guild's activities, management, and policies; and Metro General is considered to be the sole beneficiary of the guild (i.e., Metro General has transferred certain resources to the guild, and substantially all of the guild's resources are held for the benefit of Metro General). Although Metro General is considered to be the sole beneficiary of the auxiliary (i.e., Metro General has assigned certain of its functions to the hospital auxiliary, which operates primarily for the benefit of Metro General), Metro General does *not* have control over the auxiliary.

66. (b) The revenues of a hospital are generally separated into three broad classifications: (1) patient service revenue, (2) other revenue, and (3) nonoperating gains. Patient service revenues are charges assessed for services provided to patients. This revenue would include fees for intensive care, surgery, nursing services, laboratory work, etc. Other revenues include amounts transferred from donor-restricted funds; tuition from nursing students; and cafeteria, gift shop, and parking lot revenues. Nonoperating gains generally include *gifts, bequests,* and investment income.

67. (c) The hospital's fixed assets should be reported as part of the enterprise fund fixed assets in the business-type activities column (i.e., $1,200,000

+ \$500,000 = \$1,700,000). There are only four columns in the government-wide statement of net assets: governmental activities, business-type activities, primary government total (sum of previous two), and component units. (See Chapter 21.) Alternatively, the hospital could be a discretely presented component unit, but as that option isn't included in the answer choices, we must assume that a blended presentation is appropriate.

68. (c) Abbey's patient service is determined by subtracting the charity care from the patient service revenue that would have been recorded at Abbey's established rate for all healthcare services provided (i.e., \$6,000,000 – \$1,000,000 = \$5,000,000). Charity care is not included in patient service revenues because these services were provided free of charge and, thus, were never expected to result in cash flows. On the other hand, the discounts to third party payors are reported as *deductions* from patient service revenues to determine *net* patient service revenue. Note that the amount that would be reported as *net* patient service revenue is \$4,500,000 (i.e., \$5,000,000 – \$500,000).

Colleges and Universities

69. (c) Assets with *internal* restrictions (i.e., designation by the governing board) are quasi-endowments. Endowment, term-endowment, and restricted current signify resources with *donor* restrictions.

70. (b) Tuition and fees are recorded at standard established rates, with amounts waived (such as scholarships or tuition remissions) recorded as expenditures. Actual refunds of tuition or fees should be recorded as a reduction of revenues. Therefore, Unity should include \$2,930,000 (\$3,000,000 – \$70,000) in the unrestricted current funds as revenues from tuition and fees.

71. (b) If the Board may change the designation, the assets are not restricted.

Unrestricted assets (including the \$300,000)	\$15,000,000
Liabilities	9,000,000
Unrestricted net assets	\$ 6,000,000

72. (a) The fund groups generally used by colleges and universities are (1) current funds, (2) loan funds, (3) endowment and similar funds, (4) annuity and life income funds, (5) plant funds, and (6) agency funds. Loan funds and plant funds are not included in the current funds group as they are separately disclosed.

VHWO Accounting

73. (c) Nongovernmental nonprofit organizations, including voluntary health and welfare organizations (VHWOs), use the accrual basis of accounting for all external reporting purposes.

74. (d) Voluntary health and welfare organizations record fixed asset and depreciation transactions in the Land, Building, and Equipment Fund. Two entries should be recorded in this fund in connection with the sale of the equipment. The following entry should be made to record the sale:

Cash	36,000	
Accumulated Depreciation—Equipment (\$42,000 – \$30,000)	12,000	
Equipment		42,000
Gain on Sale of Equipment		6,000

In addition, the following entry should be made to reduce the Net Assets—Expended account and increase the Net Assets—Unexpended account for the net book value of the equipment sold:

Net Assets—Expended	30,000	
Net Assets—Unexpended		30,000

The Net Assets—Expended account represents the net book value of fixed assets not represented by indebtedness. It is debited to reduce it for the net book value of the equipment sold. The Net Assets—Unexpended account represents the assets available for future expenditure for plant. It is credited for the same amount in this entry. The logic of this credit is explained below. The Net Assets—Unexpended account (the assets available for future expenditure for plant) must increase by the \$36,000 cash received from the sale. To accomplish this, the account is credited for (1) the \$30,000 book value of the equipment sold per the preceding entry, and (2) the \$6,000 gain on the sale when the gain is closed out to this account at year-end.

75. (b) Nongovernmental nonprofit organizations, including voluntary health and welfare organizations (VHWOs), use the accrual basis of accounting for all external reporting purposes.

76. (a) The contributions to the building fund are included as support in the statement of activities of a voluntary health and welfare organization.

PERFORMANCE BY SUBTOPICS

Each category below parallels a subtopic covered in Chapter 20. Record the number and percentage of questions you correctly answered in each subtopic area.

Definitions

Question #	Correct √
1	
2	
3	
4	
5	
# Questions	5
# Correct	______
% Correct	______

Financial Statements—General

Question #	Correct √
6	
7	
8	
9	
# Questions	4
# Correct	______
% Correct	______

Statement of Financial Position

Question #	Correct √
10	
11	
# Questions	2
# Correct	______
% Correct	______

Statement of Activities

Question #	Correct √
12	
13	
14	
# Questions	3
# Correct	______
% Correct	______

Statement of Cash Flows

Question #	Correct √
15	
16	
17	
18	
# Questions	4
# Correct	______
% Correct	______

Contributions

Question #	Correct √
19	
20	
21	
22	
23	
24	
25	
26	
# Questions	8
# Correct	______
% Correct	______

Investments

Question #	Correct √
27	
28	
# Questions	2
# Correct	______
% Correct	______

Depreciation

Question #	Correct √
29	
30	
# Questions	2
# Correct	______
% Correct	______

Healthcare Entities

Question #	Correct √
31	
32	
33	
34	
35	
36	
37	
38	
# Questions	8
# Correct	______
% Correct	______

Colleges and Universities

Question #	Correct √
39	
40	
41	
42	
43	
44	
45	
46	
# Questions	8
# Correct	______
% Correct	______

VWHO Accounting

Question #	Correct √
47	
48	
49	
# Questions	3
# Correct	______
% Correct	______

SIMULATION SOLUTIONS

Solution 20-3

Research

Industry Standards

No5.126

.126 The primary purpose of a statement of cash flows is to provide relevant information about the cash receipts and cash payments of an organization during a period. Section C25, "Cash Flows Statement," discusses how that information helps investors, creditors, and others and establishes standards for the information to be provided in a statement of cash flows of a business enterprise [and a not-for-profit organization. Illustrations of both direct and indirect methods of reporting cash flows are found in paragraph .135, Exhibits 135A and 135B.] [FAS117, ¶29]

Responses 1-4

1. U Contributions receivable should be at least $40,000, to include the unrestricted $28,000 and the restricted $12,000 of year 2 promised contributions that are uncollected.

2. U The year 1 promises to contribute cash in year 2 and the bus purchase cash are both assets released from restrictions.

3. C The year 1 promises to contribute cash of $22,000 are restricted by time only.

4. O Temporarily restricted cash is composed of uncollected year 2 promises to give in future years. At most this is ($28,000 + $12,000) $40,000. The $25,000 matching funds advance is a liability, as the conditions of the potential contributor are apparently not met.

Responses 5-11

5. L Permanently restricted contributions for the year are the debt security endowment, at its fair value at time of receipt.

6. D The only revenues that Community had during the year are the admission fees to the music festival.

7. E Investment income includes interest earned plus the change in fair value from time of receipt to the balance sheet date. ($9,000 – $1,000)

8. O Program expenses are those connected with the NPO's mission. These include reading materials distributed to children, instructor salaries, the director of community activities' salary, and a portion of the space rental.

9. B The printing and mailing costs for pledge cards are the only general fund-raising expenses.

10. A There is no unrestricted income from long-term investments.

11. A There are no contributed voluntary services that qualify to be included on the statement of activities (i.e., that result from an employer-employee type of relationship).

Responses 12-19

12. O Cash flows from operating activities include most contributions; certain donor-restricted cash that must be used for long-term purposes is included in financing activities.

13. O Cash flows from operating activities include most contributions; certain donor-restricted cash that must be used for long-term purposes is included in financing activities.

14. I Transactions involving investments as well as property, plant, and equipment generally are classified as investing activities.

15. F Principal repayments are cash flows used by financing activities.

16. I Cash paid for, and received from, transactions involving investments and property, plant, and equipment generally is classified as investing.

17. O Interest and dividends received are cash flows from operating activities.

18. O Interest payments are cash flows used by operating activities.

19. O Interest and dividends received are cash flows from operating activities.

Solution 20-4

Research

General Standards

C67.109

.109 Contributions of services shall be recognized if the services received (a) create or enhance non-financial assets or (b) require specialized skills, are provided by individuals possessing those skills, and would typically need to be purchased if not provided by donation. Services requiring specialized skills are provided by accountants, architects, carpenters, doctors, electricians, lawyers, nurses, plumbers, teachers, and other professionals and craftsmen. Contributed services and promises to give services that do not meet the above criteria shall not be recognized. [FAS116, ¶9]

Responses 1-6

1. E Board designated assets are unrestricted. Only donor restrictions "restrict" assets for external reporting purposes.

2. A Income from board-designated assets is unrestricted revenue.

3. C The donation is restricted only until the donor's conditions are met.

4. A As Alpha does not have an accounting policy that implies a time restriction on gifts of long-lived assets, the building expansion funds are unrestricted when the building is built.

5. A The measurable fair value of donated services that would otherwise be purchased are recorded as both revenue and expense if (1) non-financial assets are created or enhanced, (2) the performance of the services is controlled by the NPO, and (3) special skills are required. All of these conditions are met. As the terms of the inherent restriction (to purchase accounting services) is met within the period of donation, this is an unrestricted donation.

6. D The donation is subject to the donor's restriction, a requirement that cannot be fulfilled with the passage of time or the accomplishment of a specific objective.

CPA Exam Week Checklist

What to pack for exam week:

1. CPA exam registration material
2. Hotel confirmation
3. Cash and/or a major credit card
4. Alarm clock—Don't rely on a hotel wake-up call
5. Comfortable clothing that can be layered to suit varying temperatures
6. A watch
7. Appropriate review materials, pencils, erasers, and pencil sharpener
8. Healthy snack foods

Evenings before exam sections:

1. Read through your Bisk Education chapter outlines for the next day's section(s).
2. Eat lightly and monitor your intake of alcohol and caffeine. Get a good night's rest.
3. Do not try to cram. A brief review of your notes will help to focus your attention on important points and remind you that you are well prepared, but too much cramming can shatter your self-confidence. If you have reviewed conscientiously, you are already well-prepared for the CPA exam.

The morning of each exam section:

1. Eat a satisfying breakfast. It will be several hours before your next meal. Eat enough to ward off hunger, but not so much that you feel uncomfortable.
2. Dress appropriately. Wear layers you can take off to suit varying temperatures in the room.
3. Arrive at the exam center thirty minutes early. Check in as soon as you are allowed to do so.

More helpful exam information is included in the **Practical Advice** appendix in this volume.

APPENDIX A
PRACTICE EXAMINATION

Editor's Note: There is only one practice (or final) examination. Do not take this exam until you are ready for it. If you did not mark the answers on the diagnostic exam, it can be used as a second "final" exam.

Testlet 1 MULTIPLE CHOICE QUESTIONS (40 to 50 minutes)

1. On January 1, year 2, Victor Company purchased for $85,000 a machine having a useful life of ten years and an estimated salvage value of $5,000. The machine was depreciated by the straight-line method. On July 1, year 7, the machine was sold for $45,000. For the year ended December 31, year 7, how much gain should Victor record on the sale?
a. $0
b. $1,000
c. $4,000
d. $6,750 (9911)

2. According to the FASB conceptual framework, which of the following is an essential characteristic of an asset?
a. The claims to an asset's benefit are legally enforceable
b. An asset is tangible
c. An asset is obtained at a cost
d. An asset provides future benefits (2694)

3. Brock Corp.'s transactions for the current year ended December 31 included the following:

- Acquired 50% of Hoag Corp.'s common stock for $225,000 cash which was borrowed from a bank.
- Issued 5,000 shares of its preferred stock for land having a fair value of $400,000.
- Issued 500 of its 11% debenture bonds, due in 3 years, for $490,000 cash.
- Purchased a patent for $275,000 cash.
- Paid $150,000 toward a bank loan.
- Sold investment securities for $995,000.

Brock's net cash provided by investing activities for the year was
a. $370,000
b. $495,000
c. $595,000
d. $770,000 (9911)

4. Which is the most appropriate financial statement to use to determine if a company obtained financing during a year by issuing debt or equity securities?
a. Balance sheet
b. Statement of cash flows
c. Statement of changes in stockholders' equity
d. Income statement (7620)

5. On January 2, City of Walton issued $500,000, 10-year, 7% general obligation bonds. Interest is payable annually, beginning January 2 of the following year. What amount of bond interest is Walton required to report in the statement of revenue, expenditures, and changes in fund balance of its governmental funds at the close of this fiscal year, September 30?
a. $0
b. $17,500
c. $26,250
d. $35,000 (7757)

6. The following financial ratios and calculations were based on information from Kohl Co.'s financial statements for the current year:

Accounts receivable turnover
Ten times during the year

Total assets turnover
Two times during the year

Average receivables during the year
$200,000

What was Kohl's average total assets for the year?
a. $2,000,000
b. $1,000,000
c. $ 400,000
d. $ 200,000 (7760)

7. The following condensed balance sheet is presented for the partnership of Smith and Jones, who share profits and losses in the ratio of 60:40, respectively:

Other assets	$ 450,000	Accounts payable	$ 120,000
Smith, loan	20,000	Smith, capital	195,000
	$ 470,000	Jones, capital	155,000
			$ 470,000

The partners have decided to liquidate the partnership. If the other assets are sold for $385,000, what amount of the available cash should be distributed to Smith?
a. $136,000
b. $156,000
c. $159,000
d. $195,000 (4852)

8. The following data pertain to Cowl Inc. for the current year ended December 31:

Net sales	$ 600,000
Net income	150,000
Total assets, January 1	2,000,000
Total assets, December 31	3,000,000

What was Cowl's rate of return on assets?
a. 5%
b. 6%
c. 20%
d. 24% (6142)

9. On December 31 of the current year, Jet Co. received two $10,000 notes receivable from customers in exchange for services rendered. On both notes, interest is calculated on the outstanding principal balance at the annual rate of 3% and payable at maturity. The note from Hart Corp., made under customary trade terms, is due in nine months and the note from Maxx Inc. is due in five years. The market interest rate for similar notes on this date was 8%. The compound interest factors to convert future values into present values at 8% follow:

Present value of $1 due in nine months:	.944
Present value of $1 due in five years:	.680

At what amounts should these two notes receivable be reported in Jet's December 31 balance sheet?

	Hart	*Maxx*
a.	$ 9,440	$6,800
b.	$ 9,652	$7,820
c.	$10,000	$6,800
d.	$10,000	$7,820

(2582)

10. Bren Co.'s beginning inventory at January 1 was understated by $26,000, and its ending inventory was overstated by $52,000. As a result, Bren's cost of goods sold for the year was
a. Understated by $26,000
b. Overstated by $26,000
c. Understated by $78,000
d. Overstated by $78,000 (5305)

11. Strand Inc., provides an incentive compensation plan under which its president receives a bonus equal to 10% of the corporation's income in excess of $200,000 before income tax but after deduction of the bonus. If income before income tax and bonus is $640,000 and the tax rate is 40%, the amount of the bonus would be
a. $40,000
b. $44,000
c. $58,180
d. $64,000 (9911)

12. Mint Co.'s cash balance in its balance sheet is $1,300,000, of which $300,000 is identified as a compensating balance. In addition, Mint has classified cash of $250,000 that has been restricted for future expansion plans as "other assets." Which of the following should Mint disclose in notes to its financial statements?

	Compensating balance	*Restricted cash*
a.	Yes	Yes
b.	Yes	No
c.	No	Yes
d.	No	No

(7619)

13. Gray Co. was granted a patent on January 2, Year 1, and appropriately capitalized $45,000 of related costs. Gray was amortizing the patent over its estimated useful life of fifteen years. During year 4, Gray paid $15,000 in legal costs in successfully defending an attempted infringement of the patent. After the legal action was completed, Gray sold the patent to the plaintiff for $75,000. Gray's policy is to take no amortization in the year of disposal. In its year 4 income statement, what amount should Gray report as gain from sale of patent?
a. $15,000
b. $24,000
c. $27,000
d. $39,000 (6115)

14. On January 2, Gant Co. purchased a franchise with a useful life of five years for $60,000 and an annual fee of 1% of franchise revenues. Franchise revenues were $20,000 during the year. Gant projects future revenues of $40,000 next year and $60,000 per year for the following three years. Gant uses the straight-line method of amortization. What amount should Gant report as intangible asset-franchise, net of related amortization in its December 31 balance sheet?
a. $48,000
b. $48,160
c. $49,920
d. $56,000 (7618)

15. During a period of inflation in which an asset account remains constant, which of the following occurs?
a. A purchasing power gain, if the item is a monetary asset
b. A purchasing power gain, if the item is a nonmonetary asset
c. A purchasing power loss, if the item is a monetary asset
d. A purchasing power loss, if the item is a nonmonetary asset (4874)

16. Crane Mfg. leases a machine from Frank Leasing. Ownership of the machine returns to Frank after the 15-year lease expires. The machine is expected to have an economic life of 17 years. At this time, Frank is unable to predict the collectibility of the lease payments to be received from Crane. The present value of the minimum lease payments exceeds 90% of the fair value of the machine. What is the appropriate classification of this lease for Crane?
a. Operating
b. Leveraged
c. Capital
d. Installment (7605)

Items 17 and 18 are based on the following:

Scroll, Inc., a wholly owned subsidiary of Pirn, Inc., began operations on January 1 of the current year. The following information is from the condensed year-end income statements of Pirn and Scroll:

	Pirn	Scroll
Sales to Scroll	$ 100,000	$ --
Sales to others	400,000	300,000
	500,000	300,000
Cost of goods sold:		
Acquired from Pirn	--	(80,000)
Acquired from others	(350,000)	(190,000)
Gross profit	150,000	30,000
Depreciation	(40,000)	(10,000)
Other expenses	(60,000)	(15,000)
Income from operations	50,000	5,000
Gain on sale of equipment to Scroll	(12,000)	--
Income before income taxes	$ 38,000	$ 5,000

- Sales by Pirn to Scroll are made on the same terms as those made to third parties.
- Equipment purchased by Scroll from Pirn for $36,000 on January 1 is depreciated using the straight-line method over four years.

17. In Pirn's December 31 consolidating worksheet, how much intercompany profit should be eliminated from Scroll's inventory?
a. $30,000
b. $20,000
c. $10,000
d. $ 6,000 (2575)

18. What amount should be reported as depreciation expense in Pirn's year-end consolidated income statement?
a. $50,000
b. $47,000
c. $44,000
d. $41,000 (2576)

19. Which of the following payments by a company should be disclosed in the notes to the financial statements as a related party transaction?

I. Royalties paid to a major stockholder as consideration for patents purchased from the shareholder
II. Officers' salaries

a. I only
b. II only
c. Both I and II
d. Neither I nor II (7616)

20. Busy Corp. prepared the following reconciliation between pretax accounting income and taxable income for the year ended December 31:

Pretax accounting income	$ 250,000
Taxable income	(150,000)
Difference	$ 100,000
Analysis of difference:	
Interest on municipal bonds	$ 25,000
Excess of tax over book depreciation	75,000
	$ 100,000

Busy's effective income tax rate for the year is 30%. The depreciation difference will reverse in equal amounts over the next three years at an enacted tax rate of 40%. In Busy's income statement, what amount should be reported as the current portion of its provision for income taxes?
a. $45,000
b. $67,500
c. $75,000
d. $82,500 (2628)

21. On November 15, Year 1, Celt Inc., a U.S. company, ordered merchandise F.O.B. shipping point from a German company for 100,000 euros. The merchandise was shipped and invoiced to Celt on December 10, Year 1. Celt paid the invoice on January 10, Year 2. The spot rates for euros on the respective dates are as follows:

November 15, Year 1	$.991
December 10, Year 1	.975
December 31, Year 1	.935
January 10, Year 2	.895

In Celt's December 31, Year 1 income statement, the foreign exchange gain is
a. $9,600
b. $8,000
c. $4,000
d. $1,600 (1334)

22. For a bond issue which sells for less than its face amount, the market rate of interest is
a. Dependent on rate stated on the bond
b. Equal to rate stated on the bond
c. Less than rate stated on the bond
d. Higher than rate stated on the bond (1870)

23. The calculation of the income recognized in the third year of a five-year construction contract accounted for using the percentage of completion method includes the ratio of
a. Costs incurred in year 3 to total billings
b. Costs incurred in year 3 to total estimated costs
c. Total costs incurred to date to total billings
d. Total costs incurred to date to total estimated costs (7752)

24. How should the effect of a change in accounting principle that is inseparable from the effect of a change in accounting estimate be reported?
a. As a component of income from continuing operations
b. By restating the financial statements of all prior periods presented
c. As a correction of an error
d. By footnote disclosure only (6476)

25. Which of the following qualifies as an operating segment?
a. Corporate headquarters, which oversees $1 billion in sales for the entire company
b. North American segment, whose assets are 12% of the company's assets of all segments, and management reports to the chief operating officer
c. South American segment, whose results of operations are reported directly to the chief operating officer, and has 5% of the company's assets, 9% of revenues, and 8% of the profits
d. Eastern Europe segment, which reports its results directly to the manager of the European division, and has 20% of the company's assets, 12% of revenues, and 11% of profits (7784)

26. Property taxes levied in fiscal year 1 to finance the general fund budget of fiscal year 2 should be reported as general fund revenues in fiscal year 2
a. Regardless of the fiscal year in which collected.
b. For the amount collected before the end of fiscal year 2 or shortly thereafter.
c. For the amount collected before the end of fiscal year 2 only.
d. For the amount collected in fiscal year 1 only. (2751)

27. A city taxes merchants for various central district improvements. Which of the following accounting methods assist(s) in assuring that these revenues are expended legally?

	Fund accounting	Budgetary accounting
a.	Yes	No
b.	No	Yes
c.	No	No
d.	Yes	Yes (7609)

28. Which of the following ratios should be used in evaluating the effectiveness with which the company uses its assets?

	Receivables turnover	*Dividend payout ratio*
a.	Yes	Yes
b.	No	No
c.	Yes	No
d.	No	Yes (1762)

29. Hunt Community Development Agency (HCDA), a financially independent authority, provides loans to commercial businesses operating in Hunt County. This year, HCDA made loans totaling $500,000. How should HCDA classify the disbursements of loans on the cash flow statement?
a. Operating activities
b. Noncapital financing activities
c. Capital and related financing activities
d. Investing activities (6987)

30. Allan Rowe established a $100,000 endowment, the income from which is to be paid to Elm Hospital for general operating purposes. The present value of the income is estimated at $95,000. Elm does not control the endowment's principal. Rowe appointed West National Bank as trustee. What journal entry is required by Elm to record the establishment of the endowment?

		Debit	*Credit*
a.	Beneficiary Interest in Trust	$95,000	
	Nonexpendable Endowment: Net Assets		$95,000
b.	Beneficiary Investment in Trust	$95,000	
	Permanently Restricted Revenues: Contributions		$95,000
c.	Beneficiary Interest in Trust	$100,000	
	Permanently Restricted Revenues: Contributions		$100,000
d.	Memorandum entry only	--	--

(1420)

Testlet 2 MULTIPLE CHOICE QUESTIONS (40 to 50 minutes)

1. Reporting inventory at the lower-of-cost-or-market is a departure from the accounting principle of
a. Historical cost
b. Consistency
c. Conservatism
d. Full disclosure (4818)

2. On August 31, Wood Corp. issued 100,000 shares of its $20 par value common stock for the net assets of Pine, Inc., in a business combination accounted for by the purchase method. The market value of Wood's common stock on August 31 was $36 per share. Wood paid a fee of $160,000 to the consultant who arranged this acquisition. Costs of registering and issuing the equity securities amounted to $80,000. No goodwill was involved in the purchase. What amount should Wood capitalize as the cost of acquiring Pine's net assets?
a. $3,600,000
b. $3,680,000
c. $3,760,000
d. $3,840,000 (1269)

3. On January 1, year 3, Vick Company purchased a trademark for $400,000, having an estimated useful life of 16 years. In January of year 7, Vick paid $60,000 for legal fees in a successful defense of the trademark. Trademark amortization expense for the year ended December 31, year 7, should be
a. $0
b. $25,000
c. $28,750
d. $30,000 (9911)

4. Poe Inc. had the following bank reconciliation at March 31 of the current year:

Balance per bank statement, 3/31	$ 46,500
Add: Deposit in transit	10,300
	56,800
Less: Outstanding checks	(12,600)
Balance per books, 3/31	$ 44,200

Data per bank for the month of April:	
Deposits	$ 58,400
Disbursements	49,700

All reconciling items at March 31 cleared the bank in April. Outstanding checks at April 30 totaled $7,000. There were no deposits in transit at April 30. What is the cash balance per books at April 30?
a. $48,200
b. $52,900
c. $55,200
d. $58,500 (0875)

5. Company J acquired all of the outstanding common stock of Company K in exchange for cash. The acquisition price exceeds the fair value of net assets acquired. How should Company J determine the amounts to be reported for the plant and equipment and long-term debt acquired from Company K?

	Plant and equipment	*Long-term debt*
a.	K's carrying amount	K's carrying amount
b.	K's carrying amount	Fair value
c.	Fair value	K's carrying amount
d.	Fair value	Fair value

(2019)

6. On January 2 of the current year, Loch Co. established a noncontributory defined benefit pension plan covering all employees and contributed $400,000 to the plan. At December 31, Loch determined that the service and interest costs on the plan were $720,000 for the year. The expected and the actual rate of return on plan assets for the year was 10%. There are no other components of Loch's pension expense. What amount should Loch report as accrued pension cost in its December 31 year-end balance sheet?
a. $280,000
b. $320,000
c. $360,000
d. $720,000 (6902)

7. The following assets were among those that appeared on Baird Co.'s books at the end of the year:

Demand bank deposits	$650,000
Net long-term receivables	400,000
Patents and trademarks	150,000

In preparing constant dollar financial statements, how much should Baird classify as monetary assets?
a. $1,200,000
b. $1,050,000
c. $ 800,000
d. $ 650,000 (1245)

8. Rice Co. was incorporated on January 1 of the current year with $500,000 from the issuance of stock and borrowed funds of $75,000. During this first year of operations, net income was $25,000. On December 15, Rice paid a $2,000 cash dividend. No additional activities affected owners' equity in the year. At December 31, Rice's liabilities had increased to $94,000. In Rice's December 31 balance sheet, total assets should be reported at
a. $598,000
b. $600,000
c. $617,000
d. $692,000 (3239)

9. Which of the following statements regarding inventory accounting systems is true?
a. A disadvantage of the perpetual inventory system is that the inventory dollar amounts used for interim reporting purposes are estimated amounts.
b. A disadvantage of the periodic inventory system is that the cost of good sold amount used for financial reporting purposes includes both the cost of inventory sold and inventory shortages.
c. An advantage of the perpetual inventory system is that the record keeping required to maintain the system is relatively simple.
d. An advantage of the periodic inventory system is that it provides a continuous record of the inventory balance. (7759)

10. Jent Corp. purchased bonds at a discount of $10,000. Subsequently, Jent sold these bonds at a premium of $14,000. During the period that Jent held this investment, amortization of the discount amounted to $2,000. What amount should Jent report as gain on the sale of bonds?
a. $12,000
b. $22,000
c. $24,000
d. $26,000 (4858)

11. When the cash proceeds from a bond issued with detachable stock purchase warrants exceeds the sum of the par value of the bonds and the fair value of the warrants, the excess should be credited to
a. Additional paid-in capital
b. Retained earnings
c. Premium on bonds payable
d. Detachable stock warrants outstanding (9911)

12. Rose Co. sells one product and uses the last-in, first-out method to determine inventory cost. Information for the month of January follows:

	Total Units	*Unit Cost*
Beginning inventory, 1/1	8,000	$8.20
Purchases, 1/5	12,000	7.90
Sales	10,000	

Rose has determined that at January 31 the replacement cost of its inventory was $8 per unit and the net realizable value was $8.80 per unit. Rose's normal profit margin is $1 per unit. Rose applies the lower of cost or market rule to total inventory and records any resulting loss. At January 31, what should be the net carrying amount of Rose's inventory?
a. $79,000
b. $79,800
c. $80,000
d. $81,400 (7612)

13. Tomson Co. installed new assembly line production equipment at a cost of $175,000. Tomson had to rearrange the assembly line and remove a wall to install the equipment. The rearrangement cost $12,000 and the wall removal cost $3,000. The rearrangement did not increase the life of the assembly line but it did make it more efficient. What amount of these costs should be capitalized by Tomson?
a. $175,000
b. $178,000
c. $187,000
d. $190,000 (7764)

14. Bean Co. included interest expense and transactions classified as extraordinary items in its determination of segment profit, which Bean's chief financial officer considered in determining the segment's operating budget. Bean is required to report the segment's financial data under SFAS No. 131, Disclosures about Segments of an Enterprise and Related Information. Which of the following items should Bean disclose in reporting segment data?

	Interest expense	*Extraordinary items*
a.	No	No
b.	No	Yes
c.	Yes	No
d.	Yes	Yes

(7621)

15. Cado Co.'s payroll for the month ended January 31 is summarized as follows:

Total wages	$100,000
Amount of wages subject to payroll taxes:	
FICA	80,000
Unemployment	20,000
Payroll tax rates:	
FICA for employer and employee	7% each
Unemployment	3%

In its January 31 balance sheet, what amount should Cado accrue as its share of payroll taxes?
a. $ 6,200
b. $10,000
c. $11,800
d. $17,000 (7606)

16. Deck Co. had 120,000 shares of common stock outstanding at January 1 of the current year. On July 1, it issued 40,000 additional shares of common stock. Outstanding all year were 10,000 shares of nonconvertible cumulative preferred stock. What is the number of shares that Deck should use to calculate earnings per share?
a. 140,000
b. 150,000
c. 160,000
d. 170,000 (6904)

17. On June 30, of the previous year, Lomond, Inc. issued twenty $10,000, 7% bonds at par. Each bond was convertible into 200 shares of common stock. On January 1 of the current year, 10,000 shares of common stock were outstanding. The bondholders converted all the bonds on July 1 of the current year. The following amounts were reported in Lomond's income statement for the current year ended December 31:

Revenues	$ 977,000
Operating expenses	(920,000)
Interest on bonds	(7,000)
Income before income tax	50,000
Income tax at 30%	(15,000)
Net income	$ 35,000

What amount should Lomond report as its current year basic earnings per share?
a. $2.50
b. $2.85
c. $2.92
d. $3.50 (2632)

18. In governmental accounting, a fund is

I. The basic accounting unit
II. Used to assist in ensuring fiscal compliance

a. I only
b. II only
c. Both I and II
d. Neither I nor II (7610)

19. Pharm, a nongovernmental not-for-profit organization, is preparing its year-end financial statements. Which of the following statements is required?
a. Statement of changes in financial position
b. Statement of cash flows
c. Statement of changes in fund balance
d. Statement of revenue, expenses and changes in fund balance (6995)

20. Which of the following statements regarding foreign exchange gains and losses is correct?
a. An exchange gain occurs when the exchange rate increases between the date a payable is recorded and the date of cash payment.
b. An exchange gain occurs when the exchange rate increases between the date a receivable is recorded and the date of cash receipt.
c. An exchange loss occurs when the exchange rate decreases between the date a payable is recorded and the date of the cash payment.
d. An exchange loss occurs when the exchange rate increases between the date a receivable is recorded and the date of the cash receipt. (7604)

21. During the current year, both Raim Co. and Cane Co. suffered losses due to the flooding of the Mississippi River. Raim is located two miles from the river and sustains flood losses every two to three years. Cane, which has been located fifty miles from the river for the past twenty years, has never before had flood losses. How should the flood losses be reported in each company's year-end income statement?

	Raim	*Cane*
a.	As a component of income from continuing operations	As an extraordinary item
b.	As a component of income from continuing operations	As a component of income from continuing operations
c.	As an extraordinary item	As a component of income from continuing operations
d.	As an extraordinary item	As an extraordinary item

(6124)

22. Which of the following should be recognized for the amount of deferred tax consequences attributable to temporary differences that will result in taxable amounts in future years?

	Deferred tax asset	*Deferred tax liability*
a.	Yes	Yes
b.	Yes	No
c.	No	Yes
d.	No	No

(3622)

23. In an exchange with commercial substance, Slate Co. and Talse Co. exchanged similar plots of land with fair values in excess of carrying amounts. In addition, Slate received cash from Talse to compensate for the difference in land values. As a result of the exchange, Slate should recognize
a. A gain equal to the difference between the fair value of the total consideration received and the carrying amount of the land given up
b. A gain in an amount determined by the ratio of cash received to total consideration
c. A loss in an amount determined by the ratio of cash received to total consideration
d. **Neither** a gain **nor** a loss (5/95, FAR, #30, amended, 5566)

24. Which of the following would be reported in the income statement of a proprietorship?

	Proprietor's draw	*Depreciation*
a.	Yes	Yes
b.	Yes	No
c.	No	Yes
d.	No	No

(7615)

25. On December 31, Pell, Inc., sold a machine to Flax, and simultaneously leased it back for one year. Pertinent information at this date is as follows:

Sales price	$360,000
Carrying amount	315,000
Estimated remaining useful life	12 years
Present value of lease rentals ($3,000 for 12 months @ 12%)	34,100

At December 31, how much should Pell report as deferred revenue from the sale of the machine?

a. $0
b. $10,900
c. $34,100
d. $45,000 (9911)

26. Both Curry City and the state have a general sales tax on all merchandise. Curry City's tax rate is 2 percent and the state's rate is 4 percent. Merchants are required by law to remit all sales tax collected each month to the state by the 15th of the following month. By law, the state has 45 days to process the collections and to make disbursements to the various jurisdictions for which it acts as an agent. Sales tax collected by merchants in Curry total $450,000 in May and $600,000 in June. Both merchants and the state make remittances in accordance with statutes. What amount of sales tax revenue for May and June is included in the June 30 year-end financial statements of the state and Curry?

	State	*Curry*
a.	$1,050,000	$0
b.	$1,050,000	$350,000
c.	$ 700,000	$350,000
d.	$ 300,000	$150,000

(6907)

27. On December 31 of the previous year, Dahlia, a nongovernmental not-for-profit organization, purchased a vehicle with $15,000 unrestricted cash and received a donated second vehicle having a fair value of $12,000. Dahlia expects each vehicle to provide it with equal service value over each of the next five years and then to have no residual value. Dahlia has an accounting policy implying a time restriction on gifts of long-lived assets. In Dahlia's current year statement of activities, what depreciation expense should be included under changes in unrestricted net assets?

a. $0
b. $2,400
c. $3,000
d. $5,400 (7607)

28. On January 2 of the current year, Yardley Co. sold a plant to Ivory Inc. for $1,500,000. On that date, the plant's carrying cost was $1,000,000. Ivory gave Yardley $300,000 cash and a $1,200,000 note, payable in 4 annual installments of $300,000 plus 12% interest. Ivory made the first principal and interest payment of $444,000 on December 31. Yardley uses the installment method of revenue recognition. In its current year income statement, what amount of realized gross profit should Yardley report?

a. $344,000
b. $200,000
c. $148,000
d. $100,000 (4083)

29. Pine City's year end is June 30. Pine levies property taxes in January of each year for the calendar year. One-half of the levy is due in May and one-half is due in October. Property tax revenue is budgeted for the period in which payment is due. The following information pertains to Pine's property taxes for the period from July 1, year 1, to June 30, year 2:

	Calendar year	
	Year 1	Year 2
Levy	$2,000,000	$2,400,000
Collected in:		
May	950,000	1,100,000
July	50,000	60,000
October	920,000	
December	80,000	

The $40,000 balance due for the May year 2 installments was expected to be collected in August of year 2. What amount should Pine recognize for property tax revenue for the year ended June 30, year 2?

a. $2,160,000
b. $2,200,000
c. $2,360,000
d. $2,400,000 (2653)

30. In year 1, Gamma, a not-for-profit organization, deposited at a bank $1,000,000 given by a donor to purchase endowment securities. The securities were purchased January 2, year 2. At December 31, year 1, the bank recorded $2,000 interest on the deposit. In accordance with the bequest, this $2,000 was used to finance ongoing program expenses in March of year 2. At December 31, year 1, what amount of the bank balance should be included as current assets in Gamma's classified balance sheet?

a. $0
b. $ 2,000
c. $1,000,000
d. $1,002,000 (6304)

Testlet 3 MULTIPLE CHOICE QUESTIONS (40 to 50 minutes)

1. In a statement of cash flows, if used equipment is sold at a gain, the amount shown as a cash inflow from investing activities equals the carrying amount of the equipment
a. Plus the gain
b. Plus the gain and less the amount of tax attributable to the gain
c. Plus both the gain and the amount of tax attributable to the gain
d. With no addition or subtraction (4546)

2. On January 1 of the current year, Poe Corp. sold a machine for $900,000 to Saxe Corp., its wholly owned subsidiary. Poe paid $1,100,000 for this machine, which had accumulated depreciation of $250,000. Poe estimated a $100,000 salvage value and depreciated the machine on the straight-line method over 20 years, a policy which Saxe continued. In Poe's December 31 consolidated balance sheet, this machine should be included in cost and accumulated depreciation as

	Cost	*Accumulated depreciation*
a.	$1,100,000	$300,000
b.	$1,100,000	$290,000
c.	$ 900,000	$ 40,000
d.	$ 850,000	$ 42,500

(1268)

3. At year end, Rim Co. held several investments with the intent of selling them in the near term. The investments consisted of $100,000, 8%, five-year bonds, purchased for $92,000, and equity securities purchased for $35,000. At year end, the bonds were selling on the open market for $105,000 and the equity securities had a market value of $50,000. What amount should Rim report as trading securities in its year-end balance sheet?
a. $ 50,000
b. $127,000
c. $142,000
d. $155,000 (7751)

4. Macklin Co. entered into a franchise agreement with Heath Co. for an initial fee of $50,000. Macklin received $10,000 when the agreement was signed. The balance was to be paid at a rate of $10,000 per year, starting the next year. All services were performed by Macklin and the refund period had expired. Operations started in the current year. What amount should Macklin recognize as revenue in the current year?
a. $0
b. $10,000
c. $20,000
d. $50,000 (7770)

5. In a statement of cash flows (indirect method), which of the following are subtracted from net income to determine net cash flow from operating activities?

	Increase in accrued interest payable	*Depreciation expense*
a.	Yes	Yes
b.	Yes	No
c.	No	Yes
d.	No	No (1966)

6. During the current year, Rand Co. purchased $960,000 of inventory. The cost of goods sold for the year was $900,000, and the ending inventory at December 31 was $180,000. What was the inventory turnover for the year?
a. 6.4
b. 6.0
c. 5.3
d. 5.0 (1253)

7. Hahn Co. prepared financial statements on the cash basis of accounting. The cash basis was modified so that an accrual of income taxes was reported. Are these financial statements in accordance with the modified cash basis of accounting?
a. Yes
b. No, because the modifications are illogical
c. No, because there is no substantial support for recording income taxes
d. No, because the modifications result in financial statements equivalent to those prepared under the accrual basis of accounting (7060)

8. The replacement cost of an inventory item is below the net realizable value and above the net realizable value less the normal profit margin. The original cost of the inventory item is above the replacement cost and below the net realizable value. As a result, under the lower-of-cost-or-market method, the inventory item should be valued at the
a. Replacement cost
b. Original cost
c. Net realizable value
d. Net realizable value less the normal profit margin (9911)

9. How would the amortization of discount on bonds payable affect each of the following?

	Carrying amount of bond	*Net income*
a.	Increase	Decrease
b.	Increase	Increase
c.	Decrease	Decrease
d.	Decrease	Increase (1890)

10. On January 3, Quarry Co. purchased a manufacturing machine for $864,000. The machine had an estimated eight-year useful life and a $72,000 estimated salvage value. Quarry expects to manufacture 1,800,000 units over the life of the machine. During the year, Quarry manufactured 300,000 units. Quarry uses the units-of-production depreciation method. In its December 31 balance sheet, what amount of accumulated depreciation should Quarry report for the machine?

a. $ 99,000
b. $108,000
c. $132,000
d. $144,000 (7617)

11. During December of the previous year, Nile Co. incurred special insurance costs but did not record these costs until payment was made during the current year. These insurance costs related to inventory that had been sold by December 31 of the previous year. What is the effect of the omission on Nile's accrued liabilities and retained earnings at December 31 of the previous year?

	Accrued liabilities	*Retained earnings*
a.	No effect	No effect
b.	No effect	Overstated
c.	Understated	Overstated
d.	Understated	No effect

(7614)

12. Wagner, a holder of a $1,000,000 Palmer, Inc. bond, collected the interest due on March 31 of the current year, and then sold the bond to Seal, Inc. for $975,000. On that date, Palmer, a 75% owner of Seal, had a $1,075,000 carrying amount for this bond. What was the effect of Seal's purchase of Palmer's bond on the retained earnings and minority interest amounts reported in Palmer's March 31 consolidated balance sheet?

	Retained earnings	*Minority interest*
a.	$100,000 increase	$0
b.	$ 75,000 increase	$ 25,000 increase
c.	$0	$ 25,000 increase
d.	$0	$100,000 increase

(2571)

13. Japes City issued $1,000,000 general obligation bonds at 101 to build a new city hall. As part of the bond issue, the city also paid a $500 underwriter fee and $2,000 in debt issue costs. What amount should Japes City report as other financing sources?

a. $1,010,000
b. $1,008,000
c. $1,007,500
d. $1,000,000 (6994)

14. According to the FASB conceptual framework, which of the following statements conforms to the realization concept?

a. Equipment depreciation was assigned to a production department and then to product unit costs.
b. Depreciated equipment was sold in exchange for a note receivable.
c. Cash was collected on accounts receivable.
d. Product unit costs were assigned to cost of goods sold when the units were sold. (4511)

15. Murphy Co. had 200,000 shares outstanding of $10 par common stock on March 30 of the current year. Murphy reacquired 30,000 of those shares at a cost of $15 per share, and recorded the transaction using the cost method on April 15. Murphy reissued the 30,000 shares at $20 per share, and recognized a $50,000 gain on its income statement on May 20. Which of the following statements is correct?

a. Murphy's comprehensive income for the current year is correctly stated.
b. Murphy's net income for the current year is overstated.
c. Murphy's net income for the current year is understated.
d. Murphy should have recognized a $50,000 loss on its income statement for the current year. (7775)

16. Cobb Co. purchased 10,000 shares (2% ownership) of Roe Co. on February 12 of the current year. Cobb received a stock dividend of 2,000 shares on March 31 when the carrying amount per share on Roe's books was $35 and the market value per share was $40. Roe paid a cash dividend of $1.50 per share on September 15. In Cobb's income statement for the year ended October 31, what amount should Cobb report as dividend income?

a. $98,000
b. $88,000
c. $18,000
d. $15,000 (4417)

17. Home Care, Inc., a nongovernmental voluntary health and welfare organization, received two contributions in the current year. One contribution of $250,000 was restricted for use as general support in the following year. The other contribution of $200,000 carried no donor restrictions. What amount should Home Care report as temporarily restricted contributions in its current year statement of activities?

a. $450,000
b. $250,000
c. $200,000
d. $0 (7611)

18. On January 2 of the current year, Boulder Co. assigned its patent to Castle Co. for royalties of 10% of patent-related sales. The assignment is for the remaining four years of the patent's life. Castle guaranteed Boulder a minimum royalty of $100,000 over the life of the patent and paid Boulder $50,000 against future royalties during the year. Patent-related sales for the year were $300,000. In its current year income statement, what amount should Boulder report as royalty revenue?
a. $ 25,000
b. $ 30,000
c. $ 50,000
d. $100,000 (7613)

19. On February 2, Flint Corp.'s board of directors voted to discontinue operations of its frozen food division and to sell the division's assets on the open market as soon as possible. The division reported net operating losses of $20,000 in January and $30,000 in February. On February 26, sale of the division's assets resulted in a gain of $90,000. What amount of gain from disposal of a business segment should Flint recognize in its income statement for the three months ended March 31?
a. $0
b. $40,000
c. $60,000
d. $90,000 (6903)

20. In a statement of activities of the People's Environmental Protection Association, a voluntary community organization, depreciation expense should
a. Not be included
b. Be included as an element of support
c. Be included as an element of other changes in net assets
d. Be included as an element of expense (5006)

21. Which of the following normally would be included in other operating revenues of a hospital?

	Revenues from educational programs	*Unrestricted gifts*
a.	No	No
b.	No	Yes
c.	Yes	No
d.	Yes	Yes

(5005)

22. An unrestricted grant received from another government to support enterprise fund operations should be reported as
a. Contributed capital
b. Nonoperating revenues
c. Operating revenues
d. Revenues and expenditures (7608)

23. Jan Corp. amended its defined benefit pension plan, granting a total credit of $100,000 to four employees for services rendered prior to the plan's adoption. The employees, A, B, C, and D, are expected to retire from the company as follows:

"A" will retire after three years.
"B" and "C" will retire after five years.
"D" will retire after seven years.

What is the amount of prior service cost amortization in the first year?
a. $0
b. $ 5,000
c. $20,000
d. $25,000 (6782)

24. On June 1 of the current year, Ichor Company entered into a ten-year noncancellable lease with Gillie, Inc., for a machine owned by Gillie. The machine had a fair value of $180,000 at inception of the lease. Ownership of the machine is transferred to Ichor upon expiration of the lease. The present value of the ten $30,000 annual lease payments, based on Ichor's incremental borrowing rate of 12%, is $190,000. The lease agreement specifies that all executory costs are assumed by Ichor. How much should Ichor record as an asset and corresponding liability at the inception of the lease?
a. $0
b. $180,000
c. $190,000
d. $300,000 (9911)

25. On January 1 of the current year, Jambon purchased equipment for use in developing a new product. Jambon uses the straight-line depreciation method. The equipment could provide benefits over a 10-year period. However, the new product development is expected to take five years, and the equipment can be used only for this project. Jambon's current year expense equals
a. The total cost of the equipment.
b. One-fifth of the cost of the equipment.
c. One-tenth of the cost of the equipment.
d. Zero. (2540)

26. On January 2, Basketville City purchased equipment with a useful life of three years to be used by its water and sewer enterprise fund. Which of the following is the correct treatment for the asset?
a. Record the purchase of the equipment as an expenditure
b. Capitalize; depreciation is optional
c. Capitalize; depreciation is required
d. Capitalize; depreciation is not permitted (7755)

27. On December 31 of the previous and current year, Taft Corporation had 100,000 shares of common stock and 50,000 shares of noncumulative and nonconvertible preferred stock issued and outstanding. Additional information for the current year follows:

Stockholder's equity at 12/31	$4,500,000
Net income year ended 12/31	1,200,000
Dividends on preferred stock year ended 12/31	300,000
Market price per share of common stock at 12/31	72

The price-earnings ratio on common stock at December 31 was

a. 5 to 1
b. 6 to 1
c. 8 to 1
d. 9 to 1 (1259)

28. Which basis of accounting should a voluntary health and welfare organization use?

a. Accrual basis for some resources and modified accrual basis for resources
b. Modified accrual basis
c. Accrual basis
d. Cash basis (9205)

29. Gains resulting from the process of translating a foreign entity's financial statements from the functional currency, which has not experienced significant inflation, to U.S. dollars should be included as a(an)

a. Other comprehensive income item
b. Deferred credit
c. Component of income from continuing operations
d. Extraordinary item (9060)

30. KLU Broadcast Co. entered into an agreement to exchange unsold advertising time for travel and lodging services with Hotel Co. As of June 30, travel and lodging services of $10,000 were used by KLU. However, the advertising service had not been provided. How should KLU account for travel and lodging in its June 30 financial statements?

a. Revenue and expense is recognized when the agreement is complete.
b. An asset and revenue for $10,000 is recognized.
c. An expense and liability of $10,000 is recognized.
d. Not reported (7622)

SIMULATIONS

Testlet 4 (30 to 40 minutes)

Research Task | Scenario | Additional Information | Income Statement

Research Question: What criteria should be met to classify an event or transaction as an extraordinary item?

Paragraph Reference Answer: ________________

Research Task | Scenario | Additional Information | Income Statement

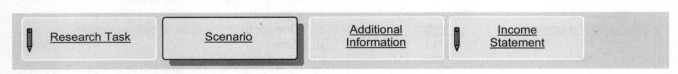

The following condensed trial balance of Probe Co., a publicly held company, has been adjusted except for income tax expense.

Probe Co.
CONDENSED TRIAL BALANCE

	12/31, Year 3 Balances Dr. (Cr.)	12/31, Year 2 Balances Dr. (Cr.)	Net change Dr. (Cr.)
Cash	$ 473,000	$ 817,000	$(344,000)
Accounts receivable, net	670,000	610,000	60,000
Property, plant, and equipment	1,070,000	995,000	75,000
Accumulated depreciation	(345,000)	(280,000)	(65,000)
Dividends payable	(25,000)	(10,000)	(15,000)
Income taxes payable	35,000	(150,000)	185,000
Deferred income tax liability	(42,000)	(42,000)	--
Bonds Payable	(500,000)	(1,000,000)	500,000
Unamortized premium on bonds	(71,000)	(150,000)	79,000
Common stock	(350,000)	(150,000)	(200,000)
Additional paid-in capital	(430,000)	(375,000)	(55,000)
Retained earnings	(185,000)	(265,000)	80,000
Sales	(2,420,000)		
Cost of sales	1,863,000		
Selling and administrative expenses	220,000		
Interest income	(14,000)		
Interest expense	46,000		
Depreciation	88,000		
Loss on sale of equipment	7,000		
Gain on flood damage	(90,000)		
	$ 0	$ 0	$ 300,000

Research Task	Scenario	Additional Information	Income Statement

Additional information:

- During year 3 equipment with an original cost of $50,000 was sold for cash, and equipment costing $125,000 was purchased.
- Insurance reimbursements exceeded the carrying amount of a warehouse and its contents destroyed in a year 3 flood. The flood was the first recorded flood at the warehouse's location.
- Probe's tax payments during year 3 were debited to *Income Taxes Payable.* For the year ended December 31, year 2, Probe recorded a deferred income tax liability of $42,000 based on temporary differences of $120,000 and an enacted tax rate of 35%. Probe's year 3 financial statement income before income taxes was greater than its year 3 taxable income, due entirely to temporary differences, by $60,000. Probe's cumulative net taxable temporary differences at December 31, year 3, were $180,000. Probe's enacted tax rate for the current and future years is 30%.
- 60,000 shares of common stock, $2.50 par, were outstanding on December 31, year 2. Probe issued an additional 80,000 shares on April 1, year 3.
- There were no changes to retained earnings other than dividends declared.

Prepare Probe Co.'s multiple-step income statement for the year ended December 31, year 3, with earnings per share information and supporting computations for current and deferred income tax expense. (9911)

Research Task | Scenario | Additional Information | Income Statement

Probe Co.
INCOME STATEMENT
For the Year Ended December 31, Year 3

Sales		
Cost of sales		
Gross profit		
Selling and administrative expenses		
Depreciation		
Operating income		
Other income (expenses):		
Interest income		
Interest expense		
Loss on sale of equipment		
Income before income tax and extraordinary item		
Income tax:		
Current		
Deferred		
Income before extraordinary item		
Extraordinary item:		
Gain on flood damage, net of income taxes of $27,000		
Net income		
Earnings per share:		
Earnings before extraordinary item		
Extraordinary item		
Net income		

Testlet 5 (40 to 50 minutes)

Research Task | Scenario | Additional Information | Statement of Cash Flows

Research Question: What are the three classifications of cash receipts that are reported on a statement of cash flows?

Paragraph Reference Answer: ________________

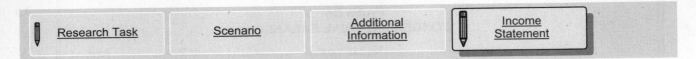

Research Task	Scenario	Additional Information	Statement of Cash Flows

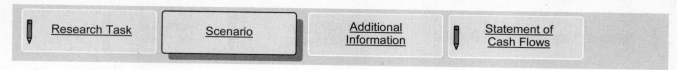

Presented below are the balance sheet accounts of Kern Inc. as of December 31, year 8 and year 7, and their net changes.

Assets	Year 8	Year 7	Net change
Cash	$ 471,000	$ 307,000	$ 164,000
Marketable equity securities, at cost	150,000	250,000	(100,000)
Allowance to reduce marketable equity securities to market	(10,000)	(25,000)	15,000
Accounts receivable, net	550,000	515,000	35,000
Inventories	810,000	890,000	(80,000)
Investment in Word Corp., at equity	420,000	390,000	30,000
Property, plant, and equipment	1,145,000	1,070,000	75,000
Accumulated depreciation	(345,000)	(280,000)	(65,000)
Patent, net	109,000	118,000	(9,000)
Total assets	$3,300,000	$3,235,000	$ 65,000

Liabilities and Stockholders' Equity			
Accounts payable and accrued liabilities	$ 845,000	$ 960,000	$(115,000)
Note payable, long-term	600,000	900,000	(300,000)
Deferred tax liability	190,000	190,000	--
Common stock, $10 par value	850,000	650,000	200,000
Additional paid-in capital	230,000	170,000	60,000
Retained earnings	585,000	365,000	220,000
Total liabilities and stockholder's equity	$3,300,000	$3,235,000	$ 65,000

Research Task	Scenario	Additional Information	Statement of Cash Flows

Additional information:

- On January 2, year 8, Kern sold equipment costing $45,000, with a carrying amount of $28,000, for $18,000 cash.
- On March 31, year 8, Kern sold one of its marketable equity security holdings for $119,000 cash. There were no other transactions involving marketable equity securities.
- On April 15, year 8, Kern issued 20,000 shares of its common stock for cash at $13 per share.
- On July 1, year 8, Kern purchased equipment for $120,000 cash.
- Kern's net income for year 8 is $305,000. Kern paid a cash dividend of $85,000 on October 26, year 8.
- Kern acquired a 20% interest in Word Corp.'s common stock during year 5. There was no goodwill attributable to the investment which is appropriately accounted for by the equity method. Word reported net income of $150,000 for the year ended December 31, year 8. No dividend was paid on Word's common stock during year 8.

Prepare a statement of cash flows for Kern Inc. for the year ended December 31, year 8, using the indirect method. A worksheet is not required.

(3422)

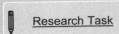

Research Task	Scenario	Additional Information	Statement of Cash Flows

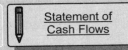

Kern Inc.
Statement of Cash Flows
For the Year Ended December 31, Year 8
Increase (Decrease) in Cash

Cash flows from operating activities:		
Net income		
Adjustments to reconcile net income to net cash provided by		
operating activities:		
Depreciation		
Amortization of patent		
Loss on sale of equipment		
Equity in income of Word Corp.		
Gain on sale of marketable equity securities		
Decrease in allowance to reduce marketable equity securities to market		
Increase in accounts receivable		
Decrease in inventories		
Decrease in accounts payable and accrued liabilities		
Net cash provided by operating activities		
Cash flows from investing activities:		
Sale of marketable equity securities		
Sale of equipment		
Purchase of equipment		
Net cash provided by investing activities		
Cash flows from financing activities:		
Issuance of common stock		
Cash dividend paid		
Payment on note payable		
Net cash used in financing activities		
Net increase in cash		
Cash at beginning of year		307,000
Cash at end of year		

MULTIPLE CHOICE ANSWERS (1 point each; 90 points total)

Solution 1

1. (c) The machine had a depreciable basis of \$80,000 (\$85,000 cost – \$5,000 salvage value) and was depreciated at a rate of \$8,000 per year (\$80,000 / 10-year useful life). At the time of sale, Victor depreciated the machine for 5.5 years and its carrying amount was equal to \$41,000, i.e., [\$85,000 – (5.5 × \$8,000)]. Thus a \$4,000 gain (\$45,000 – \$41,000) should be recognized.

2. (d) SFAC 6, par. 26, states, "An asset has three essential characteristics: (1) it embodies a probable future benefit that involves a capacity, singly or in combination with other assets, to contribute directly or indirectly to future net cash inflows, (2) a particular entity can obtain the benefit and control others' access to it, and (3) the transaction or other event giving rise to the entity's right to or control of the benefit has already occurred." The legal enforceability of a claim to a benefit is not a prerequisite for a benefit to qualify as an asset if the entity has the ability to obtain and control the benefit in other ways

(par. 26). Assets may be intangible and they may be acquired without cost (par. 26).

3. (b) The purchase of the investment securities for cash which was borrowed from a bank is **not** a noncash investing and financing transaction because the asset was not acquired by assuming a directly related liability. Examples of acquiring assets by assuming directly related liabilities include purchasing a building by incurring a mortgage to the seller and obtaining an asset by entering into a capital lease. On the other hand, the acquisition of the land by issuing preferred stock is a noncash investing and financing transaction. The proceeds from the issuance of the bonds payable and payment toward the bank loan are to be classified as financing activities.

Purchase of investment securities for cash	$(225,000)
Purchase of a patent for cash	(275,000)
Proceeds from sale of investment securities	995,000
Net cash provided by investing activities	$ 495,000

4. (b) The primary purpose of a statement of cash flows is to provide relevant information about the cash receipts and cash payments of an enterprise during a period. The information provided in a statement of cash flows helps investors, creditors, and others to assess the effects on an enterprise's financial position of both its cash and non-cash investing and financing transactions during the period. Related disclosures should report the effects of investing and financing transactions that affect an enterprise's financial position, but do **not** directly affect cash flows during the period. Neither the balance sheet nor the income statement would show changes in the balances of debt or equity accounts. The statement of changes in stockholders' equity would not indicate changes in debt accounts.

5. (a) Interest on general long-term debt, usually accounted for in debt service funds, normally are recorded as an expenditure on its due date rather than being accrued prior to its due date.

6. (b)

Net credit sales / average net receivables =
  accounts receivable turnover
Net credit sales / $200,000 = 10
Net credit sales = $2,000,000
Total assets turnover = total sales (net credit sales in
  this case) / average total assets
2 = 2,000,000 / average total assets
Average total assets = $2,000,000 / 2
Average total assets = $1,000,000

7. (a) Smith's capital balance of $195,000 is reduced by his $20,000 loan *from* the partnership ($195,000 – $20,000). (in 000's)

	Cash	Other assets	Liabs	Smith (60%)	Jones (40%)
Balances before realization	$ 0	$ 450	$120	$175	$155
Sale of other assets	385	(450)	0	(39)	(26)
Balances after realization	385	$ 0	120	136	129
Pay liabilities	(120)		(120)	0	0
Balances	$265		$ 0	$136	$129

8. (b) Rate of Return on Assets = Net Income / Average Total Assets

$$\frac{\$150{,}000}{(\$2{,}000{,}000 + \$3{,}000{,}000) / 2} = \$150{,}000 / \$2{,}500{,}000 = \mathbf{6\%}$$

9. (d) Both notes were received on the balance sheet date. Since the note from Hart arose from a transaction with a customer in the normal course of business and is due in customary trade terms not exceeding one year, it can be reported at its face amount of $10,000 despite the fact that the 3% stated interest rate of the note differs from the prevailing market interest rate of 8% for similar notes at the transaction date [APB 21, ¶3(a)]. On the other hand, the note from Maxx is due in more than one year. Therefore, the note from Maxx cannot be reported at its face amount because the 3% stated interest rate of the note differs from the prevailing market interest rate of 8% for similar notes at the transaction date. Because neither the fair value of the services performed by Jet nor the fair value of the note received from Maxx is indicated, the note is reported at its present value, determined by discounting all future cash payments of the note at the prevailing (i.e., market) rate of interest for a note of this type.

Principal amount	$10,000
Interest on outstanding principal balance due on maturity date [($10,000 × 3%) × 5]	1,500
Amount due on maturity date	11,500
Present value factor of $1 at 8% for 5 periods	× 0.680
Present value of note received from Maxx	$ 7,820

10. (c) An understatement of beginning inventory understates the cost of goods available for sale, thereby understating cost of goods sold. An overstatement of ending inventory also understates cost of goods sold. Therefore, cost of goods sold for the year is understated by the sum of the understatement of beginning inventory and the overstatement of ending inventory.

11. (a) Where B = Bonus:

B = 0.10($640,000 – $200,000 – B)
B = $44,000 – 0.1B; 1.1 B = $44,000
B = $40,000

12. (a) A compensating balance is a legally restricted deposit held against borrowing arrangements with a lending institution. SFAS No. 47 requires that the combined aggregate amount of maturities and sinking fund requirements for all long-term borrowings be disclosed for each of the five years following the date of the latest balance sheet period. Restricting cash to be used for future expansion would be a significant accounting policy of Mint Co. All significant accounting policies followed by an enterprise should be disclosed in its financial statements. No specific disclosure format is required. APB 22 prefers a *separate* note, or a summary preceding the notes entitled *Summary of Significant Accounting Policies.* The accounting policy disclosures should identify and describe the principles and methods that materially affect the financial position and operations.

13. (b) The cost of a successful legal defense of an existing patent is capitalized because it offers probable future benefits.

Cost of patent year 1	$ 45,000
Amortization (3 yrs. × $45,000/15)	(9,000)
Carrying value 12/31, year 3	36,000
Capitalization of legal costs	15,000
Carrying value of patent year 4	$ 51,000

Proceeds from sale	$ 75,000
Carrying value of patent	(51,000)
Gain from sale	$ 24,000

14. (a) A franchise represents a special right to operate under the name and guidance of another enterprise over a limited geographic area. A franchise is always externally purchased; it cannot be internally developed. Capitalize all significant costs incurred to acquire the franchise (e.g., purchase price, legal fees, etc.). If the acquisition cost of the franchise requires future cash payments, these payments should be capitalized at their present value using an appropriate interest rate. On the other hand, periodic service fees charged as a percentage of revenues are not capitalized; these costs represent a current operating expense of the franchisee.

15. (c) Purchasing power *losses* result from holding monetary assets during a period of inflation because the fixed amount of money will purchase fewer goods and services following a period of inflation. The holding of nonmonetary items during a period of changing prices does not give rise to purchasing power gains or losses.

16. (c) The question states that the present value of the minimum lease payments exceeds 90% of the fair value of the machine, and also give information that the lease term is equal to or greater than 75% of the estimated life of the asset (15/17 = 88%). The criteria to classify and account for the lease as a capital lease is that at the date of the lease agreement (date of lease inception), the lease must satisfy at least one of the following four criteria: The lease transfers ownership of the property to the lessee by the end of the lease; the lease contains a bargain purchase option; the lease term is equal to 75% or more of the estimated economic life of the leased property (as determined at the inception of the lease); or the present value of the minimum lease payments (excluding executory costs) equals or exceeds 90% of the fair value of the leased property at lease inception. Even though there is no transfer of ownership, the lease meets two of the four criteria to be classified as a capital lease.

17. (d) When one company sells merchandise to an affiliate at a price above cost, the ending inventory of the purchasing affiliate contains an element of unrealized gross profit. The gross profit is not realized to the economic entity until the inventory is sold to an unaffiliated company. The unrealized gross profit in inventory must be eliminated in the preparation of consolidated financial statements.

Scroll's ending inventory acquired from Pirn ($100,000 – $80,000)	$20,000
Times: Pirn's gross profit percentage [100% – ($350,000 / $500,000)]	× 30%
Unrealized intercompany profit in Scroll's ending inventory	$ 6,000

18. (b) The cost of the equipment to the purchasing affiliate exceeds the carrying amount of the equipment to the consolidated entity by the gain recognized on the sale by the selling affiliate. Consolidated depreciation expense must be based upon the cost of the equipment to the consolidated entity. Therefore, consolidated depreciation expense must be reduced by the excess depreciation recorded by the purchasing affiliate [i.e., ($40,000 + $10,000) – ($12,000 / 4) = $47,000].

19. (a) Financial statements should include disclosures of material related party transactions, other than compensation arrangements, expense allowances, and other similar items in the ordinary course of business. Officers' salaries are compensation arrangements in the ordinary course of business. Transactions (such as the sale of the patent, and the

resulting royalties) involving related parties cannot be presumed to be carried out on an arm's-length basis, as the requisite conditions of competitive, free market dealings may not exist.

20. (a)

Pretax financial income	$250,000
Permanent difference—interest	(25,000)
Temporary difference—excess tax depreciation	(75,000)
Taxable income	150,000
Tax rate	30%
Current provision	$ 45,000

21. (c) Whenever a **transaction** is denominated (i.e., payable) in a foreign currency, changes in the translation rate of the foreign currency with respect to the entity's functional currency (i.e., the dollar in this case) will result in a transaction gain or loss. The gain or loss should be recognized in income in the period(s) the rate changes, and the related asset or liability (i.e., accounts payable in this case) should be adjusted accordingly. Likewise, if the transaction is finally settled at a rate different from that reflected in the related asset or liability, gain or loss will also be recognized. The purchase and the related payable should not have been recorded until 12/10, year 1, because no liability had been incurred until the merchandise was shipped (i.e., the merchandise was ordered F.O.B. shipping point).

Initial obligation, 12/10, year 1, in $US (100,000 euros × $0.975)	$ 97,500
Amount payable, 12/31, year 1 (100,000 euros × $0.935)	(93,500)
Foreign exchange gain recognized, year 1	$ 4,000

Amount payable, 12/31, year 1 (above)	$ 93,500
Amount of settlement, 1/10, year 2 (100,000 euros × $0.895)	(89,500)
Foreign exchange gain recognized, year 2	$ 4,000

22. (d) A bond issue will sell for less than its face amount (i.e., at a discount) when the nominal or stated interest rate is less than the market rate [or, when the market rate of interest is higher than the nominal rate].

23. (d) The ratio used for the percentage of completion method is incurred costs to date over total expected costs. Progress billings are not generally accepted as a method of recognizing income because billings do not necessarily relate to work actually performed on a contract. Costs incurred in year 3 to total estimated costs are not part of the cost of completion ratio.

24. (a) When a change in accounting estimate and a change in accounting principle are inseparable, the change should be accounted for as a change in estimate, which is a component of income from continuing operations. A change in estimate does not require the restatement of prior period financial statements. Corrections of errors are reported as prior-period adjustments and prior-period financial statements are restated. Material effects of a change in estimate on income before extraordinary items, net income, and related per share amounts should be disclosed. Footnote disclosure only is not proper accounting treatment of a change in estimate.

25. (b) Operating segments have three characteristics. The description in answer a contains no characteristics that would qualify it as an operating segment. The description in answer b meets all three characteristics of an operating segment as well as the quantitative thresholds criteria. Even though the description in answer c meets the characteristics of an operating segment, it does not meet the quantitative thresholds criteria. The description in answer d meets the quantitative thresholds criteria but does not meet all three characteristics of an operating segment.

26. (b) Governmental funds use the modified accrual basis of accounting, under which, revenues are recognized when they become measurable and available for use. "Available for use" means that the revenues will be collected within the current period or collected early enough in the next period to be used to pay for expenditures incurred in the current period. The property taxes collected before the end of fiscal year 2 or shortly thereafter should be reported as revenues in fiscal year 2.

27. (d) In the absence of a profit motive, a net income bottom line, or other performance indicators, governments are subjected to a variety of restrictions and controls. The most important are overall restrictions on the use of resources (which leads to fund accounting) and exercise of expenditure control through the annual budget (which leads to budgetary accounting)

28. (c) The receivables turnover is computed by dividing net credit sales by net average receivables. This calculation provides information related to how effectively an enterprise uses its assets because it provides a measure of how many times the receivables have been turned into cash during the year. The dividend payout ratio is computed by dividing dividends per common share by earnings per share. This ratio is an index showing whether an enterprise pays out most of its earnings in dividends or reinvests the earnings internally; it provides no information related to how effectively the enterprise uses its assets.

29. (a) Hunt Community Development Agency provides loans as its operating activity, not as financing or investing activities.

30. (b) The establishment of an endowment requires a nonprofit organization (NPO) to recognize restricted contribution revenue. The NPO includes an asset in its balance sheet. When a beneficiary has an unconditional right to specific cash flows from trust, the beneficiary interest is measured and subsequently remeasured at fair value, using a valuation technique such as the present value of the estimated expected future cash flows. (SFAS 136, ¶15).

Solution 2

1. (a) The accounting principle of historical cost requires assets as well as liabilities to be recorded and carried on the books at cost. Therefore, reporting inventory at the lower-of-cost-or-market is a departure from this principle.

2. (c) Wood's investment in Pine should be recorded at the fair value of the common shares issued to effect the combination. The bargained exchange price is $3,600,000 since the mode of payment by Wood will be 100,000 shares of its common stock having a fair value of $36 per share. In addition, Wood will pay a $160,000 finder's fee to a consultant who arranged the acquisition. Any direct costs of the combination, such as the finder's fee, are included, along with the bargained exchange price, in calculating the total acquisition cost because such costs are a necessary element in carrying out an acquisition. On the other hand, the $80,000 cost of registering and issuing the common stock is considered to be a cost of the securities rather than a cost of the acquisition. As such, the $80,000 should be accounted for as a reduction in the additional paid-in capital figure of the issued shares. ($3,600,000 + $160,000 = $3,760,000).

3. (d)

Amortization of original cost ($400,000 /16 years)	$25,000
Amortization of legal defense cost, ($60,000 / 12 remaining years)	5,000
Total amortization expense, year 7	$30,000

4. (a) The cash balance per books at April 30, is computed by subtracting the outstanding checks at April 30, from the balance per bank.

Cash balance per bank 3/31	$ 46,500
Add: Deposits per bank, April	58,400
Less: Disbursements per bank, April	(49,700)
Cash balance per bank, 4/30	55,200
Less: Outstanding checks, 4/30	(7,000)
Cash balance per books, 4/30	$ 48,200

5. (d) The acquisition corporation allocates the cost of the acquired company to the assets acquired and the liabilities assumed. All identifiable assets acquired and liabilities assumed are assigned a portion of the cost, normally equal to their fair values at the date of acquisition. The excess of the acquisition price over the fair value of the net identifiable assets acquired is goodwill.

6. (a)

Service and interest costs	$ 720,000
Less: Contributions	(400,000)
Less: Actual return on plan assets (10% of $400,000)	(40,000)
Accrued pension cost	$ 280,000

7. (b) Monetary assets represent a claim to receive a fixed sum of money or an amount determinable without reference to future prices of specific goods and services. The demand bank deposits and net long-term receivables are monetary assets as they represent claims to receive a fixed sum of money, the amounts of which can be determined without reference to future prices of specific goods and services. All assets that are not monetary are nonmonetary. The patents and trademarks do not represent a claim to receive cash, and hence are classified as nonmonetary assets.

8. (c) Total assets equal the sum of liabilities and stockholders' equity.

Total liabilities, 12/31 (given)		$ 94,000
Proceeds from stock issue	$ 500,000	
Net income for current year	25,000	
Cash dividend declared	(2,000)	
Total stockholders' equity, 12/31		523,000
Total liabilities and stockholders' equity (and thus total assets) at 12/31		$617,000

9. (b) In the periodic system cost of goods sold (CGS) is a residual amount obtained by subtracting the ending inventory from the sum of beginning inventory and net purchases. The periodic system is characterized by no entries being made to the inventory account during the period. This amount would also include shortages as well as items actually sold, thus inaccurately reporting the true cost of goods sold. In a perpetual inventory system, record keeping is not simple; inventory dollar amounts are not estimated. The balance in the inventory account at any time reveals the inventory that should be on hand.

10. (b) Since the bond was purchased at a discount, the initial carrying value of the bond investment is $10,000 less than the face amount. The amortization of the discount increases the bond investment and so, on the date of sale the bond investment is carried on Jent Corp.'s books at $8,000 less (i.e., $10,000 – 2,000) than the face amount. Therefore, the sale of the bond at a premium (i.e., at $14,000 more than the face amount of the bond) results in recognition of a gain (i.e., $8,000 + $14,000).

11. (c) The proceeds from the sale of debt with stock purchase warrants should be allocated between the two instruments based on the relative fair values of the debt security without the warrants and the warrants themselves. The portion of the proceeds so allocated to the warrants is accounted for as paid-in capital. The remainder is allocated to the face amount of the bond, and to the extent remaining, to premium on bonds payable.

12. (c) The market *maximum,* or *ceiling,* should not exceed the net realizable value (NRV), which is the estimated selling price in the ordinary course of business less reasonably predictable costs of completion and disposal. Market minimum, or floor should not be less than the net realizable value minus normal profit.

Market:	
Ceiling (NRV)	$8.80
Replacement cost	8.00
Floor (NRV minus normal profit)	7.80

LIFO charges Cost of Goods Sold with the latest acquisition costs, while ending inventories are reported at the older costs of the earliest units. The 10,000 units sold reduce the 1/5 purchases, leaving 8,000 units from the beginning inventory and 2,000 units purchased on 1/5.

Cost [(8,000 × $8.20) + (2,000 × $7.90)]	$81,400
Market (10,000 × $8.00)	80,000

$80,000 is the lowest of cost or market.

13. (d) Assets are to be recorded at their acquisition cost. Acquisition cost is defined as the cash price, or its equivalent, plus all other costs reasonably necessary to bring it to the location and to make it ready for its intended use.

Cost	$175,000
Rearrangement	12,000
Removal of wall	3,000
Total amount to be capitalized	$190,000

14. (d) An enterprise shall report a measure of profit or loss and total assets for each reportable segment. These measures are generally based upon the measures as reported to, and used by, the chief operating decision maker, and may include revenues from external customers; revenues from transactions with other operating segments of the same enterprise; interest revenue; interest expense; depreciation, depletion, and amortization expense; unusual items; equity in the net income of investees accounted for by the equity method; income tax expense or benefit; extraordinary items; and significant other noncash items.

15. (a) ($80,000 × .07) + ($20,000 × .03) = ($5,600 + $600) = $6,200

16. (a) For EPS, the denominator is the weighted-average number of common shares outstanding during the period. This number will include common shares outstanding the entire period, shares issued during the period, and shares where all of the conditions of issuance have been met. In this case, there is no need for a diluted EPS adjustment because the preferred stock is not convertible.

Common shares outstanding on January 1		120,000
Common shares issued on July 1	$40,000	
Times: Weight factor for shares issued in July (1/2 year)	× 50%	20,000
Weighted-average number of shares outstanding		140,000

17. (c) To reflect the actual conversion on July 1, 4,000 additional common shares are added to the 10,000 common shares outstanding since the beginning of the year, resulting in 12,000 weighted average common shares outstanding. Basic EPS = $35,000 / 12,000 = $2.92 per share.

10,000 × 12/12	10,000
4,000 × 6/12	2,000
Weighted average common shares o/s	12,000

18. (c) A specific governmental unit is not accounted for through a single accounting entity. Instead, the accounts of a government are divided into several funds. A fund is a fiscal and accounting entity with a self-balancing set of accounts recording cash and other financial resources, together with all related liabilities and residual equities and balances, and changes therein, that are segregated for the purpose of carrying on specific activities or attaining certain objectives in accordance with special regulations, restrictions, or limitations.

19. (b) SFAS 117 requires nonprofit organizations to present, at a minimum, a statement of

financial position, a statement of activities, and a statement of cash flows.

20\. (b) Receivable: Rate increase results in a gain (receive more at settlement), rate decrease results in a loss (receive less at settlement). Payable: Rate increase results in a loss (pay more at settlement), rate decrease results in a gain (pay less at settlement).

21\. (a) Generally, for an event to be classified as extraordinary, it must be both unusual in nature and infrequent of occurrence. As Raim sustains flood losses every two to three years, neither of these conditions is met. For Cane, the flood loss is both unusual and infrequent.

22\. (c) A deferred tax liability is recognized for the amount of deferred tax consequences attributable to temporary differences that will result in taxable amounts in future years. The liability is the amount of taxes that will be payable on those taxable amounts in future years based on the provisions of the tax law. On the other hand, a deferred tax asset is recognized for the amount of deferred tax consequences attributable to temporary differences that will result in tax deductions in future years which will reduce taxes payable in those future years.

23\. (a) In general, accounting for nonmonetary transactions should be based on the fair values of the assets involved. The acquisition is recorded at the fair value of the asset surrendered or the FV of the asset received, whichever is more clearly determinable, and gains or losses should be recognized. The amount would be the difference between the fair value received and the carrying value of the consideration given up.

24\. (c) A sole proprietorship's equity consists of a single proprietor's equity account, *Owner's Equity* or *Net Worth*. This is the sum of the beginning capital balance, plus additional investments during the period, plus net income (or minus net loss) minus withdrawals. The proprietor's draw is not reported separately on the income statement, but rather is included in *Owner's Equity* or *Net Worth*. Depreciation is not included in the *Owner's Equity* or *Net Worth* account. It is reported on the income statement of a proprietorship.

25\. (a) Gains or losses on sale-leaseback transactions generally are deferred and amortized over the term of the lease. There are two exceptions to this general rule: (1) where the seller-lessee retains only a minor portion of the use of the property, or (2) where the seller-lessee retains more than a minor portion of the use but less than substantially all. For purposes of these tests, a minor portion is defined as 10% or less of the use of the asset; thus, if the present value of lease rentals during the leaseback period is 10% or less than the fair value of the property, the seller-lessee is deemed to have retained only a minor interest in the property (SFAS 28, ¶3). In this case, the sale and leaseback are accounted for as two separate transactions (i.e., the entire gain is recognized upon sale of the property). In this problem, the present value of the lease payments ($34,100) was less than 10% of the fair value of the property (i.e., 10% of $360,000 = $36,000).

26\. (c) Under the modified basis of accounting, governments accrue sales tax revenue when it is measurable and available for use. "Available for use" means that the revenues will be collected within the current period or early enough in the next period (i.e., within 60 days or so) to be used to pay for expenditures incurred in the current period. All of these revenues will be collected within 60 days. Curry City's portion of the total is not reported as revenues in the state's financial statements. Curry's portion is reported in the state's books in an agency fund (which does not have operating accounts) in an account such as *Due to City*.

27\. (d) ($15,000 + $12,000 – $0) / 5 = $5,400)

28\. (b) The gross profit on the sale of the plant is $500,000 (i.e., the $1,500,000 sales price minus the $1,000,000 cost). Thus, the gross profit margin ratio to be applied to the annual installment payments is 1/3 (i.e., $500,000 / $1,500,000). During the year, Yardley received (1) $300,000 at the time of sale, (2) the first annual installment on the note of $300,000, and (3) interest of $144,000 (i.e., $1,200,000 × 12%). The amount of realized gross profit that Yardley should recognize from the installment sale is the sum of the down payment and first installment on the note times the gross profit margin ratio [($300,000 + $300,000) × 1/3 = <u>$200,000</u>]. The $144,000 of interest received in the year is recognized separately as interest income.

29\. (b) Governmental funds use the modified accrual basis of accounting, under which revenues are recognized when they become measurable and available for use. "Available for use" means that the revenues will be collected within the current period or collected early enough in the next period (e.g., within 60 days or so) to be used to pay for expenditures incurred in the current period. Therefore, for fiscal year 2, Pine should recognize property tax revenue of <u>$2,200,000</u>. This amount is comprised of (1) $1,000,000 (i.e., $920,000 + $80,000) of property taxes levied in January of year 1 that were collected in October and December and (2) $1,200,000 (i.e.,

$1,100,000 + $60,000 + $40,000) of property taxes levied in January of year 2 that were collected in May, July, and August.

30. (b) Assets restricted to a particular use assume the liquidity of that use. Endowment funds are typically long-term assets. (Endowment implies a permanent restriction.)

Solution 3

1. (a) In the statement of cash flows, proceeds from the sale of used equipment should be reported as a cash inflow due to an investing activity. Since the equipment was sold at a gain, the amount of the proceeds would equal the equipment's carrying amount plus the gain recognized on disposal. The income tax effect of the gain on disposal does not affect the amount reported in the investing section because all income taxes are to be classified as an operating activity on a statement of cash flows (see SFAS 95, ¶91-92).

2. (a) In the consolidated balance sheet, the machine's cost and accumulated depreciation must be based upon the cost of the machine to the consolidated entity. Therefore, the machine is reported at its cost to the consolidated entity of $\underline{\$1{,}100{,}000}$, and thus, the balance of the machine's accumulated depreciation is $\underline{\$300{,}000}$ [$250,000 + ($1,100,000 – $100,000) / 20].

3. (d) Trading securities can be debt and/or equity securities that are bought and held principally for the purpose of selling in the near term. Trading securities are reported at fair value and unrealized holding gains and losses are included in current earnings.

4. (d) Initial franchise fees from franchise sales ordinarily must be recognized (with provision for estimated uncollectible amounts) when all material services or conditions relating to the sale have been substantially performed or satisfied by the franchisor.

5. (d) When accrued interest payable increases during a period, interest expense on a cash basis is less than interest expense on an accrual basis, because cash interest payments are less than interest expense reported on an accrual basis. To convert net income to net cash flow from operating activities, the increase in accrued interest payable must be added. Depreciation is a noncash expense which was deducted in arriving at net income. Thus, it must be added back to net income to determine net cash flow from operating activities.

6. (b) To determine the inventory turnover for the year, the beginning inventory at January 1 must first be determined by working backwards through the cost of goods sold schedule. The inventory turnover for the year can then be computed.

Cost of goods sold for the year	$ 900,000
Add: Ending inventory, 12/31	180,000
Goods available for sale	1,080,000
Less: Purchases for the year	(960,000)
Beginning inventory, 1/1	$ 120,000

$$\textit{Inventory turnover} = \frac{\textit{Cost of goods sold}}{\textit{Average inventory}}$$

$$\frac{\$900{,}000}{\$120{,}000 + \$180{,}000) / 2}$$

7. (a) According to SAS 62, a comprehensive basis of accounting other than generally accepted accounting principles is one of the following: (1) a basis of accounting used to comply with regulatory requirements; (2) a basis used for tax purposes; (3) a cash basis; (4) a definite set of criteria having substantial support, such as the price-level basis of accounting.

Cash basis does not attempt to match revenues and the expenses associated with those revenues, therefore conversion of income statement amounts from the cash basis to the accrual basis would be in accordance with the modified cash basis of accounting.

8. (a) ARB 43, Chap. 4, requires valuation of inventory items at the lower of cost or replacement cost (commonly referred to as market). For purposes of this rule, however, market cannot exceed the net realizable value (ceiling) of the good (i.e., selling price less expected costs to sell), and market should not be less than this net realizable value reduced by an allowance for a normal profit margin (floor). In this problem, the replacement cost is between the ceiling and floor amounts, and so it is compared to cost. Because the original cost is greater than replacement cost, the item will be carried at replacement cost.

9. (a) When bonds are issued at a discount, the *Discount on Bonds Payable* account is a contra-liability account to *Bonds Payable,* i.e., it reduces the carrying amount of the bonds. Thus, as the bond

discount is amortized, the carrying amount of the bonds increases. The bond discount amortization increases the interest expense on the bonds, and so net income decreases.

10. (c) Units-of-output depreciation takes into account salvage value and the number of units produced by the asset. Cost – salvage/expected output × current output:

$$\frac{\$864{,}000 - \$72{,}000}{1{,}800{,}000} = \frac{\$792{,}000}{\$1{,}800{,}000} = \$0.44 \times 300{,}000 = \$132{,}000$$

11. (c) Accrual accounting recognized and reports the effects of transactions and other events on the assets and liabilities of a business enterprise in the time periods to which they relate rather than only when cash is received of paid. Accrual accounting attempts to match revenues and the expenses associated with those revenues in order to determine net income for an accounting period. The insurance costs were not recorded during the period to which they relate, so the accrued liabilities is understated. Because the expense was not included in the inventory that was sold, the COGS was less than it should have been, and as a result, the retained earnings were overstated.

12. (a) An investment by one member of a consolidated group of companies in the bonds of another member of that group is, in substance, the same thing as the purchase by a member of its own bonds. Although the bonds cannot physically be retired, since two separate entities are involved in the transaction, from a consolidated viewpoint, the transaction is treated as a constructive retirement of the bonds to the extent of the investment in the bonds. Thus, the consolidated financial statements will reflect any gain or loss on the retirement of bonds in the year of purchase. This is true despite the fact that the books of the affiliates involved in the transaction continue to reflect the *Investment in Bonds* and *Bond Payable* accounts, respectively. Thus, the consolidated entity in question recognizes a gain of $100,000 (i.e., $1,075,000 carrying amount of bond – $975,000 cost to subsidiary) on the bond retirement. Gains and losses on the early retirement of bonds can only be reflected on the books of the issuer. Thus, Palmer, the parent company, is attributed the entire $100,000 gain on the retirement, thereby increasing consolidated *Retained Earnings* by the same amount. Since no portion of the gain on retirement is attributed to the subsidiary, the amount reported in the consolidated financial statements for the 25% minority interest in the subsidiary is unaffected by the intercompany bond transaction.

13. (a) GASB 34 requires long-term debt issued ($1,000,000) to be reported as an other financing source. Premiums ($10,000) and discounts are reported as other financing sources and uses, respectively. Debt issue costs paid out of proceeds are reported as expenditures. Therefore, the city should report the entire $1,010,000 as an other financing source, not net of expenditures.

14. (b) Per SFAC 6, par. 143, "Realization in the most precise sense means the process of converting noncash resources and rights into money and is most precisely used in accounting and financial reporting to refer to sales of assets for cash or *claims to cash.*" Thus, the sale of the depreciated equipment for a note (i.e., a claim to cash) conforms to the realization concept. None of the transactions in the other choices involve the conversion of a noncash resource or right into cash or claims to cash.

15. (b) The net income for the current year is overstated, because no gains or losses are recognized on treasury stock transactions.

16. (c) Cobb owns only a 2% interest in Roe. Thus, Cobb does not have the ability to exercise significant influence over Roe by virtue of the investment, and the investment should be accounted for under the cost method. Therefore, Cobb should report the cash dividend received from Roe as dividend income. No income is recognized from the receipt of the stock dividend from Roe, since Cobb's proportionate interest in Roe has not changed and Roe's underlying assets and liabilities have also not changed.

Shares of Roe purchased 2/12	10,000
Add: Shares of Roe from stock dividend, 3/31	2,000
Shares of Roe held, 9/15	12,000
Times: Cash dividend per share	× $1.50
Dividend income, year ended 10/31	$ 18,000

17. (b) Entities are required to classify net assets based upon the existence or absence of donor-imposed restrictions. Thus, net assets are classified into at least three categories: permanently restricted, temporarily restricted, and unrestricted. A temporary restriction is a donor-imposed restriction that will lapse upon occurrence of conditions specified by the donor. The allowable use of the income of a temporarily restricted asset may also be restricted by the terms of the donation.

18. (b) Revenue generally is recognized when both the earnings process is complete and an exchange has taken place. Deferred revenue is revenue collected, but not yet earned. Royalty revenue to Boulder would be $30,000 ($300,000 × .10).

The remaining $20,000 balance of Castle's payment against future royalties is deferred revenue.

19. (b) SFAS 144, ¶43 states, "In the period in which a component of an entity either has been disposed of or is classified as held for sale, the income statement of a business enterprise for current and prior periods shall report the results of operations of the component...in discontinued operations...in the periods(s) in which they occur."

Gain from sale of division assets on Feb 26	$ 90,000
Less: Operating loss during the fiscal year	(50,000)
Gain on disposal of segment, before income taxes	$ 40,000

20. (d) SFAS 93 requires all (nongovernmental) nonprofit organizations to recognize depreciation in external financial statements.

21. (c) Operating revenues include "Net Patient Revenue" and "Other Revenues." Other revenues of a hospital are defined as amounts generated from *activities that are major and central to ongoing operations other than patient services.* This classification includes activities from gift shops, cafeterias, education programs, snack bars, newsstands, parking lots, etc. However, unrestricted gifts are not included and are classified as "Nonoperating Gains," a separate and distinct section of the operating statement.

22. (b) Interest income, interest expense, gain or loss on sales of capital assets, grants to or from other governments, operating transfers to or from other funds, and residual equity transfers are examples of transactions that are reported as nonoperating revenue.

23. (c) The cost of retroactive benefits generated by a plan amendment is amortized by assigning an equal amount to each year of future service for each employee active at the date of the amendment expected to receive benefits under the plan. SFAS 87 permits the use of simplified methods, including the use of the straight-line method that amortizes the cost over the average remaining service life of the active participants. The average remaining service life is 5 years, calculated by adding the expected remaining years of service of the participants (3 + 5 + 5 + 7 = 20 years) and dividing by the number of participants (4). The total credit of $100,000 would thus be amortized over 5 years, at $20,000 per year. If instead the amortization is calculated by prorating for each year over the next 7 years, during the first year 4 participants remain in active service; 4/20($100,000) = $20,000. In this problem, during each of the first three years the amortization is the same under either method.

24. (b) Because ownership of the machine is transferred to the lessee upon expiration of the lease, SFAS 13 provides that the lessee account for the lease as a capital lease. As a result, the lessee, at the inception of the lease, records the asset and the corresponding liability at an amount equal to the lesser of the asset's fair value at the inception date or the present value of the minimum lease payments, or $180,000.

25. (a) The costs of equipment or facilities that are acquired or constructed for R&D activities and have alternative future uses (in R&D or otherwise) should be capitalized when acquired or constructed. However, the cost of equipment or facilities that are acquired or constructed for a particular R&D project and have no alternative future uses (in other R&D projects or otherwise) are expensed as R&D costs at the time the costs are incurred (SFAS 2, ¶11).

26. (c) Depreciation of fixed assets is required and is not optional in an enterprise fund. Enterprise funds must be used to account for a government's business-type operations that are financed and operated like private businesses—where the government's intent is that all costs (expenses, including depreciation) of providing goods or services to the general public on a continuing basis are to be financed or recovered primarily through user charges. Fixed assets are not treated as expenditures in an enterprise fund.

27. (c) To determine the price-earnings ratio on common stock, the current year earnings per share must first be computed, as follows:

EPS=Net income to common stockholders / Weighted average common shares = (Net income – Preferred dividend requirement / Weighted average common shares = ($1,200,000 – $300,000 / 100,000 shares = $9.00

Price earnings ratio = Market price per share / EPS = $72 /$9.00 = 8 to 1.

28. (c) Nongovernmental nonprofit organizations, including voluntary health and welfare organizations (VHWOs), use the accrual basis of accounting for all external reporting purposes.

29. (a) If an entity's functional currency is the foreign currency, which has not experienced significant inflation, translation adjustments result from the process of **translating** that entity's financial statements into the reporting currency (SFAS 52).

Translation adjustments (gains or losses) are not included in net income, but in other comprehensive income.

30. (c) Advanced payments received from customers and others are liabilities until the transaction is completed. The travel and lodging services that were used by KLU is a liability because use of the services indicated a payment in advance for the advertising time to be provided at a later date. Use of the services is an expense.

PERFORMANCE BY SUBTOPICS

Practice exam Testlet and question numbers corresponding to each chapter of the Financial Accounting & Reporting text are listed below. To assess your preparedness for the CPA exam, record the number and percentage of questions you correctly answered in each topic area. Multiple choice questions are worth one point each. The point distribution approximates that of the exam.

Chapter 1: Overview

Question #	Correct √
1:2	
2:1	
3:8	
# Points	3
# Correct	______
% Correct	______

Chapter 2: Cash, Marketable Securities & Receivables

Question #	Correct √
1:7	
1:8	
2:7	
3:5	
3:14	
# Points	5
# Correct	______
% Correct	______

Chapter 3: Inventory

Question #	Correct √
1:9	
2:8	
2:12	
3:7	
# Points	4
# Correct	______
% Correct	______

Chapter 4: Property, Plant & Equipment

Question #	Correct √
1:1	
2:9	
2:23	
3:9	
# Points	4
# Correct	______
% Correct	______

Chapter 5: Intangible Assets, R&D Costs & Other Assets

Question #	Correct √
1:10	
1:11	
2:5	
3:26	
# Points	4
# Correct	______
% Correct	______

Chapter 6: Bonds

Question #	Correct √
1:12	
2:10	
2:11	
3:10	
# Points	4
# Correct	______
% Correct	______

Chapter 7: Liabilities

Question #	Correct √
1:23	
2:15	
3:30	
# Points	3
# Correct	______
% Correct	______

Chapter 8: Leases

Question #	Correct √
1:15	
2:18	
3:23	
# Points	3
# Correct	______
% Correct	______

Chapter 9: Postemployment Benefits

Question #	Correct √
2:4	
3:20	
# Points	2
# Correct	______
% Correct	______

Chapter 10: Owners' Equity

Question #	Correct √
1:13	
2:13	
2:19	
3:11	
# Points	4
# Correct	______
% Correct	______

Chapter 11: Reporting the Results of Operations

Question #	Correct √
1:16	
1:19	
1:20	
2:20	
2:29	
3:6	
3:12	
3:19	
# Points	8
# Correct	______
% Correct	______

Chapter 12: Reporting: Special Areas

Question #	Correct √
1:14	
1:22	
2:6	
2:14	
3:13	
3:15	
# Points	6
# Correct	______
% Correct	______

Chapter 13: Accounting for Income Taxes

Question #	Correct √
1:21	
2:21	
# Points	2
# Correct	______
% Correct	______

Chapter 14: Statement of Cash Flows

Question #	Correct √
1:3	
1:25	
3:1	
3:3	
# Points	4
# Correct	______
% Correct	______

Chapter 15: Financial Statement Analysis

Question #	Correct √
1:5	
1:6	
1:27	
2:16	
2:27	
3:4	
3:22	
# Points	7
# Correct	______
% Correct	______

Chapter 16: Foreign Operations

Question #	Correct √
1:29	
2:22	
3:28	
# Points	3
# Correct	______
% Correct	______

Chapter 17: Consolidated Financial Statements

Question #	Correct √
1:17	
1:18	
2:2	
2:3	
3:2	
3:16	
# Points	6
# Correct	______
% Correct	______

Chapter 18: Governmental Overview

Question #	Correct √
1:24	
1:26	
2:17	
3:21	
# Points	4
# Correct	
% Correct	

Chapter 19: Governmental Funds & Transactions

Question #	Correct √
1:4	
2:24	
2:25	
3:17	
3:27	
# Questions	5
# Correct	
% Correct	

Chapter 20: Nonprofit Accounting

Question #	Correct √
1:28	
1:30	
2:26	
2:28	
2:30	
3:18	
3:24	
3:25	
3:29	
# Questions	9
# Correct	
% Correct	

PERFORMANCE BY AICPA CONTENT SPECIFICATION OUTLINE

Practice exam Testlet and question numbers corresponding to each section of the AICPA Content Specification Outline are listed below. To assess your preparedness for the CPA exam, record the number and percentage of questions you correctly answered in each topic area. Multiple choice questions are worth one point each. The point distribution approximates that of the exam.

CSO I: Concepts and Standards for Financial Statements (17% - 23%)

Question #	Correct √
1:2	
1:3	
1:6	
1:8	
1:22	
1:25	
1:27	
2:1	
2:3	
2:6	
3:1	
3:3	
3:4	
3:6	
3:8	
3:23	
# Points	17
# Correct	
% Correct	

CSO II: Typical items: Recognition, Measurement, Valuation, and Presentation in Financial Statements in Conformity With GAAP (27% - 33%)

Question #	Correct √
1:1	
1:7	
1:9	
1:10	
1:11	
1:12	
1:13	
1:14	
2:5	
2:7	
2:8	
2:9	
2:10	
2:11	
2:12	
2:13	
2:14	
2:15	
2:19	
3:5	
3:7	
3:9	
3:10	
3:11	
3:12	
3:13	
3:14	
3:15	
# Points	28
# Correct	
% Correct	

CSO III: Specific Types of Transactions and Events: Recognition, Measurement, Valuation, and Presentation in Financial Statements in Conformity With GAAP (27% - 33%)

Question #	Correct √
1:15	
1:16	
1:17	
1:18	
1:19	
1:20	
1:21	
1:23	
1:29	
2:2	
2.4	
2:16	
2:18	
2:20	
2:21	
2:22	
2:23	
2:27	
2:29	
3:2	
3:16	
3:19	
3:22	
3:26	
3:27	
3:28	
3:30	
# Points	27
# Correct	
% Correct	

CSO IV: Accounting and Reporting for Governmental Entities (8% - 12%)

Question #	Correct √
1:4	
1:24	
1:26	
2:17	
2:24	
2:25	
3:17	
3:18	
3:21	
3:24	
# Points	10
# Correct	
% Correct	

CSO V: Accounting and Reporting for Nongovernmental Not-for-Profit Organizations (8% - 12%)

Question #	Correct √
1:28	
1:30	
2:26	
2:28	
2:30	
3:20	
3:25	
3:29	
# Points	8
# Correct	
% Correct	

SIMULATION SOLUTIONS

Solution 4

Research

APB30, par 20

20. Extraordinary items are events and transactions that are distinguished by their unusual nature and by the infrequency of their occurrence. Thus, both of the following criteria should be met to classify an event or transaction as an extraordinary item:

a. Unusual nature—the underlying event or transaction should possess a high degree of abnormality and be of a type clearly unrelated to, or only incidentally related to, the ordinary and typical activities of the entity, taking into account the environment in which the entity operates. (See discussion in paragraph 21.)

b. Infrequency of occurrence—the underlying event or transaction should be of a type that would not reasonably be expected to recur in the foreseeable future, taking into account the environment in which the entity operates.

Multiple-Step Income Statement

Probe Co.
Income Statement
For the Year Ended December 31, Year 3

	A	B	
Sales		$2,420,000	1
Cost of sales		1,863,000	2
Gross profit		557,000	3
Selling and administrative expenses	$220,000		4
Depreciation	88,000	308,000	5
Operating income		249,000	6
Other income (expenses):			
Interest income	14,000		7
Interest expense	(46,000)		8
Loss on sale of equipment	(7,000)	(39,000)	9
Income before income tax and extraordinary item		210,000	10
Income tax:			
Current	45,000		11
Deferred	12,000	57,000	12
Income before extraordinary item		153,000	13
Extraordinary item:			
Gain on flood damage, net of income taxes of $27,000		63,000	14
Net income		$ 216,000	15
Earnings per share:			
Earnings before extraordinary item		$ 1.275	16
Extraordinary item		.525	17
Net income		$ 1.800	18

1B. Sales given in scenario information.

2B. Cost of sales given in scenario information.

3B. Sales less cost of sales ($,420,000 – $1,863,000).

4A. Selling and administrative expenses given in scenario information.

5A. Depreciation given in scenario information.

5B. Total selling & administrative expenses plus depreciation ($220,000 + $88,000).

6B. Gross profit less expenses ($557,000 – $308,000).

7A. Interest income given in scenario information.

8A. Interest expense given in scenario information.

9A. Loss on sale of equipment given in scenario information.

9B. Total other income less expenses ($14,000 – $46,000 – $7,000).

10B. Sum of operating income and other income (expenses) ($249,000 – $39,000).

11A. Current income tax.

Income before income tax and extraordinary item	$210,000
Differences between financial statement and taxable income	(60,000)
Income subject to tax	150,000
Income tax rate	× 30%
Income tax excluding extraordinary item (current income tax expense)	$ 45,000

12A. Deferred income tax.

Cumulative temporary differences—12/31, year 3	$180,000
Income tax rate	× 30%
Deferred tax liability—12/31, year 3	54,000
Deferred tax liability—12/31, year 2	(42,000)
Deferred income tax expense for year 3	$ 12,000

12B. Total income taxes (current plus deferred) ($45,000 + $12,000).

13B. Income less taxes ($210,000 – $57,000).

14B. Gain on flood damage less taxes ($90,000 × .7).

15B. Income adjusted for extraordinary items ($153,000 + $63,000).

16B. Earnings per share before extraordinary item.

Earnings per share:	
January thru March	
60,000 × 3 months	180,000
April thru December	
140,000 × 9 months	$1,260,000
Total	1,440,000
	/ 12
Weighted average number of shares outstanding for year 3	120,000
Income before extraordinary item	$ 153,000
Earnings per share ($153,000 / 120,000)	$ 1.275

17B. Extraordinary item per share: Extraordinary item divided by weighted average number of shares outstanding for year 3 ($63,000 / 120,000).

18B. Net income per share: Net income divided by weighted average number of shares outstanding for year 3 ($216,000 / 120,000)

Solution 5

Research

FAS 95 Summary

This Statement establishes standards for cash flow reporting. It supersedes APB Opinion No. 19, Reporting Changes in Financial Position, and requires a statement of cash flows as part of a full set of financial statements for all business enterprises in place of a statement of changes in financial position.

This Statement requires that a statement of cash flows classify cash receipts and payments according to whether they stem from operating, investing, or financing activities and provides definitions of each category.

Statement of Cash Flows

Kern Inc.
Statement of Cash Flows
For the Year Ended December 31, Year 8
Increase (Decrease) in Cash

Cash flows from operating activities:			
Net income	$ 305,000		1
Adjustments to reconcile net income to net cash provided by operating activities:			
Depreciation	82,000 [1]		2
Amortization of patent	9,000		3
Loss on sale of equipment	10,000		4
Equity in income of Word Corp.	(30,000) [2]		5
Gain on sale of marketable equity securities	(19,000)		6
Decrease in allowance to reduce marketable equity securities to market	(15,000)		7
Increase in accounts receivable	(35,000)		8
Decrease in inventories	80,000		9
Decrease in accounts payable and accrued liabilities	(115,000)		10
Net cash provided by operating activities		$ 272,000	11
Cash flows from investing activities:			
Sale of marketable equity securities	$ 119,000		12
Sale of equipment	18,000		13
Purchase of equipment	(120,000)		14
Net cash provided by investing activities		17,000	15
Cash flows from financing activities:			
Issuance of common stock	$ 260,000 [3]		16
Cash dividend paid	(85,000)		17
Payment on note payable	(300,000)		18
Net cash used in financing activities		(125,000)	19
Net increase in cash		164,000	20
Cash at beginning of year [Info given in worksheet – 0 points]		307,000	21
Cash at end of year		$ 471,000	22

1. Given in Additional Information.

2. Net increase in accumulated depreciation — $ 65,000
   Accumulated depreciation on equipment sold — 17,000
   Depreciation year — $ 82,000

3. Net change in patent given in scenario.

4. Equipment sold for cash — $ 18,000
   Carrying value of equipment — 28,000
   Loss on sale of equipment — $ 10,000

5. Reported net income for Word Corp. — $ 150,000
   Kern's ownership — × 20%
   Equity in income of Word Corp. — $ 30,000

6. Marketable equity securities balance 12/31, year 8 — $ 150,000
   Marketable equity securities balance 12/31, year 7 — 250,000
   Change in marketable equity securities — $(100,000)
   Cash sale of marketable equity securities — 119,000
   Gain on sale of marketable equity securities — $ 19,000

7. Change in allowance to reduce marketable equity securities to market given in scenario.

8. Increase in accounts receivable given in scenario.

9. Decrease in inventories given in scenario.

10. Decrease in accounts payable and accrued liabilities given in scenario.

11. Sum of adjustments to reconcile net income to net cash provided by operating activities plus net income.

12. Sale of marketable equity securities given in additional information.

13. Sale of equipment given in additional information.

14. Purchase of equipment given in additional information.

15. Sum of cash flows from investing activities.

16. Issuance of common stock, 20,000 shares for cash at $13 per share — $ 260,000

17. Cash dividend paid given in additional information.

18. Payment on note payable given in scenario.

19. Sum of cash used in financing activities.

20. Net cash provided by operating activities — $ 272,000
    Net cash provided by investing activities — 17,000
    Net cash used in financing activities — (125,000)
    Net increase in cash — $ 164,000

21. Cash at beginning of year – given in scenario.

22. Net increase in cash — $ 164,000
    Plus cash at beginning of year — 307,000
    Cash at end of year — $ 471,00

Video Description

CPA 4135 Intensive Financial Accounting & Reporting
This unbeatable instructor guides you through the intricacies of the material, providing a comprehensive review of accounting for business, governmental and nonprofit enterprises. Many helpful hints and memory aids are included. Topics include investments in debt and equity securities, comprehensive income, derivative instruments, hedging activities, accounting changes, discontinued operations, statement of cash flows, accounting for income taxes, segment reporting, inventory, bonds, contingencies, troubled debt restructuring, leases, pensions, stockholders' equity, consolidated statements, fund accounting for state and local governments, nonprofit health care, nonprofit colleges and universities, and other nonprofit organizations! During this program, Bob Monette discusses numerous multiple choice questions related to business enterprises and to governmental and nonprofit enterprises. Also included in this video are one governmental accounting problem and one nonprofit accounting problem.

Each section of the Bisk CPA Review has an intensive video program associated with it. These Intensive video programs are designed for a final, intensive review, after a candidate has already done considerable work. If time permits, use the Intensive program for the section you are studying at the very beginning of your review (for an overview) and set it aside until the final review two weeks before your exam. Intensive video programs contain concise, informative lectures, as well as CPA exam tips, tricks, and techniques that will help you to learn the material needed to pass the exam.

Call our customer representatives toll-free at 1 (800) 874-7877 for more details about videos.

Subject to Change Without Notice

APPENDIX B
PRACTICAL ADVICE

Your first step toward an effective CPA Review program is to **study** the material in this appendix. It has been carefully developed to provide you with essential information that will help you succeed on the CPA exam. This material will assist you in organizing an efficient study plan and will demonstrate effective techniques and strategies for taking the CPA exam.

SECTION	CONTENTS	PAGE
1	General Comments on the CPA Exam	B-2
	State Boards of Accountancy	B-4
	Computer-Based Testing (CBT)	B-5
	The Nondisclosed Exam	B-9
	Ten Attributes of Examination Success	B-10
2	Examination Strategies	B-12
3	Examination Grading Orientation	B-17
4	The Solutions Approach™	B-24
5	Content Specification Outline	B-29
6	Authoritative Pronouncements Cross-References	B-31

SECTION ONE: GENERAL COMMENTS ON THE CPA EXAM

The difficulty and comprehensiveness of the CPA exam is a well-known fact to all candidates. However, success on the CPA exam is a **reasonable, attainable** goal. You should keep this point in mind as you study this appendix and develop your study plan. A positive attitude toward the examination, combined with determination and discipline, will enhance your opportunity to pass.

Purpose of the CPA Exam

The CPA exam is designed as a licensing requirement to measure the technical competence of CPA candidates. Although licensing occurs at the state level, the exam is uniform at all sites and has national acceptance. In other words, passing the CPA exam in one jurisdiction generally allows a candidate to obtain a reciprocal certificate or license, if they meet all the requirements imposed by the jurisdiction from which reciprocity is sought.

Boards of accountancy also rely upon other means to ensure that candidates possess the necessary technical and character attributes, including interviews, letters of reference, affidavits of employment, ethics examinations, and educational requirements. Boards' contact information is listed in this section of the **Practical Advice** appendix and on the web site of the National Association of the State Boards of Accountancy (http://www.nasba.org).

The CPA exam essentially is an academic examination that tests the breadth of material covered by good accounting curricula. It emphasizes the body of knowledge required for the practice of public accounting. It is to your advantage to take the exam as soon as possible after completing the formal education requirements.

We recommend that most candidates study for two examination sections at once, since there is a **synergistic** learning effect to be derived through preparing for more than one part. That is, all sections of the exam share some common subjects (particularly Financial Accounting & Reporting and Auditing & Attestation); so as you study for one section, you are also studying for the others. This advice will be different for different candidates. Candidates studying full-time may find that studying for all four sections at once is most beneficial. Some candidates with full-time jobs and family responsibilities may find that studying for a single exam section at once is best for them.

Score

A passing score for each exam section is 75 points. The objective responses are scored electronically. The written communication response (essay) portions of simulations (essay elements) are graded manually. Scores are released to candidates during the next exam window by boards of accountancy. Scores are not available from the testing sites.

Format

The CPA exam is split into four sections of differing length.

1. **Financial Accounting & Reporting**—This section covers generally accepted accounting principles for business enterprises and governmental and nonprofit organizations. This section's name frequently is abbreviated as FAR or FARE. (4 hours)

2. **Auditing & Attestation**—This section covers the generally accepted auditing standards, procedures, and related topics. The CPA's professional responsibility is no longer tested in this area. This section's name often is abbreviated as AUD. (4½ hours)

3. **Regulation**—This section covers the CPA's professional responsibility to the public and the profession, the legal implications of business transactions generally confronted by CPAs, and federal taxation. This section's name commonly is abbreviated as REG. (3 hours)

4. **Business Environment & Concepts**—This section covers business organizations, economic concepts, financial management, planning, measurement, and information technology. This section's name typically is abbreviated as BEC. The AICPA has announced that initially, it will not test

candidates using simulations in this section. The AICPA has not specified when simulations will first appear in this exam section. (2½ hours)

Schedule

There are four exam windows annually; the first one starts in January. A candidate may sit for any particular exam section only once during a window. Between windows there is a dark period of about a month when the exam is not administered. Once a candidate has a passing score for one section, that candidate has a certain length of time (typically 18 months) to pass the other three exam sections, or lose the credit for passing that first exam section. Candidates should check with the governing Board of Accountancy concerning details on the length of time to pass all four sections. Exam sites typically are open Mondays through Fridays; some are open on Saturdays as well.

January	February	March
April	May	June
July	August	September
October	November	December

Writing Skills Content

Written communication responses (commonly called essays) are used to assess candidates' writing skills. Additional information is included in the **Writing Skills** section. Only those writing samples that generally are responsive to the topic will be graded. If the response is off topic or offers advice that is clearly incorrect, no credit will be given for the response.

Written communication responses are scored holistically. Scores are based on three general writing criteria:

1. Organization
2. Development
3. Expression

Reference Materials

All the material you need to review to pass the CPA exam is in your Bisk Education *CPA Comprehensive Review* texts! However, should you desire more detailed coverage in any area, you may consult the actual promulgations. Individual copies of recent pronouncements are available from the FASB, AICPA, SEC, etc. To order printed materials from the **FASB** or **AICPA** contact:

FASB Order Department
P.O. Box 5116
Norwalk, CT 06856-5116
Telephone (203) 847-0700

AICPA Order Department
P.O. Box 1003
New York, NY 10108-1003
Telephone (800) 334-6961

www.aicpa.org

The AICPA has made available, to candidates with their Notice to Schedule (NTS), a **free** six-month's subscription to some of the databases used in the exam. Bisk Education is unable to fill orders for these subscriptions; they are available only through the AICPA exam web site (www.cpa-exam.org).

If you do not yet have your NTS, the FASB offers a student discount that varies depending on the publication. The AICPA offers a 30% educational discount, which students may claim by submitting proof of their eligibility (e.g., copy of ID card or teacher's letter). AICPA members get a 20% discount and delivery time is speedier because members may order by phone. Unamended, full-text FASB statements are available without charge in PDF format on the FASB Web site (www.fasb.org/st). Bear in mind that these statements are not provided in a searchable format, nor are they the only authoritative literature used in the research element of simulations.

STATE BOARDS OF ACCOUNTANCY

Certified Public Accountants are licensed to practice by individual State Boards of Accountancy. Application forms and requirements to sit for the CPA exam should be requested from your individual State Board. IT IS EXTREMELY IMPORTANT THAT YOU COMPLETE THE APPLICATION FORM CORRECTLY AND RETURN IT TO YOUR STATE BOARD BEFORE THE DEADLINE. Errors and/or delays may result in the rejection of your application. Be extremely careful in filling out the application and be sure to enclose all required materials. Requirements as to education, experience, internship, and other matters vary. If you have not already done so, take a moment to call the appropriate board for specific and current requirements. Complete the application in a timely manner. Some states arrange for an examination administrator, such CPA Examination Services [a division of the National Association of State Boards of Accountancy (NASBA), (800) CPA-EXAM (272-3926)], to handle candidate registration, examination administration, etc.

It may be possible to sit for the exam in another state as an out-of-state candidate. Candidates wishing to do so should also contact the Board of Accountancy in the state where they plan to be certified. NASBA has links (**http://www.nasba.org**) to many state board sites.

At least 45 days before you plan to sit for the exam, check to see that your application to sit for the exam has been processed. DON'T ASSUME THAT YOU ARE PROPERLY REGISTERED UNLESS YOU HAVE RECEIVED YOUR NOTICE TO SCHEDULE (NTS). You must present your NTS and proper identification to be admitted to the testing room at an exam site. Contact the applicable board of accountancy if you have any doubts about what constitutes proper ID.

The AICPA publishes a booklet entitled *Uniform CPA Examination Candidate Bulletin: Information for Applicants,* usually distributed by Boards of Accountancy to candidates upon receipt or acceptance of their applications. To request a complimentary copy, contact your **state board** or the **AICPA,** Examination Division, 1211 Avenue of the Americas, New York, NY 10036. This publication is also available on the AICPA's exam web site: www.cpa-exam.org.

Candidates requiring medication during the exam should make sure to notify the state board and other examining entities as appropriate during registration.

Contacting Your State Board

CPA Examination Services, a division of the National Association of State Boards of Accountancy (NASBA) administers the examination for 25 states. Contact CPA Examination Services at (800) CPA-EXAM (272-3926), (615) 880-4250, or www.nasba.org.

CO	CT	DE	FL	GA	HI	IA	IN	KS	LA	MA	ME	MI	MN	MO	MT
NE	NH	NJ	NM	NY	OH	PA	PR	RI	SC	TN	UT	VA	VT	WI	

Castle Worldwide at (800) 655-4845 administers the examination for WA.

Following are the telephone numbers for the boards in the other states.

AK	(907) 465-2580	IL	(217) 333-1565	OK	(405) 521-2397
AL	(334) 242-5700	KY	(502) 595-3037	OR	(503) 378-4181
AR	(501) 682-1520	MD	(410) 333-6322	SD	(605) 367-5770
AZ	(602) 255-3648	MS	(601) 354-7320	TX	(512) 305-7850
CA	(916) 263-3680	NC	(919) 733-4222	VI	(340) 773-2226
DC	(202) 442-4461	ND	(800) 532-5904	WV	(304) 558-3557
GU	(671) 477-1050	NE	(402) 471-3595	WY	(307) 777-7551
ID	(208) 334-2490	NV	(775) 786-0231		

The web sites for the state boards that administer the exam themselves are listed here. Each address has www. as a prefix, except WY. The Bisk Education web site **(www.cpaexam.com)** has links to the AICPA and NASBA. These numbers and addresses are subject to change without notice. Bisk Education doesn't assume responsibility for their accuracy.

AK	dced.state.ak.us/occ/pcpa.htm	MT	discoveringmontana.com/dli/bsd
AL	asbpa.state.al.us	NE	nol.org/home/BPA
AZ	accountancy.state.az.us	NV	accountancy/state.nv.us
AR	state.ar.us/asbpa	NH	state.nh.us/accountancy
CA	dca.ca.gov/cba	NC	state.nc.us/cpabd
DC	dcra.org/acct/newboa.shtm	ND	state.nd.us/ndsba
FL	myflorida.com	OK	state.ok.us/~oab
GU	guam.net/gov/gba	OR	boa.state.or.us/boa.html
ID	state.id.us/boa	SD	state.sd.us/dcr/accountancy
IL	illinois-cpa-exam.com/cpa.htm	TX	tsbpa.state.tx.us
KY	state.ky.us/agencies/boa	UT	commerce.state.ut.us
MD	dllr.state.md.us/license/occprof/account.html	VI	usvi.org/dlca/licensing/cpa.html
MN	boa.state.mn.us	WV	state.wv.us/wvboa
MS	msbpa.state.ms.us	WY	cpaboard.state.wy.us

COMPUTER-BASED TESTING (CBT)

The information presented here is intended to give candidates an overall idea of what their exam will be like. This information is as accurate as possible; however, circumstances are subject to change after this publication goes to press. Candidates should check the AICPA's web site (www.cpa-exam.org) 45 days before their exam for the most recent bulletin.

Registration Process

To sit for the exam, candidates apply to the appropriate state board of accountancy. Some state boards contract with NASBA's service to handle candidate applications. Once a state board or its agent determines that a candidate is eligible to sit for the exam, the board informs NASBA of candidate eligibility and NASBA adds the candidate to its database. With a national database, NASBA is able to ensure that no candidate can sit for the same exam section more than once during a single exam window. Within 24 hours, NASBA sends Prometric a notice to schedule (NTS). At that point, a candidate can schedule a date and time to sit for the exam with Prometric. With a NTS, a candidate also can subscribe to electronic databases of professional literature for free through the AICPA's exam website, www.cpa-exam.org. Please note that at Prometric's call center, Monday tends to have the longest wait times.

Scheduling

Candidates to whom taking the exam on a particular day is important should plan to schedule their exam dates **45 days** in advance. Upon receipt of the NTS, candidates have a limited amount of time to sit for the specified exam sections; this time is set by states. The exam is called on-demand because candidates may sit at anytime for any available date in the open window.

Candidate Medical Condition

If any medical conditions exist that need to be considered during the exam, candidates should supply information about that situation when scheduling. Ordinarily, candidates may not bring anything into the exam room—including prescription medications.

Granting of Credit

Once candidates have been granted credit for one exam section, they typically have 18 months to pass the three other exam sections. As this issue is decided by 54 boards of accountancy which are independent of each other, the length of time varies among jurisdictions. With CBT implementation, the AICPA uses the term *granting of credit* as opposed to the former term, *conditioning.* Candidates who conditioned in paper-and-pencil exams should contact the appropriate accountancy board regarding its transition conditioning policies.

Prometric

Prometric, a commercial testing center, has facilities at different security levels; the CPA exam is administered only at locations that have the highest restrictions. In other words, not all Prometric facilities may administer the CPA exam. These locations have adjustable chairs, 17-inch monitors, and uninterruptible power supplies (UPS). Prometric generally is closed on Sundays. A few locations are open on Saturdays. Candidates can register either at individual Prometric locations or through Prometric's national call center (800-864-8080). Candidates also may schedule, reschedule, cancel, or confirm an exam as well as find the closest testing location online at www.prometric.com.

Prometric doesn't score the exam. Candidates do not know their scores when they leave the exam site. Prometric sends a result file to NASBA that includes candidate responses, attendance information, and any incident reports.

Incident Reports

Prometric prepares an incident report for any unusual circumstances that occur during the exam. While Prometric has UPS available at qualified testing centers, if some problem similar to a power outage should occur, an incident report is included with the information that Prometric sends to NASBA after the candidate is finished with the exam. An incident report would be filed for such events as missing scratch sheets or a mid-testlet absence from the testing room.

Exam Day

On the day of their exam, candidates sign in and confirm their appointments. An administrator checks notices to schedule and **two** forms of identification. Digital photos are created. Candidates stow their belongings in designated locations. Candidates may not bring purses, watches, bottles of water, tissues, etc. into the exam room. Each candidate may receive six pages of scratch paper. Candidates may exchange used sheets for six more sheets. Candidates must account for the six pages at the conclusion of the exam. After the exam, candidates complete a survey to provide feedback.

Fees

States inform candidates of the total applicable fee. The total fee includes fees for NASBA, AICPA, Prometric, the state board, and the digital photo. Cancellations in advance generally result in a partially refunded fee. Cancellations (as opposed to a missed appointment) with no notice result in no refund. If a candidate misses an appointment, there generally is a $35 to $50 rescheduling fee unless due to circumstances beyond the candidate's control. Those situations are decided on a case-by-case basis. Some states structure their fees to provide incentive for taking more than one exam section in the same exam window.

Testing Room

Ordinarily, candidates are not permitted to bring any supplies into the testing room, including pencils, water, or aspirin. Candidates requiring medication during the exam should make sure to notify the state board as appropriate during the registration process. Exam proctors supply "scratch" or note paper. These pages must be returned to proctors before leaving the examination site.

Testlets

Multiple choice questions and simulations are grouped into testlets. A testlet typically has either from 24 to 30 multiple choice questions or a single simulation. The typical exam has three multiple choice testlets and two simulation testlets. Candidates may not pick the order in which they answer testlets. In other words, candidates cannot choose to answer the simulation testlets first and then the multiple choice question testlets. Within any one testlet, questions cover the entire content specification outline and are presented in random order.

Adaptive Testing

Each testlet is designed to cover all of the topics for an exam section. After the first testlet is finished, the software selects a second testlet based on the candidate's performance on the first testlet. If a candidate did well on the first testlet, the second testlet will be a little more difficult than average. Conversely, if a candidate did poorly on the first testlet, the second testlet will be a little less difficult than average. The examiners plan on adaptive testing eventually allowing for less questions, resulting in more time for testing skills.

Initially, testlets with different levels of difficulty will have the same number of questions; however, the point value of a question from an "easy" testlet will be less than a question from a "difficult" testlet. Thus, some candidates may think that they are not doing well because they are finding the questions difficult; when in reality, they are getting difficult questions because of exceptional performance on previous testlets. Other candidates may think that they are doing well because they are finding the questions easy; when in reality, they are getting easy questions because of poor performance on previous testlets.

The BEC exam section is not yet adaptive. The AICPA has not announced when this will change.

Breaks

Once a testlet is started, a candidate ordinarily may not leave the workstation until that testlet is finished. Once a testlet is finished, a candidate may not return to it to change responses. After each testlet, a candidate has the option to take a break, but the clock still is running; a candidate's time responding to questions is reduced by the amount of time spent on breaks.

For a well-prepared candidate, time should not be an issue. Candidates will receive a five or ten minute warning. The software stops accepting exam responses at the end of the exam time automatically. All information entered before that time is scored.

Multiple Choice Questions

If there are six answer options and a candidate is told to choose one, the software will allow the selection of a second option and automatically unselect the previously selected option. If there are six answer options and a candidate is told to choose two, the software will not allow the selection of a third option without the candidate unselecting one of the other selected options.

In Bisk Education's printed book, letter answers appear next to each answer option to simplify indicating the correct answer. In the exam, a radio button appears instead of this letter. During the exam, candidates will indicate their response by clicking the appropriate radio button with a mouse device.

Simulations

A simulation is a collection of related items. A single simulation likely will have several response types. In other words, objective and essay responses may be included in the same simulation. Simulations typically are 20% or less of the exam score. The BEC exam section currently does not have simulations. Rather than announcing when simulations will first appear in the BEC section, the AICPA examiners are re-considering whether to have BEC simulations. BEC simulations are not expected until 2008, at earliest.

Simulation Appearance Simulations generally appear as a collection of tabbed pages. Each tab requiring a candidate response will be designated by a pencil icon that changes appearance when any response is entered on that tab. Candidates should be alert to the fact that the altered icon does not indicate that all responses on that tab are entered, but rather that one response is entered.

Scenario Elements Simulations generally have one or two scenarios providing the basis for answers to all of the questions in the simulations.

Objective Response Elements Simulations may require candidates to select answers from drop-down lists or to enter numbers into worksheets or tax forms. Tax forms or schedules may appear on the REG exam section, but not all simulations on tax topics will include tax forms. Candidates don't need to know how to create a spreadsheet from scratch to earn full points on the exam; they do need to know how to categorize, determine value, and add to a previously constructed worksheet.

Written Communication Elements Written communication elements are hand-graded. The "essay" score focuses primarily on writing skills. The essay content must be on topic to earn the full point value, but the examiners plan to focus on testing content in the objective response questions. Candidates should use their own words in essays; cut-and-paste excerpts from the standards may result in a zero-point score for this element.

Word Processor Tool There is a word processor tool with limited features in some simulations. The word processor tool has cut, paste, copy, do, and undo features. Spell check likely will be available. The word processor intentionally does **not** have bold, underline, or bullet features; the examiners don't want candidates spending much time on formatting.

Spreadsheet Tool The exam has a blank spreadsheet for use like a piece of electronic scratch paper. Anything in such a spreadsheet generally is not graded. In other words, if a candidate calculates an amount in a spreadsheet, it must be transferred to the appropriate answer location in order to earn points.

Research Elements At least one simulation in the FAR, AUD, and REG exam sections will have a research element, probably for one point. With an estimated two simulations per exam section, this means that the point value on any one of these three exam sections for the research element of a simulation will total two percent of that section's point value, at most. The initial BEC exam section simulations will not have research elements. The AICPA has not announced yet when simulations, let alone research elements, first will appear in the BEC exam section.

A research element involves a search of an electronic database of authoritative literature for guidance. The examiners devise research questions with references unlikely to be known, requiring candidates to search the material. No written analysis of the reference is required; candidates merely provide the most appropriate reference(s) to a research question. Each research question will specify the number of references to provide.

The research skill evaluation distills down to the ability to structure a search of an electronic database and select the appropriate guidance from the "hits" generated by that search. Candidates may search using **either** Boolean protocols or the table of contents of the relevant guidance. Qualified candidates may get a **free** six month subscription to the databases used in the FAR and AUD exam sections from the AICPA and NASBA. Any difficulties candidates encounter in accepting the joint AICPA-NASBA offer should be brought to the attention of AICPA or NASBA. Qualified candidates may subscribe at www.cpa-exam.org. Only candidates who have applied to take the exam, been deemed eligible by one of the 54 boards of accountancy, and have a valid Notice to Schedule (NTS) may have access to this complimentary package of professional literature. Further information may be found at www.cpa-exam.org. For further inquiries after subscribing at this site, candidates may contact either: AICPA, 212.596.6111; or NASBA, 615.880.4237.

Tutorial

The AICPA provides a web-based tutorial for the CBT. This tutorial has samples of all the different types of simulation elements. The examiners believe that an hour spent with this tutorial will eliminate any point value loss due merely to unfamiliarity with the CBT system. It is important that you become familiar with the latest version of the AICPA testing software. The simulations use both a word processor and a spreadsheet program; however, these applications are not Microsoft Excel™ or Word™. It may be unsettling to encounter an unfamiliar interface on your exam day.

Advice to Candidates

Arrive at the testing center **at least** ½ hour before your appointment. Midweek appointments probably will be easiest to schedule. If taking the exam on a certain day is important, **schedule 45 days in advance.** Prometric doesn't overbook like airlines do—that is why there is a rescheduling fee for missed appointments.

Don't go to the exam without spending at least an hour with the practice materials (also called a tutorial) available on the AICPA exam web-site. This tutorial is intended to familiarize candidates with the features of the exam software, so that when they take the exam, they are not worried about functionality and, hence, can concentrate on the content. The AICPA does **not** intend its tutorial to demonstrate content. The Bisk Education editors recommend viewing this tutorial at least a month before taking the exam and again a second time a week before your exam date.

THE NONDISCLOSED EXAM

Exam Disclosure

The Uniform CPA Examination is nondisclosed. This means that candidates are not allowed to receive a copy of their examination questions after the test. Also, candidates are required to sign a statement of confidentiality in which they promise not to reveal questions or answers. Only the AICPA have access to the test questions and answers. (In the past, the AICPA has released a small number of questions with unofficial answers from each nondisclosed exam; it makes no guarantees that it will continue this practice.) Bisk Education's editors update the diagnostic, study, and practice questions, based upon content changes, items from previously disclosed tests, and the teaching expertise of our editors. Due to the nondisclosure requirements, Bisk Education's editors are no longer able to address questions about specific examination questions, although we continue to supply help with similar study problems and questions in our texts.

The AICPA no longer discloses the exam in order to increase consistency, facilitate computer administration of the test, and improve examination quality by pretesting questions. Because the examination is no longer completely changed every year, statistical equating methods are more relevant, and the usefulness of specific questions as indicators of candidates' knowledge can be tested.

Time Management

Approximately 20% of the multiple choice questions in every section of every exam are questions that are being pretested. These questions are not included in candidates' final grades; they are presented only so that the Board of Examiners may evaluate them for effectiveness and possible ambiguity. The Scholastic Achievement Test and the Graduate Record Exam both employ similar but not identical strategies: those tests include an extra section that is being pretested, and test-takers do not know which section is the one which will not be graded. On the Uniform CPA Examination, however, the extra questions are mixed in among the graded questions. This makes time management even more crucial. Candidates who are deciding how much time to spend on a difficult multiple choice question must keep in mind that there is a 20% chance that the answer to the question will not affect them either way. Also, candidates should not allow a question that seems particularly difficult or confusing to shake their confidence or affect their attitude towards the rest of the test; it may not even count. This experimental 20% works against candidates who are not sure whether they have answered enough questions to earn 75%. Candidates should try for a safety margin, so that they will have accumulated enough correct answers to pass, even though some of their correctly answered questions will not be scored.

Post-Exam Diagnostics

The AICPA Board of Examiners' Advisory Grading Service provides boards of accountancy with individual diagnostic reports for all candidates along with the candidates' grades. The accountancy boards may mail the diagnostic reports to candidates along with their grades. Candidates should contact the state board in their jurisdiction to find out its policy on this issue. Grades are mailed in the first month of the next exam window; the examiners plan to reduce this waiting time gradually as they speed up the grading process.

Question Re-Evaluation

Candidates who believe that an examination question contains errors that will affect the grading should contact the AICPA Examinations Division, in accordance with the AICPA's *Uniform CPA Examination Candidate Bulletin: Information for Applicants* within **four days** of taking the examination. The Advisory Grading Service asks candidates to be as precise as possible about the question and their reason for believing that it should be re-evaluated, and, if possible, to supply references to support their position. Since candidates are not able to keep a copy of examination questions, it is important to remember as much detail as possible about a disputed question.

TEN ATTRIBUTES OF EXAMINATION SUCCESS

1. **Positive Mental Attitude**
2. **Development of a Plan**
3. **Adherence to the Plan**
4. **Time Management**
5. **Knowledge**
6. **Examination Strategies**
7. **Examination Grading**
8. **Solutions Approach™**
9. **Focus on Ultimate Objective—Passing!**
10. **Examination Confidence**

We believe that successful CPA candidates possess these ten characteristics that contribute to their ability to pass the exam. Because of their importance, we will consider each attribute individually.

1. Positive Mental Attitude

Preparation for the CPA exam is a long, intense process. A positive mental attitude, above all else, can be the difference between passing and failing.

2. Development of a Plan

The significant commitment involved in preparing for the exam requires a plan. We have prepared a study plan in the preceding **Getting Started** section. Take time to read this plan. **Amend it to your situation.** Whether you use our study plan or create your own, the importance of this attribute can't be overlooked.

3. Adherence to the Plan

You cannot expect to accomplish a successful and comprehensive review without adherence to your study plan.

4. Time Management

We all lead busy lives and the ability to budget study time is a key to success. We have outlined steps to budgeting time in the **Personalized Training Plan** found in the **Getting Started** section.

5. Knowledge

There is a distinct difference between understanding the material and knowing the material. A superficial understanding of accounting, auditing, and the business environment is not enough. You must know the material likely to be tested on the exam. Your Bisk Education text is designed to help you acquire the working knowledge that is essential to exam success.

6. Examination Strategies

You should be familiar with the format of the CPA exam and know exactly what you will do when you enter the examination room. In Section Two, we discuss the steps you should take from the time you enter the testing room, until you hand in your note (or scratch) sheets. Planning in advance how you will spend your examination time will save you time and confusion on exam day.

7. Examination Grading

An understanding of the CPA exam written communication (essay) grading procedure will help you to maximize grading points on the exam. Remember that your objective is to score 75 points on each section. Points are assigned to essay questions by the human grader who reads your exam. In essence, your job is to satisfy the grader by writing answers that closely conform to the grading guide. In Section Three, we explain AICPA grading procedures and show you how to tailor your answer to the grading guide and thus earn more points on the exam.

8. Solutions Approach™

The Solutions Approach™ is an efficient, systematic method of organizing and solving questions found on the CPA exam. This Approach will permit you to organize your thinking and your written answers in a logical manner that will maximize your exam score. Candidates who do not use a systematic answering method often neglect to show all their work on free form response questions—work that could earn partial credit if it were presented to the grader in an orderly fashion. The Solutions Approach™ will help you avoid drawing "blanks" on the exam; with it, you always know where to begin.

Many candidates have never developed an effective problem-solving methodology in their undergraduate studies. The "cookbook" approach, in which students work problems by following examples, is widespread among accounting schools. Unfortunately, it is not an effective problem-solving method for the CPA exam or for problems you will encounter in your professional career. Our Solutions Approach™ teaches you to derive solutions independently, without an example to guide you.

Our **Solutions Approach™** and grader orientation skills, when developed properly, can be worth at least 10 to 15 points for most candidates. These 10 to 15 points can often make the difference between passing and failing.

The **Solutions Approach™** for objective questions and essays is outlined in Section Four. Examples are worked and explained.

9. Focus on the Ultimate Objective—Passing!

Your primary goal in preparing for the CPA exam is to attain a grade of 75 or better on all sections and, thus, **pass the examination**. Your review should be focused on this goal. Other objectives, such as learning new material or reviewing old material, are important only insofar as they assist you in passing the exam.

10. Examination Confidence

Examination confidence is actually a function of the other nine attributes. If you have acquired a good working knowledge of the material, an understanding of the grading system, a tactic for answering simulations, and a plan for taking the exam, you can go into the examination room **confident** that you are in control.

SECTION TWO: EXAMINATION STRATEGIES

- Overall Preparation B-12
- CPA Exam Strategies B-12
- Examination Inventory B-13
- Order of Answering Questions B-13
- Examination Time Budgeting B-13
- Page Numbering B-14
- Psychology of Examination Success B-14
- AICPA General Rules Governing Examinations B-15
- CPA Exam Week Checklist B-15

The CPA exam is more than a test of your knowledge and technical competence. It is also a test of your ability to function under psychological pressure. You easily could be thrown off balance by an unexpected turn of events during the days of the exam. Your objective is to avoid surprises and eliminate hassles and distractions that might shake your confidence. You want to be in complete control so that you can concentrate on the exam material, rather than the exam situation. By taking charge of the exam, you will be able to handle pressure in a constructive manner. The keys to control are adequate preparation and an effective examination strategy.

Overall Preparation

Advance preparation will arm you with the confidence you need to overcome the psychological pressure of the exam. As you complete your comprehensive review, you will cover most of the material that will be tested on the exam; it is unlikely that an essay, problem, or series of objective questions will deal with a topic you have not studied. But if an unfamiliar topic **is** tested, you will not be dismayed because you have learned to use the **Solutions Approach™** to derive the best possible answer from the knowledge you possess. Similarly, you will not feel pressured to write "perfect" essay answers, because you understand the grading process. You recognize that there is a limit to the points you can earn for each answer, no matter how much you write.

The components of your advance preparation program have previously been discussed in this appendix. Briefly summarizing, they include the following.

1. Comprehensive review materials such as your Bisk Education CPA Review Program.

2. A method for pre-review and ongoing self-evaluation of your level of proficiency.

3. A study plan that enables you to review each subject area methodically and thoroughly.

4. A **Solutions Approach™** for each type of examination question.

5. An understanding of the grading process and grader orientation skills.

CPA Exam Strategies

The second key to controlling the exam is to develop effective strategies for the days you take the exam. Your objective is to avoid surprises and frustrations so that you can focus your full concentration on the questions and your answers.

You should be familiar with the format of the CPA exam and know exactly what you will do when you enter the testing room. Remember to read all instructions carefully, whether general or specific to a particular question. Disregarding the instructions may mean loss of points.

On the following pages, we discuss the steps you should take on exam day. Planning in advance how you will spend your examination time will save you time and confusion.

Examination Inventory

You should spend the first few minutes of the exam planning your work. **Do not** plunge head-first into answering the questions without a plan of action. You do not want to risk running out of time, becoming frustrated by a difficult question, or losing the opportunity to answer a question that you could have answered well. Your inventory should take no longer than a minute. The time you spend will help you "settle in" to the examination and develop a feel for your ability to answer the questions.

1. Carefully read the "Instructions to Candidates."
2. Note the number and type of testlets, as well as any other information provided by the examiners.
3. Devise a time schedule on your "scratch" paper, taking into account the number and type of testlets.

Order of Answering Questions

Objective questions comprise a majority of the point value of each section. Because of their objective nature, the correct solution often is listed as one of the answer choices. (The exception is when a numeric response is required.) By solving these questions, not only do you gain confidence, but they often involve the same or a related topic to that covered in any essays that may appear in the simulations.

A very effective and efficient manner of answering the objective questions is to make **two passes** through the questions. On the first pass, you should answer those questions that you find the easiest. If you come across a question that you find difficult to solve, note it on your scratch paper and proceed to the next one. This will allow you to avoid wasting precious time and will enable your mind to clear and start anew on your **second pass.** On the second pass, you should return and solve those questions you left unanswered on the first pass. Some of these questions you may have skipped over without an attempt, while in others you may have been able to eliminate one or two of the answer choices. Either way, you should come up with an answer on the second pass, even if you have to guess! Once you leave a testlet, you may not return to it. Before leaving a testlet, make sure you have answered all of the individual questions. Be careful not to overlook any items; use particular care in simulations.

Written communication responses (commonly called essays) should be worked only through the key word outlines on the first pass. Then take a fresh look at the question and return to write your essay solution.

Examination Time Budgeting

You must **plan** how you will use your examination time and adhere faithfully to your schedule. If you budget your time carefully, you should be able to answer all parts of all questions. You should subtract a minute or two for your initial inventory on each section. Assuming you will use the **Solutions Approach™** and there will be two simulations in all sections except BEC, your time budgets may be similar to these. Your actual exam may differ from this scenario. You may benefit by taking more breaks than are included in this schedule. Be sure to adjust your time budget to accommodate the number and type of questions asked as well as your individual needs and strengths.

	Minutes			
	FAR	AUD	REG	BEC
Inventory examination	1	1	1	1
Answer multiple choice question testlet	51	58	33	49
Answer multiple choice question testlet	51	58	33	50
Answer multiple choice question testlet	51	58	33	50
Break	6	5	0	0
Answer simulation testlet	40	45	40	n/a
Answer simulation testlet	40	45	40	n/a
	240	270	180	150

Your objective in time budgeting is to avoid running out of time to answer a question. Work quickly but efficiently (i.e., use the **Solutions Approach™**). Remember that when you are answering an essay question, a partial answer is better than no answer at all. If you don't write anything, how can a grader justify giving you any points?

Page Numbering

Identify and label your scratch pages to avoid confusing yourself during the stress of the exam.

Psychology of Examination Success

As stated previously, the CPA exam is in itself a physical and mental strain. You can minimize this strain by avoiding all unnecessary distractions and inconveniences during your exam week. For example, consider the following.

- **Use the AICPA's free tutorial and sample examination** at www.cpa-exam.org at least a week before your examination. Because the exam interface is subject to change, re-visit the site to be sure that you are familiar with the current interface if you took an exam in a previous window. The site also has the most current *Uniform CPA Examination Candidate Bulletin,* a publication with useful information for candidates. These are **not** available at the test center.

- **Carefully register for the examination.** You must bring two forms of identification and your notice to schedule to the test center on the day of your exam. The name you use to make the appointment must match **exactly** your name on the identification and your notice to schedule (which also must match each other exactly).

- **Make any reservations for lodging well in advance.** If you are traveling, it's best to reserve a room for the preceding night so that you can check in, get a good night's sleep, and locate the exam site well before the exam.

- **Stick to your normal eating, sleeping, and exercise habits.** Eat lightly before the exam. Watch your caffeine and alcohol intake. If you are accustomed to regular exercise, continue a regular routine leading up to your exam day.

- **Locate the examination facilities** before the examination and familiarize yourself with the surroundings and alternate routes.

- **Arrive early for the exam.** Allow plenty of time for unexpected delays. Nothing is more demoralizing than getting caught in a traffic jam ten minutes before your exam is scheduled to begin. Your appointment time is the time that the actual examination process is scheduled to start, not the start of the test center pre-exam procedures: identification verification, digital photography, storage locker assignment, etc. The examiners recommend that you arrive **at least** 30 minutes before your scheduled appointment. If your examination doesn't begin within 30 minutes of your scheduled start time, you may have to reschedule. This means that if you show up 30 minutes after your scheduled start time, you may have to reschedule—pre-exam procedures are neither instantaneous nor factored into your scheduled appointment.

- **Avoid possible distractions,** such as friends and pre-exam conversation, immediately before the exam.

- In general, **you should not attempt serious study on the nights before exam sessions.** It's better to relax—watch a movie, exercise, or read a novel. If you feel you must study, spend half an hour or so going over the chapter outlines in the text. Some candidates develop a single page of notes for each chapter (or each exam section) throughout their review process to review for a few minutes during the evening before the exam. This single page includes only those things that are particularly troublesome for that candidate, such as the criteria for a capital lease or the economic order quantity formula.

- **Don't discuss exam answers with other candidates.** Not only have you signed a statement of confidentiality, but someone is sure to disagree with your answer, and if you are easily influenced by his or her reasoning, you can become doubtful of your own ability. If you are writing more than one exam section within a two-month exam window, you will not have the reliable feedback that only your score can provide from your first section before you sit for the second section. Wait and analyze your performance by yourself when you are in a relaxed and objective frame of mind.

- **Avoid self-evaluation** of your exam performance until after you receive your official score. The Bisk editors have heard from several candidates who were sure that they failed by a large margin, only to receive subsequent messages rejoicing in scores in the 80s and 90s. Self-evaluation without an official score is unreliable. Not all of the examiners' questions are the same point value. Further, approximately 20% of multiple choice questions are not scored; candidates have no reliable way to know which questions are not scored. Instead of speculating, focus on preparing for your next exam section.

General Rules Governing Examinations

1. Read carefully any paperwork assigned to you; make note of numbers for future reference; when it is requested, return it to the examiner. Only the examination number on your card shall be used on your exam for the purpose of identification. If a question calls for an answer involving a signature, **do not** use your own name or initials.

2. Use the exact same name as on your notice to schedule (NTS) when scheduling your appointment. Two pieces of identification are required; one must have a photo. The name on your identification must match your name on your notice to schedule **exactly.**

3. Seating during the exam is assigned by Prometric.

4. Supplies furnished by the Board remain its property and must be returned whether used or not.

5. Any reference during the examination to books or other matters or the exchange of information with other persons shall be considered misconduct sufficient to bar you from further participation in the examination.

6. The only aids most candidates are permitted to have in the examination room are supplied by the proctors. Wallets, briefcases, files, books, phones, watches, and other material brought to the examination site by candidates must be placed in a designated area before the start of the examination. Candidates get a key to a **small** storage locker. The test center is not responsible for lost items.

7. Do not leave your workstation during a testlet. Breaks are allowed only before starting and after finishing testlets.

8. Smoking is allowed only in designated areas away from the general examination area.

9. No telephone calls are permitted during the examination session.

10. Answers must be completed in the total time allotted for each exam section. The fixed time for each session must be observed by all candidates. One time warning is given five or ten minutes before the end of the exam. The testing software will end the test at the end of the specified time.

CPA Exam Week Checklist

What to pack for exam week:

1. CPA exam notice to schedule and matching identification.

2. If traveling, your hotel confirmation and an alarm clock. (Don't rely on a hotel wake-up call.)

3. Cash and/or a major credit card.

4. An inexpensive watch (will not be allowed in the testing room) to facilitate your timely arrival at the exam site.

5. Comfortable clothing that can be loosened to suit varying temperatures. What is worn into the testing room must be worn throughout the testing period; however, once at the testing center, you can remove a sweater or coat, for instance, before entering the testing room.

6. Appropriate review materials and tools for final reviews during the last days before the exam.

7. Healthy snack foods (will not be allowed in testing room).

Evenings before exam sections:

1. Read through your Bisk Education chapter outlines for the next day's section(s).

2. Eat lightly and monitor your intake of alcohol and caffeine. Get a good night's rest.

3. Do **not** try to cram. A brief review of your notes will help to focus your attention on important points and remind you that you are well prepared, but too much cramming can shatter your self-confidence. If you have reviewed conscientiously, you are already well-prepared for the CPA exam.

The morning of each exam section:

1. Eat a satisfying meal before your exam. It will be several hours before your next meal. Eat enough to ward off hunger, but not so much that you feel uncomfortable.

2. Dress appropriately. Wear layers you can loosen to suit varying temperatures in the room.

3. Arrive at the exam center at least 30 minutes early.

What to bring to the exam:

1. Appropriate identification (two forms, one with a picture) and notice to schedule (NTS). Your name on the identification must match your name on your NTS **exactly.** Use the exact same name when scheduling your appointment.

2. An inexpensive watch (to be left outside of the exam room) to ensure that you arrive 30 minutes early.

3. Take only those articles that you need to get to and from the exam site. Avoid taking any articles that are not allowed in the exam room, especially valuable ones. There are **small** storage lockers outside of the testing room to hold purses, etc. The test center is not responsible for lost items. Watches, phones, pencils, purses, tissues, candy, and gum are not allowed in the exam room. Even medication is not allowed except by previous arrangement.

During the exam:

1. Always read all instructions and follow the directions of the exam administrator. If you don't understand any written or verbal instructions, or if something doesn't seem right, ASK QUESTIONS as allowed. Remember that an error in following directions could invalidate your **entire** exam.

2. Budget your time. Always keep track of the time and avoid getting too involved with one question.

3. **Satisfy the grader.** Remember that the grader cannot read your mind. You must explain every point in written communications. Focus on key words and concepts. Tell the grader what you know, don't **worry** about any points you don't know.

4. Answer every question, even if you must guess.

5. Use **all** the allotted time. If you finish a testlet early, go back and reconsider the more difficult questions.

6. Get up and stretch between testlets, if you feel sluggish. Walk around as allowed. Breathe deeply; focus your eyes on distant objects to avoid eye strain. Do some exercises to relax muscles in the face, neck, fingers, and back.

7. Do not leave your workstation. except between testlets. Leaving your workstation during a testlet may invalidate your score.

8. Take enough time to organize written answers. Well-organized answers will impress the grader.

9. Remember that you are well-prepared for the CPA exam, and that you can **expect to pass!** A confident attitude will help you overcome examination anxiety.

SECTION THREE: EXAMINATION GRADING ORIENTATION

- Security B-17
- Objective Questions B-17
- Written Communications B-17
- Written Communication Example—Grading Guide B-18
- Importance of Key Concepts B-19
- Importance of Writing Skills B-20
- Research Questions B-20
- Research Question Example B-21
- Additional Reference Notations B-22
- Grading Implications for CPA Candidates B-23

The CPA exam is prepared and graded by the AICPA Examinations Division. It is administered by a commercial testing center, Prometric. Candidates register for the exam through various State Boards of Accountancy.

An understanding of the grading procedure will help you maximize grading points on the CPA exam. Remember that your objective is to pass the exam. You cannot afford to spend time on activities that will not affect your grade, or to ignore opportunities to increase your points. The following material abstracted from the *Information for CPA Candidates* booklet summarizes the important substantive aspects of the Uniform CPA Examination itself and the grading procedures used by the AICPA.

Security

The examination is prepared and administered under tight security measures. The candidates' anonymity is preserved throughout the examination and grading process. Unusual similarities in answers among candidates are reported to the appropriate State Boards.

Objective Questions

Objective questions consist of multiple-choice questions and objective format questions in simulations, which include: yes-no, true-false, matching, and questions requiring a numerical response. Objective questions are machine graded. It is important to understand that there is **no grade reduction** for incorrect responses to objective questions—your total objective question grade is determined solely by the number of correct answers. Thus, you **should answer every question.** If you do not know the answer, make an intelligent guess.

The point to remember is to avoid getting "bogged down" on one answer. Move along and answer all the questions. This helps you avoid leaving questions unanswered or panic-answering questions due to poor budgeting of test time.

Written Communications

Written communications appear on the computer-based exam as components of simulations. Responses are graded mainly for writing skills, but the content must answer the question that the examiners asked. Written communication questions (constructed response questions) are graded by CPAs and AICPA staff members, using the following procedures:

First Grading

The first grading is done by graders assigned to individual questions. For example, each written communication question in the Financial Accounting & Reporting section will be graded by a different grader. A grader, assigned to a single question that will be graded during the full grading session of six or seven weeks, becomes an expert in the subject matter of the question and in the evaluation of the candidates' answers. Thus, grading is objective and uniform.

The purpose of the first grading is to separate the candidates' papers into three groups: obvious passes, marginal, and obvious failures.

Second Grading

Upon completion of the first grading, a second grading is done by reviewers. Obvious passes and failures are subjected to cursory reviews as part of the grading controls. Marginal papers, however, receive an extensive review.

The graders who make the extensive reviews have had years of experience grading the CPA Examination. They have also participated in the development of the grading bases and have access to item analysis for objective questions, identifying concepts as discriminating (those included by most candidates passing the exam) or as rudimentary (those included by candidates both passing and failing the exam). An important indicator of the competence of the candidate is whether grade points were earned chiefly from discriminating concepts or from rudimentary concepts.

Third Grading

After the papers have been through the second grading for all parts of the examination, the resultant grades are listed by candidate number and compared for consistency among subjects. For example, if a candidate passes two subjects and receives a marginal grade in a third, the marginal paper will receive a third grading in the hope that the candidate, now identified as possessing considerable competence, can have the paper raised to a passing grade by finding additional points for which to grant positive credit. This third grading is done by the section head or a reviewer who did not do the second grading of the paper.

Fourth Grading

The Director of Examinations applies a fourth grading to papers that have received the third grading but have grades that are inconsistent. The Director knows that the papers have already been subjected to three gradings, and that it would be difficult to find additional points for which the candidates should be given credit. Obviously, very few candidates are passed in this manner, but this fourth grading assures that marginal candidates receive every possible consideration.

Written Communication Example—Grading Guide

Points are assigned to essay questions on the basis of **key concepts.** A key concept is an idea, thought, or option that can be clearly defined and identified. Through a grading of sample papers, a list of key concepts related to each question is accumulated. These key concepts become the **grading bases** for the question. That is, your answer will be scored according to the number of key concepts it contains. Note that you need not include **all** possible key concepts to receive full credit on a question. The total number of grading bases exceeds the point value of the question. For example, a 10-point question may have 15 or more grading bases. Thus, a candidate would not have to provide all the key concepts to get the maximum available points. Conversely, a candidate cannot receive more points even if s/he provides more than 10 key concepts.

To illustrate the grading procedure and the importance of using key concepts in your answers, we will develop a hypothetical grading guide for a question adapted from a past Auditing exam. We will assume that the entire question is worth 5 points.

Example 1—Sample Written Communication

Taylor Company, a household appliances dealer, purchases its inventories from various suppliers. Taylor has consistently stated its inventories at the lower of cost **(FIFO)** or market.

Required:

Identify the effects on both the balance sheet and the income statement of using the LIFO inventory method instead of the FIFO method over a substantial time period when purchase prices of household appliances are rising. State why these effects take place.

Now let's look at the unofficial answer. Notice that we have boldfaced the key concepts in the answer. Later, as we develop a grading guide for the answer, you will see the importance of using key concepts to tailor your answer to parallel the grading guide.

Solution: Effects of Using LIFO instead of FIFO

Inventories would be **lower** using the LIFO inventory method instead of the FIFO method over a substantial time period when purchase prices of household appliances are rising, because the **inventories are at the oldest (lower) purchase prices** instead of the most recent (higher) purchase prices. Correspondingly, the **cost of goods sold would be higher** because the cost of goods sold is at **more recent** (higher) purchase prices instead of older (lower) purchase prices. Consequently, **net income and retained earnings would be lower.**

More cash flow would generally be available using the LIFO inventory method instead of the **FIFO** method because **taxable income is decreased,** resulting generally in accrual and payment of lower income taxes. Correspondingly, **income tax expense would generally be lower.**

The grading guide consists of a list of the key concepts relevant to the question, both in key word form and in detailed phrases. Each concept is assigned a point (more than one point if it is particularly important or fundamental). A point is also given on many questions for neatness and clarity of answer (including the use of proper formats, schedules, etc.). A hypothetical grading guide for our sample question follows.

Example 2—Grading Guide for Written Communications

STATE ____________________

CANDIDATE NO. _______________

POINTS	KEY WORD CONCEPTS
2	Inventories lower:
1	Inventories at lower (oldest) purchase prices.
2	CGS higher:
1	CGS at higher (most recent) purchase prices
1	Net income and R/E lower
1	Greater cash flow:
1	Decrease in taxable income results in lower income tax expense.
1	Neatness and clarity
10	

GRADE CONVERSION CHART: POINTS TO GRADE

POINTS	1	2 3	4 5	6 7	8 9 10
GRADE	1	2	3	4	5

Importance of Key Concepts

A grading guide similar to the one in Example 2 is used to evaluate every candidate's work, with the key concepts or grading bases for each question. On the first grading, answers may be scanned first for key words, then read carefully to ascertain that no key concepts were overlooked. Each key concept in the answer increases the candidate's grade. The candidate's total grade for the question is easily determined by converting raw points, using a conversion chart. For example, a candidate who provides 8 of the 10 possible points for key concepts for this question would earn a grade of 5 for the answer. The process is repeated by the second grader and subsequent graders if necessary (i.e., borderline papers).

The point you should notice is that **key concepts earn points.** The unofficial answer closely conforms to the grading guide, making the grader's task simple. In turn, the unofficial answer also conforms to the format of the question. That is, each answer is numbered and lettered to correspond to the requirements. This should be your standard format.

There are two more points you should observe as you study the unofficial answer for our example. First, the answer is written in standard English, with clear, concise sentences and short paragraphs. A simple listing of key words is **unacceptable;** the concepts and their interrelationships must be logically presented. Secondly, remember that the unofficial answer represents the most acceptable solution to a question. This is not to say, however, that alternative answers are not considered, or that other answers are not equally as acceptable. During the accumulation of grading bases, many concepts are added to the original "correct answer." Additionally, a paper that is near the passing mark receives a third (and perhaps fourth) grading, at which time individual consideration is given to the merits of each answer.

Parenthetically, we should mention that all the Bisk Education *CPA Review* written communications and problems are solved using the unofficial AICPA answers. Thus, you have ample opportunity to accustom yourself to the favored answer format.

Importance of Writing Skills

Essay responses are graded for writing skills, but the content must answer the question that the examiner asked.

Research Questions

In their current form, research questions merely are objective questions. The only response is a reference to the professional literature. The candidate doesn't provide any commentary or analysis of the guidance. Please note the following statements from the FAQ pages of the AICPA exam website (www.cpa-exam.org).

> CPA candidates are expected to know how to use common spreadsheet and word processing functions, including writing formulae for spreadsheets. They must also have the ability to use a four-function calculator or a spreadsheet to perform standard financial calculations. In addition, candidates will be asked to use online authoritative literature. Many of the question types used in the simulations are based on familiar computer interface controls (e.g., text entry, mouse clicks, highlighting, copy and pasting). In order to become familiar with the electronic tools provided for research questions, further practice may be required.
>
> All CPA candidates are strongly encouraged to review the practice exams and tutorial at http://www.cpa-exam.org. The tutorial explains the design and operation of the computer-based test, and reviews the types of questions and responses used in the new exam. Sample tests that contain a few sample multiple-choice questions and a sample simulation for each applicable section (BEC does not currently contain simulations) are also available at www.cpa-exam.org. The sample tests use the same software that is used for the operational examination. Neither the tutorial nor the sample test will be available at the test centers.

Candidates who would like more practice with the professional literature than is provided by the research questions in the Bisk materials and the AICPA tutorial might take some of the references from the Bisk text material and locate them in the codification of standards. If you do this, use at least one reference from Bisk Chapters 1 through 17 and at least one from Bisk Chapters 18 through 20; note the differences in the abbreviations. This will also help you become familiar with the standards.

Many candidates have access to the FASB and GASB databases (and the other databases for the other exam sections) through their college or employers. When you access the FASB *Financial Accounting Research System*, please note the table of contents from which to chose. If you are using a printed codification, you will find a similar table of contents.

Original Pronouncements, as amended, including Implementation Guides and FASB Staff Positions
Original Pronouncements
Current Text
EITF Abstracts
Topical Index
FARS Reference Guide

The most advantageous areas to choose might be Original Pronouncements or Current Text. Candidates unfamiliar with the professional standards are advised to read the "How Professional Standards Is Organized" portion of the professional literature.

For candidates who have received a Notice to Schedule (NTS), the AICPA & NASBA offer complimentary six-month on-line subscription to professional audit and accounting literature. The on-line package includes AICPA Professional Standards, FASB Current Text, and FASB Original Pronouncements.

Candidates cannot avoid the research merely by answering the question. The research element of the simulation is completed when the candidate narrows the search (to answer the question asked) down to a paragraph reference. In other words, the paragraph reference is the answer that the examiners seek. The candidate doesn't provide commentary or conclusions.

Expect all FAR simulations on the CPA exam to include a research element. This type of element probably will be about 2% of the point value for an exam section with simulations. (Initially, the BEC exam section will not have simulations.) If you can search the Internet using Boolean logic and the advanced search features of an Internet search engine such as www.google.com, you probably already have sufficient skills to earn the points related to the research elements of simulations on the CPA exam.

The search can be made either by using the table of contents feature (if provided with the database of authoritative literature) or by using the search engine and Boolean operators. The design of questions probably will tend to make use of the search engine and Boolean operators the most efficient means of completing the research elements for most candidates. The three Boolean operators are OR, AND, and NOT. A brief review of these operators is provided here.

A search using "accounting OR auditing" will find all documents containing either the word "accounting" or the word "auditing." All other things being equal, a search using OR typically will find the most documents. OR typically is used to search for terms that are used as synonyms, such as "management" and "client." As more terms are combined in an OR search, more documents are included in the results.

A search using "accounting AND auditing" will find all documents containing both the word "accounting" and the word "auditing." All other things being equal, a search using AND typically will find fewer documents than a search using OR, but more than a search using NOT. As more terms are combined in an AND search, fewer documents are included in the results.

A search using "accounting NOT auditing" will find all documents containing the word "accounting" except those that also contain the word "auditing." All other things being equal, a search using NOT typically will find the fewest documents. As more terms are combined in a NOT search, fewer documents are included in the results.

Boolean operators can be combined to refine searches. For example, the following parameters would find information on letters to a client's attorney inquiring about litigation, claims, and assessments: (attorney OR lawyer) AND (letter OR inquiry).

If you get too many or too few results from a search, refine your search parameters until you find what you need. The exam doesn't limit candidates from repeating searches with refined parameters.

Research Question Example

Required: When does an exception to the general rule of determining the present value of the minimum lease payments for recording the asset and obligation under a capital lease occur?

If you have difficulty with Boolean searches, consider using the table of contents instead. Research is a very instance-specific activity; search skills are developed with practice. Any particular search will have little value for you when you are confronted with what likely will be a different research question on the exam. Use the process illustrated here to refine your Boolean search process; do not memorize the answer to this particular example.

Avoid using a search phrase such as "general rule of determining the present value of the minimum lease payments" or "recording the asset and obligation under a capital lease." The exact terms "general rule" or "asset and obligation" might not be in the reference that you seek. Also, eliminate words such as "of" and "for" unless you are seeking an exact phrase that you are sure includes them.

This leaves "exception general rule present value minimum lease payments record asset obligation capital lease." Typically, search engines default to the Boolean search connector "OR" for all words, which probably would give us many irrelevant hits with this phrase, so modify it to "exception" AND "present" AND "minimum" AND "capital."

Why not include "value" in this search phrase? If "present" is in the reference, "value" probably will be there also. If "value" is in the reference without "present," that reference is likely irrelevant. In other words, the word "value" does little to narrow the search. However, if there are too many hits using "present" AND "minimum" AND "capital," try adding another restrictive term, such as "exception." The standards are not always consistent with their use of words; the guidance might use both "exception" and "exceptions."

Why not include "lease" in the search phrase? If "minimum" AND "capital" are in the reference, "lease" probably will be there also. Again, the word "lease" does little to narrow the search.

Once you have narrowed the responses to a few hits (responses to a search) read through the most likely ones to determine which answers the question at hand.

Once you find the guidance, determine the reference from your selection of the authoritative literature menu. (In the printed version of the codification, the section numbers are in the page margins, usually the footer.)

Please note the following information from the top of the page of the FASB Statement 13 section: FASB Statements – FAS 13: Accounting for Leases – Appendix B: Basis for Conclusions – Accounting by Lessees – FAS 13, Par. 93. This is how you know that the reference is from FASB Statement 13.

The rest of the reference comes from the paragraph number. For instance, the paragraph labeled "93" reads as follows. (In the printed version of the codification, each paragraph also has a paragraph number.)

> 93. With respect to the rate of interest to be used in determining the present value of the minimum lease payments for recording the asset and obligation under a capital lease, the Board concluded the rate should generally be that which the lessee would have incurred to borrow for a similar term the funds necessary to purchase the leased asset (the lessee's incremental borrowing rate). An exception to that general rule occurs when (a) it is practicable for the lessee to ascertain the implicit rate computed by the lessor and (b) that rate is less than the lessee's incremental borrowing rate; if both of those conditions are met, the lessee shall use the implicit rate. However, if the present value of the minimum lease payments, using the appropriate rate, exceeds the fair value of the leased property at the inception of the lease, the amount recorded as the asset and obligation shall be the fair value.

Additional Reference Notations

A reference located in the General Standards (Current Text) of the FARS database is signified by a letter at the beginning of a reference (e.g., I would be for Interest, Inventory, etc.). Numbers at the beginning of a reference signifies guidance on a governmental accounting topic. A reference beginning with "2450" would relate to information on cash flows statements for a governmental entity found in the Government Accounting Research System database (GARS). The editors suggest that candidates with access to the standards browse through several of the chapters of guidance and become familiar with the standards, starting with the "FARS Reference Guide" in the FARS database, and the "Using the Codification" section in the Front Matter of the GARS database. Take some of the references from the Bisk text material and locate them in the corresponding standards; use at least one reference from Bisk chapters 1 through 17 and at least one from Bisk chapters 18 through 20; note the differences in the abbreviations.

The portion of the reference following the single letter or four digit number is the paragraph number. For instance, I67.103 refers to paragraph .103 of the FASB topic "Interest: Capitalization of Interest Costs." and reads, "The objectives of capitalizing interest are (a) to obtain a measure of acquisition cost that more closely reflects the enterprise's total investment in the asset and (b) to charge a cost that relates to the acquisition of a resource that will benefit future periods against the revenues of the periods benefited. [FAS34, ¶7]." The GARS reference shown as 2450.103 refers to paragraph .103 of the GASB topic "Cash Flows Statements," and reads, "Proprietary funds and governmental activities engaged in business-type activities should present a statement of cash flows for each period for which results of operations are reported. [GASBS 9, ¶6; GASBS 34, ¶91 and ¶138]."

Grading Implications for CPA Candidates

To summarize this review of the AICPA's grading procedure, we can offer the following conclusions that will help you to **satisfy the grader** and maximize your score:

1. Attempt an answer on every question.
2. Respond directly to the requirements of the questions.
3. Use of a well-chosen example is an easy way of expressing an understanding of the subject or supporting a conclusion.
4. Use schedules and formats favored by the AICPA examiners.
5. Answer all requirements.
6. Develop a **Solutions Approach™** to each question type.
7. Essay questions:

   Label your solutions parallel to the requirements.

   Offer reasons for your conclusions.

   Separate grading concepts into individual sentences or paragraphs.

   Do **not** present your answer in outline format.
8. Allocate your examination time based on AICPA point value, if provided.

SECTION FOUR: THE SOLUTIONS APPROACH™

- Solutions Approach™ for Written Communication Questions B-24
- Solutions Approach™ for Objective Questions B-26
- Benefits of the Solutions Approach™ B-28

The **Bisk Education Solutions Approach™** is an efficient, systematic method of organizing and solving questions found on the CPA exam. Remember that all the knowledge in the world is worthless unless you can put it into words. Conversely, a little knowledge can go a long way if you use a proper approach. The **Solutions Approach™** was developed by our Editorial Board in 1971; all subsequently developed stereotypes trace their roots from the original "Approach" that we formulated. Our **Solutions Approach™** and grader orientation skills, when properly developed, can be worth at least 10 to 15 points for most candidates. These 10 to 15 points often make the difference between passing and failing.

We will suggest a number of steps for deriving a solution that will help maximize your grade on the exam. Although you should remember the important steps in our suggested approach, don't be afraid to adapt these steps to your own taste and requirements. When you work the questions at the conclusion of each chapter, make sure you use your variation of the **Solutions Approach™**. It is also important for you to attempt to pattern the organization and format of your written solution to the unofficial answer reprinted after the text of the questions. However, DO NOT CONSULT THE UNOFFICIAL ANSWER UNTIL YOU FINISH THE QUESTION. The worst thing you can do is look at questions and then turn to the answer without working the problem. This will build false confidence and provide **no** skills in developing a **Solutions Approach™**. Therefore, in order to derive the maximum number of points from an essay solution, you should **first** apply the **Solutions Approach™** to reading and answering the question, and **secondly,** write an essay answer using an organization and format identical to that which would be used by the AICPA in writing the unofficial answer to that essay question.

Solutions Approach™ for Written Communication Questions

Our **six steps** are as follows:

1. Scan the text of the question for an overview of the subject area and content of the question.
2. Study the question requirements slowly and thoroughly. Note portions of the requirements on your scratch paper as needed.
3. Visualize the unofficial answer format based on the requirements of the question.
4. Carefully study the text of the question. Note important data on your scratch paper.
5. Outline the solution in key words and phrases. Be sure to respond to the requirements, telling the grader only what s/he needs to know. Explain the reasons for your conclusions.
6. Write the solution in the proper format based upon your key word outline. Write concise, complete sentences. Do not forget to proofread and edit your solution.

Written Communication Example

To illustrate the Solutions Approach™ for written communication questions, we consider a question from a past examination. Key words in the solution are bold.

Sample Question

Bristol Company purchased land as a site for construction of a factory. Outside contractors were engaged to:

- Construct the factory.
- Grade and pave a parking lot adjacent to the factory for the exclusive use of the factory workers.

Operations at the new location began during the year and normal factory maintenance costs were incurred after production began.

Required:

a. Distinguish between capital and revenue expenditures.

b. Indicate how expenditures for each of the following should be accounted for and reported by Bristol at the time incurred and in subsequent accounting periods.

1. Purchase of land.
2. Construction of factory.
3. Grading and paving parking lot.
4. Payment of normal factory maintenance costs.

Do not discuss capitalization of interest during construction in your response.

Applying the Solutions Approach™

Let's look at the steps you go through to arrive at your solution:

In **Step 1,** you scan the question. Do not read thoroughly, simply get an overview of the subject area and content of the question. You notice the question addresses the acquisition costs of plant assets.

In **Step 2,** you study the question requirements thoroughly. **Part a** addresses capital and revenue expenditures in general, while **Part b** refers to individual expenditures. Note key phrases and words on your scratch paper.

In **Step 3,** you visualize the format of your solution. The solution will be in paragraph form. **Part a** will define capital and revenue expenditures and discuss the differences between the two. **Part b** will discuss each individual expenditure and describe how each should be accounted for.

In **Step 4,** you carefully study the text of the question, given the requirements you want to satisfy, i.e., read the question carefully, noting the individual expenditures. You should note important information on your scratch paper.

In **Step 5,** you outline your answer in keyword form. This will include a description of each type of expenditure and an explanation of their differences in **Part a** along with individual analysis of each requirement in **Part b** plus additional key concepts you want to include in your final answer.

Outline Answer

a. Capital Expenditures—future periods
Revenue Expenditures—current period only

b. 1. Land
Capitalize
Noncurrent Asset
Original Cost
Non-depreciable

2. Factory Construction
Capitalize
Depreciate over expected life
Apply cost to inventory through Factory Overhead
Classification
Factory—noncurrent
Inventory—current
Cost of Sales—expense

3. Parking Lot
Capitalize
Depreciate over the shorter of factory life or parking lot life
Apply depreciation to inventory via factory overhead
Classification

Parking Lot improvements—Noncurrent
Inventory—current
Cost of Sales—expense

4. Factory Maintenance—Revenue Type expenditure
"Factory Cost" to be added to inventory cost via overhead
Inventory—current asset
Cost of Sales—expense

In **Step 6,** you write your solution in a format similar to the unofficial answer. Notice how clear and concise the AICPA unofficial answers are. There is no doubt as to their decision or the reasoning supporting the decision. Notice also how they answer each requirement separately and in the same order as in the question. Be sure to proofread and edit your solution.

Sample Unofficial Answer

a. Capital expenditures **benefit future periods.** Revenue expenditures **benefit the current period only.**

b. 1. The **purchase price** of the **land** should be **capitalized.** The land should be shown as a **noncurrent asset** on the balance sheet at its **original cost** and is **not subject to depreciation.**

2. The cost of constructing the factory should be **capitalized** and **depreciated** over the expected life of the factory. The **depreciation should be added to cost of inventory, via factory overhead,** as goods are produced, and **expensed as cost of sales as goods are sold.** The factory expenditures, net of accumulated depreciation, should be shown as a **noncurrent asset** on the balance sheet. Inventory should be reported as a **current asset** on the balance sheet, and cost of sales should be reported as an **expense** on the income statement.

3. The cost of grading and paving the parking lot should be **capitalized** and **depreciated** over the expected life of either the factory or parking lot, **whichever is shorter.** The depreciation should be **added to cost of inventory,** via factory overhead, as goods are produced, and **expensed as cost of sales as goods are sold.** The land improvement expenditures, net of accumulated depreciation, should be shown as a **noncurrent asset** on the balance sheet. Inventory should be reported as a **current asset** on the balance sheet, and cost of sales should be reported as an **expense** on the income statement.

4. The cost of maintaining the factory once production has begun is a **"revenue type" expenditure.** However, since it is a factory cost, it should be **added to cost of inventory, via factory overhead,** as goods are produced, and **expensed as cost of sales as goods are sold.** Inventory should be reported as a **current asset** on the balance sheet, and cost of sales should be reported as an **expense** on the income statement.

Solutions Approach™ for Objective Questions

The **Solutions Approach™** is also adaptable to objective questions. We recommend the following framework:

1. Read the "Instructions to Candidates" section on your particular exam to determine if the AICPA's standard is the same. Generally, your objective portion will be determined by the number of correct answers with no penalty for incorrect answers.

2. Read the question carefully, noting exactly what the question is asking. Negative requirements are easily missed. Note key words and when the requirement is an exception (e.g., "except for…," or "which of the following does **not**…"). Perform any intermediate calculations necessary to the determination of the correct answer.

3. Anticipate the answer by covering the possible answers and seeing if you **know** the correct answer.

4. Read the answers given.

5. Select the best alternative. Very often, one or two possible answers will be clearly incorrect. Of the other alternatives, be sure to select the alternative that **best answers the question asked.**

6. After completing all of the individual questions in a testlet, **go back** and double check that you have answered each question.

7. Answer the questions in order. This is a proven, systematic approach to objective test taking. You generally will be limited to a maximum of 2 to 2½ minutes per multiple choice question. Under no circumstances should you allow yourself to fall behind schedule. If a question is difficult, or long, be sure you remain cognizant of the time you are using. If after a minute or so you feel that it is too costly to continue on with a particular question, select the letter answer you tentatively feel is the best answer and go on to the next question. Return to these questions at a later time and attempt to finally answer them when you have time for more consideration. If you cannot find a better answer when you return to the question, use your preliminary answer because your first impressions are often correct. However, as you read other question(s), if something about these subsequent questions or answers jogs your memory, return to the previous tentatively answered question(s) and make a note of the idea for later consideration (time permitting).

A simulation is a particularly challenging format for many candidates. A simulation is a group of objective questions based on one hypothetical situation. In this case, you should skim all the related questions (but not the answer possibilities) before you begin answering, since an overall view of the problem will guide you in the work you do.

Note also that many incorrect answer choices are based on the erroneous application of one or more items in the text of the question. Thus, it is extremely important to **anticipate** the answer before you read the alternatives. Otherwise, you may be easily persuaded by an answer choice that is formulated through the incorrect use of the given data.

Let's consider a multiple choice question adapted from a past examination.

Sample Objective Question

Jel Co., a consignee, paid the freight costs for goods shipped from Dale Co., a consignor. These freight costs are to be deducted from Jel's payment to Dale when the consignment goods are sold. Until Jel sells the goods, the freight costs should be included in Jel's

a. Cost of goods sold.
b. Freight-out costs.
c. Selling expenses.
d. Accounts receivable.

Applying the Solutions Approach™

Let's look at the steps you should go through to arrive at your objective question solution.

In **Step 1,** you must carefully read the "**Instructions**" that precede your particular objective CPA exam portion.

In **Step 2,** you must read the question and its requirements carefully. Look out for questions that require you to provide those options **not** applicable, **not** true, etc...

In **Step 3,** you must anticipate the correct answer **after** reading the question **but before** reading the possible answers.

In **Step 4,** you must read the answer carefully and select the alternative that best answers the question asked. Ideally, the best alternative will immediately present itself because it roughly or exactly corresponds with the answer you anticipated before looking at the other possible choices.

In **Step 5,** you select the best alternative. If there are two close possibilities, make sure you select the **best** one in light of the **facts** and **requirements** of the question.

In **Step 6,** you must make sure you accurately mark the **correct answer** in the proper sequence. If **anything** seems wrong, stop, go back and double check.

In **Step 7,** you must make sure you answer the questions in order, with due regard to time constraints.

Sample Objective Question Solution

The answer is (d). The consignee will be reimbursed for the freight costs after the sale of the consignment goods by reducing the payment to the consignor. An amount that will be reimbursed in the future represents a receivable. The other answers are incorrect because an amount that will be reimbursed in the future should not be recorded as an expense.

Benefits of the Solutions Approach™

The **Solutions Approach™** may seem cumbersome the first time you attempt it; candidates frequently have a tendency to write as they think. It should be obvious to you that such a haphazard approach will result in a disorganized answer. The Solutions Approach™ will help you write a solution that parallels the question requirements. It will also help you recall information under the pressure of the exam. The technique assists you in directing your thoughts toward the information required for the answer. Without a Solutions Approach™, you are apt to become distracted or confused by details that are irrelevant to the answer. Finally, the Solutions Approach™ is a **faster** way to answer exam questions. You will not waste time on false starts or rewrites. The approach may seem time-consuming at first, but as you become comfortable using it, you will see that it actually saves time and results in a better answer.

We urge you to give the **Solutions Approach™** a good try by using it throughout your CPA review. As you practice, you may adapt or modify it to your own preferences and requirements. The important thing is to develop a system so that you do not approach exam questions with a storehouse of knowledge that you can not express to the graders.

SECTION FIVE: CONTENT SPECIFICATION OUTLINE

The AICPA Board of Examiners has developed a **Content Specification Outline** of each section of the exam to be tested. These outlines list the areas, groups, and topics to be tested and indicate the approximate percentage of the total test score devoted to each area. The content of the examination is based primarily on the results of two national studies of public accounting practice and the evaluation of CPA practitioners and educators.

FINANCIAL ACCOUNTING & REPORTING

I. Concepts and standards for financial statements (17% - 23%)

A. Financial accounting concepts
   1. Process by which standards are set and roles of standard-setting bodies
   2. Conceptual basis for accounting standards.

B. Financial accounting standards for presentation and disclosure in general-purpose financial statements
   1. Consolidated and combined financial statements
   2. Balance sheet
   3. Statement(s) of income, comprehensive income, and changes in equity accounts
   4. Statement of cash flows
   5. Accounting policies and other notes to financial statements

C. Other presentations of financial data (financial statements prepared in conformity with comprehensive bases of accounting other than GAAP

D. Financial statement analysis

II. Typical items: recognition, measurement, valuation, and presentation in financial statements in conformity with GAAP (27% - 33%)

A. Cash, cash equivalents, and marketable securities
B. Receivables
C. Inventories
D. Property, plant, and equipment
E. Investments
F. Intangibles and other assets
G. Payables and accruals
H. Deferred revenues
I. Notes and bonds payable
J. Other liabilities
K. Equity accounts
L. Revenue, cost, and expense accounts

III. Specific types of transactions and events: recognition, measurement, valuation, and presentation in financial statements in conformity with GAAP (27% - 33%)

A. Accounting changes and corrections of errors
B. Business combinations
C. Contingent liabilities and commitments
D. Discontinued operations
E. Earnings per share
F. Employee benefits, including stock options
G. Extraordinary items
H. Financial instruments, including derivatives
I. Foreign currency transactions and translation
J. Income taxes
K. Interest costs
L. Interim financial reporting
M. Leases
N. Non-monetary transactions

O. Related parties
P. Research and development costs
Q. Segment reporting
R. Subsequent events

IV. Accounting and reporting for governmental entities (8% - 12%)

A. Governmental accounting concepts
   1. Measurement focus and basis of accounting
   2. Fund accounting concepts and application
   3. Budgetary process
B. Format and content of governmental financial statements
   1. Government-wide financial statements
   2. Governmental funds financial statements
   3. Conversion from fund to government-wide financial statements
   4. Proprietary fund financial statements
   5. Fiduciary fund financial statements
   6. Notes to financial statements
   7. Required supplementary information, including management's discussion and analysis
   8. Comprehensive annual financial report (CAFR)
C. Financial reporting entity including blended and discrete component units
D. Typical items and specific types of transactions and events: recognition, measurement, valuation and presentation in governmental entity financial statements in conformity with GAAP
   1. Net assets
   2. Capital assets and infrastructure
   3. Transfers
   4. Other financing sources and uses
   5. Fund balance
   6. Non-exchange revenues
   7. Expenditures
   8. Special items
   9. Encumbrances
E. Accounting and financial reporting for governmental not-for-profit organizations

V. Accounting and reporting for nongovernmental not-for-profit organizations (8% - 12%)

A. Objectives, elements and formats of financial statements
   1. Statement of financial position
   2. Statement of activities
   3. Statement of cash flows
   4. Statement of functional expenses
B. Typical items and specific types of transactions and events: recognition, measurement, valuation and presentation in the financial statements of not-for-profit organizations in conformity with GAAP
   1. Revenues and contributions
   2. Restrictions on resources
   3. Expenses, including depreciation and functional expenses
   4. Investments

SECTION SIX: AUTHORITATIVE PRONOUNCEMENTS CROSS-REFERENCES

FINANCIAL ACCOUNTING & REPORTING

Pronouncement	Bisk Education Chapter Number(s)	Accounting Research Bulletins
ARB 43	1, 2, 3, 7, 10, 11	Restatement and Revision of Accounting Research Bulletins
ARB 45	12	Long-Term Construction-Type Contracts
ARB 51	17	Consolidated Financial Statements

Pronouncement	Bisk Education Chapter Number(s)	Accounting Principles Board Opinions
APB 2 & 4	13	Accounting for the Investment Credit
APB 6	4, 10	Status of Accounting Research Bulletins
APB 9	1, 11	Reporting the Results of Operations
APB 10	1, 10, 11, 12	Omnibus Opinion—1966
APB 12	10	Omnibus Opinion—1967
APB 14	6	Convertible Debt and Debt Issued With Stock Purchase Warrants
APB 18	2, 13, 17	The Equity Method of Accounting for Investments in Common Stock
APB 21	2, 6, 7	Interest on Receivables and Payables
APB 22	10, 11, 12	Disclosure of Accounting Policies
APB 23	13, 16	Accounting for Income Taxes—Special Areas
APB 25	10	Accounting for Stock Issued to Employees
APB 26	6, 7	Early Extinguishment of Debt
APB 28	11, 13	Interim Financial Reporting
APB 29	4	Accounting for Nonmonetary Transactions
APB 30	1, 11	Reporting the Results of Operations—Reporting the Effects of Disposal of a Segment of a Business, and Extraordinary, Unusual, and Infrequently Occurring Events and Transactions

Pronouncement	Bisk Education Chapter Number(s)	Statements of Financial Accounting Standards
SFAS 2	5	Accounting for Research & Development Costs
SFAS 5	7, 12, 17	Accounting for Contingencies
SFAS 6	7	Classification of Short-Term Obligations Expected to Be Refinanced
SFAS 7	11	Accounting & Reporting by Development Stage Enterprises
SFAS 13	8	Accounting for Leases
SFAS 15	7	Accounting by Debtors and Creditors for Troubled Debt Restructurings
SFAS 16	11	Prior Period Adjustments
SFAS 22	8	Changes in the Provisions of Lease Agreements Resulting From Refundings of Tax-Exempt Debt
SFAS 23	8	Inception of the Lease
SFAS 27	8	Classification of Renewals or Extensions of Existing Sales-Type or Direct Financing Leases
SFAS 28	8	Accounting for Sales With Leasebacks
SFAS 29	7	Determining Contingent Rentals
SFAS 34	4	Capitalization of Interest Cost
SFAS 37	13	Balance Sheet Classification of Deferred Income Taxes
SFAS 42	4	Determining Materiality for Capitalization of Interest Cost
SFAS 43	7	Accounting for Compensated Absences
SFAS 45	12	Accounting for Franchise Fee Revenue
SFAS 47	6, 7	Disclosure of Long-Term Obligations

Pronouncement	Bisk Education Chapter Number(s)	Statements of Financial Accounting Standards
SFAS 48	12	Revenue Recognition When Right of Return Exists
SFAS 49	7	Accounting for Product Financing Arrangements
SFAS 52	16	Foreign Currency Translation
SFAS 57	11	Related Party Disclosures
SFAS 58	4	Capitalization of Interest Cost in Financial Statements That Include Investments Accounted for by the Equity Method
SFAS 62	4	Capitalization of Interest Cost in Situations Involving Certain Tax-Exempt Borrowings and Certain Gifts and Grants
SFAS 68	5	Research and Development Arrangements
SFAS 78	6, 7	Classification of Obligations That Are Callable by the Creditor
SFAS 84	6	Induced Conversions of Convertible Debt
SFAS 86	5	Accounting for the Costs of Computer Software to Be Sold, Leased, or Otherwise Marketed
SFAS 87	9	Employers' Accounting for Pensions
SFAS 88	7, 9	Employers' Accounting for Settlements and Curtailments of Defined Benefit Pension Plans and for Termination Benefits
SFAS 89	1, 12	Financial Reporting and Changing Prices
SFAS 91	8	Accounting for Nonrefundable Fees and Costs Associated with Originating or Acquiring Loans and Initial Direct Costs of Leases
SFAS 93	20	Recognition of Depreciation by Not-for-profit Organizations
SFAS 94	2, 17	Consolidation of All Majority-Owned Subsidiaries
SFAS 95	1, 14, 20	Statement of Cash Flows
SFAS 98	8	Accounting for Leases—Sale-Leaseback Transactions Involving Real Estate; Sales-Type Leases of Real Estate; Definition of the Lease Term; Initial Direct Costs of Direct Financing Leases
SFAS 102	14	Statement of Cash Flows—Exemption of Certain Enterprises and Classification Cash Flows From Certain Securities Acquired for Resale
SFAS 104	14	Statement of Cash Flows—Net Reporting of Certain Cash Receipts and Cash Payments and Classification of Cash Flows From Hedging Transactions
SFAS 106	9	Employers' Accounting for Postretirement Benefits Other Than Pensions
SFAS 107	2	Disclosures About Fair Value of Financial Statements
SFAS 109	13	Accounting for Income Taxes
SFAS 110	9	Reporting by Defined Benefit Pension Plans of Investment Contracts
SFAS 112	7	Employers' Accounting for Postemployment Benefits
SFAS 114	2	Accounting by Creditors for Impairment of a Loan
SFAS 115	2, 17	Accounting for Certain Investments in Debt and Equity Securities
SFAS 116	4, 20	Accounting for Contributions Received and Contributions Made
SFAS 117	20	Financial Statements for Not-for-Profit Entities
SFAS 118	2	Accounting by Creditors for Impairment of a Loan—Income Recognition and Disclosures
SFAS 123R	10	Accounting for Stock-Based Compensation
SFAS 124	20	Accounting for Certain Investments Held by Not-for-Profit Organizations
SFAS 126	2	Exemption from Certain Required Disclosures about Financial Instruments for Certain Nonpublic Entities
SFAS 128	15	Earnings Per Share
SFAS 129	10	Disclosure of Information about Capital Structure

Pronouncement	Bisk Education Chapter Number(s)	Statements of Financial Accounting Standards
SFAS 130	1, 2, 9, 11, 16	Reporting Comprehensive Income
SFAS 131	11	Disclosures about Segments of an Enterprise and Related Information
SFAS 132	9	Employers' Disclosures about Pensions and Other Postretirement Benefits
SFAS 133	2, 7, 11, 16	Accounting for Derivative Instruments and Hedging Activities
SFAS 136	20	Transfers of Assets to a Not-for-profit Organization or Charitable Trust That Raises or Holds Contributions for Others
SFAS 137	2, 7, 11, 16	Deferral of Effective Date of FASB 133
SFAS 138	2	Accounting for Certain Derivative Instruments and Certain Hedging Activities (amends SFAS 133)
SFAS 140	2, 7	Accounting for Transfers and Servicing of Financial Assets and Extinguishments of Liabilities
SFAS 141	2, 17	Business Combinations
SFAS 142	5, 17	Goodwill and Other Intangible Assets
SFAS 143	7	Accounting for Asset Retirement Obligations
SFAS 144	4, 11	Accounting for Impairment or Disposal of Long-Lived Assets
SFAS 145	6, 7, 8, 11	Rescission of FASB Statements No. 4, 44, and 64, Amendment of FASB Statement No. 13, and Technical Corrections
SFAS 146	8, 9, 11	Accounting for Costs Associated With Exit or Disposal Activities
SFAS 147	17	Acquisitions of Certain Financial Institutions—an Amendment of FASB Statements No. 72 and 144 and FASB Interpretation No. 9
SFAS 148	10	Accounting for Stock-Based-Compensation, Amendment of FASB Statement No. 123
SFAS 149	14	Amendment of Statement 133 on Derivative Instruments and Hedging Activities
SFAS 150	10	Accounting for Certain Financial Instruments with Characteristics of both Liabilities and Equity
SFAS 151	3	Inventory Costs—an amendment of ARB No. 43, Chapter 4
SFAS 153	4	Exchanges of Nonmonetary Assets—an amendment of APB Opinion No. 29
SFAS 154	11	Accounting Changes and Error Corrections—a replacement of APB Opinion No. 20 and FASB Statement No. 3
SFAS 155	2	Accounting for Certain Hybrid Financial Instruments—an amendment of FASB Statements No. 133 and 146
SFAS 156	2	Accounting for Servicing of Financial Assets—an amendment of FASB Statement No. 140
SFAS 157	1	Fair Value Measurements
SFAS 158	9	Employers' Accounting for Defined Benefit Pension and Other Retirement Plans—an amendment of FASB Statements No. 87, 88, 106, and 132(R)

Pronouncement	Bisk Education Chapter Number(s)	Statements of Financial Accounting Concepts
SFAC 1	1	Objectives of Financial Reporting by Business Enterprises
SFAC 2	1	Qualitative Characteristics of Accounting Information
SFAC 5	1	Recognition and Measurement in Financial Statements of Business Enterprises
SFAC 6	1, 10, 11	Elements of Financial Statements
SFAC 7	1	Using Cash Flow Information and Present Value in Accounting Measurements

Interpretation No.	Pronouncement	FASB Interpretations
No. 1	APB 20	Accounting Changes Related to the Cost of Inventory
No. 4	SFAS 2	Applicability of SFAS 2 to Business Combinations Accounted for by the Purchase Method
No. 6	SFAS 2	Applicability of SFAS 2 to Computer Software
No. 7	SFAS 7	Applying SFAS 7 in Financial Statements of Established Operating Enterprises
No. 8	SFAS 6	Classification of a Short-Term Obligation Repaid Prior to Being Replaced by a Long-Term Security
No. 14	SFAS 5	Reasonable Estimation of the Amount of Loss
No. 18	SFAS 28	Accounting for Income Taxes in Interim Periods
No. 19	SFAS 13	Lessee Guarantee of the Residual Value of Leased Property
No. 20	APB 20	Reporting Accounting Changes under AICPA Statements of Position
No. 21	SFAS 13	Accounting for Leases in a Business Combination
No. 24	SFAS 13	Leases Involving Only Part of a Building
No. 26	SFAS 13	Accounting for Purchase of a Leased Asset by the Lessee During the Term of the Lease
No. 27	SFAS 13 & APB 30	Accounting for a Loss on a Sublease
No. 28	APB 25	Accounting for Stock Appreciation Rights and Other Variable Stock Option or Award Plans
No. 30	APB 29	Accounting for Involuntary Conversions of Nonmonetary Assets to Monetary Assets
No. 35	APB 18	Criteria for Applying the Equity Method of Accounting for Investments in Common Stock
No. 37	SFAS 52	Accounting for Translation Adjustments Upon Sale of Part of an Investment in a Foreign Entity
No. 38	APB 25	Determining the Measurement Date for Stock Option, Purchase, and Award Plans Involving Junior Stock
No. 39	APB 10 & SFAS 105	Offsetting of Amounts Related to Certain Contracts
No. 41	APB 10	Offsetting of Amounts Related to Certain Repurchase and Reverse Repurchase Agreements
No. 44	APB 25	Accounting for Certain Transactions Involving Stock Compensation
No. 45	SFAS 5, 57 & 107	Guarantor's Accounting and Disclosure Requirements for Guarantees, Including Guarantees of Indebtedness of Others

Pronouncement	Bisk Education Chapter Number(s)	Statements of the Governmental Accounting Standards Board
GASB 18	18	Accounting for Municipal Solid Waste Landfill Closure and Postclosure Care Costs
GASB 19	18	Governmental College and University Omnibus Statement
GASB 20	19	Accounting and Financial Reporting For Proprietary Funds and Other Governmental Entities That Use Proprietary Fund Accounting
GASB 21	18	Accounting for Escheat Property
GASB 22	19	Accounting for Taxpayer-Assessed Revenues in Governmental Funds
GASB 23	19	Accounting and Financial Reporting for Refundings of Debt Reported by Proprietary Activities
GASB 24	19	Accounting and Reporting for Certain Grants and Other Financial Assistance
GASB 25	18	Financial Reporting For Defined Benefit Plans and Note Disclosures for Defined Contribution Plans
GASB 26	18	Financial Reporting for Postemployment Healthcare Plans Administered by Defined Benefit Pension Plans

Pronouncement	Bisk Education Chapter Number(s)	Statements of the Governmental Accounting Standards Board
GASB 27	18	Accounting For Pensions by State and Local Employers
GASB 28	18	Accounting and Financial Reporting for Securities Lending Transactions
GASB 29	19	The Use of Not-For-Profit Accounting and Financial Reporting Principles by Governmental Entities
GASB 30	18	Risk Financing Omnibus
GASB 31	18	Accounting and Financial Reporting for Certain Investments and for External Investment Pools
GASB 32	18	Accounting and Financial Reporting for Internal Revenue Code Section 457 Deferred Compensation Plans
GASB 33	18	Nonexchange Transactions
GASB 34	18, 19	Basic Financial Statements—and Management's Discussion & Analysis—-for State and Local Governments
GASB 35	18, 19	Basic Financial Statements—and Management's Discussion & Analysis—-for Public Colleges and Universities
GASB 36	18	Recipient Reporting for Certain Shared Nonexchange Revenues
GASB 37	18, 19	Basic Financial Statements—and Management's Discussion & Analysis—for State and Local Governments: Omnibus—an Amendment of GASB Statements No. 21 and No. 34
GASB 38	18	Certain Financial Statement Note Disclosures
GASB 39	18	Determining Whether Certain Organizations Are Component Units—an amendment of GASB Statement No. 14
GASB 40	18	Deposit and Investment Risk Disclosures—an Amendment of GASB Statement No. 3
GASB 41	18	Budgetary Comparison Schedules—Perspective Differences—an Amendment of GASB Statement No. 34
GASB 42	18	Accounting and Financial Reporting for Impairmental Capital Assets and for Insurance Recoveries
GASB 43	18	Financial Reporting for Postemployment Benefit Plans Other Than Pension Plans
GASB 44	18	Economic Condition Reporting: The Statistical Section (an amendment of NCGA Statement 1)
GASB 45	18	Accounting and Financial Reporting by Employers for Postemployment Benefits Other Than Pensions
GASB 46	18	Net Assets Restricted by Enabling Legislation—an amendment of GASB Statement No. 34
GASB 47	18	Accounting for Termination Benefits

Pronouncement	Bisk Education Chapter Number(s)	Concept Statements of the Governmental Accounting Standards Board
1	18	Objectives of Financial Reporting
2	18	Service Efforts and Accomplishments Reporting

From the *Uniform CPA Examination Candidate Bulletin*:

"Accounting and auditing pronouncements are eligible to be tested on the Uniform CPA Examination in the window beginning six months after a pronouncement's *effective* date, unless early application is permitted. When early application is permitted, the new pronouncement is eligible to be tested in the window beginning six months after the *issuance* date. In this case, both the old and new pronouncements may be tested until the old pronouncement is superseded."

FYI: Question Reference Numbers

This page is included due to questions editors have received from some candidates using previous editions; however, it is not essential for your review.

In the lower right-hand corner of a multiple choice question, you may note a question reference. This reference is included primarily so that editors may trace a question to its source and readily track it from one edition to another and from one media to another.

The reference indicates the source of the question and, possibly, a similar question in the software. For instance, a question with reference 11/93, Aud., #4, 4241, was question number 4 from the November 1993 AICPA Auditing & Attestation examination. When the reference has an "R" instead of 5 or 11, the AICPA released the question from a "nondisclosed" exam without specifying the exam month. Questions marked "Editors" are questions that are modeled after AICPA questions, but are not actually from the examiners. The examiners occasionally move topics from one exam section to another. You may see a question from a former AUD exam, for instance, in the REG or BEC volume. The following abbreviations indicate former exam section titles.

BLPR	Business Law & Professional Responsibilities
AR	Accounting & Reporting
AUD	Auditing & Attestation
FAR	Financial Accounting & Reporting
BL	Business Law
PI	Accounting Practice, Part I
PII	Accounting Practice, Part II
T	Accounting Theory

At first glance, candidates may assume that very early questions are irrelevant for preparation for upcoming exams. Provided that they are updated appropriately, many early questions are excellent choices for review questions. When the exam was fully disclosed, editors noted that it was **more** likely that questions from early exams would reappear than questions from relatively recent exams. For instance, on a 1994 exam, it was more likely that an updated question from a 1988 exam would appear than an updated question from a 1993 exam. Second-guessing what questions the examiners will ask typically is more difficult and less reliable than merely learning the content eligible to be tested on the exam.

The four-digit number in these references often corresponds to a four-digit ID number in our software and online courses. Sometimes questions are removed from the software but not the book (and vice versa), so a question in the book is not necessarily in the software. Also, questions may vary slightly between the book and software. The four digit number has no significance for a candidate who is not using our software. If you need help finding a question from the book in the software using this four-digit ID number, please contact our technical support staff at support@cpaexam.com or 1-800-742-1309 and ask them to explain using the "jump" feature for questions.

More helpful exam information is included in the **Practical Advice** appendix in this volume.

APPENDIX C
WRITING SKILLS

CONTENTS

- Introduction C-1
- Writing Skills Samples C-2
- Paragraphs C-2
- Writing an Answer to an Exam Question C-5
- Diagnostic Quiz C-8
- Sentence Structure C-10
- Numbers C-15
- Capitalization C-16
- Punctuation C-16
- Spelling C-19
- Grammar C-22

INTRODUCTION

Before skipping this appendix, review at least the following writing samples and the "Writing an Answer to an Exam Question" starting on page C-5. Be sure to take the Diagnostic Quiz on C-8.

In place of essays, an assessment of written communication skills has been incorporated into the simulation portion of the examination. These skills are tested by written communications which require the candidate to write memoranda, letters to clients, or other communications an entry-level CPA would write on the job. Simulations are presented in the Financial Accounting & Reporting, Auditing & Attestation, and Regulation sections. The Business Environment & Concepts exam section eventually will have simulations, and therefore, written communication questions.

For this simulation element, candidates must read a situation description and then write an appropriate document relating to the situation. The instructions will state in what form the document should be presented and its focus. The candidate's response should provide the correct information in writing that is clear, complete, and professional. Only those writing samples that are in your own words and responsive to the topic will be graded. If the response is off-topic, or offers advice that is clearly illegal, no credit will be given for the response.

Constructed responses will be scored holistically. Scores will be based on three general writing criteria: organization, development, and expression.

1. **Organization:** The document's structure, ordering of ideas, and linking of one idea to another:

   Overview/thesis statement
   Unified paragraphs (topic and supporting sentences)
   Transitions and connectives

2. **Development:** The document's supporting evidence/information to clarify thoughts:

   Details
   Definitions
   Examples
   Rephrasing

3. **Expression:** The document's use of conventional standards of business English:

   Grammar (sentence construction, subject/verb agreement, pronouns, modifiers)
   Punctuation (final, comma)
   Word usage (incorrect, imprecise language)
   Capitalization
   Spelling

WRITING SKILLS SAMPLES

The following problems taken from past exams are answered in various ways to illustrate good, fair, and poor writing skills.

Essex Company has a compensation plan for future vacations for its employees. What conditions must be met for Essex to accrue compensation for future vacations? FAR Problem—From Chapter 7—Liabilities

Good: Essex must accrue compensation for future vacations if all of the following criteria are met. Essex's obligation relating to employees' rights to receive compensation for future vacations is attributable to employees' services already rendered. The obligation relates to rights that vest or accumulate. Payment of the vacation benefits is probable. The amount can be reasonably estimated.

Explanation: This essay is coherent, concise, and well organized. The first sentence uses the wording of the question to introduce the elements of the answer. Each point is then made clearly and concisely. There are no unnecessary words or elements. The language and vocabulary are appropriate, and there are no mistakes in grammar or spelling.

Fair: In order for Essex to accrue compensation for future vacations, they must attribute their obligation to employees services already rendered, recognize that the obligation relates to vested and accumulated rights, and that payment is probable and the amount can be reasonably estimated.

Explanation: This passage is also coherent and concise; however, it lacks the clarity and detail of the previous answer. The language is appropriate, but the grammatical construction is somewhat weak.

Poor: It is based on accrual. The employees must have vested or accumulated rights. They must be able to estimate amounts of compensation and their payment. Vested rights means that the employer must pay the employees even if he is fired or quits.

Explanation: This answer is so poorly worded and disorganized as to be virtually incoherent. There are also some grammar mistakes. The final sentence is additional information but not necessary to answer the question.

PARAGRAPHS

The kind of writing you do for the CPA exam is called **expository writing** (writing in which something is explained in straightforward terms). Expository writing uses the basic techniques we will be discussing here. Other kinds of writing (i.e., narration, description, argument, and persuasion) will sometimes require different techniques.

Consider a paragraph as a division of an essay that consists of one or more sentences, deals with one point, and begins on a new, indented line. Paragraphs provide a way to write about a subject one point or one thought at a time.

Usually, a paragraph begins with a **topic sentence.** The topic sentence communicates the main idea of the paragraph, and the remainder of the paragraph explains or illuminates that central idea. The paragraph sometimes finishes with a restatement of the topic sentence. This strategy is easily read by the exam graders.

Often the topic sentence of the first paragraph is the central idea of the entire composition. Each succeeding paragraph then breaks down this idea into subtopics with each of the new topic sentences being the central thought of that subtopic.

Let's take a look at a simple paragraph to see how it's put together.

> The deductibility of home mortgage interest has been under recent review by Congress as a way to raise revenue. There have been two major reasons for this scrutiny. First, now that consumer interest is nondeductible and investment interest is limited to net investment income, taxpayers have been motivated to rearrange their finances to maximize their tax deductions. Second, most voters do not own

homes costing more than $500,000 and, therefore, putting a cap on mortgage loans does not affect the mass of voters. Given the pressure to raise revenue, two major changes have occurred in this area.

The first sentence of the example is the **topic sentence.** The second sentence introduces the supporting examples which appear in the next two sentences beginning with *first* and *second.* The final sentence of the paragraph acts as a preview to the contents of the next paragraph.

Now, let's examine the makeup of a single paragraph answer to an essay question from a previous CPA Exam.

> Question: Dunhill fraudulently obtained a negotiable promissory note from Beeler by misrepresentation of a material fact. Dunhill subsequently negotiated the note to Gordon, a holder in due course. Pine, a business associate of Dunhill, was aware of the fraud perpetrated by Dunhill. Pine purchased the note for value from Gordon. Upon presentment, Beeler has defaulted on the note.
>
> Required: Answer the following, setting forth reasons for any conclusions stated.
>
> 1. What are the rights of Pine against Beeler?
> 2. What are the rights of Pine against Dunhill?

Examples of possible answers:

> 1. The rights of Pine against Beeler arise from Pine's having acquired the note from Gordon, who was a holder in due course. Pine himself is not a holder in due course because he had knowledge of a defense against the note. The rule wherein a transferee, not a holder in due course, acquires the rights of one by taking from a holder in due course is known as the "shelter rule." Through these rights, Pine is entitled to recover the proceeds of the note from Beeler. The defense of fraud in the inducement is a personal defense and not valid against a holder in due course.

The first sentence of the paragraph is the topic sentence in which the basic answer to the question is given. The third and fourth sentence explains the rule governing Pine's rights. (The *shelter rule* would be considered a *key phrase* in this answer.) The final sentence of the paragraph is not really necessary to answer the question but was added as an explanation of what some might mistakenly believe to be the key to the answer.

> 2. As one with the rights of a holder in due course, Pine is entitled to proceed against any person whose signature appears on the note, provided he gives notice of dishonor. When Dunhill negotiated the note to Gordon, Dunhill's signature on the note made him secondarily liable. As a result, if Pine brings suit against Dunhill, Pine will prevail because of Dunhill's secondary liability.

The first sentence of this paragraph restates the fact that Pine has the rights of a holder in due course and what these rights mean. The second sentence explains what happened when Dunhill negotiated the note, and the third sentence states the probable outcome of these results.

Note that in both answers 1. and 2., the sentences hang together in a logical fashion and lead the reader easily from one thought to the next. This is called coherence, a primary factor in considerations of conciseness and clarity.

Transitions

To demonstrate how to use **transitions** in a paragraph to carry the reader easily from one thought or example to another, let's consider a slightly longer and more detailed paragraph. The transitions are indicated in italics.

> A concerted effort to reduce book income in response to AMT could have a significant impact on corporations. *For example,* the auditor-client relationship may change. *Currently,* it isn't unusual for corporate management to argue for higher rather than lower book earnings, *while* the auditor would argue for conservative reported numbers. Such a corporate reporting posture may change as a consequence of the BURP adjustment. *Furthermore,* stock market analysts often rely on a price/earnings ratio. Lower earnings for essentially the same level of activity may have a significant effect on security prices.

The first sentence of the paragraph is the topic sentence. The next sentence, beginning with the transition *for example,* introduces the example with a broad statement. The following sentence, beginning with *currently,* gives a specific example to support the basic premise. The sentence beginning *furthermore* leads us into a final example. Without these transitions, the paragraph would be choppy and lack coherence.

What follows is a list of some transitions divided by usage. We suggest you commit some of these to memory so that you will never be at a loss as to how to tie your ideas together.

Transitional Words & Phrases

One idea plus one idea:

again	equally important	in addition	likewise	similarly
also	finally	in the same fashion	moreover	third
and	first	in the same respect	next	thirdly
and then	further	last	second	too
besides	furthermore	lastly	secondly	

To show time or place:

after a time	at that time	immediately	presently	thereafter
after a while	at the same time	in due time	second	thereupon
afterwards	before	in the meantime	shortly	to the left
as long as	earlier	lately	since	until
as soon as	eventually	later	soon	when
at last	finally	meanwhile	temporarily	while
at length	first	next	then	
	further	of late		

To contrast or qualify:

after all	at the same time	however	nevertheless	on the other hand
although true	but	in any case	nonetheless	otherwise
and yet	despite this fact	in contrast	notwithstanding	still
anyway	for all that	in spite of	on the contrary	yet

To introduce an illustration

for example	in particular	incidentally	specifically	to illustrate
for instance	in other words	indeed	that is	
in fact	in summary	namely	thus	

To indicate concession

after all	I admit
although this may be	naturally
at the same time	of course
even though	

To indicate comparison:

in a likewise manner
likewise
similarly

WRITING AN ANSWER TO AN EXAM QUESTION

Now that we have examined the makeup of an answer to an exam question, let's take another essay question from a past CPA Exam and see how to go about writing a clear, comprehensive answer, step by step, sentence by sentence. A question similar to the one that follows would very likely be one the examiners would choose to grade writing skills.

Question:

Bar Manufacturing and Cole Enterprises were arch rivals in the high technology industry, and both were feverishly working on a new product that would give the first to develop it a significant competitive advantage. Bar engaged Abel Consultants on April 1, 20X3, for one year, commencing immediately, at $7,500 a month to aid the company in the development of the new product. The contract was oral and was consummated by a handshake. Cole approached Abel and offered them a $10,000 bonus for signing, $10,000 a month for nine months, and a $40,000 bonus if Cole was the first to successfully market the new product. In this connection, Cole stated that the oral contract Abel made with Bar was unenforceable and that Abel could walk away from it without liability. In addition, Cole made certain misrepresentations regarding the dollar amount of its commitment to the project, the state of its development, and the expertise of its research staff. Abel accepted the offer.

Four months later, Bar successfully introduced the new product. Cole immediately dismissed Abel and has paid nothing beyond the first four $10,000 payments plus the initial bonus. Three lawsuits ensued: Bar sued Cole, Bar sued Abel, and Abel sued Cole.

Required: Answer the following, setting forth reasons for any conclusions stated.

Discuss the various theories on which each of the three lawsuits is based, the defenses that will be asserted, the measure of possible recovery, and the probable outcome of the litigation.

Composing an Answer:

Analyze requirements.

Plan on one paragraph for each lawsuit. Each paragraph will contain four elements: theory, defenses, recovery, and outcome.

Paragraph one:

Step 1: Begin with the first lawsuit mentioned, Bar vs. Cole. Write a topic sentence that will sum up the theory of the suit.

Topic sentence: Bar's lawsuit against Cole will be based upon the intentional tort of wrongful interference with a contractual relationship.

Step 2: Back up this statement with law and facts from the question scenario.

The primary requirement for this cause of action is a valid contractual relationship with which the defendant knowingly interferes. This requirement is met in the case of Cole.

Step 3: State defenses.

The contract is not required to be in writing since it is for exactly one year from the time of its making. It is, therefore, valid even though oral.

Step 4: Introduce subject of recovery (damages).

Cole's knowledge of the contract is obvious.

Step 5: Explain possible problems to recovery.

The principal problem, however, is damages. Since Bar was the first to market the product successfully, it would seem that damages are not present. It is possible there were actual damages incurred by Bar (for example, it hired another consulting firm at an increased price).

Step 6: Discuss possible outcome.

It also might be possible that some courts would permit the recovery of punitive damages since this is an intentional tort.

Paragraph one completed:

Bar's lawsuit against Cole will be based upon the intentional tort of wrongful interference with a contractual relationship. The primary requirement for this cause of action is a valid contractual relationship with which the defendant knowingly interferes. The requirement is met in the case of Cole. The contract is not required to be in writing since it is for exactly one year from the time of its making. It is, therefore, valid even though oral. Cole's knowledge of the contract is obvious. The principal problem, however, is damages. Since Bar was the first to market the product successfully, it would seem that damages are not present. It is possible there were actual damages incurred by Bar (for example, it hired another consulting firm at an increased price). It also might be possible that some courts would permit the recovery of punitive damages since this is an intentional tort.

Paragraph two:

Step 1: Discuss second lawsuit mentioned, Bar vs. Abel. Write a topic sentence that will sum up the theory of the suit.

Topic sentence: Bar's cause of action against Abel would be for breach of contract.

Step 2: State defenses. [Same as for first paragraph; this could be left out.]

The contract is not required to be in writing since it is for exactly one year from the time of its making. It is, therefore, valid even though oral.

Step 3: Introduce subject of recovery (damages).

Once again, [*indicating similarity and tying second paragraph to first*] damages would seem to be a serious problem.

Step 4: Explain possible problems to recovery.

Furthermore, punitive damages would rarely be available in a contract action. Finally, Bar cannot recover the same damages twice.

Step 5: Discuss possible outcome.

Hence, if it proceeds against Cole and recovers damages caused by Abel's breach of contract, it will not be able to recover a second time.

Paragraph two completed:

Bar's cause of action against Abel would be for breach of contract. [The contract is not required to be in writing since it is for exactly one year from the time of its making. It is, therefore, valid even though oral.] Once again, damages would seem to be a serious problem. Furthermore, punitive damages would rarely be available in a contract action. Finally, Bar cannot recover the same damages twice. Hence, if it proceeds against Cole and recovers damages caused by Abel's breach of contract, it will not be able to recover a second time.

Paragraph three:

Step 1: Discuss third lawsuit mentioned, Abel vs. Cole. Write a topic sentence that will sum up the theory of the suit.

Topic sentence: Abel's lawsuit against Cole will be based upon fraud and breach of contract.

Step 2: State defenses.

There were fraudulent statements made by Cole with the requisite intent and that were possibly to Abel's detriment. The breach of contract by Cole is obvious.

Step 3: Back up these statements with law and facts from the question scenario.

However, the contract that Cole induced Abel to enter into and which it subsequently breached was an illegal contract, that is, one calling for the commission of a tort.

Step 4: Explain possible problems to recovery and possible outcome.

Therefore, both parties are likely to be treated as wrongdoers, and Abel will be denied recovery.

Paragraph three completed:

Abel's lawsuit against Cole will be based upon fraud and breach of contract. There were fraudulent statements made by Cole with the requisite intent and that were possibly to Abel's detriment. The breach of contract by Cole is obvious. However, the contract that Cole induced Abel to enter into and which it subsequently breached was an illegal contract, that is, one calling for the commission of a tort. Therefore, both parties are likely to be treated as wrongdoers, and Abel will be denied recovery.

Paragraph Editing:

After you have written your essay, go back over your work to check for the six characteristics that the AICPA will be looking for; coherent organization, conciseness, clarity, use of standard English, responsiveness to the requirements of the question, and appropriateness to the reader.

DIAGNOSTIC QUIZ

The following quiz is designed to test your knowledge of standard English. The correct answers follow the quiz, along with references to the sections that cover that particular area. By identifying the sections that are troublesome for you, you will be able to assess your weaknesses and concentrate on reviewing these areas. If you simply made a lucky guess, you'd better do a review anyway.

Circle the correct choice in the brackets for items 1 through 17.

1. The company can assert any defenses against third party beneficiaries that [they have/it has] against the promisee.

2. Among those securities [which/that] are exempt from registration under the 1933 Act [are/is] a class of stock given in exchange for another class by the issuer to its existing stockholders without the [issuer's/ issuer] paying a commission.

3. This type of promise will not bind the promisor [as/because/since] there is no mutuality of obligation.

4. Under the cost method, treasury stock is presented on the balance sheet as an unallocated reduction of total [stockholders'/stockholders/stockholder's] equity.

5. Jones wished that he [was/were] not bound by the offer he made Smith, while Smith celebrated [his/him] having accepted the offer.

6. [Non-cash/Noncash] investing and financing transactions are not reported in the statement of cash flows because the statement reports only the [affects/effects] of operating, investing, and financing activities that directly [affect/effect] cash flows.

7. Since [its/it's] impossible to predict the future and because prospective financial statements can be [effected/ affected] by numerous factors, the accountant must use [judgment/judgement] to estimate when and how conditions are [likely/liable] to change.

8. A common format of bank reconciliation statements [is/are] to reconcile both book and bank balances to a common amount known as the "true balance."

9. Corporations, clubs, churches, and other entities may be beneficiaries so long as they are sufficiently identifiable to permit a determination of [who/whom] is empowered to enforce the terms of the trust.

10. None of the beneficiaries [was/were] specifically referred to in the will.

11. Either Dr. Kline or Dr. Monroe [have/has] been elected to the board of directors.

12. The letter should be signed by Bill and [me/myself].

13. Any trust [which/that] is created for an illegal purpose is invalid.

14. When the nature of relevant information is such that it cannot appear in the accounts, this [principal/ principle] dictates that such relevant information be included in the accompanying notes to the financial statements. Financial reporting is the [principal/principle] means of communicating financial information to those outside an entity.

15. The inheritance was divided [between/among] several beneficiaries.

16. Termination of an offer ends the offeree's power to [accept/except] it.

17. The consideration given by the participating creditors is [their/there] mutual promises to [accept/except] less than the full amount of [their/there] claims. Because [their/there] must be such mutual promises [between/ among] all the participating creditors, a composition or extension agreement requires the participation of at least two or more creditors.

Follow instructions for items 18 through 20.

18. The duties assigned to the interns were to accompany the seniors on field work assignments and the organization and filing of the work papers.

    Fix this sentence so that it will read more smoothly. ____________________

    ____

    ____

19. Circle the correct spelling of the following pairs of words.

    liaison laison — privilege priviledge — paralleled paraleled

    achieve acheive — occasion occassion — accommodate accomodate

20. Each set of brackets in the following example represents a possible location for punctuation. If you believe a location needs no punctuation, leave it blank; if you think a location needs punctuation, enter a comma, a colon, or a semicolon.

    If the promises supply the consideration [ ] there must be a mutuality of obligation [ ] in other words [ ] both parties must be bound.

ANSWERS TO DIAGNOSTIC QUIZ

Each answer includes a reference to the section that covers what you need to review.

1.	it has	Pronouns—Antecedents, p. C-27.
2.	that; is; issuer's	Subordinating Conjunctions, p. C-30; Verbs—Agreement, p. C-23; Nouns—Gerunds, p. C-26.
3.	because	Subordinating Conjunctions, p. C-30.
4.	stockholders'	Possessive Nouns, p. C-25.
5.	were; his	Verbs, Mood, p. C-22; Nouns—Gerunds, p. C-26.
6.	Noncash; effects; affect	Hyphen, p. C-20; Syntax: Troublesome Words, p. C-13.
7.	it's; affected; judgment, likely	Syntax: Troublesome Words, p. C-13; Spelling: Troublesome Words, p. C-22; Diction: List of Words, p. C-11.
8.	is	Verbs—Agreement, p. C-23.
9.	who	Pronouns, Who/Whom, p. C-26.
10.	were	Verbs—Agreement with Each/None, p. C-24.
11.	has	Verbs—Agreement, p. C-23.
12.	me	Pronouns, that follow prepositions, p. C-27.
13.	that	Subordinating Conjunctions, p. C-30.
14.	principle; principal	Syntax: Troublesome Words, p. C-12.
15.	among	Diction: List of Words, p. C-10.
16.	accept	Syntax: Troublesome Words, C-12

17. their; accept; their; there; among; Syntax: Troublesome Words, p. C-12; Diction: List of Words, p. C-10.

18. Two possible answers: Parallelism: p. C-15.

The duties assigned to the interns were *accompanying* the seniors on field work assignments and *organizing* and filing the work papers.

or

The duties assigned to the interns were to accompany the seniors on field work assignments and *to organize* and *file* the work papers.

19. In every case, the **first choice** is the correct spelling.
Refer to Spelling: Troublesome Words, p. C-21.

20. If the promises supply the consideration [,] there must be a mutuality of obligation [;] in other words [,] both parties must be bound. Refer to Punctuation, p. C-16.

Scoring

Count one point for each item (some numbers contain more than one item) and one point for question number 18 if your sentence came close to the parallelism demonstrated by the answer choices. There are a total of 40 points.

If you scored 37-40, you did very well. A brief review of the items you missed should be sufficient to make you feel fairly confident about your grammar skills.

If you scored 33-36, you did fairly well—better than average—but you should do a thorough review of the items you missed.

If you scored 29-32, your score was average. Since "average" will probably not make it on the CPA exam, you might want to consider a thorough grammar review, in addition to the items you missed.

If you scored below average (28 or less), you **definitely** should make grammar review a high priority when budgeting your exam study time. You should consider using resources beyond those provided here.

SENTENCE STRUCTURE

A sentence is a statement or question, consisting of a subject and a predicate. A subject, at a minimum is a noun, usually accompanied by one or more modifiers (for example, "The Trial Balance"). A predicate consists, at a minimum, of a verb. Cultivate the habit of a quick verification for a subject, predicate, capitalized first word, and ending punctuation in each sentence of an essay. A study of sentence structure is essentially a study of grammar but also moves just beyond grammar to diction, syntax, and parallelism. As we discuss how sentences are structured, there will naturally be some overlapping with grammar.

DICTION

Diction is appropriate word choice. There is no substitute for a diversified vocabulary. If you have a diversified vocabulary or "a way with words," you are already a step ahead. A good general vocabulary, as well as a good accounting vocabulary, is a prerequisite of the CPA exam. Develop your vocabulary as you review for the Exam.

An important aspect of choosing the right words is knowing the audience for whom you are choosing those "perfect words." A perfect word for accountants is not necessarily the perfect word for mechanics or lawyers or English professors. If a CPA exam question asks you to write a specific document for a reader other than another accountant or CPA, you need to be very specific but less technical than you would be otherwise.

Accounting, auditing, and related areas have a certain diction and syntax peculiar unto themselves. Promulgations, for instance, are written very carefully so as to avoid possible misinterpretations or misunderstandings. Of course, you are not expected to write like this—for the CPA exam or in other situations. Find the best word possible to explain clearly and concisely what it is you are trying to say. Often the "right word" is simply just not the "wrong word," so be certain you know the exact meaning of a word before you use it. As an accountant writing for accountants, what is most important is knowing the technical terms and the "key words" and placing them in your sentences properly and effectively. Defining or explaining key words demonstrates to graders that you understand the words you are using and not merely parroting the jargon.

The following is a list of words that frequently either are mistaken for one another or incorrectly assumed to be more or less synonymous.

Among—preposition, refers to more than two
Between—preposition, refers to two; is used for three or more if the items are considered severally and individually

> If only part of the seller's capacity to perform is affected, the seller must allocate deliveries *among* the customers, and he or she must give each one reasonable notice of the quota available to him or her.
> *Between* merchants, the additional terms become part of the contract unless one of the following applies. (This sentence is correct whether there are two merchants or many merchants.)

Amount—noun, an aggregate; total number or quantity
Number—noun, a sum of units; a countable number
Quantity—noun, an indefinite amount or number

> The checks must be charged to the account in the order of lowest *amount* to highest *amount* to minimize the *number* of dishonored checks.
> The contract is not enforceable under this paragraph beyond the *quantity* of goods shown in such writing.

Allude—verb, to state indirectly
Refer—verb, to state clearly and directly

> She *alluded* to the fact that the company's management was unscrupulous.
> She *referred* to his poor management in her report.

Bimonthly—adjective or adverb; every two months
Semimonthly—adjective or adverb; twice a month

> Our company has *bimonthly* meetings.
> We get paid *semimonthly.*

Continual—adjective, that which is repeatedly renewed after each interruption or intermission
Continuous—adjective, that which is uninterrupted in time, space, or sequence

> The *continuous* ramblings of the managing partner caused the other partners to *continually* check the time.

Cost—noun, the amount paid for an item
Price—noun, the amount set for an item
Value—noun, the relative worth, utility, or importance of an item
Worth—noun, value of an item measured by its qualities or by the esteem in which it is held

> The *cost* of that stock is too much.
> The *price* of that stock is $100 a share.
> I place no *value* on that stock.
> That stock's *worth* is overestimated.

Decide—verb, to arrive at a solution
Conclude—verb, to reach a final determination; to exercise judgment

Barbara *decided* to listen to what the accountant was saying; she then *concluded* that what he was saying was true.

Fewer—adjective, not as many; consisting or amounting to a smaller number (used of numbers; comparative of few)
Less—adjective, lower rank, degree, or importance; a more limited amount (used of quantity—for the most part)

My clients require *fewer* consultations than yours do.
My clients are *less* demanding than yours are.

Good—adjective, of a favorable character or tendency; noun, something that is good
Well—adverb, good or proper manner; satisfactorily with respect to conduct or action; adjective, being in satisfactory condition or circumstances

It was *good* [adjective] of you to help me study for the CPA exam.
The decision was for the *good* [noun] of the firm.
He performed that task *well* [adverb].
His work was *well* [adjective] respected by the other accountants.

Imply—verb, to suggest
Infer—verb, to assume; deduce

Her report seems to *imply* that my work was not up to par.
From reading her report, the manager *inferred* that my work was not up to par.

Oral—adjective, by the mouth, spoken; not written
Verbal—adjective, relating to or consisting of words
Vocal—adjective, uttered by the voice, spoken; persistence and volume of speech

Hawkins, Inc. made an *oral* agreement to the contract.
One partner gave his *verbal* consent while the other partner was very *vocal* with his objections.

State—verb, to set forth in detail; completely
Assert—verb, to claim positively, sometimes aggressively or controversially
Affirm—verb, to validate, confirm, state positively

The attorney *stated* the facts of the case.
The plaintiff asserted that his rights had been violated.
The judge *affirmed* the jury's decision.

SYNTAX

Syntax is the order of words in a sentence. Errors in syntax occur in a number of ways; the number one way is through hasty composition. The only way to catch errors in word order is to read each of your sentences carefully to make sure that the words you meant to write or type are the words that actually appear on the page and that those words are in the best possible order. The following list should help you avoid errors in both diction and syntax and gives examples where necessary.

Troublesome Words

Accept—verb, to receive or to agree to willingly
Except—verb, to take out or leave out from a number or a whole; conjunction, on any other condition but that condition

Except for the items we have mentioned, we will *accept* the conditions of the contract.

Advice—noun, information or recommendation
Advise—verb, to recommend, give advice

The *accountant advised* us to take his *advice.*

Affect—verb, to influence or change (**Note:** affect is occasionally used as a noun in technical writing only.)
Effect—noun, result or cause; verb, to cause

The effect [noun] of Ward, Inc.'s decision to cease operations affected many people.
He quickly *effected* [verb] policy changes for office procedures.

All Ready—adjectival phrase, completely prepared
Already—adverb, before now; previously

Although the tax return was *all ready* to be filed, the deadline had *already* passed.

All Right; Alright—adjective or adverb, beyond doubt; very well; satisfactory; agreeable, pleasing. (Although many grammarians insist that **alright** is not a proper form, it is widely accepted.)

Appraise—verb, set a value on
Apprise—verb, inform

Dane Corp. *apprised* him of the equipment's age, so that he could *appraise* it more accurately.

Assure—verb, to give confidence to positively
Ensure—verb, to make sure, certain, or safe
Insure—verb, to obtain or provide insurance on or for; to make certain by taking necessary measures and precautions

The accountant assured his client that he would file his return in a timely manner.
He added the figures more than once to *ensure* their accuracy.
She was advised to *insure* her diamond property.

Decedent—noun, a deceased person
Descendant—noun, proceeding from an ancestor or source

The decedent left her vast fortune to her *descendants*.

Eminent—adjective, to stand out; important
Imminent—adjective, impending

Although he was an *eminent* businessman, foreclosure on his house was *imminent.*

Its—possessive
It's—contraction, **it is**

The company held *its* board of directors meeting on Saturday. *It's* the second meeting this month.

Lay—verb, to place or set
Lie—verb, to recline

He *lies* down to rest.
He *lays* down the book.

Percent—used with numbers only
Percentage—used with words or phrases

Each employee received 2 *percent* of the profits.
They all agreed this was a small *percentage.*

Precedence—noun, the fact of preceding in time, priority of importance
Precedent—noun, established authority; adjective, prior in time, order, or significance

The board of directors meeting took *precedence* over his going away.
The president set a *precedent* when making that decision.

Principal—noun, a capital sum placed at interest; a leading figure; the corpus of an estate; adjective, first, most important
Principle—noun, a basic truth or rule

Paying interest on the loan's *principal* [noun] was explained to the company's *principals* [noun].
The principal [adjective] part of…
She refused to compromise her *principles.*

Than—conjunction, function word to indicate difference in kind, manner, or identity; preposition, in comparison with (indicates comparison)
Then—adverb, at that time; soon after that (indicates time)

BFE Corp. has more shareholders *than* Hills Corp.
First, we must write the report, and *then* we will meet with the clients.

Their—adjective, of or relating to them or themselves
There—adverb, in or at that place

There were fifty shareholders at the meeting to cast *their* votes.

Modifier Placement

Pay close attention to where modifiers are placed, especially adverbs such as **only** and **even.** In speech, inflection aids meaning but, in writing, placing modifiers improperly can be confusing and often changes the meaning. The modifier should usually be placed before the word(s) it modifies.

She *almost* finished the whole report.
She finished *almost* the whole report.

Only she finished the report.
She *only* finished the report.
She finished *only* the report.

Phrases also must be placed properly, usually, but not always, following the word or phrase they modify. Often, **reading the sentence aloud** will help you decide where the modifier belongs.

Fleming introduced a client to John with a counter-offer. (*With a counter-offer* modifies *client,* not *John,* and should be placed after *client.)*
The accountant recommended a bankruptcy petition to the client under Chapter 7. (*Under Chapter 7* modifies *bankruptcy petition,* not *the client,* and should be placed after *bankruptcy petition.)*

Split Infinitives

Infinitives are the root verb form (e.g., to be, to consider, to walk). Generally speaking, infinitives should not be split except when to do so makes the meaning clearer.

Awkward:	Management's responsibility is to clearly represent its financial position.
Better:	Management's responsibility is to represent its financial position clearly.
Exception:	Management's responsibility in the future is to better represent its financial position.

Sentence Fragments

To avoid sentence fragments, read over your work carefully. Each sentence needs at least (1) a subject and (2) a predicate.

> Unlike the case of a forged endorsement, a drawee bank charged with the recognition of its drawer-customer's signature. (The verb *is*, before the word *charged,* has been left out.)

PARALLELISM

Parallelism refers to a similarity in structure and meaning of all parts of a sentence or a paragraph. In parallelism, parts of a sentence (or a paragraph) that are parallel in meaning are also parallel in structure. Sentences that violate rules of parallelism will be difficult to read and may obscure meaning. The following are some examples of different **violations** of parallelism.

(1) A security interest can be effected through a financing statement or the creditor's taking possession of it. (The two prepositional phrases separated by **or** should be parallel.)

Corrected: A security interest can be effected through a financing statement or through possession by the creditor.

(2) The independent auditor should consider whether the scope is appropriate, adequate audit programs and working papers, appropriate conclusions, and reports prepared are consistent with results of the work performed. (The clause beginning with **whether** (which acts as the direct object of the verb **should consider**) is faulty. The items mentioned must be similarly constructed to each other.)

Corrected: The independent auditor should consider whether the scope is appropriate, audit programs and working papers are adequate, conclusions are appropriate, and reports prepared are consistent with results of the work performed.

(3) The CPA was responsible for performing the inquiry and analytical procedures and that the review report was completed in a timely manner. (The prepositional phrase beginning with **for** is faulty.)

Corrected: The CPA was responsible for performing the inquiry and analytical procedures and ensuring that the review report was completed in a timely manner.

(4) Procedures that should be applied in examining the stock accounts are as follows:

(1) Review the corporate charter…
(2) Obtain or preparing an analysis of…
(3) Determination of authorization for… (All items in a list must be in parallel structure.)

Corrected:

1. Review the corporate charter…
2. Obtain or prepare an analysis of…
3. Determine the authorization for…

There are many other types of faulty constructions that can creep into sentences—too many to detail here. Furthermore, if any of the above is not clear, syntax may be a problem for you and you might want to consider a more thorough review of this subject.

NUMBERS

1. The basic rule for writing numbers is to write out the numbers ten and under and use numerals for all the others. More formal writing may dictate writing out all round numbers and numbers under 101. Let style, context of the sentence and of the work, and common sense be your guide.

The partnership was formed 18 years ago.
Jim Bryant joined the firm four years ago.
Baker purchased 200 shares of stock.

2. When there are two numbers next to each other, alternate the styles.

three 4-year certificates of deposit　　　　5 two-party instruments

3. Never begin a sentence with numerals, such as:

1989 was the last year that Zinc Co. filed a tax return.

This example can be corrected as follows:

Nineteen hundred and eighty-nine was the last year that Zinc Co. filed a tax return. (For use only in very formal writing)
or
Zinc Co. has not filed a tax return since 1989.

CAPITALIZATION

This section mentions only areas that seem to cause particular difficulties.

1. The first word **after a colon** is capped only when it is the beginning of a complete sentence.

We discussed several possibilities at the meeting: Among them were liquidation, reorganization, and rehabilitation.
We discussed several possibilities at the meeting: liquidation, reorganization, and rehabilitation.

2. The capitalization of titles and headings is especially tricky. In general, the first word and all other important words, no matter what length they are, should be capped. Beyond this general rule, there are several variations relating to the capitalization of pronouns. The important thing here is to pick a style and use it consistently within a single document, article, etc.

For example, the following pair of headings would both be acceptable depending on the style and consistency of style:

Securities to which SFAS 115 Applies	**or**	Securities to Which SFAS 115 Applies
Issues for Property other than Cash	**or**	Issues For Property Other Than Cash

PUNCTUATION

PERIOD

Probably the two most common errors involving periods occur when incorporating quotation marks and/or parentheses with periods.

1. When a period is used with closing quotation marks, the period is always placed **inside,** regardless of whether the entire sentence is a quote or only the end of the sentence.

2. When a period is used with parentheses, the period goes **inside** the closing parenthesis if the entire sentence is enclosed in parentheses. When only the last word or words is enclosed in parentheses, the period goes **outside** the closing parenthesis.

(See Chapter 34, Contracts.)
The answer to that question is in the section on contracts (Chapter 34).

EXCLAMATION POINT

An exclamation point is used for emphasis and when issuing a command. In many cases, this is determined by the author when he or she wants to convey urgency, irony, or stronger emotion than ordinarily would be inferred.

COLON

A colon is used to introduce something in the sentence—a list of related words, phrases, or items directly related to the first part of the sentence; a quotation; a **direct** question; or an example of what was stated in the first part of the sentence. The colon takes the place of **that is** or **such as** and should never be used **with** such phrases.

> The accountant discussed two possibilities with the clients: first, a joint voluntary bankruptcy petition under Chapter 7, and second,…
>
> The following will be discussed: life insurance proceeds; inheritance; and property.
>
> My CPA accounting review book states the following: "All leases that do not meet any of the four criteria for capital leases are operating leases."

Colons are used in formal correspondence after the salutation.

> Dear Mr. Bennett:
> To Whom it May Concern:

Note: When **that is** or **such as** is followed by a numeric list, it may be followed by a colon.

When writing a sentence, if you're not sure whether or not a colon is appropriate, it probably isn't. When in doubt, change the sentence so that you're sure it doesn't need a colon.

SEMICOLON

A semicolon is used in a number of ways:

1. Use a **semicolon in place of a conjunction** when there are two or more closely related thoughts and each is expressed in a coordinate clause (a clause that could stand as a complete sentence).

   > A marketable title is one that is free from plausible or reasonable objections; it need not be perfect.

2. Use a **semicolon** as in the above example **with a conjunction** when the sentence is very long and complex. This promotes **clarity** by making the sentence easier to read.

   > Should the lease be prematurely terminated, the deposit may be retained only to cover the landlord's actual expenses or damages; ***and*** any excess must be returned to the tenant.
   >
   > An assignment establishes privity of estate between the lessor and assignee; ***[and]*** therefore, the assignee becomes personally liable for the rent.

3. When there are commas in a series of items, use a **semicolon** to separate the main items.

   > Addison, Inc. has distribution centers in Camden, Maine; Portsmouth, New Hampshire; and Rock Island, Rhode Island.

COMMA

Informal English allows much freedom in the placement or the omission of commas, and the overall trend is away from commas. However, standard, formal English provides rules for its usage. Accounting "language" can be so complex that using commas and using them correctly and appropriately is a necessity to avoid obscurity and promote clarity. Accordingly, we encourage you to learn the basics about comma placement.

What follows is not a complete set of rules for commas but should be everything you need to know about commas to make your sentences clear and concise. Because the primary purpose of the comma is to clarify meaning, it is the opinion of the authors that in the case of a complex subject such as accounting, it is better to overpunctuate than to underpunctuate. If you are concerned about overpunctuation, try to reduce an unwieldy sentence to two or more sentences.

1. Use a comma to **separate a compound sentence** (one with two or more independent coordinate clauses joined by a conjunction).

   Gil Corp. has current assets of $90,000**,** but the corporation has current liabilities of $180,000.
   Jim borrowed $60,000**,** and he used the proceeds to purchase outstanding common shares of stock.

   Note: In these examples, a comma would **not** be necessary if the **and** or the **but** were not followed by a noun or pronoun (the subject of the second clause). In other words, if by removing the conjunction, the sentence could be separated into two complete sentences, it needs a comma.

2. Use a comma after an introductory word or phrase.

   During 1992**,** Rand Co. purchased $960,000 of inventory.
   On April 1, 1993**,** Wall's inventory had a fair value of $150,000.

   Note: Writers often choose to omit this comma when the introductory phrase is very short. Again, we recommend using the comma. It will never be incorrect in this position.

3. Use a comma after an introductory adverbial clause.

   Although insurance contracts are not required by the Statute of Frauds to be in writing**,** most states have enacted statutes that now require such.

4. Use commas to separate items, phrases, or clauses in a series.

   To be negotiable, an instrument must be in writing**,** signed by the maker or drawer**,** contain an unconditional promise or order to pay a sum certain in money on demand or at a specific time**,** and be payable to order or to bearer.

   Note: Modern practice often omits the last comma in the series (in the above example, the one before **and**). Again, for the sake of clarity, we recommend using this comma.

5. In most cases, use a comma or commas to separate **a series of adjectives.**

   Silt Co. kept their inventory in an old**,** decrepit**,** brick building.
   He purchased several outstanding shares of common stock. (*No* commas are needed.)

> When in doubt as to whether or not to use a comma after a particular adjective, try inserting the word **and** between the adjectives. If it makes sense, use a comma. (In the second example, above, **several and outstanding,** or **outstanding and several** don't make sense.)

6. Use a comma or commas to set off any **word or words, phrase, or clause that interrupts the sentence** but does not change its essential meaning.

   SLD Industries**,** as drawer of the instrument**,** is only secondarily liable.

7. Use commas to set off **geographical names** and **dates.**

   Feeney Co. moved its headquarters to Miami, Florida, on August 16, 1992.

QUOTATION MARKS

Quotation marks are used with **direct quotations; direct discourse and direct questions;** and **definitions or explanations of words.** Other uses of quotation marks are used rarely in the accounting profession and, therefore, are not discussed in this review.

HYPHEN

1. Use a hyphen to separate words into syllables. It is best to check a dictionary, because some words do not split where you might imagine.

2. Modern practice does not normally hyphenate prefixes and their root words, even when both the prefix and the root word begin with vowels. A common exception is when the root word begins with a capital letter or a date or number.

prenuptial	nonexempt	semiannual
pre-1987	nonnegotiable	non-American

3. Although modern practice is moving away from using hyphens for **compound adjectives** (a noun and an adjective in combination to make a single adjective), clarity dictates that hyphens still be used in many cases.

long-term investments	two-party instrument
a noninterest-bearing note	short-term capital losses

4. Use a hyphen **only** when the compound adjective or compound adjective-adverb **precedes the noun.**

   The well-known company is going bankrupt.
   The company is well known for its quality products.

Note: There are certain word combinations that are always hyphenated, always one word, or always two words. Use the dictionary.

5. **Suspended hyphens** are used to avoid repetition in compound adjectives. For example, instead of having to write **himself or herself,** especially when these forms are being used repeatedly as they often must be in our newly nongender-biased world, use **him- or herself.**

   10-, 15-, and 18-year depreciation   first-, second-, and third-class

SPELLING

Just as many of us believe that arithmetic can be done always by our calculators, we also believe that spelling will be done by our word processors and, therefore, we needn't worry too much about it. There is no doubt that these devices are tremendous boons. However, sometimes a spell-checker cannot tell the difference between words that you have misspelled which are nonetheless real words, such as **there** and **their.** (See the list in this section of words often confused.)

Let's hit some highlights here of troublesome spellings with some brief tips that should help you become a better speller.

1. **IE** or **EI**? If you are still confused by words containing the **ie** or **ei** combinations, you'd better relearn those old rhymes we ridiculed in grade school.

   "**i** before **e** except after **c.**" (This works only for words where the ie-ei combination sounds like **ee.**)

ach**ie**ve	bel**ie**ve	ch**ie**f
ceiling	re**cei**ve	re**cei**pt

Of course there are always **exceptions** such as:

either	neither	seize	financier

When **ie** or **ei** have a different sound than **ee**, the above rule does not apply. For example:

fr**ie**nd	s**ie**ve	effic**ie**nt
for**ei**gn	sover**ei**gn	surf**ei**t

2. **Doubling final consonants.** When an ending (**suffix**) beginning with a vowel is added to a root word that ends in a single consonant, that final consonant is **usually doubled**.

lag—lagging	bid—bidding	top—topped

The exceptions generally fall under three rules.

First, double only after a short vowel and **not** after a double vowel.

big—bigger	tug—tugging	get—getting
need—needing	keep—keeping	pool—pooled

Second, a **long** vowel (one that "says its own name"), which is almost always followed by a silent **e** that must be dropped to add the suffix, is **not** doubled.

hope—hoping	tape—taped	rule—ruled

Note: Sometimes, as in the first two examples above, doubling the consonants would create entirely new words.

Third, with root words of two or more syllables ending in a single consonant, double the consonant **only** when the last syllable is the **stressed syllable.**

Double:	beg**in**—beginning, beginner	pre**fer**—preferred, preferring
	re**gret**—**regretted**, regrettable	ad**mit**—admitted, admittance
Don't Double:	pro**hi**bit—prohibited, prohibitive	**ben**efit—benefited, benefiting
	de**vel**op—developing	**pref**erence—preferable

3. **Drop** the silent **e** before adding a suffix **beginning with a vowel.**

store—storing	take—taking	value—valuing

Keep the **e** before adding a suffix **beginning with a consonant,** such as:

move—movement	achieve—achievement

Again, there are **exceptions**.

e:	mile—mileage	dye—dyeing	
No e:	argue—argument	due—duly	true—truly

4. Change **y** to **ie** before adding **s** when it is the single final vowel.

country—countries	study—studies	quantity—quantities

Change **y** to **i** before adding other endings **except s.**

busy—business	dry—drier	copy—copier

Exceptions: Keep **y** for the following:

copying	studying	trying

Y is also usually preserved when it follows another vowel.

delays	joys	played

Exceptions:

day—daily	lay—laid	pay—paid	say—said

5. **Forming Plurals.** The formation of some plurals does not follow the general rule of adding **s** or **es** to the singular. What follows are some of the more troublesome forms.

Some singular nouns that end in **o** form their plurals by adding **s**; some by adding **es**.

ratio**s**	zero**s**	hero**es**	potato**es**

Many nouns taken directly from **foreign languages** retain their original plural. Below are a few of the more common ones.

alumnus—alumni	basis—bases	crisis—crises
criterion—criteria	datum—data	matrix—matrices

Other nouns taken directly from foreign languages have **two acceptable plural forms:** the foreign language plural and the anglicized plural. Here are some of the more common:

medium—media, mediums	appendix—appendices, appendixes
formula—formulae, formulas	memorandum—memoranda, memorandums

Finally, in this foreign language category are some commonly used Latin nouns that form their plurals by adding **es.**

census—censuses	consensus—consensuses
hiatus—hiatuses	prospectus—prospectuses

Troublesome Words: Spelling

Spelling errors occur for different reasons; probably the most common reason is confusion with the spelling of similar words. The following is a list of commonly misspelled words. You will find those you may have misspelled in taking the Diagnostic Quiz, and you may recognize others you have problems with. Memorize them. (Note: some of these words may have acceptable alternative spellings; however, the spellings listed below are the preferred form.)

accommodate	bankruptcy	irrelevant	paralleled	skillful
achieve	deferred	judgment	privilege	supersede
acknowledgment	existence	liaison	receivable	surety
balance	fulfill	occasion	resistance	trial

GRAMMAR

This section on grammar is intended to be a brief overview only. Consequently, the authors have chosen to focus on items that seem to cause the most problems. If you did not do well on the Diagnostic Quiz, you would be well advised to go over all the material in this section and consider a more thorough grammar study than provided here.

VERBS

The verb is the driving force of the sentence: it is the word or words to which all other parts of the sentence relate. When trying to analyze a sentence to identify its grammatical parts or its meaning, or when attempting to amend a sentence, you should always identify the verb or verbs first. A verb expresses action or being.

Action: The accountant *visits* his clients regularly.
Being: Kyle *is* an accountant.

Voice

1. The **active voice** indicates that the subject of the sentence (the person or thing) does something. The **passive voice** indicates that the subject is acted upon.

   Active: *The accountant worked* on the client's financial statements.
   Passive: The client's financial statements *were worked on by the accountant.*

2. The most important thing to understand about voice is that it should be consistent; that is, you should avoid shifts from one voice to another, especially within the same sentence as below.

   Taylor Corporation *hired* an independent computer programmer to develop a simplified payroll application for its new computer, and an on-line, data-based microcomputer system *was developed.*

   Use the active voice for the entire sentence:

   Taylor Corporation *hired* an independent computer programmer to develop a simplified payroll application for its new computer, and he *developed* an on-line, data-based microcomputer system.

Mood

1. Common errors in syntax are made when **more than one mood** is used in a single sentence. The first example that follows begins with the **imperative** and shifts to the **indicative.** The second example corrects the sentence by using the imperative in both clauses, and the third example corrects the sentence by using the indicative in both clauses. The fourth example avoids the problem by forming two sentences.

   Pick up (imperative) that work program for me at the printer, and then we will go (indicative) to the client.
   Pick up that work program for me at the printer, and then go to the client with me.
   After you pick up that work program for me at the printer, we will go to the client.
   Pick up that work program for me at the printer. Then we will go to the client.

2. There are three moods: the indicative, the imperative, and the subjunctive. We do not examine the subjunctive. Most sentences are **indicative:**

   The percentage of completion method is justified. Declarative indicative.
   Is the percentage of completion method justified? Interrogative indicative.

3. Sentences that give a command are called **imperative** sentences:

   Pick up your books!
   Be sure to use the correct method of accounting for income taxes.

Tense

1. Tense is all about *time.* If the proper sequence of tenses is not used, confusion can arise as to what happened when. Consider:

   Not getting the raise he was expecting, John was unhappy about the additional work load. [???]
   Having not gotten the raise he was expecting, John was unhappy about the additional work load. [Much clearer]

2. The **present tense** is used to express action or a state of being that is taking place in the present. The present tense is also used to express an action or a state of being that is habitual and when a definite time in the future is stated.

   Dan *is taking* his CPA exam.
   Robin *goes* to the printer once a week.
   The new computer *arrives* on Monday.

3. The **present perfect tense** is used to indicate action that began in the past and has continued to the present.

   From the time of its founder, the CPA firm *has celebrated* April 16 with a fabulous dinner party.

4. The **future tense** is used to indicate action that takes place in the indefinite future.

   A plan of reorganization *will determine* the amount and the manner in which the creditors *will be paid*, in what form the business *will continue,* and any other necessary details.

5. The **future perfect tense** is used to indicate action that has not taken place yet but will take place before a specific future time.

   Before Susan arrives at the client's office, the client *will have prepared* the documents she needs.

6. The **past tense** is used to indicate an action that took place in the past. The **past tense** is also used to indicate a condition or state occurring at a specific time in the past.

   The predecessor auditor *resigned* last week.
   The company *contacted* its auditor the first of every new year.

7. The **past perfect tense** is used to indicate an action that is completed before another action that also took place in the past.

   The work load *had been* so heavy that she was required to work overtime. (Not *was*)

Agreement

1. The first element of agreement to examine is **verb** and **subject.** These two components must agree **in number.** Number is just one of several things to consider when examining the agreement of the components of a sentence.

2. The subject of the sentence is the noun or pronoun (person, place, or thing) doing the action stated by the verb (in the case of the active voice) or being acted upon by the verb (in the case of the passive voice). Although the subject normally precedes the verb, this is not always the case. Thus, you must be able to identify sentence elements no matter where they happen to fall. This is not a difficult matter, at least most of the time. Consider:

   (1) Lewis, Bradford, Johnson & Co. [is or are] the client with the best pay record.

   (2) For me, one of the most difficult questions on the exam [was or were] concerned with correcting weaknesses in internal controls.

In both examples, the first choice, the singular verb form, is correct. In sentence (1), Lewis, Bradford, Johnson & Co. is considered singular in number because we are talking about the company, not Lewis, Bradford, and Johnson per se. In sentence (2), the verb is also singular because **one** is the subject of the sentence, not **questions.** **Questions** is the object of the preposition **of.** If this seems confusing, rearrange the sentence so that the prepositional phrase appears first, and the agreement of subject and verb will be clearer. Thus:

Of the most difficult questions, one *was concerned* with correcting weaknesses in internal controls.

We will address special problems associated with prepositional phrases in other sections.

3. Beware of the word **number.** When it is preceded by the word **the,** it is always singular, and when it is preceded by the word **a,** it is always plural.

The number of listings generated by the new EDP system *was* astounding.
A number of listings *were generated* by the new EDP system.

4. A **compound subject,** even when made up of nouns singular in number, always takes a plural verb.

The balance sheet, the independent auditor's report, and the quarterly report *are lying* on the desk. (Not *is lying*)

5. Continuing now with **compound subjects,** let's address the problem of when there are two or more subjects—one (or more) singular and one (or more) plural. When the sentence contains subjects connected by **or** or **nor,** or **not only...but also,** the verb should agree with the subject nearer to the verb.

Either the auditors or the partner *is going* to the client.
Not only the partner but also the auditors *are going* to the client.

In the case of the first example above, which sounds awkward, simply switch the order of the subjects **(the partner; the auditors)** and use the verb **are going** to make it read better.

6. When one subject is **positive** and one is **negative,** the verb always agrees with the positive.

The partner, and not the auditors, *is going* to the client.
Not the partner but the auditors frequently go to the client.

7. You should use singular verbs with the following: each, every, everyone, everybody, anyone, anybody, either, neither, someone, somebody, no one, nobody, and one.

Anybody who wants to go *is* welcome.
Neither the accountant nor the bookkeeper ever *arrives* on time.
One never *knows* what to expect.

Watch out for the words **each** and **none.** They can trip up even careful writers.

8. Improper placement of **each** in the sentence will confuse the verb agreement.

The balance sheet, the income statement, and the statement of cash flows each [has/have] several errors.

In this example, we know that the verb must be **has** (to agree with **each**), but then again, maybe it should be **have** to agree with the subjects. The problem is that we have a sentence with a compound subject that must take a plural verb, but here it is connected with a singular pronoun (each). This is a very common error. This particular example may be fixed in one of two ways. First, if the word **each** is not really necessary in the sentence, simply drop it. Second, simply place the word **each** in a better position in the sentence. In the example below, placing the word **each** at the end of the sentence properly connects it to **errors;** also it no longer confuses verb agreement.

The balance sheet, the income statement, and the statement of cash flows *have* several errors *each.*

9. The word **none** has special problems all its own. Not too many years ago, it was the accepted rule that every time **none** was the subject of the sentence, it should take a **singular verb.** Most modern grammarians now agree that the plural may be used when followed by a prepositional phrase with a plural object (noun) or with an object whose meaning in the sentence is plural.

   None of the statements *were* correct.

   When **none** stands alone, some purists believe it should take the singular and others believe that the plural is the proper form when the meaning conveys plurality. Consequently, in the following example, either the singular or plural is generally acceptable.

   All the financial statements had been compiled, but none *was* ***or*** *were* correct.

> When in doubt, use **not one** in place of **none** (with a singular verb, of course).

NOUNS

Nouns are people, places, and things and can occur anywhere in the sentence. Make sure that, when necessary, the nouns are the same in number.

Do the exercises at the end of each chapter by answering the *questions* true or false. (Not singular *question*)
At the end of the engagement, everyone must turn in their *time sheets.* (Not singular *time sheet*)

Possessive Nouns

1. The basic rule for making a **singular noun** possessive is to add an **apostrophe and an s.** If a singular noun ends in s, **add apostrophe and an s.** To make a **plural noun** possessive, add an **apostrophe alone** when the plural ends in **s** or an **apostrophe and an s** when the plural does not end in an **s.**

Singular:	client*'s*	system*'s*	beneficiary*'s*	*Chris'*
Plural:	clients*'*	systems*'*	beneficiarie*s'*	

2. A common area of difficulty has to do with **ownership,** that is, when two or more individuals or groups are mentioned as owning something. If the ownership is **not common** to all, apostrophes appear after each individual or group. If the ownership **is common** to all, only the last individual or group in the series takes an apostrophe.

Not common to all:	The accountant's and the attorney's offices…
Common to all:	Robert, his brother, and their sons' company…

> Most of the confusion associated with possessives seems to be with the plural possessive. Remember to make the noun **plural** first and **possessive** second.

3. Modern usage tends to make possessive forms into adjectives where appropriate. Thus:

   Company's (possessive) management becomes *company* (adjective) management.
   A *two weeks'* (possessive) vacation becomes a *two weeks* or *two-week* (both adjectives) vacation.

> In most instances, either the possessive form or the adjectival form is acceptable. Go with the form that seems most appropriate for that particular sentence.

Gerunds

1. A gerund is a verb changed to a noun by adding **ing.** A noun preceding a gerund must be possessive so that it may be construed as **modifying the noun.**

   Caroline's telecommuting was approved by the partner.

   In this example, the subject of the sentence is **telecommuting,** not Caroline or Caroline's. Since we know that nouns cannot modify nouns, Caroline must become **Caroline's** to create a possessive form that can modify the noun **telecommuting.**

2. The same holds true for **gerunds** used as **objects of prepositions:**

   The partner objected to *Caroline's telecommuting.*

   In this example, **telecommuting** is the object of the preposition **to.** Caroline's is an appositive (or possessive) form modifying **telecommuting.**

PRONOUNS

Like Latin where most words have "cases" according to their function in the sentence, English **pronouns** also have cases. Sometimes you may be aware that you are using a case when determining the proper form of the pronoun and sometimes you may not.

He met *his* partner at *their* office.

1. Let's begin by tackling everybody's favorite: **who** and **whom.** We're going to take some time reviewing this one since it seems to be a major area of confusion. There is little or no confusion when **who** is clearly the **subject** of the sentence:

   Who is going with us?

   And little or no confusion when **whom** is clearly (1) the **object** of the sentence or (2) the **object** of the preposition.

   (1) Jenny audited *whom*? *Whom* did Jenny audit?

   (2) Jenny is working for *whom*? For *whom* is Jenny working?

> If you are having difficulty with **questions,** try changing them into declarative sentences (statements) and substituting another pronoun. Thus: Jenny audits **them** (objective), obviously not **they** (subjective), or Jenny is working for **her,** obviously not **she.**

2. **Who** or **whoever** is the subjective case, and **whom** or **whomever** is the objective case. Common errors occur frequently in two instances: (1) when **who or whoever** is interrupted by a parenthetical phrase and (2) when an entire clause is the subject of a preposition.

   (1) *Whoever* she decides is working with her should meet her at six o'clock.

   In this example, **she decides** is a parenthetical phrase (one that could be left out of the sentence and the sentence would still be a complete thought). When you disregard **she decides,** you can see that **whoever** is the subject of the sentence, not **she.** The error occurs when **she** is believed to be the subject and **whomever,** the object of **decides.**

   (2) Jenny will work with *whoever* shows up first.

   This example represents what seems the most problematic of all the areas relating to who or whom. We have been taught to use the objective case after the preposition (in this case **with**). So why isn't **whomever** the correct form in this example? The answer is that it would be the correct form if the sentence ended with the word **whomever.** (**Whomever** would be the object of the preposition **with.**) In this case, it is not the last word but, rather, it is the **subject** of the clause **whoever shows up first.**

Again, make the substitution of another pronoun as a test of whether to use the subjective or objective case.

Let's look at a few more examples. See if you are better able to recognize the correct form.

(1) I'm sure I will be comfortable with [*whoever/whomever*] the manager decides to assign.

(2) To [*who/whom*] should she speak regarding that matter?

(3) He always chooses [*whoever/whomever*] in his opinion is the best auditor.

(4) She usually enjoys working with [*whoever/whomever*] the partner assigns.

(5) [*Who/Whom*] should I ask to accompany me?

Let's see how well you did.

(1) **Whomever** is correct. The whole clause after the preposition **with** is the object of the preposition, and **whomever** is the object of the verb **to assign.** Turn the clause around and substitute another pronoun. Thus, **the manager decides to assign *him.***

(2) **Whom** is correct. **Whom** is the object of the preposition **to.** Make the question into a declarative sentence and substitute another pronoun. Thus, **She should speak to *him* regarding that matter.**

(3) **Whoever** is correct. The entire clause **whoever is the best auditor** is the object of the main verb **chooses. Whoever** is the subject of that clause. **In his opinion** is a parenthetical phrase and doesn't affect the rest of the sentence.

(4) **Whomever** is correct. The entire clause **whomever the partner assigns** is the object of the preposition **with,** and **whomever** is the object of the verb **assigns.** Again, turn the clause around and substitute another pronoun. Thus, **the partner assigns *him.***

(5) **Whom** is correct. **Whom** is the object of the main verb **ask.** Turn the question into a regular declarative sentence and substitute another pronoun. Thus, **I should ask *her* to accompany me.**

3. Pronouns that follow prepositions are always in the **objective case,** except when serving as the subject of a clause, as discussed above. The most popular misuse occurs when using a pronoun after the preposition **between.** (**I, he, she, they,** are never used after **between,** no matter where the prepositional phrase falls in the sentence.)

   Between you and me, I don't believe our client will be able to continue as a going concern.
   That matter is strictly between her and them.

Antecedents

1. An antecedent is the word or words for which a pronoun stands. Any time a pronoun is used, its antecedent must be clear and agree with the word or words for which it stands.

   The accountant placed *his* work in the file.

   In this example, **his** is the pronoun with **the accountant** as its antecedent. **His** agrees with **the accountant** in person and number. **His** is used so as not to repeat **the accountant.**

2. Confusion most often occurs when using indefinite pronouns such as **it, that, this,** and **which.**

   The company for *which* he works always mails *its* paychecks on Friday.

In this example, the pronouns **which** and **its** both clearly refer to **the company.** Consider the next example. Since it is not clear what the antecedent for **it** is, we can't tell for sure whether the company or the paycheck is small.

The company always mails my paycheck on Friday and *it* is a small one.

3. So far in our discussion of antecedents, we have talked about agreement in person. We have not addressed agreement in **number.** The following examples demonstrate pronouns that **do not agree** in number with their antecedents.

   The company issued quarterly financial reports to *their* shareholders. (*Its* is the correct antecedent to agree in number with *company*.)

   Each of the methods is introduced on a separate page, so that the student is made aware of *their* importance. (*Its* is the correct antecedent to agree in number with *each*.) **Note: Importance** refers to **each,** the subject of the sentence, not to **methods,** which is the object of the preposition **of.**

4. When a pronoun refers to singular antecedents that are connected by **or** or **nor**, the pronoun should be **singular.**

   Joe or Buddy has misplaced *his* workpapers.

   Neither Joe nor Buddy has misplaced *his* workpapers.

5. When a pronoun refers to a singular and a plural antecedent connected by **or** or **nor**, the pronoun should be **plural.**

   Neither Joe nor his associates can locate *their* workpapers.

6. Pronouns must also agree with their antecedents in **gender.** Because English language has no way of expressing gender-neutral in pronoun agreement, it has been the custom to use **his** as a convenience when referring to both sexes. To avoid this "gender bias" in writing, there is a growing use of a more cumbersome construction in order to be more politically correct.

   Old: When a new partner's identifiable asset contribution is less than the ownership interest *he* is to receive, the excess capital allowed *him* is considered as goodwill attributable to *him.*

   New: When a new partner's identifiable asset contribution is less than the ownership interest *he or she* is to receive, the excess capital allowed *the new partner* is considered as goodwill attributable to *him or her.*

   You will note in the above example that **he or she (he/she)** and **him or her (him/her)** have been used only once each and the antecedent **new partner** has been repeated once.

The idea is to not overload a single sentence with too many repetitions of each construction. When it seems that **he/she** constructions are overwhelming the sentence, repeat the noun antecedent where possible, even if it sounds a bit labored.

7. **Reflexive pronouns** are pronouns that are used for **emphasizing their antecedents** and should **not be used as substitutes** for regular pronouns. The reflexive pronouns are **myself, yourself, himself, herself, itself, ourselves, yourselves, and themselves.**

   The financing is being handled by the principals *themselves.* (Demonstrates emphasis)
   The partner *himself* will take care of that matter. (Demonstrates emphasis)
   My associate and *I* accept the engagement. (Not my associate and *myself*...)
   I am fine; how about *you*? (Not how about *yourself?*)

ADJECTIVES & ADVERBS

1. Most of us understand that adjectives and adverbs are **modifiers,** but many of us can't tell them apart. In fact, there are many words that can be used as either depending on their use. Consequently, differentiating adjectives from adverbs is really not very important as long as you know how to use them. Understanding, however, that **adjectives modify nouns or pronouns,** and **adverbs modify verbs** and adjectives will help you choose the correct form.

   Falcone Co. purchased *two* computers from Wizard Corp., a very *small* manufacturer. (*two* is an adjective describing the noun *computers, very* is an adverb modifying the adjective *small*, and *small* is an adjective describing the noun *manufacturer.*)

   Acme advised Mason that it would deliver the appliances on July 2 as *originally* agreed. (*originally* is an adverb describing the verb *agreed.*)

2. In writing for the CPA exam, avoid colloquial uses of the adjectives **real** and **sure.** In the following examples, adverbs are called for.

   I am *very* (not *real*) sorry that you didn't pass the exam.
   He will *surely* (not *sure*) be glad if he passes the exam.

3. **Comparisons** using adjectives frequently present problems. Remember that when comparing two things, the **comparative** (often **er)** form is used, and when comparing more than two, the **superlative** (often **est**) form is used.

   This report is *larger* than the other one.
   This report is the *largest* of them all.
   This report is *more* detailed than the others.
   This report is the *most* detailed of them all.

4. **Articles** are adjectives. **An** precedes most vowels, but when the vowel begins with a **consonant sound,** we should use **a.**

   a usual adjustment...
   a one in a million deal...

   Similarly, when **a** or **an** precedes abbreviations or initials, it is the next **sound** that we should consider, not the next letter. In other words, if the next sound is a vowel sound, **an** should be used. Usually, your reader will be reading the abbreviations or initials and not the whole term, title, etc.

   An S.A. will be used to head up the field work on this engagement.
   An F.O.B. contract is a *contract* indicating that the seller will bear that degree of risk and expense that is appropriate to the F.O.B. terms.

CONJUNCTIONS

There are three types of conjunctions: coordinating, subordinating, and correlative.

Coordinating Conjunctions

Coordinating conjunctions are conjunctions that connect equal elements in a sentence. These conjunctions include **and, but, for, yet, so, or,** and **nor.** Examples of common problems involving coordinating conjunctions:

1. Leaving out the **and,** leading to difficulties with comprehension and clarity.

   The accountant studied some of management's representations, marked what she wanted to discuss in the meeting. (The word *and* should be in the place of the comma.)

Mike's summer job entails opening the mail, stamps it with a dater, routing it to the proper person. (Should be: ...opening the mail from other offices, *stamping* it with a dater, *and* routing it to the proper person. **This example also demonstrates a lack of parallelism,** which is addressed in an earlier section.)

2. Omission of **and** is correct when the sentence is a compound sentence (meaning that it contains two independent clauses), in which case a semicolon takes the place of **and.** When the semicolon is used, the ideas of each independent clause should be closely related.

   The security is genuine; it has not been materially altered.

3. Although the rules for **or** and **nor** have become less strict over time, you should understand proper usage for the sake of comprehension and clarity. Most of us are familiar with **either**...**or** and **neither**...**nor:**

   Either the creditor must take possession *or* the debtor must sign a security agreement that describes the collateral.

The company would neither accept delivery of the water coolers, nor pay for them, because Peterson did not have the authority to enter into the contract.

Subordinating Conjunctions

Subordinating conjunctions are conjunctions that introduce subordinate elements of the sentence. The most common and the ones we want to concentrate on here are **as, since, because, that, which, when, where,** and **while.**

1. **As; Since; Because**

   Because is the only word of the three that **always** indicates cause. **Since** usually indicates **time** and, when introducing adverbial clauses, may mean either **when** or **because. As** should be avoided altogether in these constructions and used only for comparisons. We strongly recommend using the exact word to avoid any confusion, especially when clarity is essential.

   Attachment of the security interest did not occur because Pix failed to file a financing statement. (Specifically indicates *cause.*)
   Green has not paid any creditor since January 1, 1992. (Specifically indicates *time.*)

   The following example is a typical misuse of the conjunction **as** and demonstrates why **as** should not be used as a substitute for **because:**

   As the partners are contributing more capital to the company, the stock prices are going up.

   The meaning of this sentence is ambiguous. Are the stock prices going up **while** the partners are contributing capital or are the stock prices going up **because** the partners are contributing more capital?

2. **That; Which**

   Many people complain about not understanding when to use **that** and when to use **which** more than just about anything else. The rule to follow requires that you know the difference between a restrictive and a nonrestrictive clause. A **restrictive clause** is one that must remain in the sentence for the sentence to make sense. A **nonrestrictive** clause is one that may be removed from a sentence and the sentence will still make sense.

   That is used with restrictive clauses; *which* is used with nonrestrictive clauses.

   (1) An accountant who breaches his or her contract with a client may be subject to liability for damages and losses *which* the client suffers as a direct result of the breach.

(2) As a result, the accountant is responsible for errors resulting from changes *that* occurred between the time he or she prepared the statement and its effective date.

(3) A reply *that* purports to accept an offer but which adds material qualifications or conditions is not an acceptance; rather, it is a rejection and a counter-offer.

In example (1) above, the clause beginning with **which** is nonrestrictive (sentence would make sense without it). In examples (2) and (3), the clauses that follow **that** are restrictive (necessary for the meaning of the sentence).

> If you can put commas around the clause in question, it is usually nonrestrictive and thus takes **which.** Occasionally, there will be a fine line between what one might consider restrictive or nonrestrictive. In these cases, make your choice based on which sounds better and, if there is another **which** or **that** nearby, let that help your decision. (Unless truly necessary, don't have two or three uses of **which** or two or three uses of **that** in the same sentence.)

3. **When; Where**

The most common incorrect usage associated with these words occurs when they are used to define something.

(1) Exoneration is *where* the surety takes action against the debtor, which seeks to force the debtor to pay his or her debts.

(2) A fiduciary relationship is where the agent acts for the benefit of the principal.

(3) Joint liability is *when* all partners in a partnership are jointly liable for any contract actions against the partnership.

The above three examples are **faulty constructions.** The verb **to be** (**is,** in this case) must be followed by a predicate adjective (an adjective modifying the subject) or a predicate nominative (a noun meaning the same as the subject), **not** an adverbial phrase or clause. These sentences should be rewritten as follows:

(1) Exoneration is *an action* by the surety against the debtor, which seeks to force the debtor to pay his or her debts.

(2) A fiduciary relationship is *the association* of the agent and the principal whereby the agent acts for the benefit of the principal.

(3) Joint liability is *the liability* of all partners in a partnership for any contract actions against the partnership.

4. **While**

Formerly, **while** was acceptable only to denote time. Modern practice accepts **while** and **although** as nearly synonymous. In example (1), either while or although is acceptable. In example (2), **while** is **not** a proper substitution for **although.**

(1) *While/Although* Acme contends that its agreement with Mason was not binding, it is willing to deliver the goods to Mason.

(2) Under a sale or return contract, the sale is considered as completed *although* it is voidable at the buyer's election.

Correlative Conjunction

The third type of conjunction is the **correlative conjunction.** We have briefly mentioned and presented examples of **either…or** and **neither…nor** earlier in connection with nouns, verbs, and agreement. Now we want to discuss these correlatives in connection with **parallelism.**

1. **Not only** should be followed by **but (also).**

   In determining whether a mere invitation or an offer exists, the courts generally will look *not only* to the specific language *but also* to the surrounding circumstances, the custom within the industry, and the prior practice between the parties.

2. Watch out for **placement of correlatives.** Faulty placement leads to faulty construction and obstructs clarity.

   The lawyer *either* is asked to furnish specific information *or* comment as to where the lawyer's views differ from those of management.

Below is the same sentence in much clearer form. Note that the phrases introduced by *either* and *or* are now in parallel construction: *either to furnish…or to comment.*

> The lawyer is asked *either* to furnish specific information *or to* comment as to where the lawyer's views differ from those of management.

APPENDIX D
COMPOUND INTEREST TABLES

Table 1: Future Value of $1 .... D-2

Table 2: Present Value of $1 .... D-3

Table 3: Future Value of an Annuity of $1 in Arrears D-4

Table 4: Present Value of an Annuity of $1 in Arrears D-5

Table 1—Future Value of $1

$FV = PV(1 + r)^n$

r = interest rate; n = number of periods until valuation; PV = $1

	1%	2%	3%	4%	5%	6%	7%	8%	10%	12%	15%	20%	25%
n = 1	1.010000	1.020000	1.030000	1.040000	1.050000	1.060000	1.070000	1.080000	1.100000	1.120000	1.150000	1.200000	1.250000
2	1.020100	1.040400	1.060900	1.081600	1.102500	1.123600	1.144900	1.166400	1.210000	1.254400	1.322500	1.440000	1.562500
3	1.030301	1.061208	1.092727	1.124864	1.157625	1.191016	1.225043	1.259712	1.331000	1.404928	1.520875	1.728000	1.953125
4	1.040604	1.082432	1.125509	1.169859	1.215506	1.262477	1.310796	1.360489	1.464100	1.573519	1.749006	2.073600	2.441406
5	1.051010	1.104081	1.159274	1.216653	1.276282	1.338226	1.402552	1.469328	1.610510	1.762342	2.011357	2.488320	3.051758
6	1.061520	1.126162	1.194052	1.265319	1.340096	1.418519	1.500730	1.586874	1.771561	1.973823	2.313061	2.985984	3.814697
7	1.072135	1.148686	1.229874	1.315932	1.407100	1.503630	1.605781	1.713824	1.948717	2.210681	2.660020	3.583181	4.768372
8	1.082857	1.171659	1.266770	1.368569	1.477455	1.593848	1.718186	1.850930	2.143589	2.475963	3.059023	4.299817	5.960464
9	1.093685	1.195093	1.304773	1.423312	1.551328	1.689479	1.838459	1.999005	2.357948	2.773079	3.517876	5.159781	7.450581
10	1.104622	1.218994	1.343916	1.480244	1.628895	1.790848	1.967151	2.158925	2.593743	3.105848	4.045558	6.191737	9.313226
11	1.115668	1.243374	1.384234	1.539454	1.710339	1.898299	2.104852	2.331639	2.853117	3.478550	4.652391	7.430084	11.64153
12	1.126825	1.268242	1.425761	1.601032	1.795856	2.012197	2.252192	2.518170	3.138428	3.895976	5.350250	8.916101	14.55192
13	1.138093	1.293607	1.468534	1.665074	1.885649	2.132928	2.409845	2.719624	3.452271	4.363493	6.152788	10.69932	18.18989
14	1.149474	1.319479	1.512590	1.731676	1.979932	2.260904	2.578534	2.937194	3.797498	4.887112	7.075706	12.83918	22.73737
15	1.160969	1.345868	1.557967	1.800943	2.078928	2.396558	2.759032	3.172169	4.177248	5.473566	8.137062	15.40702	28.42171
16	1.172579	1.372786	1.604706	1.872981	2.182875	2.540352	2.952164	3.425943	4.594973	6.130394	9.357621	18.48843	35.52714
17	1.184304	1.400241	1.652848	1.947900	2.292018	2.692773	3.158815	3.700018	5.054471	6.866041	10.76126	22.18611	44.40892
18	1.196147	1.428246	1.702433	2.025816	2.406619	2.854339	3.379932	3.996019	5.559917	7.689965	12.37545	26.62333	55.51115
19	1.208109	1.456811	1.753506	2.106849	2.526950	3.025599	3.616528	4.315701	6.115909	8.612761	14.23177	31.94800	69.38894
20	1.220190	1.485947	1.806111	2.191123	2.653298	3.207135	3.869684	4.660957	6.727500	9.646293	16.36654	38.33760	86.73618
22	1.244716	1.545980	1.916103	2.369919	2.925261	3.603537	4.430402	5.436540	8.140275	12.10031	21.64475	55.20615	135.5253
24	1.269735	1.608437	2.032794	2.563304	3.225100	4.048934	5.072367	6.341180	9.849733	15.17863	28.62518	79.49685	211.7582
26	1.295256	1.673418	2.156591	2.772470	3.555673	4.549383	5.807353	7.396353	11.91818	19.04007	37.85680	114.4755	330.8723
28	1.321291	1.741024	2.287928	2.998703	3.920129	5.111687	6.648839	8.627106	14.42099	23.88387	50.06562	164.8447	516.9879
30	1.347849	1.811362	2.427262	3.243397	4.321942	5.743491	7.612255	10.06266	17.44940	29.95992	66.21178	237.3763	807.7936
32	1.374941	1.884541	2.575083	3.508059	4.764942	6.453386	8.715271	11.73708	21.11378	37.58172	87.56509	341.8219	1262.177
34	1.402577	1.960676	2.731905	3.794316	5.253348	7.251025	9.978113	13.69013	25.54767	47.14251	115.8048	492.2236	1972.152
36	1.430769	2.039887	2.898278	4.103932	5.791816	8.147252	11.42394	15.96817	30.91268	59.13557	153.1519	708.8019	3081.488
38	1.459527	2.122299	3.074783	4.438813	6.385478	9.154252	13.07927	18.62527	37.40435	74.17966	202.5434	1020.675	4814.825
40	1.488864	2.208040	3.262038	4.801021	7.039989	10.28572	14.97446	21.72452	45.25926	93.05096	267.8636	1469.772	7523.164
45	1.564811	2.437854	3.781596	5.841176	8.985008	13.76461	21.00245	31.92045	72.89049	163.9876	538.7694	3657.262	22958.88
50	1.644632	2.691588	4.383906	7.106683	11.46740	18.42015	29.45703	46.90161	117.3909	289.0022	1083.658	9100.439	70064.92
100	2.704814	7.244646	19.21863	50.50494	131.5013	339.3020	867.7164	2199.761	13780.61	83522.24	117×10^4	828×10^5	491×10^7

Example 1 ▸ Future Value of a Single Sum

Required: Find the future value of a $100 certificate of deposit at 8% for three years, (A) compounded annually and (B) compounded quarterly.

Solution A: Let Principal = P = $100, Interest Rate = r = 8%, Period = n = 3 years

Future Value Interest Factor at r Rate for n Periods = FVIF(r, n)

Future Value = FV = P × FVIF(r, n)

FVIF(8%, 3 years) = 1.2597 (from Table 1)

FV = $100 × 1.2597 = $125.97

Solution B: Let Principal = P = $100

Interest Rate = r = 8% / 4 quarters = 2%, Period = n = 12 quarters

Future Value Interest Factor at r Rate for n Periods = FVIF(r, n)

Future Value = FV = P × FVIF(r, n)

FVIF(2%, 12 quarters) = 1.2682 (from Table 1)

FV = $100 × 1.2682 = $126.82

Table 2—Present Value of $1

$$PV = \frac{FV}{(1 + r)^n}$$

r = discount rate; n = number of periods until payment; FV = $1

	1%	2%	3%	4%	5%	6%	7%	8%	10%	12%	15%	20%	25%
n = 1	0.990099	0.980392	0.970874	0.961538	0.952381	0.943396	0.934579	0.925926	0.909091	0.892857	0.869565	0.833333	0.800000
2	0.980296	0.961169	0.942596	0.924556	0.907029	0.889996	0.873439	0.857339	0.826446	0.797194	0.756144	0.694444	0.640000
3	0.970590	0.942322	0.915142	0.888996	0.863838	0.839619	0.816298	0.793832	0.751315	0.711780	0.657516	0.578704	0.512000
4	0.960980	0.923845	0.888487	0.854804	0.822702	0.792094	0.762895	0.735030	0.683013	0.635518	0.571753	0.482253	0.409600
5	0.951466	0.905731	0.862609	0.821927	0.783526	0.747258	0.712986	0.680583	0.620921	0.567427	0.497177	0.401878	0.327680
6	0.942045	0.887971	0.837484	0.790315	0.746215	0.704961	0.666342	0.630170	0.564474	0.506631	0.432328	0.334898	0.262144
7	0.932718	0.870560	0.813092	0.759918	0.710681	0.665057	0.622750	0.583490	0.513158	0.452349	0.375937	0.279082	0.209715
8	0.923483	0.853490	0.789409	0.730690	0.676839	0.627412	0.582009	0.540269	0.466507	0.403883	0.326902	0.232568	0.167772
9	0.914340	0.836755	0.766417	0.702587	0.644609	0.591898	0.543934	0.500249	0.424098	0.360610	0.284262	0.193807	0.134218
10	0.905287	0.820348	0.744094	0.675564	0.613913	0.558395	0.508349	0.463194	0.385543	0.321973	0.247185	0.161506	0.107374
11	0.896324	0.804263	0.722421	0.649581	0.584679	0.526788	0.475093	0.428883	0.350494	0.287476	0.214943	0.134588	0.085899
12	0.887449	0.788493	0.701380	0.624597	0.556837	0.496969	0.444012	0.397114	0.318631	0.256675	0.186907	0.112157	0.068719
13	0.878663	0.773033	0.680951	0.600574	0.530321	0.468839	0.414964	0.367698	0.289664	0.229174	0.162528	0.093464	0.054976
14	0.869963	0.757875	0.661118	0.577475	0.505068	0.442301	0.387817	0.340461	0.263331	0.204620	0.141329	0.077887	0.043980
15	0.861349	0.743015	0.641862	0.555265	0.481017	0.417265	0.362446	0.315242	0.239392	0.182696	0.122894	0.064905	0.035184
16	0.852821	0.728446	0.623167	0.533908	0.458112	0.393646	0.338735	0.291890	0.217629	0.163122	0.106865	0.054088	0.028147
17	0.844378	0.714163	0.605016	0.513373	0.436297	0.371364	0.316574	0.270269	0.197845	0.145644	0.092926	0.045073	0.022518
18	0.836017	0.700159	0.587395	0.493628	0.415521	0.350344	0.295864	0.250249	0.179859	0.130040	0.080805	0.037561	0.018014
19	0.827740	0.686431	0.570286	0.474642	0.395734	0.330513	0.276508	0.231712	0.163508	0.116107	0.070265	0.031301	0.014412
20	0.819544	0.672971	0.553676	0.456387	0.376889	0.311805	0.258419	0.214548	0.148644	0.103667	0.061100	0.026084	0.011529
22	0.803396	0.646839	0.521892	0.421955	0.341850	0.277505	0.225713	0.183941	0.122846	0.082643	0.046201	0.018114	0.007379
24	0.787566	0.621722	0.491934	0.390121	0.310068	0.246979	0.197147	0.157699	0.101526	0.065882	0.034934	0.012579	0.004722
26	0.772048	0.597579	0.463695	0.360689	0.281241	0.219810	0.172195	0.135202	0.083905	0.052521	0.026415	0.008735	0.003022
28	0.756836	0.574375	0.437077	0.333477	0.255094	0.195630	0.150402	0.115914	0.069343	0.041869	0.019974	0.006066	0.001934
30	0.741923	0.552071	0.411987	0.308319	0.231377	0.174110	0.131367	0.099377	0.057309	0.033378	0.015103	0.004213	0.001238
32	0.727304	0.530633	0.388337	0.285058	0.209866	0.154957	0.114741	0.085200	0.047362	0.026609	0.011420	0.002926	0.000792
34	0.712973	0.510028	0.366045	0.263552	0.190355	0.137912	0.100219	0.073045	0.039143	0.021212	0.008635	0.002032	0.000507
36	0.698925	0.490223	0.345032	0.243669	0.172657	0.122741	0.087535	0.062625	0.032349	0.016910	0.006529	0.001411	0.000325
38	0.685153	0.471187	0.325226	0.225285	0.156605	0.109239	0.076457	0.053690	0.026735	0.013481	0.004937	0.000980	0.000208
40	0.671653	0.452890	0.306557	0.208289	0.142046	0.097222	0.066780	0.046031	0.022095	0.010747	0.003733	0.000680	0.000133
45	0.639055	0.410197	0.264439	0.171198	0.111297	0.072650	0.047613	0.031328	0.013719	0.006098	0.001856	0.000273	0.000044
50	0.608039	0.371528	0.228107	0.140713	0.087204	0.054288	0.033948	0.021321	0.008519	0.003460	0.000923	0.000110	0.000014
100	0.369711	0.138033	0.052033	0.019800	0.007604	0.002947	0.001152	0.000455	0.000073	0.000012	0.000001	0.000000	0.000000

Note: The future value factor is equal to 1 divided by the present value factor.

Example 2 ▸ Present Value of a Single Sum

Required: Find the present value of $100 paid three years from now if the market rate of interest is 8% (A) compounded annually and (B) compounded quarterly.

Solution A: Let Principal = P = $100, Interest Rate = r = 8%, Period = n = 3 years
Present Value Interest Factor at r Rate for n Periods = PVIF(r, n)
Present Value = PV = P × PVIF(r, n)

PVIF(8%, 3 years) = 0.7938 (from Table 2)

PV = $100 × 0.7938 = $79.38

Solution B: Let Principal = P = $100, Interest Rate = r = 2%, Period = n = 12 quarters
Present Value Interest Factor at r Rate for n Periods = PVIF(r, n)
Present Value = PV = P × PVIF(r, n)

PVIF(2%, 12 quarters) = 0.7885 (from Table 2)

PV = $100 × 0.7885 = $78.85

Table 3—Future Value of Annuity of $1 in Arrears

$FV = \frac{(1 + r)^n - 1}{r}$ *r* = interest rate; *n* = number of payments

n	1%	2%	3%	4%	5%	6%	7%	8%	10%	12%	15%	20%	25%
n = 1	1.000000	1.000000	1.000000	1.000000	1.000000	1.000000	1.000000	1.000000	1.000000	1.000000	1.000000	1.000000	1.000000
2	2.010000	2.020000	2.030000	2.040000	2.050000	2.060000	2.070000	2.080000	2.100000	2.120000	2.150000	2.200000	2.250000
3	3.030100	3.060400	3.090900	3.121600	3.152500	3.183600	3.214900	3.246400	3.310000	3.374400	3.472500	3.640000	3.812500
4	4.060401	4.121608	4.183627	4.246464	4.310125	4.374616	4.439943	4.506112	4.641000	4.779328	4.993375	5.368000	5.765625
5	5.101005	5.204040	5.309136	5.416323	5.525631	5.637093	5.750739	5.866601	6.105100	6.352847	6.742381	7.441600	8.207031
6	6.152015	6.308121	6.468410	6.632976	6.801913	6.975318	7.153291	7.335929	7.715610	8.115189	8.753738	9.929920	11.25879
7	7.213535	7.434283	7.662462	7.898294	8.142009	8.393838	8.654021	8.922803	9.487171	10.08901	11.06680	12.91590	15.07349
8	8.285670	8.582969	8.892336	9.214226	9.549109	9.897468	10.25980	10.63663	11.43589	12.29969	13.72682	16.49908	19.84186
9	9.368527	9.754628	10.15911	10.58280	11.02656	11.49132	11.97799	12.48756	13.57948	14.77566	16.78584	20.79890	25.80232
10	10.46221	10.94972	11.46388	12.00611	12.57789	13.18079	13.81645	14.48656	15.93742	17.54873	20.30372	25.95868	33.25290
11	11.56683	12.16872	12.80780	13.48635	14.20679	14.97164	15.78360	16.64549	18.53117	20.65458	24.34928	32.15042	42.56613
12	12.68250	13.41209	14.19203	15.02581	15.91713	16.86994	17.88845	18.97713	21.38428	24.13313	29.00167	39.58050	54.20766
13	13.80933	14.68033	15.61779	16.62684	17.71298	18.88214	20.14064	21.49530	24.52271	28.02911	34.35192	48.49660	68.75957
14	14.94742	15.97394	17.08632	18.29191	19.59863	21.01507	22.55049	24.21492	27.97498	32.39260	40.50471	59.19592	86.94947
15	16.09690	17.29342	18.59891	20.02359	21.57856	23.27597	25.12902	27.15211	31.77248	37.27971	47.58041	72.03511	109.6868
16	17.25786	18.63929	20.15688	21.82453	23.65749	25.67253	27.88805	30.32428	35.94973	42.75328	55.71748	87.44213	138.1086
17	18.43044	20.01207	21.76159	23.69751	25.84037	28.21288	30.84022	33.75023	40.54470	48.88367	65.07510	105.9306	173.6357
18	19.61475	21.41231	23.41443	25.64541	28.13239	30.90565	33.99903	37.45024	45.59917	55.74971	75.83636	128.1167	218.0446
19	20.81090	22.84056	25.11687	27.67123	30.53900	33.75999	37.37896	41.44626	51.15909	63.43968	88.21181	154.7400	273.5558
20	22.01900	24.29737	26.87037	29.77808	33.06596	36.78559	40.99549	45.76196	57.27500	72.05244	102.4436	186.6880	342.9447
22	24.47159	27.29898	30.53678	34.24797	38.50521	43.39229	49.00574	55.45675	71.40275	92.50258	137.6317	271.0307	538.1011
24	26.97346	30.42186	34.42647	39.08260	44.50200	50.81557	58.17667	66.76476	88.49733	118.1552	184.1679	392.4843	843.0330
26	29.52563	33.67091	38.55304	44.31174	51.11345	59.15638	68.67647	79.95441	109.1818	150.3339	245.7120	567.3773	1319.489
28	32.12910	37.05121	42.93092	49.96758	58.40258	68.52811	80.69769	95.33883	134.2099	190.6989	327.1041	819.2233	2063.951
30	34.78489	40.56808	47.57542	56.08494	66.43885	79.05818	94.46078	113.2832	164.4940	241.3327	434.7452	1181.882	3227.174
32	37.49407	44.22703	52.50276	62.70147	75.29883	90.88978	110.2182	134.2135	201.1378	304.8477	577.1005	1704.110	5044.710
34	40.25770	48.03380	57.73018	69.85791	85.06696	104.1838	128.2588	158.6267	245.4767	384.5210	765.3655	2456.118	7884.609
36	43.07688	51.99437	63.27594	77.59831	95.83633	119.1209	148.9135	187.1021	299.1268	484.4631	1014.346	3539.010	12321.95
38	45.95272	56.11494	69.15945	85.97034	107.7095	135.9042	172.5610	220.3159	364.0435	609.8305	1343.622	5098.374	19255.30
40	48.88637	60.40198	75.40126	95.02551	120.7998	154.7620	199.6351	259.0565	442.5926	767.0914	1779.091	7343.858	30088.66
45	56.48108	71.89271	92.71986	121.0294	159.7002	212.7435	285.7493	386.5056	718.9048	1358.230	3585.129	18281.31	91831.50
50	64.46318	84.57940	112.7969	152.6671	209.3480	290.3359	406.5289	573.7701	1163.909	2400.018	7217.718	45497.20	280255.7
100	170.4814	312.2323	607.2877	1237.624	2610.025	5638.368	12381.66	27484.51	137796.1	696010.5	783×10^4	414×10^6	196×10^8

Note: To convert from this table to values of an annuity in advance, determine the annuity in arrears factor above for one more period and subtract 1.

Example 3 ▸ Future Value of an Annuity in Arrears

Required: Jones plans to save $300 a year for three years. If Jones deposits money at the end of each period in a savings plan that yields 24%, how much will Jones have at the end of the three years if Jones deposits (A) $75 at the end of each quarter? (B) $25 at the end of every month?

Solution A: Let Payment = P = $75, Interest Rate = r = 6%, Period = n = 12 quarters
Future Value of an Annuity Factor at r Rate for n Periods = FVAF(r, n)
Future Value of the Annuity = FVA = P × FVAF(r, n)

FVAF(6%, 12 quarters) = 16.8699 (from Table 3)

FVA = $75 × 16.8699 = $1,265.24

Solution B: Let Payment = P = $25, Interest Rate = r = 2%, Period = n = 36 months
Future Value of an Annuity Factor at r Rate for n Periods = FVAF(r, n)
Future Value of the Annuity = FVA = P × FVAF(r, n)

FVAF(2%, 36 months) = 51.9944 (from Table 3)

FVA = $25 × 51.9944 = $1,299.86

Table 4—Present Value of Annuity of $1 in Arrears

$$PV = \frac{1-(1+r)^{-n}}{r}$$ *r* = discount rate; *n* = number of payments

	1%	2%	3%	4%	5%	6%	7%	8%	10%	12%	15%	20%	25%
n = 1	0.990099	0.980392	0.970874	0.961538	0.952381	0.943396	0.934579	0.925926	0.909091	0.892857	0.869565	0.833333	0.800000
2	1.970395	1.941561	1.913470	1.886095	1.859410	1.833393	1.808018	1.783265	1.735537	1.690051	1.625709	1.527778	1.440000
3	2.940985	2.883883	2.828611	2.775091	2.723248	2.673012	2.624316	2.577097	2.486852	2.401831	2.283225	2.106482	1.952000
4	3.901966	3.807729	3.717098	3.629895	3.545950	3.465106	3.387211	3.312127	3.169865	3.037349	2.854978	2.588735	2.361600
5	4.853431	4.713459	4.579707	4.451822	4.329477	4.212364	4.100197	3.992710	3.790787	3.604776	3.352155	2.990612	2.689280
6	5.795476	5.601431	5.417192	5.242137	5.075692	4.917325	4.766540	4.622880	4.355261	4.111407	3.784483	3.325510	2.951424
7	6.728195	6.471991	6.230283	6.002055	5.786374	5.582381	5.389289	5.206370	4.868419	4.563756	4.160419	3.604592	3.161139
8	7.651678	7.325481	7.019692	6.732745	6.463213	6.209794	5.971299	5.746639	5.334926	4.967640	4.487321	3.837160	3.328911
9	8.566017	8.162237	7.786109	7.435332	7.107821	6.801692	6.515232	6.246888	5.759024	5.328250	4.771584	4.030966	3.463129
10	9.471305	8.982585	8.530203	8.110896	7.721735	7.360087	7.023582	6.710082	6.144567	5.650223	5.018768	4.192472	3.570503
11	10.36763	9.786848	9.252625	8.760477	8.306415	7.886875	7.498674	7.138964	6.495061	5.937699	5.233712	4.327060	3.656403
12	11.25508	10.57534	9.954004	9.385074	8.863252	8.383844	7.942686	7.536078	6.813692	6.194374	5.420619	4.439217	3.725122
13	12.13374	11.34837	10.63496	9.985648	9.393573	8.852683	8.357651	7.903776	7.103356	6.423549	5.583147	4.532681	3.780098
14	13.00370	12.10625	11.29607	10.56312	9.898641	9.294984	8.745468	8.244237	7.366687	6.628168	5.724475	4.610567	3.824078
15	13.86505	12.84926	11.93793	11.11839	10.37966	9.712249	9.107914	8.559479	7.606080	6.810864	5.847370	4.675473	3.859262
16	14.71787	13.57771	12.56110	11.65230	10.83777	10.10590	9.446649	8.851369	7.823709	6.973986	5.954235	4.729560	3.887410
17	15.56225	14.29187	13.16612	12.16567	11.27407	10.47726	9.763223	9.121638	8.021553	7.119631	6.047161	4.774634	3.909928
18	16.39827	14.99203	13.75351	12.65930	11.68959	10.82760	10.05909	9.371887	8.201412	7.249670	6.127965	4.812195	3.927943
19	17.22601	15.67846	14.32380	13.13394	12.08532	11.15812	10.33560	9.603600	8.364920	7.365777	6.198231	4.843496	3.942354
20	18.04555	16.35143	14.87747	13.59033	12.46221	11.46992	10.59401	9.818148	8.513564	7.469444	6.259331	4.869580	3.953883
22	19.66038	17.65805	15.93692	14.45112	13.16300	12.04158	11.06124	10.20074	8.771541	7.644646	6.358663	4.909431	3.970485
24	21.24339	18.91393	16.93554	15.24696	13.79864	12.55036	11.46933	10.52876	8.984744	7.784316	6.433771	4.937104	3.981111
26	22.79520	20.12104	17.87684	15.98277	14.37519	13.00317	11.82578	10.80998	9.160945	7.895660	6.490564	4.956323	3.987911
28	24.31644	21.28127	18.76411	16.66306	14.89813	13.40616	12.13711	11.05108	9.306566	7.984423	6.533508	4.969668	3.992263
30	25.80771	22.39646	19.60044	17.29203	15.37245	13.76483	12.40904	11.25778	9.426914	8.055184	6.565979	4.978936	3.995048
32	27.26959	23.46833	20.38877	17.87355	15.80268	14.08404	12.64655	11.43500	9.526376	8.111594	6.590533	4.985373	3.996831
34	28.70267	24.49859	21.13184	18.41120	16.19290	14.36814	12.85401	11.58693	9.608575	8.156565	6.609098	4.989842	3.997972
36	30.10751	25.48884	21.83225	18.90828	16.54685	14.62099	13.03521	11.71719	9.676508	8.192414	6.623137	4.992946	3.998702
38	31.48466	26.44064	22.49246	19.36786	16.86789	14.84602	13.19347	11.82887	9.732652	8.220994	6.633752	4.995101	3.999169
40	32.83469	27.35548	23.11477	19.79277	17.15909	15.04630	13.33171	11.92461	9.779051	8.243777	6.641778	4.996598	3.999468
45	36.09451	29.49016	24.51871	20.72004	17.77407	15.45583	13.60552	12.10840	9.862807	8.282516	6.654293	4.998633	3.999826
50	39.19612	31.42361	25.72976	21.48219	18.25593	15.76186	13.80075	12.23349	9.914814	8.304499	6.660514	4.999451	3.999943
100	63.02888	43.09835	31.59891	24.50500	19.84791	16.61755	14.26925	12.49432	9.999274	8.333234	6.666661	5.000000	4.000000

Note: To convert from this table to values of an annuity in advance, determine the annuity in arrears factor above for one less period and add 1.

Example 4 ▸ Present Value of an Annuity in Arrears and Present Value of an Annuity Due

Required: Smith can make annual mortgage payments (not including taxes, etc.) of $4,800. How much can Smith borrow at 8% interest and repay in 20 years: (A) making 20 equal payments at the end of the year? (B) making 20 equal payments at the beginning of the year?

Solution A: Let Payment = P = $4,800, Interest Rate = r = 8%, Period = n = 20 years
Present Value of an Annuity Factor at r Rate for n Periods = PVAF(r, n)
Present Value of the Annuity = PVA = P × PVAF(r, n)

PVAF(8%, 20 years) = 9.8181 (from Table 4)

Loan = PVA = $4,800 × 9.8181 = $47,126.88

Solution B: Let Payment = P = $4,800, Interest Rate = r = 8%, Period = n = 20 years
Present Value of an Annuity Factor at r Rate for n Periods = PVAF(r, n)
Present Value of the Annuity in Advance = PVAA = P × [PVAF(r, n – 1) + 1]

PVAF(8%, 19 years) = 9.6036 (from Table 4)

Loan = PVAA = $4,800 × (9.6036 + 1) = $50,897.28

Example 5 ▸ Capital Lease Obligation

Alpha Company has a 10 year capital lease with an implicit interest rate of 8%. The $40,000 payments are made at the beginning of each year.

Required: What is the capital lease obligation (the present value of the lease payments)?

Solution: Let Payment = P = $40,000, Interest Rate = r = 8%, Period = n = 10 years
Present Value of an Annuity Factor at r Rate for n Periods = PVAF(r, n)
Present Value of the Annuity in Advance = PVAA = P × [PVAF(r, n – 1) + 1]

PVAF(8%, 9 years) = 6.246888 (from Table 4)

Capital Lease Obligation = PVAA = $40,000 × (6.246888 + 1) = $289,875.52

This is the same as: Capital Lease Obligation = Initial Payment + PVA (where r = 8%, n = 9)
= Initial Payment + P × PVAF(8%, 9)
= $40,000 + $40,000 × 6.246888
= $289,875.52

Example 6 ▸ Internal Rate of Return

Beta Company is considering the purchase of a machine for $12,500. Beta expects a net year-end cash inflow of $5,000 annually over the machine's 3-year life. [The IRR is that rate at which NPV = 0. For more information on internal rate of return (IRR) and net present value (NPV), see Chapter 26 in the ARE volume.]

Required: What is this project's approximate internal rate of return?

Solution: This example involves a present single sum and an annuity. The present value of the single sum paid today is $12,500. In this situation, NPV is the present value of the purchase price (P) less the present value of the future annual cash inflow (PVA).

Let Single Payment = P = $12,500 Interest Rate = r = ?
Annual Cash Inflow = A = $5,000 Period = n = 3 years
Present Value of an Annuity Factor at r Rate for n Periods = PVAF(r, n)

NPV = P – PVA and NPV = 0 Thus, P – PVA = 0

PVA = A x PVAF(r, n) so P – [A × PVAF(r, n)] = 0 or
P = A × PVAF(r, n) or
P / A = PVAF(r, n) and substituting known values:
$12,500 / $5,000 = PVAF(r, 3 years) or
PVAF(r, 3 years) = 2.5

Looking in the 3 period row of Table 4, we find the interest rate that produces the interest factor closest to 2.5 is in the 10% column. (Examiners generally narrow the field somewhat by supplying half a dozen values instead of a whole table, but they frequently also provide values from tables that are misleading. For instance, they may supply future values of annuities or present values of single sums.)

PVAF(8%, 3 years) = 2.577097 rounds to 2.6
PVAF(10%, 3 years) = 2.486852 rounds to 2.5 Thus, r (or IRR) is about 10%.
PVAF(12%, 3 years) = 2.401831 rounds to 2.4

APPENDIX E
RECENTLY RELEASED AICPA QUESTIONS

In April 2006, the AICPA released several questions labeled as "Year 2006 CPA Exams." The FAR questions and the related unofficial solutions are reproduced here, along with the exclusive Bisk Education explanations. The AICPA did not state whether these questions were used on an exam. These questions are intended only as a study aid and should not be used to predict the content of future exams. It is extremely unlikely that released questions will appear on future examinations.

Problem 1 MULTIPLE CHOICE QUESTIONS (100 to 125 minutes)

1. Which of the following should be disclosed in a summary of significant accounting policies?

a. Basis of profit recognition on long-term construction contracts
b. Future minimum lease payments in the aggregate and for each of the five succeeding fiscal years
c. Depreciation expense
d. Composition of sales by segment

(FAR, R/06, 0012F, #1, 8068)

2. A capital projects fund for a new city courthouse recorded a receivable of $300,000 for a state grant and a $450,000 transfer from the general fund. What amount should be reported as revenue by the capital projects fund?

a. $0
b. $300,000
c. $450,000
d. $750,000 (FAR, R/06, 0111G, #2, 8069)

3. Cart Co. purchased an office building and the land on which it is located for $750,000 cash and an existing $250,000 mortgage. For realty tax purposes, the property is assessed at $960,000, 60% of which is allocated to the building. At what amount should Cart record the building?

a. $500,000
b. $576,000
c. $600,000
d. $960,000 (FAR, R/06, 0266F, #3, 8070)

4. A flash flood swept through Hat, Inc.'s warehouse on May 1. After the flood, Hat's accounting records showed the following:

Inventory, January 1	$ 35,000
Purchases, January 1 through May 1	200,000
Sales, January 1 through May 1	250,000
Inventory not damaged by flood	30,000
Gross profit percentage on sales	40%

What amount of inventory was lost in the flood?

a. $ 55,000
b. $ 85,000
c. $120,000
d. $150,000 (FAR, R/06, 0386F, #4, 8071)

5. Which of the following financial instruments is **not** considered a derivative financial instrument?

a. Interest-rate swaps
b. Currency futures
c. Stock-index options
d. Bank certificates of deposit

(FAR, R/06, 0551F, #5, 8072)

6. Dex Co. has entered into a joint venture with an affiliate to secure access to additional inventory. Under the joint venture agreement, Dex will purchase the output of the venture at prices negotiated on an arms'-length basis. Which of the following is(are) required to be disclosed about the related party transaction?

I. The amount due to the affiliate at the balance sheet date
II. The dollar amount of the purchases during the year

a. I only
b. II only
c. Both I and II
d. Neither I nor II (FAR, R/06, 0564F, #6, 8073)

7. Arpco, Inc., a for-profit provider of healthcare services, recently purchased two smaller companies and is researching accounting issues arising from the two business combinations. Which of the following accounting pronouncements are the most authoritative?

a. AICPA Statements of Position
b. AICPA Industry and Audit Guides
c. FASB Statements of Financial Accounting Concepts
d. FASB Statements of Financial Accounting Standards (FAR, R/06, 0568F, #7, 8074)

8. Which of the following should be disclosed for each reportable operating segment of an enterprise?

	Profit or loss	*Total assets*
a.	Yes	Yes
b.	Yes	No
c.	No	Yes
d.	No	No

(FAR, R/06, 0652F, #8, 8075)

9. According to the FASB conceptual framework, the quality of information that helps users increase the likelihood of correctly forecasting the outcome of past or present events is called
a. Feedback value
b. Predictive value
c. Representational faithfulness
d. Reliability (FAR, R/06, 0778F, #9, 8076)

10. During the year, Public College received the following:

An unrestricted $50,000 pledge to be paid the following year
A $25,000 cash gift restricted for scholarships
A notice from a recent graduate that the college is named as a beneficiary of $10,000 in that graduate's will

What amount of contribution revenue should Public College report in its statement of activities?
a. $25,000
b. $35,000
c. $75,000
d. $85,000 (FAR, R/06, 0784G, #10, 8077)

11. When debt is issued at a discount, interest expense over the term of debt equals the cash interest paid
a. Minus discount
b. Minus discount minus par value
c. Plus discount
d. Plus discount plus par value
(FAR, R/06, 0835F, #11, 8078)

12. On December 30, Devlin Co. sold goods to Jensen Co. for $10,000, under an arrangement in which (1) Jensen has an unlimited right of return and (2) Jensen's obligation to pay Devlin is contingent upon Jensen's reselling the goods. Past experience has shown that Jensen ordinarily resells 60% of goods and returns the other 40%. What amount should Devlin include in sales revenue for this transaction on its December 31 income statement?
a. $10,000
b. $ 6,000
c. $ 4,000
d. $0 (FAR, R/06, 0900F, #12, 8079)

13. Which of the following is a required financial statement for an investment trust fund?
a. Statement of revenues, expenditures, and changes in fiduciary net assets
b. Statement of activities
c. Statement of revenues, expenses, and changes in fiduciary net assets
d. Statement of changes in fiduciary net assets
(FAR, R/06, 0968G, #13, 8080)

14. Payne Co. prepares its statement of cash flows using the indirect method. Payne's unamortized bond discount account decreased by $25,000 during the year. How should Payne report the change in unamortized bond discount in its statement of cash flows?
a. As a financing cash inflow
b. As a financing cash outflow
c. As an addition to net income in the operating activities section
d. As a subtraction from net income in the operating activities section
(FAR, R/06, 1046F, #14, 8081)

15. A voluntary health and welfare organization received a $700,000 permanent endowment during the year. The donor stipulated that the income and investment appreciation be used to maintain its senior center. The endowment fund reported a net investment appreciation of $80,000 and investment income of $50,000. The organization spent $60,000 to maintain its senior center during the year. What amount of change in temporarily restricted net assets should the organization report?
a. $ 50,000
b. $ 70,000
c. $130,000
d. $770,000 (FAR, R/06, 1085G, #15, 8082)

16. Koby Co. entered into a capital lease with a vendor for equipment on January 2 for seven years. The equipment has no guaranteed residual value. The lease required Koby to pay $500,000 annually on January 2, beginning with the current year. The present value of an annuity due for seven years was 5.35 at the inception of the lease. What amount should Koby capitalize as leased equipment?
a. $ 500,000
b. $ 825,000
c. $2,675,000
d. $3,500,000 (FAR, R/06, 1266F, #16, 8083)

17. Godart Co. issued $4,500,000 notes payable as a scrip dividend that matured in five years. At maturity, each shareholder of Godart's three million shares will receive payment of the note principal plus interest. The annual interest rate was 10%. What amount should be paid to the stockholders at the end of the fifth year?
a. $ 450,000
b. $2,250,000
c. $4,500,000
d. $6,750,000 (FAR, R/06, 1471F, #17, 8084)

18. Standard Co. spent $10,000,000 on its new software package that is to be used only for internal use. The amount spent is for costs after the application development stage. The economic life of the product is expected to be three years. The equipment on which the package is to be used is being depreciated over five years. What amount of expense should Standard report on its income statement for the first full year?

a. $0
b. $ 2,000,000
c. $ 3,333,333
d. $10,000,000 (FAR, R/06, 1512F, #18, 8085)

19. Which of the following conditions must exist in order for an impairment loss to be recognized?

I. The carrying amount of the long-lived asset is less than its fair value.
II. The carrying amount of the long-lived asset is not recoverable.

a. I only
b. II only
c. Both I and II
d. Neither I nor II (FAR, R/06, 1565F, #19, 8086)

20. Which of the following should be disclosed in a company's financial statements related to deferred taxes?

I. The types and amounts of existing temporary differences
II. The types and amounts of existing permanent differences
III. The nature and amount of each type of operating loss and tax credit carryforward

a. I and II only
b. I and III only
c. II and III only
d. I, II, and III (FAR, R/06, 1725F, #20, 8087)

21. Nomar Co. shipped inventory on consignment to Seabright Co. that cost $20,000. Seabright paid $500 for advertising that was reimbursable from Nomar. At the end of the year, 70% of the inventory was sold for $30,000. The agreement states that a commission of 20% will be provided to Seabright for all sales. What amount of net inventory on consignment remains on the balance sheet for the first year for Nomar?

a. $0
b. $ 6,000
c. $ 6,500
d. $20,000 (FAR, R/06, 1800F, #21, 8088)

22. During the current year, a voluntary health and welfare organization receives $300,000 in unrestricted pledges. Of this amount, $100,000 has been designated by donors for use next year to support operations. If 15% of the unrestricted pledges are expected to be uncollectible, what amount of unrestricted support should the organization recognize in its current-year financial statements?

a. $300,000
b. $270,000
c. $200,000
d. $170,000 (FAR, R/06, A0008N, #22, 8089)

23. Which of the following must be included in a company's summary of significant accounting policies in the notes to the financial statements?

a. Description of current year equity transactions
b. Summary of long-term debt outstanding
c. Schedule of fixed assets
d. Revenue recognition policies (FAR, R/06, C00161F, #23, 8090)

24. Mellow Co. depreciated a $12,000 asset over five years, using the straight-line method with no salvage value. At the beginning of the fifth year, it was determined that the asset will last another four years. What amount should Mellow report as depreciation expense for Year 5?

a. $ 600
b. $ 900
c. $1,500
d. $2,400 (FAR, R/06, C02257F, #24, 8091)

25. Cantor Co. purchased a coal mine for $2,000,000. It cost $500,000 to prepare the coal mine for extraction of the coal. It was estimated that 750,000 tons of coal would be extracted from the mine during its useful life. Cantor planned to sell the property for $100,000 at the end of its useful life. During the current year, 15,000 tons of coal were extracted and sold. What would be Cantor's depletion amount per ton for the current year?

a. $2.50
b. $2.60
c. $3.20
d. $3.30 (FAR, R/06, C03042F, #25, 8092)

26. Assuming no outstanding encumbrances at year end, closing entries for which of the following situations would increase the unreserved fund balance at year end?

a. Actual revenues were **less** than estimated revenues.
b. Estimated revenues exceed actual appropriations.
c. Actual expenditures exceed appropriations.
d. Appropriations exceed actual expenditures. (FAR, R/06, 0245G, #26, 8093)

27. Which of the following is correct concerning financial statement disclosure of accounting policies?
a. Disclosures should be limited to principles and methods peculiar to the industry in which the company operates.
b. Disclosure of accounting policies is an integral part of the financial statements.
c. The format and location of accounting policy disclosures are fixed by generally accepted accounting principles.
d. Disclosures should duplicate details disclosed elsewhere in the financial statements.
(FAR, R/06, 0375F, #27, 8094)

28. An employer's obligation for postretirement health benefits that are expected to be fully provided to or for an employee must be fully accrued by the date the
a. Benefits are paid.
b. Benefits are utilized.
c. Employee retires.
d. Employee is fully eligible for benefits.
(FAR, R/06, 0487F, #28, 8095)

29. On September 30, World Co. borrowed \$1,000,000 on a 9% note payable. World paid the first of four quarterly payments of \$264,200 when due on December 30. In its income statement for the year, what amount should World report as interest expense?
a. \$0
b. \$14,200
c. \$22,500
d. \$30,000 (FAR, R/06, 0524F, #29, 8096)

30. Which of the following factors determines whether an identified segment of an enterprise should be reported in the enterprise's financial statements under SFAS No. 131, *Disclosures about Segments of an Enterprise and Related Information*?

I. The segment's assets constitute more than 10% of the combined assets of all operating segments.
II. The segment's liabilities constitute more than 10% of the combined liabilities of all operating segments.

a. I only
b. II only
c. Both I and II
d. Neither I nor II (FAR, R/06, 0716F, #30, 8097)

31. Which of the following is a research and development cost?
a. Development or improvement of techniques and processes
b. Offshore oil exploration that is the primary activity of a company
c. Research and development performed under contract for others
d. Market research related to a major product for the company (FAR, R/06, 0820F, #31, 8098)

32. Which of the following items is included in the financing activities section of the statement of cash flows?
a. Cash effects of transactions involving making and collecting loans
b. Cash effects of acquiring and disposing of investments and property, plant, and equipment
c. Cash effects of transactions obtaining resources from owners and providing them with a return on their investment
d. Cash effects of transactions that enter into the determination of net income
(FAR, R/06, 1007F, #32, 8099)

33. North Co. entered into a franchise agreement with South Co. for an initial fee of \$50,000. North received \$10,000 at the agreement's signing. The remaining balance was to be paid at a rate of \$10,000 per year, beginning the following year. North's services per the agreement were not complete in the current year. Operating activities will commence next year. What amount should North report as franchise revenue in the current year?
a. \$0
b. \$10,000
c. \$20,000
d. \$50,000 (FAR, R/06, 1178F, #33, 8100)

34. Whether recognized or unrecognized in an entity's financial statements, disclosure of the fair values of the entity's financial instruments is required when

	It is practicable to estimate those values	*Aggregated fair values are material to the entity*
a.	No	No
b.	No	Yes
c.	Yes	No
d.	Yes	Yes

(FAR, R/06, 1300F, #34, 8101)

35. Green Co. incurred leasehold improvement costs for its leased property. The estimated useful life of the improvements was 15 years. The remaining term of the nonrenewable lease was 20 years. These costs should be

a. Expensed as incurred
b. Capitalized and depreciated over 20 years
c. Capitalized and expensed in the year in which the lease expires
d. Capitalized and depreciated over 15 years

(FAR, R/06, 1350F, #35, 8102)

36. On January 1 of the current year, Lean Co. made an investment of $10,000. The following is the present value of $1.00 discounted at a 10% interest rate:

Periods	*Present value of $1.00 Discounted at 10%*
1	0.909
2	0.826
3	0.751

What amount of cash will Lean accumulate in two years?

a. $12,000
b. $12,107
c. $16,250
d. $27,002

(FAR, R/06, 1506F, #36, 8103)

37. Yellow Co. spent $12,000,000 during the current year developing its new software package. Of this amount, $4,000,000 was spent before it was at the application development stage and the package was only to be used internally. The package was completed during the year and is expected to have a four-year useful life. Yellow has a policy of taking a full-year's amortization in the first year. After the development stage, $50,000 was spent on training employees to use the program. What amount should Yellow report as an expense for the current year?

a. $1,600,000
b. $2,000,000
c. $6,012,500
d. $6,050,000

(FAR, R/06, 1518F, #37, 8104)

38. Miller Co. discovered that in the prior year, it failed to report $40,000 of depreciation related to a newly constructed building. The depreciation was computed correctly for tax purposes. The tax rate for the current year was 40%. What was the impact of the error on Miller's financial statements for the prior year?

a. Understatement of accumulated depreciation of $24,000
b. Understatement of accumulated depreciation of $40,000
c. Understatement of depreciation expense of $24,000
d. Understatement of net income of $24,000

(FAR, R/06, 1538F, #38, 8105)

39. At June 30, Almond Co.'s cash balance was $10,012 before adjustments, while its ending bank statement balance was $10,772. Check number 101 was issued June 2 in the amount of $95, but was erroneously recorded in Almond's general ledger balance as $59. The check was correctly listed in the bank statement at $95. The bank statement also included a credit memo for interest earned in the amount of $35, and a debit memo for monthly service charges in the amount of $50. What was Almond's adjusted cash balance at June 30?

a. $ 9,598
b. $ 9,961
c. $10,048
d. $10,462

(FAR, R/06, 1554F, #39, 8106)

40. Trans Co. uses a periodic inventory system. The following are inventory transactions for the month of January:

1/1	Beginning inventory	10,000 units at $3
1/5	Purchase	5,000 units at $4
1/15	Purchase	5,000 units at $5
1/20	Sales at $10 per unit	10,000 units

Trans uses the average pricing method to determine the value of its inventory. What amount should Trans report as cost of goods sold on its income statement for the month of January?

a. $ 30,000
b. $ 37,500
c. $ 40,000
d. $100,000

(FAR, R/06, 1674F, #40, 8107)

41. Porter Co. began its business last year and issued 10,000 shares of common stock at $3 per share. The par value of the stock is $1 per share. During January of the current year, Porter bought back 500 shares at $6 per share, which were reported by Porter as treasury stock. The treasury stock shares were reissued later in the current year at $10 per share. Porter used the cost method to account for its equity transactions. What amount should Porter report as paid-in capital related to its treasury stock transactions on its balance sheet for the current year?
a. $ 1,500
b. $ 2,000
c. $ 4,500
d. $20,000 (FAR, R/06, 1691F, #41, 8108)

42. New England Co. had net cash provided by operating activities of $351,000; net cash used by investing activities of $420,000; and cash provided by financing activities of $250,000. New England's cash balance was $27,000 on January 1. During the year, there was a sale of land that resulted in a gain of $25,000 and proceeds of $40,000 were received from the sale. What was New England's cash balance at the end of the year?
a. $ 27,000
b. $ 40,000
c. $208,000
d. $248,000 (FAR, R/06, 1843F, #42, 8109)

43. Which of the following assets of a nongovernmental not-for-profit charitable organization must be depreciated?
a. A freezer costing $150,000 for storing food for the soup kitchen
b. Building costs of $500,000 for construction in progress for senior citizen housing
c. Land valued at $1 million being used as the site of the new senior citizen home
d. A bulk purchase of $20,000 of linens for its nursing home (FAR, R/06, A0079N, #43, 8110)

44. Which of the following would be reported as program revenues on a local government's government-wide statement of activities?
a. Charges for services
b. Taxes levied for a specific function
c. Proceeds from the sale of a capital asset used for a specific function
d. Interest revenues

(FAR, R/06, A0095G, #44, 8111)

45. A nongovernmental not-for-profit organization borrowed $5,000, which it used to purchase a truck. In which section of the organization's statement of cash flows should the transaction be reported?
a. In cash inflow and cash outflow from investing activities
b. In cash inflow and cash outflow from financing activities
c. In cash inflow from financing activities and cash outflow from investing activities
d. In cash inflow from operating activities and cash outflow from investing activities

(FAR, R/06, A0149N, #45, 8112)

46. Janna Association, a nongovernmental not-for-profit organization, received a cash gift with the stipulation that the principal be held for at least 20 years. How should the cash gift be recorded?
a. A temporarily restricted asset
b. A permanently restricted asset
c. An unrestricted asset
d. A temporary liability

(FAR, R/06, A0156N, #46, 8113)

47. Which of the following assumptions means that money is the common denominator of economic activity and provides an appropriate basis for accounting measurement and analysis?
a. Going concern
b. Periodicity
c. Monetary unit
d. Economic entity (FAR, R/06, A0677F, #47, 8114)

48. Which of the following statements best describes an operating procedure for issuing a new Financial Accounting Standards Board (FASB) statement?
a. The emerging issues task force must approve a discussion memorandum before it is disseminated to the public.
b. The exposure draft is modified per public opinion before issuing the discussion memorandum.
c. A new statement is issued only after a majority vote by the members of the FASB.
d. A new FASB statement can be rescinded by a majority vote of the AICPA membership.

(FAR, R/06, A0711F, #48, 8115)

49. What is the present value of all future retirement payments attributed by the pension benefit formula to employee services rendered prior to that date only?
a. Service cost
b. Interest cost
c. Projected benefit obligation
d. Accumulated benefit obligation

(FAR, R/06, C03070F, #49, 8116)

50. Which of the following is a criterion for a lease to be classified as a capital lease in the books of a lessee?

a. The lease contains a bargain purchase option.
b. The lease does **not** transfer ownership of the property to the lessee.
c. The lease term is equal to 65% or more of the estimated useful life of the leased property.
d. The present value of the minimum lease payments is 70% or more of the fair market value of the leased property.

(FAR, R/06, C03117F, #50, 8117)

SIMULATION

Problem 2 (40 to 50 minutes)

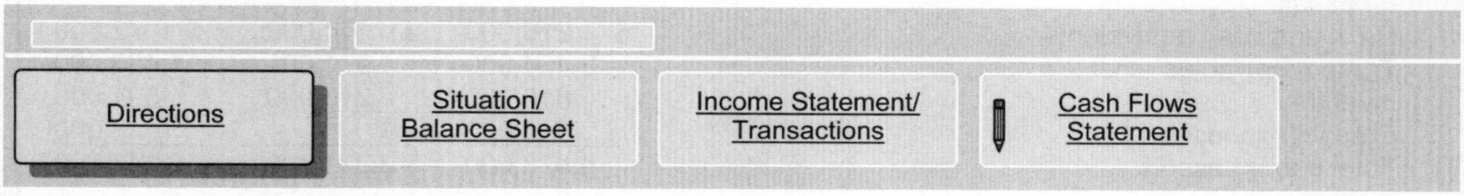

In the following simulation, you will be asked various questions regarding accounting and reporting for cash flows. You will use the content in the **Information Tabs** to complete the tasks in the **Work Tabs.** (The following pictures are for illustration only; the actual tabs in your simulation may differ from these.)

Information Tabs:

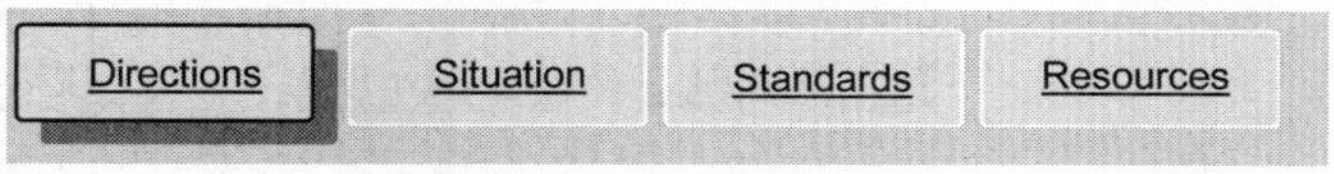

Beginning with the Directions tab at the left side of the screen, go through each of the **Information Tabs** to familiarize yourself with the simulation content. Note that the **Resources** tab will contain useful information, including formulas and definitions, to help you complete the tasks. You may want to refer to this information while you are working.

Work Tabs:

The **Work Tabs,** on the right side of the screen, contain the tasks for you to complete.

Once you complete any part of a task, the pencil for that tab will be shaded. Note that a shaded pencil does NOT indicate that you have completed the entire task.

You must complete all of the tasks in **Work Tabs** to receive full credit.

If you have difficulty answering a **Work Tab,** read the tab directions carefully.

Note: If you believe you have encountered a software malfunction, report it to the test center staff immediately.

Directions	Situation/ Balance Sheet	Income Statement/ Transactions	Cash Flows Statement

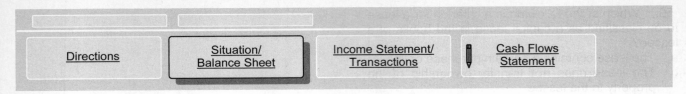

Comparative balance sheets for Bayshore Industries, Inc. as of December 31, year 2 and year 1 are presented below. Use this information to answer the subsequent questions.

Bayshore Industries, Inc.
Balance Sheets
December 31, Year 2 and Year 1

	Year 2	Year 1	Change
Assets			
Current assets			
Cash and cash equivalents	$ 216,000	$ 144,000	$ 72,000
Trade receivables – net	3,434,000	1,971,000	1,463,000
Inventory	810,000	216,000	594,000
Prepaid expenses	18,000	--	18,000
Total current assets	4,478,000	2,331,000	2,147,000
Property and equipment	7,780,000	7,740,000	40,000
Less: accumulated depreciation	576,000	455,000	121,000
Property and equipment – net	7,204,000	7,285,000	(81,000)
Intangibles, less accumulated amortization of $14,400 – year 2 and $7,200 – year 1	21,600	28,800	(7,200)
Total assets	$11,703,600	$9,644,800	$2,058,800
Liabilities and Stockholders' Equity			
Current liabilities			
Accounts payable and accrued expenses	$ 872,600	$ 396,800	$ 475,800
Line of credit	108,000	90,000	18,000
Current portion of long-term debt	29,000	27,000	2,000
Total current liabilities	1,009,600	513,800	495,800
Long-term debt	3,069,000	3,098,000	(29,000)
Total liabilities	4,078,600	3,611,800	466,800
Stockholders' equity			
Common stock	9,000	9,000	0
Additional paid-in capital	5,400,000	5,400,000	0
Retained earnings	2,216,000	624,000	1,592,000
Total stockholders' equity	7,625,000	6,033,000	1,592,000
Total liabilities and stockholders' equity	$11,703,600	$9,644,800	$2,058,800

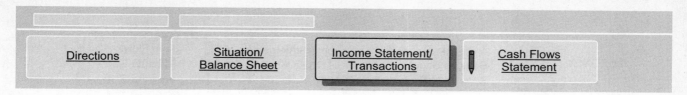

Directions	Situation/ Balance Sheet	Income Statement/ Transactions	Cash Flows Statement

The Statement of Income and Retained Earnings for Bayshore Industries, Inc. for Year 2, as well as additional information regarding the company's operations for the year, is presented below. Use this information to answer the subsequent questions.

Bayshore Industries, Inc.
Statement of Income and Retained Earnings
For the year ended December 31, Year 2

Net sales	$19,800,000
Cost of sales	9,000,000
Gross profit on sales	10,800,000
Operating expenses	
Selling expenses	3,600,000
General and administrative expenses	4,050,000
Other operating expenses	393,300
Total operating expenses	8,043,300
Operating income	2,756,700
Other income and expenses	
Gain/loss on property and equipment disposals	18,000
Interest income	9,000
Interest expense	(252,000)
Other income and expenses – net	(225,000)
Income before income taxes	2,531,700
Provision for income taxes	759,700
Net income	1,772,000
Retained earnings – beginning	624,000
Dividends paid	180,000
Retained earnings – ending	$ 2,216,000

Additional information on transactions during the year ended December 31, year 2:

All accounts receivable relate to customer sales.
All accounts payable relate to suppliers.
All fixed assets were acquired for cash.
A building with original cost of $360,000 and accumulated depreciation of $319,500 was sold for $58,500.
The company had no new debt in year 2.
Interest paid in current year was $250,000.
Cash paid for income taxes in current year were $700,000.
There were no noncash financing or investing transactions during the year.

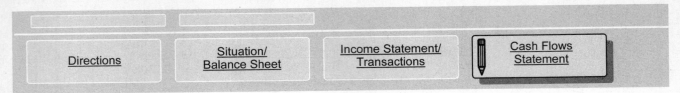

Directions | Situation/ Balance Sheet | Income Statement/ Transactions | Cash Flows Statement

Using the indirect method, prepare the portions of the Statement of Cash Flows of Bayshore Industries, Inc. shown below for the year ended December 31, Year 2. Double-click on a shaded cell in the Statement of Cash Flows below and choose an activity name from the dropdown list. (Editor's Note: The dropdown list is reproduced on the next page.) Next to each activity, enter the appropriate value. Enter negative numbers with a leading minus (–) sign. Each item in the dropdown list may be used once, more than once, or not at all. Some of the shaded cells in the table may not be used in the completion of this task. Note: To use a formula in the spreadsheet, it must be preceded by an equal sign e.g., = A1+B1.

Bayshore Industries, Inc.
Statement of Cash Flows
For the year ended December 31, Year 2

	C	
Cash flows from operating activities:		
		6
		7
		8
		9
		10
		11
		12
		13
		14
Net cash provided by operating activities	= +C6+C7+C8 +C9+C10+C11 +C12+C13+C14	
Cash flows from investing activities:		
		17
		18
		19
Net cash used in investing activities	= +C17+C18+C19	
Cash flows from financing activities:		
		22
		23
		24
		25
Net cash used by financing activities	= C22+C23+C24 +C25	
Net increase (decrease) in cash and cash equivalents	= +C16+C21+C27	
Supplemental disclosures:		
		29
		30

Dropdown Selection List

A. Increase/decrease in prepaid expenses
B. Cash paid for income taxes
C. Net income/loss
D. Depreciation and amortization expense
E. Allowance for bad debts
F. Cash collected from licensees
G. Increase/decrease in intangibles
H. Proceeds from/repayment of line of credit
I. Deferred income taxes
J. Dividends received
K. Increase/decrease in trade receivables – net
L. Increase/decrease in accounts payable and accrued expenses
M. Interest received
N. Purchases of property and equipment
O. Increase/decrease in inventory
P. Dividends paid
Q. Cash paid to suppliers and employees
R. Gain/loss on property and equipment disposals
S. Repayment of long-term debt
T. Cash received from lessees
U. Collections from customers
V. Interest paid
W. Proceeds from plant and equipment disposals
X. Proceeds from issuance of common stock
Y. Proceeds from issuance of long-term debt

Communication | Research

Bayshore Industries Inc.'s Board of Directors consists mainly of Bayshore Industries family members with no training in accounting. To them, "financing" means borrowing money, and "investing" means putting money into the bank or stock market. They have asked you to write a memorandum to them explaining what the terms "investing" and "financing" mean in the Statement of Cash Flows.

Type your communication in the response area below the horizontal line using the word processor provided.

REMINDER: Your response will be graded for both technical content and writing skills. Technical content will be evaluated for information that is helpful to the intended reader and clearly relevant to the issue. Writing skills will be evaluated for development, organization, and the appropriate expression of ideas in professional correspondence. Use a standard business memo or letter format with a clear beginning, middle, and end. Do not convey information in the form of a table, bullet point list, or other abbreviated presentation.

Communication | Research

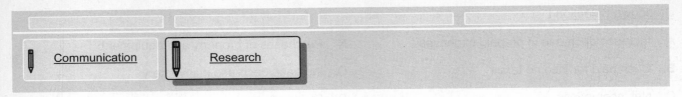

When is the acquisition of equipment reported in the operating section of the statement of cash flows?

To complete this task, first split the screen and select this tab (the RESEARCH tab) in one window and the STANDARDS tab in the other. Use the search capabilities provided by the STANDARDS tab to find the citation in either the Current Text or Original Pronouncements that addresses the issue above. Click (highlight) the appropriate citation, and then click on the TRANSFER TO ANSWER button located in the upper left of the STANDARDS tab. Your selected citation will appear in the answer space below.

Note:	A citation may include one or more paragraphs; all parts of a citation will be automatically selected.
	You do not need to delete a citation to replace it. If you try to transfer more than one citation, the previous one will be overwritten by the current selection.
	The Copy and Paste icon on the helm do **not** work with this tab. Use the TRANSFER TO ANSWER button on the Standards tab to complete the task.

Solution 1 MULTIPLE CHOICE ANSWERS

Legend for Cognitive CBT Skills

1 Understanding
2 Judgment / Application
3 Analysis

1. (a) The summary of significant accounting policies should disclose policies involving a choice of alternative acceptable polices, policies peculiar to that particular industry, and unusual applications of acceptable principles. This includes methods of profit recognition on long-term construction contracts. Financial statement disclosure of accounting policies should not duplicate details presented elsewhere as part of the financial statements. Future minimum lease payments in the aggregate and for each of the five succeeding fiscal years generally are presented in the notes to the financial statements, but not with the summary of significant accounting policies. Depreciation expense and composition of sales by segment are presented on the face of the financial statements. (Chapter 11-4-5; CBT Skill: 1; CSO: 1.2.5)

2. (b) The capital projects fund reports unrestricted grants received from other governmental units as revenue. Therefore, the $300,000 grant from the state is reported as revenue in the capital projects fund's operating statement. The capital projects fund reports long-term debt proceeds and operating transfers from other funds as other financing sources. Therefore, the $450,000 transfer from the general fund is reported as other financing sources in the capital project fund's operating statement. (Chapter 19-1-4; CBT Skill: 3; CSO: 4.1.2)

3. (c) Assets are to be recorded at their acquisition cost, which is defined as the cash price or its equivalent. The acquisition cost of the office building and the land together is $1,000,000; the total of the $750,000 cash and $250,000 mortgage. The property is assessed with 60% allocated to the building. Cart would record the building at $600,000 ($1,000,000 × 60%) and the land at the remaining $400,000. (Chapter 4-2-1; CBT Skill: 2; CSO: 2.4.0)

4. (a) The amount of inventory lost in the flood is calculated by determining the difference between the estimated ending inventory using the gross margin method and the actual physical inventory not damaged by the flood.(Chapter 3-3-1; CBT Skill: 3; CSO: 2.3.0)

Beginning inventory, January 1		$ 35,000
Purchases, January 1 through May 1		200,000
Goods available for sale		235,000
Sales, January 1 through May 1	$ 250,000	
Less: Gross margin (40% × $250,000)	(100,000)	
Less: Estimated CGS		(150,000)
Estimated ending inventory		85,000
Less: Physical ending inventory		(30,000)
Estimated flood loss		$ 55,000

5. (d) A derivative financial instrument is an instrument or contract that has three characteristics;

(1) an underlying and notional amount or payment provision, (2) zero or small investment, and (3) net settlement. Bank certificates of deposit do not contain these features. They are investments that normally require a minimum amount of deposit and can be classified as cash if the original maturity is three months or less. The other items listed are all derivative instruments. An interest rate swap is an arrangement where two companies swap interest payments, but not the principal, to limit interest rate risk. Currency futures are contracts to buy or sell a foreign currency on a specific date in the future at a price set today. Stock-index options are privileges to buy or sell a stock index security to be delivered by the derivative contract. (Chapter 2-5-1; CBT Skill: 3; CSO: 3.8.0)

6. (c) Transactions between affiliates are considered related party transactions. Related party disclosures should include, among other things, the dollar amount of purchases during the year and the amounts due from or to the affiliate at the balance sheet date. (Chapter 11-4-6; CBT Skill: 1; CSO: 3.15.0)

7. (d) SAS 69 establishes a hierarchy (five tiers) for applying accounting principles to financial statements in conformance with GAAP. FASB Statements of Financial Accounting Standards are part of the top tier (most authoritative). Both the AICPA Statements of Position and AICPA Industry and Audit Guides are in the second tier. FASB Statements of Financial Accounting Concepts are in the bottom tier. (Chapter 1-7-2; CBT Skill: 1; CSO: 1.1.1)

8. (a) SFAS 131 requires that general-purpose financial statements include selected information on an enterprise's operating segments. An enterprise is required to report a measure of segment profit or loss, segment assets and certain related items, but not segment cash flows or segment liabilities. (Chapter 11-6-1; CBT Skill: 1; CSO: 3.17.0)

9. (b) The purpose of SFAC 2 is to examine the characteristics that make accounting information useful for decision making. Information useful for decision making should be both relevant and reliable. Relevant information must be timely and must have either predictive or feedback value. Information has predictive value if it helps users increase the likelihood of correctly forecasting the outcome of past or present events. Information has feedback value if it enables users to confirm or correct prior expectations. Representational faithfulness is correspondence or agreement between a measure or description and the phenomenon that it purports to represent. Reliability exists when information represents what it purports to represent, coupled with an assurance for the user that it has representational faithfulness. (Chapter 1-6-3; CBT Skill: 1; CSO: 1.1.2)

10. (c) SFAS 116 governs contributions received and made for nonprofit entities. Contributions are unconditional donations, or gifts, of assets, including both property and services. Donated assets other than property and equipment, are reported as operating gains or revenue if unrestricted and restricted gain or revenue if restricted. Pledges are reported in the period in which they are made, net of an allowance for uncollectible amounts. Conditional pledges are not recorded until they become unconditional. Public College should report $75,000 as contribution revenue in its statement of activities; the total of the $25,000 cash gift restricted for scholarships and the $50,000 unrestricted (unconditional) pledge. The $10,000 is conditional upon the graduate's death. (Chapter 20-1-4; CBT Skill: 3; CSO: 4.5.0)

11. (c) A bond will sell at a discount (less than par) when the stated interest rate is less than the market rate. The amount of the discount will be equal to the difference between the bond payable amount and the cash received. The bond discount is recorded in a separate account in the balance sheet as a direct deduction from the face amount of the bond. The discount will be amortized over the period from the date of sale to the maturity date as interest expense. Thus, the total interest expense over the term of debt equals the cash interest paid plus the discount amount at issue. (Chapter 6-2-3; CBT Skill: 1; CSO: 2.9.0)

12. (d) Revenue from sales when the buyer has the right to return the product should be recognized at the time of sale **only** if all of several conditions are met. One condition is that the buyer has paid the seller, or is obligated to pay the seller, and the obligation is not contingent on resale of the product. While the amount of returns can be estimated based on past experience, the obligation for Jensen to pay Devlin is contingent upon Jensen reselling the goods. Thus Devlin has no sales revenue for this transaction. (Chapter 12-2-1; CBT Skill: 3; CSO: 2.12.0)

13. (d) Because an investment trust fund accounts for resources (and related liabilities) held by governments in a trustee capacity, it is considered a fiduciary fund type. Required statements for fiduciary funds are (1) statement of fiduciary net assets and (2) statement of changes in fiduciary net assets. (Chapter 18-2-4; CBT Skill: 2; CSO: 4.2.5)

14. (c) Cash flows from operating activities are generally the cash effects of transactions and other

events that enter into the determination of net income. Interest payments and interest receipts are operating activities. The decrease in unamortized bond discount represents a non-cash increase in interest expense that must be added to net income to arrive at cash flows. Cash inflows from financing activities are (1) proceeds from issuing equity instruments and (2) proceeds from issuing bonds, mortgages, notes, and from other short- or long-term borrowing. Cash outflows from financing activities include payments of dividends to owners, repayments of amounts borrowed, and other principal payments to creditors who have extended long-term credit. (Chapter 14-2-1; CBT Skill: 1; CSO: 1.2.4)

15. (b) The restricted current fund is used for available financial resources and related liabilities that are expendable only for operating purposes specified by the donor. The change in temporarily restricted assets would consist of the $80,000 investment appreciation plus the $50,000 investment income less the $60,000 spent to maintain the center. An endowment fund would be used to account for the $700,000 principal accepted with the donor stipulation that the income and investment appreciation be used to maintain the senior center. (Chapter 20-5-2; CBT Skill: 3; CSO: 5.1.2)

16. (c) A lessee must record a capital lease in an amount equal to either the fair value of the leased property at the inception date or the present value of the minimum lease payments using the present value discount rate, whichever is lower. As no fair value of the leased property was provided, the present value discount rate must be used. Koby should capitalize $500,000 × 5.35 = $2,675,000. (Chapter 8-4-1; CBT Skill: 3; CSO: 3.13.0)

17. (d) The amount paid to the stockholders at the end of the fifth year should be the accumulated annual interest, $4,500,000 × 10% × 5 yrs = $2,250,000 over the five years, plus the notes payable issue amount of $4,500,000. (Chapter 7-1-3; CBT Skill: 3; CSO: 3.6.0)

18. (c) Internal use computer software costs that are incurred in the preliminary project stage should be expensed as incurred. Costs incurred in the application development stage are capitalized and should not cease until the software project is substantially complete and ready for its intended use. Capitalization of costs should begin when both of the following occur: (1) the preliminary project stage is completed, and (2) management implicitly or explicitly authorizes and commits to funding a computer software project and it is probable that the software will be used to perform the function intended. The $10,000,000 in cost would be capitalized and then expensed over the three year economic life of the product. The amount of expense reported for the first full year would be $3,333,333. (Chapter 5-3-2; CBT Skill: 3; CSO: 2.6.0)

Editors Note: This question appears exactly as it was received from the AICPA. The AICPA provided "c", $3,333,333 derived as explained, as the correct answer. The question stating the amount spent is for costs "after" the application development stage could be taken two different ways. One is, as we presume they intended, to mean the end of the application development stage and would be better read if it stated "during" the application development stage. The second way would literally mean the costs came after the application stage, placing them in the implementation/operation stage. Costs in this stage would be expensed as incurred unless they were for upgrades or enhancements, in which case they'd be capitalized.

19. (b) SFAS 144 requires recognition of an impairment loss only if a long-term asset's, or asset group's, carrying amount is not recoverable and exceeds its fair value. (Chapter 4-4-1; CBT Skill: 1; CSO: 2.4.0)

20. (b) The recognition and measurement of a deferred tax liability or asset is based on the future effects on income taxes, as measured by the provisions of enacted tax laws, resulting from temporary differences and operating loss and tax credit carryforwards at the end of the current year. An enterprise is to identify (disclose) the types and amounts of existing temporary differences and the nature and amount of each type of operating loss and tax credit carryforward (and the remaining length of the carryforward period). (Chapter 13-4-1; CBT Skill: 2; CSO: 3.10.0)

21. (b) Goods out on consignment should be included in inventory at cost because title to the goods has not changed. Of the $20,000 inventory Nomar shipped, only 70% ($14,000) was sold by Seabright. This leaves $6,000 to be included on the balance sheet for the first year for Nomar. The $500 Seabright paid for advertising is advertising expense and not included in inventory. (Chapter 3-1-2; CBT Skill: 3; CSO: 1.2.3)

22. (d) Pledges are reported in the period in which they are made, net of an allowance for uncollectible amounts. If part of the pledge is to be applied during some future period, that part is reported as restricted revenue. Of the $300,000 in unrestricted pledges, $100,000 would be earmarked as temporarily restricted revenue because it has been designated by donors for use next year. The remaining $200,000 would be earmarked as unrestricted.

The $200,000 less 15% allowance for uncollectible amounts would leave $170,000 as the recognizable amount of unrestricted support in the current-year financial statements. (Chapter 20-1-4; CBT Skill: 3; CSO: 5.2.1)

23. (d) The summary of significant accounting policies should disclose policies involving a choice of alternative acceptable polices, policies peculiar to that particular industry, and unusual applications of acceptable principles. This includes revenue recognition policies. Financial statement disclosure of accounting policies should not duplicate details presented elsewhere as part of the financial statements. Descriptions of transactions, summaries of debt, and schedules of assets are not policies and are located elsewhere in the financial statements. (Chapter 11-4-5; CBT Skill: 1; CSO: 1.2.5)

24. (a) A change in the useful life of a depreciable asset is a change in accounting estimate. It is accounted for in the period of change if the change only affects that period, or in the current and subsequent periods if the change affects both. The straight-line depreciation method is a fixed charge method where an equal amount of depreciable cost is allocated to each period. Mellow would have originally been depreciating the asset $2,400 per year over the five years. At the beginning of the fifth year there would be $9,600 ($2,400 × 4) in accumulated depreciation and the asset would have a net book value of $2,400. This $2,400 would now be depreciated over the new remaining life span of four more years. The depreciation expense for year 5, and each of the following three years, would be $2,400 / 4 = $600. (Chapter 11-4-2; CBT Skill: 3; CSO: 3.1.0)

25. (c) Assets are to be recorded at their acquisition cost. Acquisition cost is the cash price, or its equivalent, plus all costs reasonably necessary to bring it to the location and to make it ready for its intended use. Depletion refers to periodic allocation of acquisition costs of natural resources. A per-unit depletion rate is computed by dividing the acquisition cost of the natural resource (i.e., purchase price, and other development costs), less any estimated residual value, by the estimated number of units of the resource available for extraction. (Chapter 4-3-2; CBT Skill: 3; CSO: 2.12.0)

Purchase price of coal mine	$2,000,000
Plus: Mine preparation costs	500,000
Mine total acquisition cost	$2,500,000
Less: Value at end of useful life	(100,000)
Net depletable amount	$2,400,000
Divided by: Estimated number of units available for extraction	750,000
Depletion amount per ton	$ 3.20

26. (d) Revenues are amounts received, appropriations are amounts budgeted to be spent and expenditures are amounts that have been spent. The fund balance is the fund residual account that balances the asset and liability accounts of a governmental fund (and trust funds), thus recording the amount available for expenditures. In situations in which more money is available the fund balance will increase, conversely less money available will cause a decrease. The appropriations are closed out against the unreserved fund balance. If appropriations exceed actual expenditures, more money was budgeted (available) than spent, there is in effect an increase in the unreserved fund balance at year end. If actual revenues were less than estimated revenues, there would be less money available to spend. If estimated revenues exceed actual appropriations, there is less money than budgeted (available) to spend. If actual expenditures exceed appropriations there is less money available because more was spent than was budgeted. (Chapter 19-1-2; CBT Skill: 3; CSO: 4.4.5)

27. (b) APB 22 requires disclosure of all significant accounting policies in an enterprise's financial statements. Thus disclosure of accounting policies is an integral part of the financial statements Disclosures should not be limited to principles and methods peculiar to the industry in which it operates, but instead include policies involving a choice of alternative acceptable polices, policies peculiar to that particular industry, and unusual applications of acceptable principles. There is no specific required format and location of accounting policy disclosures. Financial statement disclosure of accounting policies should not duplicate details presented elsewhere as part of the financial statements. (Chapter 11-4-5; CBT Skill: 1; CSO: 1.2.5)

28. (d) SFAS 106 requires that an employer's obligations for postretirement benefits expected to be provided to or for an employee be fully accrued by the date that employee attains full eligibility for all of the benefits expected to be received by that employee, any beneficiaries, and covered dependents (the full eligibility date), even if the employee is expected to render additional service beyond that date. (Chapter 9-4-1; CBT Skill: 1; CSO: 3.6.0)

29. (c) World's interest rate on the $1,000,000 note payable was 9%. The loan is outstanding for three months interest for the year. The interest expense is $1,000,000 × .09 × 3/12 = $22,500. (Chapter 7-1-3; CBT Skill: 3; CSO: 3.11.0)

30. (a) There are three tests to determine whether an identified segment of an enterprise should be reported in the enterprise's financial statements.

(1) The revenue test: the segment's reported revenue is 10% or more of the combined revenue of all operating segments; (2) The profit (loss) test: the absolute amount of the segment's profit or loss is 10% or more of the greater, in absolute amount, of the combined reported profit of all operating segments that did not report a loss or the combined reported loss of all operating segments that did report a loss; (3) The assets test: the segment's assets are 10% or more of the combined assets of all operating segments. (Chapter 11-6-3; CBT Skill: 1; CSO: 3.17.0)

31. (a) Research activities are those aimed at the discovery of knowledge that will be useful in developing or significantly improving products or processes and development activities are those concerned with translating research findings and other knowledge into plans or designs for new or significantly improved products, techniques, or processes. Offshore oil exploration as a primary activity is the main job function and not a R & D cost. Research and development under contract for others is a service and not a R & D cost. Market research for a product is a company expense and not a R & D cost. (Chapter 5-2-1; CBT Skill: 1; CSO: 3.16.0)

32. (c) Included in the financing activities section of the statement of cash flows are cash effects of (1) obtaining resources from owners and providing them with a return on their investment, (2) borrowing money and repaying amounts borrowed, or otherwise settling the obligation, (3) obtaining and paying for other resources obtained from creditors on long-term credit, and (4) derivatives that contain a financing component and are accounted for a fair-value or cash-flow hedges. The cash effects of transactions involving making and collecting loans and those of acquiring and disposing of investments and property, plant, and equipment would be included in the investing activities section. The cash effects of transactions and other events that enter into the determination of net income would be included in the operating activities section. (Chapter 14-2-3; CBT Skill: 1; CSO: 1.2.4)

33. (a) Initial franchise fees from franchise sales ordinarily must be recognized (with provision for estimated uncollectible amounts) when all material services or conditions relating to the sale have been substantially performed or satisfied by the franchisor. North's services per the agreement were not complete in the current year so no franchise revenue would be reported by North in the current year. (Chapter 12-5-1; CBT Skill: 3; CSO: 2.12.0)

34. (d) SFAS 107 requires that an entity shall disclose, either in the body of the financial statements or in the accompanying notes, the fair value of financial instruments for which it is practicable to estimate that value and the method(s) and significant assumptions used to estimate the fair value of financial instruments. It also states that these provisions need not be applied to immaterial items. (Chapter 2-5-3; CBT Skill: 1; CSO: 3.8.0)

35. (d) A leasehold improvement is an improvement made by the lessee to a leased property for which benefits are expected beyond the current accounting period. The cost of leasehold improvements should be capitalized and amortized over the lesser of the estimated useful life or the remaining term of the lease. If a lease has a renewal option, which the lessee intends to exercise, the leasehold improvement should be amortized over the lesser of its estimated useful life or the sum of the remaining term of the lease and the period covered by the renewal option. The leasehold improvement costs incurred by Green Co. would be capitalized and depreciated over 15 years, the estimated useful life. (Chapter 5-1-1; CBT Skill: 1; CSO: 2.4.0)

36. (b) The future value factor is equal to 1 divided by the present value factor. An investment in two years would accumulate to the principal multiplied by the future value factor. In this case the $10,000 × 1/0.826 = $12,107. (Appendix D; CBT Skill: 3; CSO: 2.5.0)

Editors Note: This question appears exactly as it was received from the AICPA. The AICPA provided "b", $12,107 derived as explained, as the correct answer. The question stated that Lean Co. made an investment on $10,000 on Jan 1 of the current year and provided no further details. Also provided is a three year table for the present value of $1.00 discounted at a 10% interest rate. In lieu of other information, you have to assume the prevailing rate of interest is 10% and you are to use the table provided.

37. (d) Internal use computer software costs that are incurred in the preliminary project stage should be expensed as incurred. Most costs incurred in the application development stage are capitalized and should not cease until the software project is substantially complete and ready for its intended use. Training costs and data conversion costs are generally expensed in the application development stage. In the post-implementation/operation stage, training and maintenance costs should be expensed as incurred while the costs of upgrades or enhancements are capitalized. The annual amortization cost is calculated by taking the remaining $8,000,000 (12,000,000 less the $4,000,000 spent) and dividing by the four-year useful life. (Chapter 5-3-2; CBT Skill: 3; CSO: 2.6.0)

Preliminary project costs	$4,000,000
Post development training costs	50,000
Year 1 amortization expense	2,000,000
Current year expense	6,050,000

38. (b) Failure to report $40,000 depreciation in the prior year would result in an understatement of accumulated depreciation of the $40,000 in the prior year financial statements. The tax rate of 40% for the current year has no bearing on the prior year financials as the tax return was correct. As such, no figures containing $24,000 would be correct. There would be a $40,000 understatement of depreciation expense and overstatement of net income. (Chapter 11-4-4; CBT Skill: 2; CSO: 3.1.0)

39. (b) A common format of the bank reconciliation statement is to reconcile both book and bank balances to a common amount known as the "true balance". (Chapter 2-2-3; CBT Skill: 3; CSO: 2.1.0)

Balance per books June 30 prior to any adjustments	$10,012
Less: Difference in check 101 for $95 but recorded at $59	(36)
Plus: Interest earned on account	35
Less: Monthly service charge	(50)
Adjusted cash balance per books	$ 9,961

40. (b) Average inventory methods assume that the cost of goods sold and ending inventory should be based on the average cost of the inventories available for sale (AFS) during the period. A weighted average method generally is used with a periodic inventory system. The weighted-average method costs inventory items on the basis of average prices paid, weighted according to the quantity purchased at each price. (Chapter 3-2-3; CBT Skill: 3; CSO: 2.3.0)

Beg. Inventory, (10,000 × $3)	$ 30,000
Jan 5 purchase, (5,000 × $4)	20,000
Jan 15 purchase, (5,000 × $5)	25,000
Total cost of goods AFS	$ 75,000
Divided by: Total units available	20,000
Weighted average cost per unit	$ 3.75
Times: Units sold during January	× 10,000
Cost of goods sold for January	$ 37,500

41. (b) Treasury stock is the corporation's common or preferred stock that has been reacquired by purchase, by settlement of an obligation to the corporation, or through donation. The cost method views the purchase and subsequent disposition of stock as one transaction. The treasury stock is recorded (debited), carried, and then reissued at acquisition cost. If the stock is reissued at a price in excess of the acquisition cost, the excess is credited to an appropriately titled paid-in capital (PIC) account. If the stock is reissued at less than the acquisition cost, the deficit is first charged against any existing balance in the treasury stock paid-in capital account and then excess, if any, is then charged against retained earnings. Porter reissued the 500 shares of treasury stock at a price ($10 per share) in excess of the acquisition cost ($6 per share). The excess ($10 – $6 = $4 per share × 500 shares = $2,000) is credited to the PIC account related to treasury stock on Porter's balance sheet for the current year. (Chapter 10-5-2; CBT Skill: 3; CSO: 2.11.0)

42. (c) A statement of cash flows should report the cash provided or used by operating, investing, and financing activities. It should also report the net effect of those flows on cash and cash equivalents during the period in such a manner that reconciles the beginning and ending cash and cash equivalents. The $40,000 sale of land proceeds already is incorporated in the cash flows from investing activities. (Chapter 14-1-3; CBT Skill: 3; CSO: 1.2.4)

Beginning cash balance, Jan 1	$ 27,000
Plus: Cash from operating activities	351,000
Less: Cash for investing activities	(420,000)
Plus: Cash for financing activities	250,000
Cash balance, Dec 31	$ 208,000

43. (a) SFAS 93 requires all non-profit organizations to recognize depreciation in general purpose financial statements. They would use the same criteria in allocating the depreciable cost of fixed assets over their estimated useful lives as commercial enterprises. The freezer is a fixed asset that the not-for-profit must depreciate. The building is under construction and thus is not yet depreciated. Land is never depreciated. The linens may be classified as supplies, not fixed assets, and thus need not be depreciated. (Chapter 20-1-7; CBT Skill: 3; CSO: 5.1.1)

44. (a) On the government-wide statement of activities, the net revenue (expense) format and net program cost format are used. Charges for services are one of the program revenues reported on a local government's government-wide statement of activities. Taxes levied, proceeds from the sale of a capital asset, and interest revenues would fall under general revenues. (Chapter 18-2-3; CBT Skill: 1; CSO: 4.2.1)

45. (c) The statement of cash flows for not-for-profit organizations reports the change in cash and cash equivalents similar to commercial enterprises. The borrowed $5,000 is classified as a cash inflow from financing activities. The purchase of the truck is

considered a cash outflow from investing activities. (Chapter 20-1-3; CBT Skill: 2; CSO: 5.1.3)

46. (a) The cash gift should be recorded as a temporarily restricted asset because the donor-imposed restriction, that the principal be held, will lapse upon occurrence of conditions specified by the donor, after the 20 years. A permanent restriction is a donor-imposed restriction that doesn't lapse. The gift is not a liability. (Chapter 20-1-2; CBT Skill: 2; CSO: 5.2.2)

47. (c) Accounting operates in an environment almost as varied as the many types of entities which accounting serves. To provide a basis for comparison, it has been necessary to formulate certain underlying environmental assumptions on which financial accounting theory is based. The monetary unit (unit-of-measure) assumption is used for the measurement and reporting of economic activity. The going concern assumption is that the business is not expected to liquidate in the near future. The periodicity assumption recognizes the necessity of providing financial accounting information on a periodic, timely basis, so that it is useful in decision making. The economic entity assumption states in order to properly report those economic events affecting an entity, the specific economic entity must be defined and separated from other entities. (Chapter 1-1-2; CBT Skill: 1; CSO: 1.1.2)

48. (c) A new Financial Accounting Standards Board (FASB) statement is issued only after a majority vote by the members of FASB. The emerging issues task force assists the FASB in improving financial reporting through the timely identification, discussion, and resolution of financial accounting issues within the framework of existing authoritative literature. It does not approve a discussion memorandum before it is disseminated to the public. A discussion memorandum is prepared before any deliberations on a new major project and thus before any exposure draft. FASB statements are not rescinded by the AICPA member's votes. (Chapter 1-7-1; CBT Skill: 1; CSO: 1.1.1)

49. (d) An accumulated benefit obligation is the actuarial present value of benefits attributed by the pension benefit formula to employee services rendered before a specified date and based on employee services and compensation prior to that date. Service and interest costs are components of the net periodic pension cost. The projected benefit obligation is the actuarial present value as of a date of all benefits attributed by the pension benefit formula to employee service rendered prior to that date. (Chapter 9-2-1; CBT Skill: 1; CSO: 3.6.0)

50. (a) If the lease contains a bargain purchase option, it must be classified as a capital lease in the books of a lessee. A lease would also be classified as a capital lease if the lease transfers ownership of the property to the lessee by the end of the lease or the lease term is equal to 75% or more of the estimated economic life of the leased property or the present value of the minimum lease payments equals or exceeds 90% of the fair value of the leased property at lease inception. (Chapter 8-2-1; CBT Skill: 1; CSO: 3.13.0)

Solution 2

Response #1: Cash Flows Statement Tab

Bayshore Industries, Inc.
Statement of Cash Flows
For the year ended December 31, Year 2

	C	
Cash flows from operating activities:		
Net income/loss	1,772,000	6
Depreciation and amortization expense	447,700	7
Increase/decrease in trade receivables – net	–1,463,000	8
Increase/decrease in inventory	–594,000	9
Increase/decrease in prepaid expenses	–18,000	10
Gain/loss on property and equipment disposals	–18,000	11
Increase/decrease in accounts payable and accrued expenses	475,800	12
		13
		14
Net cash provided by operating activities	602,500	
Cash flows from investing activities:		
Purchases of property and equipment	–400,000	17
Proceeds from plant and equipment disposals	58,500	18
		19
Net cash used in investing activities	–341,500	
Cash flows from financing activities:		
Proceeds from/repayment of line of credit	18,000	22
Repayment of long-term debt	–27,000	23
Dividends paid	–180,000	24
		25
Net cash used by financing activities	–189,000	
Net increase (decrease) in cash and cash equivalents	72,000	
Supplemental disclosures:		
Interest paid	250,000	29
Cash paid for income taxes	700,000	30

Cash Flows From Operating Activities (lines 6-14): Cash flows from operating activities are generally the cash effects of transactions and other events that enter into the determination of net income. Lines 13 and 14 are extra lines. These answers may be on any of lines 6-14, but the letter and amount must be together.

Line 6:	C, 1,772,000	Positive cash flow from net income, as shown on the statement of income and retained earnings
Line 7:	D, 447,700	Positive cash flow from the total of (1) increase in accumulated depreciation [576,000 – 455,000 = 121,000], plus (2) increase in accumulated amortization [14,400 – 7,200 = 7,200], plus (3) the accumulated depreciation on the building that was sold

Line 8:	K, -1,463,000	Negative cash flow from increase in trade receivables [3,434,000 – 1,971,000 = 1,463,000]
Line 9:	O, -594,000	Negative cash flow from increase in inventory [810,000 – 216,000 = 594,000]
Line 10:	A, -18,000	Negative cash flow from increase in prepaid expenses [18,000 – 0 = 18,000]
Line 11:	R, -18,000	Negative cash flow from gain on sale of building [58,500 sale price – 40,500 book value] (The 360,000 cost – 319,500 accumulated depreciation = 40,500 book value)
Line 12:	L, 475,800	Positive cash flow from increase in accounts payable and accrued expenses [872,000 – 396,800]

FYI (no points): Net Cash Provided by Operating Activities: 806,500

Cash Flows From Investing Activities (lines 17-19): Cash inflows from financing activities are (1) proceeds from issuing equity instruments and (2) proceeds from issuing bonds, mortgages, notes, and from other short- or long-term borrowing. Line 19 is an extra line. These answers may be on any of lines 17-19, but the letter and amount must be together.

Line 17:	N, -400,000	Negative cash flow from total increase in property and equipment [7,780,000 – (7,740,000 – 360,000 from building sold) = 400,000]
Line 18:	W, 58,500	Positive cash flow from proceeds of building sold, as provided in additional information for year 2

FYI (no points): Net Cash Provided by Investing Activities: -341,500

Cash Flows From Financing Activities (lines 22-25): Cash outflows from financing activities include payments of dividends to owners, repayments of amounts borrowed, and other principal payments to creditors who have extended long-term credit Line 25 is an extra line. These answers may be on any of lines 22-25, but the letter and amount must be together.

Line 22:	H, 18,000	Positive cash flow from increase in line of credit [108,000 – 90,000 = 18,000]
Line 23:	S, -27,000	Negative cash flow from repayment of long-term debt, as shown on the year 1 balance sheet (Note this was “current portion” of long-term debt)
Line 24:	P, -180,000	Negative cash flow from dividends paid, as shown on the statement of income and retained earnings

FYI (no points): Net Cash Provided by Financing Activities: -189,000

Supplemental Disclosures (lines 29-30): These answers may be on any of lines 29-30, but the letter and amount must be together.

Line 29:	V, 250,000	As provided in additional information for year 2
Line 30:	B, 700,000	As provided in additional information for year 2

Response #2: Communication Tab

To: **Board of Directors, Bayshore Industries Inc.**
Re: Statement of Cash Flows Investing and Financing

The purpose of a statement of cash flows is to provide information to help investors, creditors, and others make financial assessments of an enterprise. It should report the cash effects during a period of an enterprise's operations, it's investing transactions, and its financing transactions. Operating activities generally involve producing and delivering goods and providing services.

Investing activities include transactions involving the making and collecting of loans. Investing is also the acquiring and disposing of property, plant, equipment, and other productive assets. Purchases, sales, and maturities of debt and equity available-for-sale and held-to-maturity securities, along with investments in other certain equity securities are also classified as investing activities.

Financing activities include obtaining resources from owners and providing them with a return on, and return of, their investment. Financing also is the borrowing of money and repaying amounts borrowed, or otherwise settling the obligation, and obtaining and paying for other resources from creditors on long-term credit. Any cash flows from derivatives that contain a financing component and are accounted for as fair-value or cash flow hedges are also classified as financing.

One could consider investing activities those entered into to provide some return, whether on a financial instrument or an asset such as plant, property, and equipment. Financing activities are those to obtain (or repay) resources that will be used for some other purpose.

Response #3: Research Tab

FAS 95, par.24; CT 25.122

24. Certain cash receipts and payments may have aspects of more than one class of cash flows. For example, a cash payment may pertain to an item that could be considered either inventory or a productive asset. If so, the appropriate classification shall depend on the activity that is likely to be the predominant source of cash flows for the item. For example, the acquisition and sale of equipment to be used by the enterprise or rented to others generally are investing activities. However, equipment sometimes is acquired or produced to be used by the enterprise or rented to others for a short period and then sold. In those circumstances, the acquisition or production and subsequent sale of those assets shall be considered operating activities. Another example where cash receipts and payments include more than one class of cash flows involves a derivative instrument that includes a financing element at inception because the borrower's cash flows are associated with both the financing element and the derivative. For that derivative instrument, all cash inflows and outflows shall be considered cash flows from financing activities by the borrower.

Time Management

Approximately 20 percent of the multiple choice questions in every section of every exam given after November 2003 are questions that are being pre-tested. These questions are **not** included in candidates' final grades; they are presented only so that the Board of Examiners may evaluate them for effectiveness and possible ambiguity.

The Scholastic Achievement Test and the Graduate Record Exam both employ similar but not identical strategies. Those tests include an extra section, which is being pre-tested, and test-takers do not know which section is the one that will not be graded. On the Uniform CPA Examination, however, the extra questions are mixed in among the graded questions.

This makes time management crucial. Candidates who are deciding how much time to spend on a difficult multiple choice question must keep in mind that there is a 20 percent chance that the answer to the question will not affect them either way. Also, candidates should not allow a question that seems particularly difficult or confusing to shake their confidence or affect their attitude towards the rest of the test; it may not even count.

This experimental 20 percent works against candidates who are not sure whether they have answered enough questions to earn 75 points. Candidates should try for a safety margin, so that they will have accumulated enough correct answers to pass, even though some of their correctly answered questions will not be scored.

See the **Practical Advice** appendix for more information regarding the exam.

INDEX

A

Abnormal Costs 3-3
Accelerated Depreciation 4-9
Account Groups 18-39
Accountability 18-3
Accounting
  Accrual 1-16
  Assumptions 1-2
  Financial 1-2
  Model 1-3
  Principles, basic 1-2
Accounting Policies Disclosure (APB 22) 11-16
Accounts Payable 7-2
Accounts Receivable
  Adjustments 2-30
  Aging of 2-28
  Assignment of 2-35
  Definition 2-27
  Discounting 2-34
  Discounts 2-27
  Estimating uncollectibles 2-28
  Factoring 2-36
  Pledging 2-36
  Returns and allowances 2-28
  Sources of cash, as 2-34
  Valuation 2-27
Accrual 1-16
Accrual Accounting 11-18
  Prepaid expenses 5-9
Accrued Liabilities (Expenses) 7-3
Accrued Pension Cost 9-11, 9-13
Accumulated Balance of OCI 10-3, 11-10
Accumulated Benefit Obligation 9-5
Acid-Test Ratio 15-3
Acquisition
  By exchange 4-4
  Cost 3-3, 4-2
Actual Return on Plan Assets 9-7
Actuarial Gains and Losses 9-9
Actuarial Present Value 9-5
Additional Paid-In Capital 10-3
Advances & Returnable Deposits 7-3
Affiliated Companies 17-13
Agency Funds 18-6, 19-13, 20-18, 20-21
Aggregation Criteria 11-24
Allocation 1-16
Allowances 2-28
  Valuation 13-21
Amortization 1-16, 8-7, 9-6, 9-15
  Bonds 6-8
  Discount 6-3, 7-11
  Effective interest method 6-8
  Goodwill 5-3
  Intangible asset 5-3
  Premium 6-3, 7-11
  Prior service cost 9-8
  Straight-line 6-8
  Unrecognized gains or losses 9-9
  Unrecognized net obligation or asset 9-11
  Unrecognized prior service costs 9-8
Annual Budget 18-4
Annuity Contract 9-6
Annuity Fund 20-21, 20-22, 20-25
Antidilution (Antidilutive), EPS 15-6
Antiques 20-7
APB 9 .... 11-2, 11-15
APB 11 13-4
APB 12 10-8
APB 14 6-10
APB 16 .... 2-5, 17-8
APB 18 .... 2-5, 2-7, 13-29
APB 21 .... 7-10, 7-16
APB 22 11-16
APB 23 16-12
APB 25 10-17
APB 26 .... 6-11, 7-14
APB 28 .... 11-20, 13-24
APB 29 4-4
APB 30 .... 11-2, 11-7
APIC 10-3
Applicable Tax Rate 13-14
Appropriations 18-5
ARB 43 .... 1-17, 2-2, 3-2, 3-3, 7-2, 10-12, 11-2
ARB 51 .... 2-5, 2-7, 17-8, 20-11
Artwork 20-7
Asset & Liability Method 13-20
Asset Classification (NPO) 20-3
Assets 1-4
  Board-restricted 20-2
  Current 1-4, 2-2
  Donated 20-7
  Endowment 20-2
  Intangible 5-2
  Limited-use 20-18
  Long-lived, impairment 4-11
  Monetary 12-11
  Nonmonetary 12-11
  Of related organization 20-11
  Operational 1-4
  Property, plant, and equipment 4-2
  Requiring individual analysis 12-11
  Test 11-26
  Unrestricted 20-3
Assignment of Accounts Receivable 2-35
Attribution 9-6, 9-15
Available-for-Sale (AFS) Securities 2-11

B

Bad Debts 20-12
Balance Sheet 1-4, 11-6, 13-26
Bank Reconciliation 2-3
Bankruptcy 7-16
BAPCPA-2005 7-16
Basic
  Accounting principles 1-2
  Earnings per share 15-6
  Financial statements 18-8
Basis of Accounting 18-9
Benchmark Interest Rate 2-21
Benefits 9-5
Big Bath Accounting 11-6
Black-Scholes Pricing Model 10-17
Board-Restricted Assets 20-2
Bond Conversion 6-10
Bond Issue Costs 6-6
Bond Retirement 6-6
Bonds 6-2
  Acquired at a discount 6-3
  Convertible 6-10
  Payable 6-5, 17-15
  Serial 6-10
Bonus Method 10-20
Book Value Per Share 15-5

Boot 4-6
Borrower Journal Entries 6-12
Budgetary Accounting 19-2
Budgetary Comparison Schedule (BCS) 18-26
Budgets 18-7
Business Combinations 17-2
Business-Type Accounting 19-10
Business-Type Activities 18-4

C

Callable Bonds 6-2
Capital
  Assets 18-10
  Contributed 10-3
  Financial 1-15
  Lease obligations 18-29
  Leases 8-4, 8-7, 8-10
  Legal 10-3
  Physical 1-15
  Projects fund 18-6, 19-7
Cash 2-2
  Basis accounting 11-19
  Equivalents 14-2
  Flow hedge 2-17
  Flow statement 1-4, 14-2
  Flows 14-3, 20-5
  Inflows 14-5, 14-6, 14-7
  Outflows 14-5, 14-6, 14-7
  Receipts & payments 14-3
  Surrender value 5-9
Chain Discount 3-3
Chain of Interests 17-2
Chain-Link Method 3-7
Change In
  Accounting estimate 11-4, 11-13
  Accounting principle 11-4, 11-12
  Reporting entity 11-4, 11-14
Changing Prices 12-10
Chapter 7 Bankruptcy 7-16
Charitable Contributions
  (Also see Contributions) 20-7
Chief Operating Decision Maker 11-24
Claims, Bankruptcy 7-16
Collections 20-7
Colleges and Universities
  Governmental 18-32
  Nonprofit organizations 20-14
Combined
  Financial statements 17-20
Commercial Substance 4-6
Comparability 18-3
Comparison of Borrower & Investor 6-11
Compensated Absences 7-7, 7-9
Compensatory Plans 10-17
Completed Contract Method 12-4
Completeness 1-15
Completion of Production Method 12-4
Complex Capital Structure 15-13
Component Unit 18-38
  Balance sheet 18-23
  Operating statement 18-23
Composite Depreciation 4-10
Comprehensive Annual Financial Report (CAFR) 18-26
Comprehensive Income 11-8, 11-9, 11-11
  Accumulated balance 11-10
  Format 1-11, 11-10
  Interim-period reporting 11-9
Comprehensive Income (continued)
  Other comprehensive income (OCI) 11-9
  Reclassification adjustments 11-10
  Reporting 1-11, 11-8
  Reporting related income tax 11-10
Computer Software
  Internal use 5-8
  Sold, leased, or otherwise marketed 5-7
Conservatism 1-3
Consignments 12-8
Consistency 18-3
Consistency Principle 1-3
Consolidated Financial Statements 2-5
Consolidation Procedures 17-3, 17-8
Constraints 1-13
Construction Contracts (ARB 45) 12-4
Contingent Liabilities 7-8
Contingently Issuable Shares 15-11
Continuing Operations 11-2, 11-20
Contributed Capital 1-5
Contributions 20-7
  Annuity fund 20-21, 20-22
  Beneficiary 20-9
  Classification as gains or revenue 20-8
  Donated assets 20-7
  Donated services 20-7
  For others 20-8
  Life income fund 20-21, 20-22
  Pledges 20-8
  Recipient 20-9
Contributory Plan 9-6
Convertible Bonds 6-2, 6-10, 12-11
Copyrights 5-2
Correction of Errors 11-14
Cost
  Acquisition 4-2
  Constraints 1-13
  Flow assumptions 3-5, 3-8
  Historical 1-5
  Interest 4-3
  Method of accounting 2-5
  Recovery 4-8
  Recovery expense 12-15
  Recovery method 12-3
  Replacement 1-6
  Subsequent to acquisition 4-8
Cost Method 17-9
Cost of Goods Sold 12-15
Credit Risk 2-24
Cumulative 10-5
Currency
  Foreign 16-2, 16-9, 16-11
  Functional 16-2, 16-6, 16-8
  Local 16-2
  U.S. dollar 16-2
Current
  Assets 1-4, 2-2
  Liabilities 1-4
  Ratio 15-3
Current Funds
  Budgetary accounts 20-21
  Restricted 20-22, 20-24
  Restricted vs. unrestricted 20-20
  Unrestricted 20-22, 20-24
Current Maturities of Long-Term Debt 7-4
Curtailments, Pension Plans 9-14
Custodian Fund 20-24

D

Debenture Bonds ... 6-2
Debt
  Extinguishment ... 6-6, 7-13
  Retirement ... 6-6
  Securities ... 2-11
  Service fund ... 18-6, 18-30, 19-8
  To equity ratio ... 15-3
Defeasance ... 19-10
Defensive-Interval Ratio ... 15-3
Deferral ... 1-16
Deferred
  Revenues ... 7-4, 11-19, 19-3
  Tax assets ... 13-21
  Tax liabilities & assets ... 13-6, 13-13
Defined
  Benefit pension plans ... 9-5, 18-32
  Contribution pension plans ... 9-5
  Contribution plans ... 18-32
Depletion ... 4-11
Depreciation ... 4-8, 18-11, 20-10
Derivative Instruments (Derivatives) ... 2-15
  Disclosures ... 2-20
  Gains and losses ... 2-18
  Hedging ... 2-17
  Terminology ... 2-21
Detachable Stock Warrants ... 6-11
Development Stage Enterprises ... 11-17
Differences
  Permanent ... 13-10
  Temporary ... 13-6
  Timing ... 13-7
Diluted Earnings Per Share ... 15-6, 15-8
Dilutive Security ... 15-8
Direct
  Financing leases ... 8-5, 8-12
  Method for cash flows ... 14-3
  Write-off method ... 2-30
Disclosures ... 1-3, 10-6, 15-15
  Accounting policies ... 11-16
  Additional current year ... 12-12
  Bonds ... 6-5
  Combined statements ... 17-12
  Credit risk ... 2-23
  Derivatives ... 2-20
  Fair value measurements ... 1-7
  Financial instruments ... 2-23
  Hedges ... 2-20
  Impairment ... 2-34
  Investments ... 2-11
  Leases ... 8-16
  Nonprofit organization ... 20-6
  Nonprofit organization investments ... 20-10
  Notes to government financial statements ... 18-12
  Pensions ... 9-3
  Receivables ... 2-34
  Related Party ... 11-16
  Research & development ... 5-7
  Segment ... 11-23
  Separate ... 12-12
  Stock-based compensation ... 10-19
  Tax assets and liabilities ... 13-26
Discontinued Operations ... 11-5
Discount ... 6-8
Discounted Cash Flows ... 1-6
Discounting ... 2-34
Dividend Payout Ratio ... 15-6
Dividends ... 2-6, 7-3, 10-10
  Preferred stock ... 10-5
  Received deduction ... 13-29, 13-30
Dollar-Value LIFO ... 3-6
Donations (also see Contributions) ... 20-7, 20-8
Double-Declining Balance ... 4-9

E

Earnings Per Share (EPS) ... 15-6
Economic Entity Assumption ... 1-2
Educational Assistance ... 18-32
Effective Interest Method ... 6-4
Employee Bonuses ... 7-4
Employee Stock Ownership Plans ... 10-19
Enacted Change in Tax Laws ... 13-24
Enacted Tax Rate ... 13-13
Encumbrance
  Accounting ... 19-2
  System ... 18-7
Encumbrances ... 19-2
Endowment ... 20-2
Endowment Funds ... 20-2, 20-13, 20-19, 20-25
Enterprise Fund ... 18-6, 19-11
Environmental Remediation Liabilities ... 7-9
EPS (Earnings Per Share) ... 15-6
Equity ... 2-5, 2-6
  Comprehensive income ... 1-10, 11-9
  Owners' ... 1-5, 10-3
  Reclassification ... 10-15
Equity Method ... 17-10
Errors
  Classification of ... 11-15
  Correction of ... 11-14
Escheat Property ... 18-31
Estimated Revenues Account ... 18-5
Exchange ... 4-4
Expected Return on Plan Assets ... 9-6
Expenditures ... 18-5, 19-3
Expenditures Account ... 18-5
Expense ... 1-9
  Classification (NPO) ... 20-2, 20-5, 20-12, 20-15
  Life insurance ... 5-9
  Prepaid ... 5-9
  Realized ... 5-9
  Recognition ... 1-15, 11-18
External Investment Pools ... 18-36
Extinguishment of Debt ... 7-13
Extraordinary Item ... 11-7, 18-10
  Bonds ... 6-11
  Debt extinguishment ... 7-13
  Troubled debt restructuring ... 7-15

F

F.O.B. ... 2-28, 3-2
Factoring ... 2-27, 2-36
Fair Value ... 1-6, 2-15, 7-10, 10-17
Fair Value Hedge ... 2-16, 16-11
FASB Interp. 18 ... 11-20
FASB Interp. 35 ... 2-7
Fiduciary Fund ... 18-6, 18-10, 18-18
  Balance sheet ... 18-22
  Operating statement ... 18-22
Fiduciary Funds ... 19-13
FIFO ... 3-5
Financial
  Accounting, defined ... 1-2
  Assets ... 2-24
  Capital maintenance ... 1-15
  Instrument ... 2-14
  Position ... 1-3, 1-4

Financial (continued)
Statement analysis ... 15-2
Statements, defined ... 1-2
Financial Assistance, Students ... 18-32
Financial Report
Comprehensive annual ... 18-26
Infrastructure schedules ... 18-26
Users of ... 18-3
Uses of ... 18-4
Financial Reporting
Characteristics of ... 18-3
Limitations of ... 18-3
Financial Statements ... 19-16
Activities ... 20-3, 20-4, 20-14, 20-15
Cash flows ... 18-24, 20-5, 20-15
Comprehensive annual financial report ... 18-26
Consolidated ... 17-2, 17-8
Financial position ... 20-3, 20-15, 20-17, 20-22
Functional expenses ... 20-5, 20-15
Fund ... 18-9, 18-15
Governmental reporting entity ... 18-5
Government-wide ... 18-9, 18-11
Financial Trends Information ... 18-28
Financial-Components Approach ... 2-25
Financing Activities, Cash Flows ... 14-7
Finite Useful Life ... 5-3
Firm Commitment ... 2-15
First-In, First-Out (FIFO) ... 3-5
Fixed Assets ... 4-2
Disposal ... 4-12
Fixed-Percentage-of-Declining-Balance Method ... 4-9
Forecasted Transaction ... 2-15
Foreign Currency
Financial statements ... 16-2
Hedge ... 2-15, 2-17, 16-11
Items ... 11-9
Transactions ... 16-9
Foreign Operations ... 16-9, 16-11
Former Reporting Model ... 18-39
Forward Exchange Contract ... 16-10
Fractional-Year Depreciation ... 4-11
Franchise ... 5-2, 12-8
Freight Charges ... 2-28
Functional
Classification ... 20-2, 20-5, 20-15
Currency ... 16-2, 16-6, 16-8
Expenses ... 20-5
Fund
Accounting ... 18-7
Agency ... 19-13
Balance ... 18-6
Balance reserves ... 18-6
Capital projects ... 19-7
Debt service ... 19-8
Enterprise ... 19-11
Fiduciary ... 18-18, 19-13
Financial statements ... 18-15
General ... 19-4
Governmental-type ... 19-2
Internal service ... 19-10
Investment trust ... 19-13
Major ... 18-18
Pension trust ... 19-13
Permanent ... 19-9
Private-purpose trust ... 19-13
Proprietary ... 18-18, 19-10
Special revenue ... 19-6
Fund Accounting ... 20-2
Agency funds ... 20-18, 20-22
Basis of accounting ... 18-8
Colleges and universities ... 20-19
Concepts ... 20-17
Fund Accounting (contineud)
Donor-restricted funds ... 20-18
Endowment fund ... 20-2, 20-19
General funds ... 20-18
Governmental ... 18-7
Plant replacement and expansion funds ... 20-19
Property and equipment ... 20-18
Specific-purpose funds ... 20-19
Term endowment funds ... 20-19
University ... 20-14
Fund Types (NPO) ... 20-17
Fund(s)
Annuity and life income ... 20-21
Current ... 20-20
Donor-restricted ... 20-18
Endowment ... 20-2
General ... 20-18
Health care types ... 20-17
Held in trust by others ... 20-8
Plant ... 20-21
Trust and agency ... 20-21
University ... 20-20
VHWO types ... 20-24
Future Operating Losses ... 11-6

G

GAAP Hierarchy ... 1-18
Gain Contingencies ... 7-9
Gains and Losses ... 20-13
GASB 14 ... 18-38
GASB 18 ... 18-31
GASB 19 ... 18-32
GASB 21 ... 18-31
GASB 22 ... 19-3
GASB 23 ... 19-10
GASB 24 ... 18-29
GASB 25 ... 18-32
GASB 26 ... 18-32
GASB 27 ... 18-33
GASB 28 ... 18-35
GASB 29 ... 19-10
GASB 30 ... 18-35
GASB 31 ... 18-36
GASB 32 ... 18-34
GASB 33 ... 18-28
GASB 34 ... 18-8
Reporting model ... 19-13
Transition ... 19-13
GASB 35 ... 18-8
GASB 36 ... 18-28
GASB 37 ... 18-10, 18-18
GASB 38 ... 18-12
GASB 39 ... 18-38
GASB 40 ... 18-12
GASB 46 ... 18-13
GASB 47 ... 18-34
General Fund ... 18-6, 19-4
Going Concern
Assumption ... 1-2
Incorporation of ... 10-7
Goods
In transit ... 3-2
On consignment ... 3-2
Goodwill ... 5-3, 13-29, 17-2
Impairment testing ... 5-4
Method ... 10-21
Presentation ... 5-5
Governmental Accountability ... 18-2

Governmental Accounting
- Accountability ... 18-2
- Basis of accounting ... 18-8
- Budgets ... 18-7
- Capital and related financing activities ... 18-25
- Capital lease ... 18-29
- Colleges & universities ... 18-32
- Encumbrances ... 18-7, 19-2
- Environment ... 18-2
- Fiduciary funds ... 18-6, 19-13
- Financial statements ... 18-8
- Fund accounting ... 18-7
- Governmental-type funds ... 18-6, 19-2
- Grants ... 18-29
- Interfund transactions ... 19-15
- Investing activities ... 18-25
- Nature of governmental entities ... 18-2
- Noncapital financing activities ... 18-24
- Operating activities ... 18-24
- Proprietary fund ... 18-6, 19-10
- Transfers ... 19-16

Governmental College and University ... 18-32
Governmental Entities, Nonprofit Accounting by ... 19-10
Governmental Fund Accounts ... 18-5
Governmental Funds ... 18-6, 18-30
- Capital projects fund ... 19-7
- Debt service fund ... 19-8
- General fund ... 19-4
- Permanent fund ... 19-9
- Special revenue fund ... 19-6

Governmental Hospital ... 20-14
Government-Wide Financial Statements ... 18-11
- Operating statement ... 18-15
- Statement of activities ... 18-14
- Statement of net assets ... 18-14

Grants ... 19-3
Grants, Pell ... 18-32

H

Health Care Entities ... 20-12
- Fund accounting ... 20-17

Hedge of Net Investment in Foreign Operation ... 16-12
Hedging ... 2-15
Held-to-Maturity (HTM) Securities ... 2-11
Hierarchy of Accounting Qualities ... 1-14
Historical
- Collections ... 20-7
- Cost ... 1-2, 1-5, 12-10

Holding Gains and Losses ... 12-17
Hospitals and Other Health Care Entities
- For-profit ... 20-13
- Government entities ... 20-14
- Nonprofit organizations ... 20-12

I

If-Converted Method, EPS ... 15-9
Impairment ... 5-3, 5-4
- Disclosures ... 2-34
- Lease ... 8-9
- Long-lived assets ... 4-11
- Recognition ... 2-32

Impairment or Disposal ... 4-11
Income
- Comprehensive ... 11-8
- Concepts ... 11-2
- Pretax ... 13-2
- Reconciliation ... 13-4

Income (continued)
- Taxable ... 13-2
- Taxes ... 13-2

Income Determination, Unique Features
- Colleges and universities ... 20-14
- Hospitals ... 20-12

Income From Continuing Operations ... 12-10
Income Statement ... 1-9, 11-6, 13-27
- Components ... 11-5
- Format ... 11-2

Income Tax Expense ... 13-28
Income Taxes ... 13-2
Indefinite Useful Life ... 5-3
Indirect Method for Cash Flows ... 14-3
Induced Conversions ... 6-11
Installment Method ... 12-2
In-Substance Defeasance ... 7-14
Intangible Assets ... 5-2, 17-4
Intercompany
- Bonds ... 17-15
- Eliminations ... 17-13
- Receivables, payables & loans ... 17-13
- Sales of fixed assets ... 17-14
- Sales of inventory ... 17-14

Interest
- Accrual ... 6-4
- Capitalized ... 4-3
- Cost, pensions ... 9-7
- Imputed ... 7-10
- Income ... 6-3
- Method ... 2-31
- Only strip ... 2-27
- Payments ... 6-8
- Rate not stated or unreasonable ... 7-10
- Rate swap agreement ... 2-21

Interfund
- Loans ... 19-16
- Transactions ... 19-15

Interim Financial Reporting ... 11-20
Intermediary Transactions ... 20-8
Internal Service Fund ... 18-6, 19-10
Interperiod Equity ... 18-2
Intraperiod Tax Allocation ... 13-27
Intrinsic Value ... 10-17
Inventory ... 12-13
- Estimation ... 3-10
- Governmental accounting methods ... 18-38
- Turnover ratio ... 15-4

Investing Activities, Cash Flows ... 14-6
Investment Trust Fund ... 18-6, 19-13
Investments
- Acquisition cost ... 2-5
- Bond ... 6-2
- Cost method investments ... 13-29
- Cost method of accounting ... 2-5
- Deferred income taxes ... 2-8
- Defined ... 1-4
- Dividends ... 2-8
- Equity method ... 2-5, 13-29
- Financial statement presentation ... 2-10
- Goodwill ... 2-8
- Governmental ... 18-36
- Intercompany ... 2-8
- Investee's ... 2-7, 2-8
- Long-term ... 2-4, 6-2
- Losses ... 2-10
- Not-for-profit organizations ... 20-10
- Prepaid expenses ... 5-9
- Sale of bonds ... 6-5
- Special purpose funds ... 5-10

Investments (continued)
Temporary....2-4
Unrealized gains and losses....11-9
Investor Journal Entries....6-11

L

Land, Building, and Equipment Fund....20-24
Landfill....18-31
Last-In, First-Out (LIFO)....3-5
Leasehold Improvement....5-2
Leaseholds....5-2
Leases....8-2, 18-29
Capital....8-4
Direct financing....8-5, 8-12
Disclosures....8-16
Operating....8-6
Sale-leaseback....8-14
Sales-type....8-4, 8-10
Length of Operating Cycle....15-4
Lessee....8-2, 8-4, 8-6
Lessor....8-2, 8-4, 8-6
Letter of Transmittal....18-32
Liabilities....1-4, 7-2
Accrued....7-3
Contingent....7-8
Current....1-4, 7-2
Dependent on results....7-4
Disclosures....7-9, 7-10
Environmental remediation....7-9
Estimated....7-5
Long-term....1-4, 7-10
Reclassification....7-12
Valuation....7-2
LIBOR....2-21
Licenses....5-2
Life Income Funds....20-21, 20-22
Life Insurance....5-9
Liquidating Dividends....2-6, 10-11
Loan Fund....20-22, 20-25
Loan Impairment....2-32
Long-Lived Assets, Impairment....4-11
Long-Term
Contracts....12-4
Investments....2-4
Liabilities....1-4, 7-10
Loss....5-3
Losses, Impairment....4-11
Lower-of-Cost-or-Market (LCM)....3-8

M

Management Approach Method....11-23
Management's Discussion & Analysis (MD&A)....18-10
Market
Rate....6-6
Risk....2-24
Value....1-5, 2-11
Marketable Securities....2-11
Marketable Securities (NPO)....20-10
Matching....1-3, 1-16
Materiality....1-3, 1-13
Measurement, Inventory....3-2
Measuring Systems....3-2
Costs....3-3
Definition....3-2
Minimum Lease Payments....8-2
Modified Accrual....19-3
Monetary
Assets....12-10, 12-16
Liabilities....12-10, 12-16
Moving Average....3-8
Multiple-Asset Depreciation Methods....4-10
Municipal Solid Waste Landfill (MSWLF)....18-31
Museum Collections....20-7

N

Natural Resources....4-2
NCGA Statement No. 1....19-11
Net Assets, Not-For-Profit Organizations....1-5
Net Pension Cost....9-5
Net Periodic Pension Cost....9-7
Net Realizable Value....2-27
Neutrality....1-13
New Pronouncements
SFAS 155....2-16
SFAS 156....2-24
SFAS 157....1-6
SFAS 158....9-2
Noncompensatory Plans....10-16
Noncumulative....10-5
Nonexchange Transactions....18-28
Nonmonetary
Assets....12-11, 12-17
Exchanges....4-4
Liabilities....12-12
Nonprofit Accounting....20-2
Nonprofit Organizations....18-5, 20-2
Colleges and universities....20-14
Hospitals and other health care entities....20-17
Other (ONPO)....20-17
Voluntary health and welfare organizations (VHWO)....20-15
Nonreciprocal Transfers....4-5
Nonrevenue Producing Capital Assets....18-4
No-Par Value....10-4
Notes
Payable....7-2
Receivable....2-30
Not-for-Profit Accounting....19-10
Notional Amount....2-15
Number of Days'
Sales in average receivables....15-4
Supply in average inventory....15-4

O

Object Classification....20-2
Objectives of Governmental Financial Reporting....18-2
Objectivity Principle....1-3
Obligations
Asset retirement....7-13
Short-term....7-12
Off-Balance-Sheet Risk....1-8
Operating
Activities, cash flows....14-5
Leases....8-4, 8-6, 18-30
Segments....11-23
Operational Assets....1-4
Operational Efficiency....15-4
Operations
Reporting of....1-9
Other
Comprehensive Basis of Accounting (OCBOA)....11-19
Comprehensive Income (OCI)....1-5, 1-10, 2-13, 2-19, 2-21, 9-4, 9-12, 11-8, 16-6
Financing sources....18-5, 19-3

Other (continued)
- Financing uses 18-5, 19-3
- Gains/Losses 12-16
- Nonprofit Organizations (ONPO) 20-17
- Revenue 20-12
- Revenues/Expenses 12-16

Overfunded Project Benefit Obligation 9-14
Owners' Equity 1-5, 10-3, 10-21

P

Par Value 10-4
Participating 10-5
Participation Rights 10-5
Partnerships 10-20
- Liquidation 10-27
- New partner admission 10-22
- Partner withdrawal 10-25

Patents 5-2
Patient Service Revenue 20-12
Pension Trust Fund 18-6, 19-13
Pensions 9-5, 18-32
Percentage
- Of completion method 12-5
- Of-outstanding-receivables method 2-28
- Of-sales method 2-28

Periodic Inventory System 3-2
Periodicity Assumption 1-2
Permanent
- Differences 13-10, 13-12
- Fund 18-6, 19-9
- Fund restriction 20-2

Perpetual Inventory System 3-2
Physical Capital Maintenance Concept 1-15
Plant Funds 20-21, 20-24
Pledges 20-8
Pledging 2-36
Pooling Method 17-2, 17-3
Postemployment (Governmental)
- Benefits 18-32
- Healthcare 18-32

Postemployment Benefits 7-7, 7-9, 9-2
Postretirement Benefits 9-16
Preferred Stock 12-11
Premium 6-8
Prepaid
- Expenses 5-9, 11-19
- Pension cost 9-11

Present Value 1-17, 2-31, 6-2, 7-10, 8-7, 9-5
Pretax Financial Income 13-2
Price
- Earnings ratio 15-6
- Index 3-6
- Level adjusted 1-6

Prior Period Adjustments 11-15
Prior Service Cost 9-6
Private-Purpose Trust Fund 18-6, 19-13
Product Warranties & Guarantees 7-5
Profit(loss) Test 11-26
Profitability & Investment Analysis Ratios 15-5
Program Services 20-2
Projected Benefit Obligation 9-6
Promises to Give (Pledges) 20-8
Property
- Dividends 10-11
- Plant & equipment 4-2, 4-8

Proprietary Fund 18-6, 18-18, 19-10
- Balance sheet 18-19
- Cash flows statement 18-21
- Debt 19-10

Proprietary Fund (continued)
- Leases 18-30
- Operating statement 18-20

Proprietary Funds 18-10, 18-30
Public Entity Risk Pools 18-35
Purchase Method 17-2, 17-3
Purchasing Power 12-16
Push-Down Accounting 17-20

Q

Quantitative Thresholds 11-26
Quantity LIFO 3-6
Quasi-External Transactions 19-15
Quasi-Reorganization 10-9
Quick Ratio 15-3

R

Ratio Analysis 15-2
Realization 1-16, 2-6
Receivables
- For health care services 20-13
- Turnover ratio 15-4

Recent Pronouncements
- GASB 46 18-13
- GASB 47 18-34
- SFAS 151 3-3
- SFAS 153 4-4
- SFAS 154 11-12
- SFAS 155 2-16
- SFAS 156 2-24
- SFAS 157 1-6
- SFAS 158 9-2

Recognition, Defined 1-15, 1-16
Recoverable Amount 12-14
Refinancing 7-12
Refundings of Debt 19-10
Reimbursements 19-16
Related
- Organization (NPO) 20-11
- Party disclosures 11-16

Relative Sales Value Method 3-3
Relevance 1-13, 1-15, 18-3
Reliability 1-13, 1-15, 18-3
Reorganization of
- Capital structure 10-9

Replacement Cost 1-6
Reportable Segments 11-24
Representational Faithfulness 1-13
Required Supplementary Information (RSI) 18-26
Research and Development 5-5
Residual Value 8-3
Restricted Cash 2-3
Retained Earnings 1-5, 10-8
- Transactions 10-9

Retirement of Bonds 6-6
Return
- On assets 15-5
- On equity 15-5

Returns 2-28
Revenue 1-9, 12-4, 18-5, 19-10
- Classification (NPO) 20-12
- Colleges and universities 20-14
- Health care entities 20-12
- Patient service 20-12
- Realization 1-3
- Recognition 1-3, 1-15, 1-16, 11-18, 12-4
- Recognition methods 12-2

Revenue (continued)
Taxpayer assessed 19-3
Test 11-26
Revised Uniform Partnership Act (RUPA) 10-20
Right of Return 12-4
Royalties 12-9

S

Sale-Leaseback Transactions 8-14
Sales
Returns and allowances 2-28
Type leases 8-4
SAS 69 1-18
Secured Claims 7-16
Securities 2-4, 10-5
Acquisition 2-7, 2-11
Available-for-sale 2-6, 2-11
Bond 6-2
Changes 2-8, 2-13
Cost 2-5, 2-11
Cost method 2-5
Equity 2-5
Equity method 2-6
Held-to-maturity (HTM) 2-11, 6-2
Lending transactions 18-35
Marketable 2-11
Purchase by issuance 4-2
Trading 2-6, 2-11
Valuation 2-12
Securities (NPO) 20-10
Segment 9-15
Disclosures 11-23, 11-27
Disposal 9-15
Manager 11-24
Tests 11-26
Serial Bonds 6-2
Service
Cost 9-7
Efforts and Accomplishments (SEA) 18-38
Hours 4-11
Services, Donated 20-7
Settlements, Pension Plans 9-14
SFAC 1 1-12
SFAC 2 1-12
SFAC 5 1-15
SFAC 6 .... 1-4, 1-10, 1-16, 10-3
SFAC 7 1-17
SFAS 2 5-5
SFAS 3 11-22
SFAS 5 .... 7-7, 12-4
SFAS 6 .... 7-12, 19-7
SFAS 7 11-17
SFAS 13 8-2
SFAS 15 .... 7-13, 7-14
SFAS 34 4-3
SFAS 37 13-26
SFAS 43 .... 7-7, 7-9
SFAS 45 12-8
SFAS 47 7-10
SFAS 48 12-4
SFAS 52 .... 1-5, 16-2
SFAS 57 11-16
SFAS 84 6-11
SFAS 87 .... 1-5, 9-5, 9-11, 9-14
SFAS 88 .... 9-5, 9-14
SFAS 89 .... 1-2, 12-10
SFAS 93 20-10
SFAS 94 .... 2-7, 17-2
SFAS 95 .... 1-11, 14-2, 18-24, 20-5
SFAS 106 9-15
SFAS 107 2-23
SFAS 109 .... 13-4, 13-5, 16-12
SFAS 112 7-7
SFAS 114 .... 2-32, 7-15
SFAS 115 .... 1-5, 2-5, 2-11, 14-6
SFAS 116 .... 4-4, 20-7
SFAS 117 20-3
SFAS 118 .... 7-14, 7-15
SFAS 123 10-17
SFAS 124 20-10
SFAS 125 2-24
SFAS 128 15-6
SFAS 129 10-6
SFAS 130 .... 1-10, 2-14, 10-3, 11-8, 16-6
SFAS 131 11-23
SFAS 132(R) 9-3
SFAS 133 .... 2-16, 2-23, 11-9, 16-11
SFAS 136 20-8
SFAS 138 2-16
SFAS 140 .... 2-24, 2-34, 7-13
SFAS 141 .... 2-5, 17-2
SFAS 142 5-3
SFAS 143 7-13
SFAS 144 .... 4-11, 8-6, 8-9, 11-5
SFAS 145 .... 6-7, 7-14, 8-14, 11-7
SFAS 146 .... 8-3, 9-15, 11-6
SFAS 147 17-2
SFAS 148 10-19
SFAS 149 2-16
SFAS 150 10-15
SFAS 151 3-3
SFAS 153 4-6
SFAS 154 .... 11-12, 11-14
SFAS 155 2-16
SFAS 156 2-24
SFAS 157 1-6
SFAS 158 9-2
Simple Capital Structure 15-13
Sole Proprietorship 10-3
Solvency 15-2, 15-3
SOP 96-1 7-9
SOP 98-1 5-8
Special
Items 18-10
Purpose funds 5-10
Revenue fund 18-6, 19-6
Specific Identification 3-5
Statement of
Activities 18-14, 20-3, 20-14
Cash Flows 1-4, 1-11, 14-2, 18-24, 20-5
Financing activities 14-4, 14-7
Investing activities 14-4, 14-6
Operating activities 14-3, 14-5
Changes in net assets 20-4
Changes in retained earnings 10-8
Comprehensive Income 1-10
Financial position 20-3, 20-22
Functional expenses 20-5, 20-15
Retained Earnings 1-10
Revenues, expenditures, and changes in fund balances 18-17
Support, revenue, and expenses and changes in net assets 20-15
Unrestricted revenues, expenses, and other changes in unrestricted net assets 20-4
Statement-of-Changes-in-Equity 11-10
Statements of Financial Accounting Concepts (SFAC) 1-12
Stock
Common 10-4
Dividends 10-11
Issues 10-6

Stock (continued)
Option plans 10-16
Preferred 10-4
Retirement 10-14
Right(s) 2-6, 10-5
Splits 10-12
Subscription 10-6
Treasury 10-13
Warrant(s) 2-6, 10-6
Straight-Line Depreciation Method 4-8
Subsidiaries 17-8
Subsidiary Entity Records 17-20
Sum-of-the-Years' Digits Method 4-9
Supplementary Information, Measurement of 12-13
Supporting Activities 20-2

T

Tax Agency Fund 19-14
Tax Benefit
Future realization 13-23
Taxable Income 13-2
Assumptions about future 13-14
Taxpayer Assessed Revenue 19-3
Tax-Planning 13-23
Temporary
Differences 13-6, 13-12
Restriction 20-3
Term Bonds 6-2
Termination Benefits.... 9-15, 18-34
Timeliness 18-3
Times
Interest earned ratio 15-3
Preferred dividends earned ratio 15-3
Timing Sources 13-7
Trade Discount 3-3
Trademarks 5-3
Transfers & Servicing of Financial Assets 2-25
Transportation Charges 3-2
Treasury
Stock method, EPS 15-10
Troubled Debt Restructuring 7-13, 7-14
Trust Funds 18-6, 20-21

U

U.S. GAAP 16-5
Uncollectibles 2-28
Underlying 2-15
Underlying Environmental Assumptions 1-2
Understandability 18-3
Unfunded
Accrued pension cost 9-11, 9-13
Projected benefit obligation 9-7, 9-14
Unique Accounting Features
Colleges and universities 20-14
Health care entities 20-12
Unit-of-Measure Assumption 1-2
Units-of-Output 4-11
Universities (also see Colleges) 20-14
University Funds 20-20
Unrestricted Assets 20-3
Unsecured Claims 7-16
Utilities 19-11

V

Valuation 1-5
Accounts 1-4
Accounts receivable 2-27
Allowance 13-21
Stock-based compensation 10-17
Value in Use 12-11
Variable Charge Methods 4-10
Verifiability 1-13
Vested Benefit Obligation 9-7
Voluntary Health and Welfare Organizations (VHWO) 20-15
Volunteers' Services 20-7

W

Warranties 7-5
Warrants 6-11, 6-16
Wash Sales 2-27
Waste, Municipal Landfill 18-31
Weighted Average 3-8, 3-11
Welfare Organizations 20-15
Working Capital Ratio 15-2

Y

Yield on Common Stock 15-6

Z

Zero Profit 19-10

Updating Supplements

From time to time, various regulating bodies issue new pronouncements that are testable on the AICPA Exam.

In order to keep you up-to-date on the latest information, we at Bisk periodically publish updating supplements applicable to the review volume you are currently studying. Bisk Education's updating supplements are small publications available from either customer representatives or our CPA Review website (http://www.cpaexam.com/content/support.asp).

The editors recommend checking the website for new supplements a month before your exam and again a week before your exam. Version 36 (and higher) updating supplements are appropriate for candidates with the 36th edition. Information from earlier supplements (for instance, Version 35.2) are incorporated into this edition. Supplements are issued no more frequently than every three months. Supplements are not necessarily issued every three months; supplements are issued only as information appropriate for supplements becomes available.

Updating supplements for previous versions are available from the website and customer service representatives. Candidates choosing to continue using previous editions of our materials must accept responsibility for adequately updating them. Candidates should consider the strain that this will add to the already time-consuming process of studying for the exam before deciding to continue using previous versions.

Application & exam fees

CPA Examination Services
Attn: Massachusetts Coordinator
P.O. BOX 198469,
Nashville, TN 37219-8469.
— evaluation report

CPA Examination Services
P.O. BOX 440555
Nashville, TN. 37244
— Application & fees payable to CPA Examination Service